UNDERSTANDING PLAYS

Third Edition

❦

Milly S. Barranger

The University of North Carolina
Chapel Hill

PEARSON

Boston   New York   San Francisco
Mexico City   Montreal   Toronto   London   Madrid   Munich   Paris
Hong Kong   Singapore   Tokyo   Cape Town   Sydney

Series Editor: Molly Taylor
Editorial Assistant: Michael Kish
Marketing Manager: Mandee Eckersly
Production Administrator: Michael Granger
Editorial-Production Service: Omegagtype Typography, Inc.
Composition and Prepress Buyer: Linda Cox
Manufacturing Buyer: JoAnne Sweeney
Cover Administrator: Kristina Mose-Libon
Electronic Composition: Omegatype Typography, Inc.

For related titles and support materials, visit our online catalog at www.ablongman.com.

Between the time Website information is gathered and then published, it is not unusual for some sites to have closed. Also, the transcription of URLs can result in typographical errors. The publisher would appreciate notification where these occur so that they may be corrected in subsequent editions.

Library of Congress Cataloging-in-Publication Data

Barranger, Milly S.
    Understanding plays / Milly S. Barranger. — 3rd ed.
        p. cm.
    Includes bibliographical references and index.
    ISBN 0-205-38190-1
        1. Drama—History and criticism.   I. Title.

PN1721.B37 2004
808.2—dc21

                                             2003048042

Printed in the United States of America

10 9 8 7 6 5 4 3 2 1   08 07 06 05 04 03

For Heather, Lincoln, Maggy, and Lilly

CONTENTS

PREFACE

Understanding Plays, the third edition, provides a concise collection of sixteen plays that spans the range of Western writing for the theater from the Greeks to the post-moderns. In response to requests from instructors for additional materials on play-reading, critical interpretation, and performance, each chapter has new sections on production histories as well as seminal documents dealing with critical interpretation and theater practice. Where appropriate, interviews with playwrights on their creative process and comments by theater artists involved in staging the plays are incorporated in these sections, called "Critics' Notebook." Several instructors asked for materials to assist students in writing analyses of plays that they were reading or seeing on campuses and in communities. Dramaturg Gayle M. Austin has provided an exceptionally useful essay on "Play Analysis and Conceptualization: A Process" that provides strategies for writing about plays as texts for performance.

The three editions of *Understanding Plays* begin with an introductory chapter that sets forth methods and strategies for understanding dramatic texts as "pre-texts" for theatrical performance. Discussion of the "literary" text proceeds from the idea that *drama* is a special form of theatrical writing with methods, language, conventions, and characteristics of its own, unlike those found in poetry, fiction, or screenwriting. Proceeding from the premise that drama is not literary history, biography, or a history of ideas, but rather a unique form of writing for the theater, the playwright's text is approached here as dramatic writing having the potential for being performed by actors with the stage's support.

In an effort to provide ample resources for the beginning student, the third edition begins with an introduction that sets forth drama's vocabulary, methods, and conventions for generating theatrical excitement and meaning. Long

ago, Aristotle established in the *Poetics* the elements of drama and influenced our understanding of plot, action, character, language, and types of writing (tragedy and comedy) for the theater. On this foundation, modern approaches to understanding new types of dramatic writing and distinctly contemporary views of the world are introduced and explored in relation to a variety of dramatic texts written for our time. The playwrights and plays selected for this third edition are stepping stones leading to an appreciation for and understanding of world theater.

NEW FEATURES IN THIS EDITION

Understanding Plays is designed for the one-semester course in theater or literature. Of the sixteen plays included here, six are new to this edition. They are Oscar Wilde's *The Importance of Being Earnest,* Tony Kushner's *Angels in America Part One: Millennium Approaches,* Paula Vogel's *How I Learned to Drive,* Moisés Kaufman's *The Laramie Project,* David Henry Hwang's *Golden Child,* and Deb Margolin's *The Secaucas Monologue* (from *Of Mice, Bugs and Women*). Also new to this edition are commentaries by playwrights, directors, scholars, and critics that give students a variety of perspectives on the creative process and insight into critical approaches to interpreting plays as texts for performance.

The plays new to this edition serve two goals. The first is to include landmark plays written for the contemporary theater that have challenged audiences and readers to rethink the complexities of theatrical art and life in America at the millennium. Two wholly new chapters introduce documentary playwriting and the creation of solo performance texts as challenging new forms of writing and performance. The second goal expands the inclusion of multicultural artists and women playwrights whose works are changing the landscape of American playwriting. Significant works by new voices in the American theater in the last quarter of the twentieth century are represented by David Henry Hwang, Moisés Kaufman, Tony Kushner, Eduardo Machado, Deb Margolin, and Paula Vogel.

The sixteen plays found in the third edition provide a comprehensive range of writing for the theater through the ages and address issues of changing forms and styles. Included are *Hamlet* by William Shakespeare, *The Glass Menagerie* by Tennessee Williams, *The Cherry Orchard* by Anton Chekhov, *Oedipus the King* by Sophocles, *The Importance of Being Earnest* by Oscar Wilde, *The Colored Museum* by George C. Wolfe, *Angels in America Part One: The Millennium Approaches* by Tony Kushner, *Hedda Gabler* by Henrik Ibsen, *Fences* by August Wilson, *Galileo* by Bertolt Brecht, *Footfalls* by Samuel Beckett, *How I Learned to Drive* by Paula Vogel, *The Laramie Project* by Moisés Kaufman, *The Secaucas Monologue* (from *Of Mice, Bugs and Women*) by Deb Margolin, *Broken Eggs* by Eduardo Machado, and *Golden Child* by David Henry Hwang.

The seventeen chapters are divided into six parts, followed by appendices containing an essay on analyzing the play contributed by Gayle M. Austin, definitions of critical terms, resources for reading and research, and related videos, films, and web sites. Part 1 contains the introductory chapter that provides an overview of theater, drama, performance, and dramaturgy as preparation for discussions in Part 2 on the elements of drama. Aristotle's criteria found in the *Poetics* serve as a guide for discussions of play structure (*Hamlet*), character (*The Glass Menagerie*), and theatrical language (*The Cherry Orchard*). Types of dramatic writing (Part 3) begin with the traditional pathways of tragedy, comedy, farce and satire, and tragicomedy. *Oedipus the King*, *The Importance of Being Earnest*, *The Colored Museum*, and *Angels in America Part One: Millennium Approaches* represent these types of theatrical writing.

Modernism and realism are introduced in Part 4 as predominant writing styles of the twentieth century. *Hedda Gabler,* written in 1890, demonstrates Henrik Ibsen's early brand of modernism; August Wilson's *Fences,* produced in 1987, demonstrates realistic writing for the stage in our time. In opposition to realism in the modern theater is theatricalism—the yin and yang of theatrical writing styles. Epic and absurdist theater (Part 5) represent the theatricalism of epic staging and the absurdist void as seen in Bertolt Brecht's *Galileo* and Samuel Beckett's *Footfalls.*

American theater in the late twentieth century grew eclectic, contentious, minimalist, and surreal. To introduce U.S. playwriting at the millennium, Part 6 is divided into feminist drama and theory, documentary texts, solo performance texts and performance art, and intercultural texts by Latino/a and Asian American writers. Representing the impact and variety of the new writing are Tony Kushner, Paula Vogel, Moisés Kaufman, Deb Margolin, Eduardo Machado, and David Henry Hwang. An Afterword charts the waters of other dramatic writing at the millennium, namely postmodern work.

In addition to new chapters on documentary and solo performance texts, other new features are brief accounts of the performance histories of the sixteen plays and critical commentaries that feature seminal writings on theater, performance, and interpretation. Found in the "critics' notebooks" are interviews with playwrights and directors along with excerpts from essays on dramatic literature and theater theory. In addition to Aristotle, the playwrights, critics, and scholars represented here are: Gayle M. Austin, Eric Bentley, Karen Blansfield, C. W. E. Bigsby, Bertolt Brecht, Peter Brook, Bert Cardullo, Anton Chekhov, Jill Dolan, Martin Esslin, Sigmund Freud, Northrop Frye, Alexis Greene, Lynda Hart, David Henry Hwang, Henrik Ibsen, Dorinne Kondo, Tony Kushner, Bonnie Lyons, Eduardo Machado, Deb Margolin, Janelle Reinelt, Caridad Svich, David Savran, Alan Schneider, George Bernard Shaw, Roger B. Stein, J. L. Styan, Paula Vogel, Margaret Webster,

August Wilson, George C. Wolfe, and Connie K. Zaytoun.

ACKNOWLEDGMENTS

My thanks are due to a large number of colleagues for their encouragement and assistance in the preparation of the three editions of this book. In the first edition, Gayle M. Austin, Georgia State University; Barbara Clayton, University of Wisconsin–Madison; David Cook, University of Tulsa; Robert Hedley, University of Iowa; Tice Miller, University of Nebraska–Omaha; Robert Schultz, Texas A & M University; Adam Versenyí, University of North Carolina at Chapel Hill; and Jeff Warburton, University of Arizona–Tempe for their early suggestions and steadfast encouragement.

For the second edition, Gayle M. Austin, Georgia State University; William G. Biddy, Mississippi University for Women; Anthony Fichera, University of North Carolina at Chapel Hill; J. Paul Marcoux, Boston College; Joy Reilly, Ohio State University; Roger Schultz, Texas A & M University; Ed Shockley, Temple University; Adam Versenyí, University of North Carolina at Chapel Hill; and Joseph Whited, Kent State University provided helpful suggestions on revisions and new directions.

For this third edition, Gayle M. Austin, George State University; Karen Blansfield, University of North Carolina at Chapel Hill, Beverly W. Long, University of North Carolina at Chapel Hill; Bert Cardullo, University of Michigan–Ann Arbor; Larry J. Evans, Ohio State University; Kimball King, University of North Carolina at Chapel Hill; Deb Margolin, Yale School of Drama; Maaja A. Stewart, Tulane University; Curt Yehnert, Western Oregon University; and Constance K. Zaytoun, a doctoral candidate at The City University of New York Graduate Center, provided materials and made suggestions to ensure a comprehensive approach to understanding dramatic writing and performance. As always, Phyllis Ryan and Betty Futrell in the Department of Dramatic Art at the University of North Carolina at Chapel Hill require special mention for their friendship and support through three editions of this book.

For their contributions to this third edition in the form of original essays and interviews, I want to thank Gayle M. Austin of Georgia State University and performance artist Deb Margolin of the Yale School of Drama. Ben Sampson of Theatre Communications Group, New York City, expedited access to writings published by TCG that ensured the inclusiveness of this edition and Liz Woodman, Casting Society of America, expedited contacts with literary agents in the New York City area. Constance K. Zaytoun also provided editorial assistance on this book, including reference materials, web sites, and steadfast encouragement.

Also, I am most grateful for the guidance and contributions of the editors at Allyn & Bacon who introduced this book to the marketplace in 1990 and have since guided it through three editions. These untiring editors are Steve Hull and Molly Taylor, who are notable for their encouragement, persistence, and appreciation of a book that spans both theater and literature programs.

ABOUT THE AUTHOR

Milly S. Barranger is an Alumni Distinguished Professor at The University of North Carolina at Chapel Hill. She served as Chairman of the Department of Theatre at Tulane University in New Orleans and of the Department of Dramatic Art at The University of North Carolina at Chapel Hill where she was also producing director of the professional regional theater, PlayMakers Repertory Company. She is author of *Theatre: A Way of Seeing, Theatre: Past and Present,* and reference works on Jessica Tandy and Margaret Webster. She is also a co-editor of *Notable Women in the American Theatre: A Biographical Dictionary* and author of the forthcoming biography *Margaret Webster: A Life in the Theater.* She is a member of the College of Fellows of the American Theatre and the National Theatre Conference and has served as President of both the National Theatre Conference and the American Theatre Association.

PART ONE
❦
INTRODUCTION

CHAPTER 1

FROM TEXT TO PERFORMANCE

(Left to Right) Kerri Higuchi, Daniel Dae Kim, and Amy Hill in *Golden Child* by David Henry Hwang, directed by Chay Yew, East West Players, Los Angeles, 2000. (Photo by Michael Lamont, courtesy of East West Players.)

The manuscript, the words on the page, was what you started with and what you have left. The production is of great importance, has given the play the life it will know, but it is gone, in the end, and the pages are the only wall against which to throw the future or measure the past.
—Lillian Hellman,[1] Playwright

DRAMA AND PERFORMANCE

We are bombarded daily with television, videos, newsprint, films, and dramatic events. Terrorists threaten our lives and the environment, soldiers fight in faraway places, nations negotiate peace treaties, nuclear accidents and bioterrorism threaten lives, and a famous boxer divorces his glamorous actress-wife. All are subjects for novels, films, miniseries, and plays. The larger subject is human experience (real or imagined), but the means of representing experience in artistic forms differ with the artist and with the medium. A play is at once a dramatic text to be read and a script to be performed.

Plays are read daily by individuals as diverse as stage directors, designers, actors, technicians, teachers, students, critics, scholars, and the general public. In contrast to novels and poetry, a play is often the most difficult type of prose or poetry to read because it is written not only to be read, but also to be performed by actors before audiences. Like a screenplay, a play is also given life by actors although the medium and technology are significantly different. Kenneth Branagh acts Shakespeare's Hamlet or Gwyneth Paltrow appears as Rosalind in *As you Like It* for the time of the performance. In contrast, their film performances in *Shackleton* and *Shakespeare in Love,* respectively, are contained, unchanging, on videotape for all time.

Reading plays is a unique challenge. It is a different experience from *seeing* the play enacted. For one thing, readers do not have the benefit of the various interpretations of text and space that derive from directors, designers, and actors as they shape the theatrical event. As readers, we must visualize all of the elements the playwright has placed on the page to convey a story to us: its characters in action and conflict, its happening in time and space, and, at the end, the completed meaning of all that has happened.

Plays have been formally analyzed since the days of classical Greece. Aristotle's *Poetics* (c. 330 B.C.) is our first record of a critical assessment of plays presented in the ancient Greek festivals. Since Aristotle, there have been many approaches to "understanding" plays. For our purposes, we will approach the analysis of plays from the viewpoint and techniques of the playwright who creates the dramatic text. As Lillian Hellman said, the words on the page are the playwright's measure, after all is said and done, of the future and the past: "The manuscript, the words on the page, was what you started with and what you have left."[2]

Although we call the playwright's words on the printed page "drama," we also use the words "drama" and "dramatic" to describe many events ranging from riots to parades, from sports events to political speeches. These current events are life's "dramas" but not dramatic "texts."

Martin Esslin wrote that "a dramatic text, unperformed, is literature."[3] Like a novel or poem, drama, as written words, is considered a literary text. The chief ingredient that distinguishes drama from other types of literature is, precisely, its potential for being performed or enacted. The very origin of the word "drama" implies its potential for becoming a performable script. We use the words "text" or "script" to describe this written form that becomes the basis for theatrical performance.

Drama comes from the Greek *dran*, meaning "to do" or "to act." Since the word is rooted in "doing" or "enacting," we have come to understand drama as a special way of imitating human behavior and human events. Drama is like narrative in that it tells a story; but unlike narrative, or storytelling, it requires enactment before an audience. The story's events must be represented in drama, not merely told or narrated as in epic poetry.

The word *theater* has its roots in the Greek word, *theatron,* meaning "a place for seeing," or that special place where actors and audiences come together to experience a performance of the playwright's raw materials—the drama. The dramatic text is not wholly realized until the theater's artists complete for audiences what the playwright began. As Hamlet, Kenneth Branaugh must breathe life into Shakespeare's character for the text to come alive in the imagined world of Elsinore Castle.

All dramatic texts are constructs. They have in common the fact that they set forth events taking place in an imagined or fictional world, whether it be ancient Thebes or contemporary Manhattan. The dramatic text is the playwright's blueprint for setting forth physical and psychological experience—to give shape and meaning to the world as the playwright sees and understands it. Over the centuries, these blueprints have related a variety of stories not as narrations, but as imitations of imagined actions. Sophocles wrote of a king confronted by a plague-ridden kingdom (*Oedipus the King*), Sam Shepard depicted American midwesterners confronting their lost connections with the land and with one another (*Buried Child*), and Samuel Beckett presented worlds in which human beings "wait out" lifetimes (*Footfalls*).

Drama, then, is a special written way of imitating human experience. It is both a literary and a performance text. The fictional character, Hamlet, is played by the living actor. It is our purpose here to learn to *read* plays, to understand the how and why of the dramatic text, without ignoring the fact that the playwright's words have the potential to be performed in the theater. We must learn to analyze the pattern of words and scenes that have the potential for "becoming" living words and actions.

The playwright provides us with *dialogue*—words arranged in a meaningful sequence—intended to be spoken aloud and enacted by actors before audiences. Often the playwright includes descriptions of scenes, characters, objects, and movement in stage directions and dialogue. However, the actor remains the playwright's essential intermediary in that complex relationship between the drama and the performance.

DRAMATURGY

In its original Greek meaning, a *dramaturg* was simply a playwright. The word "dramaturgy" defines the playwright's craft. It involves the elements, conventions, and techniques the playwright uses to delineate general and particular truths about the human condition. Those elements involve plot, action, character, meaning, language, spectacle, space, and time. We must develop tools for understanding a writer's dramaturgical skills, which deal with plot, character, language, and so forth, so that we can read plays from all periods of theatrical, cultural, and social history. Styles, conventions, language, and techniques differ among playwrights depending on the physical theater, the writing conventions of the historical period, and the society or universe mirrored in the writer's work. Also applicable are the ever-changing cultural, social, and technological conditions under which plays have been written, produced, and performed in Western society for 2500 years.

DRAMA'S STAGES

Drama's stages are as varied as the society, culture, and artists engaged in creating the scripts and performances. In ages past, drama was staged in convenient outdoor places. The amphitheaters of Greek and Roman drama, like the stately Theatre at Epidaurus in Greece today, brought communities together on a hillside to watch the several actors and choruses in the circular area at the base of the hill perform the tragic stories taken from myth and legend. In the Middle Ages in Europe and England, the theater was again an outdoor festival staged for the public at large. Performances of plays written and produced by craft guilds were staged on platforms erected in marketplaces or on wagons, which proceeded from place to place in the medieval towns. During the Renaissance, some plays were staged in banquet halls to elite audiences and illuminated by candles and tinted reflectors; in Italy indoor playhouses were built with the first perspective scenery to create an illusion of place. However, the Elizabethan theaters in England remained largely public theaters open to the weather and a cross-section of society. Shakespeare's plays were staged in the most famous theater of the day—The Globe. Modeled on the new European theaters, indoor playhouses replaced the open-air ones in popularity by the late seventeenth century and playwriting reflected a larger concern for place and interior events. With the invention of gas light and then electricity in the nineteenth century, even more elaborate "indoor" playhouses were constructed with proscenium arches framing the stages, front curtains, and large forestages where actors could step out of the picture frame to address the audience.

In today's theaters, audiences find a variety of performance spaces. Broadway's proscenium playhouses with elaborate lighting and sound systems hold the audience at a formal remove from the stage. Arena and thrust stages seat audiences on four and three sides of a platform and establish a more intimate relationship with the audience seated in closer proximity to the actors. Arena Stage in Washington, D.C., and the Guthrie Theatre in Minneapolis are two well-known stages of these types. Then, too, large rooms (called black boxes and favored by low-budget, experimental groups) found in performing arts centers and converted warehouses and garages often press audiences into participation in the play's action about contemporary social and political issues.

There are few common denominators that define drama's stages other than the performance space, the actor, and the audience. For example, drama's stages are large and small, open-air or indoors, formal proscenium theaters or converted spaces. Some playwrights envision the play's environment in elaborate detail; others leave the void of the stage space to be filled by directors and designers. As we read plays,

we face a task unlike the experience of sitting in the theater where we experience the play in performance. As readers, we necessarily have a different experience where we depend on the mind's eye to fill in the spaces, colors, and sounds. We must sharpen our abilities to see the environments envisioned by the playwright, the interactions among characters, the effects of color and lighting, and the use of sounds and silences that contribute meaning. Our task as readers is to visualize a living world, to hear words and sounds, and to follow the story, characters, and events to their final meaning.

DRAMATIC SPACE

Drama is unique among the arts in that it imitates reality through representation rather than narration. The playwright creates a fictional universe with human beings, familiar objects, and recognizable environments. Beckett's characters' feet hurt; August Wilson's hero holds onto his baseball bat. Like Beckett and Wilson, playwrights use "real" human beings in particular spaces and times to create the illusion of fictional worlds in which recognizable events take place in time and space. We distinguish between the *performance space* (the stage) and the *dramatic space* (the playwright's fictional locale). Dramatic space—or the play's environment—is usually described in dialogue or in stage directions found in modern texts. What is exhibited in the performance space is an interpretation, or staging, of the play's physical requirements set forth in those directions or reconceived by directors and designers.

Dramatic space has essentially two characteristics. First, it is a "fictional" space—the characters' environment—described by playwrights in dialogue and stage directions. The fictional space may be the palace of Thebes (*Oedipus the King*), a nineteenth-century drawing room (*The Importance of Being Earnest*), or the bare front yard and wooden porch of the Maxon home (*Fences*). The fictional space may encompass simultaneously more than one space, such as palaces and battlefields or apartments and streets. Shakespeare's plays require locations that are miles apart, but the characters must appear in those locales within seconds. Hamlet moves from battlements, to chambers, to graveyards. Dramatic space is magical in its ability to present several locales simultaneously. Bertolt Brecht's Galileo travels many miles and journeys to many cities in his pursuit of truth and reason.

Second, dramatic space always assumes the presence of a stage and an audience and a relationship between the two. As we read plays, we are aware that they are written to be performed. While the stage where a play is produced may be almost any type—proscenium, arena, thrust, environmental—the characters may or may not be aware of the audience. In modern realistic plays, the characters are not aware that an audience is present. The pretense, or stage convention, is that a "fourth wall" exists through which the actors-as-characters cannot see, although audiences can. No character in Henrik Ibsen's *Hedda Gabler* ever acknowledges the audience. In other plays, characters directly address the audience, establishing an invisible flow of space between actor and audience. Oscar Wilde's *The Importance of Being Earnest* has many asides where characters speak directly to the audience to comment briefly on some situation. As readers, we need to be sensitive to the "look" of the characters' environment and to the intended relationship of the dramatic space to the audience.

DRAMATIC TIME

Dramatic time is a phenomenon of the text. Jan Kott wrote that "theater is a place where time is always present."[4] Once begun, the time of a performance is one-directional. It follows a linear path for the two or more hours of its duration. Dramatic time, in contrast to performance time, is free of such constraints.

Within the fictional world of the play, time can be expanded or compressed. Unlike the film editor's manipulation of images in films, the playwright does not have the advantage of editing and splicing film to carry us forward or backward in time. Rather, dramatic time can be accelerated by using gaps of days, months, and even years; or, it can be slowed down by using soliloquies and flashbacks. Whereas real or performance time moves in one direction (present to future) and the past can never be recaptured, dramatic time can violate the relentless forward motion of performance time measured by the clock. For example, events may be shown out of their chronological sequence, or they may be foreshortened so they occur more swiftly than they would in nature. Shakespeare's battles, requiring only a few minutes of swordplay on stage, would ordinarily require days or even months in real time. In Samuel Beckett's plays, characters experience the relentless passage of time because there are no major events or crises. An unchanging sameness characterizes their lives. In Samuel Beckett's *Waiting for Godot*, Vladimir and Estragon wait for Godot's arrival, which is always postponed by the messenger's announcement that "Mr. Godot told me to tell you he won't come this evening but surely tomorrow." In Beckett's plays the experience of dramatic time is cyclical—day becomes night and night becomes day—while his characters wait out their uneventful lives in patterns that are repetitive and are experienced as "waiting." In his plays, nothing happens in the traditional sense, but time erodes lives in a relentless journey toward death.

Time and space in the fictional universe of drama are highly malleable and unlike the actual time we experience in our daily lives. Consideration of dramatic time and space has always played a large part in the different theories and rules of drama. In his *Poetics*, Aristotle briefly suggested that the amount of time it takes the actors to tell the story should ideally be concurrent with the actual time it takes to perform the play. This attention to a *unity of time,* as it was later called, is still found in modern realistic plays.

In the many words written about drama over the centuries, the most attention has been given to the playwright's meanings and messages.

DRAMA'S LANDSCAPES

One critic said that "the dramatic text is incomplete without the stage's support."[5] A play's literal, figurative, and symbolic landscape is often the writer's vision of the "stage's support" of the dramatic text. *Scenography* is frequently the name given by theater practitioners to that support. They are defining the playwright's concept of the stage as a fictional environment with literal and visible dimensions as well as figurative and symbolic meanings. As readers, we seek clues in the text's dialogue and stage directions for how to imagine the "look" of the play's fictional world but the play's scenography is much more than scenic representation of literal places on stage.

Playwrights have their own kind of "literary" or "verbal" scenography. It includes the play's geography, its interior and/or exterior environs, and the symbolic meanings of those fictional worlds, whether we are visualizing Oedipus' plague-ravaged kingdom, Hamlet's haunted castle at Elsinore, or Amanda Wingfield's tattered living quarters.

The playwright's scenography has two distinct components: (1) scenery, costumes, sounds, lighting effects, colors, objects, furnishings, and special effects; (2) the symbolic, cultural, and thematic meanings of the play's fictional world. These are the playwright's scenographic materials, which we may think of as a gigantic musical score indicating the "look" and use of the stage space, as well as the meaning of this environment as fictional world.

The open-air theaters of classical, medieval, and Elizabethan times embraced large human actions that took place in cosmic space. The myths and legends of Greek tragedy show an expansive landscape with humans and gods under pressure, confronting chaos and disorder, often in contradictory and catastrophic ways. In the landscape of Sophocles' *Oedipus the King*, a plague of physical and spiritual proportions overtakes a kingdom and royal family.

The platform stage and neutral façade of the Elizabethan theater held the dramatic mirror up to human experience. It was no accidental turn of phrase when Shakespeare wrote, "All the world's a stage, And all the men and women merely players" (*As You Like It*). The dramatic landscapes of the Elizabethan playwrights touched on all places and human actions, including magical islands and battlefields. Costumes, music, and sound effects (trumpet flourishes, for instance) contributed to the analogue between life and art.

Many nineteenth-century playwrights confined their characters within a stage setting defined by three walls and a ceiling (called a box set) to depict the landscape of a repressive society that dictated lifestyle, manners, dress codes, social conventions, and mores. Others used literal journeys from lowlands to mountaintops to complement a character's journey of the soul that culminated in a spiritual epiphany. Playwrights have also used journeys from heights to depths to trace a character's moral degeneration.

The playwright's visual landscape places the dramatic material in a historical time and space. The playwright inserts notes on geography, light, color, furniture, clothing, and develops their relationship to the play's action and characters. Stage directions are a literal gold mine of this type of scenographic detail. Ibsen meticulously described in stage directions Hedda Gabler's drawing room, the scene of her social and spiritual confinement. The room is at once a fictional landscape and a symbolic universe—all contained within a recognizable 1890s middle-class drawing room located on the outskirts of a Norwegian town. Ibsen's detailed analogue to the virtual world is one type of dramatic landscape—a "slice of life" representation that reflects the everyday reality of the historical world.

More recent texts written for the realistic theater, including *The Cherry Orchard, The Glass Menagerie, Fences,* and *Broken Eggs,* use material objects, places, décor, and clothing to define the dramatic landscape. Then, there is the more complex scenography of anti-realistic writing wherein the stage and the performance are viewed as reality that demonstrates how human beings live out their life's "roles" and "act out" their charades and crises. In the work of Luigi Pirandello, Eugène Ionesco, and Jean Genet, the stage—as a place for pretense—is viewed as more "real" than our workaday lives. Writing in the 1920s, Italian playwright Luigi Pirandello understood the essence of human nature as *pretense*—the putting on of masks as social personas to play out public roles. The theater with its interactions between audience and actors was the perfect landscape to create works about playing, about theatricality, and about the human impulse to create fictions, revise reality, and to put on masks. Pirandello created the *metatheatrical* play in his "theater trilogy"—*Six Characters in Search of an Author, Each in His Own Way,* and *Tonight We Improvise*—where the playwright's essential scenographic tool is the stage itself. The emphasis of this type of dramatic writing is on theatricality and artifice rather than on a photographic landscape of middle-class life and its environs.

Another variation of the complex scenography of the post-realistic theater is found in the epic staging envisioned by Bertolt Brecht and the absurdist writing of Samuel Beckett. Brecht uses the stage's empty space as an undefined, highly flexible landscape accommodating Galileo's journey through historical conflict with religious authority and scientific investigation. Influenced by Brecht's writing and staging, playwrights Tony Kushner and Suzan-Lori Parks also envision the dramatic landscape as encompassing the real and surreal.

In absurdist writing, the stage is a landscape of emptiness and isolation. The "empty stage" (the gaping void or cavity of the physical space) becomes the playwright's scenographic landscape of existential or metaphysical proportions. The plays of Samuel Beckett present the absurdity of all human struggle as senseless, futile, and oppressive. It follows that his absurdist landscape depicts human isolation and its visual counterpart—physical emptiness. In *Waiting for Godot,* two tramps in a wasted and forlorn area inhabited by a single tree wait for Godot, who never arrives. Emptiness comprises Beckett's landscape so much so that such minimal properties as a tree (*Waiting for Godot*), a rocking chair (*Rockaby*), or a tape recorder (*Krapp's Last Tape*) take on visual significance and philosophical meaning.

DRAMA'S MEANINGS AND MESSAGES

The play reader's greatest temptation is to concentrate on the general meaning of the literary work—the novel, poem, or play—overlooking the fact that meaning is generated as the work is experienced. A play's complete meaning does not emerge in the early pages of a text or in the first moments of a performance, but quite often the seeds of the message can be found there.

In creating the dramatic text, the playwright connects the reader (and audiences) with a common humanity through the progression of the play's events. Great plays confront us with life's verities, conveying the hope, courage, despair, compassion, violence, love, hate, exploitation, and generosity experienced by all humankind. They show us the possibilities of losing our families and property through accidents, catastrophes of war, or tyranny. Plays show us ways of fulfilling ourselves in relationships or confronting despair and death. August Wilson's characters struggle to show love and affection to one another. The most enduring plays explore what it means to be human beings in special circumstances. These circumstances may be unfamiliar, like the prince dispossessed of his rightful heritage through murder, marriage, and calumny (*Hamlet*); or bizarre, like the family that has literally buried its family skeleton in the back yard (*Buried Child*); or familiar, like the unwanted ambitions of a mother for her children (*The Glass Menagerie*).

Drama's most enduring achievements, like the representative plays contained in this book, serve as reflections of ourselves, or what potentially could be ourselves in different times and circumstances. Drama's best moments lead us to discoveries and reflections about our personalities, circumstances, desires, anxieties, hopes, and dreams. Playwrights also move beyond personal concerns to discuss social and political issues that are of a certain time, yet transcend specific historical periods. Playwrights stimulate social awareness and put us in touch with our thoughts and feelings about issues. The aim of great playwrights is to expand our consciousness on old and new social and personal issues, and to endow us with *new perspectives* on our humanity and the human condition.

Plays are written as a process of unfolding and discovery. To read plays successfully is to understand essentially "how" the playwright generates meaning. Scene follows scene in meaningful patterns; dialogue communicates feelings and ideas; characters display motives and emotions; locales give social and economic contexts. "What" a play means involves the completed action, that is, all that has gone before in organized, meaningful segments that, when taken in their totality, express the writer's vision or conviction about the world. As readers, we share that unfolding—those discoveries—with audiences. We also learn to experience the developing actions, events, and relationships which, in turn, produce a coherent statement about individuals, societies, and the universe. We learn to follow the playwright's ways and means of organizing the dramatic material into a coherent whole. We discover the writer's methods for developing the psychological and physical currents of human endeavor that result in visible (and meaningful) behavior.

The same process is at work in our personal experiences. In our daily lives, we are not instantly aware that some actions have repercussions far beyond our expectations. As we begin a trip, we cannot know the full extent of what is to come, namely, our experiences. With time, we come to understand the meaning of our experiences, feelings, and actions, as well as the motives and actions of others. In some instances, meanings are elusive—sometimes impossible to pin down. The same is true in understanding the how and the why of the dramatic text. When Tom Wingfield brings the "gentleman caller" to dine with his sister Laura in Tennessee Williams' *The Glass Menagerie,* he is not aware, nor are we as readers and audiences, of the psychological damage he is imposing on Laura's fragile emotional life.

All art condenses, clarifies, and orders the chaos, disorder, and inconsequential happenings of life. The poet William Wordsworth gives shape to girlhood innocence in his "Lucy Gray" poems. The playwright Tennessee Williams organizes Tom Wingfield's memories of his chaotic and unhappy life in his mother's home. However, great plays, like great poems, confront life's complexities in such a way that they can-

not be reduced to a single meaning. Since there is usually no author's voice in drama, as there is in the novel where the writer can speak directly to the reader, we are left with layers of possible meaning based on the play's events. We can usually agree that Hamlet was given the task of avenging his father's murder, that he hesitated and ultimately achieved his objective at the cost of his life. What remains open to interpretation is the ultimate meaning or significance of the play—"what it was all about." For that reason, we can read and see *Hamlet* any number of times and continue to discover new meanings in this complex text. We want to learn to identify *how* playwrights order, clarify, and distill their imitations of real life in the dramatic text and what larger meanings emerge from these efforts.

CRITICS' NOTEBOOK

Bert Cardullo, dramaturg and scholar, has written on the role of the dramaturg that developed in German theaters in the late eighteenth century and found its way into the American resident theaters in the late twentieth century. His notes on the work of the dramaturg, published in *What Is Dramaturgy?* (1995), relate to the discussion of playwriting and performance found in this introductory chapter.

Bert Cardullo, from *What Is Dramaturgy?**

If you consult a dictionary, the meaning of the word "dramaturgy" you find there is "the craft or the techniques of dramatic composition considered collectively," and a "dramaturg" is defined simply as "a dramatist or playwright." Now we know that a playwright is a "maker" or "worker" of plays, not merely a writer of them (as a shipwright is a maker of ships and a wainwright a maker of wagons). This meaning of "playwright" is reinforced by the Greek word

*Bert Cardullo, *What Is Dramaturgy?*, American University Studies, vol. 20 (New York: Peter Lang Publishing, Inc., 1995): 3–4, 10–11.

dramaturgy (and its back formation, *dramaturg*), which is made up of the root for "action or doing" (*drame*) and the suffix for "process or working" (*-urgy*). Here we may helpfully think of the words "metallurgy"—the working of metal—and "thaumaturgy"—the working of miracles.

But let us venture on another meaning of the word "dramaturgy," which has come into usage in the American theatre fairly recently. As a result of our belated acknowledgement of European theatre practice, "dramaturgy" today denotes the multi-faceted study of a given play: its author, content, style, and interpretive possibilities, together with its historical, theatrical, and intellectual background. This study is conducted by people called "dramaturgs" in the European repertory theatre, most conspicuously in Germany, where each of the approximately 120 municipal theatres has a dramaturgical department. The dramaturg's profession was instituted in the United States during the rise of the regional theatre movement and continues to be important in ensemble theatres as well as in those regional theatres that have remained non-commercial. As critics-in-residence (also known as literary managers or literary advisors), dramaturgs perform a variety of tasks. Broadly speaking, the dramaturg's duties are (1) to select and prepare playtexts for performance; (2) to advise directors and actors; and (3) to educate the audience. To fulfill these duties, dramaturgs serve as script readers, translators, theatre historians, play adaptors or even playwrights, directorial assistants or sometimes apprentice directors, critics of works-in-progress, and talent scouts....

❧ ❧ ❧

The dramaturg is spokesman for the word if not a creator of words himself; he is the champion of ideas in a theatre—and a world—increasingly devoid of them; and he is a believer in the elusive if not ineffable spirit of well-wrought dramatic texts, which he helps to embody in beautifully shaped, infinitely shaded, and piercingly heard theatrical productions. Without the dramaturg, in fact, there is no real theatre. He is its true architect and archaeologist,

the discoverer, transmitter, and interpreter of playtexts both ancient and modern, a kind of playwright for all ages or crossroads of dramatic tradition. A dramaturg is to a play as a mechanic is to an automobile: he may not have built it, but he knows what makes it work, and this enables him to rebuild it as the theatrical occasion warrants. Playwrights—and directors as well as audiences—should be grateful, and should take advantage.

REVISITING DRAMA AND PERFORMANCE

As we have discovered, plays are at once literary texts and texts for performance. For this reason, there is a doubleness about our experience of them. In the theater itself, we experience plays in the present time and in their performance space. Literary texts (called *drama*) also contain their own versions of time and space in fictional worlds. Dramatic space, like the stage itself, is highly malleable and can portray locations that are miles apart; characters can move from locale to locale without violating our sense of the logical progression of events. One play may take place wholly in a living room; another may take place in a character's memory; another may require battlefields, castles, and graveyards. Dramatic time is likewise flexible. Within a play's fictional world, time can be compressed or expanded to reflect the passage of hours or years.

In reading plays, we progress from "what is happening next" in terms of storytelling to "what it all means." This is our final concern because plays, like the lives or realities they imitate, progress through action and events to a discovery that those human choices and happenings have special meanings in the completed action. However, "what it is all about" is not in the least a fixed message but open to reinterpretation with changing historical periods, cultures, and societies. Following the Bolshevik revolution in Russia in 1917, the ending of Anton Chekhov's *The Cherry Orchard* was "reinterpreted" as the great playwright's forecast of the political and social changes to come in the creation of the Union of Soviet Socialist Republics. Today, the ending is again reinterpreted to capture Chekhov's balanced view of humanity's struggle to survive in a changing world.

Let us begin our process of understanding plays with the *elements of drama*—play structure, character, and language—found in three masterpieces of Western playwriting: *Hamlet, The Glass Menagerie,* and *The Cherry Orchard.*

NOTES

1. Lillian Hellman, *Pentimento: A Book of Portraits* (Boston: Little, Brown, 1973): 151–152.

2. Hellman, 151–152.

3. Martin Esslin, *The Field of Drama: How the Signs of Drama Create Meaning on Stage and Screen* (London: Methuen, 1987): 24.

4. Jan Kott, *The Theater of Essence and Other Essays* (Evanston, Ill.: Northwestern University Press, 1984): 211.

5. Patrice Pavis, *Languages of the Stage: Essays on the Semiology of Theatre* (New York: Performing Arts Journal Publications, 1982): 145.

PART TWO

ELEMENTS OF DRAMA

CHAPTER 2

UNDERSTANDING PLAY STRUCTURE

Ralph Fiennes as Hamlet and Francesca Annis as Gertrude in *Hamlet*, directed by Jonathan Kent, in the Almeida Theatre Company production, Hackney Empire Theatre, London, 1995. (Photo © Robbie Jack/CORBIS.)

If art reflects life it does so with special mirrors.
—Bertolt Brecht

DRAMA'S SPECIAL MIRRORS

In writing about the practice of making plays and theater, German playwright Bertolt Brecht used the metaphor of "special mirrors" to describe the changing forms, conventions, and techniques of his day.[1] In one sense, play structure is like the *frame* of the mirror, the incasement, that gives a special shape to drama's events.

Drama is a pattern of imagined words and actions having the potential for "doing" or "becoming" living words and actions through human presence. Drama imitates human actions and circumstances (Aristotle called it *mimesis*). Dramatic structure is the overall pattern that gives a special shape to these events, either compressing or expanding the mystery of human behavior into a semblance of time, space, and living presence. Over the years, we have developed a vocabulary to describe the variety of mirrors playwrights have used to imitate the shape of human events. That common vocabulary describes play structure generally as *climactic, episodic, situational,* or *reflexive.* These terms are descriptive of plays by Sophocles, William Shakespeare, Samuel Beckett, and Suzan-Lori Parks. Others have devised such terms as the "well-made play," "anti-play," "talking pieces," and "synthetic fragments" to identify further the overall shape of a dramatic text. A play's structure, as we shall discover, gives form to the physical, psychological, and philosophical experiences contained collectively in the text's action, plot, characters, speech, and landscapes.

Suzanne K. Langer described drama thus: "Drama, though it implies past actions (the 'situation'), moves not toward the present, as narrative does, but toward something beyond; it deals essentially with commitments and consequences."[2] In Langer's view, drama is a dynamic pattern of circumstances and actions, always in the process of being completed. *How* drama's impending acts are shaped determines the labels we use—climactic, episodic, and so on.

Found in *Oedipus the King* and *Hamlet*, the older types of play structure represent compressed or expanding stories built upon cause and effect, commitments and consequences, or purposeful seeking and meaningful discovery. The *quest,* a search for or pursuit of an objective or goal, is perhaps the oldest mode for structuring a play. Sophocles' plays are excellent examples. The *journey,* a passage or progress through time from one point to the next, is probably the second oldest and found splendidly realized in Elizabethan plays. In these two instances, a play's structure may be climactic (the quest) or episodic (the journey). In both, plot and action are based on a central conflict and organized usually in a progression from confrontation to crisis to resolution.[3]

CLIMACTIC PLAY STRUCTURE

Found in classical and modern plays, climactic structure limits the characters' activities and increases pressures on them until they are forced into irreversible acts. The playwright begins late in the course of the story, near the crisis and climax, and we experience a brief time in the life of the characters, usually limited to a few hours or days. The events of the story's past weigh heavily on the present situation, and are gradually revealed even until the play's final moments. This gradual unfolding of background information is called *retrospective exposition;* it demonstrates the effects of the past on present events and lives. Sophocles' treatment of the Oedipus story gradually reveals the choices made in the past that bring the hero to the moment of discovery and terrible self-knowledge.

As the action develops in climactic structure, the characters' options are reduced. In many cases, they are aware that their choices are being limited and that they are being moved toward a crisis and turning point of present fortunes—from good to bad, or from bad to good. Climactic structure is a *cause-to-effect* arrangement of events leading to a climax and quick resolution. *Oedipus the King, Hedda Gabler,* and *Fences* are three excellent examples of climactic structure.

In *Oedipus the King,* Sophocles started at a critical point in the ancient Theban story when the plague descends upon the city Oedipus and Jocasta had been ruling for a number of years. The play's action takes less than a day and consists of Oedipus' quest for Laius's slayer—his consulting the Oracle of Apollo, his interrogation of the seer Teiresias and of a series of witnesses, ending with the old shepherd who gave him as a baby to a servant of the rulers of Corinth. The play ends when Oedipus is unmistakably revealed as the culprit and exacts a self-inflicted punishment—blindness and exile.

By starting the play late in the story (also called a *point of attack*), and by showing only the last crucial episodes before Oedipus' fall, the past and present events of the protagonist's life are revealed simultaneously. Oedipus' quest for the slayer of Laius becomes a search for the hidden reality of his own past. As that past slowly comes into focus in the light of irrefutable facts, his quest also reaches its end. Oedipus discovers himself as both the city's savior and its pollution.

The plot and action (the search for truth) also have a secondary shape: a beginning, middle, and end, in time and space. The play starts with the immediate cause (the plague) which results in Oedipus' objective to find Laius's slayer. His search for a murderer turns into an intense pursuit of truth. Complications evolve into an unexpected climax and new understanding in the resolution. The action moves quickly and methodically from purpose to understanding, cause to effect. Oedipus suffers forces he can neither control nor understand; yet, at the same time, he intelligently wills each move in his search. The action is an intensive search for Laius's killer and as Oedipus' past is unrolled before us in five episodes, his whole life is seen as a quest for his true nature, identity, and destiny. The structure also mirrors the age-old quest of all human beings to discover who they are and the meaning of what they have done.

Sophocles' arrangement of the story's events, starting his play near the end and representing the past in relation to what is happening in the present while bringing all to a resolution, has shaped dramatic writing for 2500 years. The well-made play, so popular with French writers of the nineteenth century and adapted by Henrik Ibsen and more recently by August Wilson, demonstrates the timeless appeal of climactic structure. For a play to be considered "well-made," it had to have clear exposition of the situation, late point of attack, careful preparation of events, withheld secrets, unexpected but logical reversals, mounting suspense, an obligatory scene revealing the secret and explaining the writer's social and moral viewpoints, and a logical resolution. Ibsen's *Hedda Gabler* and August Wilson's *Fences* are examples of well-made play structure and, therefore, are climactic.

Let us return to the mirror as paradigm for dramatic structure. The playwright's universal view of human beings in action and the meaning of those actions determine the play's structure. Climactic structure reflects a vision of an orderly, rational universe in which causes have effects and deeds have moral consequences. Past, present, and future have logical, traceable kinships giving rise to a dramatic structure that mirrors a rational world. For example, Sophocles' tragedies demonstrate a divinely ordered universe where humans can, through suffering, learn the meaning of their deeds. No effect is without cause, no life without meaning. The shape of Sophocles' plays, therefore, is logical and ordered according to a rational pattern whose meaning is intelligible.

EPISODIC PLAY STRUCTURE

Found in medieval plays and in the work of William Shakespeare, Bertolt Brecht, Tony Kushner, and Suzan-Lori Parks, episodic play structure traces its characters through a *journey* both physical and spiritual to a final understanding of the meaning of the *total* experience. The journey, as with any kind of travel, can always take new twists and turns, introduce new characters, and leap across years and locales. In Shakespeare's plays, events do not confine the characters because the plot and action expand to include many people and considerable time and distance. *Hamlet* takes place over several months and countries. And the expanding plot takes in a variety of events, including encounters with a ghost, a suicide, a funeral, and an ill-fated duel. In this loose structure, characters are not caught in circumstances but maneuver within them as Brecht's Galileo maneuvers to outwit the reactionary powers of seventeenth-century Italy at the dawn of a new scientific age.

Episodic play structure begins early in the story (called an *early point of attack*) and involves many people, places, and events that do not confine the characters or necessarily restrict their choices and movements. Unlike climactic structure, people are not perceived as victims of their past histories, but only of their present circumstances. Accordingly, the plot develops a variety of events and activities. There may also be more than one plot involving, for example, the stories of two families which, as in *King Lear,* eventually impact on each other in the play's resolution.

Elizabethans thought of the play (and the stage) as a "mirror held up to nature," as Shakespeare said, reflecting the behavior and sociopolitical conditions of the time. Since most Elizabethan playwrights, including Shakespeare, turned to popular romances and histories for their plots, their material did not lend itself to tight plotting of incidents. Instead, writers concentrated on the rapid and expanding progress of a story from high point to high point, opting for effects more than causes. Shakespeare emphasized the effects of Duncan's murder in *Macbeth* and of Hamlet's procrastination. In addition, we find in *Hamlet* the appearance of a ghost, the staging of a play within a play (Hamlet's "Mousetrap"), Polonius' murder, Ophelia's suicide and burial, the duel between Hamlet and Laertes and multiple deaths, and Fortinbras' martial entrance to claim the kingdom. In this type of structure, plots were composed of events (or episodes) placed end to end to tell a story about active lives—killing kings, fighting over kingdoms, usurping thrones, avenging wrongs, and so on.

Episodic plotting required little exposition, usually because not much had happened before the play began. Although many years earlier the elder Hamlet defeated the elder Fortinbras to reclaim Denmark, this information is not vital to Hamlet's situation at the play's start. What is vital is that Hamlet's uncle has recently usurped the throne and married his mother and a ghost has appeared to the palace guards. The forward movement of the plot requires Hamlet's encounter with the ghost. It is typical of episodic structure that some force occurs early in the opening scenes, or just before them, to impel the characters to act. The ghost in *Hamlet* is one such instance.

Episodic structure takes its name from the end-to-end arrangement of a series of events, each of which is completed before another begins. Usually, in Shakespeare's plays, exits mark the end of scenes together with couplets or soliloquies. Each scene has one of three functions, or a combination thereof: (1) to propel the plot toward its crisis and resolution; (2) to develop traits of character; or (3) to compare and contrast situations among the characters.

The episodes were developed within a five-part form the Elizabethans probably adopted from their classical studies of Seneca and Terence, Roman playwrights. However, within the five parts, the Elizabethans spread out the events of the plot and shaped the dramatic action to develop the highest tension during the middle of the play and revived it again toward the end. Therefore, in the Elizabethan model, the first three parts were an expanding and complicating of events leading to a climax. The fourth part included events that reduced tensions, and the final part concluded with another climactic moment and a resolution of the conflict. One reading of *Hamlet* places the first climax at the moment when Hamlet kills Polonius, resulting in an irreversible course of events from which there is no turning back; the second combines the fatal poisoning and duel. Episodic structure juxtaposes, repeats, and contrasts the play's events in a sweep of action that has repercussions for all involved.

Shakespeare's plays often ended with a public resolution of the conflict. Usually, an authority figure (a king, judge, or governor) meted out justice, married lovers, and reordered the body politic. The means of bringing about a play's ending varied; it ranged from the discovery of true identities to a trial, execution, or single combat. In *Macbeth* and *Hamlet,* a single combat decides the issue against the forces of evil. Following this type of critical event, someone in authority pronounced judgment, declaring the meaning of the action and reasserting order. Usually, these final lines were little more than ceremonial, and they were followed by the stately exit of all persons to clear the stage.

Like Shakespeare, Bertolt Brecht used episodic structure to mirror persons caught up in historical moments and making choices that had moral consequences. Brecht's epic writing, linking contrasting episodes, mirrors a world whose materialism confounds the gullible and the naive. While Brecht used historical events as background to dramatic action, he believed that art had a social function: to show society's ills in such a way as to convince audiences that social change was possible and desirable. Mother Courage, in *Mother Courage and Her Children,* according to Brecht, does not learn from her wrong choices that result in the deaths of her children and her moral and material impoverishment. Nevertheless, audiences learn from observing her choices, her children's fates, and her diminishing circumstances.

Linking episodes end to end gives an expanding shape and sequential order to activities taking place in time and space. It mirrors historical process and provides a venue for the playwright's statement about the meaning of human events for individuals, societies, and kingdoms. Shakespeare's universe is as orderly as Sophocles'. Evil will be uncovered and punished, and innocence, though temporarily tainted, will be restored in reputation even in death.

Like climactic structure, episodic structure displays order in disorder and rationality in chaos. A progression of events mirrors historical moments and comments on the potential progress of humankind in this figurative journey of life called episodic structure.

SITUATIONAL PLAY STRUCTURE

In absurdist plays of the 1950s and recent plays of the contemporary theater, *situation* shapes the action, not plot or character. Situation, presented in a concrete stage image, takes the place of the journey or the quest. The situation in *Waiting for Godot* presents two tramps waiting in a sparse landscape for a person named Godot who never arrives. What they do while they "wait" is the interest and statement of Beckett's text.

The principal absurdist writers of the postwar era—Samuel Beckett, Eugène Ionesco, and Arthur Adamov—shared a deep sense of human isolation and the irremediable nature of the human condition. In their individual views of the world's absurdity, these writers expressed the same futility and pointlessness of human effort, the impossibility of human communication, and the same inevitable failure of hope. The element of *the absurd* that informs the structure of this type of play was defined by Ionesco as "that which has no purpose, or goal, or objective."[4] Absurdist play structure must, therefore, reject logical progression and reveal the irrationality of the human condition. Dramatic conventions of previous epochs reflected an accepted moral order, a world with aims and objectives, an unquestioned belief in religious faith and secular progress. One critic explained the results of the modern loss of an integrated world picture in this way:

> The decline of religious faith, the destruction of the belief in automatic social and biological progress, the discovery of vast areas of irrational and unconscious forces within the human psyche, the loss of control over rational human development in an age of totalitarianism and weapons of mass destruction, have all contributed to the erosion of the basis for a dramatic convention in which the action proceeds within a fixed and self-evident framework of generally accepted values.[5]

To mirror the human predicament as contradictory and absurd, the older play forms were unworkable. They belonged to another age where actions were meaningful, plots clear-cut, characters recognizable, and endings tidy resolutions. In the conventional theater, action always proceeds toward a definable end. Will Oedipus make the discovery? Will Hamlet avenge the murder of his father? Will Hedda Gabler reconcile herself to middle-class life? The interest is on *what* will happen in a known framework of accepted values and a rational view of life.

The problem for absurdist writers was to find a dramatic structure to present a world devoid of clear-cut purpose with infinite possibilities for bitter truths. Situation, then, became the mirror of an unchanging reality with an infinite number of interpretations. Does Godot, so fervently and vainly awaited by Vladimir and Estragon, stand for God? Or, does Godot merely represent the ever elusive tomorrow, humanity's hope that one day something will happen that will render our existence meaningful? The force and poetic power of the play lie precisely in the impossibility of ever reaching a conclusive answer to this question.

The suspense of the absurdist play is: Will the next incident add to our understanding of *what is happening?* Although there may be an increasing number of contradictory and bewildering clues, the final question is never wholly answered. Audiences are compelled to puzzle out the meaning of what they have seen. Of this type of writing, Martin Esslin said, "All they can show is that while the solutions have evaporated the riddle of our existence remains—complex, unfathomable, and paradoxical."[6]

It would be incorrect to imply that situational plays do not have inner patterns. The situation has its own rhythms, which are like the basic rhythms of life: birth to death, day to night, summer to winter, and so on. Although the situation usually remains unchanged at the play's end, these rhythms move in a recurring cycle beginning with a situation that develops (a) increasing tension, (b) leading to some type of explosion, (c) and returning to the original situation. In the first act, *Waiting for Godot* builds toward Lucky's much-vaunted gibberish of

"philosophical wisdom," followed by the disappointing message that Godot will not come that evening. The second act builds through the return of Pozzo and Lucky with their positions of master and slave mysteriously reversed, followed by the message that once again Godot will not appear. Although developed in two parts, Beckett recycles the ending of each act so that, clearly, the situation is unchanged. (Only time has passed, for the ubiquitous tree has grown leaves between the two parts.) Moreover, the characters repeat the same dialogue, in reverse, in the final moments of each part. Estragon (I), Vladimir (II): "Well, shall we go?" Vladimir (I), Estragon (II): "Yes, let's go." Stage directions (I, II): *They do not move.*

Situational structure relates to older conventions only in the sense that it mirrors the writer's world view. Absurdist plays, emerging in Europe following the Second World War, convey a sense of alienation, of people having lost their bearings in an illogical and ridiculous world. Divorced from a rational universe mirrored in the ordered structure of climactic and episodic plays, situational structure also conveys a patterned meaning: the paradox and irrationality of the human condition.

REFLEXIVE STRUCTURE

The playwright's view of a postmodern world in the 1980s required new critical terms to describe the subversion of familiar staging and writing conventions. Borrowing their discontents from Samuel Beckett who wrote in *Endgame*, "…you're on earth, there's no cure for that," the postmoderns have substituted narrative for dialogue, signs for characters, performance for action, and fragments for plot. In a dramatic text bereft of such familiar signposts as plot, action, character, and dialogue, we find a proliferation of self-canceling images. In German playwright Heiner Müller's *Hamletmachine*, written for a postindustrial age, we ask ourselves are Hamlet and Ophelia Shakespeare's characters? Or, are these mere images labeled Hamlet and Ophelia? If so, what are we to think? What does it all mean? Are our assumptions about Shakespeare's characters being used to say something about the ego and the self in the postmodern age? Or, is the image not its own reality? Because of the many images and scene fragments, we refer to these plays as having a *reflexive structure*. The critical term comes from English grammar: a reflexive verb or pronoun is identical with its subject. It is at once alike and unlike its referent. An example of a reflexive verb is "She *dresses* herself." While we know that *Hamletmachine* is not Shakespeare's play, we are asked to reflect upon the older play, not to comment upon the past in the present, but as a mode of *self-criticism* and as an avenue of new insight.

In this century of holocaustic annihilation and pandemic disease, writers seek new dramatic forms for "imaging" contemporary history and a postindustrial world. The new structure reduces dramatic form to imagistic fragments enacted in time and space without regard for coherent, linear plot or whole characters. The performance of these texts may require hours or minutes. By "re-imaging" our survival and annihilation in disparate fragments of images, sounds, and narrative, such writers as Heiner Müller and Robert Wilson have devised a new dramatic structure for postmodern times. Their dramatic fragments are like cracked mirrors reflecting broken images of a too rapidly changing reality and the imagined horrors of the ultimate threat to humanity's survival—a nuclear explosion.

The Tragedy of Hamlet Prince of Denmark

WILLIAM SHAKESPEARE

William Shakespeare (1564–1616) was born in Strat-ford-on-Avon where he received a grammar school ed-ucation and married the twenty-six-year-old Anne Hathaway when he was eighteen. They had three chil-dren, Susanna and twins Judith and Hamnet.

Other facts about Shakespeare's life have been es-tablished. By 1587–1588, leaving his family in Strat-ford, he had moved to London where he remained until 1611, except for occasional visits to his Strat-ford home. He appears to have found work almost at once in the London theater as actor and writer. By 1592, he was regarded as a promising playwright; by 1594, he had won the patronage of the Earl of Southampton for two poems, Venus and Adonis *and* The Rape of Lucrece.

By 1594, he had joined James Burbage's theater company, The Lord Chamberlain's Men, as actor and playwright; later, he became a company shareholder and part owner of the Globe and Blackfriars theaters. He wrote over thirty plays for this company, suiting them to the talents of the great tragic actor Richard Burbage and other members of the troupe, including the popular clowns Will Kempe and Robert Armin. Near the end of his life, he retired to Stratford as a well-to-do country gentleman.

Shakespeare wrote sonnets, tragedies, comedies, history plays, and tragicomedies, including some of the greatest plays written in English: Macbeth, King Lear, The Tempest, Othello, *and* Hamlet.

CRITICAL INTRODUCTION TO *HAMLET*

Hamlet was written around 1600, performed in the 1600–1601 season, and published in 1603 as *The Tragicall Historie of Hamlet Prince of Denmarke.* It was the property of the King's Men (formerly the Lord Chamberlain's Men), as the company was renamed with the ascension of King James I to the English throne upon the death of Queen Elizabeth I.

Hamlet is an example of episodic play struc-ture. Several elementary facts account for the structure of this play, in addition to what we said earlier in this chapter about the episodic journey as a structural archetype. *Hamlet* belongs to a well-known type of Elizabethan drama known as the "revenge" play which had its own set of writing conventions. Perfect vengeance for a crime against a close relative required uncom-mon strategies for bringing about the villain's death. The revenge play required a crime, usu-ally a murder, where the vengeance fell upon the next of kin as a pious duty; the discovery of the murder by the avenger; obstacles to revenge; and the triumphant conclusion in which the mur-derer is destroyed and condemned everlastingly to hell. The revenge pattern was usually accom-panied by ghosts, madness, gore, poisonings, and violent (often bizarre) deaths.

Hamlet combines two modes of Elizabethan writing: the episodic journey and the revenge conventions. Shakespeare's play is further com-plicated by two simultaneous journeys in the figure of the hero. One is the progress of Ham-let's intellect and soul as he wrestles with the cruel paradoxes of existence. The second is his journey through successful revenge with delays owing to his ethical and psychological needs to confirm facts and to consider his actions.

On one level, the twin arcs of Hamlet's jour-ney trace his wrestling with the need for re-venge, his becoming an avenger, and the obstacles in his pathway to success. On another level, the hero's inner life, revealed in his solilo-quies, retards the usual revenge journey which is ordinarily mean, violent, and swift. Hamlet discourses on certain troubling matters. His mother, with indecent haste, has married the brother of her late husband. According to canon law, she has, therefore, committed incest ("the incestuous sheets"), for in early Christian doctrine the relatives of a husband and wife were considered "as one flesh." The Polonius family introduces complications of sexual love and filial loyalty into his discourse. And, although the ghost tells Hamlet the story of the murder and demands revenge, Hamlet delays executing revenge to verify the ghost's evidence. According to theological notions of the day, a Christian knew that the appearance of a spirit in the shape of a person recently deceased might be evil and set upon condemning one's soul to perdition.

Hamlet's revenge gains ground as he proves his uncle's guilt. Rosencrantz and Guildenstern tell him about the players and he improvises his mousetrap: "The play's the thing/ Wherein I'll catch the conscience of the King." The trap springs and Claudius reveals his guilt beyond any doubt; thus, Hamlet knows he has been visited by a true ghost, not a devil or figment of his melancholy imagination.

Thus far, Hamlet's journey has moved along the road to confirming Claudius' guilt while exploring the essence of human nature. At this point, Hamlet has one clear opportunity to take his revenge. He discovers Claudius at prayer; they are alone, but the opportunity for vengeance is unsuitable. Revenge demands hellfire for the culprit and Claudius, at prayer, "seems" to be in a state of grace which would cancel out his eternal damnation. So, Hamlet passes into his mother's chamber and there mistakenly kills Polonius.

Now, there are three avengers: Hamlet, Laertes, and Fortinbras. We must remember that Hamlet's cousin, Fortinbras, whose father was killed by Hamlet's own father in a civil war, is also seeking to avenge his parent's untimely death and to regain his own property rights lost in battle. Events now begin to accelerate. To neutralize (and terminate) Hamlet, Claudius sends him away to England with his death warrant

carried by Rosencrantz and Guildenstern. Ophelia goes mad from the weight of her losses (father and lover) and drowns herself. Hamlet unexpectedly returns, having escaped one trap, only to face another: the duel with Laertes.

This time, Ophelia's "maimed funeral rites" delay the final catastrophe. Hamlet and Laertes confront one another over the open grave. But neither avenger has satisfaction. Osric, the fashionable courtier, with his surface manners and fine clothes, is used to lay out the final mousetrap—a duel between Hamlet and Laertes. Now calamity is whole when vengeances are consummated, all the guilty are punished in one bloody ending, and Fortinbras is vindicated as well.

Viewed as a traditional revenge tragedy intersected by the hero's meditations on the quintessence of the human condition, the twin arcs of Hamlet's episodic journey through revenge and self-understanding can be easily traced. However, *Hamlet* is one of the great tragedies of all times, rising above the overly simplistic revenge motif to comment on universal human problems: on fathers and children, on mothers and sons, on love and sex, on loss and grief, on guilt and innocence, on corruption and wholesomeness, on ingratitude and loyalty, on acting and deceit, on anguish and despair, on irony and fate. The great soliloquies, some of Shakespeare's finest writing, interrupt the vengeful journey to explore these universal and timeless issues.

As one of the great figures of Western tragedy, Hamlet has proved to be the most difficult of Shakespeare's heroes to grasp. He is intelligent, witty, sensitive, grief-stricken, angry, disillusioned, contemplative, and violent. He is called upon to redeem a world (an "unweeded garden") for which he feels alienation and disgust. G. Wilson Knight summarized the play as "the story of a 'sweet prince' wrenched from life and dedicated alone to death."[7] It is Hamlet's dedication to death that marks the stages of his progress in this episodic journey of body, mind, and soul from his confrontation with the ghost on the battlements to his death in the dueling chamber.

The Tragedy of Hamlet Prince of Denmark

DRAMATIS PERSONAE

CLAUDIUS   King of Denmark
HAMLET   son to the late, and nephew to the
   present, King
POLONIUS   Lord Chamberlain
HORATIO   friend to Hamlet
LAERTES   son to Polonius
VOLTEMAND ⎫
CORNELIUS ⎪
ROSENCRANTZ ⎬   courtiers
GUILDENSTERN ⎪
OSRIC ⎪
A GENTLEMAN ⎭
A PRIEST
MARCELLUS ⎫   officers
BARNARDO ⎭
FRANCISCO   a soldier
REYNALDO   servant to Polonius
PLAYERS
TWO CLOWNS   gravediggers
FORTINBRAS   Prince of Norway
A NORWEGIAN CAPTAIN
ENGLISH AMBASSADORS
GERTRUDE, QUEEN OF DENMARK   mother to Hamlet
OPHELIA   daughter to Polonius
GHOST of Hamlet's father
LORDS, LADIES, OFFICERS, SOLDIERS, SAILORS,
   MESSENGERS, ATTENDANTS

SCENE:
Elsinore

ACT I

SCENE I

A guard platform of the castle.

Enter BARNARDO *and* FRANCISCO, *two sentinels.*

   BARNARDO
Who's there?

   FRANCISCO
Nay, answer me. Stand and unfold°¹ yourself.
   BARNARDO   5
Long live the King!°
   FRANCISCO
Barnardo?
   BARNARDO
He.   10
   FRANCISCO
You come most carefully upon your hour.
   BARNARDO
'Tis now struck twelve. Get thee to bed, Francisco.
   FRANCISCO   15
For this relief much thanks. 'Tis bitter cold,
And I am sick at heart.
   BARNARDO
Have you had quiet guard?
   FRANCISCO   20
Not a mouse stirring.
   BARNARDO
Well, good night.
If you do meet Horatio and Marcellus,
The rivals° of my watch, bid them make haste.   25

Enter HORATIO *and* MARCELLUS.

   FRANCISCO
I think I hear them. Stand, ho! Who is there?
   HORATIO
Friends to this ground.
   MARCELLUS   30
And liegemen to the Dane.°

---

¹The degree sign (°) indicates a footnote, which is keyed
to the text by the line number. Text references are printed
in **bold** type; the annotation follows in roman type.

I.i. 4 unfold disclose **6 Long live the King** (perhaps a
password, perhaps a greeting) **25 rivals** partners
31 liegemen to the Dane loyal subjects to the King of
Denmark

FRANCISCO
Give you° good night.
MARCELLUS
35 O, farewell, honest soldier.
Who hath relieved you?
FRANCISCO
Barnardo hath my place.
Give you good night. *Exit* **FRANCISCO.**
40   **MARCELLUS**
Holla, Barnardo!
BARNARDO
Say—
What, is Horatio there?
45   **HORATIO**
A piece of him.
BARNARDO
Welcome, Horatio. Welcome, good Marcellus.
MARCELLUS
50 What, has this thing appeared again tonight?
BARNARDO
I have seen nothing.
MARCELLUS
Horatio says 'tis but our fantasy,
55 And will not let belief take hold of him
Touching this dreaded sight twice seen of us;
Therefore I have entreated him along
With us to watch the minutes of this night,
That, if again this apparition come,
60 He may approve° our eyes and speak to it.
HORATIO
Tush, tush, 'twill not appear.
BARNARDO
Sit down awhile,
65 And let us once again assail your ears,
That are so fortified against our story,
What we have two nights seen.
HORATIO
Well, sit we down,
70 And let us hear Barnardo speak of this.
BARNARDO
Last night of all,
When yond same star that's westward from the
pole°
75 Had made his course t' illume that part of heaven
Where now it burns, Marcellus and myself,
The bell then beating one—

Enter **GHOST.**
MARCELLUS
Peace, break thee off. Look where it comes again.
BARNARDO   80
In the same figure like the king that's dead.
MARCELLUS
Thou art a scholar; speak to it, Horatio.
BARNARDO
Looks 'a not like the king? Mark it, Horatio.   85
HORATIO
Most like: it harrows me with fear and wonder.
BARNARDO
It would be spoke to.
MARCELLUS   90
Speak to it, Horatio.
HORATIO
What art thou that usurp'st this time of night,
Together with that fair and warlike form
In which the majesty of buried Denmark°   95
Did sometimes march? By heaven I charge thee,
speak.
MARCELLUS
It is offended.
BARNARDO   100
See, it stalks away.
HORATIO
Stay! Speak, speak. I charge thee, speak.
Exit **GHOST.**
MARCELLUS
'Tis gone and will not answer.   105
BARNARDO
How now, Horatio? You tremble and look pale.
Is not this something more than fantasy?
What think you on't?
HORATIO   110
Before my God, I might not this believe
Without the sensible and true avouch°
Of mine own eyes.
MARCELLUS
Is it not like the King?   115
HORATIO
As thou art to thyself.
Such was the very armor he had on
When he the ambitious Norway° combated:
So frowned he once, when, in an angry parle,°   120

---

33 **Give you** God give you   60 **approve** confirm   74 **pole**
polestar

95 **buried Denmark** the buried King of Denmark   112
sensible and true avouch sensory and true proof   119
Norway King of Norway   120 **parle** parley

He smote the sledded Polacks° on the ice.
'Tis strange.
    MARCELLUS
Thus twice before, and jump° at this dead hour,
125 With martial stalk hath he gone by our watch.
    HORATIO
In what particular thought to work I know not;
But, in the gross and scope° of my opinion,
This bodes some strange eruption to our state.
130   MARCELLUS
Good now, sit down, and tell me he that knows,
Why this same strict and most observant watch
So nightly toils the subject° of the land,
And why such daily cast of brazen cannon
135 And foreign mart° for implements of war,
Why such impress° of shipwrights, whose sore task
Does not divide the Sunday from the week,
What might be toward° that this sweaty haste
140 Doth make the night joint-laborer with the day?
Who is't that can inform me?
    HORATIO
That can I.
At least the whisper goes so: our last king,
145 Whose image even but now appeared to us,
Was, as you know, by Fortinbras of Norway,
Thereto pricked on by a most emulate pride,
Dared to the combat; in which our valiant Hamlet
(For so this side of our known world esteemed
150   him)
Did slay this Fortinbras, who, by a sealed compact
Well ratified by law and heraldry,°
Did forfeit, with his life, all those his lands
Which he stood seized° of, to the conqueror;
155 Against the which a moiety competent°
Was gagèd° by our King, which had returned
To the inheritance of Fortinbras,
Had he been vanquisher, as, by the same comart°
And carriage of the article designed,°
160 His fell to Hamlet. Now, sir, young Fortinbras,
Of unimprovèd° mettle hot and full,

Hath in the skirts° of Norway here and there
Sharked up° a list of lawless resolutes,°
For food and diet, to some enterprise
That hath a stomach in't° which is no other,   165
As it doth well appear unto our state,
But to recover of us by strong hand
And terms compulsatory, those foresaid lands
So by his father lost; and this, I take it,
Is the main motive of our preparations,   170
The source of this our watch, and the chief head°
Of this posthaste and romage° in the land.
    BARNARDO
I think it be no other but e'en so;
Well may it sort° that this portentous figure   175
Comes armèd through our watch so like the King
That was and is the question of these wars.
    HORATIO
A mote it is to trouble the mind's eye:
In the most high and palmy state of Rome,   180
A little ere the mightiest Julius fell,
The graves stood tenantless, and the sheeted dead
Did squeak and gibber in the Roman streets;°
As stars with trains of fire and dews of blood,
Disasters° in the sun; and the moist star,°   185
Upon whose influence Neptune's empire stands,
Was sick almost to doomsday with eclipse.
And even the like precurse° of feared events,
As harbingers° preceding still° the fates
And prologue to the omen° coming on,   190
Have heaven and earth together demonstrated
Unto our climatures° and countrymen.
Enter GHOST.
But soft, behold, lo where it comes again!
I'll cross it,° though it blast me.—Stay, illusion.
It spreads his° arms.
If thou hast any sound or use of voice,   195

121 **sledded Polacks** Poles in sledges   124 **jump** just
128 **gross and scope** general drift   133 **toils the subject**
makes the subjects toil   135 **mart** trading   136 **impress**
forced service   139 **toward** in preparation   152 **law and
heraldry** heraldic law (governing the combat)   154 **seized**
possessed   155 **moiety competent** equal portion   156
gagèd engaged, pledged   158 **comart** agreement   159
carriage of the article designed import of the agreement
drawn up   161 **unimprovèd** untried

162 **skirts** borders   163 **Sharked up** collected indiscrimi-
nately (as a shark gulps its prey)   163 **resolutes** des-
peradoes   165 **hath a stomach in't** i.e., requires courage
171 **head** fountainhead, origin   172 **romage** bustle   175
sort befit   183 **Did squeak…Roman streets** (the break in
the sense which follows this line suggests that a line has
dropped out)   185 **Disasters** threatening signs   185
moist star moon   188 **precurse** precursor, foreshadowing   189 **harbingers** forerunners   189 **still** always   190
omen calamity   192 **climatures** regions   194 **cross it**
(1) cross its path, confront it (2) make the sign of the cross
in front of it s.d. **his** i.e., its, the ghost's (though possibly
what is meant is that Horatio spreads his own arms, making a cross of himself)

Speak to me.
If there be any good thing to be done
That may to thee do ease and grace to me,
Speak to me.
200 If thou art privy to thy country's fate,
Which happily° foreknowing may avoid,
O, speak!
Or if thou hast uphoarded in thy life
Extorted° treasure in the womb of earth,
205 For which, they say, you spirits oft walk in death,
The cock crows.
Speak of it. Stay and speak. Stop it, Marcellus.
        MARCELLUS
Shall I strike at it with my partisan°?
        HORATIO
210 Do, if it will not stand.
        BARNARDO
'Tis here.
        HORATIO
'Tis here.
215   MARCELLUS
'Tis gone.
Exit GHOST.
We do it wrong, being so majestical,
To offer it the show of violence,
For it is as the air, invulnerable,
220 And our vain blows malicious mockery.
        BARNARDO
It was about to speak when the cock crew.
        HORATIO
And then it started, like a guilty thing
225 Upon a fearful summons. I have heard,
The cock, that is the trumpet to the morn,
Doth with his lofty and shrill-sounding throat
Awake the god of day, and at his warning,
Whether in sea or fire, in earth or air,
230 Th' extravagant and erring° spirit hies
To his confine; and of the truth herein
This present object made probation.°
        MARCELLUS
It faded on the crowing of the cock.
235 Some say that ever 'gainst° that season comes
Wherein our Savior's birth is celebrated,
This bird of dawning singeth all night long,
And then, they say, no spirit dare stir abroad,

The nights are wholesome, then no planets strike,°
No fairy takes,° nor witch hath power to charm: 240
So hallowed and so gracious is that time.
        HORATIO
So have I heard and do in part believe it.
But look, the morn in russet mantle clad
Walks o'er the dew of yon high eastward hill.   245
Break we our watch up, and by my advice
Let us impart what we have seen tonight
Unto young Hamlet, for upon my life
This spirit, dumb to us, will speak to him.
Do you consent we shall acquaint him with it,   250
As needful in our loves, fitting our duty?
        MARCELLUS
Let's do't, I pray, and I this morning know
Where we shall find him most convenient.
(*Exeunt.*)

SCENE II

The castle.

Flourish.° Enter CLAUDIUS, KING OF DENMARK, GER-
TRUDE THE QUEEN, COUNCILORS, POLONIUS *and his
son* LAERTES, HAMLET, *cum aliis*° (*including* VOLTE-
MAND *and* CORNELIUS).

        KING
Though yet of Hamlet our dear brother's death
The memory be green, and that it us befitted
To bear our hearts in grief, and our whole
        kingdom   5
To be contracted in one brow of woe,
Yet so far hath discretion fought with nature
That we with wisest sorrow think on him
Together with remembrance of ourselves.
Therefore our sometime sister,° now our Queen,   10
Th' imperial jointress° to this warlike state,
Have we, as 'twere, with a defeated joy,
With an auspicious° and a dropping eye,
With mirth in funeral, and with dirge in marriage,
In equal scale weighing delight and dole,   15
Taken to wife. Nor have we herein barred
Your better wisdoms, which have freely gone.
With this affair along. For all, our thanks.

---

239 **strike** exert an evil influence   240 **takes** bewitches
I.ii. s.d. **Flourish** fanfare of trumpets s.d. **cum aliis** with
others (Latin)   10 **our sometime sister** my (the royal
"we") former sister-in-law   11 **jointress** joint tenant,
partner   13 **auspicious** joyful

---

201 **happily** haply, perhaps   204 **Extorted** ill-won   208
partisan pike (a long-handled weapon)   230 **extravagant and erring** out of bounds and wandering   232 **probation** proof   235 **'gainst** just before

Now follows that you know young Fortinbras,
20 Holding a weak supposal of our worth,
Or thinking by our late dear brother's death
Our state to be disjoint and out of frame,°
Colleaguèd with this dream of his advantage,°
He hath not failed to pester us with message,
25 Importing the surrender of those lands
Lost by his father, with all bands of law,
To our most valiant brother. So much for him.
Now for ourself and for this time of meeting.
Thus much the business is: we have here writ
30 To Norway, uncle of young Fortinbras—
Who, impotent and bedrid, scarcely hears
Of this his nephew's purpose—to suppress
His further gait° herein, in that the levies,
The lists, and full proportions° are all made
35 Out of his subject;° and we here dispatch
You, good Cornelius, and you, Voltemand,
For bearers of this greeting to old Norway,
Giving to you no further personal power
To business with the King, more than the scope
40 Of these delated articles° allow.
Farewell, and let your haste commend your duty.
    CORNELIUS, VOLTEMAND
In that, and all things, will we show our duty.
    KING
45 We doubt it nothing. Heartily farewell.
    Exit VOLTEMAND *and* CORNELIUS.
And now, Laertes, what's the news with you?
You told us of some suit. What is't, Laertes?
You cannot speak of reason to the Dane
And lose your voice.° What wouldst thou beg,
50   Laertes,
That shall not be my offer, not thy asking?
The head is not more native° to the heart,
The hand more instrumental to the mouth,
Than is the throne of Denmark to thy father.
55 What wouldst thou have, Laertes?
    LAERTES
My dread lord,
Your leave and favor to return to France,
From whence, though willingly I came to
60   Denmark
To show my duty in your coronation,

Yet now I must confess, that duty done,
My thoughts and wishes bend again toward
    France
And bow them to your gracious leave and pardon. 65
    KING
Have you your father's leave? What says Polonius?
    POLONIUS
He hath, my lord, wrung from me my slow leave 70
By laborsome petition, and at last
Upon his will I sealed my hard consent.°
I do beseech you give him leave to go.
    KING
Take thy fair hour, Laertes. Time be thine, 75
And thy best graces spend it at thy will.
But now, my cousin° Hamlet, and my son—
    HAMLET
(*Aside*) A little more than kin, and less than kind!°
    KING 80
How is it that the clouds still hang on you?
    HAMLET
Not so, my lord. I am too much in the sun.°
    QUEEN
Good Hamlet, cast thy nighted color off, 85
And let thine eye look like a friend on Denmark.
Do not forever with thy vailèd° lids
Seek for thy noble father in the dust.
Thou knowist 'tis common; all that lives must die,
Passing through nature to eternity. 90
    HAMLET
Ay, madam, it is common.°
    QUEEN
If it be,
Why seems it so particular with thee? 95
    HAMLET
Seems, madam? Nay, it is. I know not "seems."
'Tis not alone my inky cloak, good mother,
Nor customary suits of solemn black,
Nor windy suspiration° of forced breath, 100
No, nor the fruitful river in the eye,
Nor the dejected havior of the visage,
Together with all forms, moods, shapes of grief,

72 **Upon his...hard consent** to his desire I gave my reluctant consent 77 **cousin** kinsman 79 **kind** (pun on the meanings "kindly" and "natural"; though doubly related—**more than kin**—Hamlet asserts that he neither resembles Claudius in nature or feels kindly toward him) 83 **sun** sunshine of royal favor (with a pun on "son") 87 **vailèd** lowered 92 **common** (1) universal (2) vulgar 100 **windy suspiration** heavy sighing

22 **frame** order 23 **advantage** superiority 33 **gait** proceeding 34 **proportions** supplies for war 35 **Out of his subject** i.e., out of old Norway's subjects and realm 40 **delated articles** detailed documents 49 **lose your voice** waste your breath 52 **native** related

That can denote me truly. These indeed seem,
105 For they are actions that a man might play,
But I have that within which passes show;
These but the trappings and the suits of woe.
          KING
'Tis sweet and commendable in your nature,
110   Hamlet,
To give these mourning duties to your father,
But you must know your father lost a father,
That father lost, lost his, and the survivor bound
In filial obligation for some term
115 To do obsequious° sorrow. But to persever
In obstinate condolement° is a course
Of impious stubbornness. 'Tis unmanly grief.
It shows a will most incorrect to heaven,
A heart unfortified, a mind impatient,
120 An understanding simple and unschooled.
For what we know must be and is as common
As any the most vulgar° thing to sense,
Why should we in our peevish opposition
Take it to heart? Fie, 'tis a fault to heaven,
125 A fault against the dead, a fault to nature,
To reason most absurd, whose common theme
Is death of fathers, and who still hath cried,
From the first corse° till he that died today,
"This must be so." We pray you throw to earth
130 This unprevailing° woe, and think of us
As of a father, for let the world take note
You are the most immediate to our throne,
And with no less nobility of love
Than that which dearest father bears his son
135 Do I impart toward you. For your intent
In going back to school in Wittenberg,
It is most retrograde° to our desire,
And we beseech you, bend you° to remain
Here in the cheer and comfort of our eye,
140 Our chiefest courtier, cousin, and our son.
          QUEEN
Let not thy mother lose her prayers, Hamlet.
I pray thee stay with us, go not to Wittenberg.
          HAMLET
145 I shall in all my best obey you, madam.
          KING
Why, 'tis a loving and a fair reply.
Be as ourself in Denmark. Madam, come.

This gentle and unforced accord of Hamlet
Sits smiling to my heart, in grace whereof   150
No jocund health that Denmark drinks today,
But the great cannon to the clouds shall tell,
And the King's rouse° the heaven shall bruit°
      again,
Respeaking earthly thunder. Come away.   155
Flourish. Exeunt all but HAMLET.
          HAMLET
O that this too too sullied° flesh would melt,
Thaw, and resolve itself into a dew,
Or that the Everlasting had not fixed
His canon° 'gainst self-slaughter. O God, God,   160
How weary, stale, flat, and unprofitable
Seem to me all the uses of this world!
Fie on't, ah, fie, 'tis an unweeded garden
That grows to seed. Things rank and gross in
      nature   165
Possess it merely.° That it should come to this:
But two months dead, nay, not so much, not two,
So excellent a king, that was to this
Hyperion° to a satyr, so loving to my mother
That he might not beteem° the winds of heaven   170
Visit her face too roughly. Heaven and earth,
Must I remember? Why, she would hang on him
As if increase of appetite had grown
By what it fed on; and yet within a month—
Let me not think on't; frailty, thy name is   175
      woman—
A little month, or ere those shoes were old
With which she followed my poor father's body
Like Niobe,° all tears, why she, even she—
O God, a beast that wants discourse of reason°   180
Would have mourned longer—married with my
      uncle,
My father's brother, but no more like my father
Than I to Hercules. Within a month,
Ere yet the salt of most unrighteous tears   185
Had left the flushing° in her gallèd eyes,

---

115 **obsequious** suitable to obsequies (funerals) 116
condolement mourning 122 **vulgar** common 128
corse corpse 130 **unprevailing** unavailing 137 **retro-**
grade contrary 138 **bend you** incline

153 **rouse** deep drink 153 **bruit** announce noisily 157
sullied (Q2 has **sallied,** here modernized to **sullied,**
which makes sense and is therefore given; but the Folio
reading, **solid,** which fits better with **melt,** is quite possibly correct) 160 **canon** law 166 **merely** entirely 169
Hyperion the sun god, a model of beauty 170 **beteem**
allow 179 **Niobe** (a mother who wept profusely at the
death of her children) 180 **wants discourse of reason**
lacks reasoning power 186 **left the flushing** stopped
reddening

She married. O, most wicked speed, to post°
With such dexterity to incestuous° sheets!
It is not, nor it cannot come to good.
190　But break my heart, for I must hold my tongue.
Enter HORATIO, MARCELLUS, *and* BARNARDO.
　　HORATIO
Hail to your lordship!
　　HAMLET
I am glad to see you well.
195　Horatio—or I do forget myself.
　　HORATIO
The same, my lord, and your poor servant ever.
　　HAMLET
Sir, my good friend, I'll change° that name
200　with you.
And what make you from Wittenberg, Horatio?
Marcellus.
　　MARCELLUS
My good lord!
205　　HAMLET
I am very glad to see you. (*To* BARNARDO)
Good even, sir.
But what, in faith, make you from Wittenberg?
　　HORATIO
210　A truant disposition, good my lord.
　　HAMLET
I would not hear your enemy say so,
Nor shall you do my ear that violence
To make it truster° of your own report
215　Against yourself. I know you are no truant.
But what is your affair in Elsinore?
We'll teach you to drink deep ere you depart.
　　HORATIO
My lord, I came to see your father's funeral.
220　　HAMLET
I prithee do not mock me, fellow student.
I think it was to see my mother's wedding.
　　HORATIO
Indeed, my lord, it followed hard upon.
225　　HAMLET
Thrift, thrift, Horatio. The funeral baked meats
Did coldly furnish forth the marriage tables.
Would I had met my dearest° foe in heaven

Or ever I had seen that day, Horatio!
My father, methinks I see my father.　　230
　　HORATIO
Where, my lord?
　　HAMLET
In my mind's eye, Horatio.
　　HORATIO　　235
I saw him once. 'A° was a goodly king.
　　HAMLET
'A was a man, take him for all in all,
I shall not look upon his like again.
　　HORATIO　　240
My lord, I think I saw him yesternight.
　　HAMLET
Saw? Who?
　　HORATIO
My lord, the King your father.　　245
　　HAMLET
The King my father?
　　HORATIO
Season your admiration° for a while
With an attent ear till I may deliver　　250
Upon the witness of these gentlemen
This marvel to you.
　　HAMLET
For God's love let me hear!
　　HORATIO　　255
Two nights together had these gentlemen,
Marcellus and Barnardo, on their watch
In the dead waste and middle of the night
Been thus encountered. A figure like your father,
Armèd at point exactly, cap-a-pe,°　　260
Appears before them, and with solemn march
Goes slow and stately by them. Thrice he walked
By their oppressed and fear-surprisèd eyes,
Within his truncheon's length,° whilst they,
　　distilled°　　265
Almost to jelly with the act° of fear,
Stand dumb and speak not to him. This to me
In dreadful° secrecy impart they did,
And I with them the third night kept the watch,
Where, as they had delivered, both in time,　　270
Form of the thing, each word made true and good,

---

187 **post** hasten　188 **incestuous** (canon law considered marriage with a deceased brother's widow to be incestuous)　199 **change** exchange　214 **truster** believer　228 **dearest** most intensely felt

236 **'A** he　249 **Season your admiration** control your wonder　260 **cap-a-pe** head to foot　264 **truncheon's length** space of a short staff　265 **distilled** reduced　266 **act** action　268 **dreadful** terrified

The apparition comes. I knew your father.
These hands are not more like.
   HAMLET
275 But where was this?
   MARCELLUS
My lord, upon the platform where we watched.
   HAMLET
Did you not speak to it?
280 HORATIO
My lord, I did;
But answer made it none. Yet once methought
It lifted up it° head and did address
Itself to motion like as it would speak:
285 But even then the morning cock crew loud,
And at the sound it shrunk in haste away
And vanished from our sight.
   HAMLET
'Tis very strange.
290 HORATIO
As I do live, my honored lord, 'tis true,
And we did think it writ down in our duty
To let you know of it.
   HAMLET
295 Indeed, indeed, sirs, but this troubles me.
Hold you the watch tonight?
   ALL
We do, my lord.
   HAMLET
300 Armed, say you?
   ALL
Armed, my lord.
   HAMLET
From top to toe?
305 ALL
My lord, from head to foot.
   HAMLET
Then saw you not his face.
   HORATIO
310 O, yes, my lord. He wore his beaver° up.
   HAMLET
What, looked he frowningly?
   HORATIO
315 A countenance more in sorrow than in anger.
   HAMLET
Pale or red?
   HORATIO
Nay, very pale.

   HAMLET
And fixed his eyes upon you?   320
   HORATIO
Most constantly.
   HAMLET
I would I had been there.
   HORATIO   325
It would have much amazed you.
   HAMLET
Very like, very like. Stayed it long?
   HORATIO
While one with moderate haste might tell° a 330
 hundred.
   BOTH
Longer, longer.
   HORATIO
Not when I saw't.   335
   HAMLET
His beard was grizzled,° no?
   HORATIO
It was as I have seen it in his life,
A sable silvered.°   340
   HAMLET
I will watch tonight.
Perchance 'twill walk again.
   HORATIO
I warr'nt it will.   345
   HAMLET
If it assume my noble father's person,
I'll speak to it though hell itself should gape
And bid me hold my peace. I pray you all,
If you have hitherto concealed this sight,   350
Let it be tenable° in your silence still,
And whatsomever else shall hap tonight,
Give it an understanding but no tongue;
I will requite your loves. So fare you well.
Upon the platform 'twixt eleven and twelve 355
I'll visit you.
   ALL
Our duty to your honor.
   HAMLET
Your loves, as mine to you. Farewell.   360
Exeunt (all but HAMLET).
My father's spirit—in arms? All is not well.
I doubt° some foul play. Would the night were
 come!

---

283 **it** its 310 **beaver** visor, face guard

330 **tell** count 337 **grizzled** gray 340 **sable silvered**
black mingled with white 351 **tenable** held 362 **doubt**
suspect

Till then sit still, my soul. Foul deeds will rise,
365 Though all the earth o'erwhelm them, to men's
        eyes.
Exit.

SCENE III

A room.

Enter LAERTES *and* OPHELIA, *his sister.*

LAERTES
My necessaries are embarked. Farewell.
And, sister, as the winds give benefit
And convoy° is assistant, do not sleep,
5 But let me hear from you.
    OPHELIA
Do you doubt that?
    LAERTES
For Hamlet, and the trifling of his favor,
10 Hold it a fashion and a toy° in blood,
A violet in the youth of primy° nature,
Forward,° not permanent, sweet, not lasting,
The perfume and suppliance° of a minute,
No more.
15   OPHELIA
No more but so?
    LAERTES
Think it no more.
For nature crescent° does not grow alone
20 In thews° and bulk, but as this temple° waxes,
The inward service of the mind and soul
Grows wide withal. Perhaps he loves you now,
And now no soil nor cautel° doth besmirch
The virtue of his will; but you must fear,
25 His greatness weighed,° his will is not his own.
For he himself is subject to his birth.
He may not, as unvalued° persons do,
Carve for himself; for on his choice depends
The safety and health of this whole state;
30 And therefore must his choice be circumscribed
Unto the voice and yielding of that body
Whereof he is the head. Then if he says he loves
        you,

It fits your wisdom so far to believe it
As he in his particular act and place   35
May give his saying deed, which is no further
Than the main voice of Denmark goes withal.
Then weigh what loss your honor may sustain
If with too credent° ear you list his songs,
Or lose your heart, or your chaste treasure open   40
To his unmastered importunity.
Fear it, Ophelia, fear it, my dear sister,
And keep you in the rear of your affection,
Out of the shot and danger of desire.
The chariest maid is prodigal enough   45
If she unmask her beauty to the moon.
Virtue itself scapes not calumnious strokes.
The canker° galls the infants of the spring
Too oft before their buttons° be disclosed,
And in the morn and liquid dew of youth   50
Contagious blastments are most imminent.
Be wary then; best safety lies in fear;
Youth to itself rebels, though none else near.
    OPHELIA
I shall the effect of this good lesson keep   55
As watchman to my heart, but, good my brother,
Do not, as some ungracious° pastors do,
Show me the steep and thorny way to heaven,
Whiles, like a puffed and reckless libertine,
Himself the primrose path of dalliance treads   60
And recks not his own rede.°
Enter POLONIUS.
    LAERTES
O, fear me not.
I stay too long. But here my father comes.
A double blessing is a double grace;   65
Occasion smiles upon a second leave.
    POLONIUS
Yet here, Laertes? Aboard, aboard, for shame!
The wind sits in the shoulder of your sail,
And you are stayed for. There—my blessing with   70
        thee,
And these few precepts in thy memory
Look thou character.° Give thy thoughts no tongue,
Nor any unproportioned° thought his act.   75
Be thou familiar, but by no means vulgar.
Those friends thou hast, and their adoption tried,

I.iii. 4 **convoy** conveyance   10 **toy** idle fancy   11 **primy**
springlike   12 **Forward** premature   13 **suppliance** di-
version   19 **crescent** growing   20 **thews** muscles and sinews   20 **temple** i.e., the body   23 **cautel** deceit   25
greatness weighed high rank considered   27 **unvalued**
of low rank

39 **credent** credulous   48 **canker** cankerworm   49 **buttons** buds   57 **ungracious** lacking grace   61 **recks not
his own rede** does not heed his own advice   73 **character** inscribe   75 **unproportioned** unbalanced

Grapple them unto thy soul with hoops of steel,
But do not dull thy palm with entertainment
80 Of each new-hatched, unfledged courage.° Beware
Of entrance to a quarrel; but being in,
Bear't that th' opposèd may beware of thee.
Give every man thine ear, but few thy voice;
Take each man's censure,° but reserve thy
85   judgment.
Costly thy habit as thy purse can buy,
But not expressed in fancy; rich, not gaudy,
For the apparel oft proclaims the man,
And they in France of the best rank and station
90 Are of a most select and generous, chief in that.°
Neither a borrower nor a lender be,
For loan oft loses both itself and friend,
And borrowing dulleth edge of husbandry.°
This above all, to thine own self be true,
95 And it must follow, as the night the day,
Thou canst not then be false to any man.
Farewell. My blessing season this° in thee!
     LAERTES
Most humbly do I take my leave, my lord.
100   POLONIUS
The time invites you. Go, your servants tend.°
     LAERTES
Farewell, Ophelia, and remember well
What I have said to you.
105   OPHELIA
'Tis in my memory locked,
And you yourself shall keep the key of it.
     LAERTES
Farewell.
     Exit LAERTES.
110   POLONIUS
What is't, Ophelia, he hath said to you?
     OPHELIA
So please you, something touching the Lord
     Hamlet.
115   POLONIUS
Marry,° well bethought.
'Tis told me he hath very oft of late
Given private time to you, and you yourself

Have of your audience been most free and
     bounteous.   120
If it be so—as so 'tis put on me,
And that in way of caution—I must tell you
You do not understand yourself so clearly
As it behooves my daughter and your honor.
What is between you? Give me up the truth.   125
     OPHELIA
He hath, my lord, of late made many tenders°
Of his affection to me.
     POLONIUS
Affection pooh! You speak like a green girl,   130
Unsifted° in such perilous circumstance.
Do you believe his tenders, as you call them?
     OPHELIA
I do not know, my lord, what I should think.
     POLONIUS   135
Marry, I will teach you. Think yourself a baby
That you have ta'en these tenders for true pay
Which are not sterling. Tender yourself more
     dearly,
Or (not to crack the wind of the poor phrase)   140
Tend'ring it thus you'll tender me a fool.°
     OPHELIA
My lord, he hath importuned me with love
In honorable fashion.
     POLONIUS   145
Ay, fashion you may call it. Go to, go to.
     OPHELIA
And hath given countenance to his speech, my
     lord,
With almost all the holy vows of heaven.   150
     POLONIUS
Ay, springes to catch woodcocks.° I do know,
When the blood burns, how prodigal the soul
Lends the tongue vows. These blazes, daughter,
Giving more light than heat, extinct in both,   155
Even in their promise, as it is a-making,
You must not take for fire. From this time
Be something scanter of your maiden presence.
Set your entreatments° at a higher rate
Than a command to parley. For Lord Hamlet,   160

80 **courage** gallant youth 84 **censure** opinion 90 **Are of…in that** show their fine taste and their gentlemanly instincts more in that than in any other point of manners (Kittredge) 93 **husbandry** thrift 97 **season this** make fruitful this (advice) 101 **tend** attend 116 **Marry** (a light oath, from "By the Virgin Mary")

127 **tenders** offers (in line 132 it has the same meaning, but in line 137 Polonius speaks of **tenders** in the sense of counters or chips: in line 141 **Tend'ring** means "holding," and tender means "give," "present") 131 **Unsifted** untried 141 **tender me a fool** (1) present me with a fool (2) present me with a baby 152 **springes to catch woodcocks** snares to catch stupid birds 159 **entreatments** interviews

Believe so much in him that he is young,
And with a larger tether may he walk
Than may be given you. In few, Ophelia,
Do not believe his vows, for they are brokers,°
165 Not of that dye° which their investments° show,
But mere implorators° of unholy suits,
Breathing like sanctified and pious bonds,°
The better to beguile. This is for all:
I would not, in plain terms, from this time forth
170 Have you so slander° any moment leisure
As to give words or talk with the Lord Hamlet.
Look to't, I charge you. Come your ways.

    OPHELIA
I shall obey, my lord. (*Exeunt.*)

SCENE IV

A guard platform.

Enter HAMLET, HORATIO, *and* MARCELLUS.

    HAMLET
The air bites shrewdly;° it is very cold.
    HORATIO
It is a nipping and an eager° air.
5   HAMLET
What hour now?
    HORATIO
I think it lacks of twelve.
    MARCELLUS
10 No, it is struck.
    HORATIO
Indeed? I heard it not. It then draws near the season
Wherein the spirit held his wont to walk.
A flourish of trumpets, and two pieces go off.
15 What does this mean, my lord?
    HAMLET
The King doth wake° tonight and takes his rouse,°
Keeps wassail, and the swagg'ring upspring°
    reels,
20 And as he drains his draughts of Rhenish° down
The kettledrum and trumpet thus bray out
The triumph of his pledge.°

    HORATIO
Is it a custom?
    HAMLET   25
Ay, marry, is't,
But to my mind, though I am native here
And to the manner born, it is a custom
More honored in the breach than the observance.
This heavy-headed revel east and west   30
Makes us traduced and taxed of° other nations.
They clepe° us drunkards and with swinish phrase
Soil our addition,° and indeed it takes
From our achievements, though performed at   35
    height,
The pith and marrow of our attribute.°
So oft it chances in particular men
That for some vicious mole° of nature in them,
As in their birth, wherein they are not guilty,   40
(Since nature cannot choose his origin)
By the o'ergrowth of some complexion,°
Oft breaking down the pales° and forts of reason,
Or by some habit that too much o'erleavens°
The form of plausive° manners, that (these men,   45
Carrying, I say, the stamp of one defect,
Being nature's livery, or fortune's star°)
Their virtues else, be they as pure as grace,
As infinite as man may undergo,
Shall in the general censure° take corruption   50
From that particular fault. The dram of evil
Doth all the noble substance of a doubt,
To his own scandal.°
Enter GHOST.
    HORATIO
Look, my lord, it comes.   55
    HAMLET
Angels and ministers of grace defend us!
Be thou a spirit of health° or goblin damned,
Bring with thee airs from heaven or blasts from
    hell,
Be thy intents wicked or charitable,   60

---

164 **brokers** procurers   165 **dye** i.e., kind   165 **invest-ments** garments   166 **implorators** solicitors   167 **bonds** pledges   170 **slander** disgrace   **I.iv.** 2 **shrewdly** bitterly 4 **eager** sharp   17 **wake** hold a revel by night   17 **takes his rouse** carouses   18 **upspring** (a dance)   20 **Rhenish** Rhine wine   22 **The triumph of his pledge** the achieve-ment (of drinking a wine cup in one draught) of his toast

31 **taxed of** blamed by   32 **clepe** call   34 **addition** repu-tation (literally, "title of honor")   37 **attribute** reputation 39 **mole** blemish   42 **complexion** natural disposition 43 **pales** enclosures   44 **o'er-leavens** mixes with, cor-rupts   45 **plausive** pleasing   47 **nature's livery, or for-tune's star** nature's equipment (i.e., "innate"), or a person's destiny determined by the stars   50 **general censure** pop-ular judgment   51–53 **The dram…own scandal** (though the drift is clear, there is no agreement as to the exact meaning of these lines)   58 **spirit of health** good spirit

Thou com'st in such a questionable° shape
That I will speak to thee. I'll call these Hamlet,
King, father, royal Dane. O, answer me!
65 Let me not burst in ignorance, but tell
Why thy canonized° bones, hearsèd in death,
Have burst their cerements,° why the sepulcher
Wherein we saw thee quietly interred
Hath oped his ponderous and marble jaws
70 To cast thee up again. What may this mean
That thou, dead corse, again in complete steel,
Revisits thus the glimpses of the moon,
Making night hideous, and we fools of nature
So horridly to shake our disposition°
75 With thoughts beyond the reaches of our souls?
Say, why is this? Wherefore? What should we do?
GHOST *beckons* HAMLET.
    HORATIO
It beckons you to go away with it,
As if it some impartment° did desire
80 To you alone.
    MARCELLUS
Look with what courteous action
It waves you to a more removèd ground.
But do not go with it.
85   HORATIO
No, by no means.
    HAMLET
It will not speak. Then I will follow it.
    HORATIO
90 Do not, my lord.
    HAMLET
Why, what should be the fear?
I do not set my life at a pin's fee,
And for my soul, what can it do to that,
95 Being a thing immortal as itself?
It waves me forth again. I'll follow it.
    HORATIO
What if it tempt you toward the flood, my lord,
Or to the dreadful summit of the cliff
100 That beetles° o'er his base into the sea,
And there assume some other horrible form,
Which might deprive your sovereignty of reason°
And draw you into madness? Think of it.

The very place puts toys° of desperation,
Without more motive, into every brain   105
That looks so many fathoms to the sea
And hears it roar beneath.
    HAMLET
It waves me still.
Go on; I'll follow thee.   110
    MARCELLUS
You shall not go, my lord.
    HAMLET
Hold off your hands.
    HORATIO   115
Be ruled. You shall not go.
    HAMLET
My fate cries out
And makes each petty artere° in this body
As hardy as the Nemean lion's nerve.°   120
Still am I called! Unhand me, gentlemen.
By heaven, I'll make a ghost of him that lets° me!
I say, away! Go on. I'll follow thee.
Exit GHOST, *and* HAMLET.
    HORATIO
He waxes desperate with imagination.   125
    MARCELLUS
Let's follow. 'Tis not fit thus to obey him.
    HORATIO
Have after! To what issue will this come?
    MARCELLUS   130
Something is rotten in the state of Denmark.
    HORATIO
Heaven will direct it.
    MARCELLUS
Nay, let's follow him. (*Exeunt.*)   135

SCENE V

The battlements.

Enter GHOST, *and* HAMLET

    HAMLET
Whither wilt thou lead me?
Speak; I'll go no further.
    GHOST
Mark me.   5
    HAMLET
I will.

---

62 **questionable** (1) capable of discourse (2) dubious   66
canonized buried according to the canon or ordinance of
the church   67 **cerements** waxed linen shroud   74 **shake
our disposition** disturb us   79 **impartment** communication   100 **beetles** juts out   102 **deprive your sovereignty
of reason** destroy the sovereignty of your reason

104 **toys** whims, fancies 119 **artere** artery 120 **Nemean
lion's nerve** sinews of the mythical lion slain by Hercules
122 **lets** hinders

GHOST

My hour is almost come,

10 When I to sulf'rous and tormenting flames

Must render up myself.

HAMLET

Alas, poor ghost.

GHOST

15 Pity me not, but lend thy serious hearing

To what I shall unfold.

HAMLET

Speak. I am bound to hear.

GHOST

20 So art thou to revenge, when thou shalt hear.

HAMLET

What?

GHOST

I am thy father's spirit,

25 Doomed for a certain term to walk the night,

And for the day confined to fast in fires,

Till the foul crimes° done in my days of nature

Are burnt and purged away. But that I am forbid

To tell the secrets of my prison house,

30 I could a tale unfold whose lightest word

Would harrow up thy soul, freeze thy young
blood,

Make thy two eyes like stars start from their
spheres,°

35 Thy knotted and combinèd locks to part,

And each particular hair to stand an end

Like quills upon the fearful porpentine.°

But this eternal blazon° must not be

To ears of flesh and blood. List, list, O, list!

40 If thou didst ever thy dear father love—

HAMLET

O God!

GHOST

45 Revenge his foul and most unnatural murder.

HAMLET

Murder?

GHOST

Murder most foul, as in the best it is,

But this most foul, strange, and unnatural.

50 HAMLET

Haste me to know't, that I, with wings as swift

As meditation° or the thoughts of love,

May sweep to my revenge.

GHOST

I find thee apt,   55

And duller shouldst thou be than the fat weed

That roots itself in ease on Lethe wharf,°

Wouldst thou not stir in this. Now, Hamlet, hear.

'Tis given out that, sleeping in my orchard,

A serpent stung me. So the whole ear of Denmark 60

Is by a forgèd process° of my death

Rankly abused. But know, thou noble youth,

The serpent that did sting thy father's life

Now wears his crown.

HAMLET   65

O my prophetic soul!

My uncle?

GHOST

Ay, that incestuous, that adulterate° beast,

With witchcraft of his wits, with traitorous gifts— 70

O wicked wit and gifts, that have the power

So to seduce!—won to his shameful lust

The will of my most seeming-virtuous queen.

O Hamlet, what a failing-off was there,

From me, whose love was of that dignity   75

That it went hand in hand even with the vow

I made to her in marriage, and to decline

Upon a wretch whose natural gifts were poor

To those of mine.

But virtue, as it never will be moved,   80

Though lewdness° court it in a shape of heaven,

So lust, though to a radiant angel linked,

Will sate itself in a celestial bed

And prey on garbage.

But soft, methinks I scent the morning air;   85

Brief let me be. Sleeping within my orchard,

My custom always of the afternoon,

Upon my secure° hour thy uncle stole

With juice of cursed hebona° in a vial,

And in the porches of my ears did pour   90

The leperous distillment, whose effect

Holds such an enmity with blood of man

That swift as quicksilver it courses through

The natural gates and alleys of the body,

And with a sudden vigor it doth posset°   95

I.v. 27 **crimes** sins   34 **spheres** (in Ptolemaic astronomy, each planet was fixed in a hollow transparent shell concentric with the earth)   37 **fearful porpentine** timid porcupine   38 **eternal blazon** revelation of eternity

52 **meditation** thought   57 **Lethe wharf** bank of the river of forgetfulness in Hades   61 **forgèd process** false account   69 **adulterate** adulterous   81 **lewdness** lust   88 **secure** unsuspecting   89 **hebona** a poisonous plant   95 **posset** curdle

And curd, like eager° droppings into milk,
The thin and wholesome blood. So did it mine,
And a most instant tetter° barked about
Most lazarlike° with vile and loathsome crust
100 All my smooth body.
     Thus was I, sleeping, by a brother's hand
Of life, of crown, of queen at once dispatched,
Cut off even in the blossoms of my sin,
Unhouseled, disappointed, unaneled,°
105 No reck'ning made, but sent to my account
With all my imperfections on my head.
O, horrible! O, horrible! Most horrible!
If thou hast nature in thee, bear it not.
Let not the royal bed of Denmark be
110 A couch for luxury° and damnèd incest.
But howsomever thou pursues this act,
Taint not thy mind, nor let thy soul contrive
Against thy mother aught. Leave her to heaven
And to those thorns that in her bosom lodge
115 To prick and sting her. Fare thee well at once.
The glowworm shows the matin° to be near
And 'gins to pale his uneffectual fire.
Adieu, adieu, adieu. Remember me. (*Exit.*)
    HAMLET
120 O all you host of heaven! O earth! What else?
And shall I couple hell? O fie! Hold, hold, my heart,
And you, my sinews, grow not instant old,
But bear me stiffly up. Remember thee?
125 Ay, thou poor ghost, whiles memory holds a seat
In this distracted globe.° Remember thee?
Yea, from the table° of my memory
I'll wipe away all trivial fond° records,
All saws° of books, all forms, all pressures° past
130 That youth and observation copied there,
And thy commandment all alone shall live
Within the book and volume of my brain,
Unmixed with baser matter. Yes, by heaven!
O most pernicious woman!
135 O villain, villain, smiling, damnèd villain!
My tables—meet it is I set it down
That one may smile, and smile, and be a villain.
At least I am sure it may be so in Denmark.
    (*Writes.*)

---

96 **eager** acid 98 **tatter** scab 99 **lazarlike** leperlike
104 **Unhouseled, disappointed, unaneled** without the
sacrament of communion, unabsolved, without extreme
unction 110 **luxury** lust 116 **matin** morning 126 **globe**
i.e., his head 127 **table** tablet, notebook 128 **fond** foolish 129 **saws** maxims 129 **pressures** impressions

So, uncle, there you are. Now to my word:
It is "Adieu, adieu, remember me."   140
I have sworn't.
    HORATIO *and* MARCELLUS
(*Within*) My lord, my lord!
Enter HORATIO *and* MARCELLUS.
    MARCELLUS
Lord Hamlet!   145
    HORATIO
Heavens secure him!
    HAMLET
So be it!
    MARCELLUS   150
Illo, ho, ho,° my lord!
    HAMLET
Hillo, ho, ho, boy! Come, bird, come.
    MARCELLUS
How is't, my noble lord?   155
    HORATIO
What news, my lord?
    HAMLET
O, wonderful!
    HORATIO   160
Good my lord, tell it.
    HAMLET
No, you will reveal it.
    HORATIO
Not I, my lord, by heaven.   165
    MARCELLUS
Nor I, my lord.
    HAMLET
How say you then? Would heart of man once
    think it?   170
But you'll be secret?
    BOTH
Ay, by heaven, my lord.
    HAMLET
There's never a villain dwelling in all Denmark   175
But he's an arrant knave.
    HORATIO
There needs no ghost, my lord, come from the
    grave
To tell us this.   180
    HAMLET
Why, right, you are in the right;
And so, without more circumstance° at all,

---

151 **Illo, ho, ho** (falconer's call to his hawk) 183 **circumstance** details

I hold it fit that we shake hands and part:
185 You, as your business and desire shall point you,
For every man hath business and desire
Such as it is, and for my own poor part,
Look you, I'll go pray.

HORATIO
190 These are but wild and whirling words, my lord.

HAMLET
I am sorry they offend you, heartily;
Yes, faith, heartily;

HORATIO
195 There's no offense, my lord.

HAMLET
Yes, by Saint Patrick, but there is, Horatio,
And much offense too. Touching this vision here,
It is an honest ghost,° that let me tell you.
For your desire to know what is between us,
200 O'ermaster't as you may. And now, good friends,
As you are friends, scholars, and soldiers,
Give me one poor request.

HORATIO
205 What is't, my lord? We will.

HAMLET
Never make known what you have seen tonight.

BOTH
My lord, we will not.

210 HAMLET
Nay, but swear't.

HORATIO
In faith,
My lord, not I.

215 MARCELLUS
Nor I, my lord—in faith.

HAMLET
Upon my sword.

MARCELLUS
220 We have sworn, my lord, already.

HAMLET
Indeed, upon my sword, indeed.

GHOST cries under the stage.

GHOST
Swear.

225 HAMLET
Ha, ha, boy, sayist thou so? Art thou there,
truepenny?°
Come on. You hear this fellow in the cellarage.
Consent to swear.

HORATIO   230
Propose the oath, my lord.

HAMLET
Never to speak of this that you have seen.
Swear by my sword.

GHOST   235
(Beneath) Swear.

HAMLET
Hic et ubique?° then we'll shift our ground;
Come hither, gentlemen,
And lay your hands again upon my sword.   240
Never to speak of this that you have heard.
Swear by my sword.

GHOST
(Beneath) Swear by his sword.

HAMLET   245
Well said, old mole! Canst work i' th' earth so
fast?
A worthy pioner!° Once more remove, good
friends.

HORATIO   250
O day and night, but this is wondrous strange!

HAMLET
And therefore as a stranger give it welcome
There are more things in heaven and earth,
Horatio,   255
Then are dreamt of in you, philosophy.
But come:
Here as before, never, so help you mercy,
How strange or odd some'er I bear myself
(As I perchance hereafter shall think meet   260
To put an antic disposition° on),
That you, at such times seeing me, never shall
With arms encumb'red° thus, or this headshake,
Or by pronouncing of some doubtful phrase,
As "Well, well, we know," or "We could, and if we 265
would,"
Or "If we list to speak," or "There be, an if they
might,"
Or such ambiguous giving out, to note
That you know aught of me—this do swear,   270
So grace and mercy at your most need help you.

GHOST
(Beneath) Swear. (They swear.)

HAMLET
Rest, rest, perturbed spirit. So, gentlemen,   275

---

198 **honest ghost** i.e., not a demon in his father's shape
227 **truepenny** honest fellow

238 **hic et ubique** here and everywhere (Latin)   248 **pioner** digger of mines   261 **antic dispostion** fantastic behavior   263 **encumb'rd** folded

With all my love I do commend me° to you,
And what so poor a man as Hamlet is
May do t' express his love and friending to you,
God willing, shall not lack. Let us go in together,
280 And still your fingers on your lips, I pray.
The time is out of joint. O cursèd spite,
That ever I was born to set it right!
Nay, come, let's go together. (*Exeunt.*)

ACT II

SCENE I

A room.

Enter old POLONIUS, *with his man* REYNALDO.

POLONIUS
Give him this money and these notes, Reynaldo.
REYNALDO
I will, my lord.
5   POLONIUS
You shall do marvell's° wisely, good Reynaldo,
Before you visit him, to make inquire
Of his behavior.
REYNALDO
10 My lord, I did intend it.
POLONIUS
Marry, well said, very well said. Look you sir,
Inquire me first what Danskers° are in Paris,
And how, and who, what means, and where they
15   keep,°
What company, at what expense; and finding
By this encompassment° and drift of question
That they do know my son, come you more nearer
Than your particular demands° will touch it.
20 Take you as 'twere some distant knowledge of
      him,
As thus, "I know his father and his friends,
And in part him," Do you mark this, Reynaldo?
REYNALDO
25 Ay, very well, my lord.
POLONIUS
"And in part him, but," you may say, "not well,
But if't be he I mean, he's very wild,
30 Addicted so and so." And there put on him

What forgeries° you please; marry, none so rank
As may dishonor him—take heed of that—
But, sir, such wanton, wild, and usual slips
As are companions noted and most known
To youth and liberty.   35
REYNALDO
As gaming, my lord.
POLONIUS
Ay, or drinking, fencing, swearing, quarreling.
Drabbing.° You may go so far.   40
REYNALDO
My lord, that would dishonor him.
POLONIUS
Faith, no, as you may season it in the charge.
You must not put another scandal on him,   45
That he is open to incontinency.°
That's not my meaning. But breathe his faults so
      quaintly°
That they may seem the taints of liberty,
The flash and outbreak of a fiery mind,   50
A savageness in unreclaimèd blood,
Of general assault.°
REYNALDO
But, my good lord—
POLONIUS   55
Wherefore should you do this?
REYNALDO
Ay, my lord,
I would know that.
POLONIUS   60
Marry, sir, here's my drift,
And I believe it is a fetch of warrant.°
You laying these slight sullies on my son
As 'twere a thing a little soiled i' th' working,
Mark you,   65
Your party in converse, him you would sound,
Having ever seen in the prenominate crimes°
The youth you breathe of guilty, be assured
He closes with you in this consequence:°
"Good sir," or so, or "friend," or "gentleman"—   70
According to the phrase or the addition°
Of man and country—

---

31 **forgeries** inventions   40 **Drabbing** wenching   46 **incontinency** habitual licentiousness   48 **quaintly** ingeniously, delicately   52 **Of general assault** common to all men   62 **fetch of warrant** justifiable device   67 **Having …crimes** if he has ever seen in the aforementioned crimes   69 **He closes…this consequence** he falls in with you in this conclusion   71 **addition** title

---

276 **commend me** entrust myself   **II.i.** 6. **marvell's** marvelous(ly)   13 **Danskers** Danes   15 **keep** dwell   17 **encompassment** circling   19 **demands** questions

REYNALDO
Very good, my lord.

75 POLONIUS
And then, sir, does 'a° this—'a does—
What was I about to say? By the mass, I was about
to say something! Where did I leave?

REYNALDO
80 At "closes in the consequence," at "friend
or so," and "gentleman."

POLONIUS
At "closes in the consequence"—Ay, marry!
He closes thus: "I know the gentleman;
85 I saw him yesterday, or t'other day,
Or then, or then, with such or such, and, as you
say,
There was 'a gaming, there o'ertook in's rouse,
There falling out at tennis"; or perchance,
90 "I saw him enter such a house of sale,"
Videlicet,° a brothel, or so forth.
See you now—
Your bait of falsehood take this carp of truth,
And thus do we of wisdom and of reach,°
95 With windlasses° and with assays of bias,°
By indirections find directions out.
So, by my former lecture and advice,
Shall you my son. You have me, have you not?

REYNALDO
100 My lord, I have.

POLONIUS
God bye ye, fare ye well.

REYNALDO
Good my lord.

105 POLONIUS
Observe his inclination in yourself.°

REYNALDO
I shall, my lord.

POLONIUS
110 And let him ply his music.

REYNALDO
Well, my lord.

POLONIUS
Farewell. (*Exit* REYNALDO.)
Enter OPHELIA.
115 How now, Ophelia, what's the matter?

OPHELIA
O my lord, my lord, I have been so affrighted!

POLONIUS
With what, i' th' name of God?

OPHELIA
My lord, as I was sewing in my closet,° 120
Lord Hamlet, with his doublet all unbraced,°
No hat upon his head, his stockings fouled,
Ungartered, and down-gyvèd° to his ankle,
Pale as his shirt, his knees knocking each other, 125
And with a look so piteous in purport,°
As if he had been loosèd out of hell
To speak of horrors—he comes before me.

POLONIUS
Mad for thy love? 130

OPHELIA
My lord, I do not know,
But truly I do fear it.

POLONIUS
What said he? 135

OPHELIA
He took me by the wrist and held me hard;
Then goes he to the length of all his arm,
And with his other hand thus o'er his brow
He falls to such perusal of my face 140
As 'a would draw it. Long stayed he so.
At last, a little shaking of mine arm,
And thrice his head thus waving up and down,
He raised a sigh so piteous and profound
As it did seem to shatter all his bulk 145
And end his being. That done, he lets me go,
And, with his head over his shoulder turned,
He seemed to find his way without his eyes,
For out o' doors he went without their helps,
And to the last bended their light on me. 150

POLONIUS
Come, go with me. I will go seek the King.
This is the very ecstasy° of love,
Whose violent property fordoes° itself
And leads the will to desperate undertakings 155
As oft as any passions under heaven
That does afflict our natures. I am sorry.
What, have you given him any hard words of late?

OPHELIA
No, my good lord; but as you did command, 160

76 'a he   91 Videlicet namely   94 reach far-reaching
awareness(?)   95 windlasses circuitous courses   95 assays of bias indirect attempts (metaphor from bowling;
bias = curved course)   106 in yourself for yourself

121 closet private room   122 doublet all unbraced
jacket entirely unlaced   124 down-gyvèd hanging down
like fetters   126 purport expression   153 ecstasy madness   154 property fordoes quality destroys

I did repel his letters and denied
His access to me.
      POLONIUS
That hath made him mad.
165 I am sorry that with better heed and judgment
I had not quoted° him. I feared he did but trifle
And meant to wrack thee; but beshrew my
      jealousy.°
By heaven, it is as proper° to our age
170 To cast beyond ourselves° in our opinions
As it is common for the younger sort
To lack discretion. Come, go we to the King.
This must be known, which, being kept close,
      might move
175 More grief to hide than hate to utter love.°
Come. (*Exeunt.*)

SCENE II

The castle.

Flourish. Enter KING *and* QUEEN, ROSENCRANTZ, *and*
GUILDENSTERN (*with others*).

      KING
Welcome, dear Rosencrantz and Guildenstern.
Moreover that° we much did long to see you,
The need we have to use you did provoke
5 Our hasty sending. Something have you heard
Of Hamlet's transformation: so call it,
Sith° nor th' exterior nor the inward man
Resembles that it was. What it should be,
More than his father's death, that thus hath put
10   him
So much from th' understanding of himself,
I cannot dream of. I entreat you both
That, being of so° young days brought up with
     him,
15 And sith so neighbored to his youth and havior,°
That you vouchsafe your rest° here in our court
Some little time, so by your companies

To draw him on to pleasures, and to gather
So much as from occasion you may glean,
Whether aught to us unknown afflicts him thus,   20
That opened° lies within our remedy.
      QUEEN
Good gentlemen, he hath much talked of you,
And sure I am, two men there is not living
To whom he more adheres. If it will please you   25
To show us so much gentry° and good will
As to expend your time with us awhile
For the supply and profit of our hope,
Your visitation shall receive such thanks
As fits a king's remembrance.   30
      ROSENCRANTZ
Both your Majesties
Might, by the sovereign power you have of us,
Put your dread pleasures more into command
Than to entreaty.   35
      GUILDENSTERN
But we both obey,
And here give up ourselves in the full bent°
To lay our service freely at your feet,   40
To be commanded.
      KING
Thanks, Rosencrantz and gentle Guildenstern.
      QUEEN
Thanks, Guildenstern and gentle Rosencrantz.
And I beseech you instantly to visit   45
My too much changèd son. Go, some of you,
And bring these gentlemen where Hamlet is.
      GUILDENSTERN
Heavens make our presence and our practices
Pleasant and helpful to him!   50
      QUEEN
Ay, amen!
Exeunt ROSENCRANTZ *and* GUILDENSTERN (*with some
     Attendants*).
Enter POLONIUS.
      POLONIUS
Th' ambassadors from Norway, my good lord,
Are joyfully returned.   55
      KING
Thou still° hast been the father of good news.
      POLONIUS
Have I, my lord? Assure you, my good liege,
I hold my duty, as I hold my soul,   60

---

166 quoted noted   **168 beshrew my jealousy** curse on
my suspicions   **169 proper** natural   **170 To cast beyond
ourselves** to be overcalculating   **172–75 Come, go…ut-
ter love** (the general meaning is that while telling the
King of Hamlet's love may anger the King, more grief
would come from keeping it secret)   **II.ii. 3 Moreover
that** beside the fact that   **7 Sith** since   **13 of so** from
such   **15 youth and havior** behavior in his youth   **16
vouchsafe your rest** consent to remain

21 opened revealed   **26 gentry** courtesy   **39 in the full
bent** entirely (the figure is of a bow bent to its capacity)
57 still always

Both to my God and to my gracious king;
And I do think, or else this brain of mine
Hunts not the trail of policy so sure°
As it hath used to do, that I have found
65 The very cause of Hamlet's lunacy.
  KING
O, speak of that! That do I long to hear.
  POLONIUS
Give first admittance to th' ambassadors.
70 My news shall be the fruit to that great feast.
  KING
Thyself do grace to them and bring them in.
(*Exit* POLONIUS.)
He tells me, my dear Gertrude, he hath found
The head and source of all your son's distemper.
75   QUEEN
I doubt° it is no other but the main,°
His father's death and our o'erhasty marriage.
  KING
Well, we shall sift him.
Enter POLONIUS, VOLTEMAND, *and* CORNELIUS.
80 Welcome, my good friends.
Say, Voltemand, what from our brother Norway?
  VOLTEMAND
Most fair return of greetings and desires.
Upon our first,° he sent out to suppress
85 His nephew's levies, which to him appeared
To be a preparation 'gainst the Polack;
But better looked into, he truly found
It was against your Highness, whereat grieved,
That so his sickness, age, and impotence
90 Was falsely borne in hand,° sends out arrests
On Fortinbras; which he, in brief, obeys,
Receives rebuke from Norway, and in fine,°
Makes vow before his uncle never more
To give th' assay° of arms against your Majesty.
95 Whereon old Norway, overcome with joy,
Gives him threescore thousand crowns in annual
    fee
And his commission to employ those soldiers,
So levied as before, against the Polack,
100 With an entreaty, herein further shown,
(*Gives a paper.*)
That it might please you to give quiet pass
Through your dominions for this enterprise,

On such regards of safety and allowance°
As therein are set down.
  KING   105
It likes us well;
And at our more considered time° we'll read,
Answer, and think upon this business.
Meantime, we thank you for your well-took labor.
Go to your rest; at night we'll feast together.   110
Most welcome home!
Exeunt AMBASSADORS.
  POLONIUS
This business is well ended.
My liege and madam, to expostulate°
What majesty should be, what duty is,   115
Why day is day, night night, and time is time.
Were nothing but to waste night, day, and time.
Therefore, since brevity is the soul of wit,°
And tediousness the limbs and outward
    flourishes,   120
I will be brief. Your noble son is mad.
Mad call I it, for, to define true madness,
What is't but to be nothing else but mad?
But let that go.
  QUEEN   125
More matter, with less art.
  POLONIUS
Madam, I swear I use no art at all.
That he's mad, 'tis true: 'tis true 'tis pity,
And pity 'tis 'tis true—a foolish figure.°   130
But farewell it, for I will use no art.
Mad let us grant him then; and now remains
That we find out the cause of this effect,
Or rather say, the cause of this defect,
For this effect defective comes by cause.   135
Thus it remains, and the remainder thus.
Perpend.°
I have a daughter: have, while she is mine,
Who in her duty and obedience, mark,
Hath given me this. Now gather, and surmise.   140
(*Reads the letter.*)
"To the celestial, and my soul's idol, the most
    beautified Ophelia"—
That's an ill phrase, a vile phrase; "beautified" is a
    vile phrase. But you shall hear. Thus:
"In her excellent white bosom, these, &c."   144

---

63 **Hunts not...so sure** does not follow clues of political
doings with such sureness 76 **doubt** suspect 76 **main**
principal point 84 **first** first audience 90 **borne in
hand** deceived 92 **in fine** finally 94 **assay** trial

103 **regards of safety and allowance** i.e., conditions 107
considered time time proper for considering 114 **ex-
postulate** discuss 118 **wit** wisdom, understanding 130
figure figure of rhetoric 137 **Perpend** consider carefully

QUEEN
ne this from Hamlet to her?
POLONIUS
madam, stay awhile. I will be faithful.
150 Doubt thou the stars are fire,
Doubt that the sun doth move;
Doubt° truth to be a liar,
But never doubt I love.
O dear Ophelia, I am ill at these numbers.° I have
155 not art to reckon my groans; but that I love thee
best, O most best, believe it. Adieu.
Thine evermore, most dear lady, whilst this
machine° is to him, Hamlet."
This in obedience hath my daughter shown me,
160 And more above° hath his solicitings,
As they fell out by time, by means, and place,
All given to mine ear.
        KING
But how hath she
165 Received his love?
        POLONIUS
What do you think of me?
        KING
As of a man faithful and honorable.
170   POLONIUS
I would fain prove so. But what might you think,
When I had seen this hot love on the wing
(As I perceived it, I must tell you that,
Before my daughter told me), what might you,
175 Or my dear Majesty your Queen here, think,
If I had played the desk or table book,°
Or given my heart a winking,° mute and dumb,
Or looked upon this love with idle sight?
What might you think? No, I went round to work
180 And my young mistress thus I did bespeak:
"Lord Hamlet is a prince, out of thy star.°
This must not be." And then I prescripts gave her,
That she should lock herself from his resort,
Admit no messengers, receive no tokens.
185 Which done, she took the fruits of my advice,
And he, repellèd, a short tale to make,
Fell into a sadness, then into a fast,
Thence to a watch,° thence into a weakness,

Thence to a lightness,° and, by this declension,
Into the madness wherein now he raves,   190
And all we mourn for.
        KING
Do you think 'tis this?
        QUEEN
It may be, very like.   195
        POLONIUS
Hath there been such a time, I would fain know
        that,
That I have positively said " 'Tis so,"
When it proved otherwise?   200
        KING
Not that I know.
        POLONIUS
(Pointing to his head and shoulder) Take this from this,
        if this be otherwise.   205
If circumstances lead me, I will find
Where truth is hid, though it were hid indeed
Within the center.°
        KING
How may we try it further?   210
        POLONIUS
You know sometimes he walks four hours
        together
Here in the lobby.
        QUEEN   215
So he does indeed.
        POLONIUS
At such a time I'll loose my daughter to him.
Be you and I behind an arras° then.
Mark the encounter. If he love her not,   220
And be not from his reason fall'n thereon,
Let me be no assistant for a state
But keep a farm and carters.
        KING
We will try it.   225
Enter HAMLET reading on a book.
        QUEEN
But look where sadly the poor wretch comes
        reading.
        POLONIUS
Away, I do beseech you both, away.   230
Exit KING and QUEEN.
I'll board him presently.° O, give me leave.
How does my good Lord Hamlet?

---

152 **Doubt** suspect   154 **ill at these numbers** unskilled
in verses   158 **machine** complex device (here, his body)
160 **more above** in addition   176 **played the desk or table book** i.e., been a passive recipient of secrets   177
winking closing of the eyes   181 **star** sphere   188 **watch**
wakefulness

189 **lightness** mental derangement   208 **center** center of
the earth   219 **arras** tapestry hanging in front of a wall
231 **board him presently** accost him at once

HAMLET
Well, God-a-mercy.

235 **POLONIUS**
Do you know me, my lord?

HAMLET
Excellent well. You are a fishmonger.°

POLONIUS
240 Not I, my lord.

HAMLET
Then I would you were so honest a man.

POLONIUS
Honest, my lord?

245 **HAMLET**
Ay, sir. To be honest, as this world goes, is to be
one man picked out of ten thousand.

POLONIUS
That's very true, my lord.

250 **HAMLET**
For if the sun breed maggots in a dead dog, being
a good kissing carrion°—Have you a daughter?

POLONIUS
I have, my lord.

255 **HAMLET**
Let her not walk i' th' sun. Conception° is a
blessing, but as your daughter may conceive,
friend, look to't.

POLONIUS
260 (*Aside*) How say you by that? Still harping on my
daughter. Yet he knew me not at first. 'A said I
was a fishmonger. 'A is far gone, far gone. And
truly in my youth I suffered much extremity for
love, very near this. I'll speak to him
265 again.—What do you read, my lord?

HAMLET
Words, words, words.

POLONIUS
What is the matter, my lord?

270 **HAMLET**
Between who?

POLONIUS
I mean the matter° that you read, my lord.

HAMLET
Slanders, sir; for the satirical rogue says here that   275
old men have gray beards, that their faces are
wrinkled, their eyes purging thick amber and
plum-tree gum, and that they have a plentiful
lack of wit, together with most weak hams. All
which, sir, though I most powerfully and potently   280
believe, yet I hold it not honesty° to have it thus
set down; for you yourself, sir, should be old as I
am if, like a crab, you could go backward.

POLONIUS
(*Aside*) Though this be madness, yet there is   285
method in't. Will you walk out of the air, my lord?

HAMLET
Into my grave.

POLONIUS
Indeed, that's out of the air. (*Aside*). How   290
pregnant° sometimes his replies are! A happiness°
that often madness hits on, which reason and
sanity could not so prosperously be delivered of. I
will leave him and suddenly contrive the means
of meeting between him and my daughter.—My   295
lord, I will take my leave of you.

HAMLET
You cannot take from me anything that I will
more willingly part withal—except
my life, except my life, except my life.   300

Enter GUILDENSTERN *and* ROSENCRANTZ.

POLONIUS
Fare you well, my lord.

HAMLET
These tedious old fools!

POLONIUS   305
You go to seek the Lord Hamlet? There he is.

ROSENCRANTZ
(*To* POLONIUS) God save you, sir!

Exit POLONIUS.

GUILDENSTERN
My honored lord!   310

ROSENCRANTZ
My most dear lord!

HAMLET
My excellent good friends! How dost thou,
Guildenstern? Ah, Rosencrantz! Good lads, how   315
do you both?

ROSENCRANTZ
As the indifferent° children of the earth.

---

238 **fishmonger** dealer in fish (slang for a procurer)   252
a good kissing carrion (perhaps the meaning is "a good
piece of flesh to kiss," but many editors emend good to
god, taking the word to refer to the sun)   256 **Conception** (1) understanding (2) becoming pregnant   273 **matter** (Polonius means "subject matter," but Hamlet
pretends to take the word in the sense of "quarrel"

281 **honesty** decency   291 **pregnant** meaningful   291
happiness apt turn of phrase   318 **indifferent** ordinary

GUILDENSTERN

320 Happy in that we are not overhappy. On
Fortune's cap we are not the very button.

HAMLET

Nor the soles of her shoe?

ROSENCRANTZ

325 Neither, my lord.

HAMLET

Then you live about her waist, or in the middle of
her favors?

GUILDENSTERN

330 Faith, her privates° we.

HAMLET

In the secret parts of Fortune? O, most true! She is
a strumpet. What news?

ROSENCRANTZ

335 None, my lord, but that the world's grown honest.

HAMLET

Then is doomsday near. But your news is not
true. Let me question more in particular. What
have you, my good friends, deserved at the hands
340 of Fortune that she sends you to prison hither?

GUILDENSTERN

Prison, my lord?

HAMLET

Denmark's a prison.

ROSENCRANTZ

345 Then is the world one.

HAMLET

A goodly one, in which there are many confines,
wards,° and dungeons, Denmark being one o' th'
350 worst.

ROSENCRANTZ

We think not so, my lord.

HAMLET

Why, then 'tis none to you, for there is nothing
355 either good or bad but thinking makes it so. To
me it is a prison.

ROSENCRANTZ

Why then your ambition makes it one. 'Tis too
narrow for your mind.

HAMLET

360 O God, I could be bounded in a nutshell and
count myself a king of infinite space, were it not
that I have bad dreams.

GUILDENSTERN

365 Which dreams indeed are ambition, for the very

substance of the ambitious is merely the shadow
of a dream.

HAMLET

A dream itself is but a shadow.

ROSENCRANTZ   370

Truly, and I hold ambition of so airy and light a
quality that it is but a shadow's shadow.

HAMLET

Then are our beggars bodies, and our monarchs
and outstretched heroes the beggars' shadows.°   375
Shall we to th' court? For, by my fay,° I cannot
reason.

BOTH

We'll wait upon you.

HAMLET   380

No such matter. I will not sort you with the rest of
my servants, for, to speak to you like an honest
man, I am most dreadfully attended. But in the
beaten way of friendship, what make you at
Elsinore?   385

ROSENCRANTZ

To visit you, my lord; no other occasion.

HAMLET

Beggar that I am, I am even poor in thanks, but I
thank you; and sure, dear friends, my thanks are   390
too dear a halfpenny.° Were you not sent for? Is it
your own inclining? Is it a free visitation? Come,
come, deal justly with me. Come, come; nay,
speak.

GUILDENSTERN   395

What should we say, my lord?

HAMLET

Why anything—but to th' purpose. You were sent
for, and there is a kind of confession in your
looks, which your modesties have not craft   400
enough to color. I know the good King and
Queen have sent for you.

ROSENCRANTZ

To what end, my lord?

HAMLET   405

That you must teach me. But let me conjure you
by the rights of our fellowship, by the consonancy
of our youth, by the obligation of our
everpreserved love, and by what more dear a
better proposer can charge you withal, be even   410

---

330 **privates** ordinary men (with a pun on "private
parts") 349 **wards** cells

374–76 **Then are...beggars' shadows** i.e., by your logic,
beggars (lacking ambition) are substantial, and great men
are elongated shadows 376 **fay** faith 391 **too dear a
halfpenny** i.e., not worth a halfpenny

and direct with me, whether you were sent for or
no.

ROSENCRANTZ
(*Aside to* GUILDENSTERN) What say you?

415   HAMLET
(*Aside*) Nay then, I have an eye of you.—If you
love me, hold not off.

GUILDENSTERN
My lord, we were sent for.

420   HAMLET
I will tell you why; so shall my anticipation
prevent your discovery,° and your secrecy to the
King and Queen molt no feather. I have of late,
but wherefore I know not, lost all my mirth,
425 forgone all custom of exercises; and indeed, it
goes so heavily with my disposition that this
goodly frame, the earth, seems to me a sterile
promontory; this most excellent canopy, the air,
look you, this brave o'erhanging firmament, this
430 majestical roof fretted° with golden fire: why, it
appeareth nothing to me but a foul and pestilent
congregation of vapors. What a piece of work is a
man, how noble in reason, how infinite in
faculties, in form and moving how express° and
435 admirable, in action how like an angel, in
apprehension how like a god: the beauty of the
world, the paragon of animals; and yet to me,
what is this quintessence of dust? Man delights
not me; nor woman neither, though by your
440 smiling you seem to say so.

ROSENCRANTZ
My lord, there was no such stuff in my thoughts.

HAMLET
Why did ye laugh then, when I said "Man
445 delights not me"?

ROSENCRANTZ
To think, my lord, if you delight not in man, what
lenten° entertainment the players shall receive
from you. We coted° them on the way, and hither
450 are they coming to offer you service.

HAMLET
He that plays the king shall be welcome; his
Majesty shall have tribute of me; the adventurous
knight shall use his foil and target°; the lover shall
455 not sigh gratis; the humorous man° shall end his

part in peace; the clown shall make those laugh
whose lungs are tickle o' th' sere° and the lady
shall say her mind freely, or° the blank verse shall
halt° for't. What players are they?

ROSENCRANTZ   460
Even those you were wont to take such delight in,
the tragedians of the city.

HAMLET
How chances it they travel? Their residence, both
in reputation and profit, was better both ways.   465

ROSENCRANTZ
I think their inhibition° comes by the means of the
late innovation.°

HAMLET
Do they hold the same estimation they did when I 470
was in the city? Are they so followed?

ROSENCRANTZ
No indeed, are they not.

HAMLET
How comes it? Do they grow rusty?   475

ROSENCRANTZ
Nay, their endeavor keeps in the wonted pace,
but there is, sir, an eyrie° of children, little eyases,
that cry out on the top of question° and are most
tyrannically° clapped for't. These are now the 480
fashion, and so berattle the common stages° (so
they call them) that many wearing rapiers are
afraid of goosequills° and dare scarce come
thither.

HAMLET   485
What, are they children? Who maintains 'em?
How are they escoted?° Will they pursue the
quality° no longer than they can sing? Will they
not say afterwards, if they should grow
themselves to common players (as it is most like, 490
if their means are no better), their writers do them
wrong to make them exclaim against their own
succession?°

---

457 **tickle o' th' sere** on hair trigger (**sere** = part of the
gunlock)   458 **or** else   459 **halt** limp   467 **inhibition**
hindrance   468 **innovation** (probably an allusion to the
companies of child actors that had become popular and
were offering serious competition to the adult actors)
478 **eyrie** nest   478–79 **eyases, that...of question** unfledged hawks that cry shrilly above others in matters of
debate   480 **tyrannically** violently   481 **berattle the
common stages** cry down the public theaters (with the
adult acting companies)   483 **goosequills** pens (of satirists who ridicule the public theaters and their
audiences)   487 **escoted** financially supported   488 **quality** profession of acting   493 **succession** future

---

422 **prevent your discovery** forestall your disclosure
430 **fretted** adorned   434 **express** exact   448 **lenten**
meager   449 **coted** overtook   454 **target** shield   455
humorous man i.e., eccentric man (among stock characters in dramas were men dominated by a "humor" or
odd trait)

ROSENCRANTZ

495 Faith, there has been much to-do on both sides,
and the nation holds it no sin to tarre° them to
controversy. There was, for a while, no money bid
for argument° unless the poet and the player
went to cuffs in the question.

500 HAMLET

Is't possible?

GUILDENSTERN

O, there has been much throwing about of brains.

HAMLET

505 Do the boys carry it away?

ROSENCRANTZ

Ay, that they do, my lord—Hercules and his
load° too.

HAMLET

510 It is not very strange, for my uncle is King of
Denmark, and those that would make mouths at
him while my father lived give twenty, forty,
fifty, a hundred ducats apiece for his picture in
little. 'Sblood,° there is something in this more
515 than natural, if philosophy could find it out.
A flourish.

GUILDENSTERN

There are the players.

HAMLET

Gentlemen, you are welcome to Elsinore. Your
520 hands, come then. Th' appurtenance of welcome
is fashion and ceremony. Let me comply° with
you in this garb,° lest my extent° to the players
(which I tell you must show fairly outwards)
should more appear like entertainment than
525 yours. You are welcome. But my uncle-father and
aunt-mother are deceived.

GUILDENSTERN

In what, my dear lord?

HAMLET

530 I am but mad north-northwest:° when the wind is
southerly I know a hawk from a handsaw.°

Enter POLONIUS.

POLONIUS

Well be with you, gentlemen.

HAMLET

Hark you, Guildenstern, and you too; at each ear   535
a hearer. That great baby you see there is not yet
out of his swaddling clouts.

ROSENCRANTZ

Happily° he is the second time come to them, for
they say an old man is twice a child.   540

HAMLET

I will prophesy he comes to tell me of the players.
Mark it.—You say right, sir; a Monday morning,
'twas then indeed.

POLONIUS   545

My lord, I have news to tell you.

HAMLET

My lord, I have news to tell you. When Roscius°
was an actor in Rome—

POLONIUS   550

The actors are come hither, my lord.

HAMLET

Buzz, buzz.°

POLONIUS

Upon my honor—   555

HAMLET

Then came each actor on his ass—

POLONIUS

The best actors in the world, either for tragedy,
comedy, history, pastoral, pastoral-comical,   560
historical-pastoral, tragical-historical,
tragical-comical-historical-pastoral; scene
individable,° or poem unlimited.° Seneca° cannot
be too heavy, nor Plautus° too light. For the law
of writ and the liberty,° these are the only men.   565

HAMLET

O Jeptha, judge of Israel,° what a treasure hadst
thou!

496 **tarre** incite   498 **argument** plot of a play   507–08 **Hercules and his load** i.e., the whole world (with a reference to the Globe Theatre, which had a sign that represented Hercules bearing the globe)   514 **'Sblood** by God's blood   521 **comply** be courteous   522 **garb** outward show   522 **extent** behavior   530 **north-northwest** i.e., on one point of the compass only   531 **hawk from a handsaw** (**hawk** can refer not only to a bird but to a kind of pickax; **handsaw**—a carpenter's tool—may involve a similar pun on "hernshaw," a heron)

539 **Happily** perhaps   548 **Roscius** (a famous Roman comic actor)   553 **Buzz, buzz** (an interjection, perhaps indicating that the news is old)   563 **scene individable** plays observing the unities of time, place, and action   563 **poem unlimited** plays not restricted by the tenets of criticism   563 **Seneca** (Roman tragic dramatist)   564 **Plautus** (Roman comic dramatist)   565 **For the law of writ and the liberty** (perhaps "for sticking to the text and for improvising"; perhaps "for classical plays and for modern loosely written plays")   567 **Jeptha, judge of Israel** (the title of a ballad on the Hebrew judge who sacrificed his daughter; see Judges 11)

POLONIUS

570 What a treasure had he, my lord?

HAMLET

Why,

"One fair daughter, and no more,
The which he lovèd passing well."

575 POLONIUS

(*Aside*) Still on my daughter.

HAMLET

Am I not i' th' right, old Jeptha?

POLONIUS

580 If you call me Jeptha, my lord, I have a daughter
that I love passing well.

HAMLET

Nay, that follows not.

POLONIUS

585 What follows, then, my lord?

HAMLET

Why,

"As by lot, God wot,"
and then, you know,

590 "It came to pass, as most like it was."
The first row of the pious chanson° will show you
more, for look where my abridgment° comes.
Enter the PLAYERS.
You are welcome, masters, welcome, all. I am
glad to see thee well. Welcome, good friend. O,

595 old friend, why, thy face is valanced° since I saw
thee last. Comist thou to beard me in Denmark?
What, my young lady° and mistress? By'r Lady,
your ladyship is nearer to heaven than when I
saw you last by the altitude of a chopine.° Pray

600 God your voice, like a piece of uncurrent gold, be
not cracked within the ring.°—Masters, you are
all welcome. We'll e'en to't like French falconers,
fly at anything we see. We'll have a speech
straight. Come, give us a taste of your quality.

605 Come, a passionate speech.

PLAYER

What speech, my good lord?

HAMLET

I heard thee speak me a speech once, but it was
never acted, or if it was, not above once, for the 610
play, I remember, pleased not the million; 'twas
caviary to the general,° but it was (as I received it,
and others, whose judgments in such matters
cried in the top of° mine) an excellent play, well
digested in the scenes, set down with as much 615
modesty as cunning.° I remember one said there
were no sallets° in the lines to make the matter
savory; nor no matter in the phrase that might
indict the author of affectation, but called it an
honest method, as wholesome as sweet, and by 620
very much more handsome than fine.° One
speech in't I chiefly loved. 'Twas Aeneas' tale to
Dido, and thereabout of it especially when he
speaks of Priam's slaughter. If it live in your
memory, begin at this line—let me see, let me see: 625

"The rugged Pyrrhus, like th' Hyrcanian
beast°—"

'Tis not so; it begins with Pyrrhus:

"The rugged Pyrrhus, he whose sable° arms,
Black as his purpose, did the night resemble 630
When he lay couchèd in th' ominous horse,°
Hath now this dread and black complexion
     smeared
With heraldry more dismal.° Head to foot
Now is he total gules, horridly tricked° 635
With blood of father, mothers, daughters, sons,
Baked and impasted° with the parching streets,
That lend a tyrannous and a damnèd light
To their lord's murder. Roasted in wrath and fire,
And thus o'ersizèd° with coagulate gore, 640
With eyes like carbuncles, the hellish Pyrrhus
Old grandsire Priam seeks."

So, proceed you.

---

591 **row of the pious chanson** stanza of the scriptural
song 592 **abridgment** (1) i.e., entertainers, who abridge
the time (2) interrupts 595 **valanced** fringed (with a
beard) 597 **young lady** i.e., boy for female roles 599
chopine thick-soled shoe 600–01 **like a piece…the ring**
(a coin was unfit for legal tender if a crack extended from
the edge through the ring enclosing the monarch's head.
Hamlet, punning on *ring,* refers to the change of voice
that the boy actor will undergo)

612 **caviary to the general** i.e., too choice for the multitude 614 **in the top of** overtopping 616 **modesty as
cunning** restraint as art 617 **sallets** salads, spicy jests
621 **more handsome than fine** well-proportioned rather
than ornamented 626–27 **Hyrcanian beast** i.e., tiger
(Hyrcania was in Asia) 629 **sable** black 631 **ominous
horse** i.e., wooden horse at the siege of Troy 634 **dismal**
ill-omened 635 **total gules, horridly tricked** all red,
horridly adorned 637 **impasted** encrusted 640 **o'ersizèd**
smeared over

POLONIUS
645 Fore God, my lord, well spoken, with good accent
and good discretion.
PLAYER
"Anon he finds him,
Striking too short at Greeks. His antique sword,
650 Rebellious to his arm, lies where it falls,
Repugnant to command.° Unequal matched,
Pyrrhus at Priam drives, in rage strikes wide,
But with the whiff and wind of his fell sword
Th' unnervèd father falls. Then senseless Ilium,°
655 Seeming to feel this blow, with flaming top
Stoops to his base,° and with a hideous crash
Takes prisoner Pyrrhus' ear. For lo, his sword,
Which was declining on the milky head
Of reverend Priam, seemed i' th' air to stick.
660 So as a painted tyrant° Pyrrhus stood,
And like a neutral to his will and matter°
Did nothing.
But as we often see, against° some storm,
A silence in the heavens, the rack° stand still,
665 The bold winds speechless, and the orb below
As hush as death, anon the dreadful thunder
Doth rend the region, so after Pyrrhus' pause,
A rousèd vengeance sets him new awork,
And never did the Cyclops' hammers fall
670 On Mars's armor, forged for proof eterne,°
With less remorse than Pyrrhus' bleeding sword
Now falls on Priam.
Out, out, thou strumpet Fortune! All you gods,
In general synod° take away her power,
675 Break all the spokes and fellies° from her wheel,
And bowl the round nave° down the hill of
       heaven,
As low as to the fiends."
POLONIUS
680 This is too long.
HAMLET
It shall to the barber's, with your beard.— Prithee
say on. He's for a jig or a tale of bawdry, or he
sleeps. Say on; come to Hecuba.

PLAYER   685
"But who (ah woe!) had seen the mobled°
queen—"
HAMLET
"The mobled queen"?
POLONIUS   690
That's good. "Mobled queen" is good.
PLAYER
"Run barefoot up and down, threat'ning the
       flames
With bisson rheum;° a clout° upon that head   695
Where late the diadem stood, and for a robe,
About her lank and all o'erteemèd° loins,
A blanket in the alarm of fear caught up—
Who this had seen, with tongue in venom steeped
'Gainst Fortune's state would treason have   700
       pronounced.
But if the gods themselves did see her then,
When she saw Pyrrhus make malicious sport
In mincing with his sword her husband's limbs,
The instant burst of clamor that she made   705
(Unless things mortal move them not at all)
Would have made milch° the burning eyes of
       heaven
And passion in the gods."
POLONIUS   710
Look, whe'r° he has not turned his color, and has
tears in's eyes. Prithee no more.
HAMLET
'Tis well. I'll have thee speak out the rest of this
soon. Good my lord, will you see the players well 715
bestowed?° Do you hear? Let them be well used,
for they are the abstract and brief chronicles of the
time. After your death you were better have a bad
epitaph than their ill report while you live.
POLONIUS   720
My lord, I will use them according to their desert.
HAMLET
God's bodkin,° man, much better! Use every man
after his desert, and who shall scape whipping?
Use them after your own honor and dignity. The   725
less they deserve, the more merit is in your
bounty. Take them in.

651 **Repugnant to command** disobedient   654 **senseless
Ilium** insensate Troy   656 **Stoops to his base** collapses
(**his** = its)   660 **painted tyrant** tyrant in a picture   661
matter task   663 **against** just before   664 **rack** clouds
670 **proof eterne** eternal endurance   674 **synod** council
675 **fellies** rims   676 **nave** hub

686 **mobled** muffled   695 **bisson rheum** blinding tears
695 **clout** rag   697 **o'erteemèd** exhausted with childbear-
ing   707 **milch** moist (literally, "milk-giving")   711 **whe'r**
whether   716 **bestowed** housed   723 **God's bodkin** by
God's little body

POLONIUS
Come, sirs.
730   **HAMLET**
Follow him, friends. We'll hear a play tomorrow.
(*Aside to* PLAYER) Dost thou hear me, old friend?
Can you play *The Murder of Gonzago?*
        PLAYER
735   Ay, my lord.
        HAMLET
We'll ha't tomorrow night. You could for a need
study a speech of some dozen or sixteen lines
which I would set down and insert in't, could you
740   not?
        PLAYER
Ay, my lord.
        HAMLET
Very well. Follow that lord, and look you mock
745   him not. My good friends, I'll leave you till night.
You are welcome to Elsinore.
Exeunt POLONIUS *and* PLAYERS.
        ROSENCRANTZ
Good my lord.
Exeunt (ROSENCRANTZ *and* GUILDENSTERN).
        HAMLET
750   Ay, so, God bye to you.—Now I am alone.
O, what a rogue and peasant slave
am I!
Is it not monstrous that this player here,
But in a fiction, in a dream of passion,°
755   Could force his soul so to his own conceit°
That from her working all his visage wanned,
Tears in his eyes, distraction in his aspect,
A broken voice, and his whole function° suiting
With forms° to his conceit? And all for nothing!
760   For Hebuca!
What's Hecuba to him, or he to Hecuba,
That he should weep for her? What would he do
Had he the motive and the cue for passion
That I have? He would drown the stage with tears
765   And cleave the general ear with horrid speech,
Make mad the guilty and appall the free,°
Confound the ignorant, and amaze indeed
The very faculties of eyes and ears.
Yet I,

A dull and muddy-mettled° rascal, peak   770
Like john-a-dreams,° unpregnant of° my cause,
And can say nothing. No, not for a king,
Upon whose property and most dear life
A damned defeat was made. Am I a coward?
Who calls me villain? Breaks my pate across?   775
Plucks off my beard and blows it in my face?
Tweaks me by the nose? Gives me the lie i' th'
        throat
As deep as to the lungs? Who does me this?
Ha, 'swounds,° I should take it, for it cannot be   780
But I am pigeon-livered° and lack gall
To make oppression bitter, or ere this
I should ha' fatted all the region kites°
With this slave's offal. Bloody, bawdy villain!
Remorseless, treacherous, lecherous, kindless°   785
        villain!
O, vengeance!
Why, what an ass am I! This is most brave,°
That I, the son of a dear father murdered,
Prompted to my revenge by heaven and hell,   790
Must, like a whore, unpack my heart with words
And fall a-cursing like a very drab,°
A stallion!° Fie upon't, foh! About,° my brains.
Hum—
I have heard that guilty creatures sitting at a play 795
Have by the very cunning of the scene
Been struck so to the soul that presently°
They have proclaimed their malefactions.
For murder, though it have no tongue, will speak
With most miraculous organ. I'll have these players 800
Play something like the murder of my father
Before mine uncle. I'll observe his looks,
I'll tent° him to the quick. If 'a do blench,°
I know my course. The spirit that I have seen
May be a devil, and the devil hath power   805
T' assume a pleasing shape, yea, and perhaps
Out of my weakness and my melancholy,

---

770 **muddy-mettled** weak-spirited   770–71 **peak/Like John-a-dreams** mope like a dreamer   771 **unpregnant of** unquickened by   780 **'swounds** by God's wounds   781 **pigeon-livered** gentle as a dove   783 **region kites** kites (scavenger birds) of the sky   785 **kindless** unnatural   788 **brave** fine   792 **drab** prostitute   793 **stallion** male prostitute (perhaps one should adopt the Folio reading, **scullion** = kitchen wench)   793 **About** to work   797 **presently** immediately   803 **tent** probe   803 **blench** flinch

---

754 **dream of passion** imaginary emotion   755 **conceit** imagination   758 **function** action   759 **forms** bodily expressions   766 **appall the free** terrify (make pale?) the guiltless

As he is very potent with such spirits,
Abuses me to damn me. I'll have grounds
810 More relative° than this. The play's the thing
Wherein I'll catch the conscience of the King.
(*Exit.*)

ACT III

SCENE I

The castle.

Enter KING *and* QUEEN, POLONIUS, OPHELIA, ROSEN-
CRANTZ, GUILDENSTERN, LORDS.

    KING
And can you by no drift of conference°
Get from him why he puts on this confusion,
Grating so harshly all his days of quiet
5 With turbulent and dangerous lunacy?
    ROSENCRANTZ
He does confess he feels himself distracted,
But from what cause 'a will by no means speak.
    GUILDENSTERN
10 Nor do we find him forward to be sounded,°
But with a crafty madness keeps aloof
When we would bring him on to some confession
Of his true state.
    QUEEN
15 Did he receive you well?
    ROSENCRANTZ
Most like a gentleman.
    GUILDENSTERN
But with much forcing of his disposition.°
20   ROSENCRANTZ
Niggard of question,° but of our demands
Most free in his reply.
    QUEEN
Did you assay° him
25 To any pastime?
    ROSENCRANTZ
Madam, it so fell out that certain players
We o'erraught° on the way; of these we told him,
And there did seem in him a kind of joy

To hear of it. They are here about the court,   30
And, as I think, they have already order
This night to play before him.
    POLONIUS
'Tis most true,
And he beseeched me to entreat your Majesties   35
To hear and see the matter.
    KING
With all my heart, and it doth much content me
To hear him so inclined.
Good gentlemen, give him a further edge   40
And drive his purpose into these delights.
    ROSENCRANTZ
We shall, my lord.
Exeunt ROSENCRANTZ *and* GUILDENSTERN.
    KING
Sweet Gertrude, leave us too,   45
For we have closely° sent for Hamlet hither,
That he, as 'twere by accident, may here
Affront° Ophelia.
Her father and myself (lawful espials°)
Will so bestow ourselves that, seeing unseen,   50
We may of their encounter frankly judge
And gather by him, as he is behaved,
If't be th' affliction of his love or no
That thus he suffers for.
    QUEEN   55
I shall obey you.
And for your part, Ophelia, I do wish
That your good beauties be the happy cause
Of Hamlet's wildness. So shall I hope your virtues
Will bring him to his wonted way again,   60
To both your honors.
    OPHELIA
Madam, I wish it may.
(*Exit* QUEEN.)
    POLONIUS
Ophelia, walk you here.—Gracious, so please you,   65
We will bestow ourselves. (*To* OPHELIA) Read on
    this book,
That show of such an exercise may color°
Your loneliness. We are oft to blame in this,
'Tis too much proved, that with devotion's visage   70
And pious action we do sugar o'er
The devil himself.

---

810 **relative** (probably "pertinent," but possibly "able to
be related plausibly")   III.i. 2 **drift of conference** management of conversation   10 **forward to be sounded**
willing to be questioned   19 **forcing of his disposition**
effort   21 **Niggard of question** uninclined to talk   24
assay tempt   28 **o'erraught** overtook

46 **closely** secretly   48 **Affront** meet face to face   49 **es-
pials** spies   68 **exercise may color** act of devotion may
give a plausible hue to (the book is one of devotion)

KING
(*Aside*) O, 'tis too true.
75 How smart a lash that speech doth give my
      conscience!
The harlot's cheek, beautied with plast'ring art,
Is not more ugly to the thing that helps it
Than is my deed to my most painted word.
80 O heavy burden!
      POLONIUS
I hear him coming. Let's withdraw, my lord.
(*Exeunt* KING *and* POLONIUS.)
Enter HAMLET.
      HAMLET
To be, or not to be: that is the question:
85 Whether 'tis nobler in the mind to suffer
The slings and arrows of outrageous fortune,
Or to take arms against a sea of troubles,
And by opposing end them. To die, to sleep—
No more—and by a sleep to say we end
90 The heartache, and the thousand natural shocks
That flesh is heir to! 'Tis a consummation
Devoutly to be wished. To die, to sleep—
To sleep—perchance to dream: ay, there's the
      rub,°
95 For in that sleep of death what dreams may come
When we have shuffled off this mortal coil,°
Must give us pause. There's the respect°
That makes calamity of so long life:°
For who would bear the whips and scorns of time,
100 Th' oppressor's wrong, the proud man's
      contumely,
The pangs of despised love, the law's delay,
The insolence of office, and the spurns
That patient merit of th' unworthy takes,
105 When he himself might his quietus° make
With a bare bodkin?° Who would fardels° bear,
To grunt and sweat under a weary life,
But that the dread of something after death,
The undiscovered country, from whose bourn°
110 No traveler returns, puzzles the will,
And makes us rather bear those ills we have,
Than fly to others that we know not of?

Thus conscience° does make cowards of us all,
And thus the native hue of resolution
Is sicklied o'er with the pale cast° of thought, 115
And enterprises of great pitch° and moment,
With this regard° their current turn awry,
And lose the name of action.—Soft you now,
The fair Ophelia!—Nymph, in thy orisons°
Be all my sins remembered. 120
      OPHELIA
Good my lord,
How does your honor for this many a day?
      HAMLET
I humbly thank you; well, well, well. 125
      OPHELIA
My lord, I have remembrances of yours
That I have longèd long to redeliver.
I pray you now, receive them.
      HAMLET 130
No, not I,
I never gave you aught.
      OPHELIA
My honored lord, you know right well you did,
And with them words of so sweet breath 135
      composed
As made these things more rich. Their perfume
      lost,
Take these again, for to the noble mind
Rich gifts wax poor when givers prove unkind. 140
There, my lord.
      HAMLET
Ha, ha! Are you honest?°
      OPHELIA
My lord? 145
      HAMLET
Are you fair?
      OPHELIA
What means your lordship?
      HAMLET 150
That if you be honest and fair, your honesty
should admit no discourse to your beauty.°
      OPHELIA
Could beauty, my lord, have better commerce
than with honesty? 155

---

94 **rub** impediment (obstruction to a bowler's ball) 96
coil (1) turmoil (2) a ring of rope (here the flesh encircling
the soul) 97 **respect** consideration 98 **makes calamity
of so long life** (1) makes calamity so long-lived (2) makes
living so long a calamity 105 **quietus** full discharge (a
legal term) 106 **bodkin** dagger 106 **fardels** burdens
109 **bourn** region

113 **conscience** self-consciousness, introspection 115
cast color 116 **pitch** height (a term from falconry) 117
regard consideration 119 **orisons** prayers 144 **Are you
honest** (1) are you modest (2) are you chaste (3) have you
integrity 151–52 **your honesty...to your beauty** your
modesty should permit no approach to your beauty

HAMLET

Ay, truly; for the power of beauty will sooner
transform honesty from what it is to a bawd° than
the force of honesty can translate beauty into his
160 likeness. This was sometime a paradox, but now
the time gives it proof. I did love you once.

OPHELIA

Indeed, my lord, you made me believe so.

HAMLET

165 You should not have believed me, for virtue
cannot so inoculate° our old stock but we shall
relish of it.° I loved you not.

OPHELIA

I was the more deceived.

170 HAMLET

Get thee to a nunnery. Why wouldst thou be a
breeder of sinners? I am myself indifferent
honest,° but yet I could accuse me of such things
that it were better my mother had not borne me: I
175 am very proud, revengeful, ambitious, with more
offenses at my beck° than I have thoughts to put
them in, imagination to give them shape, or time
to act them in. What should such fellows as I do
crawling between earth and heaven? We are
180 arrant knaves all; believe none of us. Go thy ways
to a nunnery. Where's your father?

OPHELIA

At home, my lord.

HAMLET

185 Let the doors be shut upon him, that he may play
the fool nowhere but in's own house. Farewell.

OPHELIA

O help him, you sweet heavens!

HAMLET

190 If thou dost marry, I'll give thee this plague for
thy dowry: be thou as chaste as ice, as pure as
snow, thou shalt not escape calumny. Get thee to
a nunnery. Go, farewell. Or if thou wilt needs
marry, marry a fool, for wise men know well
195 enough what monsters° you make of them. To a
nunnery, go,° and quickly too. Farewell.

OPHELIA

Heavenly powers, restore him!

HAMLET

200 I have heard of your paintings, well enough.

---

158 **bawd** procurer   166 **inoculate** graft   167 **relish of it**
smack of it (our old sinful nature)   172–73 **indifferent
honest** moderately virtuous   176 **beck** call   195 **monsters** horned beasts, cuckolds

God hath given you one face, and you make
yourselves another. You jig and amble, and you
lisp; you nickname God's creatures and make
your wantonness your ignorance.° Go to, I'll no
more on't; it hath made me mad. I say we will   205
have no moe° marriage. Those that are married
already—all but one—shall live. The rest shall
keep as they are. To a nunnery, go. (*Exit.*)

OPHELIA

O what a noble mind is here o'erthrown!   210
The courtier's, soldier's, scholar's, eye, tongue,
    sword,
Th' expectancy and rose° of the fair state,
The glass of fashion, and the mold of form,°
Th' observed of all observers, quite, quite down! 215
And I, of ladies most deject and wretched,
That sucked the honey of his musicked vows,
Now see that noble and most sovereign reason
Like sweet bells jangled, out of time and harsh,
That unmatched form and feature of blown° youth 220
Blasted with ecstasy.° O, woe is me
T' have seen what I have seen, see what I see!
Enter KING *and* POLONIUS.

KING

Love? His affections° do not that way tend,
Nor what he spake, though it lacked form a little, 225
Was not like madness. There's something in his
    soul
O'er which his melancholy sits on brood,
And I do doubt° the hatch and the disclose
Will be some danger; which for to prevent,   230
I have in quick determination
Thus set it down: he shall with speed to England
For the demand of our neglected tribute.
Haply the seas, and countries different,
With variable objects, shall expel   235
This something-settled° matter in his heart,
Whereon his brains still beating puts him thus
From fashion of himself. What think you on't?

POLONIUS

It shall do well. But yet do I believe   240
The origin and commencement of his grief

203–04 **make your wantonness your ignorance** excuse
your wanton speech by pretending ignorance   206 **moe**
more   213 **expectancy and rose** i.e., fair hope   214 **The
glass...of form** the mirror of fashion, and the pattern of
excellent behavior   220 **blown** blooming   221 **ecstasy**
madness   224 **affections** inclinations   229 **doubt** fear
236 **something-settled** somewhat settled

Sprung from neglected love. How now, Ophelia?
You need not tell us what Lord Hamlet said;
We heard it all. My lord, do as you please,
245 But if you hold it fit, after the play,
Let his queen mother all alone entreat him
To show his grief. Let her be round° with him,
And I'll be placed, so please you, in the ear
Of all their conference. If she find him not,°
250 To England send him, or confine him where
Your wisdom best shall think.

      KING
It shall be so.
Madness in great ones must not unwatched go.
Exeunt.

SCENE II

The castle.

Enter HAMLET *and three of the* PLAYERS.

      HAMLET
Speak the speech, I pray you, as I pronounced it
to you, trippingly on the tongue. But if you
mouth it, as many of our players do, I had as lief
5 the town crier spoke my lines. Nor do not saw the
air too much with your hand, thus, but use all
gently, for in the very torrent, tempest, and (as I
may say) whirlwind of your passion, you must
acquire and beget a temperance that may give it
10 smoothness. O, it offends me to the soul to hear a
robustious periwig-pated° fellow tear a passion to
tatters, to very rags, to split the ears of the
groundlings,° who for the most part are capable
of° nothing but inexplicable dumb shows° and
15 noise. I would have such a fellow whipped for
o'erdoing Termagant. It out-herods Herod.° Pray
you avoid it.

      PLAYER
I warrant your honor.
20   HAMLET
Be not too tame neither, but let your own

---

247 **round** blunt   249 **find him not** does not find him out
III.ii. 11 **robustious periwig-pated** boisterous wig-
headed   13 **groundlings** those who stood in the pit of
the theater (the poorest and presumably most ignorant of
the audience)   13–14 **are capable of** are able to understand 14 **dumb shows** (it had been the fashion for actors
to preface plays or parts of plays with silent mime)   16
Termagant…Herod (boisterous characters in the old
mystery plays)

---

discretion be your tutor. Suit the action to the
word, the word to the action, with this special
observance, that you o'erstep not the modesty of
nature. For anything so o'erdone is from° the   25
purpose of playing, whose end, both at the first
and now, was and is, to hold, as 'twere, the
mirror up to nature; to show virtue her own
feature, scorn her own image, and the very age
and body of the time his form and pressure.°   30
Now, this overdone, or come tardy off, though it
makes the unskillful laugh, cannot but make the
judicious grieve, the censure of the which one
must in your allowance o'erweigh a whole theater
of others. O, there be players that I have seen   35
play, and heard others praise, and that highly
(not to speak it profanely), that neither having th'
accent of Christians, nor the gait of Christian,
pagan, nor man, have so strutted and bellowed
that I have thought some of Nature's   40
journeymen° had made men, and not made them
well, they imitated humanity so abominably.

      PLAYER
I hope we have reformed that indifferently° with
us, sir.   45
      HAMLET
O, reform it altogether! And let those that play
your clowns speak no more than is set down for
them, for there be of them that will themselves
laugh, to set on some quantity of barren   50
spectators to laugh too, though in the meantime
some necessary question of the play be then to be
considered. That's villainous and shows a most
pitiful ambition in the fool that uses it. Go make
you ready.   55
Exit PLAYERS.
Enter POLONIUS, GUILDENSTERN, *and* ROSENCRANTZ.
How now, my lord? Will the King hear this piece
of work?
      POLONIUS
And the Queen too, and that presently.
      HAMLET   60
Bid the players make haste. (*Exit* POLONIUS.)
Will you two help to hasten them?
      ROSENCRANTZ
Ay, my lord. (*Exeunt they two.*)

---

25 **from** contrary to   30 **pressure** image, impress   41
journeymen workers not yet masters of their craft   44
indifferently tolerably

HAMLET
65 What, ho, Horatio!
Enter HORATIO.
    HORATIO
Here, sweet lord, at your service.
    HAMLET
70 Horatio, thou art e'en as just a man
As e'er my conversation coped withal.°
    HORATIO
O, my dear lord——
    HAMLET
75 Nay, do not think I flatter.
For what advancement° may I hope from thee,
That no revenue hast but thy good spirits
To feed and clothe thee? Why should the poor be
    flattered?
80 No, let the candied° tongue lick absurd pomp,
And crook the pregnant° hinges of the knee
Where thrift° may follow fawning. Dost thou hear?
Since my dear soul was mistress of her choice
85 And could of men distinguish her election,
S' hath sealed thee° for herself, for thou hast been
As one, in suff'ring all, that suffers nothing,
A man that Fortune's buffets and rewards
Hast ta'en with equal thanks; and blest are those
90 Whose blood° and judgment are so well
    commeddled°
That they are not a pipe for Fortune's finger
To sound what stop she please. Give me that man
That is not passion's slave, and I will wear him
95 In my heart's core, ay, in my heart of heart,
As I do thee. Something too much of this—
There is a play tonight before the King.
One scene of it comes near the circumstance
Which I have told thee, of my father's death.
100 I prithee, when thou seest that act afoot,
Even with the very comment° of thy soul
Observe my uncle. If his occulted° guilt
Do not itself unkennel in one speech,
It is a damnèd ghost that we have seen,
105 And my imaginations are as foul
As Vulcan's stithy.° Give him heedful note,
For I mine eyes will rivet to his face,

And after we will both our judgments join
In censure of his seeming.°
    HORATIO   110
Well, my lord.
If 'a steal aught the whilst this play is playing,
And scape detecting, I will pay the theft.
Enter Trumpets and Kettledrums, KING, QUEEN,
POLONIUS, OPHELIA, ROSENCRANTZ, GUILDENSTERN,
*and other Lords attendant with his Guard carrying
torches. Danish March. Sound a Flourish.*
    HAMLET
They are coming to the play: I must be idle;° Get   115
you a place.
    KING
How fares our cousin Hamlet?
    HAMLET
Excellent, i' faith, of the chameleon's dish;° I eat   120
the air, promise-crammed; you cannot feed
capons so.
    KING
I have nothing with this answer, Hamlet; these
words are not mine.   125
    HAMLET
No, nor mine now.
(*To* POLONIUS) My lord, you played once i' th'
university, you say?
    POLONIUS   130
That did I, my lord, and was accounted a good
actor.
    HAMLET
What did you enact?
    POLONIUS   135
I did enact Julius Caesar. I was killed i' th'
Capitol; Brutus killed me.
    HAMLET
It was a brute part of him to kill so capital a calf
there. By the players ready?   140
    ROSENCRANTZ
Ay, my lord. They stay upon your patience.
    QUEEN
Come hither, my dear Hamlet, sit by me.
    HAMLET   145
No, good mother. Here's metal more attractive.°
    POLONIUS
(*To the* KING) O ho! Do you mark that?

71 **coped withal** met with   76 **advancement** promotion
80 **candied** sugared, flattering   81 **pregnant** (1) pliant
(2) full of promise of good fortune   82 **thrift** profit   86
S' hath sealed thee she (the soul) has set a mark on you
90 **blood** passion   91 **commeddled** blended   101 **very
comment** deepest wisdom   102 **occulted** hidden

106 **stithy** forge, smithy   109 **censure of his seeming**
judgment on his looks   115 **be idle** play the fool   120
the chameleon's dish air (on which chameleons were
thought to live)   146 **attractive** magnetic

150   HAMLET
Lady, shall I lie in your lap? (*He lies at* OPHELIA'S
feet.)
OPHELIA
No, my lord.
HAMLET
155 I mean, my head upon your lap?
OPHELIA
Ay, my lord.
HAMLET
Do you think I meant country matters?°
160 OPHELIA
I think nothing, my lord.
HAMLET
That's a fair thought to lie between maids' legs.
OPHELIA
165 What is, my lord?
HAMLET
Nothing.
OPHELIA
You are merry, my lord.
170 HAMLET
Who, I?
OPHELIA
Ay, my lord.
HAMLET
175 O God, your only jig-maker!° What should a man
do but be merry? For look you how cheerfully my
mother looks, and my father died within's two
hours.
OPHELIA
180 Nay, 'tis twice two months, my lord.
HAMLET
So long? Nay then, let the devil wear black, for I'll
have a suit of sables.° O heavens! Die two months
ago, and not forgotten yet? Then there's hope a
185 great man's memory may outlive his life half a
year. But, by'r Lady, 'a must build churches then,
or else shall 'a suffer not thinking on, with the
hobbyhorse,° whose epitaph is "For O, for O, the
hobbyhorse is forgot!"
The trumpets sound. Dumb show follows: Enter a
King and a Queen very lovingly, the Queen embracing

him, and he her. She kneels; and makes show of
protestation unto him. He takes her up, and declines
his head upon her neck. He lies him down upon a bank
of flowers. She, seeing him asleep, leaves him. Anon
come in another man: takes off his crown, kisses it,
pours poison in the sleeper's ears, and leaves him. The
Queen returns, finds the King dead, makes passionate
action. The poisoner, with some three or four, come in
again, seem to condole with her. The dead body is carried
away. The poisoner woos the Queen with gifts; she seems
harsh awhile, but in the end accepts love. (*Exeunt.*)
190 OPHELIA
What means this, my lord?
HAMLET
Marry, this is miching mallecho;° it means
mischief.
195 OPHELIA
Belike this show imports the argument° of the
play.
Enter PROLOGUE.
HAMLET
We shall know by this fellow. The players cannot
keep counsel; they'll tell all. 200
OPHELIA
Will 'a tell us what this show meant?
HAMLET
Ay, or any show that you will show him. Be not
you ashamed to show, he'll not shame to tell you 205
what it means.
OPHELIA
You are naught,° you are naught; I'll mark the
play.
PROLOGUE 210
For us, and for our tragedy,
Here stooping to your clemency,
We beg your hearing patiently. (*Exit.*)
HAMLET
Is this a prologue, or the posy of a ring?° 215
OPHELIA
'Tis brief, my lord.
HAMLET
As a woman's love.
Enter (*two* PLAYERS *as*) *King and Queen.*
PLAYER KING 220
Full thirty times hath Phoebus' cart° gone round

159 **country matters** rustic doings (with a pun on the vulgar word for the pudendum)   175 **jig-maker** composer
of songs and dances (often a Fool, who performed them)
183 **sables** (pun on "black" and "luxurious furs")   188
hobbyhorse mock horse worn by a performer in the morris dance

193 **miching mallecho** sneaking mischief   196 **argument**
plot   208 **naught** wicked, improper   215 **posy of a ring**
motto inscribed in a ring   221 **Phoebus' cart** the sun's
chariot

Neptune's salt wash° and Tellus'° orbéd ground,
And thirty dozen moons with borrowed sheen
About the world have times twelve thirties been,
225 Since love our hearts, and Hymen did our hands,
Unite commutual in most sacred bands.

PLAYER QUEEN

So many journeys may the sun and moon
Make us again count o'er ere love be done!
230 But woe is me, you are so sick of late,
So far from cheer and from your former state,
That I distrust° you. Yet, though I distrust,
Discomfort you, my lord, it nothing must.
For women fear too much, even as they love,
235 And women's fear and love hold quantity,
In neither aught, or in extremity.°
Now what my love is, proof° hath made you
       know,
And as my love is sized, my fear is so.
240 Where love is great, the littlest doubts are fear;
Where little fears grow great, great love grows
       there.

PLAYER KING

Faith, I must leave thee, love, and shortly too;
245 My operant° powers their functions leave to do:
And thou shalt live in this fair world behind,
Honored, beloved, and haply one as kind
For husband shalt thou—

PLAYER QUEEN

250 O, confound the rest!
Such love must needs be treason in my breast.
In second husband let me be accurst!
None wed the second but who killed the first.

HAMLET

255 (*Aside*) That's wormwood.°

PLAYER QUEEN

The instances° that second marriage move°
Are base respects of thrift,° but none of love.
A second time I kill my husband dead
260 When second husband kisses me in bed.

PLAYER KING

I do believe you think what now you speak,
But what we do determine oft we break.
Purpose is but the slave to memory,
Of violent birth, but poor validity,°   265
Which now like fruit unripe sticks on the tree,
But fall unshaken when they mellow be.
Most necessary 'tis that we forget
To pay ourselves what to ourselves is debt.
What to ourselves in passion we propose,   270
The passion ending, doth the purpose lose.
The violence of either grief or joy
Their own enactures° with themselves destroy;
Where joy most revels, grief doth most lament;
Grief joys, joy grieves, on slender accident.   275
This world is not for aye, nor 'tis not strange
That even our loves should with our fortunes
       change,
For 'tis a question left us yet to prove,
Whether love lead fortune, or else fortune love.   280
The great man down, you mark his favorite flies;
The poor advanced makes friends of enemies;
And hitherto doth love on fortune tend,
For who not needs shall never lack a friend;
And who in want a hollow friend doth try,   285
Directly seasons him° his enemy.
But, orderly to end where I begun,
Our wills and fates do so contrary run
That our devices still are overthrown;
Our thoughts are ours, their ends none of our   290
       own.
So think thou wilt no second husband wed,
But die thy thoughts when thy first lord is dead.

PLAYER QUEEN

Nor earth to me give food, nor heaven light,   295
Sport and repose lock from me day and night,
To desperation turn my trust and hope,
An anchor's° cheer in prison be my scope,
Each opposite that blanks° the face of joy
Meet what I would have well, and it destroy: 300
Both here and hence pursue me lasting strife,
If, once a widow, ever I be wife!

HAMLET

If she should break it now!

PLAYER KING   305

'Tis deeply sworn. Sweet, leave me here awhile;

---

222 **Neptune's salt wash** the sea   222 **Tellus** Roman
goddess of the earth   232 **distrust** am anxious about
235–36 **And women's…in extremity** (perhaps the idea is
that women's anxiety is great or little in proportion to
their love. The previous line, unrhymed, may be a false
start that Shakespeare neglected to delete)   237 **proof**
experience   245 **operant** active   255 **wormwood** a bitter
herb   257 **instances** motives   257 **move** induce   258 **respects of thrift** considerations of profit

265 **validity** strength   273 **enactures** acts   286 **seasons
him** ripens him into   298 **anchor's** anchorite's, hermit's
299 **opposite that blanks** adverse thing that blanches

My spirits grow dull, and fain I would beguile
The tedious day with sleep.
    PLAYER QUEEN
Sleep rock thy brain,
310 (*He*) *sleeps.*
And never come mischance between us twain!
Exit.
    HAMLET
Madam, how like you this play?
    QUEEN
315 The lady doth protest too much, methinks.
    HAMLET
O, but she'll keep her word.
    KING
Have you heard the argument?° Is there no
320 offense in't?
    HAMLET
No, no, they do but jest, poison in jest; no offense
i' th' world.
    KING
325 What do you call the play?
    HAMLET
The Mousetrap. Marry, how? Tropically.° This play
is the image of a murder done in Vienna:
Gonzago is the Duke's name; his wife, Baptista.
330 You shall see anon. 'Tis a knavish piece of work,
but what of that? Your Majesty, and we that have
free° souls, it touches us not. Let the galled jade
winch;° our withers are unwrung.
Enter LUCIANUS.
This is one Lucianus, nephew to the King.
335   **OPHELIA**
You are as good as a chorus, my lord.
    HAMLET
I could interpret° between you and your love, if I
could see the puppets dallying.
340   **OPHELIA**
You are keen,° my lord, you are keen.
    HAMLET
It would cost you a groaning to take off mine
edge.
345   **OPHELIA**
Still better, and worse.

    HAMLET
So you mistake° your husbands.—Begin,
murderer. Leave thy damnable faces and begin.
Come, the croaking raven doth bellow for revenge. 350
    LUCIANUS
Thoughts black, hands apt, drugs fit, and time
agreeing.
Confederate season,° else no creature seeing, 355
Thou mixture rank, of midnight weeds collected,
With Hecate's ban° thrice blasted, thrice infected,
Thy natural magic and dire property°
On wholesome life usurps immediately.
Pours the poison in his ears.
    HAMLET 360
'A poisons him i' th' garden for his estate. His
name's Gonzago. The story is extant, and written
in very choice Italian. You shall see anon how the
murderer gets the love of Gonzago's wife.
    OPHELIA 365
The King rises.
    HAMLET
What, frighted with false fire?°
    QUEEN
How fares my lord? 370
    POLONIUS
Give o'er the play.
    KING
Give me some light. Away!
    POLONIUS 375
Lights, lights, lights!
Exeunt all but HAMLET *and* HORATIO.
    HAMLET
Why, let the strucken deer go weep,
The hart ungallèd play:
For some must watch, while some must sleep; 380
Thus runs the world away.
Would not this, sir, and a forest of feathers°—if the
rest of my fortunes turn Turk° with me—with two
Provincial roses° on my razed° shoes, get me a
fellowship in a cry° of players? 385

324 **argument** plot   327 **Tropically** figuratively (with a
pun on "trap")   332 **free** innocent   332–33 **galled jade
winch** chafed horse wince   338 **interpret** (like a showman
explaining the action of puppets)   341 **keen** (1) sharp
(2) sexually aroused

348 **mistake** err in taking   355 **Confederate season** the
opportunity allied with me   357 **Hecate's ban** the curse
of the goddess of sorcery   358 **property** nature   368
false fire blank discharge of firearms   382 **feathers**
(plumes were sometimes part of a costume)   383 **turn
Turk** i.e., go bad, treat me badly   384 **Provincial roses**
rosettes like the roses of Provence (?)   384 **razed** ornamented with slashes   385 **cry** pack, company

HORATIO

Half a share.

HAMLET

A whole one, I.

390 For thou dost know, O Damon dear,

This realm dismantled was

Of Jove himself, and now reigns here

A very, very—pajock.°

HORATIO

395 You might have rhymed.°

HAMLET

O good Horatio, I'll take the ghost's word for a

thousand pound. Didst perceive?

HORATIO

400 Very well, my lord.

HAMLET

Upon the talk of poisoning?

HORATIO

I did very well note him.

405 **HAMLET**

Ah ha! Come, some music! Come, the recorders!°

For if the King like not the comedy,

Why then, belike he likes it not, perdy.°

Come, some music!

Enter ROSENCRANTZ *and* GUILDENSTERN.

410 **GUILDENSTERN**

Good my lord, vouchsafe me a word with you.

HAMLET

Sir, a whole history.

GUILDENSTERN

415 The King, sir—

HAMLET

Ay, sir, what of him?

GUILDENSTERN

Is in his retirement marvelous distemp'red.

420 **HAMLET**

With drink, sir?

GUILDENSTERN

No, my lord, with choler.°

HAMLET

425 Your wisdom should show itself more richer to

signify this to the doctor, for for me to put him to

his purgation would perhaps plunge him into

more choler.

GUILDENSTERN

Good my lord, put your discourse into some   430

frame,° and start not so wildly from my affair.

HAMLET

I am tame, sir; pronounce.

GUILDENSTERN

The Queen, your mother, in most great affliction   435

of spirit hath sent me to you.

HAMLET

You are welcome.

GUILDENSTERN

Nay, good my lord, this courtesy is not of the   440

right breed. If it shall please you to make me a

wholesome answer, I will do your mother's

commandment: if not, your pardon and my

return shall be the end of my business.

HAMLET   445

Sir, I cannot.

ROSENCRANTZ

What, my lord?

HAMLET

Make you a wholesome° answer; my wit's   450

diseased. But, sir, such answer as I can make, you

shall command, or rather, as you say, my mother.

Therefore no more, but to the matter. My mother,

you say—

ROSENCRANTZ   455

Then thus she says: your behavior hath struck her

into amazement and admiration.°

HAMLET

O wonderful son, that can so astonish a mother!

But is there no sequel at the heels of this mother's   460

admiration? Impart.

ROSENCRANTZ

She desires to speak with you in her closet ere

you go to bed.

HAMLET   465

We shall obey, were she ten times our mother.

Have you any further trade with us?

ROSENCRANTZ

My lord, you once did love me.

HAMLET   470

And do still, by these pickers and stealers.°

ROSENCRANTZ

Good my lord, what is your cause of distemper?

---

393 **pajock** peacock   395 **You might have rhymed** i.e.,
rhymed "was" with "ass"   406 **recorders** flutelike
instruments   408 **perdy** by God (French: **par dieu**)   423
choler anger (but Hamlet pretends to take the word in its
sense of "biliousness")

431 **frame** order, control   450 **wholesome** sane   457 **admiration** wonder   471 **pickers and stealers** i.e., hands
(with reference to the prayer; "Keep my hands from picking and stealing")

You do surely bar the door upon your own
475 liberty, if you deny your griefs to your friend.

HAMLET

Sir, I lack advancement.°

ROSENCRANTZ

How can that be, when you have the voice of the
480 King himself for your succession in Denmark?

Enter the PLAYERS *with recorders.*

HAMLET

Ay, sir, but "while the grass grows"—the
proverb° is something musty. O, the recorders.
Let me see one. To withdraw° with you—why do
485 you go about to recover the wind° of me as if you
would drive me into a toil?°

GUILDENSTERN

O my lord, if my duty be too bold, my love is too
unmannerly.°

490 HAMLET

I do not understand that. Will you play upon this
pipe?

GUILDENSTERN

My lord, I cannot.

495 HAMLET

I pray you.

GUILDENSTERN

Believe me, I cannot.

HAMLET

500 I beseech you.

GUILDENSTERN

I know no touch of it, my lord.

HAMLET

It is as easy as lying. Govern these ventages° with
505 your fingers and thumb, give it breath with your
mouth, and it will discourse most eloquent music.
Look you, these are the stops.

GUILDENSTERN

But these cannot I command to any utt'rance of
510 harmony; I have not the skill.

HAMLET

Why, look you now, how unworthy a thing you
make of me! You would play upon me; you
would seem to know my stops; you would pluck

out the heart of my mystery; you would sound 515
me from my lowest note to the top of my
compass;° and there is much music, excellent
voice, in this little organ,° yet cannot you make it
speak. 'Sblood, do you think I am easier to be
played on than a pipe? Call me what instrument 520
you will, though you can fret° me, you cannot
play upon me.

Enter POLONIUS.

God bless you, sir!

POLONIUS

My lord, the Queen would speak with you, and 525
presently.

HAMLET

Do you see yonder cloud that's almost in shape of
a camel?

POLONIUS 530

By th' mass and 'tis, like a camel indeed.

HAMLET

Methinks it is like a weasel.

POLONIUS

It is backed like a weasel. 535

HAMLET

Or like a whale.

POLONIUS

Very like a whale.

HAMLET 540

Then I will come to my mother by and by. (*Aside*)
They fool me to the top of my bent.°—I will come
by and by.°

POLONIUS

I will say so. (*Exit.*) 545

HAMLET

"By and by" is easily said. Leave me, friends.

Exeunt all but HAMLET.

'Tis now the very witching time of night,
When churchyards yawn, and hell itself breathes
out
Contagion to this world. Now could I drink hot 550
blood
And do such bitter business as the day
Would quake to look on. Soft, now to my mother.
O heart, lose not thy nature; let not ever 555

---

477 **advancement** promotion 483 **proverb** ("While the
grass groweth, the horse starveth") 484 **withdraw** speak
in private 485 **recover the wind** get on the windward
side (as in hunting) 486 **toil** snare 488–89 **if my duty
…too unmannerly** i.e., if these questions seem rude, it is
because my love for you leads me beyond good manners. 504 **ventages** vents, stops on a recorder

517 **compass** range of voice 518 **organ** i.e., the recorder
521 **fret** vex (with a pun alluding to the frets, or ridges,
that guide the fingering on some instruments) 542
They fool…my bent they compel me to play the fool to
the limit of my capacity 543 **by and by** very soon

The soul of Nero° enter this firm bosom.
Let me be cruel, not unnatural;
I will speak daggers to her, but use none.
My tongue and soul in this be hypocrites:
565 How in my words somever she be shent,°
To give them seals° never, my soul, consent! (*Exit.*)

SCENE III

The castle.

Enter KING, ROSENCRANTZ, *and* GUILDENSTERN.

    KING
I like him not, nor stands it safe with us
To let his madness range. Therefore prepare you.
I your commission will forthwith dispatch,
5 And he to England shall along with you.
The terms° of our estate may not endure
Hazard so near's° as doth hourly grow
Out of his brows.
    GUILDENSTERN
10 We will ourselves provide.
Most holy and religious fear it is
To keep those many many bodies safe
That live and feed upon your Majesty.
    ROSENCRANTZ
15 The single and peculiar° life is bound
With all the strength and armor of the mind
To keep itself from noyance,° but much more
That spirit upon whose weal depends and rests
The lives of many. The cess of majesty°
20 Dies not alone, but like a gulf° doth draw
What's near it with it; or it is a massy wheel
Fixed on the summit of the highest mount,
To whose huge spokes ten thousand lesser things
Are mortised and adjoined, which when it falls,
25 Each small annexment, petty consequence,
Attends° the boist'rous ruin. Never alone
Did the King sigh, but with a general groan.
    KING
Arm° you, I pray you, to this speedy voyage,
30 For we will fetters put about this fear,
Which now goes too free-footed.

---

556 **Nero** (Roman emperor who had his mother murdered) 560 **shent** rebuked 561 **give them seals** confirm them with deeds **III.iii.** 6 **terms** conditions 7 **near's** near us 15 **peculiar** individual, private 17 **noyance** injury 19 **cess of majesty** cessation (death) of a king 20 **gulf** whirlpool 26 **Attends** waits on, participates in 29 **Arm** prepare

    ROSENCRANTZ
We will haste us.
Exeunt Gentlemen.
Enter POLONIUS.
    POLONIUS
My lord, he's going to his mother's closet.°   35
Behind the arras I'll convey myself
To hear the process.° I'll warrant she'll tax him
    home,°
And, as you said, and wisely was it said,
'Tis meet that some more audience than a mother,   40
Since nature makes them partial, should o'erhear
The speech of vantage.° Fare you well, my liege.
I'll call upon you ere you go to bed
And tell you what I know.
    KING   45
Thanks, dear my lord.
Exit POLONIUS.
O, my offense is rank, it smells to heaven;
It hath the primal eldest curse° upon't,
A brother's murder. Pray can I not,
Though inclination be as sharp as will.   50
My stronger guilt defeats my strong intent,
And like a man to double business bound
I stand in pause where I shall first begin,
And both neglect. What if this cursèd hand
Were thicker than itself with brother's blood,   55
Is there not rain enough in the sweet heavens
To wash it white as snow? Whereto serves mercy
But to confront° the visage of offense?
And what's in prayer but this twofold force,
To be forestallèd ere we come to fall,   60
Or pardoned being down? Then I'll look up.
My fault is past. But, O, what form of prayer
Can serve my turn? "Forgive me my foul murder"?
That cannot be, since I am still possessed   65
Of those effects° for which I did the murder,
My crown, mine own ambition, and my queen.
May one be pardoned and retain th' offense?
In the corrupted currents of this world
Offense's gilded hand may shove by justice,   70
And oft 'tis seen the wicked prize itself
Buys out the law. But 'tis not so above.
There is no shuffling°; there the action lies

---

35 **closet** private room 37 **process** proceedings 37–38 **tax him home** censure him sharply 42 **of vantage** from an advantageous place 48 **primal eldest curse** (curse of Cain, who killed Abel) 58 **confront** oppose 66 **effects** things gained 73 **shuffling** trickery

In his true nature, and we ourselves compelled,
75 Even to the teeth and forehead of our faults,
To give in evidence. What then? What rests?°
Try what repentance can. What can it not?
Yet what can it when one cannot repent?
O wretched state! O bosom black as death!
80 O limèd soul,° that struggling to be free
Art more engaged!° Help, angels! Make assay.°
Bow, stubborn knees, and, heart with strings of
       steel,
Be soft as sinews of the newborn babe.
85 All may be well. (*He kneels.*)
       Enter HAMLET.
              HAMLET
Now might I do it pat, now 'a is a-praying,
And now I'll do't. And so 'a goes to heaven,
And so am I revenged. That would be scanned.°
90 A villain kills my father, and for that
I, his sole son, do this same villain send
To heaven.
Why, this is hire and salary, not revenge.
'A took my father grossly, full of bread,°
95 With all his crimes broad blown,° as flush° as
       May;
And how his audit° stands, who knows save
       heaven?
But in our circumstance and course of thought,
100 'Tis heavy with him; and am I then revenged,
To take him in the purging of his soul,
When he is fit and seasoned for his passage?
No.
Up, sword, and know thou a more horrid hent.°
105 When he is drunk asleep, or in his rage,
Or in th' incestuous pleasure of his bed,
At game a-swearing, or about some act
That has no relish° of salvation in't—
Then trip him, that his heels may kick at heaven,
110 And that his soul may be as damned and black
As hell, whereto it goes. My mother stays.
This physic° but prolongs thy sickly days. (*Exit.*)

76 **rests** remains   80 **limèd** caught (as with birdlime, a sticky substance spread on boughs to snare birds)   81 **engaged** ensnared   81 **assay** an attempt   89 **would be scanned** ought to be looked into   94 **bread** i.e., worldly gratification   95 **crimes broad blown** sins in full bloom   95 **flush** vigorous   97 **audit** account   104 **hent** grasp (here, occasion for seizing)   108 **relish** flavor   112 **physic** (Claudius' purgation by prayer, as Hamlet thinks in line 101)

              KING
(*Rises*) My words fly up, my thoughts remain
       below.   115
Words without thoughts never to heaven go. (*Exit.*)

SCENE IV

The Queen's closet.

Enter (QUEEN) GERTRUDE *and* POLONIUS.

              POLONIUS
'A will come straight. Look you lay home° to him.
Tell him his pranks have been too broad° to bear
       with,
And that your Grace hath screened and stood   5
       between
Much heat and him. I'll silence me even here.
Pray you be round with him.
              HAMLET
(*Within*) Mother, Mother, Mother!   10
              QUEEN
I'll warrant you; fear me not.
Withdraw; I hear him coming.
(POLONIUS *hides behind the arras.*)
Enter HAMLET.
              HAMLET
Now, Mother, what's the matter?   15
              QUEEN
Hamlet, thou hast thy father much offended.
              HAMLET
Mother, you have my father much offended.
              QUEEN   20
Come, come, you answer with an idle° tongue.
              HAMLET
Go, go, you question with a wicked tongue.
              QUEEN
Why, how now, Hamlet?   25
              HAMLET
What's the matter now?
              QUEEN
Have you forgot me?
              HAMLET   30
No, by the rood,° not so!
You are the Queen, your husband's brother's wife,
And, would it were not so, you are my mother.
              QUEEN
Nay, then I'll set those to you that can speak.   35

III.iv. 2 lay home thrust (rebuke) him sharply   **3 broad** unrestrained   **21 idle** foolish   **31 rood** cross

HAMLET
Come, come, and sit you down. You shall not budge.
You go not till I set you up a glass°
40 Where you may see the inmost part of you!
QUEEN
What wilt thou do? Thou wilt not murder me?
Help, ho!
POLONIUS
45 (*Behind*) What, ho! Help!
HAMLET
(*Draws*) How now? A rat? Dead for a ducat, dead!
(*Makes a pass through the arras and*) kills **POLONIUS.**
POLONIUS
(*Behind*) O, I am slain!
50 **QUEEN**
O me, what hast thou done?
HAMLET
Nay, I know not. Is it the King?
QUEEN
55 O, what a rash and bloody deed is this!
HAMLET
A bloody deed—almost as bad, good Mother,
As kill a king, and marry with his brother.
QUEEN
60 As kill a king?
HAMLET
Ay, lady, it was my word.
(*Lifts up the arras and sees* POLONIUS.)
Thou wretched, rash, intruding fool, farewell!
I took thee for thy better. Take thy fortune.
65 Thou find'st to be too busy is some danger.—
Leave wringing of your hands. Peace, sit you down
And let me wring your heart, for so I shall
If it be made of penetrable stuff,
70 If damnèd custom have not brazed° it so
That it be proof° and bulwark against sense.°
QUEEN
What have I done that thou dar'st wag thy tongue
In noise so rude against me?
75 **HAMLET**
Such an act
That blurs the grace and blush of modesty,
Calls virtue hypocrite, takes off the rose
From the fair forehead of an innocent love,
80 And sets a blister° there, makes marriage vows

39 **glass** mirror   70 **brazed** hardened like brass   71 **proof**
armor   71 **sense** feeling   80 **sets a blister** brands (as a
harlot)

As false as dicers' oaths. O, such a deed
As from the body of contraction° plucks
The very soul, and sweet religion makes
A rhapsody° of words! Heaven's face does glow
O'er this solidity and compound mass   85
With heated visage, as against the doom
Is thoughtsick at the act.°
QUEEN
Ay me, what act,
That roars so loud and thunders in the index?°   90
HAMLET
Look here upon this picture, and on this,
The counterfeit presentment° of two brothers.
See what a grace was seated on this brow:
Hyperion's curls, the front° of Jove himself,   95
An eye like Mars, to threaten and command,
A station° like the herald Mercury
New lighted on a heaven-kissing hill—
A combination and a form indeed
Where every god did seem to set his seal   100
To give the world assurance of a man.
This was your husband. Look you now what
    follows.
Here is your husband, like a mildewed ear
Blasting his wholesome brother. Have you eyes? 105
Could you on this fair mountain leave to feed,
And batten° on this moor? Ha! Have you eyes?
You cannot call it love, for at your age
The heyday° in the blood is tame, it's humble,
And waits upon the judgment, and what   110
    judgment
Would step from this to this? Sense° sure you
    have,
Else could you not have motion, but sure that
    sense   115
Is apoplexed,° for madness would not err,
Nor sense to ecstasy° was neer so thralled
But it reserved some quantity of choice
To serve in such a difference. What devil was't
That thus hath cozened you at hoodman-blind?°   120
Eyes without feeling, feeling without sight,

82 **contraction** marriage contract   84 **rhapsody** senseless
string   84–87 **Heaven's face...the act** i.e., the face of
heaven blushes over this earth (compounded of four elements), the face hot, as if Judgment Day were near, and it
is thoughtsick at the act   90 **index** prologue   93 **counterfeit presentment** represented image   95 **front** forehead   97 **station** bearing   107 **batten** feed gluttonously
109 **heyday** excitement   112 **Sense** feeling   116 **apoplexed** paralyzed   117 **ecstasy** madness

Ears without hands or eyes, smelling sans° all,
Or but a sickly part of one true sense
Could not so mope.°
125 O shame, where is thy blush? Rebellious hell,
If thou canst mutine in a matron's bones,
To flaming youth let virtue be as wax
And melt in her own fire. Proclaim no shame
When the compulsive ardor° gives the charge,
130 Since frost itself as actively doth burn,
And reason panders will.°

    QUEEN
O Hamlet, speak no more.
Thou turn'st mine eyes into my very soul,
135 And there I see such black and grainèd° spots
As will not leave their tinct.°

    HAMLET
Nay, but to live
In the rank sweat of an enseamèd° bed,
140 Stewed in corruption, honeying and making love
Over the nasty sty—

    QUEEN
O, speak to me no more.
These words like daggers enter in my ears.
145 No more, sweet Hamlet.

    HAMLET
A murderer and a villain,
A slave that is not twentieth part the tithe°
Of your precedent lord, a vice° of kings,
150 A cutpurse of the empire and the rule,
That from a shelf the precious diadem stole
And put it in his pocket—

    QUEEN
No more.

Enter GHOST.

155   HAMLET
A king of shreds and patches—
Save me and hover o'er me with your wings,
You heavenly guards! What would your gracious
    figure?

    QUEEN   160
Alas, he's mad.

    HAMLET
Do you not come your tardy son to chide,
That, lapsed in time and passion, lets go by
Th' important acting of your dread command?   165
O, say!

    GHOST
Do not forget. This visitation
Is but to whet thy almost blunted purpose.
But look, amazement on thy mother sits.   170
O, step between her and her fighting soul!
Conceit° in weakest bodies strongest works.
Speak to her, Hamlet.

    HAMLET
How is it with you, lady?   175

    QUEEN
Alas, how is't with you,
That you do bend your eye on vacancy,
And with th' incorporal° air do hold discourse?
Forth at your eyes your spirits wildly peep,   180
And as the sleeping soldiers in th' alarm
Your bedded hair° like life in excrements°
Start up and stand an end.° O gentle son,
Upon the heat and flame of thy distemper
Sprinkle cool patience. Whereon do you look?   185

    HAMLET
On him, on him! Look you, how pale he glares!
His form and cause conjoined, preaching to
    stones,
Would make them capable.°—Do not look upon   190
    me,
Lest with this piteous action you convert
My stern effects.° Then what I have to do
Will want true color; tears perchance for blood.

    QUEEN   195
To whom do you speak this?

    HAMLET
Do you see nothing there?

    QUEEN
Nothing at all; yet all that is I see.   200

    HAMLET
Nor did you nothing hear?

---

120 **cozened you at hoodman-blind** cheated you at blindman's buff 122 **sans** without 124 **mope** be stupid 129 **compulsive ardor** compelling passion 131 **reason panders will** reason acts as a procurer for desire 135 **grainèd** dye in grain (fast dyed) 136 **tinct** color 139 **enseamèd** (perhaps "soaked in grease," i.e., sweaty; perhaps "much wrinkled") 148 **tithe** tenth part 149 **vice** (like the Vice, a fool and mischief-maker in the old morality plays)

172 **Conceit** imagination 179 **incorporal** bodiless 182 **bedded hair** hairs laid flat 182 **excrements** outgrowths (here, the hair) 183 **an end** on end 190 **capable** receptive 192–93 **convert/My stern effects** divert my stern deeds

QUEEN

No, nothing but ourselves.

205   HAMLET

Why, look you there! Look how it steals away!
My father, in his habit° as he lived!
Look where he goes even now out at the portal!

Exit GHOST.

QUEEN

210 This is the very coinage of your brain.
This bodiless creation ecstasy
Is very cunning in.

HAMLET

Ecstasy?

215 My pulse as yours doth temperately keep time
And makes as healthful music. It is not madness
That I have uttered. Bring me to the test,
And I the matter will reword, which madness
Would gambol° from. Mother, for love of grace,

220 Lay not that flattering unction° to your soul,
That not your trespass but my madness speaks.
It will but skin and film the ulcerous place
Whiles rank corruption, mining° all within,
Infects unseen. Confess yourself to heaven,

225 Repent what's past, avoid what is to come,
And do not spread the compost° on the weeds
To make them ranker. Forgive me this my virtue.
For in the fatness of these pursy° times
Virtue itself of vice must pardon beg,

230 Yea, curb° and woo for leave to do him good.

QUEEN

O Hamlet, thou hast cleft my heart in twain.

HAMLET

O, throw away the worser part of it,

235 And live the purer with the other half.
Good night—but go not to my uncle's bed.
Assume a virtue, if you have it not.
That monster custom, who all sense doth eat,
Of habits devil, is angel yet in this,

240 That to the use° of actions fair and good
He likewise gives a frock or livery°
That aptly is put on. Refrain tonight,

And that shall lend a kind of easiness
To the next abstinence; the next more easy;
For use almost can change the stamp of nature,   245
And either° the devil, or throw him out
With wondrous potency. Once more, good night,
And when you are desirous to be blest,
I'll blessing beg of you.—For this same lord,
I do repent; but heaven hath pleased it so,   250
To punish me with this, and this with me,
That I must be their° scourge and minister.
I will bestow° him and will answer well
The death I gave him. So again, good night.
I must be cruel only to be kind.   255
Thus bad begins, and worse remains behind.
One word more, good lady.

QUEEN

What shall I do?

HAMLET   260

Not this, by no means, that I bid you do:
Let the bloat King tempt you again to bed,
Pinch wanton on your cheek, call you his mouse,
And let him, for a pair of reechy° kisses,
Or paddling in your neck with his damned   265
    fingers,
Make you to ravel° all this matter out,
That I essentially am not in madness,
But mad in craft. 'Twere good you let him know,
For who that's but a queen, fair, sober, wise,   270
Would from a paddock,° from a bat, a gib,°
Such dear concernings hide? Who would do so?
No, in despite of sense and secrecy,
Unpeg the basket on the house's top,
Let the birds fly, and like the famous ape,   275
To try conclusions,° in the basket creep
And break your own neck down.

QUEEN

Be thou assured, if words be made of breath,
And breath of life, I have no life to breathe   280
What thou hast said to me.

HAMLET

I must to England; you know that?

---

207 **habit** garment (Q1, though a "bad" quarto, is probably correct in saying that at line 156 the ghost enters "in his nightgown," i.e., dressing gown) 219 **gambol** start away 220 **unction** ointment 223 **mining** undermining 226 **compost** fertilizing substance 228 **pursy** bloated 230 **curb** bow low 240 **use** practice 241 **livery** characteristic garment (punning on "habits" in line 239)

246 **either** (probably a word is missing after **either**; among suggestions are "master," "curb," and "house"; but possibly **either** is a verb meaning "make easier") 252 **their** i.e., the heavens' 253 **bestow** stow, lodge 264 **reechy** foul (literally "smoky") 267 **ravel** unravel, reveal 271 **paddock** toad 271 **gib** tomcat 276 **To try conclusions** to make experiments

QUEEN

285 Alack,
I had forgot. 'Tis so concluded on.

HAMLET

There's letters sealed, and my two school fellows
Whom I will trust as I will adders fanged,
290 They bear the mandate° they must sweep my way
And marshal me to knavery. Let it work;
For 'tis the sport to have the enginer
Hoist with his own petar,° and 't shall go hard
But I will delve one yard below their mines
295 And blow them at the moon. O, 'tis most sweet
When in one line two crafts° directly meet.
This man shall set me packing:
I'll lug the guts into the neighbor room.
Mother, good night. Indeed, this counselor
300 Is now most still, most secret, and most grave,
Who was in life a foolish prating knave.
Come, sir, to draw toward an end with you.
Good night, Mother.

(*Exit the* QUEEN. *Then exit* HAMLET, *tugging in*
POLONIUS.)

ACT IV

SCENE I

The castle.

Enter KING *and* QUEEN, *with* ROSENCRANTZ *and* GUIL-
DENSTERN.

KING

There's matter in these sighs. These profound
heaves
You must translate; 'tis fit we understand them.
5 Where is your son?

QUEEN

Bestow this place on us a little while.
(*Exeunt* ROSENCRANTZ *and* GUILDENSTERN.)
Ah, mine own lord, what have I seen tonight!

KING

10 What, Gertrude? How does Hamlet?

QUEEN

Mad as the sea and wind when both contend
Which is the mightier. In his lawless fit,
Behind the arras hearing something stir,

Whips out his rapier, cries, "A rat, a rat!"   15
And in this brainish apprehension° kills
The unseen good old man.

KING

O heavy deed!
It had been so with us, had we been there.   20
His liberty is full of threats to all,
To you yourself, to us, to every one.
Alas, how shall this bloody deed be answered?
It will be laid to us, whose providence°
Should have kept short, restrained, and out of   25
haunt°
This mad young man. But so much was our love
We would not understand what was most fit,
But, like the owner of a foul disease,
To keep it from divulging, let it feed   30
Even on the pith of life. Where is he gone?

QUEEN

To draw apart the body he hath killed;
O'er whom his very madness, like some ore
Among a mineral° of metals base,   35
Shows itself pure. 'A weeps for what is done.

KING

O Gertrude, come away!
The sun no sooner shall the mountains touch
But we will ship him hence, and this vile deed   40
We must with all our majesty and skill
Both countenance and excuse. Ho, Guildenstern!
Enter ROSENCRANTZ *and* GUILDENSTERN.
Friends both, go join you with some further aid:
Hamlet in madness hath Polonius slain,
And from his mother's closet hath he dragged   45
him.
Go seek him out; speak fair, and bring the body
Into the chapel. I pray you haste in this.
Exeunt ROSENCRANTZ *and* GUILDENSTERN.
Come, Gertrude, we'll call up our wisest friends
And let them know both what we mean to do   50
And what's untimely done…°
Whose whisper o'er the world's diameter,
As level as the cannon to his blank°
Transports his poisoned shot, may miss our name

IV.i. 16 **brainish apprehension** mad imagination 24
providence foresight   25–26 **out of haunt** away from association with others   34–35 **ore/Among a mineral** vein
of gold in a mine   51 **done…** (evidently something has
dropped out of the text. Capell's conjecture, "So, haply
slander," is usually printed)   53 **blank** white center of a
target

290 **mandate** command   293 **petar** bomb   296 **crafts**
(1) boats (2) acts of guile, crafty schemes

55 And hit the woundless° air. O, come away!
   My soul is full of discord and dismay. (*Exeunt.*)

SCENE II

The castle.

Enter HAMLET.

HAMLET
Safely stowed.
   GENTLEMEN
(*Within*) Hamlet! Lord Hamlet!
   HAMLET
5 But soft, what noise? Who calls on Hamlet? O, here
   they come.
   Enter ROSENCRANTZ *and* GUILDENSTERN.
   ROSENCRANTZ
What have you done, my lord, with the dead
body?
10   HAMLET
Compounded it with dust, whereto 'tis kin.
   ROSENCRANTZ
Tell us where 'tis, that we may take it thence
And bear it to the chapel.
15   HAMLET
Do not believe it.
   ROSENCRANTZ
Believe what?
   HAMLET
20 That I can keep your counsel and not mine own.
   Besides, to be demanded of° a sponge, what
   replication° should be made by the son of a king?
      ROSENCRANTZ
Take you me for a sponge, my lord?
25   HAMLET
Ay, sir, that soaks up the King's countenance,° his
rewards, his authorities. But such officers do the
King best service in the end. He keeps them, like
an ape, in the corner of his jaw, first mouthed, to
30 be last swallowed. When he needs what you have
gleaned, it is but squeezing you and, sponge, you
shall be dry again.
   ROSENCRANTZ
I understand you not, my lord.
35   HAMLET
I am glad of it: a knavish speech sleeps in a
foolish ear.

   ROSENCRANTZ
My lord, you must tell us where the body is and
go with us to the King.   40
   HAMLET
The body is with the King, but the King is not
with the body. The King is a thing——
   GUILDENSTERN
A thing, my lord?   45
   HAMLET
Of nothing. Bring me to him.
Hide fox, and all after.° (*Exeunt.*)

SCENE III

The castle.

Enter KING *and two or three.*

   KING
I have sent to seek him and to find the body:
How dangerous is it that this man goes loose!
Yet must not we put the strong law on him:
He's loved of the distracted° multitude,   5
Who like not in their judgment, but their eyes,
And where 'tis so, th' offender's scourge is
   weighed,
But never the offense. To bear° all smooth and
   even,   10
This sudden sending him away must seem
Deliberate pause.° Diseases desperate grown
By desperate appliance are relieved,
Or not at all.
Enter ROSENCRANTZ, (GUILDENSTERN,) *and all the rest.*
How now? What hath befall'n?   15
   ROSENCRANTZ
Where the dead body is bestowed, my lord,
We cannot get from him.
   KING
But where is he?   20
   ROSENCRANTZ
Without, my lord; guarded, to know your pleasure.
   KING
Bring him before us.   25
   ROSENCRANTZ
Ho! Bring in the lord.
They enter.

---

55 **woundless** invulnerable **IV.ii. 21 demanded of** questioned by **22 replication** reply **26 countenance** favor

48 **Hide fox, and all after** (a cry in a game such as hide-
and-seek; Hamlet runs from the stage) **IV.iii. 5 distracted** bewildered, senseless **9 bear** carry out **12 pause**
planning

KING
Now, Hamlet, where's Polonius?

30 **HAMLET**
At supper.

KING
At supper? Where?

HAMLET
35 Not where he eats, but where 'a is eaten. A certain
convocation of politic° worms are e'en at him.
Your worm is your only emperor for diet. We fat
all creatures else to fat us, and we fat ourselves
for maggots. Your fat king and your lean beggar
40 is but variable service°—two dishes, but to one
table. That's the end.

KING
Alas, alas!

HAMLET
45 A man may fish with the worm that hath eat of a
king, and eat of the fish that hath fed of that
worm.

KING
What dost thou mean by this?

50 **HAMLET**
Nothing but to show you how a king may go a
progress° through the guts of a beggar.

KING
Where is Polonius?

55 **HAMLET**
In heaven. Send thither to see. If your messenger
find him not there, seek him i' th' other place
yourself. But if indeed you find him not within
this month, you shall nose him as you go up the
60 stairs into the lobby.

KING
(*To* ATTENDANTS) *Go seek him there.*

HAMLET
'A will stay till you come.
(*Exeunt* ATTENDANTS.)

65 **KING**
Hamlet, this deed, for thine especial safety,
Which we do tender° as we dearly grieve
For that which thou hast done, must send thee
    hence
70 With fiery quickness. Therefore prepare thyself.
The bark is ready and the wind at help,
Th' associates tend,° and everything is bent
For England.

HAMLET
For England?   75

KING
Ay, Hamlet.

HAMLET
Good.

KING   80
So is it, if thou knew'st our purposes.

HAMLET
I see a cherub° that sees them. But come, for
England! Farewell, dear Mother.

KING   85
Thy loving father, Hamlet.

HAMLET
My mother—father and mother is man and wife,
man and wife is one flesh, and so, my mother.
Come, for England! (*Exit*)   90

KING
Follow him at foot;° tempt him with speed aboard.
Delay it not; I'll have him hence tonight.
Away! For everything is sealed and done
That else leans° on th' affair. Pray you make haste. 95
(*Exeunt all but the* KING.)
And, England, if my love thou hold'st at aught—
As my great power thereof may give thee sense,
Since yet thy cicatrice° looks raw and red
After the Danish sword, and thy free awe°
Pays homage to us—thou mayst not coldly set 100
Our sovereign process,° which imports at full
By letters congruing to that effect
The present° death of Hamlet. Do it, England,
For like the hectic° in my blood he rages,
And thou must cure me. Till I know 'tis done, 105
Howe'er my haps,° my joys were ne'er begun.
(*Exit.*)

SCENE IV

A plain in Denmark.

Enter FORTINBRAS *with his Army over the stage.*

FORTINBRAS
Go, Captain, from me greet the Danish king.
Tell him that by his license Fortinbras
Craves the conveyance of° a promised march

---

36 **politic** statesmanlike, shrewd   40 **variable service**
different courses   52 **progress** royal journey   67 **tender**
hold dear   72 **tend** wait

83 **cherub** angel of knowledge   92 **at foot** closely   95
leans depends   98 **cicatrice** scar   99 **free awe** uncom-
pelled submission   100–01 **coldly set/Our sovereign
process** regard slightly our royal command   103 **present**
instant   104 **hectic** fever   105 **haps** chances, fortunes
IV.iv. 4 conveyance of escort for

5 Over his kingdom. You know the rendezvous.
   If that his Majesty would aught with us,
   We shall express our duty in his eye;°
   And let him know so.

     CAPTAIN
10 I will do't, my lord.

     FORTINBRAS
   Go softly° on.
   (*Exeunt all but the* CAPTAIN.)
   Enter HAMLET, ROSENCRANTZ, OTHERS.

     HAMLET
   Good sir, whose powers° are these?

15   **CAPTAIN**
   They are of Norway, sir.

     HAMLET
   How purposed, sir, I pray you?

     CAPTAIN
20 Against some part of Poland.

     HAMLET
   Who commands them, sir?

     CAPTAIN
   The nephew to old Norway, Fortinbras.

25   **HAMLET**
   Goes it against the main° of Poland, sir,
   Or for some frontier?

     CAPTAIN
   Truly to speak, and with no addition,°
30 We go to gain a little patch of ground
   That hath in it no profit but the name.
   To pay five ducats, five, I would not farm it,
   Nor will it yield to Norway or the Pole
   A ranker° rate, should it be sold in fee.°

35   **HAMLET**
   Why, then the Polack never will defend it.

     CAPTAIN
   Yes, it is already garrisoned.

     HAMLET
40 Two thousand souls and twenty thousand ducats
   Will not debate° the question of this straw.
   This is th' imposthume° of much wealth and peace,
   That inward breaks, and shows no cause without
45 Why the man dies. I humbly thank you, sir.

     CAPTAIN
   God bye you, sir. (*Exit.*)

     ROSENCRANTZ
   Will't please you go, my lord?

     HAMLET
   I'll be with you straight. Go a little before.   50
   (*Exeunt all but* HAMLET.)
   How all occasions do inform against me
   And spur my dull revenge! What is a man,
   If his chief good and market° of his time
   Be but to sleep and feed? A beast, no more.
   Sure he that made us with such large discourse,°   55
   Looking before and after, gave us not
   That capability and godlike reason
   To fust° in us unused. Now, whether it be
   Bestial oblivion,° or some craven scruple
   Of thinking too precisely on th' event°—   60
   A thought which, quartered, hath but one part
     wisdom
   And ever three parts coward—I do not know
   Why yet I live to say, "This thing's to do,"
   Sith I have cause, and will, and strength, and   65
     means
   To do't. Examples gross° as earth exhort me.
   Witness this army of such mass and charge,°
   Led by a delicate and tender prince,
   Whose spirit, with divine ambition puffed,   70
   Makes mouths at the invisible event,°
   Exposing what is mortal and unsure
   To all that fortune, death, and danger dare,
   Even for an eggshell. Rightly to be great
   Is not° to stir without great argument,°   75
   But greatly° to find quarrel in a straw
   When honor's at the stake. How stand I then,
   That have a father killed, a mother stained,
   Excitements° of my reason and my blood,
   And let all sleep, while to my shame I see   80
   The imminent death of twenty thousand men
   That for a fantasy and trick of fame°
   Go to their graves like beds, fight for a plot
   Whereon the numbers cannot try the cause,
   Which is not tomb enough and continent°   85
   To hide the slain? O, from this time forth,

---

53 **market** profit   55 **discourse** understanding   58 **fust** grow moldy   59 **oblivion** forgetfulness   60 **event** outcome   67 **gross** large, obvious   68 **charge** expense   71 **Makes mouths at the invisible event** makes scornful faces (is contemptuous of) the unseen outcome   75 **not** (the sense seems to require "not not")   75 **argument** reason   76 **greatly** i.e., nobly   79 **Excitements** incentives   82 **fantasy and trick of fame** illusion and trifle of reputation   85 **continent** receptacle, container

---

7 **in his eye** before his eyes (i.e., in his presence)   12 **softly** slowly   14 **powers** forces   26 **main** main part   29 **with no addition** plainly   34 **ranker** higher   34 **in fee** outright   41 **debate** settle   42 **imposthume** abscess, ulcer

My thoughts be bloody, or be nothing worth!
(*Exit.*)

SCENE V

The castle.

Enter HORATIO, (QUEEN) GERTRUDE, *and a*
GENTLEMAN.

QUEEN
I will not speak with her.
GENTLEMAN
She is importunate, indeed distract.
5 Her mood will needs be pitied.
QUEEN
What would she have?
GENTLEMAN
She speaks much of her father, says she hears
10 There's tricks i' th' world, and hems, and beats
    her heart,
Spurns enviously at straws,° speaks things in
    doubt°
That carry but half sense. Her speech is nothing,
15 Yet the unshapèd use of it doth move
The hearers to collection;° they yawn° at it,
And botch the words up fit to their own thoughts,
Which, as her winks and nods and gestures yield
    them
20 Indeed would make one think there might be
    thought,
Though nothing sure, yet much unhappily.
HORATIO
'Twere good she were spoken with, for she may
    strew
25 Dangerous conjectures in ill-breeding minds.
QUEEN
Let her come in. (*Exit* GENTLEMAN.)
(*Aside*) To my sick soul (as sin's true nature is)
30 Each toy seems prologue to some great amiss;°
So full of artless jealousy° is guilt
It spills° itself in fearing to be spilt.
Enter OPHELIA (*distracted*).

OPHELIA
Where is the beauteous majesty of Denmark?
QUEEN   35
How now, Ophelia?
OPHELIA
(*She sings.*) How should I your truelove know
From another one?
By his cockle hat° and staff   40
And his sandal shoon.°
QUEEN
Alas, sweet lady, what imports this song?
OPHELIA
Say you? Nay, pray you mark.   45
He is dead and gone, lady, (*Song*)
He is dead and gone;
At his head a grass-green turf,
At his heels a stone.
O, ho!   50
QUEEN
Nay, but Ophelia—
OPHELIA
Pray you mark.
(*Sings.*) White his shroud as the mountain snow— 55
Enter KING.
QUEEN
Alas, look here, my lord.
OPHELIA
Larded° all with sweet flowers (*Song*)
Which bewept to the grave did not go   60
With truelove showers.
KING
How do you, pretty lady?
OPHELIA
Well, God dild° you! They say the owl was a   65
baker's daughter.° Lord, we know what we are,
but know not what we may be. God be at your
table!
KING
Conceit° upon her father.   70
OPHELIA
Pray let's have no words of this, but when they
ask you what it means, say you this:

IV.v. 12 **Spurns enviously at straws** objects spitefully to
insignificant matters   12–13 **in doubt** uncertainly   15–16
Yet the…to collection i.e., yet the formless manner of it
moves her listeners to gather up some sort of meaning
16 **yawn** gape (?)   30 **amiss** misfortune   31 **artless jealousy** crude suspicion   32 **spills** destroys

40 **cockle hat** (a cockleshell on the hat was the sign of a
pilgrim who had journeyed to shrines overseas. The association of lovers and pilgrims was a common one)   41
shoon shoes   59 **Larded** decorated   65 **dild** yield, i.e.,
reward   66 **baker's daughter** (an allusion to a tale of a
baker's daughter who begrudged bread to Christ and
was turned into an owl)   70 **Conceit** brooding

Tomorrow is Saint Valentine's day.° (*Song*)
75 All in the morning betime,
And I a maid at your window,
To be your Valentine.
Then up he rose and donned his clothes
And dupped° the chamber door,
80 Let in the maid, that out a maid
Never departed more.
      KING
Pretty Ophelia.
      OPHELIA
85 Indeed, la, without an oath, I'll make an end on't:
(*Sings.*) By Gis° and by Saint Charity,
Alack, and fie for shame!
Young men will do't if they come to't,
By Cock,° they are to blame.
90 Quoth she, "Before you tumbled me,
You promised me to wed."
He answers:
"So would I 'a' done, by yonder sun,
An thou hadst not come to my bed."
95   KING
How long hath she been thus?
      OPHELIA
I hope all will be well. We must be patient, but I
cannot choose but weep to think they would lay
100 him i' th' cold ground. My brother shall know of
it; and so I thank you for your good counsel.
Come, my coach! Good night, ladies, good night.
Sweet ladies, good night, good night. (*Exit.*)
      KING
105 Follow her close; give her good watch, I pray you.
(*Exit* HORATIO.)
O, this is the poison of deep grief, it springs
All from her father's death—and now behold!
O Gertrude, Gertrude,
When sorrows come, they come not single spies,
110 But in battalions: first, her father slain;
Next, your son gone, and he most violent author
Of his own just remove; the people muddied,°
Thick and unwholesome in their thoughts and
      whispers
115 For good Polonius' death, and we have done but
      greenly°

In huggermugger° to inter him; poor Ophelia
Divided from herself and her fair judgment,
Without the which we are pictures or mere beasts;
Last, and as much containing as all these,   120
Her brother is in secret come from France,
Feeds on his wonder,° keeps himself in clouds,
And wants not buzzers° to infect his car
With pestilent speeches of his father's death,
Wherein necessity, of matter beggared,°   125
Will nothing stick° our person to arraign
In ear and ear. O my dear Gertrude, this,
Like to a murd'ring piece,° in many places
Gives me superfluous death. (*A noise within.*)
Enter a MESSENGER.
      QUEEN   130
Alack, what noise is this?
      KING
Attend, where are my Switzers?° Let them guard
      the door.
What is the matter?   135
      MESSENGER
Save yourself, my lord.
The'ocean, overpeering of his list,°
Eats not the flats with more impiteous haste
Than young Laertes, in a riotous head,°   140
O'erbears your officers. The rabble call him lord,
And, as the world were now but to begin,
Antiquity forgot, custom not known,
The ratifiers and props of every word,
They cry, "Choose we! Laertes shall be king!"   145
Caps, hands, and tongues applaud it to the clouds,
"Laertes shall be king! Laertes king!" *A noise within.*
      QUEEN
How cheerfully on the false trail they cry!   150
O, this is counter,° you false Danish dogs!
Enter LAERTES *with others.*
      KING
The doors are broke.
      LAERTES
Where is this king?—Sirs, stand you all without.   155

---

74 **Saint Valentine's day** Feb. 14 (the notion was that a
bachelor would become the true love of the first girl he
saw on this day) 79 **dupped** opened (did up) 86 **Gis**
(contraction of "Jesus") 89 **Cock** (1) God (2) phallus
112 **muddied** muddled

116 **greenly** foolishly 117 **huggermugger** secret haste
122 **wonder** suspicion 123 **wants not buzzers** does not
lack talebearers 125 **of matter beggared** unprovided
with facts 126 **Will nothing stick** will not hesitate 128
murd'ring piece (a cannon that shot a kind of shrapnel)
133 **Switzers** Swiss guards 138 **list** shore 140 **in a riotous head** with a rebellious force 151 **counter** (a hound
runs counter when he follows the scent backward from
the prey)

ALL
No, let's come in.
        LAERTES
I pray you give me leave.
160   ALL
We will, we will.
        LAERTES
I thank you. Keep the door.
(*Exeunt his* FOLLOWERS.) O thou vile King,
165 Give me my father.
        QUEEN
Calmly, good Laertes.
        LAERTES
That drop of blood that's calm proclaims me
170   bastard,
Cries cuckold° to my father, brands the harlot
Even here between the chaste unsmirchèd brow
Of my true mother.
        KING
175 What is the cause, Laertes,
That thy rebellion looks so giantlike?
Let him go, Gertrude. Do not fear° our person.
There's such divinity doth hedge a king
That treason can but peep to° what it would,
180 Acts little of his will. Tell me, Laertes,
Why thou art thus incensed. Let him go, Gertrude.
Speak, man.
        LAERTES
Where is my father?
185   KING
Dead.
        QUEEN
But not by him.
        KING
190 Let him demand his fill.
        LAERTES
How came he dead? I'll not be juggled with.
To hell allegiance, vows to the blackest devil,
195 Conscience and grace to the profoundest pit!
I dare damnation. To this point I stand,
That both the worlds I give to negligence,°
Let come what comes, only I'll be revenged
Most throughly for my father.
        KING
200 Who shall stay you?

        LAERTES
My will, not all the world's.
And for my means, I'll husband them° so well
They shall go far with little.
        KING   205
Good Laertes,
If you desire to know the certainty
Of your dear father, is't writ in your revenge
That swoopstake° you will draw both friend and
        foe,   210
Winner and loser?
        LAERTES
None but his enemies.
        KING
Will you know them then?   215
        LAERTES
To his good friends thus wide I'll ope my arms
And like the kind life-rend'ring pelican°,
Repast° them with my blood.
        KING   220
Why, now you speak
Like a good child and a true gentleman.
That I am guiltless of your father's death,
And am most sensibly° in grief for it,
It shall as level to your judgment 'pear   225
As day does to your eye.
A noise within: "Let her come in."
        LAERTES
How now? What noise is that?
Enter OPHELIA.
O heat, dry up my brains; tears seven times salt   230
Burn out the sense and virtue° of mine eye!
By heaven, thy madness shall be paid with weight
Till our scale turn the beam.° O rose of May,
Dear maid, kind sister, sweet Ophelia!
O heavens, is't possible a young maid's wits   235
Should be as mortal as an old man's life?
Nature is fine° in love, and where 'tis fine,
It sends some precious instance° of itself
After the thing it loves.
        OPHELIA   240
They bore him barefaced on the bier (*Song*)
Hey non nony, nony, hey nony

171 **cuckold** man whose wife is unfaithful   177 **fear** fear for   179 **peep to** i.e., look at from a distance   197 **That both…to negligence** i.e., I care not what may happen (to me) in this world or the next

203 **husband them** use them economically   209 **swoopstake** in a clean sweep   218 **pelican** (thought to feed its young with its own blood)   219 **Repast** feed   224 **sensibly** acutely   231 **virtue** power   233 **turn the beam** weigh down the bar (of the balance)   237 **fine** refined, delicate   238 **instance** sample

And in his grave rained many a tear—
Fare you well, my dove!

245   **LAERTES**
Hadst thou thy wits, and didst persuade revenge,
It could not move thus.

OPHELIA
You must sing "A-down a-down, and you call
250 him a-down-a." O, how the wheel° becomes it! It
is the false steward, that stole his master's
daughter.

LAERTES
This nothing's more than matter.°

255   **OPHELIA**
There's rosemary, that's for remembrance. Pray
you, love, remember. And there is pansies, that's
for thoughts.

LAERTES
260 A document° in madness,
thoughts and remembrance fitted.

OPHELIA
There's fennel° for you, and columbines. There's
rue for you, and here's some for me. We may call
265 it herb of grace o' Sundays. O, you must wear
your rue with a difference. There's a daisy. I
would give you some violets, but they withered
all when my father died. They say 'a made a good
end.
270 (*Sings*) For bonny sweet Robin is all my joy.

LAERTES
Thought and affliction, passion, hell itself, She
turns to favor° and to prettiness.

OPHELIA
275 And will 'a not come again?
And will 'a not come again?
No, no, he is dead,
Go to the deathbed,
He never will come again.
280 His beard was as white as snow,

All flaxen was his poll.°
He is gone, he is gone,
And we cast away moan.
God 'a' mercy on his soul!
And of all Christian souls, I pray God. God bye   285
   you.
(*Exit.*)

LAERTES
Do you see this, O God?

KING
Laertes, I must commune with your grief,   290
Or you deny me right. Go but apart,
Make choice of whom your wisest friends you will,
And they shall hear and judge 'twixt you and me.
If by direct or by collateral° hand   295
They find us touched,° we will our kingdom give,
Our crown, our life, and all that we call ours,
To you in satisfaction; but if not,
Be you content to lend your patience to us,
And we shall jointly labor with your soul   300
To give it due content.

LAERTES
Let this be so.
His means of death, his obscure funeral—
No trophy, sword, nor hatchment° o'er his bones,   305
No noble rite nor formal ostentation°—
Cry to be heard, as 'twere from heaven to earth,
That I must call't in question.

KING
So you shall;   310
And where th' offense is, let the great ax fall.
I pray you go with me. (*Exeunt.*)

SCENE VI

The castle.

Enter **HORATIO** *and* **OTHERS.**

HORATIO
What are they that would speak with me?

GENTLEMAN
Seafaring men, sir. They say they have letters for
you.   5

---

250 **wheel** (of uncertain meaning, but probably a turn or dance of Ophelia's, rather than Fortune's wheel)   254 **This nothing's more than matter** this nonsense has more meaning than matters of consequence   260 **document** lesson   263 **fennel** (the distribution of flowers in the ensuing lines has symbolic meaning, but the meaning is disputed. Perhaps **fennel**, flattery; **columbines**, cuckoldry; **rue**, sorrow for Ophelia and repentance for the Queen; **daisy**, dissembling; **violets**, faithfulness. For other interpretations, see J. W. Lever in *Review of English Studies*, New Series 3 [1952], pp. 123–29)   273 **favor** charm, beauty

281 **All flaxen was his poll** white as flax was his head   295 **collateral** indirect   296 **touched** implicated   305 **hatchment** tablet bearing the coat of arms of the dead   306 **ostentation** ceremony

HORATIO

Let them come in. (*Exit* ATTENDANT.) I do not
know from what part of the world I should be
greeted, if not from Lord Hamlet.

10   **SAILOR**

God bless you, sir.

HORATIO

Let Him bless thee too.

SAILOR

15 'A shall, sir, an't please Him. There's a letter for
you, sir—it came from th' ambassador that was
bound for England—if your name be Horatio, as I
am let to know it is.

HORATIO

20 (*Reads the letter.*) "Horatio, when thou shalt have
overlooked° this, give these fellows some means
to the King. They have letters for him. Ere we
were two days old at sea, a pirate of very warlike
appointment° gave us chase. Finding ourselves
25 too slow of sail, we put on a compelled valor, and
in the grapple I boarded them. On the instant
they got clear of our ship; so I alone became their
prisoner. They have dealt with me like thieves of
mercy, but they knew what they did: I am to do a
30 good turn for them. Let the King have the letters I
have sent, and repair thou to me with as much
speed as thou wouldest fly death. I have words to
speak in thine ear will make thee dumb; yet are
they much too light for the bore° of the matter.
35 These good fellows will bring thee where I am.
Rosencrantz and Guildenstern hold their course
for England. Of them I have much to tell thee.
Farewell. He that thou knowest thine, HAMLET."
Come, I will give you way for these your letters,
40 And do't the speedier that you may direct me
To him from whom you brought them. (*Exeunt.*)

SCENE VII

The castle.

Enter KING *and* LAERTES.

    KING

Now must your conscience my acquittance seal,
And you must put me in your heart for friend,
Sith you have heard, and with a knowing ear,

That he which hath your noble father slain   5
Pursued my life.

    LAERTES

It well appears. But tell me
Why you proceeded not against these feats
So criminal and so capital° in nature,   10
As by your safety, greatness, wisdom, all things
    else,
You mainly° were stirred up.

    KING

O, for two special reasons,   15
Which may to you perhaps seem much
    unsinewed,°
But yet to me they're strong. The Queen his
    mother
Lives almost by his looks, and for myself—   20
My virtue or my plague, be it either which—
She is so conjunctive° to my life and soul,
That, as the star moves not but in his sphere,
I could not but by her. The other motive
Why to a public count° I might not go   25
Is the great love the general gender° bear him,
Who, dipping all his faults in their affection,
Would, like the spring that turneth wood to
    stone,°
Convert his gyves° to graces; so that my arrows,   30
Too slightly timbered° for so loud a wind,
Would have reverted to my bow again,
And not where I had aimed them.

    LAERTES

And so have I a noble father lost,   35
A sister driven into desp'rate terms,°
Whose worth, if praises may go back again,°
Stood challenger on mount of all the age
For her perfections. But my revenge will come.

    KING   40

Break not your sleeps for that. You must not think
That we are made of stuff so flat and dull
That we can let our beard be shook with danger,
And think it pastime. You shortly shall hear more.
I loved your father, and we love ourself,   45

IV.vi. 21 **overlooked** surveyed   24 **appointment** equipment   34 **bore** caliber (here, "importance")

IV.vii. 10 **capital** deserving death   13 **mainly** powerfully
17 **unsinewed** weak   22 **conjunctive** closely united   25
count reckoning   26 **general gender** common people
28–29 **spring that turneth wood to stone** (a spring in
Shakespeare's county was so charged with lime that it
would petrify wood placed in it)   30 **gyves** fetters   31
timbered shafted   36 **terms** conditions   37 **go back
again** revert to what is past

And that, I hope, will teach you to imagine—
Enter a MESSENGER *with letters.*
How now? What news?
    MESSENGER
Letters, my lord, from Hamlet:
50 These to your Majesty; this to the Queen.
    KING
From Hamlet? Who brought them?
    MESSENGER
Sailors, my lord, they say; I saw them not.
55 They were given me by Claudio; he received them
Of him that brought them.
    KING
Laertes, you shall hear them.—
Leave us. (*Exit* MESSENGER.)
60 (*Reads.*) "High and mighty, you shall know I am
set naked° on your kingdom. Tomorrow shall I
beg leave to see your kingly eyes; when I shall
(first asking your pardon thereunto) recount the
occasion of my sudden and more strange return.
65 HAMLET."
What should this mean? Are all the rest come
    back?
Or is it some abuse,° and no such thing?
    LAERTES
70 Know you the hand?
    KING
'Tis Hamlet's character.° "Naked"!
And in a postscript here, he says "alone."
Can you devise° me?
75   LAERTES
I am lost in it, my lord. But let him come.
It warms the very sickness in my heart
That I shall live and tell him to his teeth,
"Thus didst thou."
80   KING
If it be so, Laertes
(As how should it be so? How otherwise?),
Will you be ruled by me?
    LAERTES
85 Ay, my lord,
So you will not o'errule me to a peace.
    KING
To thine own peace. If he be now returned,
As checking at° his voyage, and that he means
90 No more to undertake it, I will work him

To an exploit now ripe in my device,
Under the which he shall not choose but fall;
And for his death no wind of blame shall breathe,
But even his mother shall uncharge the practice°
And call it accident.   95
    LAERTES
My lord, I will be ruled;
The rather if you could devise it so
That I might be the organ.
    KING   100
It falls right.
You have been talked of since your travel much,
And that in Hamlet's hearing, for a quality
Wherein they say you shine. Your sum of parts
Did not together pluck such envy from him   105
As did that one, and that, in my regard,
Of the unworthiest siege.°
    LAERTES
What part is that, my lord?
    KING   110
A very riband in the cap of youth,
Yet needful too, for youth no less becomes
The light and careless livery that it wears
Than settled age his sables and his weeds,°
Importing health and graveness. Two months since 115
Here was a gentleman of Normandy.
I have seen myself, and served against, the French,
And they can° well on horseback, but this gallant
Had witchcraft in't. He grew unto his seat,   120
And to such wondrous doing brought his horse
As had he been incorpsed and deminatured
With the brave beast. So far he topped my thought
That I, in forgery° of shapes and tricks,
Come short of what he did.   125
    LAERTES
A Norman was't?
    KING
A Norman.
    LAERTES   130
Upon my life, Lamord.
    KING
The very same.
    LAERTES
I know him well. He is the brooch° indeed   135
And gem of all the nation.

---

61 **naked** destitute   68 **abuse** deception   72 **character** handwriting   74 **devise** advise   89 **checking at** turning away from (a term in falconry)

94 **uncharge the practice** not charge the device with treachery   107 **siege** rank   114 **sables and his weeds** i.e., sober attire   119 **can** do   124 **forgery** invention   135 **brooch** ornament

KING
He made confession° of you,
And gave you such a masterly report,
140 For art and exercise in your defense,
And for your rapier most especial,
That he cried out 'twould be a sight indeed
If one could match you. The scrimers° of their
    nation
145 He swore had neither motion, guard, nor eye,
If you opposed them. Sir, this report of his
Did Hamlet so envenom with his envy
That he could nothing do but wish and beg
Your sudden coming o'er to play with you.
150 Now, out of this——
    LAERTES
What out of this, my lord?
    KING
Laertes, was your father dear to you?
155 Or are you like the painting of a sorrow,
A face without a heart?
    LAERTES
Why ask you this?
    KING
160 Not that I think you did not love your father,
But that I know love is begun by time,
And that I see, in passages of proof,°
Time qualifies° the spark and fire of it.
There lives within the very flame of love
165 A kind of wick or snuff° that will abate it,
And nothing is at a like goodness still,°
For goodness, growing to a plurisy,°
Dies in his own too-much. That we would do
We should do when we would, for this "would"
170   changes,
And hath abatements and delays as many
As there are tongues, are hands, are accidents,
And then this "should" is like a spendthrift sigh,°
That hurts by easing. But to the quick° of th'
175   ulcer—
Hamlet comes back; what would you undertake
To show yourself in deed your father's son
More than in words?

LAERTES
To cut his throat i' th' church!   180
    KING
No place indeed should murder sanctuarize;°
Revenge should have no bounds. But, good
    Laertes,
Will you do this? Keep close within your chamber.   185
Hamlet returned shall know you are come home.
We'll put on those° shall praise your excellence
And set a double varnish on the fame
The Frenchman gave you, bring you in fine°
    together   190
And wager on your heads. He, being remiss,
Most generous, and free from all contriving,
Will not peruse the foils, so that with ease,
Or with a little shuffling, you may choose
A sword unbated,° and, in a pass of practice,°   195
Requite him for your father.
    LAERTES
I will do't,
And for that purpose I'll anoint my sword.
I bought an unction of a mountebank,°   200
So mortal that, but dip a knife in it,
Where it draws blood, no cataplasm° so rare,
Collected from all simples° that have virtue°
Under the moon, can save the thing
from death   205
That is but scratched withal. I'll touch my point
With this contagion, that, if I gall him slightly,
It may be death.
    KING
Let's further think of this,   210
Weigh what convenience both of time and means
May fit us to our shape.° If this should fail,
And that our drift look through° our bad
    performance,
'Twere better not assayed. Therefore this project   215
Should have a back or second, that might hold
If this did blast in proof.° Soft, let me see.
We'll make a solemn wager on your cunnings—
I ha't!
When in your motion you are hot and dry—   220

---

138 **confession** report   143 **scrimers** fencers   162 **passages of proof** proved cases   163 **qualifies** diminishes
165 **snuff** residue of burnt wick (which dims the light)
166 **still** always   167 **plurisy** fullness, excess   173
spendthrift sigh (sighing provides ease, but because it
was thought to thin the blood and so shorten life it was
spendthrift)   174 **quick** sensitive flesh

182 **sanctuarize** protect   187 **We'll put on those** we'll incite persons who   189 **in fine** finally   195 **unbated** not
blunted   195 **pass of practice** treacherous thrust   200
mountebank quack   202 **cataplasm** poultice   203 **simples** medicinal herbs   203 **virtue** power (to heal)   212
shape role   213 **drift look through** purpose show
through   217 **blast in proof** burst (fail) in performance

As make your bouts more violent to that end—
And that he calls for drink, I'll have prepared him
A chalice for the nonce,° whereon but sipping,
If he by chance escape your venomed stuck,°
225 Our purpose may hold there.—But stay, what
    noise?
Enter QUEEN.
    QUEEN
One woe doth tread upon another's heel.
So fast they follow. Your sister's drowned,
230   Laertes.
    LAERTES
Drowned! O, where?
    QUEEN
There is a willow grows askant° the brook,
235 That shows his hoar° leaves in the glassy stream:
Therewith° fantastic garlands did she make
Of crowflowers, nettles, daisies, and long purples,
That liberal° shepherds give a grosser name,
But our cold maids do dead men's fingers call
240   them.
There on the pendent boughs her crownet° weeds
Clamb'ring to hang, an envious sliver° broke,
When down her weedy trophies and herself
Fell in the weeping brook. Her clothes spread
245   wide,
And mermaidlike awhile they bore her up,
Which time she chanted snatches of old lauds,°
As one incapable° of her own distress,
Or like a creature native and indued°
250 Unto that element. But long it could not be
Till that her garments, heavy with their drink,
Pulled the poor wretch from her melodious lay
To muddy death.
    LAERTES
255 Alas, then she is drowned?
    QUEEN
Drowned, drowned.
    LAERTES
Too much of water hast thou, poor Ophelia,
260 And therefore I forbid my tears; but yet
It is our trick;° nature her custom holds,
Let shame say what it will: when these are gone,

The woman° will be out. Adieu, my lord.
I have a speech o' fire, that fain would blaze,
But that this folly drowns it. (*Exit.*)   265
    KING
Let's follow, Gertrude.
How much I had to do to calm his rage!
Now fear I this will give it start again;
Therefore let's follow. (*Exeunt.*)   270

ACT V

SCENE I

A churchyard.

Enter TWO CLOWNS.°

    CLOWN
Is she to be buried in Christian burial when she
willfully seeks her own salvation?
    OTHER
I tell thee she is. Therefore make her grave   5
straight.° The crowner° hath sate on her, and
finds it Christian burial.
    CLOWN
How can that be, unless she drowned herself in
her own defense?   10
    OTHER
Why, 'tis found so.
    CLOWN
It must be *se offendendo;*° it cannot be else. For here
lies the point: if I drown myself wittingly, it   15
argues an act, and an act hath three branches—it
is to act, to do, to perform. Argal,° she drowned
herself wittingly.
    OTHER
Nay, but hear you, Goodman Delver.   20
    CLOWN
Give me leave. Here lies the water—good. Here
stands the man—good. If the man go to this water
and drown himself, it is, will he nill he,° he goes;
mark you that. But if the water come to him and   25
drown him, he drowns not himself. Argal, he that
is not guilty of his own death, shortens not his
own life.

223 **nonce** occasion   224 **stuck** thrust   234 **askant** aslant
235 **hoar** silver-gray   236 **Therewith** i.e., with willow
twigs   238 **liberal** free-spoken, coarse-mouthed   241
crownet coronet   242 **envious sliver** malicious branch
247 **lauds** hymns   248 **incapable** unaware   249 **indued**
in harmony with   261 **trick** trait, way

263 **woman** i.e., womanly part of me   **V.i.** s.d. **Clowns**
rustics   6 **straight** straightway   6 **crowner** coroner   14
se offendendo (blunder for *se defendendo,* a legal term
meaning "in self-defense")   17 **Argal** (blunder for Latin
ergo, "therefore")   24 **will he nill he** will he or will he
not (whether he will or will not)

OTHER

30 But is this law?

CLOWN

Ay marry, is't—crowner's quest° law.

OTHER

Will you ha' the truth on't? If this had not been a

35 gentlewoman, she should have been buried out o'
Christian burial.

CLOWN

Why, there thou say'st. And the more pity that
great folk should have count'nance° in this world

40 to drown or hang themselves more than their
even-Christen.° Come, my spade. There is no
ancient gentlemen but gard'ners, ditchers, and
gravemakers. They hold up° Adam's profession.

OTHER

45 Was he a gentleman?

CLOWN

'A was the first ever bore arms.°

OTHER

Why, he had none.

50 CLOWN

What, art a heathen? How dost thou understand
the Scripture? The Scripture says Adam digged.
Could he dig without arms? I'll put another
question to thee. If thou answerest me not to the

55 purpose, confess thyself—

OTHER

Go to.

CLOWN

What is he that builds stronger than either the

60 mason, the shipwright, or the carpenter?

OTHER

The gallowsmaker, for that frame outlives a
thousand tenants.

CLOWN

65 I like thy wit well, in good faith. The gallows does
well. But how does it well? It does well to those
that do ill. Now thou dost ill to say the gallows is
built stronger than the church. Argal, the gallows
may do well to thee. To't again, come.

70 OTHER

Who builds stronger than a mason, a shipwright,
or a carpenter?

CLOWN

Ay, tell me that, and unyoke.°

OTHER

75 Marry, now I can tell.

CLOWN

To't.

OTHER

Mass,° I cannot tell.

80 *Enter* HAMLET *and* HORATIO *afar off.*

CLOWN

Cudgel thy brains no more about it, for your dull
ass will not mend his pace with beating. And
when you are asked this question next, say "a
gravemaker." The houses he makes lasts till

85 doomsday. Go, get thee in, and fetch me a stoup°
of liquor.

(*Exit* OTHER CLOWN.)

In youth when I did love, did love, (*Song*)
Methought it was very sweet

90 To contract—O—the time for—a—my behove,°
O, methought there—a—was nothing—a—meet.

HAMLET

Has this fellow no feeling of his business? 'A
sings in gravemaking.

95 HORATIO

Custom hath made it in him a property of
easiness.°

HAMLET

'Tis e'en so. The hand of little employment hath

100 the daintier sense.°

CLOWN

But age with his stealing steps (*Song*)
Hath clawed me in his clutch,
And hath shipped me into the land,

105 As if I had never been such.

(*Throws up a skull.*)

HAMLET

That skull had a tongue in it, and could sing once.
How the knave jowls° it to the ground, as if
'twere Cain's jawbone, that did the first murder!

110 This might be the pate of a politician, which this
ass now o'erreaches,° one that would circumvent
God, might it not?

HORATIO

It might, my lord.

115 HAMLET

Or, of a courtier, which could say "Good morrow,

---

32 **quest** inquest   39 **count'nance** privilege   41 **even-
Christen** fellow Christian   43 **hold up** keep up   47 **bore
arms** had a coat of arms (the sign of a gentleman)   74
unyoke i.e., stop work for the day

80 **Mass** by the mass   86 **stoup** tankard   90 **behove**
advantage   96–97 **in him a property of easiness** easy for
him   99–100 **hath the daintier sense** is more sensitive
(because it is not calloused)   108 **jowls** hurls   111 **o'erreaches** (1) reaches over (2) has the advantage over

sweet lord! How dost thou, sweet lord?" This might be my Lord Such-a-one, that praised my Lord Such-a-one's horse when 'a went to beg it,
120 might it not?

HORATIO
Ay, my lord.

HAMLET
Why, e'en so, and now my Lady Worm's,
125 chapless,° and knocked about the mazzard° with a sexton's spade. Here's fine revolution, an we had the trick to see't. Did these bones cost no more the breeding but to play at loggets° with them? Mine ache to think on't.

130 **CLOWN**
A pickax and a spade, a spade, (*Song*)
For and a shrouding sheet;
O, a pit of clay for to be made
For such a guest is meet.
(*Throws up another skull.*)

135 **HAMLET**
There's another. Why may not that be the skull of a lawyer? Where be his quiddities° now, his quillities,° his cases, his tenures,° and his tricks? Why does he suffer this mad knave now to knock
140 him about the sconce° with a dirty shovel, and will not tell him of his action of battery? Hum! This fellow might be in's time a great buyer of land, with his statutes, his recognizances, his fines,° his double vouchers, his recoveries. Is this
145 the fine° of his fines, and the recovery of his recoveries, to have his fine pate full of fine dirt? Will his vouchers vouch him no more of his purchases, and double ones too, than the length and breadth of a pair of indentures?° The very
150 conveyances° of his lands will scarcely lie in this box, and must th' inheritor himself have no more, ha?

HORATIO
Not a jot more, my lord.

---

125 **chapless** lacking the lower jaw   125 **mazzard** head   128 **loggets** (a game in which small pieces of wood were thrown at an object)   137 **quiddities** subtle arguments (from Latin **quidditas**, "whatness")   138 **quillities** fine distinctions   138 **tenures** legal means of holding land   140 **sconce** head   143–44 **his statutes, his recognizances, his fines** his documents giving a creditor control of a debtor's land, his bonds of surety, his documents changing an entailed estate into fee simple (unrestricted ownership)   145 **fine** end   149 **indentures** contracts   150 **conveyances** legal documents for the transference of land

HAMLET 155
Is not parchment made of sheepskins?

HORATIO
Ay, my lord, and of calveskins too.

HAMLET
They are sheep and calves which seek out assurance° in that. I will speak to this fellow. 160
Whose grave's this, sirrah?

CLOWN
Mine, sir.
(*Sings.*) O, a pit of clay for to be made 165
For such a guest is meet.

HAMLET
I think it be thine indeed, for thou liest in't.

CLOWN
You lie out on't, sir, and therefore 'tis not yours. 170
For my part, I do not lie in't, yet it is mine.

HAMLET
Thou dost lie in't, to be in't and say it is thine. 'Tis for the dead, not for the quick;° therefore, thou liest.

CLOWN 175
'Tis a quick lie, sir; 'twill away again from me to you.

HAMLET
What man dost thou dig it for?

CLOWN 180
For no man, sir.

HAMLET
What woman then?

CLOWN
For none neither. 185

HAMLET
Who is to be buried in't?

CLOWN
One that was a woman, sir: but, rest her soul, she's dead. 190

HAMLET
How absolute° the knave is! We must speak by the card,° or equivocation° will undo us. By the Lord, Horatio, this three years I have took note of it, the age is grown so picked° that the toe of the 195 peasant comes so near the heel of the courtier he galls his kibe.° How long hast thou been a gravemaker?

---

160 **assurance** safety   174 **quick** living   192 **absolute** positive, decided   192–93 **by the card** by the compass card, i.e., exactly   193 **equivocation** ambiguity   195 **picked** refined   197 **kibe** sore on the back of the heel

CLOWN

200 Of all the days i' th' year, I came to't that day that
our last king Hamlet overcame Fortinbras.

HAMLET

How long is that since?

CLOWN

205 Cannot you tell that? Every fool can tell that. It
was that very day that young Hamlet was born—
he that is mad, and sent into England.

HAMLET

Ay, marry, why was he sent into England?

CLOWN

210 Why, because 'a was mad. 'A shall recover his
wits there; or, if 'a do not, 'tis no great matter
there.

HAMLET

215 Why?

CLOWN

'Twill not be seen in him there. There the men are
as mad as he.

HAMLET

220 How came he mad?

CLOWN

Very strangely, they say.

HAMLET

How strangely?

CLOWN

225 Faith, e'en with losing his wits.

HAMLET

Upon what ground?

CLOWN

230 Why, here in Denmark. I have been sexton here,
man and boy, thirty years.

HAMLET

How long will a man lie i' th' earth ere he rot?

CLOWN

235 Faith, if 'a be not rotten before 'a die (as we have
many pocky corses° nowadays that will scarce
hold the laying in), 'a will last you some eight
year or nine year. A tanner will last you nine year.

HAMLET

240 Why he, more than another?

CLOWN

Why, sir, his hide is so tanned with his trade that
'a will keep out water a great while, and your
water is a sore decayer of your whoreson dead
245 body. Here's a skull now hath lien you i' th' earth
three and twenty years.

HAMLET

Whose was it?

CLOWN

250 A whoreson mad fellow's it was. Whose do you
think it was?

HAMLET

Nay, I know not.

CLOWN

255 A pestilence on him for a mad rogue! 'A poured a
flagon of Rhenish on my head once. This same
skull, sir, was, sir, Yorick's skull, the King's jester.

HAMLET

This?

CLOWN

260 E'en that.

HAMLET

Let me see. (*Takes the skull.*) Alas, poor Yorick! I
knew him, Horatio, a fellow of infinite jest, of
most excellent fancy. He hath borne me on his
265 back a thousand times. And now how abhorred in
my imagination it is! My gorge rises at it. Here
hung those lips that I have kissed I know not how
oft. Where be your gibes now? Your gambols,
your songs, your flashes of merriment that were
270 wont to set the table on a roar? Not one now to
mock your own grinning? Quite chapfall'n°?
Now get you to my lady's chamber, and tell her,
let her paint an inch thick, to this favor° she must
come. Make her laugh at that. Prithee, Horatio,
275 tell me one thing.

HORATIO

What's that, my lord?

HAMLET

Dost thou think Alexander looked o' this fashion
280 i' th' earth?

HORATIO

E'en so.

HAMLET

And smelt so? Pah! (*Puts down the skull.*)
285

HORATIO

E'en so, my lord.

HAMLET

To what base uses we may return, Horatio! Why
may not imagination trace the noble dust of
290 Alexander till 'a find it stopping a bunghole?

HORATIO

'Twere to consider too curiously,° to consider so.

---

236 **pocky corses** bodies of persons who had been infected with the pox (syphilis)

272 **chapfall'n** (1) down in the mouth (2) jawless   274 **favor** facial appearance

HAMLET

295 No, faith, not a jot, but to follow him thither with
modesty enough,° and likelihood to lead it; as
thus: Alexander died, Alexander was buried,
Alexander returneth to dust; the dust is earth; of
earth we make loam; and why of that loam
300 whereto he was converted might they not stop a
beer barrel?
Imperious Caesar, dead and turned to clay,
Might stop a hole to keep the wind away.
O, that that earth which kept the world in awe
305 Should patch a wall t' expel the winter's flaw!°
But soft, but soft awhile! Here comes the King.
Enter KING, QUEEN, LAERTES, *and a coffin, with*
LORDS *attendant* (*and a* DOCTOR *of Divinity*).
The Queen, the courtiers. Who is this they follow?
And with such maimèd° rites? This doth betoken
The corse they follow did with desp'rate hand
310 Fordo it° own life. 'Twas of some estate.°
Couch° we awhile, and mark. (*Retires with* HORATIO.)

LAERTES

What ceremony else?

HAMLET

315 That is Laertes,
A very noble youth. Mark.

LAERTES

What ceremony else?

DOCTOR

320 Her obsequies have been as far enlarged
As we have warranty. Her death was doubtful,°
And, but that great command o'ersways the order,
She should in ground unsanctified been lodged
Till the last trumpet. For charitable prayers,
325 Shards,° flints, and pebbles should be thrown on
her.
Yet here she is allowed her virgin crants,°
Her maiden strewments,° and the bringing home
Of bell and burial.

330 LAERTES

Must there no more be done?

DOCTOR

No more be done.
We should profane the service of the dead

To sing a requiem and such rest to her   335
As to peace-parted souls.

LAERTES

Lay her i' th' earth,
And from her fair and unpolluted flesh
May violets spring! I tell thee, churlish priest,   340
A minist'ring angel shall my sister be
When thou liest howling!

HAMLET

What, the fair Ophelia?

QUEEN   345

Sweets to the sweet! Farewell.
(*Scatters flowers.*)
I hoped thou shouldst have been my Hamlet's
wife.
I thought thy bride bed to have decked, sweet
maid,   350
And not have strewed thy grave.

LAERTES

O, treble woe
Fall ten times treble on that cursèd head
Whose wicked deed thy most ingenious sense°   355
Deprived thee of! Hold off the earth awhile,
Till I have caught her once more in mine arms.
(*Leaps in the grave.*)
Now pile your dust upon the quick and dead
Till of this flat a mountain you have made
T'o'ertop old Pelion° or the skyish head   360
Of blue Olympus.

HAMLET

(*Coming forward*) What is he whose grief
Bears such an emphasis, whose phrase of sorrow
Conjures the wand'ring stars,° and makes them   365
stand
Like wonder-wounded hearers? This is I,
Hamlet the Dane.

LAERTES

The devil take thy soul! (*Grapples with him.*)°   370

355 **most ingenious sense** finely endowed mind   360
Pelion (according to classical legend, giants in their fight
with the gods sought to reach heaven by piling Mount
Pelion and Mount Ossa on Mount Olympus)   365
wand'ring stars planets   370 s.d. **Grapples with him**
(Q1, a bad quarto, presumably reporting a version that
toured, has a previous direction saying "Hamlet leaps in
after Laertes." Possibly he does so, somewhat hysterically. But such a direction—absent from the two good
texts, Q2 and F—makes Hamlet the aggressor, somewhat
contradicting his next speech. Perhaps Laertes leaps out
of the grave to attack Hamlet)

293 **curiously** minutely   295–296 **with modesty enough**
without exaggeration   305 **flaw** gust   308 **maimèd** incomplete   310 **Fordo it** destroy its   310 **estate** high rank
311 **Couch** hide   321 **doubtful** suspicious   325 **Shards**
broken pieces of pottery   327 **crants** garlands   328 **strewments** i.e., of flowers

HAMLET

Thou pray'st not well.

I prithee take thy fingers from my throat,

For, though I am not splenitive° and rash,

375 Yet have I in me something dangerous,

Which let thy wisdom fear. Hold off thy hand.

KING

Pluck them asunder.

QUEEN

380 Hamlet, Hamlet!

ALL

Gentlemen!

HORATIO

Good my lord, be quiet.

(*Attendants part them.*)

385   **HAMLET**

Why, I will fight with him upon this theme

Until my eyelids will no longer wag.

QUEEN

O my son, what theme?

390   **HAMLET**

I loved Ophelia. Forty thousand brothers

Could not with all their quantity of love

Make up my sum. What wilt thou do for her?

KING

395 O, he is mad, Laertes.

QUEEN

For love of God forbear him.

HAMLET

'Swounds, show me what thou't do.

Woo't weep? Woo't fight? Woo't fast? Woo't tear

400   thyself?

Woo't drink up eisel?° Eat a crocodile?

I'll do't. Dost thou come here to whine?

To outface me with leaping in her grave?

Be buried quick with her, and so will I.

405 And if thou prate of mountains, let them throw

Millions of acres on us, till our ground,

Singeing his pate against the burning zone,°

Make Ossa like a wart! Nay, an thou'lt mouth,

I'll rant as well as thou.

410   **QUEEN**

This is mere madness;

And thus a while the fit will work on him.

Anon, as patient as the female dove

When that her golden couplets are disclosed,°

His silence will sit drooping.   415

HAMLET

Hear you, sir.

What is the reason that you use me thus?

I loved you ever. But it is no matter.

Let Hercules himself do what he may,   420

The cat will mew, and dog will have his day.

KING

I pray thee, good Horatio, wait upon him.

Exit HAMLET *and* HORATIO.

(*To* LAERTES) Strengthen your patience

in our last night's speech.   425

We'll put the matter to the present push.°

Good Gertrude, set some watch over your son.

This grave shall have a living° monument.

An hour of quiet shortly shall we see;

Till then in patience our proceeding be. (*Exeunt.*)   430

SCENE II

The castle.

Enter HAMLET *and* HORATIO.

HAMLET

So much for this, sir; now shall you see the other.

You do remember all the circumstance?

HORATIO

Remember it, my lord!   5

HAMLET

Sir, in my heart there was a kind of fighting

That would not let me sleep. Methought I lay

Worse than the mutines in the bilboes.° Rashly

(And praised be rashness for it) let us know,   10

Our indiscretion sometime serves us well

When our deep plots do pall,° and that should

    learn us

There's a divinity that shapes our ends,

Rough-hew them how we will.   15

HORATIO

That is most certain.

HAMLET

Up from my cabin,

My sea gown scarfed about me, in the dark   20

---

414 **golden couplets are disclosed** (the dove lays two eggs, and the newly hatched [disclosed] young are covered with golden down)   426 **present push** immediate test   428 **living** lasting (with perhaps also a reference to the plot against Hamlet's life)   **V.ii.** 9 **mutines in the bilboes** mutineers in fetters   12 **pall** fail

374 **splenitive** fiery (the spleen was thought to be the seat of anger)   401 **eisel** vinegar   407 **burning zone** sun's orbit

Groped I to find out them, had my desire,
Fingered° their packet, and in fine° withdrew
To mine own room again, making so bold,
My fears forgetting manners, to unseal
25 Their grand commission; where I found,
    Horatio—
Ah, royal knavery!—an exact command,
Larded° with many several sorts of reasons,
Importing Denmark's health, and England's too,
30 With, ho, such bugs and goblins in my life,°
That on the supervise,° no leisure bated,°
No, not to stay the grinding of the ax,
My head should be struck off.
    HORATIO
35 Is't possible?
    HAMLET
Here's the commission; read it at more leisure.
But wilt thou hear now how I did proceed?
    HORATIO
40 I beseech you.
    HAMLET
Being thus benetted round with villains,
Or° I could make a prologue to my brains,
They had begun the play. I sat me down,
45 Devised a new commission, wrote it fair.
I once did hold it, as our statists° do,
A baseness to write fair,° and labored much
How to forget that learning, but, sir, now
It did me yeoman's service. Wilt thou know
50 Th' effect° of what I wrote?
    HORATIO
Ay, good my lord.
    HAMLET
An earnest conjuration from the King,
55 As England was his faithful tributary,
As love between them like the palm might flourish,
As peace should still her wheaten garland wear
And stand a comma° 'tween their amities,
60 And many suchlike as's of great charge,°
That on the view and knowing of these contents,
Without debatement further, more or less,

He should those bearers put to sudden death,
Not shriving° time allowed.
    HORATIO   65
How was this sealed?
    HAMLET
Why, even in that was heaven ordinant.°
I had my father's signet in my purse,
Which was the model° of that Danish seal,   70
Folded the writ up in the form of th' other,
Subscribed it, gave't th' impression, placed it
    safely,
The changeling never known. Now, the next day
Was our sea fight, and what to this was sequent   75
Thou knowest already.
    HORATIO
So Guildenstern and Rosencrantz go to't.
    HAMLET
Why, man, they did make love to this   80
    employment.
They are not near my conscience; their defeat
Does by their own insinuation° grow.
'Tis dangerous when the baser nature comes
Between the pass° and fell° incensèd points   85
Of mighty opposites.
    HORATIO
Why, what a king is this!
    HAMLET
Does it not, think thee, stand me now upon°—   90
He that hath killed my king, and whored my
    mother,
Popped in between th' election° and my hopes,
Thrown out his angle° for my proper life,°
And with such coz'nage°—is't not perfect   95
    conscience
To quit° him with this arm? And is't not to be
    damned
To let this canker of our nature come
In further evil?   100
    HORATIO
It must be shortly known to him from England
What is the issue of the business there.
    HAMLET
It will be short; the interim's mine,

---

22 **Fingered** stole 22 **in fine** finally 28 **Larded** enriched 30 **such bugs and goblins in my life** such bugbears and imagined terrors if I were allowed to live 31 **supervise** reading 31 **leisure bated** delay allowed 43 **Or** ere 46 **statists** statesmen 47 **fair** clearly 50 **effect** purport 59 **comma** link 60 **great charge** (1) serious exhortation (2) heavy burden (punning on **as's** and "asses")

64 **shriving** absolution 68 **ordinant** ruling 70 **model** counterpart 83 **insinuation** meddling 85 **pass** thrust 85 **fell** cruel 90 **stand me now upon** become incumbent upon me 93 **election** (the Danish monarchy was elective) 94 **angle** fishing line 94 **my proper life** my own life 95 **coz'nage** trickery 97 **quit** pay back

105 And a man's life's no more than to say "one."
But I am very sorry, good Horatio,
That to Laertes I forgot myself,
For by the image of my cause I see
The portraiture of his. I'll court his favors.
110 But sure the bravery° of his grief did put me
Into a tow'ring passion.

HORATIO
Peace, who comes here?
Enter young OSRIC, *a courtier.*

OSRIC
115 Your lordship is right welcome back to Denmark.

HAMLET
I humbly thank you, sir. (*Aside to* HORATIO) Dost
know this waterfly?

HORATIO
120 (*Aside to* HAMLET) No, my good lord.

HAMLET
(*Aside to* HORATIO) Thy state is the more
gracious, for 'tis a vice to know him. He hath
much land, and fertile. Let a beast be lord of
125 beasts, and his crib shall stand at the king's mess.°
'Tis a chough,° but, as I say, spacious° in the
possession of dirt.

OSRIC
Sweet lord, if your lordship were at leisure, I
130 should impart a thing to you from his Majesty.

HAMLET
I will receive it, sir, with all diligence of spirit.
Put your bonnet to his right use. 'Tis for the head.

135 OSRIC
I thank your lordship, it is very hot.

HAMLET
No, believe me, 'tis very cold; the wind is
northerly.

140 OSRIC
It is indifferent cold, my lord, indeed.

HAMLET
But yet methinks it is very sultry and hot for my
complexion.°

145 OSRIC
Exceedingly, my lord; it is very sultry, as 'twere
—I cannot tell how. But, my lord, his Majesty
bade me signify to you that 'a has laid a great
wager on your head. Sir, this is the matter—

HAMLET   150
I beseech you remember.
(HAMLET *moves him to put on his hat.*)

OSRIC
Nay, good my lord; for my ease, in good faith. Sir,
here is newly come to court Laertes—believe me,
an absolute gentleman, full of most excellent   155
differences,° of very soft society and great
showing. Indeed, to speak feelingly° of him, he is
the card° or calendar of gentry; for you shall find
in him the continent° of what part a gentleman
would see.   160

HAMLET
Sir, his definement° suffers no perdition° in you,
though, I know, to divide him inventorially
would dozy° th' arithmetic of memory, and yet
but yaw neither in respect of his quick sail.° But, 165
in the verity of extolment, I take him to be a soul
of great article,° and his infusion° of such dearth
and rareness as, to make true diction° of him, his
semblable° is his mirror, and who else would
trace him, his umbrage,° nothing more.   170

OSRIC
Your lordship speaks most infallibly of him.

HAMLET
The concernancy,° sir? Why do we wrap the
gentleman in our more rawer breath?   175

OSRIC
Sir?

HORATIO
Is't not possible to understand in another tongue?
You will to't,° sir, really.   180

HAMLET
What imports the nomination of this gentleman?

OSRIC
Of Laertes?

HORATIO   185
(*Aside to* HAMLET) His purse is empty already.
All's golden words are spent.

---

110 **bravery** bravado   125 **mess** table   126 **chough** jack-
daw (here, chatterer)   126 **spacious** well off   144 **complexion** temperament

156 **differences** distinguishing characteristics   157 **feel-
ingly** justly   158 **card** chart   159 **continent** summary
162 **definement** description   162 **perdition** loss   164
dozy dizzy   164–65 **and yet…quick sail** i.e., and yet
only stagger despite all (**yaw neither**) in trying to over-
take his virtues   167 **article** (literally, "item," but here
perhaps "traits" or "importance")   167 **infusion** essential quality   168 **diction** description   169 **semblable**
likeness   170 **umbrage** shadow   174 **concernancy**
meaning   180 **will to't** will get there

HAMLET
Of him, sir.

190 **OSRIC**
I know you are not ignorant——

HAMLET
I would you did, sir; yet, in faith, if you did, it
would not much approve° me. Well, sir?

195 **OSRIC**
You are not ignorant of what excellence Laertes
is——

HAMLET
I dare not confess that, lest I should compare with
200 him in excellence; but to know a man well were to
know himself.

OSRIC
I mean, sir, for his weapon; but in the imputation°
laid on him by them, in his meed° he's
205 unfellowed.

HAMLET
What's his weapon?

OSRIC
Rapier and dagger.

210 **HAMLET**
That's two of his weapons—but well.

OSRIC
The King, sir, hath wagered with him six Barbary
horses, against the which he has impawned,° as I
215 take it, six French rapiers and poniards, with their
assigns,° as girdle, hangers,° and so. Three of the
carriages,° in faith, are very dear to fancy, very
responsive° to the hilts, most delicate carriages,
and of very liberal conceit.°

220 **HAMLET**
What call you the carriages?

HORATIO
(*Aside to* **HAMLET**) I knew you must be edified by
the margent° ere you had done.

225 **OSRIC**
The carriages, sir, are the hangers.

HAMLET
The phrase would be more germane to the matter
if we could carry a cannon by our sides. I would it

might be hangers till then. But on! Six Barbary   230
horses against six French swords, their assigns,
and three liberal-conceited carriages—that's the
French bet against the Danish. Why is this all
impawned, as you call it?

OSRIC   235
The King, sir, hath laid, sir, that in a dozen passes
between yourself and him he shall not exceed you
three hits; he hath laid on twelve for nine, and it
would come to immediate trial if your lordship
would vouchsafe the answer.   240

HAMLET
How if I answer no?

OSRIC
I mean, my lord, the opposition of your person in
trial.   245

HAMLET
Sir, I will walk here in the hall. If it please his
Majesty, it is the breathing time of day with me.°
Let the foils be brought, the gentleman willing,
and the King hold his purpose. I will win for him   250
an I can; if not, I will gain nothing but my shame
and the odd hits.

OSRIC
Shall I deliver you e'en so?

HAMLET   255
To this effect, sir, after what flourish your nature
will.

OSRIC
I commend my duty to your lordship.

HAMLET   260
Yours, yours. (*Exit* **OSRIC.**) He does well to
commend it himself; there are no tongues else
for's turn.

HORATIO
This lapwing° runs away with the shell on his   265
head.

HAMLET
'A did comply, sir, with his dug° before 'a sucked
it. Thus he, and many more of the same breed that
I know the drossy age dotes on, only got the tune   270
of the time and, out of an habit of encounter,° a

---

194 **approve** commend   203 **imputation** reputation   204
meed merit   214 **impawned** wagered   216 **assigns** ac-
companiments   216 **hangers** straps hanging the sword
to the belt   217 **carriages** (an affected word for hangers)
218 **responsive** corresponding   219 **liberal conceit** elaborate design   224 **margent** i.e., marginal (explanatory)
comment

248 **breathing time of day with me** time when I take exercise   265 **lapwing** (the new-hatched lapwing was
thought to run around with half its shell on its head)
268 **'A did comply, sir, with his dug** he was ceremoniously polite to his mother's breast   271 **out of an habit
of encounter** out of his own superficial way of meeting
and conversing with people

kind of yeasty° collection, which carries them
through and through the most fanned and
winnowed opinions; and do but blow them to
275 their trial, the bubbles are out.°
Enter a LORD.

LORD
My lord, his Ma'esty commended him to you by
young Osric, who brings back to him that you
attend him in the hall. He sends to know if your
280 pleasure hold to play with Laertes, or that you
will take longer time.

HAMLET
I am constant to my purposes; they follow the
King's pleasure. If his fitness speaks, mine is
285 ready; now or whensoever, provided I be so able
as now.

LORD
The King and Queen and all are coming down.

HAMLET
290 In happy time.

LORD
The Queen desires you to use some gentle
entertainment° to Laertes before you fall to play.

HAMLET
295 She well instructs me. (*Exit* LORD.)

HORATIO
You will lose this wager, my lord.

HAMLET
I do not think so. Since he went into France I have
300 been in continual practice. I shall win at the odds.
But thou wouldst not think how ill all's here
about my heart. But it is no matter.

HORATIO
Nay, good my lord——

305 HAMLET
It is but foolery, but it is such a kind of
gaingiving° as would perhaps trouble a woman.

HORATIO
If your mind dislike anything, obey it. I will
310 forestall their repair hither and say you are not fit.

HAMLET
Not a whit, we defy augury. There is special
providence in the fall of a sparrow.° If it be now,

'tis not to come; if it be not to come, it will be
now; if it be not now, yet it will come. The 315
readiness is all. Since no man of aught he leaves
knows, what is't to leave betimes?° Let be.
A table prepared. (Enter) TRUMPETS, DRUMS, *and*
OFFICERS *with cushions;* KING, QUEEN, (OSRIC,) *and all
the* STATE, (*with*) *foils, daggers, (and stoups of wine
borne in); and* LAERTES.

KING
Come, Hamlet, come, and take this hand from me.
(*The* KING *puts* LAERTES' *hand into* HAMLET'S.)

HAMLET 320
Give me your pardon, sir. I have done you wrong,
But pardon't, as you are a gentleman.
This presence° knows, and you must needs have
    heard,
How I am punished with a sore distraction. 325
What I have done
That might your nature, honor, and exception°
Roughly awake, I here proclaim was madness.
Was't Hamlet wronged Laertes? Never Hamlet.
If Hamlet from himself be ta'en away, 330
And when he's not himself does wrong Laertes,
Then Hamlet does it not, Hamlet denies it.
Who does it then? His madness. If't be so,
Hamlet is of the faction° that is wronged;
His madness is poor Hamlet's enemy. 335
Sir, in this audience,
Let my disclaiming from a purposed evil
Free me so far in your most generous thoughts
That I have shot my arrow o'er the house
And hurt my brother. 340

LAERTES
I am satisfied in nature,
Whose motive in this case should stir me most
To my revenge. But in my terms of honor 345
I stand aloof, and will no reconcilement
Till by some elder masters of known honor
I have a voice and precedent° of peace
To keep my name ungored. But till that time
I do receive your offered love like love, 350
And will not wrong it.

HAMLET
I embrace it freely,
And will this brother's wager frankly play.
Give us the foils. Come on. 355

---

272 **yeasty** frothy   275 **the bubbles are out** i.e., they are
blown away (the reference is to the "yeasty collection")
292–93 **to use some gentle entertainment** to be courteous
307 **gaingiving** misgiving   313 **the fall of a sparrow** (cf.
Matthew 10:29 "Are not two sparrows sold for a far-
thing? and one of them shall not fall on the ground without your Father")

317 **betimes** early   323 **presence** royal assembly   327 **exception** disapproval   334 **faction** party, side   348 **voice
and precedent** authoritative opinion justified by precedent

LAERTES
Come, one for me.
HAMLET
I'll be your foil,° Laertes. In mine ignorance
360 Your skill shall, like a star i' th' darkest night,
Stick fiery off° indeed.
LAERTES
You mock me, sir.
HAMLET
365 No, by this hand.
KING
Give me the foils, young Osric. Cousin Hamlet,
You know the wager?
HAMLET
370 Very well, my lord.
Your grace has laid the odds o' th' weaker side.
KING
I do not fear it, I have seen you both;
But since he is bettered,° we have therefore odds.
375 **LAERTES**
This is too heavy; let me see another.
HAMLET
This likes me well. These foils have all a length?
Prepare to play.
OSRIC
380 Ay, my good lord.
KING
Set me the stoups of wine upon that table.
If Hamlet give the first or second hit,
Or quit° in answer of the third exchange,
385 Let all the battlements their ordnance fire.
The King shall drink to Hamlet's better breath,
And in the cup an union° shall be throw
Richer than that which four successive kings
In Denmark's crown have worn. Give me the
390 cups,
And let the kettle° to the trumpet speak,
The trumpet to the cannoneer without,
The cannons to the heavens, the heaven to earth,
"Now the King drinks to Hamlet." Come, begin.
Trumpets the while.
395 And you, the judges, bear a wary eye.
HAMLET
Come on, sir.
LAERTES
Come, my lord. *They play.*

HAMLET   400
One.
LAERTES
No.
HAMLET
Judgment?   405
OSRIC
A hit, a very palpable hit.
Drum, trumpets, and shot. Flourish; a piece goes off.
LAERTES
Well, again.
KING   410
Stay, give me drink. Hamlet, this pearl is thine.
Here's to thy health. Give him the cup.
HAMLET
I'll play this bout first; set it by awhile.
Come. (*They play.*) Another hit. What say you? 415
LAERTES
A touch, a touch; I do confess't.
KING
Our son shall win.
QUEEN   420
He's fat,° and scant of breath.
Here, Hamlet, take my napkin, rub thy brows.
The Queen carouses to thy fortune, Hamlet.
HAMLET
Good madam!   425
KING
Gertrude, do not drink.
QUEEN
I will, my lord; I pray you pardon me. (*Drinks.*)
KING   430
(*Aside*) It is the poisoned cup; it is too late.
HAMLET
I dare not drink yet, madam—by and by.
QUEEN
Come, let me wipe thy face.   435
LAERTES
My lord, I'll hit him now.
KING
I do not think't.
LAERTES   440
(*Aside*) And yet it is almost against my conscience.
HAMLET
Come for the third, Laertes. You do but dally.
I pray you pass with your best violence;
I am sure you make a wanton° of me.   445

359 **foil** (1) blunt sword (2) background (of metallic leaf)
for a jewel   361 **Stick fiery off** stand out brilliantly   374
bettered has improved (in France)   384 **quit** repay, hit
back   387 **union** pearl   391 **kettle** kettledrum

421 **fat** (1) sweaty (2) out of training   445 **wanton** spoiled
child

LAERTES
Say you so? Come on. (*They play.*)

OSRIC
Nothing neither way.

450 LAERTES
Have at you now!
In scuffling they change rapiers, (and both are wounded).

KING
Part them. They are incensed.

HAMLET
455 Nay, come—again! (*The* QUEEN *falls.*)

OSRIC
Look to the Queen there, ho!

HORATIO
They bleed on both sides. How is it, my lord?

460 OSRIC
How is't, Laertes?

LAERTES
Why, as a woodcock to mine own springe,° Osric.
I am justly killed with mine own treachery.

465 HAMLET
How does the Queen?

KING
She sounds° to see them bleed.

QUEEN
470 No, no, the drink, the drink! O my dear Hamlet!
The drink, the drink! I am poisoned. (*Dies.*)

HAMLET
O villainy! Ho! Let the door be locked.
Treachery! Seek it out. (LAERTES *falls.*)

475 LAERTES
It is here, Hamlet. Hamlet, thou art slain;
No medicine in the world can do thee good.
In thee there is not half an hour's life.
The treacherous instrument is in thy hand,
480 Unbated and envenomed. The foul practice°
Hath turned itself on me. Lo, here I lie,
Never to rise again. Thy mother's poisoned.
I can no more. The King, the King's to blame.

HAMLET
485 The point envenomed too?
Then, venom, to thy work. *Hurts the* KING.

ALL
Treason! Treason!

KING
490 O, yet defend me, friends. I am but hurt.

HAMLET
Here, thou incestuous, murd'rous, damnèd
Dane,
Drink off his potion. Is thy union here?
Follow my mother. KING *dies.*   495

LAERTES
He is justly served.
It is a poison tempered° by himself.
Exchange forgiveness with me, noble Hamlet.
Mine and my father's death come not upon thee,   500
Nor thine on me! (*Dies.*)

HAMLET
Heaven make thee free of it! I follow thee.
I am dead, Horatio. Wretched Queen, adieu!
You that look pale and tremble at this chance,   505
That are but mutes,° or audience to this act,
Had I but time (as this fell sergeant,° Death,
Is strict in his arrest) O, I could tell you—
But let it be. Horatio, I am dead;
Thou livest; report me and my cause aright   510
To the unsatisfied.°

HORATIO
Never believe it.
I am more an antique Roman° than a Dane.
Here's yet some liquor left.   515

HAMLET
As th' art a man,
Give me the cup. Let go. By heaven, I'll ha't!
O God, Horatio, what a wounded name,
Things standing thus unknown, shall live behind   520
    me!
If thou didst ever hold me in thy heart,
Absent thee from felicity° awhile,
And in this harsh world draw thy breath in pain,
To tell my story. *A march afar off.* (*Exit* OSRIC.)   525
What warlike noise is this?
Enter OSRIC.

OSRIC
Young Fortinbras, with conquest come from
    Poland,
To th' ambassadors of England gives   530
This warlike volley.

HAMLET
O, I die, Horatio!

498 **tempered** mixed   506 **mutes** performers who have
no words to speak   507 **fell sergeant** dread sheriff's officer   511 **unsatisfied** uninformed   514 **antique Roman**
(with reference to the old Roman fashion of suicide)   523
felicity i.e., the felicity of death

463 **springe** snare   468 **sounds** swoons   480 **practice**
deception

The potent poison quite o'ercrows° my spirit.
535 I cannot live to hear the news from England,
But I do prophesy th' election lights
On Fortinbras. He has my dying voice.
So tell him, with th' occurrents,° more and less,
Which have solicited°—the rest is silence. (*Dies.*)
540   HORATIO
Now cracks a noble heart. Good night, sweet
        Prince,
And flights of angels sing thee to thy rest.
(*March within.*)
Why does the drum come hither?
Enter FORTINBRAS, *with the* AMBASSADORS *with*
DRUM, COLORS, *and* ATTENDANTS.
545   FORTINBRAS
Where is this sight?
         HORATIO
What is it you would see?
If aught of woe or wonder, cease your search.
550   FORTINBRAS
This quarry° cries on havoc.° O proud Death,
What feast is toward° in thine eternal cell
That thou so many princes at a shot
So bloodily hast struck?
555   AMBASSADOR
The sight is dismal;
And our affairs from England come too late.
The ears are senseless that should give us hearing
To tell him his commandment is fulfilled,
560 That Rosencrantz and Guildenstern are dead.
Where should we have our thanks?
         HORATIO
Not from his° mouth,
Had it th' ability of life to thank you.
565 He never gave commandment for their death.
But since, so jump° upon this bloody question,
You from the Polack wars, and you from England,
Are here arrived, give order that these bodies
High on a stage° be placèd to the view,
570 And let me speak to th' yet unknowing world
How these things came about. So shall you hear
Of carnal, bloody, and unnatural acts,

Of accidental judgments, casual° slaughters,
Of deaths put on by cunning and forced cause,
And, in this upshot, purposes mistook   575
Fall'n on th' inventors' heads. All this can I
Truly deliver.
         FORTINBRAS
Let us haste to hear it,
And call the noblest to the audience.   580
For me, with sorrow I embrace my fortune.
I have some rights of memory° in this kingdom,
Which now to claim my vantage doth invite me.
         HORATIO
Of that I shall have also cause to speak,   585
And from his mouth whose voice will draw on°
        more.
But let this same be presently performed,
Even while men's minds are wild, lest more
        mischance   590
On° plots and errors happen.
         FORTINBRAS
Let four captains
Bear Hamlet like a soldier to the stage,
For he was likely, had he been put on,°   595
To have proved most royal; and for his passage°
The soldiers' music and the rite of war
Speak loudly for him.
Take up the bodies. Such a sight as this
Becomes the field,° but here shows much amiss.   600
Go, bid the soldiers shoot.
*Exeunt marching; after the which a peal of ordnance
are shot off.*

FINIS

🐦 🐦 🐦

PERFORMING *HAMLET*

Hamlet is the most frequently performed of
Shakespeare's plays. Richard Burbage created
the long and complex role of the title character,
and, according to tradition, Shakespeare himself
played the ghost in the Globe Theater production in 1601–02. Since then, the play has had an
almost uninterrupted career on the English-
speaking stage.

---

534 **o'ercrows** overpowers (as a triumphant cock crows
over its weak opponent)   538 **occurrents** occurrences
539 **solicited** incited   551 **quarry** heap of slain bodies
551 **cries on havoc** proclaims general slaughter   552 **toward** in preparation   563 **his** (Claudius')   566 **jump** precisely 569 **stage** platform

573 **casual** not humanly planned, chance   582 **rights of
memory** remembered claims   586 **voice will draw on** vote
will influence   591 **On** on top of   595 **put on** advanced (to
the throne)   596 **passage** death   600 **field** battlefield

Celebrated actors playing Hamlet after Burbage began with Thomas Betterton in the 1661 London revival of Shakespeare's play. He acted "the best part that ever man acted," according to diarist Samuel Pepys. The next great performer, David Garrick, who first acted the role in 1742 and played Hamlet for the next thirty years, followed Betterton's active, robust Prince. Garrick also played a drastically reduced text (only restoring some 629 lines in 1772) and rewrote the ending to conform to neoclassical principles. Ophelia's funeral is omitted; the Queen is not poisoned onstage (the audience is informed that her guilt has driven her mad); and the King is killed in a duel with Hamlet.

Under the influence of the romantic critics in the early nineteenth century, actors, such as John Philip Kemble and Edmund Kean, moved away from playing Hamlet as a man of action and portrayed the Prince as sensitive, distracted, and oftentimes irresolute. American actor Edwin Booth rounded out the nineteenth-century romantic tradition by playing Hamlet as a man devoted to his father, anguished by his mother's remarriage, and remorseful over his part in the deaths of Claudius and Laertes. The great English actor-manager Henry Irving added an interpretation of Hamlet as a man overpowered by his love for Ophelia and staged the play for spectacle and illusionism. His popular version ran for an unprecedented 200 nights. He introduced the celebrated actress Ellen Terry as Ophelia in 1878. Her luminous performance defined the role for the next generations of actresses.

American actor John Barrymore first defined the twentieth-century playing of Hamlet on the New York stage in 1922 for 101 performances. Barrymore's virile, intense, and sophisticated Hamlet feigned the character's madness and introduced a seemingly incestuous relationship with Gertrude. Margaret Webster, who was on stage with him as a Court lady in the London revival, said that he made "all other Hamlets seem stodgy by comparison."

John Gielgud, who first played the role at the Old Vic in London in 1929–30 and for a record-breaking season in New York in 1936–37, created a "modern" Hamlet. The handsome Gielgud stressed the romantic sensitivity, the youthfulness, and sudden flashes of steely determination of the Prince and spoke Shakespeare's lines with intelligence and elegance of diction. After the run of 155 performances (and again in New York), Gielgud was called the finest classical actor of his generation.

Following John Gielgud, modern Hamlets seen both on stage and in film have been played by Laurence Olivier, Maurice Evans, Paul Scofield, Michael Redgrave, Richard Burton, David Warner, Kenneth Branagh, and Ralph Fiennes, and by Olivier and Branagh in film. There was a *G. I. Hamlet* performed by Maurice Evans for American troops during the Second World War; modern-dress stage productions (Richard Burton in a black turtleneck sweater); disillusioned, apathetic, and rebellious student-Hamlets (David Warner); and boyish, reluctant, anti-heroic Hamlets (Simon Russell Beale).

For over four hundred years, Shakespeare's great text has survived the tampering, the cutting, the restorations, the scenic spectacles, and costumes from all ages. Still aiming to play the Prince of Denmark today, actors accept the challenge almost daily to mine the ambiguous nature of perhaps Shakespeare's greatest character—certainly his most complex.

CRITICS' NOTEBOOK

These two approaches to understanding Shakespeare's masterful play introduce modern scholars and stage directors who treat the Elizabethan text as a living event of complex humanity. Margaret Webster and Peter Brook discuss the impact of Shakespeare's work on readers and theatergoers. Born in New York City and trained as an actor in London, Margaret Webster became the first woman to direct Shakespeare's plays on Broadway, to critical acclaim. She wrote *Shakespeare Without Tears* to persuade readers that the Bard's work, written for actors and audiences, had dramatic values that swept through theaters for four hundred years with the joyful mystery of life and the bitter release of death.

Director Peter Brook has staged productions of *Love's Labour's Lost, A Midsummer Night's Dream, Measure for Measure, The Tempest,* and *Hamlet* to critical acclaim. Celebrated internationally for his inventive staging of Shakespeare's plays and for grasping the ageless truths of Shakespeare's work, Brook is represented here by his essay on *Shakespearean Realism.*

Margaret Webster,
from *Shakespeare Without Tears**

❧

In reviewing thus briefly the potentialities of Shakespeare's plays in our contemporary theater I have not attempted to supply a ready-to-wear solution for any of their problems but simply to point out certain aspects of those problems. In doing so, I am acutely aware of the danger of generalizations. Every producer, designer, director, every company of actors, will bring qualities of mind and spirit to bear on the texts which will illuminate them from a different angle. Every play, self-evidently, requires a particularized treatment. Each separate text presents its own specific difficulties; settings and costumes must be considered in relation to the mood and emotional pattern of each. The musical accompaniment, whether it be indicated or required by the script itself, or added to it as a supplementary factor, must equally be devised to enhance and vivify the essential spirit of each play. So the actors' personal gifts or shortcomings must be welded together into an interpretative whole, not violating the author's intention, but translating it anew into the living language which is shared by actors and audience alike. No part of the theater is machine-made, and no part may be governed by mathematical formulas. Human fallibility being what it is, none of us may be assured of encompassing our vision; all we can do is to try to bring this vision into focus

with Shakespeare himself and pursue it with such integrity as we may.

If a modern producer were dealing with an author with thirty-seven plays to his credit, most of them successes and a dozen or so smash hits, he would at least listen with respect to what that author had to say and take some trouble to appreciate the workings of his mind. Shakespeare is still one of Broadway's most successful playwrights. His pay checks, if he still received them, would top the lists of Dramatists' Guild members. Every year or two a major motion-picture company acquires one or another of his scripts and his name appears regularly on TV credit titles though what happens on the screen thereafter may not always do him credit. His royalties from amateur rights alone would be worth a fortune. Surely so durable a dramatist rates a little investigation, perhaps even a trifle of respect, from those who exploit his works....

It is, of course, essential that we should interpret Shakespeare to our audiences through the medium of our common experience and our common humanity. And these channels of communication are precisely what the director must use to reach the heart of the plays themselves. He must learn to know the human beings who people them, all of them, from King Lear to the Third Citizen. Who are they? What are they like? They have a certain background, sometimes of historical fact, sometimes of tale or legend; they have an Elizabethan background in Shakespeare's Elizabethan mind. These we shall want to understand, for they will bring light into shadowed places. But, above all, what qualities in their minds and hearts do we share? What is their kinship with us? What is it in their blood which we also feel to be in our own?

The tangible things by which they are surrounded, the hats and cloaks they wear, the weapons they use, their food and drink, may belong almost exclusively to Shakespeare's England. Even the conventions of love and honor, hate and merriment, may differ from our own. But we can still lay our hands upon the pulse of each one of them; Shylock's speech may still stand for the universality of man, annihilating

*Margaret Webster, *Shakespeare Without Tears* (New York: McGraw-Hill Company, 1942): 218–221.

the gap of time as easily as the division of race. We too have "organs, dimensions, senses; affections, passions." We are "subject to the same diseases, healed by the same means, warmed and cooled by the same winter and summer.... If you prick us do we not bleed? If you tickle us do we not laugh? If you poison us do we not die? and if you wrong us, shall we not revenge?" It is always a sense of closeness at which the director should aim, rather than an emphasis of separation.

But he should not underrate either the author or the audience. There is no need to assume that they can be brought into accord only by such devices as dressing Hotspur in Air Force uniform or translating Ancient Rome into terms of South Side Chicago. Many directors and designers are rightly anxious that their theater should be "contemporary" in its approach. But Shakespeare is not merely local, and the attempt to make him so can become precious and pretentious unless it is used with discretion. The timeliness of the plays is more than costume deep; their truth is universal, and the analogies of external circumstances no more than a fortuitous, though sometimes poignant, reminder that the returning paths of history have been trodden by many feet.

With Shakespeare, as with any classic playwright, the importance of the settings is not exactly what it might be in the case of a new play in a contemporary idiom. The designer, like the director, has an interpretative function. But he will not be able to start from scratch, as with an original script; he will have to face precedents and comparisons. Neither director nor designer should let this trap him into mistaking novelty for penetration nor eccentricity for vitality. It is the truth of the vision which matters.

But the designer has, I think, a greater contribution to make than the convinced Globolators allow. We must transport our audiences into a world of illusion and we must appeal to their eyes as well as their ears. It is part of the theater's legitimate business to draw the eye with visual beauty. Shakespeare's men knew this. Although they had few scenic resources and no opportunity for lighting effects, they made up the decorative deficiency by lavish expenditure on "props" and costume.

We are well equipped to satisfy the eyes of our audience; but we must do it by going a little deeper than "something pretty to look at." Sets and costumes are a part of the interpretative vision and they can translate it by the simplest of means. But even if we decide to strip our stages of all redundant decoration, we should still preserve a rhythm and harmony of composition. Our settings do not have to be harsh or ugly because they are economical and austere. A man may carry away a picture in his mind even when the words have faded. It may be the impression of a background, a flight of steps, a shaft of light, a crimson curtain; it may be a group, a massing of people in action or repose. We must see to it that all these things have significance; there is drama in the pictorial composition on which the curtain rises, in a combination of color or of light and shadow. Equally, there is drama in the tension of an actor's body, as he listens, as he waits, as he stands in thought or as he unleashes action; in a gesture, an attitude or a piece of business silently executed. For the actor too, must interpret to the eye and must be given a costume which will most vividly help him to do so....

I once talked with a group of college students after a performance of HAMLET which had been received with tremendous enthusiasm. I asked them what it was that had appealed to them most. One said it was the sound of the words themselves, another the color and glamour and pictorial drama, a third the excitement of the story itself, the fights and the thrill of action; but the fourth expressed a different point of view. "It's funny," he said, "but while you're there you don't think—you forget about everything. But when you come away, you realize you've been through something—something that's made you different—an experience."

I do not believe that this experience has lost its validity or ever will lose it. It is a part of our inheritance. For three hundred and fifty years Shakespeare has been, for the English-speaking peoples, the voice of hope and love and laughter; he has comforted our griefs and spoken our triumphs with the sound of trumpets. He is beyond the divisions and barriers of contention; for there is singularly little hatred in the plays, and infinite understanding. It would be a barren world which ever felt that it had gone beyond his wisdom and compassion.

Nor shall we outgrow him as long as we have the ears to hear his own magnificent challenge: "What a piece of work is a man! how noble in reason! how infinite in faculties! in form and moving how express and admirable! in action how like an angel, in apprehension how like a god! the beauty of the world! the paragon of animals!" We cannot part company from him unless we abrogate our kinship with the angels.

And Shakespeare in the theater is a source of wealth we cannot afford to lose. Everyone can draw from it—the poet, the philosopher, the businessman, the truck driver, or the college student. Each will take from the plays as much as his mind and heart will carry, just as everyone concerned in producing or acting them will bring to their service all he has, and find it fully absorbed. Shakespeare's stamp and seal of honor has been set on every actor who has won a lasting reputation and on every theater company of enduring accomplishment. Shakespeare is not only the glory of the language which we speak; he is part of the stuff from which our civilization has been forged. It is for the theater to accept the high responsibility of preserving his living work; then only can we claim our rightful share in his immortality.

Peter Brook, "Shakespearean Realism"*

🐛

Everyone has a sort of shrewd suspicion that all great art is "real," but nobody agrees on what the word means. As a result, the very precise work involved in staging a play can easily get muddled by a large band of people valiantly seeking completely different things.

Any child today knows that at any given moment through his living room disembodied images are invisibly floating toward the televi-

sion set; he knows that the substance he breathes called air (which he cannot see but believes exists) is throbbing with equally concealed vibrations of musicians, comedians and BBC announcers. As he grows older, he learns about the subconscious. Long before he is out of school, he is aware that his father's stolid silences may be concealing a volcanic flow of pent-up hates, that his sister's blithe chatter may be a counterpoint to an inner rumble of obsessive guilt.

By the time he is old enough to be a theatregoer he will have already learned from films if not from life that space and time are loose and meaningless terms: that with a cut the mind can flick from yesterday to Australia.

So he will realize that the distinction between the realistic play and the poetic one, between the naturalistic and the stylized is artificial and very old-fashioned. He will see that the problem of the play that takes place in a living room or in a kitchen is no longer that it is *too* realistic but that it is not realistic at all. He will realize that although the chairs and tables are undoubtedly genuine, everything else smells false. He will sense that the so-called real dialogue and the so-called real acting do not actually capture that totality of information, visible and invisible, that corresponds to what he instinctively knows as reality.

So we come to Shakespeare. For centuries our practical understanding of Shakespeare has been blocked by the false notion that Shakespeare was a writer of far-fetched plots which he decorated with genius. Too long we have considered Shakespeare in separate compartments, dividing the story from the characters, the verse from the philosophy. Today we are beginning to see that Shakespeare forged a style in advance of any style anywhere, before or *since,* that enabled him, in a very compact space of time, by a superb and conscious use of varied means, to create a realistic image of life.

Let me take a far-fetched parallel. Picasso began to paint portraits with several eyes and noses the day he felt that to paint a profile—or to paint full face—was a form of lie. He set out to find a technique with which to capture a larger

*Peter Brook, "Shakespearean Realism" from *The Shifting Point: Theatre, Film, Opera 1946–1987* (New York: Harper & Row Publishers, 1987): 83–86.

slice of the truth. Shakespeare, knowing that man is living his everyday life and at the same time is living intensely in the invisible world of his thoughts and feelings, developed a method through which we can see at one and the same time the look on the man's face and the vibrations of his brain. We can hear the particular rhythm of speech and choice of slang by which we would know him at once as a character in real life, with a name, as though we met him on the street. But in the street his face might be blank and his tongue silent—Shakespeare's verse gives density to the portrait. This is the purpose of the striking metaphor, the purple passage, the ringing phrase. It can no longer be held for one second that such plays are "stylized," "formalized" or "romantic" as opposed to "realistic."

Our problem is to bring the actor, slowly, step by step, toward an understanding of this remarkable invention, this curious structure of free verse and prose which a few hundred years ago was already the Cubism of the theatre. We must wean the actor away from a false belief: that there is a heightened playing for the classics, a more real playing for the works of today. We must get him to see that the challenge of the verse play is that he must bring to it an even deeper search for truth, for truth of emotion, truth of ideas, and truth of character—all quite separate and yet all interwoven—and then as an artist find, with objectivity, the form that gives these meanings life.

The problem for the actor is to find a way of dealing with verse. If he approaches it too emotionally, he can end up in empty bombast; if he approaches it too intellectually, he can lose the ever-present humanity; if he is too literal, he gains the commonplace and loses the true meaning. Here are great problems, related to technique, imagination, and living experience that have to be solved in creating an ensemble. Eventually, we want to have actors who know with such certainty that there is no contradiction between the heightened and the real that they can slide effortlessly between the gears of verse and prose, following the modulations of the text.

We must move the productions and the settings away from all that played so vital a part in the postwar Stratford renaissance—away from romance, away from fantasy, away from decoration. Then they were necessary for shaking the ugliness and the boredom off these well-worn texts. Now we must look beyond an outer liveliness to an inner one. Outer splendor can be exciting but has little relation with modern life: on the inside lie themes and issues, rituals and conflicts which are as valid as ever. Any time the Shakespearean meaning is caught, it is "real" and so contemporary.

In the same way, in a country that has become very theatre-conscious, and which happens also to possess such a fantastic heritage, one question must be why no present-day English dramatist approaches the beginnings of Shakespearean power and freedom. Why, we must ask in the mid-twentieth century, are we more timid and more constipated in the ambition and scope of our thinking than the Elizabethans?

When we perform the classics, we know that their deepest reality will never speak for itself. Our efforts and our technique are to make them speak clearly through us. I think our responsibility toward the modern drama is to see that the reality of everyday life will not speak for itself either. We can record it, film it, jot it down, but we will be far from catching its nature. We see that Shakespeare in his day found the answer in his verse and prose structure related to the peculiar freedom of the Elizabethan stage. This can teach us something, and it is no coincidence that the modern theatre is moving toward open stages and is using surrealism of behavior in the place of verse as a technique for cracking open surface appearances. Our great opportunity and our challenge in Stratford and London is to endeavor to relate our work on Shakespeare and our work on modern plays to the search for a new style—dreadful word, I would prefer to say anti-style—which would enable dramatists to synthesize the self-contained achievements of the Theatre of the Absurd, the epic theatre and the naturalistic theatre. This is where our thinking must go and where our experiments must thrust.

REVISITING PLAY STRUCTURE

A play's structure is largely shaped by two factors: how the writer perceives human experience and by established writing conventions he or she may adopt, reject, reconstruct, or alter in the creation of a play. A play's structure is also influenced in large measure by the society and by the theater conventions of its day. For example, Sophocles' methods of organizing human activities in *Oedipus the King* reflect not only the writer's vision of humanity's relation to the universe but also his understanding of the festival requirements for play production. The controlled, orderly development of Oedipus' unrelenting quest for truth reflects a moral philosophy grounded in cause and effect; that is, all acts have predictable consequences. Moreover, the conventions of the fifth-century Greek theatre required that the principal episodes be separated by choral odes, and that the episodes include the messenger's report, the arias of suffering, and confrontations between hero and others. Climactic (classical) structure takes its name from the ever-contracting circle of the hero's choices which leads quickly to discovery and resolution.

In contrast, Elizabethan playwrights developed an expanding progression of events as a variation on the medieval idea of "life as a journey" between birth and death. Like the Greeks, they also perceived an orderly world whose theater was a mirror held up to a divinely appointed universe. Mirroring a cosmic order, episodic structure is expansive, encompassing many characters, events, locations, and years. It conforms to a kind of fluid staging where any and all can happen—from shipwrecks to battles to love scenes. There are leaps in time, gaps between events, and variety in characters and circumstances. Action becomes journey in the present, not confrontation with the past.

Playwrights of modern realism, like Henrik Ibsen and August Strindberg, adhered largely to the older compressed play structure to demonstrate the causes and effects of heredity and environment on individuals and societies. Climactic play structure continues to be popular among writers for our commercial theatre because of its compressed action and limited number of characters.

However, in its self-conscious departure from the past, our modern age has also evolved eclectic forms to mirror its disjunctions: epic (for episodic), situational (for absurd), and reflexive (for postmodern). African American Pulitzer-Prize-winning playwright Suzan-Lori Parks adds repetition and revision ("Rep & Rev"), which are integral to the Jazz aesthetic to define the central element of her work. In a departure from traditional linear storytelling, she creates a writing style and structure that looks and sounds like a musical score in such works as *The Death of the Last Black Man in the Whole Entire World*, *The America Play*, and *Topdog/Underdog*.

Shakespeare's Hamlet calls upon the players to hold "the mirror up to nature; to show virtue her own feature, scorn her own image, and the very age and body of the time his form and pressure." In one sense, he is pointing to the effective use of drama's key elements: play structure, character, and language. Drama requires flexibility of forms, effective creation of character, and compelling language. Tennessee Williams's *The Glass Menagerie* and Anton Chekhov's *The Cherry Orchard* continue our discussion of character and language in drama.

NOTES

1. Bertolt Brecht, "A Short Organon for the Theater," *Brecht on Theater: The Development of an Aesthetic*, trans. and ed. John Willett (New York: Hill and Wang, 1964): 204.
2. Suzanne K. Langer, *Feeling and Form: A Theory of Art* (New York: Charles Scribner's Sons, 1953): 307.
3. For my understanding of climactic and episodic play structure, I am indebted to Bernard Becker-

man's fine discussion in *Dynamics of Drama: Theory and Method of Analysis* (New York: Drama Book Specialists, 1979): 186–209.

4. Eugène Ionesco, *Notes and Counter Notes: Writings on the Theater*, trans. Donald Watson (New York: Grove Press, 1964): 257.

5. Martin Esslin, "The Theater of the Absurd," *Theater in the Twentieth Century*, ed. Robert W. Corrigan (New York: Grove Press, 1963): 233.

6. Esslin 244.

7. G. Wilson Knight, *The Wheel of Fire: Interpretations of Shakespearean Tragedy* (New York: Meridian Books, 1957): 46.

CHAPTER 3

UNDERSTANDING CHARACTER

Calista Flockhart as Laura Wingfield and Kevin Kilner as The Gentleman Caller, in *The Glass Menagerie* by Tennessee Williams, directed by Frank Galati, Roundabout Theatre Company, New York City, 1994. (Photo © Carol Rosegg.)

*My chief aim in playwriting is the creation of character.
I have always had a deep feeling for the mystery in life,
and essentially my plays have been an effort to explore
the beauty and meaning in the confusion of living.*
—Tennessee Williams[1]

CHARACTER'S DOUBLENESS

Drama is unique among the representational arts in that it represents "reality" by using real human beings—actors-as-characters—to create its fictional universe. There is a doubleness inherent in drama's characters. While fictions of the playwright's imagination, they are given life by actors. Tom Wingfield is the "fictitious" young man depicted by the "real" John Malkovich. The playwright visualizes the fictional character's clothes, habitat, thoughts, speech, and actions. Moreover, the more skilled the playwright, the more complex the characters and their situations. For instance, characters have complex personalities; they represent a class of individuals, such as kings or blue-collar workers, and they signify the human predicament from the writer's historical and philosophical perspective.

We have said that drama is essentially mimetic action. However, action springs from character. It is a product of the characters' motivations and circumstances. In some plays, those motivations and circumstances are more complex than in others. The great dramatic characters—Oedipus, Hamlet, Hedda Gabler, Amanda Wingfield—are not easily deciphered in what they say and what they do. We are constantly compelled to question their motives and to review them in light of developing situations. An assertion in an early scene can be proved or discredited by subsequent events. For example, as the plots progress, Claudius' innocence is discredited as is Amanda Wingfield's selflessness.

What do we look for in characters' speech, gestures, and actions to determine *who* they are and *what* they are doing? Martin Esslin said that much depends on the dialectic between what the characters know or do not know, and what the audience knows that the characters may not know.[2] This type of dramatic irony is one of the most ancient dramatic devices. Oedipus blindly insists on learning the full truth, which we already know, and Laertes knows that he has a poisoned foil but Hamlet does not. In both instances, the reader or audience (and other characters) has information that the central characters do not, but, eventually, the situation will be made known to them.

Dramatic character, thus, is defined, in part, by *who* does *what* (and *why*) and to *whom* under specific *circumstances.* In other words, the meaning of a character's behavior and choices ultimately derives from situation or circumstances.

CLASSICAL VERSUS MODERN CHARACTERS

Drama's characters are credible images of active human beings. To be credible, their manners and dress must fit their period, place, and social class. Their speech must suit their age, sex, personality, class, and circumstances. Their actions must be rooted in situation. In writing about character, Aristotle drew a relationship between character and plot. In *The Poetics*, plot was the chief element of drama ("the soul of tragedy"). This suggests that plot reveals character; in other words, we *are* what we *do* in given situations. Oedipus pursues the cause of the plague with the same moral determination he showed in fleeing Corinth. The modern critic Francis Fergusson defined dramatic character another way—as "will in action," or as "focused psychic energy."[3] This definition recognizes a play's dynamics as being charged by a character's choices—what Fergusson called the "shifting life of the psyche." Characters interact with other characters and, typically, this interaction results in some form of conflict. Oedipus clashes with Teiresias, Hamlet with Claudius, Tom Wingfield with his mother, and so forth.

As it relates to character, conflict is both general and particular. We may see a character against God, against nature, against society, against the unknown, against another character, and against himself or herself. Or, there may be a combination of forces at work. The conflict in *Oedipus the King* is most simply defined as one between man and fate. The conflict in *The Importance of Being Earnest* is between the lovers and society's marriage codes represented by Lady Brackwell. In *The Glass Menagerie,* the conflict is between two generations in an inhospitable world. In our own lives, our daily conflicts are for the most part superficial. When our parents refuse to lend us the family car for an important occasion, conflict is established between our desires and parental authority. Like drama's characters, however, we often attempt to overcome the obstacles by determined will in action.

Dramatic conflict is most often resolved by the removal of obstacles. Over the centuries, patterns have emerged in dramatic writing. In tragedy, like *Oedipus the King,* Oedipus is heroically uncompromising when confronted with obstacles to his will and, therefore, doomed. In comedy, the character's will is either successful (Gwendolyn Fairfax gets her Ernest) or frustrated (Madame Ranevskaia in *The Cherry Orchard*). Dramatic action is the movement of opposing forces toward a resolution of conflict in the hero's death (in tragedy), in triumph (in comedy), or in the villain's defeat (in both).

The playwright's success depends on skill in weaving character and event together in a believable and convincing pattern of choice and behavior. In Brecht's play, Galileo has to choose between dying as a martyr and surviving as a coward; he chooses to live. Galileo's fear of physical pain was enough to make him recant his "truths" before the Inquisition. However, his passion for food, pleasure, and scientific truth resulted in the preservation of his life and his writings, and the induction of a new scientific age for humankind.

The influence of Charles Darwin, Karl Marx, Sigmund Freud, and their followers is often visible in characters' choices and actions in plays written since the late nineteenth century. For example, characters' fates are often determined by issues of heredity and environment, by their fitness to survive in a hostile world, by their neuroses as a result of unresolved conflicts, and by economic factors where character becomes a function of society's materialism. In the postmodern world, character, if it exists at all, is a fragmented image of a total life. In Heiner Müller's *Hamletmachine,* Ophelia seated in a wheelchair in the deep sea surrounded by fish, debris, and dead bodies captures *in a single image* the modern character's inadequacy, confinement, and doom. The image also comments on Shakespeare's version of Ophelia's death by drowning.

PORTRAITS

In drama, characters are traditionally defined by their physical characteristics, speech, and dress; their socioeconomic status; their psychological makeup; and their moral or ethical choices. There are several ways to approach understanding drama's characters. First, we observe what playwrights say about them in stage directions and, second, we hear or read what characters say about one another in dialogue. Third, we note general types—physical and psychological. Fourth, we construe the moral or ethical choices that determine their destinies.

In modern plays, a character's appearance is usually described in stage directions that establish physical characteristics: gender, age, physique, clothing, and class, with some implication about the character's psychological makeup. As each character enters in *Hedda Gabler,* Ibsen describes in detail the character's sex, age, size, complexion, demeanor, and clothing. Of his heroine, he writes:

> She is a woman of twenty-nine. Distinguished, aristocratic face and figure. Her complexion is pale and opalescent. Her eyes are steel-grey, with an expression of cold, calm serenity. Her hair is of a handsome auburn color, but is not especially abundant. She is dressed in an elegant, somewhat loose-fitting morning gown. (1)

As we progress through Ibsen's text, we realize that he has provided, in a brief passage, crucial facts about his heroine. In 1890, a woman marrying at twenty-nine would already have been considered a spinster. Why did an attractive, vibrant woman delay marriage against all convention and then make a peremptory marriage to the conventional George Tesman? Hedda's aristocratic background as General Gabler's daughter makes her an "outsider" in the middle-class Tesman household. Her steel-grey eyes and cold expression highlight her psychological remoteness from her circumstances as Mrs. George Tesman—wife and mother-to-be. In literature, abundant hair has long been associated with fertility; Hedda's "not especially" abundant hair hints at her inability to assimilate herself into the gender role she is expected to fulfill as a married woman in the 1890s. Her psychological denial of who she is and what she has become will surface in her destructive and life-denying acts.

Over fifty years later, but in the same tradition of writing for the theater, Tennessee Williams described his matriarch in *The Glass Menagerie:*

> AMANDA WINGFIELD *(the mother) A little woman of great but confused vitality clinging frantically to another time and place. Her characterization must be carefully created, not copied from type. She is not paranoiac, but her life is paranoia. There is much to admire in Amanda, and as much to love and pity as there is to laugh at. Certainly she has endurance and a kind of heroism, and though her foolishness makes her unwittingly cruel at times, there is tenderness in her slight person.*

The kinds of facts provided by Ibsen and Williams in stage directions were gathered in earlier plays from a character's social rank (king, soldier, doctor, servant), clothing (luxurious, raggedy, military), and demeanor and speech (manners, attitude, vocabulary). Oedipus is a king whom the city elders *address* as the "first of men," a superior being, one who takes aggressive charge of a difficult situation. Hamlet's mother urges him to forego his mourning clothes and his grief over his father's untimely death. Hamlet himself *describes* his "inky cloak," his customary suit of solemn black, and his tears as but outward "trappings" of his profound grief over his father's death compounded by his mother's premature marriage to his uncle. Hamlet's disturbed thoughts are expressed in his soliloquy beginning, "Oh, that this too too solid flesh would melt,/Thaw, and resolve itself into a dew!" and ending with the ominous forecast that "it cannot come to good."

Playwrights, including Shakespeare, also use stereotypes, a practice dating from Greek and Roman comedy, to capture easily recognizable types of human foolishness. Stereotypical characters display *general* types of behavior outwardly noted by their dress and physical appearance. Character types from Italy's *commedia dell'arte*—professional companies dating from the 1500s specializing in improvisational comedy—such as the doctor, pedant, miser, rogue, braggart, parasite, and trickster, were identified by their general characteristics of greed, crabbiness, pedantry, quackery, craftiness, cowardice, and selfishness. Also, *commedia* characters remained true to their attitudes, costumes, and masks, which made it easy to identify the Capitano or Dottore and to follow their antics. Although *commedia* masks, costumes, and improvisational performance style were rarely assimilated into other periods of theater history, its character types were. Shakespeare's Falstaff, Molière's Harpagon, and Richard Brinsley Sheridan's gossipmongers Lady Sneerwell and Mr. Snake testify to the importance of broad stereotypes in capturing timeless human folly, especially in comedy.

A COMMON HUMANITY

Around the middle of the eighteenth century, changes in social and ethical considerations caused philosophers and writers to look upon human beings—a common humanity—with greater sympathy than had been true of their ancestors. Tragicomedy first showed us comic characters for whom we could feel deep sympathy and, later, domestic tragedies showed common people who suffered with dignity.

Behind the changing vision that only the sufferings of the great merit our awe are two hundred years of social and political thought that reduced human aspirations and sufferings to a common denominator. We have come to see human beings as less than heroic but still deserving of our attention and respect. Domestic or bourgeois drama of the mid-eighteenth century undermined the concept of the tragic hero as an individual of great rank and deeds. Instead of showing a heroic figure engaged in deeds of universal importance, it showed ordinary people in relation to their society, thus paving the way for our commonplace heroes—Arthur Miller's Willy Loman (*Death of a Salesman*) or August Wilson's Troy Maxson (*Fences*). These are decent, though deficient, characters who are at the end of the proverbial rope. They are not kings and princes, but they exhibit joy and pain as universal human traits even though they are salesmen and garbage collectors.

A great deal has been written about the loss of the concept of the heroic in modern times. There are several signposts on this road to our reduced and nonheroic stature. Charles Darwin's *The Origin of Species* (1859), from which we get such catch phrases as "natural selection" and "the survival of the fittest," reduced human beings to the product of "accidental variations" and substituted for a cosmic order a savage struggle for existence. Although Darwin (1809–1882) was ambivalent about how a supreme creator fit into this picture, he argued that all forms of life gradually developed from a common ancestry and that the evolution of species is explained by the "survival of the fittest." Darwin's theories implied that heredity and environment were the twin causes of everything humanity is or does. Since behavior is determined by factors largely beyond our control, individuals cannot truly be held responsible for what they do, nor for their destinies. If blame is to be assigned, it must go to a society that has allowed undesirable hereditary and environmental factors to exist. Therefore, we find modern playwrights assigning to society the earlier role of cosmic forces. Darwin's theories both contributed to humanity's loss of a privileged status in the universe and strengthened the idea of human progress through science and education.

While Darwin studied the progress of humankind "up from the apes," in the 1860s Karl Marx (1818–1883) studied the evolution of societies. Marx attributed our new sense of alienation and loss of identity to economic forces. Marx, like Darwin, reasoned that human beings were not really in control of their lives or responsible for their misfortunes and destinies. Blame rested with the twin exploiters: economic materialism and capitalistic societies whose singular purpose was the acquisition of wealth.

At the beginning of the twentieth century, Sigmund Freud (1856–1939) turned to the mind in an effort to free us from an inner tyranny—the unconscious. In *The Interpretation of Dreams* (1900), Freud turned his attention toward powerful psychological forces and to dreams as keys to human behavior. Freud's explanation of human behavior, with its emphasis on the unconscious mind—that reservoir of suppressed desires, complexes, drives, and impulses—led to distrust of our motives and actions.

These three explorers of genetics, environment, economics, and neuroses have had a pervasive influence on modern writers and on approaches to the creation of dramatic character. New backgrounds, subjects, motives, and actions took hold in realistic and nonrealistic plays, beginning in the 1880s. Plays, dating from the late nineteenth century, which stressed the influence of heredity and environment on the motives and actions of such characters as Hedda Gabler, for example, convey the intellectual influence of the Darwinian universe. Brecht's Mother Courage, whose function and misfortune in society is wholly economic, can be traced to the influence of Karl Marx. And the inner conflicts (or neuroses) of Tennessee Williams's Amanda Wingfield and Blanche DuBois have their origins in the findings of Sigmund Freud.

In 1949, Arthur Miller became the spokesman for the dignity and worthiness of ordinary individuals who have replaced persons of rank and nobility in modern drama. In his essay, "Tragedy and the Common Man," written while *Death of a Salesman* was running successfully on Broadway, Miller argued that kings had been replaced in modern plays by ordinary individuals prepared to secure at any cost a "sense of personal dignity." This compulsion belongs to all of us, not just to an Oedipus or a Hamlet. Miller asserted that moderns act against a scheme of things that degrades them and, in the process, generate a "fear" (similar to classical catharsis) in their assault on accepted ways and seemingly stable environments. The most ordinary of human beings may take on stature to the extent they are willing to battle to secure a rightful place in their world. "The quality in such plays that does shake us, however, derives from the underlying fear of being displaced, the disaster inherent in being torn away from our chosen image of what and who we are in this world.... In fact, it is the common man who knows this fear best."[4] Fighting for personal dignity and a refuge even in a hostile environment, Blanche DuBois of Mississippi cries out for her sister Stella to resist the "subhuman" quality of her life with the "survivor of the stone age"—Stanley Kowalski—in Tennessee Williams's *A Streetcar Named Desire*. "Don't—don't hang back with the brutes!" Blanche says in a moment of insight and courage before her defeat by overwhelming forces in the Kowalski household. Seen in this light, Blanche fights a battle she cannot possibly win, but her struggle is total and without reservation. We can identify with her spirit and struggle in a new kind of heroism for modern times.

"WHO'S THERE?"

When the guard in *Hamlet* challenges his comrade-in-arms with "Who's there?," he raises the central question about character for the contemporary theater. Arthur Miller's "common man" became obsolete as the absurdists raised questions about the human condition that moved beyond social, economic, and psychological concerns. No longer concerned with the causes of behavior and society's influences, the absurdists concerned themselves with the condition of being human in a world devoid of purpose and meaning.

Absurdist writers (and Anton Chekhov before them) first clearly combined human anguish with comic techniques of improbable situations and bizarre characters. In general, major absurdist writers, such as Beckett, Ionesco, and Pinter,

are preoccupied with the loneliness of people in a world without the certainties afforded by a supreme being or by human rationalism. This loneliness is heightened by our awareness of an inability to communicate, for language has become meaningless, and human existence is threatened in the nuclear age. As Ionesco said in *Notes and Counter Notes*, when "man is cut off from his religious or metaphysical roots, he is lost, all his struggles become senseless, futile and oppressive."[5] Absurdist writers *present* situations showing life's senselessness and oppressiveness. The common factors in their plays are nightmarish situations, incoherent dialogue, mechanical characters, and human anguish.

The philosophical uncertainty about instability of character or identity ("Who's there?") was stated for the theater as early as 1888 in August Strindberg's Preface to *Miss Julie*: "...I have made my people somewhat "characterless".... Because they are modern characters, living in a period of transition more feverishly hysterical than its predecessor at least, I have drawn my figures vacillating, disintegrated, a blend of old and new...."[6]

In Strindberg's *A Dream Play* (1902), his characters literally "split, double and multiply; they evaporate, crystallise, scatter, and converge."[7] Strindberg's view of the instability of character—what he called "characterless"—continued in the 1920s in the work of Italian playwright Luigi Pirandello to arrive fully developed in plays written by the absurdists, beginning in the late 1940s. In Ionesco's plays there is a loss of unity of character and coherent identity. "Personality doesn't exist," wrote Ionesco in *Victims of Duty*. In the absurdists' postwar writing, there are no beginnings and no endings, no causes and no effects, no identity and certainty of self. This does not mean that amazement at the very fact of being is lost. Rather, it becomes more intensified as we perceive the uncertainties and incongruities of existence. Ionesco made this point:

> ...the fact of being astonishes us, in a world that now seems all illusion and pretense, in which all human behavior tells of absurdity and all history of ab-

solute futility; all reality and all language appear to lose their articulation, to disintegrate and collapse, so what possible reaction is there left, when everything has ceased to matter, but laugh at it all?[8]

POSTMODERN DISSOLUTION

Postmodernism was a term used in the 1980s to declare that a long history of artistic achievement had come to an end. In discussions of art, architecture, dance, music, and theater, "modernism" was declared obsolete. Ruling in its place is a world whose boundaries and values have collapsed. While the absurdists argued a loss of certainty and identity in the modern world, postmoderns, like playwright Heiner Müller, defend the individual as victimized and oppressed by technological societies. Nevertheless, in the struggle, Müller anticipates the defeat and disappearance of the individual as he or she is torn apart by the contradictions of existence. The postmodern condition is viewed as schizoid. Even the writer is no longer detached—outside of the text—or whole, as evidenced in Müller's *Hamletmachine,* completed in 1977, in which a photograph of the author is torn apart on stage in demonstration of this premise. Müller calls his new play form consisting of disparate scenes without coherent, linear plots, "synthetic fragments." In postmodern dramaturgy, characters are schizoid "masks" the playwright can talk through—general types with individual names, such as Hamlet reconstituted as "the intellectual in conflict with history," or Ophelia as "the European terrorist."

For postmodernists, like Germany's Heiner Müller or America's Robert Wilson and Suzan-Lori Parks, there is a dissolution of the ego which has been central to dramatic character since the Greeks. For recognizable human beings, postmoderns substitute surreal, grotesque, gory, or cartoonlike characters as masks or images through which they, as writers, can talk to us. "That's why I prefer drama—because of the masks," said Müller. "I can say one thing and say the contrary. I have a need to get rid of contradictions and that is easier to do with drama."[9]

Nonetheless, in the mainstream of writing from the Greeks to the moderns, dramatic character has been portrayed as a whole, recognizable persona. Tennessee Williams provides this more traditional approach to the creation of character in *The Glass Menagerie.*

The Glass Menagerie

TENNESSEE WILLIAMS

Tennessee Williams (1911–1983) was born Thomas Lanier Williams III in Columbus, Mississippi, the son of a traveling salesman and an Episcopalian minister's daughter. The family, including siblings Rose Isabel and Walter Dakin, moved to St. Louis in 1918 where Williams grew up. He was educated at Missouri University, Washington University (St. Louis), and later at the University of Iowa where he received his B.A. degree.

In 1939, Story magazine published his short story, "The Field of Blue Children," the first work to appear under the name "Tennessee" Williams, which was probably a nickname given to him in college because of his southern accent. Earlier that year, he won a Group Theater prize with American Blues *(one-acts) and attracted the interest of New York agent Audrey Wood, who represented him for the next thirty-two years.*

In 1945 The Glass Menagerie *marked Williams's first major success and established him as an important American playwright. Two years later with the resounding Broadway success of* A Streetcar Named Desire *(winner of the Pulitzer Prize for Drama), Williams was acclaimed as the "new" Eugene O'Neill. Other major plays followed:* Summer and Smoke *(1948),* The Rose Tattoo *(1951),* Camino Real *(1953),* Cat on a Hot Tin Roof *(1955, winner of a second Pulitzer Prize for Drama),* Sweet Bird of Youth *(1959), and* The Night of the Iguana *(1961). Though his later plays, such as* Small Craft Warnings *(1972) and* Vieux Carré *(1977), failed to please critics, he continued to write until his death. In 1969, Williams was awarded the Gold Medal for Literature by the American Academy of Arts and Letters and the National Institute of Arts and Letters, and he received the Presidential Medal for the Arts by then-President Jimmy Carter.*

Several of Williams's early, unpublished plays written in the late 1930s (Not About Nightingales, Spring Storm, *and* Stairs to the Roof) *have recently been published and also produced with various successes.* Not About Nightingales *reached Broadway in 1999 to critical acclaim.*

Williams is our preeminent American playwright, having added at least five major plays to the modern repertoire along with some of the great dramatic roles: Amanda Wingfield, Blanche DuBois, Stanley Kowalski, Alma Winemiller, Serafina Delle Rose, Big Daddy Pollitt, and Alexandra del Lago.

CRITICAL INTRODUCTION TO
THE GLASS MENAGERIE

The Glass Menagerie, written in 1944 and originally titled *The Gentleman Caller,* is one of the great plays of the American theater whose central characters—Amanda, Tom, and Laura—are emotionally and economically maimed individuals. In the play's action, they become powerful images of human alienation and despair. The play's events trace, in seven scenes, Tom's memories of his family in the 1930s through the crisis leading up to his escape from his stultifying home and job. The Wingfield family is physically isolated in a St. Louis tenement building. (Their apartment faces on an alleyway and is entered by a fire escape.) The father, whose photograph hangs on the living room wall, abandoned his wife and two children long ago. As Tom says of his father, "He was a telephone man who fell in love with long distances...."

Williams's characters are a blend of self-absorbing needs and desperate courage. His "menagerie" is comprised of the oppressed, the fragile, and the needful. Amanda Wingfield reincarnates pride, pretensions, disappointment, perseverance, and desperation. She clings to her illusions of a more gentle life in the Mississippi

Delta and of the exhilaration of receiving seventeen gentlemen callers in one youthful day. Her daughter Laura, physically impaired from a childhood illness, has retreated in young adulthood into her own fantasy world. Like a piece from her glass animal collection from which the play takes its title, Laura is too fragile to come into contact with the harsh realities of a world where her need for love, companionship, and self-esteem are unlikely to be fulfilled. Tom, who carries the playwright's name, escapes his life of boredom by going to movies night after night. He finally chooses the merchant marine over his oppressive life of familial entrapment.

The fourth character is the "gentleman caller" who brings the reality of the outside world into their lives. In one brief evening, he introduces hope, warmth, sympathy, companionship, and finally disillusionment into their lives. He is a "nice, ordinary, young man" who comes to dinner at Tom's invitation urged on by his mother to provide an eligible suitor for his sister. However, the outsider becomes the playwright's catalyst for demonstrating to his narrator Tom, the gap between what is and what ought to be. Williams described the dinner guest as "the long-delayed but always expected something we live for." After the gentleman caller departs, nothing will ever again be the same for the Wingfield family. While Amanda keeps up the pretense that there will be others, Laura and Tom can no longer sustain their illusions about the life their mother imagines is just around the corner for them: success and marriage. Tom escapes to freedom, though not from his guilt for abandoning his family; and the candles, which illuminate the real world of unpaid electric bills, are forever snuffed out in Laura's life as she retreats further from reality into a world inhabited by glass replicas of animals which can be fondled and loved, but can never wound or frighten.

Williams called this play about human desperation and courage a "memory" play. Tom, the poet-narrator, exists both without and within the play. In seven scenes, he narrates his memories of another time, place, occasion, and family. Dressed as a merchant seaman, a sign of

his apartness, he sets the beginning scene: "I am the narrator of the play, and also a character in it." As narrator, he controls time past and present. The drama is enriched by the imaginative freedom of the narrator to choose scenes, seemingly at will, and to tell his story of illusion and despair. By using the device of a narrator, the harsh reality of the Wingfield family's impoverished existence is softened and blurred because they are, in one sense, creatures of Tom's imagination. In the same way, Amanda and Laura's illusions soften and blur their perceptions of reality. To one, southern gentility and mores are the operable way of life; to the other, isolation in daydreams provides refuge from a frightening world.

To reinforce the slightly unreal presentation of the play's world, Williams originally called for such expressionistic staging devices as the use of projections or "legends" to label scenes (these were omitted from the original production) and the use of a scrim ("the transparent fourth wall of the building") to ascend out of sight of the audience after the opening scene and to descend again during Tom's final speech. The scrim was to remind audiences that the play was the invention of a dramatic character and should be viewed as events projected from memory and distanced by time.

However, the social and psychological dimensions of the characters are wholly clear (and realistic) in Williams's exploration of the "beauty and meaning in the confusion of living." Tom Wingfield is oppressed by the suffocating realities of his daily life at the warehouse and in his mother's home. Amanda desperately sets herself the task of marrying Laura off in an act both selfish and cruel. Amanda is concerned that Laura must have a husband to secure her future well-being. Laura, shy and handicapped, retreats from her mother's ambitions into an imaginative world of glass animals whose fragility and uniqueness replicate her own. In the end, both siblings escape the dangerous world of burning human needs; only their strategies differ. Moreover, the fact that the Wingfield home is entered by a fire escape is no accidental poetic image. In scene seven, Tom exits the smoldering embers of his mother's and sister's desperation.

The story as told by Tom-the-poet is likewise *his* glass menagerie. The images from his past are fragile, distorted by memory and vulnerable to time. They even have names: Amanda, Laura, Tom. As Williams says of him, he is "a poet with a job in a warehouse. His nature is not remorseless, but to escape from a trap he has to act without pity." But, in telling the story from afar, Tom makes an effort to explain and ameliorate his sense of guilt for abandoning, like his father before him, his familial responsibilities in the name of peace and freedom.

Williams's characters, such as we find in *The Glass Menagerie,* carry a knowledge that pain and defeat await them both in the real and in the imagined world. For them, there is no escape from life's anguish and loneliness. Nevertheless, Williams celebrates courage and compassion in his maimed and anguished characters. Despite her selfishness, Amanda has tried to help her children; despite her infirmity, Laura has tried to adjust to the world outside; despite his frustrations, Tom has attempted to be a responsible son and brother. They have consistently failed. The knowledge of their failure and of their courage to go on despite failure is Williams's celebration of humanity's endurance and quiet nobility.

The Glass Menagerie

Nobody, not even the rain, has such small hands.
—e. e. cummings

SCENE

An Alley in St. Louis
    Part I.   *Preparation for a Gentleman Caller.*
    Part II.   *The Gentleman Calls.*
    Time: *Now and the Past.*

THE CHARACTERS

AMANDA WINGFIELD (*the mother*) A little woman of great but confused vitality clinging frantically to another time and place. Her characterization must be carefully created, not copied from type. She is not paranoiac, but her life is paranoia. There is much to admire in Amanda, and as much to love and pity as there is to laugh at. Certainly she has endurance and a kind of heroism, and though her foolishness makes her unwittingly cruel at times, there is tenderness in her slight person.

LAURA WINGFIELD (*her daughter*) Amanda, having failed to establish contact with reality, continues to live vitally in her illusions, but Laura's situation is even graver. A childhood illness has left her crippled, one leg slightly shorter than the other, and held in a brace. This defect need not be more than suggested on the stage. Stemming from this, Laura's separation increases till she is like a piece of her own glass collection, too exquisitely fragile to move from the shelf.

TOM WINGFIELD (*her son*) And the narrator of the play. A poet with a job in a warehouse. His nature is not remorseless, but to escape from a trap he has to act without pity.

JIM O'CONNOR (*the gentleman caller*) A nice, ordinary, young man.

SCENE ONE

The Wingfield apartment is in the rear of the building, one of those vast hive-like conglomerations of cellular living-units that flower as warty growths in overcrowded urban centers of lower middle-class population and are symptomatic of the impulse of this largest and fundamentally enslaved section of American society to avoid fluidity and differentiation and to exist and function as one interfused mass of automatism.

The apartment faces an alley and is entered by a fire escape, a structure whose name is a touch of accidental poetic truth, for all of these huge buildings are always burning with the slow and implacable fires of human desperation. The fire escape is part of what we see—that is, the landing of it and steps descending from it.

The scene is memory and is therefore nonrealistic. Memory takes a lot of poetic license. It omits some details; others are exaggerated, according to the emotional value of the articles it touches, for memory is seated predominantly in the heart. The interior is therefore rather dim and poetic.

At the rise of the curtain, the audience is faced with the dark, grim rear wall of the Wingfield tenement. This building is flanked on both sides by dark, narrow alleys which run into murky canyons of tangled clotheslines, garbage cans, and the sinister latticework of neighboring fire escapes. It is up and down these side alleys that exterior entrances and exits are made during the play. At the end of TOM'S opening commentary, the dark tenement wall slowly becomes transparent and reveals the interior of the ground-floor Wingfield apartment.

Nearest the audience is the living room, which also serves as a sleeping room for LAURA, the sofa unfolding to make her bed. Just beyond, separated from the living room by a wide arch or second proscenium with transparent faded portieres (or second curtain), is the dining room. In an old-fashioned whatnot in the living room are seen scores of transparent glass animals. A blown-up photograph of the father hangs on the wall of the living room, to the left of the archway. It is the face of a very handsome young man in a doughboy's First World War cap. He is gallantly smiling, ineluctably smiling, as if to say "I will be smiling forever."

Also hanging on the wall, near the photograph, are a typewriter keyboard chart and a Gregg shorthand diagram. An upright typewriter on a small table stands beneath the charts.

The audience hears and sees the opening scene in the dining room through both the transparent fourth wall of the building and the transparent gauze portieres of the dining-room arch. It is during this revealing scene that the fourth wall slowly ascends, out of sight. This transparent exterior wall is not brought down again until the very end of the play, during Tom's final speech.

The narrator is an undisguised convention of the play. He takes whatever license with dramatic convention is convenient to his purposes.

TOM *enters, dressed as a merchant sailor, and strolls across to the fire escape. There he stops and lights a cigarette. He addresses the audience.*

TOM: Yes, I have tricks in my pocket, I have things up my sleeve. But I am the opposite of a stage magician. He gives you illusion that has the appearance of truth. I give you truth in the pleasant disguise of illusion.

To begin with, I turn back time. I reverse it to that quaint period, the thirties, when the huge middle class of America was matriculating in a school for the blind. Their eyes had failed them, or they had failed their eyes, and so they were having their fingers pressed forcibly down on the fiery Braille alphabet of a dissolving economy.

In Spain there was revolution. Here there was only shouting and confusion. In Spain there was Guernica. Here there were disturbances of labor, sometimes pretty violent, in otherwise peaceful cities such as Chicago,

Cleveland, Saint Louis…

This is the social background of the play. *Music begins to play.*

The play is memory. Being a memory play, it is dimly lighted, it is sentimental, it is not realistic. In memory everything seems to happen to music. That explains the fiddle in the wings.

I am the narrator of the play, and also a character in it. The other characters are my mother, Amanda, my sister, Laura, and a gentleman caller who appears in the final scenes. He is the most realistic character in the play, being an emissary from a world of reality that we were somehow set apart from. But since I have a poet's weakness for symbols, I am using this character also as a symbol; he is the long-delayed but always expected something that we live for. There is a fifth character in the play who doesn't appear except in this larger-than-life-size photograph over the mantel. This is our father who left us a long time ago. He was a telephone man who fell in love with long distances; he gave up his job with the telephone company and skipped the light fantastic out of town…

The last we heard of him was a picture postcard from Mazatlan, on the Pacific coast of Mexico, containing a message of two words: "Hello—Goodbye!" and no address.

I think the rest of the play will explain itself…

AMANDA'S *voice becomes audible through the portieres.*

Legend on screen: "Ou sont les neiges."

TOM *divides the portieres and enters the dining room.* AMANDA *and* LAURA *are seated at a drop-leaf table. Eating is indicated by gestures without food or utensils.* AMANDA *faces the audience.* TOM *and* LAURA *are seated in profile. The interior has lit up softly and through the scrim we see* AMANDA *and* LAURA *seated at the table.*

AMANDA (*calling*): Tom?

TOM: Yes, Mother.

AMANDA: We can't say grace until you come to the table!

TOM: Coming, Mother. (*He bows slightly and withdraws, reappearing a few moments later in his place at the table.*)

AMANDA (*to her son*): Honey, don't *push* with your *fingers*. If you have to push with something, the thing to push with is a crust of bread. And chew—chew! Animals have secretions in their stomachs which enable them to digest food without mastication, but human beings are supposed to chew their food before they swallow it down. Eat food leisurely, son, and really enjoy it. A well-cooked meal has lots of delicate flavors that have to be held in the mouth for appreciation. So chew your food and give your salivary glands a chance to function!

TOM *deliberately lays his imaginary fork down and pushes his chair back from the table.*

TOM: I haven't enjoyed one bite of this dinner because of your constant directions on how to eat it. It's you that make me rush through meals with your hawklike attention to every bite I take. Sickening—spoils my appetite—all this discussion of—animals' secretion—salivary glands—mastication!

AMANDA (*lightly*): Temperament like a Metropolitan star!

TOM *rises and walks toward the living room.* You're not excused from the table.

TOM: I'm getting a cigarette.

AMANDA: You smoke too much.

LAURA *rises.*

LAURA: I'll bring in the blanc mange.

TOM *remains standing with his cigarette by the portieres.*

AMANDA (*rising*): No, sister, no, sister—you be the lady this time and I'll be the darky.

LAURA: I'm already up.

AMANDA: Resume your seat, little sister—I want you to stay fresh and pretty—for gentlemen callers!

LAURA (*sitting down*): I'm not expecting any gentlemen callers.

AMANDA (*crossing out to the kitchenette, airily*): Sometimes they come when they are least expected! Why, I remember one Sunday afternoon in Blue Mountain—

She enters the kitchenette.

TOM: I know what's coming!

LAURA: Yes. But let her tell it.

TOM: Again?

LAURA: She loves to tell it.

AMANDA *returns with a bowl of dessert.*

AMANDA: One Sunday afternoon in Blue Mountain—your mother received—*seventeen!*—gentlemen callers! Why, sometimes there weren't chairs enough to accommodate them all. We had to send the nigger over to bring in folding chairs from the parish house.

TOM (*remaining at the portieres*): How did you entertain those gentlemen callers?

AMANDA: I understood the art of conversation!

TOM: I bet you could talk.

AMANDA: Girls in those days *knew* how to talk, I can tell you.

TOM: Yes?

Image on screen: Amanda as a girl on a porch, greeting callers.

AMANDA: They knew how to entertain their gentlemen callers. It wasn't enough for a girl to be possessed of a pretty face and a graceful figure—although I wasn't slighted in either respect. She also needed to have a nimble wit and a tongue to meet all occasions.

TOM: What did you talk about?

AMANDA: Things of importance going on in the world! Never anything coarse or common or vulgar.

She addresses TOM *as though he were seated in the vacant chair at the table though he remains by the portieres. He plays this scene as though reading from a script.*

My callers were gentlemen—all! Among my callers were some of the most prominent young planters of the Mississippi Delta—planters and sons of planters!

TOM *motions for music and a spot of light on* AMANDA. *Her eyes lift, her face glows, her voice becomes rich and elegiac.*

Screen legend: "Ou sont les neiges d'antan?" There was young Champ Laughlin who later became vice-president of the Delta Planters Bank. Hadley Stevenson who was drowned in Moon Lake and left his widow one hundred and fifty thousand in Government bonds. There were the Cutrere broth-ers, Wesley and Bates. Bates was one of my bright particular beaux! He got in a quarrel with that wild Wainwright boy. They shot it out on the floor of Moon Lake Casino. Bates was shot through the stomach. Died in the ambulance on his way to Memphis. His widow was also well provided-for, came into eight or ten thousand acres, that's all. She married him on the rebound—never loved her—carried my picture on him the night he died! And there was that boy that every girl in the Delta had set her cap for! That beautiful, brilliant young Fitzhugh boy from Greene County!

TOM: What did he leave his widow?

AMANDA: He never married! Gracious, you talk as though all of my old admirers had turned up their toes to the daisies!

TOM: Isn't this the first you've mentioned that still survives?

AMANDA: That Fitzhugh boy went North and made a fortune—came to be known as the Wolf of Wall Street! He had the Midas touch, whatever he touched turned to gold! And I could have been Mrs. Duncan J. Fitzhugh, mind you! But—I picked your *father*!

LAURA (*rising*): Mother, let me clear the table.

AMANDA: No, dear, you go in front and study your typewriter chart. Or practice your shorthand a little. Stay fresh and pretty!—It's almost time for our gentlemen callers to start arriving. (*She flounces girlishly toward the kitchenette.*) How many do you suppose we're going to entertain this afternoon?

TOM *throws down the paper and jumps up with a groan.*

LAURA (*alone in the dining room*): I don't believe we're going to receive any, Mother.

AMANDA (*reappearing airily*): What? No one —not one? You must be joking!

LAURA *nervously echoes her laugh. She slips in a fugitive manner through the half-open portieres and draws them gently behind her. A shaft of very clear light is thrown on her face against the faded tapestry of the curtains. Faintly the music of "The Glass Menagerie" is heard as she contin-ues, lightly:*

Not one gentleman caller? It can't be true! There must be a flood, there must have been a tornado!

LAURA: It isn't a flood, it's not a tornado, Mother. I'm just not popular like you were in Blue Mountain....

TOM *utters another groan.* LAURA *glances at him with a faint, apologetic smile. Her voice catches a little:*

Mother's afraid I'm going to be an old maid. *The scene dims out with the "Glass Menagerie" music.*

SCENE TWO

On the dark stage the screen is lighted with the image of blue roses. Gradually LAURA'S *figure becomes ap-parent and the screen goes out. The music subsides.*

LAURA *is seated in the delicate ivory chair at the small clawfoot table. She wears a dress of soft violet material for a kimono—her hair is tied back from her forehead with a ribbon. She is washing and polishing her collection of glass.* AMANDA *appears on the fire escape steps. At the sound of her ascent,* LAURA *catches her breath, thrusts the bowl of ornaments away, and seats herself stiffly before the diagram of the typewriter keyboard as though it held her spell-bound. Something has happened to* AMANDA. *It is written in her face as she climbs to the landing: a look that is grim and hopeless and a little absurd. She has on one of those cheap or imitation velvety-looking cloth coats with imitation fur collar. Her hat is five or six years old, one of those dreadful cloche hats that were worn in the late Twenties, and she is clutching an enormous black patent-leather pocketbook with nickel clasps and initials. This is her full-dress outfit, the one she usually wears to the D.A.R. Before enter-ing she looks through the door. She purses her lips, opens her eyes very wide, rolls them upward and shakes her head. Then she slowly lets herself in the door. Seeing her mother's expression* LAURA *touches her lips with a nervous gesture.*

LAURA: Hello, Mother, I was—(*She makes a ner-vous gesture toward the chart on the wall.* AMANDA *leans against the shut door and stares at* LAURA *with a martyred look.*)

AMANDA: Deception? Deception? (*She slowly re-moves her hat and gloves, continuing the sweet suffering stare. She lets the hat and gloves fall on the floor—a bit of acting.*)

LAURA (*shakily*): How was the D.A.R. meeting?

AMANDA *slowly opens her purse and removes a dainty white handkerchief which she shakes out delicately and delicately touches to her lips and nostrils.*

Didn't you go to the D.A.R. meeting, Mother?

AMANDA (*faintly, almost inaudibly*): —No.—No. (*then more forcibly:*) I did not have the strength—to go to the D.A.R. In fact, I did not have the courage! I wanted to find a hole in the ground and hide myself in it forever! (*She crosses slowly to the wall and removes the diagram of the typewriter keyboard. She holds it in front of her for a second, staring at it sweetly and sorrowfully—then bites her lips and tears it in two pieces.*)

LAURA (*faintly*): Why did you do that, Mother?

AMANDA *repeats the same procedure with the chart of the Gregg Alphabet.*

Why are you—

AMANDA: Why? Why? How old are you, Laura?

LAURA: Mother, you know my age.

AMANDA: I thought that you were an adult; it seems that I was mistaken. (*She crosses slowly to the sofa and sinks down and stares at* LAURA.)

LAURA: Please don't stare at me, Mother.

AMANDA *closes her eyes and lowers her head. There is a ten-second pause.*

AMANDA: What are we going to do, what is going to become of us, what is the future?

There is another pause.

LAURA: Has something happened, Mother?

AMANDA *draws a long breath, takes out the handkerchief again, goes through the dabbing process.*

Mother, has—something happened?

AMANDA: I'll be all right in a minute, I'm just bewildered—(*She hesitates.*)—by life....

LAURA: Mother, I wish that you would tell me what's happened!

AMANDA: As you know, I was supposed to be inducted into my office at the D.A.R. this afternoon.

Screen image: A swarm of typewriters.

But I stopped off at Rubicam's Business College to speak to your teachers about your having a cold and ask them what progress they thought you were making down there.

LAURA: Oh....

AMANDA: I went to the typing instructor and introduced myself as your mother. She didn't know who you were. "Wingfield," she said, "We don't have any such student enrolled at the school!"

I assured her she did, that you had been going to classes since early in January.

"I wonder," she said, "If you could be talking about that terribly shy little girl who dropped out of school after only a few days' attendance?"

"No," I said, "Laura, my daughter, has been going to school every day for the past six weeks!"

"Excuse me," she said. She took the attendance book out and there was your name, unmistakably printed, and all the dates you were absent until they decided that you had dropped out of school.

I still said, "No, there must have been some mistake! There must have been some mix-up in the records!"

And she said, "No—I remember her perfectly now. Her hands shook so that she couldn't hit the right keys! The first time we gave a speed test, she broke down completely—was sick at the stomach and almost had to be carried into the wash room! After that morning she never showed up any more. We phoned the house but never got any answer"—While I was working at Famous-Barr, I suppose, demonstrating those—

She indicates a brassiere with her hands.

Oh! I felt so weak I could barely keep on my feet! I had to sit down while they got me a glass of water! Fifty dollars' tuition, all of our plans—my hopes and ambitions for you—just gone up the spout, just gone up the spout like that.

LAURA *draws a long breath and gets awkwardly to her feet. She crosses to the Victrola and winds it up.*

What are you doing?

LAURA: Oh! (*She releases the handle and returns to her seat.*)

AMANDA: Laura, where have you been going when you've gone out pretending that you were going to business college?

LAURA: I've just been going out walking.

AMANDA: That's not true.

LAURA: It is. I just went walking.

AMANDA: Walking? Walking? In winter? Deliberately courting pneumonia in that light coat? Where did you walk to, Laura?

LAURA: All sorts of places—mostly in the park.

AMANDA: Even after you'd started catching that cold?

LAURA: It was the lesser of two evils, Mother.
Screen image: Winter scene in a park.
I couldn't go back there. I—threw up—on the floor!

AMANDA: From half past seven till after five every day you mean to tell me you walked around in the park, because you wanted to make me think that you were still going to Rubicam's Business College?

LAURA: It wasn't as bad as it sounds. I went inside places to get warmed up.

AMANDA: Inside where?

LAURA: I went in the art museum and the bird houses at the Zoo. I visited the penguins every day! Sometimes I did without lunch and went to the movies. Lately I've been spending most of my afternoons in the Jewel Box, that big glass house where they raise the tropical flowers.

AMANDA: You did all this to deceive me, just for deception? (LAURA *looks down.*) Why?

LAURA: Mother, when you're disappointed, you get that awful suffering look on your face, like the picture of Jesus' mother in the museum!

AMANDA: Hush!

LAURA: I couldn't face it.
There is a pause. A whisper of strings is heard.
Legend on screen: "The Crust of Humility."

AMANDA (*hopelessly fingering the huge pocketbook*): So what are we going to do the rest of our lives? Stay home and watch the parades go by? Amuse ourselves with the glass menagerie, darling? Eternally play those worn-out phonograph records your father left as a painful reminder of him? We won't have a business career—we've given that up because it gave us nervous indigestion! (*She laughs wearily.*) What is there left but dependency all our lives? I know so well what becomes of unmarried women who aren't prepared to occupy a position. I've seen such pitiful cases in the South—barely tolerated spinsters living upon the grudging patronage of sister's husband or brother's wife!—stuck away in some little mousetrap of a room—encouraged by one in-law to visit another—little birdlike women without any nest—eating the crust of humility all their life! Is that the future that we've mapped out for ourselves? I swear it's the only alternative I can think of! (*She pauses.*) It isn't a very pleasant alternative, is it? (*She pauses again.*) Of course—some girls do marry.

LAURA *twists her hands nervously.*
Haven't you ever liked some boy?

LAURA: Yes. I liked one once. (*She rises.*) I came across his picture a while ago.

AMANDA (*with some interest*): He gave you his picture?

LAURA: No, it's in the yearbook.

AMANDA (*disappointed*): Oh—a high school boy.
Screen image: Jim as the high school hero bearing a silver cup.

LAURA: Yes. His name was Jim. (*She lifts the heavy annual from the claw-foot table.*) Here he is in *The Pirates of Penzance.*

AMANDA (*absently*): The what?

LAURA: The operetta the senior class put on. He had a wonderful voice and we sat across the aisle from each other Mondays, Wednesdays and Fridays in the Aud. Here he is with the silver cup for debating! See his grin?

AMANDA (*absently*): He must have had a jolly disposition.

LAURA: He used to call me—Blue Roses.
Screen image: Blue roses.

AMANDA: Why did he call you such a name as that?

LAURA: When I had that attack of pleurosis—he asked me what was the matter when I came back. I said pleurosis—he thought that I said Blue Roses! So that's what he always called me after that. Whenever he saw me, he'd holler, "Hello, Blue Roses!" I didn't care for the girl that he went out with. Emily Meisenbach. Emily was the best-dressed girl at Soldan. She never struck me, though, as being sincere…. It says in the Personal Section—they're engaged. That's—six years ago! They must be married by now.

AMANDA: Girls that aren't cut out for business careers usually wind up married to some nice man. (*She gets up with a spark of revival.*) Sister, that's what you'll do!

LAURA *utters a startled, doubtful laugh. She reaches quickly for a piece of glass.*

LAURA: But, Mother—

AMANDA: Yes? (*She goes over to the photograph.*)

LAURA (*in a tone of frightened apology*): I'm—crippled!

AMANDA: Nonsense! Laura, I've told you never, never to use that word. Why, you're not crippled, you just have a little defect—hardly noticeable, even! When people have some slight disadvantage like that, they cultivate other things to make up for it—develop charm—and vivacity—and—*charm!* That's all you have to do! (*She turns again to the photograph.*) One thing your father had plenty of—was *charm!*

The scene fades out with music.

SCENE THREE

Legend on screen: "After the fiasco—"
TOM *speaks from the fire escape landing.*

TOM: After the fiasco at Rubicam's Business College, the idea of getting a gentleman caller for Laura began to play a more and more important part in Mother's calculations. It became an obsession. Like some archetype of the universal unconscious, the image of the gentleman caller haunted our small apartment….

Screen image: A young man at the door of a house with flowers.

An evening at home rarely passed without some allusion to this image, this specter, this hope…. Even when he wasn't mentioned, his presence hung in Mother's preoccupied look and in my sister's frightened, apologetic manner—hung like a sentence passed upon the Wingfields!

Mother was a woman of action as well as words. She began to take logical steps in the planned direction. Late that winter and in the early spring—realizing that extra money would be needed to properly feather the nest and plume the bird—she conducted a vigorous campaign on the telephone, roping in subscribers to one of those magazines for matrons called *The Homemaker's Companion,* the type of journal that features the serialized sublimations of ladies of letters who think in terms of delicate cuplike breasts, slim, tapering waists, rich, creamy thighs, eyes like wood smoke in autumn, fingers that soothe and caress like strains of music, bodies as powerful as Etruscan sculpture.

Screen image: The cover of a glamor magazine.

AMANDA *enters with the telephone on a long extension cord. She is spotlighted in the dim stage.*

AMANDA: Ida Scott? This is Amanda Wingfield! We *missed* you at the D.A.R. last Monday! I said to myself: She's probably suffering with that sinus condition! How is that sinus condition?

Horrors! Heaven have mercy!—You're a Christian martyr, yes, that's what you are, a Christian martyr!

Well, I just now happened to notice that your subscription to the *Companion's* about to expire! Yes, it expires with the next issue, honey!—just when that wonderful new serial by Bessie Mae Hopper is getting off to such an exciting start. Oh, honey, it's something that you can't miss! You remember how *Gone with the Wind* took everybody by storm? You simply couldn't go out if you hadn't read it. All everybody *talked* was Scarlett O'Hara. Well, this is a book that critics already compare to *Gone with the Wind.* It's the *Gone with the Wind* of the post-World-War generation!—What?—Burning?—Oh, honey, don't let them burn, go take a look in the oven and I'll hold the wire! Heavens—I think she's hung up!

The scene dims out.

Legend on screen: "You think I'm in love with Continental Shoemakers?"

Before the lights come up again, the violent voices of TOM *and* AMANDA *are heard. They are quarreling behind the portieres. In front of them stands* LAURA *with clenched hands and panicky expression. A clear pool of light is on her figure throughout this scene.*

TOM: What in Christ's name am I—

AMANDA (*shrilly*): Don't you use that—

TOM: —supposed to do!

AMANDA: —expression! Not in my—

TOM: Ohhh!

AMANDA: —presence! Have you gone out of your senses?

TOM: I have, that's true, *driven* out!

AMANDA: What is the matter with you, you—big—big—IDIOT!

TOM: Look!—I've got no thing, no single thing—

AMANDA: Lower your voice!

TOM: —in my life here that I can call my OWN! Everything is—

AMANDA: Stop that shouting!

TOM: Yesterday you confiscated my books! You had the nerve to—

AMANDA: I took that horrible novel back to the library—yes! That hideous book by that insane Mr. Lawrence.

TOM laughs wildly.

I cannot control the output of diseased minds or people who cater to them—

TOM laughs still more wildly.

BUT I WON'T ALLOW SUCH FILTH BROUGHT INTO MY HOUSE! No, no, no, no, no!

TOM: House, house! Who pays rent on it, who makes a slave of himself to—

AMANDA (*fairly screeching*): Don't you DARE to—

TOM: No, no, *I* mustn't say things! *I've* got to just—

AMANDA: Let me tell you—

TOM: I don't want to hear any more!

He tears the portieres open. The dining-room area is lit with a turgid smoky red glow. Now we see AMANDA; *her hair is in metal curlers and she is wearing a very old bathrobe, much too large for her slight figure, a relic of the faithless Mr. Wingfield. The upright typewriter now stands on the drop-leaf table, along with a wild disarray of manuscripts. The quarrel was probably precipitated by* AMANDA'S *interruption of* TOM'S *creative labor. A chair lies overthrown on the floor. Their gesticulating shadows are cast on the ceiling by the fiery glow.*

AMANDA: You *will* hear more, you—

TOM: No, I won't hear more, I'm going out!

AMANDA: You come right back in—

TOM: Out, out, out! Because I'm—

AMANDA: Come back here, Tom Wingfield! I'm not through talking to you!

TOM: Oh, go—

LAURA (*desperately*): —Tom!

AMANDA: You're going to listen, and no more insolence from you! I'm at the end of my patience!

He comes back toward her.

TOM: What do you think I'm at? Aren't I supposed to have any patience to reach the end of, Mother? I know, I know. It seems unimportant to you, what I'm *doing*—what I *want* to do—having a little *difference* between them! You don't think that—

AMANDA: I think you've been doing things that you're ashamed of. That's why you act like this. I don't believe that you go every night to the movies. Nobody goes to the movies night after night. Nobody in their right minds goes to the movies as often as you pretend to. People don't go to the movies at nearly midnight, and movies don't let out at two A.M. Come in stumbling. Muttering to yourself like a maniac! You get three hours' sleep and then go to work. Oh, I can picture the way you're doing down there. Moping, doping, because you're in no condition.

TOM (*wildly*): No, I'm in no condition!

AMANDA: What right have you got to jeopardize your job? Jeopardize the security of us all? How do you think we'd manage if you were—

TOM: Listen! You think I'm crazy about the *warehouse*? (*He bends fiercely toward her slight figure.*) You think I'm in love with the Continental Shoemakers? You think I want to spend fifty-five *years* down there in that—*celotex interior!* with—*fluorescent—tubes!* Look! I'd rather somebody picked up a crowbar and battered out my brains—than go back mornings! I *go!* Every time you come in yelling that God-damn *"Rise and Shine!" "Rise and Shine!"* I say to myself, "How *lucky dead* people are!" But I get up. I *go!* For sixty-five dollars a month I give up all that I dream of doing and being *ever!* And you say self— *self's* all I ever think of. Why, listen, if self is what I thought of, Mother, I'd be where he is—GONE! (*He points to his father's picture.*) As far as the system of transportation reaches! (*He starts past her. She grabs his arm.*) Don't grab at me, Mother!

AMANDA: Where are you going?

TOM: I'm going to the *movies!*

AMANDA: I don't believe that lie!

TOM *crouches toward her, overtowering her tiny figure. She backs away, gasping.*

TOM: I'm going to opium dens! Yes, opium dens, dens of vice and criminals' hang-outs, Mother. I've joined the Hogan Gang, I'm a hired assassin, I carry a tommy gun in a violin case! I run a string of cat houses in the Valley! They call me Killer, Killer Wingfield, I'm leading a double-life, a simple, honest warehouse worker by day, by night a dynamic *czar* of the *underworld, Mother.* I go to gambling casinos, I spin away fortunes on the roulette table! I wear a patch over one eye and a false mustache, sometimes I put on green whiskers. On those occasions they call me—*El Diablo!* Oh, I could tell you many things to make you sleepless! My enemies plan to dynamite this place. They're going to blow us all sky-high some night! I'll be glad, very happy, and so will you! You'll go up, up on a broomstick, over Blue Mountain with seventeen gentlemen callers! You ugly—babbling old—*witch....*

He goes through a series of violent, clumsy movements, seizing his overcoat, lunging to the door, pulling it fiercely open. The women watch him, aghast. His arm catches in the sleeve of the coat as he struggles to pull it on. For a moment he is pinioned by the bulky garment. With an outraged groan he tears the coat off again, splitting the shoulder of it, and hurls it across the room. It strikes against the shelf of LAURA's glass collection, and there is a tinkle of shattering glass. LAURA cries out as if wounded. Music.

Screen legend: "The Glass Menagerie."

LAURA (*shrilly*): My glass!—menagerie.... (*She covers her face and turns away.*)

But AMANDA *is still stunned and stupefied by the "ugly witch" so that she barely notices this occurrence. Now she recovers her speech.*

AMANDA (*in an awful voice*): I won't speak to you—until you apologize!

She crosses through the portieres and draws them together behind her. TOM *is left with* LAURA. LAURA *clings weakly to the mantel with her face averted.* TOM *stares at her stupidly for a moment. Then he crosses to the shelf. He drops awkwardly on his knees to collect the fallen glass, glancing at* LAURA *as if he would speak but couldn't.*

"The Glass Menagerie" music steals in as the scene dims out.

SCENE FOUR

The interior of the apartment is dark. There is a faint light in the alley. A deep-voiced bell in a church is tolling the hour of five.

TOM *appears at the top of the alley. After each solemn boom of the bell in the tower, he shakes a little noisemaker or rattle as if to express the tiny spasm of man in contrast to the sustained power and dignity of the Almighty. This and the unsteadiness of his advance make it evident that he has been drinking. As he climbs the few steps to the fire escape landing light steals up inside.* LAURA *appears in the front room in a nightdresss. She notices that* TOM'S *bed is empty.* TOM *fishes in his pockets for his door key, removing a motley assortment of articles in the search, including a shower of movie ticket stubs and an empty bottle. At last he finds the key, but just as he is about to insert it, it slips from his fingers. He strikes a match and crouches below the door.*

TOM (*bitterly*): One crack—and it falls through!

LAURA *opens the door.*

LAURA: Tom! Tom, what are you doing?

TOM: Looking for a door key.

LAURA: Where have you been all this time?

TOM: I have been to the movies.

LAURA: All this time at the movies?

TOM: There was a very long program. There was a Garbo picture and a Mickey Mouse and a travelogue and a newsreel and a preview of coming attractions. And there was an organ solo and a collection for the Milk Fund—simultaneously—which ended up in a terrible fight between a fat lady and an usher!

LAURA (*innocently*): Did you have to stay through everything?

TOM: Of course! And, oh, I forgot! There was a big stage show! The headliner on this stage show was Malvolio the Magician. He performed wonderful tricks, many of them, such as pouring water back and forth between pitchers. First it turned to wine and then it turned to beer and then it turned to whisky. I know it was whisky it finally turned into because he needed somebody to come up out of the audience to help him, and I came up—both shows! It was Kentucky Straight Bourbon. A very generous fellow, he gave souvenirs. (*He pulls from his back pocket a shimmering rainbow-colored scarf.*) He gave me this. This is his magic scarf. You can have it, Laura. You wave it over a canary cage and you get a bowl of goldfish. You wave it over the goldfish bowl and they fly away canaries.... But the wonderfullest trick of all was the coffin trick. We nailed him into a coffin and he got out of the coffin without removing one nail. (*He has come inside.*) There is a trick that would come in handy for me—get me out of this two-by-four situation! (*He flops onto the bed and starts removing his shoes.*)

LAURA: Tom—shhh!

TOM: What're you shushing me for?

LAURA: You'll wake up Mother.

TOM: Goody, goody! Pay 'er back for all those "Rise an' Shines." (*He lies down, groaning.*) You know it don't take much intelligence to get yourself into a nailed-up coffin, Laura. But who in hell ever got himself out of one without removing one nail?

As if in answer, the father's grinning photograph lights up. The scene dims out. Immediately following, the church bell is heard striking six. At the sixth stroke the alarm clock goes off in AMANDA'S *room, and after a few moments we hear her calling: "Rise and Shine! Rise and Shine!* LAURA, *go tell your brother to rise and shine!"*

TOM (*sitting up slowly*): I'll rise—but I won't shine.

The light increases.

AMANDA: Laura, tell your brother his coffee is ready.

LAURA *slips into the front room.*

LAURA: Tom!—It's nearly seven. Don't make Mother nervous.

He stares at her stupidly.

(*beseechingly:*) Tom, speak to Mother this morning. Make up with her, apologize, speak to her!

TOM: She won't to me. It's her that started not speaking.

LAURA: If you just say you're sorry she'll start speaking.

TOM: Her not speaking—is that such a tragedy?

LAURA: Please—please!

AMANDA (*calling from the kitchenette*): Laura, are you going to do what I asked you to do, or do I have to get dressed and go out myself?

LAURA: Going, going—soon as I get on my coat!

She pulls on a shapeless felt hat with a nervous, jerky movement, pleadingly glancing at TOM. *She rushes awkwardly for her coat. The coat is one of* AMANDA'S, *inaccurately made-over, the sleeves too short for* LAURA.

Butter and what else?

AMANDA (*entering from the kitchenette*): Just butter. Tell them to charge it.

LAURA: Mother, they make such faces when I do that.

AMANDA: Sticks and stones can break our bones, but the expression on Mr. Garfinkel's face won't harm us! Tell your brother his coffee is getting cold.

LAURA (*at the door*): Do what I asked you, will you, will you, Tom?

He looks sullenly away.

AMANDA: Laura, go now or just don't go at all!

LAURA (*rushing out*): Going—going!

> *A second later she cries out.* TOM *springs up and crosses to the door.* TOM *opens the door.*

TOM: Laura?

LAURA: I'm all right. I slipped, but I'm all right.

AMANDA (*peering anxiously after her*): If anyone breaks a leg on those fire-escape steps, the landlord ought to be sued for every cent he possesses! (*She shuts the door. Now she remembers she isn't speaking to* TOM *and returns to the other room.*) *As* TOM *comes listlessly for his coffee, she turns her back to him and stands rigidly facing the window on the gloomy gray vault of the areaway. Its light on her face with its aged but childish features is cruelly sharp, satirical as a Daumier print. The music of "Ave Maria," is heard softly.*

> TOM *glances sheepishly but sullenly at her averted figure and slumps at the table. The coffee is scalding hot; he sips it and gasps and spits it back in the cup. At his gasp,* AMANDA *catches her breath and half turns. Then she catches herself and turns back to the window.* TOM *blows on his coffee, glancing sidewise at his mother. She clears her throat.* TOM *clears his. He starts to rise, sinks back down again, scratches his head, clears his throat again.* AMANDA *coughs.* TOM *raises his cup in both hands to blow on it, his eyes staring over the rim of it at his mother for several moments. Then he slowly sets the cup down and awkwardly and hesitantly rises from the chair.*

TOM (*hoarsely*): Mother. I—I apologize, Mother.

> AMANDA *draws a quick, shuddering breath. Her face works grotesquely. She breaks into childlike tears.*

I'm sorry for what I said, for everything that I said, I didn't mean it.

AMANDA (*sobbingly*): My devotion has made me a witch and so I make myself hateful to my children!

TOM: *No, you don't.*

AMANDA: I worry so much, don't sleep, it makes me nervous!

TOM (*gently*): I understand that.

AMANDA: I've had to put up a solitary battle all these years. But you're my right-hand bower! Don't fall down, don't fail!

TOM (*gently*): I try, Mother.

AMANDA (*with great enthusiasm*): Try and you will succeed! (*The notion makes her breathless.*) Why, you—you're just *full* of natural endowments! Both of my children—they're *unusual* children! Don't you think I know it? I'm so—*proud!* Happy and—feel I've—so much to be thankful for but—promise me one thing, son!

TOM: What, Mother?

AMANDA: Promise, son, you'll—never be a drunkard!

TOM (*turns to her grinning*): I will never be a drunkard, Mother.

AMANDA: That's what frightened me so, that you'd be drinking! Eat a bowl of Purina!

TOM: Just coffee, Mother.

AMANDA: Shredded wheat biscuit?

TOM: No. No, Mother, just coffee.

AMANDA: You can't put in a day's work on an empty stomach. You've got ten minutes—don't gulp! Drinking too-hot liquids makes cancer of the stomach…. Put cream in.

TOM: No, thank you.

AMANDA: To cool it.

TOM: No! No, thank you, I want it black.

AMANDA: I know, but it's not good for you. We have to do all that we can to build ourselves up. In these trying times we live in, all that we have to cling to is—each other…. That's why it's so important to—Tom, I—I sent out your sister so I could discuss something with you. If you hadn't spoken I would have spoken to you. (*She sits down.*)

TOM (*gently*): What is it, Mother, that you want to discuss?

AMANDA: *Laura!*

> TOM *puts his cup down slowly.*
> *Legend on screen: "Laura." Music: "The Glass Menagerie."*

TOM: —Oh.—Laura…

AMANDA (*touching his sleeve*): You know how Laura is. So quiet but—still water runs deep! She notices things and I think she—broods about them.

> TOM *looks up.*

A few days ago I came in and she was crying.

TOM: What about?

AMANDA: You.

TOM: Me?

AMANDA: She has an idea that you're not happy here.

TOM: What gave her that idea?

AMANDA: What gives her any idea? However, you do act strangely. I—I'm not criticizing, understand *that!* I know your ambitions do not lie in the warehouse, that like everybody in the whole wide world—you've had to—make sacrifices, but—Tom—Tom— life's not easy, it calls for—Spartan endurance! There's so many things in my heart that I cannot describe to you! I've never told you but I—*loved* your father....

TOM (*gently*): I know that, Mother.

AMANDA: And you—when I see you taking after his ways! Staying out late—and—well, you *had* been drinking the night you were in that—terrifying condition! Laura says that you hate the apartment and that you go out nights to get away from it! Is that true, Tom?

TOM: No. You say there's so much in your heart that you can't describe to me. That's true of me, too. There's so much in my heart that I can't describe to you! So let's respect each other's—

AMANDA: But, why—*why*, Tom—are you always so *restless*? Where do you *go* to, nights?

TOM: I—go to the movies.

AMANDA: Why do you go to the movies so much, Tom?

TOM: I go to the movies because—I like adventure. Adventure is something I don't have much of at work, so I go to the movies.

AMANDA: But, Tom, you go to the movies *entirely* too *much!*

TOM: I like a lot of adventure.

> AMANDA *looks baffled, then hurt. As the familiar inquisition resumes,* TOM *becomes hard and impatient again.* AMANDA *slips back into her querulous attitude toward him.*
> *Image on screen:* A sailing vessel with Jolly Roger.

AMANDA: Most young men find adventure in their careers.

TOM: Then most young men are not employed in a warehouse.

AMANDA: The world is full of young men employed in warehouses and offices and factories.

TOM: Do all of them find adventure in their careers?

AMANDA: They do or they do without it! Not everybody has a craze for adventure.

TOM: Man is by instinct a lover, a hunter, a fighter, and none of those instincts are given much play at the warehouse!

AMANDA: Man is by instinct! Don't quote instinct to me! Instinct is something that people have got away from! It belongs to animals! Christian adults don't want it!

TOM: What do Christian adults want, then, Mother?

AMANDA: Superior things! Things of the mind and the spirit! Only animals have to satisfy instincts! Surely your aims are somewhat higher than theirs! Than monkeys—pigs—

TOM: I reckon they're not.

AMANDA: You're joking. However, that isn't what I wanted to discuss.

TOM (*rising*): I haven't much time.

AMANDA (*pushing his shoulders*): Sit down.

TOM: You want me to punch in red at the warehouse, Mother?

AMANDA: You have five minutes. I want to talk about Laura.
> *Screen legend:* "Plans and Provisions."

TOM: All right! What about Laura?

AMANDA: We have to be making some plans and provisions for her. She's older than you, two years, and nothing has happened. She just drifts along doing nothing. It frightens me terribly how she just drifts along.

TOM: I guess she's the type that people call home girls.

AMANDA: There's no such type, and if there is, it's a pity! That is unless the home is hers, with a husband!

TOM: What?

AMANDA: Oh, I can see the handwriting on the wall as plain as I see the nose in front of my face! It's terrifying! More and more you remind me of your father! He was out all hours without explanation!—Then *left! Goodbye!* And me with the bag to hold. I saw that letter you got from the Merchant Marine. I know what you're dreaming of. I'm not standing here blindfolded. (*She pauses.*) Very well, then. Then *do* it! But not till there's somebody to take your place.

TOM: What do you mean?

AMANDA: I mean that as soon as Laura has got somebody to take care of her, married, a home of her own, independent—why, then you'll be free to go wherever you please, on land, on sea, whichever way the wind blows you! But until that time you've got to look out for your sister. I don't say me because I'm old and don't matter! I say for your sister because she's young and dependent.

I put her in business college—a dismal failure! Frightened her so it made her sick at the stomach. I took her over to the Young People's League at the church. Another fiasco. She spoke to nobody, nobody spoke to her. Now all she does is fool with those pieces of glass and play those worn-out records. What kind of a life is that for a girl to lead?

TOM: What can I do about it?

AMANDA: Overcome selfishness! Self, self, self is all that you ever think of! TOM *springs up and crosses to get his coat. It is ugly and bulky. He pulls on a cap with earmuffs.*

Where is your muffler? Put your wool muffler on!

He snatches it angrily from the closet, tosses it around his neck and pulls both ends tight.

Tom! I haven't said what I had in mind to ask you.

TOM: I'm too late to—

AMANDA (*catching his arm—very importunately; then shyly*): Down at the warehouse, aren't there some—nice young men?

TOM: No!

AMANDA: There *must* be—*some*…

TOM: Mother—(*He gestures.*)

AMANDA: Find out one that's clean-living— doesn't drink and ask him out for sister!

TOM: What?

AMANDA: For *sister!* To *meet!* Get *acquainted!*

TOM (*stamping to the door*): Oh, my go-osh!

AMANDA: Will you?

He opens the door. She says, imploringly:

Will you?

(*He starts down the fire escape.*)

Will you? Will you, dear?

TOM (*calling back*): Yes!

AMANDA *closes the door hesitantly and with a troubled but faintly hopeful expression.*

Screen image: The cover of a glamor magazine.

The spotlight picks up AMANDA *at the phone.*

AMANDA: Ella Cartwright? This is Amanda Wingfield! How are you, honey? How is that kidney condition?

There is a five-second pause.

Horrors!

There is another pause.

You're a Christian martyr, yes, honey, that's what you are, a Christian martyr! Well, I just now happened to notice in my little red book that your subscription to the *Companion* has just run out! I knew that you wouldn't want to miss out on the wonderful serial starting in this new issue. It's by Bessie Mae Hopper, the first thing she's written since *Honeymoon for Three*. Wasn't that a strange and interesting story? Well, this one is even lovelier, I believe. It has a sophisticated society background. It's all about the horsey set on Long Island!

The light fades out.

SCENE FIVE

Legend on the screen: "Annunciation."

Music is heard as the light slowly comes on.

It is early dusk of a spring evening. Supper has just been finished in the Wingfield apartment. AMANDA *and* LAURA, *in light-colored dresses, are removing dishes from the table in the dining room, which is shadowy, their movements formalized almost as a dance or ritual, their moving forms as pale and silent as moths.* TOM, *in white shirt and trousers, rises from the table and crosses toward the fire escape.*

AMANDA (*as he passes her*): Son, will you do me a favor?

TOM: What?

AMANDA: Comb your hair! You look so pretty when your hair is combed!

TOM *slouches on the sofa with the evening paper. Its enormous headline reads: "Franco Triumphs."*

There is only one respect in which I would like you to emulate your father.

TOM: What respect is that?

AMANDA: The care he always took of his appearance. He never allowed himself to look untidy.

He throws down the paper and crosses to the fire escape.

Where are you going?

TOM: I'm going out to smoke.

AMANDA: You smoke too much. A pack a day at fifteen cents a pack. How much would that amount to in a month? Thirty times fifteen is how much, Tom? Figure it out and you will be astounded at what you could save. Enough to give you a night-school course in accounting at Washington U.! Just think what a wonderful thing that would be for you, son!

TOM *is unmoved by the thought.*

TOM: I'd rather smoke. (*He steps out on the landing, letting the screen door slam.*)

AMANDA (*sharply*): I know! That's the tragedy of it....

(*Alone, she turns to look at her husband's picture.*)

Dance music: "The World Is Waiting for the Sunrise!"

TOM (*to the audience*): Across the alley from us was the Paradise Dance Hall. On evenings in spring the windows and doors were open and the music came outdoors. Sometimes the lights were turned out except for a large glass sphere that hung from the ceiling. It would turn slowly about and filter the dusk with delicate rainbow colors. Then the orchestra played a waltz or a tango, something that had a slow and sensuous rhythm. Couples would come outside, to the relative privacy of the alley. You could see them kissing behind ash pits and telephone poles. This was the compensation for lives that passed like mine, without any change or adventure. Adventure and change were imminent in this year. They were waiting around the corner for all these kids. Suspended in the mist over Berchtesgaden, caught in the folds of Chamberlain's umbrella. In Spain there was Guernica! But here there was only hot swing music and liquor, dance halls, bars, and movies, and sex that hung in the gloom like a chandelier and flooded the world with brief, deceptive rainbows.... All the world was waiting for bombardments!

AMANDA *turns from the picture and comes outside.*

AMANDA (*sighing*): A fire escape landing's a poor excuse for a porch. (*She spreads a newspaper on a step and sits down, gracefully and demurely as if she were settling into a swing on a Mississippi veranda.*)

What are you looking at?

TOM: The moon.

AMANDA: Is there a moon this evening?

TOM: It's rising over Garfinkel's Delicatessen.

AMANDA: So it is! A little silver slipper of a moon. Have you made a wish on it yet?

TOM: Um-hum.

AMANDA: What did you wish for?

TOM: That's a secret.

AMANDA: A secret, huh? Well, I won't tell mine either. I will be just as mysterious as you.

TOM: I bet I can guess what yours is.

AMANDA: Is my head so transparent?

TOM: You're not a sphinx.

AMANDA: No, I don't have secrets. I'll tell you what I wished for on the moon. Success and happiness for my precious children! I wish for that whenever there's a moon, and when there isn't a moon, I wish for it, too.

TOM: I thought perhaps you wished for a gentleman caller.

AMANDA: Why do you say that?

TOM: Don't you remember asking me to fetch one?

AMANDA: I remember suggesting that it would be nice for your sister if you brought home some nice young man from the warehouse. I think that I've made that suggestion more than once.

TOM: Yes, you have made it repeatedly.

AMANDA: Well?

TOM: We are going to have one.

AMANDA: What?

TOM: A gentleman caller!

The annunciation is celebrated with music.

AMANDA *rises*.

Image on screen: A caller with a bouquet.

AMANDA: You mean you have asked some nice young man to come over?

TOM: Yep. I've asked him to dinner.

AMANDA: You really did?

TOM: I did!

AMANDA: You did, and did he—*accept?*

TOM: He did!

AMANDA: Well, well—well, well! That's—lovely!

TOM: I thought that you would be pleased.

AMANDA: It's definite then?

TOM: Very definite.

AMANDA: Soon?

TOM: Very soon.

AMANDA: For heaven's sake, stop putting on and tell me some things, will you?

TOM: What things do you want me to tell you?

AMANDA: *Naturally* I would like to know when he's *coming!*

TOM: He's coming tomorrow.

AMANDA: Tomorrow?

TOM: Yep. Tomorrow.

AMANDA: But, Tom!

TOM: Yes, Mother?

AMANDA: Tomorrow gives me no time!

TOM: Time for what?

AMANDA: Preparations! Why didn't you phone me at once, as soon as you asked him, the minute that he accepted? Then, don't you see, I could have been getting ready!

TOM: You don't have to make any fuss.

AMANDA: Oh, Tom, Tom, Tom, of course I have to make a fuss! I want things nice, not sloppy! Not thrown together. I'll certainly have to do some fast thinking, won't I?

TOM: I don't see why you have to think at all.

AMANDA: You just don't know. We can't have a gentleman caller in a pigsty! All my wedding silver has to be polished, the monogrammed table linen ought to be laundered! The windows have to be washed and fresh curtains put up. And how about clothes? We have to *wear* something, don't we?

TOM: Mother, this boy is no one to make a fuss over!

AMANDA: Do you realize he's the first young man we've introduced to your sister? It's terrible, dreadful, disgraceful that poor little sister has never received a single gentleman caller! Tom, come inside! (*She opens the screen door.*)

TOM: What for?

AMANDA: I want to ask you some things.

TOM: If you're going to make such a fuss, I'll call it off, I'll tell him not to come!

AMANDA: You certainly won't do anything of the kind. Nothing offends people worse than broken engagements. It simply means I'll have to work like a Turk! We won't be brilliant, but we will pass inspection. Come on inside.

TOM *follows her inside, groaning.*

Sit down.

TOM: Any particular place you would like me to sit?

AMANDA: Thank heavens I've got that new sofa! I'm also making payments on a floor lamp I'll have sent out! And put the chintz covers on, they'll brighten things up! Of course I'd hoped to have these walls re-papered.... What is the young man's name?

TOM: His name is O'Connor.

AMANDA: That, of course, means fish—tomorrow is Friday! I'll have that salmon loaf—with Durkee's dressing! What does he do? He works at the warehouse?

TOM: Of course! How else would I—

AMANDA: Tom, he—doesn't drink?

TOM: Why do you ask me that?

AMANDA: Your father *did!*

TOM: Don't get started on that!

AMANDA: He *does* drink, then?

TOM: Not that I know of!

AMANDA: Make sure, be certain! The last thing I want for my daughter's a boy who drinks!

TOM: Aren't you being a little bit premature? Mr. O'Connor has not yet appeared on the scene!

AMANDA: But will tomorrow. To meet your sister, and what do I know about his character? Nothing! Old maids are better off than wives of drunkards!

TOM: Oh, my God!

AMANDA: Be still!

TOM (*leaning forward to whisper*): Lots of fellows meet girls whom they don't marry!

AMANDA: Oh, talk sensibly, Tom—and don't be sarcastic!
She has gotten a hairbrush.

TOM: What are you doing?

AMANDA: I'm brushing that cowlick down! (*She attacks his hair with the brush.*) What is this young man's position at the warehouse?

TOM (*submitting grimly to the brush and the interrogation*): This young man's position is that of a shipping clerk, Mother.

AMANDA: Sounds to me like a fairly responsible job, the sort of a job *you* would be in if you just had more *get-up.* What is his salary? Have you any idea?

TOM: I would judge it to be approximately eighty-five dollars a month.

AMANDA: Well—not princely, but—

TOM: Twenty more than I make.

AMANDA: Yes, how well I know! But for a family man, eighty-five dollars a month is not much more than you can just get by on....

TOM: Yes, but Mr. O'Connor is not a family man.

AMANDA: He might be, mightn't he? Some time in the future?

TOM: I see. Plans and provisions.

AMANDA: You are the only young man that I know of who ignores the fact that the future becomes the present, the present the past, and the past turns into everlasting regret if you don't plan for it!

TOM: I will think that over and see what I can make of it.

AMANDA: Don't be supercilious with your mother! Tell me some more about this— what do you call him?

TOM: James D. O'Connor. The D. is for Delaney.

AMANDA: Irish on *both* sides! *Gracious!* And doesn't drink?

TOM: Shall I call him up and ask him right this minute?

AMANDA: The only way to find out about those things is to make discreet inquiries at the proper moment. When I was a girl in Blue Mountain and it was suspected that a young man drank, the girl whose attentions he had been receiving, if any girl *was,* would sometimes speak to the minister of his church, or rather her father would if her father was liv-

ing, and sort of feel him out on the young man's character. That is the way such things are discreetly handled to keep a young woman from making a tragic mistake!

TOM: Then how did you happen to make a tragic mistake?

AMANDA: That innocent look of your father's had everyone fooled! He *smiled*—the world was *enchanted!* No girl can do worse than put herself at the mercy of a handsome appearance! I hope that Mr. O'Connor is not too good-looking.

TOM: No, he's not too good-looking. He's covered with freckles and hasn't too much of a nose.

AMANDA: He's not right-down homely, though?

TOM: Not right-down homely. Just medium homely, I'd say.

AMANDA: Character's what to look for in a man.

TOM: That's what I've always said, Mother.

AMANDA: You've never said anything of the kind and I suspect you would never give it a thought.

TOM: Don't be so suspicious of me.

AMANDA: At least I hope he's the type that's up and coming.

TOM: I think he really goes in for self-improvement.

AMANDA: What reason have you to think so?

TOM: He goes to night school.

AMANDA (*beaming*): Splendid! What does he do, I mean study?

TOM: Radio engineering and public speaking!

AMANDA: Then he has visions of being advanced in the world! Any young man who studies public speaking is aiming to have an executive job some day! And radio engineering? A thing for the future! Both of these facts are very illuminating. Those are the sort of things that a mother should know concerning any young man who comes to call on her daughter. Seriously or—not.

TOM: One little warning. He doesn't know about Laura. I didn't let on that we had dark ulterior motives. I just said, why don't you come and have dinner with us? He said okay and that was the whole conversation.

AMANDA: I bet it was! You're eloquent as an oyster. However, he'll know about Laura when he gets here. When he sees how lovely and sweet and pretty she is, he'll thank his lucky stars he was asked to dinner.

TOM: Mother, you mustn't expect too much of Laura.

AMANDA: What do you mean?

TOM: Laura seems all those things to you and me because she's ours and we love her. We don't even notice she's crippled any more.

AMANDA: Don't say crippled! You know that I never allow that word to be used!

TOM: But face facts, Mother. She is and—that's not all—

AMANDA: What do you mean "not all"?

TOM: Laura is very different from other girls.

AMANDA: I think the difference is all to her advantage.

TOM: Not quite all—in the eyes of others—strangers—she's terribly shy and lives in a world of her own and those things make her seem a little peculiar to people outside the house.

AMANDA: Don't say peculiar.

TOM: Face the facts. She is.

The dance hall music changes to a tango that has a minor and somewhat ominous tone.

AMANDA: In what way is she peculiar—may I ask?

TOM (*gently*): She lives in a world of her own—a world of little glass ornaments, Mother….

He gets up. AMANDA *remains holding the brush, looking at him, troubled.*

She plays old phonograph records and—that's about all—

(*He glances at himself in the mirror and crosses to the door.*)

AMANDA (*sharply*): Where are you going?

TOM: I'm going to the movies. (*He goes out the screen door.*)

AMANDA: Not to the movies, every night to the movies! (*She follows quickly to the screen door.*) I don't believe you always go to the movies! *He is gone.* AMANDA *looks worriedly after him for a moment. Then vitality and optimism return and she turns from the door, crossing to the portieres.*

Laura! Laura!

LAURA *answers from the kitchenette.*

LAURA: Yes, Mother.

AMANDA: Let those dishes go and come in front! LAURA *appears with a dish towel.* AMANDA *speaks to her gaily.* Laura, come here and make a wish on the moon!

Screen image: The Moon.

LAURA (*entering*): Moon—moon?

AMANDA: A little silver slipper of a moon. Look over your left shoulder, Laura, and make a wish!

LAURA *looks faintly puzzled as if called out of sleep.* AMANDA *seizes her shoulders and turns her at an angle by the door.*

Now! Now, darling, *wish!*

LAURA: What shall I wish for, Mother?

AMANDA (*her voice trembling and her eyes suddenly filling with tears*): Happiness! Good fortune! *The sound of the violin rises and the stage dims out.*

SCENE SIX

The light comes up on the fire escape landing. TOM *is leaning against the grill, smoking.*

Screen image: The high school hero.

TOM: And so the following evening I brought Jim home to dinner. I had known Jim slightly in high school. In high school Jim was a hero. He had tremendous Irish good nature and vitality with the scrubbed and polished look of white chinaware. He seemed to move in a continual spotlight. He was a star in basketball, captain of the debating club, president of the senior class and the glee club and he sang the male lead in the annual light operas. He was always running or bounding, never just walking. He seemed always at the point of defeating the law of gravity. He was shooting with such velocity through his adolescence that you would logically expect him to arrive at nothing short of the White House by the time he was thirty. But Jim apparently ran into more interference after his graduation from Soldan. His speed had definitely slowed. Six years after he left high school he was holding a job that wasn't much better than mine.

Screen image: The Clerk.

He was the only one at the warehouse with whom I was on friendly terms. I was valuable to him as someone who could remember his former glory, who had seen him win basketball games and the silver cup in debating. He knew of my secret practice of retiring to a cabinet of the washroom to work on poems when business was slack in the warehouse. He called me Shakespeare. And while the other boys in the warehouse regarded me with suspicious hostility, Jim took a humorous attitude toward me. Gradually his attitude affected the others, their hostility wore off and they also began to smile at me as people smile at an oddly fashioned dog who trots across their path at some distance.

I knew that Jim and Laura had known each other at Soldan, and I had heard Laura speak admiringly of his voice. I didn't know if Jim remembered her or not. In high school Laura had been as unobtrusive as Jim had been astonishing. If he did remember Laura, it was not as my sister, for when I asked him to dinner, he grinned and said, "You know, Shakespeare, I never thought of you as having folks!"

He was about to discover that I did....

Legend on screen: "The accent of a coming foot."

The light dims out on TOM *and comes up in the Wingfield living room—a delicate lemony light. It is about five on a Friday evening of late spring which comes "scattering poems in the sky."*

AMANDA *has worked like a Turk in preparation for the gentleman caller. The results are astonishing. The new floor lamp with its rose silk shade is in place, a colored paper lantern conceals the broken light fixture in the ceiling, new billowing white curtains are at the windows, chintz covers are on the chairs and sofa, a pair of new sofa pillows make their initial appearance. Open boxes and tissue paper are scattered on the floor.*

LAURA *stands in the middle of the room with lifted arms while* AMANDA *crouches before her, adjusting the hem of a new dress, devout and ritualistic. The dress is colored and designed by memory. The arrangement of* LAURA'S *hair is changed; it is softer and more becoming. A fragile, unearthly prettiness has come out in* LAURA: *she is like a piece of translucent glass touched by light, given a momentary radiance, not actual, not lasting.*

AMANDA (*impatiently*): Why are you trembling?

LAURA: Mother, you've made me so nervous!

AMANDA: How have I made you nervous?

LAURA: By all this fuss! You make it seem so important!

AMANDA: I don't understand you, Laura. You couldn't be satisfied with just sitting home, and yet whenever I try to arrange something for you, you seem to resist it. (*She gets up.*) Now take a look at yourself. No, wait! Wait just a moment—I have an idea!

LAURA: What is it now?

AMANDA *produces two powder puffs which she wraps in handkerchiefs and stuffs in* LAURA'S *bosom.*

LAURA: Mother, what are you doing?

AMANDA: They call them "Gay Deceivers"!

LAURA: I won't wear them!

AMANDA: You will!

LAURA: Why should I?

AMANDA: Because, to be painfully honest, your chest is flat.

LAURA: You make it seem like we were setting a trap.

AMANDA: All pretty girls are a trap, a pretty trap, and men expect them to be.

Legend on screen: "A pretty trap."

Now look at yourself, young lady. This is the prettiest you will ever be! (*She stands back to admire Laura.*) I've got to fix myself now! You're going to be surprised by your mother's appearance!

AMANDA *crosses through the portieres, humming gaily.* LAURA *moves slowly to the long mirror and stares solemnly at herself. A wind blows the white curtains inward in a slow, graceful motion and with a faint, sorrowful sighing.*

AMANDA (*from somewhere behind the portieres*): It isn't dark enough yet.

LAURA *turns slowly before the mirror with a troubled look.*

Legend on screen: "This is my sister: Celebrate her with strings!" Music plays.

AMANDA (*laughing, still not visible*): I'm going to show you something. I'm going to make a spectacular appearance!

LAURA: What is it, Mother?

AMANDA: Possess your soul in patience—you will see! Something I've resurrected from that old trunk! Styles haven't changed so terribly much after all…. (*She parts the portieres.*) Now just look at your mother! (*She wears a girlish frock of yellowed voile with a blue silk sash. She carries a bunch of jonquils—the legend of her youth is nearly revived. Now she speaks feverishly:*) This is the dress in which I led the cotillion. Won the cakewalk twice at Sunset Hill, wore one Spring to the Governor's Ball in Jackson! See how I sashayed around the ballroom, Laura? (*She raises her skirt and does a mincing step around the room.*) I wore it on Sundays for my gentlemen callers! I had it on the day I met your father…. I had malaria fever all that Spring. The change of climate from East Tennessee to the Delta—weakened resistance. I had a little temperature all the time—not enough to be serious—just enough to make me restless and giddy! Invitations poured in—parties all over the Delta! "Stay in bed," said Mother, "you have a fever!"—but I just wouldn't. I took quinine but kept on going, going! Evenings, dances! Afternoons, long, long rides! Picnics—lovely! So lovely, that country in May—all lacy with dogwood, literally flooded with jonquils! That was the spring I had the craze for jonquils. Jonquils became an absolute obsession. Mother said, "Honey, there's no more room for jonquils." And still I kept on bringing in more jonquils. Whenever, wherever I saw them, I'd say, "Stop! Stop! I see jonquils!" I made the young men help me gather the jonquils! It was a joke, Amanda and her jonquils. Finally there were no more vases to hold them, every available space was filled with jonquils. No vases to hold them? All right, I'll hold them myself! And then I—(*She stops in front of the picture. Music plays.*) met your father! Malaria fever and jonquils and then—this—boy…. (*She switches on the rose-colored lamp.*) I hope they get here before it starts to rain. (*She crosses the room and places the jonquils in a bowl on the table.*) I gave your brother a little extra change so he and Mr. O'Connor could take the service car home.

LAURA (*with an altered look*): What did you say his name was?

AMANDA: O'Connor.

LAURA: What is his first name?

AMANDA: I don't remember. Oh, yes, I do. It was—Jim!

LAURA *sways slightly and catches hold of a chair.*

Legend on screen: "Not Jim!"

LAURA (*faintly*): Not—Jim!

AMANDA: Yes, that was it, it was Jim! I've never known a Jim that wasn't nice!

The music becomes ominous.

LAURA: Are you sure his name is Jim O'Connor?

AMANDA: Yes. Why?

LAURA: Is he the one that Tom used to know in high school?

AMANDA: He didn't say so. I think he just got to know him at the warehouse.

LAURA: There was a Jim O'Connor we both knew in high school—(*then, with effort*) If that is the one that Tom is bringing to dinner—you'll have to excuse me, I won't come to the table.

AMANDA: What sort of nonsense is this?

LAURA: You asked me once if I'd ever liked a boy. Don't you remember I showed you this boy's picture?

AMANDA: You mean the boy you showed me in the yearbook?

LAURA: Yes, that boy.

AMANDA: Laura, Laura, were you in love with that boy?

LAURA: I don't know, Mother. All I know is I couldn't sit at the table if it was him!

AMANDA: It won't be him! It isn't the least bit likely. But whether it is or not, you will come to the table. You will not be excused.

LAURA: I'll have to be, Mother.

AMANDA: I don't intend to humor your silliness, Laura. I've had too much from you and your brother, both! So just sit down and compose yourself till they come. Tom has forgotten his key so you'll have to let them in, when they arrive.

LAURA (*panicky*): Oh, Mother—*you* answer the door!

AMANDA (*lightly*): I'll be in the kitchen—busy!

LAURA: Oh, Mother, please answer the door, don't make me do it!

AMANDA (*crossing into the kitchenette*): I've got to fix the dressing for the salmon. Fuss, fuss— silliness!–over a gentleman caller!

The door swings shut. LAURA *is left alone.*
Legend on screen: "Terror!"
She utters a low moan and turns off the lamp— sits stiffly on the edge of the sofa, knotting her fingers together.
Legend on screen: "The Opening of a Door!"
TOM *and* JIM *appear on the fire escape steps and climb to the landing. Hearing their approach,* LAURA *rises with a panicky gesture. She retreats to the portieres. The doorbell rings.* LAURA *catches her breath and touches her throat. Low drums sound.*

AMANDA (*calling*): Laura, sweetheart! The door!
LAURA *stares at it without moving.*

JIM: I think we just beat the rain.

TOM: Uh-huh. (*He rings again, nervously. Jim whistles and fishes for a cigarette.*)

AMANDA (*very, very gaily*): Laura, that is your brother and Mr. O'Connor! Will you let them in, darling?
LAURA *crosses toward the kitchenette door.*

LAURA (*breathlessly*): Mother—you go to the door!
AMANDA *steps out of the kitchenette and stares furiously at* LAURA. *She points imperiously at the door.*

LAURA: Please, please!

AMANDA (*in a fierce whisper*): What is the matter with you, you silly thing?

LAURA (*desperately*): Please, you answer it, *please!*

AMANDA: I told you I wasn't going to humor you, Laura. Why have you chosen this moment to lose your mind?

LAURA: Please, please, please, you go!

AMANDA: You'll have to go to the door because I can't!

LAURA (*despairingly*): I can't either!

AMANDA: *Why?*

LAURA: I'm *sick!*

AMANDA: I'm sick, too—of your nonsense! Why can't you and your brother be normal people? Fantastic whims and behavior!
TOM *gives a long ring.*
Preposterous goings on! Can you give me one reason—(*She calls out lyrically.*) *Coming! just one second!*—why you should be afraid to open a door? Now you answer it, Laura!

LAURA: Oh, oh, oh…. (*She returns through the portieres, darts to the Victrola, winds it frantically and turns it on.*)

AMANDA: Laura Wingfield, you march right to that door!

LAURA: Yes—yes, Mother!
A faraway, scratchy rendition of "Dardanella" softens the air and gives her strength to move through it. She slips to the door and draws it cautiously open. TOM *enters with the caller,* JIM O'CONNOR.

TOM: Laura, this is Jim. Jim, this is my sister, Laura.

JIM (*stepping inside*): I didn't know that Shakespeare had a sister!

LAURA (*retreating, stiff and trembling, from the door*): How—how do you do?

JIM (*heartily, extending his hand*): Okay!
LAURA *touches it hesitantly with hers.*

JIM: Your hand's *cold*, Laura!

LAURA: Yes, well—I've been playing the Victrola….

JIM: Must have been playing classical music on it! You ought to play a little hot swing music to warm you up!

LAURA: Excuse me—I haven't finished playing the Victrola…. (*She turns awkwardly and hurries into the front room. She pauses a second by the Victrola. Then she catches her breath and darts through the portieres like a frightened deer.*)

JIM (*grinning*): What was the matter?

TOM: Oh—with Laura? Laura is—terribly shy.

JIM: Shy, huh? It's unusual to meet a shy girl nowadays. I don't believe you ever mentioned you had a sister.

TOM: Well, now you know. I have one. Here is the *Post Dispatch.* You want a piece of it?

JIM: Uh-huh.

TOM: What piece? The comics?

JIM: Sports! (*He glances at it.*) Ole Dizzy Dean is on his bad behavior.

TOM (*uninterested*): Yeah? (*He lights a cigarette and goes over to the fire-escape door.*)

JIM: Where are *you* going?

TOM: I'm going out on the terrace.

JIM (*going after him*): You know, Shakespeare—I'm going to sell you a bill of goods!

TOM: What goods?

JIM: A course I'm taking.

TOM: Huh?

JIM: In public speaking! You and me, we're not the warehouse type.

TOM: Thanks—that's good news. But what has public speaking got to do with it?

JIM: It fits you for—executive positions!

TOM: Awww.

JIM: I tell you it's done a helluva lot for me.
Image on screen: Executive at his desk.

TOM: In what respect?

JIM: In every! Ask yourself what is the difference between you an' me and men in the office down front? Brains?—No!—Ability?—No! Then what? Just one little thing—

TOM: What is that one little thing?

JIM: Primarily it amounts to—social poise! Being able to square up to people and hold your own on any social level!

AMANDA (*from the kitchenette*): Tom?

TOM: Yes, Mother?

AMANDA: Is that you and Mr. O'Connor?

TOM: Yes, Mother.

AMANDA: Well, you just make yourselves comfortable in there.

TOM: Yes, Mother.

AMANDA: Ask Mr. O'Connor if he would like to wash his hands.

JIM: Aw, no—no—thank you—I took care of that at the warehouse. Tom—

TOM: Yes?

JIM: Mr. Mendoza was speaking to me about you.

TOM: Favorably?

JIM: What do you think?

TOM: Well—

JIM: You're going to be out of a job if you don't wake up.

TOM: I am waking up—

JIM: You show no signs.

TOM: The signs are interior.
Image on screen: The sailing vessel with the Jolly Roger again.

TOM: I'm planning to change. (*He leans over the fire-escape rail, speaking with quiet exhilaration. The incandescent marquees and signs of the first-run movie houses light his face from across the alley. He looks like a voyager.*) I'm right at the point of committing myself to a future that doesn't include the warehouse and Mr. Mendoza or even a night-school course in public speaking.

JIM: What are you gassing about?

TOM: I'm tired of the movies.

JIM: Movies!

TOM: Yes, movies! Look at them—(*a wave toward the marvels of Grand Avenue*) All of those glamorous people—having adventures—hogging it all, gobbling the whole thing up! You know what happens? People go to the *movies* instead of *moving!* Hollywood characters are supposed to have all the adventures for everybody in America, while everybody in America sits in a dark room and watches them have them! Yes, until there's a war. That's when adventure becomes available to the masses! *Everyone's* dish, not only Gable's! Then the people in the dark room come out of the dark room to have some adventures themselves—goody, goody! It's our turn now, to go to the South Sea Island—to make a safari—to be exotic, far-off! But I'm not patient. I don't want to wait till then. I'm tired of the movies and I am *about* to *move!*

JIM (*incredulously*): Move?

TOM: Yes.

JIM: When?

TOM: Soon!

JIM: Where? Where?
The music seems to answer the question, while TOM *thinks it over. He searches in his pockets.*

TOM: I'm starting to boil inside. I know I seem dreamy, but inside—well, I'm boiling!

Whenever I pick up a shoe, I shudder a little thinking how short life is and what I am doing! Whatever that means, I know it doesn't mean shoes—except as something to wear on a traveler's feet! (*He finds what he has been searching for in his pockets and holds out a paper to Jim.*) Look—

JIM: What?

TOM: I'm a member.

JIM (*reading*): The Union of Merchant Seamen.

TOM: I paid my dues this month, instead of the light bill.

JIM: You will regret it when they turn the lights off.

TOM: I won't be here.

JIM: How about your mother?

TOM: I'm like my father. The bastard son of a bastard! Did you notice how he's grinning in his picture in there? And he's been absent going on sixteen years!

JIM: You're just talking, you drip. How does your mother feel about it?

TOM: Shhh! Here comes Mother! Mother is not acquainted with my plans!

AMANDA (*coming through the portieres*): Where are you all?

TOM: On the terrace, Mother.

They start inside. She advances to them. TOM *is distinctly shocked at her appearance. Even* JIM *blinks a little. He is making his first contact with girlish Southern vivacity and in spite of the night-school course in public speaking is somewhat thrown off the beam by the unexpected outlay of social charm. Certain responses are attempted by* JIM *but are swept aside by* AMANDA'S *gay laughter and chatter.* TOM *is embarrassed but after the first shock* JIM *reacts very warmly. He grins and chuckles, is altogether won over.*

Image on screen: Amanda as a girl.

AMANDA (*coyly smiling, shaking her girlish ringlets*): Well, well, well, so this is Mr. O'Connor. Introductions entirely unnecessary. I've heard so much about you from my boy. I finally said to him, Tom—good gracious!—why don't you bring this paragon to supper? I'd like to meet this nice young man at the warehouse!—instead of just hearing him sing your praises so much! I don't know why my son is so stand-offish—that's not Southern behavior!

Let's sit down and—I think we could stand a little more air in here! Tom, leave the door open. I felt a nice fresh breeze a moment ago. Where has it gone to? Mmm, so warm already! And not quite summer, even. We're going to burn up when summer really gets started. However, we're having—we're having a very light supper. I think light things are better fo' this time of year. The same as light clothes are. Light clothes an' light food are what warm weather calls fo'. You know our blood gets so thick during th' winter—it takes a while fo' us to *adjust* ou'selves!—when the season changes.... It's come so quick this year. I wasn't prepared. All of a sudden—heavens! Already summer! I ran to the trunk an' pulled out this light dress—terribly old! Historical almost! But feels so good—so good an' co-ol, y' know....

TOM: Mother—

AMANDA: Yes, honey?

TOM: How about—supper?

AMANDA: Honey, you go ask Sister if supper is ready! You know that Sister is in full charge of supper! Tell her you hungry boys are waiting for it. (*to* JIM) Have you met Laura?

JIM: She—

AMANDA: Let you in? Oh, good, you've met already! It's rare for a girl as sweet an' pretty as Laura to be domestic! But Laura is, thank heavens, not only pretty but also very domestic. I'm not at all. I never was a bit. I never could make a thing but angel-food cake. Well, in the South we had so many servants. Gone, gone, gone. All vestige of gracious living! Gone completely! I wasn't prepared for what the future brought me. All of my gentlemen callers were sons of planters and so of course I assumed that I would be married to one and raise my family on a large piece of land with plenty of servants. But man proposes—and woman accepts the proposal! To vary that old, old saying a little bit—I married no planter! I married a man who worked for the telephone company! That gallantly smiling gentleman over there! (*She points to the picture.*) A telephone man who—fell in love with long-distance! Now he travels and I don't even know where! But what am I going on for about my—tribulations? Tell me yours—I hope you don't have any! Tom?

TOM (*returning*): Yes, Mother?

AMANDA: Is supper nearly ready?

TOM: It looks to me like supper is on the table.

AMANDA: Let me look—(*She rises prettily and looks through the portieres.*) Oh, lovely! But where is Sister?

TOM: Laura is not feeling well and she says that she thinks she'd better not come to the table.

AMANDA: What? Nonsense! Laura? Oh, Laura!

LAURA (*from the kitchenette, faintly*): Yes, Mother.

AMANDA: You really must come to the table. We won't be seated until you come to the table! Come in, Mr. O'Connor. You sit over there, and I'll…. Laura? Laura Wingfield! You're keeping us waiting, honey! We can't say grace until you come to the table!

The kitchenette door is pushed weakly open and LAURA *comes in. She is obviously quite faint, her lips trembling, her eyes wide and staring. She moves unsteadily toward the table.*

Screen legend: "Terror!"

Outside a summer storm is coming on abruptly. The white curtains billow inward at the windows and there is a sorrowful murmur from the deep blue dusk.

LAURA *suddenly stumbles; she catches at a chair with a faint moan.*

TOM: Laura!

AMANDA: Laura!

There is a clap of thunder.

Screen legend: "Ah!"

(*despairingly*) Why, Laura, you *are* ill, darling! Tom, help your sister into the living room, dear! Sit in the living room, Laura—rest on the sofa. Well! (*to* JIM *as* TOM *helps his sister to the sofa in the living room*) Standing over the hot stove made her ill! I told her that it was just too warm this evening, but—

TOM *comes back to the table.*

Is Laura all right now?

TOM: Yes.

AMANDA: What *is* that? Rain? A nice cool rain has come up! (*She gives* JIM *a frightened look.*) I think we may—have grace—now…

(TOM *looks at her stupidly.*) Tom, honey—you say grace!

TOM: Oh… "For these and all thy mercies—"

They bow their heads, AMANDA *stealing a nervous glance at* JIM. *In the living room* LAURA, *stretched on the sofa, clenches her hand to her lips, to hold back a shuddering sob.*

God's Holy Name be praised—

The scene dims out.

SCENE SEVEN

It is half an hour later. Dinner is just being finished in the dining room. LAURA *is still huddled upon the sofa, her feet drawn under her, her head resting on a pale blue pillow, her eyes wide and mysteriously watchful. The new floor lamp with its shade of rose-colored silk gives a soft, becoming light to her face, bringing out the fragile, unearthly prettiness which usually escapes attention. From outside there is a steady murmur of rain, but it is slackening and soon stops; the air outside becomes pale and luminous as the moon breaks through the clouds. A moment after the curtain rises, the lights in both rooms flicker and go out.*

JIM: Hey, there, Mr. Light Bulb!

AMANDA *laughs nervously.*

Legend on screen: "Suspension of a public service."

AMANDA: Where was Moses when the lights went out? Ha-ha. Do you know the answer to that one, Mr. O'Connor?

JIM: No, Ma'am, what's the answer?

AMANDA: In the dark!

JIM *laughs appreciatively.*

Everybody sit still. I'll light the candles. Isn't it lucky we have them on the table? Where's a match? Which of you gentlemen can provide a match?

JIM: Here.

AMANDA: Thank you, Sir.

JIM: Not at all, Ma'am!

AMANDA (*as she lights the candles*): I guess the fuse has burnt out. Mr. O'Connor, can you tell a burnt-out fuse? I know I can't and Tom is a total loss when it comes to mechanics. *They rise from the table and go into the kitchenette, from where their voices are heard.* Oh, be careful you don't bump into something. We don't want our gentleman caller to break his neck. Now wouldn't that be a fine howdy-do?

JIM: Ha-ha! Where is the fuse-box?

AMANDA: Right here next to the stove. Can you see anything?

JIM: Just a minute.

AMANDA: Isn't electricity a mysterious thing? Wasn't it Benjamin Franklin who tied a key to a kite? We live in such a mysterious universe, don't we? Some people say that science clears up all the mysteries for us. In my opinion it only creates more! Have you found it yet?

JIM: No, Ma'am. All these fuses look okay to me.

AMANDA: Tom!

TOM: Yes, Mother?

AMANDA: That light bill I gave you several days ago. The one I told you we got the notices about?

Legend on screen: "Ha!"

TOM: Oh—yeah.

AMANDA: You didn't neglect to pay it by any chance?

TOM: Why, I—

AMANDA: Didn't! I might have known it!

JIM: Shakespeare probably wrote a poem on that light bill, Mrs. Wingfield.

AMANDA: I might have known better than to trust him with it! There's such a high price for negligence in this world!

JIM: Maybe the poem will win a ten-dollar prize.

AMANDA: We'll just have to spend the remainder of the evening in the nineteenth century, before Mr. Edison made the Mazda lamp!

JIM: Candlelight is my favorite kind of light.

AMANDA: That shows you're romantic! But that's no excuse for Tom. Well, we got through dinner. Very considerate of them to let us get through dinner before they plunged us into everlasting darkness, wasn't it, Mr. O'Connor?

JIM: Ha-ha!

AMANDA: Tom, as a penalty for your carelessness you can help me with the dishes.

JIM: Let me give you a hand.

AMANDA: Indeed you will not!

JIM: I ought to be good for something.

AMANDA: Good for something? (*Her tone is rhapsodic.*) You? Why, Mr. O'Connor, nobody, *nobody's* given me this much entertainment in years—as you have!

JIM: Aw, now, Mrs. Wingfield!

AMANDA: I'm not exaggerating, not one bit! But Sister is all by her lonesome. You go keep her company in the parlor! I'll give you this lovely old candelabrum that used to be on the altar at the Church of the Heavenly Rest. It was melted a little out of shape when the church burnt down. Lightning struck it one spring. Gypsy Jones was holding a revival at the time and he intimated that the church was destroyed because the Episcopalians gave card parties.

JIM: Ha-ha.

AMANDA: And how about you coaxing Sister to drink a little wine? I think it would be good for her! Can you carry both at once?

JIM: Sure. I'm Superman!

AMANDA: Now, Thomas, get into this apron!

JIM comes into the dining room, carrying the candelabrum, its candles lighted, in one hand and a glass of wine in the other. The door of the kitchenette swings closed on AMANDA'S gay laughter; the flickering light approaches the portieres. LAURA sits up nervously as JIM enters. She can hardly speak from the almost intolerable strain of being alone with a stranger.

Screen legend: "I don't suppose you remember me at all!"

At first, before JIM'S warmth overcomes her paralyzing shyness, LAURA'S voice is thin and breathless, as though she had just run up a steep flight of stairs. JIM'S attitude is gently humorous. While the incident is apparently unimportant, it is to LAURA the climax of her secret life.

JIM: Hello there, Laura.

LAURA (*faintly*): Hello.

She clears her throat.

JIM: How are you feeling now? Better?

LAURA: Yes. Yes, thank you.

JIM: This is for you. A little dandelion wine.
(*He extends the glass toward her with extravagant gallantry.*)

LAURA: Thank you.

JIM: Drink it—but don't get drunk!
He laughs heartily. LAURA *takes the glass uncertainly; she laughs shyly.*
Where shall I set the candles?

LAURA: Oh—oh, anywhere…

JIM: How about here on the floor? Any objections?

LAURA: No.

JIM: I'll spread a newspaper under to catch the drippings. I like to sit on the floor. Mind if I do?

LAURA: Oh, no.

JIM: Give me a pillow!

LAURA: What?

JIM: A pillow?

LAURA: Oh… (*She hands him one quickly.*)

JIM: How about you? Don't you like to sit on the floor?

LAURA: Oh—yes.

JIM: Why don't you, then?

LAURA: I—will.

JIM: Take a pillow!
LAURA *does. She sits on the floor on the other side of the candelabrum.* JIM *crosses his legs and smiles engagingly at her.* I can't hardly see you sitting way over there.

LAURA: I can—see you.

JIM: I know, but that's not fair, I'm in the limelight.
LAURA *moves her pillow closer.*
Good! Now I can see you! Comfortable?

LAURA: Yes.

JIM: So am I. Comfortable as a cow! Will you have some gum?

LAURA: No, thank you.

JIM: I think that I will indulge, with your permission. (*He musingly unwraps a stick of gum and holds it up.*) Think of the fortune made by the guy that invented the first piece of chewing gum. Amazing, huh? The Wrigley Building is one of the sights of Chicago—I saw it when I went up to the Century of Progress. Did you take in the Century of Progress?

LAURA: No, I didn't.

JIM: Well, it was quite a wonderful exposition. What impressed me most was the Hall of Science. Gives you an idea of what the future will be in America, even more wonderful than the present time is! (*There is a pause.* JIM *smiles at her.*) Your brother tells me you're shy. Is that right, Laura?

LAURA: I—don't know.

JIM: I judge you to be an old-fashioned type of girl. Well, I think that's a pretty good type to be. Hope you don't think I'm being too personal—do you?

LAURA (*hastily, out of embarrassment*): I believe I will take a piece of gum, if you—don't mind. (*Clearing her throat*) Mr. O'Connor, have you—kept up with your singing?

JIM: Singing? Me?

LAURA: Yes. I remember what a beautiful voice you had.

JIM: When did you hear me sing?
LAURA *does not answer, and in the long pause which follows a man's voice is heard singing offstage.*

VOICE:
O blow, ye winds, heigh-ho,
A-roving I will go!
I'm off to my love
With a boxing glove—
Ten thousand miles away!

JIM: You say you've heard me sing?

LAURA: Oh, yes! Yes, very often… I—don't suppose—you remember me—at all?

JIM (*smiling doubtfully*): You know I have an idea I've seen you before. I had that idea soon as you opened the door. It seemed almost like I was about to remember your name. But the name that I started to call you—wasn't a name! And so I stopped myself before I said it.

LAURA: Wasn't it—Blue Roses?

JIM (*springing up, grinning*): Blue Roses! My gosh, yes—Blue Roses! That's what I had on my tongue when you opened the door! Isn't it funny what tricks your memory plays? I didn't connect you with high school somehow or other. But that's where it was; it was high school. I didn't even know you were Shakespeare's sister! Gosh, I'm sorry.

LAURA: I didn't expect you to. You—barely knew me!

JIM: But we did have a speaking acquaintance, huh?

LAURA: Yes, we—spoke to each other.

JIM: When did you recognize me?

LAURA: Oh, right away!

JIM: Soon as I came in the door?

LAURA: When I heard your name I thought it was probably you. I knew that Tom used to know you a little in high school. So when you came in the door—well, then I was—sure.

JIM: Why didn't you *say* something, then?

LAURA (*breathlessly*): I didn't know what to say, I was—too surprised!

JIM: For goodness' sakes! You know, this sure is funny!

LAURA: Yes! Yes, isn't it, though…

JIM: Didn't we have a class in something together?

LAURA: Yes, we did.

JIM: What class was that?

LAURA: It was—singing—chorus!

JIM: Aw!

LAURA: I sat across the aisle from you in the Aud.

JIM: Aw.

LAURA: Mondays, Wednesdays, and Fridays.

JIM: Now I remember—you always came in late.

LAURA: Yes, it was so hard for me, getting upstairs. I had that brace on my leg—it clumped so loud!

JIM: I never heard any clumping.

LAURA (*wincing at the recollection*): To me it sounded like—thunder!

JIM: Well, well, well, I never even noticed.

LAURA: And everybody was seated before I came in. I had to walk in front of all those people. My seat was in the back row. I had to go clumping all the way up the aisle with everyone watching!

JIM: You shouldn't have been self-conscious.

LAURA: I know, but I was. It was always such a relief when the singing started.

JIM: Aw, yes, I've placed you now! I used to call you Blue Roses. How is it that I got started calling you that?

LAURA: I was out of school a little while with pleurosis. When I came back you asked me what was the matter. I said I had pleuro-sis—you thought I said *Blue Roses*. That's what you always called me after that!

JIM: I hope you didn't mind.

LAURA: Oh, no—I liked it. You see, I wasn't acquainted with many—people....

JIM: As I remember you sort of stuck by yourself.

LAURA: I—I—never have much luck at—making friends.

JIM: I don't see why you wouldn't.

LAURA: Well, I—started out badly.

JIM: You mean being—

LAURA: Yes, it sort of—stood between me—

JIM: You shouldn't have let it!

LAURA: I know, but it did, and—

JIM: You were shy with people!

LAURA: I tried not to be but never could—

JIM: Overcome it?

LAURA: No, I—I never could!

JIM: I guess being shy is something you have to work out of kind of gradually.

LAURA (*sorrowfully*): Yes—I guess it—

JIM: Takes time!

LAURA: Yes—

JIM: People are not so dreadful when you know them. That's what you have to remember! And everybody has problems, not just you, but practically everybody has got some problems. You think of yourself as having the only problems, as being the only one who is disappointed. But just look around you and you will see lots of people as disappointed as you are. For instance, I hoped when I was going to high school that I would be further along at this time, six years later, than I am now. You remember that wonderful write-up I had in *The Torch*?

LAURA: Yes! (*She rises and crosses to the table.*)

JIM: It said I was bound to succeed in anything I went into!

LAURA *returns with the high school yearbook.*
Holy Jeez! *The Torch!*
He accepts it reverently. They smile across the book with mutual wonder. LAURA *crouches beside him and they begin to turn the pages.* LAURA'S *shyness is dissolving in his warmth.*

LAURA: Here you are in *The Pirates of Penzance!*

JIM (*wistfully*): I sang the baritone lead in that operetta.

LAURA (*raptly*): So—*beautifully!*

JIM (*protesting*): Aw—

LAURA: Yes, yes—beautifully—beautifully!

JIM: You heard me?

LAURA: All three times!

JIM: No!

LAURA: Yes!

JIM: All three performances?

LAURA (*looking down*): Yes.

JIM: Why?

LAURA: I—wanted to ask you to—autograph my program.
She takes the program from the back of the year-book and shows it to him.

JIM: Why didn't you ask me to?

LAURA: You were always surrounded by your own friends so much that I never had a chance to.

JIM: You should have just—

LAURA: Well, I—thought you might think I was—

JIM: Thought I might think you was—what?

LAURA: Oh—

JIM (*with a reflective relish*): I was beleaguered by females in those days.

LAURA: You were terribly popular!

JIM: Yeah—

LAURA: You had such a—friendly way—

JIM: I was spoiled in high school.

LAURA: Everybody—liked you!

JIM: Including you?

LAURA: I—yes, I—did, too—(*She gently closes the book in her lap.*)

JIM: Well, well, well! Give me that program, Laura.
She hands it to him. He signs it with a flourish.
There you are— better late than never!

LAURA: Oh, I—what a—surprise!

JIM: My signature isn't worth very much right now. But some day—maybe—it will increase in value! Being disappointed is one thing and being discouraged is something else. I am disappointed but I am not discouraged. I'm twenty-three years old. How old are you?

LAURA: I'll be twenty-four in June.

JIM: That's not old age!

LAURA: No, but—

JIM: You finished high school?

LAURA (*with difficulty*): I didn't go back.

JIM: You mean you dropped out?

LAURA: I made bad grades in my final examinations. (*She rises and replaces the book and the program on the table. Her voice is strained.*) How is—Emily Meisenbach getting along?

JIM: Oh, that kraut-head!

LAURA: Why do you call her that?

JIM: That's what she was.

LAURA: You're not still—going with her?

JIM: I never see her.

LAURA: It said in the "Personal" section that you were—engaged!

JIM: I know, but I wasn't impressed by that—propaganda!

LAURA: It wasn't—the truth?

JIM: Only in Emily's optimistic opinion!

LAURA: Oh—
Legend: "What have you done since high school?"
JIM *lights a cigarette and leans indolently back on his elbows smiling at* LAURA *with a warmth and charm which lights her inwardly with altar candles. She remains by the table, picks up a piece from the glass menagerie collection, and turns it in her hands to cover her tumult.*

JIM (*after several reflective puffs on his cigarette*): What have you done since high school?
She seems not to hear him.
Huh?
LAURA *looks up.*
I said what have you done since high school, Laura?

LAURA: Nothing much.

JIM: You must have been doing something these six long years.

LAURA: Yes.

JIM: Well, then, such as what?

LAURA: I took a business course at business college—

JIM: How did that work out?

LAURA: Well, not very—well—I had to drop out, it gave me—indigestion—
JIM *laughs gently.*

JIM: What are you doing now?

LAURA: I don't do anything—much. Oh, please don't think I sit around doing nothing! My glass collection takes up a good deal of time.

Glass is something you have to take good care of.

JIM: What did you say—about glass?

LAURA: Collection I said—I have one—(*She clears her throat and turns away again, acutely shy.*)

JIM (*abruptly*): You know what I judge to be the trouble with you? Inferiority complex! Know what that is? That's what they call it when someone low-rates himself! I understand it because I had it, too. Although my case was not so aggravated as yours seems to be. I had it until I took up public speaking, developed my voice, and learned that I had an aptitude for science. Before that time I never thought of myself as being outstanding in any way whatsoever! Now I've never made a regular study of it, but I have a friend who says I can analyze people better than doctors that make a profession of it. I don't claim that to be necessarily true, but I can sure guess a person's psychology, Laura! (*He takes out his gum.*) Excuse me, Laura. I always take it out when the flavor is gone. I'll use this scrap of paper to wrap it in. I know how it is to get it stuck on a shoe. (*He wraps the gum in paper and puts it in his pocket.*) Yep—that's what I judge to be your principal trouble. A lack of confidence in yourself as a person. You don't have the proper amount of faith in yourself. I'm basing that fact on a number of your remarks and also on certain observations I've made. For instance that clumping you thought was so awful in high school. You say that you even dreaded to walk into class. You see what you did? You dropped out of school, you gave up an education because of a clump, which as far as I know was practically non-existent! A little physical defect is what you have. Hardly noticeable even! Magnified thousands of times by imagination! You know what my strong advice to you is? Think of yourself as *superior* in some way!

LAURA: In what way would I think?

JIM: Why, man alive, Laura! Just look about you a little. What do you see? A world full of common people! All of 'em born and all of 'em going to die! Which of them has one-tenth of your good points! Or mine! Or anyone else's, as far as that goes—gosh! Everybody excels in some one thing. Some in many! (*He unconsciously glances at himself in the mirror.*) All you've got to do is discover in *what!* Take me, for instance. (*He adjusts his tie at the mirror.*) My interest happens to lie in electro-dynamics. I'm taking a course in radio engineering at night school, Laura, on top of a fairly responsible job at the warehouse. I'm taking that course and studying public speaking.

LAURA: Ohhhh.

JIM: Because I believe in the future of television! (*Turning his back to her.*) I wish to be ready to go up right along with it. Therefore I'm planning to get in on the ground floor. In fact I've already made the right connections and all that remains is for the industry itself to get under way! Full steam—(*His eyes are starry.*) Knowledge—Zzzzzp! Money—Zzzzzzp!— Power! That's the cycle democracy is built on!

His attitude is convincingly dynamic. LAURA *stares at him, even her shyness eclipsed in her absolute wonder. He suddenly grins.*

I guess you think I think a lot of myself!

LAURA: No—o-o-o, I—

JIM: Now how about you? Isn't there something you take more interest in than anything else?

LAURA: Well, I do—as I said—have my—glass collection—

A peal of girlish laughter rings from the kitchenette.

JIM: I'm not right sure I know what you're talking about. What kind of glass is it?

LAURA: Little articles of it, they're ornaments mostly! Most of them are little animals made out of glass, the tiniest little animals in the world. Mother calls them a glass menagerie! Here's an example of one, if you'd like to see it! This one is one of the oldest. It's nearly thirteen.

Music: "The Glass Menagerie."

He stretches out his hand.

Oh, be careful—if you breathe, it breaks!

JIM: I'd better not take it. I'm pretty clumsy with things.

LAURA: Go on, I trust you with him! (*She places the piece in his palm.*) There now—you're holding him gently! Hold him over the light, he loves the light! You see how the light shines through him?

JIM: It sure does shine!

LAURA: I shouldn't be partial, but he is my favorite one.

JIM: What kind of a thing is this one supposed to be?

LAURA: Haven't you noticed the single horn on his forehead?

JIM: A unicorn, huh?

LAURA: Mmmm-hmmm!

JIM: Unicorns—aren't they extinct in the modern world?

LAURA: I know!

JIM: Poor little fellow, he must feel sort of lonesome.

LAURA (*smiling*): Well, if he does, he doesn't complain about it. He stays on a shelf with some horses that don't have horns and all of them seem to get along nicely together.

JIM: How do you know?

LAURA (*lightly*): I haven't heard any arguments among them!

JIM (*grinning*): No arguments, huh? Well, that's a pretty good sign! Where shall I set him?

LAURA: Put him on the table. They all like a change of scenery once in a while!

JIM: Well, well, well, well—(*He places the glass piece on the table, then raises his arms and stretches.*) Look how big my shadow is when I stretch!

LAURA: Oh, oh, yes—it stretches across the ceiling!

JIM (*crossing to the door*): I think it's stopped raining. (*He opens the fire-escape door and the background music changes to a dance tune.*) Where does the music come from?

LAURA: From the Paradise Dance Hall across the alley.

JIM: How about cutting the rug a little, Miss Wingfield?

LAURA: Oh, I—

JIM: Or is your program filled up? Let me have a look at it. (*He grasps an imaginary card.*) Why, every dance is taken! I'll just have to scratch some out.

Waltz music: "La Golondrina."
Ahhh, a waltz! (*He executes some sweeping turns by himself, then holds his arms toward* LAURA.)

LAURA (*breathlessly*): I—can't dance!

JIM: There you go, that inferiority stuff!

LAURA: I've never danced in my life!

JIM: Come on, try!

LAURA: Oh, but I'd step on you!

JIM: I'm not made out of glass.

LAURA: How—how—how do we start?

JIM: Just leave it to me. You hold your arms out a little.

LAURA: Like this?

JIM (*taking her in his arms*): A little bit higher. Right. Now don't tighten up, that's the main thing about it—relax.

LAURA (*laughing breathlessly*): It's hard not to.

JIM: Okay.

LAURA: I'm afraid you can't budge me.

JIM: What do you bet I can't? (*He swings her into motion.*)

LAURA: Goodness, yes, you can!

JIM: Let yourself go, now, Laura, just let yourself go.

LAURA: I'm—

JIM: Come on!

LAURA: —trying!

JIM: Not so stiff—easy does it!

LAURA: I know but I'm—

JIM: Loosen th' backbone! There now, that's a lot better.

LAURA: Am I?

JIM: Lots, lots better! (*He moves her about the room in a clumsy waltz.*)

LAURA: Oh, my!

JIM: Ha-ha!

LAURA: Oh, my goodness!

JIM: Ha-ha-ha!
They suddenly bump into the table, and the glass piece on it falls to the floor. JIM *stops the dance.* What did we hit on?

LAURA: Table.

JIM: Did something fall off it? I think—

LAURA: Yes.

JIM: I hope that it wasn't the little glass horse with the horn!

LAURA: Yes. (*She stoops to pick it up.*)

JIM: Aw, aw, aw. Is it broken?

LAURA: Now it is just like all the other horses.

JIM: It's lost its—

LAURA: Horn! It doesn't matter. Maybe it's a blessing in disguise.

JIM: You'll never forgive me. I bet that that was your favorite piece of glass.

LAURA: I don't have favorites much. It's no tragedy, Freckles. Glass breaks so easily. No matter how careful you are. The traffic jars the shelves and things fall off them.

JIM: Still I'm awfully sorry that I was the cause.

LAURA (*smiling*): I'll just imagine he had an operation. The horn was removed to make him feel less—freakish!

They both laugh.

Now he will feel more at home with the other horses, the ones that don't have horns....

JIM: Ha-ha, that's very funny! (*Suddenly he is serious.*) I'm glad to see that you have a sense of humor. You know—you're—well—very different! Surprisingly different from anyone else I know! (*His voice becomes soft and hesitant with a genuine feeling.*) Do you mind me telling you that?

LAURA *is abashed beyond speech.*

I mean it in a nice way—

LAURA *nods shyly, looking away.*

You make me feel sort of—I don't know how to put it! I'm usually pretty good at expressing things, but—this is something that I don't know how to say!

LAURA *touches her throat and clears it—turns the broken unicorn in her hands. His voice becomes softer.*

Has anyone ever told you that you were pretty?

There is a pause, and the music rises slightly. LAURA looks up slowly, with wonder, and shakes her head.

Well, you are! In a very different way from anyone else. And all the nicer because of the difference, too.

His voice becomes low and husky. LAURA turns away, nearly faint with the novelty of her emotions.

I wish that you were my sister. I'd teach you to have some confidence in yourself. The different people are not like other people,
but being different is nothing to be ashamed of. Because other people are not such wonderful people. They're one hundred times one thousand. You're one times one! They walk all over the earth. You just stay here. They're common as weeds, but—you—well, you're—*Blue Roses!*

Image on screen: Blue Roses.

The music changes.

LAURA: But blue is wrong for—roses....

JIM: It's right for you! You're—pretty!

LAURA: In what respect am I pretty?

JIM: In all respects—believe me! Your eyes—your hair—are pretty! Your hands are pretty! (*He catches hold of her hand.*) You think I'm making this up because I'm invited to dinner and have to be nice. Oh, I could do that! I could put on an act for you, Laura, and say lots of things without being very sincere. But this time I am. I'm talking to you sincerely. I happened to notice you had this inferiority complex that keeps you from feeling comfortable with people. Somebody needs to build your confidence up and make you proud instead of shy and turning away and—blushing. Somebody—ought to—*kiss* you, Laura!

His hand slips slowly up her arm to her shoulder as the music swells tumultuously. He suddenly turns her about and kisses her on the lips. When he releases her, LAURA sinks on the sofa with a bright, dazed look. JIM backs away and fishes in his pocket for a cigarette.

Legend on screen: "A souvenir."

Stumblejohn!

He lights the cigarette, avoiding her look. There is a peal of girlish laughter from AMANDA in the kitchenette. LAURA slowly raises and opens her hand. It still contains the little broken glass animal. She looks at it with a tender, bewildered expression.

Stumblejohn! I shouldn't have done that—that was way off the beam. You don't smoke, do you?

She looks up, smiling, not hearing the question. He sits beside her rather gingerly. She looks at him speechlessly—waiting. He coughs decorously and moves a little farther aside as he con-

siders the situation and senses her feelings, dimly, with perturbation. He speaks gently.
Would you—care for a—mint?
She doesn't seem to hear him but her look grows brighter even.
Peppermint? Life Saver? My pocket's a regular drugstore—wherever I go.... (*He pops a mint in his mouth. Then he gulps and decides to make a clean breast of it. He speaks slowly and gingerly.*) Laura, you know, if I had a sister like you, I'd do the same thing as Tom. I'd bring out fellows and—introduce her to them. The right type of boys—of a type to—appreciate her. Only—well—he made a mistake about me. Maybe I've got no call to be saying this. That may not have been the idea in having me over. But what if it was? There's nothing wrong about that. The only trouble is that in my case—I'm not in a situation to—do the right thing. I can't take down your number and say I'll phone. I can't call up next week and—ask for a date. I thought I had better explain the situation in case you—misunderstood it and—I hurt your feelings....
There is a pause. Slowly, very slowly, LAURA'S look changes, her eyes returning slowly from his to the glass figure in her palm. AMANDA utters another gay laugh in the kitchenette.
LAURA (*faintly*): You—won't—call again?
JIM: No, Laura, I can't. (*He rises from the sofa.*) As I was just explaining, I've—got strings on me. Laura, I've—been going steady! I go out all the time with a girl named Betty. She's a home-girl like you, and Catholic, and Irish, and in a great many ways we—get along fine. I met her last summer on a moonlight boat trip up the river to Alton, on the *Majestic*. Well—right away from the start it was—love!
Legend: Love!
LAURA *sways slightly forward and grips the arm of the sofa. He fails to notice, now enrapt in his own comfortable being.*
Being in love has made a new man of me!
Leaning stiffly forward, clutching the arm of the sofa, LAURA struggles visibly with her storm. But JIM is oblivious; she is a long way off.

The power of love is really pretty tremendous! Love is something that—changes the whole world, Laura!
The storm abates a little and LAURA leans back. He notices her again.
It happened that Betty's aunt took sick, she got a wire and had to go to Centralia. So Tom—when he asked me to dinner—I naturally just accepted the invitation, not knowing that you—that he—that I—(*He stops awkwardly.*)
Huh—I'm a stumblejohn!
He flops back on the sofa. The holy candles on the altar of LAURA'S face have been snuffed out. There is a look of almost infinite desolation. JIM glances at her uneasily.
I wish that you would—say something.
She bites her lip which was trembling and then bravely smiles. She opens her hand again on the broken glass figure. Then she gently takes his hand and raises it level with her own. She carefully places the unicorn in the palm of his hand, then pushes his fingers closed upon it.
What are you—doing that for? You want me to have him? Laura?
She nods.
What for?
LAURA: A—souvenir....
She rises unsteadily and crouches beside the Victrola to wind it up.
Legend on screen: "Things have a way of turning out so badly!" Or image: "Gentleman caller waving goodbye—gaily."
At this moment AMANDA rushes brightly back into the living room. She bears a pitcher of fruit punch in an old-fashioned cut-glass pitcher, and a plate of macaroons. The plate has a gold border and poppies painted on it.
AMANDA: Well, well, well! Isn't the air delightful after the shower? I've made you children a little liquid refreshment.
(*She turns gaily to JIM.*) Jim, do you know that song about lemonade?

"Lemonade, lemonade
made in the shade and stirred with a spade—
Good enough for any old maid!"

JIM (*uneasily*): Ha-ha! No—I never heard it.

AMANDA: Why, Laura! You look so serious!

JIM: We were having a serious conversation.

AMANDA: Good! Now you're better acquainted!

JIM (*uncertainly*): Ha-ha! Yes.

AMANDA: You modern young people are much more serious-minded than my generation. I was so gay as a girl!

JIM: You haven't changed, Mrs. Wingfield.

AMANDA: Tonight I'm rejuvenated! The gaiety of the occasion, Mr. O'Connor! (*She tosses her head with a peal of laughter, spilling some lemonade.*) Oooo! I'm baptizing myself!

JIM: Here—let me—

AMANDA (*setting the pitcher down*): There now. I discovered we had some maraschino cherries. I dumped them in, juice and all!

JIM: You shouldn't have gone to that trouble, Mrs. Wingfield.

AMANDA: Trouble, trouble? Why, it was loads of fun! Didn't you hear me cutting up in the kitchen? I bet your ears were burning! I told Tom how outdone with him I was for keeping you to himself so long a time! He should have brought you over much, much sooner! Well, now that you've found your way, I want you to be a very frequent caller! Not just occasional but all the time. Oh, we're going to have a lot of gay times together! I see them coming! Mmm, just breathe that air! So fresh, and the moon's so pretty! I'll skip back out—I know where my place is when young folks are having a—serious conversation!

JIM: Oh, don't go out, Mrs. Wingfield. The fact of the matter is I've got to be going.

AMANDA: Going, now? You're joking! Why, it's only the shank of the evening, Mr. O'Connor!

JIM: Well, you know how it is.

AMANDA: You mean you're a young workingman and have to keep workingmen's hours. We'll let you off early tonight. But only on the condition that next time you stay later. What's the best night for you? Isn't Saturday night the best night for you workingmen?

JIM: I have a couple of time-clocks to punch, Mrs. Wingfield. One at morning, another one at night!

AMANDA: My, but you *are* ambitious! You work at night, too?

JIM: No, Ma'am, not work but—Betty!

He crosses deliberately to pick up his hat. The band at the Paradise Dance Hall goes into a tender waltz.

AMANDA: Betty? Betty? Who's—Betty!

There is an ominous cracking sound in the sky.

JIM: Oh, just a girl. The girl I go steady with!

He smiles charmingly. The sky falls.

Legend: "The Sky Falls."

AMANDA (*a long-drawn exhalation*): Ohhhh... Is it a serious romance, Mr. O'Connor?

JIM: We're going to be married the second Sunday in June.

AMANDA: Ohhhh—how nice! Tom didn't mention that you were engaged to be married.

JIM: The cat's not out of the bag at the warehouse yet. You know how they are. They call you Romeo and stuff like that. (*He stops at the oval mirror to put on his hat. He carefully shapes the brim and the crown to give a discreetly dashing effect.*) It's been a wonderful evening, Mrs. Wingfield. I guess this is what they mean by Southern hospitality.

AMANDA: It really wasn't anything at all.

JIM: I hope it don't seem like I'm rushing off. But I promised Betty I'd pick her up at the Wabash depot, an' by the time I get my jalopy down there her train'll be in. Some women are pretty upset if you keep 'em waiting.

AMANDA: Yes, I know—the tyranny of women! (*She extends her hand.*) Goodbye, Mr. O'Connor. I wish you luck—and happiness—and success! All three of them, and so does Laura! Don't you, Laura?

LAURA: Yes!

JIM (*taking LAURA's hand*): Goodbye, Laura. I'm certainly going to treasure that souvenir. And don't you forget the good advice I gave you. (*He raises his voice to a cheery shout.*) So long, Shakespeare! Thanks again, ladies. Good night!

He grins and ducks jauntily out. Still bravely grimacing, AMANDA closes the door on the gentleman caller. Then she turns back to the room with a puzzled expression. She and LAURA don't dare to face each other. LAURA *crouches beside the Victrola to wind it.*

AMANDA (*faintly*): Things have a way of turning out so badly. I don't believe that I would play the Victrola. Well, well—well! Our gentleman caller was engaged to be married! (*She raises her voice.*) Tom!

TOM (*from the kitchenette*): Yes, Mother?

AMANDA: Come in here a minute. I want to tell you something awfully funny.

TOM (*entering with a macaroon and a glass of the lemonade*): Has the gentleman caller gotten away already?

AMANDA: The gentleman caller has made an early departure. What a wonderful joke you played on us!

TOM: How do you mean?

AMANDA: You didn't mention that he was engaged to be married.

TOM: Jim? Engaged?

AMANDA: That's what he just informed us.

TOM: I'll be jiggered! I didn't know about that.

AMANDA: That seems very peculiar.

TOM: What's peculiar about it?

AMANDA: Didn't you call him your best friend down at the warehouse?

TOM: He is, but how did I know?

AMANDA: It seems extremely peculiar that you wouldn't know your best friend was going to be married!

TOM: The warehouse is where I work, not where I know things about people!

AMANDA: You don't know things anywhere! You live in a dream; you manufacture illusions!
He crosses to the door.
Where are you going?

TOM: I'm going to the movies.

AMANDA: That's right, now that you've had us make such fools of ourselves. The effort, the preparations, all the expense! The new floor lamp, the rug, the clothes for Laura! All for what? To entertain some other girl's fiancé! Go to the movies, go! Don't think about us, a mother deserted, an unmarried sister who's crippled and has no job! Don't let anything interfere with your selfish pleasure! Just go, go, go—to the movies!

TOM: All right, I will! The more you shout about my selfishness to me the quicker I'll go, and I won't go to the movies!

AMANDA: Go, then! Go to the moon—you selfish dreamer!
TOM *smashes his glass on the floor. He plunges out on the fire escape, slamming the door.* LAURA *screams in fright. The dance-hall music becomes louder.* TOM *stands on the fire escape, gripping the rail. The moon breaks through the storm clouds, illuminating his face.*
Legend on screen: "And so goodbye…."
TOM'S *closing speech is timed with what is happening inside the house. We see, as though through soundproof glass, that* AMANDA *appears to be making a comforting speech to* LAURA, *who is huddled upon the sofa. Now that we cannot hear the mother's speech, her silliness is gone and she has dignity and tragic beauty.* LAURA'S *hair hides her face until, at the end of the speech, she lifts her head to smile at her mother.* AMANDA'S *gestures are slow and graceful, almost dancelike, as she comforts her daughter. At the end of her speech she glances a moment at the father's picture—then withdraws through the portieres. At the close of* TOM'S *speech,* LAURA *blows out the candles, ending the play.*

TOM: I didn't go to the moon, I went much further—for time is the longest distance between two places. Not long after that I was fired for writing a poem on the lid of a shoebox. I left Saint Louis. I descended the steps of this fire escape for a last time and followed, from then on, in my father's footsteps, attempting to find in motion what was lost in space. I traveled around a great deal. The cities swept about me like dead leaves, leaves that were brightly colored but torn away from the branches. I would have stopped, but I was pursued by something. It always came upon me unawares, taking me altogether by surprise. Perhaps it was a familiar bit of music. Perhaps it was only a piece of transparent glass. Perhaps I am walking along a street at night, in some strange city, before I have found companions. I pass the lighted window of a shop where perfume is sold. The window is filled with pieces of colored glass, tiny transparent bottles in delicate colors, like bits of a shattered rainbow. Then all at once my sister touches my shoulder. I turn around and look into her eyes. Oh, Laura, Laura, I tried to leave you behind me, but I am more faithful than I intended to be! I reach for a cigarette, I cross the street, I run into the movies or a bar, I buy a drink, I speak to the nearest stranger—anything that can blow your candles out!

LAURA *bends over the candles.*

For nowadays the world is lit by lightning! Blow out your candles, Laura—and so goodbye....

She blows the candles out.

PRODUCTION NOTES (PLAYWRIGHT'S)

Being a "memory play," *The Glass Menagerie* can be presented with unusual freedom of convention. Because of its considerably delicate or tenuous material, atmospheric touches and subtleties of direction play a particularly important part. Expressionism and all other unconventional techniques in drama have only one valid aim, and that is a closer approach to truth. When a play employs unconventional techniques, it is not, or certainly shouldn't be, trying to escape its responsibility of dealing with reality, or interpreting experience, but is actually or should be attempting to find a closer approach, a more penetrating and vivid expression of things as they are. The straight realistic play with its genuine Frigidaire and authentic icecubes, its characters who speak exactly as its audience speaks, corresponds to the academic landscape and has the same virtue of a photographic likeness. Everyone should know nowadays the unimportance of the photographic in art: that truth, life, or reality is an organic thing which the poetic imagination can represent or suggest, in essence, only through transformation, through changing into other forms than those which were merely present in appearance.

These remarks are not meant as a preface only to this particular play. They have to do with a conception of a new, plastic theater which must take the place of the exhausted theater of realistic conventions if the theater is to resume vitality as a part of our culture.

THE SCREEN DEVICE: There is *only one important difference between the original and the acting version of the play* and that is the *omission* in the latter of the device that I tentatively included in my *original* script. This device was the use of a screen on which were projected magic-lantern slides bearing images or titles. I do not regret the omission of this device from the original Broadway production. The extraordinary power of Miss Taylor's* performance made it suitable to have the utmost simplicity in the physical production. But I think it may be interesting to some readers to see how this device was conceived. So I am putting it into the published manuscript. These images and legends, projected from behind, were cast on a section of wall between the front-room and dining-room areas, which should be indistinguishable from the rest when not in use.

The purpose of this will probably be apparent. It is to give accent to certain values in each scene. Each scene contains a particular point (or several) which is structurally the most important. In an episodic play, such as this, the basic structure or narrative line may be obscured from the audience; the effect may seem fragmentary rather than architectural. This may not be the fault of the play so much as a lack of attention in the audience. The legend or image upon the screen will strengthen the effect of what is merely allusion in the writing and allow the primary point to be made more simply and lightly than if the entire responsibility were on the spoken lines. Aside from this structural value, I think the screen will have a definite emotional appeal, less definable but just as important. An imaginative producer or director may invent many other uses for this device than those indicated in the present script. In fact the possibilities of the device seem much larger to me than the instance of this play can possibly utilize.

---

*Actress Laurette Taylor created the role of Amanda Wingfield.

THE MUSIC: Another extra-literary accent in this play is provided by the use of music. A single recurring tune, "The Glass Menagerie," is used to give emotional emphasis to suitable passages. This tune is like circus music, not when you are on the grounds or in the immediate vicinity of the parade, but when you are at some distance and very likely thinking of something else. It seems under those circumstances to continue almost interminably and it weaves in and out of your preoccupied consciousness; then it is the lightest, most delicate music in the world and perhaps the saddest. It expresses the surface vivacity of life with the underlying strain of immutable and inexpressible sorrow. When you look at a piece of delicately spun glass you think of two things: how beautiful it is and how easily it can be broken. Both of those ideas should be woven into the recurring tune, which dips in and out of the play as if it were carried on a wind that changes. It serves as a thread of connection and allusion between the narrator with his separate point in time and space and the subject of his story. Between each episode it returns as reference to the emotion, nostalgia, which is the first condition of the play. It is primarily Laura's music and therefore comes out most clearly when the play focuses upon her and the lovely fragility of glass which is her image.

THE LIGHTING: The lighting in the play is not realistic. In keeping with the atmosphere of memory, the stage is dim. Shafts of light are focused on selected areas or actors, sometimes in contradistinction to what is the apparent center. For instance, in the quarrel scene between Tom and Amanda, in which Laura has no active part, the clearest pool of light is on her figure. This is also true of the supper scene, when her silent figure on the sofa should remain the visual center. The light upon Laura should be distinct from the others, having a peculiar pristine clarity such as light used in early religious portraits of female saints or madonnas. A certain correspondence to light in religious paintings, such as El Greco's,* where the figures are radiant in atmo-

sphere that is relatively dusky, could be effectively used throughout the play. (It will also permit a more effective use of the screen.) A free, imaginative use of light can be of enormous value in giving a mobile, plastic quality to plays of a more or less static nature.

Tennessee Williams

PERFORMING *THE GLASS MENAGERIE*

The luminous actress Laurette Taylor (1884–1946) created the role of Amanda Wingfield in the 1944–45 Chicago and New York premieres of *The Glass Menagerie.* Her performance has cast a long shadow over all other performances of Tennessee Williams's enduring Southern belle fallen on hard times. In the now-legendary original production, actor-producer-director Eddie Dowling directed and played Tom in the play, originally called *The Gentleman Caller.* Julie Haydon played Laura, Anthony Ross, the Gentleman Caller, and the peerless, though troubled, Laurette Taylor whom Konstantin Stanislavski hailed as America's greatest actress, played Amanda. Long considered a hopeless alcoholic, Taylor was ostensibly in retirement from the stage when Eddie Dowling, persuaded that she was the one to play Amanda, brought her the script by the strangely named and unknown playwright—Tennessee Williams. Now renamed *The Glass Menagerie,* the production opened in a Chicago snowstorm on December 26, 1944, but two formidable critics had made it to the theater—Claudia Cassidy for the *Chicago Tribune* and Ashton Stevens for the *Chicago Herald American.* Despite their unanimous praise for the play and the "miraculously electrical" portrayal by Laurette Taylor, now compared to the great European actress Eleonora Duse, ticket buyers stayed away. Faced with the closing of a powerful and beautiful play, the Chicago critics and columnists joined forces to exhort their readers to come out and support a rare theatrical event. By the third week, the collective impact of their exhortations was decisive. The play was bound for Broadway in March of 1945 and theatrical history for the play, playwright, and the incandescent Laurette Taylor.

*A seventeenth-century Spanish painter.

Other notable actresses of the American stage have played Williams's most enduring heroine: Helen Hayes, Jessica Tandy, Maureen Stapleton, Julie Harris, Joanne Woodward, and in film and on television Helen Hayes, Katherine Hepburn, and Joanne Woodward. The play continues to receive numerous revivals in regional, campus, and community theaters throughout the United States. Williams's poetic work is timeless, his tortured, fragile family unforgettable, and Laurette Taylor's performance "immortal."

CRITICS' NOTEBOOK:

Writings on Tennessee Williams by friends, producers, directors, scholars, and critics have taken on the aspect of a publishing industry. The playwright invited producer and author Lyle Leverich to write his authorized biography and Leverich published the first of two volumes in 1995, entitled *Tom: The Unknown Tennessee,* which ends with the success of *The Glass Menagerie.* Leverich died shortly following the publication of the first volume. The second volume is being completed, in part, from the biographer's notes. Other biographies have been written by the playwright's brother, Dakin Williams (with Shepherd Mead), called *Tennessee Williams: An Intimate Biography* (1983) and by Donald Spoto, titled *The Kindness of Strangers: The Life of Tennessee Williams* (1985). Williams himself wrote his *Memoirs* in 1975. All of the biographies include accounts of the Chicago and subsequent New York productions of *The Glass Menagerie.*

In addition to the eloquence of his plays, the voice of the playwright is also heard in an extraordinary number of interviews that he gave during his lifetime. Albert J. Devlin collected thirty-five interviews from five decades of the playwright's life and published them as *Conversations with Tennessee Williams* (1986). Such notable scholars as Judith Thompson, Gerald Weales, Nancy M. Tischler, Ronald Hayman, David Savran, Mel Gussow, W. Kenneth Holditch, Richard Freeman Leavitt, and Brenda Murphy have written and edited books and collections on Williams. Roger B. Stein's essay on *The Glass Menagerie,* found in *Tennessee Williams: A Collection of Critical Essays* (1977), edited by Stephen S. Stanton, remains one of the most insightful interpretations of Tennessee Williams's first successful full-length play.

Roger B. Stein, *The Glass Menagerie* Revisited: Catastrophe without Violence*

The Glass Menagerie (1945) was Tennessee Williams' first major theatrical success. Over the years he has written much, some of high quality indeed, but nothing better than this play which established him as an important post-war playwright. "The dramatist of frustration," John Gassner dubbed him in 1948 after *Streetcar,* but unlike most of his later plays, *The Glass Menagerie* projects not a series of violent confrontations leading to catastrophe but a vision of lonely human beings who fail to make contact, who are isolated from each other and from society, and who seem ultimately abandoned in the universe.

What holds the play together are Tom's remembrance of things past, not plot or characterization. Tom, the poet-narrator and author's surrogate, called "Shakespeare" in the warehouse, organizes the drama symbolically through language and image. This is the "new plastic theater" of which Williams spoke in his production notes, a revelation not through dramatic struggle but through the allusive power of the word, the accretion of symbolic clusters which bear the meaning, reinforced dramaturgically through lighting, music, the distancing devices of a narrator and, as originally planned, of screen images.

The glass menagerie is itself the most obvious organizing symbol. It embodies the fragility of Laura's world, her search for beauty; it registers sensitively changes in lighting and stands in vivid contrast to the harshness of the outer world which can (and does) shatter it so easily. The unicorn can become the gift to Jim the Gentleman

*Roger B. Stein, "*The Glass Managerie* Revisited: Catastrophe without Violence," in *Western Humanities Review,* 18 (Spring 1964): 141–153.

Caller, whose anticipation and appearance form the plot of the play, only when it has lost its mythical uniqueness, the horn, when dream becomes momentarily possibility before it is obliterated at the end. The magic of Prince Charming's kiss can not work ("Stumblejohn," he brands himself in the published version of the play, taking on for the moment Laura's crippled condition). The "little silver slipper of a moon" on which Amanda has asked Laura to wish becomes an ironic image of Laura's isolated condition, but Amanda, wrapped up in her own illusions and selling magazine subscriptions and brassieres (like the "Gay Deceivers" with which she tries to stuff Laura before Jim appears) prefers to believe not in Tom's favorite D. H. Lawrence, but in Cinderella and courtly love and *Gone With the Wind,* the novel to which she compares Bessie May Harper's latest effort in *The Homemaker's Companion.* The ironies of the allusive imagery proliferate: Amanda's heroic efforts as homemaker are unsuccessful (the father appears only as a happy doughboy photographic image), and Margaret Mitchell's depression romance about the desirable Scarlett O'Hara in a lost Eden, a South fantasized in the national imagination during the Depression, only makes Laura look more forlorn. Finally one may note that the title image itself of *Gone With the Wind* underlines the evanescent quality of this dream and all of the Wingfields' illusions. As such, it points directly to the last line of the play and Tom's injunction to "Blow out your candles, Laura."

❧ ❧ ❧

But *The Glass Menagerie* is built upon more than the poignant plot of illusion and frustration in the lives of little people. Williams has deepened the losses of individuals by pointing to social and even spiritual catastrophe. The time of the play is 1939, as the narrative frame makes explicit both at the beginning and the end. The life of illusion is not confined to the Wingfields alone. As Tom says, "the huge middle class of America was matriculating in a school for the blind." What he calls the "social background" of the play has an important role. The international backdrop is Guernica and the song America

sings is "The World Is Waiting for the Sunrise," for the sober truth is that America is still in the depression and on the brink of war. The note of social disaster runs throughout the drama, fixing the lives of individuals against the larger canvas.

Amanda's anxieties are in large part economic and there is money behind many of their illusions: her mythical suitors were all wealthy men, as are her magazine heroes; she computes the money Tom would save by giving up smoking. When Tom complains of the grimness of life in the shoe factory, she replies, "Try and you will succeed!" If this is another of Amanda's illusions, it is one shared by her fellow Americans, for "try and you will succeed" is the traditional motto of the American dream of success, the theme of confident self-reliance canonized in the romances of Horatio Alger.

It is not Amanda, however, but Jim, the emissary from reality, who is the chief spokesman for the American dream. To Jim the warehouse is not a prison but a rung on the ladder toward success. He believes in self-improvement through education, and the lecture on self-confidence which he reads to Laura is part of the equipment of the future executive. He is awed by the fortune made in chewing gum and rhapsodizes on the theme of the future material progress of America: "All that remains is for the industry to get itself under way! Full stream— *Knowledge—Zzzzz! Money—Zzzzzp! Power!* That's the cycle democracy is built on!"

Yet when the theme of success is superimposed upon the lives of the characters, the social irony emerges. Father was not the successful businessman, but a telephone man who "fell in love with long distances." Tom, the substitute father, refuses to pay the light bill, plunges his family into darkness, and then runs out, and Amanda sells subscriptions and brassieres only at the loss of her dignity. Jim's own dream of success seems to have reached its peak in high school. (Williams later explored this theme more fully in *Cat on a Hot Tin Roof.*) The trek upward through the depression years is disappointing, but the indomitable optimist is not discouraged.

The experience of the 1930s did not turn Williams into a proletarian writer or social realist, but it did open up for him a darker vision of American life which he suggests to his audience but which is denied to his characters, still "matriculating in a school for the blind": a belief that the American dream is itself a sham and a failure. In his essay "The Catastrophe of Success," Williams said that "the Cinderella story is our favorite national myth, the cornerstone of the film industry if not of the Democracy itself." The social catastrophe inherent in *The Glass Menagerie* lies precisely in the fact that Laura is *not* Cinderella: the silver slipper does not finally fit, and Jim is not Prince Charming but one of the innumerable Americans who would soon be moving overseas in troop ships. As Tom says at the end, "for nowadays the world is lit by lightning! Blow out your candles, Laura—and so goodbye...." The world which had been waiting for the sunrise burst with bombardments instead, and the lives of the Wingfields at the end are absorbed in the larger social tragedy.

REVISITING DRAMATIC CHARACTER

Drama's characters, like the novel's, are fictional. However, they differ from those found in the novel for the chief reason that they are created to be given life by actors. At all times there are two levels of humanness at work in drama's characters. One level involves the story's characters as individualized forms of motives and actions in special circumstances. The second concerns dramatic characters as images of humanity having the potential to be given life by actors.

Drama's characters can be understood, first, as general types of humanity by observing gender, age, profession, clothing, manners, gestures, and speech. Second, since characters are also individualized images of humanity, we must carefully assess what they say and what they do to understand their particular habits, motives, and acts. As we said, drama's action springs from character. After all, in the old way of thinking about drama as an imitation of an action or of human events, those doing the imitating are characters, or reflected human beings. They may be as complex as Hamlet or as vulner-able as Laura Wingfield. Yet, their speech, gestures, and actions determine who they are and what their acts mean in the special circumstances devised by the playwright.

Over the centuries, drama's central characters have changed from royalty to commoners—from kings and princes to traveling salesmen and blue-collar workers. The change of social class and universal deeds is a result of changing intellectual and social thought. Since the mid-eighteenth century, new subjects, social classes, milieus, events, and commentaries have been introduced into plays, bringing about significant changes in the types and circumstances of those human beings represented in drama. Topics of heredity, environment, economics, and the unconscious have replaced older notions of cosmic forces and mysterious fates at work in our lives. As subject matter is reduced so, too, is a character's stature. Consequently, we argue in modern times for the dignity and worth of ordinary individuals in an effort to define a new kind of heroism for the modern world.

Since 1950, avant garde writers have placed their representative characters in an absurd world devoid of purpose and meaning. A recognizable humanity—individuals like those we encounter in our everyday lives—is exchanged for mechanical characters whose struggles are senseless, futile, and oppressive. The loss of a coherent unity of character and purpose is concomitant with the loss of coherent plots and meaningful actions. The postmodernists, rejecting the absurdist paradigms of senselessness and purposelessness, have dissolved the ego which we can still discover in Samuel Beckett's character May in *Footfalls*. In postmodernist texts, a recognizable humanity is replaced by masks and icons through which writers can speak of the contradictions of social history. An example of this contradiction is the terrorist who destroys people and societies in an apocalyptic vision of preservation.

However, avant garde writers remain in the minority. Fully dimensional characters like those created by Tennessee Williams are representative of the mainstream approach to creating (or "fleshing out") dramatic character. The Wingfield family—Amanda, Tom, Laura—is Williams's articulation of the beauty, pain, vulnerability, and desperation to be found in the confusion of living. In Williams's dramatic world, as in the plays of other mainstream contemporary playwrights, character is still defined by situation, motives, feelings, gestures, choices, actions, and words. Our next discussion deals with an understanding of the playwright's language—the verbal text—which differs remarkably from the language of poetry and the novel.

NOTES

1. R. C. Lewis, "A Playwright Named Tennessee," *The New York Times Magazine,* 7 Dec. 1947: 67.
2. Martin Esslin, *The Field of Drama: How Signs of Drama Create Meaning on Stage & Screen* (New York: Methuen, 1987): 84–85.
3. Francis Fergusson, *The Idea of a Theater: A Study of Ten Plays: The Art of Drama in Changing Perspectives* (Princeton, N.J.: Princeton University Press, 1968): 255.
4. Arthur Miller, "Tragedy and the Common Man," *The New York Times,* 27 Feb. 1949: II, 1, 3.
5. Eugène Ionesco, *Notes and Counter Notes: Writings on the Theatre,* trans. Donald Watson (New York: Grove Press, 1964): 257.
6. August Strindberg, "Preface to *Miss Julie"* in *Six Plays of Strindberg,* trans. Elizabeth Sprigge (Garden City, N.Y.: Doubleday & Company, 1955): 65.
7. August Strindberg, "Author's Note to A *Dream Play,"* in *Six Plays by Strindberg,* trans. Elizabeth Sprigge (Garden City, N.Y.: Doubleday & Company, 1955): 193.
8. Ionesco 163.
9. Heiner Müller, "19 Answers," *Hamletmachine and Other Texts for the Stage,* ed. and trans. Carl Weber (New York: Performing Arts Journal Publications, 1984): 138.

CHAPTER 4

UNDERSTANDING LANGUAGE

Penelope Wilton as Md. Ranyevskaya and Alec McGowen as Gaev in *The Cherry Orchard* by Anton Chekhov, directed by Adrian Noble, Royal Shakespeare Company production, Barbican Theatre, London, 1995. (Photo © Robbie Jack/CORBIS.)

> POLONIUS: *What do you read, my lord?*
> HAMLET: *Words, words, words.*
> —William Shakespeare

THE VERBAL TEXT

The language of a play is most often thought of as *words* that appear on the printed page as dialogue the actor makes into living speech exchanged between characters or delivered as solo acts of speech in soliloquies or monologues. Martin Esslin called the play's dialogue the "verbal text."[1] In fact, the verbal text is more than dialogue, for it designates the spoken and the unspoken, the verbal and the nonverbal, the sounds and silences, the signs and symbols, of human communication.

George Steiner defined *drama* as "language under such high pressure of feeling that the words carry a necessary and immediate connotation of gesture."[2] Drama's words convey feelings and gestures; they can be active and reactive. The opening dialogue of Shakespeare's *Hamlet* is keenly active as two guards challenge one another on the battlements at midnight:

> BERNARDO: Who's there?
> FRANCISCO: Nay, answer me.
> Stand and unfold yourself. (1.1)

Having seen a ghostly figure while guarding the castle at Elsinore, the soldiers are cautious and frightened. Bernardo's question ("Who's there?") challenges Francisco, demanding identification. Francisco behaves likewise. He is frightened and demands to be answered ("Nay, answer me."). In modern speech he is saying to Bernardo, "No, *you* identify yourself to *me*!" Each soldier is actively using language to challenge the identity of the other in a threatening situation. They want information and their words also convey the menacing use of their weapons.

In contrast to the confrontational dialogue of the guards in *Hamlet,* Anton Chekhov's dialogue in *The Cherry Orchard,* written in 1903, is reactive or mainly passive responses to people and situations. The opening moments of *The Cherry Orchard* reveal in the predawn light two individuals who have waited all night for the arrival of the estate's owner and her entourage from Paris. The servant Dooniasha with candle in hand awakens Lopakhin, a rich merchant, with the news that the train has arrived at the station. In their first lines of dialogue, the characters "react" to place, time, and situation—the fact of the train's arrival, the family's imminent appearance, the time of day, and their night's vigil.

> LOPAKHIN: The train's arrived, thank God. What time is it?
> DOONIASHA: It's nearly two. (*Blows out the candle.*) It's light already.
> LOPAKHIN: How late was the train then? Two hours at least. (*Yawns and stretches.*) How stupid I am! What a fool I've made of myself! Came here on purpose to go to the station and meet them—and then overslept!... Dropped off to sleep in the chair. Annoying ...I wish you'd woken me up.
> DOONIASHA: I thought you'd gone. (*Listens.*) Sounds as if they're coming. (1)

LANGUAGE AS ORGANIZATION

The language of a play organizes our perceptions of the elements of drama, such as plot, character, and meaning. It is enhanced by sounds, silences, gestures, lighting, costume, scenery, movement, and music. Unlike our random conversations in restaurants and coffee shops, the playwright's language is written to be spoken by actors on stage before audiences. Therefore, the playwright's use of language is highly selective and purposeful.

All speech in drama produces meaning on several levels, as it does in real life. First, the language of the play is the playwright's means of providing background information, of developing plot and action, and of expressing the characters' conscious thoughts and feelings. Second, it conveys the characters' subconscious feelings in latent or hidden meanings embedded in words and/or gestures. Chekhov's use of language is often deceptive, for his characters frequently avoid or hide their true feelings.

In reading a Chekhov play, we have to be especially careful to distinguish between what a character *does* and what that same character *says*. Chekhov did not intend to confuse readers and audiences, but he believed there were contradictions between our words and our actions. He believed that while people went about their daily routines of eating, drinking, working, and amusing themselves, their lives were taking shape and they were being made happy or unhappy. For example, in *The Cherry Orchard*, Lopakhin contemplates proposing marriage to Varia, Madame Ranyevskaia's adopted daughter; the couple talks around the subject with restrained emotions while routinely packing to leave the estate, but Lopakhin exits without proposing and they go their separate ways forever.

CONVENTIONS OF STAGE LANGUAGE

Unlike conversations in real life, the playwright uses certain accepted conventions to convey a character's interior thoughts. Shakespeare's poetic dialogue allows Hamlet to express his feelings and thoughts in blank verse (unrhymed iambic pentameter), often in some of the most eloquent soliloquies found in the English language. Many of Shakespeare's lines and phrases have become a part of a commonplace vocabulary. For example,

To be, or not to be—that is the question.

The play's the thing....

—Frailty, thy name is woman!

Thus conscience does make cowards of us all....

These are lines from the great soliloquies where Hamlet, alone on stage, speaks his thoughts aloud for audiences to overhear his internal debates and subsequent decisions.

As a soliloquy demonstrates, drama's language is highly selective, often complex, and charged with verbal nuance and gesture. It is a vehicle for characters to speak aloud thoughts, choices, and motives. It also involves implied meanings and assumptions relating to historical time and place, such as the assumed "majesty of kings" among Shakespeare's characters. Stage language is designed to be given life in the theater by actors as characters. Its purpose is to express ideas, feelings, attitudes, intentions, and, finally, the meaning of the play's completed action. This is why we say a play's language is selective and purposeful and highly unlike our random daily conversations.

It is true that the words we use to communicate to the world around us also accomplish many of the same things as stage language: We express ideas, attitudes, feelings, and intentions. We also surround ourselves in daily life with music; we "dress" for special occasions like weddings, rock concerts, or job interviews; and we invent scenarios to get us through such awkward periods as meeting strangers, dealing with irate parents, or impressing VIPs. However, there is an important difference between a play's language, constructed to be spoken by an actor in the theater, and everyday conversation. The playwright selects the language (verbal and nonverbal) that appears on the text's printed page and the actor projects the living quality of the playwright's words. By avoiding the randomness of everyday conversation, stage language shapes the play's action, directs the plot, and controls the characters' experiences in action, plot, and resolution.

While a play's language is carefully arranged by the playwright, there are also other theatrical influences on the verbal text. Directors, actors, and designers—through the use of movement, costumes, scenery, lighting, and sound—collaborate with the playwright to create a meaningful pattern of communication.

As we study the various possibilities of drama's language, we become attuned to its verbal and nonverbal characteristics. Let us begin with the stage directions (the *didascalia*) the reader of a modern text encounters on the printed page. Next, let us consider verbal and nonverbal elements, including sounds, silences, subtext, and stage properties. The printed text, approved by the playwright before publication, contains all the writer's stage directions, notes, exits and entrances, sounds, music, and so on. These notations are an effort to preserve the ephemeral qualities of the text-as-performance.

Stage Directions

Before the printing press and a general readership for plays, stage directions (if they existed at all) were used solely by theater personnel. In modern editions of *Hamlet*, we find such sparse directions as *"A flourish," "Exeunt," "Aside," "Dies,"* and *"Exit Ghost."* It is assumed that these directions were added later to Shakespeare's original promptbook by playwright or players and printed with various emendations in the first and second quartos (published 1603 and 1604) and in the first Folio, or first collection of Shakespeare's complete works, printed in 1623, twenty-three years after the first performance of *Hamlet*.

The modern playwrights include stage directions at the beginning of each act and provide information about how they imagine details of the three-dimensional stage space; that is, Hedda Gabler's drawing room or Amanda Wingfield's tenement apartment. Stage directions are largely for the reader's information, for audiences experience the play's environment visually and aurally. Stage directions include facts about geography, weather conditions, décor, dress, atmosphere, stage properties, music cues, and general impressions of place or environment. The modern reader has the advantage of knowing how Chekhov visualized the opening scene of *The Cherry Orchard*, for he described in detail the room, called the "nursery," and the cherry trees that can be seen outside the windows.

> *A room which used to be the children's bedroom and is still referred to as the "nursery." There are several doors: one of them leads into* ANIA'S *room. It is early morning: the sun is just coming up. The windows of the room are shut, but through them the cherry trees can be seen in blossom. It is May, but in the orchard there is morning frost.* (1)

On the other hand, Shakespeare and his contemporaries were not very interested in the specifics of environment as a factor that shaped human events, nor was the Elizabethan stage compatible with overly decorated settings. Shakespeare placed all indications of time, place, weather, and mood in the dialogue of minor characters who provided the background information at the play's beginning as they captured the audience's attention preparatory to the entrance of the principals. These are called "weather lines." Within eleven lines at the beginning of *Hamlet*, the two guards give us a sense of place (castle battlements), time ("'Tis now struck twelve"), weather ("'Tis bitter cold"), mood ("I'm sick at heart"), and what's happening ("not a mouse stirring").

In play analysis, stage directions must not be ignored, for they provide crucial information and raise questions to be answered as action and plot develop. For example, why are the guards in *Hamlet* uneasy and relieved to report that not a "mouse is stirring"? We learn shortly about the ghost's appearance and then follow all the complicated events associated with the ghost's reappearance to Hamlet.

In Shakespeare's plays, stage directions are chiefly embedded in dialogue. In Chekhov's plays, written 300 years later, the directions are separated from the dialogue and often prefatory to the action. In *The Cherry Orchard*, we learn in the initial stage directions that the cherry trees are in blossom and are part of the play's scenic background. As the play's complications unfold, choices about these trees and the land where they are located will determine the future of the Ranyevskaia estate.

Verbal Language

As we look at the page of a play, we are aware of *words* as key elements for making things happen in the theater. Language or dialogue on a printed page has the potential for bringing human presence and activity onto the stage. Words spoken by actors convey plot, action, character, emotions, relationships, ideas, motives, sounds, and commentary. Words also individualize characters by giving them speech patterns, regional dialects, and vocabularies special to social classes and to professions.

In modern language theory, words are at once signs and symbols. As signs, words can create a picture of an object (called an *icon*), such as a throne or a sword. Othello uses words as iconic signs when he says to his opponents, "Keep up your bright *swords,* for the dew will rust them" (1.2). A second type is the *index* sign (the gesture), such as an actor's pointing to a person or object. In *Hamlet,* Claudius literally gestures for "lights" (torches and candles) to end the mockery of the play-within-the-play and to cast away the shadows of his crime. The third type is the *symbol* which is more familiar to us as readers of literature. Symbols have multiple meanings, depending on their dramatic or literary contexts. Symbols differ from signs in that they have complex connections to their referents. The poet Robert Frost wrote of the "road not taken." As a poetic symbol, Frost's "road" is not simply a pathway through the woods that divided in two directions, forcing the individual to choose between them. Frost's "two roads that diverged in a yellow wood" are symbols for any choice in life between two alternatives which appear, at the time, equally attractive, but which in later years will have made a significant difference on the kinds of life experiences one has had. Like Frost's road, symbols have ranged over the centuries from flags (for nations), roses (for love), doves (for peace), night (for death), to stars (for permanency), and so on.

In the theater, unlike in poetry, symbols can be both verbal and nonverbal. The cherry orchard itself is a complex symbol. The orchard is a symbol of tradition and beauty, but it is also an object of much debate regarding how to save the estate and a way of life. Chekhov also used symbolic sounds to enhance a play's meaning. The sound of a snapped string midway in *The Cherry Orchard* becomes an aural symbol foreshadowing the pain and loss to come at the play's end.

Signs and symbols create the rich texture of dramatic language. The reader must catch all nuances of verbal and nonverbal meaning. For example, Chekhov titled his play *The Cherry Orchard;* play titles always carry a large burden of a playwright's intentions. The orchard, as symbol, is variously interpreted as the passing of the old way of life in provincial Russia, circa 1900. Through the four acts of the play, the orchard symbolizes the many ways Chekhov's characters deal with or fail to deal with life's demands. In the final stage direction as the orchard is destroyed, it becomes a symbol of social change: the passing of a way of life and the start of a new and different world.

Nonverbal Language

In addition to words—the verbal text—the theater's language communicates to us through many other means: the actors' presence, sounds, lighting effects, movement, silences, gestures, activity, inactivity, color, music, songs, costumes, scenic devices, stage properties, and film projections or images. During a performance, the stage is filled with these simultaneous aspects of the play's theatrical life that enlarge the verbal text. In stage directions, the playwright indicates sounds, silences, colors, activities, and so on. It remains, however, for the theater's collaborators—writer, director, designers, and actors—to make nonverbal language effective on stage. In *The Cherry Orchard,* the sound of the snapped string and the thud of an ax against a tree at the play's end are nonverbal means of communicating the destruction of the family's treasure and their way of life. The final stage direction in *The Cherry Orchard* is one of the most renown in the history of Western drama.

> *(A distant sound is heard, coming as if out of the sky, like the sound of a string snapping, slowly and sadly dying away. Silence ensues, broken only by the sound of an axe striking a tree in the orchard far away.) (4)*

In imagining such a powerful and symbolic moment, the playwright knows that without the skills of the theater's sound designer, the aural effect will not have its full symbolic meaning and theatrical impact.

In one sense, the reader's job is more difficult than the audience's. What the audience experiences, we must imagine based wholly upon the verbal text, that is, upon the words we read, not the sounds we hear and the sights we see.

Sounds and Silences

The end of *The Cherry Orchard* demonstrates how sounds are some of the theater's most powerful nonverbal effects and, consequently, some of the writer's most effective tools. Shakespeare used trumpets to announce the entrance of the court in *Hamlet* and thunder machines to simulate the storms in *Macbeth* and *King Lear*, for example. With modern sound technology, almost any effect is possible—from passing trains to marching bands to the fading sound of a snapped string. As readers, we have to recreate these sounds in the mind's ear just as we visualize the play's action in the mind's eye. The task is not easy. Sounds are sometimes alternated with silences, words with pauses, activity with inactivity. Readers must be attuned to the absence of words and be prepared to understand pauses and silences just as we comprehend the meaning of a character's words and actions. The last scene of *The Cherry Orchard* shows how Chekhov juxtaposed sounds with silences to achieve another level of meaning. In the family's hurried departure from the estate that has been sold at auction, Feers, the elderly valet, has been forgotten and left behind. His final speech is framed between stage directions calling for offstage sounds of doors being locked and carriages driving away and the distant sound of a breaking string that fades away to silence before the sound of the ax is heard striking a tree in the orchard.

Discovering that he has been forgotten, Feers talks to himself in fragmented dialogue punctuated by frequent pauses. These pauses, or brief silences, indicate the winding down of a single life and also of a way of life that the family's departure signifies. The fact that Feers is alone, locked in the house, sick and dying, tells us more vividly than any narration that "life has passed him by." At the end of *The Cherry Orchard*, we hear and see a world in transition.

Subtext

The notion of *subtext* is a post-Chekhovian concept used by actors, directors, and critics in the modern theater to identify a character's inner thoughts, feelings, and intentions not explicitly expressed in dialogue. In performance, the subtext—the inner life of a character—is supplied by the actor. In playwriting, subtext—the inner life of the work and its implied meanings—is often an outgrowth of characters avoiding directness. In imitation of "real life," modern playwrights create characters who rarely say simply and directly what they truly mean because people in real life often avoid being too direct for many reasons: out of politeness, shyness, subterfuge, boredom, or style. Moreover, people rarely reveal their personal problems to one another, but rather camouflage their anxieties with verbal trivia. In the proposal scene (4) in *The Cherry Orchard*, Varia and Lopakhin, rather than confront their feelings, talk about luggage, weather, work, distances, train schedules, but not about marriage. *The Cherry Orchard* illustrates how broken speech, the irrelevant remark, or the avoided topic can indirectly allude to passion, to dreams, and to lost hopes. In contrast, Shakespeare wrote Hamlet's soliloquies to *reveal* the inner content of the prince's thoughts and feelings.

Subtext is underlying, unspoken thoughts, emotions, and implications separate from spoken words (dialogue). As in life, the meaning of the words spoken in drama, especially in modern times, is usually charged with latent or hidden meanings. What is going on between characters is ultimately derived from the given situation. In Chekhov's play, the family waits to learn from Lopakhin and Gayev the outcome of the estate's auction (3). Upon their return, the two men are reluctant to share their information and feelings. Gayev hides his distress over the loss of the estate behind complaints of hunger and fatigue. Lopakhin, who has bought the estate, tries to suppress his joy (the son of a serf now owns the estate!) and to delay the inevitable announcement which will bring pain to the family.

Finally, subtext is a collaboration between writer and actor that reveals the character's inner life, but the collaboration begins with the verbal text. As readers, we seek out clues to inner feelings and responses in language and stage directions. For example, Madame Ranyevskaia's spendthrift nature is underscored when she gives a beggar a gold coin, choosing it over a silver piece when, as Varia says, "There's nothing in the house for people to eat, and you gave him a gold piece" (2). The gesture is grand and typical of an individual who has for years borrowed and spent with no thought for the day of reckoning.

In modern writing, characters usually retain deep feelings and thoughts but either avoid talking about them or lack the vocabulary to articulate their painful thoughts and feelings. Hence, we must be aware of the gap between the expressed and the unexpressed that contributes to the inner life of the play.

Stage Properties

From earliest times, playwrights have made use of large and small movable objects in the theater to enliven audience interest, to aid the actor's work, to further the storyline, and to resolve the play's ending. Greek playwrights used a crane-like device (the *mechane*) to lower and raise gods and humans into the playing space, wagons (the *ekkyklema*) for displaying the dead, and perhaps even chariots for spectacular entrances. The Elizabethans used set pieces, costumes, and properties, such as thrones, cages, beds, crowns, swords, and skulls, to enhance the telling of the story. These objects were also introduced into the verbal text and used by the characters. One of the most famous instances is the use of a skull in the gravedigger's scene in *Hamlet* (5.1). The gravedigger's act of tossing up a skull from the grave he is preparing to receive Ophelia's body results in Hamlet's meditation on the impermanency of life and the famous "Alas, poor Yorick!" speech. The skull's presence in the actor's hand rivets the audience's attention to the subject of death and mortality. The skull, as a stage property, adds to the rich language of the theater as both an iconic sign of death and a symbol of mortality.

By the nineteenth century, stage language was influenced by the new "realism" and by a theater technology unknown in Shakespeare's day. The concern for stage realism resulted in reproducing speech, dress, and behavior appropriate to a character's socioeconomic background and psychological makeup. To enhance the illusion of a candid representation on stage of everyday reality (as the audience would understand or recognize it) and to maintain language's symbolic ambiguity and richness, playwrights made use of "real" objects, such as furniture, table lamps, books, pistols, stoves, keys, and family portraits, appropriate to the stage environment and action. They further endowed ordinary objects logically found in the environment with symbolic meanings. In some realistic plays, for example, table lamps and sunlight glimpsed through windows became symbols of "throwing light on a subject," or of a character's new understanding.

In *Hedda Gabler*, written in 1890 at the height of stage realism as a new writing and performance style, Henrik Ibsen used personal and decorative objects found in the Tesman home as symbols of the neurotic and destructive forces at work within his heroine. For example, Hedda's dueling pistols inherited from her father, General Gabler, and the wood-burning stove are part of the drawing room decor. The pistols and the stove are at once ordinary and symbolic objects. The pistols can be discharged and the stove presumably has fire in it, but both are symbolic of Hedda's destructive nature fueled by her boredom, jealousy, and neurotic inability to adapt to the proscribed gender role of her day—housewife and mother. As symbols of her destructiveness, the dueling pistols are associated with the former lifestyle of General Gabler's daughter, now the scholarly George Tesman's wife, and are part of her personal possessions kept in the drawing room. One pistol plays a part in Eilif Lovborg's accidental death and the other in Hedda's suicide. The stove is used by Hedda in a jealous rage to burn her former lover's manuscript and destroy his life's work.

In *The Cherry Orchard*, Varia, Madame Ranyevskaia's adopted daughter, housekeeper, and general factotum, wears the household keys fastened to her belt at all times. They complete her costume, but are literal signs of her authority and responsibility in the household. When Lopakhin announces that he has bought the estate at auction, Varia removes the keys from her belt and without comment throws them on the floor at Lopakhin's feet (3). The keys are familiar objects, but Varia's gesture turns them into an eloquent statement about the change of the estate's ownership, the material loss and gain, and the psychological pain and pleasure of those involved in the transfer of ownership. In terms of stage realism, the keys are ordinary signs of the character's social status and symbolic of the family's ownership of the estate. As they are cast down, they symbolize the family's change of fortune.

Stage properties are powerful nonverbal means (both signs and symbols) of enhancing the play's visual impact, of endowing the stage picture with ordinary yet richly meaningful objects, and of reinforcing the play's final meaning. They are three-dimensional elements of the theater's language.

The Cherry Orchard

Anton Chekhov

Anton Pavlovich Chekhov (1860–1904) was born in southern Russia, the grandson of a serf and the son of a grocer. He studied medicine at Moscow University but never practiced regularly because of ill health and literary interests. During his student years, he wrote short stories to earn money and was soon accepted into literary circles. He began his playwriting career in the 1880s with one-act farces, The Marriage Proposal *and* The Bear. The Sea Gull, *written in 1896, was his first full-length play to capture the serious attention of theater managers, but it was a colossal failure when produced in St. Petersburg. Two years later, it was a brilliant success with the new Moscow Art Theater and established his reputation as a major playwright.*

Chekhov's career was defined by his association with the Moscow Art Theater between 1898 and 1904. He redefined stage realism by writing plays without direct, purposive action which chronicled the lives of rural Russians. Director Konstantin Stanislavski's methods of interpreting the inner truth of Chekhov's characters and the mood of his plays resulted in one of the great theatrical collaborations.

During his last years, Chekhov lived in Yalta, where he had gone for his health, and made occasional trips to Moscow to see his plays. He married the Moscow Art Theater's leading actress, Olga Knipper, for whom he had written parts in his last three plays. He died of tuberculosis at a German spa in 1904 and was buried in Moscow.

During his short career, Chekhov wrote four masterpieces of modern stage realism: The Sea Gull, Uncle Vanya, The Three Sisters, *and* The Cherry Orchard.

CRITICAL INTRODUCTION TO
THE CHERRY ORCHARD

Anton Chekhov wrote plays that chronicled the lives of ordinary people in rural Russia at the turn of the century. In doing so, he created a new type of realistic dramaturgy distinguished by understated plots and disjointed dialogue that mirrored the stagnant lives of provincial gentry, doctors, writers, tutors, servants, hangers-on, merchants, and government officials. He depicted them as going about their daily routines of working, eating, drinking, talking, reading, falling in and out of love, and playing cards and billiards while their lives were subtly altered for better or for worse. Banal conversation and unspectacular lives are the fabric of Chekhov's art. The dramatic action of a Chekhov play is contained within the inconsequential and habitual routines of living and surviving.

Of his different writing style, Chekhov said:

> *After all, in real life, people don't spend every moment in shooting one another, hanging themselves, or making declarations of love. They do not spend all their time saying clever things. They are more occupied with eating, drinking, flirting, and saying stupidities, and these are the things which ought to be shown on the stage.... People eat their dinner, just eat their dinner, and all the time their happiness is taking form, or their lives are being destroyed.[3]*

Chekhov's approach to writing for the theater in the 1890s set a standard and style that continue to influence playwrights today. *The Cherry Orchard*, which many consider his masterpiece, conveys the perfection of Chekhov's unique dramaturgy: Seemingly purposeless activities and aimless dialogue gradually reveal the lives of rural Russians living on the estates owned by their families for centuries. For example, Madame Ranyevskaia returns to her estate after some years in Paris only to find that it has been mortgaged to pay her debts and is to be sold at auction. Half-hearted attempts are made by her relatives to collect money owed her by a neighboring landowner, but he is also in financial straits. For a time, they rely on an uncertain legacy from a wealthy relative, or a rich marriage for the daughter Ania. As the head of the family, Madame Ranyevskaia seems incapable of coping with her financial situation and the looming reality of the loss of the estate at auction. The only realistic proposal for saving the estate comes from Lopakhin, a wealthy merchant whose father was a serf on the estate. In the first act, Lopakhin suggests cutting down the famous cherry orchard (for it no longer produces income) and dividing the land into acreage for summer cottages to create a modern-day "subdivision." The family rejects the idea of destroying such beauty and tradition, but they have no plan of action.

Chekhov contains the action of the play—loss and gain—within a realistic framework of the family's arrival and departure. Their arrival at the beginning and their departure at the end are realistic means of bringing disparate people together to demonstrate their hopes and dreams among the most ordinary activities, such as eating, drinking, playing billiards, talking, and daydreaming. However, in *The Cherry Orchard,* time passes and the characters do nothing to take control of their lives (and to save the estate). Things are put off until "tomorrow" and unrealistic strategies are discussed. In the meantime, the play is climaxed by the sale of the estate (which takes place off stage and whose outcome is reported). Chekhov's aim was to divert attention away from the "big" theatrical moments of nineteenth-century melodrama (suicides, murders, duels, auctions) and to examine the reactions of recognizable characters to how their lives are being shaped by events over which they have exercised little, if any, control. His concept of stage realism was to define the play's environment, make use of indirect action and dialogue, and present characters whose happiness or unhappiness grows out of inconsequential events.

Chekhov avoided large "stage" moments of confrontation and physical action. For Chekhov, ordinary moments more accurately reflected the day-to-day reality of our lives rather than sordid murders, ghosts, battles, and so on. To universalize his statement about what it is to experience lives of commonplace routines, disappointments, and habituation, Chekhov added to indirect action and understated dialogue, such nonverbal sound effects as the distant "breaking string," to remind us that time passes, lives take shape, and people are made happy or unhappy as their worlds change.

The Cherry Orchard

A COMEDY IN FOUR ACTS

CHARACTERS IN THE PLAY

RANYEVSKAIA, Liubov Andryeevna (Liuba), a landowner

ANIA (Anichka), her daughter, aged 17

VARIA (Varvara Mihailovna), her adopted daughter, aged 24

GAYEV, Leonid Andryeevich (Lionia), brother of Mme. Ranyevskaia

LOPAKHIN, Yermolai Aleksyeevich, a businessman

TROFIMOV, Piotr Serghyeevich (Pyetia), a student

SIMEONOV-PISHCHIK, Boris Borisovich, a landowner

CHARLOTTA IVANOVNA, a German governess

YEPIHODOV, Semion Pantelyeevich, a clerk on Ranyevskaia's estate

DOONIASHA (Avdotyia Fiodorovna), a parlourmaid

FEERS (Feers Nikolayevich), a man-servant, aged 87

YASHA, a young man-servant

A TRAMP

STATION-MASTER

POST-OFFICE CLERK

GUESTS, SERVANTS

The action takes place on the estate of Mme. Ranyevskaia.

ACT ONE

A room which used to be the children's bedroom and is still referred to as the 'nursery'. There are several doors: one of them leads into ANIA'S *room. It is early morning: the sun is just coming up. The windows of the room are shut, but through them the cherry trees can be seen in blossom. It is May, but in the orchard there is morning frost.*

Enter DOONIASHA, *carrying a candle, and* LO-PAKHIN *with a book in his hand.*

LOPAKHIN: The train's arrived, thank God. What time is it?

DOONIASHA: It's nearly two. (*Blows out the candle.*) It's light already.

LOPAKHIN: How late was the train then? Two hours at least. (*Yawns and stretches.*) How stupid I am! What a fool I've made of myself! Came here on purpose to go to the station and meet them—and then overslept!… Dropped off to sleep in the chair. Annoying …I wish you'd woken me up.

DOONIASHA: I thought you'd gone. (*Listens.*) Sounds as if they're coming.

LOPAKHIN (*also listens*): No…. They'll have to get their luggage out, and all that…. (*Pause.*) Liubov Andryeevna has been abroad for five years, I don't know what she's like now…. She used to be a good soul. An easy-going, simple kind of person. I remember when I was a boy of about fifteen, my father—he had a small shop in the village then—hit me in the face and made my nose bleed…. We had come to the manor for something or other, and he'd been drinking, I remember it as if it happened yesterday: Liubov Andryeevna—she was still young and slender then—brought me in and took me to the washstand in this very room, the nursery it was then. 'Don't cry, little peasant,' she said, 'it'll be better before you're old enough to get married'…. (*Pause.*) 'Little peasant'…. She was right enough, my father was a peasant. Yet here I am—all dressed up in a white waistcoat and brown shoes…. But you can't make a silk purse out of a sow's ear. I am rich, I've got a lot of money, but anyone can see I'm just a peasant, anyone who takes the trouble to think about me and look under my skin. (*Turning over pages in the book.*) I've been reading this book, and I haven't understood a word of it. I fell asleep reading it. (*Pause.*)

DOONIASHA: The dogs didn't sleep all night: they know their masters are coming.

LOPAKHIN: What's the matter, Dooniasha?

DOONIASHA: My hands are trembling. I feel as if I'm going to faint.

LOPAKHIN: You're too refined and sensitive, Dooniasha. You dress yourself up like a lady, and you do your hair like one, too. That won't do, you know. You must remember your place.

Enter YEPIHODOV *with a bunch of flowers; he wears a jacket and brightly polished high boots which squeak loudly; as he comes in, he drops the flowers.*

YEPIHODOV (*picks up the flowers*): The gardener sent these. He says they're to go in the dining-room. (*Hands the flowers to* DOONIASHA.)

LOPAKHIN: And bring me some kvass.

DOONIASHA: Very well.

YEPIHODOV: There's a frost outside, three degrees of it, and the cherry trees are covered with bloom. I can't approve of this climate of ours, you know. (*Sighs.*) No, I can't. It doesn't contribute to—to things, I mean. And do you know, Yermolai Aleksyeevich, I bought myself a pair of boots the day before yesterday, and they squeak so terribly…well, I mean to say, it's utterly impossible, you know.… What can I put on them?

LOPAKHIN: Oh, leave me alone. You make me tired.

YEPIHODOV: Every day something or other unpleasant happens to me. But I don't complain; I'm accustomed to it, I even laugh at it.

Enter DOONIASHA; *she serves* LOPAKHIN *with kvass.*

I'll leave you now. (*Bumps into a chair which falls over.*)

You see! (*Triumphantly.*) You can see for yourself what it is, I mean to say…so to speak.… It's simply extraordinary! (*Goes out.*)

DOONIASHA: I want to tell you a secret, Yermolai Aleksyeevich. Yepihodov proposed to me.

LOPAKHIN: Ah!

DOONIASHA: I don't know what to do.… He's a quiet man, but sometimes he gets talking, and then you can't understand anything he says. It sounds nice, it sounds very moving, but you just can't understand it. I think I like him a little, and he's madly in love with me. He's an unlucky sort of person, something unpleasant seems to happen to him every day. That's why they tease him and call him 'two-and-twenty misfortunes'.

LOPAKHIN (*listens*): I think I can hear them coming.…

DOONIASHA: Coming!… Oh, dear! I don't know what's the matter with me.… I feel cold all over.

LOPAKHIN: Yes, they really are coming! Let's go and meet them at the door. I wonder if she'll recognize me? We haven't met for five years.

DOONIASHA (*agitated*): I'm going to faint.… Oh, I'm fainting!…

The sound of two coaches driving up to the house is heard. LOPAKHIN *and* DOONIASHA *go out quickly. The stage is empty. Then there are sounds of people arriving in the adjoining room.* FEERS, *leaning on a stick, crosses the stage hurriedly: he has been to the station to meet Liubov Andryeevna. He is dressed in an old-fashioned livery coat and a top hat and is muttering to himself, though it is impossible to make out what he is saying. The noises off stage become louder. A voice says: 'Let's go through here'. Enter* LIUBOV ANDRYEEVNA, ANIA *and* CHARLOTTA IVANOVNA, *leading a small dog, all in travelling clothes,* VARIA, *wearing an overcoat and a kerchief over her head,* GAYEV, SIMEONOV-PISHCHIK, LOPAKHIN, DOONIASHA, *carrying a bundle and an umbrella, and other servants with luggage.*

ANIA: Let's go through here. You remember what room this is, Mamma?

LIUBOV ANDRYEEVNA (*joyfully, through her tears*): The nursery!

VARIA: How cold it is! My hands are quite numb. (*To* LIUBOV ANDRYEEVNA.) Your rooms are just as you left them, Mamma dear, the white one, and the mauve one.

LIUBOV ANDRYEEVNA: The nursery, my dear, my beautiful room!… I used to sleep here when

I was little.... (*Cries.*) And now I feel as if I were little again.... (*She kisses her brother, then* VARIA, *then her brother again.*) And Varia is just the same as ever, looking like a nun. I recognized Dooniasha, too. (*Kisses* DOONIASHA.)

GAYEV: The train was two hours late. Just think of it! What efficiency!

CHARLOTTA (*to* PISHCHIK): My dog actually eats nuts.

PISHCHIK (*astonished*): Fancy that!

They all go out except ANIA *and* DOONIASHA.

DOONIASHA: We've waited and waited for you.... (*Helps* ANIA *to take off her hat and coat.*)

ANIA: I haven't slept for four nights.... I'm frozen.

DOONIASHA: You went away during Lent and it was snowing and freezing then, but now it's spring-time. Darling! (*She laughs and kisses her.*) I could hardly bear waiting for you, my pet, my precious.... But I must tell you at once, I can't wait a minute longer....

ANIA (*without enthusiasm*): What is it this time?...

DOONIASHA: Yepihodov, the clerk, proposed to me just after Easter.

ANIA: You never talk about anything else.... (*Tidies her hair.*) I've lost all my hairpins.... (*She is very tired and can hardly keep on her feet.*)

DOONIASHA: I really don't know what to think. He loves me...he does love me so!

ANIA (*looking through the door into her room, tenderly*): My own room, my own windows, just as if I had never been away! I'm home again! Tomorrow I'm going to get up and run straight into the garden! Oh, if only I could go to bed and sleep now! I couldn't sleep all the way back, I was so worried.

DOONIASHA: Piotr Serghyeevich arrived the day before yesterday.

ANIA (*joyfully*): Pyetia!

DOONIASHA: He's sleeping in the bath-house, and living there, too. 'I wouldn't like to inconvenience them,' he said. (*Looks at her watch.*) I ought to wake him up, but Varvara Mihailovna told me not to. 'Don't you wake him,' she said.

Enter VARIA *with a bunch of keys at her waist.*

VARIA: Dooniasha, make some coffee, quick! Mamma is asking for coffee.

DOONIASHA: It'll be ready in a moment. (*Goes out.*)

VARIA: Thank God, you've arrived. You're home again. (*Embracing her.*) My darling's come back! My precious!

ANIA: If you only knew the things I had to put up with!

VARIA: I can just imagine it.

ANIA: I left just before Easter: it was cold then. Charlotta never stopped talking, never left off doing her silly conjuring tricks all the way. Why did you make me take Charlotta?

VARIA: But how could you go alone, darling? At seventeen!

ANIA: When we arrived in Paris it was cold and snowing. My French was awful. Mamma was living on the fifth floor, and when I got there she had visitors. There were some French ladies there and an old priest with a little book, and the room was full of cigarette smoke, so untidy and uncomfortable. Suddenly I felt so sorry for Mamma, so sorry, that I took her head between my hands, and just couldn't let it go.... Afterwards Mamma cried and was very sweet to me.

VARIA (*tearfully*): I can hardly bear listening to you....

ANIA: She had already sold her villa near Mentone, and she had nothing left, positively nothing. And I hadn't any money left either, not a penny: I had hardly enough to get to Paris. And Mamma couldn't grasp that! In station restaurants she would order the most expensive dishes and tip the waiters a rouble each. Charlotta was just the same. And Yasha expected a full-course dinner for himself: it was simply dreadful. You know, Yasha is Mamma's valet, we brought him with us.

VARIA: Yes, I've seen the wretch.

ANIA: Well, how are things going? Have we paid the interest?

VARIA: Far from it.

ANIA: Oh dear! Oh dear!

VARIA: The estate will be up for sale in August.

ANIA: Oh dear!

LOPAKHIN (*puts his head through the door and bleats*): Me-e-e.... (*Disappears.*)

VARIA (*tearfully*): I'd like to give him this.... (*Clenches her fist.*)

ANIA (*her arms round* VARIA, *dropping her voice*): Varia, has he proposed to you?

VARIA *shakes her head.*

But he loves you.... Why don't you talk it over with him, what are you waiting for?

VARIA: I don't believe anything will come of it. He's too busy, he's no time to think of me.... He takes no notice of me at all. I'd rather he didn't come, it makes me miserable to see him. Everyone's talking of our wedding, everyone's congratulating me, but in fact there's nothing in it, it's all a kind of dream. (*In a changed tone of voice.*) You've got a new broach, a bee, isn't it?

ANIA (*sadly*): Mamma bought it for me. (*She goes into her room and now speaks gaily, like a child.*) You know, I went up in a balloon in Paris!

VARIA: My darling's home again! My precious girl!

(DOONIASHA *returns with a coffee-pot and prepares coffee.*)

VARIA (*standing by* ANIA'S *door*): You know, dearest, as I go about the house doing my odd jobs, I'm always dreaming and dreaming. If only we could marry you to some rich man, I feel my mind would be at ease. I'd go away then, first to a hermitage, then on to Kiev, to Moscow...walking from one holy place to another. I'd go on and on. Oh, what a beautiful life!

ANIA: The birds are singing in the garden. What time is it?

VARIA: It must be gone two. Time you went to bed, darling. (*Goes into* ANIA'S *room.*) A beautiful life!

Enter YASHA, *carrying a travelling rug and a small bag.*

YASHA (*crossing the stage, in an affectedly genteel voice*): May I go through here?

DOONIASHA: I can hardly recognize you, Yasha. You've changed so abroad.

YASHA: Hm! And who are you?

DOONIASHA: When you left here, I was no bigger than this.... (*Shows her height from the floor with her hand.*) I'm Dooniasha, Fiodor Kosoyedov's daughter. You can't remember!

YASHA: Hm! Quite a little peach! (*Looks round, puts his arms round her; she cries out and drops a saucer.* YASHA *goes out quickly.*)

VARIA (*in the doorway, crossly*): What's going on here?

DOONIASHA (*tearfully*): I've broken a saucer.

VARIA: That's a good omen.

ANIA (*coming out of her room*): We ought to warn Mamma that Pyetia is here.

VARIA: I gave orders not to wake him.

ANIA (*pensively*): It was six years ago that father died, and then, only a month after that, little brother Grisha was drowned in the river. He was only seven, such a pretty little boy! Mamma couldn't bear it and went away... she never looked back. (*Shivers.*) How well I understand her! If she only knew how I understand her! (*Pause.*) And, of course, Pyetia Trofimov was Grisha's tutor, he might remind her....

Enter FEERS, *wearing a jacket and a white waistcoat.*

FEERS (*goes to the coffee-pot, preoccupied*): Madam will have her coffee here. (*Puts on white gloves.*) Is the coffee ready?

(*To* DOONIASHA, *severely.*) What about the cream?

DOONIASHA: Oh, my goodness! (*Goes out quickly.*)

FEERS (*fussing around the coffee-pot*): The girl's daft ...(*Mutters.*) From Paris.... The master used to go to Paris years ago.... Used to go by coach.... (*Laughs.*)

VARIA: Feers, what are you laughing at?

FEERS: What can I get you, Madam? (*Happily.*) The mistress is home again! Home at last! I don't mind if I die now.... (*Weeps with joy.*)

Enter LIUBOV ANDRYEEVNA, LOPAKHIN, GAYEV *and* SIMEONOV-PISHCHIK, *the last wearing a long peasant coat of finely-woven cloth and wide trousers tucked inside high boots.* GAYEV, *as he comes in, moves his arms and body as if he were playing billiards.*

LIUBOV ANDRYEEVNA: How does it go now? Let me think.... I pot the red.... I go in off into the middle pocket!

GAYEV: I pot into the corner pocket...Years ago you and I slept in this room, little brother and sister together; and now I'm fifty-one, strange as it may seem.

LOPAKHIN: Yes, time flies.

GAYEV: What?

LOPAKHIN: Time flies, I say.

GAYEV: This place smells of patchouli....

ANIA: I think I'll go to bed. Good-night, Mamma. (*Kisses her.*)

LIUBOV ANDRYEEVNA: My precious child! (*Kisses her hands.*) You're glad to be home, aren't you? I still feel dazed.

ANIA: Good-night, Uncle.

GAYEV (*kisses her face and hands*): God bless you! How like your mother you are! (*To his sister.*) You looked exactly like her at her age, Liuba.

ANIA *shakes hands with* LOPAKHIN *and* PISHCHIK, *goes out and shuts the door after her.*

LIUBOV ANDRYEEVNA: She's very tired.

PISHCHIK: It's a long journey.

VARIA (*to* LOPAKHIN *and* PISHCHIK): Well, gentlemen? It's past two, time to break up the party.

LIUBOV ANDRYEEVNA (*laughs*): You're just the same, Varia. (*Draws* VARIA *to her and kisses her.*) Let me have some coffee, then we'll all go. (FEERS *places a cushion under her feet.*) Thank you, my dear. I've got into the habit of drinking coffee. I drink it day and night. Thank you, my dear old friend. (*Kisses* FEERS.)

VARIA: I'd better see if all the luggage is there. (*Goes out.*)

LIUBOV ANDRYEEVNA: Is it really me sitting here? (*Laughs.*) I feel like dancing and flinging my arms about. (*Hides her face in her hands.*) What if I'm just dreaming? God, how I love my own country! I love it so much, I could hardly see it from the train, I was crying all the time. (*Through tears.*) However, I must drink my coffee. Thank you, Feers, thank you, my dear old friend. I am so glad I found you still alive.

FEERS: The day before yesterday.

GAYEV: He doesn't hear very well.

LOPAKHIN: I've got to leave for Kharkov soon after four. What a nuisance! I'd like to have a good look at you, to have a talk.... You look as lovely as ever.

PISHCHIK (*breathing heavily*): She looks prettier. In her Parisian clothes...enough to turn anybody's head!

LOPAKHIN: Your brother here—Leonid Andryeevich—says that I'm a country bumpkin, a tight-fisted peasant, but I don't take any notice of that. Let him say what he likes. The only thing I want is for you to have faith in me as you did before. Merciful God! My father was your father's serf, and your grandfather's, too, but you did so much for me in the past that I forget everything and love you as if you were my own sister...more than my own sister.

LIUBOV ANDRYEEVNA: I just can't sit still, I simply can't! (*She jumps up and walks about the room in great agitation.*) This happiness is too much for me. You can laugh at me, I'm foolish.... My dear bookcase! (*Kisses bookcase.*) My own little table!

GAYEV: You know, old Nanny died while you were away.

LIUBOV ANDRYEEVNA (*Sits down and drinks coffee*): Yes, I know. May the Kingdom of Heaven be hers. They wrote to tell me.

GAYEV: Anastasiy died, too. Petrooshka Kosoy has left me and is working for the police in town. (*Takes a box of boiled sweets from his pocket and puts one in his mouth.*)

PISHCHIK: My daughter, Dashenka, sends her greetings to you.

LOPAKHIN: I feel I'd like to tell you something nice, something jolly. (*Glances at his watch.*) I'll have to go in a moment, there's no time to talk. However, I could tell you in a few words. You know, of course, that your cherry orchard is going to be sold to pay your debts. The auction is to take place on the twenty-second of August, but there's no need for you to worry. You can sleep in peace, my dear; there's a way out. This is my plan, please listen carefully. Your estate is only twenty miles from town, and the railway line is not far away. Now, if your cherry orchard and the land along the river are divided into plots and leased out for summer residences you'll have a yearly income of at least twenty-five thousand roubles.

GAYEV: But what nonsense!

LIUBOV ANDRYEEVNA: I don't quite understand you, Yermolai Aleksyeevich.

LOPAKHIN: You'll charge the tenants at least twenty-five roubles a year for a plot of one acre, and if you advertise now, I'm prepared to stake any amount you like that you won't have a spot of land unoccupied by the autumn: it will be snatched up. In fact, I really feel I must congratulate you, you're saved after all! It's a marvellous situation and the river's deep enough for bathing. But, of course, the place will have to be cleaned up, put in order. For instance, all the old outbuildings will have to be pulled down, as well as this house which is no good to anybody. The old cherry orchard should be cut down, too.

LIUBOV ANDRYEEVNA: Cut down? My dear man, forgive me, you don't seem to understand. If there's one thing interesting, one thing really outstanding in the whole county, it's our cherry orchard.

LOPAKHIN: The only outstanding thing about this orchard is that it's very large. It only produces a crop every other year, and then there's nobody to buy it.

GAYEV: This orchard is actually mentioned in the Encyclopaedia.

LOPAKHIN (*glancing at his watch*): If you can't think clearly about it, or come to a decision, the cherry orchard and the whole estate as well will be sold by auction. You must decide! There's no other way out, I assure you. There's no other way.

FEERS: In the old days, forty or fifty years ago, the cherries were dried, preserved, marinaded, made into jam, and sometimes…

GAYEV: Be quiet, Feers.

FEERS: And sometimes, whole cartloads of dried cherries were sent to Moscow and Kharkov. The money they fetched! And the dried cherries in those days were soft, juicy, sweet, tasty…. They knew how to do it then …they had a recipe….

LIUBOV ANDRYEEVNA: And where is that recipe now?

FEERS: Forgotten. No one can remember it.

PISHCHIK (*to* LIUBOV ANDRYEEVNA): What was it like in Paris? Did you eat frogs?

LIUBOV ANDRYEEVNA: I ate crocodiles.

PISHCHIK: Fancy that!

LOPAKHIN: Up to just recently there were only gentry and peasants living in the country, but now there are all these summer residents. All the towns, even quite small ones, are surrounded with villas. And probably in the course of the next twenty years or so, these people will multiply tremendously. At present they merely drink tea on the verandah, but they might start cultivating their plots of land, and then your cherry orchard would be gay with life and wealth and luxury….

GAYEV (*indignantly*): What nonsense! *Enter* VARIA *and* YASHA.

VARIA: Here are two telegrams for you, Mamma dear. (*Picks out a key and unlocks an old bookcase with a jingling noise.*) Here they are.

LIUBOV ANDRYEEVNA: They are from Paris. (*Tears them up without reading them.*) I've finished with Paris.

GAYEV: Do you know, Liuba, how old this bookcase is? A week ago I pulled out the bottom drawer, and I found some figures burnt in the wood. It was made exactly a hundred years ago. What do you think of that, eh? We ought to celebrate its anniversary. An inanimate object, true, but still—a bookcase!

PISHCHIK (*astonished*): A hundred years! Fancy that!

GAYEV: Yes…. This is a valuable piece of furniture. (*Feeling round the bookcase with his hands.*) My dear, venerable bookcase! I salute you! For more than a hundred years you have devoted yourself to the highest ideals of goodness and justice. For a hundred years you have never failed to fill us with an urge to useful work; several generations of our family have had their courage sustained and their faith in a better future fortified by your silent call; you have fostered in us the ideal of public good and social consciousness. *Pause.*

LOPAKHIN: Yes….

LIUBOV ANDRYEEVNA: You're just the same, Lionia.

GAYEV (*slightly embarrassed*): I pot into the corner pocket! I pot into the middle pocket!…

LOPAKHIN (*glances at his watch*): Well, it's time for me to be going.

YASHA (*brings medicine to* LIUBOV ANDRYEEVNA): Would you care to take your pills now?

PISHCHIK: Don't take medicines, my dear…they don't do you any good…or harm either. Let me have them. (*Takes the box from her, pours the pills into the palm of his hand, blows on them, puts them all into his mouth and takes a drink of kvass.*) There!

LIUBOV ANDRYEEVNA (*alarmed*): But you're mad!

PISHCHIK: I've taken all the pills.

LOPAKHIN: What a digestion!

All laugh.

FEERS: His honour came to see us in Holy Week, and ate half-a-bucketful of salt cucumbers. (*Mutters.*)

LIUBOV ANDRYEEVNA: What is it he's saying?

VARIA: He's been muttering for the last three years. We're accustomed to it.

YASHA: It's his age….

CHARLOTTA IVANOVNA, *very thin and tightly laced in a white dress, with a lorgnette at her waist, passes across the stage.*

LOPAKHIN: Forgive me, Charlotta Ivanovna, I haven't yet had time to say how d'you do to you. (*Tries to kiss her hand.*)

CHARLOTTA (*withdrawing her hand*): If you were permitted to kiss a lady's hand, you'd want to kiss her elbow next, and then her shoulder.

LOPAKHIN: I'm unlucky today.

All laugh.

Charlotta Ivanovna, do a trick for us.

CHARLOTTA: There's no need to, now. I want to go to bed. (*Goes out.*)

LOPAKHIN: I'll see you in three weeks' time. (*Kisses* LIUBOV ANDRYEEVNA'S *hand.*) Meanwhile, good-bye. Time to go. (*To* GAYEV.) Au revoir. (*Embraces* PISHCHIK.) Au revoir. (*Shakes hands with* VARIA, *then with* FEERS *and* YASHA.) I don't want to go, really. (*To* LIUBOV ANDRYEEVNA.) If you think over this question of country villas and come to a decision, let me know, and I'll get you a loan of fifty thousand or more. Think it over seriously.

VARIA (*crossly*): Will you ever go away?

LOPAKHIN: I'm going, I'm going. (*Goes out.*)

GAYEV: What a boor! I beg your pardon…. Varia's going to marry him, he's Varia's precious fiancé.

VARIA: Place don't say anything uncalled for, Uncle dear.

LIUBOV ANDRYEEVNA: Well, Varia, I shall be very glad. He's a good man.

PISHCHIK: He's a man…let's admit it…a most admirable fellow…. My Dashenka says so, too…she says all sorts of things…. (*He drops asleep and snores, but wakes up again at once.*) Incidentally, my dear, will you lend me two hundred and forty roubles? I've got to pay the interest on the mortgage tomorrow….

VARIA (*in alarm*): We haven't got it, we really haven't!

LIUBOV ANDRYEEVNA: It's quite true, I have nothing.

PISHCHIK: It'll turn up. (*Laughs.*) I never lose hope. Sometimes I think everything's lost, I'm ruined, and then—lo and behold!—a railway line is built through my land, and they pay me for it! Something or other is sure to happen, tomorrow, if not today. Perhaps Dashenka will win two hundred thousand roubles. She's got a lottery ticket.

LIUBOV ANDRYEEVNA: I've finished my coffee; now I can go and rest.

FEERS (*brushing* GAYEV, *admonishing him*): You've put on the wrong pair of trousers again! What am I to do with you?

VARIA (*in a low voice*): Ania's asleep. (*Quietly opens a window.*) The sun has risen, it's warmer already. Look, Mamma dear, how wonderful the trees are! Heavens, what lovely air! The starlings are singing!

GAYEV (*opens another window*): The orchard is all white. You haven't forgotten, Liuba? How straight this long avenue is—quite straight, just like a ribbon that's been stretched taut. It glitters on moonlit nights. Do you remember? You haven't forgotten?

LIUBOV ANDRYEEVNA (*looks through the window at the orchard*): Oh, my childhood, my innocent childhood! I used to sleep in this nursery; I used to look on to the orchard from here, and I woke up happy every morning. In those days the orchard was just as it is now, nothing has changed. (*Laughs happily.*) All, all white! Oh, my orchard! After the dark, stormy autumn and the cold winter, you are young and joyous again; the angels have not forsaken you! If only this burden could be taken from me, if only I could forget my past!

GAYEV: Yes, and now the orchard is going to be sold to pay our debts, strange as it seems....

LIUBOV ANDRYEEVNA: Look, there's Mother walking through the orchard...in a white dress! (*Laughs happily.*) It is her!

GAYEV: Where?

VARIA: Bless you, Mamma dear!

LIUBOV ANDRYEEVNA: It's no one, I only imagined it. Over there, you see, on the right, by the turning to the summer house there's a small white tree and it's bending over...it looks like a woman.

Enter TROFIMOV. *He is dressed in a shabby student's uniform, and wears glasses.*

LIUBOV ANDRYEEVNA: What a wonderful orchard! Masses of white blossom, the blue sky....

TROFIMOV: Liubov Andryeevna! (*She turns to him.*) I'll just make my bow and go at once. (*Kisses her hand warmly.*) I was told to wait until the morning, but it was too much for my patience.

LIUBOV ANDRYEEVNA *looks at him, puzzled.*

VARIA (*through tears*): This is Pyetia Trofimov.

TROFIMOV: Pyetia Trofimov, I used to be tutor to your Grisha. Have I really changed so much?

LIUBOV ANDRYEEVNA *puts her arms round him and weeps quietly.*

GAYEV (*embarrassed*): Now, now, Liuba....

VARIA (*weeps*): Didn't I tell you to wait until tomorrow, Pyetia?

LIUBOV ANDRYEEVNA: My Grisha...my little boy...Grisha...my son....

VARIA: There's nothing for it, Mamma darling. It was God's will.

TROYFIMOV (*gently, with emotion*): Don't, don't...

LIUBOV ANDRYEEVNA (*quietly weeping*): My little boy was lost...drowned.... What for? What for, my friend? (*More quietly.*) Ania's asleep there, and here I am, shouting and making a scene. Well, Pyetia? How is it you've lost your good looks? Why have you aged so?

TROFIMOV: A peasant woman in the train called me 'that moth-eaten gent'.

LIUBOV ANDRYEEVNA: In those days you were quite a boy, a nice young student, and now your hair is thin, you wear glasses.... Are you still a student? (*Walks to the door.*)

TROFIMOV: I expect I shall be a student to the end of my days.

LIUBOV ANDRYEEVNA (*kisses her brother, then* VARIA): Well, go to bed now. You have aged, too, Leonid.

PISHCHIK (*following her*): So you're going to bed now? Och, my gout! I'd better stay the night here. And tomorrow morning, Liubov Andryeevna, my dear, I'd like to borrow those two hundred and forty roubles.

GAYEV: How the fellow keeps at it!

PISHCHIK: Two hundred and forty roubles.... You see, I've got to pay the interest on the mortgage.

LIUBOV ANDRYEEVNA: I have no money, my dear.

PISHCHIK: I'll pay you back, my dear lady. It's a trifling amount, after all.

LIUBOV ANDRYEEVNA: Very well, then. Leonid will give you the money. You give him the money, Leonid.

GAYEV: I'll be delighted; anything he wants, of course!

LIUBOV ANDRYEEVNA: What else can we do? He needs it. He'll pay it back.

LIUBOV ANDRYEEVNA, TROFIMOV, PISHCHIK and FEERS *go out,* GAYEV, VARIA *and* YASHA *remain.*

GAYEV: My sister hasn't lost her habit of throwing money away. (*To* YASHA.) Out of the way, my man, you smell of the kitchen.

YASHA (*with a sneer*): I see you're just the same as you used to be, Leonid Andryeevich.

GAYEV: What's that? (*To* VARIA.) What did he say?

VARIA (*to* YASHA): Your mother's come from the village, she's been sitting in the servants' hall since yesterday, wanting to see you.

YASHA: I wish she'd leave me alone!

VARIA: You...aren't you ashamed of yourself?

YASHA: It's quite unnecessary. She could have come tomorrow. (YASHA *goes out.*)

VARIA: Dear Mamma is just the same as she used to be, she hasn't changed a bit. If she had her own way, she'd give away everything.

GAYEV: Yes.... You know, if a lot of cures are suggested for a disease, it means that the disease is incurable. I've been thinking and puzzling my brains, and I've thought of plenty of ways out, plenty—which means there aren't any. It would be a good thing if somebody left us some money, or if we married off our Ania to some very rich man, or if one of us went to Yaroslavl and tried our luck with the old aunt, the Countess. You know she's very rich.

VARIA (*weeping*): If only God would help us.

GAYEV: Do stop blubbering! The Countess is very rich, but she doesn't like us.... First, because my sister married a solicitor, and not a nobleman....

ANIA *appears in the doorway.*

She married a man who wasn't of noble birth...and then you can't say her behaviour's been exactly virtuous. She's a good, kind, lovable person, and I'm very fond of her, but whatever extenuating circumstances you may think of, you must admit that she's a bit easy-going morally. You can sense it in every movement....

VARIA (*in a whisper*): Ania's standing in the doorway.

GAYEV: What? (*A pause.*) Funny thing, something's got into my right eye.... I can't see properly. And on Thursday, when I was at the District Court....

ANIA *comes in.*

VARIA: Well, why aren't you asleep, Ania?

ANIA: I can't get to sleep. I just can't.

GAYEV: My dear little girl! (*Kisses* ANIA'S *face and hands.*) My dear child! (*Through tears.*) You're not just a niece to me, you're an angel, you're everything to me. Please believe me, believe...

ANIA: I believe you, Uncle. Everyone loves you, respects you...but, dear Uncle, you oughtn't to talk, you ought to try to keep quiet. What was that you were saying just now about my mother, about your own sister? Why were you saying it?

GAYEV: Yes, yes! (*He takes her hand and puts it over his face.*) You're quite right, it's dreadful! My God! My God! And the speech I made today in front of the bookcase...so foolish! And it was only after I'd finished that I realized it was foolish.

VARIA: It's true, Uncle dear, you ought to try to keep quiet. Just keep quiet, that's all.

ANIA: If you keep quiet, you'll be happier in yourself.

GAYEV: I'll be quiet. (*Kisses* ANIA'S *and* VARIA'S *hands.*) I'll be quiet. But I must tell you something important. Last Thursday I went to the District Court, and I got talking with some friends, and from what they said it looks as if it might be possible to get a loan on promissory notes, in order to pay the interest to the bank.

VARIA: If only God would help us!

GAYEV: I'll go there again on Tuesday and have another talk. (*To* VARIA.) Don't keep crying. (*To* ANIA.) Your Mother's going to have a talk with Lopakhin: he won't refuse her, of course. And after you've had a rest, you will go to Yaroslavl, to see the Countess, your grandmother. And so we'll approach the matter from three angles, and—the thing's done! We shall pay the interest, I'm sure of it. (*He puts a sweet into his mouth.*) I swear on my honour, on anything you like, that the estate will not be sold! (*Excited.*) I'll stake my happiness! Here's my hand, you can call me a good-for-nothing liar if I allow the auction to take place. I swear on my soul!

ANIA (*calmer, with an air of happiness*): How good you are, Uncle, and how sensible! (*Puts her arms round him.*) I feel calmer now. I feel so calm and happy. *Enter* FEERS.

FEERS (*reproachfully*): Leonid Andryeevich, aren't you ashamed of yourself? When are you going to bed?

GAYEV: Presently, presently. You go away, Feers. I don't need your help. Well, children dear, bye-bye now.... All the news tomorrow, you must go to bed now. (*Kisses* ANIA *and* VARIA.) You know, I'm a man of the 'eighties. People don't think much of that period, but all the same, I can say that I've suffered quite a lot in the course of my life for my convictions. It's not for nothing that the peasants love me. You have to know the peasants! You have to know from which side…

ANIA: You're starting it again, Uncle!

VARIA: You'd better keep quiet, Uncle dear.

FEERS (*sternly*): Leonid Andryeevich!

GAYEV: Coming, coming! Go to bed! In off the cushion! I pot the white!…(*Goes out;* FEERS *hobbles after him.*)

ANIA: My mind is at rest now. I don't really feel like going to Yaroslavl, I don't like Grand-mamma; but still, I'm not worrying. I'm grateful to Uncle. (*She sits down.*)

VARIA: I must get some sleep. I'm going. Oh, by the way, while you were away something unpleasant happened here. You know, there are only a few old servants living in the servants' quarters: just Yefemooshka, Polia, Yevstignei and Karp. Well, they let some tramps sleep there, and I didn't say anything about it. But some time afterwards I heard some gossip; people said I had ordered them to be fed on nothing but dried peas. Because I was mean, you see…. Yevstignei was at the bottom of it all. 'Well,' I said to myself, 'if that's how the matter stands, just you wait!' So I sent for Yevstignei. (*Yawns.*) In he comes. 'What's all this, Yevstignei,' I said to him, 'id-iot that you are.'…(*She walks up to* ANIA.) An-ichka! (*A pause.*) She's asleep!…(*Takes her arm*) Come to bed! Come! (*Leads her away.*) My darling's fallen asleep! Come….

They go towards the door. The sound of a shep-herd's pipe is heard from far away, beyond the or-chard. TROFIMOV *crosses the stage, but, seeing* VARIA *and* ANIA, *stops.*

VARIA: Sh-sh! She's asleep…asleep…Come, my dear.

ANIA (*softly, half-asleep*): I'm so tired…. I can hear bells tinkling all the time…. Uncle…dear… Mamma and Uncle….

VARIA: Come, darling, come…. (*They go into* ANIA'S *room.*)

TROFIMOV (*deeply moved*): Ania…my one bright star! My spring flower!

CURTAIN

ACT TWO

An old wayside shrine in the open country; it leans slightly to one side and has evidently been long aban-doned. Beside it there are a well, an old seat and a number of large stones which apparently served as gravestones in the past. A road leads to GAYEV'S *es-tate. On one side and some distance away is a row of dark poplars, and it is there that the cherry orchard be-gins. Further away is seen a line of telegraph poles, and beyond them, on the horizon, the vague outlines of a large town, visible only in very good, clear weather.*

The sun is about to set. CHARLOTTA, YASHA *and* DOONIASHA *are sitting on the seat;* YEPIHODOV *is standing near by, playing a guitar; all look pen-sive.* CHARLOTTA *is wearing a man's old peaked cap; she has taken a shot-gun off her shoulder and is ad-justing a buckle on the strap.*

CHARLOTTA (*thoughtfully*): I don't know how old I am. I haven't got a proper identity card, you see…and I keep on imagining I'm still quite young. When I was little, father and mother used to tour the fairs and give per-formances—very good ones they were, too. And I used to jump the *salto-mortale* and do all sorts of other tricks. When Papa and Mamma died, a German lady took me into her house and began to give me lessons. So then I grew up and became a governess. But where I come from and who I am, I don't know. Who my parents were—perhaps they weren't properly married—I don't know. (*She takes a cucumber from her pocket and be-gins to eat it.*) I don't know anything. (*Pause.*) I'm longing to talk to someone, but there isn't anyone. I haven't anyone….

YEPIHODOV (*plays the guitar and sings*): 'What care I for the noisy world?…What are friends and foes to me?' How pleasant it is to play the mandoline!

DOONIASHA: That's a guitar, not a mandoline. (*She looks at herself in a hand mirror and pow-ders her face.*)

YEPIHODOV: To a man that's crazy with love this is a mandoline. (*Sings quietly.*) 'If only my heart might be warmed by the ardour of love requited.'…

YASHA *joins in.*

CHARLOTTA: How dreadful their singing is!... Ach! It is like the jackals.

DOONIASHA (*to* YASHA): You are lucky to have been abroad!

YASHA: Of course I am. I'm bound to agree with you there. (*Yawns, then lights a cigar.*)

YEPIHODOV: Stands to reason. Abroad everything's been in full swing.... I mean to say, everything's been going on for ever so long.

YASHA: Obviously.

YEPIHODOV: Personally, I'm a cultured sort of fellow, I read all sorts of extraordinary books, you know, but somehow I can't seem to make out where I'm going, what it is I really want, I mean to say—to live or to shoot myself, so to speak. All the same, I always carry a revolver on me. Here it is. (*Shows the revolver.*)

CHARLOTTA: I have finished. Now I'm going. (*Slips the strap of the gun over her shoulder.*) Yes, you are a very clever man, Yepihodov, and rather frightening, too; the women must fall madly in love with you! Brrr! (*Walks off.*) All these clever people are so stupid, I have no one to talk to. I am so lonely, always so lonely, no one belongs to me, and...and who I am, what I exist for, nobody knows.... (*Goes out leisurely.*)

YEPIHODOV: Candidly speaking, and I do want to keep strictly to the point, by the way, but I feel I simply must explain that Fate, so to speak, treats me absolutely without mercy, just like a storm treats a small ship, as it were. I mean to say, supposing I'm wrong, for instance, then why should I wake up this morning and suddenly see a simply colossal spider sitting on my chest? like this.... (*Makes a gesture with both hands.*) Or supposing I pick up a jug to have a drink of kvass, there's sure to be something frightful inside it, such as a cockroach. (*Pause.*) Have you read Buckle? (*Pause.*) May I trouble you for a word, Avdotya Fiodorovna?

DOONIASHA: All right, carry on.

YEPIHODOV: I'd very much like to speak to you alone. (*Sighs.*)

DOONIASHA (*embarrassed*): Very well then...only will you bring me my little cape first.... It's hanging beside the wardrobe. It's rather chilly here....

YEPIHODOV: Very well, I'll bring it.... Now I know what to do with my revolver. (*Picks up his guitar and goes, twanging it.*)

YASHA: Two-and-twenty misfortunes! He's a stupid fellow, between you and me. (*Yawns.*)

DOONIASHA: I hope to God he won't shoot himself. (*Pause.*) I've got sort of anxious, worrying all the time. I came to live here with the Master and Mistress when I was still a little girl you see. Now I've got out of the way of living a simple life, and my hands are as white...as white as a young lady's. I've grown sensitive and delicate, just as if I was one of the nobility; I'm afraid of everything.... Just afraid. If you deceive me, Yasha, I don't know what will happen to my nerves.

YASHA (*kisses her*): Little peach! Mind you, a girl ought to keep herself in hand, you know. Personally I dislike it more than anything if a girl doesn't behave herself.

DOONIASHA: I love you so much, so much! You're educated, you can reason about everything. *Pause.*

YASHA (*yawns*): Y-yes.... To my way of thinking, it's like this: if a girl loves somebody, it means she's immoral. (*Pause.*) It's nice to smoke a cigar in the open air.... (*Listens.*) Someone's coming this way. Our ladies and gentlemen.... (DOONIASHA *impulsively puts her arms round him.*) Go home now, as if you'd been down to the river bathing; go by this path, or you'll meet them, and they might think I've been keeping company with you. I couldn't stand that.

DOONIASHA (*coughing softly*): My head's aching from that cigar.... (*Goes out.*)

YASHA *remains sitting by the shrine. Enter* LIUBOV ANDRYEEVNA, GAYEV *and* LOPAKHIN.

LOPAKHIN: We must decide once and for all: time won't wait. After all, my question's quite a simple one. Do you consent to lease your land for villas, or don't you? You can answer in one word: yes or no? Just one word!

LIUBOV ANDRYEEVNA: Who's been smoking such abominable cigars here? (*Sits down.*)

GAYEV: How very convenient it is having a railway here. (*Sits down.*) Here we are—we've been up to town for lunch and we're back home already. I pot the red into the middle pocket! I'd like to go indoors now and have just one game....

LIUBOV ANDRYEEVNA: You've plenty of time.

LOPAKHIN: Just one word! (*Beseechingly.*) Do give me an answer!

GAYEV (*yawns*): What do you say?

LIUBOV ANDRYEEVNA (*looking into her purse*): Yesterday I had a lot of money, but today there's hardly any left. My poor Varia is feeding everyone on milk soups to economize; the old servants in the kitchen get nothing but dried peas to eat, and here I am, spending money senselessly, I don't know why.... (*She drops the purse, scattering gold coins.*) Now I've scattered it all over the place.... (*Annoyed.*)

YASHA: Allow me, Madam, I'll pick them up in a minute. (*Gathers up the money.*)

LIUBOV ANDRYEEVNA: Thank you, Yasha.... Why did I go out to lunch? It was quite vile, that restaurant of yours, with its beastly music; and the table-cloths smelt of soap, too.... Need one drink so much, Lionia? Need one eat so much? And talk so much? Today at the restaurant you talked too much again, and it was all so pointless. About the seventies, about the decadents. And who to? Fancy talking about the decadents to the restaurant waiters!

LOPAKHIN: Yes, fancy.

GAYEV (*waving his hand*): I'm hopeless, I know. (*To* YASHA, *with irritation.*) Why are you always buzzing about in front of me?

YASHA (*laughs*): I can never hear you talk without laughing.

GAYEV (*to his sister*): Either he goes, or I do....

LIUBOV ANDRYEEVNA: Go away, Yasha, go along.

YASHA (*hands the purse to* LIUBOV ANDRYEEVNA): I'll go now. (*He can hardly restrain his laughter.*) This very minute.... (*Goes out.*)

LOPAKHIN: You know, that wealthy fellow Deriganov, he's intending to buy your estate. They say he's coming to the auction himself.

LIUBOV ANDRYEEVNA: Where did you hear that?

LOPAKHIN: They were saying so in town.

GAYEV: Our Aunt in Yaroslavl promised to send us money but when and how much it will be we don't know.

LOPAKHIN: How much will she send you? A hundred thousand? Two hundred?

LIUBOV ANDRYEEVNA: Well, hardly.... Ten or twelve thousand, perhaps. We'll be thankful for that much.

LOPAKHIN: You must forgive me for saying it, but really I've never met such feckless, unbusiness-like, queer people as you are. You are told in plain language that your estate is up for sale, and you simply don't seem to understand it.

LIUBOV ANDRYEEVNA: But what are we to do? Tell us, what?

LOPAKHIN: I keep on telling you. Every day I tell you the same thing. You must lease the cherry orchard and the land for villas, and you must do it now, as soon as possible. The auction is going to be held almost at once. Please do try to understand! Once you definitely decide to have the villas, you'll be able to borrow as much money as you like, and then you'll be out of the wood.

LIUBOV ANDRYEEVNA: Villas and summer visitors! Forgive me, but it's so vulgar.

GAYEV: I absolutely agree with you.

LOPAKHIN: Honestly, I feel I shall burst into tears, or shriek, or fall down and faint. I simply can't stand it. You've literally worn me out. (*To* GAYEV.) An old woman, that's what you are!

GAYEV: What's that?

LOPAKHIN: An old woman!

LIUBOV ANDRYEEVNA (*alarmed*): No, don't go, do stay, my dear. Please stay! Perhaps we could think of something.

LOPAKHIN: It hardly seems worth trying.

LIUBOV ANDRYEEVNA: Don't go, please! Somehow it's more cheerful with you here. (*Pause.*) I keep expecting something dreadful to happen...as if the house were going to fall down on us.

GAYEV (*in deep thought*): I cannon off the cushions! I pot into the middle pocket....

LIUBOV ANDRYEEVNA: We've sinned too much....

LOPAKHIN: Sinned, indeed! What were your sins?

GAYEV (*puts a sweet into his mouth*): They say I've eaten up my whole fortune in sweets. (*Laughs.*)

LIUBOV ANDRYEEVNA: Oh, my sins! Look at the way I've always squandered money, continually. It was sheer madness. And then I got married to a man who only knew how to get into debt. Champagne killed him—he was a terrific drinker—and then, worse luck I fell in love with someone else. We had an affair, and just at that very time—it was my first punishment, a blow straight to my heart— my little boy was drowned here, in this river…and then I went abroad. I went away for good, and never meant to return, I never meant to see the river again…I just shut my eyes and ran away in a frenzy of grief, but *he*…he followed me. It was so cruel and brutal of him! I bought a villa near Mentone because he fell ill there, you see, and for three years I never had any rest, day or night. He was a sick man, he quite wore me out; my soul seemed to dry right up. Then, last year when the villa had to be sold to pay the debts, I went to Paris, and there he robbed me and left me; he went away and lived with another woman…. I tried to poison myself… It was all so foolish, so shameful! And then suddenly I felt an urge to come back to Russia, to my own country and my little girl…. (*Wipes away her tears.*) Oh, Lord, Lord, be merciful, forgive me my sins! Don't punish me any more! (*Takes a telegram out of her pocket.*) I had this from Paris today. He's asking my forgiveness, begging me to return…. (*Tears up the telegram.*) Sounds like music somewhere. (*Listens.*)

GAYEV: That's our famous Jewish band. Do you remember, four violins, a flute and a contrabass?

LIUBOV ANDRYEEVNA: Is that still in existence? It would be nice to get them to come to the house one day, and we could have a little dance.

LOPAKHIN (*listens*): I can't hear anything…. (*Sings quietly.*) 'And the Germans, if you pay, will turn Russian into Frenchman, so they say.'… (*Laughs.*) I saw such a good play at the theatre yesterday. Very amusing.

LIUBOV ANDRYEEVNA: I'm sure it wasn't at all amusing. Instead of going to see plays, you should take a good look at yourself. Just think what a drab kind of life you lead, what a lot of nonsense you talk!

LOPAKHIN: It's perfectly true. Yes, I admit it, we lead an idiotic existence…. (*Pause.*) My Dad was a peasant, a blockhead, he didn't understand anything, and he didn't teach me anything, but just beat me when he was drunk, and always with a stick at that. As a matter of fact, I'm just as much of a fool and a halfwit myself. No one taught me anything, my writing is awful, I'm ashamed even to show it to people: it's just like a pig's.

LIUBOV ANDRYEEVNA: You ought to get married, my friend.

LOPAKHIN: Yes…. That's true.

LIUBOV ANDRYEEVNA: You ought to marry our Varia. She's a nice girl.

LOPAKHIN: Yes.

LIUBOV ANDRYEEVNA: She comes from the common folk, and she's a hard-working girl: she can work the whole day without stopping. But the main thing is that she loves you, and you've been attracted by her for a long time yourself.

LOPAKHIN: Well…. I'm quite willing…. She's a nice girl.
Pause.

GAYEV: I've been offered a job at the bank. Six thousand a year. Have you heard?

LIUBOV ANDRYEEVNA: Indeed I have. You'd better stay where you are.
Enter FEERS *with an overcoat.*

FEERS (*to* GAYEV): Will you please put it on, Sir, it's so chilly.

GAYEV (*Puts on the overcoat*): You *are* a nuisance.

FEERS: Tut, tut! You went off this morning and never told me you were going. (*Looks him over.*)

LIUBOV ANDRYEEVNA: How you've aged, Feers!

FEERS: What can I get you, Madam?

LOPAKHIN: They say, you've aged a lot.

FEERS: I've been alive a long time. They were going to marry me off before your Dad was born. (*Laughs.*) And when Freedom was granted to the people, I'd already been made a chief valet. I wouldn't take my Freedom then, I stayed with the Master and Mistress…. (*Pause.*) I remember everyone was glad at the time, but what they were glad about, no one knew.

LOPAKHIN: Oh, yes, it was a good life all right! At least, people got flogged!

FEERS (*not having heard him*): Rather! The peasants belonged to the gentry, and the gentry belonged to the peasants; but now everything's separate, and you can't understand anything.

GAYEV: Be quiet, Feers. Tomorrow I must go to town. I was promised an introduction to some general or other who'll lend us some money on a promissory note.

LOPAKHIN: Nothing will come of that. And you won't be able to pay the interest, anyway.

LIUBOV ANDRYEEVNA: He's talking through his hat. There aren't any generals. *Enter* TROFI-MOV, ANIA *and* VARIA.

GAYEV: Here come the children.

ANIA: There's Mamma.

LIUBOV ANDRYEEVNA: Come here, my dears. My dear children…. (*Embraces* ANIA *and* VARIA.) If you both only knew how much I love you! Sit down beside me, here.
All sit down.

LOPAKHIN: Our 'eternal student' is always with the young ladies.

TROFIMOV: It's none of your business, anyway.

LOPAKHIN: He'll soon be fifty, yet he's still a student.

TROFIMOV: I wish you'd drop your idiotic jokes.

LOPAKHIN: But why are you getting annoyed? You *are* a queer chap!

TROFIMOV: Why do you keep pestering me?

LOPAKHIN (*laughs*): Just let me ask you one question: what do you make of me?

TROFIMOV: My opinion of you, Yermolai Aleksyeevich, is simply this: you're a wealthy man, and before long you'll be a millionaire; and in so far as a wild beast is necessary because it devours everything in its path and so converts one kind of matter into another, you are necessary also.
Everybody laughs.

VARIA: You'd better tell us about the planets, Pyetia.

LIUBOV ANDRYEEVNA: No, let's continue what we were talking about yesterday.

TROFIMOV: What were we talking about?

GAYEV: About pride.

TROFIMOV: We talked a lot yesterday, but we didn't agree on anything. The proud man, in the sense you understand him, has something mystical about him. Maybe you're right in a way, but if we try to think it out simply, without being too far-fetched about it, the question arises—why should he be proud? Where's the sense in being proud when you consider that Man, as a species, is not very well constructed physiologically, and, in the vast majority of cases is coarse, stupid, and profoundly unhappy, too? We ought to stop all this self-admiration. We ought to—just work.

GAYEV: You'll die just the same, whatever you do.

TROFIMOV: Who knows? And anyway, what does it mean—to die? It may be that Man is possessed of a hundred senses, and only the five that are known to us perish in death, while the remaining ninety-five live on afterwards.

LIUBOV ANDRYEEVNA: How clever you are, Pyetia!

LOPAKHIN (*ironically*): Oh, awfully clever!

TROFIMOV: Humanity is perpetually advancing, always seeking to perfect its own powers. One day all the things that are beyond our grasp at present are going to fall within our reach, only to achieve this we've got to work with all our might, to help the people who are seeking after truth. Here, in Russia, very few people have started to work, so far. Nearly all the members of the intelligentsia that I know care for nothing, do nothing and are still incapable of work. They call themselves 'intelligentsia', but they still talk contemptuously to their servants, they treat the peasants as if they were animals, they study without achieving anything, they don't read anything serious, they just do nothing. As for science, they only talk about it, and they don't understand much about art either. They all look very grave and go about with grim expressions on their faces, and they only discuss important matters and philosophize. Yet all the time anyone can see that our work-people are abominably fed and have to sleep without proper beds, thirty to forty to a room, with bedbugs, bad smells, damp, and immorality everywhere. It's perfectly obvious that all our nice-sounding talk is intended only to mislead ourselves and others. Tell me then, where are the criches which we're always talking about, where are the reading rooms? We only write about them in novels, but actually there just aren't any. There's nothing but dirt, bestiality, Asiatic customs.... I'm afraid of these deadly serious faces, I don't like them; I'm afraid of serious talk. It would be better for us just to keep quiet.

LOPAKHIN: Well, let me tell you that *I'm* up soon after four every morning, and I work from morning till night. I always have money in hand, my own and other people's, and I have plenty of opportunities to learn what the people around me are like. You only have to start on a job of work to realize how few honest, decent people there are about. Sometimes, when I can't sleep, I start brooding over it. The Lord God has given us vast forests, immense fields, wide horizons; surely we ought to be giants, living in such a country as this....

LIUBOV ANDRYEEVNA: Whatever do you want giants for? They're all right in fairytales, otherwise they're just terrifying.

YEPIHODOV crosses the stage in the background, playing his guitar.

LIUBOV ANDRYEEVNA (*pensively*): There goes Yepihodov....

ANIA (*pensively*): There goes Yepihodov....

GAYEV: The sun's gone down, ladies and gentlemen.

TROFIMOV: Yes.

GAYEV (*in a subdued voice, as if reciting a poem*): Oh, glorious Nature, shining with eternal light, so beautiful, yet so indifferent to our fate... you, whom we call Mother, uniting in your-

self both Life and Death, you live and you destroy....

VARIA (*imploringly*): Uncle, dear!

ANIA: You're starting again, Uncle!

TROFIMOV: You'd better screw back off the red into the middle pocket.

GAYEV: I'll keep quiet, I'll keep quiet.

They all sit deep in thought; the silence is only broken by the subdued muttering of FEERS. Suddenly a distant sound is heard, coming as if out of the sky, like the sound of a string snapping, slowly and sadly dying away.

LIUBOV ANDRYEEVNA: What was that?

LOPAKHIN: I don't know. Somewhere a long way off a lift cable in one of the mines must have broken. But it must be somewhere very far away.

GAYEV: Or perhaps it was some bird...a heron, perhaps.

TROFIMOV: Or an owl....

LIUBOV ANDRYEEVNA (*shudders*): It sounded unpleasant, somehow....

A pause.

FEERS: It was the same before the misfortune: the owl hooted and the samovar kept singing.

GAYEV: What misfortune?

FEERS: Before they gave us Freedom.

A pause.

LIUBOV ANDRYEEVNA: Come along, my friends! Let us go home, it's getting dark. (*To ANIA.*) You've got tears in your eyes. What is it, my little one? (*Embraces her.*)

ANIA: Never mind, Mamma. It's nothing.

TROFIMOV: Someone's coming.

Enter A TRAMP in a white battered peaked cap and an overcoat; he is slightly tipsy.

THE TRAMP: Excuse me, can I get straight to the station through here?

GAYEV: You can. Follow the road.

THE TRAMP: I'm greatly obliged to you, Sir. (*Coughs.*) Lovely weather today. (*Recites.*) 'Oh, my brother, my suffering brother!... Come to mother Volga, whose groans....' (*To VARIA.*) Mademoiselle, may a starving Russian citizen trouble you for a few coppers?

VARIA *cries out, frightened.*

LOPAKHIN (*angrily*): Really, there's a limit to everything!

LIUBOV ANDRYEEVNA (*at a loss what to do*): Take this…here you are. (*Searches in her purse.*) I have no silver…. Never mind, here's a gold one….

THE TRAMP: I'm deeply grateful to you! (*Goes off.*) *Laughter.*

VARIA (*frightened*): I'm going…. I'm going…. Oh, Mamma dear, you know there's no food in the house, and you gave him all that!

LIUBOV ANDRYEEVNA: Well, what can you do with a fool like me? I'll give you all I've got when we get home. Yermolai Aleksyeevich, you'll lend me some more, won't you?

LOPAKHIN: Certainly I will.

LIUBOV ANDRYEEVNA: Let's go on now, it's time. By the way, Varia, we almost fixed up your marriage just now. I congratulate you.

VARIA (*through her tears*): It's no laughing matter, Mamma!

LOPAKHIN: Go to a nunnery, Ohmelia!…

GAYEV: Look how my hands are trembling: I haven't played billiards for a long time.

LOPAKHIN: Ohmelia, oh nymph, remember me in thy orisons!

LIUBOV ANDRYEEVNA: Come along, everybody. It's almost supper time.

VARIA: That man scared me so. My heart keeps thumping.

LOPAKHIN: My friends, just one word, please just one word: on the twenty-second of August the cherry orchard is going to be sold. Just consider that! Just think….

All go out, except **TROFIMOV** *and* **ANIA.**

ANIA (*laughs*): Thank the tramp for this! He frightened Varia, now we are alone.

TROFIMOV: Varia's afraid—afraid we might suddenly fall in love with each other—so she follows us about all day long. She's so narrow-minded, she can't grasp that we are above falling in love. To rid ourselves of all that's petty and unreal, all that prevents us from being happy and free, that's the whole aim and meaning of our life. Forward! Let's march on irresistibly towards that bright star over there, shining in the distance! Forward! Don't fall behind, friends!

ANIA (*raising her hands*): How well you talk! (*A pause.*) It's wonderful here today.

TROFIMOV: Yes, the weather's marvellous.

ANIA: What have you done to me, Pyetia? Why is it that I don't love the cherry orchard as I used to? I used to love it so dearly, it seemed to me that there wasn't a better place in all the world than our orchard.

TROFIMOV: The whole of Russia is our orchard. The earth is great and beautiful and there are many, many wonderful places on it. (*A pause.*) Just think, Ania: your grandfather, your great grandfather and all your forefathers were serf owners—they owned living souls. Don't you see human beings gazing at you from every cherry tree in your orchard, from every leaf and every tree-trunk, don't you hear voices?… They owned living souls—and it has perverted you all, those who came before you, and you who are living now, so that your mother, your uncle and even you yourself no longer realize that you're living in debt, at other people's expense, at the expense of people you don't admit further than the kitchen. We are at least two hundred years behind the times; we still have no real background, no clear attitude to our past, we just philosophize and complain of depression, or drink vodka. Yet it's perfectly clear that to begin to live in the present, we must first atone for our past and be finished with it, and we can only atone for it by suffering, by extraordinary, unceasing exertion. You must understand this, Ania.

ANIA: The house we live in hasn't really been ours for a long time. I'll leave it, I give you my word.

TROFIMOV: Leave it, and if you have any keys to it, throw them down a well. Be free like the wind.

ANIA (*in rapture*): How well you put it!

TROFIMOV: You must believe me, Ania, you must. I'm not thirty yet, I'm young, and I'm still a student, but I've suffered so much already. As soon as the winter comes, I get half-starved, and ill, and worried, poor as a beggar, and there's hardly anywhere I haven't been to, where I haven't been driven to by Fate. And yet, always, every moment of the day and night my soul has been filled with such marvellous hopes and visions. I can see happiness, Ania, I can see it coming....

ANIA (*pensively*): The moon's coming up.

YEPIHODOV *can be heard playing his guitar, the same melancholy tune as before. The moon rises. Somewhere in the vicinity of the poplars* VARIA *is looking for* ANIA *and calling: 'Ania! Where are you?'*

TROFIMOV: Yes, the moon is rising. (*A pause.*) There it is—happiness—it's coming nearer and nearer, I seem to hear its footsteps. And if we don't see it, if we don't know when it comes, what does it matter? Other people will see it!

VARIA'S VOICE: Ania! Where are you?

TROFIMOV: That Varia again! (*Angrily.*) It's disgusting!

ANIA: Well? Let us go to the river. It's nice there.

TROFIMOV: Let's go.

TROFIMOV *and* ANIA *go out.*

VARIA'S VOICE: Ania! Ania!

CURTAIN

ACT THREE

The drawing-room of the Ranyevskaia's house. Adjoining the drawing-room at the back, and connected to it by an archway, is the ballroom. A Jewish band, the same that was mentioned in Act II, is heard playing in the hall. It is evening; the candles in a chandelier are alight. In the ballroom a party is dancing the Grand-Rond, SIMEONOV-PISHCHIK *is heard to call out: 'Promenade une paire!', then all come into the drawing-room.* PISHCHIK *and* CHARLOTTA IVANOVNA *form the leading couple, then come* TROFIMOV *and* LIUBOV ANDRYEEVNA, ANIA *with a post-office clerk,* VARIA *with the station-master, and so on.* VARIA *cries quietly and wipes away her tears as she dances.* DOONIASHA *is in the last couple. They walk across the drawing-room.* PISHCHIK *shouts: 'Grand rond balancez!' and 'Les cavaliers genoux et remerciez vos dames!'*

FEERS, *wearing a tail-coat, crosses the room with soda-water on a tray.* PISHCHIK *and* TROFIMOV *re-enter the drawing-room.*

PISHCHIK: I've got this high blood-pressure—I've had a stroke twice already, you know—and it makes dancing difficult; but if you're one of a pack, as the saying goes, you've got to wag your tail, whether you bark or not. Actually I'm as strong as a horse. My dear father—he liked his little joke, God bless him—he used to say that the ancient family of Simeonov-Pishchik was descended from the very same horse that Caligula sat in the Senate. (*Sits down.*) But the trouble is, we've no money. A hungry dog can only think about food.... (*Falls asleep and snores, but wakes up almost at once.*) Just like myself—I can't think of anything but money....

TROFIMOV: It's quite true, there *is* something horsy about your build.

PISHCHIK: Oh, well, the horse is a good animal, you can sell a horse....

From the adjoining room comes the sound of someone playing billiards. VARIA *appears in the ballroom, under the arch.*

TROFIMOV (*teasing her*): Madame Lopakhin! Madame Lopakhin!

VARIA (*angrily*): The 'moth-eaten gent'!

TROFIMOV: Yes, I am a moth-eaten gent, and I'm proud of it.

VARIA (*brooding bitterly*): So now we've hired a band—but how are we going to pay for it? (*Goes out.*)

TROFIMOV (*to* PISHCHIK): If all the energy you've wasted in the course of a life-time looking for money to pay interest on your debts—if all that energy had been used for something else, you'd probably have turned the world upside down by now.

PISHCHIK: The philosopher Nietzsche, the greatest, the most famous—a man of the highest intellect, in fact—says it's justifiable to forge bank-notes.

TROFIMOV: Have you read Nietzsche then?

PISHCHIK: Well, no.... Dashenka told me. But just now I'm in such a frightful position that I wouldn't mind forging a few bank-notes. The day after tomorrow I've got to pay three hundred and ten roubles. I've borrowed one hundred and thirty already.... (*Feels in his pockets with alarm.*) The money's gone! I've lost the money. (*Tearfully.*) Where's the money? (*With an expression of joy.*) Here it is, inside the lining! The shock's made me sweat!...

Enter LIUBOV ANDRYEEVNA *and* CHARLOTTA.

LIUBOV ANDRYEEVNA (*singing 'Lezghinka'[1] under her breath*): Why is Leonid so late? What's he doing in town? (*To* DOONIASHA.) Dooniasha, offer the musicians some tea.

TROFIMOV: I suppose the auction didn't take place.

LIUBOV ANDRYEEVNA: The band came at the wrong time, and the party started at the wrong time.... Well...never mind.... (*Sits down and sings quietly.*)

CHARLOTTA (*hands a pack of cards to* PISHCHIK): Here's a pack of cards—think of any card, now.

PISHCHIK: I've thought of one.

CHARLOTTA: Now shuffle the pack. That's right. Now give it to me, my good Monsieur Pishchik. *Ein, zwei, drei!* Now look for it. There it is, in your breast pocket.

PISHCHIK (*takes the card out of his breast-pocket*): The eight of spades, absolutely right! (*In astonishment.*) Fancy that!

CHARLOTTA (*holding the pack of cards on the palm of her hand, to* TROFIMOV): Tell me quickly, which card is on top?

TROFIMOV: Well.... Let us say, the queen of spades.

CHARLOTTA: Here it is! (*She claps her hand over the pack of cards, which disappears.*) What fine weather we're having today! (*A woman's voice, apparently coming from beneath the floor, answers her: 'Oh yes, Madam, the weather's perfectly marvellous!'*)

CHARLOTTA (*addressing the voice*): How charming you are, quite delightful!

VOICE: And I like you very much also Madam.

STATION-MASTER (*applauding*): Madame ventriloquist, well done!

PISHCHIK (*astonished*): Fancy that! Charlotta Ivanovna, how fascinating you are! I'm quite in love with you!

CHARLOTTA (*shrugging her shoulders*): In love? Do you know how to love? *Guter Mensch, aber schlechter Musikant.*

TROFIMOV (*slaps* PISHCHIK *on the shoulder*): A regular old horse!

CHARLOTTA: Attention please! Here's just one more trick. (*She takes a rug from a chair.*) Now I'm offering this very nice rug for sale.... (*Shakes it out.*) Would anyone like to buy it?

PISHCHIK (*astonished*): Just fancy!

CHARLOTTA: *Ein, zwei, drei! (She lifts up the rug and discloses* ANIA *standing behind it;* ANIA *drops a curtsey, runs to her mother, gives her a hug, then runs back into the ballroom. Everyone is delighted.*)

LOPAKHIN (*clapping*): Bravo, bravo!

CHARLOTTA: Just once more. *Ein, zwei, drei! (Lifts the rug; behind it stands* VARIA, *who bows.*)

PISHCHIK (*astonished*): Fancy that!

CHARLOTTA: Finished! (*She throws the rug over* PISHCHIK, *curtseys and runs off to the ballroom.*)

PISHCHIK (*hurries after her*): The little rascal!... Have you ever seen anything like it...have you ever.... (*Goes out.*)

LIUBOV ANDRYEEVNA: Still no Leonid. I can't understand what he's doing all this time in town. In any case, everything must be over by now, either the estate's been sold or the auction never took place. Why must he keep us in ignorance so long?

VARIA (*trying to comfort her*): Uncle bought it, dear Uncle, I'm sure he did.

TROFIMOV (*sarcastically*): Oh yes?

VARIA: Grandmamma sent him power of attorney to buy the estate in her name, and transfer the mortgage to her. She's done it for Ania's sake.... God will help us, I'm sure of it—Uncle will buy the estate.

LIUBOV ANDRYEEVNA: Grandmamma sent us fifteen thousand roubles to buy the estate in her name—she doesn't trust us, you see—but the money wouldn't even pay the interest. (*She covers her face with her hands.*) Today my fate is being decided, my fate....

TROFIMOV (*to* VARIA, *teasingly*): Madame Lopakhin!

VARIA (*crossly*): The eternal student! Why, you've been thrown out of the University twice already!

---

[1]A popular dance tune.

LIUBOV ANDRYEEVNA: Why get so cross, Varia? He does tease you about Lopakhin, but what's the harm? If you feel inclined to, why don't you marry Lopakhin: he's a nice, interesting fellow. Of course, if you don't feel like it, don't. No one's trying to force you, darling.

VARIA: I do take it very seriously, Mamma dear ...and I want to be frank with you about it...he's a nice man and I like him.

LIUBOV ANDRYEEVNA: Then marry him. What are you waiting for? I can't understand you.

VARIA: Mamma darling, I can't propose to him myself, can I? It's two years now since everyone started talking to me about him, and everyone is still doing it, but he either says nothing, or else he just talks in a sort of bantering way. I understand what's the matter. He's getting rich, he's occupied with his business, and he's no time for me. If only I had some money, just a little, even a hundred roubles, then I'd have left everything and gone away, the farther the better. I'd have gone into a convent.

TROFIMOV: A beautiful life!

VARIA (to TROFIMOV): Of course, a student like you has to be clever! (Softly and tearfully.) How plain you've become, Pyetia, how much older you look! (To LIUBOV ANDRYEEVNA, her tearfulness gone.) The only thing I can't bear, Mamma dear, is to be without work. I must be doing something all the time.

Enter YASHA.

YASHA (with difficulty restraining his laughter): Yepihodov's broken a billiard cue!... (Goes out.)

VARIA: But why is Yepihodov here? Who allowed him to play billiards? I can't understand these people.... (Goes out.)

LIUBOV ANDRYEEVNA: Don't tease her, Pyetia. Don't you see she's upset already?

TROFIMOV: She's too much of a busy-body, she will poke her nose into other people's affairs. She wouldn't leave us alone the whole summer, neither Ania, nor me. She was afraid we might fall in love with each other. Why should she mind? Besides, I didn't show any sign of it. I'm too far removed from such trivialities. We are above love!

LIUBOV ANDRYEEVNA: And I suppose I'm below love. (In great agitation.) Why isn't Leonid back? I only want to know whether the estate's sold or not. Such a calamity seems so incredible that somehow I don't even know what to think, I feel quite lost. Honestly, I feel I could shriek out loud this very moment.... I shall be doing something silly. Help me, Pyetia. Say something, speak!

TROFIMOV: Isn't it all the same whether the estate's sold today or not? It's finished and done with long ago, there's no turning back, the bridges are burnt. You must keep calm, my dear; you mustn't deceive yourself, for once in your life you must look the truth straight in the face.

LIUBOV ANDRYEEVNA: What truth? You can see where the truth is and where it isn't, but I seem to have lost my power of vision, I don't see anything. You're able to solve all your problems in a resolute way—but, tell me, my dear boy, isn't that because you're young, because you're not old enough yet to have suffered on account of your problems? You look ahead so boldly—but isn't that because life is still hidden from your young eyes, so that you're not able to foresee anything dreadful, or expect it? You've a more courageous and honest and serious nature than we have, but do consider our position carefully, do be generous—even if only a little bit—and spare me. I was born here, you know, my father and mother lived here, and my grandfather, too, and I love this house—I can't conceive life without the cherry orchard, and if it really has to be sold, then sell me with it.... (Embraces TROFIMOV, kisses him on the forehead.) You know, my son was drowned here.... (Weeps.) Have pity on me, my dear, dear friend.

TROFIMOV: You know that I sympathize with you with all my heart.

LIUBOV ANDRYEEVNA: But you must say it differently...differently. (Takes out a handkerchief; a telegram falls on to the floor.) There's such a weight on my mind today, you can't imagine. This place is too noisy, my very soul seems to shudder with every sound, and I'm trembling all over—yet I can't go to my room for fear of being alone and quiet.... Don't blame me, Pyetia.... I love you as if you were my own child. I would willingly let Ania marry you, honestly I would, but, my dear boy, you must study, you must finish your course. You don't do anything, Fate seems to drive you from one place to another—such a strange thing.... Isn't it? Isn't it? And you should do something about your beard, make it grow somehow.... (*Laughs.*) You are a funny boy!

TROFIMOV (*picks up the telegram*): I don't want to be a dandy.

LIUBOV ANDRYEEVNA: That telegram's from Paris. I get one everyday.... Yesterday and today. That savage is ill again, and things are going badly with him.... He wants me to forgive him, implores me to return, and, really, I do feel I ought to go to Paris and stay near him for a bit. You're looking very stern, Pyetia, but what's to be done, my dear boy, what am I to do? He's ill, and lonely, and unhappy, and who's there to take care of him, to prevent him from making a fool of himself, and give him his medicine at the proper time? And anyway, why should I hide it, or keep quiet about it? I love him, of course I love him. I do, I do.... It's a millstone round my neck, and I'm going to the bottom with it—but I love him and I can't live without him. (*She presses* TROFIMOV'S *hand.*) Don't think badly of me; Pyetia, don't speak, don't say anything....

TROFIMOV (*with strong emotion*): Please—please forgive my frankness, but that man's been robbing you!

LIUBOV ANDRYEEVNA: No, no, no, you mustn't talk like that.... (*Puts her hands over her ears.*)

TROFIMOV: He's a cad, you're the only one who doesn't know it! He's a petty-minded cad, a worthless...

LIUBOV ANDRYEEVNA (*angry, but in control of herself*): You're twenty-six or twenty-seven years old, but you're still like a schoolboy in a prep school!

TROFIMOV: Never mind me!

LIUBOV ANDRYEEVNA: You ought to be a man, at your age you ought to understand people who are in love. And you ought to be able to love...to fall in love! (*Angrily.*) Yes, yes! And you're not 'pure', but you just make a fad of purity, you're a ridiculous crank, a freak....

TROFIMOV (*horrified*): What is she saying?

LIUBOV ANDRYEEVNA: 'I'm above love!' You're not above love, you're daft, as our Feers would say. Not to have a mistress at your age!...

TROFIMOV (*horrified*): This is dreadful! What's she saying? (*Walks quickly towards the ballroom, his head between his hands.*) This is dreadful.... I can't, I'm going.... (*Goes out, but returns at once.*) Everything's finished between us! (*Goes out through the door into the hall.*)

LIUBOV ANDRYEEVNA (*calls after him*): Pyetia, wait! You funny fellow, I was joking! Pyetia!
From the hall comes the sound of someone running quickly upstairs; then falling down with a crash. There are shrieks from ANIA *and* VARIA, *followed by laughter.*
What's happened?
ANIA *runs in.*

ANIA (*laughing*): Pyetia's fallen downstairs. (*Runs out.*)

LIUBOV ANDRYEEVNA: What a queer fellow he is!
The STATION-MASTER *stands in the middle of the ballroom and begins to recite 'The Sinner' by Alexyei Tolstoy. The others listen, but he has hardly had time to recite more than a few lines when the sound of a waltz reaches them from the hall, and the recitation breaks off. Everyone dances. Enter from the hall:* TROFIMOV, ANIA, VARIA.

LIUBOV ANDRYEEVNA: Now, Pyetia...there, my dear boy...I ask your forgiveness...let's dance.... (*She dances with* PYETIA.)
ANIA *and* VARIA *dance.*
Enter FEERS, *then* YASHA. FEERS *stands his walking stick by the side door.* YASHA *looks at the dancers from the drawing-room.*

YASHA: How goes it, Grandad?

FEERS: I'm not too well.... We used to have generals, barons, and admirals dancing at our balls, but now we send for the post-office clerk and the station-master, and even they don't come too willingly. I seem to have grown so weak somehow…. My old master, that's the mistress's grandfather, used to give everyone powdered sealing wax for medicine, whatever the illness was. I've been taking it every day for the last twenty years, or perhaps even longer. Maybe that's why I'm still alive.

YASHA: How you weary me, Grandad! (*Yawns.*) I wish you'd go away and die soon.

FEERS: Eh, you!…You're daft…. (*Mutters.*) TROFIMOV *and* LIUBOV ANDRYEEVNA *dance in the ballroom, then in the drawing-room.*

LIUBOV ANDRYEEVNA: Thank you. I'd like to sit down for a bit. (*Sits down.*) I'm tired.

Enter ANIA.

ANIA (*agitated*): A man in the kitchen was saying just now that the cherry orchard was sold today.

LIUBOV ANDRYEEVNA: Sold? Who to?

ANIA: He didn't say. He's gone. (*She dances with* TROFIMOV; *both go to the ballroom.*)

YASHA: There was some old man there, gossiping away. A stranger.

FEERS: And Leonid Andryeevich's not back, yet, he's still not back. He's only got his light overcoat on—his 'between-seasons' coat—and he might easily catch a cold. These youngsters!

LIUBOV ANDRYEEVNA: I feel as though I'm going to die. Yasha, go and find out who bought it.

YASHA: But the old man's been gone a long time. (*Laughs.*)

LIUBOV ANDRYEEVNA (*with a touch of annoyance*): Well, what are you laughing at? What are you so happy about?

YASHA: Yepihodov's such a comic chap—a stupid fellow. Two-and-twenty misfortunes!

LIUBOV ANDRYEEVNA: Feers, if the estate is sold, where will you go?

FEERS: I'll go wherever you order me to.

LIUBOV ANDRYEEVNA: Why are you looking like that? Are you ill? You should go to bed, you know…

FEERS: Yes…. (*With a faint smile.*) If I went to bed, who'd wait on the guests, who'd keep things going? There's no one in the house but me.

YASHA (*to* LIUBOV ANDRYEEVNA): Liubov Andryeevna! I want to ask you for something, please! If you go to Paris again, do me a favour and take me with you. It's quite impossible for me to stay here. (*Looking round, in a subdued voice.*) There's no need for me to say it: you can see it for yourself—the people are uneducated, and they're immoral, too. Besides, it's so boring, and the food they give you in the kitchen is abominable. Then this Feers keeps on walking around and muttering all sorts of silly things. Take me with you, please do!

Enter PISHCHIK.

PISHCHIK: Allow me to ask you for a dance, beautiful lady…. (LIUBOV ANDRYEEVNA *gets up to dance.*) I'll have that hundred and eighty roubles from you all the same, my charmer…. Yes, I will…. (*Dances.*) Just one hundred and eighty roubles, that's all….

They go into the ballroom.

YASHA (*sings quietly*): 'Will you understand the agitation of my soul?…'

In the ballroom a woman in check trousers and a grey top hat starts jumping in the air and throwing her arms about; there are shouts of: 'Bravo, Charlotta Ivanovna!'

DOONIASHA (*stops to powder her face*): The young mistress ordered me to dance: there are so many gentlemen and only a few ladies; but I get so dizzy from dancing, and my heart beats too fast. Feers Nikolayevich, the post-office clerk told me something just now that quite took my breath away.

The music stops.

FEERS: What did he tell you?

DOONIASHA: You are like a flower, he said.

YASHA (*yawns*): What ignorance!…(*Goes out.*)

DOONIASHA: Like a flower…. I'm so sensitive, I love it when people say nice things to me.

FEERS: You'll get your head turned all right.

Enter YEPIHODOV.

YEPIHODOV: Avdotyia Fiodorovna, you don't seem to want to look at me…as if I were some sort of insect. (*Sighs.*) What a life!

DOONIASHA: What is it you want?

YEPIHODOV: Perhaps you may be right, no doubt. (*Sighs.*) But, of course, if one looks at it from a certain point of view—if I may so express myself—forgive my frankness—you've driven me into such a state.... I know what my fate is; every day some misfortune's sure to happen to me, but I've been so long accustomed to it, that I look at life with a smile. You gave me your word, and though I...

DOONIASHA: Please, please, let's have a talk later, but now leave me alone. I feel in a kind of dream just now. (*Plays with her fan.*)

YEPIHODOV: Some misfortune or other happens to me every day, and yet—if I may so express myself—I only smile, I even laugh.
VARIA *enters from the ballroom.*

VARIA: Haven't you gone yet, Semion? What an ill-mannered fellow you are, really! (*To* DOONIASHA.) You'd better go, Dooniasha. (*To* YEPIHODOV.) First you go and play billiards and break a cue, and now you're walking about the drawing-room, like a visitor.

YEPIHODOV: Permit me to inform you that you can't start imposing penalties on me.

VARIA: I'm not imposing penalties, I'm merely telling you. All you do is to walk from one place to another, instead of getting on with your work. We keep a clerk, but what for no one knows.

YEPIHODOV (*offended*): Whether I work, walk about, eat or play billiards, the only people who are entitled to judge my actions are those who are older than me and know what they're talking about.

VARIA: You dare say that to me? (*Flying into a temper.*) You dare to say that? You're suggesting I don't know what I'm talking about? Get out of here! This very minute!

YEPIHODOV (*cowed*): I wish you'd express yourself more delicately.

VARIA (*beside herself*): Get out this minute! Out! *He goes go the door, she follows him.* Two-and-twenty misfortunes! I don't want any more of you here! I don't want ever to set eyes on you again!
YEPIHODOV *goes out; his voice is heard from outside the door: 'I'll complain about you.'* Ah, you're coming back, are you? (*She seizes the stick which* FEERS *left by the door.*) Come along,

come along...I'll show you! Ah, you're coming back...are you? There, I'll give it to you.... (*Swings the stick, and at that moment* LOPAKHIN *enters.*)

LOPAKHIN (*whom the stick did not, in fact, touch*): Thank you very much!

VARIA (*angry and sarcastic*): I beg your pardon!

LOPAKHIN: Don't mention it. Thanks for a pleasant surprise.

VARIA: It's not worth thanking me for. (*Goes to the side, then looks round and says gently.*) I haven't hurt you, have I?

LOPAKHIN: No, not at all.... There's a huge bump coming up, though.

VOICES IN THE BALLROOM: Lopakhin's arrived! Yermolai Aleksyeevich!

PISHCHIK: Look here, you can see him, you can hear him!... (*Embraces* LOPAKHIN.) You smell of cognac, my dear fellow, my bonny boy! We're making merry here, too.
Enter LIUBOV ANDRYEEVNA.

LIUBOV ANDRYEEVNA: It's you, Yermolai Aleksyeevich? Why have you been so long? Where is Leonid?

LOPAKHIN: Leonid Andryeevich returned with me, he's coming along.

LIUBOV ANDRYEEVNA (*agitated*): Well, what happened? Was there an auction? Speak, tell me!

LOPAKHIN (*embarrassed, fearing to betray his joy*): The auction was over by four o'clock.... We missed our train and had to wait until half-past nine. (*With a deep sigh.*) Ugh! My head's going round....
Enter GAYEV; *he carries some parcels in his right hand and wipes away his tears with his left.*

LIUBOV ANDRYEEVNA: Lionia, what happened? Well, Lionia? (*Impatiently, with tears.*) Tell me quickly, for God's sake!...

GAYEV (*does not reply, but waves his hand at her. To* FEERS, *weeping*): Here, take this...it's some anchovies and Kerch herrings.... I've had nothing to eat all day.... What I've been through!
Through the open door leading to the billiard room comes the sound of billiard balls in play and YASHA'S *voice saying: 'Seven and eighteen'.* GAYEV'S *expression changes and he stops crying.*

I'm dreadfully tired. Come, Feers, I want to change. (*Goes out through the ballroom,* FEERS *following.*)

PISHCHIK: What happened at the auction? Come, do tell us!

LIUBOV ANDRYEEVNA: Has the cherry orchard been sold?

LOPAKHIN: It has.

LIUBOV ANDRYEEVNA: Who bought it?

LOPAKHIN: I did.

A pause.

LIUBOV ANDRYEEVNA *is overcome; only the fact that she is standing beside a table and a chair prevents her from falling.* VARIA *takes a bundle of keys off her belt, throws them on the floor in the middle of the drawing-room and walks out.*

Yes, I bought it. Wait a moment, ladies and gentlemen, do, please. I don't feel quite clear in my head, I hardly know how to talk…. (*Laughs.*) When we got to the auction, Deriganov was there already. Of course, Leonid Andryeevich only had fifteen thousand roubles, and Deriganov at once bid thirty over and above the mortgage. I could see how things were going, so I muscled in and offered forty. He bid forty-five, I bid fifty-five; he kept on adding five thousand each time and I added ten thousand each time. Well, it finished at last—I bid ninety thousand over and above the mortgage, and I got the property. Yes, the cherry orchard's mine now! Mine! (*Laughs.*) My God! the cherry orchard's mine! Come on, tell me I'm drunk, tell me I'm out of my mind, say I've imagined all this…. (*Stamps his foot.*) Don't laugh at me! If only my father and grandfather could rise from their graves and see everything that's happened …how their Yermolai, their much-beaten, half-literate Yermolai, the lad that used to run about with bare feet in the winter…how he's bought this estate, the most beautiful place on God's earth! Yes, I've bought the very estate where my father and grandfather were serfs, where they weren't even admitted to the kitchen! I must be asleep, I must be dreaming, I only think it's true… it's all just my imagination, my imagina-

tion's been wandering…. (*Picks up the keys, smiling tenderly.*) She threw these down because she wanted to show she's not mistress here any more. (*Jingles the keys.*) Well, never mind. (*The band is heard tuning up.*) Hi! you musicians, come on now, play something, I want some music! Now then, all of you, just you wait and see Yermolai Lopakhin take an axe to the cherry orchard, just you see the trees come crashing down! We're going to build a whole lot of new villas, and our children and great-grandchildren are going to see a new living world growing up here…. Come on there, let's have some music! *The band plays.* LIUBOV ANDRYEEVNA *has sunk into a chair and is crying bitterly.* (*Reproachfully.*) Why didn't you listen to me before, why didn't you? My poor, dear lady, you can't undo it now. (*With great emotion.*) Oh, if only we could be done with all this, if only we could alter this distorted unhappy life somehow!

PISHCHIK (*taking his arm, in a subdued voice*): She's crying. Come into the ballroom, leave her alone…. Come along…. (*Takes his arm and leads him away to the ballroom.*)

LOPAKHIN: Never mind! Come on, band, play up, play up! Everything must be just as *I* wish it now. (*Ironically.*) Here comes the new landowner, here comes the owner of the cherry orchard! (*He pushes a small table accidentally and nearly knocks over some candlesticks.*) Never mind, I can pay for everything! (*Goes out with* PISHCHIK.)

No one remains in the ballroom or drawing-room save LIUBOV ANDRYEEVNA, *who sits hunched up in a chair, crying bitterly. The band continues playing quietly.* ANIA *and* TROFIMOV *enter quickly;* ANIA *goes up to her mother and kneels beside her,* TROFIMOV *remains standing by the entrance to the ballroom.*

ANIA: Mamma!… Mamma, you're crying? Dear, kind, sweet Mamma, my darling precious, how I love you! God bless you, Mamma! The cherry orchard's sold, it's quite true, there isn't any cherry orchard any more, it's true…but don't cry, Mamma, you still have your life ahead of you, you still have your dear, innocent heart. You must come away with me, darling, we must get away from here! We'll plant a new orchard, even more splendid than this one—and when you see it, you'll understand everything, your heart will be filled with happiness, like the sun in the evening; and then you'll smile again, Mamma! Come with me, darling, do come!…

CURTAIN

ACT FOUR

The same setting as for Act I. There are no pictures on the walls or curtains at the windows; only a few remaining pieces of furniture are piled up in a corner, as if for sale. There is an oppressive sense of emptiness. At the back of the stage, beside the door, suitcases and other pieces of luggage have been piled together as if ready for a journey. The voices of VARIA *and* ANIA *can be heard through the door on the left, which is open.* LOPAKHIN *stands waiting;* YASHA *is holding a tray laden with glasses of champagne. In the hall* YEPIHODOV *is tying up a large box. From somewhere behind the scenes comes the low hum of voices: the peasants have called to say good-bye.* GAYEV'S *voice is heard; saying: 'Thank you, friends, thank you.'*

YASHA: The villagers have come to say good-bye. In my view, Yermolai Aleksyeevich, they're kind-hearted folk, but they haven't much understanding.
The hum subsides. LIUBOV ANDRYEEVNA *and* GAYEV *enter from the hall;* LIUBOV ANDRYEEVNA *is not crying but her face is pale and tremulous. She seems unable to speak.*

GAYEV: You gave them your purse, Liuba. You shouldn't have done that. You really shouldn't.

LIUBOV ANDRYEEVNA: I couldn't help myself, I couldn't help myself!
Both go out.

LOPAKHIN (*calls after them through the door*): Have some champagne, please do, please! Just one little glass before you go. I didn't think of bringing any from town, and I could only get one bottle at the station. Do have some,

please. (*A pause.*) Won't you have any, ladies and gentlemen? (*Walks away from the door.*) If I'd known, I wouldn't have brought any.… Then I won't have any either.
YASHA *carefully puts the tray on a chair.*
You have a drink, Yasha, if nobody else will.

YASHA: Here's to the travellers! And here's to you staying behind. (*Drinks.*) This champagne isn't the real thing, I can tell you.

LOPAKHIN: Eight roubles a bottle. (*A pause.*) It's devilishly cold here.

YASHA: The stoves weren't lit today. It doesn't matter as we're going. (*Laughs.*)

LOPAKHIN: Why are you laughing?

YASHA: Because I'm feeling glad.

LOPAKHIN: October's here, but it's still sunny and calm, as if it were summer. Good building weather. (*Looks at his watch, then at the door.*) Ladies and gentlemen, don't forget there are only forty-six minutes before the train's due to leave. That means we must start in twenty minutes. Hurry up.
TROFIMOV, *wearing an overcoat, comes in from outdoors.*

TROFIMOV: I think it's time to start. The horses are at the door. God knows where my goloshes are, they've disappeared. (*Calls through the door.*) Ania, my goloshes aren't here; I can't find them.

LOPAKHIN: And I must be off to Kharkov. I'll travel with you on the same train. I shall stay the whole winter in Kharkov: I've hung around here too long, and it's torture having no work to do. I can't be without work: I just don't know what to do with my hands; they feel limp and strange, as if they didn't belong to me.

TROFIMOV: We'll soon be gone, then you can start your useful labours again.

LOPAKHIN: Have a little drink, do.

TROFIMOV: No, thanks.

LOPAKHIN: You're going to Moscow, then?

TROFIMOV: Yes, I'll see them off to town, and then, tomorrow I'm off to Moscow.

LOPAKHIN: Well, well.… I expect the professors are holding up their lectures, waiting for your arrival!

TROFIMOV: That's none of your business.

LOPAKHIN: How many years have you been studying at the university?

TROFIMOV: I wish you'd think up something new, that's old and stale. (*Looks for his goloshes.*) Incidentally, as we're not likely to meet again, I'd like to give you a bit of advice, by way of a farewell: stop throwing your arms about! Try to get rid of that habit of making wide, sweeping gestures. Yes, and all this talk, too, about building villas, these calculations about summer residents that are going to turn into smallholders, these forecasts—they're all sweeping gestures, too.... When all's said and done, I like you, despite everything. You've a fine, sensitive soul....

LOPAKHIN (*embraces him*): Good-bye, my friend. Thank you for everything. I can let you have some money for your journey, if you need it.

TROFIMOV: Whatever for? I don't want it.

LOPAKHIN: But you haven't any!

TROFIMOV: Yes, I have, thank you. I've just had some for a translation. Here it is, in my pocket. (*Anxiously.*) But I can't see my goloshes anywhere.

VARIA (*from the other room*): Take your beastly things! (*She throws a pair of rubber goloshes into the room.*)

TROFIMOV: But why are you angry, Varia? Hm...but these aren't my goloshes!

LOPAKHIN: I had a thousand acres of poppy sown last spring, and now I've just made forty thousand net profit on it. And when they were in bloom, what a picture it was! What I want to say is that I've made the forty thousand, and now I'm offering to lend you money because I'm in a position to do it. Why are you so stuck up? I'm a peasant...I've no manners.

TROFIMOV: Your father was a peasant, mine had a chemist's shop. But there's nothing in that. LOPAKHIN *takes out his wallet.*

Leave it alone, leave it alone.... Even if you offered me two hundred thousand, I wouldn't take it. I'm a free man. And all that you value so highly and hold so dear, you rich men—and beggars, too, for that matter—none of it has the slightest power over me—it's all just so much fluff blowing about in the air. I'm strong, I'm proud, I can do without you, I can pass you by. Humanity is advancing towards the highest truth, the greatest happiness that it is possible to achieve on earth, and I am in the van!

LOPAKHIN: Will you get there?

TROFIMOV: Yes. (*A pause.*) I'll get there myself, or show others the way to get there. *The sound of an axe striking a tree is heard in the distance.*

LOPAKHIN: Well, good-bye, my friend, it's time to go. We show off in front of one another, and in the meantime life is slipping by. When I work for long hours on end, without taking any time off, I feel happier in my mind and I even imagine I know why I exist. But how many people there are in Russia, my friend, who exist to no purpose whatever! Well, never mind, perhaps it's no matter. They say, Leonid Andryeevich has taken a post at the bank, at six thousand a year. I don't expect he'll stick to it: he's too lazy....

ANIA (*in the doorway*): Mamma asks you not to cut the orchard down until she's left.

TROFIMOV: I should say not! Haven't you got any tact? (*Goes out through the hall.*)

LOPAKHIN: All right, all right.... These people! (*Follows* TROFIMOV.)

ANIA: Has Feers been taken to hospital?

YASHA: I told them to take him this morning. He's gone, I think.

ANIA (*to* YEPIHODOV, *who passes through the ball-room*): Semion Pantelyeevich, will you please find out whether Feers has been taken to hospital?

YASHA (*offended*): I told Yegor this morning. Need you ask ten times?

YEPIHODOV: This superannuated Feers—candidly speaking, I mean—he's beyond repair, he ought to go and join his ancestors. As for me, I can only envy him. (*He places a suitcase on top of a cardboard hat-box and squashes it.*) There you are, you see!...I might have known it! (*Goes out.*)

YASHA (*sardonically*): Two-and-twenty misfortunes!

VARIA (*from behind the door*): Has Feers been taken to the hospital?

ANIA: Yes.

VARIA: Why haven't they taken the letter to the doctor, then?

ANIA: I'll send someone after them with it.... (*Goes out.*)

VARIA (*from adjoining room*): Where's Yasha? Tell him, his mother is here and wants to say good-bye to him.

YASHA (*waves his hand*): She makes me lose patience with her.

While the foregoing action has been taking place, DOONIASHA *has been fussing with the luggage; now that* YASHA *is alone, she comes up to him.*

DOONIASHA: If only you'd look at me once, Yasha! You're going...you're leaving me behind!... (*She cries and throws her arms round his neck.*)

YASHA: What's the point of crying? (*Drinks champagne.*) In a week's time I'll be in Paris again. Tomorrow we'll get into an express train— and off we'll go—we shall just disappear! I can hardly believe it. Vive la France! This place doesn't suit me, I can't live here— there's nothing going on. I've seen enough of all this ignorance. I've had enough of it. (*Drinks.*) What are you crying for? Behave like a respectable girl, then there won't be any need to cry.

DOONIASHA (*looking into a hand-mirror and powdering her nose*): Write to me from Paris, won't you? You know that I've loved you, Yasha. I've loved you so much! I've got a soft heart, Yasha!

YASHA: Someone's coming. (*Pretends to be busy with a suitcase, singing quietly to himself.*)

Enter LIUBOV ANDRYEEVNA, GAYEV, ANIA *and* CHARLOTTA IVANOVNA.

GAYEV: We ought to be going. There isn't much time left. (*Looks at* YASHA.) Who's smelling of herring here?

LIUBOV ANDRYEEVNA: In ten minutes we ought to be getting into the carriage.... (*Glances round the room.*) Good-bye, dear house, old grandfather house. Winter will pass, spring will come again, and then you won't be here any more, you'll be pulled down. How much these walls have seen! (*Kisses her daughter ardently.*) My little treasure, you look simply radiant, your eyes are shining like diamonds. Are you glad? Very glad?

ANIA: Yes, very. Our new life is just beginning, Mamma!

GAYEV (*brightly*): So it is indeed, everything's all right now. Before the cherry orchard was sold everybody was worried and upset, but as soon as it was all settled finally and once for all, everybody calmed down, and felt quite cheerful, in fact.... I'm an employee of a bank now, a financier.... I pot the red...and you, Liuba, you're looking better, too, when all's said and done. There's no doubt about it.

LIUBOV ANDRYEEVNA: Yes, my nerves are better, it's true.

Someone helps her on with her hat and coat. I'm sleeping better, too. Take my things out, Yasha, it's time. (*To* ANIA.) My little girl, we'll soon be seeing each other again. I'm going to Paris—I shall live there on the money which your Grandmamma in Yaroslavl sent us to buy the estate—God bless Grandmamma!—and that money won't last long either.

ANIA: You'll come back soon, Mamma...quite soon, won't you? I shall study and pass my exams at the high school and then I'll work and help you. We'll read all sorts of books together, Mamma...won't we? (*She kisses her mother's hands.*) We'll read during the long autumn evenings, we'll read lots of books, and a new, wonderful world will open up before us.... (*Dreamily.*) Mamma, come back....

LIUBOV ANDRYEEVNA: I'll come back, my precious. (*Embraces her.*)

Enter LOPAKHIN. CHARLOTTA *quickly sings to herself.*

GAYEV: Happy Charlotta! She's singing.

CHARLOTTA (*picks up a bundle that looks like a baby in swaddling clothes.*): Bye-bye, little baby. (*A sound like a baby crying is heard.*) Be quiet, my sweet, be a good little boy. (*The 'crying' continues.*) My heart goes out to you, baby! (*Throws the bundle down.*) Are you going to find me another job, please? I can't do without one.

LOPAKHIN: We'll find you one, Charlotta Ivanovna, don't worry.

GAYEV: Everybody's leaving us, Varia's going away…we've suddenly become unwanted.

CHARLOTTA: I haven't got anywhere to live in town. I shall have to go. (*Hums.*) Oh, well, never mind.

Enter PISHCHIK.

LOPAKHIN: What a phenomenon!

PISHCHIK (*out of breath*): Och, let me get my breath…. I'm worn out…. My good friends…. Give me some water….

GAYEV: I suppose you've come to borrow money? I'd better go…. Excuse me…. (*Goes out.*)

PISHCHIK: I've not been to see you for a long time…my beautiful lady…. (*To* LOPAKHIN.) So you're here…I'm glad to see you… you're a man of great intelligence…here… take this…. (*Hands money to* LOPAKHIN.) Four hundred roubles…. I still owe you eight hundred and forty….

LOPAKHIN (*shrugs his shoulders, bewildered*): It's like a dream…. Where did you get it from?

PISHCHIK: Wait a moment…. I'm so hot…. A most extraordinary thing happened. Some English people came to see me and discovered a sort of white clay on my land…. (*To* LIUBOV ANDRYEEVNA.) Here's four hundred for you also my dear…enchantress…. (*Hands her the money.*) You'll get the rest later on. (*Takes a drink of water.*) Just now a young fellow in the train was telling me that some great philosopher or other…advises people to jump off roofs. You just jump off, he says, and that settles the whole problem. (*As though astonished at what he has just said.*) Fancy that! More water, please.

LOPAKHIN: Who were these Englishmen?

PISHCHIK: I let the land with the clay to them for twenty-four years…. And now you must excuse me, I'm in a hurry. I've got to get along as quickly as I can. I'm going to Znoikov's, then to Kardamonov's…. I owe money to all of them. (*Drinks.*) Good health to you all. I'll call again on Thursday….

LIUBOV ANDRYEEVNA: We're just on the point of moving to town, and tomorrow I'm going abroad.

PISHCHIK: What's that? (*In agitation.*) What are you going to town for? I see now…this furniture and the suitcases…. Well, never mind. (*Tearfully.*) Never mind…. These Englishmen, you know, they're men of the greatest intelligence…. Never mind…. I wish you every happiness, God be with you. Never mind, everything comes to an end eventually. (*Kisses* LIUBOV ANDRYEEVNA'S *hand.*) And when you hear that my end has come, just think of—a horse, and say: 'There used to be fellow like that once…Simeonov-Pishchik his name was—God be with him!' Wonderful weather we're having. Yes…. (*Goes out, overcome with embarrassment, but returns at once and stands in the doorway.*) Dashenka sent greetings to you. (*Goes out.*)

LIUBOV ANDRYEEVNA: Well, we can go now. I'm leaving with two worries on my mind. One is Feers—he's sick, you know. (*Glances at her watch.*) We have another five minutes or so….

ANIA: Mamma, Feers has been taken to hospital already. Yasha sent him this morning.

LIUBOV ANDRYEEVNA: The other is Varia. She's been accustomed to getting up early and working, and now, without work, she's like a fish out of water. She's got so thin and pale, and she cries a lot, poor thing. (*A pause.*) You know very well, Yermolai Aleksyeevich, that I'd been hoping to get her married to you…and everything seemed to show that you meant to marry her, too. (*Whispers to* ANIA, *who nods to* CHARLOTTA, *and they both go out.*) She loves you, and you must be fond of her, too…and I just don't know, I just don't know why you seem to keep away from each other. I don't understand it.

LOPAKHIN: Neither do I myself, I must confess. It's all so strange somehow…. If there's still time, I'm ready even now…. Let's settle it at once—and get it over! Without you here, I don't feel I shall ever propose to her.

LIUBOV ANDRYEEVNA: That's an excellent idea! You'll hardly need more than a minute, that's all. I'll call her at once.

LOPAKHIN: There's champagne here, too, quite suitable for the occasion. (*Takes a look at the glasses.*) But they're empty, someone's drunk it up. (YASHA *coughs.*) I should have said lapped it up.

LIUBOV ANDRYEEVNA (*with animation*): I'm so glad. We'll go outside. Yasha, allez! I'll call her…. (*Through the door.*) Varia, come here a moment, leave what you're doing for a minute! Varia! (*Goes out with* YASHA.)

LOPAKHIN (*glancing at his watch*): Yes…. (*A pause.*) *Suppressed laughter and whispering is heard from behind the door, and finally* VARIA *comes in and starts examining the luggage. After some time she says:*

VARIA: It's strange, I just can't find…

LOPAKHIN: What are you looking for?

VARIA: I packed the things myself, yet I can't remember….
A pause.

LOPAKHIN: Where are you going to now, Varvara Mihailovna?

VARIA: I? To the Rogulins. I've agreed to look after the house for them…to be their housekeeper, or something.

LOPAKHIN: That's at Yashnevo, isn't it? About seventy miles from here. (*A pause.*) So this is the end of life in this house….

VARIA (*examining the luggage*): But where could it be? Or perhaps I've packed it in the trunk?…Yes, life in this house has come to an end…there won't be any more….

LOPAKHIN: And I'm going to Kharkov presently…. On the next train. I've got a lot to do there. And I'm leaving Yepihodov here…. I've engaged him.

VARIA: Well!…

LOPAKHIN: Do you remember, last year about this time it was snowing already, but now it's quite still and sunny. It's rather cold, though…. About three degrees of frost.

VARIA: I haven't looked. (*A pause.*) Besides, our thermometer's broken…. (*A pause.*) *A voice is heard from outside the door: 'Yermolai Aleksyeevich!'*

LOPAKHIN (*as if he had long been expecting it*): Coming this moment! (*Goes out quickly.*) VARIA,

sitting on the floor, with her head on the bundle of clothes, sobs softly. The door opens, LIUBOV ANDRYEEVNA *enters quietly.*

LIUBOV ANDRYEEVNA: Well? (*A pause.*) We must go.

VARIA (*stops crying and wipes her eyes*): Yes, it's time, Mamma dear. I'll just be able to get to the Rogulins today, if only we don't miss the train.

LIUBOV ANDRYEEVNA (*calls through the door*): Ania, put your coat on. *Enter* ANIA, *followed by* GAYEV *and* CHARLOTTA IVANOVNA. GAYEV *wears a heavy overcoat with a hood. Servants and coachmen come into the room.* YEPIHODOV *fusses with the luggage.*
Now we can start on our journey!

ANIA (*joyfully*): Yes, our journey!

GAYEV: My friends, my dear, kind friends! Now as I leave this house for ever, how can I remain silent, how can I refrain from expressing to you, as a last farewell, the feelings which now overwhelm me….

ANIA (*imploringly*): Uncle!

VARIA: Uncle, dear, please don't!

GAYEV (*downcast*): I pot the red and follow through…. I'll keep quiet. *Enter* TROFIMOV, *then* LOPAKHIN.

TROFIMOV: Well, ladies and gentlemen, it's time to go.

LOPAKHIN: Yepihodov, my coat!

LIUBOV ANDRYEEVNA: I'll just sit down for one little minute more. I feel as if I'd never seen the walls and ceilings of this house before, and now I look at them with such longing and affection….

GAYEV: I remember when I was six years old—it was Holy Trinity day—I was sitting on this window-still, looking at Father—he was just going to church….

LIUBOV ANDRYEEVNA: Have they taken out all the luggage?

LOPAKHIN: It looks as if they have. (*To* YEPIHODOV, *as he puts on his coat.*) See that everything's all right, Yepihodov.

YEPIHODOV (*in a husky voice*): Don't worry, Yermolai Aleksyeevich!

LOPAKHIN: What are you talking like that for?

YEPIHODOV: I've just had a drink of water, I must have swallowed something.

YASHA (*with contempt*): What ignorance!

LIUBOV ANDRYEEVNA: When we leave here there won't be a soul in the place....

LOPAKHIN: Until the spring.

VARIA (*pulls an umbrella from a bundle of clothes;* LOPAKHIN *pretends to be frightened that she is going to strike him*): Now, why...why are you doing that?...I never thought of...

TROFIMOV: Ladies and gentlemen, come, let's get into the carriage. It's high time. The train will be in soon.

VARIA: Pyetia, here they are, your goloshes, beside the suitcase. (*Tearfully.*) And how dirty and worn-out they are!...

TROFIMOV (*puts them on*): Come along, ladies and gentlemen!

GAYEV (*greatly embarrassed, afraid of breaking into tears*): The train, the station.... In off into the middle pocket....

LIUBOV ANDRYEEVNA: Let us go!

LOPAKHIN: Is everyone here? No one left behind? (*Locks the door on the left.*) There are some things put away there, it had better be locked up. Come along!

ANIA: Good-bye, old house! Good-bye, old life!

TROFIMOV: Greetings to the new life!...(*Goes out with* ANIA.)

VARIA *glances round the room and goes out slowly.* YASHA *and* CHARLOTTA, *with her little dog, follow.*

LOPAKHIN: And so, until the spring. Come along, ladies and gentlemen.... Au revoir! (*Goes out.*)

LIUBOV ANDRYEEVNA *and* GAYEV *are left alone. They seem to have been waiting for this moment, and now they embrace each other and sob quietly, with restraint, so as not to be heard.*

GAYEV (*with despair in his voice*): Sister, my sister....

LIUBOV ANDRYEEVNA: Oh my darling, my precious, my beautiful orchard! My life, my youth, my happiness...good-bye!...Good-bye!

ANIA'S VOICE (*gaily*): Mamma!...

TROFIMOV'S VOICE (*gaily and excitedly*): Ah-oo!...

LIUBOV ANDRYEEVNA: For the last time—to look at these walls, these windows.... Mother used to love walking up and down this room....

GAYEV: Sister, my sister!...

ANIA'S VOICE: Mamma!

TROFIMOV'S VOICE: Ah-oo!

LIUBOV ANDRYEEVNA: We're coming....

(*Both go out.*)

The stage is empty. The sound of doors being locked is heard, then of carriages driving off. It grows quiet. The stillness is broken by the dull thuds of an axe on a tree. They sound forlorn and sad.

There is a sound of footsteps and from the door on the right FEERS *appears. He is dressed, as usual, in a coat and white waistcoat, and is wearing slippers. He looks ill.*

FEERS (*walks up to the middle door and tries the handle*): Locked. They've gone.... (*Sits down on a sofa.*) They forgot about me. Never mind.... I'll sit here for a bit. I don't suppose Leonid Andryeevich put on his fur coat, I expect he's gone in his light one.... (*Sighs, preoccupied.*) I didn't see to it.... These youngsters!... (*Mutters something unintelligible.*) My life's gone as if I'd never lived.... (*Lies down.*) I'll lie down a bit. You haven't got any strength left, nothing's left, nothing.... Oh, you... you're daft!...(*Lies motionless.*)

A distant sound is heard, coming as if out of the sky, like the sound of a string snapping, slowly and sadly dying away. Silence ensues, broken only by the sound of an axe striking a tree in the orchard far away.

CURTAIN

PERFORMING *THE CHERRY ORCHARD*

Anton Chekhov set the Moscow Art Theater's 1903–04 season as his target date for completing *The Cherry Orchard.* When he finished the play, he emphasized to director Konstantin Stanislavski that "not a drama but a comedy has emerged from me, in places even a farce." Stanislavski read the new script as "a poetically tragic drama of the vanishing life of the gentry crushed by economic demands of vulgar commercialism."[4] The director's view won out in the original production and the première on January 17, 1904 of Chekhov's final play enjoyed a mediocre success but disappointment was masked by the celebration of Chekhov's forty-fourth birthday and the twenty-fifth anniversary of his literary activities.

The reviewers adopted Stanislavski's viewpoint that *The Cherry Orchard* was the social tragedy of the passing of the old order symbolized by the sale of the cherry orchard. Nonetheless, Chekhov insisted that he had written a comedy and his characters were not very serious people who quickly adapted to their predicament. He regarded self-deluding people as truly comic—both ludicrous and worthy of the audience's compassion. The shifting viewpoints within the text between the old way and the new, the serious and the comic, have challenged artists for one hundred years. All agree, however, that Madame Ranyevskaia, originally played by Chekhov's wife (Olga Knipper), is a magnificent role and has been performed on recent stages by the great actresses of the American theater—Eva Le Gallienne, Jessica Tandy, Colleen Dewhurst, and Irene Worth. The play has also been adapted to the American Confederate South by director Joshua Logan and called *The Wisteria Trees*, given naturalistic treatments by most directors including Tyrone Guthrie, and staged with a postmodern treatment in an open white setting by director Andrei Serban. For the 1977 New York Shakespeare Festival production of Chekhov's play, Serban departed from the traditional interior settings and visually depicted Chekhov's family existing in a frozen landscape of unbroken tradition and unchanging perspectives.

CRITICS' NOTEBOOK

Anton Chekhov's letters have been a great resource for understanding his approach to depicting humanity in his short stories and plays. In his letters to friends, publishers, and other writers, he detailed his thoughts on close observation of human behavior and on storytelling without villains, heroes, or moral positions.

As an actor/director, Konstantin Stanislavski wrote extensively on his work with the Moscow Art Theater and his approach to acting that became known as the Stanislavski system and as "The Method" in the United States. The Moscow Art Theater's reputation was made with Chekhov's plays depicting in realistic detail the lives of the rural landowning class in provincial Russia. Stanislavski's autobiography, *My Life in Art,* was published in 1924 and provided a record of the founding of the Moscow Art Theater and the premières of Chekhov's full-length plays, including *The Sea Gull, Uncle Vanya, The Three Sisters, Ivanov,* and *The Cherry Orchard,* between 1898 and 1904. In *My Life in Art,* Stanislavski recorded his oftentimes troubled relationship with Chekhov and their disagreements in rehearsals over Stanislavski's staging of the playwright's work. *My Life in Art* is a theatrical sourcebook for understanding the creative process that first brought Chekhov's work to the stage and established his reputation as a playwright.

Modern scholars, including J. L. Styan, have written extensively on Chekhov's brand of stage realism, with depends less on externals than on the observation of people going about commonplace activities while their futures are being irrevocably shaped.

In his three-volume study of modern drama and landmark productions of plays in modern times, J. L. Styan looked at realism and naturalism in the first volume. Henrik Ibsen, August Strindberg, George Bernard Shaw, and Anton Chekhov are set forth as the progenitors of playwriting for the modern realistic theater. Chekhov's style of writing, according to Styan, set forth a more profound drama of realism than his fellow realists in the late nineteenth-century theater.

Anton Chekhov sent his advice on playwriting to his oldest brother, Alexander Chekhov, who was a fiction writer, journalist, and editor of trade journals. Alexander Chekhov's literary abilities were quickly overtaken by those of his younger brother.

Chekhov sent the manuscript of *The Cherry Orchard* to Konstantin Stanislavski at the Moscow Art Theater on October 20, 1903. Stanislavski read the play with great enthusiasm and immediately sent Chekhov a telegram followed by a letter in which he talked about casting and even argued that Chekhov was wrong to call his play a "comedy." Stanislavski thought the play a "tragedy" regardless of the "escape into a better life you [Chekhov] might indicate in the last act." Chekhov responded on October 30, 1903 with early notes on casting the roles.

J. L. Styan on *Chekhov's Contribution to Realism**

❦

The Moscow Art Theatre went on to produce the last plays of Anton Chekhov (1860–1904), each with a structure more fragile than that of *The Seagull* with its comparatively conventional plotting. These were Chekhov's masterpieces, *Uncle Vanya* (1899), *Three Sisters* (1901) and *The Cherry Orchard* (1904). Whereas Stanislavsky largely developed his thinking about the art of the theatre after Chekhov's death, it was during the production of these plays that Chekhov increased his understanding of stage realism. He learned by experience and largely taught himself.

Three Sisters was the first play he wrote knowing who might play the parts. This factor might be thought to make it easier to write 'to the life', but in practice the availability of a company who could be counted on to indulge his experiments presented him with the greater challenge. After seeing this play in rehearsal and performance, he continued to worry at its text to get it right. *The Cherry Orchard* gave him even more trouble. He cast and recast the parts in his mind, and the play was three years in the writing. However, he was a dying man by the time it was produced, and he was spared the work of rewriting it. As a result of his agonizing, his achievement was of such a stature as called for a redefinition of naturalism, and made Ibsen's look old-fashioned. Stark Young spoke for the

*J. L. Styan, *Modern Drama in Theory and Practice 1: Realism and Naturalism* (New York: Cambridge University Press, 1983): 81–84.

post-Ibsen generation when he found that only Chekhov's plays as performed by the MAT gave him 'the thrill that comes from a sense of truth', for only they carried realism 'to an honest and spiritual depth and candour'.

❧ ❧ ❧

In his last years Chekhov knew a little of Ibsen from Moscow productions, but he made it clear that he did not approve of Ibsen's kind of realism. Doubtless Chekhov recognized the forms and trappings of the well-made play still presented in the Norwegian: the big conflicts, the *scènes à faire* and the preconceived roles and attitudes, all lacking the quiet irony with which Chekhov himself saw human behaviour. He saw *Hedda Gabler* in 1900 and thought Hedda's suicide too sensational—'Look here', he said to Stanislavsky, 'Ibsen is not really a dramatist'. At that time, Chekhov had already learned to write an objective, underplayed curtain scene. Even the most Chekhovian of Ibsen's plays, *The Wild Duck*, which Chekhov saw in 1901, he found 'uninteresting'. He saw *Ghosts* just before his death in 1904, and again the curt verdict: 'A rotten play'. It was Ibsen's lack of humour and his posture as a moralist which disturbed the Russian, whose aim was to keep his characters flexible and his mind open.

Chekhov himself pursued a unique objectivity in his naturalism. 'Freedom from force and falsehood, no matter how they manifest themselves', he wrote to his editor Pleshcheyev on 4 October 1888. He refused to moralize, and part of the discomfort of watching Chekhov on the stage comes of having no moral position to espouse. 'I have not introduced a single villain nor an angel, although I could not refuse myself buffoons; I accused nobody, justified nobody' (this in a letter of 24 October 1887). So it is that we can be angry with Mme. Ranevsky for letting the orchard slip through her fingers, like the money we twice see her give away so recklessly, but we can also understand her inability to manage a situation wholly foreign to her nature and upbringing. The well-known assertion by Chekhov that 'a writer should be as objective as a chemist' (14 January 1887) could sum up the reasons why he goes beyond Ibsen and Strindberg in his realism. Chekhov had been trained as a physician, but his pursuit of a scientific ideal of truth, one in which the writer was required to be as impersonal as a doctor examining a patient, really came of his extraordinarily sharp eye for spotting incongruity in human behaviour. This kind of objectivity forced upon the audience a role equivalent to that of a jury presented with a mass of circumstantial and contradictory evidence—it must stand back and coolly sort it out.

By the time Chekhov wrote *The Cherry Orchard*, the last vestiges of romantic sensationalism had disappeared from his playwriting. There is no shot fired on or off the stage, no death of one of the characters to upset the balance of interest. Epihodov's pistol is all for laughter, and Charlotta's hunting gun amusingly illuminates her character. Every love scene in the play, Anya with Trofimov, Yasha with Dunyasha, Varya with Lopakhin, is designed for an incisive moment of comic irony. The triumph of Lopakhin, who becomes the new owner of the very estate where his family had formerly worked as serfs, is undercut by his drunken good humour, and any grand and knowing statement in his public announcement of the purchase in act III is not to be found. There is no villain, no hero, no moral, just a calm and amused treatment of a potentially enormous and explosive situation, that of the breaking up of the old order and the disintegration of a whole class of society. In form and style, *The Cherry Orchard* was a final rejection of the ways of the nineteenth-century stage and drama.

Anton Chekhov's Letter on Playwriting (April 11, 1889)*

❦

Try to be original in your play and as clever as possible; but don't be afraid to show yourself foolish; we must have freedom of thinking, and

only he is an emancipated thinker who is not afraid to write foolish things. Don't round things out, don't polish—but be awkward and imprudent. Brevity is the sister of talent. Remember, by the way that declarations of love, the infidelity of husbands and wives; widows', orphans', and all other tears, have long since been written up. The subject ought to be new, but there need be no "fable." and the main thing is—father and mother must eat. Write. Flies purify the air, and plays—the morals.

Anton Chekhov Writes to Konstantin Stanislavski*

Yalta October 30, 1903

Dear Konstantin Sergeyevich,

Many thanks for the letter and thank you for the telegram too. Letters are very precious to me because in the first place I'm all alone and in the second I sent the play off three weeks ago and didn't receive your letter until yesterday, and if it hadn't been for my wife [Olga Knipper] I'd have known nothing and could have imagined any number of things. As I worked on Lopakin, I thought of him as your role. If for any reason he doesn't appeal to you, take Gayev. Lopakin may be a merchant, but he is a decent person in every sense; his behavior must be entirely proper, cultivated and free of pettiness or clowning. I had the feeling you could do a brilliant job of this role, the central role of the play. If you take Gayev, give Lopakin to [Alexander] Vishnevsky. He won't be an artistic Lopakin, but he won't be a petty one either. [Vasily] Luzhsky would make an unfeeling foreigner of the role, [Leonid] Leonidov would turn it into a cute little kulak.

I very much want to go to Moscow, but I don't see how I can break away from here. It's growing cold, and I almost never leave the house. I'm not used to being out of doors and

*Anton Chekhov, *Letters on the Short Story, the Drama and other Literary Topics*, selected and edited by Louis S. Friedland (New York: Minton, Balch & Co., 1924): 170.

Letters of Anton Chekhov, trans. Michael Henry Heim with Simon Karlinsky (New York: Harper & Row Publishers, 1973): 460–461.

keep coughing. It's not Moscow or the trip I'm afraid of: it's the layover in Sevastopol that lasts from two o'clock until eight—and in the most boring company imaginable....

Yours, A. Chekhov

REVISITING STAGE LANGUAGE

Language in the theater is often deceptive. On the printed page, words follow one another in a simple format of consecutive lines set down as dialogue to indicate different characters as they speak to one another. Nonetheless, language written for the stage is complex and multifaceted. It is not merely the spoken word written by the playwright as dialogue, though when we read a play we tend to equate theater language with words and words with the playwright's text and meaning. Playwrights do not communicate through words alone. The language of a play involves communication among characters and audiences in a highly complex system of words, signs, symbols, sounds, and silences. In some instances, characters use language not to reveal information so much as to conceal their feelings and intentions. In addition, the theater's technology, depending on the historical period, enters into the communication system between the theater's artists and audiences.

Playwrights and critics have spoken about the uniqueness of language written for the theater and how it differs from the language of poetry and fiction. The key to the success of the playwright's words on the page is *performability*. The words of the drama must have the potential for action, gesture, feeling, sound, and aliveness. The actor fills the character's words, actions, gestures, and intentions with a living presence.

The collaboration between playwright Anton Chekov and director/actor Konstantin Stanislavski resulted in the creation of modern theatrical realism that emphasized careful attention to details of environment and truthful behavior that were recreated in production as life being lived on stage. Realism in writing and production became the dominant literary and performance style of theater in the twentieth century and beyond.

NOTES

1. Martin Esslin, *The Field of Drama: How the Signs of Drama Create Meaning on Stage & Screen* (New York: Methuen, 1987): 82.
2. George Steiner, *The Death of Tragedy* (New York: Oxford University Press, 1963): 275.
3. Maurice Valency, *The Breaking String: The Plays of Anton Chekhov* (New York: Oxford University Press, 1966): 249.
4. Ernest J. Simmons, *Chekhov: A Biography* (Boston: Little, Brown & Co., 1962): 604.

PART THREE

TYPES OF
DRAMATIC WRITING

CHAPTER 5

❦

TRAGEDY

Kiyosumi Niihari as Oedipus in *Oedipus the King* by Sophocles, directed and designed by Tadashi Suzuki, co-produced by the Shizuoka Performing Arts Center, Japan, and The Professional Training Program in Theatre at the University of Delaware, Hartshorn Theatre, Newark, DE, 2002. (Photo by William Browning.)

> *It is not the theme of the play to which we respond, but the* action—*the through-action of the protagonist, and the attendant support of the secondary characters, this support lent through their congruent actions.*
> —David Mamet[1]

ORIGINS OF THEATER AND DRAMA

Until very recently, approaches to play analysis had their roots in Aristotle's *Poetics,* a fragmentary treatise of the fourth century B.C. that remains the starting point for most discussions of drama. Aristotle (384–322 B.C.), the first theorist of drama, introduced to the Western world two essential ways of understanding plays. The first concerned how drama "imitated" human experience and involved such terms as plot, action, character, language, universal meanings, and visual effects. The second concerned the types of plays performed in the theater festivals of his time and earlier, namely, tragedy, comedy, and satyr plays.

Drama as an imitation of human action will be our starting point for understanding two major types of writing for the Western theater—tragedy and comedy.

Many anthropologists and theater historians trace the origins of theater and drama to ritual dances and mimes performed by masked dancers during fertility rites and ceremonies calling to the gods for success in war, hunting, and farming. The rain dance ceremonies of Native Americans of the Southwest were intended to ensure that the tribal gods would send rain to make crops grow. Early societies acted out patterns of life, death, and rebirth associated with the welfare of the village until these ceremonies became formalized dramatic rituals. Imitation, costumes, masks, makeup, gesture, dance, music, and pantomime were some of the theatrical elements in early rituals. Children at play reenact these ancient beginnings of art when they "play at" being someone or something other than themselves. Aristotle wrote that deep within human nature lies an instinct for imitation that gives us pleasure and knowledge. In play, children experiment with and learn roles they will experience in their adult lives; they im-itate adult behavior, thereby fitting themselves into as yet unfamiliar worlds.

Unlike childhood games, primitive rituals concerned practical matters: the tribe's protection and welfare. Theater betrays its origins in ancient tribal ceremonies enacting life, death, and rebirth because plays are largely imitations of living, dying, and surviving. They enact situations of joy and sorrow, struggle and conquest; they mirror our questions and tentative answers about life. From uncertain ritual origins evolved the great plays of Western drama, the greatest being, from Aristotle's perspective, *Oedipus the King* by Sophocles.

Of all the arts, Aristotle thought of drama as the most direct response to humanity's deep need to imitate experience. We have already traced the source of the word *drama* from the Greek *dran,* meaning "to do," "act," or "perform." Aristotle put it more succinctly when he defined drama as an "imitation of an action." This statement has large implications for understanding plays. Even though drama began as a preverbal activity—for example, an early society's celebration with mime, music, and dance of a successful hunt—for all practical purposes, Western drama's history begins with Greek tragedies and comedies from the fifth century B.C.

ARISTOTLE'S DEFINITIONS

In *The Poetics,* Aristotle set out to distinguish between two types of writing: epic poetry and drama. Although both present "imitations of human beings in action," they differ greatly in the way in which they imitate human events. Epic poems, such as Homer's *Iliad* and *Odyssey,* narrate and describe. Drama, such as Sophocles' *Oedipus the King* and *Antigone,* shows and enacts. In Aristotle's words, drama "presents all characters as living and moving before us."

Aristotle's concept of "imitation" (*mimesis*) begins with the playwright's deliberate selection and arrangement of events, words, and images into a pattern that makes up a meaningful and whole course of human events. In his famous definition, the dramatic pattern of imitation is an action (*praxis*) that represents nature as the Greeks understood it: the sum of all the changeless laws under which we manifest our "human nature." Art imitates nature to help us understand ourselves and the world around us.

In *The Poetics*, Aristotle set down a detailed analysis of tragedy which he had deduced from the plays he observed in the Greek festivals. To these he added his theory of imitation which assumes the significance of content in drama—what we call drama's meanings and messages. Third, he added his theory of *catharsis*, or purgation, attributed to tragedy in which audiences experience emotions of pity and fear as they witness human suffering.

DRAMA'S ELEMENTS AND WRITING CONVENTIONS

Aristotle theorized that drama was made up of six elements and set them down in order of their importance in his view: plot, character, thought, language, spectacle or visual effects, and choral odes. He began with plot, calling it the "soul of tragedy." *Plot*, sometimes called the "story," is the order of events as the author arranges them. A plot may be simple or complex, compressed or diffuse. The plot of *Oedipus the King* is compressed, charting Oedipus' relentless search for the cause of the city's plague—the murderer of the former king. The plot of *Hamlet* is diffuse as the hero wanders in a roundabout fashion to avenge his father's murder. More recently, plots have subordinated storytelling to the creation of a sense of active human presence. *The Cherry Orchard* and *How I Learned to Drive* minimize plot in favor of the interaction of character and situation in a succession of scenes that carry the characters to a decisive event that ends the play. For example, in *The Cherry Orchard* that decisive event is the auction of the Ranevskaya estate. Many Renaissance plays have two or more plots moving

simultaneously toward a resolution. More recent plays are essentially plotless. *Footfalls* presents a concrete stage image of habituated modern life. *The America Play* substitutes a collage of powerful images of a world approaching Armageddon.

Clearly over the centuries, the types of plots that Aristotle envisioned have varied with writers and cultures. However, plays that are built on the principle of cause and effect, like *Oedipus the King, Hamlet, The Importance of Being Earnest, Hedda Gabler,* and *Fences,* have plots that can be divided for analysis into four parts: (1) *exposition,* the beginning of the play that introduces characters with their past and present situations; (2) *complication,* developing relationships and changing fortunes of the characters in a "compounding" of the plot; (3) *reversal* (*peripety* or *peripeteia*), or the point at which the hero's fortunes change from good to bad in tragedy or from bad to good in comedy. Reversal is accompanied by the hero's recognition (*anagnorisis*) in which there is a change from ignorance to knowledge; and (4) *resolution,* tying up loose ends, showing painful actions (such as deaths or wounds) or joyful events (such as weddings or reunions), and providing answers to unanswered questions.

Other common terms in plot analysis are *crisis* and *climax*. Crisis is the complication by which the outcome of the plot is irreversibly determined; the climax is the point in the play at which tension is highest and audience emotions are most intense. The tension often continues to build, engaging the audience's interests and emotions until the end. Also, there is *recognition*, the central character's realization that his or her fortune has decisively turned and that he or she shares in the responsibility for that change. The climax usually coincides either with the crisis or with the recognition, as in *Oedipus the King*.

Aristotle considered the best plot to be a concentrated compiling of events leading to reversal, catastrophe, and recognition. In this type of dramatic storytelling, the unfolding of past events leads to the present crisis. In *Oedipus the King,* past circumstances keep coming to light until, near the end, the two shepherds from Mount Cithaeron stand together before Oedipus in the moment of truth. In the course of

Sophocles' play, the powerful king is reduced to a blind beggar. In the action of the play, Oedipus did not outrun his past or the gods' will.

Aristotle's traditional plot analysis does not work equally well for all plays, not even for all older plays. For some of the most original modern plays, it does not work at all. Nothing (or almost nothing) precedes the complication in Bertolt Brecht's *Galileo*. In Beckett's *Waiting for Godot*, waiting is the essential action, not the occurrence of life-changing sequential events. Indeed, the history of modern drama reads like a continuing revolt against the very idea of traditional writing and storytelling. Nonetheless, mastering traditional plot analysis is important in understanding plays that use it as well as those that dispense with it.

Following Aristotle's celebration of plot as the imitation of human endeavor, *character,* or the story's personalities, is introduced as the second most important element. The suggestion is that plot reveals character, that we are defined by what we choose to confront or to avoid. Character represents what Francis Fergusson called the "changing life of the psyche."[2] These changes come through interactions of one psyche with another, namely, one character with another. In drama, the interaction of characters is typically in the form of *conflict.* The conflict in *Oedipus the King* is most simply defined as one between humans and gods: human reason versus supernatural prediction. As in plot, conflict in character may be simple or complex. It may be as simple as Cinderella's conflict with her jealous stepsisters in the fairy tale, or as complex as Hamlet's inner turmoil over the necessity to avenge his father's murder. It may be sexual, domestic, political, philosophical, or metaphysical. Conflict creates suspense, making us wonder what will happen next, who will win or lose. It is integral to *dramatic action,* which is defined as the movement of opposing forces toward a resolution of their opposition in the hero's death and/or the villain's defeat.

THEORIES OF TRAGEDY

Reflecting on plays written by Sophocles and Euripides, Aristotle perceived of characters in tragedy as individuals of high renown, usually from illustrious families. One of the ironies in Sophocles' play is that Oedipus, thinking he may be lowborn, is a prince of the House of Thebes. In his interpretation of character, Aristotle was most concerned that an individual's personality profile develop out of moral choices made in given situations and under extreme pressures. The tragic hero usually does some deed and suffers as a consequence because, in Aristotle's view, *actions have consequences in the moral world.* This was also Sophocles' view. Moreover, Aristotle urged that the tragic hero, or protagonist, be credible; that is, he or she should be neither utterly villainous nor eminently virtuous. The reversal of circumstances is, therefore, brought about not by vice or corruption, but by some great error—usually a misjudgment—on the hero's part. The Greeks called this error or frailty *hamartia.* Some critics have called this trait the hero's "tragic flaw," pointing to acts of pride or ambition. However, the concept of grave error does not imply a single trait, such as rashness or pride, but a combination of character traits that results in deeds growing out of errors in judgment. Oedipus, for example, is prone to rashness, physical violence, anger, pride, and compassion. He tries to avoid the prophecy that he will destroy his parents, but his haste and misjudgment lead him into actions that destroy Laius and Jocasta, his father and mother. As a responsible ruler, he determines to save the city of Thebes from the pollution and, despite warnings, comes face to face with himself as an incestuous murderer and the cause of the plague. He then accepts responsibility for who and what he is.

Generally, the classical formula illustrates the tragic hero committing some deed that causes great unintended suffering; and then, by seeing the consequences, the hero learns the true nature of his or her choices and acts. In the best classical tragedies, the hero is an important person with certain admirable qualities who makes some portentous mistake that results in great suffering and often death. Calamity is not the result of external or irrational forces but of the hero's misjudgment. Oedipus, under the erroneous impression that Polybus and Merope are his parents, flees from them when he learns that he will kill his father and marry his mother. His decision to flee Corinth is commendable, but it happens to be a great mistake because it brings him to his real parents and the subsequent disasters. As a dramatic character, Oedipus is credible: He is self-assured, quick-tempered, violent, and proud.

Universal truths, language, spectacle, and choral odes/music/song complete Aristotle's elements of drama. "Thought," general maxims, or characters' arguments are derived both from viewing the consequences of human choices, although fictional, and from the hero's ability to reflect on the meaning of his or her choices. The blind Oedipus appears, finally, before us in full understanding of the implications of his deeds: "contaminated, cursed,/ Unclean in heaven's sight." Hamlet surmises, "There is special providence in the fall of a sparrow." In *Waiting for Godot*, Beckett's Vladimir concludes, "We are not saints, but we have kept our appointment. How many people can boast as much?" His cohort, Estragon, replies, "Billions."

Since the playwright's meanings are usually conveyed through actions and words, Aristotle describes language as one of drama's conveyers of meaning. Songs or choral odes, also central to classical Greek plays, provided variations on spoken dialogue by introducing different rhythms and harmonies. Finally, spectacle, or the production of spectacular visual effects, was, for Aristotle, the least important of drama's elements since these effects depended on the "art of the stage machinist" (today's stage technician) rather than the playwright.

Oedipus the King has long been celebrated as the most satisfying of Greek tragedies. A model of tragic writing for the theater, Sophocles' play exemplifies those classical elements and conventions examined here as basic to understanding Western playwriting.

Oedipus the King

SOPHOCLES

Sophocles (496?–406 B.C.) was one of four classical Greek playwrights whose work survives today. He wrote perhaps the greatest Greek tragedy, Oedipus the King, *in 427 B.C., along with two other plays dealing with the story of the House of Thebes. They are* Antigone, *written earlier in 441 B.C., and* Oedipus at Colonus, *written in 406 B.C., the year of Sophocles' death, and produced posthumously in the Festival of Dionysus.*

Born in Colonus, Sophocles is said to have written 120 plays. In the annual competition among playwrights held in the Dionysian Festival in Athens, he won eighteen first prizes. He is the second of the three great Athenian tragedians whose work has survived. Aeschylus was thirty years older and Euripides some fifteen years younger. Sophocles' young adulthood coincided with the flowering of Athenian civilization between the defeat of the Persians in 480 B.C. and the surrender to Sparta at the end of the Peloponnesian War in 404 B.C. He was an aristocrat and was active in political and military affairs. Only seven of his plays are extant today.

CRITICAL INTRODUCTION TO *OEDIPUS THE KING*

To fifth-century Athenians, a theatrical performance was a religious, civic, and entertaining occasion. The theater was a setting for the worship of Dionysus, god of fertility, wine, and rebirth. The Greater or City Dionysia in Athens, celebrated for five or six days every spring, was the most important of the Dionysian festivals held throughout Greece. Three playwrights were chosen a year in advance to compete for first prize with four plays each (a tetralogy), including three tragedies (a trilogy), sometimes but not always related in subject matter or theme, and a satyr play, which burlesqued parts

of myths. By Sophocles' day, the trilogy had been abandoned, resulting in three playwrights competing in a single day and concentrating on writing the single play.

The origins of Greek tragedy cannot be clearly traced. *Tragedy* means literally "goat song," and was perhaps a choral song improvised and sung for the prize of a goat. Historians generally agree that tragedy as we know it in the works of Aeschylus, Sophocles, and Euripides grew out of choral contests delivered in honor of Dionysus. The choral odes with their combination of song, dance, and recitative provided Greek drama with its most characteristic trait. In the earliest tragedies, the lyrical element, sung by the chorus, must have predominated over dialogue. By the fifth century B.C., the chorus had become a community voice, a kind of audience representative on stage—concerned but ignorant, reacting to events, affected by what happens but participating as a bystander or eyewitness. They watched, listened, and reacted but did not initiate events.

Tradition also records the existence of Thespis, a sixth-century figure who may have been the first individual to step out of the chorus and take a solo part, or to exchange dialogue with the chorus. Hence, Thespis is credited with being the first actor. Aristotle credits Aeschylus with introducing the second actor—a virtual prerequisite for the development of dialogue and complex plots. Sophocles added the third actor. Aeschylus is also credited with reducing the size of the theatrical chorus from fifty to twelve or fifteen. The chorus moved in slow and stately measures accompanied by the flute, chanting odes usually reflecting on the events immediately preceding or giving background on the myth in general. In dialogue passages, the choral leader (*coryphaeus*) probably spoke for the entire chorus. The odes were divided into stanzas, called *strophes* and *antistrophes*, delivered as the chorus moved first in one direction and then in the opposite. The odes alternated with *episodes* in which several actors told the story and moved the plot forward. The first episode was called the *prologos* and the last the *exodos*; there were typically five episodes in a tragedy. The odes separated the episodes, adding dimensions of myth, memory, emotion, and background information.

The physical theater and its conventions, for which Sophocles wrote, were to a large degree inflexible. We must remember that the physical theater always influences the playwright's work, resulting in peculiarities of writing throughout the centuries. We know some facts about the Theater of Dionysus during the age of Aeschylus, Sophocles, and Euripides. The theater was located at the base of a hillside. The audience—perhaps as large as 15,000—sat on benches rising in half circles on the southern slope of the Acropolis. In time, plays were performed before a long, low wooden building (*skene*) that served as background for the action and as a dressing room for the actors. In front of the scene building was the main circular acting area, called the *orchestra* or dancing circle, with an altar for Dionysus in the center. Whether or not there was a low, raised stage in front of the building and separating the main action from the choral action, we do not know. Most historians think it was an unlikely feature in the fifth century B.C. The platform stage became a known feature in later stage architecture but its existence was debatable at the time of Sophocles. Both actors and chorus wore masks to indicate age, temperament, and sex. Since men played women's parts and actors often played several parts, masks also had a practical function. The actors wore ankle-length, colorful robes (*chitons*), resembling garments worn by well-dressed Athenians. The playwright had to take into account the number of speaking actors available to him at any given time, although there could be actors in nonspeaking roles, like palace guards. The actors had to be highly trained professionals because the performance of several plays, lasting most of the daylight hours, made great demands on their voices and physical stamina.

In Sophocles' time, playwrights usually dramatized a traditional story (for example, the legend surrounding the House of Thebes). In Sophocles' treatment the old Theban myth of humanity's vain effort to circumvent divine will is a suspenseful revelation of the fateful continuity of the past into the present. There is the pathos of innocent ignorance and impotence which affects aristocrat and shepherd alike. Oedipus is ignorant of who he is and what he has done in all innocence. The structure of the story is *retrospective:* The gradual revelation of past events creates the present. Every step Oedipus takes to solve the old murder mystery of who killed Laius, every one of the chance disclosures, brings him closer both to the solution he seeks and to the self-discovery he does not expect. When the last piece falls into place, the detective has become the criminal, his success has become his doom, and his ignorance has become tragic knowledge.

The plot is heavily ironic, introducing the technique of *dramatic irony* of which Sophocles was a master. Dramatic irony operates whenever there are circumstances in plot or character of which the speaker is ignorant or misunderstands. The more unfortunate the significance of the character's ignorance, the more poignant the tragic irony. Oedipus' early words to the Theban citizens are, "There is not one of you who knows my pain." On the surface we hear the king's concern for his stricken people and his involvement in the city's fate, but, because we know the Theban myth, we also perceive the dreadful accuracy of his description of himself.

The knowledgeable reader is alert to the persistent ironies in Oedipus' story: He curses Laius's murderer, promising to take revenge for the dead king, "As I would for my own father"—Laius is his biological father; his berating of Teiresias, the blind seer, for his arrogance and complicity in Laius's murder hints at his own blindness; his accusation that Jocasta does not want the truth of Oedipus' identity revealed because she fears she has married a peasant

Oedipus the King

TRANSLATED BY DAVID GRENE

CHARACTERS

OEDIPUS   King of Thebes
JOCASTA   His Wife
CREON   His Brother-in-Law
TEIRESIAS   An Old Blind Prophet
A PRIEST
FIRST MESSENGER
SECOND MESSENGER
A HERDSMAN
A CHORUS OF OLD MEN OF THEBES

SCENE

*In front of the palace of Oedipus at Thebes. To the right of
the stage near the altar stands the* PRIEST *with a crowd of
children.* OEDIPUS *emerges from the central door.*

OEDIPUS

Children, young sons and daughters of old
    Cadmus,
why do you sit here with your suppliant crowns?
The town is heavy with a mingled burden
of sounds and smells, of groans and hymns and
    incense;
I did not think it fit that I should hear
of this from messengers but came myself,—
I Oedipus whom all men call the Great.
(*He turns to the* PRIEST.)
You're old and they are young; come, speak for
    them.
What do you fear or want, that you sit here
    suppliant? Indeed I'm willing to give all
that you may need; I would be very hard
should I not pity suppliants like these.
    PRIEST
O ruler of my country, Oedipus,
you see our company around the altar;
you see our ages; some of us, like these,
who cannot yet fly far, and some of us
heavy with age; these children are the chosen

among the young, and I the priest of Zeus.
Within the market place sit others crowned
with suppliant garlands, at the double shrine
of Pallas and the temple where Ismenus
gives oracles by fire. King, you yourself
have seen our city reeling like a wreck
already; it can scarcely lift its prow
out of the depths, out of the bloody surf.
A blight is on the fruitful plants of the earth,
A blight is on the cattle in the fields,
a blight is on our women that no children
are born to them; a God that carries fire,
a deadly pestilence, is on our town,
strikes us and spares not, and the house of
    Cadmus
is emptied of its people while black Death
grows rich in groaning and in lamentation.
We have not come as suppliants to this altar
because we thought of you as of a God,
but rather judging you the first of men
in all the chances of this life and when
we mortals have to do with more than man.
You came and by your coming saved our city,
freed us from tribute which we paid of old
to the Sphinx, cruel singer. This you did
in virtue of no knowledge we could give you,
in virtue of no teaching; it was God
that aided you, men say, and you are held
with God's assistance to have saved our lives.
Now Oedipus, Greatest in all men's eyes,
here falling at your feet we all entreat you,
find us some strength for rescue.
Perhaps you'll hear a wise word from some God,
perhaps you will learn something from a man
(for I have seen that for the skilled of practice
the outcome of their counsels live the most).
Noblest of men, go, and raise up our city,
go,—and give heed. For now this land of ours
calls you its savior since you saved it once.
So, let us never speak about your reign

202

as of a time when first our feet were set
secure on high, but later fell to ruin.
Raise up our city, save it and raise it up.
Once you have brought us luck with happy omen;
be no less now in fortune.
If you will rule this land, as now you rule it,
better to rule it full of men than empty.
For neither tower nor ship is anything
when empty, and none live in it together.

OEDIPUS

I pity you, children. You have come full of
    longing,
but I have known the story before you told it
only too well. I know you are all sick,
yet there is not one of you, sick though you are,
that is as sick as I myself.
Your several sorrows each have single scope
and touch but one of you. My spirit groans
for city and myself and you at once.
You have not roused me like a man from sleep;
know that I have given many tears to this,
gone many ways wandering in thought,
but as I thought I found only one remedy
and that I took. I send Menoeceus' son
Creon, Jocasta's brother, to Apollo,
to his Pythian temple,
that he might learn there by what act or word
I could save this city. As I count the days,
it vexes me what ails him; he is gone
far longer than he needed for the journey.
But when he comes, then, may I prove a villain,
if I shall not do all the God commands.

PRIEST

Thanks for your gracious words. Your servants
    here
signal that Creon is this moment coming.

OEDIPUS

His face is bright. O holy Lord Apollo,
grant that his news too may be bright for us
and bring us safety.

PRIEST

It is happy news,
I think, for else his head would not be crowned
with sprigs of fruitful laurel.

OEDIPUS

                        We will know soon,
he's within hail. Lord Creon, my good brother,
what is the word you bring us from the God?
(CREON enters.)

CREON

A good word,—for things hard to bear themselves
if in the final issue all is well
I count complete good fortune.

OEDIPUS

                        What do you mean?
What you have said so far
leaves me uncertain whether to trust or fear.

CREON

If you will hear my news before these others
I am ready to speak, or else to go within.

OEDIPUS

Speak it to all;
the grief I bear, I bear it more for these
than for my own heart.

CREON

                        I will tell you, then,
what I heard from the God.
King Phoebus in plain words commanded us
to drive out a pollution from our land,
pollution grown ingrained within the land;
drive it out, said the God, not cherish it,
till it's past cure.

OEDIPUS

                        What is the rite
of purification? How shall it be done?

CREON

By banishing a man, or expiation
of blood by blood, since it is murder guilt
which holds our city in this destroying storm.

OEDIPUS

Who is this man whose fate the God pronounces?

CREON

My Lord, before you piloted the state
we had a king called Laius.

OEDIPUS

I know of him by hearsay. I have not seen him.

CREON

The God commanded clearly: let some one
punish with force this dead man's murderers.

OEDIPUS

Where are they in the world? Where would a trace
of this old crime be found? It would be hard
to guess where.

CREON

                        The clue is in this land;
that which is sought is found;
the unheeded thing escapes:
so said the God.

OEDIPUS

Was it at home,
or in the country that death came upon him,
or in another country travelling?

CREON

He went, he said himself, upon an embassy,
but never returned when he set out from home.

OEDIPUS

Was there no messenger, no fellow traveller
who knew what happened? Such a one might tell
something of use.

CREON

They were all killed save one. He fled in terror
and he could tell us nothing in clear terms
of what he knew, nothing, but one thing only.

OEDIPUS

What was it?
If we could even find a slim beginning
in which to hope, we might discover much.

CREON

This man said that the robbers they encountered
were many and the hands that did the murder
were many; it was no man's single power.

OEDIPUS

How could a robber dare a deed like this
were he not helped with money from the city,
money and treachery?

CREON

That indeed was thought.
But Laius was dead and in our trouble
there was none to help.

OEDIPUS

What trouble was so great to hinder you
inquiring out the murder of your king?

CREON

The riddling Sphinx induced us to neglect
mysterious crimes and rather seek solution
of troubles at our feet.

OEDIPUS

I will bring this to light again. King Phoebus
fittingly took this care about the dead,
and you too fittingly
And justly you will see in me an ally,
a champion of my country and the God.
For when I drive pollution from the land
I will not serve a distant friend's advantage,
but act in my own interest. Whoever
he was that killed the king may readily
wish to dispatch me with his murderous
hand;

so helping the dead king I help myself.
Come, children, take your suppliant boughs and
go;
up from the altars now. Call the assembly
and let it meet upon the understanding
that I'll do everything. God will decide
whether we prosper or remain in sorrow.

PRIEST

Rise, children—it was this we came to seek,
which of himself the king now offers us.
May Phoebus who gave us the oracle
come to our rescue and stay the plague.

(*Exeunt all but the* CHORUS.)

CHORUS
Strophe

What is the sweet spoken word of God from the
shrine of Pytho rich in gold
that has come to glorious Thebes?
I am stretched on the rack of doubt, and terror and
trembling hold
my heart, O Delian Healer, and I worship full of
fears
for what doom you will bring to pass, new or
renewed in the revolving years.
Speak to me, immortal voice,
child of golden Hope.

Antistrophe

First I call on you, Athene, deathless daughter of
Zeus,
and Artemis, Earth Upholder,
who sits in the midst of the market place in the
throne which men call Fame,
and Phoebus, the Far Shooter, three averters of
Fate,
come to us now, if ever before, when ruin rushed
upon the state,
you drove destruction's flame away
out of our land.

Strophe

Our sorrows defy number;
all the ship's timbers are rotten;
taking of thought is no spear for the driving away
of the plague.
There are no growing children in this famous land;
there are no women bearing the pangs of
childbirth.
You may see them one with another, like birds swift
on the wing,
quicker than fire unmastered,
speeding away to the coast of the Western God.

Antistrophe

In the unnumbered deaths
of its people the city dies;
those children that are born lie dead on the naked
    earth
unpitied, spreading contagion of death; and grey
    haired mothers and wives
everywhere stand at the altar's edge, suppliant,
    moaning;
the hymn to the healing God rings out but with it
    the wailing voices are blended.
From these our sufferings grant us, O golden
    Daughter of Zeus,
glad-faced deliverance.

Strophe

There is no clash of brazen shields but our fight is
    with the War God,
a War God ringed with the cries of men, a savage
    God who burns us;
grant that he turn in racing course backwards out
    of our country's bounds
to the great palace of Amphitrite or where the
    waves of the Thracian sea
deny the stranger safe anchorage.
Whatsoever escapes the night
at last the light of day revisits;
so smite the War God, Father Zeus,
beneath your thunderbolt,
for you are the Lord of lightning, the lightning that
    carries fire.

Antistrophe

And your unconquered arrow shafts, winged by
    the golden corded bow,
Lycean King, I beg to be at our side for help;
and the gleaming torches of Artemis with which
    she scours the Lycean hills,
and I call on the God with the turban of gold, who
    gave his name to this country of ours,
the Bacchic God with the wind flushed face,
Evian One, who travel
with the Maenad company,
combat the God that burns us
with your torch of pine;
for the God that is our enemy is a God unhonoured
    among the Gods.

(OEDIPUS *returns.*)

OEDIPUS

For what you ask me—if you will hear my words,
and hearing welcome them and fight the plague,
you will find strength and lightening of your load.

Hark to me; what I say to you, I say
as one that is a stranger to the story
as stranger to the deed. For I would not
be far upon the track if I alone
were tracing it without a clue. But now,
since after all was finished, I became
a citizen among you, citizens—
now I proclaim to all the men of Thebes:
who so among you knows the murderer
by whose hand Laius, son of Labdacus,
died—I command him to tell everything
to me,—yes, though he fears himself to take the
    blame
on his own head; for bitter punishment
he shall have none, but leave this land
    unharmed.
Or if he knows the murderer, another,
a foreigner, still let him speak the truth.
For I will pay him and be grateful, too.
But if you shall keep silence, if perhaps
some one of you, to shield a guilty friend,
or for his own sake shall reject my words—
hear what I shall do then:
I forbid that man, whoever he be, my land,
my land where I hold sovereignty and throne;
and I forbid any to welcome him
or cry him greeting or make him a sharer
in sacrifice or offering to the Gods,
or give him water for his hands to wash.
I command all to drive him from their homes,
since he is our pollution, as the oracle
of Pytho's God proclaimed him now to me.
So I stand forth a champion of the God
and of the man who died.
Upon the murderer I invoke this curse—
whether he is one man and all unknown,
or one of many—may he wear out his life
in misery to miserable doom!
If with my knowledge he lives at my hearth
I pray that I myself may feel my curse.
On you I lay my charge to fulfill all this
for me, for the God, and for this land of ours
destroyed and blighted, by the God forsaken.
Even were this no matter of God's ordinance
it would not fit you so to leave it lie,
unpurified, since a good man is dead
and one that was a king. Search it out.
Since I am now the holder of his office,
and have his bed and wife that once was his,
and had his line not been unfortunate

we would have common children—(fortune
    leaped
upon his head)—because of all these things,
I fight in his defense as for my father,
and I shall try all means to take the murderer
of Laius the son of Labdacus
the son of Polydorus and before him
of Cadmus and before him of Agenor.
Those who do not obey me, may the Gods
grant no crops springing from the ground they
    plough
nor children to their women! May a fate
like this, or one still worse than this consume them!
For you whom these words please, the other
    Thebans,
may Justice as your ally and all the Gods
live with you, blessing you now and for ever!

CHORUS
As you have held me to my oath, I speak:
I neither killed the king nor can declare
the killer; but since Phoebus set the quest
it is his part to tell who the man is.

OEDIPUS
Right; but to put compulsion on the Gods
against their will—no man can do that.

CHORUS
May I then say what I think second best?

OEDIPUS
If there's a third best, too, spare not to tell it.

CHORUS
I know that what the Lord Teiresias
sees, is most often what the Lord Apollo
sees. If you should inquire of this from him
you might find out most clearly.

OEDIPUS
Even in this my actions have not been sluggard.
On Creon's word I have sent two messengers
and why the prophet is not here already
I have been wondering.

CHORUS
                  His skill apart
there is besides only an old faint story.

OEDIPUS
What is it?
I look at every story.

CHORUS
                  It was said
that he was killed by certain wayfarers.

OEDIPUS
I heard that, too, but no one saw the killer.

CHORUS
Yet if he has a share of fear at all,
his courage will not stand firm, hearing your
    curse.

OEDIPUS
The man who in the doing did not shrink
will fear no word.

CHORUS
                Here comes his prosecutor:
led by your men the godly prophet comes
in whom alone of mankind truth is native
(*Enter* TEIRESIAS, *led by a little boy.*)

OEDIPUS
Teiresias, you are versed in everything,
things teachable and things not to be spoken,
things of the heaven and earth-creeping things.
You have no eyes but in your mind you know
with what a plague our city is afflicted.
My lord, in you alone we find a champion,
in you alone one that can rescue us.
Perhaps you have not heard the messengers,
but Phoebus sent in answer to our sending
an oracle declaring that our freedom
from this disease would only come when we
should learn the names of those who killed King
    Laius,
and kill them or expel from our country.
Do not begrudge us oracles from birds,
or any other way of prophecy
within your skill; save yourself and the city,
save me; redeem the debt of our pollution
that lies on us because of this dead man.
We are in your hands; pains are most nobly taken
to help another when you have means and power.

TEIRESIAS
Alas, how terrible is wisdom when
it brings no profit to the man that's wise!
This I knew well, but had forgotten it,
else I would not have come here.

OEDIPUS
                    What is this?
How sad you are now you have come!

TEIRESIAS
                    Let me
go home. It will be easiest for us both
to bear our several destinies to the end
if you will follow my advice.

OEDIPUS
                  You'd rob us
of this your gift of prophecy? You talk

as one who had no care for law nor love
for Thebes who reared you.
        TEIRESIAS
Yes, but I see that even your own words
miss the mark; therefore I must fear for mine.
        OEDIPUS
For God's sake if you know of anything,
do not turn from us; all of us kneel to you,
all of us here, your suppliants.
        TEIRESIAS
All of you here know nothing. I will not
bring to the light of day my troubles, mine—
rather than call them yours.
        OEDIPUS
                        What do you mean?
You know of something but refuse to speak.
Would you betray us and destroy the city?
        TEIRESIAS
I will not bring this pain upon us both,
neither on you nor on myself. Why is it
you question me and waste your labour? I
will tell you nothing.
        OEDIPUS
You would provoke a stone! Tell us, you villain,
tell us, and do not stand there quietly
unmoved and balking at the issue.
        TEIRESIAS
You blame my temper but you do not see
your own that lives within you; it is me
you chide.
        OEDIPUS
Who would not feel his temper rise
at words like these with which you shame our
    city?
        TEIRESIAS
Of themselves things will come, although I hide
    them
and breathe no word of them.
        OEDIPUS
                        Since they will come
tell them to me.
        TEIRESIAS
                        I will say nothing further.
Against this answer let your temper rage
as wildly as you will.
        OEDIPUS
                        Indeed I am
so angry I shall not hold back a jot
of what I think. For I would have you know
I think you were complotter of the deed

and doer of the deed save in so far
as for the actual killing. Had you had eyes
I would have said alone you murdered him.
        TEIRESIAS
Yes? Then I warn you faithfully to keep
the letter of your proclamation and
from this day forth to speak no word of greeting
to these nor me; you are the land's pollution.
        OEDIPUS
How shamelessly you started up this taunt!
How do you think you will escape?
        TEIRESIAS
                                        I have.
I have escaped; the truth is what I cherish
and that's my strength.
        OEDIPUS
                        And who has taught you truth?
Not your profession surely!
        TEIRESIAS
                                You have taught me,
for you have made me speak against my will.
        OEDIPUS
Speak what? Tell me again that I may learn it
    better.
        TEIRESIAS
Did you not understand before or would you
provoke me into speaking?
        OEDIPUS
                                I did not grasp it,
not so to call it known. Say it again.
        TEIRESIAS
I say you are the murderer of the king
whose murderer you seek.
        OEDIPUS
                                Not twice you shall
say calumnies like this and stay unpunished.
        TEIRESIAS
Shall I say more to tempt your anger more?
        OEDIPUS
As much as you desire; it will be said
in vain.
        TEIRESIAS
                I say that with those you love best
you live in foulest shame unconsciously
and do not see where you are in calamity.
        OEDIPUS
Do you imagine you can always talk
like this, and live to laugh at it hereafter?
        TEIRESIAS
Yes, if the truth has anything of strength.

saw his wisdom and in that test
he saved the city. So he will not be condemned by
　　my mind.
(*Enter* CREON.)

CREON

Citizens, I have come because I heard
deadly words spread about me, that the king
accuses me. I cannot take that from him.
If he believes that in these present troubles
he has been wronged by me in word or deed
I do not want to live on with the burden
of such a scandal on me. The report
injures me doubly and most vitally—
for I'll be called a traitor to my city
and traitor also to my friends and you.

CHORUS

Perhaps it was a sudden gust of anger
that forced that insult from him, and no judgment.

CREON

But did he say that it was in compliance
with schemes of mine that the seer told him lies?

CHORUS

Yes, he said that, but why, I do not know.

CREON

Were his eyes straight in his head? Was his mind
　　right
when he accused me in this fashion?

CHORUS

I do not know; I have no eyes to see
what princes do. Here comes the king himself.
(*Enter* OEDIPUS.)

OEDIPUS

You, sir, how is it you come here? Have you so
　　much
brazen-faced daring that you venture in
my house although you are proved manifestly
the murderer of that man, and though you
　　tried,
openly, highway robbery of my crown?
For God's sake, tell me what you saw in me,
what cowardice or what stupidity,
that made you lay a plot like this against me?
Did you imagine I should not observe
the crafty scheme that stole upon me or
seeing it, take no means to counter it?
Was it not stupid of you to make the attempt,
to try to hunt down royal power without
the people at your back or friends? For only
with the people at your back or money can
the hunt end in the capture of a crown.

CREON

Do you know what you're doing? Will you listen
to words to answer yours, and then pass judgment?

OEDIPUS

You're quick to speak, but I am slow to grasp you,
for I have found you dangerous,—and my foe.

CREON

First of all hear what I shall say to that.

OEDIPUS

At least don't tell me that you are not guilty.

CREON

If you think obstinacy without wisdom
a valuable possession, you are wrong.

OEDIPUS

And you are wrong if you believe that one,
a criminal, will not be punished only
because he is my kinsman.

CREON

　　　　　　　　　　　　　　This is but just—
but tell me, then, of what offense I'm guilty?

OEDIPUS

Did you or did you not urge me to send
to this prophetic mumbler?

CREON

　　　　　　　　　　　　　　I did indeed,
and I shall stand by what I told you.

OEDIPUS

How long ago is it since Laius….

CREON

What about Laius? I don't understand.

OEDIPUS

Vanished—died—was murdered?

CREON

　　　　　　　　　　　　　　It is long,
a long, long time to reckon.

OEDIPUS

　　　　　　　　　　　　Was this prophet
in the profession then?

CREON

　　　　　　　　　　He was, and honoured
as highly as he is today.

OEDIPUS

At that time did he say a word about me?

CREON

Never, at least when I was near him.

OEDIPUS

You never made a search for the dead man?

CREON

We searched, indeed, but never learned of
　　anything.

OEDIPUS
Why did our wise old friend not say this then?
CREON
I don't know; and when I know nothing, I
usually hold my tongue.
OEDIPUS
You know this much,
and can declare this much if you are loyal.
CREON
What is it? If I know, I'll not deny it.
OEDIPUS
That he would not have said that I killed Laius
had he not met you first.
CREON
You know yourself
whether he said this, but I demand that I
should hear as much from you as you from me.
OEDIPUS
Then hear,—I'll not be proved a murderer.
CREON
Well, then. You're married to my sister.
OEDIPUS
Yes,
that I am not disposed to deny.
CREON
You rule
this country giving her an equal share
in the government?
OEDIPUS
Yes, everything she wants
she has from me.
CREON
And I, as thirdsman to you,
am rated as the equal of you two?
OEDIPUS
Yes, and it's there you've proved yourself false
friend.
CREON
Not if you will reflect on it as I do.
Consider, first, if you think any one
would choose to rule and fear rather than rule
and sleep untroubled by a fear if power
were equal in both cases. I, at least,
I was not born with such a frantic yearning
to be a king—but to do what kings do.
And so it is with every one who has learned
wisdom and self-control. As it stands now,
the prizes are all mine—and without fear.
But if I were the king myself, I must
do much that went against the grain.

How should despotic rule seem sweeter to me
than painless power and an assured authority?
I am not so besotted yet that I
want other honours than those that come with
profit.
Now every man's my pleasure; every man greets
me;
now those who are your suitors fawn on me,—
success for them depends upon my favour.
Why should I let all this go to win that?
My mind would not be traitor if it's wise;
I am no treason lover, of my nature,
nor would I ever dare to join a plot.
Prove what I say. Go to the oracle
at Pytho and inquire about the answers,
if they are as I told you. For the rest,
if you discover I laid any plot
together with the seer, kill me, I say,
not only by your vote but by my own.
But do not charge me on obscure opinion
without some proof to back it. It's not just
lightly to count your knaves as honest men,
nor honest men as knaves. To throw away
an honest friend is, as it were, to throw
your life away, which a man loves the best.
In time you will know all with certainty;
time is the only test of honest men,
one day is space enough to know a rogue.
CHORUS
His words are wise, king, if one fears to fall.
Those who are quick of temper are not safe.
OEDIPUS
When he that plots against me secretly
moves quickly, I must quickly counterplot.
If I wait taking no decisive measure
his business will be done, and mine be spoiled.
CREON
What do you want to do then? Banish me?
OEDIPUS
No, certainly; kill you, not banish you.[1]
CREON
I do not think that you've your wits about you.

[1]Two lines omitted here owing to the confusion in the dialogue consequent on the loss of a third line. The lines as they said in Jebb's edition (1902) are:

OED.: That you may show what manner of thing is envy.
CREON: You speak as one that will not yield or trust.
[OED. lost line.]

OEDIPUS

For my own interests, yes.

CREON

But for mine, too,

you should think equally.

OEDIPUS

You are a rogue.

CREON

Suppose you do not understand?

OEDIPUS

But yet

I must be ruler.

CREON

Not if you rule badly.

OEDIPUS

O, city, city!

CREON

I too have some share

in the city; it is not yours alone.

CHORUS

Stop, my lords! Here—and in the nick of time

I see Jocasta coming from the house;

with her help lay the quarrel that now stirs you.

(*Enter* JOCASTA.)

JOCASTA

For shame! Why have you raised this foolish
    squabbling

brawl? Are you not ashamed to air your private

griefs when the country's sick? Go in, you,
    Oedipus,

And you, too, Creon, into the house. Don't
    magnify

your nothing troubles.

CREON

Sister, Oedipus,

your husband, thinks he has the right to do

terrible wrongs—he has but to choose between

two terrors: banishing or killing me.

OEDIPUS

He's right, Jocasta; for I find him plotting

with knavish tricks against my person.

CREON

That God may never bless me! May I die

accursed, if I have been guilty of

one tittle of the charge you bring against me!

JOCASTA

I beg you, Oedipus, trust him in this,

spare him for the sake of this his oath to God,

for my sake, and the sake of those who stand
    here.

CHORUS

Be gracious, be merciful,

we beg of you.

OEDIPUS

In what would you have me yield?

CHORUS

He has been no silly child in the past.

He is strong in his oath now.

Spare him.

OEDIPUS

Do you know what you ask?

CHORUS

Yes.

OEDIPUS

Tell me then.

CHORUS

He has been your friend before all men's eyes; do
    not cast him

away dishonoured on an obscure conjecture.

OEDIPUS

I would have you know that this request of yours

really requests my death or banishment.

CHORUS

May the Sun God, king of Gods, forbid! May I die
    without God's

blessing, without friends' help, if I had any such
    thought. But my

spirit is broken by my unhappiness for my wasting
    country; and

this would but add troubles amongst ourselves to
    the other

troubles.

OEDIPUS

Well, let him go then—if I must die ten times
    for it,

or be sent out dishonoured into exile.

It is your lips that prayed for him I pitied,

not his; wherever he is, I shall hate him.

CREON

I see you sulk in yielding and you're dangerous

when you are out of temper; natures like yours

are justly heaviest for themselves to bear.

OEDIPUS

Leave me alone! Take yourself off, I tell you.

CREON

I'll go, you have not known me, but they have,

and they have known my innocence.

(*Exit*)

CHORUS

Won't you take him inside, lady?

JOCASTA

Yes, when I've found out what was the matter.

CHORUS

There was some misconceived suspicion of a story, and on the
other side the sting of injustice.

JOCASTA

So, on both sides?

CHORUS

Yes.

JOCASTA

What was the story?

CHORUS

I think it best, in the interests of the country, to leave it
where it ended.

OEDIPUS

You see where you have ended, straight of judgment
although you are, by softening my anger.

CHORUS

Sir, I have said before and I say again—be sure that I would have
been proved a madman, bankrupt in sane council, if I should put
you away, you who steered the country I love safely when she
was crazed with troubles. God grant that now, too, you may
prove a fortunate guide for us.

JOCASTA

Tell me, my lord, I beg of you, what was it
that roused your anger so?

OEDIPUS

Yes, I will tell you.
I honour you more than I honour them.
It was Creon and the plots he laid against me.

JOCASTA

Tell me—if you can clearly tell the quarrel—

OEDIPUS

Creon says
that I'm the murderer of Laius.

JOCASTA

Of his own knowledge or on information?

OEDIPUS

He sent this rascal prophet to me, since
he keeps his own mouth clean of any guilt.

JOCASTA

Do not concern yourself about this matter;
listen to me and learn that human beings

have no part in the craft of prophecy.
Of that I'll show you a short proof.
There was an oracle once that came to Laius,—
I will not say that it was Phoebus' own,
but it was from his servants—and it told him
that it was fate that he should die a victim
at the hands of his own son, a son to be born
of Laius and me. But, see now, he,
the king, was killed by foreign highway robbers
at a place where three roads meet—so goes the
story;
and for the son—before three days were out
after his birth King Laius pierced his ankles
and by the hands of others cast him forth
upon a pathless hillside. So Apollo
failed to fulfill his oracle to the son,
that he should kill his father, and to Laius
also proved false in that the thing he feared,
death at his son's hands, never came to pass.
So clear in this case were the oracles,
so clear and false. Give them no heed, I say;
what God discovers need of, easily
he shows to us himself.

OEDIPUS

O dear Jocasta,
as I hear this from you, there comes upon me
a wandering of the soul—I could run mad.

JOCASTA

What trouble is it, that you turn again
and speak like this?

OEDIPUS

I thought I heard you say
that Laius was killed at a crossroads.

JOCASTA

Yes, that was how the story went and still
that word goes round.

OEDIPUS

Where is this place, Jocasta,
where he was murdered?

JOCASTA

Phocis is the country
and the road splits there, one of two roads from
Delphi,
another comes from Daulia.

OEDIPUS

How long ago is this?

JOCASTA

The news came to the city just before
you became king and all men's eyes looked to you.
What is it, Oedipus, that's in your mind?

OEDIPUS

What have you designed, O Zeus, to do with me?

JOCASTA

What is the thought that troubles your heart?

OEDIPUS

Don't ask me yet—tell me of Laius—
How did he look? How old or young was he?

JOCASTA

He was a tall man and his hair was grizzled
already—nearly white—and in his form
not unlike you.

OEDIPUS

O God, I think I have
called curses on myself in ignorance.

JOCASTA

What do you mean? I am terrified
when I look at you.

OEDIPUS

I have a deadly fear
that the old seer had eyes. You'll show me more
if you can tell me one more thing.

JOCASTA

I will.
I'm frightened,—but if I can understand,
I'll tell you all you ask.

OEDIPUS

How was his company?
Had he few with him when he went this journey,
or many servants, as would suit a prince?

JOCASTA

In all there were but five, and among them
a herald; and one carriage for the king.

OEDIPUS

It's plain—it's plain—who was it told you this?

JOCASTA

The only servant that escaped safe home.

OEDIPUS

Is he at home now?

JOCASTA

No, when he came home again
and saw you king and Laius was dead,
he came to me and touched my hand and begged
that I should send him to the fields to be
my shepherd and so he might see the city
as far off as he might. So I
sent him away. He was an honest man,
as slaves go, and was worthy of far more
than what he asked of me.

OEDIPUS

O, how I wish that he could come back quickly!

JOCASTA

He can. Why is your heart so set on this?

OEDIPUS

O dear Jocasta, I am full of fears
that I have spoken far too much; and therefore
I wish to see this shepherd.

JOCASTA

He will come;
but, Oedipus, I think I'm worthy too
to know what it is that disquiets you.

OEDIPUS

It shall not be kept from you, since my mind
has gone so far with its forebodings. Whom
should I confide in rather than you, who is there
of more importance to me who have passed
through such a fortune?
Polybus was my father, king of Corinth,
and Merope, the Dorian, my mother.
I was held greatest of the citizens
in Corinth till a curious chance befell me
as I shall tell you—curious, indeed,
but hardly worth the store I set upon it.
There was a dinner and at it a man,
a drunken man, accused me in his drink
of being bastard. I was furious
but held my temper under for that day.
Next day I went and taxed my parents with it;
they took the insult very ill from him,
the drunken fellow who had uttered it.
So I was comforted for their part, but
still this thing rankled always, for the story
crept about widely. And I went at last
to Pytho, though my parents did not know.
But Phoebus sent me home again unhonoured
in what I came to learn, but he foretold
other and desperate horrors to befall me,
that I was fated to lie with my mother,
and show to daylight an accursed breed
which men would not endure, and I was doomed
to be murderer of the father that begot me.
When I heard this I fled, and in the days
that followed I would measure from the stars
the whereabouts of Corinth—yes, I fled
to somewhere where I should not see fulfilled
the infamies told in that dreadful oracle.
And as I journeyed I came to the place
where, as you say, this king met with his death.
Jocasta, I will tell you the whole truth.
When I was near the branching of the
    crossroads,

going on foot, I was encountered by
a herald and a carriage with a man in it,
just as you tell me. He that led the way
and the old man himself wanted to thrust me
out of the road by force. I became angry
and struck the coachman who was pushing me.
When the old man saw this he watched his
    moment,
and as I passed he struck me from his carriage,
full on the head with his two pointed goad.
But he was paid in full and presently
my stick had struck him backwards from the car
and he rolled out of it. And then I killed them
all. If it happened there was any tie
of kinship twixt this man and Laius,
who is then now more miserable than I,
what man on earth so hated by the Gods,
since neither citizen nor foreigner
may welcome me at home or even greet me,
but drive me out of doors? And it is I,
I and no other have so cursed myself.
And I pollute the bed of him I killed
by the hands that killed him. Was I not born evil?
Am I not utterly unclean? I had to fly
and in my banishment not even see
my kindred nor set foot in my own country,
or otherwise my fate was to be yoked
in marriage with my mother and kill my father,
Polybus who begot me and had reared me.
Would not one rightly judge and say that on me
these things were sent by some malignant God?
O no, no, no—O holy majesty
of God on high, may I not see that day!
May I be gone out of men's sight before
I see the deadly taint of this disaster
come upon me.

    CHORUS
Sir, we too fear these things. But until you see this
man face to face and hear his story, hope.

    OEDIPUS
Yes, I have just this much of hope—to wait until
the herdsman comes.

    JOCASTA
And when he comes, what do you want with him?

    OEDIPUS
I'll tell you; if I find that his story is the same as
yours, I at least will be clear of this guilt.

    JOCASTA
Why what so particularly did you learn from my
story?

    OEDIPUS
You said that he spoke of highway *robbers* who
killed Laius. Now if he uses the same number, it
was not I who killed him. One man cannot be the
same as many. But if he speaks of a man
travelling alone, then clearly the burden of the
guilt inclines towards me.

    JOCASTA
Be sure, at least, that this was how he told the
story. He cannot unsay it now, for every one in
the city heard it—not I alone. But, Oedipus, even
if he diverges from what he said then, he shall
never prove that the murder of Laius squares
rightly with the prophecy—for Loxias declared
that the king should be killed by his own son.
And that poor creature did not kill him
surely,—for he died himself first. So as far as
prophecy goes, henceforward I shall not look to
the right hand or the left.

    OEDIPUS
Right. But yet, send some one for the peasant to
bring him here; do not neglect it.

    JOCASTA
I will send quickly. Now let me go indoors. I will
do nothing except what pleases you.
(*Exeunt.*)

    CHORUS
    Strophe
May destiny ever find me
pious in word and deed
prescribed by the laws that live on high:
laws begotten in the clear air of heaven,
whose only father is Olympus;
no mortal nature brought them to birth,
no forgetfulness shall lull them to sleep;
for God is great in them and grows not old.
    Antistrophe
Insolence breeds the tyrant, insolence
if it is glutted with a surfeit, unseasonable,
    unprofitable,
climbs to the roof-top and plunges
sheer down to the ruin that must be,
and there its feet are no service.
But I pray that the God may never
abolish the eager ambition that profits the state.
For I shall never cease to hold the God as our
    protector.
    Strophe
If a man walks with haughtiness
of hand or word and gives no heed

to Justice and the shrines of Gods
despises—may an evil doom
smite him for his ill-starred pride of heart!—
if he reaps gains without justice
and will not hold from impiety
and his fingers itch for untouchable things.
When such things are done, what man shall
contrive
to shield his soil from the shafts of the God?
When such deeds are held in honour,
why should I honour the Gods in the dance?
Antistrophe
No longer to the holy place,
to the navel of earth I'll go
to worship, nor to Abae
nor to Olympia,
unless the oracles are proved to fit,
for all men's hands to point at.
O Zeus, if you are rightly called
the sovereign lord, all-mastering,
let this not escape you nor your ever-living
power!
The oracles concerning Laius
are old and dim and men regard them not.
Apollo is nowhere clear in honour; God's service
perishes.
(*Enter* JOCASTA *carrying garlands.*)

JOCASTA

Princes of the land, I have had the thought to go
to the Gods' temples, bringing in my hand
garlands and gifts of incense, as you see.
For Oedipus excites himself too much
at every sort of trouble, not conjecturing,
like a man of sense, what will be from what was,
but he is always at the speaker's mercy,
when he speaks terrors. I can do no good
by my advice, and so I came as suppliant
to you, Lycaean Apollo, who are nearest.
These are the symbols of my prayer and this
my prayer: grant us escape free of the curse.
Now when we look to him we are all afraid;
he's pilot of our ship and he is frightened.
(*Enter* MESSENGER.)

MESSENGER

Might I learn from you, sirs, where is the house of
Oedipus? Or best of all, if you know, where is the
king himself?

CHORUS

This is his house and he is within doors. This lady
is his wife and mother of his children.

MESSENGER

God bless you, lady, and God bless your
household! God bless Oedipus' noble wife!

JOCASTA

God bless you, sir, for your kind greeting!
What
do you want of us that you have come here?
What have you to tell us?

MESSENGER

Good news, lady. Good for your house and for
your husband.

JOCASTA

What is your news? Who sent you to us?

MESSENGER

I come from Corinth and the news I bring will
give you pleasure. Perhaps a little pain too.

JOCASTA

What is this news of double meaning?

MESSENGER

The people of the Isthmus will choose Oedipus to
be their king. That is the rumour there.

JOCASTA

But isn't their king still old Polybus?

MESSENGER

No. He is in his grave. Death has got him.

JOCASTA

Is that the truth? Is Oedipus' father dead?

MESSENGER

May I die myself if it be otherwise!

JOCASTA (*to a servant*)

Be quick and run to the King with the news! O
oracles of the Gods, where are you now? It was
from this man Oedipus fled, lest he should be his
murderer! And now he is dead, in the course of
nature, and not killed by Oedipus.
(*Enter* OEDIPUS.)

OEDIPUS

Dearest Jocasta, why have you sent for me?

JOCASTA

Listen to this man and when you hear reflect
what is the outcome of the holy oracles of the
Gods.

OEDIPUS

Who is he? What is his message for me?

JOCASTA

He is from Corinth and he tells us that your
father
Polybus is dead and gone.

OEDIPUS

What's this you say, sir? Tell me yourself.

MESSENGER
Since this is the first matter you want clearly told:
Polybus has gone down to death. You may be
sure of it.

OEDIPUS
By treachery or sickness?

MESSENGER
A small thing will put old bodies asleep.

OEDIPUS
So he died of sickness, it seems,—poor old man!

MESSENGER
Yes, and of age—the long years he had measured.

OEDIPUS
Ha! Ha! O dear Jocasta, why should one
look to the Pythian hearth? Why should one look
to the birds screaming overhead? They
    prophesied
that I should kill my father! But he's dead,
and hidden deep in earth, and I stand here
who never laid a hand on spear against him,—
unless perhaps he died of longing for me,
and thus I am his murderer. But they,
the oracles, as they stand—he's taken them
away with him, they're dead as he himself is,
and worthless.

JOCASTA
                                    That I told you before now.

OEDIPUS
You did, but I was misled by my fear.

JOCASTA
Then lay no more of them to heart, not one.

OEDIPUS
But surely I must fear my mother's bed?

JOCASTA
Why should man fear since chance is all in all
for him, and he can clearly foreknow nothing?
Best to live lightly, as one can, unthinkingly.
As to your mother's marriage bed,—don't fear it.
Before this, in dreams too, as well as oracles,
many a man has lain with his own mother.
But he to whom such things are nothing bears
his life most easily.

OEDIPUS
All that you say would be said perfectly
if she were dead; but since she lives I must
still fear, although you talk so well, Jocasta.

JOCASTA
Still in your father's death there's light of comfort?

OEDIPUS
Great light of comfort; but I fear the living.

MESSENGER
Who is the woman that makes you afraid?

OEDIPUS
Merope, old man, Polybus' wife.

MESSENGER
What about her frightens the queen and you?

OEDIPUS
A terrible oracle, stranger, from the Gods.

MESSENGER
Can it be told? Or does the sacred law
forbid another to have knowledge of it?

OEDIPUS
O no! Once on a time Loxias said
that I should lie with my own mother and
take on my hands the blood of my own father.
And so for these long years I've lived away
from Corinth; it has been to my great happiness;
but yet it's sweet to see the face of parents.

MESSENGER
This was the fear which drove you out of Corinth?

OEDIPUS
Old man, I did not wish to kill my father.

MESSENGER
Why should I not free you from this fear, sir,
since I have come to you in all goodwill?

OEDIPUS
You would not find me thankless if you did.

MESSENGER
Why, it was just for this I brought the news,—
to earn your thanks when you had come safe home.

OEDIPUS
No, I will never come near my parents.

MESSENGER
                                                Son,
it's very plain you don't know what you're doing.

OEDIPUS
What do you mean, old man? For God's sake, tell
    me.

MESSENGER
If your homecoming is checked by fears like these.

OEDIPUS
Yes, I'm afraid that Phoebus may prove right.

MESSENGER
The murder and the incest?

OEDIPUS
                                        Yes, old man;
that is my constant terror.

MESSENGER
                                        Do you know
that all your fears are empty?

OEDIPUS

How is that,
if they are father and mother and I their son?

MESSENGER

Because Polybus was no kin to you in blood.

OEDIPUS

What, was not Polybus my father?

MESSENGER

No more than I but just so much.

OEDIPUS

How can
my father be my father as much as one
that's nothing to me?

MESSENGER

Neither he nor I
begat you.

OEDIPUS

Why then did he call me son?

MESSENGER

A gift he took you from these hands of mine.

OEDIPUS

Did he love so much what he took from another's
hand?

MESSENGER

His childlessness before persuaded him.

OEDIPUS

Was I a child you bought or found when I
was given to him?

MESSENGER

On Cithaeron's slopes
in the twisting thickets you were found.

OEDIPUS

And why
were you a traveller in those parts?

MESSENGER

I was
in charge of mountain flocks.

OEDIPUS

You were a shepherd?
A hireling vagrant?

MESSENGER

Yes, but at least at that time
the man that saved your life, son.

OEDIPUS

What ailed me when you took me in your arms?

MESSENGER

In that your ankles should be witnesses.

OEDIPUS

Why do you speak of that old pain?

MESSENGER

I loosed you;
the tendons of your feet were pierced and
fettered,—

OEDIPUS

My swaddling clothes brought me a rare disgrace.

MESSENGER

So that from this you're called your present name.

OEDIPUS

Was this my father's doing or my mother's?
For God's sake, tell me.

MESSENGER

I don't know, but he
who gave you to me has more knowledge than I.

OEDIPUS

You yourself did not find me then? You took me
from someone else?

MESSENGER

Yes, from another shepherd.

OEDIPUS

Who was he? Do you know him well enough
to tell?

MESSENGER

He was called Laius' man.

OEDIPUS

You mean the king who reigned here in the old
days?

MESSENGER

Yes, he was that man's shepherd.

OEDIPUS

Is he alive
still, so that I could see him?

MESSENGER

You who live here
would know that best.

OEDIPUS

Do any of you here
know of this shepherd whom he speaks about
in town or in the fields? Tell me. It's time
that this was found out once for all.

CHORUS

I think he is none other than the peasant
whom you have sought to see already; but
Jocasta here can tell us best of that.

OEDIPUS

Jocasta, do you know about this man
whom we have sent for? Is he the man he
mentions?

JOCASTA
Why ask of whom he spoke? Don't give it heed;
nor try to keep in mind what has been said.
It will be wasted labour.
OEDIPUS
                                    With such clues
I could not fail to bring my birth to light.
JOCASTA
I beg you—do not hunt this out—I beg you,
if you have any care for your own life.
What I am suffering is enough.
OEDIPUS
                                              Keep up
your heart, Jocasta. Though I'm proved a slave,
thrice slave, and though my mother is thrice
slave, you'll not be shown to be of lowly lineage.
JOCASTA
O be persuaded by me, I entreat you;
do not do this.
OEDIPUS
I will not be persuaded to let be
the chance of finding out the whole thing clearly.
JOCASTA
It is because I wish you well that I
give you this counsel—and it's the best counsel.
OEDIPUS
Then the best counsel vexes me, and has
for some while since.
JOCASTA
                              O Oedipus, God help you!
God keep you from the knowledge of who you
    are!
OEDIPUS
Here, some one, go and fetch the shepherd for me;
and let her find her joy in her rich family!
JOCASTA
O Oedipus, unhappy Oedipus!
that is all I can call you, and the last thing
that I shall ever call you.
(Exit.)
CHORUS
Why has the queen gone, Oedipus, in wild
grief rushing from us? I am afraid that trouble
will break out of this silence.
OEDIPUS
Break out what will! I at least shall be
willing to see my ancestry, though humble.
Perhaps she is ashamed of my low birth,
for she has all a woman's high-flown pride.

But I account myself a child of Fortune,
beneficent Fortune, and I shall not be
dishonoured. She's the mother from whom I
    spring;
the months, my brothers, marked me, now as
    small,
and now again as mighty. Such is my breeding,
and I shall never prove so false to it,
as not to find the secret of my birth.
CHORUS
Strophe
If I am a prophet and wise of heart
you shall not fail, Cithaeron,
by the limitless sky, you shall not!—
to know at tomorrow's full moon
that Oedipus honours you,
as native to him and mother and nurse at once;
and that you are honoured in dancing by us, as
    finding favour in sight of our king.
Apollo, to whom we cry, find these things
    pleasing!
Antistrophe
Who was it bore you, child? One of
the long-lived nymphs who lay with Pan—
the father who treads the hills?
Or was she a bride of Loxias, your mother? The
    grassy slopes
are all of them dear to him. Or perhaps Cyllene's
    king
or the Bacchants' God that lives on the tops
of the hills received you a gift from some
one of the Helicon Nymphs, with whom he mostly
    plays?
(Enter an old man, led by OEDIPUS' servants.)
OEDIPUS
If some one like myself who never met him
may make a guess,—I think this is the herdsman,
whom we were seeking. His old age is consonant
with the other. And besides, the men who bring him
I recognize as my own servants. You
perhaps may better me in knowledge since
you've seen the man before.
CHORUS
                                        You can be sure
I recognize him. For if Laius
had ever an honest shepherd, this was he.
OEDIPUS
You, sir, from Corinth, I must ask you first,
is this the man you spoke of?

MESSENGER

                              This is he
before your eyes.

OEDIPUS

                    Old man, look here at me
and tell me what I ask you. Were you ever
a servant of King Laius?

HERDSMAN

                              I was,—
no slave he bought but reared in his own house.

OEDIPUS

What did you do as work? How did you live?

HERDSMAN

Most of my life was spent among the flocks.

OEDIPUS

In what part of the country did you live?

HERDSMAN

Cithaeron and the places near to it.

OEDIPUS

And somewhere there perhaps you knew this
    man?

HERDSMAN

What was his occupation? Who?

OEDIPUS

                              This man here,
have you had any dealings with him?

HERDSMAN

                                    No—
not such that I can quickly call to mind.

MESSENGER

That is no wonder, master. But I'll make him
remember what he does not know. For I know,
that he well knows the country of Cithaeron, how
he with two flocks, I with one kept company for
three years—each year half a year—from spring
till autumn time and then when winter came I
drove my flocks to our fold home again and he to
Laius' steadings. Well—am I right or not in what I
said we did?

HERDSMAN

You're right—although it's a long time ago.

MESSENGER

Do you remember giving me a child
to bring up as my foster child?

HERDSMAN

                              What's this?
Why do you ask this question?

MESSENGER

                              Look old man,
here he is—here's the man who was that child!

HERDSMAN

Death take you! Won't you hold your tongue?

OEDIPUS

                                    No, no,
do not find fault with him, old man. Your words
are more at fault than his.

HERDSMAN

                    O best of masters,
how do I give offense?

OEDIPUS

                              When you refuse
to speak about the child of whom he asks you.

HERDSMAN

He speaks out of his ignorance, without meaning.

OEDIPUS

If you'll not talk to gratify me, you
will talk with pain to urge you.

HERDSMAN

                              O please, sir,
don't hurt an old man, sir.

OEDIPUS

(to the servants)

                              Here, one of you,
twist his hands behind him.

HERDSMAN

                    Why, God help me, why?
What do you want to know?

OEDIPUS

                    You gave a child
to him,—the child he asked you of?

HERDSMAN

                                    I did.
I wish I'd died the day I did.

OEDIPUS

                              You will
unless you tell me truly.

HERDSMAN

                              And I'll die
far worse if I should tell you.

OEDIPUS

                              This fellow
is bent on more delays, as it would seem.

HERDSMAN

O no, no! I have told you that I gave it.

OEDIPUS

Where did you get this child from? Was it your
    own or did you
get it from another?

HERDSMAN

                                    Not
my own at all; I had it from some one.

OEDIPUS
One of these citizens? or from what house?

HERDSMAN
O master, please—I beg you, master, please
don't ask me more.

OEDIPUS
                                    You're a dead man if I
ask you again.

HERDSMAN
                                    It was one of the children
of Laius.

OEDIPUS
                      A slave? Or born in wedlock?

HERDSMAN
O God, I am on the brink of frightful speech.

OEDIPUS
And I of frightful hearing. But I must hear.

HERDSMAN
The child was called his child; but she within,
your wife would tell you best how all this
    was.

OEDIPUS
She gave it to you?

HERDSMAN
                                    Yes, she did, my lord.

OEDIPUS
To do what with it?

HERDSMAN
                                    Make away with it.

OEDIPUS
She was so hard—its mother?

HERDSMAN
                                    Aye, through fear
of evil oracles.

OEDIPUS
                                    Which?

HERDSMAN
                                    They said that he
should kill his parents.

OEDIPUS
                      How was it that you
gave it away to this old man?

HERDSMAN
                                    O master,
I pitied it, and thought that I could send it
off to another country and this man
was from another country. But he saved it
for the most terrible troubles. If you are
the man he says you are, you're bred to
    misery.

OEDIPUS
O, O, O, they will all come,
all come out clearly! Light of the sun, let me
look upon you no more after today!
I who first saw the light bred of a match
accursed, and accursed in my living
with them I lived with, cursed in my killing.
(*Exeunt all but the* CHORUS.)

CHORUS
Strophe
O generation of men, how I
count you as equal with those who live
not at all!
What man, what man on earth wins more
of happiness than a seeming
and after that turning away?
Oedipus, you are my pattern of this,
Oedipus, you and your fate!
Luckless Oedipus, whom of all men
I envy not at all.

    Antistrophe
In as much as he shot his bolt
beyond the others and won the prize
of happiness complete—
O Zeus—and killed and reduced to nought
the hooked taloned maid of the riddling speech,
standing a tower against death for my land:
hence he was called my king and hence
was honoured the highest of all
honours; and hence he ruled
in the great city of Thebes.

    Strophe
But now whose tale is more miserable?
Who is there lives with a savager fate?
Whose troubles so reverse his life as his?
O Oedipus, the famous prince
for whom a great haven
the same both as father and son
sufficed for generation,
how, O how, have the furrows ploughed
by your father endured to bear you, poor wretch,
and hold their peace so long?

    Antistrophe
Time who sees all has found you out
against your will; judges your marriage
        accursed,
begetter and begot at one in it.
O child of Laius,
would I had never seen you.
I weep for you and cry

a dirge of lamentation.
To speak directly, I drew my breath
from you at the first and so now I lull
my mouth to sleep with your name.
(*Enter a* SECOND MESSENGER.)

SECOND MESSENGER
O Princes always honoured by our country,
what deeds you'll hear of and what horrors see,
what grief you'll feel, if you as true born Thebans
care for the house of Labdacus's sons.
Phasis nor Ister cannot purge this house,
I think, with all their streams, such things
it hides, such evils shortly will bring forth
into the light, whether they will or not;
and troubles hurt the most
when they prove self-inflicted.

CHORUS
What we had known before did not fall short
of bitter groaning's worth; what's more to tell?

SECOND MESSENGER
Shortest to hear and tell—our glorious queen
Jocasta's dead.

CHORUS
                                        Unhappy woman! How?

SECOND MESSENGER
By her own hand. The worst of what was done
you cannot know. You did not see the sight.
Yet in so far as I remember it
you'll hear the end of our unlucky queen.
When she came raging into the house she went
straight to her marriage bed, tearing her hair
with both her hands, and crying upon Laius
long dead—Do you remember, Laius,
that night long past which bred a child for us
to send you to your death and leave
a mother making children with her son?
And then she groaned and cursed the bed in
        which
she brought forth husband by her husband,
        children
by her own child, an infamous double bond.
How after that she died I do not know,—
for Oedipus distracted us from seeing.
He burst upon us shouting and we looked
to him as he paced frantically around,
begging us always: Give me a sword, I say,
to find this wife no wife, this mother's womb,
this field of double sowing whence I sprang
and where I sowed my children! As he raved
some god showed him the way—none of us there.

Bellowing terribly and led by some
invisible guide he rushed on the two doors,—
wrenching the hollow bolts out of their sockets,
he charged inside. There, there, we saw his wife
hanging, the twisted rope around her neck.
When he saw her, he cried out fearfully
and cut the dangling noose. Then, as she lay,
poor woman, on the ground, what happened after,
was terrible to see. He tore the brooches—
the gold chased brooches fastening her robe—
away from her and lifting them up high
dashed them on his own eyeballs, shrieking out
such things as: they will never see the crime
I have committed or had done upon me!
Dark eyes, now in the days to come look on
forbidden faces, do not recognize
those whom you long for—with such imprecations
he struck his eyes again and yet again
with the brooches. And the bleeding eyeballs
        gushed
and stained his beard—no sluggish oozing drops
but a black rain and bloody hail poured down.
So it has broken—and not on one head
but troubles mixed for husband and for wife.
The fortune of the days gone by was true
good fortune—but today groans and destruction
and death and shame—of all ills can be named
not one is missing.

CHORUS
Is he now in any ease from pain?

SECOND MESSENGER
                                        He shouts
for some one to unbar the doors and show him
to all the men of Thebes, his father's killer,
his mother's—no I cannot say the word,
it is unholy—for he'll cast himself,
out of the land, he says, and not remain
to bring a curse upon his house, the curse
he called upon it in his proclamation. But
he wants for strength, aye, and some one to guide
        him;
his sickness is too great to bear. You, too,
will be shown that. The bolts are opening.
Soon you will see a sight to waken pity
even in the horror of it.
(*Enter the blinded* OEDIPUS.)

CHORUS
This is a terrible sight for men to see!
I never found a worse!
Poor wretch, what madness came upon you!

What evil spirit leaped upon your life
to your ill-luck—a leap beyond man's strength!
Indeed I pity you, but I cannot
look at you, though there's much I want to ask
and much to learn and much to see.
I shudder at the sight of you.

OEDIPUS
O, O,
where am I going? Where is my voice
borne on the wind to and fro?
Spirit, how far have you sprung?

CHORUS
To a terrible place whereof men's ears
may not hear, nor their eyes behold it.

OEDIPUS
Darkness!
Horror of darkness enfolding, resistless,
    unspeakable visitant sped by an ill wind in
    haste!
madness and stabbing pain and memory
of evil deeds I have done!

CHORUS
In such misfortunes it's no wonder
if double weighs the burden of your grief.

OEDIPUS
My friend,
you are the only one steadfast, the only one that
    attends on me;
you still stay nursing the blind man.
Your care is not unnoticed. I can know
your voice, although this darkness is my world.

CHORUS
Doer of dreadful deeds, how did you dare
so far to do despite to your own eyes?
what spirit urged you to it?

OEDIPUS
It was Apollo, friends, Apollo,
that brought this bitter bitterness, my sorrows to
    completion.
But the hand that struck me
was none but my own.
Why should I see
whose vision showed me nothing sweet to see?

CHORUS
These things are as you say.

OEDIPUS
What can I see to love?
What greeting can touch my ears with joy?
Take me away, and haste—to a place out of the
    way!

Take me away, my friends, the greatly miserable,
the most accursed, whom God too hates
above all men on earth!

CHORUS
Unhappy in your mind and your misfortune,
would I had never known you!

OEDIPUS
Curse on the man who took
the cruel bonds from off my legs, as I lay in the
    field.
He stole me from death and saved me,
no kindly service.
Had I died then
I would not be so burdensome to friends.

CHORUS
I, too, could have wished it had been so.

OEDIPUS
Then I would not have come
to kill my father and marry my mother
    infamously.
Now I am godless and child of impurity,
begetter in the same seed that created my
    wretched self.
If there is any ill worse than ill,
that is the lot of Oedipus.

CHORUS
I cannot say your remedy was good;
you would be better dead than blind and living.

OEDIPUS
What I have done here was best done; don't tell
    me
otherwise, do not give me further counsel.
I do not know with what eyes I could look
upon my father when I die and go
under the earth, nor yet my wretched mother—
those two to whom I have done things deserving
worse punishment than hanging. Would the sight
of children, bred as mine are, gladden me?
No, not these eyes, never. And my city,
its towers and sacred places of the Gods,
of these I robbed my miserable self
when I commanded all to drive *him* out,
the criminal since proved by God impure
and of the race of Laius.
To this guilt I bore witness against myself—
with what eyes shall I look upon my people?
No. If there were a means to choke the fountain
of hearing I would not have stayed my hand
from locking up my miserable carcase,
seeing and hearing nothing; it is sweet

to keep our thoughts out of the range of hurt.
Cithaeron, why did you receive me? why
having received me did you not kill me straight?
And so I had not shown to men my birth.
O Polybus and Corinth and the house,
the old house that I used to call my father's—
what fairness you were nurse to, and what
    foulness
festered beneath! Now I am found to be
a sinner and a son of sinners. Crossroads,
and hidden glade, oak and the narrow way
at the crossroads, that drank my father's blood
offered you by my hands, do you remember
still what I did as you looked on, and what
I did when I came here? O marriage, marriage!
you bred me and again when you had bred
bred children of your child and showed to men
brides, wives and mothers and the foulest
    deeds
that can be in this world of ours.
Come—it's unfit to say what is unfit
to do.—I beg of you in God's name hide me
somewhere outside your country, yes, or kill me,
or throw me into the sea, to be forever
out of your sight. Approach and deign to touch
    me
for all my wretchedness, and do not fear.
No man but I can bear my evil doom.

CHORUS

Here Creon comes in fit time to perform
or give advice in what you ask of us.
Creon is left sole ruler in your stead.

OEDIPUS

Creon! Creon! What shall I say to him?
How can I justly hope that he will trust me?
In what is past I have been proved towards him
an utter liar.
(*Enter* CREON.)

CREON

                     Oedipus, I've come
not so that I might laugh at you nor taunt you
with evil of the past. But if you still
are without shame before the face of men
reverence at least the flame that gives all life,
our Lord the Sun, and do not show unveiled
to him pollution such that neither land
nor holy rain nor light of day can welcome.
(*To a* SERVANT.)
Be quick and take him in. It is most decent
that only kin should see and hear the troubles
of kin.

OEDIPUS

           I beg you, since you've torn me from
my dreadful expectations and have come
in a most noble spirit to a man
that has used you vilely—do a thing for me.
I shall speak for your own good, not for my own.

CREON

What do you need that you would ask of me?

OEDIPUS

Drive me from here with all the speed you can
to where I may not hear a human voice.

CREON

Be sure, I would have done this had not I
wished first of all to learn from the God the course
of action I should follow.

OEDIPUS

                  But his word
has been quite clear to let the parricide,
the sinner, die.

CREON

             Yes, that indeed was said.
But in the present need we had best discover
what we should do.

OEDIPUS

             And will you ask about
a man so wretched?

CREON

             Now even you will trust
the God.

OEDIPUS

   So. I command you—and will beseech you—
to her that lies inside that house give burial
as you would have it; she is yours and rightly
you will perform the rites for her. For me—
never let this my father's city have me
living a dweller in it. Leave me live
in the mountains where Cithaeron is, that's called
my mountain, which my mother and my father
while they were living would have made my tomb.
So I may die by their decree who sought
indeed to kill me. Yet I know this much:
no sickness and no other thing will kill me.
I would not have been saved from death if not
for some strange evil fate. Well, let my fate
go where it will.
              Creon, you need not care
about my sons; they're men and so wherever
they are, they will not lack a livelihood.
But my two girls—so sad and pitiful—

whose table never stood apart from mine,
and everything I touched they always shared—
Creon, have a thought for them! And most
I wish that you might suffer me to touch them
and sorrow with them.
(*Enter* ANTIGONE *and* ISMENE, OEDIPUS' *two daughters.*)
O my lord! O true noble Creon! Can I
really be touching them, as when I saw?
What shall I say?
Yes, I can hear them sobbing—my two darlings!
and Creon has had pity and has sent me
what I loved most?
Am I right?
CREON
You're right: it was I gave you this
because I knew from old days how you loved them
as I see now.
OEDIPUS
God bless you for it, Creon,
and may God guard you better on your road
than he did me!
O children,
where are you? Come here, come to my hands,
a brother's hands which turned your father's eyes,
those bright eyes you knew once, to what you see,
a father seeing nothing, knowing nothing,
begetting you from his own source of life.
I weep for you—I cannot see your faces—
I weep when I think of the bitterness
there will be in your lives, how you must live
before the world. At what assemblages
of citizens will you make one? to what
gay company will you go and not come home
in tears instead of sharing in the holiday?
And when you're ripe for marriage, who will he
be;
the man who'll risk to take such infamy
as shall cling to my children, to bring hurt
on them and those that marry with them? What
curse is not there? "Your father killed his father
and sowed the seed where he had sprung
himself
and begot you out of the womb that held him."
These insults you will hear. Then who will marry
you?
No one, my children; clearly you are doomed
to waste away in barrenness unmarried.
Son of Menocceus, since you are all the father
left these two girls, and we, their parents, both
are dead to them—do not allow them wander

like beggars, poor and husbandless.
They are of your own blood.
And do not make them equal with myself
in wretchedness; for you can see them now
so young, so utterly alone, save for you only.
Touch my hand, noble Creon, and say yes.
If you were older, children, and were wiser,
there's much advice I'd give you. But as it is,
let this be what you pray: give me a life
wherever there is opportunity
to live, and better life than was my father's.
CREON
Your tears have had enough of scope; now go
within the house.
OEDIPUS
I must obey, though bitter of heart.
CREON
In season, all is good.
OEDIPUS
Do you know on what conditions I obey?
CREON
You tell me them,
and I shall know them when I hear.
OEDIPUS
That you shall send me out
to live away from Thebes.
CREON
That gift you must ask of the God.
OEDIPUS
But I'm now hated by the Gods.
CREON
So quickly you'll obtain your prayer.
OEDIPUS
You consent then?
CREON
What I do not mean, I do not use to say.
OEDIPUS
Now lead me away from here.
CREON
Let go the children, then, and come.
OEDIPUS
Do not take them from me.
CREON
Do not seek to be master in everything,
for the things you mastered did not follow you
throughout your life.
(*As* CREON *and* OEDIPUS *go out.*)
CHORUS
You that live in my ancestral Thebes, behold this
Oedipus,—

him who knew the famous riddles and was a man
    most masterful;
not a citizen who did not look with envy on his
    lot—
see him now and see the breakers of misfortune
    swallow him!
Look upon that last day always. Count no mortal
    happy till
he has passed the final limit of his life secure from
    pain.

PERFORMING *OEDIPUS THE KING*

Since the first actor entered the Theater of Dionysus in Athens between 430–427 B.C. to play Oedipus in Sophocles' play, the role has been perceived as daunting. The three plays that tell the Theban story are often produced together today in the order of events: *Oedipus the King, Oedipus at Colonus,* and *Antigone.* By the time Sophocles was writing for the festival, the presentation of thematically related trilogies, like Aeschylus' *Oresteia,* had been abandoned. In fact, what is logically a trilogy of three plays is not.

Once the Greeks began to revive favorite plays by their master playwrights, *Oedipus* was one of the most popular. The Roman playwright Seneca followed on the popularity of the Greek original with one of his own, also called *Oedipus,* which contained explicit scenes of violence and horror (for example, Jocasta rips open her womb at the play's end).

The Oedipus story intrigued later playwrights. Pierre Corneille (1659), John Dryden (1679), Voltaire (1718), William Butler Yeats (1923), and Jean Cocteau (1931) created adaptations. In 1912, the German director Max Reinhardt produced *Oedipus Rex* at the Theater Royal, Covent Garden (London), with John Martin-Harvey in the title role. In the vast opera house, Reinhardt used the orchestra floor as the Greek *orchestra* and filled the proscenium opening with black screens and a pair of massive, burnished copper doors in the staging of a pre-Hellenic, savage rendering of Sophocles' play.

Modern actors and directors have produced both the three Theban plays together and the single *Oedipus the King.* The young Laurence Olivier played a double-bill of tragedy and comedy at the Old Vic, London, in the 1945–46 season as Oedipus in the Yeats translation, followed by Puff in Richard Brinsley Sheridan's comedy *The Critic.* Opening night was electric. Olivier's Oedipus was a handsome nobleman consumed by his half-understood quest. The actor shocked audiences with two chilling cries—one offstage and the other onstage as he reentered the stage with blood streaming from his eyes and his garments spattered with dark stains. Critics called his screams unearthly and inhuman.

Peter Brook chose Seneca's version of *Oedipus,* adapted by Ted Hughes, to stage as a primitive rite at the Royal National Theater, London, in 1968. The actors performed in contemporary dress. John Gielgud as Oedipus wore a black turtleneck sweater and Irene Worth as Jocasta appeared in a long dark dress. Brook stressed the archetypal images of the play and Irene Worth performed the ultimate symbolic ritual prescribed for her by Seneca: she impaled herself through the womb on the sword in a ritual of human sacrifice and expiation. Brook ended the production with the sudden, unexpected unveiling of a huge golden phallus in a blaze of golden light as a symbol of the Pantheon of godheads.

Other modern productions of *Oedipus* have been staged by Tyrone Guthrie with recreations of traditional masks and chitons at the Stratford Shakespeare Festival in Canada with Douglas Campbell in the title role (1955), and by Czechoslovakian director-designer Josef Svoboda at the Smetana Theater in Prague (1963). Svoboda created a vast, endless staircase with rising platforms to visualize the emotional turbulence of the play.

Sophocles' play lends itself to the traditional and to the experimental. The work is staged regularly by Greek companies in the theater at Epidaurus and elsewhere.

CRITICS' NOTEBOOK

The history of dramatic theory and criticism begins with Aristotle's fragmentary treatises on comedy, epic, and tragedy. In *The Poetics,* the philosopher-teacher looked back on a body of plays written by greater and lesser writers of classical Greece. He established critical concerns for the nature of drama as imitation and for tragedy and comedy as forms of writing for the theater. Aristotle's observations have remained the most influential comments on Western drama and have shaped dramatic criticism through the ages. Even though Bertolt Brecht and others challenged Aristotle's theory of dramatic writing in the mid-twentieth century, *The Poetics* remains the guidepost for delineating alternatives to new play forms in the twenty-first century. For Aristotle, Sophocles' *Oedipus the King* was the most perfect play written for the theater of his time.

Aristotle was Plato's most brilliant student and eventually began his own school, called the Lyceum. His students recorded and carefully preserved his lectures, which have influenced almost every brand of philosophy, science, and the arts. Although unfinished, *The Poetics* remains a document of immense importance to the beginnings of literary criticism. The sections on tragedy, reprinted here, chart his critical thinking on how one of Greece's greatest playwrights shaped the elements of his play to make a statement about human fallibility.

Sigmund Freud, the father of psychoanalytic theory and the most celebrated psychiatrist of the twentieth century, explored the symbolic meaning of dreams in his landmark study called *The Interpretation of Dreams* (1900–1930). As he researched the unconscious, he made connections between the meaning of world myths, great literature, and the lives of all human beings. Freud believed that the mythic material underlying Sophocles' *Oedipus the King* provided a vocabulary and insight into the deepest psychological development of human beings; that is, the early relationship between parents and children. Freud's "Oedipus Complex" has entered the popular culture as a means of explaining the love/hate relationships between parents and children.

Aristotle, on Tragedy, from *The Poetics* (c. 334–323 B.C.)*
Translated by S. H. Butcher
[ELEMENTS OF TRAGEDY]

❦

Tragedy, then, is an imitation of an action that is serious, complete, and of a certain magnitude; in language embellished with each kind of artistic ornament, the several kinds being found in separate parts of the play; in the form of action, not of narrative; through pity and fear effecting the proper purgation of these emotions. By 'language embellished,' I mean language into which rhythm, 'harmony,' and song enter. By 'the several kinds in separate parts,' I mean, that some parts are rendered through the medium of verse alone, others again with the aid of song.

Now as tragic imitation implies persons acting, it necessarily follows, in the first place, that Spectacular equipment will be a part of Tragedy. Next, Song and Diction, for these are the medium of imitation. By 'Diction' I mean the mere metrical arrangement of the words; as for 'Song,' it is a term whose sense every one understands.

Again, Tragedy is the imitation of an action; and an action implies personal agents, who necessarily possess certain distinctive qualities both of character and thought; for it is by these that we qualify actions themselves, and these—thought and character—are the two natural causes from which actions spring, and on actions again all success or failure depends. Hence, the Plot is the imitation of the action—for by plot I here mean the arrangement of the incidents. By Character I mean that in virtue of which we ascribe certain qualities to the agents. Thought is required wherever a statement is proved, or, it may be, a general truth enunciated. Every Tragedy, therefore, must have six parts, which parts determine its quality—namely, Plot, Character, Diction, Thought, Spectacle, Song.

Aristotle's Theory of Poetry and Fine Arts, trans. S. H. Butcher. 4th edition (Mineola, NY: Dover Publications, 1951): 7–69.

Two of the parts constitute the medium of imitation, one the manner, and three the objects of imitation. And these complete the list. These elements have been employed, we may say, by the poets to a man; in fact, every play contains Spectacular elements as well as Character, Plot, Diction, Song, and Thought.

But most important of all is the structure of the incidents. For Tragedy is an imitation, not of men, but of an action and of life, and life consists in action, and its end is a mode of action, not a quality. Now character determines men's qualities, but it is by their actions that they are happy or the reverse. Dramatic action, therefore, is not with a view to the representation of character: character comes in as subsidiary to the actions. Hence the incidents and the plot are the end of a tragedy; and the end is the chief thing of all. Again, without action there cannot be a tragedy; there may be without character. The tragedies of most of our modern poets fail in the rendering of character; and of poets in general this is often true. It is the same in painting; and here lies the difference between Zeuxis and Polygnotus. Polygnotus delineates character well: the style of Zeuxis is devoid of ethical quality. Again, if you string together a set of speeches expressive of character, and well finished in point of diction and thought, you will not produce the essential tragic effect nearly so well as with a play which, however deficient in these respects, yet has a plot and artistically constructed incidents. Besides which, the most powerful elements of emotional interest in Tragedy—Peripeteia or Reversal of the Situation and Recognition scenes—are parts of the plot. A further proof is, that novices in the art attain to finish of diction and precision of portraiture before they can construct the plot. It is the same with almost all the early poets.

The Plot, then, is the first principle, and, as it were, the soul of a tragedy: Character holds the second place. A similar fact is seen in painting. The most beautiful colours, laid on confusedly, will not give as much pleasure as the chalk outline of a portrait. Thus Tragedy is the imitation of an action, and of the agents mainly with a view to the action.

Third in order is Thought,—that is, the faculty of saying what is possible and pertinent in given circumstances. In the case of oratory, this is the function of the political art and of the art of rhetoric: and so indeed the older poets make their characters speak the language of civic life; the poets of our time, the language of the rhetoricians. Character is that which reveals moral purpose, showing what kind of things a man chooses or avoids. Speeches, therefore, which do not make this manifest, or in which the speaker does not choose or avoid anything whatever, are not expressive of character. Thought, on the other hand, is found where something is proved to be or not to be, or a general maxim is enunciated.

Fourth among the elements enumerated comes Diction; by which I mean, as has been already said, the expression of the meaning in words; and its essence is the same both in verse and prose.

Of the remaining elements Song holds the chief place among the embellishments.

The Spectacle has, indeed, an emotional attraction of its own, but, of all the parts, it is the least artistic, and connected least with the art of poetry. For the power of Tragedy, we may be sure, is felt even apart from representation and actors. Besides, the production of spectacular effects depends more on the art of the stage machinist than on that of the poet.

[ON PLOT OR FABLE]

These principles being established, let us now discuss the proper structure of the Plot, since this is the first and most important thing in Tragedy.

Now, according to our definition, Tragedy is an imitation of an action that is complete, and whole, and of a certain magnitude; for there may be a whole that is wanting in magnitude. A whole is that which has a beginning, a middle, and an end. A beginning is that which does not itself follow anything by causal necessity, but after which something naturally is or comes to be. An end, on the contrary, is that which itself naturally follows some other thing, either by necessity, or as a rule, but has nothing following it. A middle is that which follows something as some other thing follows it. A well constructed plot, therefore, must neither begin nor end at haphazard, but conform to these principles.

[ON UNITY]

Unity of plot does not, as some persons think, consist in the unity of the hero. For infinitely various are the incidents in one man's life which cannot be reduced to unity; and so, too, there are many actions of one man out of which we cannot make one action. Hence the error, as it appears, of all poets who have composed a Heracleid, a Theseid, or other poems of the kind. They imagine that as Heracles was one man, the story of Heracles must also be a unity. But Homer, as in all else he is of surpassing merit, here too—whether from art or natural genius—seems to have happily discerned the truth. In composing the Odyssey he did not include all the adventures of Odysseus—such as his wound on Parnassus, or his feigned madness at the mustering of the host—incidents between which there was no necessary or probable connexion: but he made the Odyssey, and likewise the Iliad, to centre round an action that in our sense of the word is one. As therefore, in the other imitative arts, the imitation is one when the object imitated is one, so the plot, being an imitation of an action, must imitate one action and that a whole, the structural union of the parts being such that, if any one of them is displaced or removed, the whole will be disjointed and disturbed. For a thing whose presence or absence makes no visible difference, is not an organic part of the whole.

[ON PROBABILITY]

It is, moreover, evident from what has been said, that it is not the function of the poet to relate what has happened, but what may happen,—what is possible according to the law of probability or necessity. The poet and the historian differ not by writing in verse or in prose. The work of Herodotus might be put into verse, and it would still be a species of history, with metre no less than without it. The true difference is that one relates what has happened, the other what may happen. Poetry, therefore, is a more philosophical and a higher thing than history: for poetry tends to express the universal, history the particular. By the universal I mean how a person of a certain type will on occasion speak or act, according to the law of probability or necessity....

But again, Tragedy is an imitation not only of a complete action, but of events inspiring fear or pity. Such an effect is best produced when the events come on us by surprise; and the effect is heightened when, at the same time, they follow as cause and effect. The tragic wonder will then be greater than if they happened of themselves or by accident; for even coincidences are most striking when they have an air of design. We may instance the statue of Mitys at Argos, which fell upon his murderer while he was a spectator at a festival, and killed him. Such events seem not to be due to mere chance. Plots, therefore, constructed on these principles are necessarily the best.

[ON SIMPLE AND COMPLEX PLOTS]

Plots are either Simple or Complex, for the actions in real life, of which the plots are an imitation, obviously show a similar distinction. An action which is one and continuous in the sense above defined, I call Simple, when the change of fortune takes place without Reversal of the Situation and without Recognition.

A Complex action is one in which the change is accompanied by such Reversal, or by Recognition, or by both. These last should arise from the internal structure of the plot, so that what follows should be the necessary or probable result of the preceding action. It makes all the difference whether any given event is a case of *propter hoc* or *post hoc.*

Reversal of the Situation is a change by which the action veers round to its opposite, subject always to our rule of probability or necessity. Thus in the Oedipus, the messenger comes to cheer Oedipus and free him from his alarms about his mother, but by revealing who he is, he produces the opposite effect....

Recognition, as the name indicates, is a change from ignorance to knowledge, producing love or hate between the persons destined by the poet for good or bad fortune. The best form of recognition is coincident with a Reversal of the Situation, as in the Oedipus.... But the recognition which is most intimately connected with the plot and action is, as we have said, the recognition of persons. This recognition, combined with Reversal, will produce either pity or fear; and actions producing these effects are those which, by our definition, Tragedy represents. Moreover, it is upon such situations that the issues of good or bad fortune will depend. Recognition, then, being between persons, it may happen that one person only is recognised by the other—when the latter is already known—or it may be necessary that the recognition should be on both sides. Thus Iphigenia is revealed to Orestes by the sending of the letter; but another act of recognition is required to make Orestes known to Iphigenia.

Two parts, then, of the Plot—Reversal of the Situation and Recognition—turn upon surprises. A third part is the Scene of Suffering. The Scene of Suffering is a destructive or painful action, such as death on the stage, bodily agony, wounds and the like.

[ON PITY AND FEAR]

A perfect tragedy should, as we have seen, be arranged not on the simple but on the complex plan. It should, moreover, imitate actions which excite pity and fear, this being the distinctive mark of tragic imitation. It follows plainly, in the first place, that the change of fortune presented must not be the spectacle of a virtuous man brought from prosperity to adversity: for this moves neither pity nor fear; it merely shocks us. Nor, again, that of a bad man passing from adversity to prosperity: for nothing can be more alien to the spirit of Tragedy; it possesses no single tragic quality; it neither satisfies the moral sense nor calls forth pity or fear. Nor, again,

should the downfall of the utter villain be exhibited. A plot of this kind would, doubtless, satisfy the moral sense, but it would inspire neither pity nor fear; for pity is aroused by unmerited misfortune, fear by the misfortune of a man like ourselves. Such an event, therefore, will be neither pitiful nor terrible.

[ON CHARACTER]

There remains, then, the character between these two extremes,—that of a man who is not eminently good and just, yet whose misfortune is brought about not by vice or depravity, but by some error or frailty. He must be one who is highly renowned and prosperous,—a personage like Oedipus, Thyestes, or other illustrious men of such families.

A well constructed plot should, therefore, be single in its issue, rather than double as some maintain. The change of fortune should be not from bad to good, but, reversely, from good to bad. It should come about as the result not of vice, but of some great error or frailty, in a character either such as we have described, or better rather than worse....

Fear and pity may be aroused by spectacular means; but they may also result from the inner structure of the piece, which is the better way, and indicates a superior poet. For the plot ought to be so constructed that, even without the aid of the eye, he who hears the tale told will thrill with horror and melt to pity at what takes place. This is the impression we should receive from hearing the story of the Oedipus....

[CHORUS]

The Chorus too should be regarded as one of the actors; it should be an integral part of the whole, and share in the action, in the manner not of Euripides but of Sophocles. As for the later poets, their choral songs pertain as little to the subject of the piece as to that of any other tragedy. They are, therefore, sung as mere interludes,—a practice first begun by Agathon....

Sigmund Freud, on The Oedipus Complex*
Translated by James Strachey

❦

In my experience, which is already extensive, the chief part in the mental lives of all children who later become psychoneurotics is played by their parents. Being in love with the one parent and hating the other are among the essential constituents of the stock of psychical impulses which is formed at that time and which is of such importance in determining the symptoms of the later neurosis. It is not my belief, however, that psychoneurotics differ sharply in this respect from other human beings who remain normal—that they are able, that is, to create something absolutely new and peculiar to themselves. It is far more probable—and this is confirmed by occasional observations on normal children—that they are only distinguished by exhibiting on a magnified scale feelings of love and hatred to their parents which occur less obviously and less intensely in the minds of most children.

This discovery is confirmed by a legend that has come down to us from classical antiquity: a legend whose profound and universal power to move can only be understood if the hypothesis I have put forward in regard to the psychology of children has an equally universal validity. What I have in mind is the legend of King Oedipus and Sophocles' drama which bears his name....

Oedipus Rex is what is known as a tragedy of destiny. Its tragic effect is said to lie in the contrast between the supreme will of the gods and the vain attempts of mankind to escape the evil that threatens them. The lesson which, it is said, the deeply moved spectator should learn from the tragedy is submission to the divine will and realization of his own impotence. Modern dramatists have accordingly tried to achieve a similar tragic effect by weaving the same contrast

into a plot invented by themselves. But the spectators have looked on unmoved while a curse or an oracle was fulfilled in spite of all the efforts of some innocent man: later tragedies of destiny have failed in their effect.

If *Oedipus Rex* moves a modern audience no less than it did the contemporary Greek one, the explanation can only be that its effect does not lie in the contrast between destiny and human will, but is to be looked for in the particular nature of the material on which that contrast is exemplified. There must be something which makes a voice within us ready to recognize the compelling force of destiny in *Oedipus,* while we can dismiss as merely arbitrary such dispositions as are laid down in [Grillparzer's] *Die Ahnfrau* or other modern tragedies of destiny. And a factor of this kind is in fact involved in the story of King Oedipus. His destiny moves us only because it might have been ours—because the oracle laid the same curse upon us before our birth as upon him. It is the fate of all of us, perhaps, to direct our first sexual impulse towards our mother and our first hatred and our first murderous wish against our father. Our dreams convince us that that is so. King Oedipus, who slew his father Laïus and married his mother Jocasta, merely shows us the fulfillment of our own childhood wishes. But, more fortunate than he, we have meanwhile succeeded, in so far as we have not become psychoneurotics, in detaching our sexual impulses from our mothers and in forgetting our jealousy of our fathers. Here is one in whom these primaeval wishes of our childhood have been fulfilled, and we shrink back from him with the whole force of the repression by which those wishes have since that time been held down within us. While the poet, as he unravels the past, brings to light the guilt of Oedipus, he is at the same time compelling us to recognize our own inner minds, in which those same impulses, though suppressed, are still to be found....

There is an unmistakable indication in the text of Sophocles' tragedy itself that the legend of Oedipus sprang from some primaeval dream-material which had as its content the distressing disturbance of a child's relation to his parents

*Sigmund Freud, *The Interpretation of Dreams,* written 1900–1930. This passage is taken from the eighth edition, published in 1930.

owing to the first stirrings of sexuality. At a point when Oedipus, though he is not yet enlightened, has begun to feel troubled by his recollection of the oracle, Jocasta consoles him by referring to a dream which many people dream, though, as she thinks, it has no meaning:

> Many a man ere now in dreams hath lain
> With her who bore him. He hath least annoy
> Who with such omens troubleth not his mind.

Today, just as then, many men dream of having sexual relations with their mothers, and speak of the fact with indignation and astonishment. It is clearly the key to the tragedy and the complement to the dream of the dreamer's father being dead. The story of Oedipus is the reaction of the imagination to these two typical dreams. And just as these dreams, when dreamt by adults, are accompanied by feelings of repulsion, so too the legend must include horror and self-punishment. Its further modification originates once again in a misconceived secondary revision of the material, which has sought to exploit it for theological purposes. The attempt to harmonize divine omnipotence with human responsibility must naturally fail in connection with this subject-matter just as with any other.

REVISITING GREEK TRAGEDY

Play analysis begins with the philosopher Aristotle's theories of dramatic writing, based on the practices of the early Greek playwrights. Aristotle's *Poetics,* a treatise on poetry and drama, is our earliest analytical model for understanding dramatic texts, in particular tragedy and comedy. Aristotle is our first dramatic theorist and critic whose methods have proved insightful and useful through the centuries. In modern times, other methods of analysis have emerged as societies, cultures, and writing styles have changed.

Aristotle's approach defines drama as an imitation (mimetic) of a human action and sets forth elements ranging from plot and character to universal meanings, visual effects, music, and song. Moreover, he identified for all time two types or genres of writing that imitate the antipodes of human experience: tragedy and comedy. In his assessment, *Oedipus the King* was the finest example of tragic writing within his experience.

As a model play, *Oedipus the King* illustrates drama's basic elements as laid down by Aristotle: plot, imitative action, character, thought, language (dialogue and choral odes), and spectacle or visual effects. In addition, Aristotle analyzed dramatic plots pointing to reversals and scenes of recognition as effective strategies for creating satisfactory endings.

Finally, in our study of dramatic writing, Sophocles' *Oedipus the King* exemplifies one of the two earliest types of Western writing about the extremes of human experience. Comedy is the second.

NOTES

1. David Mamet, *Writing in Restaurants* (New York: Viking Penguin, Inc., 1986): 8.
2. Francis Fergusson, *The Idea of Theater: The Art of Drama in Changing Perspective* (New Jersey: Princeton University Press, 1949): 255.

CHAPTER 6

❦

COMEDY

John Gielgud as John Worthing in *The Importance of Being Earnest* by Oscar Wilde, directed by John Gielgud, Broadway, 1947. (Photo by Vandamm Studio.)

...we should treat all the trivial things of life very seriously, and all the serious things of life with sincere and studied triviality.

—Oscar Wilde

ORIGINS OF COMEDY

Aristotle's few scattered references to comedy in *The Poetics* tell us that comedy was of later origin than tragedy, grew out of improvisations of phallic songs, and imitated lowborn persons acting and doing as distinguished from tragedy's noble persons. Comedy originated in early phallic rites with dances, songs, and parades of phallic symbols associated with tribal fertility rites dedicated to the well-being of the community. Eventually, comedy emerged in Greece as a dramatic form and dramatized the ludicrous or some absurd ugliness in human nature that was not truly destructive of self or others. The comic poets became an official part of the Greek festivals around 487–486 B.C. and evolved a writing and performance style, including a chorus, similar to tragedy.

Aristophanes (448?–380? B.C.) is the only surviving comic writer of the fifth century B.C., with eleven plays of social and political satire, and Menander (342–291 B.C.) is represented by one surviving complete play, *The Grouch,* a comedy of contemporary life and manners, along with fragments of other plays.

The Greek comic writers were followed in Roman times by Plautus and Terence, who depicted the affairs of the merchant class in plots that turned on mistaken identity, misunderstandings, and deliberate deceptions. Plautus (Titus Maccius Plautus) wrote *The Twin Menaechmi,* whose broad, farcical plot is based on mistaken identity involving identical twins; Terence (Publius Terentius Afer) wrote a more refined comedy dealing with disagreements between lovers or conflicts between parents and children. Terence's *Andria* concerns a young man's efforts to marry the girl he loves instead of the wife his father intends. Terence's plays end with a genial tolerance for humanity's foibles. Both comic writers used clearly defined character types, including the clever trickster, the parasite, courtesan, and the cowardly soldier. These character types of Roman comedy defied the centuries and appeared in other guises in the *commedia dell'arte* of the Italian improvisational companies and in comedies by Shakespeare, Molière, and William Wycherley.

THEORIES OF COMEDY

In contrast to tragic action, which commonly shows a noble individual committing a great mistake, followed by intense suffering, awareness, and usually death, comic action exposes human folly and celebrates human survival. The English poet, Lord Byron, put the matter thus: "All tragedies are finished by death,/All comedies are ended by marriage." Although it is an oversimplification, the couplet contains some truth about these two principal types of dramatic writing. Tragedy has the gravity, grief, and finality that we often associate with death, and comedy has the joy and celebration of new life that we associate with marriage and reunion. The most familiar comic plot is the one in which obstructive parents try to keep young lovers apart, but the lovers find a way to overcome parental opposition and all join in the marriage festivities. Commenting on comic structure, Northrop Frye wrote, "What normally happens is that a young man wants a young woman, that his desire is resisted by some opposition, usually paternal, and that near the end of the play some twist in the plot enables the hero to have his will."[1]

The same writing techniques that apply to tragedy also apply to comedy: comic action, plot, hero, reversals, recognition, resolution, and so on. Comic action dramatizes a train of events manifested on the stage by a diversity of activities engaging subjects of human folly and triumph. Comedy is not a mere matter of jokes, one-liners, or funny bits of business, like slipping on a banana peel or receiving the unexpected pie in the face. Comic action has consequences in the social world for the group; tragedy has consequences in the moral world for the individual. The central figure in comedy ranges from a miser determined to hoard his money for all eternity to a clever young lover determined to marry the woman he loves. Whereas tragedy concentrates on the single life that is destroyed in its ripeness, comedy dramatizes the renewal of the self within the context of social relationships. The tragic figure is isolated from society partly by birth, partly by a noble sensibility, and partly by a tragic act. The comic figure's passionate isolation is held up as human folly by a society that celebrates moderation and good-natured acceptance of human foibles. Comedy suggests that selfhood is found in joining with the life flow of common humanity, not in the assertion of individuality.

Ordinarily, there are two types of self-assertion (and central figures) in comedy: One is the ridiculous figure, like the miser, who tries to impede or stop the flow of happiness or well-being of others. The second is the individual who removes, by whatever machinations, the obstacles to happiness and well-being. The first type values worn-out habits and repeats rigid behavior; the second overcomes frustrations for the tolerant, high-spirited, generous, and life-giving. Comedy, therefore, delights in overcoming humanity's foibles represented by individuals who are grotesque and rigid of mind and spirit. The feeble old man lusting after the beautiful young girl is one of comedy's age-old grotesques.

Over the centuries, comic playwrights have displayed a range of character types (miser, hypocrite, fool, impostor, parasite), variety in word usage (puns, malapropisms), and amusing activities (disguises, mistaken identities, paranoia, obsessions, sexual intrigues). The characters who hold to mechanical behavior and outworn values are ludicrously out of place in the world of people who joyously live and let live. Since Aristophanes and Menander, comedy has always held up for ridicule society's crustaceans—pedants, hypocrites, fools, misers, braggarts, hypochondriacs, gluttons. It is all good-natured social criticism, smiling tolerantly like Puck in Shakespeare's *A Midsummer Night's Dream* who says, "Lord, what fools these mortals be!"

The comic plot is usually more involved and less plausible than the plot of a tragedy. There are comic reversals, arbitrary workings of fortune or chance, and unexpected or unlikely happenings. In Oscar Wilde's nineteenth-century comedy, *The Importance of Being Earnest,* the plot turns on a handbag. Wilde contrives a number of old clichès in the brisk and joyful comedy: a formidable relative, love at (or before) first sight, imposters, mistaken identity, overheard conversations, a forgotten menial who solves the family mystery, and a lost infant restored. Wilde exploits our pleasure in his masterful comedy by devising complications of love and a resolution based on "What's in a name?"

In comedy, unexpected letters arrive unmasking a hypocrite, and long-lost relatives turn up giving validity to the ingenue's respectable parentage, thereby resolving gross complications in the spirit of the writer's *comic vision* which devalues the rigidly consistent and the antisocial. Comedy, according to Frye, usually moves toward a happy ending ("All's well that ends well"), but the ending emphasizes the social world more so than the moral one. The society that emerges at the play's end represents a less restrained, freer society. It is understood that the newly married couple will live happily ever after or that the reunited husband and wife will get along in a more tolerant manner.

The primary action of the comic plot is to overcome the rigid behavior of comedy's laughably inflexible characters, such as misers, hypocrites, jealous husbands, or stern parents. Comedy usually begins, therefore, with a rigid circumstance; for example, the miser, crying poverty, withholds money from his children. After various doings and reversals in the comic action, a new—presumably natural, obliging, fertile, and flexible—society is formed, often centered around young lovers who are to be married with their parents' blessing and with celebrations, dances, and feasts engaging the entire community at the play's end.

Just as self-knowledge is crucial to the meaning of the tragic hero's disastrous career, so, too, in comedy there is self-recognition: Troublesome persons usually find their better natures and join in the fun. Comic self-knowledge recognizes that the troublesome individual's behavior has been aberrational, that he or she has a better nature, and as reward for reform is restored to dignity and a new position in a revitalized society. Whereas the tragic hero awakens to the fact that he or she has made a terrible error in judgment and that life has been sacrificed, the comic hero puts aside in some measure his or her inflexible individuality and submits to the will of the partner or to the social group.

As forms of dramatic writing, tragedy and comedy represent two parts of humanity's experience and spiritual life. Throughout history, tragedy has been attributed more prestige than comedy, but comedy (with its laughter and joy) has been indispensable to our survival in a world threatened by terrorism, nuclear accidents, and global warming. The best comedy is good-natured while it is critical of the mean-spirited and foolish. To paraphrase Puck, "mortals can be fools." The comic writer's vision of humanity is rarely cynical, although it is unsympathetic to mean and foolish persons. It attributes human error to folly, not to ill will or irremediable corruption, and is forgiving in its statements about human endurance and social survival.

ENGLISH COMEDY AND NEOCLASSICAL THEORY

Comedy from Aristophanes to Oscar Wilde has been a blend of satire and fantasy, physical farce and subtle wordplay. Sometimes one element outweighs another, but by the late nineteenth century, English comedy owed more to subtle wordplay and social intrigue than to boisterous farce and fantasy realms of lost children and enchanted islands.

By the late Renaissance in England, the writing of comedy was divided between the romantic comedies of Shakespeare and the neoclassical plays of Ben Jonson, differing largely in their comic character types and the lovers' pathways to marriage. Jonson wrote "comedies of humours," named after the particular humour or body fluid believed to determine excessive character traits, such as an obsession with gold (*The Alchemist*) and a passion for deception (*Volpone*). Moreover, Jonson observed neoclassical decorum, including attention to the "critics' rules": unities of time, place, and action; characters restricted to the middle or lower classes; elevated language; and sophisticated ideas. The nuances found in neoclassical writing, along with the introduction of actresses to the stage, dictated the changes in English comic writing after the return of Charles II to the throne of England and the emergence of writers devoted to the new classical comedy; chief among them was William Congreve. The new comedy in England was called a "comedy of manners."

THE COMEDY OF MANNERS

The comedies written between 1660 and 1700, called comedies of manners, revealed the foibles of a brittle, fun-loving, and witty upper class in London and mirrored the polite behavior and foibles of the society that watched the plays. English comic writers were less interested in reforming society than in depicting its faults with the aim of laughter, not sentimentality or tears. Games of fortune and marriage replaced the older comic struggles for true love. They were played in contemporary drawing rooms by the beautiful people (and their crotchety parents and older relatives) for suitable marriages, with conformity to acceptable social ranks and beneficial financial arrangements being the twin aims of the negotiations. William Congreve's *The Way of the World,* written in 1700, depicted the London scene, sophisticated attitudes toward marriage, and cautious emotional attachments between the hero and heroine playing games of marriage and fortune. Oscar Wilde's *The Importance of Being Earnest* is the direct descendant of these earlier comedies of manners *sans* the idealism and moralizing that followed in the sentimental comedies of the eighteenth century.

The Importance of Being Earnest
A Trivial Play for Serious People

OSCAR WILDE

Oscar Wilde (1854–1900) was born Oscar Fingal O'Flahertie Wills Wilde in Dublin. His father was Ireland's leading eye and ear surgeon and his mother, known by her penname Speranza, was a poet of the Free Ireland movement and an authority on Celtic folklore. Wilde attended Trinity College, Dublin, and matriculated to Oxford University where he distinguished himself as a classical scholar, wit, and poet. He won the coveted Newdigate Prize for poetry. By the early 1880s, he was established in London's smart social life as the colorful advocate of the aesthetic movement that art must serve the needs of art. Wilde was chiefly identified by his brilliant conversation, his picturesque dress (he favored velvet coats, knee breeches, black silk stockings, pale green ties, and floppy hats), and his opinions that life should follow the rules of art. He embarked on a lecture tour of the United States in 1882 and two years later married Constance Lloyd; they had two sons—Cyril and Vyvyan.

Working as editor and reviewer, Wilde published his controversial novel, The Picture of Dorian Gray, *which was hailed as brilliant but morally subversive. He then turned to writing for the stage in his most productive period. In* Lady Windermere's Fan *(1892), he found his comedic style in a well-crafted and witty play about upper-class British society in which the heroine's reputation rests on the discreet recovery of a fan.* A Woman of No Importance *(1893) and* An Ideal Husband *(1895) established Wilde's reputation as a writer of a comedy of wit and manners dominated by the upper-class drawing room, brittle self-centered characters, lively dialogue, and mechanical plotting brilliantly relieved by the sharp picture of polite society's manners and the machinations among the dowagers, dandies, and eligible daughters to preserve the status quo of wealth and sterling reputation. His masterpiece,* The Importance of Being Earnest, *was staged in 1895 to the delight of West End audiences, but scandal and court trials immediately followed and the comedy was withdrawn from production after fewer than one hundred performances.*

The events of Wilde's private life shattered his brilliant career. His homosexual tendencies were long known in his immediate circle of friends but were brought into the open by his involvement with Lord Alfred Douglas ("Bosie"), son of the embittered Marquess of Queensbury. Queensbury accused Wilde of sodomy (famously known as the crime of "gross indecency" in Victorian England) and Wilde sued him for slander. The first of two sensational trials began and at the close of the second Oscar Wilde was convicted of sodomy, a crime whose penalty was prison for two years with hard labor. The society that had cultivated him now abandoned Wilde; his wife divorced him and changed the family name to Holland. While in prison he wrote The Ballad of Reading Gaol *(published under his prison name C.3.3.) and* De Profundis, *which recorded his humiliation and despair. Released from prison in 1897 and penniless, he went to France where he lived under the name Sebastian Melmoth and died within three years; he was forty-six. Since then, his grave in the Père Lachaise Cemetery in Paris has become a place of literary pilgrimage. The Oscar Wilde Centennial was celebrated in England and the United States in the year 2000 with lectures and publications on his life and work.*

CRITICAL INTRODUCTION TO *THE IMPORTANCE OF BEING EARNEST*

Oscar Wilde's comic masterpiece belongs to the green world of family tradition, pride of birth, forceful women, polished gentlemen, power games at tea tables, the secrets of Bunburyism, and Victorian codes of respectability reaffirmed.

Invited to write on a modern subject and with an advance of £50 in his pocket, Wilde originally wrote a play in four acts but reduced it to three acts at the request of the actor-manager George Alexander, who had already programmed a one-act curtain-raiser to precede the play. His "Play of Modern Life" is crafted around the fundamental question of John Worthing's birth, parentage, and eligibility for marriage. The question itself defines the self-contained world of upper Victorian society in the 1890s—a world of proper breeding, inherited money, and guarded reputation. The play's complications are romantic love imperiled by the least departure from social and moral norms. John Worthing's questionable parentage makes him an ineligible suitor for Lady Bracknell's daughter until a handbag identifies him as the long-lost son of Lady Bracknell's sister who, by amazing circumstance, was christened with the names "Ernest John."

It would be incorrect to assume from a contemporary vantage point that Oscar Wilde was writing an anarchic comedy or questioning the values of English society. Wilde wrote to entertain his audiences and to do so by mirroring their lifestyle, manners, and conversation: no one struggles to earn a living, no politics are discussed, servants are plentiful, and there are no references to social ills—poverty, crime, lower classes, pornography, prostitution, and birth control. Wilde's plays, like Noël Coward's stylish comedies in a later era, exist in a social and moral vacuum in a long-ago and partial world. What, then, has made *The Importance of Being Earnest* a virtually guaranteed box office success on stage and in films for over a hundred years?

One critic thinks that the secret of its longevity lies in its flawless dramatic construction. Another considers that Wilde's play rises above caricature in the scintillating epigrams and the individualism displayed by his women and men. Another views Wilde's "plays of modern life" as depictions of the behavior of London's elite as a matter of power, and therefore of politics rather than of morality.[2]

"The good ended happily," says Miss Prism, discussing her lost manuscript of a novel, "and the bad unhappily. That is what Fiction means." For many years, critics have attributed the longevity of Wilde's social comedy to the well-crafted plot with its comic types (the contentious lovers, dragon-like parent, timid governess, and laconic butler), comic reversals, secrets, recognition scene, and unambiguous ending to the influence of the well-made play (the *pièce bien faite* popularized in France by Eugène Scribe and others). In this formulaic writing, character (although sharply drawn) is subordinated to incident that is usually the result of blind chance rather than human manipulation. Lady Bracknell is the formidable parent; John Worthing and Algernon Moncrieff are polished Englishmen, although studies in contrast—one is the fluid talker and the other is ponderously earnest. The young women, adept at feminine wiles, are pretty, engaging, and intelligent. Gwendolen Fairfax and Cecily Cardew are only slightly different in their backgrounds; together, they are Wilde's version of the modern "new" woman whose femininity and emotional strengths are on display in their manipulations of their suitors, governesses, and authority figures.

Wilde's characters do not develop and change in the various circumstances of the play. Rather, external circumstances, not inner forces, guide the plot to a satisfying resolution, but not without the help of physical objects to complicate and further the plot. Wilde relies on realistic three-dimensional objects to force revelations and complicate the plot. John Worthing's engraved cigarette case forces him to admit the existence of his ward. The railway timetables are conveniently placed to betray Bunbury's location. Cucumber sandwiches and later muffins are eaten to give comic interest to the contentious scenes. The grand scene of recognition that establishes John Worthing's true identity is the result not so much of Miss Prism's confession as the physical existence of the famous handbag with identifying scratches and Prism's initials on the lock. Wilde's skill in tightly contriving the plot is rivaled and surpassed only by the brilliance of the epigrammatic dialogue that expresses the surface glitter of the comedy and explains the audience's pleasure at being drawn into the world of the play.

In all of his writings, Oscar Wilde has been celebrated for his wit, epigrammatic dialogue, and paradoxical humor. Shortly before writing *The Importance of Being Earnest* (subtitled "A Trivial Play for Serious People"), Wilde had argued the philosophy of the play that "we should treat all the trivial things of life very seriously, and all the serious things of life with sincere and studied triviality." The confusion of meaning in the use of the terms *trivial* and *serious* undermines our usual understanding of the words and allows us to find new truths in the old usages. The pun on Ernest/Earnest is but one example of Wilde's paradoxical inversions. The pun on "e(a)rnest" seems to contain the opposite meanings of seriousness of purpose and truthfulness. However, when Jack is unmasked as parading another name, he discovers his lies to be true and his truth lies. He is both Ernest and John, having been christened Ernest John Moncrieff.[3]

Oscar Wilde had learned in the drawing rooms that he frequented to tease his public with paradox. He applied his epigrammatic twists and turns of phrases (and convoluted meanings) to ordinary elements of an upper-class lifestyle, including smoking, dining, parentage, governesses, and marriage proposals. In her interrogation of John Worthing's person and background, Lady Bracknell asks, "Do you smoke?" When he admits that he does, she counters with: "I'm glad to hear it. A man should always have an occupation of some kind." The serious context of the trivial question is turned topsy-turvy as a man's smoking habits are viewed with far more seriousness than his occupation in life.

Wilde's play continually undermines the qualities of truth, seriousness, identity, nature, and so on, so crucial to the moralistic well-made plays of the 1890s. As such, it would appear to be a subversive play; nonetheless, Wilde subjects the seriousness of contemporary society and culture to a playful critique. While Wilde's first-night audience perceived the charming playfulness of the play and an early reviewer called it a "paper balloon," Wilde's prosecutors clearly perceived the subversive potential of the "trivial" play. He juxtaposed nature and culture and found culture triumphant in its power to transform nature, mask identities, and alter almost anything, including fashion, names, and sexual ethics.

Wilde viewed social codes as a form of self-deceit and founded on hypocrisy. Herein lies the delicious dimension of paradox in Wilde's writing, confusing what London's elite did and what it said it did. Indeed, in his public life, Wilde gave the appearance of being a happily married Victorian father whereas in reality he led a double life. The true meaning of Bunburyism is the secret life that allows men (and women) to politely defy social rules of conduct without risk and consequences. In the play, the fictional Bunbury is John Worthing's and Algernon's means of escaping into the countryside or avoiding Lady Bracknell's tedious dinner parties. The consequences of Bunburyism are romantic complications to be sorted out in the play's final revelations that clear the path for the lovers to be united with parental blessing. At all times Miss Prism's definition of fiction is never in doubt, nor is the outcome of the play: "The good end happily and the bad unhappily."

Underlying the cheerful ruse of fiction and fantasy in *The Importance of Being Earnest* is the harsh reality of the playwright's destruction once his double life was exposed to society and to the criminal courts. It is unwise in an analysis of this play to make too much of the fact that in 1895 "earnest" was a code word for homosexual and Bunbury a pun on "buns," suggesting anal sex. Wilde was writing a comedy of manners laced with some possible in-jokes for his male friends, not concealing a homosexual text within the larger play. Wilde was too much engaged in mirroring the arbitrary social world of his audience with clever dialogue and inventive circumstances to risk a more somber statement about sexual duality. *The Importance of Being Earnest* is a public fiction and not a private exposition of the not-so-secret life of Oscar Wilde.

Once Oscar Wilde's double life was made public, he was martyred and branded an outcast, imprisoned and impoverished for his breach of society's rigid social and sexual codes. However, in his plays of modern life, his characters skirt the dangers inherent in disobedience and titillate Victorian audiences with social disasters averted by the clever manipulations of the playwright where the punning on Ernest/earnest affirms the values of the play's green world—true love, parental approval, proper breeding, inherited wealth, and marriage with society's blessing.

Algernon's advice to his friend echoes the philosophy, writing, and life of the playwright:

"The truth is rarely pure and never simple. Modern life would be tedious if it were either, and modern literature a complete impossibility!" Oscar Wilde's masterful comedy is never simple or tedious; its truthfulness lies in highlighting the paradox between its austere ethical codes of Victorian society and the arbitrary behavior of that social world, especially in matters of sexual politics.

The Importance of Being Earnest

THE PERSONS OF THE PLAY

JOHN WORTHING, J.P.

ALGERNON MONCRIEFF

REV. CANON CHASUBLE, D.D.

MERRIMAN, Butler

LANE, Manservant

LADY BRACKNELL

HON. GWENDOLEN FAIRFAX

CECILY CARDEW

MISS PRISM, Governess

THE SCENES OF THE PLAY

ACT I

ALGERNON MONCRIEFF'S *Flat in Half-Moon Street, W.*

ACT II

The Garden at the Manor House, Woolton

ACT III

Drawing-Room at the Manor House, Woolton

TIME

The Present

ACT I

Scene—Morning-room in Algernon's flat in Half-Moon Street. The room is luxuriously and artistically furnished. The sound of a piano is heard in the adjoining room.

LANE is arranging afternoon tea on the table, and after the music has ceased, ALGERNON enters.

ALGERNON: Did you hear what I was playing, Lane?

LANE: I didn't think it polite to listen, sir.

ALGERNON: I'm sorry for that, for your sake. I don't play accurately—any one can play accurately—but I play with wonderful expression. As far as the piano is concerned, sentiment is my forte. I keep science for Life.

LANE: Yes, sir.

ALGERNON: And, speaking of the science of Life, have you got the cucumber sandwiches cut for Lady Bracknell?

LANE: Yes, sir. (*Hands them on a salver.*)

ALGERNON (*inspects them, takes two, and sits down on the sofa*): Oh!... by the way, Lane, I see from your book that on Thursday night, when Lord Shoreman and Mr. Worthing were dining with me, eight bottles of champagne are entered as having been consumed.

LANE: Yes, sir; eight bottles and a pint.

ALGERNON: Why is it that at a bachelor's establishment the servants invariably drink the champagne? I ask merely for information.

LANE: I attribute it to the superior quality of the wine, sir. I have often observed that in married households the champagne is rarely of a first-rate brand.

ALGERNON: Good heavens! Is marriage so demoralizing as that?

LANE: I believe it *is* a very pleasant state, sir. I have had very little experience of it myself up to the present. I have only been married once. That was in consequence of a misunderstanding between myself and a young person.

ALGERNON (*languidly*): I don't know that I am much interested in your family life, Lane.

LANE: No, sir; it is not a very interesting subject. I never think of it myself.

ALGERNON: Very natural, I am sure. That will do, Lane, thank you.

LANE: Thank you, sir.

(*LANE goes out.*)

ALGERNON: Lane's views on marriage seem somewhat lax. Really, if the lower orders don't set us a good example, what on earth is the use of them? They seem, as a class, to have absolutely no sense of moral responsibility.

(*Enter* LANE.)

LANE: Mr. Ernest Worthing.

(*Enter* JACK. LANE *goes out.*)

ALGERNON: How are you, my dear Ernest? What brings you up to town?

JACK: Oh, pleasure, pleasure! What else should bring one anywhere? Eating as usual, I see, Algy!

ALGERNON (*stiffly*): I believe it is customary in good society to take some slight refreshment at five o'clock. Where have you been since last Thursday?

JACK (*sitting down on the sofa*): In the country.

ALGERNON: What on earth do you do there?

JACK (*pulling off his gloves*): When one is in town one amuses oneself. When one is in the country one amuses other people. It is excessively boring.

ALGERNON: And who are the people you amuse?

JACK (*airily*): Oh, neighbours, neighbours.

ALGERNON: Got nice neighbours in your part of Shropshire?

JACK: Perfectly horrid! Never speak to one of them.

ALGERNON: How immensely you must amuse them! (*Goes over and takes sandwich.*) By the way, Shropshire is your county, is it not?

JACK: Eh? Shropshire? Yes, of course. Hallo! Why all these cups? Why cucumber sandwiches? Why such reckless extravagance in one so young? Who is coming to tea?

ALGERNON: Oh! merely Aunt Augusta and Gwendolen.

JACK: How perfectly delightful!

ALGERNON: Yes, that is all very well; but I am afraid Aunt Augusta won't quite approve of your being here.

JACK: May I ask why?

ALGERNON: My dear fellow, the way you flirt with Gwendolen is perfectly disgraceful. It is almost as bad as the way Gwendolen flirts with you.

JACK: I am in love with Gwendolen. I have come up to town expressly to propose to her.

ALGERNON: I thought you had come up for pleasure?… I call that business.

JACK: How utterly unromantic you are!

ALGERNON: I really don't see anything romantic in proposing. It is very romantic to be in love. But there is nothing romantic about a definite proposal. Why, one may be accepted. One usually is, I believe. Then the excitement is all over. The very essence of romance is uncertainty. If ever I get married, I'll certainly try to forget the fact.

JACK: I have no doubt about that, dear Algy. The Divorce Court was specially invented for people whose memories are so curiously constituted.

ALGERNON: Oh! there is no use speculating on that subject. Divorces are made in Heaven— (JACK *puts out his hand to take a sandwich.* ALGERNON *at once interferes.*) Please don't touch the cucumber sandwiches. They are ordered specially for Aunt Augusta. (*Takes one and eats it.*)

JACK: Well, you have been eating them all the time.

ALGERNON: That is quite a different matter. She is my aunt. (*Takes plate from below.*) Have some bread and butter. The bread and butter is for Gwendolen. Gwendolen is devoted to bread and butter.

JACK (*advancing to table and helping himself*): And very good bread and butter it is too.

ALGERNON: Well, my dear fellow, you need not eat as if you were going to eat it all. You behave as if you were married to her already. You are not married to her already, and I don't think you ever will be.

JACK: Why on earth do you say that?

ALGERNON: Well, in the first place girls never marry the men they flirt with. Girls don't think it right.

JACK: Oh, that is nonsense!

ALGERNON: It isn't. It is a great truth. It accounts for the extraordinary number of bachelors that one sees all over the place. In the second place, I don't give my consent.

JACK: Your consent!

ALGERNON: My dear fellow, Gwendolen is my first cousin. And before I allow you to marry her, you will have to clear up the whole question of Cecily. (*Rings bell.*)

JACK: Cecily! What on earth do you mean? What do you mean, Algy, by Cecily! I don't know any one of the name of Cecily.

(*Enter* LANE.)

ALGERNON: Bring me that cigarette case Mr. Worthing left in the smoking-room the last time he dined here.

LANE: Yes, sir.

(LANE *goes out*.)

JACK: Do you mean to say you have had my cigarette case all this time? I wish to goodness you had let me know. I have been writing frantic letters to Scotland Yard about it. I was very nearly offering a large reward.

ALGERNON: Well, I wish you would offer one. I happen to be more than usually hard up.

JACK: There is no good offering a large reward now that the thing is found.

(*Enter* LANE *with the cigarette case on a salver*. ALGERNON *takes it at once*. LANE *goes out*.)

ALGERNON: I think that is rather mean of you, Ernest, I must say. (*Opens case and examines it*.) However, it makes no matter, for, now that I look at the inscription inside, I find that the thing isn't yours after all.

JACK: Of course it's mine. (*Moving to him*.) You have seen me with it a hundred times, and you have no right whatsoever to read what is written inside. It is a very ungentlemanly thing to read a private cigarette case.

ALGERNON: Oh! it is absurd to have a hard and fast rule about what one should read and what one shouldn't. More than half of modern culture depends on what one shouldn't read.

JACK: I am quite aware of the fact, and I don't propose to discuss modern culture. It isn't the sort of thing one should talk of in private. I simply want my cigarette case back.

ALGERNON: Yes; but this isn't your cigarette case. This cigarette case is a present from some one of the name of Cecily, and you said you didn't know any one of that name.

JACK: Well, if you want to know, Cecily happens to be my aunt.

ALGERNON: Your aunt!

JACK: Yes. Charming old lady she is, too. Lives at Tunbridge Wells. Just give it back to me, Algy.

ALGERNON (*retreating to back of sofa*): But why does she call herself little Cecily if she is your aunt and lives at Tunbridge Wells? (*Reading*.) "From little Cecily with her fondest love."

JACK (*moving to sofa and kneeling upon it*): My dear fellow, what on earth is there in that? Some aunts are tall, some aunts are not tall. That is a matter that surely an aunt may be allowed to decide for herself. You seem to think that every aunt should be exactly like your aunt! That is absurd! For Heaven's sake give me back my cigarette case. (*Follows* ALGERNON *round the room*.)

ALGERNON: Yes. But why does your aunt call you her uncle? "From little Cecily, with her fondest love to her dear Uncle Jack." There is no objection, I admit, to an aunt being a small aunt, but why an aunt, no matter what her size may be, should call her own nephew her uncle, I can't quite make out. Besides, your name isn't Jack at all; it is Ernest.

JACK: It isn't Ernest; it's Jack.

ALGERNON: You have always told me it was Ernest. I have introduced you to every one as Ernest. You answer to the name of Ernest. You look as if your name was Ernest. You are the most earnest-looking person I ever saw in my life. It is perfectly absurd your saying that your name isn't Ernest. It's on your cards. Here is one of them. (*Taking it from case*.) "Mr. Ernest Worthing, B.4, The Albany." I'll keep this as a proof that your name is Ernest if ever you attempt to deny it to me, or to Gwendolen, or to any one else. (*Puts the card in his pocket*.)

JACK: Well, my name is Ernest in town and Jack in the country, and the cigarette case was given to me in the country.

ALGERNON: Yes, but that does not account for the fact that your small Aunt Cecily, who lives at Tunbridge Wells, calls you her dear uncle. Come, old boy, you had much better have the thing out at once.

JACK: My dear Algy, you talk exactly as if you were a dentist. It is very vulgar to talk like a dentist when one isn't a dentist. It produces a false impression,

ALGERNON: Well, that is exactly what dentists always do. Now, go on! Tell me the whole thing. I may mention that I have always suspected you of being a confirmed and secret Bunburyist; and I am quite sure of it now.

JACK: Bunburyist? What on earth do you mean by a Bunburyist?

ALGERNON: I'll reveal to you the meaning of that incomparable expression as soon as you are kind enough to inform me why you are Ernest in town and Jack in the country.

JACK: Well, produce my cigarette case first.

ALGERNON: Here it is. (*Hands cigarette case.*) Now produce your explanation, and pray make it improbable. (*Sits on sofa.*)

JACK: My dear fellow, there is nothing improbable about my explanation at all. In fact it's perfectly ordinary. Old Mr. Thomas Cardew, who adopted me when I was a little boy, made me in his will guardian to his granddaughter, Miss Cecily Cardew. Cecily, who addresses me as her uncle from motives of respect that you could not possibly appreciate, lives at my place in the country under the charge of her admirable governess, Miss Prism.

ALGERNON: Where is that place in the country, by the way?

JACK: That is nothing to you, dear boy. You are not going to be invited.... I may tell you candidly that the place is not in Shropshire.

ALGERNON: I suspected that, my dear fellow! I have Bunburyed all over Shropshire on two separate occasions. Now, go on. Why are you Ernest in town and Jack in the country?

JACK: My dear Algy, I don't know whether you will be able to understand my real motives. You are hardly serious enough. When one is placed in the position of guardian, one has to adopt a very high moral tone on all subjects. It's one's duty to do so. And as a high moral tone can hardly be said to conduce very much to either one's health or one's happiness, in order to get up to town I have always pretended to have a younger brother of the name of Ernest, who lives in the Albany, and gets into the most dreadful scrapes. That, my dear Algy, is the whole truth pure and simple.

ALGERNON: The truth is rarely pure and never simple. Modern life would be very tedious if it were either, and modern literature a complete impossibility!

JACK: That wouldn't be at all a bad thing.

ALGERNON: Literary criticism is not your forte, my dear fellow. Don't try it. You should leave that to people who haven't been at a University. They do it so well in the daily papers. What you really are is a Bunburyist. I was quite right in saying you were a Bunburyist. You are one of the most advanced Bunburyists I know.

JACK: What on earth do you mean?

ALGERNON: You have invented a very useful younger brother called Ernest, in order that you may be able to come up to town as often as you like. I have invented an invaluable permanent invalid called Bunbury, in order that I may be able to go down into the country whenever I choose. Bunbury is perfectly invaluable. If it wasn't for Bunbury's extraordinary bad health, for instance, I wouldn't be able to dine with you at Willis's to-night, for I have been really engaged to Aunt Augusta for more than a week.

JACK: I haven't asked you to dine with me anywhere to-night.

ALGERNON: I know. You are absurdly careless about sending out invitations. It is very foolish of you. Nothing annoys people so much as not receiving invitations.

JACK: You had much better dine with your Aunt Augusta.

ALGERNON: I haven't the smallest intention of doing anything of the kind. To begin with, I dined there on Monday, and once a week is quite enough to dine with one's own relations. In the second place, whenever I do dine there I am always treated as a member of the family, and sent down with either no woman at all, or two. In the third place, I know perfectly well whom she will place me next to, to-night. She will place me next Mary Farquhar, who always flirts with her own husband across the dinner-table. That is not very pleasant. Indeed, it is not even decent…and that sort of thing is enormously on the increase. The amount of women in London who flirt with their own husbands is perfectly scandalous. It looks so bad. It is simply washing one's clean linen in public. Besides, now that I know you to be a confirmed Bunburyist I naturally want to talk to you about Bunburying. I want to tell you the rules.

JACK: I'm not a Bunburyist at all. If Gwendolen accepts me, I am going to kill my brother, indeed I think I'll kill him in any case. Cecily is a little too much interested in him. It is rather a bore. So I am going to get rid of Ernest. And I strongly advise you to do the same with Mr.…with your invalid friend who has the absurd name.

ALGERNON: Nothing will induce me to part with Bunbury, and if you ever get married, which seems to me extremely problematic, you will be very glad to know Bunbury. A man who marries without knowing Bunbury has a very tedious time of it.

JACK: That is nonsense. If I marry a charming girl like Gwendolen, and she is the only girl I ever saw in my life that I would marry, I certainly won't want to know Bunbury.

ALGERNON: Then your wife will. You don't seem to realize, that in married life three is company and two is none.

JACK (*sententiously*): That, my dear young friend, is the theory that the corrupt French Drama has been propounding for the last fifty years.

ALGERNON: Yes, and that the happy English home has proved in half the time.

JACK: For heaven's sake, don't try to be cynical. It's perfectly easy to be cynical.

ALGERNON: My dear fellow, it isn't easy to be anything nowadays. There's such a lot of beastly competition about. (*The sound of an electric bell is heard.*) Ah! that must be Aunt Augusta. Only relatives, or creditors, ever ring in that Wagnerian manner. Now, if I get her out of the way for ten minutes, so that you can have an opportunity for proposing to Gwendolen, may I dine with you to-night at Willis's?

JACK: I suppose so, if you want to.

ALGERNON: Yes, but you must be serious about it. I hate people who are not serious about meals. It is so shallow of them.

(*Enter* LANE.)

LANE: Lady Bracknell and Miss Fairfax.

(ALGERNON *goes forward to meet them. Enter* LADY BRACKNELL *and* GWENDOLEN.)

LADY BRACKNELL: Good afternoon, dear Algernon, I hope you are behaving very well.

ALGERNON: I'm feeling very well, Aunt Augusta.

LADY BRACKNELL: That's not quite the same thing. In fact the two things rarely go together. (*Sees* JACK *and bows to him with icy coldness.*)

ALGERNON (*to* GWENDOLEN): Dear me, you are smart!

GWENDOLEN: I am always smart! Am I not, Mr. Worthing?

JACK: You're quite perfect, Miss Fairfax.

GWENDOLEN: Oh! I hope I am not that. It would leave no room for developments, and I intend to develop in many directions. (GWENDOLEN *and* JACK *sit down together in the corner.*)

LADY BRACKNELL: I'm sorry if we are a little late, Algernon, but I was obliged to call on dear Lady Harbury. I hadn't been there since her poor husband's death. I never saw a woman so altered; she looks quite twenty years younger. And now I'll have a cup of tea, and one of those nice cucumber sandwiches you promised me.

ALGERNON: Certainly, Aunt Augusta. (*Goes over to tea-table.*)

LADY BRACKNELL: Won't you come and sit here, Gwendolen?

GWENDOLEN: Thanks, mamma, I'm quite comfortable where I am.

ALGERNON (*picking up empty plate in horror*): Good heavens! Lane! Why are there no cucumber sandwiches? I ordered them specially.

LANE (*gravely*): There were no cucumbers in the market this morning, sir. I went down twice.

ALGERNON: No cucumbers!

LANE: No, sir. Not even for ready money.

ALGERNON: That will do, Lane, thank you.

LANE: Thank you, sir.

(*Goes out.*)

ALGERNON: I am greatly distressed, Aunt Augusta, about there being no cucumbers, not even for ready money.

LADY BRACKNELL: It really makes no matter, Algernon. I had some crumpets with Lady Harbury, who seems to me to be living entirely for pleasure now.

ALGERNON: I hear her hair has turned quite gold from grief.

LADY BRACKNELL: It certainly has changed its colour. From what cause I, of course, cannot say. (ALGERNON *crosses and hands tea.*) Thank you. I've quite a treat for you to-night, Algernon. I am going to send you down with Mary Farquhar. She is such a nice woman, and so attentive to her husband. It's delightful to watch them.

ALGERNON: I am afraid, Aunt Augusta, I shall have to give up the pleasure of dining with you to-night after all.

LADY BRACKNELL (*frowning*): I hope not, Algernon. It would put my table completely out. Your uncle would have to dine upstairs. Fortunately he is accustomed to that.

ALGERNON: It is a great bore, and, I need hardly say, a terrible disappointment to me, but the fact is I have just had a telegram to say that my poor friend Bunbury is very ill again. (*Exchanges glances with* JACK.) They seem to think I should be with him.

LADY BRACKNELL: It is very strange. This Mr. Bunbury seems to suffer from curiously bad health.

ALGERNON: Yes; poor Bunbury is a dreadful invalid.

LADY BRACKNELL: Well, I must say, Algernon, that I think it is high time that Mr. Bunbury made up his mind whether he was going to live or to die. This shilly-shallying with the question is absurd. Nor do I in any way approve of the modern sympathy with invalids. I consider it morbid. Illness of any kind is hardly a thing to be encouraged in others. Health is the primary duty of life. I am always telling that to your poor uncle, but he never seems to take much notice…as far as any improvement in his ailment goes. I should be much obliged if you would ask Mr. Bunbury, from me, to be kind enough not to have a relapse on Saturday, for I rely on you to arrange my music for me. It is my last reception, and one wants something that will encourage conversation, particularly at the end of the season when every one has practically said whatever they had to say, which, in most cases, was probably not much.

ALGERNON: I'll speak to Bunbury, Aunt Augusta, if he is still conscious, and I think I can promise you he'll be all right by Saturday. Of course the music is a great difficulty. You see, if one plays good music, people don't listen, and if one plays bad music people don't talk. But I'll run over the programme I've drawn out, if you will kindly come into the next room for a moment.

LADY BRACKNELL: Thank you, Algernon. It is very thoughtful of you. (*Rising, and following* ALGERNON.) I'm sure the programme will be delightful, after a few expurgations. French songs I cannot possibly allow. People always seem to think that they are improper, and either look shocked, which is vulgar, or laugh, which is worse. But German sounds a thoroughly respectable language, and indeed, I believe is so. Gwendolen, you will accompany me.

GWENDOLEN: Certainly, mamma.

(LADY BRACKNELL *and* ALGERNON *go into the music-room,* GWENDOLEN *remains behind.*)

JACK: Charming day it has been, Miss Fairfax.

GWENDOLEN: Pray don't talk to me about the weather, Mr. Worthing. Whenever people talk to me about the weather, I always feel quite certain that they mean something else. And that makes me so nervous.

JACK: I do mean something else.

GWENDOLEN: I thought so. In fact, I am never wrong.

JACK: And I would like to be allowed to take advantage of Lady Bracknell's temporary absence.…

GWENDOLEN: I would certainly advise you to do so. Mamma has a way of coming back suddenly into a room that I have often had to speak to her about.

JACK (*nervously*): Miss Fairfax, ever since I met you I have admired you more than any girl …I have ever met since…I met you.

GWENDOLEN: Yes, I am quite well aware of the fact. And I often wish that in public, at any rate, you had been more demonstrative. For me you have always had an irresistible fascination. Even before I met you I was far from indifferent to you. (JACK *looks at her in amazement*.) We live, as I hope you know, Mr. Worthing, in an age of ideals. The fact is constantly mentioned in the more expensive monthly magazines, and has reached the provincial pulpits, I am told; and my ideal has always been to love some one of the name of Ernest. There is something in that name that inspires absolute confidence. The moment Algernon first mentioned to me that he had a friend called Ernest, I knew I was destined to love you.

JACK: You really love me, Gwendolen?

GWENDOLEN: Passionately!

JACK: Darling! You don't know how happy you've made me.

GWENDOLEN: My own Ernest!

JACK: But you don't really mean to say that you couldn't love me if my name wasn't Ernest?

GWENDOLEN: But your name is Ernest.

JACK: Yes, I know it is. But supposing it was something else? Do you mean to say you couldn't love me then?

GWENDOLEN (*glibly*): Ah! that is clearly a metaphysical speculation, and like most metaphysical speculations has very little reference at all to the actual facts of real life, as we know them.

JACK: Personally, darling, to speak quite candidly, I don't much care about the name of Ernest…. I don't think the name suits me at all.

GWENDOLEN: It suits you perfectly. It is a divine name. It has a music of its own. It produces vibrations.

JACK: Well, really, Gwendolen, I must say that I think there are lots of other much nicer names. I think Jack, for instance, a charming name.

GWENDOLEN: Jack?… No, there is very little music in the name Jack, if any at all, indeed. It does not thrill. It produces absolutely no vibrations…. I have known several Jacks, and they all, without exception, were more than usually plain. Besides, Jack is a notorious domesticity for John! And I pity any woman who is married to a man called John. She would probably never be allowed to know the entrancing pleasure of a single moment's solitude. The only really safe name is Ernest.

JACK: Gwendolen, I must get christened at once—I mean we must get married at once. There is no time to be lost.

GWENDOLEN: Married, Mr. Worthing?

JACK (*astounded*): Well…surely. You know that I love you, and you led me to believe, Miss Fairfax, that you were not absolutely indifferent to me.

GWENDOLEN: I adore you. But you haven't proposed to me yet. Nothing has been said at all about marriage. The subject has not even been touched on.

JACK: Well…may I propose to you now?

GWENDOLEN: I think it would be an admirable opportunity. And to spare you any possible disappointment, Mr. Worthing, I think it only fair to tell you quite frankly beforehand that I am fully determined to accept you.

JACK: Gwendolen!

GWENDOLEN: Yes, Mr. Worthing, what have you got to say to me?

JACK: You know what I have got to say to you.

GWENDOLEN: Yes, but you don't say it.

JACK: Gwendolen, will you marry me? (*Goes on his knees.*)

GWENDOLEN: Of course I will, darling. How long you have been about it! I am afraid you have had very little experience in how to propose.

JACK: My own one, I have never loved any one in the world but you.

GWENDOLEN: Yes, but men often propose for practice. I know my brother Gerald does.

All my girl-friends tell me so. What wonderfully blue eyes you have, Ernest! They are quite, quite, blue. I hope you will always look at me just like that, especially when there are other people present.

(*Enter* LADY BRACKNELL.)

LADY BRACKNELL: Mr. Worthing! Rise, sir, from this semi-recumbent posture. It is most indecorous.

GWENDOLEN: Mamma! (*He tries to rise; she restrains him.*) I must beg you to retire. This is no place for you. Besides, Mr. Worthing has not quite finished yet.

LADY BRACKNELL: Finished what, may I ask?

GWENDOLEN: I am engaged to Mr. Worthing, mamma. (*They rise together.*)

LADY BRACKNELL: Pardon me, you are not engaged to any one. When you do become engaged to some one, I, or your father, should his health permit him, will inform you of the fact. An engagement should come on a young girl as a surprise, pleasant or unpleasant, as the case may be. It is hardly a matter that she could be allowed to arrange for herself.... And now I have a few questions to put to you, Mr. Worthing. While I am making these inquiries, you, Gwendolen, will wait for me below in the carriage.

GWENDOLEN (*reproachfully*): Mamma!

LADY BRACKNELL: In the carriage, Gwendolen! (GWENDOLEN *goes to the door. She and* JACK *blow kisses to each other behind* LADY BRACKNELL'S *back.* LADY BRACKNELL *looks vaguely about as if she could not understand what the noise was. Finally turns round.*) Gwendolen, the carriage!

GWENDOLEN: Yes, mamma.

(*Goes out, looking back at* JACK.)

LADY BRACKNELL (*sitting down*): You can take a seat, Mr. Worthing.

(*Looks in her pocket for note-book and pencil.*)

JACK: Thank you, Lady Bracknell, I prefer standing.

LADY BRACKNELL (*pencil and note-book in hand*): I feel bound to tell you that you are not down on my list of eligible young men, although I have the same list as the dear Duchess of Bolton has. We work together, in fact. However, I am quite ready to enter your name, should your answers be what a really affectionate mother requires. Do you smoke?

JACK: Well, yes, I must admit I smoke.

LADY BRACKNELL: I am glad to hear it. A man should always have an occupation of some kind. There are far too many idle men in London as it is. How old are you?

JACK: Twenty-nine.

LADY BRACKNELL: A very good age to be married at. I have always been of opinion that a man who desires to get married should know either everything or nothing. Which do you know?

JACK (*after some hesitation*): I know nothing, Lady Bracknell.

LADY BRACKNELL: I am pleased to hear it. I do not approve of anything that tampers with natural ignorance. Ignorance is like a delicate exotic fruit; touch it and the bloom is gone. The whole theory of modern education is radically unsound. Fortunately in England, at any rate, education produces no effect whatsoever. If it did, it would prove a serious danger to the upper classes, and probably lead to acts of violence in Grosvenor Square. What is your income?

JACK: Between seven and eight thousand a year.

LADY BRACKNELL (*makes a note in her book*): In land, or in investments?

JACK: In investments, chiefly.

LADY BRACKNELL: That is satisfactory. What between the duties expected of one during one's lifetime, and the duties exacted from one after one's death, land has ceased to be either a profit or a pleasure. It gives one position, and prevents one from keeping it up. That's all that can be said about land.

JACK: I have a country house with some land, of course, attached to it, about fifteen hundred acres, I believe; but I don't depend on that for my real income. In fact, as far as I can make out, the poachers are the only people who make anything out of it.

LADY BRACKNELL: A country house! How many bedrooms? Well, that point can be cleared up afterwards. You have a town house, I hope? A girl with a simple, unspoiled nature, like Gwendolen, could hardly be expected to reside in the country.

JACK: Well, I own a house in Belgrave Square, but it is let by the year to Lady Bloxham. Of course, I can get it back whenever I like, at six months' notice.

LADY BRACKNELL: Lady Bloxham? I don't know her.

JACK: Oh, she goes about very little. She is a lady considerably advanced in years.

LADY BRACKNELL: Ah, nowadays that is no guarantee of respectability of character. What number in Belgrave Square?

JACK: 149.

LADY BRACKNELL (*shaking her head*): The unfashionable side. I thought there was something. However, that could easily be altered.

JACK: Do you mean the fashion, or the side?

LADY BRACKNELL (*sternly*): Both, if necessary, I presume. What are your politics?

JACK: Well, I am afraid I really have none. I am a Liberal Unionist.

LADY BRACKNELL: Oh, they count as Tories. They dine with us. Or come in the evening, at any rate. Now to minor matters. Are your parents living?

JACK: I have lost both my parents.

LADY BRACKNELL: To lose one parent, Mr. Worthing, may be regarded as a misfortune; to lose both looks like carelessness. Who was your father? He was evidently a man of some wealth. Was he born in what the Radical papers call the purple of commerce, or did he rise from the ranks of the aristocracy?

JACK: I am afraid I really don't know. The fact is, Lady Bracknell, I said I had lost my parents. It would be nearer the truth to say that my parents seem to have lost me.... I don't actually know who I am by birth. I was…well, I was found.

LADY BRACKNELL: Found!

JACK: The late Mr. Thomas Cardew, an old gentleman of a very charitable and kindly disposition, found me, and gave me the name of Worthing, because he happened to have a first-class ticket for Worthing in his pocket at the time. Worthing is a place in Sussex. It is a seaside resort.

LADY BRACKNELL: Where did the charitable gentleman who had a first-class ticket for this seaside resort find you?

JACK (*gravely*): In a hand-bag.

LADY BRACKNELL: A hand-bag?

JACK (*very seriously*): Yes, Lady Bracknell. I was in a hand-bag—a somewhat large, black leather hand-bag, with handles to it—an ordinary hand-bag in fact.

LADY BRACKNELL: In what locality did this Mr. James, or Thomas, Cardew come across this ordinary hand-bag?

JACK: In the cloak-room at Victoria Station. It was given to him in mistake for his own.

LADY BRACKNELL: The cloak-room at Victoria Station?

JACK: Yes. The Brighton line.

LADY BRACKNELL: The line is immaterial. Mr. Worthing, I confess I feel somewhat bewildered by what you have just told me. To be born, or at any rate bred, in a hand-bag, whether it had handles or not, seems to me to display a contempt for the ordinary decencies of family life that reminds one of the worst excesses of the French Revolution. And I presume you know what that unfortunate movement led to? As for the particular locality in which the hand-bag was found, a cloak-room at a railway station might serve to conceal a social indiscretion—has probably, indeed, been used for that purpose before now—but it could hardly be regarded as an assured basis for a recognised position in good society.

JACK: May I ask you then what you would advise me to do? I need hardly say I would do anything in the world to ensure Gwendolen's happiness.

LADY BRACKNELL: I would strongly advise you, Mr. Worthing, to try and acquire some relations as soon as possible, and to make a definite effort to produce at any rate one parent, of either sex, before the season is quite over.

JACK: Well, I don't see how I could possibly manage to do that. I can produce the hand-bag at any moment. It is in my dressing-room at home. I really think that should satisfy you, Lady Bracknell.

LADY BRACKNELL: Me, sir! What has it to do with me? You can hardly imagine that I and Lord Bracknell would dream of allowing our only daughter—a girl brought up with the utmost care—to marry into a cloak-room, and form an alliance with a parcel? Good morning, Mr. Worthing!

(LADY BRACKNELL *sweeps out in majestic indignation.*)

JACK: Good morning! (ALGERNON, *from the other room, strikes up the Wedding March.* JACK *looks perfectly furious, and goes to the door.*) For goodness' sake don't play that ghastly tune, Algy. How idiotic you are!

(*The music stops and* ALGERNON *enters cheerily.*)

ALGERNON: Didn't it go off all right, old boy? You don't mean to say Gwendolen refused you? I know it is a way she has. She is always refusing people. I think it is most ill-natured of her.

JACK: Oh, Gwendolen is as right as a trivet. As far as she is concerned, we are engaged. Her mother is perfectly unbearable. Never met such a Gorgon.... I don't really know what a Gorgon is like, but I am quite sure that Lady Bracknell is one. In any case, she is a monster, without being a myth, which is rather unfair.... I beg your pardon, Algy, I suppose I shouldn't talk about your own aunt in that way before you.

ALGERNON: My dear boy, I love hearing my relations abused. It is the only thing that makes me put up with them at all. Relations are simply a tedious pack of people, who haven't got the remotest knowledge of how to live, nor the smallest instinct about when to die.

JACK: Oh, that is nonsense!

ALGERNON: It isn't!

JACK: Well, I won't argue about the matter. You always want to argue about things.

ALGERNON: That is exactly what things were originally made for.

JACK: Upon my word, if I thought that, I'd shoot myself.... (*A pause.*) You don't think there is any chance of Gwendolen becoming like her mother in about a hundred and fifty years, do you, Algy?

ALGERNON: All women become like their mothers. That is their tragedy. No man does. That's his.

JACK: Is that clever?

ALGERNON: It is perfectly phrased! and quite as true as any observation in civilized life should be.

JACK: I am sick to death of cleverness. Everybody is clever nowadays. You can't go anywhere without meeting clever people. The thing has become an absolute public nuisance. I wish to goodness we had a few fools left.

ALGERNON: We have.

JACK: I should extremely like to meet them. What do they talk about?

ALGERNON: The fools? Oh! about the clever people, of course.

JACK: What fools!

ALGERNON: By the way, did you tell Gwendolen the truth about your being Ernest in town, and Jack in the country?

JACK (*in a very patronizing manner*): My dear fellow, the truth isn't quite the sort of thing one tells to a nice, sweet, refined girl. What extraordinary ideas you have about the way to behave to a woman!

ALGERNON: The only way to behave to a woman is to make love to her, if she is pretty, and to some one else, if she is plain.

JACK: Oh, that is nonsense.

ALGERNON: What about your brother? What about the profligate Ernest?

JACK: Oh, before the end of the week I shall have got rid of him. I'll say he died in Paris of apoplexy. Lots of people die of apoplexy, quite suddenly, don't they?

ALGERNON: Yes, but it's hereditary, my dear fellow. It's a sort of thing that runs in families. You had much better say a severe chill.

JACK: You are sure a severe chill isn't hereditary, or anything of that kind?

ALGERNON: Of course it isn't!

JACK: Very well, then. My poor brother Ernest to carried off suddenly, in Paris, by a severe chill. That gets rid of him.

ALGERNON: But I thought you said that...Miss Cardew was a little too much interested in your poor brother Ernest? Won't she feel his loss a good deal?

JACK: Oh, that is all right. Cecily is not a silly romantic girl, I am glad to say. She has got a capital appetite, goes long walks, and pays no attention at all to her lessons.

ALGERNON: I would rather like to see Cecily.

JACK: I will take very good care you never do. She is excessively pretty, and she is only just eighteen.

ALGERNON: Have you told Gwendolen yet that you have an excessively pretty ward who is only just eighteen?

JACK: Oh! one doesn't blurt these things out to people. Cecily and Gwendolen are perfectly certain to be extremely great friends. I'll bet you anything you like that half an hour after they have met, they will be calling each other sister.

ALGERNON: Women only do that when they have called each other a lot of other things first. Now, my dear boy, if we want to get a good table at Willis's, we really must go and dress. Do you know it is nearly seven?

JACK (irritably): Oh! it always is nearly seven.

ALGERNON: I'm hungry.

JACK: I never knew you when you weren't....

ALGERNON: What shall we do after dinner? Go to a theatre?

JACK: Oh no! I loathe listening.

ALGERNON: Well, let us go to the Club?

JACK: Oh, no! I hate talking.

ALGERNON: Well, we might trot round to the Empire at ten?

JACK: Oh, no! I can't bear looking at things. It is so silly.

ALGERNON: Well, what shall we do?

JACK: Nothing!

ALGERNON: It is awfully hard work doing nothing. However, I don't mind hard work where there is no definite object of any kind.

(Enter LANE.)

LANE: Miss Fairfax.

(Enter GWENDOLEN. LANE goes out.)

ALGERNON: Gwendolen, upon my word!

GWENDOLEN: Algy, kindly turn your back. I have something very particular to say to Mr. Worthing.

ALGERNON: Really, Gwendolen, I don't think I can allow this at all.

GWENDOLEN: Algy, you always adopt a strictly immoral attitude towards life. You are not quite old enough to do that. (ALGERNON retires to the fireplace.)

JACK: My own darling!

GWENDOLEN: Ernest, we may never be married. From the expression on mamma's face I fear we never shall. Few parents nowadays pay any regard to what their children say to them. The old-fashioned respect for the young is fast dying out. Whatever influence I ever had over mamma, I lost at the age of three. But although she may prevent us from becoming man and wife, and I may marry some one else, and marry often, nothing that she can possibly do can alter my eternal devotion to you.

JACK: Dear Gwendolen!

GWENDOLEN: The story of your romantic origin, as related to me by mamma, with unpleasing comments, has naturally stirred the deeper fibres of my nature. Your Christian name has an irresistible fascination. The simplicity of your character makes you exquisitely incomprehensible to me. Your town address at the Albany I have. What is your address in the country?

JACK: The Manor House, Woolton, Hertfordshire. (ALGERNON, who has been carefully listening, smiles to himself, and writes the address on his shirt-cuff. Then picks up the Railway Guide.)

GWENDOLEN: There is a good postal service, I suppose? It may be necessary to do something desperate. That of course will require serious consideration. I will communicate with you daily.

JACK: My own one!

GWENDOLEN: How long do you remain in town?

JACK: Till Monday.

GWENDOLEN: Good! Algy, you may turn round now.

ALGERNON: Thanks, I've turned round already.

GWENDOLEN: You may also ring the bell.

JACK: You will let me see you to your carriage, my own darling?

GWENDOLEN: Certainly.

JACK (*to* LANE, *who now enters*): I will see Miss Fairfax out.

LANE: Yes, sir.

(JACK *and* GWENDOLEN *go off.*)

(LANE *presents several letters on a salver to* ALGERNON. *It is to be surmised that they are bills, as* ALGERNON, *after looking at the envelopes, tears them up.*)

ALGERNON: A glass of sherry, Lane.

LANE: Yes, sir.

ALGERNON: To-morrow, Lane, I'm going Bun-burying.

LANE: Yes, sir.

ALGERNON: I shall probably not be back till Monday. You can put up my dress clothes, my smoking jacket, and all the Bunbury suits…

LANE: Yes, sir. (*Handing sherry.*)

ALGERNON: I hope to-morrow will be a fine day, Lane.

LANE: It never is, sir.

ALGERNON: Lane, you're a perfect pessimist.

LANE: I do my best to give satisfaction, sir.

(*Enter* JACK. LANE *goes off.*)

JACK: There's a sensible, intellectual girl! the only girl I ever cared for in my life. (ALGERNON *is laughing immoderately.*) What on earth are you so amused at?

ALGERNON: Oh, I'm a little anxious about poor Bunbury, that is all.

JACK: If you don't take care, your friend Bunbury will get you into a serious scrape some day.

ALGERNON: I love scrapes. They are the only things that are never serious.

JACK: Oh, that's nonsense, Algy. You never talk anything but nonsense.

ALGERNON: Nobody ever does.

(JACK *looks indignantly at him, and leaves the room.* ALGERNON *lights a cigarette, reads his shirt-cuff, and smiles.*)

ACT DROP

ACT II

Scene—Garden at the Manor House. A flight of grey stone steps leads up to the house. The garden, an old-fashioned one, full of roses. Time of year, July. Basket chairs, and a table covered with books, are set under a large yew-tree.

MISS PRISM *discovered seated at the table.* CECILY *is at the back, watering flowers.*

MISS PRISM (*calling*): Cecily, Cecily! Surely such a utilitarian occupation as the watering of flowers is rather Moulton's duty than yours? Especially at a moment when intellectual pleasures await you. Your German grammar is on the table. Pray open it at page fifteen. We will repeat yesterday's lesson.

CECILY (*coming over very slowly*): But I don't like German. It isn't at all a becoming language. I know perfectly well that I look quite plain after my German lesson.

MISS PRISM: Child, you know how anxious your guardian is that you should improve yourself in every way. He laid particular stress on your German, as he was leaving for town yesterday. Indeed, he always lays stress on your German when he is leaving for town.

CECILY: Dear Uncle Jack is so very serious! Sometimes he is so serious that I think he cannot be quite well.

MISS PRISM (*drawing herself up*): Your guardian enjoys the best of health, and his gravity of demeanour is especially to be commended in one so comparatively young as he is. I know no one who has a higher sense of duty and responsibility.

CECILY: I suppose that is why he often looks a little bored when we three are together.

MISS PRISM: Cecily! I am surprised at you. Mr. Worthing has many troubles in his life. Idle merriment and triviality would be out of place in his conversation. You must remember his constant anxiety about that unfortunate young man his brother.

CECILY: I wish Uncle Jack would allow that unfortunate young man, his brother, to come down here sometimes. We might have a good influence over him, Miss Prism. I am sure you certainly would. You know German, and geology, and things of that kind influence a man very much. (CECILY *begins to write in her diary.*)

MISS PRISM (*shaking her head*): I do not think that even I could produce any effect on a character that according to his own brother's admission is irretrievably weak and vacillating. Indeed I am not sure that I would desire to reclaim him. I am not in favour of this modern mania for turning bad people into good people at a moment's notice. As a man sows so let him reap. You must put away your diary, Cecily. I really don't see why you should keep a diary at all.

CECILY: I keep a diary in order to enter the wonderful secrets of my life. If I didn't write them down, I should probably forget all about them.

MISS PRISM: Memory, my dear Cecily, is the diary that we all carry about with us.

CECILY: Yes, but it usually chronicles the things that have never happened, and couldn't possibly have happened. I believe that Memory is responsible for nearly all the three-volume novels that Mudie sends us.

MISS PRISM: Do not speak slightingly of the three-volume novel, Cecily. I wrote one myself in earlier days.

CECILY: Did you really, Miss Prism? How wonderfully clever you are! I hope it did not end happily? I don't like novels that end happily. They depress me so much.

MISS PRISM: The good ended happily, and the bad unhappily. That is what Fiction means.

CECILY: I suppose so. But it seems very unfair. And was your novel ever published?

MISS PRISM: Alas! no. The manuscript unfortunately was abandoned. (CECILY *starts*.) I use the word in the sense of lost or mislaid. To your work, child, these speculations are profitless.

CECILY (*smiling*): But I see dear Dr. Chasuble coming up through the garden.

MISS PRISM (*rising and advancing*): Dr. Chasuble! This is indeed a pleasure.

(*Enter* CANON CHASUBLE.)

CHASUBLE: And how are we this morning? Miss Prism, you are, I trust, well?

CECILY: Miss Prism has just been complaining of a slight headache. I think it would do her so much good to have a short stroll with you in the Park, Dr. Chasuble.

MISS PRISM: Cecily, I have not mentioned anything about a headache.

CECILY: No, dear Miss Prism, I know that, but I felt instinctively that you had a headache. Indeed I was thinking about that, and not about my German lesson, when the Rector came in.

CHASUBLE: I hope, Cecily, you are not inattentive.

CECILY: Oh, I am afraid I am.

CHASUBLE: That is strange. Were I fortunate enough to be Miss Prism's pupil, I would hang upon her lips. (MISS PRISM *glares*.) I spoke metaphorically.—My metaphor was drawn from bees. Ahem! Mr. Worthing, I suppose, has not returned from town yet?

MISS PRISM: We do not expect him till Monday afternoon.

CHASUBLE: Ah yes, he usually likes to spend his Sunday in London. He is not one of those whose sole aim is enjoyment, as, by all accounts, that unfortunate young man his brother seems to be. But I must not disturb Egeria and her pupil any longer.

MISS PRISM: Egeria? My name is Laetitia, Doctor.

CHASUBLE (*bowing*): A classical allusion merely, drawn from the Pagan authors. I shall see you both no doubt at Evensong?

MISS PRISM: I think, dear Doctor, I will have a stroll with you. I find I have a headache after all, and a walk might do it good.

CHASUBLE: With pleasure, Miss Prism, with pleasure. We might go as far as the schools and back.

MISS PRISM: That would be delightful. Cecily, you will read your Political Economy in my absence. The chapter on the Fall of the Rupee you may omit. It is somewhat too sensational. Even these metallic problems have their melodramatic side.

(*Goes down the garden with* DR. CHASUBLE.)

CECILY (*picks up books and throws them back on table*): Horrid Political Economy! Horrid Geography! Horrid, horrid German!

(*Enter* MERRIMAN *with a card on a salver.*)

MERRIMAN: Mr. Ernest Worthing has just driven over from the station. He has brought his luggage with him.

CECILY (*takes the card and reads it*): "Mr. Ernest Worthing, B.4, The Albany, W." Uncle Jack's brother! Did you tell him Mr. Worthing was in town?

MERRIMAN: Yes, Miss. He seemed very much disappointed. I mentioned that you and Miss Prism were in the garden. He said he was anxious to speak to you privately for a moment.

CECILY: Ask Mr. Ernest Worthing to come here. I suppose you had better talk to the housekeeper about a room for him.

MERRIMAN: Yes, Miss.

(MERRIMAN *goes off.*)

CECILY: I have never met any really wicked person before. I feel rather frightened. I am so afraid he will look just like every one else.

(*Enter* ALGERNON, *very gay and debonair.*)
He does!

ALGERNON (*raising his hat*): You are my little cousin Cecily, I'm sure.

CECILY: You are under some strange mistake. I am not little. In fact, I believe I am more than usually tall for my age. (ALGERNON *is rather taken aback.*) But I am your cousin Cecily. You, I see from your card, are Uncle Jack's brother, my cousin Ernest, my wicked cousin Ernest.

ALGERNON: Oh! I am not really wicked at all, cousin Cecily. You mustn't think that I am wicked.

CECILY: If you are not, then you have certainly been deceiving us all in a very inexcusable manner. I hope you have not been leading a double life, pretending to be wicked and being really good all the time. That would be hypocrisy.

ALGERNON (*looks at her in amazement*): Oh! Of course I have been rather reckless.

CECILY: I am glad to hear it.

ALGERNON: In fact, now you mention the subject, I have been very bad in my own small way.

CECILY: I don't think you should be so proud of that, though I am sure it must have been very pleasant.

ALGERNON: It is much pleasanter being here with you.

CECILY: I can't understand how you are here at all. Uncle Jack won't be back till Monday afternoon.

ALGERNON: That is a great disappointment. I am obliged to go up by the first train on Monday morning. I have a business appointment that I am anxious…to miss?

CECILY: Couldn't you miss it anywhere but in London?

ALGERNON: No: the appointment is in London.

CECILY: Well, I know, of course, how important it is not to keep a business engagement, if one wants to retain any sense of the beauty of life, but still I think you had better wait till Uncle Jack arrives. I know he wants to speak to you about your emigrating.

ALGERNON: About my what?

CECILY: Your emigrating. He has gone up to buy your outfit.

ALGERNON: I certainly wouldn't let Jack buy my outfit. He has no taste in neckties at all.

CECILY: I don't think you will require neckties. Uncle Jack is sending you to Australia.

ALGERNON: Australia! I'd sooner die.

CECILY: Well, he said at dinner on Wednesday night, that you would have to choose between this world, the next world, and Australia.

ALGERNON: Oh, well! The accounts I have received of Australia and the next world, are not particularly encouraging. This world is good enough for me, cousin Cecily.

CECILY: Yes, but are you good enough for it?

ALGERNON: I'm afraid I'm not that. That is why I want you to reform me. You might make that your mission, if you don't mind, Cousin Cecily.

CECILY: I'm afraid I've no time, this afternoon.

ALGERNON: Well, would you mind my reforming myself this afternoon?

CECILY: It is rather Quixotic of you. But I think you should try.

ALGERNON: I will. I feel better already.

CECILY: You are looking a little worse.

ALGERNON: That is because I am hungry.

CECILY: How thoughtless of me. I should have remembered that when one is going to lead an entirely new life, one requires regular and wholesome meals. Won't you come in?

ALGERNON: Thank you. Might I have a button-hole first? I never have any appetite unless I have a buttonhole first.

CECILY: A Maréchal Niel? (*Picks up scissors.*)

ALGERNON: No, I'd sooner have a pink rose.

CECILY: Why? (*Cuts a flower.*)

ALGERNON: Because you are like a pink rose, Cousin Cecily.

CECILY: I don't think it can be right for you to talk to me like that. Miss Prism never says such things to me.

ALGERNON: Then Miss Prism is a short-sighted old lady. (CECILY *puts the rose in his button-hole.*) You are the prettiest girl I ever saw.

CECILY: Miss Prism says that all good looks are a snare.

ALGERNON: They are a snare that every sensible man would like to be caught in.

CECILY: Oh, I don't think I would care to catch a sensible man. I shouldn't know what to talk to him about.

(*They pass into the house.* MISS PRISM *and* DR. CHA-SUBLE *return.*)

MISS PRISM: You are too much alone, dear Dr. Chasuble. You should get married. A misan-thrope I can understand—a womanthrope, never!

CHASUBLE (*with a scholar's shudder*): Believe me, I do not deserve so neologistic a phrase. The precept as well as the practice of the Primitive Church was distinctly against matrimony.

MISS PRISM (*sententiously*): That is obviously the reason why the Primitive Church has not lasted up to the present day. And you do not seem to realize, dear Doctor, that by persis-tently remaining single, a man converts himself into a permanent public tempta-tion. Men should be more careful; this very celibacy leads weaker vessels astray.

CHASUBLE: But is a man not equally attractive when married?

MISS PRISM: No married man is ever attractive except to his wife.

CHASUBLE: And often, I've been told, not even to her.

MISS PRISM: That depends on the intellectual sympathies of the woman. Maturity can al-ways be depended on. Ripeness can be trusted. Young women are green. (DR. CHA-SUBLE *starts.*) I spoke horticulturally. My metaphor was drawn from fruits. But where is Cecily?

CHASUBLE: Perhaps she followed us to the schools.

(*Enter* JACK *slowly from the back of the garden. He is dressed in the deepest mourning, with crepe hatband and black gloves.*)

MISS PRISM: Mr. Worthing!

CHASUBLE: Mr. Worthing?

MISS PRISM: This is indeed a surprise. We did not look for you till Monday afternoon.

JACK (*shakes* MISS PRISM's *hand in a tragic manner*): I have returned sooner than I expected. Dr. Chasuble, I hope you are well?

CHASUBLE: Dear Mr. Worthing, I trust this garb of woe does not betoken some terrible ca-lamity?

JACK: My brother.

MISS PRISM: More shameful debts and extrava-gance?

CHASUBLE: Still leading his life of pleasure?

JACK (*shaking his head*): Dead!

CHASUBLE: Your brother Ernest dead?

JACK: Quite dead.

MISS PRISM: What a lesson for him! I trust he will profit by it.

CHASUBLE: Mr. Worthing, I offer you my sincere condolence. You have at least the consola-tion of knowing that you were always the most generous and forgiving of brothers.

JACK: Poor Ernest! He had many faults, but it is a sad, sad blow.

CHASUBLE: Very sad indeed. Were you with him at the end?

JACK: No. He died abroad; in Paris, in fact. I had a telegram last night from the manager of the Grand Hotel.

CHASUBLE: Was the cause of death mentioned?

JACK: A severe chill, it seems.

MISS PRISM: As a man sows, so shall he reap.

CHASUBLE (*raising his hand*): Charity, dear Miss Prism, charity! None of us are perfect. I my-self am peculiarly susceptible to draughts. Will the interment take place here?

JACK: No. He seems to have expressed a desire to be buried in Paris.

CHASUBLE: In Paris! (*Shakes his head.*) I fear that hardly points to any very serious state of mind at the last. You would no doubt wish me to make some slight allusion to this tragic domestic affliction next Sunday. (JACK *presses his hand convulsively.*) My sermon on the meaning of the manna in the wilderness can be adapted to almost any occasion, joyful, or, as in the present case, distressing. (*All sigh.*) I have preached it at harvest celebrations, christenings, confirmations, on days of humiliation and festal days. The last time I delivered it was in the Cathedral, as a charity sermon on behalf of the Society for the Prevention of Discontent among the Upper Orders. The Bishop, who was present, was much struck by some of the analogies I drew.

JACK: Ah! that reminds me, you mentioned christenings I think, Dr. Chasuble? I suppose you know how to christen all right? (DR. CHASUBLE *looks astounded.*) I mean, of course, you are continually christening, aren't you?

MISS PRISM: It is, I regret to say, one of the Rector's most constant duties in this parish. I have often spoken to the poorer classes on the subject. But they don't seem to know what thrift is.

CHASUBLE: But is there any particular infant in whom you are interested, Mr. Worthing? Your brother was, I believe, unmarried, was he not?

JACK: Oh yes.

MISS PRISM (*bitterly*): People who live entirely for pleasure usually are.

JACK: But it is not for any child, dear Doctor. I am very fond of children. No! the fact is, I would like to be christened myself, this afternoon, if you have nothing better to do.

CHASUBLE: But surely, Mr. Worthing, you have been christened already?

JACK: I don't remember anything about it.

CHASUBLE: But have you any grave doubts on the subject?

JACK: I certainly intend to have. Of course I don't know if the thing would bother you in any way, or if you think I am a little too old now.

CHASUBLE: Not at all. The sprinkling, and, indeed, the immersion of adults is a perfectly canonical practice.

JACK: Immersion!

CHASUBLE: You need have no apprehensions. Sprinkling is all that is necessary, or indeed I think advisable. Our weather is so changeable. At what hour would you wish the ceremony performed?

JACK: Oh, I might trot round about five if that would suit you.

CHASUBLE: Perfectly, perfectly! In fact I have two similar ceremonies to perform at that time. A case of twins that occurred recently in one of the outlying cottages on your own estate. Poor Jenkins the carter, a most hard-working man.

JACK: Oh! I don't see much fun in being christened along with other babies. It would be childish. Would half-past five do?

CHASUBLE: Admirably! Admirably! (*Takes out watch.*) And now, dear Mr. Worthing, I will not intrude any longer into a house of sorrow. I would merely beg you not to be too much bowed down by grief. What seem to us bitter trials are often blessings in disguise.

MISS PRISM: This seems to me a blessing of an extremely obvious kind.

(*Enter* CECILY *from the house.*)

CECILY: Uncle Jack! Oh, I am pleased to see you back. But what horrid clothes you have got on! Do go and change them.

MISS PRISM: Cecily!

CHASUBLE: My child! my child! (CECILY *goes towards* JACK; *he kisses her brow in a melancholy manner.*)

CECILY: What is the matter, Uncle Jack? Do look happy! You look as if you had a toothache, and I have got such a surprise for you. Who do you think is in the dining-room? Your brother!

JACK: Who?

CECILY: Your brother Ernest. He arrived about half an hour ago.

JACK: What nonsense! I haven't got a brother.

CECILY: Oh, don't say that. However badly he may have behaved to you in the past he is still your brother. You couldn't be so heartless as to disown him. I'll tell him to come out. And you will shake hands with him, won't you, Uncle Jack? (*Runs back into the house.*)

CHASUBLE: These are very joyful tidings.

MISS PRISM: After we had all been resigned to his loss, his sudden return seems to me peculiarly distressing.

JACK: My brother is in the dining-room? I don't know what it all means. I think it is perfectly absurd.

(*Enter* ALGERNON *and* CECILY *hand in hand. They come slowly up to* JACK.)

JACK: Good heavens! (*Motions* ALGERNON *away.*)

ALGERNON: Brother John, I have come down from town to tell you that I am very sorry for all the trouble I have given you, and I intend to lead a better life in the future. (JACK *glares at him and does not take his hand.*)

CECILY: Uncle Jack, you are not going to refuse your own brother's hand?

JACK: Nothing will induce me to take his hand. I think his coming down here disgraceful. He knows perfectly well why.

CECILY: Uncle Jack, do be nice. There is some good in every one. Ernest has just been telling me about his poor invalid friend Mr. Bunbury whom he goes to visit so often. And surely there must be much good in one who is kind to an invalid, and leaves the pleasures of London to sit by a bed of pain.

JACK: Oh! he has been talking about Bunbury, has he?

CECILY: Yes, he has told me all about poor Mr. Bunbury, and his terrible state of health.

JACK: Bunbury! Well, I won't have him talk to you about Bunbury or about anything else. It is enough to drive one perfectly frantic.

ALGERNON: Of course I admit that the faults were all on my side. But I must say that I think that Brother John's coldness to me is peculiarly painful. I expected a more enthusiastic welcome, especially considering it is the first time I have come here.

CECILY: Uncle Jack, if you don't shake hands with Ernest I will never forgive you.

JACK: Never forgive me?

CECILY: Never, never, never!

JACK: Well, this is the last time I shall ever do it. (*Shakes with* ALGERNON *and glares.*)

CHASUBLE: It's pleasant, is it not, to see so perfect a reconciliation? I think we might leave the two brothers together.

MISS PRISM: Cecily, you will come with us.

CECILY: Certainly, Miss Prism. My little task of reconciliation is over.

CHASUBLE: You have done a beautiful action today, dear child.

MISS PRISM: We must not be premature in our judgments.

CECILY: I feel very happy.

(*They all go off except* JACK *and* ALGERNON.)

JACK: You young scoundrel, Algy, you must get out of this place as soon as possible. I don't allow any Bunburying here.

(*Enter* MERRIMAN.)

MERRIMAN: I have put Mr. Ernest's things in the room next to yours, sir. I suppose that is all right?

JACK: What?

MERRIMAN: Mr. Ernest's luggage, sir. I have unpacked it and put it in the room next to your own.

JACK: His luggage?

MERRIMAN: Yes, sir. Three portmanteaus, a dressing-case, two hatboxes, and a large luncheon-basket.

ALGERNON: I am afraid I can't stay more than a week this time.

JACK: Merriman, order the dog-cart at once. Mr. Ernest has been suddenly called back to town.

MERRIMAN: Yes, sir. (*Goes back into the house.*)

ALGERNON: What a fearful liar you are, Jack. I have not been called back to town at all.

JACK: Yes, you have.

ALGERNON: I haven't heard any one call me.

JACK: Your duty as a gentleman calls you back.

ALGERNON: My duty as a gentleman has never interfered with my pleasures in the smallest degree.

JACK: I can quite understand that.

ALGERNON: Well, Cecily is a darling.

JACK: You are not to talk of Miss Cardew like that. I don't like it.

ALGERNON: Well, I don't like your clothes. You look perfectly ridiculous in them. Why on earth don't you go up and change? It is perfectly childish to be in deep mourning for a man who is actually staying for a whole week with you in your house as a guest. I call it grotesque.

JACK: You are certainly not staying with me for a whole week as a guest or anything else. You have got to leave…by the four-five train.

ALGERNON: I certainly won't leave you so long as you are in mourning. It would be most unfriendly. If I were in mourning you would stay with me, I suppose. I should think it very unkind if you didn't.

JACK: Well, will you go if I change my clothes?

ALGERNON: Yes, if you are not too long. I never saw anybody take so long to dress, and with such little result.

JACK: Well, at any rate, that is better than being always over-dressed as you are.

ALGERNON: If I am occasionally a little over-dressed, I make up for it by being always immensely over-educated.

JACK: Your vanity is ridiculous, your conduct an outrage, and your presence in my garden utterly absurd. However, you have got to catch the four-five, and I hope you will have a pleasant journey back to town. This Bunburying, as you call it, has not been a great success for you.

(*Goes into the house.*)

ALGERNON: I think it has been a great success. I'm in love with Cecily, and that is everything. (*Enter* CECILY *at the back of the garden. She picks up the can and begins to water the flowers.*) But I must see her before I go, and make arrangements for another Bunbury. Ah, there she is.

CECILY: Oh, I merely came back to water the roses. I thought you were with Uncle Jack.

ALGERNON: He's gone to order the dog-cart for me.

CECILY: Oh, is he going to take you for a nice drive?

ALGERNON: He's going to send me away.

CECILY: Then have we got to part?

ALGERNON: I am afraid so. It's very painful parting.

CECILY: It is always painful to part from people whom one has known for a very brief space of time. The absence of old friends one can endure with equanimity. But even a momentary separation from any one to whom one has just been introduced is almost unbearable.

ALGERNON: Thank you.

(*Enter* MERRIMAN.)

MERRIMAN: The dog-cart is at the door, sir.

(ALGERNON *looks appealingly at* CECILY.)

CECILY: It can wait, Merriman…for…five minutes.

MERRIMAN: Yes, Miss.

(*Exit* MERRIMAN.)

ALGERNON: I hope, Cecily, I shall not offend you if I state quite frankly and openly that you seem to me to be in every way the visible personification of absolute perfection.

CECILY: I think your frankness does you great credit, Ernest. If you will allow me, I will copy your remarks into my diary. (*Goes over to table and begins writing in diary.*)

ALGERNON: Do you really keep a diary? I'd give anything to look at it. May I?

CECILY: Oh no. (*Puts her hand over it.*) You see, it is simply a very young girl's record of her own thoughts and impressions, and consequently meant for publication. When it appears in volume form I hope you will order a copy. But pray, Ernest, don't stop. I delight in taking down from dictation. I have reached "absolute perfection." You can go on. I am quite ready for more.

ALGERNON (*somewhat taken aback*): Ahem! Ahem!

CECILY: Oh, don't cough, Ernest. When one is dictating one should speak fluently and not cough. Besides, I don't know how to spell a cough. (*Writes as* ALGERNON *speaks.*)

ALGERNON (*speaking very rapidly*): Cecily, ever since I first looked upon your wonderful and incomparable beauty, I have dared to love you wildly, passionately, devotedly, hopelessly.

CECILY: I don't think that you should tell me that you love me wildly, passionately, devotedly, hopelessly. Hopelessly doesn't seem to make much sense, does it?

ALGERNON: Cecily!

(*Enter* MERRIMAN.)

MERRIMAN: The dog-cart is waiting, sir.

ALGERNON: Tell it to come round next week, at the same hour.

MERRIMAN (*looks at* CECILY, *who makes no sign*): Yes, sir.

(MERRIMAN *retires*.)

CECILY: Uncle Jack would be very much annoyed if he knew you were staying on till next week, at the same hour.

ALGERNON: Oh, I don't care about Jack. I don't care for anybody in the whole world but you. I love you, Cecily. You will marry me, won't you?

CECILY: You silly boy! Of course. Why, we have been engaged for the last three months.

ALGERNON: For the last three months?

CECILY: Yes, it will be exactly three months on Thursday.

ALGERNON: But how did we become engaged?

CECILY: Well, ever since dear Uncle Jack first confessed to us that he had a younger brother who was very wicked and bad, you of course have formed the chief topic of conversation between myself and Miss Prism. And of course a man who is much talked about is always very attractive. One feels there must be something in him, after all. I daresay it was foolish of me, but I fell in love with you, Ernest.

ALGERNON: Darling! And when was the engagement actually settled?

CECILY: On the 14th of February last. Worn out by your entire ignorance of my existence, I determined to end the matter one way or the other, and after a long struggle with myself I accepted you under this dear old tree here. The next day I bought this little ring in your name, and this is the little bangle with the true lover's knot I promised you always to wear.

ALGERNON: Did I give you this? It's very pretty, isn't it?

CECILY: Yes, you've wonderfully good taste, Ernest. It's the excuse I've always given for your leading such a bad life. And this is the box in which I keep all your dear letters. (*Kneels at table, opens box, and produces letters tied up with blue ribbon*.)

ALGERNON: My letters! But, my own sweet Cecily, I have never written you any letters.

CECILY: You need hardly remind me of that, Ernest. I remember only too well that I was forced to write your letters for you. I wrote always three times a week, and sometimes oftener.

ALGERNON: Oh, do let me read them, Cecily?

CECILY: Oh, I couldn't possibly. They would make you far too conceited. (*Replaces box*.) The three you wrote me after I had broken off the engagement are so beautiful, and so badly spelled, that even now I can hardly read them without crying a little.

ALGERNON: But was our engagement ever broken off?

CECILY: Of course it was. On the 22nd of last March. You can see the entry if you like. (*Shows diary*.) "To-day I broke off my engagement with Ernest. I feel it is better to do so. The weather still continues charming."

ALGERNON: But why on earth did you break it off? What had I done? I had done nothing at all. Cecily, I am very much hurt indeed to hear you broke it off. Particularly when the weather was so charming.

CECILY: It would hardly have been a really serious engagement if it hadn't been broken off at least once. But I forgave you before the week was out.

ALGERNON (*crossing to her, and kneeling*): What a perfect angel you are, Cecily.

CECILY: You dear romantic boy. (*He kisses her, she puts her fingers through his hair*.) I hope your hair curls naturally, does it?

ALGERNON: Yes, darling, with a little help from others.

CECILY: I am so glad.

ALGERNON: You'll never break off our engagement again, Cecily?

CECILY: I don't think I could break it off now that I have actually met you. Besides, of course, there is the question of your name.

ALGERNON: Yes, of course. (*Nervously*.)

CECILY: You must not laugh at me, darling, but it had always been a girlish dream of mine to love some one whose name was Ernest.

(ALGERNON *rises*, CECILY *also.*) There is something in that name that seems to inspire absolute confidence. I pity any poor married woman whose husband is not called Ernest.

ALGERNON: But, my dear child, do you mean to say you could not love me if I had some other name?

CECILY: But what name?

ALGERNON: Oh, any name you like—Algernon—for instance…

CECILY: But I don't like the name of Algernon.

ALGERNON: Well, my own dear, sweet, loving little darling, I really can't see why you should object to the name of Algernon. It is not at all a bad name. In fact, it is rather an aristocratic name. Half of the chaps who get into the Bankruptcy Court are called Algernon. But seriously, Cecily…(*moving to her*) if my name was Algy, couldn't you love me?

CECILY (*rising*): I might respect you, Ernest, I might admire your character, but I fear that I should not be able to give you my undivided attention.

ALGERNON: Ahem! Cecily! (*Picking up hat.*) Your Rector here is, I suppose, thoroughly experienced in the practice of all the rites and ceremonials of the Church?

CECILY: Oh, yes. Dr. Chasuble is a most learned man. He has never written a single book, so you can imagine how much he knows.

ALGERNON: I must see him at once on a most important christening—I mean on most important business.

CECILY: Oh!

ALGERNON: I shan't be away more than half an hour.

CECILY: Considering that we have been engaged since February the 14th, and that I only met you to-day for the first time, I think it is rather hard that you should leave me for so long a period as half an hour. Couldn't you make it twenty minutes?

ALGERNON: I'll be back in no time. (*Kisses her and rushes down the garden.*)

CECILY: What an impetuous boy he is! I like his hair so much I must enter his proposal in my diary.

(*Enter* MERRIMAN.)

MERRIMAN: A Miss Fairfax has just called to see Mr. Worthing. On very important business, Miss Fairfax states.

CECILY: Isn't Mr. Worthing in his library?

MERRIMAN: Mr. Worthing went over in the direction of the Rectory some time ago.

CECILY: Pray ask the lady to come out here; Mr. Worthing is sure to be back soon. And you can bring tea.

MERRIMAN: Yes, Miss.

(*Goes out.*)

CECILY: Miss Fairfax! I suppose one of the many good elderly women who are associated with Uncle Jack in some of his philanthropic work in London. I don't quite like women who are interested in philanthropic work. I think it is so forward of them.

(*Enter* MERRIMAN.)

MERRIMAN: Miss Fairfax.

(*Enter* GWENDOLEN. *Exit* MERRIMAN.)

CECILY (*advancing to meet her*): Pray let me introduce myself to you. My name is Cecily Cardew.

GWENDOLEN: Cecily Cardew? (*Moving to her and shaking hands.*) What a very sweet name! Something tells me that we are going to be great friends. I like you already more than I can say. My first impressions of people are never wrong.

CECILY: How nice of you to like me so much after we have known each other such a comparatively short time. Pray sit down.

GWENDOLEN (*still standing up*): I may call you Cecily, may I not?

CECILY: With pleasure!

GWENDOLEN: And you will always call me Gwendolen, won't you?

CECILY: If you wish.

GWENDOLEN: Then that is all quite settled, is it not?

CECILY: I hope so. (*A pause. They both sit down together.*)

GWENDOLEN: Perhaps this might be a favourable opportunity for my mentioning who I am. My father is Lord Bracknell. You have never heard of papa, I suppose?

CECILY: I don't think so.

GWENDOLEN: Outside the family circle, papa, I am glad to say, is entirely unknown. I think that is quite as it should be. The home seems to me to be the proper sphere for the man. And certainly once a man begins to neglect his domestic duties he becomes painfully effeminate, does he not? And I don't like that. It makes men so very attractive. Cecily, mamma, whose views on education are remarkably strict, has brought me up to be extremely shortsighted; it is part of her system; so do you mind my looking at you through my glasses?

CECILY: Oh! not at all, Gwendolen. I am very fond of being looked at.

GWENDOLEN (*after examining* CECILY *carefully through a lorgnette*): You are here on a short visit, I suppose.

CECILY: Oh no! I live here.

GWENDOLEN (*severely*): Really? Your mother, no doubt, or some female relative of advanced years, resides here also?

CECILY: Oh no! I have no mother, nor, in fact, any relations.

GWENDOLEN: Indeed?

CECILY: My dear guardian, with the assistance of Miss Prism, has the arduous task of looking after me.

GWENDOLEN: Your guardian?

CECILY: Yes, I am Mr. Worthing's ward.

GWENDOLEN: Oh! It is strange he never mentioned to me that he had a ward. How secretive of him! He grows more interesting hourly. I am not sure, however, that the news inspires me with feelings of unmixed delight. (*Rising and going to her.*) I am very fond of you, Cecily; I have liked you ever since I met you! But I am bound to state that now that I know that you are Mr. Worthing's ward, I cannot help expressing a wish you were—well, just a little older than you seem to be—and not quite so very alluring in appearance. In fact, if I may speak candidly—

CECILY: Pray do! I think that whenever one has anything unpleasant to say, one should always be quite candid.

GWENDOLEN: Well, to speak with perfect candour, Cecily, I wish that you were fully forty-two, and more than usually plain for your age. Ernest has a strong upright nature. He is the very soul of truth and honor. Disloyalty would be as impossible to him as deception. But even men of the noblest possible moral character are extremely susceptible to the influence of the physical charms of others. Modern, no less than Ancient History, supplies us with many most painful examples of what I refer to. If it were not so, indeed, History would be quite unreadable.

CECILY: I beg your pardon, Gwendolen, did you say Ernest?

GWENDOLEN: Yes.

CECILY: Oh, but it is not Mr. Ernest Worthing who is my guardian. It is his brother—his elder brother.

GWENDOLEN (*sitting down again*): Ernest never mentioned to me that he had a brother.

CECILY: I am sorry to say they have not been on good terms for a long time.

GWENDOLEN: Ah! that accounts for it. And now that I think of it I have never heard any man mention his brother. The subject seems distasteful to most men. Cecily, you have lifted a load from my mind. I was growing almost anxious. It would have been terrible if any cloud had come across a friendship like ours, would it not? Of course you are quite, quite sure that it is not Mr. Ernest Worthing who is your guardian?

CECILY: Quite sure. (*A pause.*) In fact, I am going to be his.

GWENDOLEN (*inquiringly*): I beg your pardon?

CECILY (*rather shy and confidingly*): Dearest Gwendolen, there is no reason why I should make a secret of it to you. Our little country newspaper is sure to chronicle the fact next week. Mr. Ernest Worthing and I are engaged to be married.

GWENDOLEN (*quite politely, rising*): My darling Cecily, I think there must be some slight error. Mr. Ernest Worthing is engaged to me. The announcement will appear in the *Morning Post* on Saturday at the latest.

CECILY (*very politely, rising*): I am afraid you must be under some misconception. Ernest proposed to me exactly ten minutes ago. (*Shows diary.*)

GWENDOLEN (*examines diary through her lorgnettte carefully*): It is very curious, for he asked me to be his wife yesterday afternoon at 5:30. If you would care to verify the incident, pray do so. (*Produces diary of her own.*) I never travel without my diary. One should always have something sensational to read in the train. I am so sorry, dear Cecily, if it is any disappointment to you, but I am afraid I have the prior claim.

CECILY: It would distress me more than I can tell you, dear Gwendolen, if it caused you any mental or physical anguish, but I feel bound to point out that since Ernest proposed to you he clearly has changed his mind.

GWENDOLEN (*meditatively*): If the poor fellow has been entrapped into any foolish promise I shall consider it my duty to rescue him at once, and with a firm hand.

CECILY (*thoughtfully and sadly*): Whatever unfortunate entanglement my dear boy may have got into, I will never reproach him with it after we are married.

GWENDOLEN: Do you allude to me, Miss Cardew, as an entanglement? You are presumptuous. On an occasion of this kind it becomes more than a moral duty to speak one's mind. It becomes a pleasure.

CECILY: Do you suggest, Miss Fairfax, that I entrapped Ernest into an engagement? How dare you? This is no time for wearing the shallow mask of manners. When I see a spade I call it a spade.

GWENDOLEN (*satirically*): I am glad to say that I have never seen a spade. It is obvious that our social spheres have been widely different.

(*Enter* MERRIMAN, *followed by the footman. He carries a salver, table cloth, and plate stand.* CECILY *is about to retort. The presence of the servants exercises a restraining influence, under which both girls chafe.*)

MERRIMAN: Shall I lay tea here as usual, Miss?

CECILY (*sternly, in a calm voice*): Yes, as usual.

(MERRIMAN *begins to clear table and lay cloth. A long pause.* CECILY *and* GWENDOLEN *glare at each other.*)

GWENDOLEN: Are there many interesting walks in the vicinity, Miss Cardew?

CECILY: Oh! yes! a great many. From the top of one of the hills quite close one can see five counties.

GWENDOLEN: Five counties! I don't think I should like that; I hate crowds.

CECILY (*sweetly*): I suppose that is why you live in town? (GWENDOLEN *bites her lip, and beats her foot nervously with her parasol.*)

GWENDOLEN (*looking round*): Quite a well-kept garden this is, Miss Cardew.

CECILY: So glad you like it, Miss Fairfax.

GWENDOLEN: I had no idea there were any flowers in the country.

CECILY: Oh, flowers are as common here, Miss Fairfax, as people are in London.

GWENDOLEN: Personally I cannot understand how anybody manages to exist in the country, if anybody who is anybody does. The country always bores me to death.

CECILY: Ah! This is what the newspapers call agricultural depression, is it not? I believe the aristocracy are suffering very much from it just at present. It is almost an epidemic amongst them, I have been told. May I offer you some tea, Miss Fairfax?

GWENDOLEN (*with elaborate politeness*): Thank you. (*Aside.*) Detestable girl! But I require tea!

CECILY (*sweetly*): Sugar?

GWENDOLEN (*superciliously*): No, thank you. Sugar is not fashionable any more. (CECILY *looks angrily at her, takes up the tongs and puts four lumps of sugar into the cup.*)

CECILY (*severely*): Cake or bread and butter?

GWENDOLEN (*in a bored manner*): Bread and butter, please. Cake is rarely seen at the best houses nowadays.

CECILY (*cuts a very large slice of cake, and puts it on the tray*): Hand that to Miss Fairfax.

(MERRIMAN *does so, and goes out with footman.*

GWENDOLEN *drinks the tea and makes a grimace. Puts down cup at once, reaches out her hand to the bread and butter, looks at it, and finds it is cake. Rises in indignation.*)

GWENDOLEN: You have filled my tea with lumps of sugar, and though I asked most distinctly for bread and butter, you have given me cake. I am known for the gentleness of my disposition, and the extraordinary sweetness of my nature, but I warn you, Miss Cardew, you may go too far.

CECILY (*rising*): To save my poor, innocent, trusting boy from the machinations of any other girl there are no lengths to which I would not go.

GWENDOLEN: From the moment I saw you I distrusted you. I felt that you were false and deceitful. I am never deceived in such matters. My first impressions of people are invariably right.

CECILY: It seems to me, Miss Fairfax, that I am trespassing on your valuable time. No doubt you have many other calls of a similar character to make in the neighbourhood.

(*Enter* JACK.)

GWENDOLEN (*catching sight of him*): Ernest! My own Ernest!

JACK: Gwendolen! Darling! (*Offers to kiss her.*)

GWENDOLEN (*drawing back*): A moment! May I ask if you are engaged to be married to this young lady? (*Points to* CECILY.)

JACK (*laughing*): To dear little Cecily! Of course not! What could have put such an idea into your pretty little head?

GWENDOLEN: Thank you. You may! (*Offers her cheek.*)

CECILY (*very sweetly*): I knew there must be some misunderstanding, Miss Fairfax. The gentleman whose arm is at present round your waist is my guardian, Mr. John Worthing.

GWENDOLEN: I beg your pardon?

CECILY: This is Uncle Jack.

GWENDOLEN (*receding*): Jack! Oh!

(*Enter* ALGERNON.)

CECILY: Here is Ernest.

ALGERNON (*goes straight over to* CECILY *without noticing any one else*): My own love! (*Offers to kiss her.*)

CECILY (*drawing back*): A moment, Ernest! May I ask you—are you engaged to be married to this young lady?

ALGERNON (*looking round*): To what young lady? Good heavens! Gwendolen!

CECILY: Yes: to good heavens, Gwendolen, I mean to Gwendolen.

ALGERNON (*laughing*): Of course not! What could have put such an idea into your pretty little head?

CECILY: Thank you. (*Presenting her cheek to be kissed.*) You may. (ALGERNON *kisses her.*)

GWENDOLEN: I felt there was some slight error, Miss Cardew. The gentleman who is now embracing you is my cousin, Mr. Algernon Moncrieff.

CECILY (*breaking away from Algernon*): Algernon Moncrieff! Oh!

(*The two girls move towards each other and put their arms round each other's waists as if for protection.*)

CECILY: Are you called Algernon?

ALGERNON: I cannot deny it.

CECILY: Oh!

GWENDOLEN: Is your name really John?

JACK (*standing rather proudly*): I could deny it if I liked. I could deny anything if I liked. But my name certainly is John. It has been John for years.

CECILY (*to* GWENDOLEN): A gross deception has been practised on both of us.

GWENDOLEN: My poor wounded Cecily!

CECILY: My sweet wronged Gwendolen!

GWENDOLEN (*slowly and seriously*): You will call me sister, will you not? (*They embrace.* JACK *and* ALGERNON *groan and walk up and down.*)

CECILY (*rather brightly*): There is just one question I would like to be allowed to ask my guardian.

GWENDOLEN: An admirable idea! Mr. Worthing, there is just one question I would like to be permitted to put to you. Where is your brother Ernest? We are both engaged to be married to your brother Ernest, so it is a matter of some importance to us to know where your brother Ernest is at present.

JACK (*slowly and hesitatingly*): Gwendolen—Cecily—it is very painful for me to be forced to speak the truth. It is the first time in my life that I have ever been reduced to such a painful position, and I am really quite inexperienced in doing anything of the kind. However, I will tell you quite frankly that I have no brother Ernest. I have no brother at all. I never had a brother in my life, and I certainly have not the smallest intention of ever having one in the future.

CECILY (*surprised*): No brother at all?

JACK (*cheerily*): None!

GWENDOLEN (*severely*): Had you never a brother of any kind?

JACK (*pleasantly*): Never. Not even of any kind.

GWENDOLEN: I am afraid it is quite clear, Cecily, that neither of us is engaged to be married to anyone.

CECILY: It is not a very pleasant position for a young girl suddenly to find herself in. Is it?

GWENDOLEN: Let us go into the house. They will hardly venture to come after us there.

CECILY: No, men are so cowardly, aren't they?

(*They retire into the house with scornful looks.*)

JACK: This ghastly state of things is what you call Bunburying, I suppose?

ALGERNON: Yes, and a perfectly wonderful Bunbury it is. The most wonderful Bunbury I have ever had in my life.

JACK: Well, you've no right whatsoever to Bunbury here.

ALGERNON: That is absurd. One has a right to Bunbury anywhere one chooses. Every serious Bunburyist knows that.

JACK: Serious Bunburyist! Good heavens!

ALGERNON: Well, one must be serious about something, if one wants to have any amusement in life. I happen to be serious about Bunburying. What on earth you are serious about I haven't got the remotest idea. About everything, I should fancy. You have such an absolutely trivial nature.

JACK: Well, the only small satisfaction I have in the whole of this wretched business is that your friend Bunbury is quite exploded. You won't be able to run down to the country quite so often as you used to do, dear Algy. And a very good thing too.

ALGERNON: Your brother is a little off colour, isn't he, dear Jack? You won't be able to disappear to London quite so frequently as your wicked custom was. And not a bad thing, either.

JACK: As for your conduct towards Miss Cardew, I must say that your taking in a sweet, simple, innocent girl like that is quite inexcusable. To say nothing of the fact that she is my ward.

ALGERNON: I can see no possible defence at all for your deceiving a brilliant, clever, thoroughly experienced young lady like Miss Fairfax. To say nothing of the fact that she is my cousin.

JACK: I wanted to be engaged to Gwendolen, that is all. I love her.

ALGERNON: Well, I simply wanted to be engaged to Cecily. I adore her.

JACK: There is certainly no chance of your marrying Miss Cardew.

ALGERNON: I don't think there is much likelihood, Jack, of you and Miss Fairfax being united.

JACK: Well, that is no business of yours.

ALGERNON: If it was my business, I wouldn't talk about it. (*Begins to eat muffins.*) It is very vulgar to talk about one's business. Only people like stockbrokers do that, and then merely at dinner parties.

JACK: How can you sit there, calmly eating muffins when we are in this horrible trouble, I can't make out. You seem to me to be perfectly heartless.

ALGERNON: Well, I can't eat muffins in an agitated manner. The butter would probably get on my cuffs. One should always eat muffins quite calmly. It is the only way to eat them.

JACK: I say it's perfectly heartless your eating muffins at all, under the circumstances.

ALGERNON: When I am in trouble, eating is the only thing that consoles me. Indeed, when I am in really great trouble, as any one who knows me intimately will tell you, I refuse everything except food and drink. At the present moment I am eating muffins because I am unhappy. Besides, I am particularly fond of muffins. (*Rising.*)

JACK (*rising*): Well, there is no reason why you should eat them all in that greedy way. (*Takes muffins from Algernon.*)

ALGERNON (*offering tea-cake*): I wish you would have tea-cake instead. I don't like tea-cake.

JACK: Good heavens! I suppose a man may eat his own muffins in his own garden.

ALGERNON: But you have just said it was perfectly heartless to eat muffins.

JACK: I said it was perfectly heartless of you, under the circumstances. That is a very different thing.

ALGERNON: That may be. But the muffins are the same. (*He seizes the muffin-dish from* JACK.)

JACK: Algy, I wish to goodness you would go.

ALGERNON: You can't possibly ask me to go without having some dinner. It's absurd. I never go without my dinner. No one ever does, except vegetarians and people like that. Besides I have just made arrangements with Dr. Chasuble to be christened at a quarter to six under the name of Ernest.

JACK: My dear fellow, the sooner you give up that nonsense the better. I made arrangements this morning with Dr. Chasuble to be christened myself at 5:30, and I naturally will take the name of Ernest. Gwendolen would wish it. We can't both be christened Ernest. It's absurd. Besides, I have a perfect right to be christened if I like. There is no evidence at all that I have ever been christened by anybody. I should think it extremely probable I never was, and so does Dr. Chasuble. It is entirely different in your case. You have been christened already.

ALGERNON: Yes, but I have not been christened for years.

JACK: Yes, but you have been christened. That is the important thing.

ALGERNON: Quite so. So I know my constitution can stand it. If you are not quite sure about your ever having been christened, I must say I think it rather dangerous your venturing on it now. It might make you very unwell. You can hardly have forgotten that someone very closely connected with you was very nearly carried off this week in Paris by a severe chill.

JACK: Yes, but you said yourself that a severe chill was not hereditary.

ALGERNON: It usen't to be, I know—but I daresay it is now. Science is always making wonderful improvements in things.

JACK (*picking up the muffin-dish*): Oh, that is nonsense; you are always talking nonsense.

ALGERNON: Jack, you are at the muffins again! I wish you wouldn't. There are only two left. (*Takes them.*) I told you I was particularly fond of muffins.

JACK: But I hate tea-cake.

ALGERNON: Why on earth then do you allow tea-cake to be served up for your guests? What ideas you have of hospitality!

JACK: Algernon! I have already told you to go. I don't want you here. Why don't you go!

ALGERNON: I haven't quite finished my tea yet! and there is still one muffin left. (JACK *groans, and sinks into a chair.* ALGERNON *continues eating.*)

ACT DROP

ACT III

Scene—Drawing-room at the Manor House.

GWENDOLEN *and* CECILY *are at the window, looking out into the garden.*

GWENDOLEN: The fact that they did not follow us at once into the house, as any one else would have done, seems to me to show that they have some sense of shame left.

CECILY: They have been eating muffins. That looks like repentance.

GWENDOLEN (*after a pause*): They don't seem to notice us at all. Couldn't you cough?

CECILY: But I haven't got a cough.

GWENDOLEN: They're looking at us. What effrontery!

CECILY: They're approaching. That's very forward of them.

GWENDOLEN: Let us preserve a dignified silence.

CECILY: Certainly. It's the only thing to do now.

(*Enter* JACK *followed by* ALGERNON. *They whistle some dreadful popular air from a British Opera.*)

GWENDOLEN: This dignified silence seems to produce an unpleasant effect.

CECILY: A most distasteful one.

GWENDOLEN: But we will not be the first to speak.

CECILY: Certainly not.

GWENDOLEN: Mr. Worthing, I have something very particular to ask you. Much depends on your reply.

CECILY: Gwendolen, your common sense is invaluable. Mr. Moncrieff, kindly answer me the following question. Why did you pretend to be my guardian's brother?

ALGERNON: In order that I might have an opportunity of meeting you.

CECILY (*to* GWENDOLEN): That certainly seems a satisfactory explanation, does it not?

GWENDOLEN: Yes, dear, if you can believe him.

CECILY: I don't. But that does not affect the wonderful beauty of his answer.

GWENDOLEN: True. In matters of grave importance, style, not sincerity is the vital thing. Mr. Worthing, what explanation can you offer to me for pretending to have a brother? Was it in order that you might have an opportunity of coming up to town to see me as often as possible?

JACK: Can you doubt it, Miss Fairfax?

GWENDOLEN: I have the gravest doubts upon the subject. But I intend to crush them. This is not the moment for German scepticism. (*Moving to* CECILY.) Their explanations appear to be quite satisfactory, especially Mr. Worthing's. That seems to me to have the stamp of truth upon it.

CECILY: I am more than content with what Mr. Moncrieff said. His voice alone inspires one with absolute credulity.

GWENDOLEN: Then you think we should forgive them?

CECILY: Yes. I mean no.

GWENDOLEN: True! I had forgotten. There are principles at stake that one cannot surrender. Which of us should tell them? The task is not a pleasant one.

CECILY: Could we not both speak at the same time?

GWENDOLEN: An excellent idea! I nearly always speak at the same time as other people. Will you take the time from me?

CECILY: Certainly. (GWENDOLEN *beats time with uplifted finger.*)

GWENDOLEN and CECILY (*speaking together*): Your Christian names are still an insuperable barrier. That is all!

JACK and ALGERNON (*speaking together*): Our Christian names! Is that all? But we are going to be christened this afternoon.

GWENDOLEN (*to* JACK): For my sake you are prepared to do this terrible thing?

JACK: I am.

CECILY (*to* ALGERNON): To please me you are ready to face this fearful ordeal?

ALGERNON: I am!

GWENDOLEN: How absurd to talk of the equality of the sexes! Where questions of self-sacrifice are concerned, men are infinitely beyond us.

JACK: We are. (*Clasps hands with* ALGERNON.)

CECILY: They have moments of physical courage of which we women know absolutely nothing.

GWENDOLEN (*to* JACK): Darling!

ALGERNON (*to* CECILY): Darling! (*They fall into each other's arms.*)

(*Enter* MERRIMAN. *When he enters he coughs loudly, seeing the situation.*)

MERRIMAN: Ahem! Ahem! Lady Bracknell!

JACK: Good heavens!

(*Enter* LADY BRACKNELL. *The couples separate in alarm. Exit* MERRIMAN.)

LADY BRACKNELL: Gwendolen! What does this mean?

GWENDOLEN: Merely that I am engaged to be married to Mr. Worthing, mamma.

LADY BRACKNELL: Come here. Sit down. Sit down immediately. Hesitation of any kind is a sign of mental decay in the young, of physical weakness in the old. (*Turns to* JACK.) Apprised, sir, of my daughter's sudden flight by her trusty maid, whose confidence I purchased by means of a small coin, I followed her at once by a luggage train. Her unhappy father is, I am glad to say, under the impression that she is attending a more than usually lengthy lecture by the University Extension Scheme on the Influence of a Permanent Income on Thought. I do not propose to undeceive him. Indeed I have never undeceived him on any question. I would consider it wrong. But of course, you will clearly understand that all communication between yourself and my daughter must cease immediately from this moment. On this point, as indeed on all points, I am firm.

JACK: I am engaged to be married to Gwendolen, Lady Bracknell!

LADY BRACKNELL: You are nothing of the kind, sir. And now as regards Algernon!... Algernon!

ALGERNON: Yes, Aunt Augusta.

LADY BRACKNELL: May I ask if it is in this house that your invalid friend Mr. Bunbury resides?

ALGERNON (*stammering*): Oh! No! Bunbury doesn't live here. Bunbury is somewhere else at present. In fact, Bunbury is dead.

LADY BRACKNELL: Dead! When did Mr. Bunbury die? His death must have been extremely sudden.

ALGERNON (*airily*): Oh! I killed Bunbury this afternoon. I mean poor Bunbury died this afternoon.

LADY BRACKNELL: What did he die of?

ALGERNON: Bunbury? Oh, he was quite exploded.

LADY BRACKNELL: Exploded! Was he the victim of a revolutionary outrage? I was not aware that Mr. Bunbury was interested in social legislation. If so, he is well punished for his morbidity.

ALGERNON: My dear Aunt Augusta, I mean he was found out! The doctors found out that Bunbury could not live, that is what I mean—so Bunbury died.

LADY BRACKNELL: He seems to have had great confidence in the opinion of his physicians. I am glad, however, that he made up his mind at the last to some definite course of action, and acted under proper medical advice. And now that we have finally got rid of this Mr. Bunbury, may I ask, Mr. Worthing, who is that young person whose hand my nephew Algernon is now holding in what seems to me a peculiarly unnecessary manner?

JACK: That lady is Miss Cecily Cardew, my ward.
   (**LADY BRACKNELL** *bows coldly to* **CECILY.**)

ALGERNON: I am engaged to be married to Cecily, Aunt Augusta.

LADY BRACKNELL: I beg your pardon?

CECILY: Mr. Moncrieff and I are engaged to be married, Lady Bracknell.

LADY BRACKNELL (*with a shiver, crossing to the sofa and sitting down*): I do not know whether there is anything peculiarly exciting in the air of this particular part of Hertfordshire, but the number of engagements that go on seems to me considerably above the proper average that statistics have laid down for our guidance. I think some preliminary inquiry on my part would not be out of place. Mr. Worthing, is Miss Cardew at all connected with any of the larger railway stations in London? I merely desire information. Until yesterday I had no idea that there were any families or persons whose origin was a Terminus. (**JACK** *looks perfectly furious, but restrains himself.*)

JACK (*in a clear, cold voice*): Miss Cardew is the granddaughter of the late Mr. Thomas Cardew of 149 Belgrave Square, S.W.; Gervase Park, Dorking, Surrey; and the Sporran, Fifeshire, N.B.

LADY BRACKNELL: That sounds not unsatisfactory. Three addresses always inspire confidence, even in tradesmen. But what proof have I of their authenticity?

JACK: I have carefully preserved the Court Guides of the period. They are open to your inspection, Lady Bracknell.

LADY BRACKNELL (*grimly*): I have known strange errors in that publication.

JACK: Miss Cardew's family solicitors are Messrs. Markby, Markby, and Markby.

LADY BRACKNELL: Markby, Markby, and Markby? A firm of the very highest position in their profession. Indeed I am told that one of the Mr. Markbys is occasionally to be seen at dinner parties. So far I am satisfied.

JACK (*very irritably*): How extremely kind of you, Lady Bracknell! I have also in my possession, you will be pleased to hear, certificates of Miss Cardew's birth, baptism, whooping cough, registration, vaccination, confirmation, and the measles; both the German and the English variety.

LADY BRACKNELL: Ah! A life crowded with incident, I see; though perhaps somewhat too exciting for a young girl. I am not myself in favour of premature experiences. (*Rises, looks at her watch.*) Gwendolen! the time approaches for our departure. We have not a moment to lose. As a matter of form, Mr.

Worthing, I had better ask you if Miss Cardew has any little fortune?

JACK: Oh! about a hundred and thirty thousand pounds in the Funds. That is all. Good-bye, Lady Bracknell. So pleased to have seen you.

LADY BRACKNELL (*sitting down again*): A moment, Mr. Worthing. A hundred and thirty thousand pounds! And in the Funds! Miss Cardew seems to me a most attractive young lady, now that I look at her. Few girls of the present day have any really solid qualities, any of the qualities that last, and improve with time. We live, I regret to say, in an age of surfaces. (*To* CECILY.) Come over here, dear. (CECILY *goes across.*) Pretty child! your dress is sadly simple, and your hair seems almost as Nature might have left it. But we can soon alter all that. A thoroughly experienced French maid produces a really marvellous result in a very brief space of time. I remember recommending one to young Lady Lancing, and after three months her own husband did not know her.

JACK (*aside*): And after six months nobody knew her.

LADY BRACKNELL (*glares at* JACK *for a few moments. Then bends, with a practised smile, to* CECILY): Kindly turn round, sweet child. (CECILY *turns completely round.*) No, the side view is what I want. (CECILY *presents her profile.*) Yes, quite as I expected. There are distinct social possibilities in your profile. The two weak points in our age are its want of principle and its want of profile. The chin a little higher, dear. Style largely depends on the way the chin is worn. They are worn very high, just at present. Algernon!

ALGERNON: Yes, Aunt Augusta!

LADY BRACKNELL: There are distinct social possibilities in Miss Cardew's profile.

ALGERNON: Cecily is the sweetest, dearest, prettiest girl in the whole world. And I don't care twopence about social possibilities.

LADY BRACKNELL: Never speak disrespectfully of Society, Algernon. Only people who can't get into it do that. (*To* CECILY.) Dear child, of course you know that Algernon has nothing but his debts to depend upon. But I do not approve of mercenary marriages. When I married Lord Bracknell I had no fortune of any kind. But I never dreamed for a moment of allowing that to stand in my way. Well, I suppose I must give my consent.

ALGERNON: Thank you, Aunt Augusta.

LADY BRACKNELL: Cecily, you may kiss me!

CECILY (*kisses her*): Thank you, Lady Bracknell.

LADY BRACKNELL: You may also address me as Aunt Augusta for the future.

CECILY: Thank you, Aunt Augusta.

LADY BRACKNELL: The marriage, I think, had better take place quite soon.

ALGERNON: Thank you, Aunt Augusta.

CECILY: Thank you, Aunt Augusta.

LADY BRACKNELL: To speak frankly, I am not in favour of long engagements. They give people the opportunity of finding out each other's character before marriage, which I think is never advisable.

JACK: I beg your pardon for interrupting you, Lady Bracknell, but this engagement is quite out of the question. I am Miss Cardew's guardian, and she cannot marry without my consent until she comes of age. That consent I absolutely decline to give.

LADY BRACKNELL: Upon what grounds may I ask? Algernon is an extremely, I may almost say, an ostentatiously, eligible young man. He has nothing, but he looks everything. What more can one desire?

JACK: It pains me very much to have to speak frankly to you, Lady Bracknell, about your nephew, but the fact is that I do not approve at all of his moral character. I suspect him of being untruthful. (ALGERNON *and* CECILY *look at him in indignant amazement.*)

LADY BRACKNELL: Untruthful! My nephew Algernon? Impossible! He is an Oxonian.

JACK: I fear there can be no possible doubt about the matter. This afternoon during my temporary absence in London on an important question of romance, he obtained admission to my house by means of the false pretence of being my brother. Under an assumed name he drank, I've just been informed by my butler, an entire pint bottle of my Perrier-

Jouet, Brut, '89, a wine I was specially reserving for myself. Continuing his disgraceful deception, he succeeded in the course of the afternoon in alienating the affections of my only ward. He subsequently stayed to tea, and devoured every single muffin. And what makes his conduct all the more heartless is, that he was perfectly well aware from the first that I have no brother, that I never had a brother, and that I don't intend to have a brother, not even of any kind. I distinctly told him so myself yesterday afternoon.

LADY BRACKNELL: Ahem! Mr. Worthing, after careful consideration I have decided entirely to overlook my nephew's conduct to you.

JACK: That is very generous of you, Lady Bracknell. My own decision, however, is unalterable. I decline to give my consent.

LADY BRACKNELL (*to* CECILY): Come here, sweet child. (CECILY *goes over.*) How old are you, dear?

CECILY: Well, I am really only eighteen, but I always admit to twenty when I go to evening parties.

LADY BRACKNELL: You are perfectly right in making some slight alteration. Indeed, no woman should ever be quite accurate about her age. It looks so calculating…. (*In a meditative manner.*) Eighteen, but admitting to twenty at evening parties. Well, it will not be very long before you are of age and free from the restraints of tutelage. So I don't think your guardian's consent is, after all, a matter of any importance.

JACK: Pray excuse me, Lady Bracknell, for interrupting you again, but it is only fair to tell you that according to the terms of her grandfather's will Miss Cardew does not come legally of age till she is thirty-five.

LADY BRACKNELL: That does not seem to me to be a grave objection. Thirty-five is a very attractive age. London society is full of women of the very highest birth who have, of their own free choice, remained thirty-five for years. Lady Dumbleton is an instance in point. To my own knowledge she has been thirty-five ever since she arrived at the age of forty, which was many years

ago now. I see no reason why our dear Cecily should not be even still more attractive at the age you mention than she is at present. There will be a large accumulation of property.

CECILY: Algy, could you wait for me till I was thirty-five?

ALGERNON: Of course I could, Cecily. You know I could.

CECILY: Yes, I felt it instinctively, but I couldn't wait all that time. I hate waiting even five minutes for anybody. It always makes me rather cross. I am not punctual myself, I know, but I do like punctuality in others, and waiting, even to be married, is quite out of the question.

ALGERNON: Then what is to be done, Cecily?

CECILY: I don't know, Mr. Moncrieff.

LADY BRACKNELL: My dear Mr. Worthing, as Miss Cardew states positively that she cannot wait till she is thirty-five—a remark which I am bound to say seems to me to show a somewhat impatient nature—I would beg of you to reconsider your decision.

JACK: But my dear Lady Bracknell, the matter is entirely in your own hands. The moment you consent to my marriage with Gwendolen, I will most gladly allow your nephew to form an alliance with my ward.

LADY BRACKNELL (*rising and drawing herself up*): You must be quite aware that what you propose is out of the question.

JACK: Then a passionate celibacy is all that any of us can look forward to.

LADY BRACKNELL: That is not the destiny I propose for Gwendolen. Algernon, of course, can choose for himself. (*Pulls out her watch.*) Come, dear (GWENDOLEN *rises*), we have already missed five, if not six, trains. To miss any more might expose us to comment on the platform.

(*Enter* DR. CHASUBLE.)

CHASUBLE: Everything is quite ready for the christenings.

LADY BRACKNELL: The christenings, sir! Is not that somewhat premature?

CHASUBLE (*looking rather puzzled, and pointing to* JACK *and* ALGERNON): Both these gentlemen have expressed a desire for immediate baptism.

LADY BRACKNELL: At their age? The idea is grotesque and irreligious! Algernon, I forbid you to be baptized. I will not hear of such excesses. Lord Bracknell would be highly displeased if he learned that that was the way in which you wasted your time and money.

CHASUBLE: Am I to understand then that there are to be no christenings at all this afternoon?

JACK: I don't think that, as things are now, it would be of much practical value to either of us, Dr. Chasuble.

CHASUBLE: I am grieved to hear such sentiments from you, Mr. Worthing. They savour of the heretical views of the Anabaptists, views that I have completely refuted in four of my unpublished sermons. However, as your present mood seems to be one peculiarly secular, I will return to the church at once. Indeed, I have just been informed by the pew-opener that for the last hour and a half Miss Prism has been waiting for me in the vestry.

LADY BRACKNELL (*starting*): Miss Prism! Did I hear you mention a Miss Prism?

CHASUBLE: Yes, Lady Bracknell. I am on my way to join her.

LADY BRACKNELL: Pray allow me to detain you for a moment. This matter may prove to be one of vital importance to Lord Bracknell and myself. Is this Miss Prism a female of repellent aspect, remotely connected with education?

CHASUBLE (*somewhat indignantly*): She is the most cultivated of ladies, and the very picture of respectability.

LADY BRACKNELL: It is obviously the same person. May I ask what position she holds in your household?

CHASUBLE (*severely*): I am a celibate, madam.

JACK (*interposing*): Miss Prism, Lady Bracknell, has been for the last three years Miss Cardew's esteemed governess and valued companion.

LADY BRACKNELL: In spite of what I hear of her, I must see her at once. Let her be sent for.

CHASUBLE (*looking off*): She approaches; she is nigh.

(*Enter* MISS PRISM *hurriedly.*)

MISS PRISM: I was told you expected me in the vestry, dear Canon. I have been waiting for you there for an hour and three-quarters. (*Catches sight of* LADY BRACKNELL, *who has fixed her with a stony glare.* MISS PRISM *grows pale and quails. She looks anxiously round as if desirous to escape.*)

LADY BRACKNELL (*in a severe, judicial voice*): Prism! (MISS PRISM *bows her head in shame.*) Come here, Prism! (MISS PRISM *approaches in a humble manner.*) Prism! Where is that baby? (*General consternation. The Canon starts back in horror.* ALGERNON *and* JACK *pretend to be anxious to shield* CECILY *and* GWENDOLEN *from hearing the details of a terrible public scandal.*) Twenty-eight years ago, Prism, you left Lord Bracknell's house, Number 104, Upper Grosvenor Street, in charge of a perambulator that contained a baby of the male sex. You never returned. A few weeks later, through the elaborate investigations of the Metropolitan police, the perambulator was discovered at midnight standing by itself in a remote corner of Bayswater. It contained the manuscript of a three-volume novel of more than usually revolting sentimentality. (MISS PRISM *starts in involuntary indignation.*) But the baby was not there. (*Every one looks at* MISS PRISM.) Prism! Where is that baby? (*A pause.*)

MISS PRISM: Lady Bracknell, I admit with shame that I do not know. I only wish I did. The plain facts of the case are these. On the morning of the day you mention, a day that is for ever branded on my memory, I prepared as usual to take the baby out in its perambulator. I had also with me a somewhat old, but capacious hand-bag in which I had intended to place the manuscript of a work of fiction that I had written during my few unoccupied hours. In a moment of mental abstraction, for which I never can forgive myself, I deposited the manuscript in the bassinette, and placed the baby in the hand-bag.

JACK (*who has been listening attentively*): But where did you deposit the hand-bag?

MISS PRISM: Do not ask me, Mr. Worthing.

JACK: Miss Prism, this is a matter of no small importance to me. I insist on knowing where you deposited the hand-bag that contained that infant.

MISS PRISM: I left it in the cloak-room of one of the larger railway stations in London.

JACK: What railway station?

MISS PRISM (*quite crushed*): Victoria. The Brighton line. (*Sinks into a chair.*)

JACK: I must retire to my room for a moment. Gwendolen, wait here for me.

GWENDOLEN: If you are not too long, I will wait here for you all my life.

(*Exit* JACK *in great excitement.*)

CHASUBLE: What do you think this means, Lady Bracknell?

LADY BRACKNELL: I dare not even suspect, Dr. Chasuble. I need hardly tell you that in families of high position strange coincidences are not supposed to occur. They are hardly considered the thing.

(*Noises heard overhead as if some one was throwing trunks about. Every one looks up.*)

CECILY: Uncle Jack seems strangely agitated.

CHASUBLE: Your guardian has a very emotional nature.

LADY BRACKNELL: This noise is extremely unpleasant. It sounds as if he was having an argument. I dislike arguments of any kind. They are always vulgar, and often convincing.

CHASUBLE (*looking up*): It has stopped now. (*The noise is redoubled.*)

LADY BRACKNELL: I wish he would arrive at some conclusion.

GWENDOLEN: This suspense is terrible. I hope it will last.

(*Enter* JACK *with a hand-bag of black leather in his hand.*)

JACK (*rushing over to* MISS PRISM): Is this the hand-bag, Miss Prism? Examine it carefully before you speak. The happiness of more than one life depends on your answer.

MISS PRISM (*calmly*): It seems to be mine. Yes, here is the injury it received through the up-

setting of a Gower Street omnibus in younger and happier days. Here is the stain on the lining caused by the explosion of a temperance beverage, an incident that occurred at Leamington. And here, on the lock, are my initials. I had forgotten that in an extravagant mood I had had them placed there. The bag is undoubtedly mine. I am delighted to have it so unexpectedly restored to me. It has been a great inconvenience being without it all these years.

JACK (*in a pathetic voice*): Miss Prism, more is restored to you than this hand-bag. I was the baby you placed in it.

MISS PRISM (*amazed*): You?

JACK (*embracing her*): Yes…mother!

MISS PRISM (*recoiling in indignant astonishment*): Mr. Worthing! I am unmarried!

JACK: Unmarried! I do not deny that is a serious blow. But after all, who has the right to cast a stone against one who has suffered? Cannot repentance wipe out an act of folly? Why should there be one law for men, and another for women? Mother, I forgive you. (*Tries to embrace her again.*)

MISS PRISM (*still more indignant*): Mr. Worthing, there is some error. (*Pointing to* LADY BRACKNELL.) There is the lady who can tell you who you really are.

JACK (*after a pause*): Lady Bracknell, I hate to seem inquisitive, but would you kindly inform me who I am?

LADY BRACKNELL: I am afraid that the news I have to give you will not altogether please you. You are the son of my poor sister, Mrs. Moncrieff, and consequently Algernon's elder brother.

JACK: Algy's elder brother! Then I have a brother after all. I knew I had a brother! I always said I had a brother! Cecily—how could you have ever doubted that I had a brother? (*Seizes hold of* ALGERNON.) Dr. Chasuble, my unfortunate brother. Miss Prism, my unfortunate brother. Gwendolen, my unfortunate brother. Algy, you young scoundrel, you will have to treat me with more respect in the future. You have never behaved to me like a brother in all your life.

ALGERNON: Well, not till to-day, old boy, I admit. I did my best, however, though I was out of practice. (*Shakes hands.*)

GWENDOLEN (*to* JACK): My own! But what own are you? What is your Christian name, now that you have become some one else?

JACK: Good heavens!… I had quite forgotten that point. Your decision on the subject of my name is irrevocable, I suppose?

GWENDOLEN: I never change, except in my affections.

CECILY: What a noble nature you have, Gwendolen!

JACK: Then the question had better be cleared up at once. Aunt Augusta, a moment. At the time when Miss Prism left me in the hand-bag, had I been christened already?

LADY BRACKNELL: Every luxury that money could buy, including christening, had been lavished on you by your fond and doting parents.

JACK: Then I was christened! That is settled. Now, what name was I given? Let me know the worst.

LADY BRACKNELL: Being the eldest son you were naturally christened after your father.

JACK (*irritably*): Yes, but what was my father's Christian name?

LADY BRACKNELL (*meditatively*): I cannot at the present moment recall what the General's Christian name was. But I have no doubt he had one. He was eccentric, I admit. But only in later years. And that was the result of the Indian climate, and marriage, and indigestion, and other things of that kind.

JACK: Algy! Can't you recollect what our father's Christian name was?

ALGERNON: My dear boy, we were never even on speaking terms. He died before I was a year old.

JACK: His name would appear in the Army Lists of the period, I suppose, Aunt Augusta?

LADY BRACKNELL: The General was essentially a man of peace, except in his domestic life. But I have no doubt his name would appear in any military directory.

JACK: The Army Lists of the last forty years are here. These delightful records should have been my constant study. (*Rushes to bookcase and tears the books out.*) M. Generals…Mallam, Maxbohm, Magley, what ghastly names they have—Markby, Migsby, Mobbs, Moncrieff! Lieutenant 1840, Captain, Lieutenant-Colonel, Colonel, General 1869, Christian names, Ernest John. (*Puts book very quietly down and speaks quite calmly.*) I always told you, Gwendolen, my name was Ernest, didn't I? Well, it is Ernest after all. I mean it naturally is Ernest.

LADY BRACKNELL: Yes, I remember now that the General was called Ernest. I knew I had some particular reason for disliking the name.

GWENDOLEN: Ernest! My own Ernest! I felt from the first that you could have no other name!

JACK: Gwendolen, it is a terrible thing for a man to find out suddenly that all his life he has been speaking nothing but the truth. Can you forgive me?

GWENDOLEN: I can. For I feel that you are sure to change.

JACK: My own one!

CHASUBLE (*to* MISS PRISM): Laetitia! (*Embraces her.*)

MISS PRISM (*enthusiastically*): Frederick! At last!

ALGERNON: Cecily! (*Embraces her.*) At last!

JACK: Gwendolen! (*Embraces her.*) At last!

LADY BRACKNELL: My nephew, you seem to be displaying signs of triviality.

JACK: On the contrary, Aunt Augusta, I've now realised for the first time in my life the vital Importance of Being Earnest.

TABLEAU
CURTAIN

PERFORMING *THE IMPORTANCE OF BEING EARNEST*

By 1895 when *The Importance of Being Earnest* opened at the prestigious St. James's Theatre in London, commercial producers had transformed the proscenium playhouses in the West End into gatherings for the wealthy upper and middle classes. In the refurbished theaters, tickets prices were higher and long runs encouraged to maximize profits. The leading actor-managers were Henry Irving, George Alexander, Squire and Marie Bancroft, Charles Kean, and Herbert Beerbohm Tree. Under their scrutiny, the commercial theater of the 1890s became the chief social activity of the day and a lucrative business.

By the time George Alexander took over the management of St. James's Theatre in 1890, there were new copyright laws in Britain, Europe, and America that made it possible for writers to earn a living in the theater. Under the new laws (legislated in 1887 and 1891), playwrights could expect regular royalties from performances and publication of their plays. Many, like Oscar Wilde, turned to the theater in the early 1890s as a way of making money.

When the curtain rose on *The Importance of Being Earnest* in 1895, Algernon's flat in Mayfair (I) and then the Manor House in Hertfordshire (II and III) were depicted in three-dimensional scenery with careful attention paid to fashionable furnishings, costumes, and properties, especially silver cigarette cases, cucumber sandwiches, and worn handbags. Florence Alexander, the producer's wife, organized the costumes, ensuring that the latest women's fashions were visible on stage and women were reputed to attend the play before shopping for their dresses and evening gowns.

Since that first opening-night, John Worthing and Lady Bracknell have been favorite roles for actors and actresses. George Alexander played the original John Worthing and Rose LeClercq the first Lady Bracknell. Learning that Wilde wanted the actors to play the comedy as naturally as possible, Alexander played it lightly but with deadly seriousness, to heighten the comedy and to avoid caricature. In 1930, John Gielgud played John Worthing opposite Edith Evans as Lady Bracknell to great acclaim in a visually beautiful production with elegant costumes and heavy, ornate furnishings that set the style for modern productions that followed. Director Tyrone Guthrie called it "the high-water mark in the production of artificial comedy of our epoch."[4]

When writing a book on acting, called *An Actor in His Time*, Gielgud reminded his reader that *The Importance of Being Earnest* had to be played very strictly, like chamber music. He said, "You must not indulge your self, or caricature. You must play it with your tongue in cheek, like a solemn charade. The muffin scene, for instance, very easily degenerates into a knock-about. I discovered this years after I thought I had finished with the play forever. [Rehearsing the second act for a benefit at Oxford, he concluded]...I believe I've been wrong about this scene whenever I played it. I think it must be acted very slowly. We began at half the pace and got many many more laughs out of it by eating the muffins with real solemnity...."[5]

The Importance of Being Earnest has since been staged many times in England and in the United States in commercial and nonprofit theaters and made into films. In 1952, a film featured Michael Redgrave and Edith Evans as John Worthing and Lady Bracknell, and, as recently as 2002, Colin Firth and Judi Dench appeared in these roles in another film version of Wilde's play. The classic comedy is a *tour de force* for actors and continually adored by stage and film audiences and critics.

CRITICS' NOTEBOOK

Oscar Wilde's life and work have intrigued artists, critics, scholars, and biographers since the 1890s. Richard Ellman's *Oscar Wilde* (1987) is considered the definitive biography on the playwright; Ellman also edited *Oscar Wilde: Twentieth Century Views* (1969), an interesting and accessible collection of essays. Wilde's grandson, Merlin Holland, compiled *The Wilde Album* (1997) with text and previously unpublished family photographs. Elaine Showalter's fascinating *Sexual Anarchy: Gender and Culture at the Fin de Siècle* (1991) analyzes the interrelations between culture and gender in the life and literature of the 1890s and reflects upon present issues. A growing literature looks specifically at Oscar Wilde's homosexuality in his life and work. Ed Cohen's *Talk on the Wilde Side* (1993) and Alan Sinfield's *The Wilde Century* (1994) situate Wilde's work and life in the conflicting views toward homosexuality in the late nineteenth century.

For our purposes in understanding the writing of comedy in general and the dazzling comic masterpiece of Oscar Wilde, we want to turn again to Aristotle's *Poetics* to look at the earliest critique of comedy. Although most of what Aristotle wrote on comedy has been lost, he says that comedy grew out of the mimes and improvisations of the leaders of songs sung and danced during early phallic rites. Details of these pre-dramatic rites are unclear. Aristotle associates the beginnings of comedy with the writer Epicharmus, who lived in Syracuse, at the time a Dorian colony on the island of Sicily. What we do know is that comedy was sufficiently developed to be given a place at the City Dionysia, Athens, in 487 B.C. Of fifth-century Old Comedy performed there, only eleven plays by Aristophanes have survived.

We also want to examine the later work of Northrop Frye in his elegant essay, "The Mythos of Spring: Comedy," originally published in *The Anatomy of Criticism* (1957). Frye's writing on comedy has become a seminal work of dramatic criticism.

Aristotle on Comedy*
Translated by S. H. Butcher

[ART AS IMITATION]

❦

Epic poetry and Tragedy, Comedy also and Dithyrambic poetry, and the music of the flute and of the lyre in most of their forms, are all in their general conception modes of imitation. They differ, however, from one another in three respects, the medium, the objects, the manner or mode of imitation, being in each case distinct.

Aristotle's Theory of Poetry and Fine Arts, trans. S. H. Butcher. 4th edition (Mineola, NY: Dover Publications, 1951): 7–69.

Since the objects of imitation are men in action, and these men must be either of a higher or a lower type (for moral character mainly answers to these divisions, goodness and badness being the distinguishing marks of moral differences), it follows that we must represent men either as better than in real life, or as worse, or as they are. It is the same in painting. Polygnotus depicted men as nobler than they are, Pauson as less noble, Dionysius drew them true to life.

…The same distinction marks off Tragedy from Comedy; for Comedy aims at representing men as worse, Tragedy as better than in actual life.

There is still a third difference—the manner in which each of these objects may be imitated. For the medium being the same, and the objects the same, the poet may imitate by *narration*—in which case he can either take another personality as Homer does, or speak in his own person, unchanged—or he may present all his characters as living and moving before us.

[ORIGINS OF DRAMA]

These, then, as we said at the beginning, are the three differences which distinguish artistic imitation,—the medium, the objects, and the manner. So that from one point of view, Sophocles is an imitator of the same kind as Homer—for both imitate higher types of character; from another point of view, of the same kind as Aristophanes—for both imitate persons acting and doing. Hence, some say, the name of 'drama' is given to such poems, as representing action. For the same reason the Dorians claim the invention both of Tragedy and Comedy. The claim to Comedy is put forward by the Megarians,—not only by those of Greece proper, who allege that it originated under their democracy, but also by the Megarians of Sicily, for the poet Epicharmus, who is much earlier than Chionides and Magnes, belonged to that country.

❧ ❧ ❧

Poetry in general seems to have sprung from two causes, each of them lying deep in our nature. First, the instinct of imitation is implanted in man from childhood, one difference between him and other animals being that he is the most imitative of living creatures, and through imitation learns his earliest lessons; and no less universal is the pleasure felt in things imitated. We have evidence of this in the facts of experience. Objects which in themselves we view with pain, we delight to contemplate when reproduced with minute fidelity: such as the forms of the most ignoble animals and of dead bodies. The cause of this again is, that to learn gives the liveliest pleasure, not only to philosophers but to men in general; whose capacity, however, of learning is more limited. Thus the reason why men enjoy seeing a likeness is, that in contemplating it they find themselves learning or inferring, and saying perhaps, 'Ah, that is he.' For if you happen not to have seen the original, the pleasure will be due not to the imitation as such, but to the execution, the colouring, or some such other cause.

Imitation, then, is one instinct of our nature. Next, there is the instinct for 'harmony' and rhythm, metres being manifestly sections of rhythm. Persons, therefore, starting with this natural gift developed by degrees their special aptitudes, till their rude improvisations gave birth to Poetry.

Poetry now diverged in two directions, according to the individual character of the writers. The graver spirits imitated noble actions, and the actions of good men. The more trivial sort imitated the actions of meaner persons, at first composing satires, as the former did hymns to the gods and the praises of famous men. A poem of the satirical kind cannot indeed be put down to any author earlier than Homer; though many such writers probably there were. But from Homer onward, instances can be cited,— his own Margites, for example, and other similar compositions. The appropriate metre was also here introduced; hence the measure is still called the iambic or lampooning measure, being that in which people lampooned one another. Thus the older poets were distinguished as writers of heroic or of lampooning verse.

As, in the serious style, Homer is preeminent among poets, for he alone combined dramatic form with excellence of imitation, so he too first laid down the main lines of Comedy, by dramatising the ludicrous instead of writing personal satire. His Margites bears the same relation to Comedy that the Iliad and Odyssey do to Tragedy. But when Tragedy and Comedy came to light, the two classes of poets still followed their natural bent: the lampooners became writers of Comedy, and the Epic poets were succeeded by Tragedians, since the drama was a larger and higher form of art....

[ORIGINS OF COMEDY]

...Tragedy—as also Comedy—was at first mere improvisation. The one originated with the authors of the Dithyramb, the other with those of the phallic songs, which are still in use in many of our cities. Tragedy advanced by slow degrees; each new element that showed itself was in turn developed. Having passed through many changes, it found its natural form, and there it stopped.

🐦 🐦 🐦

Comedy is, as we have said, an imitation of characters of a lower type,—not, however, in the full sense of the word bad, the Ludicrous being merely a subdivision of the ugly. It consists in some defect or ugliness which is not painful or destructive. To take an obvious example, the comic mask is ugly and distorted, but does not imply pain.

The successive changes through which Tragedy passed, and the authors of these changes, are well known, whereas Comedy has had no history, because it was not at first treated seriously. It was late before the Archon granted a comic chorus to a poet; the performers were till then voluntary. Comedy had already taken definite shape when comic poets, distinctively so called, are heard of. Who furnished it with masks, or prologues, or increased the number of actors,— these and other similar details remain unknown.

As for the plot, it came originally from Sicily; but of Athenian writers Crates was the first who, abandoning the 'iambic' or lampooning form, generalised his themes and plots.

Northrop Frye, from "The Mythos of Spring: Comedy"*

❦

It will be most convenient to work out the theory of comic construction of drama…. What normally happens is that a young man wants a young woman, that his desire is resisted by some opposition, usually paternal, and that near the end of the play some twist in the plot enables the hero to have his will. In this simple pattern there are several complex elements. In the first place, the movement of comedy is usually a movement from one kind of society to another. At the beginning of the play the obstructing characters are in charge of the play's society, and the audience recognizes that they are usurpers. At the end of the play the device in the plot that brings hero and heroine together causes a new society to crystallize around the hero, and the moment when this crystallization occurs is the point of resolution in the action, the comic discovery, *anagnorisis* or *cognitio.*

The appearance of this new society is frequently signalized by some kind of party or festive ritual, which either appears at the end of the play or is assumed to take place immediately afterward. Weddings are most common, and sometimes so many of them occur, as in the quadruple wedding at the end of [Shakespeare's] *As You Like It,* that they suggest the wholesale pairing off that takes place in a dance, which is another common conclusion, and the normal one for the masque….

Comedy usually moves toward a happy ending, and the normal response of the audience to a happy ending is "this should be,"

*Northrop Frye, "The Mythos of Spring: Comedy," in *The Anatomy of Criticism* (Princeton, N.J.: Princeton University Press, 1957): 164–167.

which sounds like a moral judgment. So it is, except that it is not moral in the restricted sense, but social….

The society emerging at the conclusion of comedy represents, by contrast, a kind of moral norm, or pragmatically free society…. We are simply given to understand that the newly-married couple will live happily ever after, or that at any rate they will get along in a relatively un-humorous and clear-sighted manner….

REVISITING COMEDY

Comedy emerged in early societies apparently out of the need to confront the ludicrous in human nature and to celebrate humanity's procreative urges. As one of two principal dramatic forms found throughout the long history of writing for the theater, comedy exposes human folly and celebrates human survival. Unlike writers of tragedy, comic playwrights have focused on the social world and its values of moderation, benevolence, and good humor in all things. Therefore, the central characters of comedy have largely been those fools, rogues, and pranksters who have defied society's norms, been exposed as aberrations, and reformed of their waywardness by humanity's common sense. As a form of dramatic writing, comedy represents the aspect of human experience that affirms moderation, compassion, love, common sense, and good-natured foolery.

Oscar Wilde's *The Importance of Being Earnest* provides an example of comic writing that subjects the seriousness of upper-class Victorian society and culture to a playful critique of manners, social codes, and lifestyles. The development of Wilde's traditional play-construction begins, not unlike *Oedipus the King,* with a quest (for a name) and proceeds through complication to recognition in the form of a handbag. Wilde's "serious play for trivial people" emphasizes the seriousness of modern life in the trivialities of society's demands on youth and their elders.

Farce, satire, and tragicomedy—offshoots of comic writing for the theater from earliest to modern times—emphasize other comedic facets of human experience and continue our discussion of types of dramatic writing for the next two chapters.

NOTES

1. Northrop Frye, "The Mythos of Spring: Comedy," *The Anatomy of Criticism* (Princeton, N.J.: Princeton University Press, 1957): 163.

2. Arnott, p. 539; Ian Small, ed., *Lady Windermere's Fan* (London: A. and C. Black, 1980): 7.

3. Dan Rebellato, ed., *The Importance of Being Earnest* (London: Nick Hern Books, Ltd., 1995): xxi–xxii.

4. Jonathan Croall, *Gielgud: A Theatrical Life 1904–2000* (New York: Continuum International Publishing Group, Inc., 2001): 266.

5. John Gielgud, with John Miller and Jon Powell, *Gielgud: An Actor in His Time* (New York: Clarkson N. Potter, Inc., Publisher, 1979): 158.

CHAPTER 7

FARCE AND SATIRE

SOLDIER WITH A SECRET

A scene from the New York Shakespeare Festival production of *The Colored Museum.* (Photo © Martha Swope.)

Farce is tragedy played at about a hundred and twenty revolutions a minute.

—John Mortimer[1]

BACKGROUND

Farce is a simplified dramatic form derived from comedy and the human psychology that seeks out fun for fun's sake along with the fulfillment of socially unacceptable fantasies. It is not uncommon for us to say of a real-life occurrence, "It's a farce!" We mean that something or someone is outrageous. One critic called farce a "veritable structure of absurdities."[2] Farce as a dramatic form permits us the social outrage but spares us the consequences of society's punishments.

Farce is best defined as a comedy of situation. In farce, such exaggerated physical and visual activities as slips on a banana peel, pies in the face, and mistaken identities develop out of a situation. Extreme and ludicrous happenings (without serious consequences) are substituted for comedy's traditional concerns for social values. The writer of farce sees life as aggressive, mechanical, and coincidental, and entertains us with seemingly endless variations on a single situation. In a typical farce situation, the would-be adulterous lovers are momentarily trapped in a bedroom as the deceived wife or husband arrives unexpectedly. The situation is accompanied by much pounding on the bedroom door, efforts on the lovers' part to retrieve their clothing, followed by inventive escapes from the all too obvious situation, and sometimes the beating and humiliation of the intruder.

The "psychology of farce," as Eric Bentley called it, is that special opportunity for the fulfillment of our unmentionable wishes without taking responsibility for our actions or suffering the guilt.[3] Secure in a darkened theater or movie house, we can watch our most treasured, unmentionable wishes fulfilled before our eyes. Charlie Chaplin, "the little tramp," defeats the bully who can bend lamp posts with his bare hands in the film *Easy Street*. Woody Allen's awkward, unattractive lover gets the beautiful heroine in *Manhattan* and Jim Carrey in *Ace Ventura, Pet Detective* sets out to find the kidnapped mascot of the Dolphins' football team and has many mishaps before rescuing the animal.

FARCE AND COMEDY

Because farce grows out of an improbable, absurd situation, its principal characters are comedy's familiar types taken to extremes. In general, farce's characters are in broad outlines variations on the fool, the knave, and the prankster. Shakespeare's Puck—the embodiment of the spirit of mischief—is the knave of farce. Mischief frequently drives the farcical hero into pranks, both lowly and sophisticated. Fools have frequented farce since Greek and Roman comedy and the "masks" of the Italian *commedia dell'arte* of the fifteenth century. Wearing their own literal character masks, Harlequin, Brighella, Dottore, and Pantalone are the fools and pranksters of *commedia* who have found other names and shapes in farce over the centuries. Sir Toby Belch (*Twelfth Night*), Puck (*A Midsummer Night's Dream*), Dogberry (*Much Ado About Nothing*), and Launcelot Gobbo (*The Merchant of Venice*) are but a few of Shakespeare's farcical characters. They are monuments to human stupidity and mischievousness, reminding us that the human race has its rare intellect and virtues along with its fools and impostors.

Farce as a subform of comedy recklessly abandons us in a fantasy world of violence (without harm), adultery (without consequences), and brutality (without risk). In his study, *Jokes and Their Relationship to the Unconscious*, Sigmund Freud pointed out that our humorous, waking fantasies, like our dreams, bypass taboos established by our innate "cultural censor."[4] Our fantasies—call them imagined pranks—permit more primitive, antisocial impulses to express themselves in ways that both our conscious and our unconscious would habitually forbid. We regress to forms of pleasure that are normally inhibited and rejected as childish, uncivilized, or socially unacceptable. Jokes permit the delights of nonsense talk or uninhibited references to sex and vicarious indulgence of the body and all of its functions. They give free rein to our hostilities against the curbs on our behavior demanded by proper social behavior. Like Freud's interpretations of jokes, farce is a fantasy of humor acting out on stage our impulses on the one hand to pleasure and self-indulgence and on the other to aggression and hostility.

Writers associated with the theater of the absurd, such as Eugène Ionesco and Samuel Beckett, exploit the practical joke to comment on the ridiculousness of lives lived in a universe without meaning. Hence, in absurdist writing, the practical joke played upon humans is simply existence itself, which a malignant universe has apparently wished upon a variety of helpless and squirming victims. Their antics and sufferings provide both the laughter and horror of these plays. Ionesco subtitled *The Chairs,* written in 1952, a "tragic farce." Ionesco's characters are not young lovers but an elderly couple. The play's situation expands like a gigantic snowball which breaks apart in a cacophony of catcalls and hoots from an imaginary audience. The couple's great scene of triumph at the play's end is the filling of an empty stage with chairs and more chairs for imaginary guests of increasing importance. At the climax, when the Orator himself arrives (he is a real actor) to deliver a message conceived by the Old Man, the couple fling themselves into a watery grave before the Orator speaks. But, in an ironic reversal, the Orator is mute and delivers no intelligible message. Ionesco substitutes the audience's expected farcical satisfactions with a bitter and puzzled laughter. Jessica Milner Davis calls it the "horror of the practical joke."[5] Ionesco, in describing his own work in *Notes and Counter Notes,* called farce "the extreme exaggeration of parody," which in its broad and outrageous effects takes us back to the "unendurable."[6] In the context of the existential, farce becomes a means of facing up to a universe that has lost its meaning and purpose.

In one sense, farce is drama's safety valve; it releases the steam of our antisocial wishes (and fantasies) for revenge, aggression, violence, disruption, and offense. Today, the best examples of farce are found in the films of Charlie Chaplin, the Marx Brothers, W. C. Fields, Woody Allen, John Cleese, Eddie Murphy, and Chevy Chase and in plays by Georges Feydeau, Eugène Ionesco, Neil Simon, Alan Ayckbourn, and Penn and Teller. Farce has also been part of some of the world's great comedies, including those of Shakespeare and Molière. For example, the "mechanicals'" preparation for and performance of the *Pyramis and Thisbe* play in *A Midsummer Night's Dream* is farce. The humor grows out of situation: Wholly incompetent amateurs rehearse a play to be performed at court. Their rehearsal is a series of blunders and their performance is an artistic disaster, but the bumpkins are received with good humor and indulgence rather than punishment.

Farce has its place in drama's forms, for it is one facet of human psychology. The situation in farce becomes hopelessly embroiled until circumstances and human indulgence free the characters without harm from their selfishness, stupidities, or escapades.

Farce is not unrelated to satire, and *vice versa.* In almost all of the world's great comedies are to be found elements of both farce and satire.

SATIRE AND SOCIETY

Satire is also a subform of comedy that exposes, criticizes, and censors humanity's vices and cruelties with humor, wit, irony, and even cynicism. Its aim is corrective, that is, through laughter and ridicule to hold human greed, hypocrisy, and evil up for examination and moral judgment. The good of society is the ultimate goal in the satirist's attack on human folly and vice. There is a reformative subtext in the satirist's work as those who are harmful to society's well-being are exposed, ridiculed, and often cast-out, meaning sent to prison or to exile from the society that they set out to harm. The work of the French playwright Molière frequently contains satirical elements in his great comedies, such as *Tartuffe* and *The Misanthrope. Tartuffe,* for instance, exposes religious hypocrisy and censors its title character (the supposedly pious priest) for excessive greed and thievery that threaten to bring harm to the innocent and gullible alike. He is exposed and taken to prison by the King's officers.

Satire uses wit (sophisticated language) and exaggeration to expose or attack evil and harmful foolishness. Over the centuries, satirical writing has attacked and ridiculed a specific figure (the religious hypocrite Tartuffe, for example) or taken aim at a harmful social group (the gossipmongers in Richard Brinsley Sheridan's *The School for Scandal*).

Modern satire has its roots in Old Comedy and the satyr plays of the early Greek festivals. Aristophanes (c. 448–380 B.C.E.) wrote plays known as Old Comedy (as opposed to the later New Comedy of Menander) and established satirical comedy as a means of ridiculing celebrities, politicians, and cultural conditions with characters who were often recognizable personalities. The philosopher Socrates and the playwright Euripides, along with politicians and generals, were among the many prominent Athenians satirized in the plays of Aristophanes. The modern equivalent to Greek Old Comedy is political satire found in films (*Wag the Dog*), in comic strips (*Doonesbury*), in television programs (*Saturday Night Live*), in the routines of stand-up comic/satirists found on *Comedy Central,* and in the diatribes of Jon Stewart, Lewis Black, Dennis Miller, Bill Maher, Ellen DeGeneres, and Sandra Bernhardt against the establishment.

Satire's linguistic origins are to be found in the Greek satyr plays of the fifth century, which were written to accompany the tragic plays and performed as an afterpiece to the tragedies. The satyr play takes its name from the chorus costumed as half-beast, half human companions of Dionysus with the father of the satyrs, Silenus, as the choral leader. The satyr play most often was a burlesque treatment of mythology (often ridiculing the gods and heroes) in boisterous action and dance accompanied by indecent language and gesture.

Given the serious origins of satire as afterpieces to the great tragedies in the Greek festivals that debunked the gods and heroes of myth and were followed by the later comedies of Aristophanes that commented on contemporary society, politics, and literature, satire has always reflected a seriousness of purpose, that is, to correct and reform. As a dramatic form, satire is always closely aligned with the freedoms within a society that allow for public criticism and open debate on political, religious, and social issues in such public places as theaters, meeting halls, and television studios. When societies legislate against ridicule of political heads of state and suppress their satirists with threats of imprisonment or worse, then satire disappears and its sister form, farce, reverts to domestic trifles. The great democracies of the Western world have always tolerated satire as a means of holding the dramatic mirror up to social ills, public tyrants, governmental abuse, corrupt politicians and have taken to heart the carefully crafted solutions of playwrights to society's ills and political extremists.

The twentieth century has been a great age of satirical writing in the United States. Satirical plays, novels, films, television programs, comic strips, and nightclub acts reached a crescendo during the presidency of William Jefferson Clinton and the presidential election of 2001. When contemporary American playwrights have addressed issues of social scrutiny in satirical plays, the issues have been unionization (Marc Blitzstein's *The Cradle Will Rock*), discrimination (George C. Wolfe's *The Colored Museum*), and environmental concerns (Mark Hollmann's and Greg Kotis' *Urinetown: The Musical*).

In *The Colored Museum,* George C. Wolfe utilizes the techniques of farce and the moral scrutiny of satire in his examination of African-American history and literature.

The Colored Museum

GEORGE C. WOLFE

George C. Wolfe (1954–) is author of The Colored Museum, *an adaptation of* Spunk, *and the books for the musicals* Jelly's Last Jam, The Wild Party, *and* Harlem Song. *He grew up in Frankfurt, Kentucky. His father worked for the state's department of corrections and his mother was the principal of a black private school attended by the four Wolfe children. Just as his father and siblings, Wolfe attended Kentucky State University, but only for a year. He transferred to Pomona College in California and majored in theater, where he began writing and staging plays. Following graduation, he worked at the Innercity Cultural Center in Los Angeles, where he taught and directed. In 1979 Wolfe moved to New York and taught acting at the City College of New York before enrolling in the musical theater program at New York University, where he received the Master of Fine Arts degree. There, he made contact with Stephen Sondheim, Arthur Laurents, and Richard Maltby, who became early champions of his work.*

Wolfe's first big break came when Playwrights Horizons produced Paradise, *his wacky view of colonialization, which failed, but his next venture was* The Colored Museum, *which took familiar African-American stereotypes and turned them inside out and upside down. This popular production opened at the Crossroads Theater, New Jersey, in 1986, transferred to the New York Shakespeare Festival Public Theater, and established Wolfe as a new, distinctive presence in the American theater. Named one of three Artistic Associates at the New York Shakespeare Festival, he scored another success with* Spunk, *an adaptation of three stories by Harlem Renaissance writer Zora Neale Hurston.*

In 1987, he was librettist for Duke Ellington's opera, Queenie Pie, *which premiered at the American Music Theater Festival and at the John F. Kennedy Center in Washington, D.C. In 1992 Wolfe*

wrote the book for and directed Jelly's Last Jam, *the life of Jelly Roll Morton, for Broadway. In 1993, he staged Tony Kushner's* Angels in America: Millennium Approaches *and* Perestroika *for Broadway and was named Producer of the Joseph Papp Public Theater/New York Shakespeare Festival. He won the Village Voice "Obie" award for* The Colored Museum *and Antoinette Perry "Tony" awards for direction of* Jelly's Last Jam *and* Angels in America: Millennium Approaches. *He recently directed the Broadway premiere of Suzan-Lori Parks's* Topdog/Underdog, Elaine Stritch: At Liberty, *and the all-new production of* Harlem Song *at the Apollo Theater.*

"The major influence in my work is the culture I come from," Wolfe said. "The storytelling, the language, the energies of defying.... I no longer view myself as being a subculture [in America], a minority, an alternative. I am the party. I am the Jam."[7]

CRITICAL INTRODUCTION TO *THE COLORED MUSEUM*

George C. Wolfe's *The Colored Museum* takes its structure from the musical revue (there are eleven vignettes) and its outrageous treatment of stereotypes and social icons from farce. With uncompromising wit and a frenetic style, Wolfe says the unthinkable about the history and present-day contradictions of African-Americans in the United States. He leaves society's sacred taboos in ruins for both blacks and whites at the play's end.

The setting (and situation) is an antiseptic modern museum displaying exhibits of "colored" history, beginning with the slave trade and ending with contemporary Harlem. Wolfe's strategy is not to present a museum-quality display of black history in the United States, but as a farceur and satirist, he sets about to annihilate the audience's politically correct responses and attitudes and set them on a path for social reform. For example, the opening sketch presents an airline stewardess, dressed in a hot-pink outfit, welcoming her Savannah-bound passengers to "celebrity slaveship" where they are expected to obey a "Fasten Shackles" seat-belt sign and are warned that they are about to "suffer a few hundred years" in exchange for receiving a "complex culture." Thus, Wolfe establishes the outrageous playfulness of traditional farce with a personal seriousness that theater is a place for ideas and truths about society and the human condition.

The other exhibits (displayed on a revolving stage that brings them into view without interruption) comprise displays of contemporary African-Americans torn between their cultural legacy of oppression and revolt and the exigencies of living in the present. A Josephine Baker–like chanteuse, named Lala, finds her carefully created Gallicized show-business image haunted by the "little girl" she thought she had left for dead in the backwoods of Mississippi. A woman dressing for a date is traumatized when her two wigs atop her makeup table (one is a sixties' "Afro"; the other is a "Barbie Doll dipped in chocolate") come alive to debate the identity conflict they have represented in their owner's life for twenty years. A glamorous couple who admittedly cannot live "inside yesterday's pain" resolve to retreat from their past into a world of narcissistic glamor and choose to live with the beautiful people reflected in *Ebony Magazine.* They discover only the "kind of pain that comes from feeling no pain at all." A corporate type tries to throw the icons of his childhood (carried in a "Saks Fifth Avenue" shopping bag) into a trash can along with his inner adolescent self dressed in late-sixties' street style. As he attempts to eradicate his past, he discards his Afro-comb; Eldridge Cleaver's book, *Soul on Ice;* political campaign buttons of Angela Davis; and albums by Jimi Hendrix, The Jackson Five, and The Temptations. Finally, he strangles The Kid in an effort "to kill his own rage." He announces, "I have no history. I have no past," but the ado-

lescent experience within rises again from the depths where he has been temporarily left for dead with the other detritus of the corporate executive's life.

The central exhibit of *The Colored Museum* is "The Last Mama-on-the-Couch Play," a play-within-the-play, in which Wolfe shatters the pretensions of black acting styles along with the generational conflicts of 1950s' black-American drama in which families are preoccupied with middle-class aspirations. The target is Lorraine Hansberry's award-winning drama, *A Raisin in the Sun,* along with the performances of Claudia McNeil, Sidney Poitier, and Ruby Dee in the 1959 Broadway production. An elegant announcer, dressed in black-tie, promises a "searing, domestic drama that tears at the very fabric of racist America." Wolfe's scene satirizes a pretentious, latter-day form of black theater (blamed on the Juilliard School of Drama in New York City) that turns into an all-black Broadway musical that spirals into an indictment of the white audience's eternal relationship to the black performer. With farcical style and satirical wit, Wolfe has torn at the fabric of racist America by revealing the cultural blind spots of blacks and whites alike: the black millionaire basketball player, soul food, sensitive family dramas, and performers (especially tap dancers and blues singers).

The playwright's themes are resolved in the final monologue, which belongs to Topsy Washington (named for the character in *Uncle Tom's Cabin* and the seat of government) who imagines a gigantic Manhattan party "somewhere between 125th Street and infinity" where Nat Turner sips champagne out of Eartha Kitt's slipper, Angela Davis and Aunt Jemima share a plate of "greens" while they talk about South Africa, and Bert Williams and Malcolm X discuss existentialism "as it relates to the shuffle-ball-change." As this fantasy merges present and past, it snowballs into a "defying logic." Topsy decides to put her rage about the past behind her so she can "go about the business of being me" and celebrate her own "madness and colored contradictions." As music, other characters, and projected images rise up from history around Topsy, Wolfe's intention becomes clear: while the baggage of slavery cannot really be banished, we have been liberated from the shackles of the past by Wolfe's fearless and sustained Freudian joke that has bypassed social taboos and cultural censors. The exhibits in Wolfe's "colored museum" stress that we are our past, but our present-day awareness liberates us into a vital selfhood.

The vulnerability of black identity and African-American pride to exploitation and even destruction by the majority culture is the basic statement of *The Colored Museum*. To the charge that he has fostered stereotypes and not smashed them, Wolfe responded, "That's a manifestation of a slave mentality. Because you're still obsessing about how the dominant culture is going to judge you and I refuse to give anybody that kind of power over my thought process and creativity." He continued,

> *The culture I come from is very specific and very exact and what I choose to write about is specifically about that. But what it's really, ultimately dealing with is the human condition.*[8]

The Colored Museum

THE CAST: An ensemble of five, two men and three women, all black, who perform all the characters that inhabit the exhibits.*

THE STAGE: White walls and recessed lighting. A starkness befitting a museum where the myths and madness of black/Negro/colored Americans are stored.

Built into the walls are a series of small panels, doors, revolving walls, and compartments from which actors can retrieve key props and make quick entrances.

A revolve is used, which allows for quick transitions from one exhibit to the next.

MUSIC: All of the music for the show should be prerecorded. Only the drummer, who is used in *Git on Board*, and then later in *Permutations* and *The Party*, is live.

THERE IS NO INTERMISSION

THE EXHIBITS

Git on Board
Cookin' with Aunt Ethel
The Photo Session
Soldier with a Secret
The Gospel According to Miss Roj
The Hairpiece
The Last Mama-on-the-Couch Play
Symbiosis
Lala's Opening
Permutations
The Party

THE CHARACTERS

Git on Board
  MISS PAT
Cookin' with Aunt Ethel
  AUNT ETHEL
The Photo Session
  GIRL
  GUY
Soldier with a Secret
  JUNIE ROBINSON
The Gospel According to Miss Roj
  MISS ROJ
  WAITER
The Hairpiece
  THE WOMAN
  JANINE
  LAWANDA
The Last Mama-on-the-Couch Play
  NARRATOR
  MAMA
  WALTER-LEE-BEAU-WILLIE-JONES
  LADY IN PLAID
  MEDEA JONES
Symbiosis
  THE MAN
  THE KID
Lala's Opening
  LALA LAMAZING GRACE
  ADMONIA
  FLO'RANCE
  THE LITTLE GIRL
Permutations
  NORMAL JEAN REYNOLDS
The Party
  TOPSY WASHINGTON
  MISS PAT
  MISS ROJ
  LALA LAMAZING GRACE
  THE MAN (*From Symbiosis*)

*A LITTLE GIRL, seven to twelve years old, is needed for a walk-on part in *Lala's Opening*.

GIT ON BOARD

(*Blackness. Cut by drums pounding. Then slides, rapidly flashing before us. Images we've all seen before, of African slaves being captured, loaded onto ships, tortured. The images flash, flash, flash. The drums crescendo. Blackout. And then lights reveal* MISS PAT, *frozen. She is black, pert, and cute. She has a flip to her hair and wears a hot pink mini-skirt stewardess uniform.*)

(*She stands in front of a curtain which separates her from an offstage cockpit.*)

(*An electronic bell goes "ding" and* MISS PAT *comes to life, presenting herself in a friendly but rehearsed manner, smiling and speaking as she has done so many times before.*)

MISS PAT: Welcome aboard Celebrity Slaveship, departing the Gold Coast and making short stops at Bahia, Port Au Prince, and Havana, before our final destination of Savannah.

Hi. I'm Miss Pat and I'll be serving you here in Cabin A. We will be crossing the Atlantic at an altitude that's pretty high, so you must wear your shackles at all times.

(*She removes a shackle from the overhead compartment and demonstrates.*)

To put on your shackle, take the right hand and close the metal ring around your left hand like so. Repeat the action using your left hand to secure the right. If you have any trouble bonding yourself, I'd be more than glad to assist.

Once we reach the desired altitude, the Captain will turn off the "Fasten Your Shackle" sign…(*She efficiently points out the "FASTEN YOUR SHACKLE" signs on either side of her, which light up.*)…allowing you a chance to stretch and dance in the aisles a bit. But otherwise, shackles must be worn at all times.
(*The "Fasten Your Shackles" signs go off.*)

MISS PAT: Also, we ask that you please refrain from call-and-response singing between cabins as that sort of thing can lead to rebellion. And, of course, no drums are allowed on board. Can you repeat after me, "No drums." (*She gets the audience to repeat.*) With a little more enthusiasm, please. "No drums." (*After the audience repeats it.*) That was great!

Once we're airborne, I'll be by with magazines, and earphones can be purchased for the price of your first-born male.

If there's anything I can do to make this middle passage more pleasant, press the little button overhead and I'll be with you faster than you can say, "Go down, Moses." (*She laughs at her "little joke".*) Thanks for flying Celebrity and here's hoping you have a pleasant take off.
(*The engines surge, the "Fasten Your Shackle" signs go on, and over-articulate Muzak voices are heard singing as* MISS PAT *pulls down a bucket seat and "shackles-up" for takeoff.*)

VOICES:
GET ON BOARD CELEBRITY SLAVESHIP
GET ON BOARD CELEBRITY SLAVESHIP
GET ON BOARD CELEBRITY SLAVESHIP
THERE'S ROOM FOR MANY A MORE
(*The engines reach an even, steady hum. Just as* MISS PAT *rises and replaces the shackles in the overhead compartment, the faint sound of African drumming is heard.*)

MISS PAT: Hi. Miss Pat again. I'm sorry to disturb you, but someone is playing drums. And what did we just say…"No drums." It must be someone in Coach. But we here in Cabin A are not going to respond to those drums. As a matter of fact, we don't even hear them. Repeat after me. "I don't hear any drums." (*The audience repeats.*) And "I will not rebel." (*The audience repeats. The drumming grows.*)

MISS PAT: (*Placating*) OK, now I realize some of us are a bit edgy after hearing about the tragedy on board The Laughing Mary, but let me assure you Celebrity has no intention of throwing you overboard and collecting the insurance. We value you!
(*She proceeds to single out individual passengers/audience members.*)

Why, the songs *you* are going to sing in the cotton fields, under the burning heat and stinging lash, will metamorphose and give birth to the likes of James Brown and the Fabulous Flames. And you, yes *you*, are going to come up with some of the best dances. The best dances! The Watusi! The Funky Chicken! And just think of what *you* are going to mean to William Faulkner.

All right, so you're gonna have to suffer for a few hundred years, but from your pain will come a culture so complex. *And,* with this little item here…(*She removes a basketball from the overhead compartment.*)…you'll become millionaires! (*There is a roar of thunder. The lights quiver and the "Fasten Your Shackle" signs begin to flash.* MISS PAT *quickly replaces the basketball in the overhead compartment and speaks very reassuringly.*)

MISS PAT: No, don't panic. I'm here to take care of you. We're just flying through a little thunder storm. Now the only way you're going to make it through this one is if you abandon your God and worship a new one. So, on the count of three, let's all sing. One, two, three…

NOBODY KNOWS DE TROUBLE I SEEN

Oh, I forgot to mention, when singing, omit the T-H sound. "The" becomes "de". "They" becomes "dey". Got it? Good!

NOBODY KNOWS…
NOBODY KNOWS…

Oh, so you don't like that one? Well then let's try another—

SUMMER TIME
AND DE LIVIN' IS EASY

Gershwin. He comes from another oppressed people so he understands.

FISH ARE JUMPIN'…come on.
AND DE COTTON IS HIGH.

Sing, damnit!
(*Lights begin to flash, the engines surge, and there is wild drumming.* MISS PAT *sticks her head through the curtain and speaks with an off-stage* CAPTAIN.)

MISS PAT: What?
VOICE OF CAPTAIN (*O.S.*): Time warp!
MISS PAT: Time warp! (*She turns to the audience and puts on a pleasant face.*) The Captain has assured me everything is fine. We're just caught in a little time warp. (*Trying to fight her growing hysteria.*) On your right you will see the American Revolution, which will give the U.S. of A exclusive rights to your life. And on your left, the Civil War, which means you will vote Republican until F.D.R. comes along. And now we're passing over the Great Depression, which means everybody gets to live the way you've been living. (*There is a blinding flash of light, and an explosion. She screams.*) Ahhhhhhhhh! That was World War I, which is not to be confused with World War II…(*There is a larger flash of light, and another explosion.*)…Ahhhhh! Which is not to be confused with the Korean War or the Vietnam War, all of which you will play a major role in.

Oh, look, now we're passing over the sixties. Martha and Vandellas…Malcolm X. (*There is a gun shot.*)…"Julia" with Miss Diahann Carroll…and five little girls in Sunday school …(*There is an explosion.*) Martin Luther King…(*A gun shot*) Oh no! The Supremes just broke up! (*The drumming intensifies.*) Stop playing those drums. I said, stop playing those damn drums. You can't stop history! You can't stop time! Those drums will be confiscated once we reach Savannah. Repeat after me. I don't hear any drums and I will not rebel. I will not rebel! I will not re— (*The lights go out, she screams, and the sound of a plane landing and screeching to a halt is heard. After a beat, lights reveal a wasted, disheveled* MISS PAT, *but perky nonetheless.*)

MISS PAT: Hi. Miss Pat here. Things got a bit jumpy back there, but the Captain has just informed me we have safely landed in Savannah. Please check the overhead before exiting as any baggage you don't claim, we trash.

It's been fun, and we hope the next time you consider travel, it's with Celebrity.

(*Luggage begins to revolve onstage from offstage left, going past* MISS PAT *and revolving offstage right. Mixed in with the luggage are two male slaves and a woman slave, complete with luggage and I.D. tags around their necks.*)

MISS PAT: (*With routine, rehearsed pleasantness.*)
Have a nice day. Bye bye.
Button up that coat, it's kind of chilly.
Have a nice day. Bye bye.
You take care now.
See you.
Have a nice day.
Have a nice day.
Have a nice day.

COOKIN' WITH AUNT ETHEL

(*As the slaves begin to revolve off, a low-down gut-bucket blues is heard.* AUNT ETHEL, *a down-home black woman with a bandana on her head, revolves to center stage. She stands behind a big black pot and wears a reassuring grin.*)

AUNT ETHEL: Welcome to "Aunt Ethel's Down-Home Cookin' Show," where we explores the magic and mysteries of colored cuisine.

Today, we gonna be servin' ourselves up some…(*She laughs.*) I'm not gonna tell you. That's right! I'm not gonna tell you what it is till after you done cooked it. Child, on "The Aunt Ethel Show" we loves to have ourselves some fun. Well, are you ready? Here goes.
(*She belts out a hard-drivin' blues and throws invisible ingredients into the big, black pot.*)

FIRST YA ADD A PINCH OF STYLE
AND THEN A DASH OF FLAIR
NOW YA STIR IN SOME
PREOCCUPATION
WITH THE TEXTURE OF YOUR HAIR

NEXT YA ADD ALL KINDS OF
RHYTHMS
LOTS OF FEELINGS AND PIZZAZ
THEN HUNNY THROW IN SOME RAGE
TILL IT CONGEALS AND TURNS TO
JAZZ

NOW YOU COOKIN' COOKIN'
WITH AUNT ETHEL
YOU REALLY COOKIN'
COOKIN' WITH AUNT ETHEL, OH
YEAH

NOW YA ADD A HEAP OF SURVIVAL
AND HUMILITY, JUST A TOUCH
ADD SOME ATTITUDE
OOPS! I PUT TOO MUCH

AND NOW A WHOLE LOT OF HUMOR
SALTY LANGUAGE, MIXED WITH
SADNESS
THEN THROW IN A BOX OF BLUES
AND SIMMER TO MADNESS

NOW YOU COOKIN'
COOKIN' WITH AUNT ETHEL, OH
YEAH!

NOW YOU BEAT IT—REALLY WORK IT
DISCARD AND DISOWN
AND IN A FEW HUNDRED YEARS
ONCE IT'S AGED AND FULLY GROWN
YA PUT IT IN THE OVEN
TILL IT'S BLACK
AND HAS A SHEEN
OR TILL IT'S NICE AND YELLA
OR ANY SHADE IN BETWEEN

NEXT YA TAKE 'EM OUT AND COOL 'EM
'CAUSE THEY NO FUN WHEN THEY
HOT
AND WON'T YOU BE SURPRISED
AT THE CONCOCTION YOU GOT

YOU HAVE BAKED
BAKED YOURSELF A BATCH OF
NEGROES
YES YOU HAVE BAKED YOURSELF
BAKED YOURSELF A BATCH OF
NEGROES
(*She pulls from the pot a handful of Negroes, black dolls.*)

But don't ask me what to do with 'em now that you got 'em, 'cause child, that's your problem. (*She throws the dolls back into the pot.*) But in any case, yaw be sure to join Aunt Ethel next week, when we gonna be

servin' ourselves up some chitlin quiche…
some grits-under-glass,

AND A SWEET POTATO PIE
AND YOU'LL BE COOKIN'
COOKIN' WITH AUNT ETHEL
OH YEAH!
(*On* AUNT ETHEL'S *final rift, lights reveal…*)

THE PHOTO SESSION

(*…a very glamorous, gorgeous, black couple, wearing the best of everything and perfect smiles. The stage is bathed in color and bright white light. Disco music with the chant: "We're fabulous" plays in the background. As they pose, larger-than-life images of their perfection are projected on the museum walls. The music quiets and the images fade away as they begin to speak and pose.*)

GIRL: The world was becoming too much for us.
GUY: We couldn't resolve the contradictions of our existence.
GIRL: And we couldn't resolve yesterday's pain.
GUY: So we gave away our life and we now live inside *Ebony Magazine.*
GIRL: Yes, we live inside a world where everyone is beautiful, and wears fabulous clothes.
GUY: And no one says anything profound.
GIRL: Or meaningful.
GUY: Or contradictory.
GIRL: Because no one talks. Everyone just smiles and shows off their cheekbones. (*They adopt a profile pose.*)
Last month I was black and fabulous while holding up a bottle of vodka.
GUY: This month we get to be black and fabulous together.
(*They dance/pose. The "We're fabulous" chant builds and then fades as they start to speak again.*)
GIRL: There are of course setbacks.
GUY: We have to smile like this for a whole month.
GIRL: And we have no social life.
GUY: And no sex.
GIRL: And at times it feels like we're suffocating, like we're not human anymore.
GUY: And everything is rehearsed, including this other kind of pain we're starting to feel.

GIRL: The kind of pain that comes from feeling no pain at all.
(*They then speak and pose with a sudden burst of energy.*)
GUY: But one can't have everything.
GIRL: Can one?
GUY: So if the world is becoming too much for you, do like we did.
GIRL: Give away your life and come be beautiful with us.
GUY: We guarantee, no contradictions.
GIRL/GUY: Smile/click, smile/click, smile/click.
GIRL: And no pain.
(*They adopt a final pose and revolve off as the "We're fabulous" chant plays and fades into the background.*)

A SOLDIER WITH A SECRET

(*Projected onto the museum walls are the faces of black soldiers—from the Spanish-American thru to the Vietnam War. Lights slowly reveal* JUNIE ROBINSON, *a black combat soldier, posed on an onyx plinth. He comes to life and smiles at the audience. Somewhat dim-witted, he has an easy-going charm about him.*)

JUNIE: Pst. Pst. I know the secret. The secret to your pain. 'Course, I didn't always know. First I had to die, then come back to life, 'fore I had the gift.

Ya see the Cappin sent me off up ahead to scout for screamin' yella bastards. 'Course, for the life of me I couldn't understand why they'd be screamin', seein' as how we was tryin' to kill them and they us.

But anyway, I'm off lookin', when all of a sudden I find myself caught smack dead in the middle of this explosion. This blindin', burnin', scaldin' explosion. Musta been a booby trap or something, 'cause all around me is fire. Hell, I'm on fire. Like a piece of chicken dropped in a skillet of cracklin' grease. Why, my flesh was justa peelin' off of my bones.

But then I says to myself, "Junie, if yo' flesh is on fire, how come you don't feel no pain!"

And I didn't. I swear as I'm standin' here, I felt nuthin. That's when I sort of put two and two together and realized I didn't feel no whole lot of hurtin' cause I done died.

Well I just picked myself up and walked right on out of that explosion. Hell, once you know you dead, why keep on dyin', ya know?

So, like I say, I walk right outta that explosion, fully expectin' to see white clouds, Jesus, and my Mama, only all I saw was more war. Shootin' goin' on way off in this direction and that direction. And there, standin' around, was all the guys. Hubert, J.F., the Cappin. I guess the sound of the explosion must of attracted 'em, and they all starin' at me like I'm some kind of ghost.

So I yells to 'em, "Hey there Hubert! Hey there Cappin!" But they just stare. So I tells 'em how I'd died and how I guess it wasn't my time cause here I am, "Fully in the flesh and not a scratch to my bones." And they still just stare. So I took to starin' back.
(*The expression on* JUNIE'S *face slowly turns to horror and disbelief.*)

Only what I saw…well I can't exactly to this day describe it. But I swear, as sure as they was wearin' green and holdin' guns, they was each wearin' a piece of the future on their faces.

Yeah. All the hurt that was gonna get done to them and they was gonna do to folks was right there clear as day.

I saw how J. F., once he got back to Chicago, was gonna get shot dead by this po-lice, and I saw how Hubert was gonna start beatin' up on his old lady which I didn't understand, 'cause all he could do was talk on and on about how much he loved her. Each and every one of 'em had pain in his future and blood on his path. And God or the Devil one spoke to me and said, "Junie, these colored boys ain't gonna be the same after this war. They ain't gonn have no kind of happiness."

Well right then and there it come to me. The secret to their pain.

Late that night, after the medics done checked me over and found me fit for fightin', after everybody done settle down for the night, I sneaked over to where Hubert was sleepin', and with a needle I stole from the medics…pst, pst…I shot a little air into his veins. The second he died, all the hurtin-to-come just left his face.

Two weeks later I got J.F. and after that Woodrow…Jimmy Joe…I even spent all night waitin' by the latrine 'cause I knew the Cappin always made a late night visit and pst…pst…I got him.

(*Smiling, quite proud of himself.*) That's how come I died and come back to life. 'Cause just like Jesus went around healin' the sick, I'm supposed to go around healin' the hurtin' all these colored boys wearin' from the war.

Pst, pst. I know the secret. The secret to your pain. The secret to yours, and yours. Pst. Pst. Pst. Pst. (*The lights slowly fade.*)

THE GOSPEL ACCORDING TO MISS ROJ

(*The darkness is cut by electronic music. Cold, pounding, unrelenting. A neon sign which spells out THE BOTTOMLESS PIT clicks on. There is a lone bar stool. Lights flash on and off, pulsating to the beat. There is a blast of smoke and, from the haze,* MISS ROJ *appears. He is dressed in striped patio pants, white go-go boots, a halter, and cat-shaped sunglasses. What would seem ridiculous on anyone else,* MISS ROJ *wears as if it were high fashion. He carries himself with total elegance and absolute arrogance.*)

MISS ROJ: God created black people and black people created style. The name's Miss Roj …that's R.O.J. thank you and you can find me every Wednesday, Friday and Saturday nights at "The Bottomless Pit," the watering hole for the wild and weary which asks the question, "Is there life after Jherri-curl?"
(*A waiter enters, hands* MISS ROJ *a drink, and then exits.*)

Thanks, doll. *Yes,* if they be black and swish, the B.P. has seen them, which is not to suggest the Pit is lacking in cultural diversity. Oh no. There are your dinge queens, white men who like their chicken legs dark. (*He winks/flirts with a man in the audience.*) And let's not forget, "Los Muchachos de la Neighborhood." But the speciality of the house is The Snap Queens. (*He snaps his fingers.*) We are a rare breed.

For, you see, when something strikes our fancy, when the truth comes piercing through the dark, well you just can't let it pass unnoticed. No darling. You must pronounce it with a snap. (*He snaps.*)

Snapping comes from another galaxy, as do all snap queens. That's right. I ain't just your regular oppressed American Negro. No-no-no! I am an extraterrestial. And I ain't talkin' none of that shit you seen in the movies! I have real power. (*The waiter enters.* MISS ROJ *stops him.*)

Speaking of no power, will you please tell Miss Stingy-with-the-rum, that if Miss Roj had wanted to remain sober, she could have stayed home and drank Kool-aid. (*He snaps.*) Thank you.
(*The waiter exits.* MISS ROJ *crosses and sits on bar stool.*)

Yes, I was placed here on Earth to study the life habits of a deteriorating society, and child when we talkin' New York City, we are discussing the Queen of Deterioration. Miss New York is doing a slow dance with death, and I am here to warn you all, but before I do, I must know…don't you just love my patio pants? Annette Funicello immortalized them in "Beach Blanket Bingo," and I have continued the legacy. And my go-gos? I realize white after Labor Day is very gauche, but as the saying goes, if you've got it flaunt it, if you don't, front it and snap to death any bastard who dares to defy you. (*Laughing*) Oh ho! My demons are showing. Yes, my demons live at the bottom of my Bacardi and Coke.

Let's just hope for all concerned I dance my demons out before I drink them out 'cause child, dancing demons take you on a ride, but those drinkin' demons just take you, and you find yourself doing the strangest things. Like the time I locked my father in the broom closet. Seems the liquor made his tongue real liberal and he decided he was gonna baptize me with the word "faggot" over and over. Well, he's just going on and on with "faggot this" and "faggot that," all the while walking toward the broom closet to piss. Poor drunk bastard was just all turned around. So the demons just took hold of my wedges and forced me to kick the drunk son-of-a-bitch into the closet and lock the door. (*Laughter*) Three days later I remembered he was there. (*He snaps.*)
(*The waiter enters.* MISS ROJ *takes a drink and downs it.*)

Another!
(*The waiter exits.*)

(*Dancing about.*) Oh yes-yes-yes! Miss Roj is quintessential style. I corn row the hairs on my legs so that they spell out M.I.S.S. R.O.J. And I dare any bastard to fuck with me because I will snap your ass into oblivion.

I have the power, you know. Everytime I snap, I steal one beat of your heart. So if you find yourself gasping for air in the middle of the night, chances are you fucked with Miss Roj and she didn't like it.

Like the time this asshole at Jones Beach decided to take issue with my coulotte-sailor ensemble. This child, this muscle-bound Brooklyn thug in a skin-tight bikini, very skin-tight so the whole world can see that instead of a brain, God gave him an extra thick piece of sausage. You know the kind who beat up on their wives for breakfast. Well, he decided to blurt out when I walked by, "Hey look at da monkey coon in da faggit suit." Well, I walked up to the poor dear, very calmly lifted my hand, and…. (*He snaps in rapid succession.*) A heart attack, right there on the beach. (*He singles out some-*

one in the audience.) You don't believe it? Cross me! Come on! Come on! *(The waiter enters, hands* MISS ROJ *a drink.* MISS ROJ *downs it. The waiter exits.)*

(Looking around.) If this place is the answer, we're asking all the wrong questions. The only reason I come here is to communicate with my origins. The flashing lights are signals from my planet way out there. Yes, girl, even further than Flatbush. We're talking another galaxy. The flashing lights tell me how much time is left before the end.

(Very drunk and loud by now.) I hate the people here. I hate the drinks. But most of all I hate this goddamn music. That ain't music. Give me Aretha Franklin any day. *(Singing)* "Just a little respect. R.E.S.P.E.C.T." Yeah! Yeah!

Come on and dance your last dance with Miss Roj. Last call is but a drink away and each snap puts you one step closer to the end.

A high-rise goes up. You can't get no job. Come on everybody and dance. A whole race of people gets trashed and debased. Snap those fingers and dance. Some sick bitch throws her baby out the window 'cause she thinks it's the Devil. Everybody snap! *The New York Post.* Snap!

Snap for every time you walk past someone lying in the street, smelling like frozen piss and shit and you don't see it. Snap for every crazed bastard who kills himself so as to get the jump on being killed. And snap for every sick mutha-fucker who, bored with carrying around his fear, takes to shooting up other people.

Yeah, snap your fingers and dance with Miss Roj. But don't be fooled by the banners and balloons 'cause, child, this ain't no party going on. Hell no! It's a wake. And the casket's made out of stone, steel, and glass and the people are racing all over the pavement like maggots on a dead piece of meat.

Yeah, dance! But don't be surprised if there ain't no beat holding you together 'cause we traded in our drums for respectability. So now it's just words. Words rappin'. Words screechin'. Words flowin' instead of blood 'cause you know that don't work. Words cracklin' instead of fire 'cause by the time a match is struck on 125th Street and you run to mid-town, the flame has been blown away.

So come on and dance with Miss Roj and her demons. We don't ask for acceptance. We don't ask for approval. We know who we are and we move on it!

I guarantee you will never hear two fingers put together in a snap and not think of Miss Roj. That's power, baby. Patio pants and all. *(The lights begin to flash in rapid succession.)*

So let's dance! And snap! And dance! And snap!
*(*MISS ROJ *begins to dance as if driven by his demons. There is a blast of smoke and when the haze settles,* MISS ROJ *has revolved off and in place of him is a recording of Aretha Franklin singing, "Respect.")*

THE HAIRPIECE

(As "Respect" fades into the background, a vanity revolves to center stage. On this vanity are two wigs, an Afro wig, circa 1968, and a long, flowing wig, both resting on wig stands. A black WOMAN *enters, her head and body wrapped in towels. She picks up a framed picture and after a few moments of hesitation, throws it into a small trash can. She then removes one of her towels to reveal a totally bald head. Looking into a mirror on the "fourth wall," she begins applying makeup.)*

(The wig stand holding the Afro wig opens her eyes. Her name is JANINE. *She stares in disbelief at the bald woman.)*

JANINE: *(Calling to the other wig stand.)* LaWanda. LaWanda girl, wake up. *(The other wig stand, the one with the long, flowing wig, opens her eyes. Her name is* LAWANDA.)

LAWANDA: What? What is it?

JANINE: Check out girlfriend.

LAWANDA: Oh, girl, I don't believe it.

JANINE: (*Laughing*) Just look at the poor thing, trying to paint some life onto that face of hers. You'd think by now she'd realize it's the hair. It's all about the hair.

LAWANDA: What hair! She ain't got no hair! She done fried, dyed, de-chemicalized her shit to death.

JANINE: And all that's left is that buck-naked scalp of hers, sittin' up there apologizin' for being odd-shaped and ugly.

LAWANDA: (*Laughing with* JANINE.) Girl, stop!

JANINE: I ain't sayin' nuthin' but the truth.

LAWANDA/JANINE: The bitch is bald! (*They laugh.*)

JANINE: And all over some man.

LAWANDA: I tell ya, girl, I just don't understand it. I mean, look at her. She's got a right nice face, a good head on her shoulders. A good job even. And she's got to go fall in love with that fool.

JANINE: That political quick-change artist. Everytime the nigga went and changed his ideology, she went and changed her hair to fit the occasion.

LAWANDA: Well at least she's breaking up with him.

JANINE: Hunny, no!

LAWANDA: Yes child.

JANINE: Oh, girl, dish me the dirt!

LAWANDA: Well, you see, I heard her on the phone, talking to one of her girlfriends, and she's meeting him for lunch today to give him the ax.

JANINE: Well it's about time.

LAWANDA: I hear ya. But don't you worry 'bout a thing, girlfriend. I'm gonna tell you all about it.

JANINE: Hunny, you won't have to tell me a damn thing 'cause I'm gonna be there, front row, center.

LAWANDA: You?

JANINE: Yes, child, she's wearing me to lunch.

LAWANDA: (*Outraged*) I don't think so!

JANINE: (*With an attitude*) What do you mean, you don't think so?

LAWANDA: Exactly what I said, "I don't think so." Damn, Janine, get real. How the hell she gonna wear both of us?

JANINE: She ain't wearing both of us. She's wearing me.

LAWANDA: Says who?

JANINE: Says me! Says her! Ain't that right, girlfriend?
(*The* WOMAN *stops putting on makeup, looks around, sees no one, and goes back to her makeup.*)

JANINE: I said, ain't that right!
(*The* WOMAN *picks up the phone.*)

WOMAN: Hello…hello…

JANINE: Did you hear the damn phone ring?

WOMAN: No.

JANINE: Then put the damn phone down and talk to me.

WOMAN: I ah…don't understand.

JANINE: It ain't deep so don't panic. Now, you're having lunch with your boyfriend, right?

WOMAN: (*Breaking into tears.*) I think I'm having a nervous breakdown.

JANINE: (*Impatient*) I said you're having lunch with your boyfriend, right!

WOMAN: (*Scared, pulling herself together.*) Yes, right …right.

JANINE: To break up with him.

WOMAN: How did you know that?

LAWANDA: I told her.

WOMAN: (*Stands and screams.*) Help! Help!

JANINE: Sit down. I said sit your ass down! (*The* WOMAN *does.*)

JANINE: Now set her straight and tell her you're wearing me.

LAWANDA: She's the one that needs to be set straight, so go on and tell her you're wearing me.

JANINE: No, tell her you're wearing me.
(*There is a pause.*)

LAWANDA: Well?

JANINE: Well?

WOMAN: I ah…actually hadn't made up my mind.

JANINE: (*Going off*) What do you mean you ain't made up you mind! After all that fool has put you through, you gonna need all the attitude you can get and there is nothing like attitude and a healthy head of kinks to make his shit shrivel like it should!

That's right! When you wearin' me, you lettin' him know he ain't gonna get no sweet-talkin' comb through your love without some serious resistance. No-no! The kink of my head is like the kink of your heart and neither is about to be hot-pressed into surrender.

LAWANDA: That shit is so tired. The last time attitude worked on anybody was 1968. Janine girl, you need to get over it and get on with it. (*To the* WOMAN.) And you need to give the nigga a goodbye he will never forget.

I say give him hysteria! Give him emotion! Give him rage! And there is nothing like a toss of the tresses to make your emotional outburst shine with emotional flair.

You can toss me back, shake me from side to side, all the while screaming, "I want you out of my life forever!!!" And not only will I come bouncing back for more, but you just might win an Academy Award for best performance by a head of hair in a dramatic role.

JANINE: Miss hunny, please! She don't need no Barbie doll dipped in chocolate telling her what to do. She needs a head of hair that's coming from a fo' real place.

LAWANDA: Don't you dare talk about nobody coming from a "fo' real place," Miss Made-in-Taiwan!

JANINE: Hey! I ain't ashamed of where I come from. Besides, it don't matter where you come from as long as you end up in the right place.

LAWANDA: And it don't matter the grade as long as the point gets made. So go on and tell her you're wearing me.

JANINE: No, tell her you're wearing me.
(*The* WOMAN, *unable to take it, begins to bite off her fake nails, as* LAWANDA *and* JANINE *go at each other.*)

LAWANDA:
Set the bitch straight. Let her know there is no way she could even begin to compete with me. I am quality. She is kink. I am exotic. She is common. I am class and she is trash. That's right. T.R.A.S.H. We're talking three strikes and you're out. So go on and tell her you're wearing me. Go on, tell her! Tell her! Tell her!

JANINE:
Who you callin' a bitch? Why, if I had hands I'd knock you clear into next week. You think you cute. She thinks she's cute just 'cause that synthetic mop of hers blows in the wind. She looks like a fool and you look like an even bigger fool when you wear her, so go on and tell her you're wearing me. Go on, tell her! Tell her! Tell her!

(*The* WOMAN *screams and pulls the two wigs off the wig stands as the lights go to black on three bald heads.*)

THE LAST MAMA-ON-THE-COUCH PLAY

(*A* NARRATOR, *dressed in a black tuxedo, enters through the audience and stands center stage. He is totally solemn.*)

NARRATOR: We are pleased to bring you yet another Mama-on-the-Couch play. A searing domestic drama that tears at the very fabric of racist America. (*He crosses upstage center and sits on a stool and reads from a playscript.*) Act One. Scene One.
(MAMA *revolves on stage left, sitting on a couch reading a large, oversized Bible. A window is placed stage right.* MAMA'S *dress, the couch, and drapes are made from the same material. A doormat lays down center.*)

NARRATOR: Lights up on a dreary, depressing, but with middle-class aspirations tenement slum. There is a couch, with a Mama on it. Both are well worn. There is a picture of Jesus on the wall…(*A picture of Jesus is instantly revealed.*)…and a window which looks onto an abandoned tenement. It is late spring.

I GOT THE MONTH OF MAY

Here comes your favorite part. Come on, Johnny man, sing.

I GUESS YOU SAY
WHAT CAN MAKE ME FEEL THIS WAY
MY GIRL, MY GIRL, MY GIRL
TALKIN' 'BOUT

MAN: (*Exploding*) I said give it back!

KID: (*Angry*) I ain't givin' you a muthafuckin' thing!

MAN: Now you listen to me!

KID: No, you listen to me. This is the kid you're dealin' with, so don't fuck with me!
(*He hits his fist into his hand, and* THE MAN *grabs for his heart.* THE KID *repeats with two more hits, which causes the man to drop to the ground, grabbing his heart.*)

KID: Jai! Jai! Jai!

MAN: Kid, please.

KID: Yeah. Yeah. Now who's begging who.... Well, well, well, look at Mr. Cream-of-the-Crop, Mr. Colored-Man-on-Top. Now that he's making it, he no longer wants anything to do with the Kid. Well, you may put all kinds of silk ties 'round your neck and white lines up your nose, but the Kid is here to stay. You may change your women as often as you change your underwear, but the Kid is here to stay. And regardless of how much of your past that you trash, I ain't goin' no damn where. Is that clear? Is that clear?

MAN: (*Regaining his strength, beginning to stand.*) Yeah.

KID: Good. (*After a beat.*) You all right man? You all right? I don't want to hurt you, but when you start all that talk about getting rid of me, well, it gets me kind of crazy. We need each other. We are one...
(*Before* THE KID *can complete his sentence,* THE MAN *grabs him around his neck and starts to choke him violently.*)

MAN: (*As he strangles him.*) The...Ice...Age...is... upon us...and either we adjust...or we end up...extinct.
(THE KID *hangs limp in* THE MAN'S *arms.*)

MAN: (*Laughing*) Man kills his own rage. Film at eleven. (*He then dumps* THE KID *into the trash can, and closes the lid. He speaks in a contained voice.*) I have no history. I have no past. I can't. It's too much. It's much too much. I must be able to smile on cue. And watch the news with an impersonal eye. I have no stake in the madness.

Being black is too emotionally taxing; therefore I will be black only on weekends and holidays.
(*He then turns to go, but sees the Temptations album lying on the ground. He picks it up and sings quietly to himself.*)

I GUESS YOU SAY
WHAT CAN MAKE ME FEEL THIS WAY
(*He pauses, but then crosses to the trash can, lifts the lid, and just as he is about to toss the album in, a hand reaches from inside the can and grabs hold of* THE MAN'S *arm.* THE KID *then emerges from the can with a death grip on* THE MAN'S *arm.*)

KID: (*Smiling*) What's happenin'?
BLACKOUT

LALA'S OPENING

(*Roving follow spots. A timpani drum roll. As we hear the voice of the* ANNOUNCER, *outrageously glamorous images of* LALA *are projected onto the museum walls.*)

VOICE OF ANNOUNCER: From Rome to Rangoon! Paris to Prague! We are pleased to present the American debut of the one! The only! The breathtaking! The astounding! The stupendous! The incredible! The magnificient! Lala Lamazing Grace!
(*Thunderous applause as* LALA *struts on, the definitive black diva. She has long, flowing hair, an outrageous lam dress, and an affected French accent which she loses when she's upset.*)

LALA:
EVERYBODY LOVES LALA
EVERYBODY LOVES ME
PARIS! BELIN! LONDON! ROME!

NO MATTER WHERE I GO
I ALWAYS FEEL AT HOME

OHHHH
EVERYBODY LOVES LALA
EVERYBODY LOVES ME
I'M TRES MAGNIFIQUE
AND OH SO UNIQUE
AND WHEN IT COMES TO GLAMOUR
I'M CHIC-ER THAN CHIC
(*She giggles.*)

THAT'S WHY EVERYBODY
EVERYBODY
EVERYBODY-EVERYBODY-EVERYBODY
LOVES ME
*She begins to vocally reach for higher and higher
notes, until she has to point to her final note. She
ends the number with a grand flourish and bows
to thunderous applause.*)
LALA: I-love-it-l-love-it-l-love-it!

Yes, it's me! Lala Lamazing Grace and I
have come home. Home to the home I never
knew as home. Home to you, my people,
my blood, my guts.

My story is a simple one, full of fire, passion, magique. You may ask how did I, a
humble girl from the backwoods of Mississippi, come to be the ninth wonder of the
modern world. Well, I can't take all of the
credit. Part of it goes to him. *She points toward the heavens.*)

No, not the light man, darling, but God. For,
you see, Lala is a star. A very big star. Let us
not mince words, I'm a fucking meteorite.
(*She laughs.*) But He is the universe and just
like my sister, Aretha la Franklin, Lala's
roots are in the black church. (*She sings in a
showy gospel style:*)

THAT'S WHY EVERYBODY LOVES
SWING LOW SWEET CHARIOT
THAT'S WHY EVERYBODY LOVES
GO DOWN MOSES WAY DOWN IN
EGYPT LAND
THAT'S WHY EVERYBODY
EVERYBODY LOVES ME!!!

(*Once again she points to her final note and then
basks in applause.*)

Thank you. Thank you.

Now, before I dazzle you with more of my
limitless talent, tell me something, America.
(*Musical underscoring*) Why has it taken you
so long to recognize my artistry? Mother
France opened her loving arms and Lala
came running. All over the world Lala was
embraced. But here, ha! You spat at Lala.
Was I too exotic? Too much woman, or what?

Diana Ross you embrace. A two-bit nobody
from Detroit, of all places. Now, I'm not
knocking la Ross. She does the best she can
with the little she has. (*She laughs.*) But the
Paul la Robesons, the James la Baldwins, the
Josephine la Baker's, who was my god-
mother you know. The Lala Lamazing
Grace's you kick out. You drive…

AWAY
I AM GOING AWAY
HOPING TO FIND A BETTER DAY
WHAT DO YOU SAY
HEY HEY
I AM GOING AWAY
AWAY
(LALA, *caught up in the drama of the song,
doesn't see* ADMONIA, *her maid, stick her head
out from offstage.*)

(*Once she is sure* LALA *isn't looking, she wheels
onto stage right* FLO'RANCE, LALA'S *lover, who
wears a white mask/blonde hair. He is gagged
and tied to a chair.* ADMONIA *places him on
stage and then quickly exits.*)
LALA:
AU REVOIR—JE VAIS PARTIERAD
MAINTENANT
JE VEUX DIRE MAINTENANT
AU REVOIR
AU REVOIR
AU REVOIR
AU REVOIR
A-MA-VIE
(*On her last note, she sees* FLO'RANCE *and, in to-
tal shock, crosses to him.*)

LALA: Flo'rance, what the hell are you doing out here, looking like that. I haven't seen you for three days and you decide to show up now?
(*He mumbles.*)

I don't want to hear it!
(*He mumbles.*)

I said shut up!
(ADMONIA *enters from stage right and has a letter opener on a silver tray.*)
ADMONIA: Pst!
(LALA, *embarrassed by the presence of* ADMONIA *on stage, smiles apologetically at the audience.*)
LALA: Un momento.
(*She then pulls* ADMONIA *to the side.*)
LALA: Darling, have you lost your mind coming on-stage while I'm performing. And what have you done to Flo'rance? When I asked you to keep him tied up, I didn't mean to tie him up.
(ADMONIA *gives her the letter opener.*)
LALA: Why are you giving me this? I have no letters to open. I'm in the middle of my American debut. Admonia, take Flo'rance off this stage with you! Admonia!
(ADMONIA *is gone.* LALA *turns to the audience and tries to make the best of it.*)
LALA: That was Admonia, my slightly overweight black maid, and this is Flo'rance, my amour. I remember how we met, don't you Flo'rance. I was sitting in a cafè on the Left Bank, when I looked up and saw the most beautiful man staring down at me.

"Who are you," he asked. I told him my name…whatever my name was back then. Yes, I told him my name and he said, "No, that cannot be your name. Your name should dance the way your eyes dance and your lips dance. Your name should fly, like Lala." And the rest is la history.

Flo'rance molded me into the woman I am today. He is my Svengali, my reality, my all. And I thought I was all to him, until we came here to America, and he fucked that bitch. Yeah, you fucked 'em all. Anything black and breathing. And all this time, I thought you loved me for being me. (*She holds the letter opener to his neck.*)

Well, you may think you made me, but I'll have you know I was who I was, whoever that was, long before you made me what I am. So there! (*She stabs him and breaks into song.*)

OH, LOVE CAN DRIVE A WOMAN TO
MADNESS
TO PAIN AND SADNESS
I KNOW
BELIEVE ME I KNOW
I KNOW
I KNOW
(LALA *sees what she's done and is about to scream but catches herself and tries to play it off.*)
LALA: Moving right along.
(ADMONIA *enters with a telegram on a tray.*)
ADMONIA: Pst.
LALA: (*Anxious/hostile*) What is it now?
(ADMONIA *hands* LALA *a telegram.*)
LALA: (*Excited*) Oh, la telegram from one of my fans and the concert isn't even over yet. Get me the letter opener. It's in Flo'rance.
(ADMONIA *hands* LALA *the letter opener.*)
LALA: Next I am going to do for you my immortal hit song, "The Girl Inside." But first we open the telegram. (*She quickly reads it and is outraged.*) What! Which pig in la audience wrote this trash? (*Reading*) "Dear Sadie, I'm so proud. The show's wonderful, but talk less and sing more. Love, Mama."

First off, no one calls me Sadie. Sadie died the day Lala was born. And secondly, my Mama's dead. Anyone who knows anything about Lala Lamazing Grace knows that my mother and Josephine Baker were French patriots together. They infiltrated a carnival rumored to be the center of Nazi intelligence, disguised as Hottentot Siamese twins. You may laugh but it's true. Mama died a heroine. It's all in my autobiography, "Voila Lala!" So whoever sent this telegram is a liar!
(ADMONIA *promptly presents her with another telegram.*)

LALA: No doubt an apology. (*Reading*) "Dear Sadie, I'm not dead. P.S. Your child misses you." What? (*She squares off at the audience.*) Well, now, that does it! If you are my mother, which you are not. And this alleged child is my child, then that would mean I am a mother and I have never given birth. I don't know nothin' 'bout birthin' no babies! (*She laughs.*) Lala made a funny.

So whoever sent this, show me the child! Show me!
(ADMONIA *offers another telegram.*)

LALA: (*To* ADMONIA) You know you're gonna get fired! (*She reluctantly opens it.*) "The child is in the closet." What closet?

ADMONIA: Pst.
(ADMONIA *pushes a button and the center wall unit revolves around to reveal a large black door.* ADMONIA *exits, taking* FLO'RANCE *with her, leaving* LALA *alone.*)

LALA: (*Laughing*) I get it. It's a plot, isn't it. A nasty little CIA, FBI kind of plot. Well let me tell you muthafuckers one thing, there is nothing in that closet, real or manufactured, that will be a dimmer to the glimmer of Lamé the star. You may have gotten Billie and Bessie and a little piece of everyone else who's come along since, but you won't get Lala. My clothes are too fabulous! My hair is too long! My accent too French. That's why I came home to America. To prove you ain't got nothing on me!
(*The music for her next song starts, but* LALA *is caught up in her tirade, and talks/screams over the music.*)

My mother and Josephine Baker were French patriots together! I've had brunch with the Pope! I've dined with the Queen! Everywhere I go I cause riots! Hunny, I am a star! I have transcended pain! So there! (*Yelling*) Stop the music! Stop that goddamn music.
(*The music stops.* LALA *slowly walks downstage and singles out someone in the audience.*)

Darling, you're not looking at me. You're staring at that damn door. Did you pay to stare at some fucking door or be mesmerized by my talent?
(*To the whole audience:*)

Very well! I guess I am going to have to go to the closet door, fling it open, in order to dispel all the nasty little thoughts these nasty little telegrams have planted in your nasty little minds. (*Speaking directly to someone in the audience.*) Do you want me to open the closet door? Speak up, darling, this is live. (*Once she gets the person to say "yes."*) I will open the door, but before I do, let me tell you bastards one last thing. To hell with coming home and to hell with lies and insinuations! (LALA *goes into the closet and after a short pause comes running out, ready to scream, and slams the door. Traumatized to the point of no return, she tells the following story as if it were a jazz solo of rushing, shifting emotions.*)

LALA: I must tell you this dream I had last night. Simply magnifique. In this dream, I'm running naked in Sammy Davis Junior's hair. (*Crazed laughter*)

Yes! I'm caught in this larger than life, deep, dark forest of savage, nappy-nappy hair. The kinky-kinks are choking me, wrapped around my naked arms, thighs, breast, face. I can't breathe. And there was nothing in that closet!

And I'm thinking if only I has a machete, I could cut away the kinks. Remove once and for all the roughness. But then I look up and it's coming toward me. Flowing like lava. It's pomade! Ohhh, Sammy!

Yes, cakes and cakes of pomade. Making everything nice and white and smooth and shiny, like my black/white/black/white/black behiney.

Mama no!

And then spikes start cutting through the pomade. Combing the coated kink. Cutting through the kink, into me. There are bloodlines on my back. On my thighs.

It's all over. All over...all over me. All over for me.

(LALA *accidentially pulls off her wig to reveal her real hair. Stripped of her "disguise" she recoils like a scared little girl and sings.*)

MOMMY AND DADDY
MEET AND MATE
THE CHILD THAT'S BORN
IS TORN WITH LOVE AND WITH HATE
SHE RUNS AWAY TO FIND HER OWN
AND TRIES TO DENY
WHAT SHE'S ALWAYS KNOWN
THE GIRL INSIDE

(*The closet door opens.* LALA *runs away, and a* LITTLE BLACK GIRL *emerges from the closet. Standing behind her is* ADMONIA.)

(*The* LITTLE GIRL *and* LALA *are in two isolated pools of light, and mirror each other's moves until* LALA *reaches past her reflection and the* LITTLE GIRL *comes to* LALA *and they hug.* ADMONIA *then joins them as* LALA *sings. Music underscored.*)

LALA:
WHAT'S LEFT IS THE GIRL INSIDE
THE GIRL WHO DIED
SO A NEW GIRL COULD BE BORN
SLOW FADE TO BLACK

PERMUTATIONS

(*Lights up on* NORMAL JEAN REYNOLDS. *She is very Southern/country and very young. She wears a simple faded print dress and her hair, slightly mussed, is in plaits. She sits, her dress covering a large oval object.*)

NORMAL: My mama used to say, God made the exceptional, then God made the special and when God got bored, he made me. 'Course she don't say too much of nuthin' no more, not since I lay me this egg.
(*She lifts her dress to uncover a large, white egg laying between her legs.*)

Ya see it all got started when I had me sexual relations with the garbage man. Ooowee, did he smell.

No, not bad. No! He smelled of all the good things folks never shoulda thrown away. His sweat was like cantaloupe juice. His

neck was like a ripe-red strawberry. And the water that fell from his eyes was like a deep, dark, juicy-juicy grape. I tell ya, it was like fuckin' a fruit salad, only I didn't spit out the seeds. I kept them here, deep inside. And three days later, my belly commence to swell, real big like.

Well my mama locked me off in some dark room, refusin' to let me see light of day 'cause, "What would the neighbors think." At first I cried a lot, but then I grew used to livin' my days in the dark, and my nights in the dark…(*She hums.*) And then it wasn't but a week or so later, my mama off at church, that I got this hurtin' feelin' down here. Worse than anything I'd ever known. And then I started bleedin', real bad. I mean there was blood everywhere. And the pain had me howlin' like a near-dead dog. I tell ya, I was yellin' so loud, I couldn't even hear myself. Noooooooo! Noooooo! Carrying on something like that.

And I guess it was just too much for the body to take, 'cause the next thing I remember…is me coming to and there's this big white egg layin' 'tween my legs. First I thought somebody musta put it there as some kind of joke. But then I noticed that all 'round this egg were thin lines of blood that I could trace to back between my legs.

(*Laughing*) Well, when my mama come home from church she just about died. "Normal Jean, what's that thing 'tween your legs? Normal Jean, you answer me, girl!" It's not a thing, Mama. It's an egg. And I laid it.

She tried separatin' me from it, but I wasn't havin' it. I stayed in that dark room, huggin', holdin' onto it.

And then I heard it. It wasn't anything that coulda been heard 'round the world, or even in the next room. It was kinda like layin' back in the bath tub, ya know, the water just coverin' your ears…and if you lay real still and listen real close, you can hear the sound of your heart movin' the water. You ever done that? Well that's what it sounded like. A heart movin' water. And it was happenin' inside here.

Why, I'm the only person I know who ever lay themselves an egg before so that makes me special. You hear that, Mama? I'm special and so's my egg! And special things supposed to be treated like they matter. That's why everynight I count to it, so it knows nuthin' never really ends. And I sing it every song I know so that when it comes out, it's full of all kinds of feelings. And I tell it secrets and laugh with it and… (*She suddenly stops and puts her ear to the egg and listens intently.*)

Oh! I don't believe it! I thought I heard…yes! (*Excited*) Can you hear it? Instead of one heart, there's two. Two little hearts just pattering away. Boom-boom-boom. Boom-boom-boom. Talkin' to each other like old friends. Racin' toward the beginnin' of their lives.

(*Listening*) Oh, no, now there's three…four …five, six. More hearts than I can count. And they're all alive, beatin' out life inside my egg.
(*We begin to hear the heartbeats, drums, alive inside* NORMAL'S *egg.*)

Any day now, this egg is gonna crack open and what's gonna come out a be the likes of which nobody has ever seen. My babies! And their skin is gonna turn all kinds of shades in the sun and their hair a be growin' every which-a-way. And it won't matter and they won't care 'cause they know they are so rare and so special 'cause it's not everyday a bunch of babies break outta a white egg and start to live.

And nobody better not try and hurt my babies 'cause if they do, they gonna have to deal with me.

Yes, any day now, this shell's gonna crack and my babies are gonna fly. Fly! Fly! (*She laughs at the thought, but then stops and says*

the word as if it's the most natural thing in the world.)

Fly.

BLACKOUT

THE PARTY

(*Before we know what's hit us, a hurricane of energy comes bounding into the space. It is* TOPSY WASHINGTON. *Her hair and dress are a series of stylistic contradictions which are hip, black, and unencumbered.*)

(*Music, spiritual and funky, underscores.*)

TOPSY: (*Dancing about.*) Yoho! Party! Party! Turn up the music! Turn up the music!

Have yaw ever been to a party where there was one fool in the middle of the room, dancing harder and yelling louder than everybody in the entire place. Well, hunny, that fool was me!

Yes, child! The name is Topsy Washington and I love to party. As a matter of fact, when God created the world, on the seventh day, he didn't rest. No child, he partied. Yo-ho! Party! Yeah! Yeah!

But now let me tell you 'bout this function I went to the other night, way uptown. And baby when I say way uptown, I mean way-way-way-way-way-way-way-way uptown. Somewhere's between 125th Street and infinity.

Inside was the largest gathering of black/Negro/colored Americans you'd ever want to see. Over in one corner you got Nat Turner sippin' champagne out of Eartha Kitt's slipper. And over in another corner, Bert Williams and Malcom X was discussing existentialism as it relates to the shuffle-ball-change. Girl, Aunt Jemima and Angela Davis was in the kitchen sharing a plate of greens and just goin' off about South Africa.

And then Fats sat down and started to work them eighty-eights. And then Stevie joined in. And then Miles and Duke and Ella and

Jimi and Charlie and Sly and Lightin' and Count and Louie!

And then everybody joined in. I tell you all the children was just all up in there, dancing to the rhythm of one beat. Dancing to the rhythm of their own definition. Celebrating in their cultural madness.

And then the floor started to shake. And the walls started to move. And before anybody knew what was happening, the entire room lifted up off the ground. The whole place just took off and went flying through space—defying logic and limitations. Just a spinning and a spinning and a spinning until it disappeared inside of my head.

(TOPSY *stops dancing and regains her balance and begins to listen to the music in her head. Slowly we begin to hear it, too.*)

That's right, girl, there's a party goin' on inside of here. That's why when I walk down the street my hips just sashay all over the place. 'Cause I'm dancing to the music of the madness in me.

And whereas I used to jump into a rage anytime anybody tried to deny who I was, now all I got to do is give attitude, quicker than light, and then go on about the business of being me. 'Cause I'm dancing to the music of the madness in me.

(*As* TOPSY *continues to speak,* MISS ROJ, LALA, MISS PAT, *and* THE MAN *from SYMBIOSIS revolve on, frozen like soft sculptures.*)

TOPSY: And here, all this time I been thinking we gave up our drums. But, naw, we still got 'em. I know I got mine. They're here, in my speech, my walk, my hair, my God, my style, my smile, and my eyes. And everything I need to get over in this world, is inside here, connecting me to everybody and everything that's ever been.

So, hunny, don't waste your time trying to label or define me.

(*The sculptures slowly begin to come to "life" and they mirror/echo* TOPSY'S *words.*)

TOPSY/EVERYBODY: …'cause I'm not what I was ten years ago or ten minutes ago. I'm all of

that and then some. And whereas I can't live inside yesterday's pain, I can't live without it.

(*All of a sudden, madness erupts on the stage. The sculptures begin to speak all at once. Images of black/Negro/colored Americans begin to flash—images of them dancing past the madness, caught up in the madness, being lynched, rioting, partying, surviving. Mixed in with these images are all the characters from the exhibits. Through all of this* TOPSY *sings. It is a vocal and visual cacophony which builds and builds.*)

LALA: I must tell you about this dream I had last night. Simply magnifique. In this dream I'm running naked in Sammy Davis Junior's hair. Yes. I'm caught in this larger-than-life, deep, dark tangled forest of savage, nappy-nappy hair. Yes, the kinky kinks are choking me, are wrapped around my naked arms, my naked thighs, breast, and face, and I can't breathe and there was nothing in that closet.

MISS ROJ: Snap for every time you walk past someone lying in the street smelling like frozen piss and shit and you don't see it. Snap for every crazed bastard who kills himself so as to get the jump on being killed. And snap for every sick muthafucker who, bored with carrying about his fear, takes to shooting up other people.

THE MAN: I have no history. I have no past. I can't. It's too much. It's much too much. I must be able to smile on cue and watch the news with an impersonal eye. I have no stake in the madness. Being black is too emotionally taxing, therefore I will be black only on weekends and holidays.

MISS PAT: Stop playing those drums. I said stop playing those damn drums. You can't stop history. You can't stop time. Those drums will be confiscated once we reach Savannah, so give them up now. Repeat after me: I don't hear any drums and I will not rebel. I will not rebel.

TOPSY: (*Singing*)
THERE'S MADNESS IN ME
AND THAT MADNESS SETS ME FREE

THERE'S MADNESS IN ME
AND THAT MADNESS SETS ME FREE
THERE'S MADNESS IN ME
AND THAT MADNESS SETS ME FREE
THERE'S MADNESS IN ME
AND THAT MADNESS SETS ME FREE
THERE'S MADNESS IN ME
AND THAT MADNESS SETS ME FREE

TOPSY: My power is in my...

EVERYBODY: Madness!

TOPSY: And my colored contradictions.

(*The sculptures freeze with a smile on their faces as we hear the voice of* MISS PAT.)

VOICE OF MISS PAT: Before exiting, check the overhead as any baggage you don't claim, we trash.

BLACKOUT

PERFORMING *THE COLORED MUSEUM*

The award-winning *The Colored Museum* established George C. Wolfe as a new, distinctive voice in the American theater. First produced at the Crossroads Theater (New Brunswick, New Jersey) in 1986 and directed by L. Kenneth Richardson, the play was performed without intermission. *The Colored Museum* had its New York premiere at the New York Shakespeare Festival the following year with Loretta Devine and Reggie Montgomery and played for seventy-seven performances.

Since the late eighties, *The Colored Museum* has received productions at Center Stage (Baltimore), the Denver Center Theater, the Detroit Repertory Theater, and the Yale Repertory Theatre. The play won the regional theater award given by the Foundation of the Dramatists' Guild/CBS New Plays Program and in 1987 Wolfe received the *Village Voice* "Obie" award for best new play.

George C. Wolfe was praised for his satire that tore at the "very fabric of racist America." The centerpiece of the ninety-minute entertainment was the sketch titled "The Last Mama-on-the-Couch," which parodied Lorraine Hansberry's 1959 breakthrough play *A Raisin in the Sun*. Wolfe not only mocks the tradition of the well-made domestic drama but he holds up for ridicule black theater and its performers (blamed on the Juilliard School of Drama and its actor-training) heavy with "300 years of oppression." The revue-like sketches that comprise *The Colored Museum* are set in an antiseptic modern museum where eleven exhibits displaying "colored" history are brought into view on a turntable. The exhibits range from contemporary African Americans to Ebony magazine fashion models to a woman named Topsy Washington who imagines a blow-out party somewhere between 125th Street in Harlem to "infinity." As her fantasy incorporates African American jazz greats, civil rights activists, and notable writers, Topsy decides to put her rage behind her and celebrate her "madness and colored contradictions." The revolt belongs not so much to Topsy but to George C. Wolfe's fearless humor and satire that liberates but not fully banishes the baggage of slavery, racism, and angst from American culture.

CRITICS' NOTEBOOK

George C. Wolfe is primarily a producer and artistic director of one of the leading nonprofit institutions in the United States: the New York Shakespeare Festival/Joseph Papp Public Theater. He is notable for his staging of *Angels in America, Jelly's Last Jam, Bring in da Noise, Bring in da Funk,* and *Topdog/Underdog* on Broadway. His early play, *The Colored Museum,* established his reputation as a playwright. Its farcical and satirical elements set the play apart from the more realistic writing of Lorraine Hansberry and August Wilson in *A Raisin in the Sun* and *Fences.*

Eric Bentley's insightful analysis of farce remains a classic essay found in *Let's Get a Divorce! And Other Modern Plays,* which indirectly illuminates Wolfe's approach to his material in *The Colored Museum.*

Furthermore, Wolfe's comments on the play in an interview with David Savran provide interesting insights into the workings of his creative imagination.

Eric Bentley from "The Psychology of Farce"*

❦

Ideally a compendium of exact information and intelligent opinion, an encyclopedia addresses itself, in fact, to the codification of current prejudices. The article on farce in the only encyclopedia of theatre in our language starts out this way:

> *Farce*, an extreme form of comedy in which laughter is raised at the expense of probability, particularly by horseplay and bodily assault. It must, however, retain its hold on humanity, even if only in depicting the grosser faults of mankind; otherwise it degenerates into travesty and burlesque.

After remarking, *en passant*, that farce died out before Molière, the writer winds round to this conclusion:

> In modern usage, the word farce is applied to a full-length play dealing with some absurd situation hingeing generally on extra-marital relations—hence the term bedroom farce. Farce has small literary merit, but great entertainment value, and owing to its lack of subtlety can be translated from one language to another more easily than comedy....

ⅈ ⅈ ⅈ

The function of "farcical" fantasies, in dreams or in plays, is not as provocation but as compensation. The violent release is comparable to the sudden relieving hiss of steam through a safety valve. Certainly, the mental energies involved are destructive, and in all comedy there remains something of destructive orgy, farce being the kind of comedy which disguises that fact least thoroughly. But the function of orgies is also that of a safety valve. An orgy—as still practiced in the Munich Carnival, for example—is an essentially temporary truancy from the family

pieties, and, like farces, if it has any appreciable effect at all, it helps those pieties to go on existing. The main point of Freud's *Civilization and its Discontents* is pertinent here: when we buy civilization, as we do, at the price of frustration, the frustrated impulses become a potential source of trouble. The pressures are enormous and perpetual. We ought to welcome any relief from them, however slight or trivial, provided it is harmless. Dreams are the commonest relief but are usually unpleasant. The most pleasurable relief is to be found in the arts, for one of which I am staking out a claim in this essay.

ⅈ ⅈ ⅈ

Farce in general enables us, seated in dark security, to enjoy the delights of complete passivity while watching on stage the most violently active creatures ever imagined by man. In that particular application of the general formula which is bedroom farce, we enjoy the adventure of adultery, ingeniously exaggerated to the nth degree, without incurring the responsibilities or suffering the guilt, without even the hint of an affront to the wife at our side....

ⅈ ⅈ ⅈ

There are two wrong ways of playing the indirectness of farce: the amateur way and the professional way. The amateur's failure is more or less total. He lacks the art to create a mask of actuality (normality, gravity, sophistication) and, as for the life beneath, he hasn't an inkling how to get at it or, perhaps even, that it is there to be got at. He concludes that, since farce is very energetic, he should bound about, and that, since it is very funny, he should be facetious; and so his furious efforts end in vacuity.

The professional is wiser. He knows he has no such weapon in his armory as funniness. He knows that being funny is a result, and that what God gave him is fantasy; and he uses this fantasy to create a mask. Professional productions of farce tend to be plausible, even elegant, but it is the habit of the professional to neglect the face beneath the mask. Though smooth, his work is hollow. There have been productions of *The Importance of Being Earnest* in which the man-

*Eric Bentley from "The Psychology of Farce" in *Let's Get a Divorce! and Other Modern Plays* (New York: Hill and Wang, 1958): vii–xvii.

ner of an upper class was very accurately rendered in voice and gesture but in which one had
no feeling of the inordinate aggression of Wilde
against Victorian civilization, if not against all
civilization.

David Savran's Interview with George C. Wolfe (August 12, 1998)*

❦

…And Americans love to create romance. White
Americans do it about Europe, you know, and
black people create this fantasy Africa that never
existed. Extraordinary Africas did exist, but not
this fantasy Africa that black Americans walk
around with. The Americans are their own sort
of bizarre creation. If you search for purity and
you're not pure, you're either going to function
from a place of delusion or inadequacy. Whereas
if you go searching for your own complexity, it's
going to be a much more fulfilling solution. So to
me that's been the goal: to try as a human being
not to choose this quality over that quality, but
to try to embrace all of them. That's so much
what The Colored Museum was all about, "I'm not
what I was ten years ago or ten minutes ago, I'm
all of that and then some."

When I first came to New York, people were
very confused by various projects that I was
writing. Because here I was this black writer
writing in all these different forms, and most of
the plays that were being done for black audiences were these socioeconomic, realistic, "Last
Mama-on-the-Couch" plays. Which was one of
the reasons I went after that. My imagination
does not work that way. It doesn't fit inside of
four walls, it just doesn't, and it never will. So I
wrote The Colored Museum not just as a person of
color, but as a form of liberation, so that after I
wrote that play, I said, "Now I can write any
play." It's why it experiments with form as much
as it does, why it collides images, to become

*David Savran, "George C. Wolfe," in The Playwrights'
Voice: American Dramatists on Memory, Writing and the
Politics of Culture (New York: Theatre Communications
Group, 1999): 347–348.

some sort of treatise in which I can say, "As a person who creates theatre, I'm going to function
completely by my own rules. I will not be placed
in a category, I will not be forced to write 'Mama,
I'm cryin' 'cause I got so much pain.'" That was
my way of freeing myself, of standing naked in
the middle of Times Square going, "This is it."

REVISITING FARCE AND SATIRE

Farce and satire have entertained theater audiences for centuries. While they are both sub-
forms of comedy and often appear as separate
forms of writing, there are elements of both
found in most comedies ranging from Ben Jonson's Volpone to Michael Frayn's Noises Off.

Farce is a clever, physical variation on humorous activities growing out of social situations. Nonetheless, farce, like comedy, has its
serious side. According to modern critics, farce
expresses our darkest secrets and fantasies
(whether personal or social) such as the license
to insult our mother-in-law or defeat the school-
yard bully by acquiring a magical prowess or to
assimilate into other cultures or even to acquire
a new identity with attitude. As Topsy Washington sings optimistically of the "power in her
madness and in her colored contradictions," she
embodies the fantasies and contradictions that
farce best exemplifies in its knock-about antics.
In addition, there are elements of satire and parody in The Colored Museum as well. Through the
staging of the eleven vignettes as a parody of
the museum experience where we give serious
contemplation to works of art, George C. Wolfe,
the satirist, demands our moral scrutiny in the
reexamination of African-American history and
literature.

In modern times, farce and satire have
achieved unlooked-for complexities. Satire has
become a vehicle whereby to examine the effi-
cacy of modern government and politicians
with an underlying seriousness that rivals the
editorial pages of our leading newspapers. In
turn, farce has expressed the endless variations
on an absurd existence without purpose or
meaning, or it has taken on the absurdities of
the historical process, or it has tackled the icons

of the dominant popular culture to test ideas within a theatrical form that permits variations on social history without harm or reprisal.

Unlike farce and satire, tragicomedy is not a subform of comedy. Writers of tragicomedy blend ideas, moods, and elements of tragedy *and* comedy in the creation of a third mode of writing, dominant for the second half of the twentieth century.

NOTES

1. John Mortimer, *Georges Feydeau: Three Boulevard Farces* (New York: Viking Penguin, Inc., 1985): 9.

2. Eric Bentley, "Farce," *The Life of the Drama* (New York: Atheneum, 1964): 219–256.

3. Eric Bentley, "The Psychology of Farce," *Let's Get a Divorce! and Other Modern Plays* (New York: Hill and Wang, 1958): vii–xx.

4. Sigmund Freud, *Jokes and Their Relation to the Unconscious*, trans. James Strachey (New York: W. W. Norton, 1963): 170–173.

5. Jessica Milner Davis, *Farce* (London: Methuen & Company, 1978): 97.

6. Eugene Ionesco, *Notes and Counter Notes*, trans. Donald Watson (London: John Calder Publishers, 1964): 26.

7. Janice C. Simpson, "A Jam Session with George C. Wolfe," *TheaterWeek* (October 26, 1992): 18–20.

8. *TheaterWeek* 20–21.

CHAPTER 8

TRAGICOMEDY AND NEW FORMS

Ellen McLaughlin as The Angel and Stephen Spinella as Prior Walter in *Angels in America, Part One: Millennium Approaches* by Tony Kushner, directed by George C. Wolfe, Broadway, 1993. (Photo © Joan Marcus.)

> Mercury: *What's that? Are you disappointed*
> *To find it's a tragedy? Well, I can easily change it.*
> *I'm a god after all. I can easily make it a comedy,*
> *And never alter a line. Is that what you'd like?...*
> *But I was forgetting—stupid of me—of course,*
> *Being a god, I know quite well what you'd like.*
> *I know exactly what's in your minds. Very well.*
> *I'll meet you half way, and make it a* tragicomedy.
> —Plautus, *Amphitryon*

THE MIXED GENRE

Mixed forms of drama were first popularized in the Roman theater, especially by the playwright Plautus who invented the term *tragicomedy* (*tragicocomoedia*) to describe his play *Amphitryon* about serious events that, through extreme plot twists, ended happily. Even though Plautus coined the term around 186 B.C., tragic plays with happy endings (Euripides' *Helen,* for example) were not called tragicomedies until the Renaissance when Italian playwrights turned to literary critics to justify their mixed form. They used such labels as "mixed plays" for tragedies with happy endings.

The popular drama in medieval times, such as the serio-comic *Second Shepherd's Play,* was often unlabeled as well. In the English Renaissance, Latin school plays, based largely on the writings of Plautus and Terence, mixed serious main plots with comic subplots and prepared the way for the rich mixture of serious and comic elements that informed the plays of William Shakespeare.

Up to the end of the seventeenth century in England and Europe, *tragicomedy* was defined as a mixture of tragedy, which went from good fortune to bad, and comedy, which reversed the order from bad fortune to good mid-way in the play. Combining serious and comic incidents, tragicomedy mixed styles, subject matter, high- and low-born characters, and language proper to tragedy and to comedy. The *ending* (up to the nineteenth century) was its principal feature: tragicomedies were potentially tragic plays with happy endings, or at least averted catastrophes. Among the many English and European play-wrights popularizing the mixed form were William Shakespeare, Thomas Heywood, John Marston, Pierre Corneille, Lope de Vega, and Tirso de Molina. Shakespeare's late plays, *Measure for Measure, Cymbeline, All's Well That Ends Well,* and *The Winter's Tale,* are some of the finest examples of the mixed form.

In the nineteenth century, melodrama (a drama with music) sounded notes of comedy with peripheral comic characters that helped the hero defeat the villain. With the advent of realism in the late nineteenth century, serious social issues overwhelmed but not wholly concealed comic elements largely based on class differences. As they set about dramatizing contradictions within the realistic world, August Strindberg, Henrik Ibsen, George Bernard Shaw, Anton Chekhov, and Luigi Pirandello predate the absurdist writers who defined "modern" tragicomedy in the mid-twentieth century as existential comedy of absurdist situations with indeterminate endings.[1]

MODERN TRAGICOMEDY

The term *modern tragicomedy* has come to designate plays with mixed moods in which the endings are neither exclusively tragic nor comic. The Russian playwright Anton Chekhov wrote plays of mixed moods in which he described the quietly desperate lives of ordinary people in rural Russia around the turn of the century. His characters included provincial gentry, writers, doctors, servants, teachers, and government and military officials. The common denominator at the end of Chekhov's full-length plays, like *The Cherry*

Orchard, is humanity's survival; that is, despite death, misfortune, and change, life goes on.

George Bernard Shaw inclined more towards the comic rather than the tragic in such plays as *Mrs. Warren's Profession, Major Barbara, Pygmalion,* and *Heartbreak House.* "I deal," he argued in the preface to *Major Barbara,* "in the tragicomic irony of the conflict between real life and the romantic imagination."[2] In *Mrs. Warren's Profession* (her profession has been that Victorian unmentionable word *prostitution*), Shaw avoids either tragedy or comedy by having his central character neither conveniently kill herself nor repent and change her way of life. It falls to her daughter Vivie (and the audience) to probe beyond the characters and the play itself to the social, political, and economic issues of Shaw's theme: the confrontation of reality and idealism. Who wins? Who loses? It's a mixed bag, as moderns say.

Luigi Pirandello, writing in Italy during the first quarter of the twentieth century, expanded our understanding of tragicomedy. Pirandello developed his theory of humor in an essay entitled *On Humor* (1908) in which he argued that we could hold independent of one another a comic and tragic perspective of character, unhappy situation, and the world. Pirandello's plays are thereby built on shifting perspectives so that the audience is made to sympathize with the characters' situation and yet made aware of the absurdity of their predicament. To dramatize these ironies, Pirandello established contrasts between the stage world of a second-rate acting company and the sordid events of the fictional characters' lives in the inner play in *Six Characters in Search of an Author* (1921). In *Henry IV* (1922), he contrasted the compassionate self-constructed private world of Henry with the cruelties of the real world beyond his confines. The clash of viewpoints between the mad and the sane, the real and the fictive, is tragicomic in Pirandello's treatment.

Pirandello's tragicomic writing was a precursor to the new variety of mixed genre associated with the absurdists of the 1950s. Samuel Beckett subtitled *Waiting for Godot* a "tragicomedy." In this play from the 1950s, two tramps entertain themselves with comic routines while they wait in a sparse landscape for someone named Godot to arrive. But Godot never comes. As they react to this situation, humor and optimism are mixed with anguish and despair. In the modern form of tragicomedy, playwrights show people coping with their anxieties and life's contradictions with little impact on their unchanging situations. Beckett's Vladimir inadvertently describes the modern tragicomic form when he says of life, "The essential doesn't change."

Critic Martin Esslin pointed out that for centuries the kind of eternal principle for writing drama (deduced from Aristotle) demanded that drama imitate nature; that it have a plot with a beginning, a middle, and a solution; and that it have consistent characters throughout the action. Many of our finest modern writers have rebelled against this aesthetic, writing plays that lack plot and creating characters that lack consistency. In *Waiting for Godot,* Pozzo appears as a self-confident tyrant at one moment and as a blind and defeated man at another. Unlike Sophocles, Beckett offers no explanation for the change except the possibility that time has passed. Samuel Beckett and Harold Pinter have written plays that start without formal exposition and end without solution.

The old forms of drama, with logically constructed plots that start with the exposition of a problem (moral, social, or philosophical) and then proceed toward a solution, presuppose, according to Esslin, a world order that is rational and familiar to human beings.[3] Consistent characters suggest that individuals have something like an immutable essence from the cradle to the grave, and that the characters inhabit a world that is unchangeable as well. With the loss of intelligible purpose in the modern world and the disappearance of consistent character, serious drama no longer can develop along well-established formulas. "We now work with a much higher number of unknown factors," Esslin wrote, "and the certainty that there is no easy solution."

Historically, the writers of tragicomedy represented the first attack on accepted forms of writing for the theater. We now recognize that the attack on traditional dramatic forms was also an attack on their contents. As we examine the works of avant garde writers in this century—the absurdists and postmodernists—we discover the merging of form and content. As playwrights demonstrate the difficulties of communication between human beings and the inadequacy of language, they create their own conventions and new theatrical forms. The "form-smashers" of the contemporary theater, as Martin Esslin called them, must establish new ways of communicating with audiences. The absurdists—Samuel Beckett, Eugène Ionesco, Harold Pinter—substituted for plot, character, and discussion the presentation of a *sense of being*. Through the use of concrete stage images, they present the *tragicomic* absurdity of human existence. Esslin concluded that the "form-smashers are not form-smashers at all; rather they are explorers who penetrate into new fields and open up new vistas. Instead of destroyers of old forms they are the bringers of new contents."

The American tradition of writing tragicomedy, inherited from Henrik Ibsen and George Bernard Shaw, tended to dramatize contradictions in a realistic world. In the last decade of the twentieth century, contemporary playwrights expressed a tragicomic vision of the human condition with comic devices, which created tragicomedy that was amusing and serious without being foolish and superficial. In a remarkable departure in his two-part epic called *Angels in America: The Millennium Approaches* and *Perestroika*, Tony Kushner introduced into the American theater a variation on tragicomic writing that is neither Shavian nor absurdist. He has argued that all art is a form of activism because it has the potential to change the individual.[4] The transforming power of art is central to Kushner's poetic and moral vision of the human condition and to his theatrical writing.

Tragicomedy has always been a transformative style of writing for the theater where the serious and devastating can be transcended. The apocalyptic announcement at the close of *Angels in America: The Millennium Approaches*—"Greetings Prophet; The Great Work begins; The Messenger has arrived."—cancels out the indeterminate endings of absurdist drama. Kushner's dramaturgy thrusts the idea of social change into a transformative theater of people, politics, history, dreams, fantasies, and angelic hosts. *Angels in America* is a remarkable variation on tragicomic writing for postmodern times.

Angels in America
A Gay Fantasia on National Themes
Part One: Millennium Approaches

❦

TONY KUSHNER

Tony Kushner (b. 1956) has been called "a man for the millennium."[5] Born in Manhattan, he grew up as a star high-school debater in Lake Charles, Louisiana, where his father managed a lumber company that the family inherited. Kushner credits his love of music to his parents who were professional musicians and his passion for theater to his mother's performance as Linda Loman in a local production of Death of a Salesman *that he saw at an early age. He holds a B.A. degree from Columbia University, New York City, in medieval studies and an M.F.A. in directing from New York University where he studied with Carl Weber, a former assistant director to Bertolt Brecht at the Berliner Ensemble.*

A Bright Room Called Day *(1984–85), his first play about the collapse of the Left in Germany after the Weimar Republic and the rise of Fascism that followed, was written while he was a switchboard operator at the United Nations Plaza Hotel in midtown Manhattan. The play was produced by a group of actors (all working the same switchboard) who formed a company called Heat & Light. Artistic director Oskar Eustis saw the play and staged it again at the Eureka Theater in San Francisco in 1987. Eustis then invited Kushner to write a play for the company and applied for a grant from the National Endowment for the Arts. The grant was awarded and Kushner began writing* Angels in America *in 1988 at a moment when great political changes were taking place in Russia, Eastern Europe, and the United States. He described the play as being about "the end of containment as ideology"—applying the analogy to communism in Eastern Europe and to the AIDS crisis in the United States.[6]*

Following productions in California and London, the first part of Angels in America *(Millennium Approaches) reached Broadway in 1993 under the direction of George C. Wolfe. It won the Pulitzer Prize for Drama and four Tony awards, including one for the playwright. The second part (Perestroika) opened on Broadway in late 1993 and won Kushner a second Tony award for best play. Tony Kushner's reputation was established as a playwright who, some say, single-handedly rescued the American theater from numbing musical spectacles and superficial comedies and dramas.*

Kushner's considerable writing includes full-length plays, adaptations, one-acts, and libretti. Productions of Slavs! Thinking About the Longstanding Problems of Virtue and Happiness *(1995 OBIE award for Best Play) followed* Angels in America, *along with* Hydriotaphia, or The Death of Dr. Browne *and* Homebody/Kabul. *His adaptations include* A Dybbuk, or Between Two Worlds *(from S. Ansky),* Stella *(from Goethe),* The Good Person of Setzuan *(from Bertolt Brecht), and* The Illusion *(from Pierre Corneille). A collection of his essays and other writings is called* Thinking about the Longstanding Problem of Virtue and Happiness. *As a director, he has staged his own plays around the country and also works by Bertolt Brecht, Caryl Churchill, Naomi Wallace, and Ellen McLaughlin. His recent projects include the libretto for* Caroline or Change *with music by composer Jeanine Tesori, a children's book (Brundibar) with Maurice Sendak, and the film version of* Angels in America, *directed by Mike Nichols for HBO.*

CRITICAL INTRODUCTION TO
ANGELS IN AMERICA, PART ONE

Word was circulating in 1991–1992 among members of the national theater community that an extraordinary, epic-length play was being developed by a new playwright whose name was Tony Kushner. By the time *Angels in America*, subtitled *A Gay Fantasia on National Themes*, reached Broadway in November of 1993, critics referred to it as a vast theatrical epic, an audacious tragicomedy, a miraculous play, and an authoritative achievement.[7] The seven-hour production, written in two parts, challenged and mesmerized audiences with its grand sweep of history, politics, sex, religion, society, and pandemic disease during the Reagan-Bush 80s.

Part One: Millennium Approaches, written in three acts, begins in the fall of 1985 with "bad news." By the end of that year in the United States, a mysterious disease, primarily afflicting gay men, had been detected by the medical profession and the Centers for Disease Control in Atlanta published a report on Kaposi's sarcoma and pneumocystic carinii. Following these alarming announcements, the U.S. government failed to earmark federal funding for AIDS (acquired immunodeficiency syndrome) research. Two years earlier, the Pasteur Institute in Paris had discovered the virus believed to be the cause of AIDS. After four years of a full-blown AIDS epidemic in the United States, Burroughs Wellcome Pharmaceutical Company and the National Cancer Institute confirmed that a drug called AZT was effective in combating the multiplication of the AIDS virus in infected T-cells, thus allowing a patient's immune system to recover somewhat. Against the protests of the National Cancer Institute, the pharmaceutical company was granted sole patent rights to produce and sell the drug, thus cutting off general public access to AZT.

In 1985, historical events converged. Mikhail Gorbachev became head of state in the Soviet Union, actor-celebrity Rock Hudson collapsed while undergoing treatment in Paris for the AIDS virus, and the Reagan administration finally responded to the national health crisis by increasing AIDS funding to $100,000 million. There were now on record 12,067 diagnosed cases of AIDS and 6,079 deaths.

The historical sweep of *Millennium Approaches* is specific to the tragedy that was sweeping the nation and the world in the mid-eighties, afflicting individuals, friends, lovers, politicians, and celebrities. The "bad news" of Act I that two central characters have AIDS becomes "in vitro" in the late winter (December to January 1985–1986) in Act II. Act III continues in January 1986 and has as its ambiguous subtitle "Not-Yet-Conscious, Forward Dawning."

Kushner's millennial work is at once cosmic and intimate. Political, social, historical, and religious analogies reverberate throughout the text as Kushner likens the march of gay people out of the closet in the mid-eighties to the European Jews migrating to America at the turn of the century and to Mormons in the nineteenth century crossing the plains of the American West. Hardship, courage, and determination characterized those migrations for religious and economic freedoms. Against the modern backdrop of historical change in the former Soviet Union and the looming Iran-Contra scandal of the Reagan administration, Kushner dramatizes the struggles between American conservatives and liberals over moral and social dilemmas in a broadly multicultural and democratic society.[8]

To dramatize these large themes, Kushner focuses on two couples (one gay and one nominally heterosexual) and on the machinations of the closeted right-wing, lawyer-politician Roy S. Cohn. In each couple, one partner abandons the other while in the political arena Roy Cohn is isolated in his rage and cynicism. Louis Ironson, a Jewish Leftist and word processor for the Second Circuit Court of Appeals, runs out on his AIDS-stricken lover Prior Walter, a Yankee WASP whose ancestors arrived on the *Mayflower* and whose body is being ravaged by the disease. The second couple is made up of husband and wife: Joe Pitt is an ambitious, conflicted Republican lawyer clerking in the Federal Court in Washington, D.C., and his long-suffering wife Harper is addicted to Valium. Once Joe's homosexual longings overpower his strict Mormon credo, he deserts his wife. The personal crisis brings his Mormon mother, Hannah Pitt, to New York City searching for her "lost" son. The lives, dreams, and hallucinations of the central characters become interlaced in subsequent scenes in both *Millennium Approaches* and *Perestroika*.

The scoundrel of the piece and Shakespearean-size villain, Roy S. Cohn, was historically the notorious legal counsel (and accomplice) to Senator Joseph R. McCarthy and his Senate investigative subcommittee in the early 1950s, who waged a national witch-hunt for suspected Communists in the government and the entertainment industry. It is a known fact that Roy Cohn held illegal conferences with the judge during the trials of Ethel and Julius Rosenberg for treason, after which they were found guilty and executed. Despite his many protestations, he was a closeted homosexual who died of AIDS in August of 1986. Tony Kushner admits that for the purposes of the play, the character of Roy Cohn is a work of dramatic fiction.[9]

Kushner's audacious dramaturgy freely mixes realistic scenes with appearances by historical figures in new contexts. There are also scenes made up of dreams and hallucinations. The *fantasia* of the subtitle refers to the nonlinear structure of the theatrical epic and allows for the shifting relationships among the characters. The righteous Mormon mother, Hannah Pitt, becomes Prior Walter's best friend; Belize, an African-American drag queen and an earlier lover of Prior Walter, becomes Roy Cohn's nurse; Joe Pitt has an affair with Louis, who eventually rejects him; the ghost of Ethel Rosenberg returns to say Kaddish (the Jewish prayer for the dead) over Roy Cohn's body; and the somersaulting angel badgers Prior Walter into assuming the prophet's mantle, which he casts off for a secular one at the end of *Perestroika*.

The two parts of *Angels in America* begin in the mode of tragedy in *Millennium Approaches* and move toward a darkly comic resolution in *Perestroika*. It's a pattern of large dramatic writing that we have seen in Aeschylus' *Oresteia*, which moves from Agamemnon's brutal death at the hands of Clytemnestra and her lover to the wrathful vengeance of the Furies to Orestes' re-

lease from the painful cycle of vengeance through the ministrations of the goddess Athena. Not unlike the *Oresteia*, Part One of Kushner's play is a tragedy of political and celestial proportions. There is a collective breakdown: individuals flee their responsibilities, governments neglect their citizens, a plague is scorching the earth, and God has been absent from heaven since April 18, 1906, the day of the great San Francisco earthquake. The dying, abandonments, betrayals, disappointments, chaos, and celestial visitations—all part of the tragic world of Part One—are brought to a crescendant moment when the angel crashes with an apocalyptic roar through the ceiling of Prior Walter's Manhattan apartment in a Steven Spielberg–like (Prior's words) annunciation:

> *Greetings, Prophet;*
> *The Great Work begins:*
> *The Messenger has arrived.*

Throughout history, angels have been the subject of theological debate as to their corporeal nature and sexuality. Kushner's angel is derived from Walter Benjamin's image of the angel of history blown forward by a great storm as she/he looks regretfully back at the debris of the age.[10] Prior Walter, suffering from AIDS and Louis's desertion, explains that angels "commemorate death" while holding out the hope of "a world without dying." These "angelic" and very human contradictions are woven throughout the play: despair and hope, abjection and deliverance, pain and ecstasy.

Among its many attributes, *Angels in America* is also a work of political theater armed with left-wing discourse on democracy and individualism, reason and progress. Kushner raises questions with audiences about democracy and the politics of difference in America: How do we reconcile differences of religion, politics, gender, race, and sexual orientation in a multicultural society? How do we establish justice for all? How do we as a society progress and effect social change for the good of all Americans?

To dramatize these questions, Kushner's body politic is represented by characters illustrating the contradictions of American life, including different religions and ethnicities, corrupt power brokers and minimum wage workers, dysfunctional couples and reconstituted families, and so on. The character types represent individuals struggling with identity and discrimination in contemporary American life. Finally, Kushner weaves into the mix the traditions of prophecy and transcendence in Western civilization related to sweeping social change and progress. As Janelle Reinelt points out, Kushner abandons as an answer the now bankrupt Marxism and produces instead a kind of liberal pluralism, or benign tolerance. She calls it "a promise but no program."[11] Nonetheless, David Savran in his celebrated essay on *Angels in America* explains the popularity of Kushner's discourse: "Like other apocalyptic discourses…the millennialism of *Angels* reassures an 'audience that knows it has lost control over events' not by enabling it to 'regain…control,' but by letting it know 'that history is nevertheless controlled by an underlying order and that it has a purpose that is nearing fulfillment.'"[12]

The first part of *Angels in America* ends on a note, as one critic says, of "luminous ambiguity."[13] Kushner has positioned his play in the traditions of Western dramatic literature usually associated with Aeschylus, Sophocles, Shakespeare, Brecht, and others. Parallels are found in the blindness/sight opposition with Prior Walter as a new kind of Teiresias, the blind prophet. Like Teiresias, Oedipus, and Gloucester, he is the emblem of the tragic subject who is blind to truth but once he loses his sight, he sees clearly. The character of Roy Cohn has been drawn in the press as a Shakespearean villain, namely a Richard III, and the political kingdom as the domain of Ronald Reagan and his minions. The focus on the presence/absence of God reminds us of the absurdist writing of Beckett, Ionesco, and Stoppard. Nonetheless, the tragic elements and serious literary echoes are offset by irony and parody. In the hospital Prior Walter quips in a Blanche DuBois moment that he has "always depended upon the kindness of strangers," and Hannah Pitt rebukes him with "That's

a stupid thing to say." As he experiences the blaze of triumphal music and rainbow lighting effects heralding the Angel's appearance, Prior Walter, even in his terror, ironizes: "*Very* Steven Spielberg." In addition, the familiar elements of Shakespeare's romantic comedies and problem plays that reverse the order of tragic occurrence into reconciliation are present in *Angels in America*. There are the ill-matched lovers, characters finding themselves in strange places, apparitions and ghosts, repentant lovers, word-plays (lesion/legion), low-comic jokes, and families reunited in new affiliations.[14]

Part Two: Perestroika (the Russian word for "rebuilding") takes place in January–February 1986, in heaven (or hell/purgatory), and four years later before the Bethesda Fountain located in New York City's Central Park. As Kushner's dramatic world spins forward, the entire universe of this vast play is redeemed not by prophets but by ordinary human "angels" in America who champion tolerance, compliance, forgiveness, grace, and hope. Louis sees "the whole world changing and moving ahead"; Harper envisions "…a kind of painful progress.… Longing for what we've left behind, and dreaming ahead"; and, beneath the commemorative fountain for Civil War dead, Prior Walter pronounces a benediction for humanity and the body politic: "We won't die secret deaths anymore. The world only spins forward. We will be citizens. The time has come.… The Great Work Begins."

Prior Walter's guarded optimism about the future has been, as James Fisher suggests, won though terrible personal ordeals and belief in the power of humanity to survive.[15] The final moments of *Perestroika* replicate Kushner's reading of British socialist and literary critic Raymond Williams's essay "Walking Backward into the Future," written in 1985.[16] Looking backward, Prior Walter has survived four years with the disease but the world spins forward with the living and he continues as one of those legions. Tony Kushner's sweeping play, finally, articulates his own positive theory of history and the condition of things.

Angels in America
A Gay Fantasia on National Themes
Part One: Millennium Approaches

THE CHARACTERS

ROY M. COHN, *a successful New York lawyer and unofficial power broker.*

JOSEPH PORTER PITT, *chief clerk for Justice Theodore Wilson of the Federal Court of Appeals, Second Circuit.*

HARPER AMATY PITT, *Joe's wife, an agoraphobic with a mild Valium addiction.*

LOUIS IRONSON, *a word processor working for the Second Circuit Court of Appeals.*

PRIOR WALTER, *Louis's boyfriend. Occasionally works as a club designer or caterer, otherwise lives very modestly but with great style off a small trust fund.*

HANNAH PORTER PITT, *Joe's mother, currently residing in Salt Lake City, living off her deceased husband's army pension.*

BELIZE, *a former drag queen and former lover of Prior's. A registered nurse. Belize's name was originally Norman Arriaga; Belize is a drag name that stuck.*

THE ANGEL, *four divine emanations, Fluor, Phosphor, Lumen and Candle; manifest in One: the Continental Principality of America. She has magnificent steel-gray wings.*

OTHER CHARACTERS IN PART ONE

RABBI ISIDOR CHEMELWITZ, *an orthodox Jewish rabbi, played by the actor playing Hannah.*

MR. LIES, *Harper's imaginary friend, a travel agent, who in style of dress and speech suggests a jazz musician; he always wears a large lapel badge emblazoned "IOTA" (The International Order of Travel Agents). He is played by the actor playing Belize.*

THE MAN IN THE PARK, *played by the actor playing Prior.*

THE VOICE, *the voice of The Angel.*

HENRY, *Roy's doctor, played by the actor playing Hannah.*

EMILY, *a nurse, played by the actor playing The Angel.*

MARTIN HELLER, *a Reagan Administration Justice Department flackman, played by the actor playing Harper.*

SISTER ELLA CHAPTER, *a Salt Lake City real-estate saleswoman, played by the actor playing The Angel.*

PRIOR 1, *the ghost of a dead Prior Walter from the 13th century, played by the actor playing Joe. He is a blunt, gloomy medieval farmer with a guttural Yorkshire accent.*

PRIOR 2, *the ghost of a dead Prior Walter from the 17th century, played by the actor playing Roy. He is a Londoner, sophisticated, with a High British accent.*

THE ESKIMO, *played by the actor playing Joe.*

THE WOMAN IN THE SOUTH BRONX, *played by the actor playing The Angel.*

ETHEL ROSENBERG, *played by the actor playing Hannah.*

PLAYWRIGHT'S NOTES

A DISCLAIMER: Roy M. Cohn, the character, is based on the late Roy M. Cohn (1927–1986), who was all too real; for the most part the acts attributed to the character Roy, such as his illegal conferences with Judge Kaufmann during the trial of Ethel Rosenberg, are to be found in the historical record. But this Roy is a work of dramatic fiction; his words are my invention, and liberties have been taken.

A NOTE ABOUT STAGING: The play benefits from a pared-down style of presentation, with minimal scenery and scene shifts done rapidly (no blackouts!), employing the cast as well as stagehands—which makes for an actor-driven event, as this must be. The moments of magic—the appearance and disappearance of Mr. Lies and the ghosts, the Book hallucination, and the ending— are to be fully realized, as bits of wonderful *theatrical* illusion—which means it's OK if the wires show, and maybe it's good that they do, but the magic should at the same time be thoroughly amazing.

In a murderous time
the heart breaks and breaks
and lives by breaking.
—Stanley Kunitz
"The Testing-Tree"

ACT ONE: BAD NEWS
October–November 1985

SCENE 1

The last days of October. Rabbi Isidor Chemelwitz alone onstage with a small coffin. It is a rough pine box with two wooden pegs, one at the foot and one at the head, holding the lid in place. A prayer shawl embroidered with a Star of David is draped over the lid, and by the head a yarzheit candle is burning

RABBI ISIDOR CHEMELWITZ: (*He speaks sonorously, with a heavy Eastern European accent, unapologetically consulting a sheet of notes for the family names*): Hello and good morning. I am Rabbi Isidor Chemelwitz of the Bronx Home for Aged Hebrews. We are here this morning to pay respects at the passing of Sarah Ironson, devoted wife of Benjamin Ironson, also deceased, loving and caring mother of her sons Morris, Abraham, and Samuel, and her daughters Esther and Rachel; beloved grandmother of Max,

Mark, Louis, Lisa, Maria…uh…Lesley, Angela, Doris, Luke and Eric. (*Looks more closely at paper*) Eric? This is a Jewish name? (*Shrugs*) Eric. A large and loving family. We assemble that we may mourn collectively this good and righteous woman.
(*He looks at the coffin*)
    This woman. I did not know this woman. I cannot accurately describe her attributes, nor do justice to her dimensions. She was…Well, in the Bronx Home of Aged Hebrews are many like this, the old, and to many I speak but not to be frank with this one. She preferred silence. So I do not know her and yet I know her. She was…
(*He touches the coffin*)
    …not a person but a whole kind of person, the ones who crossed the ocean, who brought with us to America the villages of Russia and Lithuania—and how we struggled, and how we fought, for the family, for the Jewish home, so that you would not grow up *here,* in this strange place, in the melting pot where nothing melted. Descendants of this immigrant woman, you do not grow up in America, you and your children and their children with the goyische names. You do not live in America. No such place exists. Your clay is the clay of some Litvak shtetl, your air the air of the steppes—because she carried the old world on her back across the ocean, in a boat, and she put it down on Grand Concourse Avenue, or in Flatbush, and she worked that earth into your bones, and you pass it to your children, this ancient, ancient culture and home.
(*Little pause*)
    You can never make that crossing that she made, for such Great Voyages in this world do not any more exist. But every day of your lives the miles that voyage between that place and this one you cross. Every day. You understand me? In you that journey is.
    So…
    She was the last of the Mohicans, this one was. Pretty soon…all the old will be dead.

SCENE 2

Same day. Roy and Joe in Roy's office. Roy at an impressive desk, bare except for a very elaborate phone system, rows and rows of flashing buttons which bleep and beep and whistle incessantly, making chaotic music underneath Roy's conversations. Joe is sitting, waiting. Roy conducts business with great energy, impatience and sensual abandon: gesticulating, shouting, cajoling, crooning, playing the phone, receiver and hold button with virtuosity and love.

ROY (*Hitting a button*): Hold. (*To Joe*) I wish I was an octopus, a fucking octopus. Eight loving arms and all those suckers. Know what I mean?

JOE: No, I...

ROY (*Gesturing to a deli platter of little sandwiches on his desk*): You want lunch?

JOE: No, that's OK really I just...

ROY (*Hitting a button*): Ailene? Roy Cohn. Now what kind of a greeting is...I thought we were friends, Ai.... Look Mrs. Soffer you don't have to get.... You're upset. You're yelling. You'll aggravate your condition, you shouldn't yell, you'll pop little blood vessels in your face if you yell.... No that was a joke, Mrs. Soffer, I was joking.... I already apologized sixteen times for that, Mrs. Soffer, you.... (*While she's fulminating. Roy covers the mouthpiece with his hand and talks to Joe*) This'll take a minute, *eat* already, what is this tasty sandwich here it's—(*He takes a bite of a sandwich*) Mmmmm, liver or some.... Here.

(*He pitches the sandwich to Joe, who catches it and returns it to the platter.*)

ROY (*Back to Mrs. Soffer*): Uh huh, uh huh.... No, I already told you, it wasn't a vacation, it was business, Mrs. Soffer, I have clients in Haiti, Mrs. Soffer, I...Listen, Ailene, YOU THINK I'M THE ONLY GODDAM LAWYER IN HISTORY EVER MISSED A COURT DATE? Don't make such a big fucking.... Hold. (*He hits the hold button*) You HAG!

JOE: If this is a bad time....

ROY: *Bad* time? This is a *good* time! (*Button*) Baby doll, get me.... Oh fuck, wait.... (*Button, button*) Hello? Yah. Sorry to keep you hold-ing, Judge Hollins, I.... Oh *Mrs.* Hollins, sorry dear deep voice you got. Enjoying your visit? (*Hand over mouthpiece again, to Joe*) She sounds like a truckdriver and he sounds like Kate Smith, very confusing. Nixon appointed him, all the geeks are Nixon appointees.... (*To Mrs. Hollins*) Yeah yeah right good so how many tickets dear? Seven. For what, *Cats, 42nd Street*, what? No you wouldn't like *La Cage*, trust me, I know. Oh for godsake.... Hold. (*Button, button*) Baby doll, seven for *Cats* or something, anything hard to get, I don't give a fuck what and neither will they. (*Button; to Joe*) You see *La Cage*?

JOE: No, I....

ROY: Fabulous. Best thing on Broadway. Maybe ever. (*Button*) Who? Aw, Jesus H. Christ, Harry, *no*, Harry, Judge John Francis Grimes, Manhattan Family Court. Do I have to do every goddam thing myself? *Touch* the bastard, Harry, and don't call me on this line again, I told you not to...

JOE (*Starting to get up*): Roy, uh, should I wait outside or...

ROY (*To Joe*): Oh sit. (*To Harry*) You hold. I pay you to hold fuck you Harry you jerk. (*Button*) Half-wit dick-brain. (*Instantly philosophical*) I see the universe, Joe, as a kind of sandstorm in outer space with winds of mega-hurricane velocity, but instead of grains of sand it's shards and splinters of glass. You ever feel that way? Ever have one of those days?

JOE: I'm not sure I....

ROY: So how's life in Appeals? How's the Judge?

JOE: He sends his best.

ROY: He's a good man. Loyal. Not the brightest man on the bench, but he has manners. And a nice head of silver hair.

JOE: He gives me a lot of responsibility.

ROY: Yeah, like writing his decisions and signing his name.

JOE: Well...

ROY: He's a nice guy. And you cover admirably.

JOE: Well, thanks, Roy, I...

ROY (*Button*): Yah? Who is *this*? Well who the fuck are *you*? Hold— (*Button*) Harry? Eighty-seven grand, something like that.

Fuck him. Eat me. New Jersey, chain of porno film stores in, uh, Weehawken. That's—Harry, that's the beauty of the law. (*Button*) So, baby doll, what? *Cats?* Bleah. (*Button*) *Cats!* It's about cats. Singing cats, you'll love it. Eight o'clock, the theatre's always at eight. (*Button*) Fucking tourists. (*Button, then to Joe*) Oh live a little, Joe, *eat* something for Christ sake—

JOE: Um, Roy, could you…

ROY: What? (*To Harry*) Hold a minute. (*Button*) Mrs. Soffer? Mrs.….(*Button*) God-fucking-dammit to hell, where is…

JOE (*Overlapping*): Roy, I'd really appreciate it if…

ROY (*Overlapping*): Well she was here a minute ago, baby doll, see if…
(*The phone starts making three different beeping sounds, all at once.*)

ROY (*Smashing buttons*): Jesus fuck this goddam thing…

JOE (*Overlapping*): I really wish you wouldn't…

ROY (*Overlapping*): Baby doll? Ring the Post get me Suzy see if…
(*The phone starts whistling loudly.*)

ROY: CHRIST!

JOE: *Roy.*

ROY (*Into receiver*): Hold. (*Button; to Joe*) What?

JOE: Could you please not take the Lord's name in vain?
(*Pause*)
    I'm sorry. But please. At least while I'm…

ROY (*Laughs, then*): Right. Sorry. Fuck.
    Only in America. (*Punches a button*) Baby doll, tell 'em all to fuck off. Tell 'em I died. You handle Mrs. Soffer. Tell her it's on the way. Tell her I'm schtupping the judge. I'll call her back. I *will* call her. I *know* how much I borrowed. She's got four hundred times that stuffed up her…. Yeah, tell her I said that. (*Button. The phone is silent*)
    So, Joe.

JOE: I'm sorry Roy, I just…

ROY: No no no no, principles count, I respect principles, I'm not religious but I like God and God likes me. Baptist, Catholic?

JOE: Mormon.

ROY: Mormon. Delectable. Absolutely. Only in America. So, Joe. Whattya think?

JOE: It's…well…

ROY: Crazy life.

JOE: Chaotic.

ROY: Well but God bless chaos. Right?

JOE: Ummm…

ROY: Huh. Mormons. I knew Mormons, in, um, Nevada.

JOE: Utah, mostly.

ROY: No, these Mormons were in Vegas.
    So. So, how'd you like to go to Washington and work for the Justice Department?

JOE: Sorry?

ROY: How'd you like to go to Washington and work for the Justice Department? All I gotta do is pick up the phone, talk to Ed, and you're in.

JOE: In…what, exactly?

ROY: Associate Assistant Something Big. Internal Affairs, heart of the woods, something nice with clout.

JOE: Ed…?

ROY: Meese. The Attorney General.

JOE: Oh.

ROY: I just have to pick up the phone…

JOE: I have to think.

ROY: Of course.
    (*Pause*)
    It's a great time to be in Washington, Joe.

JOE: Roy, it's incredibly exciting…

ROY: And it would mean something to me. You understand?
    (*Little pause.*)

JOE: I…can't say how much I appreciate this Roy, I'm sort of…well, stunned, I mean…. Thanks, Roy. But I have to give it some thought. I have to ask my wife.

ROY: Your wife. Of course.

JOE: But I really appreciate…

ROY: Of course. Talk to your wife.

SCENE 3

Later that day. Harper at home, alone. She is listening to the radio and talking to herself, as she often does. She speaks to the audience.

HARPER: People who are lonely, people left alone, sit talking nonsense to the air, imagining…beautiful systems dying, old fixed orders spiraling apart…

When you look at the ozone layer, from outside, from a spaceship, it looks like a pale blue halo, a gentle, shimmering aureole encircling the atmosphere encircling the earth. Thirty miles above our heads, a thin layer of three-atom oxygen molecules, product of photosynthesis, which explains the fussy vegetable preference for visible light, its rejection of darker rays and emanations. Danger from without. It's a kind of gift, from God, the crowning touch to the creation of the world: guardian angels, hands linked, make a spherical net, a blue-green nesting orb, a shell of safety for life itself. But everywhere, things are collapsing, lies surfacing, systems of defense giving way…. This is why, Joe, this is why I shouldn't be left alone.

(Little pause)

I'd like to go traveling. Leave you behind to worry. I'll send postcards with strange stamps and tantalizing messages on the back. "Later maybe." "Nevermore…"

(Mr. Lies, a travel agent, appears.)

HARPER: Oh! You startled me!

MR. LIES: Cash, check or credit card?

HARPER: I remember you. You're from Salt Lake. You sold us the plane tickets when we flew here. What are you doing in Brooklyn?

MR. LIES: You said you wanted to travel…

HARPER: And here you are. How thoughtful.

MR. LIES: Mr. Lies. Of the International Order of Travel Agents. We mobilize the globe, we set people adrift, we stir the populace and send nomads eddying across the planet. We are adepts of motion, acolytes of the flux. Cash, check or credit card. Name your destination.

HARPER: Antarctica, maybe. I want to see the hole in the ozone. I heard on the radio…

MR. LIES (He has a computer terminal in his briefcase): I can arrange a guided tour. Now?

HARPER: Soon. Maybe soon. I'm not safe here you see. Things aren't right with me. Weird stuff happens…

MR. LIES: Like?

HARPER: Well, like you, for instance. Just appearing. Or last week…well never mind.

People are like planets, you need a thick skin. Things get to me, Joe stays away and now…. Well look. My dreams are talking back to me.

MR. LIES: It's the price of rootlessness. Motion sickness. The only cure: to keep moving.

HARPER: I'm undecided. I feel…that something's going to give. It's 1985. Fifteen years till the third millennium. Maybe Christ will come again. Maybe seeds will be planted, maybe there'll be harvests then, maybe early figs to eat, maybe new life, maybe fresh blood, maybe companionship and love and protection, safety from what's outside, maybe the door will hold, or maybe…maybe the troubles will come, and the end will come, and the sky will collapse and there will be terrible rains and showers of poison light, or maybe my life is really fine, maybe Joe loves me and I'm only crazy thinking otherwise, or maybe not, maybe it's even worse than I know, maybe…I want to know, maybe I don't. The suspense, Mr. Lies, it's killing me.

MR. LIES: I suggest a vacation.

HARPER (Hearing something): That was the elevator. Oh God, I should fix myself up, I…. You have to go, you shouldn't be here…you aren't even real.

MR. LIES: Call me when you decide…

HARPER: Go!

(The Travel Agent vanishes as Joe enters.)

JOE: Buddy?

Buddy? Sorry I'm late. I was just…out. Walking. Are you mad?

HARPER: I got a little anxious.

JOE: Buddy kiss.

(They kiss.)

JOE: Nothing to get anxious about.

So. So how'd you like to move to Washington?

SCENE 4

Same day. Louis and Prior outside the funeral home, sitting on a bench, both dressed in funereal finery, *talking. The funeral service for Sarah Ironson has just concluded and Louis is about to leave for the cemetery.*

LOUIS: My grandmother actually saw Emma Goldman speak. In Yiddish. But all Grandma could remember was that she spoke well and wore a hat.

What a weird service. That rabbi…

PRIOR: A definite find. Get his number when you go to the graveyard. I want him to bury me.

LOUIS: Better head out there. Everyone gets to put dirt on the coffin once it's lowered in.

PRIOR: Oooh. Cemetery fun. Don't want to miss that.

LOUIS: It's an old Jewish custom to express love. Here, Grandma, have a shovelful. Latecomers run the risk of finding the grave completely filled.

She was pretty crazy. She was up there in that home for ten years, talking to herself. I never visited. She looked too much like my mother.

PRIOR (*Hugs him*): Poor Louis. I'm sorry your grandma is dead.

LOUIS: Tiny little coffin, huh?

Sorry I didn't introduce you to…. I always get so closety at these family things.

PRIOR: Butch. You get butch. (*Imitating*) "Hi Cousin Doris, you don't remember me I'm Lou, Rachel's boy." Lou, not Louis, because if you say Louis they'll hear the sibilant S.

LOUIS: I don't have a…

PRIOR: I don't blame you, hiding. Bloodlines. Jewish curses are the worst. I personally would dissolve if anyone ever looked me in the eye and said "Feh." Fortunately WASPs don't say "Feh." Oh and by the way, darling, cousin Doris is a dyke.

LOUIS: No.

Really?

PRIOR: You don't notice anything. If I hadn't spent the last four years fellating you I'd swear you were straight.

LOUIS: You're in a pissy mood. Cat still missing?

(*Little pause.*)

PRIOR: Not a furball in sight. It's your fault.

LOUIS: It is?

PRIOR: I warned you, Louis. Names are important. Call an animal "Little Sheba" and you can't expect it to stick around. Besides, it's a dog's name.

LOUIS: I wanted a dog in the first place, not a cat. He sprayed my books.

PRIOR: He was a female cat.

LOUIS: Cats are stupid, high-strung predators. Babylonians sealed them up in bricks. Dogs have brains.

PRIOR: Cats have intuition.

LOUIS: A sharp dog is as smart as a really dull two-year-old child.

PRIOR: Cats know when something's wrong.

LOUIS: Only if you stop feeding them.

PRIOR: They know. That's why Sheba left, because she knew.

LOUIS: Knew what?

(*Pause.*)

PRIOR: I did my best Shirley Booth this morning, floppy slippers, housecoat, curlers, can of Little Friskies; "Come back, Little Sheba, come back…." To no avail. Le chat, elle ne reviendra jamais, jamais…

(*He removes his jacket, rolls up his sleeve, shows Louis a dark purple spot on the underside of his arm near the shoulder*)

See.

LOUIS: That's just a burst blood vessel.

PRIOR: Not according to the best medical authorities.

LOUIS: What?

(*Pause*)

Tell me.

PRIOR: K.S., baby. Lesion number one. Lookit. The wine-dark kiss of the angel of death.

LOUIS (*Very softly, holding Prior's arm*): Oh please…

PRIOR: I'm a lesionnaire. The Foreign Lesion. The American Lesion. Lesionnaire's disease.

LOUIS: Stop.

PRIOR: My troubles are lesion.

LOUIS: Will you *stop*.

PRIOR: Don't you think I'm handling this well? I'm going to die.

LOUIS: Bullshit.

PRIOR: Let go of my arm.

LOUIS: No.

PRIOR: Let go.

LOUIS (*Grabbing Prior, embracing him ferociously*): No.

PRIOR: I can't find a way to spare you baby. No wall like the wall of hard scientific fact. K.S. Wham. Bang your head on that.

LOUIS: Fuck you. (*Letting go*) Fuck you fuck you fuck you.

PRIOR: Now that's what I like to hear. A mature reaction.

Let's go see if the cat's come home. Louis?

LOUIS: When did you find this?

PRIOR: I couldn't tell you.

LOUIS: Why?

PRIOR: I was scared, Lou.

LOUIS: Of what?

PRIOR: That you'll leave me.

LOUIS: Oh.

(*Little pause.*)

PRIOR: Bad timing, funeral and all, but I figured as long as we're on the subject of death…

LOUIS: I have to go bury my grandma.

PRIOR: Lou?

(*Pause*)

Then you'll come home?

LOUIS: Then I'll come home.

SCENE 5

Same day, later on. Split scene. Joe and Harper at home; Louis at the cemetery with Rabbi Isidor Chemelwitz and the little coffin.

HARPER: Washington?

JOE: It's an incredible honor, buddy, and…

HARPER: I have to think.

JOE: Of course.

HARPER: Say no.

JOE: You said you were going to think about it.

HARPER: I don't want to move to Washington.

JOE: Well I do.

HARPER: It's a giant cemetery, huge white graves and mausoleums everywhere.

JOE: We could live in Maryland. Or Georgetown.

HARPER: We're happy here.

JOE: That's not really true, buddy, we…

HARPER: Well happy enough! Pretend-happy. That's better than nothing.

JOE: It's time to make some changes, Harper.

HARPER: No changes. Why?

JOE: I've been chief clerk for four years. I make twenty-nine thousand dollars a year. That's ridiculous. I graduated fourth in my class and I make less than anyone I know. And I'm…I'm tired of being a clerk, I want to go where something good is happening.

HARPER: Nothing good happens in Washington. We'll forget church teachings and buy furniture at…at *Conran's* and become yuppies. I have too much to do here.

JOE: Like what?

HARPER: I *do* have things…

JOE: What things?

HARPER: I have to finish painting the bedroom.

JOE: You've been painting in there for over a year.

HARPER: I know, I…. It just isn't done because I never get time to finish it.

JOE: Oh that's…that doesn't make sense. You have all the time in the world. You could finish it when I'm at work.

HARPER: I'm afraid to go in there alone.

JOE: Afraid of what?

HARPER: I heard someone in there. Metal scraping on the wall. A man with a knife, maybe.

JOE: There's no one in the bedroom, Harper.

HARPER: Not now.

JOE: Not this morning either.

HARPER: How do you know? You were at work this morning. There's something creepy about this place. Remember *Rosemary's Baby*?

JOE: *Rosemary's Baby*?

HARPER: Our apartment looks like that one. Wasn't that apartment in Brooklyn?

JOE: No, it was…

HARPER: Well, it looked like this. It did.

JOE: Then let's move.

HARPER: Georgetown's worse. *The Exorcist* was in Georgetown.

JOE: The devil, everywhere you turn, huh, buddy.

HARPER: Yeah. Everywhere.

JOE: How many pills today, buddy?

HARPER: None. One. Three. Only three.

LOUIS (*Pointing at the coffin*): Why are there just two little wooden pegs holding the lid down?

RABBI ISIDOR CHEMELWITZ: So she can get out easier if she wants to.

LOUIS: I hope she stays put.

 I pretended for years that she was already dead. When they called to say she had died it was a surprise. I abandoned her.

RABBI ISIDOR CHEMELWITZ: "Sharfervi di tson fun a shlang iz an umdankbar kind!"

LOUIS: I don't speak Yiddish.

RABBI ISIDOR CHEMELWITZ: Sharper than the serpent's tooth is the ingratitude of children. Shakespeare. *Kenig Lear.*

LOUIS: Rabbi, what does the Holy Writ say about someone who abandons someone he loves at a time of great need?

RABBI ISIDOR CHEMELWITZ: Why would a person do such a thing?

LOUIS: Because he has to.

 Maybe because this person's sense of the world, that it will change for the better with struggle, maybe a person who has this neo-Hegelian positivist sense of constant historical progress towards happiness or perfection or something, who feels very powerful because he feels connected to these forces, moving uphill all the time... maybe that person can't, um, incorporate sickness into his sense of how things are supposed to go. Maybe vomit...and sores and disease...really frighten him, maybe... he isn't so good with death.

RABBI ISIDOR CHEMELWITZ: The Holy Scriptures have nothing to say about such a person.

LOUIS: Rabbi, I'm afraid of the crimes I may commit.

RABBI ISIDOR CHEMELWITZ: Please, mister. I'm a sick old rabbi facing a long drive home to the Bronx. You want to confess, better you should find a priest.

LOUIS: But I'm not a Catholic, I'm a Jew.

RABBI ISIDOR CHEMELWITZ: Worse luck for you, bubbulah. Catholics believe in forgiveness. Jews believe in Guilt. (*He pats the coffin tenderly*)

LOUIS: You just make sure those pegs are in good and tight.

RABBI ISIDOR CHEMELWITZ: Don't worry, mister. The life she had, she'll stay put. She's better off.

JOE: Look, I know this is scary for you. But try to understand what it means to me. Will you try?

HARPER: Yes.

JOE: Good. Really try.

 I think things are starting to change in the world.

HARPER: But I don't want...

JOE: Wait. For the good. Change for the good. America has rediscovered itself. Its sacred position among nations. And people aren't ashamed of that like they used to be. This is a great thing. The truth restored. Law restored. That's what President Reagan's done, Harper. He says "Truth exists and can be spoken proudly." And the country responds to him. We become better. More good. I need to be a part of that, I need something big to lift me up. I mean, six years ago the world seemed in decline, horrible, hopeless, full of unsolvable problems and crime and confusion and hunger and...

HARPER: But it still seems that way. More now than before. They say the ozone layer is...

JOE: Harper...

HARPER: And today out the window on Atlantic Avenue there was a schizophrenic traffic cop who was making these...

JOE: Stop it! I'm trying to make a point.

HARPER: So am I.

JOE: You aren't even making sense, you...

HARPER: My point is the world seems just as...

JOE: It only seems that way to you because you never go out in the world, Harper, and you have emotional problems.

HARPER: I do so get out in the world.

JOE: You don't. You stay in all day, fretting about imaginary...

HARPER: I get out. I do. You don't know what I do.

JOE: You don't stay in all day.

HARPER: No.

JOE: Well.... Yes you do.

HARPER: That's what you think.

JOE: Where do you go?

HARPER: Where do *you* go? When you walk.

 (*Pause, then angrily*) And I DO NOT have emotional problems.

JOE: I'm sorry.

HARPER: And if I do have emotional problems it's from living with you. Or…

JOE: I'm sorry buddy, I didn't mean to…

HARPER: Or if you do think I do then you should never have married me. You have all these secrets and lies.

JOE: I want to be married to you, Harper.

HARPER: You shouldn't. You never should.
(*Pause*)
Hey buddy. Hey buddy.

JOE: Buddy kiss…
(*They kiss.*)

HARPER: I heard on the radio how to give a blowjob.

JOE: What?

HARPER: You want to try?

JOE: You really shouldn't listen to stuff like that.

HARPER: Mormons can give blowjobs.

JOE: *Harper.*

HARPER (*Imitating his tone*): *Joe.*
It was a little Jewish lady with a German accent.
This is a good time. For me to make a baby.
(*Little pause. Joe turns away.*)

HARPER: Then they went on to a program about holes in the ozone layer. Over Antarctica. Skin burns, birds go blind, icebergs melt. The world's coming to an end.

SCENE 6

First week of November. In the men's room of the offices of the Brooklyn Federal Court of Appeals; Louis is crying over the sink; Joe enters.

JOE: Oh, um…. Morning.

LOUIS: Good morning, counselor.

JOE (*He watches Louis cry*): Sorry, I…I don't know your name.

LOUIS: Don't bother. Word processor. The lowest of the low.

JOE (*Holding out hand*): Joe Pitt. I'm with Justice Wilson…

LOUIS: Oh, I know that. Counselor Pitt. Chief Clerk.

JOE: Were you…are you OK?

LOUIS: Oh, yeah. Thanks. What a nice man.

JOE: Not so nice.

LOUIS: What?

JOE: Not so nice. Nothing. You sure you're…

LOUIS: Life sucks shit. Life…just sucks shit.

JOE: What's wrong?

LOUIS: Run in my nylons.

JOE: Sorry…?

LOUIS: Forget it. Look, thanks for asking.

JOE: Well…

LOUIS: I mean it really is nice of you.
(*He starts crying again*)
Sorry, sorry, sick friend…

JOE: Oh, I'm sorry.

LOUIS: Yeah, yeah, well, that's sweet.
Three of your colleagues have preceded you to this baleful sight and you're the first one to ask. The others just opened the door, saw me, and fled. I hope they had to pee real bad.

JOE (*Handing him a wad of toilet paper*): They just didn't want to intrude.

LOUIS: Hah. Reaganite heartless macho asshole lawyers.

JOE: Oh, that's unfair.

LOUIS: What is? Heartless? Macho? Reaganite? Lawyer?

JOE: I voted for Reagan.

LOUIS: You did?

JOE: Twice.

LOUIS: Twice? Well, oh boy. A Gay Republican.

JOE: Excuse me?

LOUIS: Nothing.

JOE: I'm not…
Forget it.

LOUIS: Republican? Not Republican? Or…

JOE: What?

LOUIS: What?

JOE: Not gay. I'm not gay.

LOUIS: Oh. Sorry.
(*Blows his nose loudly*) It's just…

JOE: Yes?

LOUIS: Well, sometimes you can tell from the way a person sounds that…I mean you *sound* like a…

JOE: No I don't. Like what?

LOUIS: Like a Republican.
(*Little pause. Joe knows he's being teased; Louis knows he knows. Joe decides to he a little brave.*)

JOE (*Making sure no one else is around*): Do I? Sound like a…?

LOUIS: What? Like a…? Republican, or…? Do I?

JOE: Do you what?

LOUIS: Sound like a…?

JOE: Like a…?

I'm…confused.

LOUIS: Yes.

My name is Louis. But all my friends call me Louise. I work in Word Processing. Thanks for the toilet paper.

(*Louis offers Joe his hand, Joe reaches, Louis feints and pecks Joe on the cheek, then exits.*)

SCENE 7

A week later. Mutual dream scene. Prior is at a fantastic makeup table, having a dream, applying the face. Harper is having a pill-induced hallucination. She has these from time to time. For some reason, Prior has appeared in this one. Or Harper has appeared in Prior's dream. It is bewildering.

PRIOR (*Alone, putting on makeup, then examining the results in the mirror; to the audience*): "I'm ready for my closeup, Mr. DeMille."

One wants to move through life with elegance and grace, blossoming infrequently but with exquisite taste, and perfect timing, like a rare bloom, a zebra orchid…. One wants…. But one so seldom gets what one wants, does one? No. One does not. One gets fucked. Over. One…dies at thirty, robbed of…decades of majesty.

Fuck this shit. Fuck this shit.

(*He almost crumbles; he pulls himself together; he studies his handiwork in the mirror*)

I look like a corpse. A corpsette. Oh my queen; you know you've hit rock-bottom when even drag is a drag.

(*Harper appears.*)

HARPER: Are you…. Who are you?

PRIOR: Who are you?

HARPER: What are you doing in my hallucination?

PRIOR: I'm not in your hallucination. You're in my dream.

HARPER: You're wearing makeup.

PRIOR: So are you.

HARPER: But you're a man.

PRIOR (*Feigning dismay, shock, he mimes slashing his throat with his lipstick and dies, fabulously tragic. Then*): The hands and feet give it away.

HARPER: There must be some mistake here. I don't recognize you. You're not…. Are you my…some sort of imaginary friend?

PRIOR: No. Aren't you too old to have imaginary friends?

HARPER: I have emotional problems. I took too many pills. Why are you wearing makeup?

PRIOR: I was in the process of applying the face, trying to make myself feel better—I swiped the new fall colors at the Clinique counter at Macy's. (*Showing her*)

HARPER: You stole these?

PRIOR: I was out of cash; it was an emotional emergency!

HARPER: Joe will be so angry. I promised him. No more pills.

PRIOR: These pills you keep alluding to?

HARPER: Valium. I take Valium. Lots of Valium.

PRIOR: And you're dancing as fast as you can.

HARPER: I'm not *addicted*. I don't believe in addiction, and I never…well, I *never* drink. And I *never* take drugs.

PRIOR: Well, smell *you*, Nancy Drew.

HARPER: Except Valium.

PRIOR: Except Valium; in wee fistfuls.

HARPER: It's terrible. Mormons are not supposed to be addicted to anything. I'm a Mormon.

PRIOR: I'm a homosexual.

HARPER: Oh! In my church we don't believe in homosexuals.

PRIOR: In my church we don't believe in Mormons.

HARPER: What church do…oh! (*She laughs*) I get it.

I don't understand this. If I didn't ever see you before and I don't think I did then I don't think you should be here, in this hallucination, because in my experience the mind, which is where hallucinations come from, shouldn't be able to make up anything that wasn't there to start with, that didn't enter it from experience, from the

real world. Imagination can't create anything new, can it? It only recycles bits and
pieces from the world and reassembles
them into visions…. Am I making sense
right now?

PRIOR: Given the circumstances, yes.

HARPER: So when we think we've escaped the
unbearable ordinariness and, well, untruth-
fulness of our lives, it's really only the same
old ordinariness and falseness rearranged
into the appearance of novelty and truth.
Nothing unknown is knowable. Don't you
think it's depressing?

PRIOR: The limitations of the imagination?

HARPER: Yes.

PRIOR: It's something you learn after your second theme party: It's All Been Done Before.

HARPER: The world. Finite. Terribly, terribly….
Well…
    This is the most depressing hallucina-
tion I've ever had.

PRIOR: Apologies. I do try to be amusing.

HARPER: Oh, well, don't apologize, you…. I can't
expect someone who's really sick to entertain me.

PRIOR: How on earth did you know…

HARPER: Oh that happens. This is the very
threshhold of revelation sometimes. You
can see things…how sick you are. Do you
see anything about me?

PRIOR: Yes.

HARPER: What?

PRIOR: You are amazingly unhappy.

HARPER: Oh big deal. You meet a Valium addict
and you figure out she's unhappy. That
doesn't count. Of course I…. Something
else. Something surprising.

PRIOR: Something surprising.

HARPER: Yes.

PRIOR: Your husband's a homo.
    (Pause.)

HARPER: Oh, ridiculous.
    (Pause, then very quietly)
        Really?

PRIOR (Shrugs): Threshhold of revelation.

HARPER: Well I don't like your revelations. I
don't think you intuit well at all. Joe's a very
normal man, he…

Oh God. Oh God. He…. Do homos
take, like, lots of long walks?

PRIOR: Yes. We do. In stretch pants with lavender
coifs. I just looked at you, and there was…

HARPER: A sort of blue streak of recognition.

PRIOR: Yes.

HARPER: Like you knew me incredibly well.

PRIOR: Yes.

HARPER: Yes.
    I have to go now, get back, something
just…fell apart.
    Oh God, I feel so sad…

PRIOR: I…I'm sorry. I usually say, "Fuck the
truth," but mostly, the truth fucks you.

HARPER: I see something else about you…

PRIOR: Oh?

HARPER: Deep inside you, there's a part of you,
the most inner part, entirely free of disease.
I can see that.

PRIOR: Is that…. That isn't true.

HARPER: Threshhold of revelation.
    Home…
    (She vanishes.)

PRIOR: People come and go so quickly here…
    (To himself in the mirror) I don't think
there's any uninfected part of me. My heart
is pumping polluted blood. I feel dirty.
    (He begins to wipe makeup off with his hands,
smearing it around. A large gray feather falls from
up above. Prior stops smearing the makeup and
looks at the feather. He goes to it and picks it up.)

A VOICE (It is an incredibly beautiful voice): Look
up!

PRIOR (Looking up, not seeing anyone): Hello?

A VOICE: Look up!

PRIOR: Who is that?

A VOICE: Prepare the way!

PRIOR: I don't see any…
    (There is a dramatic change in lighting, from
above.)

A VOICE:
        Look up, look up,
        prepare the way
        the infinite descent
        A breath in air
        floating down
        Glory to…
    (Silence.)

PRIOR: Hello? Is that it? Helloooo!
> What the fuck…? (*He holds himself*)
> Poor me. Poor poor me. Why me? Why poor poor me? Oh I don't feel good right now. I really don't.

SCENE 8

That night. Split scene. Harper and Joe at home; Prior and Louis in bed.

HARPER: Where were you?

JOE: Out.

HARPER: Where?

JOE: Just out. Thinking.

HARPER: It's late.

JOE: I had a lot to think about.

HARPER: I burned dinner.

JOE: Sorry.

HARPER: Not my dinner. My dinner was fine. Your dinner. I put it back in the oven and turned everything up as high as it could go and I watched till it burned black. It's still hot. Very hot. Want it?

JOE: You didn't have to do that.

HARPER: I know. It just seemed like the kind of thing a mentally deranged sex-starved pill-popping housewife would do.

JOE: Uh huh.

HARPER: So I did it. Who knows anymore what I have to do?

JOE: How many pills?

HARPER: A bunch. Don't change the subject.

JOE: I won't talk to you when you…

HARPER: No. No. Don't do that! I'm…I'm fine, pills are not the problem, not our problem, I WANT TO KNOW WHERE YOU'VE BEEN! I WANT TO KNOW WHAT'S GOING ON!

JOE: Going on with what? The job?

HARPER: Not the job.

JOE: I said I need more time.

HARPER: Not the job!

JOE: Mr. Cohn, I talked to him on the phone, he said I had to hurry…

HARPER: Not the…

JOE: But I can't get you to talk sensibly about anything so…

HARPER: SHUT UP!

JOE: Then what?

HARPER: Stick to the subject.

JOE: I don't know what that is. You have something you want to ask me? Ask me. Go.

HARPER: I…can't. I'm scared of you.

JOE: I'm tired, I'm going to bed.

HARPER: Tell me without making me ask. Please.

JOE: This is crazy, I'm not…

HARPER: When you come through the door at night your face is never exactly the way I remembered it. I get surprised by something …mean and hard about the way you look. Even the weight of you in the bed at night, the way you breathe in your sleep seems unfamiliar.
> You terrify me.

JOE (*Cold*): I know who you are.

HARPER: Yes. I'm the enemy. That's easy. That doesn't change.
> You think you're the only one who hates sex; I do; I hate it with you; I do. I dream that you batter away at me till all my joints come apart, like wax, and I fall into pieces. It's like a punishment. It was wrong of me to marry you. I knew you…(*She stops herself*) It's a sin, and it's killing us both.

JOE: I can always tell when you've taken pills because it makes you red-faced and sweaty and frankly that's very often why I don't want to…

HARPER: Because…

JOE: Well, you aren't pretty. Not like this.

HARPER: I have something to ask you.

JOE: Then ASK! ASK! What in hell are you…

HARPER: Are you a homo?
> (*Pause*)
> Are you? If you try to walk out right now I'll put your dinner back in the oven and turn it up so high the whole building will fill with smoke and everyone in it will asphyxiate. So help me God I will.
> Now answer the question.

JOE: What if I…
> (*Small pause.*)

HARPER: Then tell me, please. And we'll see.

JOE: No. I'm not.
> I don't see what difference it makes.

LOUIS: Jews don't have any clear textual guide to the afterlife; even that it exists. I don't think much about it. I see it as a perpetual rainy Thursday afternoon in March. Dead leaves.

PRIOR: Eeeugh. Very Greco-Roman.

LOUIS: Well for us it's not the verdict that counts, it's the act of judgment. That's why I could never be a lawyer. In court all that matters is the verdict.

PRIOR: You could never be a lawyer because you are oversexed. You're too distracted.

LOUIS: Not distracted; *ab*stracted. I'm trying to make a point:

PRIOR: Namely:

LOUIS: It's the judge in his or her chambers, weighing, books open, pondering the evidence, ranging freely over categories: good, evil, innocent, guilty; the judge in the chamber of circumspection, not the judge on the bench with the gavel. The shaping of the law, not its execution.

PRIOR: The point, dear, the point…

LOUIS: That it should be the questions and shape of a life, its total complexity gathered, arranged and considered, which matters in the end, not some stamp of salvation or damnation which disperses all the complexity in some unsatisfying little decision—the balancing of the scales…

PRIOR: I like this; very zen; it's…reassuringly incomprehensible and useless. We who are about to die thank you.

LOUIS: You are not about to die.

PRIOR: It's not going well, really…two new lesions. My leg hurts. There's protein in my urine, the doctor says, but who knows what the fuck that portends. Anyway it shouldn't be there, the protein. My butt is chapped from diarrhea and yesterday I shat blood.

LOUIS: I really hate this. You don't tell me…

PRIOR: You get too upset, I wind up comforting you. It's easier…

LOUIS: Oh thanks.

PRIOR: If it's bad I'll tell you.

LOUIS: Shitting blood sounds bad to me.

PRIOR: And I'm telling you.

LOUIS: And I'm handling it.

PRIOR: Tell me some more about justice.

LOUIS: I *am* handling it.

PRIOR: Well Louis you win Trooper of the Month.

(Louis starts to cry.)

PRIOR: I take it back. You aren't Trooper of the Month. This isn't working…

Tell me some more about justice.

LOUIS: You are not about to die.

PRIOR: Justice…

LOUIS: …is an immensity, a confusing vastness. Justice is God.

Prior?

PRIOR: Hmmm?

LOUIS: You love me.

PRIOR: Yes.

LOUIS: What if I walked out on this?

Would you hate me forever?

(Prior kisses Louis on the forehead.)

PRIOR: Yes.

JOE: I think we ought to pray. Ask God for help. Ask him together…

HARPER: God won't talk to me. I have to make up people to talk to me.

JOE: You have to keep asking.

HARPER: I forgot the question.

Oh yeah. God, is my husband a…

JOE *(Scary)*: Stop it. Stop it. I'm warning you.

Does it make any difference? That I might be one thing deep within, no matter how wrong or ugly that thing is, so long as I have fought, with everything I have, to kill it. What do you want from me? What do you want from me, Harper? More than that? For God's sake, there's nothing left, I'm a shell. There's nothing left to kill.

As long as my behavior is what I know it has to be. Decent. Correct. That alone in the eyes of God.

HARPER: No, no, not that, that's Utah talk, Mormon talk, I hate it, Joe, tell me, say it…

JOE: All I will say is that I am a very good man who has worked very hard to become good and you want to destroy that. You want to destroy me, but I am not going to let you do that.

(Pause.)

HARPER: I'm going to have a baby.

JOE: Liar.

HARPER: You liar.

A baby born addicted to pills. A baby who does not dream but who hallucinates, who stares up at us with big mirror eyes and who does not know who we are. *(Pause.)*

JOE: Are you really…

HARPER: No. Yes. No. Yes. Get away from me. Now we both have a secret.

PRIOR: One of my ancestors was a ship's captain who made money bringing whale oil to Europe and returning with immigrants—Irish mostly, packed in tight, so many dollars per head. The last ship he captained foundered off the coast of Nova Scotia in a winter tempest and sank to the bottom. He went down with the ship—la Grande Geste—but his crew took seventy women and kids in the ship's only longboat, this big, open rowboat, and when the weather got too rough, and they thought the boat was overcrowded, the crew started lifting people up and hurling them into the sea. Until they got the ballast right. They walked up and down the longboat, eyes to the waterline, and when the boat rode low in the water they'd grab the nearest passenger and throw them into the sea. The boat was leaky, see; seventy people; they arrived in Halifax with nine people on board.

LOUIS: Jesus.

PRIOR: I think about that story a lot now. People in a boat, waiting, terrified, while implacable, unsmiling men, irresistibly strong, seize…maybe the person next to you, maybe you, and with no warning at all, with time only for a quick intake of air you are pitched into freezing, turbulent water and salt and darkness to drown.

I like your cosmology, baby. While time is running out I find myself drawn to anything that's suspended, that lacks an ending—but it seems to me that it lets you off scot-free.

LOUIS: What do you mean?

PRIOR: No judgment, no guilt or responsibility.

LOUIS: For me.

PRIOR: For anyone. It was an editorial "you."

LOUIS: Please get better. Please.

Please don't get any sicker.

SCENE 9

Third week in November. Roy and Henry, his doctor, in Henry's office.

HENRY: Nobody knows what causes it. And nobody knows how to cure it. The best theory is that we blame a retro-virus, the Human Immunodeficiency Virus. Its presence is made known to us by the useless antibodies which appear in reaction to its entrance into the bloodstream through a cut, or an orifice. The antibodies are powerless to protect the body against it. Why, we don't know. The body's immune system ceases to function. Sometimes the body even attacks itself. At any rate it's left open to a whole horror house of infections from microbes which it usually defends against.

Like Kaposi's sarcomas. These lesions. Or your throat problem. Or the glands.

We think it may also be able to slip past the blood-brain barrier into the brain. Which is of course very bad news.

And it's fatal in we don't know what percent of people with suppressed immune responses. *(Pause.)*

ROY: This is very interesting, Mr. Wizard, but why the fuck are you telling me this? *(Pause.)*

HENRY: Well, I have just removed one of three lesions which biopsy results will probably tell us is a Kaposi's sarcoma lesion. And you have a pronounced swelling of glands in your neck, groin, and armpits—lymphadenopathy is another sign. And you have oral candidiasis and maybe a little more fungus under the fingernails of two digits on your right hand. So that's why…

ROY: This disease…

HENRY: Syndrome.

ROY: Whatever. It afflicts mostly homosexuals and drug addicts.

HENRY: Mostly. Hemophiliacs are also at risk.

ROY: Homosexuals and drug addicts. So why are you implying that I...

(Pause)

What are you implying, Henry?

HENRY: I don't...

ROY: I'm not a drug addict.

HENRY: Oh come on Roy.

ROY: What, what, come on Roy what? Do you think I'm a junkie, Henry, do you see tracks?

HENRY: This is absurd.

ROY: Say it.

HENRY: Say what?

ROY: Say, "Roy Cohn, you are a..."

HENRY: Roy!

ROY: "You are a...." Go on. Not "Roy Cohn you are a drug fiend." "Roy Marcus Cohn, you are a..."

Go on, Henry, it starts with an "H."

HENRY: Oh I'm not going to...

ROY: *With an "H,"* Henry, and it isn't "Hemophiliac." Come on...

HENRY: What are you doing, Roy?

ROY: No, say it. I mean it. Say: "Roy Cohn, you are a homosexual."

(Pause)

And I will proceed, systematically, to destroy your reputation and your practice and your career in New York State, Henry. Which you know I can do.

(Pause.)

HENRY: Roy, you have been seeing me since 1958. Apart from the facelifts I have treated you for everything from syphilis...

ROY: From a whore in Dallas.

HENRY: From syphilis to venereal warts. In your rectum. Which you may have gotten from a whore in Dallas, but it wasn't a female whore.

(Pause.)

ROY: So say it.

HENRY: Roy Cohn, you are...

You have had sex with men, many many times, Roy, and one of them, or any number of them, has made you very sick. You have AIDS.

ROY: AIDS.

Your problem, Henry, is that you are hung up on words, on labels, that you be-

lieve they mean what they seem to mean. AIDS. Homosexual. Gay. Lesbian. You think these are names that tell you who someone sleeps with, but they don't tell you that.

HENRY: No?

ROY: No. Like all labels they tell you one thing and one thing only: where does an individual so identified fit in the food chain, in the pecking order? Not ideology, or sexual taste, but something much simpler: clout. Not who I fuck or who fucks me, but who will pick up the phone when I call, who owes me favors. This is what a label refers to. Now to someone who does not understand this, homosexual is what I am because I have sex with men. But really this is wrong. Homosexuals are not men who sleep with other men. Homosexuals are men who in fifteen years of trying cannot get a pissant antidiscrimination bill through City Council. Homosexuals are men who know nobody and who nobody knows. Who have zero clout. Does this sound like me, Henry?

HENRY: No.

ROY: No. I have clout. A lot. I can pick up this phone, punch fifteen numbers, and you know who will be on the other end in under five minutes, Henry?

HENRY: The President.

ROY: Even better, Henry. His wife.

HENRY: I'm impressed.

ROY: I don't want you to be impressed. I want you to understand. This is not sophistry. And this is not hypocrisy. This is reality. I have sex with men. But unlike nearly every other man of whom this is true, I bring the guy I'm screwing to the White House and President Reagan smiles at us and shakes his hand. Because *what* I am is defined entirely by *who* I am. Roy Cohn is not a homosexual. Roy Cohn is a heterosexual man, Henry, who fucks around with guys.

HENRY: OK, Roy.

ROY: And what is my diagnosis, Henry?

HENRY: You have AIDS, Roy.

ROY: No, Henry, no. AIDS is what homosexuals have. I have liver cancer.

(Pause.)

HENRY: Well, whatever the fuck you have, Roy, it's very serious, and I haven't got a damn thing for you. The NIH in Bethesda has a new drug called AZT with a two-year waiting list that not even I can get you onto. So get on the phone, Roy, and dial the fifteen numbers, and tell the First Lady you need in on an experimental treatment for liver cancer, because you can call it any damn thing you want, Roy, but what it boils down to is very bad news.

ACT TWO: IN VITRO
December 1985–January 1986

SCENE 1

Night, the third week in December. Prior alone on the floor of his bedroom; he is much worse.

PRIOR: Louis, Louis, please wake up, oh God.
    (Louis runs in.)
PRIOR: I think something horrible is wrong with me I can't breathe…
LOUIS (*Starting to exit*): I'm calling the ambulance.
PRIOR: No, wait, I…
LOUIS: *Wait?* Are you fucking crazy? Oh God you're on fire, your head is on fire.
PRIOR: It hurts, it hurts…
LOUIS: I'm calling the ambulance.
PRIOR: I don't want to go to the hospital, I don't want to go to the hospital please let me lie here, just…
LOUIS: No, no, God, Prior, stand up…
PRIOR: DON'T TOUCH MY LEG!
LOUIS: We have to…oh God this is so crazy.
PRIOR: I'll be OK if I just lie here Lou, really, if I can only sleep a little…
    (Louis exits.)
PRIOR: Louis?
    NO! NO! Don't call, you'll send me there and I won't come back, please, please Louis I'm begging, baby, please…
    (Screams) LOUIS!!
LOUIS (*From off; hysterical*): WILL YOU SHUT THE FUCK UP!
PRIOR (*Trying to stand*): Aaaah. I have…to go to the bathroom. Wait. Wait, just…oh. Oh God. *(He shits himself)*

LOUIS (*Entering*): Prior? They'll be here in…
    Oh my God.
PRIOR: I'm sorry, I'm sorry.
LOUIS: What did…? What?
PRIOR: I had an accident.
    (Louis goes to him.)
LOUIS: This is blood.
PRIOR: Maybe you shouldn't touch it…me.… I…
    (He faints)
LOUIS (*Quietly*): Oh help. Oh help. Oh God oh God oh God help me I can't I can't I can't.

SCENE 2

Same night. Harper is sitting at home, all alone, with no lights on. We can barely see her. Joe enters, but he doesn't turn on the lights.

JOE: Why are you sitting in the dark? Turn on the light.
HARPER: *No.* I heard the sounds in the bedroom again. I know someone was in there.
JOE: No one was.
HARPER: Maybe actually in the bed, under the covers with a knife.
    Oh, boy. Joe. I, um, I'm thinking of going away. By which I mean: I think I'm going off again. You…you know what I mean?
JOE: Please don't. Stay. We can fix it. I pray for that. This is my fault, but I can correct it. You have to try too.…
    (He turns on the light. She turns it off again.)
HARPER: When you pray, what do you pray for?
JOE: I pray for God to crush me, break me up into little pieces and start all over again.
HARPER: Oh. Please. Don't pray for that.
JOE: I had a book of Bible stories when I was a kid. There was a picture I'd look at twenty times every day: Jacob wrestles with the angel. I don't really remember the story, or why the wrestling—just the picture. Jacob is young and very strong. The angel is…a beautiful man, with golden hair and wings, of course. I still dream about it. Many nights. I'm.… It's me. In that struggle. Fierce, and unfair. The angel is not human, and it holds nothing back, so how could anyone human win, what kind of a fight is

that? It's not just. Losing means your soul thrown down in the dust, your heart torn out from God's. But you can't not lose.

HARPER: In the whole entire world, you are the only person, the only person I love or have ever loved. And I love you terribly. Terribly. That's what's so awfully, irreducibly real. I can make up anything but I can't dream that away.

JOE: Are you…are you really going to have a baby?

HARPER: It's my time, and there's no blood. I don't really know. I suppose it wouldn't be a great thing. Maybe I'm just not bleeding because I take too many pills. Maybe I'll give birth to a pill. That would give a new meaning to pill-popping, huh?

I think you should go to Washington. Alone. Change, like you said.

JOE: I'm not going to leave you, Harper.

HARPER: Well maybe not. But I'm going to leave you.

SCENE 3

One AM, the next morning. Louis and a nurse, Emily, are sitting in Prior's room in the hospital.

EMILY: He'll be all right now.

LOUIS: No he won't.

EMILY: No. I guess not. I gave him something that makes him sleep.

LOUIS: Deep asleep?

EMILY: Orbiting the moons of Jupiter.

LOUIS: A good place to be.

EMILY: Anyplace better than here. You his…uh?

LOUIS: Yes. I'm his uh.

EMILY: This must be hell for you.

LOUIS: It is. Hell. The After Life. Which is not at all like a rainy afternoon in March, by the way, Prior. A lot more vivid than I'd expected. Dead leaves, but the crunchy kind. Sharp, dry air. The kind of long, luxurious dying feeling that breaks your heart.

EMILY: Yeah, well we all get to break our hearts on this one.

He seems like a nice guy. Cute.

LOUIS: Not like this.

Yes, he is. Was. Whatever.

EMILY: Weird name. Prior Walter. Like, "The Walter before this one."

LOUIS: Lots of Walters before this one. Prior is an old old family name in an old old family. The Walters go back to the Mayflower and beyond. Back to the Norman Conquest. He says there's a Prior Walter stitched into the Bayeux tapestry.

EMILY: Is that impressive?

LOUIS: Well, it's old. Very old. Which in some circles equals impressive.

EMILY: Not in my circle. What's the name of the tapestry?

LOUIS: The Bayeux tapestry. Embroidered by La Reine Mathilde.

EMILY: I'll tell my mother. She embroiders. Drives me nuts.

LOUIS: Manual therapy for anxious hands.

EMILY: Maybe you should try it.

LOUIS: Mathilde stitched while William the Conqueror was off to war. She was capable of…more than loyalty. Devotion.

She waited for him, she stitched for years. And if he had come back broken and defeated from war, she would have loved him even more. And if he had returned mutilated, ugly, full of infection and horror, she would still have loved him; fed by pity, by a sharing of pain, she would love him even more, and even more, and she would never, never have prayed to God, please let him die if he can't return to me whole and healthy and able to live a normal life.… If he had died, she would have buried her heart with him.

So what the fuck is the matter with me? (*Little pause*)

Will he sleep through the night?

EMILY: At least.

LOUIS: I'm going.

EMILY: It's one AM. Where do you have to go at…

LOUIS: I know what time it is. A walk. Night air, good for the.… The park.

EMILY: Be careful.

LOUIS: Yeah. Danger.

Tell him, if he wakes up and you're still on, tell him goodbye, tell him I had to go.

SCENE 4

An hour later. Split scene: Joe and Roy in a fancy (straight) bar; Louis and a Man in the Rambles in Central Park. Joe and Roy are sitting at the bar; the place is brightly lit. Joe has a plate of food in front of him but he isn't eating. Roy occasionally reaches over the table and forks small bites off Joe's plate. Roy is drinking heavily, Joe not at all. Louis and the Man are eyeing each other, each alternating interest and indifference.

JOE: The pills were something she started when she miscarried or…no, she took some before that. She had a really bad time at home, when she was a kid, her home was really bad. I think a lot of drinking and physical stuff. She doesn't talk about that, instead she talks about…the sky falling down, people with knives hiding under sofas. Monsters. Mormons. Everyone thinks Mormons don't come from homes like that, we aren't supposed to behave that way, but we do. It's not lying, or being two-faced. Everyone tries very hard to live up to God's strictures, which are very…um…

ROY: Strict.

JOE: I shouldn't be bothering you with this.

ROY: No, please. Heart to heart. Want another…. What is that, seltzer?

JOE: The failure to measure up hits people very hard. From such a strong desire to be good they feel very far from goodness when they fail.

    What scares me is that maybe what I really love in her is the part of her that's farthest from the light, from God's love; maybe I was drawn to that in the first place. And I'm keeping it alive because I need it.

ROY: Why would you need it?

JOE: There are things…. I don't know how well we know ourselves. I mean, what if? I know I married her because she…because I loved it that she was always wrong, always doing something wrong, like one step out of step. In Salt Lake City that stands out. I never stood out, on the outside, but inside, it was hard for me. To pass.

ROY: Pass?

JOE: Yeah.

ROY: Pass as what?

JOE: Oh. Well…. As someone cheerful and strong. Those who love God with an open heart unclouded by secrets and struggles are cheerful; God's easy simple love for them shows in how strong and happy they are. The saints.

ROY: But you had secrets? Secret struggles…

JOE: I wanted to be one of the elect, one of the Blessed. You feel you ought to be, that the blemishes are yours by choice, which of course they aren't. Harper's sorrow, that really deep sorrow, she didn't choose that. But it's there.

ROY: You didn't put it there.

JOE: No.

ROY: You sound like you think you did.

JOE: I am responsible for her.

ROY: Because she's your wife.

JOE: That. And I do love her.

ROY: Whatever. She's your wife. And so there are obligations. To her. But also to yourself.

JOE: She'd fall apart in Washington.

ROY: Then let her stay here.

JOE: She'll fall apart if I leave her.

ROY: Then bring her to Washington.

JOE: I just can't, Roy. She needs me.

ROY: Listen, Joe. I'm the best divorce lawyer in the business.

    (Little pause.)

JOE: Can't Washington wait?

ROY: You do what you need to do, Joe. What *you* need. *You.* Let her life go where it wants to go. You'll both be better for that. *Somebody* should get what they want.

MAN: What do you want?

LOUIS: I want you to fuck me, hurt me, make me bleed.

MAN: I want to.

LOUIS: Yeah?

MAN: I want to hurt you.

LOUIS: Fuck me.

MAN: Yeah?

LOUIS: Hard.

MAN: Yeah? You been a bad boy?

    (Pause. Louis laughs, softly.)

LOUIS: Very bad. Very bad.

MAN: You need to be punished, boy?

LOUIS: Yes. I do.

MAN: Yes what?

(Little pause.)

LOUIS: Um, I…

MAN: Yes *what*, boy?

LOUIS: Oh. Yes Sir.

MAN: I want you to take me to your place, boy.

LOUIS: No, I can't do that.

MAN: No *what*?

LOUIS: No Sir, I can't, I…

I don't live alone, sir.

MAN: Your lover know you're out with a man tonight, boy?

LOUIS: No Sir, he…

My lover doesn't know.

MAN: Your lover know you…

LOUIS: Let's change the subject, OK? Can we go to your place?

MAN: I live with my parents.

LOUIS: Oh.

ROY: Everyone who makes it in this world makes it because somebody older and more powerful takes an interest. The most precious asset in life, I think, is the ability to be a good son. You have that, Joe. Somebody who can be a good son to a father who pushes them farther than they would otherwise go. I've had many fathers, I owe my life to them, powerful, powerful men. Walter Winchell, Edgar Hoover. Joe McCarthy most of all. He valued me because I am a good lawyer, but he loved me because I was and am a good son. He was a very difficult man, very guarded and cagey; I brought out something tender in him. He would have died for me. And me for him. Does this embarrass you?

JOE: I had a hard time with my father.

ROY: Well sometimes that's the way. Then you have to find other fathers, substitutes, I don't know. The father-son relationship is central to life. Women are for birth, beginning, but the father is continuance. The son offers the father his life as a vessel for carrying forth his father's dream. Your father's living?

JOE: Um, dead.

ROY: He was…what? A difficult man?

JOE: He was in the military. He could be very unfair. And cold.

ROY: But he loved you.

JOE: I don't know.

ROY: No, no, Joe, he did, I know this. Sometimes a father's love has to be very, very hard, unfair even, cold to make his son grow strong in a world like this. This isn't a good world.

MAN: Here, then.

LOUIS: I…. Do you have a rubber?

MAN: I don't use rubbers.

LOUIS: You should. (*He takes one from his coat pocket*) Here.

MAN: I don't use them.

LOUIS: Forget it, then. (*He starts to leave*)

MAN: No, wait.

Put it on me. Boy.

LOUIS: Forget it, I have to get back. Home. I must be going crazy.

MAN: Oh come on please he won't find out.

LOUIS: It's cold. Too cold.

MAN: It's never too cold, let me warm you up. Please?

(They begin to fuck.)

MAN: Relax.

LOUIS (*A small laugh*): Not a chance.

MAN: It…

LOUIS: What?

MAN: I think it broke. The rubber. You want me to keep going? (*Little pause*) Pull out? Should I…

LOUIS: Keep going.

Infect me.

I don't care. I don't care.

(Pause. The Man pulls out.)

MAN: I…um, look, I'm sorry, but I think I want to go.

LOUIS: Yeah.

Give my best to mom and dad.

(The Man slaps him.)

LOUIS: Ow!

(They stare at each other.)

LOUIS: It was a joke.

(The Man leaves.)

ROY: How long have we known each other?

JOE: Since 1980.

ROY: Right. A long time. I feel close to you, Joe. Do I advise you well?

JOE: You've been an incredible friend, Roy, I…

ROY: I want to be family. Familia, as my Italian friends call it. La Familia. A lovely word. It's important for me to help you, like I was helped.

JOE: I owe practically everything to you, Roy.

ROY: I'm dying, Joe. Cancer.

JOE: Oh my God.

ROY: Please. Let me finish.

Few people know this and I'm telling you this only because…. I'm not afraid of death. What can death bring that I haven't faced? I've lived; life is the worst. (*Gently mocking himself*) Listen to me, I'm a philosopher.

Joe. You must do this. You must must must. Love; that's a trap. Responsibility; that's a trap too. Like a father to a son I tell you this: Life is full of horror; nobody escapes, nobody; save yourself. Whatever pulls on you, whatever needs from you, threatens you. Don't be afraid; people are so afraid; don't be afraid to live in the raw wind, naked, alone…. Learn at least this: What you are capable of. Let nothing stand in your way.

SCENE 5

Three days later. Prior and Belize in Prior's hospital room. Prior is very sick but improving. Belize has just arrived.

PRIOR: Miss Thing.

BELIZE: Ma cherie bichette.

PRIOR: Stella.

BELIZE: Stella for star. Let me see. (*Scrutinizing Prior*) You look like shit, why yes indeed you do, comme la merde!

PRIOR: Merci.

BELIZE (*Taking little plastic bottles from his bag, handing them to Prior*): Not to despair, Belle Reeve. Lookie! Magic goop!

PRIOR (*Opening a bottle, sniffing*): Pooh! What kinda crap is that?

BELIZE: Beats me. Let's rub it on your poor blistered body and see what it does.

PRIOR: This is not Western medicine, these bottles…

BELIZE: Voodoo cream. From the botanica 'round the block.

PRIOR: And you a registered nurse.

BELIZE (*Sniffing it*): Beeswax and cheap perfume. Cut with Jergen's Lotion. Full of good vibes and love from some little black Cubana witch in Miami.

PRIOR: Get that trash away from me, I am immune-suppressed.

BELIZE: I *am* a health professional. I *know* what I'm doing.

PRIOR: It stinks. Any word from Louis?

(*Pause. Belize starts giving Prior a gentle massage.*)

PRIOR: Gone.

BELIZE: He'll be back. I know the type. Likes to keep a girl on edge.

PRIOR: It's been…

(*Pause.*)

BELIZE (*Trying to jog his memory*): How long?

PRIOR: I don't remember.

BELIZE: How long have you been here?

PRIOR (*Getting suddenly upset*): I don't remember, I don't give a fuck. I want Louis. I want my fucking boyfriend, where the fuck is he? I'm dying, I'm dying, where's Louis?

BELIZE: Shhhh, shhh…

PRIOR: This is a very strange drug, this drug. Emotional lability, for starters.

BELIZE: Save a tab or two for me.

PRIOR: Oh no, not this drug, ce n'est pas pour la joyeux noël et la bonne année, this drug she is serious poisonous chemistry, ma pauvre bichette.

And not just disorienting. I hear things. Voices.

BELIZE: Voices.

PRIOR: A voice.

BELIZE: Saying what?

(*Pause.*)

PRIOR: I'm not supposed to tell.

BELIZE: You better tell the doctor. Or I will.

PRIOR: No no don't. Please. I want the voice; it's wonderful. It's all that's keeping me alive. I don't want to talk to some intern about it.
    You know what happens? When I hear it, I get hard.

BELIZE: Oh my.

PRIOR: Comme ça. (*He uses his arm to demonstrate*) And you know I am slow to rise.

BELIZE: My jaw aches at the memory.

PRIOR: And would you deny me this little solace—betray my concupiscence to Florence Nightingale's storm troopers?

BELIZE: Perish the thought, ma bébé.

PRIOR: They'd change the drug just to spoil the fun.

BELIZE: You and your boner can depend on me.

PRIOR: Je t'adore, ma belle nègre.

BELIZE: All this girl-talk shit is politically incorrect, you know. We should have dropped it back when we gave up drag.

PRIOR: I'm sick, I get to be politically incorrect if it makes me feel better. You sound like Lou.
    (*Little pause*)
    Well, at least I have the satisfaction of knowing he's in anguish somewhere. I loved his anguish. Watching him stick his head up his asshole and eat his guts out over some relatively minor moral conundrum—it was the best show in town. But Mother warned me: if they get overwhelmed by the little things…

BELIZE: They'll be belly-up bustville when something big comes along.

PRIOR: Mother warned me.

BELIZE: And they do come along.

PRIOR: But I didn't listen.

BELIZE: No. (*Doing Hepburn*) Men are beasts.

PRIOR (*Also Hepburn*): The absolute lowest.

BELIZE: I have to go. If I want to spend my whole lonely life looking after white people I can get underpaid to do it.

PRIOR: You're just a Christian martyr.

BELIZE: Whatever happens, baby, I will be here for you.

PRIOR: Je t'aime.

BELIZE: Je t'aime. Don't go crazy on me, girlfriend, I already got enough crazy queens for one lifetime. For two. I can't be bothering with dementia.

PRIOR: I promise.

BELIZE (*Touching him; softly*): Ouch.

PRIOR: Ouch. Indeed.

BELIZE: Why'd they have to pick on you?
    And eat more, girlfriend, you really do look like shit.
    (*Belize leaves.*)

PRIOR (*After waiting a beat*): He's gone. Are you still…

VOICE: I can't stay. I will return.

PRIOR: Are you one of those "Follow me to the other side" voices?

VOICE: No. I am no nightbird. I am a messenger…

PRIOR: You have a beautiful voice, it sounds…like a viola, like a perfectly tuned, tight string, balanced, the truth…. Stay with me.

VOICE: Not now. Soon I will return, I will reveal myself to you; I am glorious, glorious; my heart, my countenance and my message. You must prepare.

PRIOR: For what? I don't want to…

VOICE: No death, no:
    A marvelous work and a wonder we undertake, an edifice awry we sink plumb and straighten, a great Lie we abolish, a great error correct, with the rule, sword and broom of Truth!

PRIOR: What are you talking about, I…

VOICE:
    I am on my way; when I am manifest, our Work begins:
        Prepare for the parting of the air,
        The breath, the ascent,
        Glory to…

SCENE 6

The second week of January. Martin, Roy and Joe in a fancy Manhattan restaurant.

MARTIN: It's a revolution in Washington, Joe. We have a new agenda and finally a real leader. They got back the Senate but we have the courts. By the nineties the Supreme Court will be block-solid Republican appointees, and the Federal bench—Republican judges like land mines, everywhere, everywhere they turn. Affirmative action? Take it to court. Boom! Land mine. And we'll get our way on just about everything: abortion, defense, Central America, family values, a live investment climate. We have the White House locked till the year 2000. And beyond. A permanent fix on the Oval Office? It's possible. By '92 we'll get the Senate back, and in ten years the South is going to give us the House. It's really the end of Liberalism. The end of New Deal Socialism. The end of ipso facto secular humanism. The dawning of a genuinely American political personality. Modeled on Ronald Wilson Reagan.

JOE: It sounds great, Mr. Heller.

MARTIN: Martin. And Justice is the hub. Especially since Ed Meese took over. He doesn't specialize in Fine Points of the Law. He's a flatfoot, a cop. He reminds me of Teddy Roosevelt.

JOE: I can't wait to meet him.

MARTIN: Too bad, Joe, he's been dead for sixty years!
(There is a little awkwardness. Joe doesn't respond.)

MARTIN: Teddy Roosevelt. You said you wanted to.... Little joke. It reminds me of the story about the…

ROY *(Smiling, but nasty)*: Aw shut the fuck up Martin.
   (To Joe) You see that? Mr. Heller here is one of the mighty, Joseph, in D.C. he sitteth on the right hand of the man who sitteth on the right hand of The Man. And yet I can say "shut the fuck up" and he will take no offense. Loyalty. He…
   Martin?

MARTIN: Yes, Roy?

ROY: Rub my back.

MARTIN: Roy…

ROY: No no really, a sore spot, I get them all the time now, these…. Rub it for me darling, would you do that for me?
(Martin rubs Roy's back. They both look at Joe.)

ROY *(To Joe)*: How do you think a handful of Bolsheviks turned St. Petersburg into Leningrad in one afternoon? *Comrades.* Who do for each other. Marx and Engels. Lenin and Trotsky. Josef Stalin and Franklin Delano Roosevelt.
(Martin laughs.)

ROY: *Comrades,* right Martin?

MARTIN: This man, Joe, is a Saint of the Right.

JOE: I know, Mr. Heller, I…

ROY: And you see what I mean, Martin? He's special, right?

MARTIN: Don't embarrass him, Roy.

ROY: Gravity, decency, smarts! His strength is as the strength of ten because his heart is pure! *And* he's a Royboy, one hundred percent.

MARTIN: We're on the move, Joe. On the move.

JOE: Mr. Heller, I…

MARTIN *(Ending backrub)*: We can't wait any longer for an answer.
(Little pause.)

JOE: Oh. Um, I…

ROY: Joe's a married man, Martin.

MARTIN: Aha.

ROY: With a wife. She doesn't care to go to D.C., and so Joe cannot go. And keeps us dangling. We've seen that kind of thing before, haven't we? These men and their wives.

MARTIN: Oh yes. Beware.

JOE: I really can't discuss this under…

MARTIN: Then *don't* discuss. Say yes, Joe.

ROY: Now.

MARTIN: Say yes I will.

ROY: Now.
   Now. I'll hold my breath till you do, I'm turning blue waiting…. *Now,* goddammit!

MARTIN: Roy, calm down, it's not…

ROY: Aw, fuck it. *(He takes a letter from his jacket pocket, hands it to Joe)*
   Read. Came today.
(Joe reads the first paragraph, then looks up.)

JOE: Roy. This is…Roy, this is terrible.

ROY: You're telling me.
   A letter from the New York State Bar Association, Martin.
   They're gonna try and disbar me.

MARTIN: Oh my.

JOE: Why?

ROY: Why, Martin?

MARTIN: Revenge.

ROY: The whole Establishment. Their little rules. Because I know no rules. Because I don't see the Law as a dead and arbitrary collection of antiquated dictums, thou shall, thou shalt not, because, because I know the Law's a pliable, breathing, sweating...*organ*, because, because...

MARTIN: Because he borrowed half a million from one of his clients.

ROY: Yeah, well, there's that.

MARTIN: *And* he forgot to *return* it.

JOE: Roy, that's.... You borrowed money from a client?

ROY: I'm deeply ashamed.
(*Little pause.*)

JOE (*Very sympathetic*): Roy, you know how much I admire you. Well I mean I know you have unorthodox ways, but I'm sure you only did what you thought at the time you needed to do. And I have faith that...

ROY: Not so damp, please. I'll deny it was a loan. She's got no paperwork. Can't prove a fucking thing.
(*Little pause. Martin studies the menu.*)

JOE (*Handing back the letter, more official in tone*): Roy I really appreciate your telling me this, and I'll do whatever I can to help.

ROY (*Holding up a hand, then, carefully*): I'll tell you what you can do.
I'm about to be tried, Joe, by a jury that is not a jury of my peers. The disbarment committee: genteel gentleman Brahmin lawyers, country-club men. I offend them, to these men...I'm what, Martin, some sort of filthy little Jewish troll?

MARTIN: Oh well, I wouldn't go so far as...

ROY: Oh well I would.
Very fancy lawyers, these disbarment committee lawyers, fancy lawyers with fancy corporate clients and complicated cases. Antitrust suits. Deregulation. Environmental control. Complex cases like these need justice Department cooperation like flowers need the sun. Wouldn't you say that's an accurate assessment, Martin?

MARTIN: I'm not here, Roy. I'm not hearing any of this.

ROY: No. Of course not.
Without the light of the sun, Joe, these cases, and the fancy lawyers who represent them, will wither and die.
A well-placed friend, someone in the Justice Department, say, can turn off the sun. Cast a deep shadow on my behalf. Make them shiver in the cold. If they overstep. They would fear that.
(*Pause.*)

JOE: Roy. I don't understand.

ROY: You do.
(*Pause.*)

JOE: You're not asking me to...

ROY: Sssshhhh. Careful.

JOE (*A beat, then*): Even if I said yes to the job, it would be illegal to interfere. With the hearings. It's unethical. No. I can't.

ROY: Unethical.
Would you excuse us, Martin?

MARTIN: Excuse you?

ROY: Take a walk, Martin. For real.
(*Martin leaves.*)

ROY: Un-ethical. Are you trying to embarrass me in front of my friend?

JOE: Well it is unethical, I can't...

ROY: Boy, you are really something. What the fuck do you think this is, Sunday School?

JOE: No, but Roy this is...

ROY: This is...this is gastric juices churning, this is enzymes and acids, this is intestinal is what this is, bowel movement and blood-red meat—this stinks, this is politics, Joe, the game of being alive. And you think you're.... What? Above that? Above alive is what? Dead! In the clouds! You're on earth, goddammit! Plant a foot, stay a while.
I'm sick. They smell I'm weak. They want blood this time. I must have eyes in Justice. In Justice you will protect me.

JOE: Why can't Mr. Heller...

ROY: Grow up, Joe. The administration can't get involved.

JOE: But I'd be part of the administration. The same as him.

ROY: Not the same. Martin's Ed's man. And Ed's Reagan's man. So Martin's Reagan's man.
And you're mine.

(Little pause. He holds up the letter)
      This will never be. Understand me?
(He tears the letter up)
      I'm gonna be a lawyer, Joe, I'm gonna
be a lawyer, Joe, I'm gonna be a goddam
motherfucking legally licensed member of
the bar lawyer, just like my daddy was, till
my last bitter day on earth, Joseph, until the
day I die.
(Martin returns.)
ROY: Ah, Martin's back.
MARTIN: So are we agreed?
ROY: Joe?
      (Little pause.)
JOE: I will think about it.
      (To Roy) I will.
ROY: Huh.
MARTIN: It's the fear of what comes after the do-
      ing that makes the doing hard to do.
ROY: Amen.
MARTIN: But you can almost always live with
      the consequences.

SCENE 7

*That afternoon. On the granite steps outside the Hall
of Justice, Brooklyn. It is cold and sunny. A Sabrett
wagon is selling hot dogs. Louis, in a shabby overcoat, is sitting on the steps contemplatively eating
one. Joe enters with three hot dogs and a can of Coke.*

JOE: Can I…?
LOUIS: Oh sure. Sure. Crazy cold sun.
JOE *(Sitting)*: Have to make the best of it.
      How's your friend?
LOUIS: My…? Oh. He's worse. My friend is
      worse.
JOE: I'm sorry.
LOUIS: Yeah, well. Thanks for asking. It's nice.
      You're nice. I can't believe you voted for
      Reagan.
JOE: I hope he gets better.
LOUIS: Reagan?
JOE: Your friend.
LOUIS: He won't. Neither will Reagan.
JOE: Let's not talk politics, OK?
LOUIS *(Pointing to Joe's lunch)*: You're eating *three*
      of those?

JOE: Well… I'm…hungry.
LOUIS: They're really terrible for you. Full of rat-
      poo and beetle legs and wood shavings 'n'
      shit.
JOE: Huh.
LOUIS: And…um…irridium, I think. Something
      toxic.
JOE: You're eating one.
LOUIS: Yeah, well, the shape, I can't help myself,
      plus I'm *trying* to commit suicide, what's
      your excuse?
JOE: I don't have an excuse. I just have Pepto-
      Bismol.
      *(Joe takes a bottle of Pepto-Bismol and chugs it.
      Louis shudders audibly.)*
JOE: Yeah I know but then I wash it down with
      Coke.
      *(He does this. Louis mimes barfing in Joe's lap.
      Joe pushes Louis's head away.)*
JOE: Are you *always* like this?
LOUIS: I've been worrying a lot about his kids.
JOE: Whose?
LOUIS: Reagan's. Maureen and Mike and little
      orphan Patti and Miss Ron Reagan Jr., the
      you-should-pardon-the-expression hetero-
      sexual.
JOE: Ron Reagan Jr. is *not*…. You shouldn't just
      make these assumptions about people.
      How do you know? About him? What he
      is? You don't know.
LOUIS *(Doing Tallulah)*: Well darling he never
      sucked *my* cock but…
JOE: Look, if you're going to get vulgar…
LOUIS: No no really I mean…. What's it like to be
      the child of the Zeitgeist? To have the Amer-
      ican Animus as your dad? It's not really a
      family, the Reagans, I read *People*, there aren't
      any connections there, no love, they don't
      ever even speak to each other except through
      their agents. So what's it like to be Reagan's
      kid? Enquiring minds want to know.
JOE: You can't believe everything you…
LOUIS *(Looking away)*: But…I think we all know
      what that's like. Nowadays. No connec-
      tions. No responsibilities. All of us…falling
      through the cracks that separate what we
      owe to our selves and…and what we owe
      to love.

JOE: You just…. Whatever you feel like saying or doing, you don't care, you just…do it.

LOUIS: Do what?

JOE: It. Whatever. Whatever it is you want to do.

LOUIS: Are you trying to tell me something?

(Little pause, sexual. They stare at each other. Joe looks away.)

JOE: No, I'm just observing that you…

LOUIS: Impulsive.

JOE: Yes, I mean it must be scary, you…

LOUIS *(Shrugs)*: Land of the free. Home of the brave. Call me irresponsible.

JOE: It's kind of terrifying.

LOUIS: Yeah, well, freedom is. Heartless, too.

JOE: Oh you're not heartless.

LOUIS: You don't know.

Finish your weenie.

(He pats Joe on the knee, starts to leave.)

JOE: Um…

(Louis turns, looks at him. Joe searches for something to say.)

JOE: Yesterday was Sunday but I've been a little unfocused recently and I thought it was Monday. So I came here like I was going to work. And the whole place was empty. And at first I couldn't figure out why, and I had this moment of incredible…fear and also…. It just flashed through my mind: The whole Hall of Justice, it's empty, it's deserted, it's gone out of business. Forever. The people that make it run have up and abandoned it.

LOUIS *(Looking at the building)*: Creepy.

JOE: Well yes but. I felt that I was going to scream. Not because it was creepy, but because the emptiness felt so *fast.*

And…well, good. A…happy scream.

I just wondered what a thing it would be…if overnight everything you owe anything to, justice, or love, had really gone away. Free.

It would be…heartless terror. Yes. Terrible, and…

Very great. To shed your skin, every old skin, one by one and then walk away, unencumbered, into the morning.

(Little pause. He looks at the building)

I can't go in there today.

LOUIS: Then don't.

JOE *(Not really hearing Louis)*: I can't go in, I need…

(He looks for what he needs. He takes a swig of Pepto-Bismol)

I can't *be* this anymore. I need…a change, I should just…

LOUIS *(Not a come-on, necessarily; he doesn't want to be alone)*: Want some company? For whatever?

(Pause. Joe looks at Louis and looks away, afraid. Louis shrugs.)

LOUIS: Sometimes, even if it scares you to death, you have to be willing to break the law. Know what I mean?

(Another little pause.)

JOE: Yes.

(Another little pause.)

LOUIS: I moved out. I moved out on my…

I haven't been sleeping well.

JOE: Me neither.

(Louis goes up to Joe, licks his napkin and dabs at Joe's mouth.)

LOUIS: Antacid moustache.

(Points to the building) Maybe the court won't convene. Ever again. Maybe we are free. To do whatever.

Children of the new morning, criminal minds. Selfish and greedy and loveless and blind. Reagan's children.

You're scared. So am I. Everybody is in the land of the free. God help us all.

SCENE 8

Late that night. Joe at a payphone phoning Hannah at home in Salt Lake City.

JOE: Mom?

HANNAH: Joe?

JOE: Hi.

HANNAH: You're calling from the street. It's…it must be four in the morning. What's happened?

JOE: Nothing, nothing, I…

HANNAH: It's Harper. Is Harper…. Joe? Joe?

JOE: Yeah, hi. No, Harper's fine. Well, no, she's…not fine. How are you, Mom?

HANNAH: What's happened?

JOE: I just wanted to talk to you. I, uh, wanted to try something out on you.

HANNAH: Joe, you haven't...have you been drinking, Joe?

JOE: Yes ma'am. I'm drunk.

HANNAH: That isn't like you.

JOE: No. I mean, who's to say?

HANNAH: Why are you out on the street at four AM? In that crazy city. It's dangerous.

JOE: Actually, Mom, I'm not on the street. I'm near the boathouse in the park.

HANNAH: What park?

JOE: Central Park.

HANNAH: CENTRAL PARK! Oh my Lord. What on earth are you doing in Central Park at this time of night? Are you...

Joe, I think you ought to go home right now. Call me from home.
(*Little pause*)
Joe?

JOE: I come here to watch, Mom. Sometimes. Just to watch.

HANNAH: Watch what? What's there to watch at four in the...

JOE: Mom, did Dad love me?

HANNAH: What?

JOE: Did he?

HANNAH: You ought to go home and call from there.

JOE: Answer.

HANNAH: Oh now really. This is maudlin. I don't like this conversation.

JOE: Yeah, well, it gets worse from here on.
(*Pause.*)

HANNAH: Joe?

JOE: Mom. Momma. I'm a homosexual, Momma. Boy, did that come out awkward.
(*Pause*)
Hello? Hello?
I'm a homosexual.
(*Pause*)
Please, Momma. Say something.

HANNAH: You're old enough to understand that your father didn't love you without being ridiculous about it.

JOE: What?

HANNAH: You're ridiculous. You're being ridiculous.

JOE: I'm...
What?

HANNAH: You really ought to go home now to your wife. I need to go to bed. This phone call.... We will just forget this phone call.

JOE: Mom.

HANNAH: No more talk. Tonight. This...
(*Suddenly very angry*) Drinking is a sin! A sin! I raised you better than that. (*She hangs up*)

SCENE 9

The following morning, early. Split scene. Harper and Joe at home; Louis and Prior in Prior's hospital room. Joe and Louis have just entered. This should be fast and obviously furious; overlapping is fine; the proceedings may be a little confusing but not the final results.

HARPER: Oh God. Home. The moment of truth has arrived.

JOE: Harper.

LOUIS: I'm going to move out.

PRIOR: The fuck you are.

JOE: Harper. Please listen. I still love you very much. You're still my best buddy; I'm not going to leave you.

HARPER: No, I don't like the sound of this. I'm leaving.

LOUIS: I'm leaving.
I already have.

JOE: Please listen. Stay. This is really hard. We have to talk.

HARPER: We are talking. Aren't we. Now please shut up. OK?

PRIOR: Bastard. Sneaking off while I'm flat out here, that's low. If I could get up now I'd beat the holy shit out of you.

JOE: Did you take pills? How many?

HARPER: No pills. Bad for the...(*Pats stomach*)

JOE: You aren't pregnant. I called your gynecologist.

HARPER: I'm seeing a new gynecologist.

PRIOR: You have no right to do this.

LOUIS: Oh, that's ridiculous.

PRIOR: No right. It's criminal.

JOE: Forget about that. Just listen. You want the truth. This is the truth.

I knew this when I married you. I've known this I guess for as long as I've known anything, but...I don't know, I thought maybe that with enough effort and will I could change myself...but I can't...

PRIOR: Criminal.

LOUIS: There oughta be a law.

PRIOR: There is a law. You'll see.

JOE: I'm losing ground here, I go walking, you want to know where I walk, I...go to the park, or up and down 53rd Street, or places where.... And I keep swearing I won't go walking again, but I just can't.

LOUIS: I need some privacy.

PRIOR: That's new.

LOUIS: Everything's new, Prior.

JOE: I try to tighten my heart into a knot, a snarl, I try to learn to live dead, just numb, but then I see someone I want, and it's like a nail, like a hot spike right through my chest, and I know I'm losing.

PRIOR: Apartment too small for three? Louis and Prior comfy but not Louis and Prior and Prior's disease?

LOUIS: Something like that.
   I won't be judged by you. This isn't a crime, just—the inevitable consequence of people who run out of—whose limitations...

PRIOR: Bang bang bang. The court will come to order.

LOUIS: I mean let's talk practicalities, schedules; I'll come over if you want, spend nights with you when I can, I can...

PRIOR: Has the jury reached a verdict?

LOUIS: I'm doing the best I can.

PRIOR: Pathetic. Who cares?

JOE: My whole life has conspired to bring me to this place, and I can't despise my whole life. I think I believed when I met you I could save you, you at least if not myself, but...
   I don't have any sexual feelings for you, Harper. And I don't think I ever did.
   (Little pause.)

HARPER: I think you should go.

JOE: Where?

HARPER: Washington. Doesn't matter.

JOE: What are you talking about?

HARPER: Without me.
   Without me, Joe. Isn't that what you want to hear?
   (Little pause.)

JOE: Yes.

LOUIS: You can love someone and fail them. You can love someone and not be able to...

PRIOR: You *can*, theoretically, yes. A person can, maybe an editorial "you" can love, Louis, but not *you*, specifically you, I don't know, I think you are excluded from that general category.

HARPER: You were going to save me, but the whole time you were spinning a lie. I just don't understand that.

PRIOR: A person could theoretically love and maybe many do but we both know now you can't.

LOUIS: I do.

PRIOR: You can't even say it.

LOUIS: I love you, Prior.

PRIOR: I repeat. Who cares?

HARPER: This is so scary, I want this to stop, to go back...

PRIOR: We have reached a verdict, your honor. This man's heart is deficient. He loves, but his love is worth nothing.

JOE: Harper...

HARPER: Mr. Lies, I want to get away from here. Far away. Right now. Before he starts talking again. Please, please...

JOE: As long as I've known you Harper you've been afraid of...of men hiding under the bed, men hiding under the sofa, men with knives.

PRIOR (*Shattered; almost pleading; trying to reach him*): I'm dying! You stupid fuck! Do you know what that is! Love! Do you know what love means? We lived together four-and-a-half years, you animal, you idiot.

LOUIS: I have to find some way to save myself.

JOE: Who are these men? I never understood it. Now I know.

HARPER: What?

JOE: It's me.

HARPER: It is?

PRIOR: GET OUT OF MY ROOM!

JOE: I'm the man with the knives.

HARPER: You are?

PRIOR: If I could get up now I'd kill you. I would. Go away. Go away or I'll scream.

HARPER: Oh God…

JOE: I'm sorry…

HARPER: It is you.

LOUIS: Please don't scream.

PRIOR: Go.

HARPER: I recognize you now.

LOUIS: Please…

JOE: Oh. Wait, I…. Oh!

(He covers his mouth with his hand, gags, and removes his hand, red with blood)

I'm bleeding.

(Prior screams.)

HARPER: Mr. Lies.

MR. LIES *(Appearing, dressed in Antarctic explorer's apparel)*: Right here.

HARPER: I want to go away. I can't see him anymore.

MR. LIES: Where?

HARPER: Anywhere. Far away.

MR. LIES: Absolutamento.

(Harper and Mr. Lies vanish. Joe looks up, sees that she's gone.)

PRIOR *(Closing his eyes)*: When I open my eyes you'll be gone.

(Louis leaves.)

JOE: Harper?

PRIOR *(Opening his eyes)*: Huh. It worked.

JOE *(Calling)*: Harper?

PRIOR: I hurt all over. I wish I was dead.

SCENE 10

The same day, sunset. Hannah and Sister Ella Chapter, a real-estate saleswoman, Hannah Pitt's closest friend, in front of Hannah's house in Salt Lake City.

SISTER ELLA CHAPTER: Look at that view! A view of heaven. Like the living city of heaven, isn't it, it just fairly glimmers in the sun.

HANNAH: Glimmers.

SISTER ELLA CHAPTER: Even the stone and brick it just glimmers and glitters like heaven in the sunshine. Such a nice view you get, perched up on a canyon rim. Some kind of beautiful place.

HANNAH: It's just Salt Lake, and you're selling the house *for* me, not *to* me.

SISTER ELLA CHAPTER: I like to work up an enthusiasm for my properties.

HANNAH: Just get me a good price.

SISTER ELLA CHAPTER: Well, the market's off.

HANNAH: At least fifty.

SISTER ELLA CHAPTER: Forty'd be more like it.

HANNAH: Fifty.

SISTER ELLA CHAPTER: Wish you'd wait a bit.

HANNAH: Well I can't.

SISTER ELLA CHAPTER: Wish you would. You're about the only friend I got.

HANNAH: Oh well now.

SISTER ELLA CHAPTER: Know why I decided to like you? I decided to like you 'cause you're the only unfriendly Mormon I ever met.

HANNAH: Your wig is crooked.

SISTER ELLA CHAPTER: Fix it.

(Hannah straightens Sister Ella's wig.)

SISTER ELLA CHAPTER: New York City. All they got there is tiny rooms.

I always thought: People ought to stay put. That's why I got my license to sell real estate. It's a way of saying: Have a house! Stay put! It's a way of saying traveling's no good. Plus I needed the cash. *(She takes a pack of cigarettes out of her purse, lights one, offers pack to Hannah)*

HANNAH: Not out here, anyone could come by.

There's been days I've stood at this ledge and thought about stepping over.

It's a hard place, Salt Lake: baked dry. Abundant energy; not much intelligence. That's a combination that can wear a body out. No harm looking someplace else. I don't need much room.

My sister-in-law Libby thinks there's radon gas in the basement.

SISTER ELLA CHAPTER: Is there gas in the…

HANNAH: Of course not. Libby's a fool.

SISTER ELLA CHAPTER: 'Cause I'd have to include that in the description.

HANNAH: There's no gas, Ella. *(Little pause)* Give a puff. *(She takes a furtive drag of Ella's cigarette)* Put it away now.

SISTER ELLA CHAPTER: So I guess it's goodbye.

HANNAH: You'll be all right, Ella, I wasn't ever much of a friend.

SISTER ELLA CHAPTER: I'll say something but don't laugh, OK? This is the home of saints, the godliest place on earth, they say, and I think they're right. That mean there's no evil here? No. Evil's everywhere. Sin's everywhere. But this…is the spring of sweet water in the desert, the desert flower. Every step a Believer takes away from here is a step fraught with peril. I fear for you, Hannah Pitt, because you are my friend. Stay put. This is the right home of saints.

HANNAH: Latter-day saints.

SISTER ELLA CHAPTER: Only kind left.

HANNAH: But still. Late in the day…for saints and everyone. That's all. That's all.

Fifty thousand dollars for the house, Sister Ella Chapter; don't undersell. It's an impressive view.

ACT THREE: NOT-YET-CONSCIOUS, FORWARD DAWNING
January 1986

SCENE 1

Late night, three days after the end of Act Two. The stage is completely dark. Prior is in bed in his apartment, having a nightmare. He wakes up, sits up and switches on a nightlight. He looks at his clock. Seated by the table near the bed is a man dressed in the clothing of a 13th-century British squire.

PRIOR (*Terrified*): Who are you?

PRIOR 1: My name is Prior Walter.
    (*Pause.*)

PRIOR: My name is Prior Walter.

PRIOR 1: I know that.

PRIOR: Explain.

PRIOR 1: You're alive. I'm not. We have the same name. What do you want me to explain?

PRIOR: A ghost?

PRIOR 1: An ancestor.

PRIOR: Not *the* Prior Walter? The Bayeux tapestry Prior Walter?

PRIOR 1: His great-great grandson. The fifth of the name.

PRIOR: I'm the thirty-fourth, I think.

PRIOR 1: Actually the thirty-second.

PRIOR: Not according to Mother.

PRIOR 1: She's including the two bastards, then; I say leave them out. I say no room for bastards. The little things you swallow…

PRIOR: Pills.

PRIOR 1: Pills. For the pestilence. I too…

PRIOR: Pestilence…. You too what?

PRIOR 1: The pestilence in my time was much worse than now. Whole villages of empty houses. You could look outdoors and see Death walking in the morning, dew dampening the ragged hem of his black robe. Plain as I see you now.

PRIOR: You died of the plague.

PRIOR 1: The spotty monster. Like you, alone.

PRIOR: I'm not alone.

PRIOR 1: You have no wife, no children.

PRIOR: I'm gay.

PRIOR 1: So? Be gay, dance in your altogether for all I care, what's that to do with not having children?

PRIOR: Gay homosexual, not bonny, blithe and …never mind.

PRIOR 1: I had twelve. When I died.
    (*The second ghost appears, this one dressed in the clothing of an elegant 17th-century Londoner.*)

PRIOR 1 (*Pointing to Prior 2*): And I was three years younger than him.
    (*Prior sees the new ghost, screams.*)

PRIOR: Oh God another one.

PRIOR 1: Prior Walter. Prior to you by some seventeen others.

PRIOR: He's counting the bastards.

PRIOR: Are we having a convention?

PRIOR 1: We've been sent to declare her fabulous incipience. They love a well-paved entrance with lots of heralds, and…

PRIOR 1: The messenger come. Prepare the way. The infinite descent, a breath in air…

PRIOR 2: They chose us, I suspect, because of the mortal affinities. In a family as long-descended as the Walters there are bound to be a few carried off by plague.

PRIOR 1: The spotty monster.

PRIOR 2: Blackjack. Came from a water pump, half the city of London, can you imagine? His came from fleas. Yours, I understand, is the lamentable consequence of venery...

PRIOR 1: Fleas on rats, but who knew that?

PRIOR: Am I going to die?

PRIOR 2: We aren't allowed to discuss...

PRIOR 1: When you do, you don't get ancestors to help you through it. You may be surrounded by children but you die alone.

PRIOR: I'm afraid.

PRIOR 1: You should be. There aren't even torches, and the path's rocky, dark and steep.

PRIOR 2: Don't alarm him. There's good news before there's bad.
    We two come to strew rose petal and palm leaf before the triumphal procession. Prophet. Seer. Revelator. It's a great honor for the family.

PRIOR 1: He hasn't got a family.

PRIOR 2: I meant for the Walters, for the family in the larger sense.

PRIOR (*Singing*):
    All I want is a room somewhere,
    Far away from the cold night air...

PRIOR 2 (*Putting a hand on Prior's forehead*): Calm, calm, this is no brain fever...
    (*Prior calms down, but keeps his eyes closed. The lights begin to change. Distant Glorious Music.*)

PRIOR 1 (*Low chant*): Adonai, Adonai,
    Olam ha-yichud,
    Zefirot, Zazahot,
    Ha-adam, ha-gadol
    Daughter of Light,
    Daughter of Splendors,
    Fluor! Phosphor!
    Lumen! Candle!

PRIOR 2 (*Simultaneously*):
    Even now,
    From the mirror-bright halls of heaven,
    Across the cold and lifeless infinity of space,
    The Messenger comes
    Trailing orbs of light,
    Fabulous, incipient,
    Oh Prophet,
    To you...

PRIOR 1 AND PRIOR 2:
    Prepare, prepare,
    The Infinite Descent,
    A breath, a feather,
    Glory to...
    (*They vanish.*)

SCENE 2

The next day. Split scene. Louis and Belize in a coffee shop. Prior is at the outpatient clinic at the hospital with Emily, the nurse; she has him on a pentamidine IV drip.

LOUIS: Why has democracy succeeded in America? Of course by succeeded I mean comparatively, not literally, not in the present, but what makes for the prospect of some sort of radical democracy spreading outward and growing up? Why does the power that was once so carefully preserved at the top of the pyramid by the original framers of the Constitution seem drawn inexorably downward and outward in spite of the best effort of the Right to stop this? I mean it's the really hard thing about being Left in this country, the American Left can't help but trip over all these petrified little fetishes: freedom, that's the worst; you know, *Jeane Kirkpatrick* for God's sake will go on and on about freedom and so what does that mean, the word freedom, when she talks about it, or human rights; you have Bush talking about human rights, and so what are these people talking about, they might as well be talking about the mating habits of Venusians, these people don't begin to know what, ontologically, freedom is or human rights, like they see these bourgeois property-based Rights-of-Man-type rights but that's not enfranchisement, not democracy, not what's implicit, what's potential within the idea, not the idea with blood in it. That's just liberalism, the worst kind of liberalism, really, bourgeois tolerance, and what I think is that what AIDS shows us is the limits of tolerance, that it's not enough to be tolerated, because when the shit hits the fan you find out how much tolerance is worth. Nothing. And underneath all the tolerance is intense, passionate hatred.

BELIZE: Uh huh.

LOUIS: Well don't you think that's true?

BELIZE: Uh huh. It is.

LOUIS: *Power* is the object, not being tolerated. Fuck assimilation. But I mean in spite of all this the thing about America, I think, is that ultimately we're different from every other nation on earth, in that, with people here of every race, we can't.... Ultimately what defines us isn't race, but politics. Not like any European country where there's an insurmountable fact of a kind of racial, or ethnic, monopoly, or monolith, like all Dutchmen, I mean Dutch people, are well, Dutch, and the Jews of Europe were never Europeans, just a small problem. Facing the monolith. But here there are so many small problems, it's really just a collection of small problems, the monolith is missing. Oh, I mean, of course I suppose there's the monolith of White America. White Straight Male America.

BELIZE: Which is not unimpressive, even among monoliths.

LOUIS: Well, no, but when the race thing gets taken care of, and I don't mean to minimalize how major it is, I mean I know it is, this is a really, really incredibly racist country but it's like, well, the British. I mean, all these blue-eyed pink people. And it's just weird, you know, I mean I'm not all that Jewish-looking, or...well, maybe I am but, you know, in New York, everyone is...well, not everyone, but so many are but so but in England, in London I walk into bars and I feel like Sid the Yid, you know I mean like Woody Allen in *Annie Hall,* with the payess and the gabardine coat, like never, never anywhere so much—I mean, not actively despised, not like they're Germans, who I think are still terribly anti-Semitic, and racist too, I mean black-racist, they pretend otherwise but, anyway, in London, there's just...and at one point I met this black gay guy from Jamaica who talked with a lilt but he said his family'd been living in London since before the Civil War—the American one—and how the English never let him forget for a minute that he wasn't blue-eyed and pink and I said yeah, me too, these people are anti-Semites and he said yeah but the British Jews have the clothing business all sewed up and blacks there can't get a foothold. And it was an incredibly awkward moment of just.... I mean here we were, in this bar that was gay but it was a pub, you know, the beams and the plaster and those horrible little, like, two-day-old fish and egg sandwiches—and just so British, so old, and I felt, well, there's no way out of this because both of us are, right now, too much immersed in this history, hope is dissolved in the sheer age of this place, where race is what counts and there's no real hope of change—it's the racial destiny of the Brits that matters to them, not their political destiny, whereas in America...

BELIZE: Here in America race doesn't count.

LOUIS: No, no, that's not.... I mean you *can't* be hearing that...

BELIZE: I...

LOUIS: It's—look, race, yes, but ultimately race here is a political question, right? Racists just try to use race here as a tool in a political struggle. It's not really about race. Like the spiritualists try to use that stuff, are you enlightened, are you centered, channeled, whatever, this reaching out for a spiritual past in a country where no indigenous spirits exist—only the Indians, I mean Native American spirits and we killed them off so now, there are no gods here, no ghosts and spirits in America, there are no angels in America, no spiritual past, no racial past, there's only the political, and the decoys and the ploys to maneuver around the inescapable battle of politics, the shifting downwards and outwards of political power to the people...

BELIZE: POWER to the People! AMEN! (*Looking at his watch*) *OH MY GOODNESS!* Will you look at the time, I gotta...

LOUIS: Do you....You think this is, what, racist or naive or something?

BELIZE: Well it's certainly *something*. Look, I just remembered I have an appointment…

LOUIS: What? I mean I really don't want to, like, speak from some position of privilege and…

BELIZE: I'm sitting here, thinking, eventually he's *got* to run out of steam, so I let you rattle on and on saying about maybe seven or eight things I find really offensive.

LOUIS: What?

BELIZE: But I know you, Louis, and I know the guilt fueling this peculiar tirade is obviously already swollen bigger than your hemorrhoids.

LOUIS: I don't have hemorrhoids.

BELIZE: I hear different. May I finish?

LOUIS: Yes, but I don't have hemorrhoids.

BELIZE: So finally, when I…

LOUIS: Prior told you, he's an asshole, he shouldn't have…

BELIZE: You promised, Louis. Prior is not a subject.

LOUIS: You brought him up.

BELIZE: I brought up hemorrhoids.

LOUIS: So it's indirect. Passive-aggressive.

BELIZE: Unlike, I suppose, banging me over the head with your theory that America doesn't have a race problem.

LOUIS: Oh be fair I never said that.

BELIZE: Not exactly, but…

LOUIS: I said…

BELIZE: …but it was close enough, because if it'd been that blunt I'd've just walked out and…

LOUIS: You deliberately misinterpreted! I…

BELIZE: Stop interrupting! I haven't been able to…

LOUIS: Just let me…

BELIZE: NO! What, *talk?* You've been running your mouth non-stop since I got here, yaddadda yaddadda blah blah blah, up the hill, down the hill, playing with your MONOLITH…

LOUIS (*Overlapping*): Well, you could have joined in at any time instead of…

BELIZE (*Continuing over Louis*): …and girlfriend it is truly an awesome spectacle but I got better things to do with my time than sit here listening to this racist bullshit just because I feel sorry for you that…

LOUIS: I am not a racist!

BELIZE: Oh come on…

LOUIS: So maybe I am a racist but…

BELIZE: Oh I really hate that! It's no fun picking on you Louis; you're so guilty, it's like throwing darts at a glob of jello, there's no satisfying hits, just quivering, the darts just blop in and vanish.

LOUIS: I just think when you are discussing lines of oppression it gets very complicated and…

BELIZE: Oh is that a fact? You know, we black drag queens have a rather intimate knowledge of the complexity of the lines of…

LOUIS: *Ex*-black drag queen.

BELIZE: Actually ex-ex.

LOUIS: You're doing drag again?

BELIZE: I don't…. Maybe. I don't have to tell you. Maybe.

LOUIS: I think it's sexist.

BELIZE: I didn't ask you.

LOUIS: Well it is. The gay community, I think, has to adopt the same attitude towards drag as black women have to take towards black women blues singers.

BELIZE: Oh my we *are* walking dangerous tonight.

LOUIS: Well, it's all internalized oppression, right, I mean the masochism, the stereotypes, the…

BELIZE: Louis, are you deliberately trying to make me hate you?

LOUIS: No, I…

BELIZE: I mean, are you deliberately transforming yourself into an arrogant, sexual-political Stalinist-slash-racist flag-waving thug for my benefit?

(*Pause.*)

LOUIS: You know what I think?

BELIZE: What?

LOUIS: You hate me because I'm a Jew.

BELIZE: I'm leaving.

LOUIS: It's true.

BELIZE: You have no basis except your…

Louis, it's good to know you haven't changed; you are still an honorary citizen of the Twilight Zone, and after your pale, pale white polemics on behalf of racial insensitivity you have a flaming *fuck* of a lot of nerve calling me an anti-Semite. Now I really gotta go.

LOUIS: You called me Lou the Jew.

BELIZE: That was a joke.

LOUIS: I didn't think it was funny. It was hostile.

BELIZE: It was three years ago.

LOUIS: So?

BELIZE: You just called yourself Sid the Yid.

LOUIS: That's not the same thing.

BELIZE: Sid the Yid is different from Lou the Jew.

LOUIS: Yes.

BELIZE: Someday you'll have to explain that to me, but right now…

> You hate me because you hate black people.

LOUIS: I do not. But I do think most black people are anti-Semitic.

BELIZE: "Most black people." *That's* racist, Louis, and *I* think most Jews…

LOUIS: Louis Farrakhan.

BELIZE: Ed Koch.

LOUIS: Jesse Jackson.

BELIZE: Jackson. Oh really, Louis, this is…

LOUIS: Hymietown! Hymietown!

BELIZE: Louis, you voted for Jesse Jackson. You send checks to the Rainbow Coalition.

LOUIS: I'm ambivalent. The checks bounced.

BELIZE: All your checks bounce, Louis; you're ambivalent about everything.

LOUIS: What's that supposed to mean?

BELIZE: You may be dumber than shit but I refuse to believe you can't figure it out. Try.

LOUIS: I was never ambivalent about Prior. I love him. I do. I really do.

BELIZE: Nobody said different.

LOUIS: Love and ambivalence are…. Real love isn't ambivalent.

BELIZE: "Real love isn't ambivalent." I'd swear that's a line from my favorite bestselling paperback novel, *In Love with the Night Mysterious*, except I don't think you ever read it. (*Pause.*)

LOUIS: I never read it, no.

BELIZE: You ought to. Instead of spending the rest of your life trying to get through *Democracy in America*. It's about this white woman whose Daddy owns a plantation in the Deep South in the years before the Civil War—the American one—and her name is Margaret, and she's in love with her Daddy's number-one slave, and his name is Thaddeus, and she's married but her white slave-owner husband has AIDS: Antebellum Insufficiently Developed Sexorgans. And there's a lot of hot stuff going down when Margaret and Thaddeus can catch a spare torrid ten under the cotton-picking moon, and then of course the Yankees come, and they set the slaves free, and the slaves string up old Daddy, and so on. Historical fiction. Somewhere in there I recall Margaret and Thaddeus find the time to discuss the nature of love; her face is reflecting the flames of the burning plantation—you know, the way white people do—and his black face is dark in the night and she says to him, "Thaddeus, real love isn't ever ambivalent."

(*Little pause. Emily enters and turns off IV drip.*)

BELIZE: Thaddeus looks at her; he's contemplating her thesis; and he isn't sure he agrees.

EMILY (*Removing IV drip from Prior's arm*): Treatment number…(*Consulting chart*) four.

PRIOR: Pharmaceutical miracle. Lazarus breathes again.

LOUIS: Is he….How bad is he?

BELIZE: You want the laundry list?

EMILY: Shirt off, let's check the…

(*Prior takes his shirt off. She examines his lesions.*)

BELIZE: There's the weight problem and the shit problem and the morale problem.

EMILY: Only six. That's good. Pants.

(*He drops his pants. He's naked. She examines.*)

BELIZE: And. He thinks he's going crazy.

EMILY: Looking good. What else?

PRIOR: Ankles sore and swollen, but the leg's better. The nausea's mostly gone with the little orange pills. BM's pure liquid but not bloody anymore, for now, my eye doctor says everything's OK, for now, my dentist says "Yuck!" when he sees my fuzzy tongue, and now he wears little condoms on his thumb and forefinger. And a mask. So what? My dermatologist is in Hawaii and my mother…well leave my mother out of it. Which is usually where my mother is, out of it. My glands are like walnuts, my weight's holding steady for week two, and a friend died two days ago of bird tuberculosis; bird tuberculosis; that scared me and I didn't go to the funeral today because he was an Irish Catholic and it's probably open casket and I'm afraid of…something, the bird TB or seeing him or…. So I guess I'm doing OK. Except for of course I'm going nuts.

EMILY: We ran the toxoplasmosis series and there's no indication…

PRIOR: I know, I know, but I feel like something terrifying is on its way, you know, like a missile from outer space, and it's plummeting down towards the earth, and I'm ground zero, and…I am generally known where I am known as one cool, collected queen. And I am ruffled.

EMILY: There's really nothing to worry about. I think that shochen bamromim hamtzeh menucho nechono al kanfey haschino.

PRIOR: What?

EMILY: Everything's fine. Bemaalos k'doshim ut'horim kezohar horokeea mazhirim…

PRIOR: Oh I don't understand what you're…

EMILY: Es nishmas Prior sheholoch leolomoh, baavur shenodvoo z'dokoh Fad hazkoras nishmosoh.

PRIOR: Why are you doing that?! Stop it! Stop it!

EMILY: Stop what?

PRIOR: You were just…weren't you just speaking in Hebrew or something.

EMILY: *Hebrew? (Laughs)* I'm basically Italian-American. No. I didn't speak in Hebrew.

PRIOR: Oh no, oh God please I really think I…

EMILY: Look, I'm sorry, I have a waiting room full of…. I think you're one of the lucky ones, you'll live for years, probably you're pretty healthy for someone with no immune system. Are you seeing someone? Loneliness is a danger. A therapist?

PRIOR: No, I don't need to see anyone, I just…

EMILY: Well think about it. You aren't going crazy. You're just under a lot of stress. No wonder…(*She starts to write in his chart*) (*Suddenly there is an astonishing blaze of light, a huge chord sounded by a gigantic choir, and a great book with steel pages mounted atop a molten-red pillar pops up from the stage floor. The book opens, there is a large Aleph inscribed on its pages, which bursts into flames. Immediately*

the book slams shut and disappears instantly under the floor as the lights become normal again. Emily notices none of this, writing. Prior is agog.)

EMILY (*Laughing, exiting*): Hebrew…
    (*Prior flees.*)

LOUIS: Help me.

BELIZE: I beg your pardon?

LOUIS: You're a nurse, give me something, I…don't know what to do anymore, I…. Last week at work I screwed up the Xerox machine like permanently and so I…then I tripped on the subway steps and my glasses broke and I cut my forehead, here, see, and now I can't see much and my forehead…it's like the Mark of Cain, stupid, right, but it won't heal and every morning I see it and I think, Biblical things, Mark of Cain, Judas Iscariot and his silver and his noose, people who…in betraying what they love betray what's truest in themselves, I feel…nothing but cold for myself, just cold, and every night I miss him, I miss him so much but then…those sores, and the smell and… where I thought it was going…, I could be …I could be sick too, maybe I'm sick too. I don't know.

    Belize. Tell him I love him. Can you do that?

BELIZE: I've thought about it for a very long time, and I still don't understand what love is. Justice is simple. Democracy is simple. Those things are unambivalent. But love is very hard. And it goes bad for you if you violate the hard law of love.

LOUIS: I'm dying.

BELIZE: He's dying. You just wish you were.

    Oh cheer up, Louis. Look at that heavy sky out there.

LOUIS: Purple.

BELIZE: *Purple?* Boy, what kind of a homosexual are you, anyway? That's not purple, Mary, that color up there is (*Very grand*) mauve.

    All day today it's felt like Thanksgiving. Soon, this…ruination will be blanketed white. You can smell it—can you smell it?

LOUIS: Smell what?

BELIZE: Softness, compliance, forgiveness, grace.

LOUIS: No…

BELIZE: I can't help you learn that. I can't help you, Louis. You're not my business. (*He exits*) (*Louis puts his head in his hands, inadvertently touching his cut forehead.*)

LOUIS: Ow FUCK! (*He stands slowly, looks towards where Belize exited.*) Smell what? (*He looks both ways to be sure no one is watching, then inhales deeply, and is surprised.*) Huh. Snow.

SCENE 3

Same day. Harper in a very white, cold place, with a brilliant blue sky above; a delicate snowfall. She is dressed in a beautiful snowsuit. The sound of the sea, faint.

HARPER: Snow! Ice! Mountains of ice! Where am I? I…I feel better, I do, I…feel better. There are ice crystals in my lungs, wonderful and sharp. And the snow smells like cold, crushed peaches. And there's something… some current of blood in the wind, how strange, it has that iron taste.

MR. LIES: Ozone.

HARPER: Ozone! Wow! Where am I?

MR. LIES: The Kingdom of Ice, the bottommost part of the world.

HARPER (*Looking around, then realizing*): Antarctica. This is Antarctica!

MR. LIES: Cold shelter for the shattered. No sorrow here, tears freeze.

HARPER: Antarctica, Antarctica, oh boy oh boy, LOOK at this, I…. Wow, I must've really snapped the tether, huh?

MR. LIES: Apparently…

HARPER: That's great. I want to stay here forever. Set up camp. Build things. Build a city, an enormous city made up of frontier forts, dark wood and green roofs and high gates made of pointed logs and bonfires burning on every street corner. I should build by a river. Where are the forests?

MR. LIES: No timber here. Too cold. Ice, no trees.

HARPER: Oh details! I'm sick of details! I'll plant them and grow them. I'll live off caribou fat, I'll melt it over the bonfires and drink it

from long, curved goat-horn cups. It'll be great. I want to make a new world here. So that I never have to go home again.

MR. LIES: As long as it lasts. Ice has a way of melting…

HARPER: No. Forever. I can have anything I want here—maybe even companionship, someone who has…desire for me. You, maybe.

MR. LIES: It's against the by-laws of the International Order of Travel Agents to get involved with clients. Rules are rules. Anyway, I'm not the one you really want.

HARPER: There isn't anyone…maybe an Eskimo. Who could ice-fish for food. And help me build a nest for when the baby comes.

MR. LIES: There are no Eskimo in Antarctica. And you're not really pregnant. You made that up.

HARPER: Well all of this is made up. So if the snow feels cold I'm pregnant. Right? Here, I can be pregnant. And I can have any kind of a baby I want.

MR. LIES: This is a retreat, a vacuum, its virtue is that it lacks everything; deep-freeze for feelings. You can be numb and safe here, that's what you came for. Respect the delicate ecology of your delusions.

HARPER: You mean like no Eskimo in Antarctica.

MR. LIES: Correcto. Ice and snow, no Eskimo. Even hallucinations have laws.

HARPER: Well then who's that? (*The Eskimo appears.*)

MR. LIES: An Eskimo.

HARPER: An antarctic Eskimo. A fisher of the polar deep.

MR. LIES: There's something wrong with this picture. (*The Eskimo beckons.*)

HARPER: I'm going to like this place. It's my own National Geographic Special! Oh! Oh! (*She holds her stomach*) I think…I think I felt her kicking. Maybe I'll give birth to a baby covered with thick white fur, and that way she won't be cold. My breasts will be full of hot cocoa so she doesn't get chilly. And if it gets really cold, she'll have a pouch I can crawl into. Like a marsupial. We'll mend together. That's what we'll do; we'll mend.

SCENE 4

Same day. An abandoned lot in the South Bronx. A homeless Woman is standing near an oil drum in which a fire is burning. Snowfall. Trash around. Hannah enters dragging two heavy suitcases.

HANNAH: Excuse me? I said excuse me? Can you tell me where I am? Is this Brooklyn? Do you know a Pineapple Street? Is there some sort of bus or train or…?

I'm lost, I just arrived from Salt Lake. City. Utah? I took the bus that I was told to take and I got off—well it was the very last stop, so I had to get off, and I *asked* the driver was this Brooklyn, and he nodded yes but he was from one of those foreign countries where they think it's good manners to nod at everything even if you have no idea what it is you're nodding at, and in truth I think he spoke no English at all, which I think would make him ineligible for employment on public transportation. The public being English-speaking, mostly. Do you speak English?

(*The Woman nods.*)

HANNAH: I was supposed to be met at the airport by my son. He didn't show and I don't wait more than three and three-quarters hours for *anyone*. I should have been patient, I guess, I…. Is this…

WOMAN: Bronx.

HANNAH: Is that…. The *Bronx?* Well how in the name of Heaven did I get to the Bronx when the bus driver said…

WOMAN (*Talking to herself*): Slurp slurp slurp will you STOP that disgusting slurping! YOU DISGUSTING SLURPING FEEDING ANIMAL! Feeding yourself, just feeding yourself, what would it matter, to you or to ANYONE, if you just stopped. Feeding. And DIED?

(*Pause.*)

HANNAH: Can you just tell me where I…

WOMAN: Why was the Kosciusko Bridge named after a Polack?

HANNAH: I don't know what you're…

WOMAN: That was a joke.

HANNAH: Well what's the punchline?

WOMAN: I don't know.

HANNAH (*Looking around desperately*): Oh for pete's sake, is there anyone else who…

WOMAN (*Again, to herself*): Stand further off you fat loathsome whore, you can't have any more of this soup, slurp slurp slurp you animal, and the—I know you'll just go pee it all away and where will you do that? Behind what bush? It's FUCKING COLD out here and I…

Oh that's right, because it was supposed to have been a tunnel!

That's not very funny.

Have you read the prophecies of Nostradamus?

HANNAH: Who?

WOMAN: Some guy I went out with once somewhere, Nostradamus. Prophet, outcast, eyes like…. Scary shit, he…

HANNAH: Shut up. Please. Now I want you to stop jabbering for a minute and pull your wits together and tell me how to get to Brooklyn. Because you know! And you are going to tell me! Because there is no one else around to tell me and I am wet and cold and I am very angry! So I am sorry you're psychotic but just make the effort—take a deep breath—DO IT!

(*Hannah and the Woman breathe together.*)

HANNAH: That's good. Now exhale.

(*They do.*)

HANNAH: Good. Now how do I get to Brooklyn?

WOMAN: Don't know. Never been. Sorry. Want some soup?

HANNAH: Manhattan? Maybe you know…I don't suppose you know the location of the Mormon Visitor's…

WOMAN: 65th and Broadway.

HANNAH: How do you…

WOMAN: Go there all the time. Free movies. Boring, but you can stay all day.

HANNAH: Well…. So how do I…

WOMAN: Take the D Train. Next block make a right.

HANNAH: Thank you.

WOMAN: Oh yeah. In the new century I think we will all be insane.

SCENE 5

Same day. Joe and Roy in the study of Roy's brown-stone. Roy is wearing an elegant bathrobe. He has made a considerable effort to look well. He isn't well, and he hasn't succeeded much in looking it.

JOE: I can't. The answer's no. I'm sorry.

ROY: Oh, well, apologies…

    I can't see that there's anyone asking for apologies.

    (*Pause.*)

JOE: I'm sorry, Roy.

ROY: Oh, well, apologies.

JOE: My wife is missing, Roy. My mother's coming from Salt Lake to…to help look, I guess. I'm supposed to be at the airport now, picking her up but…. I just spent two days in a hospital, Roy, with a bleeding ulcer, I was spitting up blood.

ROY: Blood, huh? Look, I'm very busy here and…

JOE: It's just a job.

ROY: A job? A *job? Washington!* Dumb Utah Mormon hick shit!

JOE: Roy…

ROY: *WASHINGTON!* When Washington called me I was younger than you, you think I said "Aw fuck no I can't go I got two fingers up my asshole and a little moral nosebleed to boot!" When Washington calls you my pretty young punk friend you go or you can go fuck yourself sideways 'cause the train has pulled out of the station, and you are *out*, nowhere, out in the cold. Fuck you, Mary Jane, get outta here.

JOE: Just let me…

ROY: Explain? Ephemera. You broke my heart. Explain that. Explain that.

JOE: I love you. Roy.

    There's so much that I want, to be… what you see in me, I want to be a participant in the world, in your world, Roy, I want to be capable of that, I've tried, really I have but…I can't do this. Not because I don't believe in you, but because I believe in you so much, in what you stand for, at heart, the order, the decency. I would give anything to protect you, but…. There are laws I can't break. It's too ingrained. It's not me. There's enough damage I've already done.

    Maybe you were right, maybe I'm dead.

ROY: You're not dead, boy, you're a sissy.

    You love me; that's moving, I'm moved. It's nice to be loved. I warned you about her, didn't I, Joe? But you don't listen to me, why, because you say Roy is smart and Roy's a friend but Roy…well, he isn't nice, and you wanna be nice. Right? A nice, nice man!

(*Little pause*)

    You know what my greatest accomplishment was, Joe, in my life, what I am able to look back on and be proudest of? And I have helped make Presidents and unmake them and mayors and more goddam judges than anyone in NYC ever—AND several million dollars, tax-free—and what do you think means the most to me?

    You ever hear of Ethel Rosenberg? Huh, Joe, huh?

JOE: Well, yeah, I guess I…. Yes.

ROY: Yes. Yes. You have heard of Ethel Rosenberg. Yes. Maybe you even read about her in the history books.

    If it wasn't for me, Joe, Ethel Rosenberg would be alive today, writing some personal-advice column for *Ms.* magazine. She isn't. Because during the trial, Joe, I was on the phone every day, talking with the judge…

JOE: Roy…

ROY: Every day, doing what I do best, talking on the telephone, making sure that timid Yid nebbish on the bench did his duty to America, to history. That sweet unprepossessing woman, two kids, boo-hoo-hoo, reminded us all of our little Jewish mamas—she came this close to getting life; I pleaded till I wept to put her in the chair. Me. I did that. I would have fucking pulled the switch if they'd have let me. Why? Because I fucking hate traitors. Because I fucking hate communists. Was it legal? Fuck legal. Am I a nice man? Fuck nice. They say terrible things about me in the *Nation*. Fuck the *Nation*. You want to be Nice, or you want to be Effective? Make the law, or subject to it. Choose. Your wife chose. A week from today, she'll be back. SHE knows how to get what SHE wants. Maybe I ought to send *her* to Washington.

JOE: I don't believe you.

ROY: Gospel.

JOE: You can't possibly mean what you're saying. Roy, you were the Assistant United States Attorney on the Rosenberg case, ex-parte communication with the judge during the trial would be...censurable, at least, probably conspiracy and...in a case that resulted in execution, it's...

ROY: What? Murder?

JOE: You're not well is all.

ROY: What do you mean, not well? Who's not well?

(Pause.)

JOE: You said...

ROY: No I didn't. I said what?

JOE: Roy, you have cancer.

ROY: No I don't.

(Pause.)

JOE: You told me you were dying.

ROY: What the fuck are you talking about, Joe? I never said that. I'm in perfect health. There's not a goddam thing wrong with me. *(He smiles)*

    Shake?

(Joe hesitates. He holds out his hand to Roy. Roy pulls, Joe into a close, strong clinch.)

ROY *(More to himself than to Joe)*: It's OK that you hurt me because I love you, baby Joe. That's why I'm so rough on you.

(Roy releases Joe. Joe backs away a step or two.)

ROY: Prodigal son. The world will wipe its dirty hands all over you.

JOE: It already has, Roy.

ROY: Now go.

(Roy shoves Joe, hard. Joe turns to leave. Roy stops him, turns him around.)

ROY *(Smoothing Joe's lapels, tenderly)*: I'll always be here, waiting for you...

(Then again, with sudden violence, he pulls Joe close, violently.)

What did you want from me, what was all this, what do you want, treacherous ungrateful little...

(Joe, very close to belting Roy, grabs him by the front of his robe, and propels him across the length of the room. He holds Roy at arm's length, the other arm ready to hit.)

ROY *(Laughing softly, almost pleading to be hit)*: Transgress a little, Joseph.

(Joe releases Roy.)

ROY: There are so many laws; find one you can break.

(Joe hesitates, then leaves, backing out. When Joe has gone, Roy doubles over in great pain, which he's been hiding throughout the scene with Joe.)

ROY: Ah, Christ...

    Andy! Andy! Get in here! Andy!

(The door opens, but it isn't Andy. A small Jewish Woman dressed modestly in a fifties hat and coat stands in the doorway. The room darkens.)

ROY: Who the fuck are you? The new nurse?

(The figure in the doorway says nothing. She stares at Roy. A pause. Roy looks at her carefully, gets up, crosses to her. He crosses back to the chair, sits heavily.)

ROY: Aw, fuck. Ethel.

ETHEL ROSENBERG *(Her manner is friendly, her voice is ice-cold)*: You don't look good, Roy.

ROY: Well, Ethel. I don't feel good.

ETHEL ROSENBERG: But you lost a lot of weight. That suits you. You were heavy back then. Zaftig, mit hips.

ROY: I haven't been that heavy since 1960. We were all heavier back then, before the body thing started. Now I look like a skeleton. They stare.

ETHEL ROSENBERG: The shit's really hit the fan, huh, Roy?

(Little pause. Roy nods.)

ETHEL ROSENBERG: Well the fun's just started.

ROY: What is this, Ethel, Halloween? You trying to scare me?

(Ethel says nothing.)

ROY: Well you're wasting your time! I'm scarier than you any day of the week! So beat it, Ethel! BOOO! BETTER DEAD THAN RED!

Somebody trying to shake me up? HAH HAH! From the throne of God in heaven to the belly of hell, you can all fuck yourselves and then go jump in the lake because I'M NOT AFRAID OF YOU OR DEATH OR HELL OR ANYTHING!

ETHEL ROSENBERG: Be seeing you soon, Roy. Julius sends his regards.

ROY: Yeah, well send this to Julius!

(*He flips the bird in her direction, stands and moves towards her. Halfway across the room he slumps to the floor, breathing laboriously, in pain.*)

ETHEL ROSENBERG: You're a very sick man, Roy.

ROY: Oh God…ANDY!

ETHEL ROSENBERG: Hmmm. He doesn't hear you, I guess. We should call the ambulance. (*She goes to the phone*)

Hah! Buttons! Such things they got now.

What do I dial, Roy?

(*Pause. Roy looks at her, then:*)

ROY: 911.

ETHEL ROSENBERG (*Dials the phone*): It sings!

(*Imitating dial tones*) La la la…

Huh.

Yes, you should please send an ambulance to the home of Mister Roy Cohn, the famous lawyer.

What's the address, Roy?

ROY (*A beat, then*): 244 East 87th.

ETHEL ROSENBERG: 244 East 87th Street. No apartment number, he's got the whole building.

My name? (*A beat*) Ethel Greenglass Rosenberg.

(*Small smile*) Me? No I'm not related to Mr. Cohn. An old friend.

(*She hangs up*)

They said a minute.

ROY: I have all the time in the world.

ETHEL ROSENBERG: You're immortal.

ROY: I'm immortal. Ethel. (*He forces himself to stand.*)

I have *forced* my way into history. I ain't never gonna die.

ETHEL ROSENBERG (*A little laugh, then*): History is about to crack wide open. Millennium approaches.

SCENE 6

Late that night. Prior's bedroom. Prior 1 watching Prior in bed, who is staring back at him, terrified. Tonight Prior 1 is dressed in weird alchemical robes and hat over his historical clothing and he carries a long palm-leaf bundle.

PRIOR 1: Tonight's the night! Aren't you excited? Tonight she arrives! Right through the roof! Ha-adam, Ha-gadol…

PRIOR 2 (*Appearing, similarly attired*): Lumen! Phosphor! Fluor! Candle! An unending billowing of scarlet and…

PRIOR: Look. Garlic. A mirror. Holy water. A crucifix. FUCK OFF! Get the fuck out of my room! GO!

PRIOR 1 (*To Prior 2*): Hard as a hickory knob, I'll bet.

PRIOR 2: We all tumesce when they approach. We wax full, like moons.

PRIOR 1: Dance.

PRIOR: Dance?

PRIOR 1: Stand up, dammit, give us your hands, dance!

PRIOR 2: Listen…

(*A lone oboe begins to play a little dance tune.*)

PRIOR 2: Delightful sound. Care to dance?

PRIOR: Please leave me alone, please just let me sleep…

PRIOR 2: Ah, he wants someone familiar. A partner who knows his steps. (*To Prior*) Close your eyes. Imagine…

PRIOR: I don't…

PRIOR 2: Hush. Close your eyes.

(*Prior does.*)

PRIOR 2: Now open them.

(*Prior does. Louis appears. He looks gorgeous. The music builds gradually into a full-blooded, romantic dance tune.*)

PRIOR: Lou.

LOUIS: Dance with me.

PRIOR: I can't, my leg, it hurts at night…Are you…a ghost, Lou?

LOUIS: No. Just spectral. Lost to myself. Sitting all day on cold park benches. Wishing I could be with you. Dance with me, babe…

(*Prior stands up. The leg stops hurting. They begin to dance. The music is beautiful.*)

PRIOR 1 (*To Prior 2*): Hah. Now I see why he's got no children. He's a sodomite.

PRIOR 2: Oh be quiet, you medieval gnome, and let them dance.

PRIOR 1: I'm not interfering, I've done my bit. Hooray, hooray, the messenger's come, now I'm blowing off. I don't like it here.
(*Prior 1 vanishes.*)

PRIOR 2: The twentieth century. Oh dear, the world has gotten so terribly, terribly old.
(*Prior 2 vanishes. Louis and Prior waltz happily. Lights fade back to normal. Louis vanishes. Prior dances alone.*
Then suddenly, the sound of wings fills the room.)

SCENE 7

Split scene: Prior alone in his apartment; Louis alone in the park.
    Again, a sound of beating wings.

PRIOR: Oh don't come in here don't come in... LOUIS!!
    No. My name is Prior Walter, I am...the scion of an ancient line, I am...abandoned I ...no, my name is...is...Prior and I live... *here and now,* and...in the dark, in the dark, the Recording Angel opens its hundred eyes and snaps the spine of the Book of Life and...hush! Hush!
    I'm talking nonsense, I...
    No more mad scene, hush, hush...
(*Louis in the park on a bench. Joe approaches, stands at a distance. They stare at each other, then Louis turns away.*)

LOUIS: Do you know the story of Lazarus?

JOE: Lazarus?

LOUIS: Lazarus. I can't remember what happens, exactly.

JOE: I don't.... Well, he was dead, Lazarus, and Jesus breathed life into him. He brought him back from death.

LOUIS: Come here often?

JOE: No. Yes. Yes.

LOUIS: Back from the dead. You believe that really happened?

JOE: I don't know anymore what I believe.

LOUIS: This is quite a coincidence. Us meeting.

JOE: I followed you.
    From work. I...followed you here.
(*Pause.*)

LOUIS: You followed me.
    You probably saw me that day in the washroom and thought: there's a sweet guy, sensitive, cries for friends in trouble.

JOE: Yes.

LOUIS: You thought maybe I'll cry for you.

JOE: Yes.

LOUIS: Well I fooled you. Crocodile tears. Nothing...(*He touches his heart, shrugs.*)
(*Joe reaches tentatively to touch Louis's face.*)

LOUIS (*Pulling back*): What are you doing? Don't do that.

JOE (*Withdrawing his hand*): Sorry. I'm sorry.

LOUIS: I'm...just not...I think, if you touch me, your hand might fall off or something. Worse things have happened to people who have touched me.

JOE: Please.
    Oh, boy...
    Can I...
    I...want...to touch you. Can I please just touch you...um, here?
(*He puts his hand on one side of Louis's face. He holds it there.*)
    I'm going to hell for doing this.

LOUIS: Big deal. You think it could be any worse than New York City?
(*He puts his hand on Joe's hand. He takes Joe's hand away from his face, holds it for a moment, then*) Come on.

JOE: Where?

LOUIS: Home. With me.

JOE: This makes no sense. I mean I don't know you.

LOUIS: Likewise.

JOE: And what you do know about me you don't like.

LOUIS: The Republican stuff?

JOE: Yeah, well for starters.

LOUIS: I don't not like that. I *hate* that.

JOE: So why on earth should we...
(*Louis goes to Joe and kisses him.*)

LOUIS: Strange bedfellows. I don't know. I never made it with one of the damned before.

I would really rather not have to spend tonight alone.

JOE: I'm a pretty terrible person, Louis.

LOUIS: Lou.

JOE: No, I really really am. I don't think I deserve being loved.

LOUIS: There? See? We already have a lot in common.

(*Louis stands, begins to walk away. He turns, looks back at Joe. Joe follows. They exit.*)

(*Prior listens. At first no sound, then once again, the sound of beating wings, frighteningly near.*)

PRIOR: That sound, that sound, it…. What is that, like birds or something, like a *really* big bird, I'm frightened, I…no, no fear, find the anger, find the…anger, my blood is clean, my brain is fine, I can handle pressure, I am a gay man and I am used to pressure, to trouble, I am tough and strong and…. Oh. Oh my goodness. I…(*He is washed over by an intense sexual feeling*) Ooohhhh…. I'm hot, I'm…so…aw Jeez what is going on here I…must have a fever I…

(*The bedside lamp flickers wildly as the bed begins to roll forward and back. There is a deep bass creaking and groaning from the bedroom ceiling, like the timbers of a ship under immense stress, and from above a fine rain of plaster dust.*)

PRIOR: OH!

PLEASE, OH PLEASE! Something's coming in here, I'm scared, I don't like this at all, something's approaching and I…. OH!

(*There is a great blaze of triumphal music, heralding. The light turns an extraordinary harsh, cold, pale blue, then a rich, brilliant warm golden color, then a hot, bilious green, and then finally a spectacular royal purple. Then silence.*)

PRIOR (*An awestruck whisper*): God almighty… *Very* Steven Spielberg.

(*A sound, like a plummeting meteor, tears down from very, very far above the earth, hurtling at an incredible velocity towards the bedroom; the* light seems to be sucked out of the room as the projectile approaches; as the room reaches darkness, we hear a terrifying CRASH as something immense strikes earth; the whole building shudders and a part of the bedroom ceiling, lots of plaster and lathe and wiring, crashes to the floor. And then in a shower of unearthly white light, spreading great opalescent gray-silver wings, the Angel descends into the room and floats above the bed.)

ANGEL:

Greetings, Prophet;
The Great Work begins:
The Messenger has arrived.

(*Blackout.*)

END OF PART ONE

PERFORMING *ANGELS IN AMERICA*

Angels in America began, Tony Kushner says, as an attempt to write a play about being a gay man in the United States in the mid-eighties but was eventually written on a larger political/historical canvas of a changing East European and American society.[17]

Kushner began work on the two parts of *Angels in America* in 1988. Commissioned by Oskar Eustis and the Eureka Theater Company in San Francisco, *Part One: Millennium Approaches* was directed there by David Esbjornson in 1991. During that time, *Perestroika* was performed as a staged reading. The Eureka Theater production of *Millennium Approaches* was followed by the sensational London production at the Royal National Theater directed by Declan Donellan. Once again in the United States, Parts One and Two, directed by Oskar Eustis with Tony Taccone, were presented together for the first time in 1992 at the Mark Taper Forum in Los Angeles as a seven-hour epic, subtitled "A Gay Fantasia on National Themes." Newly directed by George C. Wolfe, *Angels in America* opened with Part One in Broadway's Walter Kerr Theater in April 1993 and was followed by Part Two in November 1993.

From the outset, Stephen Spinella, Kathleen Chalfant, and Ellen McLaughlin as Prior Walter,

Hannah Pitt, and The Angel, remained with the productions, with the exception of the London productions that had all-British casts. Ron Leibman and Joe Mantello (playing Roy Cohn and Louis Ironson) joined the cast in Los Angeles, and David Marshall Grant, Marcia Gay Harden, and Jeffrey Wright (Joe Pitt, Harper Pitt, and Belize) appeared on Broadway in Parts One and Two. The cast of eight actors played twenty-one roles in *Millennium Approaches* with the women playing the cross-dressing roles. For example, Kathleen Chalfant, playing Hannah Pitt, doubles as the orthodox Jewish rabbi, Roy Cohn's doctor, and also as Ethel Rosenberg.

Kushner's dramaturgy overlaps scenes of dreams and hallucinations with moments of theatrical magic. In a note on the staging of *Millennium Approaches*, Kushner asks that the magic be fully realized—"it's OK if the wires show."[18] In Part One, a large, gray feather floats gently down to Prior Walter; Mr. Lies appears to Harper dressed as an Antarctic explorer and later Harper, dressed in Arctic gear, encounters an Eskimo; ancestral ghosts appear to Prior Walter and a great book bursts into flames in his presence; and, finally, the Angel crashes through the ceiling of Prior Walter's bedroom spreading great opalescent gray-silver wings as she floats above his bed.

The early directors of *Angels in America* staged subtly different productions. George C. Wolfe brought polish, inventiveness, and theatrics to the Broadway production in its commercial venue. Known for his epic staging of the work of Bertolt Brecht, British director Mark Wing-Davy staged the 1994 San Francisco production as a starker work. The audiences for these two productions differed as remarkably as their communities. There was the festive Broadway crowd holding an expensive ticket and an intensely quieter and more diverse crowd in San Francisco. Both productions and the many others that came after demonstrated that Kushner's text has an enormous potential for artists of different backgrounds staging the play for different audiences and communities.[19]

Kushner's fierce call for gay Americans to be treated with tolerance and compassion also argues that they should seize the strings of power in the war against intolerance and AIDS. Two outsized characters convey this message with bravado and eloquence. Matching the theatrical power of Ron Liebman, although perhaps not his over-the-top bravura performance, is Stephen Spinella as Prior Walter, the AIDS patient who is visited by the Angel at the end of Part One and becomes the prophet of survival for his afflicted and abandoned people in Part Two.

Finally, *Angels in America* exists in theatrical history alongside other contemporary productions requiring extraordinary commitments from their artists and audiences. John Barton's *Tantalus*, a ten-part cycle on the Trojan War, its prelude and aftermath, was produced in 2000 under the direction of Sir Peter Hall at the Denver Theater Center. The ten-hour production used materials from myth and surviving fragments from the era to tell the story of the Trojan War, beginning with the punishment of Tantalus for stealing secrets from the Olympian gods and disseminating them on earth. Tom Stoppard's three-part text, called *The Coast of Utopia*, is a theatrical treatise on the intellectual forebears of the Russian revolution with such historical figures as Turgenev, Marx, Bakunin, and Herzen. The three parts were staged over nine hours at the Royal National Theatre (London) in 2002.

Angels in America stands alongside these contemporary productions of epic proportion. Kushner's seven-hour play on "national themes" combines political theater with epic dramaturgy in a call for social change and progress in millennial America.

CRITICS' NOTEBOOK

Some of the most effective writing on Tony Kushner can be found in interviews with the playwright in which he explains the political and philosophical influences on his work along with his own collection called *Thinking about the Longstanding Problems of Virtue and Happiness: Essays, a Play, Two Poems and a Prayer* (1995). David Savran interviewed Kushner in *The Playwright's Voice: American Dramatists on Memory,*

Writing and the Politics of Culture (1999) and Robert Vorlicky edited *Tony Kushner in Conversation* (1998) with an afterword written by Kushner.

The majority of books on Kushner followed the success of *Angels in America* and include Deborah R. Geis and Steven F. Kruger's *Approaching the Millennium: Essay on Angels in America* (1997) and James Fisher's *The Theater of Tony Kushner: Living Past Hope* (2001). Other writers and scholars have focused on Kushner's writings in the framework of the literature of male homosexuality and gay identity. Among those studies are John M. Clum's *Acting Gay: Male Homosexuality in Modern Drama* (1994), Robert McRuer's *The Queer Renaissance: Contemporary American Literature and the Reinvention of Lesbian and Gay Identities* (1997), and David Román's *Acts of Intervention: Performance, Gay Culture, and AIDS* (1998).

In 1994, critic David Savran interviewed Tony Kushner in New York City as part of a series of conversations with fifteen American playwrights. This segment from the interview addresses the essential question about Kushner's understanding of the aftermath of pain and loss.

Janelle Reinelt writes cogently of the political arguments in Tony Kushner's text in her notes on staging *Angels in America* as politically engaged, left-wing theater with a dramaturgy based on epic principles.

David Savran, from an Interview with Tony Kushner*

Savran: That's the question of the play: what is there beyond pain? Is Utopia even imaginable?

Kushner: And the loss. It's the thing that I don't understand at all, which I think is under-theo-

rized and under-represented in the problematics of the left. If our lives are in fact shaped by trauma and loss—and as I get older it seems to me that life is very, very profoundly shaped by loss and death—how do you address that? And how does one progress in the face of that? That's the question that the AIDS epidemic has asked. Because there is nothing more optimistic than America, in the most awful way (like "Up with People"). It makes so many people queasy and it's the subject of so much sarcasm because it seems so dumb. But identity is shaped, even racial identity. If there weren't bigots, there wouldn't be a politics of race. That there has to be a politics of difference speaks to the presence of enormous oppression and violence and terror. What do we do? It's an interesting thing because the more we know about history, the more we realize—and this is an important thing about sadomasochism—that it really does return, it never ends. You can just see in our present moment a thousand future Sarajevos. You just know that when you're ninety, if you live so long, they'll still be fighting. Even after the Holocaust, the monsters are still among us. And can you forgive? That's why I ask this question of forgiveness because its possibility is also, I think, under-theorized and under-expressed.

Janelle Reinelt, from "Notes on *Angels in America* as American Epic Theater"*

Louis makes most of the political arguments in the script. He puts the discourse of democracy in play, although Roy Cohn also speaks a powerful political discourse. If considered abstractly, as a kind of "red thread" through the playtext, this democratic discourse emerges as a series of questions: how to reconcile difference, how to establish justice, how to effect so-

*David Savran, "Tony Kushner," in *The Playwright's Voice: American Dramatists on Memory, Writing and the Politics of Culture* (New York: Theatre Communications Group, 1999): 107.

*Janelle Reinelt, "Notes on *Angels in America* as American Epic Theater," in *Approaching the Millennium: Essays on Angels in America*, eds. Deborah R. Geis and Steven F. Kruger (Ann Arbor: The University of Michigan Press, 1997): 235–236.

cial change, how to effect personal change, how to progress? This dimension of the social, of the body politic, is represented on the bodies of characters struggling for personal solutions to the contradictions of American life. They become sites for the traffic of history and the ideology of democracy: Mormon history, Red-baiting history, Jewish history, "family values history," sin and guilt through history, traditions of prophecy and transcendence. Incidents in the lives of the characters are typical of many contemporary Americans, and every character, from Hannah to Belize, Joe to Harper, represents one of these types. The social gestus of the playtexts seems to be disconnecting from identity, a kind of cutting loose from moorings, a not-very-Marxist letting go of fiercely held convictions or practices, or the refusal of great regressive temptations (most forcefully materialized in the person of the Angel) as the various characters "travel," or put themselves in motion away from the contexts and subject positions that have held them in place. By the end of *Perestroika*, and just barely, one sees the outline for a different society. And that is all there can really be—a glimmer. Otherwise, any firmer answer, any true solution, seems prescriptive and preachy, trite or sentimental, and ultimately false. Of course, *Angels* comes perilously close to that trap all through its text. In this regard, however, *Angels is* more closely related to *Good Person of Setzuan* than to the more sentimental parable, *Caucasian Chalk Circle*. Brecht posits a world in which Shui Ta is necessary and subjectivity is hopelessly split, throwing the dilemma back to the audience to "fix." In *Chalk Circle* Azdak, the mythical judge who made justice possible but then disappeared, and may never have been real in the first place (it's a "story"), offers more of a prescription: the land should be planted for the good of all, private property notwithstanding. No prescriptions end *Angels in America*. The last scene leaves Louis and Belize fighting about politics, their differences unresolved; it leaves Harper suspended on a *"jumbo jet, airborne"* (2:144). Prior Walter remains alive, perhaps because of

the AZT Belize commandeered from Roy Cohn, but has not been cured. The final gesture is toward a possibility of healing and progress, but the details have to be worked out in human space/time within the American national context. Not an easy task.

Epic theater needs to construct the experience of ideological contradiction as the mode of subjectivity it projects for spectators rather than the ideological totalization implied in *supporter, judgment, empathy,* or even *detachment*. This is an epic play *if* the spectators engage the problems and understand the constraints operating on the nation and on themselves as social subjects. It is an epic play *if* some sense of what might be done next is suggested but not spelled out. It is an epic play *if* it does not let spectators off the hook by allowing too much psychological investment in particular characters or too much good feeling of resolution at the end.

REVISITING DRAMA AND SOCIETY

Roman playwrights popularized *tragicomedy*, a mixed dramatic form, which looked ahead to flexible writing conventions where serious plays closed with averted catastrophes or indeterminate endings. In modern times, tragicomedy, with its mixed moods and varied responses of happiness and unhappiness, anguish and despair, found favor with playwrights concerned with representing the static, uneventful quality of our lives or with changing perspectives on the root causes of human travail. Anton Chekhov records the lives of quiet desperation of Russian provincials; Luigi Pirandello pinpoints the bewildering contradictions of life in Italian drawing rooms; and Samuel Beckett cites "accursed time" as the only change in an unchanging existential situation.

Contemporary playwrights introduced new forms (new ways of dramatizing) and new contents (new ways of perceiving) into the theater of the late twentieth century. Many of these fresh theatrical structures, based on the flexibility of the older mixed forms, often served a serious ethical and social purpose while they examined our responses to the condition of being human in an unknowable and amazing world. Tony Kushner's *Angels in America: A Gay Fantasia on National Themes* provoked a radical rethinking of American political drama and transformative writing for the theater. The serious issues of life in America in the last decade of the twentieth century—politics, religion, sexuality, racism, pandemic disease, and paranoia—are wrenched in all their seriousness into a comedic statement about humanity's will to survive and, despite the odds, effect progress and change.

On the cusp of the twentieth century such playwrights as Henrik Ibsen, August Strindberg, and Anton Chekhov introduced a new writing style for the modern theater. It was dubbed *realism* to describe writing and performance styles rooted in changing views of the world. Discussions of modernism and stage realism in the works of Henrik Ibsen and August Wilson prepare the way for the eclecticism of contemporary writing and performance at the new millennium.

NOTES

1. Eric Bentley, *The Life of Drama* (New York: Applause Theatre Books, 1990): 350–351.
2. George Bernard Shaw, Preface to *Major Barbara* (New York: Dodd, Mead, and Company, 1957): 203.
3. Martin Esslin, "New Form in the Theatre," *Reflections: Essays on Modern Theatre* (Garden City, NY: Doubleday, 1969): 3–10.
4. Rhornylly B. Forbes, "Interviews Playwright Tony Kushner on Activism, the Millennium, and AIDS Today," *Arts & Understanding* (June 2001): 45.
5. Susan Cheever, "An Angel Sat Down at His Table," *The New York Times* (September 13, 1992): H7.
6. Cheever, H7.
7. Robert Brustein, "Robert Brustein on Theater: *Angels in America*," *The New Republic* (May 24, 1993):

29; David Richards, "'Angels' Finds A Poignant Hope," *The New York Times* (November 28, 1993): II, 1; Jack Kroll, "Heaven and Earth on Broadway," *Newsweek* (December 6, 1993): 83; John Lahr, "The Theater: Earth Angels," *The New Yorker* (December 13, 1993): 129–132.
8. James Fisher, *The Theater of Tony Kushner: Living Past Hope* (New York: Routledge, 2001): 56.
9. Tony Kushner, *Angels in America: A Gay Fantasia on National Themes Part One: Millennium Approaches* (New York: Theatre Communications Group, 1993): 5.
10. David Savran, "Ambivalence, Utopia, and a Queer Sort of Materialism: How *Angels in America* Reconstructs the Nation," *Theatre Journal*, 47 (1995): 210. See also Walter Benjamin, "Theses on the Philosophy of History," in *Illuminations*, ed. Hannah Arendt, trans. Harry Zohn (New York: Schocken Books, 1969): 257–258.
11. Janelle Reinelt, "Notes on *Angels in America* as American Epic Theater," in *Approaching the Millennium: Essays on* Angels in America, ed. Deborah R. Geis and Steven F. Kruger (Ann Arbor: The University of Michigan Press, 1997): 242.
12. Savran, 221. See also Barry Brummett, *Contemporary Apocalyptic Rhetoric* (New York: Praeger, 1991): 37–38.
13. Jack Kroll, "A Seven-Hour Gay Fantasia," *Newsweek* (November 23, 1993): 83.
14. I am indebted to David Savran's discussion of literary resonances in *Angels in America* found in his essay on "Ambivalence, Utopia, and a Queer Sort of Materialism: How *Angels in America* Reconstructs the Nation," p. 209.
15. Fisher, 58.
16. Raymond Williams, "Walking Backwards into the Future," in *Resources of Hope, Culture, Democracy, Socialism.* Ed. Robin Gale. (New York: Verso, 1989): 283. See also Fisher, 57.
17. David Cuthbert, "Close Look at a Tony Winner," *The Times-Picayune* (June 10, 1993): E7.
18. Kushner, *Angels in America Part One*, 5.
19. Reinelt, 235–236.

PART FOUR

UNDERSTANDING MODERN
WRITING STYLES

CHAPTER 9

UNDERSTANDING MODERNISM

Kate Burton as Hedda in *Hedda Gabler* by Henrik Ibsen, directed by Nicholas Martin, Broadway, 2001. (Photo by Richard Feldman/Williamstown Theatre Festival.)

> *It was not really my intention to deal in this play [Hedda Gabler]*
> *with so-called social problems. What I principally wanted to do was to*
> *depict human beings, human emotions, and human destinies, upon a*
> *groundwork of certain of the social conditions and principles of the*
> *present day.*[1]
>
> —Henrik Ibsen

BACKGROUND

"Modernism" entered our theatrical vocabulary in 1952 when Joseph Wood Krutch, in a series of lectures, defined *modernism* as the self-conscious belief that, beginning in the second half of the nineteenth century, artists, scholars, scientists, sociologists, and philosophers believed that they had made a "radical break with the past and looked forward to a future discontinuous with it."[2] Before him, the German philosopher G. W. F. Hegel diagnosed "modernity" as a system of social relations dominated by the "force of division and difference."[3] Some scholars have argued that modernism came into being in the drama during the Renaissance as a result of a bold intellectual effort to create an artistic reality in which human beings could fix and mirror themselves on the basis of interpersonal relationships alone.[4] The motto, of course, became: "Man is the measure of all things." The medieval concept of a harmonious world, embracing heaven and earth, was eroded during the Renaissance. Humankind became the measure of all things against the scale of what people can imagine and do within the frame of human experience.

With the collapse of a harmonious world picture, the dissonances as seen by the classicists, the romantics, and the moderns took on various shapes and debates. By the late seventeenth century, humanity was perceived as arrested "between" freedom and obligation, will and decision. Neoclassical thinkers and writers tried to bridge the disharmony between people and society by demanding that individuals choose between obligation and desire, responsibility and freedom, subordinating personal wishes to social structures. The great neoclassical tragedies by French playwright Jean Racine (*Phèdre, Bérénice,* and *Britannicus*) showed the destructive clashes between feelings and reason, instinct and obligation. Rejecting the limitations (and tyranny) of neoclassical choice, the nineteenth-century romantics revolted against society's restrictions and codes set up to minimize the conflicting choices leading to the happy life. They celebrated personal freedoms, instincts, and desires. They encouraged individuals to throw off society's shackles and explore freely physical and spiritual worlds. Romanticism became synonymous with radical idealism, passionate nationalism, spontaneous feeling, and unequivocal faith in the visionary imagination. "Restless striving" became the form and content of romantic drama with Johann Wolfgang von Goethe's *Faust* (Part 1, 1808) as the penultimate representation of romantic experience.

The dramatic revolt against romanticism's "unreal" or distorted picture of ordinary human striving emerged full-blown in the 1860s as *realism.* Like other styles of writing and performance that preceded it, realism contained its own image of truth for readers and audiences. For the realists, dramatic "truth" was a recognizable happening that could be verified by observing ordinary life. In rebellion against artificial situations and preposterous ideals associated with romanticism, the realists set about to put on stage only what they could verify by observing ordinary life. In the nineteenth century, this usually meant middle-class life and language, along with a highly defined stage action that depicted discernible social problems of the day. The results were such quintessential realistic plays as Henrik Ibsen's *A Doll's House* (1879) and George Bernard Shaw's *Mrs. Warren's Profession* (1893).

FRAGMENTATION

Modernism, as we think of it today, engaged the belief that "modern" ideas, doubts, and attitudes were somehow radically different and discontinuous with those held in the past. The viewpoint recognized the deterioration of a harmonious world such as found in classical Greek culture and the Middle Ages. The general tone of these newly held beliefs and ideas conveyed a condition of intellectual and moral paralysis. As early as 1835, Georg Büchner's hero in *Danton's Death* asserted a modernist tone: "There's no hope in death; it's only a less complicated form of decay than life—that's the only difference!"

Early modernists, like Büchner, perceived a crack in the structure of the world. They represented on stage a dissociation of milieu, character, and action. Characters like Ibsen's Hedda Gabler and Strindberg's Miss Julie are "modern," for they are forever out of sync with their surroundings and other characters, conventions, and expectations. T. S. Eliot called this condition a dissociation of sensibility. One facet of modernism in the theater has been the dramatist's efforts to expose the disconnections (one critic called them broken connections) among individuals, their lifestyles, and their aspirations.

"Modernist" methods and ideas evolved, as Krutch pointed out, from the playwrights' self-conscious break with the past. For two decades, Henrik Ibsen's plays were the key to modernism in drama before he was supplanted by the earlier, rediscovered German playwright Georg Büchner. However, the sense of modernism associated with a new wave of writers beginning in the nineteenth century—Georg Büchner, Henrik Ibsen, August Strindberg, and George Bernard Shaw—inspired new subjects and writing styles that we take for granted today.

MODERNIST THEORY

Essentially, in the late nineteenth century, a chasm opened up between the past and the present (and the future). The past, in many disguises, became the enemy of growth, change, and well-being. In play after play, the stolid convictions of the past as represented by individuals, classes, and societies became inimical to individual freedoms. Ibsen's villains, for example, are rigidly conventional voices from the past: the minister's edicts in *Ghosts,* the Rosmers' lingering ideals in *Rosmersholm,* the self-serving town council in *An Enemy of the People,* the male-dominated society in *A Doll's House.* Ibsen's "modern" individuals—Mrs. Alving, Johannes Rosmer, Thomas Stockmann, Hedda Gabler, Rebecca West—exist in defiance of their inherited middle-class values and social conditioning. They are either defeated by the weight of past convictions, beliefs, ideals, or they end in ambiguity as does Nora Helmer in *A Doll's House.* For example, Nora turns her back on husband, children, and home in an assertion of a new-found personal freedom, but Ibsen leaves the audience with the question, "Will her convictions be enough to ensure her survival in the world?"

The heart of the matter in understanding "modernism" is neither the playwright's realistic treatment of a contemporary situation, which was the dominant mode of the new writing and performance style, nor the implied criticism of Victorian sexual morality. Of crucial importance was the sense of *discontinuity* between the old and the new worlds and the impossibility of communication across the chasm that separated one from the other (the past from the future).

How did the implications and the consequences of this conviction that a radical break was being made with the past convey itself in the work of the new dramatists? The radical new writers generated their statements about discontinuity in many ways. Though not explaining his plays or committing himself personally on such public issues as women's rights, Ibsen was a revolutionary. He deliberately and often sensationally exposed society's outmoded and corrupt practices that denied human liberties. He exposed society's responsibility for industrial accidents (*Pillars of Society*), advocated human rights (*A Doll's House*), and raised controversial sexual issues (*Ghosts*). On the one hand, these plays can be seen as the work of a liberal social reformer of his day, and now somewhat dated. On the other hand, there are many contemporary realities generating attendant fears, misinformation, and social ostracism. We are never far away from Ibsen's world.

In his middle years Ibsen went even further with his conscious break with society's mores and outworn convictions. In his exploration of social corruption and society's victims, he moved steadily away from the sociological and toward the psychological and metaphysical. *Hedda Gabler,* his masterpiece, introduces attitudes and subtleties that widened the chasm between the past and the future. In *Hedda Gabler,* Ibsen's modernism is transcendent.

Hedda Gabler

HENRIK IBSEN

Henrik Ibsen (1828–1906), frequently spoken of as the "father of modern drama," was born in Skien, Norway, and became an apothecary's apprentice. He tried to become a doctor, but failed his studies in Christiania (Oslo) and turned to writing and the theater. He published his first play, Catiline, *a verse tragedy celebrating his country's past glories, in 1849. He became stage manager and resident playwright with the National Theatre in Bergen and later artistic director of the Norwegian Theater in Oslo. In this capacity, he gained a knowledge of literature and stagecraft.*

Economic hardship and the award of a government grant for foreign travel drove Ibsen to Italy in 1864 where he wrote Brand *(1865) and* Peer Gynt *(1867) which brought him international fame. For twenty-seven years, he remained with his wife and son in self-imposed exile in Rome, Dresden, and Munich. During this time, he wrote his influential prose plays,* A Doll's House, Ghosts, An Enemy of the People, The Wild Duck, Rosmersholm, *and* Hedda Gabler. *Championed by producers and critics in England and Europe, these plays changed the direction of nineteenth-century theater. In 1891, Ibsen returned to Norway, and in 1899 completed* When We Dead Awaken, *the play novelist James Joyce considered his finest. He died in Oslo in 1906.*

As one of the progenitors of modern drama, Ibsen wrote plays dealing with problems of contemporary middle-class life and with the plight of individuals victimized by repressive societies. Although his social doctrines are no longer revolutionary, his portraits of humanity in conflict and dissolution remain timeless.

CRITICAL INTRODUCTION
TO *HEDDA GABLER*

We have long associated modernism in drama with a realistic representation of contemporary society and issues. Ibsen pioneered in dramatic realism in the cycle of plays from *Pillars of Society* in 1877 to *Hedda Gabler* in 1890. As a modernist, Ibsen perceived the contradictions in our nature and in society. The issues and ideas in the foreground of his plays often mask (even obscure) the inner life of his characters. While *A Doll's House* is about the question of "human rights," as Ibsen himself said, it is also about human appetites for power and exploitation and their victims. Within the context of the Helmer household, we have other issues played out: patriarchy, submission, and rebellion. The institution of marriage becomes the paradigmatic situation for knowing ourselves and our world. Nora says, "I must stand on my own feet if I am to find out the truth about myself and about life." Her husband replies that "first and foremost you are a wife and mother." Her answer is, "I don't believe that any longer. I believe that before all else I am a human being first and foremost…or…that I must try to become one." Ibsen's play moved past ideology into the realm of broken connections; that is, we do not know ourselves and we no longer recognize the world around us.

Although *Ghosts,* written in 1881, shocked Victorian sensibilities with its examination of sexual morality and inherited disease, the surface issues are undermined by the web of self-deception and ignorance in which Mrs. Alving, the heroine, is caught. She is ruled by inherited, unexamined ideas ("the ghosts"), and she has failed to know herself. Nor is *Hedda Gabler* a mere sociological study of a deeply neurotic woman whose aggressiveness masks her sexual frigidity. On one level, Hedda is a deeply frustrated, aristocratic woman entrapped in a bourgeois existence. Her revenge upon her former lover Eilert Lœvborg and the destruction of his manuscript and then of herself are identifiable pathology. But they are more. Written a decade before Sigmund Freud's first work on psychoanalysis, *Hedda Gabler* takes us into the dark, inner recesses of modern neurosis. She exists in a condition of unresolved conflict with herself, with others, and with society. The action of the play delineates the condition of Hedda's deep-rooted conflict and its ending in dissolution. For example, her society has carved out her gender role as wife, mother, and stay-at-home. There are no other outlets for her energy and creativity in this male-dominated society. Moreover, she is pregnant, which further constricts her possibilities for enterprising activities. Wrapped in keen intelligence and a sense of class, she insults, manipulates, and destroys. She is aware that she cannot create like the brilliant scholar Eilert Lœvborg or selflessly nurture another's creativity like her friend Thea Elvsted. Instead, she pursues a course of destruction. Hedda threatens to burn her friend's hair and does indeed burn Lœvborg's unpublished manuscript. It is true that she rationalizes her motives to a degree. For example, she does not want a rival for her husband's career (and income), nor does she want competition for her ex-lover from another woman. However, her explanations for her insults, demands, and threats are not wholly convincing. Moreover, we cannot fully understand her need to assert control over Lœvborg as she sends him on an impossible mission to attend Judge Brack's stag party where she gambles that he will not succumb to his old alcoholism. She sends him off with the famous injunction, "Come back with vine leaves in your hair." Deep within her psyche, she knows that he is incapable of fulfilling her vision of Dionysian splendor, which is a vague romantic ideal of ecstasy and power. What is unclear is whose powers are being tested: Hedda's or Lœvborg's.

As a "modern" heroine, Hedda exists in a condition of unresolved conflict. Her aims and motives have a secret, personal logic of their own. She gets what she thinks she wants (husband, house, piano, admirer), but nothing satisfies her. In effect, as Richard Gilman said of her, Hedda is unable to *live*.[5] At the deepest level, she is not so much caught in a particular set of determining circumstances as she is an "ill-adapted creature" struggling to know what to do in her limited, bourgeois existence. She is surrounded by the self-destructive, unhappy Lœvborg, the dull Tesman, the salacious Judge Brack, and by two selfless women, Thea Elvsted and her husband's unmarried aunt. The fatal pistol shot is Hedda's anguished rejection of the boundaries and impasse of her life.

This type of character, new to the world of drama in 1890, implies the premise that there is a secret, sometimes unconscious, world of aims, methods, and desires that is often much more important and powerful than the rational, surface one. The chasm between Hedda's inner logic and that of the world around her becomes manifest in her suicide. Having manipulated Lœvborg's death, she is then cut off from the comraderie of her husband and Mrs. Elvsted as they undertake the reconstruction of Lœvborg's lost manuscript from his notes. Moreover, Hedda is subject to Judge Brack's salacious intentions because he knows that Lœvborg was wounded by one of Hedda's dueling pistols and threatens her with public scandal if she is not malleable to his wishes. To alleviate her condition, she shuts herself off in the music room and kills herself with the remaining dueling pistol. The astonished Brack has the famous last line of the play: "But, good God! People don't *do* such things!" His incredulity and bewilderment over Hedda's definitive act are a measure of Ibsen's modernist portrait of undetected and unknowable human conflict and desperation.

Hedda Gabler is a benchmark play in our understanding of modernism. With *Hedda Gabler,* Ibsen makes an important recognition: Human beings do not necessarily use logical methods to achieve rationally justifiable ends. Moderns eroded the older view of human behavior that one was either rational or irrational. Indeed, most *modern* literature assumes that the richest, most significant aspects of human experience are to be found in the realm of the irrational.

This is but one example of the broken connections between past and present. Ibsen, the modernist, depicted the chasm between the rational and the irrational in the twisting and turning of his conflicted heroine. Neurotic conflict in dramatic character is one signpost on the road to defining modernism as a deepening of the chasm between past and future perceptions of human behavior.

Hedda Gabler

CHARACTERS

GEORGE TESMAN research graduate in cultural
   history
HEDDA his wife
MISS JULIANA TESMAN his aunt
MRS. ELVSTED
JUDGE BRACK
EILERT LŒVBORG
BERTHA a maid

*The action takes place in Tesman's villa in the fash-
ionable quarter of town.*

ACT ONE

*A large drawing-room, handsomely and tastefully
furnished; decorated in dark colours. In the rear wall
is a broad open doorway, with curtains drawn back
to either side. It leads to a smaller room, decorated in
the same style as the drawing-room. In the right-
hand wall of the drawing-room a folding door leads
out to the hall. The opposite wall, on the left, contains
french windows, also with curtains drawn back on
either side. Through the glass we can see part of a veranda, and trees in autumn colours. Downstage
stands an oval table, covered by a cloth and surrounded by chairs. Downstage right, against the
wall, is a broad stove tiled with dark porcelain; in
front of it stand a high-backed armchair, a cushioned
footrest and two footstools. Upstage right, in an al-
cove, is a corner sofa, with a small, round table.
Downstage left, a little away from the wall, is another sofa. Upstage of the french windows, a piano.
On either side of the open doorway in the rear wall
stand what-nots holding ornaments of terra-cotta
and majolica. Against the rear wall of the smaller
room can be seen a sofa, a table and a couple of chairs.
Above this sofa hangs the portrait of a handsome old
man in general's uniform. Above the table a lamp
hangs from the ceiling, with a shade of opalescent,
milky glass. All round the drawing-room bunches of
flowers stand in vases and glasses. More bunches lie
on the tables. The floors of both rooms are covered
with thick carpets. Morning light. The sun shines in
through the french windows.*

MISS JULIANA TESMAN, *wearing a hat and carrying
a parasol, enters from the hall, followed by* BERTHA,
who is carrying a bunch of flowers wrapped in paper.
MISS TESMAN *is about sixty-five, of pleasant and
kindly appearance. She is neatly but simply dressed
in grey outdoor clothes.* BERTHA, *the maid, is rather
simple and rustic-looking. She is getting on in years.*

MISS TESMAN (*stops just inside the door, listens, and
says in a hushed voice*): Well, fancy that!
They're not up yet!

BERTHA (*also in hushed tones*): What did I tell you,
miss? The boat didn't get in till midnight.
And when they did turn up—Jesus, miss,
you should have seen all the things madam
made me unpack before she'd go to bed!

MISS TESMAN: Ah, well. Let them have a good
lie in. But let's have some nice fresh air
waiting for them when they do come
down. (*Goes to the french windows and throws
them wide open.*)

BERTHA (*bewildered at the table, the bunch of flowers
in her hand*): I'm blessed if there's a square
inch left to put anything. I'll have to let it lie
here, miss. (*Puts it on the piano.*)

MISS TESMAN: Well, Bertha dear, so now you
have a new mistress. Heaven knows it
nearly broke my heart to have to part with
you.

BERTHA (*snivels*): What about me, Miss Juju?
How do you suppose I felt? After all the
happy years I've spent with you and Miss
Rena?

MISS TESMAN: We must accept it bravely, Bertha. It was the only way. George needs you to take care of him. He could never manage without you. You've looked after him ever since he was a tiny boy.

BERTHA: Oh, but, Miss Juju, I can't help thinking about Miss Rena, lying there all helpless, poor dear. And that new girl! She'll never learn the proper way to handle an invalid.

MISS TESMAN: Oh, I'll manage to train her. I'll do most of the work myself, you know. You needn't worry about my poor sister, Bertha dear.

BERTHA: But, Miss Juju, there's another thing. I'm frightened madam may not find me suitable.

MISS TESMAN: Oh, nonsense, Bertha. There may be one or two little things to begin with—

BERTHA: She's a real lady. Wants everything just so.

MISS TESMAN: But of course she does! General Gabler's daughter! Think of what she was accustomed to when the general was alive. You remember how we used to see her out riding with her father? In that long black skirt? With the feather in her hat?

BERTHA: Oh, yes, miss. As if I could forget! But, Lord! I never dreamed I'd live to see a match between her and Master Georgie.

MISS TESMAN: Neither did I. By the way, Bertha, from now on you must stop calling him Master Georgie. You must say Dr. Tesman.

BERTHA: Yes, madam said something about that too. Last night—the moment they'd set foot inside the door. Is it true, then, miss?

MISS TESMAN: Indeed it is. Just fancy, Bertha, some foreigners have made him a doctor. It happened while they were away. I had no idea till he told me when they got off the boat.

BERTHA: Well, I suppose there's no limit to what he won't become. He's that clever. I never thought he'd go in for hospital work, though.

MISS TESMAN: No, he's not that kind of doctor. (*Nods impressively.*) In any case, you may soon have to address him by an even grander title.

BERTHA: You don't say! What might that be, miss?

MISS TESMAN (*smiles*): Ah! If you only knew! (*Moved.*) Dear God, if only poor Joachim could rise out of his grave and see what his little son has grown into! (*Looks round.*) But, Bertha, why have you done this? Taken the chintz covers off all the furniture!

BERTHA: Madam said I was to. Can't stand chintz covers on chairs, she said.

MISS TESMAN: But surely they're not going to use this room as a parlour?

BERTHA: So I gathered, miss. From what madam said. He didn't say anything. The Doctor.

GEORGE TESMAN *comes into the rear room from the right, humming, with an open, empty travelling-bag in his hand. He is about thirty-three, of medium height and youthful appearance, rather plump, with an open, round, contented face, and fair hair and beard. He wears spectacles, and is dressed in comfortable indoor clothes.*

MISS TESMAN: Good morning! Good morning, George!

TESMAN (*in open doorway*): Auntie Juju! Dear Auntie Juju! (*Comes forward and shakes her hand.*) You've come all the way out here! And so early! What?

MISS TESMAN: Well, I had to make sure you'd settled in comfortably.

TESMAN: But you can't have had a proper night's sleep.

MISS TESMAN: Oh, never mind that.

TESMAN: But you got home safely?

MISS TESMAN: Oh, yes. Judge Brack kindly saw me home.

TESMAN: We were so sorry we couldn't give you a lift. But you saw how it was—Hedda had so much luggage—and she insisted on having it all with her.

MISS TESMAN: Yes, I've never seen so much luggage.

BERTHA (*to* TESMAN): Shall I go and ask madam if there's anything I can lend her a hand with?

TESMAN: Er—thank you, Bertha, no, you needn't bother. She says if she wants you for anything she'll ring.

BERTHA (*over to right*): Oh. Very good.

TESMAN: Oh, Bertha—take this bag, will you?

BERTHA (*takes it*): I'll put it in the attic. *She goes out into the hall.*

TESMAN: Just fancy, Auntie Juju, I filled that whole bag with notes for my book. You know, it's really incredible what I've managed to find rooting through those archives. By Jove! Wonderful old things no one even knew existed—

MISS TESMAN: I'm sure you didn't waste a single moment of your honeymoon, George dear.

TESMAN: No, I think I can truthfully claim that. But, Auntie Juju, do take your hat off. Here. Let me untie it for you. What?

MISS TESMAN (*as he does so*): Oh dear, oh dear! It's just as if you were still living at home with us.

TESMAN (*turns the hat in his hand and looks at it*): I say! What a splendid new hat!

MISS TESMAN: I bought it for Hedda's sake.

TESMAN: For Hedda's sake? What?

MISS TESMAN: So that Hedda needn't be ashamed of me, in case we ever go for a walk together.

TESMAN (*pats her cheek*): You still think of everything, don't you, Auntie Juju? (*Puts the hat down on a chair by the table.*) Come on, let's sit down here on the sofa. And have a little chat while we wait for Hedda. *They sit. She puts her parasol in the corner of the sofa.*

MISS TESMAN (*clasps both his hands and looks at him*): Oh, George, it's so wonderful to have you back, and be able to see you with my own eyes again! Poor dear Joachim's own son!

TESMAN: What about me? It's wonderful for me to see you again, Auntie Juju. You've been a mother to me. And a father, too.

MISS TESMAN: You'll always keep a soft spot in your heart for your old aunties, won't you, George dear?

TESMAN: I suppose Auntie Rena's no better? What?

MISS TESMAN: Alas, no. I'm afraid she'll never get better, poor dear. She's lying there just as she has for all these years. Please God I may be allowed to keep her for a little longer. If I lost her I don't know what I'd do. Especially now I haven't you to look after.

TESMAN (*pats her on the back*): There, there, there!

MISS TESMAN (*with a sudden change of mood*): Oh, but, George, fancy you being a married man! And to think it's you who've won Hedda Gabler! The beautiful Hedda Gabler! Fancy! She was always so surrounded by admirers.

TESMAN (*hums a little and smiles contentedly*): Yes, I suppose there are quite a few people in this town who wouldn't mind being in my shoes. What?

MISS TESMAN: And what a honeymoon! Five months! Nearly six.

TESMAN: Well, I've done a lot of work, you know. All those archives to go through. And I've had to read lots of books.

MISS TESMAN: Yes, dear, of course. (*Lowers her voice confidentially.*) But tell me, George—haven't you any—any extra little piece of news to give me?

TESMAN: You mean, arising out of the honeymoon?

MISS TESMAN: Yes.

TESMAN: No, I don't think there's anything I didn't tell you in my letters. My doctorate, of course—but I told you about that last night, didn't I?

MISS TESMAN: Yes, yes, I didn't mean that kind of thing. I was just wondering—are you—are you expecting—?

TESMAN: Expecting what?

MISS TESMAN: Oh, come on, George, I'm your old aunt!

TESMAN: Well, actually—yes, I am expecting something.

MISS TESMAN: I knew it!

TESMAN: You'll be happy to learn that before very long I expect to become a—professor.

MISS TESMAN: Professor?

TESMAN: I think I may say that the matter has been decided. But, Auntie Juju, you know about this.

MISS TESMAN (*gives a little laugh*): Yes, of course. I'd forgotten. (*Changes her tone.*) But we were talking about your honeymoon. It must have cost a dreadful amount of money, George?

TESMAN: Oh well, you know, that big research grant I got helped a good deal.

MISS TESMAN: But how on earth did you manage to make it do for two?

TESMAN: Well, to tell the truth it was a bit tricky. What?

MISS TESMAN: Especially when one's travelling with a lady. A little bird tells me that makes things very much more expensive.

TESMAN: Well, yes, of course it does make things a little more expensive. But Hedda has to do things in style, Auntie Juju. I mean, she has to. Anything less grand wouldn't have suited her.

MISS TESMAN: No, no, I suppose not. A honeymoon abroad seems to be the vogue nowadays. But tell me, have you had time to look round the house?

TESMAN: You bet. I've been up since the crack of dawn.

MISS TESMAN: Well, what do you think of it?

TESMAN: Splendid. Absolutely splendid. I'm only wondering what we're going to do with those two empty rooms between that little one and Hedda's bedroom.

MISS TESMAN (laughs slyly): Ah, George dear, I'm sure you'll manage to find some use for them—in time.

TESMAN: Yes, of course, Auntie Juju, how stupid of me. You're thinking of my books? What?

MISS TESMAN: Yes, yes, dear boy. I was thinking of your books.

TESMAN: You know, I'm so happy for Hedda's sake that we've managed to get this house. Before we became engaged she often used to say this was the only house in town she felt she could really bear to live in. It used to belong to Mrs. Falk—you know, the Prime Minister's widow.

MISS TESMAN: Fancy that! And what a stroke of luck it happened to come into the market. Just as you'd left on your honeymoon.

TESMAN: Yes, Auntie Juju, we've certainly had all the luck with us. What?

MISS TESMAN: But, George dear, the expense! It's going to make a dreadful hole in your pocket, all this.

TESMAN (a little downcast): Yes, I—I suppose it will, won't it?

MISS TESMAN: Oh, George, really!

TESMAN: How much do you think it'll cost? Roughly, I mean? What?

MISS TESMAN: I can't possibly say till I see the bills.

TESMAN: Well, luckily Judge Brack's managed to get it on very favourable terms. He wrote and told Hedda so.

MISS TESMAN: Don't you worry, George dear. Anyway, I've stood security for all the furniture and carpets.

TESMAN: Security? But dear, sweet Auntie Juju, how could you possibly stand security?

MISS TESMAN: I've arranged a mortgage on our annuity.

TESMAN (jumps up): What? On your annuity? And—Auntie Rena's?

MISS TESMAN: Yes. Well, I couldn't think of any other way.

TESMAN (stands in front of her): Auntie Juju, have you gone completely out of your mind? That annuity's all you and Auntie Rena have.

MISS TESMAN: All right, there's no need to get so excited about it. It's a pure formality, you know. Judge Brack told me so. He was so kind as to arrange it all for me. A pure formality; those were his very words.

TESMAN: I dare say. All the same—

MISS TESMAN: Anyway, you'll have a salary of your own now. And, good heavens, even if we did have to fork out a little—tighten our belts for a week or two—why, we'd be happy to do so for your sake.

TESMAN: Oh, Auntie Juju! Will you never stop sacrificing yourself for me?

MISS TESMAN (gets up and puts her hands on his shoulders): What else have I to live for but to smooth your road a little, my dear boy? You've never had any mother or father to turn to. And now at last we've achieved our goal. I won't deny we've had our little difficulties now and then. But now, thank the good Lord, George dear, all your worries are past.

TESMAN: Yes, it's wonderful really how everything's gone just right for me.

MISS TESMAN: Yes! And the enemies who tried to bar your way have been struck down. They have been made to bite the dust. The man who was your most dangerous rival has had the mightiest fall. And now he's lying there in the pit he dug for himself, poor misguided creature.

TESMAN: Have you heard any news of Eilert? Since I went away?

MISS TESMAN: Only that he's said to have published a new book.

TESMAN: What! Eilert Lœvborg? You mean—just recently? What?

MISS TESMAN: So they say. I don't imagine it can be of any value, do you? When your new book comes out, that'll be another story. What's it going to be about?

TESMAN: The domestic industries of Brabant in the Middle Ages.

MISS TESMAN: Oh, George! The things you know about!

TESMAN: Mind you, it may be some time before I actually get down to writing it. I've made these very extensive notes, and I've got to file and index them first.

MISS TESMAN: Ah, yes! Making notes; filing and indexing; you've always been wonderful at that. Poor dear Joachim was just the same.

TESMAN: I'm looking forward so much to getting down to that. Especially now I've a home of my own to work in.

MISS TESMAN: And above all, now that you have the girl you set your heart on, George dear.

TESMAN (*embraces her*): Oh, yes, Auntie Juju, yes! Hedda's the loveliest thing of all! (*Looks towards the doorway.*) I think I hear her coming. What?

HEDDA *enters the rear room from the left, and comes into the drawing-room. She is a woman of twenty-nine. Distinguished, aristocratic face and figure. Her complexion is pale and opalescent. Her eyes are steel-grey, with an expression of cold, calm serenity. Her hair is of a handsome auburn colour, but is not especially abundant. She is dressed in an elegant, somewhat loose-fitting morning gown.*

MISS TESMAN (*goes to greet her*): Good morning, Hedda dear! Good morning!

HEDDA (*holds out her hand*): Good morning, dear Miss Tesman. What an early hour to call. So kind of you.

MISS TESMAN (*seems somewhat embarrassed*): And has the young bride slept well in her new home?

HEDDA: Oh—thank you, yes. Passably well.

TESMAN (*laughs*): Passably? I say, Hedda, that's good! When I jumped out of bed, you were sleeping like a top.

HEDDA: Yes. Fortunately. One has to accustom oneself to anything new, Miss Tesman. It takes time. (*Looks left.*) Oh, that maid's left the french windows open. This room's flooded with sun.

MISS TESMAN (*goes towards the windows*): Oh—let me close them.

HEDDA: No, no, don't do that. Tesman dear, draw the curtains. This light's blinding me.

TESMAN (*at the windows*): Yes, yes, dear. There, Hedda, now you've got shade and fresh air.

HEDDA: This room needs fresh air. All these flowers—! But my dear Miss Tesman, won't you take a seat?

MISS TESMAN: No, really not, thank you. I just wanted to make sure you have everything you need. I must see about getting back home. My poor dear sister will be waiting for me.

TESMAN: Be sure to give her my love, won't you? Tell her I'll run over and see her later today.

MISS TESMAN: Oh yes, I'll tell her that. Oh, George—(*Fumbles in the pocket of her skirt.*) I almost forgot. I've brought something for you.

TESMAN: What's that, Auntie Juju? What?

MISS TESMAN (*pulls out a flat package wrapped in newspaper and gives it to him*): Open and see, dear boy.

TESMAN (*opens the package*): Good heavens! Auntie Juju, you've kept them! Hedda, this is really very touching. What?

HEDDA (*by the what-nots, on the right*): What is it, Tesman?

TESMAN: My old shoes! My slippers, Hedda!

HEDDA: Oh, them. I remember you kept talking about them on our honeymoon.

TESMAN: Yes, I missed them dreadfully. (*Goes over to her.*) Here, Hedda, take a look.

HEDDA (*goes away towards the stove*): Thanks, I won't bother.

TESMAN (*follows her*): Fancy, Hedda, Auntie Rena's embroidered them for me. Despite her being so ill. Oh, you can't imagine what memories they have for me.

HEDDA (*by the table*): Not for me.

MISS TESMAN: No, Hedda's right there, George.

TESMAN: Yes, but I thought since she's one of the family now—

HEDDA (*interrupts*): Tesman, we really can't go on keeping this maid.

MISS TESMAN: Not keep Bertha?

TESMAN: What makes you say that, dear? What?

HEDDA (*points*): Look at that! She's left her old hat lying on the chair.

TESMAN (*appalled, drops his slippers on the floor*): But, Hedda—!

HEDDA: Suppose someone came in and saw it?

TESMAN: But, Hedda—that's Auntie Juju's hat.

HEDDA: Oh?

MISS TESMAN (*picks up the hat*): Indeed it's mine. And it doesn't happen to be old, Hedda dear.

HEDDA: I didn't look at it very closely, Miss Tesman.

MISS TESMAN (*tying on the hat*): As a matter of fact, it's the first time I've worn it. As the good Lord is my witness.

TESMAN: It's very pretty, too. Really smart.

MISS TESMAN: Oh, I'm afraid it's nothing much really. (*Looks round.*) My parasol. Ah, there it is. (*Takes it.*) This is mine, too. (*Murmurs*) Not Bertha's.

TESMAN: A new hat and a new parasol! I say, Hedda, fancy that!

HEDDA: Very pretty and charming.

TESMAN: Yes, isn't it? What? But, Auntie Juju, take a good look at Hedda before you go. Isn't she pretty and charming?

MISS TESMAN: Dear boy, there's nothing new in that. Hedda's been a beauty ever since the day she was born. (*Nods and goes right.*)

TESMAN (*follows her*): Yes, but have you noticed how strong and healthy she's looking? And how she's filled out since we went away?

MISS TESMAN (*stops and turns*): Filled out?

HEDDA (*walks across the room*): Oh, can't we forget it?

TESMAN: Yes, Auntie Juju—you can't see it so clearly with that dress on. But I've good reason to know—

HEDDA (*by the french windows, impatiently*): You haven't good reason to know anything.

TESMAN: It must have been the mountain air up there in the Tyrol—

HEDDA (*curtly, interrupts him*): I'm exactly the same as when I went away.

TESMAN: You keep on saying so. But you're not. I'm right, aren't I, Auntie Juju?

MISS TESMAN (*has folded her hands and is gazing at her*): She's beautiful—beautiful. Hedda is beautiful. (*Goes over to* HEDDA, *takes her head between her hands, draws it down and kisses her hair.*) God bless and keep you, Hedda Tesman. For George's sake.

HEDDA (*frees herself politely*): Oh—let me go, please.

MISS TESMAN (*quietly, emotionally*): I shall come and see you both every day.

TESMAN: Yes, Auntie Juju, please do. What?

MISS TESMAN: Good-bye! Good-bye!

She goes out into the hall. TESMAN *follows her. The door remains open.* TESMAN *is heard sending his love to* AUNT RENA *and thanking* MISS TESMAN *for his slippers. Meanwhile* HEDDA *walks up and down the room, raising her arms and clenching her fists as though in desperation. Then she throws aside the curtains from the french windows and stands there, looking out. A few moments later* TESMAN *returns and closes the door behind him.*

TESMAN (*picks up his slippers from the floor*): What are you looking at Hedda?

HEDDA (*calm and controlled again*): Only the leaves. They're so golden and withered.

TESMAN (*wraps up the slippers and lays them on the table*): Well, we're in September now.

HEDDA (*restless again*): Yes. We're already into September.

TESMAN: Auntie Juju was behaving rather oddly, I thought, didn't you? Almost as though she was in church or something. I wonder what came over her. Any idea?

HEDDA: I hardly know her. Does she often act like that?

TESMAN: Not to the extent she did today.

HEDDA (*goes away from the french windows*): Do you think she was hurt by what I said about the hat?

TESMAN: Oh, I don't think so. A little at first, perhaps—

HEDDA: But what a thing to do, throw her hat down in someone's drawing-room. People don't do such things.

TESMAN: I'm sure Auntie Juju doesn't do it very often.

HEDDA: Oh well, I'll make it up with her.

TESMAN: Oh Hedda, would you?

HEDDA: When you see them this afternoon invite her to come out here this evening.

TESMAN: You bet I will! I say, there's another thing which would please her enormously.

HEDDA: Oh?

TESMAN: If you could bring yourself to call her Auntie Juju. For my sake, Hedda? What?

HEDDA: Oh no, really, Tesman, you mustn't ask me to do that. I've told you so once before. I'll try to call her Aunt Juliana. That's as far as I'll go.

TESMAN (*after a moment*): I say, Hedda, is anything wrong? What?

HEDDA: I'm just looking at my old piano. It doesn't really go with all this.

TESMAN: As soon as I start getting my salary we'll see about changing it.

HEDDA: No, no, don't let's change it. I don't want to part with it. We can move it into that little room and get another one to put in here.

TESMAN (*a little downcast*): Yes, we—might do that.

HEDDA (*picks up the bunch of flowers from the piano*): These flowers weren't here when we arrived last night.

TESMAN: I expect Auntie Juju brought them.

HEDDA: Here's a card. (*Takes it out and reads.*) 'Will come back later today.' Guess who it's from?

TESMAN: No idea. Who? What?

HEDDA: It says: 'Mrs. Elvsted.'

TESMAN: No, really? Mrs. Elvsted! She used to be Miss Rysing, didn't she?

HEDDA: Yes. She was the one with that irritating hair she was always showing off. I hear she used to be an old flame of yours.

TESMAN (*laughs*): That didn't last long. Anyway, that was before I got to know you, Hedda. By Jove, fancy her being in town!

HEDDA: Strange she should call. I only knew her at school.

TESMAN: Yes. I haven't seen her for—oh, heaven knows how long. I don't know how she manages to stick it out up there in the north. What?

HEDDA (*thinks for a moment, then says suddenly*): Tell me, Tesman, doesn't he live somewhere up in those parts? You know—Eilert Lœvborg?

TESMAN: Yes, that's right. So he does.

BERTHA *enters from the hall.*

BERTHA: She's here again, madam. The lady who came and left the flowers. (*Points.*) The ones you're holding.

HEDDA: Oh, is she? Well, show her in.

BERTHA *opens the door for* MRS. ELVSTED *and goes out.* MRS. ELVSTED *is a delicately built woman with gentle, attractive features. Her eyes are light blue, large, and somewhat prominent, with a frightened, questioning expression. Her hair is extremely fair, almost flaxen, and is exceptionally wavy and abundant. She is two or three years younger than* HEDDA. *She is wearing a dark visiting dress, in good taste but not quite in the latest fashion.*

HEDDA (*goes cordially to greet her*): Dear Mrs. Elvsted, good morning! How delightful to see you again after all this time!

MRS. ELVSTED (*nervously, trying to control herself*): Yes, it's many years since we met.

TESMAN: And since *we* met. What?

HEDDA: Thank you for your lovely flowers.

MRS. ELVSTED: I wanted to come yesterday afternoon. But they told me you were away—

TESMAN: You've only just arrived in town, then? What?

MRS. ELVSTED: I got here yesterday, around midday. Oh, I became almost desperate when I heard you weren't here.

HEDDA: Desperate? Why?

TESMAN: My dear Mrs. Rysing—Elvsted—

HEDDA: There's nothing wrong, I hope?

MRS. ELVSTED: Yes, there is. And I don't know anyone else here whom I can turn to.

HEDDA (*puts the flowers down on the table*): Come and sit with me on the sofa—

MRS. ELVSTED: Oh, I feel too restless to sit down.

HEDDA: You must. Come along, now.

She pulls MRS. ELVSTED *down on to the sofa and sits beside her.*

TESMAN: Well? Tell us. Mrs.—er—

HEDDA: Has something happened at home?

MRS. ELVSTED: Yes—that is, yes and no. Oh, I do hope you won't misunderstand me—

HEDDA: Then you'd better tell us the whole story, Mrs. Elvsted.

TESMAN: That's why you've come. What?

MRS. ELVSTED: Yes—yes, it is. Well, then—in case you don't already know—Eilert Lœvborg is in town.

HEDDA: Lœvborg here?

TESMAN: Eilert back in town? Fancy, Hedda, did you hear that?

HEDDA: Yes, of course I heard.

MRS. ELVSTED: He's been here a week. A whole week! In this city. Alone. With all those dreadful people—

HEDDA: But, my dear Mrs. Elvsted, what concern is he of yours?

MRS. ELVSTED (*gives her a frightened look and says quickly*): He's been tutoring the children.

HEDDA: Your children?

MRS. ELVSTED: My husband's. I have none.

HEDDA: Oh, you mean your stepchildren.

MRS. ELVSTED: Yes.

TESMAN (*gropingly*): But was he sufficiently—I don't know how to put it—sufficiently regular in his habits to be suited to such a post? What?

MRS. ELVSTED: For the past two to three years he has been living irreproachably.

TESMAN: You don't say! Hedda, do you hear that?

HEDDA: I hear.

MRS. ELVSTED: Quite irreproachably, I assure you. In every respect. All the same—in this big city—with money in his pockets—I'm so dreadfully frightened something may happen to him.

TESMAN: But why didn't he stay up there with you and your husband?

MRS. ELVSTED: Once his book had come out, he became restless.

TESMAN: Oh, yes—Auntie Juju said he's brought out a new book.

MRS. ELVSTED: Yes, a big new book about the history of civilization. A kind of general survey. It came out a fortnight ago. Everyone's been buying it and reading it—it's created a tremendous stir—

TESMAN: Has it really? It must be something he's dug up, then.

MRS. ELVSTED: You mean from the old days?

TESMAN: Yes.

MRS. ELVSTED: No, he's written it all since he came to live with us.

TESMAN: Well, that's splendid news, Hedda. Fancy that!

MRS. ELVSTED: Oh, yes! If only he can go on like this!

HEDDA: Have you met him since you came here?

MRS. ELVSTED: No, not yet. I had such dreadful difficulty finding his address. But this morning I managed to track him down at last.

HEDDA (*looks searchingly at her*): I must say I find it a little strange that your husband—hm—

MRS. ELVSTED (*starts nervously*): My husband! What do you mean?

HEDDA: That he should send you all the way here on an errand of this kind. I'm surprised he didn't come himself to keep an eye on his friend.

MRS. ELVSTED: Oh, no, no—my husband hasn't the time. Besides, I—er—wanted to do some shopping here.

HEDDA (*with a slight smile*): Ah. Well, that's different.

MRS. ELVSTED (*gets up quickly, restlessly*): Please, Mr. Tesman, I beg you—be kind to Eilert Lœvborg if he comes here. I'm sure he will. I mean, you used to be such good friends in the old days. And you're both studying the same subject, as far as I can understand. You're in the same field, aren't you?

TESMAN: Well, we used to be, anyway.

MRS. ELVSTED: Yes—so I beg you earnestly, do please, please, keep an eye on him. Oh, Mr. Tesman, do promise me you will.

TESMAN: I shall be only too happy to do so, Mrs. Rysing.

HEDDA: Elvsted.

TESMAN: I'll do everything for Eilert that lies in my power. You can rely on that.

MRS. ELVSTED: Oh, how good and kind you are! (*Presses his hands.*) Thank you, thank you, thank you. (*Frightened.*) My husband's so fond of him, you see.

HEDDA (*gets up*): You'd better send him a note, Tesman. He may not come to you of his own accord.

TESMAN: Yes, that'd probably be the best plan, Hedda. What?

HEDDA: The sooner the better. Why not do it now?

MRS. ELVSTED (*pleadingly*): Oh yes, if only you would!

TESMAN: I'll do it this very moment. Do you have his address, Mrs.—er—Elvsted?

MRS. ELVSTED: Yes. (*Takes a small piece of paper from her pocket and gives it to him.*)

TESMAN: Good, good. Right, well, I'll go inside and—(*Looks round.*) Where are my slippers? Oh yes, here. (*Picks up the package and is about to go.*)

HEDDA: Try to sound friendly. Make it a nice long letter.

TESMAN: Right, I will.

MRS. ELVSTED: Please don't say anything about my having seen you.

TESMAN: Good heavens, no, of course not. What? *He goes out through the rear room to the right.*

HEDDA (*goes over to* MRS. ELVSTED, *smiles, and says softly*): Well! Now we've killed two birds with one stone.

MRS. ELVSTED: What do you mean?

HEDDA: Didn't you realize I wanted to get him out of the room?

MRS. ELVSTED: So that he could write the letter?

HEDDA: And so that I could talk to you alone.

MRS. ELVSTED (*confused*): About this?

HEDDA: Yes, about this.

MRS. ELVSTED (*in alarm*): But there's nothing more to tell, Mrs. Tesman. Really there isn't.

HEDDA: Oh, yes, there is. There's a lot more. I can see that. Come along, let's sit down and have a little chat. *She pushes* MRS. ELVSTED *down into the armchair by the stove and seats herself on one of the footstools.*

MRS. ELVSTED (*looks anxiously at her watch*): Really, Mrs. Tesman, I think I ought to be going now.

HEDDA: There's no hurry. Well? How are things at home?

MRS. ELVSTED: I'd rather not speak about that.

HEDDA: But, my dear, you can tell me. Good heavens, we were at school together.

MRS. ELVSTED: Yes, but you were a year senior to me. Oh, I used to be terribly frightened of you in those days.

HEDDA: Frightened of me?

MRS. ELVSTED: Yes, terribly frightened. Whenever you met me on the staircase you used to pull my hair.

HEDDA: No, did I?

MRS. ELVSTED: Yes. And once you said you'd burn it all off.

HEDDA: Oh, that was only in fun.

MRS. ELVSTED: Yes, but I was so silly in those days. And then afterwards—I mean, we've drifted so far apart. Our backgrounds were so different.

HEDDA: Well, now we must try to drift together again. Now listen. When we were at school we used to call each other by our Christian names—

MRS. ELVSTED: No, I'm sure you're mistaken.

HEDDA: I'm sure I'm not. I remember it quite clearly. Let's tell each other our secrets, as we used to in the old days. (*Moves closer on her footstool.*) There, now. (*Kisses her on the cheek.*) You must call me Hedda.

MRS. ELVSTED (*squeezes her hands and pats them*): Oh, you're so kind. I'm not used to people being so nice to me.

HEDDA: Now, now, now. And I shall call you Tora, the way I used to.

MRS. ELVSTED: My name is Thea.

HEDDA: Yes, of course. Of course. I meant Thea. (*Looks at her sympathetically.*) So you're not used to kindness, Thea? In your own home?

MRS. ELVSTED: Oh, if only I had a home! But I haven't. I've never had one.

HEDDA (*looks at her for a moment*): I thought that was it.

MRS. ELVSTED (*stares blankly and helplessly*): Yes—yes—yes.

HEDDA: I can't remember exactly, but didn't you first go to Mr. Elvsted as a housekeeper?

MRS. ELVSTED: Governess, actually. But his wife—at the time, I mean—she was an invalid, and had to spend most of her time in bed. So I had to look after the house, too.

HEDDA: But in the end, you became mistress of the house.

MRS. ELVSTED (*sadly*): Yes, I did.

HEDDA: Let me see. Roughly how long ago was that?

MRS. ELVSTED: When I got married, you mean?

HEDDA: Yes.

MRS. ELVSTED: About five years.

HEDDA: Yes; it must be about that.

MRS. ELVSTED: Oh, those five years! Especially the last two or three. Oh, Mrs. Tesman, if you only knew—!

HEDDA (*slaps her hand gently*): Mrs. Tesman? Oh, Thea!

MRS. ELVSTED: I'm sorry, I'll try to remember. Yes—if you had any idea—

HEDDA (*casually*): Eilert Lœvborg's been up there, too, for about three years, hasn't he?

MRS. ELVSTED (*looks at her uncertainly*): Eilert Lœvborg? Yes, he has.

HEDDA: Did you know him before? When you were here?

MRS. ELVSTED: No, not really. That is—I knew him by name, of course.

HEDDA: But up there, he used to visit you?

MRS. ELVSTED: Yes, he used to come and see us every day. To give the children lessons. I found I couldn't do that as well as manage the house.

HEDDA: I'm sure you couldn't. And your husband—? I suppose being a magistrate he has to be away from home a good deal?

MRS. ELVSTED: Yes. You see, Mrs.—you see, Hedda, he has to cover the whole district.

HEDDA (*leans against the arm of* MRS. ELVSTED'S *chair*): Poor, pretty little Thea! Now you must tell me the whole story. From beginning to end.

MRS. ELVSTED: Well—what do you want to know?

HEDDA: What kind of a man is your husband, Thea? I mean, as a person. Is he kind to you?

MRS. ELVSTED (*evasively*): I'm sure he does his best to be.

HEDDA: I only wonder if he isn't too old for you. There's more than twenty years between you, isn't there?

MRS. ELVSTED (*irritably*): Yes, there's that, too. Oh, there are so many things. We're different in every way. We've nothing in common. Nothing whatever.

HEDDA: But he loves you, surely? In his own way?

MRS. ELVSTED: Oh, I don't know. I think he just finds me useful. And then I don't cost much to keep. I'm cheap.

HEDDA: Now you're being stupid.

MRS. ELVSTED (*shakes her head*): It can't be any different. With him. He doesn't love anyone except himself. And perhaps the children—a little.

HEDDA: He must be fond of Eilert Lœvborg, Thea.

MRS. ELVSTED (*looks at her*): Eilert Lœvborg? What makes you think that?

HEDDA: Well, if he sends you all the way down here to look for him—(*Smiles almost imperceptibly.*) Besides, you said so yourself to Tesman.

MRS. ELVSTED (*with a nervous twitch*): Did I? Oh yes, I suppose I did. (*Impulsively, but keeping her voice low.*) Well, I might as well tell you the whole story. It's bound to come out sooner or later.

HEDDA: But, my dear Thea—?

MRS. ELVSTED: My husband had no idea I was coming here.

HEDDA: What? Your husband didn't know?

MRS. ELVSTED: No, of course not. As a matter of fact, he wasn't even there. He was away at the assizes. Oh, I couldn't stand it any longer, Hedda! I just couldn't. I'd be so dreadfully lonely up there now.

HEDDA: Go on.

MRS. ELVSTED: So I packed a few things. Secretly. And went.

HEDDA: Without telling anyone?

MRS. ELVSTED: Yes. I caught the train and came straight here.

HEDDA: But, my dear Thea! How brave of you!

MRS. ELVSTED (*gets up and walks across the room*): Well, what else could I do?

HEDDA: But what do you suppose your husband will say when you get back?

MRS. ELVSTED (*by the table, looks at her*): Back there? To him?

HEDDA: Yes. Surely—?

MRS. ELVSTED: I shall never go back to him.

HEDDA (*gets up and goes closer*): You mean you've left your home for good?

MRS. ELVSTED: Yes. I didn't see what else I could do.

HEDDA: But to do it so openly!

MRS. ELVSTED: Oh, it's no use trying to keep a thing like that secret.

HEDDA: But what do you suppose people will say?

MRS. ELVSTED: They can say what they like. (*Sits sadly, wearily on the sofa.*) I had to do it.

HEDDA (*after a short silence*): What do you intend to do now? How are you going to live?

MRS. ELVSTED: I don't know. I only know that I must live wherever Eilert Lœvborg is. If I am to go on living.

HEDDA (*moves a chair from the table, sits on it near* MRS. ELVSTED *and strokes her hands*): Tell me, Thea, how did this—friendship between you and Eilert Lœvborg begin?

MRS. ELVSTED: Oh, it came about gradually. I developed a kind of—power over him.

HEDDA: Oh?

MRS. ELVSTED: He gave up his old habits. Not because I asked him to. I'd never have dared to do that. I suppose he just noticed I didn't like that kind of thing. So he gave it up.

HEDDA (*hides a smile*): So you've made a new man of him! Clever little Thea!

MRS. ELVSTED: Yes—anyway, he says I have. And he's made a—sort of—real person of me. Taught me to think—and to understand all kinds of things.

HEDDA: Did he give you lessons, too?

MRS. ELVSTED: Not exactly lessons. But he talked to me. About—oh, you've no idea—so many things! And then he let me work with him. Oh, it was wonderful. I was so happy to be allowed to help him.

HEDDA: Did he allow you to help him?

MRS. ELVSTED: Yes. Whenever he wrote anything we always—did it together.

HEDDA: Like good friends?

MRS. ELVSTED (*eagerly*): Friends! Yes—why, Hedda that's exactly the word he used! Oh, I ought to feel so happy. But I can't. I don't know if it will last.

HEDDA: You don't seem very sure of him.

MRS. ELVSTED (*sadly*): Something stands between Eilert Lœvborg and me. The shadow of another woman.

HEDDA: Who can that be?

MRS. ELVSTED: I don't know. Someone he used to be friendly with in—in the old days. Someone he's never been able to forget.

HEDDA: What has he told you about her?

MRS. ELVSTED: Oh, he only mentioned her once, casually.

HEDDA: Well! What did he say?

MRS. ELVSTED: He said when he left her she tried to shoot him with a pistol.

HEDDA (*cold, controlled*): What nonsense. People don't do such things. The kind of people we know.

MRS. ELVSTED: No. I think it must have been that red-haired singer he used to—

HEDDA: Ah yes, very probably.

MRS. ELVSTED: I remember they used to say she always carried a loaded pistol.

HEDDA: Well then, it must be her.

MRS. ELVSTED: But, Hedda, I hear she's come back, and is living here. Oh, I'm so desperate—!

HEDDA (*glances towards the rear room*): Ssh! Tesman's coming. (*Gets up and whispers.*) Thea, we mustn't breathe a word about this to anyone.

MRS. ELVSTED (*jumps up*): Oh, no, no! Please don't!

GEORGE TESMAN *appears from the right in the rear room with a letter in his hand, and comes into the drawing-room.*

TESMAN: Well, here's my little epistle all signed and sealed.

HEDDA: Good. I think Mrs. Elvsted wants to go now. Wait a moment—I'll see you as far as the garden gate.

TESMAN: Er—Hedda, do you think Bertha could deal with this?

HEDDA (*takes the letter*): I'll give her instructions.
  BERTHA *enters from the hall.*
BERTHA: Judge Brack is here and asks if he may
  pay his respects to madam and the Doctor.
HEDDA: Yes, ask him to be so good as to come in.
  And—wait a moment—drop this letter in
  the post box.
BERTHA (*takes the letter*): Very good, madam. *She
  opens the door for* JUDGE BRACK, *and goes out.*
  JUDGE BRACK *is forty-five; rather short, but
  well built, and elastic in his movements. He has
  a roundish face with an aristocratic profile. His
  hair, cut short, is still almost black, and is carefully barbered. Eyes lively and humorous. Thick
  eyebrows. His moustache is also thick, and is
  trimmed square at the ends. He is wearing outdoor clothes which are elegant but a little too
  youthful for him. He has a monocle in one eye;
  now and then he lets it drop.*
BRACK (*hat in hand, bows*): May one presume to
  call so early?
HEDDA: One may presume.
TESMAN (*shakes his hand*): You're welcome here
  any time. Judge Brack—Mrs. Rysing.
  HEDDA *sighs.*
BRACK (*bows*): Ah—charmed—
HEDDA (*looks at him and laughs*): What fun to be
  able to see you by daylight for once, Judge.
BRACK: Do I look—different?
HEDDA: Yes. A little younger, I think.
BRACK: Too kind.
TESMAN: Well, what do you think of Hedda?
  What? Doesn't she look well? Hasn't she
  filled out—?
HEDDA: Oh, do stop it. You ought to be thanking
  Judge Brack for all the inconvenience he's
  put himself to—
BRACK: Nonsense, it was a pleasure—
HEDDA: You're a loyal friend. But my other
  friend is pining to get away. Au revoir,
  Judge. I won't be a minute.
  Mutual salutations. MRS. ELVSTED *and* HEDDA
  go out through the hall.
BRACK: Well, is your wife satisfied with every-
  thing?
TESMAN: Yes, we can't thank you enough.
  That is—we may have to shift one or two
  things around, she tells me. And we're

short of one or two little items we'll have to
  purchase.
BRACK: Oh? Really?
TESMAN: But you mustn't worry your head about
  that. Hedda says she'll get what's needed. I
  say, why don't we sit down? What?
BRACK: Thanks, just for a moment. (*Sits at the table.*) There's something I'd like to talk to you
  about, my dear Tesman.
TESMAN: Oh? Ah yes, of course. (*Sits.*) After the
  feast comes the reckoning. What?
BRACK: Oh, never mind about the financial
  side—there's no hurry about that. Though I
  could wish we'd arranged things a little less
  palatially.
TESMAN: Good heavens, that'd never have done.
  Think of Hedda, my dear chap. You know
  her. I couldn't possibly ask her to live like a
  petty bourgeois.
BRACK: No, no—that's just the problem.
TESMAN: Anyway, it can't be long now before
  my nomination comes through.
BRACK: Well, you know, these things often take
  time.
TESMAN: Have you heard any more news?
  What?
BRACK: Nothing definite. (*Changing the subject*).
  Oh, by the way, I have one piece of news for
  you.
TESMAN: What?
BRACK: Your old friend Eilert Lœvborg is back in
  town.
TESMAN: I know that already.
BRACK: Oh? How did you hear that?
TESMAN: She told me. That lady who went out
  with Hedda.
BRACK: I see. What was her name? I didn't catch
  it.
TESMAN: Mrs. Elvsted.
BRACK: Oh, the magistrate's wife. Yes, Lœvborg's
  been living up near them, hasn't he?
TESMAN: I'm delighted to hear he's become a de-
  cent human being again.
BRACK: Yes, so they say.
TESMAN: I gather he's published a new book,
  too. What?
BRACK: Indeed he has.
TESMAN: I hear it's created rather a stir.

BRACK: Quite an unusual stir.

TESMAN: I say, isn't that splendid news! He's such a gifted chap—and I was afraid he'd gone to the dogs for good.

BRACK: Most people thought he had.

TESMAN: But I can't think what he'll do now. How on earth will he manage to make ends meet? What?

As he speaks his last words HEDDA *enters from the hall.*

HEDDA (*to* BRACK, *laughs slightly scornfully*): Tesman is always worrying about making ends meet.

TESMAN: We were talking about poor Eilert Lœvborg, Hedda dear.

HEDDA (*gives him a quick look*): Oh, were you? (*Sits in the armchair by the stove and asks casually.*) Is he in trouble?

TESMAN: Well, he must have run through his inheritance long ago by now. And he can't write a new book every year. What? So I'm wondering what's going to become of him.

BRACK: I may be able to enlighten you there.

TESMAN: Oh?

BRACK: You mustn't forget he has relatives who wield a good deal of influence.

TESMAN: Relatives? Oh, they've quite washed their hands of him, I'm afraid.

BRACK: They used to regard him as the hope of the family.

TESMAN: Used to, yes. But he's put an end to that.

HEDDA: Who knows? (*With a little smile.*) I hear the Elvsteds have made a new man of him.

BRACK: And then this book he's just published—

TESMAN: Well, let's hope they find something for him. I've just written him a note. Oh, by the way, Hedda, I asked him to come over and see us this evening.

BRACK: But, my dear chap, you're coming to me this evening. My bachelor party. You promised me last night when I met you at the boat.

HEDDA: Had you forgotten, Tesman?

TESMAN: Good heavens, yes, I'd quite forgotten.

BRACK: Anyway, you can be quite sure he won't turn up here.

TESMAN: Why do you think that? What?

BRACK (*a little unwillingly, gets up and rests his hands on the back of his chair*): My dear Tesman—and you, too, Mrs. Tesman—there's something I feel you ought to know.

TESMAN: Concerning Eilert?

BRACK: Concerning him and you.

TESMAN: Well, my dear judge, tell us please!

BRACK: You must be prepared for your nomination not to come through quite as quickly as you hope and expect.

TESMAN (*jumps up uneasily*): Is anything wrong? What?

BRACK: There's a possibility that the appointment may be decided by competition—

TESMAN: Competition! Hedda, fancy that!

HEDDA (*leans further back in her chair*): Ah! How interesting!

TESMAN: But who else—? I say, you don't mean—?

BRACK: Exactly. By competition with Eilert Lœvborg.

TESMAN (*clasps his hands in alarm*): No, no, but this is inconceivable! It's absolutely impossible! What?

BRACK: Hm. We may find it'll happen, all the same.

TESMAN: No, but—Judge Brack, they couldn't be so inconsiderate towards me! (*Waves his arms.*) I mean, by Jove, I—I'm a married man! It was on the strength of this that Hedda and I *got* married! We've run up some pretty hefty debts. And borrowed money from Auntie Juju! I mean, good heavens, they practically promised me the appointment. What?

BRACK: Well, well, I'm sure you'll get it. But you'll have to go through a competition.

HEDDA (*motionless in her armchair*): How exciting, Tesman. It'll be a kind of duel, by Jove.

TESMAN: My dear Hedda, how can you take it so lightly?

HEDDA (*as before*): I'm not. I can't wait to see who's going to win.

BRACK: In any case, Mrs. Tesman, it's best you should know how things stand. I mean before you commit yourself to these little items I hear you're threatening to purchase.

HEDDA: I can't allow this to alter my plans.

BRACK: Indeed? Well, that's your business. Good-bye. (*To* TESMAN) I'll come and collect you on the way home from my afternoon walk.

TESMAN: Oh, yes, yes. I'm sorry. I'm all upside down just now.

HEDDA (*lying in her chair, holds out her hand*): Good-bye, Judge. See you this afternoon.

BRACK: Thank you. Good-bye, good-bye.

TESMAN (*sees him to the door*): Good-bye, my dear Judge. You will excuse me, won't you?

JUDGE BRACK *goes out through the hall.*

TESMAN (*pacing up and down*): Oh, Hedda! One oughtn't to go plunging off on wild adventures. What?

HEDDA (*looks at him and smiles*): Like you're doing?

TESMAN: Yes. I mean, there's no denying it, it was a pretty big adventure to go off and get married and set up house merely on expectation.

HEDDA: Perhaps you're right.

TESMAN: Well, anyway, we have our home, Hedda. My word, yes! The home we dreamed of. And set our hearts on. What?

HEDDA (*gets up slowly, wearily*): You agreed that we should enter society. And keep open house. That was the bargain.

TESMAN: Yes. Good heavens, I was looking forward to it all so much. To seeing you play hostess to a select circle! By Jove! What? Ah, well, for the time being we shall have to make do with each other's company, Hedda. Perhaps have Auntie Juju in now and then. Oh dear, this wasn't at all what you had in mind—

HEDDA: I won't be able to have a liveried footman. For a start.

TESMAN: Oh no, we couldn't possibly afford a footman.

HEDDA: And the bay mare you promised me—

TESMAN (*fearfully*): Bay mare!

HEDDA: I mustn't even think of that now.

TESMAN: Heaven forbid!

HEDDA (*walks across the room*): Ah, well. I still have one thing left to amuse myself with.

TESMAN (*joyfully*): Thank goodness for that. What's that, Hedda? What?

HEDDA (*in the open doorway, looks at him with concealed scorn*): My pistols, George darling.

TESMAN (*alarmed*): Pistols!

HEDDA (*her eyes cold*): General Gabler's pistols.

She goes into the rear room and disappears.

TESMAN (*runs to the doorway and calls after her*): For heaven's sake, Hedda dear, don't touch those things. They're dangerous. Hedda—please—for my sake! What?

ACT TWO

The same as in Act One, except that the piano has been removed and an elegant little writing-table, with a bookcase, stands in its place. By the sofa on the left a smaller table has been placed. Most of the flowers have been removed. MRS. ELVSTED'S *bouquet stands on the larger table, downstage. It is afternoon.*

HEDDA, *dressed to receive callers, is alone in the room. She is standing by the open french windows, loading a revolver. The pair to it is lying in an open pistol-case on the writing-table.*

HEDDA (*looks down into the garden and calls*): Good afternoon, Judge.

BRACK (*in the distance, below*): Afternoon, Mrs. Tesman.

HEDDA (*raises the pistol and takes aim*): I'm going to shoot you, Judge Brack.

BRACK (*shouts from below*): No, no, no! Don't aim that thing at me!

HEDDA: This'll teach you to enter houses by the back door.

She fires.

BRACK (*below*): Have you gone completely out of your mind?

HEDDA: Oh dear! Did I hit you?

BRACK (*still outside*): Stop playing these silly tricks.

HEDDA: All right, Judge. Come along in.

JUDGE BRACK, *dressed for a bachelor party, enters through the french windows. He has a light overcoat on his arm.*

BRACK: For God's sake, haven't you stopped fooling around with those things yet? What are you trying to hit?

HEDDA: Oh, I was just shooting at the sky.

BRACK (*takes the pistol gently from her hand*): By your leave, ma'am. (*Looks at it.*) Ah, yes—I know this old friend well. (*Looks around.*) Where's the case? Oh, yes. (*Puts the pistol in *the case and closes it.*) That's enough of that little game for today.

HEDDA: Well, what on earth *am* I to do?

BRACK: You haven't had any visitors?

HEDDA (*closes the french windows*): Not one. I suppose the best people are all still in the country.

BRACK: Your husband isn't home yet?

HEDDA (*locks the pistol-case away in a drawer of the writing-table*): No. The moment he'd finished eating he ran off to his auntie's. He wasn't expecting you so early.

BRACK: Ah, why didn't I think of that? How stupid of me.

HEDDA (*turns her head and looks at him*): Why stupid?

BRACK: I'd have come a little sooner.

HEDDA (*walks across the room*): There'd have been no one to receive you. I've been in my room since lunch, dressing.

BRACK: You haven't a tiny crack in the door through which we might have negotiated?

HEDDA: You forgot to arrange one.

BRACK: Another stupidity.

HEDDA: Well, we'll have to sit down here. And wait. Tesman won't be back for some time.

BRACK: Sad. Well, I'll be patient.

> HEDDA *sits on the corner of the sofa.* BRACK *puts his coat over the back of the nearest chair and seats himself, keeping his hat in his hand. Short pause. They look at each other.*

HEDDA: Well?

BRACK (*in the same tone of voice*): Well?

HEDDA: I asked first.

BRACK (*leans forward slightly*): Yes, well, now we can enjoy a nice, cosy little chat—Mrs. Hedda.

HEDDA (*leans further back in her chair*): It seems ages since we had a talk. I don't count last night or this morning.

BRACK: You mean: *à deux?*

HEDDA: Mm—yes. That's roughly what I meant.

BRACK: I've been longing so much for you to come home.

HEDDA: So have I.

BRACK: You? Really, Mrs. Hedda? And I thought you were having such a wonderful honeymoon.

HEDDA: Oh, yes. Wonderful!

BRACK: But your husband wrote such ecstatic letters.

HEDDA: He! Oh, yes! He thinks life has nothing better to offer than rooting around in libraries and copying old pieces of parchment, or whatever it is he does.

BRACK (*a little maliciously*): Well, that is his life. Most of it, anyway.

HEDDA: Yes, I know. Well, it's all right for him. But for me! Oh no, my dear Judge. I've been bored to death.

BRACK (*sympathetically*): Do you mean that? Seriously?

HEDDA: Yes. Can you imagine? Six whole months without ever meeting a single person who was one of us, and to whom I could talk about the kind of things we talk about.

BRACK: Yes, I can understand. I'd miss that, too.

HEDDA: That wasn't the worst, though.

BRACK: What was?

HEDDA: Having to spend every minute of one's life with—with the same person.

BRACK (*nods*): Yes. What a thought! Morning; noon; *and*—

HEDDA (*coldly*): As I said: every minute of one's life.

BRACK: I stand corrected. But dear Tesman is such a clever fellow, I should have thought one ought to be able—

HEDDA: Tesman is only interested in one thing, my dear Judge. His special subject.

BRACK: True.

HEDDA: And people who are only interested in one thing don't make the most amusing company. Not for long, anyway.

BRACK: Not even when they happen to be the person one loves?

HEDDA: Oh, don't use that sickly, stupid word.

BRACK (*starts*): But, Mrs. Hedda—!

HEDDA (*half laughing, half annoyed*): You just try it, Judge. Listening to the history of civilization morning, noon and—

BRACK (*corrects her*): Every minute of one's life.

HEDDA: All right. Oh, and those domestic industries of Brabant in the Middle Ages! That really is beyond the limit.

BRACK (*looks at her searchingly*): But, tell me—if you feel like this why on earth did you—? Hm—

HEDDA: Why on earth did I marry George Tesman?

BRACK: If you like to put it that way.

HEDDA: Do you think it so very strange?

BRACK: Yes—and no, Mrs. Hedda.

HEDDA: I'd danced myself tired, Judge. I felt my time was up—(*Gives a slight shudder.*) No, I mustn't say that. Or even think it.

BRACK: You've no rational cause to think it.

HEDDA: Oh—cause, cause—(*Looks searchingly at him.*) After all, George Tesman—well, I mean, he's a very respectable man.

BRACK: Very respectable, sound as a rock. No denying that.

HEDDA: And there's nothing exactly ridiculous about him. Is there?

BRACK: Ridiculous? N-no, I wouldn't say that.

HEDDA: Mm. He's very clever at collecting material and all that, isn't he? I mean, he may go quite far in time.

BRACK (*looks at her a little uncertainly*): I thought you believed, like everyone else, that he would become a very prominent man.

HEDDA (*looks tired*): Yes, I did. And when he came and begged me on his bended knees to be allowed to love and to cherish me, I didn't see why I shouldn't let him.

BRACK: No, well—if one looks at it like that—

HEDDA: It was more than my other admirers were prepared to do, Judge dear.

BRACK (*laughs*): Well, I can't answer for the others. As far as I myself am concerned, you know I've always had a considerable respect for the institution of marriage. As an institution.

HEDDA (*lightly*): Oh, I've never entertained any hopes of you.

BRACK: All I want is to have a circle of friends whom I can trust, whom I can help with advice or—or by any other means, and into whose houses I may come and go as a— trusted friend.

HEDDA: Of the husband?

BRACK (*bows*): Preferably, to be frank, of the wife. And of the husband too, of course. Yes, you know, this kind of triangle is a delightful arrangement for all parties concerned.

HEDDA: Yes, I often longed for a third person while I was away. Oh, those hours we spent alone in railway compartments—

BRACK: Fortunately your honeymoon is now over.

HEDDA (*shakes her head*): There's a long, long way still to go. I've only reached a stop on the line.

BRACK: Why not jump out and stretch your legs a little, Mrs. Hedda?

HEDDA: I'm not the jumping sort.

BRACK: Aren't you?

HEDDA: No. There's always someone around who—

BRACK (*laughs*): Who looks at one's legs?

HEDDA: Yes. Exactly.

BRACK: Well, but surely—

HEDDA (*with a gesture of rejection*): I don't like it. I'd rather stay where I am. Sitting in the compartment. *À deux.*

BRACK: But suppose a third person were to step into the compartment?

HEDDA: That would be different.

BRACK: A trusted friend—someone who understood—

HEDDA: And was lively and amusing—

BRACK: And interested in—more subjects than one—

HEDDA (*sighs audibly*): Yes, that'd be a relief.

BRACK (*hears the front door open and shut*): The triangle is completed.

HEDDA (*half under her breath*): And the train goes on.

GEORGE TESMAN, *in grey walking dress with a soft felt hat, enters from the hall. He has a number of paper-covered books under his arm and in his pockets.*

TESMAN (*goes over to the table by the corner sofa*): Phew! It's too hot to be lugging all this around. (*Puts the books down.*) I'm positively sweating, Hedda. Why, hullo, hullo! You here already, Judge? What? Bertha didn't tell me.

BRACK (*gets up*): I came in through the garden.

HEDDA: What are all those books you've got there?

TESMAN (*stands glancing through them*): Oh, some new publications dealing with my special subject. I had to buy them.

HEDDA: Your special subject?

BRACK: His special subject, Mrs. Tesman.

BRACK *and* HEDDA *exchange a smile.*

HEDDA: Haven't you collected enough material on your special subject?

TESMAN: My dear Hedda, one can never have too much. One must keep abreast of what other people are writing.

HEDDA: Yes. Of course.

TESMAN (*rooting among the books*): Look—I bought a copy of Eilert Lœvborg's new book, too. (*Holds it out to her.*) Perhaps you'd like to have a look at it, Hedda? What?

HEDDA: No, thank you. Er—yes, perhaps I will, later.

TESMAN: I glanced through it on my way home.

BRACK: What's your opinion—as a specialist on the subject?

TESMAN: I'm amazed how sound and balanced it is. He never used to write like that. (*Gathers his books together.*) Well, I must get down to these at once. I can hardly wait to cut the pages. Oh, I've got to change, too. (*To* BRACK) We don't have to be off just yet, do we? What?

BRACK: Heavens, no. We've plenty of time yet.

TESMAN: Good, I needn't hurry, then. (*Goes with his books, but stops and turns in the doorway.*) Oh, by the way, Hedda, Auntie Juju won't be coming to see you this evening.

HEDDA: Won't she? Oh—the hat, I suppose.

TESMAN: Good heavens, no. How could you think such a thing of Auntie Juju? Fancy—! No, Auntie Rena's very ill.

HEDDA: She always is.

TESMAN: Yes, but today she's been taken really bad.

HEDDA: Oh, then it's quite understandable that the other one should want to stay with her. Well, I shall have to swallow my disappointment.

TESMAN: You can't imagine how happy Auntie Juju was in spite of everything. At your looking so well after the honeymoon!

HEDDA (*half beneath her breath, as she rises*): Oh, these everlasting aunts!

TESMAN: What?

HEDDA (*goes over to the french windows*): Nothing.

TESMAN: Oh. All right. (*Goes into the rear room and out of sight.*)

BRACK: What was that about the hat?

HEDDA: Oh, something that happened with Miss Tesman this morning. She'd put her hat down on a chair. (*Looks at him and smiles.*) And I pretended to think it was the servant's.

BRACK (*shakes his head*): But, my dear Mrs. Hedda, how could you do such a thing? To that poor old lady?

HEDDA (*nervously, walking across the room*): Sometimes a mood like that hits me. And I can't stop myself. (*Throws herself down in the armchair by the stove.*) Oh, I don't know how to explain it.

BRACK (*behind her chair*): You're not really happy. That's the answer.

HEDDA (*stares ahead of her*): Why on earth should I be happy? Can you give me a reason?

BRACK: Yes. For one thing you've got the home you always wanted.

HEDDA (*looks at him*): You really believe that story?

BRACK: You mean it isn't true?

HEDDA: Oh, yes, it's partly true.

BRACK: Well?

HEDDA: It's true I got Tesman to see me home from parties last summer—

BRACK: It was a pity my home lay in another direction.

HEDDA: Yes. Your interests lay in another direction, too.

BRACK (*laughs*): That's naughty of you, Mrs. Hedda. But to return to you and George—

HEDDA: Well, we walked past this house one evening. And poor Tesman was fidgeting in his boots trying to find something to talk about. I felt sorry for the great scholar—

BRACK (*smiles incredulously*): Did you? Hm.

HEDDA: Yes, honestly I did. Well, to help him out of his misery, I happened to say quite frivolously how much I'd love to live in this house.

BRACK: Was that all?

HEDDA: That evening, yes.

BRACK: But—afterwards?

HEDDA: Yes. My little frivolity had its consequences, my dear Judge.

BRACK: Our little frivolities do. Much too often, unfortunately.

HEDDA: Thank you. Well, it was our mutual admiration for the late Prime Minister's house that brought George Tesman and me together on common ground. So we got engaged, and we got married, and we went on our honeymoon, and—Ah well, Judge, I've—made my bed and I must lie in it, I was about to say.

BRACK: How utterly fantastic! And you didn't really care in the least about the house?

HEDDA: God knows I didn't.

BRACK: Yes, but now that we've furnished it so beautifully for you?

HEDDA: Ugh—all the rooms smell of lavender and dried roses. But perhaps Auntie Juju brought that in.

BRACK (laughs): More likely the Prime Minister's widow, rest her soul.

HEDDA: Yes, it's got the odour of death about it. It reminds me of the flowers one has worn at a ball—the morning after. (Clasps her hands behind her neck, leans back in the chair and looks up at him.) Oh, my dear Judge, you've no idea how hideously bored I'm going to be out here.

BRACK: Couldn't you find some—occupation, Mrs. Hedda? Like your husband?

HEDDA: Occupation? That'd interest me?

BRACK: Well—preferably.

HEDDA: God knows what. I've often thought— (Breaks off.) No, that wouldn't work either.

BRACK: Who knows? Tell me about it.

HEDDA: I was thinking—if I could persuade Tesman to go into politics, for example.

BRACK (laughs): Tesman! No, honestly, I don't think he's quite cut out to be a politician.

HEDDA: Perhaps not. But if I could persuade him to have a go at it?

BRACK: What satisfaction would that give you? If he turned out to be no good? Why do you want to make him do that?

HEDDA: Because I'm bored. (After a moment.) You feel there's absolutely no possibility of Tesman becoming Prime Minister, then?

BRACK: Well, you know, Mrs. Hedda, for one thing he'd have to be pretty well off before he could become that.

HEDDA (gets up impatiently): There you are! (Walks across the room.) It's this wretched poverty that makes life so hateful. And ludicrous. Well, it is!

BRACK: I don't think that's the real cause.

HEDDA: What is, then?

BRACK: Nothing really exciting has ever happened to you.

HEDDA: Nothing serious, you mean?

BRACK: Call it that if you like. But now perhaps it may.

HEDDA (tosses her head): Oh, you're thinking of this competition for that wretched professorship? That's Tesman's affair. I'm not going to waste my time worrying about that.

BRACK: Very well, let's forget about that, then. But suppose you were to find yourself faced with what people call—to use the conventional phrase—the most solemn of human responsibilities? (Smiles.) A new responsibility, little Mrs. Hedda.

HEDDA (angrily): Be quiet! Nothing like that's going to happen.

BRACK (warily): We'll talk about it again in a year's time. If not earlier.

HEDDA (curtly): I've no leanings in that direction, Judge. I don't want any—responsibilities.

BRACK: But surely you must feel some inclination to make use of that—natural talent which every woman—

HEDDA (over by the french windows): Oh, be quiet, I say! I often think there's only one thing for which I have any natural talent.

BRACK (goes closer): And what is that, if I may be so bold as to ask?

HEDDA (stands looking out): For boring myself to death. Now you know. (Turns, looks towards the rear room and laughs.) Talking of boring, here comes the professor.

BRACK (quietly, warningly): Now, now, now, Mrs. Hedda!

GEORGE TESMAN, *in evening dress, with gloves and hat in his hand, enters through the rear room from the right.*

TESMAN: Hedda, hasn't any message come from Eilert? What?

HEDDA: No.

TESMAN: Ah, then we'll have him here presently. You wait and see.

BRACK: You really think he'll come?

TESMAN: Yes, I'm almost sure he will. What you were saying about him this morning is just gossip.

BRACK: Oh?

TESMAN: Yes, Auntie Juju said she didn't believe he'd ever dare to stand in my way again. Fancy that!

BRACK: Then everything in the garden's lovely.

TESMAN (*puts his hat, with his gloves in it, on a chair, right*): Yes, but you really must let me wait for him as long as possible.

BRACK: We've plenty of time. No one'll be turning up at my place before seven or half past.

TESMAN: Ah, then we can keep Hedda company a little longer. And see if he turns up. What?

HEDDA (*picks up* BRACK'S *coat and hat and carries them over to the corner sofa*): And if the worst comes to the worst, Mr. Lœvborg can sit here and talk to me.

BRACK (*offering to take his things from her*): No, please. What do you mean by 'if the worst comes to the worst'?

HEDDA: If he doesn't want to go with you and Tesman.

TESMAN (*looks doubtfully at her*): I say, Hedda, do you think it'll be all right for him to stay here with you? What? Remember Auntie Juju isn't coming.

HEDDA: Yes, but Mrs. Elvsted is. The three of us can have a cup of tea together.

TESMAN: Ah, that'll be all right.

BRACK (*smiles*): It's probably the safest solution as far as he's concerned.

HEDDA: Why?

BRACK: My dear Mrs. Tesman, you always say of my little bachelor parties that they should only be attended by men of the strongest principles.

HEDDA: But Mr. Lœvborg is a man of principle now. You know what they say about a reformed sinner—

BERTHA *enters from the hall.*

BERTHA: Madam, there's a gentleman here who wants to see you—

HEDDA: Ask him to come in.

TESMAN (*quietly*): I'm sure it's him. By Jove. Fancy that!

EILERT LŒVBORG *enters from the hall. He is slim and lean, of the same age as* TESMAN, *but looks older and somewhat haggard. His hair and beard are of a blackish-brown; his face is long and pale, but with a couple of reddish patches on his cheekbones. He is dressed in an elegant and fairly new black suit, and carries black gloves and a top-hat in his hand. He stops just inside the door and bows abruptly. He seems somewhat embarrassed.*

TESMAN (*goes over and shakes his hand*): My dear Eilert! How grand to see you again after all these years!

EILERT LŒVBORG (*speaks softly*): It was good of you to write, George. (*Goes near to* HEDDA.) May I shake hands with you, too, Mrs. Tesman?

HEDDA (*accepts his hand*): Delighted to see you, Mr. Lœvborg. (*With a gesture.*) I don't know if you two gentlemen—

LŒVBORG (*bows slightly*): Judge Brack, I believe.

BRACK (*also with a slight bow*): Correct. We—met some years ago—

TESMAN (*puts his hands on* LŒVBORG's *shoulders*): Now, you're to treat this house just as though it were your own home, Eilert. Isn't that right, Hedda? I hear you've decided to settle here again. What?

LŒVBORG: Yes, I have.

TESMAN: Quite understandable. Oh, by the by— I've just bought your new book. Though to tell the truth I haven't found time to read it yet.

LŒVBORG: You needn't bother.

TESMAN: Oh? Why?

LŒVBORG: There's nothing much in it.

TESMAN: By Jove, fancy hearing that from you!

BRACK: But everyone's praising it.

LŒVBORG: That was exactly what I wanted to happen. So I only wrote what I knew everyone would agree with.

BRACK: Very sensible.

TESMAN: Yes, but my dear Eilert—

LŒVBORG: I want to try to re-establish myself. To begin again—from the beginning.

TESMAN (*a little embarrassed*): Yes, I—er—suppose you do. What?

LŒVBORG (*smiles, puts down his hat and takes a package wrapped in paper from his coat pocket*): But when this gets published—George Tesman—read it. This is my real book. The one in which I have spoken with my own voice.

TESMAN: Oh, really? What's it about?

LŒVBORG: It's the sequel.

TESMAN: Sequel? To what?

LŒVBORG: To the other book.

TESMAN: The one that's just come out?

LŒVBORG: Yes.

TESMAN: But my dear Eilert, that covers the subject right to the present day.

LŒVBORG: It does. But this is about the future.

TESMAN: The future! But, I say, we don't know anything about that.

LŒVBORG: No. But there are one or two things that need to be said about it. (*Opens the package.*) Here, have a look.

TESMAN: Surely that's not your handwriting?

LŒVBORG: I dictated it. (*Turns the pages.*) It's in two parts. The first deals with the forces that will shape our civilization. (*Turns further on towards the end.*) And the second indicates the direction in which that civilization may develop.

TESMAN: Amazing! I'd never think of writing about anything like that.

HEDDA (*by the french windows, drumming on the pane*): No. You wouldn't.

LŒVBORG (*puts the pages back into their cover and lays the package on the table*): I brought it because I thought I might possibly read you a few pages this evening.

TESMAN: I say, what a kind idea! Oh, but this evening—? (*Glances at* BRACK.) I'm not quite sure whether—

LŒVBORG: Well, some other time, then. There's no hurry.

BRACK: The truth is, Mr. Lœvborg, I'm giving a little dinner this evening. In Tesman's honour, you know.

LŒVBORG (*looks round for his hat*): Oh—then I mustn't—

BRACK: No, wait a minute. Won't you do me the honour of joining us?

LŒVBORG (*curtly, with decision*): No, I can't. Thank you so much.

BRACK: Oh, nonsense. Do—please. There'll only be a few of us. And I can promise you we shall have some good sport, as Hed—as Mrs. Tesman puts it.

LŒVBORG: I've no doubt. Nevertheless—

BRACK: You could bring your manuscript along and read it to Tesman at my place. I could lend you a room.

TESMAN: Well, yes, that's an idea. What?

HEDDA (*interposes*): But, Tesman, Mr. Lœvborg doesn't want to go. I'm sure Mr. Lœvborg would much rather sit here and have supper with me.

LŒVBORG (*looks at her*): With you, Mrs. Tesman?

HEDDA: And Mrs. Elvsted.

LŒVBORG: Oh. (*Casually.*) I ran into her this afternoon.

HEDDA: Did you? Well, she's coming here this evening. So you really must stay, Mr. Lœvborg. Otherwise she'll have no one to see her home.

LŒVBORG: That's true. Well—thank you, Mrs. Tesman, I'll stay then.

HEDDA: I'll just tell the servant.

She goes to the door which leads into the hall, and rings. BERTHA *enters.* HEDDA *talks softly to her and points towards the rear room.* BERTHA *nods and goes out.*

TESMAN (*to* LŒVBORG *as* HEDDA *does this*): I say, Eilert. This new subject of yours—the—er—future—is that the one you're going to lecture about?

LŒVBORG: Yes.

TESMAN: They told me down at the bookshop that you're going to hold a series of lectures here during the autumn.

LŒVBORG: Yes, I am. I—hope you don't mind, Tesman.

TESMAN: Good heavens, no! But—?

LŒVBORG: I can quite understand it might queer your pitch a little.

TESMAN (*dejectedly*): Oh well, I can't expect you to put them off for my sake.

LŒVBORG: I'll wait till your appointment's been announced.

TESMAN: You'll wait! But—but—aren't you going to compete with me for the post? What?

LŒVBORG: No. I only want to defeat you in the eyes of the world.

TESMAN: Good heavens! Then Auntie Juju was right after all! Oh, I knew it, I knew it! Hear that, Hedda? Fancy! Eilert *doesn't* want to stand in our way.

HEDDA (*curtly*): Our? Leave me out of it, please.

She goes towards the rear room, where BERTHA *is setting a tray with decanters and glasses on the table.* HEDDA *nods approval, and comes back into the drawing-room.* BERTHA *goes out.*

TESMAN (*while this is happening*): Judge Brack, what do you think about all this? What?

BRACK: Oh, I think honour and victory can be very splendid things—

TESMAN: Of course they can. Still—

HEDDA (*looks at* TESMAN, *with a cold smile*): You look as if you'd been hit by a thunderbolt.

TESMAN: Yes, I feel rather like it.

BRACK: There was a black cloud looming up, Mrs. Tesman. But it seems to have passed over.

HEDDA (*points towards the rear room*): Well, gentlemen, won't you go in and take a glass of cold punch?

BRACK (*glances at his watch*): One for the road. Yes, why not?

TESMAN: An admirable suggestion, Hedda. Admirable! Oh, I feel so relieved!

HEDDA: Won't you have one, too, Mr. Lœvborg?

LŒVBORG: No, thank you. I'd rather not.

BRACK: Great heavens, man, cold punch isn't poison. Take my word for it.

LŒVBORG: Not for everyone, perhaps.

HEDDA: I'll keep Mr. Lœvborg company while you drink.

TESMAN: Yes, Hedda dear, would you?

He and BRACK *go into the rear room, sit down, drink punch, smoke cigarettes and talk cheerfully during the following scene.* EILERT LŒVBORG *remains standing by the stove.* HEDDA *goes to the writing-table.*

HEDDA (*raising her voice slightly*): I've some photographs I'd like to show you, if you'd care to see them. Tesman and I visited the Tyrol on our way home.

She comes back with an album, places it on the table by the sofa and sits in the upstage corner of the sofa. EILERT LŒVBORG *comes towards her, stops, and looks at her. Then he takes a chair and sits down on her left, with his back towards the rear room.*

HEDDA (*opens the album*): You see these mountains, Mr. Lœvborg? That's the Ortler group. Tesman has written the name underneath. You see: 'The Ortler Group near Meran.'

LŒVBORG (*has not taken his eyes from her; says softly, slowly*): Hedda—Gabler!

HEDDA (*gives him a quick glance*): Ssh!

LŒVBORG (*repeats softly*): Hedda Gabler!

HEDDA (*looks at the album*): Yes, that used to be my name. When we first knew each other.

LŒVBORG: And from now on—for the rest of my life—I must teach myself never to say: Hedda Gabler.

HEDDA (*still turning the pages*): Yes, you must. You'd better start getting into practice. The sooner the better.

LŒVBORG: (*bitterly*): Hedda Gabler married? And to George Tesman!

HEDDA: Yes. Well—that's life.

LŒVBORG: Oh, Hedda, Hedda! How could you throw yourself away like that?

HEDDA (*looks sharply at him*): Stop it.

LŒVBORG: What do you mean?

TESMAN *comes in and goes towards the sofa.*

HEDDA (*hears him coming and says casually*): And this, Mr. Lœvborg, is the view from the Ampezzo valley. Look at those mountains. (*Glances affectionately up at* TESMAN.) What did you say those curious mountains were called, dear?

TESMAN: Let me have a look. Oh, those are the Dolomites.

HEDDA: Of course. Those are the Dolomites, Mr. Lœvborg.

TESMAN: Hedda, I just wanted to ask you, can't we bring some punch in here? A glass for you, anyway. What?

HEDDA: Thank you, yes. And a biscuit or two, perhaps.

TESMAN: You wouldn't like a cigarette?

HEDDA: No.

TESMAN: Right.

He goes into the rear room and over to the right. BRACK *is seated there, glancing occasionally at* HEDDA *and* LŒVBORG.

LŒVBORG (*softly, as before*): Answer me, Hedda. How could you do it?

HEDDA (*apparently absorbed in the album*): If you go on calling me Hedda I won't talk to you any more.

LŒVBORG: Mayn't I even when we're alone?

HEDDA: No. You can think it. But you mustn't say it.

LŒVBORG: Oh, I see. Because you love George Tesman.

HEDDA (*glances at him and smiles*): Love? Don't be funny.

LŒVBORG: You don't love him?

HEDDA: I don't intend to be unfaithful to him. That's not what I want.

LŒVBORG: Hedda—just tell me one thing—

HEDDA: Ssh!

TESMAN *enters from the rear room, carrying a tray.*

TESMAN: Here we are! Here come the refreshments.

He puts the tray down on the table.

HEDDA: Why didn't you ask the servant to bring it in?

TESMAN (*fills the glasses*): I like waiting on you, Hedda.

HEDDA: But you've filled both glasses. Mr. Lœvborg doesn't want to drink.

TESMAN: Yes, but Mrs. Elvsted'll be here soon.

HEDDA: Oh yes, that's true. Mrs. Elvsted—

TESMAN: Had you forgotten her? What?

HEDDA: We're so absorbed with these photographs. (*Shows him one.*) You remember this little village?

TESMAN: Oh, that one down by the Brenner Pass. We spent a night there—

HEDDA: Yes, and met all those amusing people.

TESMAN: Oh yes, it was there, wasn't it? By Jove, if only we could have had you with us, Eilert! Ah, well.

He goes back into the other room and sits down with BRACK.

LŒVBORG: Tell me one thing, Hedda.

HEDDA: Yes?

LŒVBORG: Didn't you love me either? Not—just a little?

HEDDA: Well now, I wonder? No, I think we were just good friends. (*Smiles.*) You certainly poured your heart out to me.

LŒVBORG: You begged me to.

HEDDA: Looking back on it, there was something beautiful and fascinating—and brave—about the way we told each other everything. That secret friendship no one else knew about.

LŒVBORG: Yes, Hedda, yes! Do you remember? How I used to come up to your father's house in the afternoon—and the General sat by the window and read his newspapers—with his back towards us—

HEDDA: And we sat on the sofa in the corner—

LŒVBORG: Always reading the same illustrated magazine—

HEDDA: We hadn't any photograph album.

LŒVBORG: Yes, Hedda. I regarded you as a kind of confessor. Told you things about myself which no one else knew about—then. Those days and nights of drinking and—oh, Hedda, what power did you have to make me confess such things?

HEDDA: Power? You think I had some power over you?

LŒVBORG: Yes—I don't know how else to explain it. And all those—oblique questions you asked me—

HEDDA: You knew what they meant.

LŒVBORG: But that you could sit there and ask me such questions! So unashamedly—

HEDDA: I thought you said they were oblique.

LŒVBORG: Yes, but you asked them so unashamedly. That you could question me about—about that kind of thing!

HEDDA: You answered willingly enough.

LŒVBORG: Yes—that's what I can't understand—looking back on it. But tell me, Hedda—

what you felt for me—wasn't that—love? When you asked me those questions and made me confess my sins to you, wasn't it because you wanted to wash me clean?

HEDDA: No, not exactly.

LŒVBORG: Why did you do it, then?

HEDDA: Do you find it so incredible that a young girl, given the chance in secret, should want to be allowed a glimpse into a forbidden world of whose existence she is supposed to be ignorant?

LŒVBORG: So that was it?

HEDDA: One reason. One reason—I think.

LŒVBORG: You didn't love me, then. You just wanted—knowledge. But if that was so, why did you break it off?

HEDDA: That was your fault.

LŒVBORG: It was you who put an end to it.

HEDDA: Yes, when I realized that our friendship was threatening to develop into something—something else. Shame on you, Eilert Lœvborg! How could you abuse the trust of your dearest friend?

LŒVBORG (clenches his fist): Oh, why didn't you do it? Why didn't you shoot me dead? As you threatened to!

HEDDA: I was afraid. Of the scandal.

LŒVBORG: Yes, Hedda. You're a coward at heart.

HEDDA: A dreadful coward. (Changes her tone.) Luckily for you. Well, now you've found consolation with the Elvsteds.

LŒVBORG: I know what Thea's been telling you.

HEDDA: I dare say you told her about us.

LŒVBORG: Not a word. She's too silly to understand that kind of thing.

HEDDA: Silly?

LŒVBORG: She's silly about that kind of thing.

HEDDA: And I'm a coward. (Leans closer to him, without looking him in the eyes, and says quietly) But let me tell you something. Something you don't know.

LŒVBORG (tensely): Yes?

HEDDA: My failure to shoot you wasn't my worst act of cowardice that evening.

LŒVBORG (looks at her for a moment, realizes her meaning, and whispers passionately): Oh,

Hedda! Hedda Gabler! Now I see what was behind those questions. Yes! It wasn't knowledge you wanted! It was life!

HEDDA (flashes a look at him and says quietly): Take care! Don't you delude yourself!

It has begun to grow dark. BERTHA, from outside, opens the door leading into the hall.

HEDDA (closes the album with a snap and cries, smiling): Ah, at last! Come in, Thea dear!

MRS. ELVSTED enters from the hall, in evening dress. The door is closed behind her.

HEDDA (on the sofa, stretches out her arms towards her): Thea darling, I thought you were never coming!

MRS. ELVSTED makes a slight bow to the gentlemen in the rear room as she passes the open doorway, and they to her. Then she goes to the table and holds out her hand to HEDDA. EILERT LŒVBORG has risen from his chair. He and MRS. ELVSTED nod silently to each other.

MRS. ELVSTED: Perhaps I ought to go in and say a few words to your husband?

HEDDA: Oh, there's no need. They're happy by themselves. They'll be going soon.

MRS. ELVSTED: Going?

HEDDA: Yes, they're off on a spree this evening.

MRS. ELVSTED (quickly, to LŒVBORG): You're not going with them?

LŒVBORG: No.

HEDDA: Mr. Lœvborg is staying here with us.

MRS. ELVSTED (takes a chair and is about to sit down beside him): Oh, how nice it is to be here!

HEDDA: No, Thea darling, not there. Come over here and sit beside me. I want to be in the middle.

MRS. ELVSTED: Yes, just as you wish.

She goes round the table and sits on the sofa, on HEDDA's right. LŒVBORG sits down again in his chair.

LŒVBORG (after a short pause, to HEDDA): Isn't she lovely to look at?

HEDDA (strokes her hair gently): Only to look at?

LŒVBORG: Yes. We're just good friends. We trust each other implicitly. We can talk to each other quite unashamedly.

HEDDA: No need to be oblique?

MRS. ELVSTED (*nestles close to* HEDDA *and says quietly*): Oh, Hedda, I'm so happy. Imagine— he says I've inspired him!

HEDDA (*looks at her with a smile*): Dear Thea! Does he really?

LŒVBORG: She has the courage of her convictions, Mrs. Tesman.

MRS. ELVSTED: I? Courage?

LŒVBORG: Absolute courage. Where friendship is concerned.

HEDDA: Yes. Courage. Yes. If only one had that—

LŒVBORG: Yes?

HEDDA: One might be able to live. In spite of everything. (*Changes her tone suddenly.*) Well, Thea darling, now you're going to drink a nice glass of cold punch.

MRS. ELVSTED: No thank you. I never drink anything like that.

HEDDA: Oh. You, Mr. Lœvborg?

LŒVBORG: Thank you, I don't either.

MRS. ELVSTED: No, he doesn't, either.

HEDDA (*looks into his eyes*): But if I want you to.

LŒVBORG: That doesn't make any difference.

HEDDA (*laughs*): Have I no power over you at all? Poor me!

LŒVBORG: Not where this is concerned.

HEDDA: Seriously, I think you should. For your own sake.

MRS. ELVSTED: Hedda!

LŒVBORG: Why?

HEDDA: Or perhaps I should say for other people's sake.

LŒVBORG: What do you mean?

HEDDA: People might think you didn't feel absolutely and unashamedly sure of yourself. In your heart of hearts.

MRS. ELVSTED (*quietly*): Oh, Hedda, no!

LŒVBORG: People can think what they like. For the present.

MRS. ELVSTED (*happily*): Yes, that's true.

HEDDA: I saw it so clearly in Judge Brack a few minutes ago.

LŒVBORG: Oh. What did you see?

HEDDA: He smiled so scornfully when he saw you were afraid to go in there and drink with them.

LŒVBORG: Afraid! I wanted to stay here and talk to you.

MRS. ELVSTED: That was only natural, Hedda.

HEDDA: But the Judge wasn't to know that. I saw him wink at Tesman when you showed you didn't dare to join their wretched little party.

LŒVBORG: Didn't dare! Are you saying I didn't dare?

HEDDA: I'm not saying so. But that was what Judge Brack thought.

LŒVBORG: Well, let him.

HEDDA: You're not going, then?

LŒVBORG: I'm staying with you and Thea.

MRS. ELVSTED: Yes, Hedda, of course he is.

HEDDA (*smiles, and nods approvingly to* LŒVBORG): Firm as a rock! A man of principle! That's how a man should be! (*Turns to* MRS. ELVSTED *and strokes her cheek.*) Didn't I tell you so this morning when you came here in such a panic—?

LŒVBORG (*starts*): Panic?

MRS. ELVSTED (*frightened*): Hedda! But—Hedda!

HEDDA: Well, now you can see for yourself. There's no earthly need for you to get scared to death just because—(*Stops.*) Well! Let's all three cheer up and enjoy ourselves.

LŒVBORG: Mrs. Tesman, would you mind explaining to me what this is all about?

MRS. ELVSTED: Oh, my God, my God, Hedda, what are you saying? What are you doing?

HEDDA: Keep calm. That horrid Judge has his eye on you.

LŒVBORG: Scared to death, were you? For my sake?

MRS. ELVSTED (*quietly, trembling*): Oh, Hedda! You've made me so unhappy!

LŒVBORG (*looks coldly at her for a moment. His face is distorted*): So that was how much you trusted me.

MRS. ELVSTED: Eilert dear, please listen to me—

LŒVBORG (*takes one of the glasses of punch, raises it and says quietly, hoarsely*): Skoal, Thea! *He empties the glass, puts it down and picks up one of the others.*

MRS. ELVSTED (*quietly*): Hedda, Hedda! Why did you want this to happen?

HEDDA: *I*—want it? Are you mad?

LŒVBORG: Skoal to you, too, Mrs. Tesman. Thanks for telling me the truth. Here's to the truth!
He empties his glass and refills it.

HEDDA (*puts her hand on his arm*): Steady. That's enough for now. Don't forget the party.

MRS. ELVSTED: No, no, no!

HEDDA: Ssh! They're looking at you.

LŒVBORG (*puts down his glass*): Thea, tell me the truth—

MRS. ELVSTED: Yes!

LŒVBORG: Did your husband know you were following me?

MRS. ELVSTED: Oh, Hedda!

LŒVBORG: Did you and he have an agreement that you should come here and keep an eye on me? Perhaps he gave you the idea? After all, he's a magistrate. I suppose he needed me back in his office. Or did he miss my companionship at the card-table?

MRS. ELVSTED (*quietly, sobbing*): Eilert, Eilert!

LŒVBORG (*seizes a glass and is about to fill it*): Let's drink to him, too.

HEDDA: No more now. Remember you're going to read your book to Tesman.

LŒVBORG (*calm again, puts down his glass*): That was silly of me, Thea. To take it like that, I mean. Don't be angry with me, my dear. You'll see—yes, and they'll see, too—that though I fell, I—I have raised myself up again. With your help, Thea.

MRS. ELVSTED (*happily*): Oh, thank God!
BRACK *has meanwhile glanced at his watch. He and* TESMAN *get up and come into the drawing-room.*

BRACK (*takes his hat and overcoat*): Well, Mrs. Tesman, it's time for us to go.

HEDDA: Yes, I suppose it must be.

LŒVBORG (*gets up*): Time for me, too, Judge.

MRS. ELVSTED (*quietly, pleadingly*): Eilert, please don't!

HEDDA (*pinches her arm*): They can hear you.

MRS. ELVSTED (*gives a little cry*): Oh!

LŒVBORG (*to* BRACK): You were kind enough to ask me to join you.

BRACK: Are you coming?

LŒVBORG: If I may.

BRACK: Delighted.

LŒVBORG (*puts the paper package in his pocket and says to* TESMAN): I'd like to show you one or two things before I send it off to the printer.

TESMAN: I say, that'll be fun. Fancy—! Oh, but, Hedda, how'll Mrs. Elvsted get home? What?

HEDDA: Oh, we'll manage somehow.

LŒVBORG (*glances over towards the ladies*): Mrs. Elvsted? I shall come back and collect her, naturally. (*Goes closer.*) About ten o'clock, Mrs. Tesman? Will that suit you?

HEDDA: Yes. That'll suit me admirably.

TESMAN: Good, that's settled. But you mustn't expect me back so early, Hedda.

HEDDA: Stay as long as you c—as long as you like, dear.

MRS. ELVSTED (*trying to hide her anxiety*): Well then, Mr. Lœvborg, I'll wait here till you come.

LŒVBORG (*his hat in his hand*): Pray do, Mrs. Elvsted.

BRACK: Well, gentlemen, now the party begins. I trust that, in the words of a certain fair lady, we shall enjoy good sport.

HEDDA: What a pity the fair lady can't be there, invisible.

BRACK: Why invisible?

HEDDA: So as to be able to hear some of your uncensored witticisms, your honour.

BRACK (*laughs*): Oh, I shouldn't advise the fair lady to do that.

TESMAN (*laughs, too*): I say, Hedda, that's good. What!

BRACK: Well, good night, ladies, good night!

LŒVBORG (*bows farewell*): About ten o'clock then.
BRACK, LŒVBORG *and* TESMAN *go out through the hall. As they do so,* BERTHA *enters from the rear room with a lighted lamp. She puts it on the drawing-room table, then goes out the way she came.*

MRS. ELVSTED (*has got up and is walking uneasily to and fro*): Oh, Hedda, Hedda! How is all this going to end?

HEDDA: At ten o'clock, then. He'll be here. I can see him. With a crown of vine leaves in his hair. Burning and unashamed!

MRS. ELVSTED: Oh, I do hope so!

HEDDA: Can't you see? Then he'll be himself again! He'll be a free man for the rest of his days!

MRS. ELVSTED: Please God you're right.

HEDDA: That's how he'll come! (*Gets up and goes closer.*) You can doubt him as much as you like. I believe in him! Now we'll see which of us—

MRS. ELVSTED: You're after something, Hedda.

HEDDA: Yes, I am. For once in my life I want to have the power to shape a man's destiny.

MRS. ELVSTED: Haven't you that power already?

HEDDA: No, I haven't. I've never had it.

MRS. ELVSTED: What about your husband?

HEDDA: Him! Oh, if you could only understand how poor I am. And you're allowed to be so rich, so rich! (*Clasps her passionately.*) I think I'll burn your hair off after all!

MRS. ELVSTED: Let me go! Let me go! You frighten me, Hedda!

BERTHA (*in the open doorway*): I've laid tea in the dining-room, madam.

HEDDA: Good, we're coming.

MRS. ELVSTED: No, no, no! I'd rather go home alone! Now—at once!

HEDDA: Rubbish! First you're going to have some tea, you little idiot. And then—at ten o'clock—Eilert Lœvborg will come. With a crown of vine leaves in his hair!

She drags MRS. ELVSTED *almost forcibly towards the open doorway.*

ACT THREE

The same. The curtains are drawn across the open doorway, and also across the french windows. The lamp, half turned down, with a shade over it, is burning on the table. In the stove, the door of which is open, a fire has been burning, but it is now almost out. MRS. ELVSTED, *wrapped in a large shawl and with her feet resting on a footstool, is sitting near the stove, huddled in the armchair.* HEDDA *is lying asleep on the sofa, fully dressed, with a blanket over her.*

MRS. ELVSTED (*after a pause, suddenly sits up in her chair and listens tensely. Then she sinks wearily back again and sighs.*): Not back yet! Oh, God! Oh, God! Not back yet!

BERTHA tiptoes cautiously in from the hall. She has a letter in her hand.

MRS. ELVSTED (*turns and whispers*): What is it? Has someone come?

BERTHA (*quietly*): Yes, a servant's just called with this letter.

MRS. ELVSTED (*quickly, holding out her hand*): A letter! Give it to me!

BERTHA: But it's for the Doctor, madam.

MRS. ELVSTED: Oh, I see.

BERTHA: Miss Tesman's maid brought it. I'll leave it here on the table.

MRS. ELVSTED: Yes, do.

BERTHA (*puts down the letter*): I'd better put the lamp out. It's starting to smoke.

MRS. ELVSTED: Yes, put it out. It'll soon be daylight.

BERTHA (*puts out the lamp*): It's daylight already, madam.

MRS. ELVSTED: Yes. Broad day. And not home yet.

BERTHA: Oh dear, I was afraid this would happen.

MRS. ELVSTED: Were you?

BERTHA: Yes. When I heard that a certain gentleman had returned to town, and saw him go off with them. I've heard all about him.

MRS. ELVSTED: Don't talk so loud. You'll wake your mistress.

BERTHA (*looks at the sofa and sighs*): Yes. Let her go on sleeping, poor dear. Shall I put some more wood on the fire?

MRS. ELVSTED: Thank you, don't bother on my account.

BERTHA: Very good.

She goes quietly out through the hall.

HEDDA (*wakes as the door closes and looks up*): What's that?

MRS. ELVSTED: It was only the maid.

HEDDA (*looks round*): What am I doing here? Oh, now I remember. (*Sits up on the sofa, stretches herself and rubs her eyes.*) What time is it, Thea?

MRS. ELVSTED: It's gone seven.

HEDDA: When did Tesman get back?

MRS. ELVSTED: He's not back yet.

HEDDA: Not home yet?

MRS. ELVSTED (*gets up*): No one's come.

HEDDA: And we sat up waiting for them till four o'clock.

MRS. ELVSTED: God! How I waited for him!

HEDDA (*yawns and says with her hand in front of her mouth*): Oh, dear. We might have saved ourselves the trouble.

MRS. ELVSTED: Did you manage to sleep?

HEDDA: Oh, yes. Quite well, I think. Didn't you get any?

MRS. ELVSTED: Not a wink. I couldn't, Hedda. I just couldn't.

HEDDA (*gets up and comes over to her*): Now, now, now. There's nothing to worry about. I know what's happened.

MRS. ELVSTED: What? Please tell me.

HEDDA: Well, obviously the party went on very late—

MRS. ELVSTED: Oh dear, I suppose it must have. But—

HEDDA: And Tesman didn't want to come home and wake us all up in the middle of the night. (*Laughs.*) Probably wasn't too keen to show his face either, after a spree like that.

MRS. ELVSTED: But where could he have gone?

HEDDA: I should think he's probably slept at his aunts'. They keep his old room for him.

MRS. ELVSTED: No, he can't be with them. A letter came for him just now from Miss Tesman. It's over there.

HEDDA: Oh? (*Looks at the envelope.*) Yes, it's Auntie Juju's handwriting. Well, he must still be at Judge Brack's, then. And Eilert Lœvborg is sitting there, reading to him. With a crown of vine leaves in his hair.

MRS. ELVSTED: Hedda, you're only saying that. You don't believe it.

HEDDA: Thea, you really are a little fool.

MRS. ELVSTED: Perhaps I am.

HEDDA: You look tired to death.

MRS. ELVSTED: Yes. I am tired to death.

HEDDA: Go to my room and lie down for a little. Do as I say, now; don't argue.

MRS. ELVSTED: No, no. I couldn't possibly sleep.

HEDDA: Of course you can.

MRS. ELVSTED: But your husband'll be home soon. And I must know at once—

HEDDA: I'll tell you when he comes.

MRS. ELVSTED: Promise me, Hedda?

HEDDA: Yes, don't worry. Go and get some sleep.

MRS. ELVSTED: Thank you. All right, I'll try.

She goes out through the rear room. HEDDA *goes to the french windows and draws the curtains. Broad daylight floods into the room. She goes to the writing-table, takes a small hand-mirror from it and arranges her hair. Then she goes to the door leading into the hall and presses the bell. After a few moments,* BERTHA *enters.*

BERTHA: Did you want anything, madam?

HEDDA: Yes, put some more wood on the fire. I'm freezing.

BERTHA: Bless you, I'll soon have this room warmed up. (*She rakes the embers together and puts a fresh piece of wood on them. Suddenly she stops and listens.*) There's someone at the front door, madam.

HEDDA: Well, go and open it. I'll see to the fire.

BERTHA: It'll burn up in a moment.

She goes out through the hall. HEDDA *kneels on the footstool and puts more wood in the stove. After a few seconds,* GEORGE TESMAN *enters from the hall. He looks tired, and rather worried. He tiptoes towards the open doorway and is about to slip through the curtains.*

HEDDA (*at the stove, without looking up*): Good morning.

TESMAN (*turns*): Hedda! (*Comes nearer.*) Good heavens, are you up already? What?

HEDDA: Yes, I got up very early this morning.

TESMAN: I was sure you'd still be sleeping. Fancy that!

HEDDA: Don't talk so loud. Mrs. Elvsted's asleep in my room.

TESMAN: Mrs. Elvsted? Has she stayed the night here?

HEDDA: Yes. No one came to escort her home.

TESMAN: Oh. No, I suppose not.

HEDDA (*closes the door of the stove and gets up*): Well. Was it fun?

TESMAN: Have you been anxious about me? What?

HEDDA: Not in the least. I asked if you'd had fun.

TESMAN: Oh yes, rather! Well, I thought, for once in a while—! The first part was the best; when Eilert read his book to me. We arrived over an hour too early—what about that, eh? Fancy—! Brack had a lot of things to see to, so Eilert read to me.

HEDDA (*sits at the right-hand side of the table*): Well? Tell me about it.

TESMAN (*sits on a footstool by the stove*): Honestly, Hedda, you've no idea what a book that's going to be. It's really one of the most remarkable things that's ever been written. By Jove!

HEDDA: Oh, never mind about the book—

TESMAN: I'm going to make a confession to you, Hedda. When he'd finished reading a sort of beastly feeling came over me.

HEDDA: Beastly feeling?

TESMAN: I found myself envying Eilert for being able to write like that. Imagine that, Hedda!

HEDDA: Yes. I can imagine.

TESMAN: What a tragedy that with all those gifts he should be so incorrigible.

HEDDA: You mean he's less afraid of life than most men?

TESMAN: Good heavens, no. He just doesn't know the meaning of the word moderation.

HEDDA: What happened afterwards?

TESMAN: Well, looking back on it, I suppose you might almost call it an orgy, Hedda.

HEDDA: Had he vine leaves in his hair?

TESMAN: Vine leaves? No, I didn't see any of them. He made a long, rambling oration in honour of the woman who'd inspired him to write this book. Yes, those were the words he used.

HEDDA: Did he name her?

TESMAN: No. But I suppose it must be Mrs. Elvsted. You wait and see!

HEDDA: Where did you leave him?

TESMAN: On the way home. We left in a bunch—the last of us, that is—and Brack came with us to get a little fresh air. Well, then, you see, we agreed we ought to see Eilert home. He'd had a drop too much.

HEDDA: You don't say?

TESMAN: But now comes the funny part, Hedda. Or I should really say the tragic part. Oh, I'm almost ashamed to tell you. For Eilert's sake, I mean—

HEDDA: Why, what happened?

TESMAN: Well, you see, as we were walking towards town I happened to drop behind for a minute. Only for a minute—er—you understand—

HEDDA: Yes, yes—?

TESMAN: Well then, when I ran on to catch them up, what do you think I found by the roadside. What?

HEDDA: How on earth should I know?

TESMAN: You mustn't tell anyone, Hedda. What? Promise me that—for Eilert's sake. (*Takes a package wrapped in paper from his coat pocket.*) Just fancy! I found this.

HEDDA: Isn't this the one he brought here yesterday?

TESMAN: Yes! The whole of that precious, irreplaceable manuscript! And he went and lost it! Didn't even notice! What about that? Tragic.

HEDDA: But why didn't you give it back to him?

TESMAN: I didn't dare to, in the state he was in.

HEDDA: Didn't you tell any of the others?

TESMAN: Good heavens, no. I didn't want to do that. For Eilert's sake, you understand.

HEDDA: Then no one else knows you have his manuscript?

TESMAN: No. And no one must be allowed to know.

HEDDA: Didn't it come up in the conversation later?

TESMAN: I didn't get a chance to talk to him any more. As soon as we got into the outskirts of town, he and one or two of the others gave us the slip. Disappeared, by Jove!

HEDDA: Oh? I suppose they took him home.

TESMAN: Yes, I imagine that was the idea. Brack left us, too.

HEDDA: And what have you been up to since then?

TESMAN: Well, I and one or two of the others—awfully jolly chaps, they were—went back to where one of them lived and had a cup of morning coffee. Morning-after-coffee—what? Ah, well. I'll just lie down for a bit and give Eilert time to sleep it off, poor chap, then I'll run over and give this back to him.

HEDDA (*holds out her hand for the package*): No, don't do that. Not just yet. Let me read it first.

TESMAN: Oh no, really, Hedda dear, honestly, I daren't do that.

HEDDA: Daren't?

TESMAN: No—imagine how desperate he'll be when he wakes up and finds his manuscript's missing. He hasn't any copy, you see. He told me so himself.

HEDDA: Can't a thing like that be rewritten?

TESMAN: Oh no, not possibly, I shouldn't think. I mean, the inspiration, you know—

HEDDA: Oh, yes, I'd forgotten that. (*Casually.*) By the way, there's a letter for you.

TESMAN: Is there? Fancy that!

HEDDA (*holds it out to him*): It came early this morning.

TESMAN: I say, it's from Auntie Juju! What on earth can it be? (*Puts the package on the other footstool, opens the letter, reads it and jumps up.*) Oh, Hedda! She says poor Auntie Rena's dying.

HEDDA: Well, we've been expecting that.

TESMAN: She says if I want to see her I must go quickly. I'll run over at once.

HEDDA (*hides a smile*): Run?

TESMAN: Hedda dear, I suppose you wouldn't like to come with me? What about that, eh?

HEDDA (*gets up and says wearily and with repulsion*): No, no, don't ask me to do anything like that. I can't bear illness or death. I loathe anything ugly.

TESMAN: Yes, yes. Of course. (*In a dither.*) My hat? My overcoat? Oh yes, in the hall. I do hope I won't get there too late, Hedda! What?

HEDDA: You'll be all right if you run.

BERTHA *enters from the hall.*

BERTHA: Judge Brack's outside and wants to know if he can come in.

TESMAN: At this hour? No, I can't possibly receive him now.

HEDDA: I can. (*To* BERTHA) Ask his honour to come in.

BERTHA *goes.*

HEDDA (*whispers quickly*): The manuscript, Tesman. *She snatches it from the footstool.*

TESMAN: Yes, give it to me.

HEDDA: No, I'll look after it for now.
She goes over to the writing-table and puts it in the bookcase. TESMAN *stands dithering, unable to get his gloves on.* JUDGE BRACK *enters from the hall.*

HEDDA (*nods to him*): Well, you're an early bird.

BRACK: Yes, aren't I? (*To* TESMAN) Are you up and about, too?

TESMAN: Yes, I've got to go and see my aunts. Poor Auntie Rena's dying.

BRACK: Oh dear, is she? Then you mustn't let me detain you. At so tragic a—

TESMAN: Yes, I really must run. Good-bye! Good-bye!
He runs out through the hall.

HEDDA (*goes nearer*): You seem to have had excellent sport last night—Judge.

BRACK: Indeed yes, Mrs. Hedda. I haven't even had time to take my clothes off.

HEDDA: *You* haven't either?

BRACK: As you see. What's Tesman told you about last night's escapades?

HEDDA: Oh, only some boring story about having gone and drunk coffee somewhere.

BRACK: Yes, I've heard about that coffee-party. Eilert Lœvborg wasn't with them, I gather?

HEDDA: No, they took him home first.

BRACK: Did Tesman go with him?

HEDDA: No, one or two of the others, he said.

BRACK (*smiles*): George Tesman is a credulous man, Mrs. Hedda.

HEDDA: God knows. But—has something happened?

BRACK: Well, yes, I'm afraid it has.

HEDDA: I see. Sit down and tell me.
She sits on the left of the table, BRACK *at the long side of it, near her.*

HEDDA: Well?

BRACK: I had a special reason for keeping track of my guests last night. Or perhaps I should say some of my guests.

HEDDA: Including Eilert Lœvborg?

BRACK: I must confess—yes.

HEDDA: You're beginning to make me curious.

BRACK: Do you know where he and some of my other guests spent the latter half of last night, Mrs. Hedda?

HEDDA: Tell me. If it won't shock me.

BRACK: Oh, I don't think it'll shock you. They found themselves participating in an exceedingly animated *soirée.*

HEDDA: Of a sporting character?

BRACK: Of a highly sporting character.

HEDDA: Tell me more.

BRACK: Lœvborg had received an invitation in advance—as had the others. I knew all about that. But he had refused. As you know, he's become a new man.

HEDDA: Up at the Elvsteds', yes. But he went?

BRACK: Well, you see, Mrs. Hedda, last night at my house, unhappily, the spirit moved him.

HEDDA: Yes, I hear he became inspired.

BRACK: Somewhat violently inspired. And as a result, I suppose, his thoughts strayed. We men, alas, don't always stick to our principles as firmly as we should.

HEDDA: I'm sure you're an exception, Judge Brack. But go on about Lœvborg.

BRACK: Well, to cut a long story short, he ended up in the establishment of a certain Mademoiselle Danielle.

HEDDA: Mademoiselle Danielle?

BRACK: She was holding the *soirée*. For a selected circle of friends and admirers.

HEDDA: Has she got red hair?

BRACK: She has.

HEDDA: A singer of some kind?

BRACK: Yes—among other accomplishments. She's also a celebrated huntress—of men, Mrs. Hedda. I'm sure you've heard about her. Eilert Lœvborg used to be one of her most ardent patrons. In his salad days.

HEDDA: And how did all this end?

BRACK: Not entirely amicably, from all accounts. Mademoiselle Danielle began by receiving him with the utmost tenderness and ended by resorting to her fists.

HEDDA: Against Lœvborg?

BRACK: Yes. He accused her, or her friends, of having robbed him. He claimed his pocketbook had been stolen. Among other things. In short, he seems to have made a bloodthirsty scene.

HEDDA: And what did this lead to?

BRACK: It led to a general free-for-all, in which both sexes participated. Fortunately, in the end the police arrived.

HEDDA: The police, too?

BRACK: Yes. I'm afraid it may turn out to be rather an expensive joke for Master Eilert. Crazy fool!

HEDDA: Oh?

BRACK: Apparently he put up a very violent resistance. Hit one of the constables on the ear and tore his uniform. He had to accompany them to the police station.

HEDDA: Where did you learn all this?

BRACK: From the police.

HEDDA (*to herself*): So that's what happened. He didn't have a crown of vine leaves in his hair.

BRACK: Vine leaves, Mrs. Hedda?

HEDDA (*in her normal voice again*): But, tell me, Judge, why do you take such a close interest in Eilert Lœvborg?

BRACK: For one thing it'll hardly be a matter of complete indifference to me if it's revealed in court that he came there straight from my house.

HEDDA: Will it come to court?

BRACK: Of course. Well, I don't regard that as particularly serious. Still, I thought it my duty, as a friend of the family, to give you and your husband a full account of his nocturnal adventures.

HEDDA: Why?

BRACK: Because I've a shrewd suspicion that he's hoping to use you as a kind of screen.

HEDDA: What makes you think that?

BRACK: Oh, for heaven's sake, Mrs. Hedda, we're not blind. You wait and see. This Mrs. Elvsted won't be going back to her husband just yet.

HEDDA: Well, if there were anything between those two there are plenty of other places where they could meet.

BRACK: Not in anyone's home. From now on every respectable house will once again be closed to Eilert Lœvborg.

HEDDA: And mine should be, too, you mean?

BRACK: Yes. I confess I should find it more than irksome if this gentleman were to be granted unrestricted access to this house. If he were superfluously to intrude into—

HEDDA: The triangle?

BRACK: Precisely. For me it would be like losing a home.

HEDDA (*looks at him and smiles*): I see. You want to be the cock of the walk.

BRACK (*nods slowly and lowers his voice*): Yes, that is my aim. And I shall fight for it with—every weapon at my disposal.

HEDDA (*as her smile fades*): You're a dangerous man, aren't you? When you really want something.

BRACK: You think so?

HEDDA: Yes, I'm beginning to think so. I'm deeply thankful you haven't any kind of hold over me.

BRACK (*laughs equivocally*): Well, well, Mrs. Hedda—perhaps you're right. If I had, who knows what I might not think up?

HEDDA: Come, Judge Brack. That sounds almost like a threat.

BRACK (*gets up*): Heaven forbid! In the creation of a triangle—and its continuance—the question of compulsion should never arise.

HEDDA: Exactly what I was thinking.

BRACK: Well, I've said what I came to say. I must be getting back. Good-bye, Mrs. Hedda. (*Goes towards the french windows.*)

HEDDA (*gets up*): Are you going out through the garden?

BRACK: Yes, it's shorter.

HEDDA: Yes. And it's the back door, isn't it?

BRACK: I've nothing against back doors. They can be quite intriguing—sometimes.

HEDDA: When people fire pistols out of them, for example?

BRACK (*in the doorway, laughs*): Oh, people don't shoot tame cocks.

HEDDA (*laughs, too*): I suppose not. When they've only got one.

They nod good-bye, laughing. He goes. She closes the french windows behind him, and stands for a moment, looking out pensively. Then she walks across the room and glances through the curtains in the open doorway. Goes to the writing-table, takes LŒVBORG's *package from the bookcase and is about to turn through the pages when* BERTHA *is heard remonstrating loudly in the hall.* HEDDA *turns and listens. She hastily puts the package back in the drawer, locks it and puts the key on the inkstand.* EILERT LŒVBORG, *with his overcoat on and his hat in his hand, throws the door open. He looks somewhat confused and excited.*

LŒVBORG (*shouts as he enters*): I must come in, I tell you! Let me pass!

He closes the door, turns, sees HEDDA, *controls himself immediately and bows.*

HEDDA (*at the writing table*): Well, Mr. Lœvborg, this is rather a late hour to be collecting Thea.

LŒVBORG: And an early hour to call on you. Please forgive me.

HEDDA: How do you know she's still here?

LŒVBORG: They told me at her lodgings that she has been out all night.

HEDDA (*goes to the table*): Did you notice anything about their behaviour when they told you?

LŒVBORG (*looks at her, puzzled*): Notice anything?

HEDDA: Did they sound as if they thought it—strange?

LŒVBORG (*suddenly understands*): Oh, I see what you mean. I'm dragging her down with me. No, as a matter of fact I didn't notice anything. I suppose Tesman isn't up yet?

HEDDA: No, I don't think so.

LŒVBORG: When did he get home?

HEDDA: Very late.

LŒVBORG: Did he tell you anything?

HEDDA: Yes. I gather you had a merry party at Judge Brack's last night.

LŒVBORG: He didn't tell you anything else?

HEDDA: I don't think so. I was so terribly sleepy—

MRS. ELVSTED *comes through the curtains in the open doorway.*

MRS. ELVSTED (*runs towards him*): Oh, Eilert! At last!

LŒVBORG: Yes—at last. And too late.

MRS. ELVSTED: What is too late?

LŒVBORG: Everything—now. I'm finished, Thea.

MRS. ELVSTED: Oh, no, no! Don't say that!

LŒVBORG: You'll say it yourself, when you've heard what I—

MRS. ELVSTED: I don't want to hear anything!

HEDDA: Perhaps you'd rather speak to her alone? I'd better go.

LŒVBORG: No, stay.

MRS. ELVSTED: But I don't want to hear anything, I tell you!

LŒVBORG: It's not about last night.

MRS. ELVSTED: Then what—?

LŒVBORG: I want to tell you that from now on we must stop seeing each other.

MRS. ELVSTED: Stop seeing each other!

HEDDA (*involuntarily*): I knew it!

LŒVBORG: I have no further use for you, Thea.

MRS. ELVSTED: You can stand there and say that! No further use for me! Surely I can go on helping you? We'll go on working together, won't we?

LŒVBORG: I don't intend to do any more work from now on.

MRS. ELVSTED (*desperately*): Then what use have I for my life?

LŒVBORG: You must try to live as if you had never known me.

MRS. ELVSTED: But I can't!

LŒVBORG: Try to, Thea. Go back home—

MRS. ELVSTED: Never! I want to be wherever you are! I won't let myself be driven away like this! I want to stay here—and be with you when the book comes out.

HEDDA (*whispers*): Ah, yes! The book!

LŒVBORG (*looks at her*): Our book; Thea's and mine. It belongs to both of us.

MRS. ELVSTED: Oh, yes! I feel that, too! And I've a right to be with you when it comes into the world. I want to see people respect and honour you again. And the joy! The joy! I want to share it with you!

LŒVBORG: Thea—our book will never come into the world.

HEDDA: Ah!

MRS. ELVSTED: Not—?

LŒVBORG: It cannot. Ever.

MRS. ELVSTED: Eilert—what have you done with the manuscript?

HEDDA: Yes—the manuscript?

MRS. ELVSTED: Where is it?

LŒVBORG: Oh, Thea, please don't ask me that!

MRS. ELVSTED: Yes, yes—I must know. I've a right to know. Now!

LŒVBORG: The manuscript. Yes. I've torn it up.

MRS. ELVSTED (*screams*): No, no!

HEDDA (*involuntarily*): But that's not—!

LŒVBORG (*looks at her*): Not true, you think.

HEDDA (*controls herself*): Why—yes, of course it is, if you say so. It sounded so incredible—

LŒVBORG: It's true, nevertheless.

MRS. ELVSTED: Oh, my God, my God, Hedda—he's destroyed his own book!

LŒVBORG: I have destroyed my life. Why not my life's work, too?

MRS. ELVSTED: And you—did this last night?

LŒVBORG: Yes, Thea. I tore it into a thousand pieces. And scattered them out across the fjord. It's good, clean, salt water. Let it carry them away; let them drift in the current and the wind. And in a little while, they will sink. Deeper and deeper. As I shall, Thea.

MRS. ELVSTED: Do you know, Eilert—this book—all my life I shall feel as though you'd killed a little child.

LŒVBORG: You're right. It is like killing a child.

MRS. ELVSTED: But how could you? It was my child, too!

HEDDA (*almost inaudibly*): Oh—the child—!

MRS. ELVSTED (*breathes heavily*): It's all over, then. Well—I'll go now, Hedda.

HEDDA: You're not leaving town?

MRS. ELVSTED: I don't know what I'm going to do. I can't see anything except—darkness. *She goes out through the hall.*

HEDDA (*waits a moment*): Aren't you going to escort her home, Mr. Lœvborg?

LŒVBORG: I? Through the streets? Do you want me to let people see her with me?

HEDDA: Of course, I don't know what else may have happened last night. But is it so utterly beyond redress?

LŒVBORG: It isn't just last night. It'll go on happening. I know it. But the curse of it is, I don't want to live that kind of life. I don't want to start all that again. She's broken my courage. I can't spit in the eyes of the world any longer.

HEDDA (*as though to herself*): That pretty little fool's been trying to shape a man's destiny. (*Looks at him.*) But how could you be so heartless towards her?

LŒVBORG: Don't call me heartless!

HEDDA: To go and destroy the one thing that's made her life worth living? You don't call that heartless?

LŒVBORG: Do you want to know the truth, Hedda?

HEDDA: The truth?

LŒVBORG: Promise me first—give me your word—that you'll never let Thea know about this.

HEDDA: I give you my word.

LŒVBORG: Good. Well, what I told her just now was a lie.

HEDDA: About the manuscript?

LŒVBORG: Yes. I didn't tear it up. Or throw it in the fjord.

HEDDA: You didn't? But where is it, then?

LŒVBORG: I destroyed it, all the same. I destroyed it, Hedda!

HEDDA: I don't understand.

LŒVBORG: Thea said that what I had done was like killing a child.

HEDDA: Yes. That's what she said.

LŒVBORG: But to kill a child isn't the worst thing a father can do to it.

HEDDA: What could be worse than that?

LŒVBORG: Hedda—suppose a man came home one morning, after a night of debauchery, and said to the mother of his child: 'Look here. I've been wandering round all night. I've been to—such-and-such a place and such-and-such a place. And I had our child with me. I took him to—these places. And I've lost him. Just—lost him. God knows where he is or whose hands he's fallen into.'

HEDDA: I see. But when all's said and done, this was only a book—

LŒVBORG: Thea's heart and soul were in that book. It was her whole life.

HEDDA: Yes, I understand.

LŒVBORG: Well, then you must also understand that she and I cannot possibly ever see each other again.

HEDDA: Where will you go?

LŒVBORG: Nowhere. I just want to put an end to it all. As soon as possible.

HEDDA (takes a step towards him): Eilert Lœvborg, listen to me. Do it—beautifully!

LŒVBORG: Beautifully? (Smiles.) With a crown of vine leaves in my hair? The way you used to dream of me—in the old days?

HEDDA: No. I don't believe in that crown any longer. But—do it beautifully, all the same. Just this once. Goodbye. You must go now. And don't come back.

LŒVBORG: Adieu, madame. Give my love to George Tesman. (Turns to go.)

HEDDA: Wait. I want to give you a souvenir to take with you.

She goes over to the writing-table, opens the drawer and the pistol-case, and comes back to LŒVBORG *with one of the pistols.*

LŒVBORG (looks at her): This? Is this the souvenir?

HEDDA (nods slowly): You recognize it? You looked down its barrel once.

LŒVBORG: You should have used it then.

HEDDA: Here! Use it now!

LŒVBORG (puts the pistol in his breast pocket): Thank you.

HEDDA: Do it beautifully, Eilert Lœvborg. Only promise me that!

LŒVBORG: Good-bye, Hedda Gabler.

He goes out through the hall. HEDDA *stands by the door for a moment, listening. Then she goes over to the writing-table, takes out the package containing the manuscript, glances inside it, pulls some of the pages half out and looks at them. Then she takes it to the armchair by the stove and sits down with the package in her lap. After a moment, she opens the door of the stove; then she opens the packet.*

HEDDA (throws one of the pages into the stove and whispers to herself): I'm burning your child, Thea! You with your beautiful, wavy hair! (She throws a few more pages into the stove.) The child Eilert Lœvborg gave you. (Throws the rest of the manuscript in.) I'm burning it! I'm burning your child!

ACT FOUR

The same. It is evening. The drawing-room is in darkness. The small room is illuminated by the hanging lamp over the table. The curtains are drawn across the french windows. HEDDA, *dressed in black, is walking up and down in the darkened room. Then she goes into the small room and crosses to the left. A few chords are heard from the piano. She comes back into the drawing-room.*

BERTHA *comes through the small room from the right with a lighted lamp, which she places on the table in front of the corner sofa in the drawing-room. Her eyes are red with crying, and she has black ribbons on her cap. She goes quietly out, right.* HEDDA *goes over to the french windows, draws the curtains slightly to one side and looks out into the darkness.*

A few moments later, MISS TESMAN *enters from the hall. She is dressed in mourning, with a black hat and veil.* HEDDA *goes to meet her and holds out her hand.*

MISS TESMAN: Well, Hedda, here I am in the weeds of sorrow. My poor sister has ended her struggles at last.

HEDDA: I've already heard. Tesman sent me a card.

MISS TESMAN: Yes, he promised me he would. But I thought, no, I must go and break the news of death to Hedda myself—here, in the house of life.

HEDDA: It's very kind of you.

MISS TESMAN: Ah, Rena shouldn't have chosen a time like this to pass away. This is no moment for Hedda's house to be a place of mourning.

HEDDA (*changing the subject*): She died peacefully, Miss Tesman?

MISS TESMAN: Oh, it was quite beautiful! The end came so calmly. And she was so happy at being able to see George once again. And say good-bye to him. Hasn't he come home yet?

HEDDA: No. He wrote that I mustn't expect him too soon. But please sit down.

MISS TESMAN: No, thank you, Hedda dear—bless you. I'd like to. But I've so little time. I must dress her and lay her out as well as I can. She shall go to her grave looking really beautiful.

HEDDA: Can't I help with anything?

MISS TESMAN: Why, you mustn't think of such a thing! Hedda Tesman mustn't let her hands be soiled by contact with death. Or her thoughts. Not at this time.

HEDDA: One can't always control one's thoughts.

MISS TESMAN (*continues*): Ah, well, that's life. Now we must start to sew poor Rena's shroud. There'll be sewing to be done in this house, too, before long, I shouldn't wonder. But not for a shroud, praise God.

GEORGE TESMAN *enters from the hall.*

HEDDA: You've come at last! Thank heavens!

TESMAN: Are you here, Auntie Juju? With Hedda? Fancy that!

MISS TESMAN: I was just on the point of leaving, dear boy. Well, have you done everything you promised me?

TESMAN: No, I'm afraid I forgot half of it. I'll have to run over again tomorrow. My head's in a complete whirl today. I can't collect my thoughts.

MISS TESMAN: But, George dear, you mustn't take it like this.

TESMAN: Oh? Well—er—how should I?

MISS TESMAN: You must be happy in your grief. Happy for what's happened. As I am.

TESMAN: Oh, yes, yes. You're thinking of Aunt Rena.

HEDDA: It'll be lonely for you now, Miss Tesman.

MISS TESMAN: For the first few days, yes. But it won't last long, I hope. Poor dear Rena's little room isn't going to stay empty.

TESMAN: Oh? Whom are you going to move in there? What?

MISS TESMAN: Oh, there's always some poor invalid who needs care and attention.

HEDDA: Do you really want another cross like that to bear?

MISS TESMAN: Cross! God forgive you, child. It's been no cross for me.

HEDDA: But now—if a complete stranger comes to live with you—?

MISS TESMAN: Oh, one soon makes friends with invalids. And I need so much to have someone to live for. Like you, my dear. Well, I expect there'll soon be work in this house too for an old aunt, praise God!

HEDDA: Oh—please!

TESMAN: My word, yes! What a splendid time the three of us could have together if—

HEDDA: If?

TESMAN (*uneasily*): Oh, never mind. It'll all work out. Let's hope so—what?

MISS TESMAN: Yes, yes. Well, I'm sure you two would like to be alone. (*Smiles.*) Perhaps Hedda may have something to tell you, George. Good-bye. I must go home to Rena. (*Turns to the door.*) Dear God, how strange! Now Rena is with me and with poor dear Joachim.

TESMAN: Why, yes, Auntie Juju! What?

MISS TESMAN *goes out through the hall.*

HEDDA (*follows* TESMAN *coldly and searchingly with her eyes*): I really believe this death distresses you more than it does her.

TESMAN: Oh, it isn't just Auntie Rena. It's Eilert I'm so worried about.

HEDDA (*quickly*): Is there any news of him?

TESMAN: I ran over to see him this afternoon. I wanted to tell him his manuscript was in safe hands.

HEDDA: Oh? You didn't find him?

TESMAN: No, he wasn't at home. But later I met Mrs. Elvsted and she told me he'd been here early this morning.

HEDDA: Yes, just after you'd left.

TESMAN: It seems he said he'd torn the manuscript up. What?

HEDDA: Yes, he claimed to have done so.

TESMAN: You told him we had it, of course?

HEDDA: No. (*Quickly.*) Did you tell Mrs. Elvsted?

TESMAN: No. I didn't like to. But you ought to have told him. Think if he should go home and do something desperate! Give me the manuscript, Hedda. I'll run over to him with it right away. Where did you put it?

HEDDA (*cold and motionless, leaning against the armchair*): I haven't got it any longer.

TESMAN: Haven't got it? What on earth do you mean?

HEDDA: I've burned it.

TESMAN (*starts, terrified*): Burned it! Burned Eilert's manuscript!

HEDDA: Don't shout. The servant will hear you.

TESMAN: Burned it! But in heaven's name—! Oh, no, no, no! This is impossible!

HEDDA: Well, it's true.

TESMAN: But, Hedda, do you realize what you've done? That's appropriating lost property! It's against the law! By God! You ask Judge Brack and see if I'm not right.

HEDDA: You'd be well advised not to talk about it to Judge Brack or anyone else.

TESMAN: But how could you go and do such a dreadful thing? What on earth put the idea into your head? What came over you? Answer me! What?

HEDDA (*represses an almost imperceptible smile*): I did it for your sake, George.

TESMAN: For my sake?

HEDDA: When you came home this morning and described how he'd read this book to you—

TESMAN: Yes, yes?

HEDDA: You admitted you were jealous of him.

TESMAN: But, good heavens, I didn't mean it literally!

HEDDA: No matter. I couldn't bear the thought that anyone else should push you into the background.

TESMAN (*torn between doubt and joy*): Hedda—is this true? But—but—but I never realized you loved me like that! Fancy that!

HEDDA: Well, I suppose you'd better know. I'm going to have—(*Breaks off and says violently*) No, no—you better ask your Auntie Juju. She'll tell you.

TESMAN: Hedda! I think I understand what you mean. (*Clasps his hands.*) Good heavens, can it really be true? What?

HEDDA: Don't shout. The servant will hear you.

TESMAN (*laughing with joy*): The servant! I say, that's good! The servant! Why, that's Bertha! I'll run out and tell her at once!

HEDDA (*clenches her hands in despair*): Oh, it's destroying me, all this—it's destroying me!

TESMAN: I say, Hedda, what's up? What?

HEDDA (*cold, controlled*): Oh, it's all so—absurd—George.

TESMAN: Absurd? That I'm so happy? But surely—? Ah, well—perhaps I won't say anything to Bertha.

HEDDA: No, do. She might as well know, too.

TESMAN: No, no, I won't tell her yet. But Auntie Juju—I must let her know! And you—you called me George! For the first time! Fancy that! Oh, it'll make Auntie Juju so happy, all this! So very happy!

HEDDA: Will she be happy when she hears I've burned Eilert Lœvborg's manuscript—for your sake?

TESMAN: No, I'd forgotten about that. Of course, no one must be allowed to know about the manuscript. But that you're burning with love for me, Hedda, I must certainly let Auntie Juju know that. I say, I wonder if young wives often feel like that towards their husbands? What?

HEDDA: You might ask Auntie Juju about that, too.

TESMAN: I will, as soon as I get the chance. (*Looks uneasy and thoughtful again.*) But I say, you know, that manuscript. Dreadful business. Poor Eilert!

MRS. ELVSTED, *dressed as on her first visit, with hat and overcoat, enters from the hall.*

MRS. ELVSTED (*greets them hastily and tremulously*): Oh, Hedda dear, do please forgive me for coming here again.

HEDDA: Why, Thea, what's happened?

TESMAN: Is it anything to do with Eilert Lœvborg? What?

MRS. ELVSTED: Yes—I'm so dreadfully afraid he may have met with an accident.

HEDDA (*grips her arm*): You think so?

TESMAN: But, good heavens, Mrs. Elvsted, what makes you think that?

MRS. ELVSTED: I heard them talking about him at the boarding-house, as I went in. Oh, there are the most terrible rumours being spread about him in town today.

TESMAN: Er—yes, I heard about them, too. But I can testify that he went straight home to bed. Fancy—!

HEDDA: Well—what did they say in the boarding-house?

MRS. ELVSTED: Oh, I couldn't find out anything. Either they didn't know, or else—They stopped talking when they saw me. And I didn't dare to ask.

TESMAN (*fidgets uneasily*): We must hope—we must hope you misheard them, Mrs. Elvsted.

MRS. ELVSTED: No, no, I'm sure it was him they were talking about. I heard them say something about a hospital—

TESMAN: Hospital!

HEDDA: Oh no, surely that's impossible!

MRS. ELVSTED: Oh, I became so afraid. So I went up to his rooms and asked to see him.

HEDDA: Do you think that was wise, Thea?

MRS. ELVSTED: Well, what else could I do? I couldn't bear the uncertainty any longer.

TESMAN: But *you* didn't manage to find him either? What?

MRS. ELVSTED: No. And they had no idea where he was. They said he hadn't been home since yesterday afternoon.

TESMAN: Since yesterday? Fancy that!

MRS. ELVSTED: I'm sure he must have met with an accident.

TESMAN: Hedda, I wonder if I ought to go into town and make one or two enquiries?

HEDDA: No, no, don't you get mixed up in this.

JUDGE BRACK *enters from the hall, hat in hand.* BERTHA, *who has opened the door for him, closes it. He looks serious and greets them silently.*

TESMAN: Hullo, my dear Judge. Fancy seeing you!

BRACK: I had to come and talk to you.

TESMAN: I can see Auntie Juju's told you the news.

BRACK: Yes, I've heard about that, too.

TESMAN: Tragic, isn't it?

BRACK: Well, my dear chap, that depends how you look at it.

TESMAN (*looks uncertainly at him*): Has something else happened?

BRACK: Yes.

HEDDA: Another tragedy?

BRACK: That also depends on how you look at it, Mrs. Tesman.

MRS. ELVSTED: Oh, it's something to do with Eilert Lœvborg!

BRACK (*looks at her for a moment*): How did you guess? Perhaps you've heard already—?

MRS. ELVSTED (*confused*): No, no, not at all—I—

TESMAN: For heaven's sake, tell us!

BRACK (*shrugs his shoulders*): Well, I'm afraid they've taken him to the hospital. He's dying.

MRS. ELVSTED (*screams*): Oh God, God!

TESMAN: The hospital! Dying!

HEDDA (*involuntarily*): So quickly!

MRS. ELVSTED (*weeping*): Oh, Hedda! And we parted enemies!

HEDDA (*whispers*): Thea—Thea!

MRS. ELVSTED (*ignoring her*): I must see him! I must see him before he dies!

BRACK: It's no use, Mrs. Elvsted. No one's allowed to see him now.

MRS. ELVSTED: But what's happened to him? You must tell me!

TESMAN: He hasn't tried to do anything to himself? What?

HEDDA: Yes, he has. I'm sure of it.

TESMAN: Hedda, how can you—?

BRACK (*who has not taken his eyes from her*): I'm afraid you've guessed correctly, Mrs. Tesman.

MRS. ELVSTED: How dreadful!

TESMAN: Attempted suicide! Fancy that!

HEDDA: Shot himself!

BRACK: Right again, Mrs. Tesman—

MRS. ELVSTED (*tries to compose herself*): When did this happen, Judge Brack?

BRACK: This afternoon. Between three and four.

TESMAN: But, good heavens—where? What?

BRACK (*a little hesitantly*): Where? Why, my dear chap, in his rooms, of course.

MRS. ELVSTED: No, that's impossible. I was there soon after six.

BRACK: Well, it must have been somewhere else, then. I don't know exactly. I only know that they found him. He's shot himself—through the breast.

MRS. ELVSTED: Oh, how horrible! That he should end like that!

HEDDA (*to* BRACK): Through the breast, you said?

BRACK: That is what I said.

HEDDA: Not through the head?

BRACK: Through the breast, Mrs. Tesman.

HEDDA: The breast. Yes; yes. That's good, too.

BRACK: Why, Mrs. Tesman?

HEDDA: Oh—no, I didn't mean anything.

TESMAN: And the wound's dangerous, you say? What?

BRACK: Mortal. He's probably already dead.

MRS. ELVSTED: Yes, yes—I feel it! It's all over. All over. Oh Hedda—!

TESMAN: But, tell me, how did you manage to learn all this?

BRACK (*curtly*): From the police. I spoke to one of them.

HEDDA (*loudly, clearly*): Thank God! At last!

TESMAN (*appalled*): For God's sake, Hedda, what are you saying?

HEDDA: I am saying there's beauty in what he has done.

BRACK: Hm—Mrs. Tesman—

TESMAN: Beauty! Oh, but I say!

MRS. ELVSTED: Hedda, how can you talk of beauty in connection with a thing like this?

HEDDA: Eilert Lœvborg has settled his account with life. He's had the courage to do what—what he had to do.

MRS. ELVSTED: No, that's not why it happened. He did it because he was mad.

TESMAN: He did it because he was desperate.

HEDDA: You're wrong! I know!

MRS. ELVSTED: He must have been mad. The same as when he tore up the manuscript.

BRACK (*starts*): Manuscript? Did he tear it up?

MRS. ELVSTED: Yes. Last night.

TESMAN (*whispers*): Oh, Hedda, we shall never be able to escape from this.

BRACK: Hm. Strange.

TESMAN (*wanders round the room*): To think of Eilert dying like that. And not leaving behind him the thing that would have made his name endure.

MRS. ELVSTED: If only it could be pieced together again!

TESMAN: Yes, yes, yes! If only it could! I'd give anything—

MRS. ELVSTED: Perhaps it can, Mr. Tesman.

TESMAN: What do you mean?

MRS. ELVSTED (*searches in the pocket of her dress*): Look. I kept the notes he dictated it from.

HEDDA (*takes a step nearer*): Ah!

TESMAN: You kept them, Mrs. Elvsted! What?

MRS. ELVSTED: Yes, here they are. I brought them with me when I left home. They've been in my pocket ever since.

TESMAN: Let me have a look.

MRS. ELVSTED (*hands him a wad of small sheets of paper*): They're in a terrible muddle. All mixed up.

TESMAN: I say, just fancy if we could sort them out! Perhaps if we work on them together—?

MRS. ELVSTED: Oh, yes! Let's try, anyway!

TESMAN: We'll manage it. We must! I shall dedicate my life to this.

HEDDA: *You,* George? Your life?

TESMAN: Yes—well, all the time I can spare. My book'll have to wait. Hedda, you do understand? What? I owe it to Eilert's memory.

HEDDA: Perhaps.

TESMAN: Well, my dear Mrs. Elvsted, you and I'll have to pool our brains. No use crying over spilt milk, what? We must try to approach this matter calmly.

MRS. ELVSTED: Yes, yes, Mr. Tesman. I'll do my best.

TESMAN: Well, come over here and let's start looking at these notes right away. Where shall we sit? Here? No, the other room. You'll excuse us, won't you, Judge? Come along with me, Mrs. Elvsted.

MRS. ELVSTED: Oh, God! If only we can manage to do it!

TESMAN *and* MRS. ELVSTED *go into the rear room. He takes off his hat and overcoat. They sit at the table beneath the hanging lamp and absorb themselves in the notes.* HEDDA *walks across to the stove and sits in the armchair. After a moment,* BRACK *goes over to her.*

HEDDA (*half aloud*): Oh, Judge! This act of Eilert Lœvborg's—doesn't it give one a sense of release!

BRACK: Release, Mrs. Hedda? Well, it's a release for him, of course—

HEDDA: Oh, I don't mean him—I mean me! The release of knowing that someone can do something really brave! Something beautiful!

BRACK (*smiles*): Hm—my dear Mrs. Hedda—

HEDDA: Oh, I know what you're going to say. You're a *bourgeois* at heart, too, just like—ah, well!

BRACK (*looks at her*): Eilert Lœvborg has meant more to you than you're willing to admit to yourself. Or am I wrong?

HEDDA: I'm not answering questions like that from you. I only know that Eilert Lœvborg has had the courage to live according to his own principles. And now, at last, he's done something big! Something beautiful! To have the courage and the will to rise from the feast of life so early!

BRACK: It distresses me deeply, Mrs. Hedda, but I'm afraid I must rob you of that charming illusion.

HEDDA: Illusion?

BRACK: You wouldn't have been allowed to keep it for long, anyway.

HEDDA: What do you mean?

BRACK: He didn't shoot himself on purpose.

HEDDA: Not on purpose?

BRACK: No. It didn't happen quite the way I told you.

HEDDA: Have you been hiding something? What is it?

BRACK: In order to spare poor Mrs. Elvsted's feelings, I permitted myself one or two small—equivocations.

HEDDA: What?

BRACK: To begin with, he is already dead.

HEDDA: He died at the hospital?

BRACK: Yes. Without regaining consciousness.

HEDDA: What else haven't you told us?

BRACK: The incident didn't take place at his lodgings.

HEDDA: Well, that's utterly unimportant.

BRACK: Not utterly. The fact is, you see, that Eilert Lœvborg was found shot in Mademoiselle Danielle's boudoir.

HEDDA (*almost jumps up, but instead sinks back in her chair*): That's impossible. He can't have been there today.

BRACK: He was there this afternoon. He went to ask for something he claimed they'd taken from him. Talked some crazy nonsense about a child which had got lost—

HEDDA: Oh! So that was the reason!

BRACK: I thought at first he might have been referring to his manuscript. But I hear he destroyed that himself. So he must have meant his pocket-book—I suppose.

HEDDA: Yes, I suppose so. So they found him there?

BRACK: Yes; there. With a discharged pistol in his breast pocket. The shot had wounded him mortally.

HEDDA: Yes. In the breast.

BRACK: No. In the—stomach. The—lower part—

HEDDA (*looks at him with an expression of repulsion*): That, too! Oh, why does everything I touch become mean and ludicrous? It's like a curse!

BRACK: There's something else, Mrs. Hedda. It's rather disagreeable, too.

HEDDA: What?

BRACK: The pistol he had on him—

HEDDA: Yes? What about it?

BRACK: He must have stolen it.

HEDDA (*jumps up*): Stolen it! That isn't true! He didn't!

BRACK: It's the only explanation. He must have stolen it. Ssh!

TESMAN and MRS. ELVSTED *have got up from the table in the rear room and come into the drawing-room.*

TESMAN (*his hands full of papers*): Hedda, I can't see properly under that lamp. Do you think—?

HEDDA: I am thinking.

TESMAN: Do you think we could possibly use your writing-table for a little? What?

HEDDA: Yes, of course. (*Quickly.*) No, wait! Let me tidy it up first.

TESMAN: Oh, don't you trouble about that. There's plenty of room.

HEDDA: No, no, let me tidy it up first, I say. I'll take these in and put them on the piano. Here.

She pulls an object, covered with sheets of music, out from under the bookcase, puts some more sheets on top and carries it all into the rear room and away to the left. TESMAN *puts his papers on the writing-table and moves the lamp over from the corner table. He and* MRS. ELVSTED *sit down and begin working again.* HEDDA *comes back.*

HEDDA (*behind* MRS. ELVSTED'S *chair, ruffles her hair gently*): Well, my pretty Thea. And how is work progressing on Eilert Lœvborg's memorial?

MRS. ELVSTED (*looks up at her, dejectedly*): Oh, it's going to be terribly difficult to get these into any order.

TESMAN: We've got to do it. We must! After all, putting other people's papers into order is rather my specialty, what?

HEDDA goes over to the stove and sits on one of the footstools. BRACK *stands over her, leaning against the armchair.*

HEDDA (*whispers*): What was that you were saying about the pistol?

BRACK (*softly*): I said he must have stolen it.

HEDDA: Why do you think that?

BRACK: Because any other explanation is unthinkable, Mrs. Hedda. Or ought to be.

HEDDA: I see.

BRACK (*looks at her for a moment*): Eilert Lœvborg was here this morning. Wasn't he?

HEDDA: Yes.

BRACK: Were you alone with him?

HEDDA: For a few moments.

BRACK: You didn't leave the room while he was here?

HEDDA: No.

BRACK: Think again. Are you sure you didn't go out for a moment?

HEDDA: Oh—yes, I might have gone into the hall. Just for a few seconds.

BRACK: And where was your pistol-case during this time?

HEDDA: I'd locked it in that—

BRACK: Er—Mrs. Hedda?

HEDDA: It was lying over there on my writing-table.

BRACK: Have you looked to see if both the pistols are still there?

HEDDA: No.

BRACK: You needn't bother. I saw the pistol Lœvborg had when they found him. I recognized it at once. From yesterday. And other occasions.

HEDDA: Have you got it?

BRACK: No. The police have it.

HEDDA: What will the police do with this pistol?

BRACK: Try to trace the owner.

HEDDA: Do you think they'll succeed?

BRACK (*leans down and whispers*): No, Hedda Gabler. Not as long as I hold my tongue.

HEDDA (*looks nervously at him*): And if you don't?

BRACK (*shrugs his shoulders*): You could always say he'd stolen it.

HEDDA: I'd rather die!

BRACK (*smiles*): People say that. They never do it.

HEDDA (*not replying*): And suppose the pistol wasn't stolen? And they trace the owner? What then?

BRACK: There'll be a scandal, Hedda.

HEDDA: A scandal!

BRACK: Yes, a scandal. The thing you're so frightened of. You'll have to appear in court together with Mademoiselle Danielle. She'll have to explain how it all happened. Was it an accident, or was it—homicide? Was he about to take the pistol from his pocket to threaten her? And did it go off? Or did she snatch the pistol from his hand, shoot him and then put it back in his pocket? She might quite easily have done it. She's a resourceful lady, is Mademoiselle Danielle.

HEDDA: But I have nothing to do with this repulsive business.

BRACK: No. But you'll have to answer one question. Why did you give Eilert Lœvborg this pistol? And what conclusions will people draw when it is proved you did give it to him?

HEDDA (*bows her head*): That's true. I hadn't thought of that.

BRACK: Well, luckily there's no danger as long as I hold my tongue.

HEDDA (*looks up at him*): In other words, I'm in your power, Judge. From now on, you've got your hold over me.

BRACK (*whispers, more slowly*): Hedda, my dearest—believe me—I will not abuse my position.

HEDDA: Nevertheless, I'm in your power. Dependent on your will, and your demands. Not free. Still not free! (*Rises passionately.*) No. I couldn't bear that. No.

BRACK (*looks half-derisively at her*): Most people resign themselves to the inevitable, sooner or later.

HEDDA (*returns his gaze*): Possibly they do.
She goes across to the writing-table.

HEDDA (*represses an involuntary smile and says in* TESMAN's *voice*): Well, George. Think you'll be able to manage? What?

TESMAN: Heaven knows, dear. This is going to take months and months.

HEDDA (*in the same tone as before*): Fancy that, by Jove! (*Runs her hands gently through* MRS. ELVSTED's *hair.*) Doesn't it feel strange, Thea? Here you are working away with Tesman just the way you used to work with Eilert Lœvborg.

MRS. ELVSTED: Oh—if only I can inspire your husband, too!

HEDDA: Oh, it'll come. In time.

TESMAN: Yes—do you know, Hedda, I really think I'm beginning to feel a bit—well—

that way. But you go back and talk to Judge Brack.

HEDDA: Can't I be of use to you two in any way?

TESMAN: No, none at all. (*Turns his head.*) You'll have to keep Hedda company from now on, Judge, and see she doesn't get bored. If you don't mind.

BRACK (*glances at* HEDDA): It'll be a pleasure.

HEDDA: Thank you. But I'm tired this evening. I think I'll lie down on the sofa in there for a little while.

TESMAN: Yes, dear—do. What?
HEDDA *goes into the rear room and draws the curtains behind her. Short pause. Suddenly she begins to play a frenzied dance melody on the piano.*

MRS. ELVSTED (*starts up from her chair*): Oh, what's that?

TESMAN (*runs to the doorway*): Hedda dear, please! Don't play dance music tonight! Think of Auntie Rena. And Eilert.

HEDDA (*puts her head through the curtains*): And Auntie Juju. And all the rest of them. From now on I'll be quiet.
She closes the curtains behind her.

TESMAN (*at the writing-table*): It distresses her to watch us doing this. I say, Mrs. Elvsted, I've an idea. Why don't you move in with Auntie Juju? I'll run over each evening, and we can sit and work there. What?

MRS. ELVSTED: Yes, that might be the best plan.

HEDDA (*from the rear room*): I can hear what you're saying, Tesman. But how shall I spend the evenings out here?

TESMAN (*looking through his papers*): Oh, I'm sure Judge Brack'll be kind enough to come over and keep you company. You won't mind my not being here, Judge?

BRACK (*in the armchair, calls gaily*): I'll be delighted, Mrs. Tesman. I'll be here every evening. We'll have great fun together, you and I.

HEDDA (*loud and clear*): Yes, that'll suit you, won't it, Judge? The only cock on the dunghill—
A shot is heard from the rear room. TESMAN, MRS. ELVSTED *and* JUDGE BRACK *start from their chairs.*

TESMAN: Oh, she's playing with those pistols again.

He pulls the curtains aside and runs in. MRS. ELVSTED *follows him.* HEDDA *is lying dead on the sofa. Confusion and shouting.* BERTHA *enters in alarm from the right.*

TESMAN (*screams to* BRACK): She's shot herself! Shot herself in the head! Fancy that!

BRACK (*half paralysed in the armchair*): But, good God! People don't do such things!

PERFORMING *HEDDA GABLER*

Hedda Gabler has been a favorite role on English-language stages since Elizabeth Robins and Janet Achurch introduced Ibsen's heroines to London audiences in the new William Archer translations in the 1890s. Robins, an American actress, played the first Hedda on the London stage in 1891. She scored a personal triumph, convincing London audiences that "Ibsenism," as George Bernard Shaw labeled the new playwriting, was no longer an aberration, but a new brand of realism sensitive to new ideas and feminist issues. Despite Shaw's efforts, Ibsen's influence in the British theater was never as pervasive as it was in Germany and the United States.

Hedda Gabler was first performed in Munich, Germany, in 1891. The playwright was disappointed in the leading actress who did not speak naturally but declaimed her lines; audiences, in turn, hissed and whistled. A month later in Berlin, Anna Haverland in the title role pleased Ibsen but critics found the play irrational, if not annoying. For the most part, Hedda Gabler in 1890s Germany was relegated to the domain of Ibsen's "incomprehensible females."

In Russia in 1904, actress Vera Kommissarzhevskaya opened her own theater in St. Petersburg and hired Vsevelod Meyerhold, who had broken with Konstantin Stanislavski at the Moscow Art Theater, to stage *Hedda Gabler*. Known for his experiments with non-realistic staging, Meyerhold ignored Ibsen's stage directions and created a greenish-blue and white setting absent of realistic details. Seated on a white, fur-covered throne, Hedda dominated the action from center stage and the other characters were dressed in distinctively colored garments and assumed sculptural poses.

Ibsen's plays were introduced to American audiences in 1899 and were played, in turn, by Mrs. Minnie Maddern Fiske, Helena Modjeska, Eleonora Duse, and Alla Nazimova. In the late twenties, actress Eva Le Gallienne became the foremost interpreter of Ibsen's complex heroine in the United States. She played Hedda in modern dress in 1928 at her Civic Repertory Theatre on Fourteenth Street in New York City. She appeared on stage with her hair cut short, smoking a cigarette, and wearing a fashionable gown of yellow silk. By 1964, Le Gallienne had played the role six times in New York (once with the American Repertory Theatre), directed and played Hedda in two national tours, and made a full-length recording of Ibsen's play. One observer said that Le Gallienne's Hedda had "a strange, graceful beauty like a lean, aristocratic and intangibly evil cat."[6] Le Gallienne divined that Hedda's ruthlessness and cruelty should be obsessive, pathological, and devious—and, hence, dangerous.

Le Gallienne's forerunners were the cosmopolitan European actresses Eleonora Duse and Alla Nazimova. Known for her gracefulness, expressive eyes, and melancholy in repose, the Italian actress Eleonora Duse was renown for her statuesque way of playing the role with slowness and subtlety. She toured the United States and England between 1893 and 1924 and was outstanding in what were called Ibsen's chillier-blooded women found in *Hedda Gabler* and *Rosmersholm*. Alla Nazimova, the Russian-born actress known for her passionate yet subtle characterizations, presented a triple-bill of *Hedda Gabler, A Doll's House,* and *The Master Builder* in New York in 1906. Hedda Gabler was her first English-speaking part.

Since the popularity of Duse, Nazimova, and Le Gallienne as Ibsen's heroines on New York stages, Ibsen's plays have been found largely in the nonprofit resident theaters in the United States and in the national theaters in England and Europe. In Sweden, Liv Ullman played Hedda under the direction of Ingmar

Bergman; in England, Janet Suzman, Glenda Jackson, Maggie Smith, and Fiona Shaw added to the portraits of Ibsen's conflicted heroine. Glenda Jackson fixed on the "grotesque farce" of Hedda's life in the portrayal of a fierce tiger-like villainess who plays vicious games but who is unable to jar her banal world except in the moment of her self-destruction. In Stratford, Canada, Irene Worth played Hedda to critical acclaim and in the United States, Susannah York, Annette Bening, and Kate Burton again brought notoriety to Ibsen's heroine. As recently as 2001, Kate Burton appeared as Ibsen's "perplexing and beguiling heroine" in a Broadway production that one critic praised for a performance that allows Hedda's "infinite perversity" (as Henry James said) to grow out of her disappointments with life. Ben Brantley wrote that Hedda has become "electric with disappointment" in this production.[6]

Ibsen's heroine has lived on the stages of the world for over a hundred years. In all of her discontented game-playing and perverse cruelty, she continues to illumine the frustrations of smart, intelligent women entrapped and imprisoned by a circumscribed world.

CRITICS' NOTEBOOK

The playwright Henrik Ibsen wrote on his own work in notes describing the development of his plays and in letters to publishers, actors, and producers.

Writing notes in Rome in 1978, Ibsen expressed his thoughts on "modern" tragedy in which women, like Nora Helmer in *A Doll's House* and Hedda Gabler in his later play, were caught in conflicts between spiritual, moral, and societal forces and inevitably experienced catastrophe of some order.

Ibsen's champion in England was none other than critic and playwright George Bernard Shaw, who wrote his landmark essay on *The Quintessence of Ibsenism* (1891, revised in 1913) and coined the term "Ibsenism." Shaw called attention to the fact that Henrik Ibsen introduced a new "drama of ideas" into the modern realistic theater. For Shaw, "Ibsenism" was a new school

of playwriting in which the dramatic interest grew out of a "conflict of ideals" that penetrated the entire play.

Henrik Ibsen, from *Notes for the Modern Tragedy* * Translated by A. G. Chater

❦

Rome, 19. 10, 78.

There are two kinds of spiritual law, two kinds of conscience, one in man and another, altogether different, in woman. They do not understand each other; but in practical life the woman is judged by man's law, as though she were not a woman but a man.

The wife in the play ends by having no idea of what is right or wrong; natural feeling on the one hand and belief in authority on the other have altogether bewildered her.

A woman cannot be herself in the society of the present day, which is an exclusively masculine society, with laws framed by men and with a judicial system that judges feminine conduct from a masculine point of view.

She has committed forgery, and she is proud of it; for she did it out of love for her husband, to save his life. But this husband with his commonplace principles of honour is on the side of the law and regards the question with masculine eyes.

Spiritual conflicts. Oppressed and bewildered by the belief in authority, she loses faith in her moral right and ability to bring up her children. Bitterness. A mother in modern society, like certain insects who go away and die when she has done her duty in the propagation of the race. Love of life, of home, of husband and children and family. Here and there a womanly shaking-off of her thoughts. Sudden return of anxiety and terror. She must bear it all alone. The catastrophe approaches, inexorably, inevitably. Despair, conflict and destruction.

*Henrik Ibsen, "Notes for the Modern Tragedy," from *The Collected Works of Henrik Ibsen*, trans. A. G. Chater, Vol. 12 (New York: Charles Scribner's Sons, 1929): 91–92.

George Bernard Shaw, from *The Quintessence of Ibsenism**

❦

The drama was born of old from the union of two desires: the desire to have a dance and the desire to hear a story. The dance became a rant: the story became a situation. When Ibsen began to make plays, the art of the dramatist had shrunk into the art of contriving a situation. And it was held that the stranger the situation, the better the play. Ibsen saw that, on the contrary, the more familiar the situation, the more interesting the play. Shakespear had put ourselves on the stage but not our situations. Our uncles seldom murder our fathers, and cannot legally marry our mothers; we do not meet witches; our kings are not as a rule stabbed and succeeded by their stabbers; and when we raise money by bills we do not promise to pay pounds of our flesh. Ibsen supplies the want left by Shakespear. He gives us not only ourselves, but ourselves in our own situations. The things that happen to his stage figures are things that happen to us. One consequence is that his plays are much more important to us than Shakespear's. Another is that they are capable both of hurting us cruelly and of filling us with excited hopes of escape from idealistic tyrannies, and with visions of intenser life in the future.

Changes in technique follow inevitably from these changes in the subject matter of the play. When a dramatic poet can give you hopes and visions, such old maxims as that stage-craft is the art of preparation become boyish, and may be left to those unfortunate playwrights who, being unable to make anything really interesting happen on the stage, have to acquire the art of continually persuading the audience that it is going to happen presently. When he can stab people to the heart by shewing them the meanness or cruelty of something they did yes-

terday and intend to do tomorrow, all the old tricks to catch and hold their attention become the silliest of superfluities. The play called The Murder of Gonzago, which Hamlet makes the players act before his uncle, is artlessly constructed; but it produces a greater effect on Claudius than the Œdipus of Sophocles, because it is about himself. The writer who practises the art of Ibsen therefore discards all the old tricks of preparation, catastrophe, *dénouement,* and so forth without thinking about it, just as a modern rifleman never dreams of providing himself with powder horns, percussion caps, and wads: indeed he does not know the use of them. Ibsen substituted a terrible art of sharpshooting at the audience, trapping them, fencing with them aiming always at the sorest spot in their consciences. Never mislead an audience, was an old rule. But the new school will trick the spectator into forming a meanly false judgement, and then convict him of it in the next act, often to his grievous mortification. When you despise something you ought to take off your hat to, or admire and imitate something you ought to loathe, you cannot resist the dramatist who knows how to touch these morbid spots in you and make you see that they are morbid. The dramatist knows that as long as he is teaching and saving his audience, he is as sure of their strained attention as a dentist is, or the Angel of the Annunciation. And though he may use all the magic of art to make you forget the pain he causes you or to enhance the joy of the hope and courage he awakens, he is never occupied in the old work of manufacturing interest and expectation with materials that have neither novelty, significance, nor relevance to the experience or prospects of the spectators.

Hence a cry has arisen that the post-Ibsen play is not a play, and that its technique, not being the technique described by Aristotle, is not a technique at all. I will not enlarge on this: the fun poked at my friend Mr. A. B. Walkley in the prologue of Fanny's First Play need not be repeated here. But I may remind him that the new technique is new only on the modern stage. It has been used by preachers and orators ever since

*George Bernard Shaw, *The Quintessence of Ibsenism Now Completed to the Death of Ibsen* (London: The Society of Authors, 1913): 182–184.

speech was invented. It is the technique of playing upon the human conscience; and it has been practised by the playwright whenever the playwright has been capable of it. Rhetoric, irony, argument, paradox, epigram parable, the rearrangement of haphazard facts into orderly and intelligent situations: these are both the oldest and the newest arts of the drama; and your plot construction and art of preparation are only the tricks of theatrical talent and the shifts of moral sterility, not the weapons of dramatic genius. In the theatre of Ibsen we are not flattered spectators killing an idle hour with an ingenious and amusing entertainment: we are "guilty creatures sitting at a play"; and the technique of pastime is no more applicable than at a murder trial.

The technical novelties of the Ibsen and post-Ibsen plays are, then: first, the introduction of the discussion and its development until it so overspreads and interpenetrates the action that it finally assimilates it, making play and discussion practically identical; and second, as a consequence of making the spectators themselves the persons of the drama, and the incidents of their own lives its incidents, the disuse of the old stage tricks by which audiences had to be induced to take an interest in unreal people and improbable circumstances, and the substitution of a forensic technique of recrimination, disillusion, and penetration through ideals to the truth, with a free use of all the rhetorical and lyrical arts of the orator, the preacher, the pleader, and the rhapsodist.

REVISITING MODERNISM

The term *modern* has been applied to art, architecture, and writing for at least 150 years. In dramatic theory and criticism, *modernism* became associated with the new wave of realistic writers in the mid-nineteenth century, followed by the naturalists, symbolists, and expressionists.

As a way of perceiving contradictions and disconnections in experience, *modernism* was frequently synonymous with realism as the dominant "new" mode of representing experience in plays and novels. As a way of thinking about contemporary experience, modernism was also embraced by other styles of artistic expression. In drama, the symbolists departed from observing and recording outward appearance. They attempted to show the deeper contradictions of life's subjectivity and mystery by emphasizing symbols, myths, and moods. Of the French symbolist dramatists, Maurice Maeterlinck (1862–1949) was perhaps the best known. In *The Intruder* and *The Blind*, written in 1890, Maeterlinck argued that *silences* evoked the mystery and pain of existence often obscured by the hurly-burly of nineteenth-century life.

At the turn of the century, especially in Germany, expressionism reaffirmed the modernist view by portraying the disharmony between inner truth and external reality. The expressionists demonstrated the gap between social and political conditions, which mechanized and distorted human experience, and denied humanity any hope of happiness and contentment. Published in 1912, *The Beggar* by Reinhard Johannes Sorge (1892–1916) is considered the first expressionist play. It shows the struggles between old conventions and new values in the efforts of a visionary poet to achieve fulfillment in a materialistic and insensitive society.

In summary, modernist writers in the late nineteenth and early twentieth century set about to describe the chasm between past and present which resulted in people becoming alienated from their surroundings, from others, and from themselves. The chief paradigm was the dissolution of those connections between a sense of personal worth and the facts of experience. In the instance of *Hedda Gabler*, Henrik Ibsen perceived no reconciliation between Hedda's psychic tendency to dissolution and the social structures that limited her life and determined her circumstances. With the past as the chief villain responsible for the contradictions and ills of modern life, human alienation from self, others, and society emerges in the 1890s as a recurrent theme in modern literature.

Since modernism as a mode of understanding essentially emerges in the drama with realism as a new writing and performance style, the next chapter considers "modern realism"—its subjects and methods.

NOTES

1. *Ibsen Letters and Speeches,* ed. Evert Sprinchorn (New York: Hill and Wang, 1964): 297.
2. Joseph Wood Krutch, *"Modernism" in Modern Drama: A Definition and an Estimate* (Ithaca, NY: Cornell University Press, 1953): vii–ix.
3. Peter Szondi, *Theory of Modern Drama,* trans. Michael Hays (Minneapolis: University of Minnesota Press, 1987): viii.
4. Szondi 7.
5. Helen Sheehy, *Eva Le Gallienne: A Biography* (New York: Alfred A. Knopf, 1996): 172.
6. Ben Brantley, "An Unhappy Monster Made Human: The Frustrated Trophy Wife," *The New York Times* (October 5, 2001): E1, E4.

CHAPTER 10

UNDERSTANDING MODERN REALISM

James Earl Jones as Troy Maxson in *Fences* by August Wilson, directed by Lloyd Richards, Yale Repertory Theatre, New Haven, CT, 1987. (Photo by William Carter, courtesy of Yale Repertory Theatre.)

The time has come to produce plays of reality.
—Emile Zola[1]

OBSERVATIONS OF THE ORDINARY

As the image of truth verified by observing ordinary life, *realism* has been a principal style of writing and performance since the 1860s. It continues to be the representational style of choice for stage, film, and television, especially in the Broadway theater as the plays of Arthur Miller, Neil Simon, Marsha Norman, Athol Fugard, David Mamet, and August Wilson demonstrate.

Realism as a social philosophy and artistic style developed in the European theater about 1860, influenced by philosophers, naturalists, and scientists. As a revolt against writing and theater conventions of the past, especially the excesses of romantic character and situation, realism demanded that playwrights, through direct observation of the world around them, depict that world truthfully, or, as Eric Bentley wrote, give a "candid presentation of the natural world."[2] The "real" meant essentially the impersonal and objective observation of the physical world and direct scrutiny of *contemporary* life and manners. The realists focused on the observed, material world around them and on contemporary social issues.

French philosopher Auguste Comte (1798–1857), English naturalist Charles Darwin (1809–1882), and French author Emile Zola (1840–1902) were major influences on the theater of realism which depended on the "new dramatic text" for its materials and performance style. Comte argued that the key to understanding the world around us was careful observation and even experimentation to reveal causes and effects behind all events. He advocated the rigorous application of scientific methods to predict human behavior and to control society. Darwin's *The Origin of Species* (1859) examined our common ancestry and explained the evolution of species by way of "the survival of the fittest," that is, the strong versus the weak. Zola called for artists to emulate scientists both in searching out subjects and in examining them without prejudice with the aim of transferring observed reality to the stage as faithfully as possible.

Responding to the new intellectual currents, realistic playwrights emphasized details of contemporary life based on the five senses of sight, hearing, taste, smell, and touch, and brought a new kind of recognizable truth to the stage by introducing subjects and characters not previously considered acceptable, especially for tragedy. The new realism shocked audiences and created controversy by presenting such subjects as prostitution, poverty, ignorance, disease, judicial inequities, and adverse industrial conditions. The most influential playwrights in the nineteenth century who adopted the realistic mode were Henrik Ibsen, August Strindberg, George Bernard Shaw, and Anton Chekhov.

As an offshoot of the new realism, writers such as Zola, Ibsen, and Strindberg also fostered a secondary movement in the 1880s called *naturalism.* The naturalists focused more specifically on powerful forces governing human lives, especially on the twin factors of heredity and environment. Naturalism centered on the study and dissection of observable behavior along with heredity and environment as chief influences on human behavior. Heredity and environment replaced classical fate in the drama as factors determining human destiny. In this view, no individual is fully responsible for his or her actions. Rather, *genetics* and *society* assume the chief blame for criminal acts, neuroses, poverty, ignorance, injustice, illness, and prejudice. Obviously, then, scientific advances and social-educational reforms were looked upon as the hope for changing individuals and for reforming society. Sometimes it is difficult to separate the dramatic biases of realistic and naturalistic writers of this period. Playwrights like Ibsen and Strindberg fall into both camps. However, the causal factors of heredity and environment have long been the chief means of identifying the naturalistic play.

THE "NEW" DRAMATIC TEXT

Realism and naturalism, which paralleled realistic writing for twenty years (from 1870 to 1890), were closely linked as styles for effecting truthful, empirical depictions of life on stage. The movement away from the artificiality of romantic plot and character toward a drama of inner and outer truth is by and large the story of modern playwriting (and performance styles). Such playwrights as Henrik Ibsen used the conventions of the well-made play with its compressed structure, family secrets, and end-of-act crises as a vehicle to present the new subjects and characters. Ibsen's plays of social realism—*The Pillars of Society, An Enemy of the People, A Doll's House, Ghosts, Rosmersholm,* and *The Wild Duck*—established many tenets of new writing for the stage. First, the new subjects dealt with corrupt business practices, social repression, exploitation, inherited disease, neurotic behavior, conditioned mores, and outdated beliefs. Second, the new subjects spawned a new kind of tragedy and tragic hero. Modern tragedy engages heredity (the past in the present) and environment (the present) as shapers of conflict, choice, and destiny. Joseph Wood Krutch, writing in *"Modernism" in Modern Drama,* suggested that, in the new view, humanity becomes less a creature of reason than the victim of obsessions, fixations, delusions, and perversions.[3] Ibsen's heroes are victims of a past that haunts the present in the shape of conflicts between individuals and a repressive society. In *Ghosts,* written in 1881, the debilitating "ghosts" are both literal and figurative. The Alving son, Oswald, is terminally ill with a syphilitic disease inherited from his father; in appearance, he "looks like" his father and he exhibits his father's tastes for liquor and sex. In addition, inherited spiritual and social ideals impact on Mrs. Alving, the modern realistic heroine. Although a woman of courage, intelligence, and business acumen, she succumbs under pressure to an outworn system of social convention and respectability represented by the local minister. When her progressive ideals and enlightened views come into conflict with her conditioned emotional life, she is doomed to repeat the mistakes of the past. Just as Oswald has no control over the disease that consumes him, so, too, Mrs. Alving has no control over her spiritual and social inheritance. In his preface to *Miss Julie,* written in 1888, August Strindberg described the new tragic hero for the modern age:

> *Miss Julie is a modern character…a relic of the old warrior nobility now giving way to the new nobility of nerve and brain. She is a victim of the discord which a mother's "crime" has produced in a family, a victim too of the day's complaisance, of circumstances, of her own defective constitution, all of which are equivalent to the Fate or Universal Law of former days.*[4]

The "new" tragic character is reduced in social class, personal ambitions, and universal influence. Ibsen's middle-class heroes and Strindberg's neurotic aristocrats inhabit drawing rooms and servants' quarters. They struggle tragically with commonplace urges for equality, fulfillment, identity, and dignity. In recognizable and familiar ways, they fail to overcome society's strictures along with their inherited physical, spiritual, and psychological conditioning.

In the new realistic text, *dialogue* approximates everyday conversation, dispensing with verse, soliloquies, and asides. In addition, the text's signs and symbols are taken directly from the play's environment. Mrs. Alving and Oswald are visible symbols of the ghosts that pervade the play's action—victims of heredity and environment, which are forces over which they can exercise little, if any, control. Light, a timeless literary symbol for truth and understanding, takes its source in the realistic style from the physical world: sunlight through open windows or illumination from table lamps or fireplaces. In *Ghosts,* the burning orphanage built with her husband's tainted money brings truth into the Alving home by forcing Mrs. Alving to reveal her husband's promiscuity—the source of Oswald's disease. With his total collapse at the play's end, Oswald calls for the "sun." But the sunrise (truth) has come too late into this home to avoid the total collapse of the Alving world.

THE PHOTOGRAPHIC LANDSCAPES

Since environment played such a dominant role in subject matter and characters' lives in the new realism and naturalism, writers and directors made special efforts to bring accurate details into the play's physical world—living areas, clothing, furniture, decor, and light sources. As early as 1882, Ibsen insisted in a letter to the Norwegian director of *An Enemy of the People* that the staging should reflect, above all, "truthfulness to nature—the illusion that everything is real and that one is sitting and watching something that is actually taking place in real life."[5] Like other writers of the period, Ibsen's photographic sensibilities are to be found in the characters' behavior and in the detailed stage directions that describe the dramatic landscape as the "illusion of the real." The new writers brought the physical quality of real living conditions into the theater. They demanded real rooms with transparent fourth walls, and actors dressed and moving in believable fashion among familiar furnishings and using authentic properties. The illusion of the real in writing and staging practices resulted in pictorial illusion being one of the modern theater's chief stylistic characteristics.

NATURALISM'S "CASE STUDIES"

Emile Zola fathered naturalistic writing as an outgrowth of the realistic movement by advocating scientific methods as the key to all truth, social progress, and artistic endeavors. As envisioned by Zola, the new dramatic writing would illustrate the "inevitable laws of heredity and environment" and record "case studies." He urged dramatists of the new creed to observe, record, and experiment with the same detachment as scientists. Like the doctor who seeks the causes of disease, the dramatist in Zola's mandate must likewise seek out social ills (no matter how unpleasant) and examine them so that they might be corrected. The writer's task was to promote truth and experimental knowledge; the stage was also to become a replica of the real world. Zola explained that scientific methods of inquiry and analysis were to be models for the naturalists in their "research" into behavioral causes and effects. Zola further said, "[The movement] has sent us back to the study of documents, to experience, made us realize that to start anew we must take things back to the beginning, become familiar with man and nature, verify what is...."[6]

Zola's statements on naturalism are to be found in his preface to the dramatization of his novel *Thérèse Raquin* (1873), *Naturalism in the Theater* (1881), and *The Experimental Novel* (1881). Some of Zola's followers argued that a play should be a "slice of life" (like a specimen under a microscope) transferred to the stage. In their zeal to approximate scientific truth, the naturalists eventually doomed the movement because they ignored the subjectivity of artistic temperament and attempted to obliterate distinctions between art and life.

However, the naturalistic plays, written by Henrik Ibsen, August Strindberg, Henri Becque, Leo Tolstoy, and Eugène Brieux, spawned a group of directors who responded to the new staging demands. In Paris, André Antoine founded the Théâtre Libre (the "Free Theater") in 1887 and evolved production techniques for staging the new plays in environments with real furniture (borrowed from his mother's living room), clothes, rooms, and an acting style that virtually ignored the audience. The "natural" behavior of Antoine's actors complemented the new subjects, characters, and unpleasant case histories. Becque's *The Vultures* (1882) shows the fleecing of a family of women by their supposed business advisors after their father's death. Brieux's *Damaged Goods* (1902), like Ibsen's *Ghosts*, concerns syphilis and its transmission to a child, but Brieux's play attacks a society that does not legitimize birth control.

The new dramaturgy demanded new directors. Antoine was soon followed by directors in Germany, England, and Russia who staged the new plays in meticulous and graphic ways, creating acting ensembles and new scenic artists capable of replicating "real" behavior, speech, and environments.

The extremes of naturalistic writing whose subjects were often too sordid to arouse society's broad social conscience were soon reabsorbed into the more universal writing of the realists that embraced a broader landscape of characters, subjects, activities, and milieus without losing sight of the demands for careful observation of inner and outer behavior.

THE WELL-MADE PLAY

Plays have been "well made" for centuries. Sophocles wrote the play most admired by Aristotle and later generations for its perfection of taut construction and moral lesson. That play was *Oedipus the King.* The term *well-made play* (in French, *pièce bien faite*) has fallen into disrepute so much so that Lillian Hellman found it necessary to defend her playwriting against the charge of being "too well-made." She said, "The charge of too well-made I suppose means too neat, too well-put together. It's basically I think a rather foolish charge against anybody, because what is too well-made? Why should something be badly made?"[7]

Defined by modern critics as a play that adheres to an ingenious, commercially successful pattern of construction, the well-made play usually contains a dash of social thesis or moral lesson. In our time the term has become synonymous with the play that amuses but says nothing.

To dismiss the well-made play in this manner is perhaps an unjust indictment of the well-constructed play and those modern playwrights who have written them: Henrik Ibsen, George Bernard Shaw, Oscar Wilde, Lillian Hellman, Arthur Miller, Neil Simon, and so many more.

The father of the well-made play, Augustin-Eugène Scribe (1791–1861), wrote some 374 works for the Paris commercial theater and for French opera as well. Scribe defended the theater as a place of entertainment rather than a classroom or lecture hall. "You go to the theater for relaxation and amusement," he said, "not for instruction or correction. Now what most amuses you is not truth but fiction...."[8] Scribe distilled his well-made pattern of play construction from classical Greek plays, especially those of Sophocles. Some of the best French writers in the mid- to late nineteenth century, including Alexandre Dumas *fils,* Emile Augier, and Victorien Sardou, endowed Scribe's technical methods with social import, thus creating the social problem play (the *pièce à these*) which became a staple of European and American dramatic writing after 1850. The reason such writers as George Bernard Shaw, Oscar Wilde, Arthur Wing Pinero, and other socially minded dramatists adopted Scribe's techniques was that he had perfected mechanical yet tricky and theatrically satisfying methods of dealing with social and moral themes so as to make them seem amusing to a jaded and uncaring society. The best playwrights turned the well-made play to their own uses. Out of this remolding of Scribean stage devices emerged Wilde's *Lady Windermere's Fan* (1892), Pinero's *The Second Mrs. Tanqueray* (1892), and Shaw's *Mrs. Warren's Profession* (1893) and *Candida* (1897).

The most significant dramas of the late nineteenth and early twentieth centuries in France, England, and America were born out of the union of a specific and amusing technical form—the *pièce bien faite* perfected for the commercial theater by Eugène Scribe—with serious social or psychological subject matter perfected by Henrik Ibsen.

The characteristics of the well-made play are essentially nine in number and emphasize tight plotting with reversals, secrets, misunderstandings, contrived exits and entrances, and climactic events occurring only moments before the curtain comes down. Scribe's plot, like Sophocles' in *Oedipus the King,* was based on (1) a *secret* known to the audience but withheld from certain characters. The revealing of the secret in a climactic scene serves to unmask a fraudulent character or harmful condition and to restore to good fortune the suffering hero, with whom the audience sympathizes. The (2) *plot* develops a pattern of increasingly intense action and suspense prepared by exposition and enhanced by contrived entrances and exits (the unexpected visitor, for example), ominous letters, or other devices. A (3) *misunderstanding* develops among the characters. The central figure or hero experiences (4) a *series of ups and downs* in his or her fortunes, caused by a conflict with an able adversary. These events are followed by a severe and seemingly irreversible (5) *change in fortune* for the worst (called a reversal or *peripeteia*). This ebb in the hero's fortunes is followed by (6) an *obligatory scene* (or *scène à faire*) in which secrets are disclosed and misunderstandings cleared up. A logical and credible (7) denouement or *resolution* occurs in which all is satisfactorily explained.

In the well-made pattern of playwriting (8) the *play's acts* repeat the overall pattern of action so that the three or more acts repeat the shape of the entire play. Each act builds to its own (9) *climax* so that the curtain falls on the highest emotional moment of the act (the *coup de théâtre*) in which a withheld truth that contains a moral judgment is disclosed. This judgment need not necessarily be profound and in Scribe's plays it was often frankly trivial, but at least a moral dimension to the story was specified.

Eugène Scribe invented nothing. If we look closely at the episodes of *Oedipus the King*, we find the secret withheld, misunderstandings, reversals of fortune on a lesser scale for Teiresias, Creon, Jocasta, and finally in a major key for Oedipus himself. Unlike Sophocles' writing, the Scribean formula fails as great drama because the complex emotional life of the characters is always subordinate to the exigencies of plot and to external devices, such as misplaced letters. It must be admitted that pasteboard characters occasionally assume the color and conviction of life, and the artificial bravura of many roles appears emotionally convincing when the roles are interpreted by great actors.

Scribe's influence on world drama was in his technical methods. Even before 1830, Scribean drama had become an industry translated and imported to England and Norway. Henrik Ibsen, a young apprentice at the theater in Bergen between 1851 and 1856, directed some twenty-one plays by Scribe for that theater. He experimented with Scribe's methods in his early plays, written in the 1850s, and little by little transformed the Scribean formula. By opening his plays in mid-story and gradually revealing past and present events simultaneously in retrospective dialogue while propelling the narrative to an inevitable crisis, Ibsen greatly improved Scribe's static first act. He reserved the obligatory scene for his iconoclastic disclosures. In *A Doll's House* (1878), the sham of Nora Helmer's marriage is suddenly revealed to her. In *Ghosts* (1881), the depravity and hypocrisy of a son's upbringing and a mother's life are exposed beneath a lacquer of middle-class respectability.

Ibsen was to influence a long line of dramatists, including George Bernard Shaw, Lillian Hellman, and Arthur Miller. Borrowing Scribe's theatrical tricks and Ibsen's complex revelations of turbulent middle-class lives existing beneath surfaces of respectability, they created new and provocative examples of dramatic art.

The well-made play became the realistic frame in which later playwrights fit their social and psychological insights into contemporary life. August Wilson's *Fences* is an example of the continuing importance of finely tuned realistic writing for the contemporary American stage.

Fences

AUGUST WILSON

August Wilson (1945–), born Frederick August Kittel in Pittsburgh, has had seven plays produced on Broadway: Ma Rainey's Black Bottom *(1984 and 2003),* Fences *(1985),* Joe Turner's Come and Gone *(1986),* The Piano Lesson *(1988),* Two Trains Running *(1990),* Seven Guitars *(1995),* King Hedley II *(2000) and* Gem of the Ocean *(2003). His first play,* Jitney, *was written in 1979 and was followed by* Fullerton Street.

At nineteen Wilson left home to become a writer; he supported himself as a cook and stock clerk; in his spare time he read voraciously in the public library. Writing became a means for him to respond to changing race relations in America and to the violence erupting within the African-American community. In 1968, under his penname August Wilson, he co-founded Pittsburgh's Black Horizons Theater and secured a production of his first play, Black Bart and the Sacred Hills, *in St. Paul, Minnesota. In St. Paul, Wilson was hired as a scriptwriter for the Science Museum of Minnesota, which had a theater company attached to it. In 1981, after several rejections of other scripts, a draft of* Ma Rainey's Black Bottom *was accepted by The Eugene O'Neill Theater Center's National Playwrights Conference in Waterford, Connecticut, and Wilson's career was launched.*

Wilson developed a national reputation as a playwright and an association with directors Lloyd Richards and Marion McClinton who have since staged the premieres of his major plays. Both Fences *and* The Piano Lesson *have won Pulitzer Prizes for drama.*

Wilson's major plays, set in different decades of twentieth-century America, are a series in progress. He is writing a history of African Americans, probing what he perceives to be the crucial opposition in that culture between those who celebrate black America's African roots and those who deny that historical

reality. Fences, *which won the 1987 Pulitzer Prize, examines the nature and dynamics of this heritage within the framework of realistic dramaturgy.*

CRITICAL INTRODUCTION TO *FENCES*

August Wilson writes in the realistic tradition influenced by Arthur Miller, Lorraine Hansberry, and others in the modern American theater. In *Fences*, Wilson uses the well-made play model to examine the inheritance of patriarchy in the father-son conflict between fifty-three-year-old Troy Maxson and his teenage son, Cory. The conflict in this urban African-American family develops step by step to a crisis that hinges on the disclosure of crucial and traumatic incidents in the father's past and then in his present. The first act climaxes in Troy's revelation of events crucial to the shaping of his life: his break with his father, the murder that put him in a penitentiary for fifteen years, and the subsequent loss of his dream to become a professional baseball player. The second act ends with Cory, now a Marine sergeant, reconciled to the shadow of his father, now dead. As Cory's mother, Rose, explains: "That shadow wasn't nothing but you growing into yourself. You either got to grow into it or cut it down to fit you. But that's all you got to make life with. That's all you got to measure yourself against that world out there" (2.5). Rose speaks for the ironic persistence of the past in the present: "Your daddy wanted you to be everything he wasn't…and at the same time he tried to make you into everything he was" (2.5).

Wilson's central character is both victim and victimizer. Troy Maxson is victim to oppressive systems. He is victimized by his birth, his race, his father, his poverty, his employer, his society, and by his intellectual and emotional limitations. As victimizer, he takes advantage of his brother, Gabriel, whose war injuries have reduced him to a mental defective with a "metal plate" in his head. Troy bought the family house with Gabriel's army check, though Gabriel is permitted to live with them whenever he chooses. In his relationship with his son, Troy repeats his earlier experience with his own father. He also allows Cory no freedom to grow or to express his individuality. Troy loves his wife, but asserts his own freedom in a relationship with another woman after eighteen years of stultifying as a "good husband." He justifies himself to Rose: "It's not easy for me to admit that I been standing in the same place for eighteen years" (2.1). Rose answers, "I gave eighteen years of my life to stand in the same spot with you…What about my life?" (2.1). Wilson uses Troy Maxson's ambiguous moral status to question the mechanics of patriarchy and to universalize both central character and theme.

As we have seen, the well-made play generates theatrical crises. In *Fences*, Troy refuses to sign the recruitment form for his son to play college football because of his own failed struggle as a black to become a baseball player; he confesses his adultery to Rose and tells her of his child to be born to another woman; Cory attacks his father for physically abusing his mother; and Gabriel performs a ritual dance in anticipation of Troy's funeral at the play's end. The strange, mad dance, accompanied by Gabriel's howling sounds, is eerie but life-affirming. As he finishes, the stage directions suggest that "the gates of heaven stand open as wide as God's closet" (2.5). The family's love, forgiveness, and understanding of Troy Maxson find their cultural symbolism in Gabriel's atavistic ritual.

Fences is set respectively in 1957 and in 1965 in an African-American urban neighborhood. The action takes place on the front porch and in the yard of an "ancient two-story brick house set back in a small alley." The small dirt yard (which is fenced in as the play progresses) has a single tree from which hangs a homemade baseball of rags. Troy's baseball bat leans against the tree. This is the play's highly realistic environment where family and friends come and go, take their meals, experience their crises, and generally live out their unspectacular, though emotion-filled, lives. However, the play's centerpiece is the normal generational conflict between father and son. Wilson views *Fences* as a recycling of Troy's relationship with his father in his treatment of Cory. "I was trying to get at why Troy made the choices he made," Wilson said in an interview, "how they have influenced his values and how he attempts to pass those along to his son." He continued:

> *Each generation gives the succeeding generation what they think they need. One question in the play is, "Are the tools we are given sufficient to compete in a world that is different from the one our parents knew?" I think they are—it's just that we have to do different things with the tools…. Troy's flaw is that he does not recognize that the world was changing.*[9]

Writing in a realistic tradition, Wilson converts the yard "fence" into the play's controlling metaphor. The fence is *tangible* ("real" wood for the fence is sawed and hammered), but it is also Wilson's metaphor for the cultural situation of African Americans in the late fifties. Every person in the play, with the exception of Raynell, is fenced in or out by personal and/or societal strictures. When asked why Rose wants to fence in the yard in the first place, Troy's friend, Bono, says: "Some people build fences to keep people out…and some people build fences to keep people in" (2.1). The Maxson family experiences both alternatives. Society has conspired to keep them out of the mainstream of American life. For instance, Troy and Bono are "refuse workers"; they are permitted to lift garbage but not to drive the union trucks that carry the refuse. At the play's end, all of the members of the Maxson family are fenced in: in a church (Rose), in a penitentiary (Rose's stepson), in a mental hospital (Gabriel), in the Marines (Cory). Troy's daughter, Raynell, is the only potentially free person, for the winds of social change are starting to blow in the new and turbulent decade of the 1960s.

As a realistic writer, Wilson also takes his secondary metaphors (baseball and food) from the lifelong interests and habits of Troy and

Rose. Not unlike Arthur Miller's Willie Loman in *Death of a Salesman* (1949), Troy lives on lost dreams, explaining his philosophy of life with baseball jargon—a language immediate and meaningful to his philosophy of existence. For example, he announces, "Death ain't nothing but a fastball on the outside corner." Troy says about his race, "…you born with two strikes on you before you come to the plate." And, he warns Cory at each point of conflict between them: "Don't you strike out. You living with a full count. Don't you strike out."

The texture and rhythms of Troy's language underscore the uniqueness and dynamics of his character. From Rose's and Gabriel's associations with food, Wilson establishes the social organization of the Maxson family, and, by extension, African-American culture of the time.

As part of the ritual of living, food interests Wilson as a sign and symbol of the economic systems and cultural differences between black and white Americans. The family meals emanate from Rose's kitchen: chicken, biscuits, coffee, meatloaf, lima beans, and corn bread. Even the maimed Gabriel tries to be self-sufficient as he collects fruit and vegetables to sell. These small family rituals, like Troy's swinging at the rag baseball and Rose's predictable meals, illuminate the manners and life style of the urban African American in the late fifties. While the father-son conflict is a universal generational conflict, August Wilson portrays in *Fences* the daily rituals of African Americans to make a statement about black culture in America and its unique difference from white culture.

Fences

When the sins of our fathers visit us
We do not have to play host.
We can banish them with forgiveness
As God, in His Largeness and Laws.
— August Wilson

CHARACTERS

TROY MAXSON

JIM BONO   TROY's *friend*

ROSE   TROY's *wife*

LYONS   TROY's *oldest son by previous marriage*

GABRIEL   TROY's *brother*

CORY   TROY *and* ROSE's *son*

RAYNELL   TROY's *daughter*

THE PLAY

Near the turn of the century, the destitute of Europe sprang on the city with tenacious claws and an honest and solid dream. The city devoured them. They swelled its belly until it burst into a thousand furnaces and sewing machines, a thousand butcher shops and bakers' ovens, a thousand churches and hospitals and funeral parlors and moneylenders. The city grew. It nourished itself and offered each man a partnership limited only by his talent, his guile, and his willingness and capacity for hard work. For the immigrants of Europe, a dream dared and won true.

The descendants of African slaves were offered no such welcome or participation. They came from places called the Carolinas and the Virginias, Georgia, Alabama, Mississippi, and Tennessee. They came strong, eager, searching. The city rejected them and they fled and settled along the riverbanks and under bridges in shallow, ramshackle houses made of sticks and tar-paper. They collected rags and wood. They sold the use of their muscles and their bodies. They cleaned houses and washed clothes, they shined shoes, and in quiet desperation and vengeful pride, they stole, and lived in pursuit of their own dream. That
they could breathe free, finally, and stand to meet life with the force of dignity and whatever eloquence the heart could call upon.

By 1957, the hard-won victories of the European immigrants had solidified the industrial might of America. War had been confronted and won with new energies that used loyalty and patriotism as its fuel. Life was rich, full, and flourishing. The Milwaukee Braves won the World Series, and the hot winds of change that would make the sixties a turbulent, racing, dangerous, and provocative decade had not yet begun to blow full.

SETTING

The setting is the yard which fronts the only entrance to the MAXSON *household, an ancient two-story brick house set back off a small alley in a big-city neighborhood. The entrance to the house is gained by two or three steps leading to a wooden porch badly in need of paint.*

A relatively recent addition to the house and running its full width, the porch lacks congruence. It is a sturdy porch with a flat roof. One or two chairs of dubious value sit at one end where the kitchen window opens onto the porch. An old-fashioned icebox stands silent guard at the opposite end.

The yard is a small dirt yard, partially fenced, except for the last scene, with a wooden sawhorse, a pile of lumber, and other fence-building equipment set off to the side. Opposite is a tree from which hangs a ball made of rags. A baseball bat leans against the tree. Two oil drums serve as garbage receptacles and sit near the house at right to complete the setting.

ACT ONE

SCENE ONE

It is 1957. TROY *and* BONO *enter the yard, engaged in conversation.* TROY *is fifty-three years old, a large man with thick, heavy hands; it is this largeness that he strives to fill out and make an accommodation with. Together with his blackness, his largeness informs his sensibilities and the choices he has made in his life.*

Of the two men, BONO *is obviously the follower. His commitment to their friendship of thirty-odd years is rooted in his admiration of* TROY's *honesty, capacity for hard work, and his strength, which* BONO *seeks to emulate.*

It is Friday night, payday, and the one night of the week the two men engage in a ritual of talk and drink. TROY *is usually the most talkative and at times he can be crude and almost vulgar, though he is capable of rising to profound heights of expression. The men carry lunch buckets and wear or carry burlap aprons and are dressed in clothes suitable to their jobs as garbage collectors.*

BONO: Troy, you ought to stop that lying!

TROY: I ain't lying! The nigger had a watermelon this big.

> (*He indicates with his hands.*)

Talking about…"What watermelon, Mr. Rand?" I liked to fell out! "What watermelon, Mr. Rand?"…And it sitting there big as life.

BONO: What did Mr. Rand say?

TROY: Ain't said nothing. Figure if the nigger too dumb to know he carrying a watermelon, he wasn't gonna get much sense out of him. Trying to hide that great big old watermelon under his coat. Afraid to let the white man see him carry it home.

BONO: I'm like you…I ain't got no time for them kind of people.

TROY: Now what he look like getting mad cause he see the man from the union talking to Mr. Rand?

BONO: He come to me talking about…"Maxson gonna get us fired." I told him to get away from me with that. He walked away from me calling you a trouble-maker. What Mr. Rand say?

TROY: Ain't said nothing. He told me to go down the Commissioner's office next Friday. They called me down there to see them.

BONO: Well, as long as you got your complaint filed, they can't fire you. That's what one of them white fellows tell me.

TROY: I ain't worried about them firing me. They gonna fire me cause I asked a question? That's all I did. I went to Mr. Rand and asked him, "Why? Why you got the white mens driving and the colored lifting?" Told him, "what's the matter, don't I count? You think only white fellows got sense enough to drive a truck. That ain't no paper job! Hell, anybody can drive a truck. How come you got all whites driving and the colored lifting?" He told me "take it to the union." Well, hell, that's what I done! Now they wanna come up with this pack of lies.

BONO: I told Brownie if the man come and ask him any questions…just tell the truth! It ain't nothing but something they done trumped up on you cause you filed a complaint on them.

TROY: Brownie don't understand nothing. All I want them to do is change the job description. Give everybody a chance to drive the truck. Brownie can't see that. He ain't got that much sense.

BONO: How you figure he be making out with that gal be up at Taylors' all the time…that Alberta gal?

TROY: Same as you and me. Getting just as much as we is. Which is to say nothing.

BONO: It is, huh? I figure you doing a little better than me…and I ain't saying what I'm doing.

TROY: Aw, nigger, look here…I know you. If you had got anywhere near that gal, twenty minutes later you be looking to tell somebody. And the first one you gonna tell…that you gonna want to brag to…is gonna be me.

BONO: I ain't saying that. I see where you be eyeing her.

TROY: I eye all the women. I don't miss nothing. Don't never let nobody tell you Troy Maxson don't eye the women.

BONO: You been doing more than eyeing her. You done bought her a drink or two.

TROY: Hell yeah, I bought her a drink! What that mean? I bought you one, too. What that mean cause I buy her a drink? I'm just being polite.

BONO: It's alright to buy her one drink. That's what you call being polite. But when you wanna be buying two or three…that's what you call eyeing her.

TROY: Look here, as long as you known me… you ever known me to chase after women?

BONO: Hell yeah! Long as I done known you. You forgetting I knew you when.

TROY: Naw, I'm talking about since I been married to Rose.

BONO: Oh, not since you been married to Rose. Now, that's the truth, there. I can say that.

TROY: Alright then! Case closed.

BONO: I see you be walking up around Alberta's house. You supposed to be at Taylors' and you be walking up around there.

TROY: What you watching where I'm walking for? I ain't watching after you.

BONO: I seen you walking around there more than once.

TROY: Hell, you liable to see me walking anywhere! That don't mean nothing cause you see me walking around there.

BONO: Where she come from anyway? She just kinda showed up one day.

TROY: Tallahassee. You can look at her and tell she one of them Florida gals. They got some big healthy women down there. Grow them right up out the ground. Got a little bit of Indian in her. Most of them niggers down in Florida got some Indian in them.

BONO: I don't know about that Indian part. But she damn sure big and healthy. Woman wear some big stockings. Got them great big old legs and hips as wide as the Mississippi River.

TROY: Legs don't mean nothing. You don't do nothing but push them out of the way. But them hips cushion the ride!

BONO: Troy, you ain't got no sense.

TROY: It's the truth! Like you riding on Goodyears!

ROSE *enters from the house. She is ten years younger than* TROY, *her devotion to him stems from her recognition of the possibilities of her life without him: a succession of abusive men and their babies, a life of partying and running the streets, the Church, or aloneness with its attendant pain and frustration. She recognizes* TROY's *spirit as a fine and illuminating one and she either ignores or forgives his faults, only some of which she recognizes. Though she doesn't drink, her presence is an integral part of the Friday night rituals. She alternates between the porch and the kitchen, where supper preparations are under way.*

ROSE: What you all out here getting into?

TROY: What you worried about what we getting into for? This is men talk, woman.

ROSE: What I care what you all talking about? Bono, you gonna stay for supper?

BONO: No, I thank you, Rose. But Lucille say she cooking up a pot of pigfeet.

TROY: Pigfeet! Hell, I'm going home with you! Might even stay the night if you got some pigfeet. You got something in there to top them pigfeet, Rose?

ROSE: I'm cooking up some chicken. I got some chicken and collard greens.

TROY: Well, go on back in the house and let me and Bono finish what we was talking about. This is men talk. I got some talk for you later. You know what kind of talk I mean. You go on and powder it up.

ROSE: Troy Maxson, don't you start that now!

TROY: (*Puts his arm around her.*) Aw, woman… come here. Look here, Bono…when I met this woman…I got out that place, say, "Hitch up my pony, saddle up my mare… there's a woman out there for me somewhere. I looked here. Looked there. Saw Rose and latched on to her." I latched on to her and told her—I'm gonna tell you the truth—I told her, "Baby, I don't wanna marry, I just wanna be your man." Rose told me…tell him what you told me, Rose.

ROSE: I told him if he wasn't the marrying kind, then move out the way so the marrying kind could find me.

TROY: That's what she told me. "Nigger, you in my way. You blocking the view! Move out the way so I can find me a husband." I thought it over two or three days. Come back—

ROSE: Ain't no two or three days nothing. You was back the same night.

TROY: Come back, told her…"Okay, baby…but I'm gonna buy me a banty rooster and put him out there in the backyard…and when he see a stranger come, he'll flap his wings and crow…" Look here, Bono, I could watch the front door by myself…it was that back door I was worried about.

ROSE: Troy, you ought not talk like that. Troy ain't doing nothing but telling a lie.

TROY: Only thing is…when we first got married…forget the rooster…we ain't had no yard!

BONO: I hear you tell it. Me and Lucille was staying down there on Logan Street. Had two rooms with the outhouse in the back. I ain't mind the outhouse none. But when that goddamn wind blow through there in the winter…that's what I'm talking about! To this day I wonder why in the hell I ever stayed down there for six long years. But see, I didn't know I could do no better. I thought only white folks had inside toilets and things.

ROSE: There's a lot of people don't know they can do no better than they doing now. That's just something you got to learn. A lot of folks still shop at Bella's.

TROY: Ain't nothing wrong with shopping at Bella's. She got fresh food.

ROSE: I ain't said nothing about if she got fresh food. I'm talking about what she charge. She charge ten cents more than the A&P.

TROY: The A&P ain't never done nothing for me. I spends my money where I'm treated right. I go down to Bella, say, "I need a loaf of bread, I'll pay you Friday." She give it to me. What sense that make when I got money to go and spend it somewhere else and ignore the person who done right by me? That ain't in the Bible.

ROSE: We ain't talking about what's in the Bible. What sense it make to shop there when she overcharge?

TROY: You shop where you want to. I'll do my shopping where the people been good to me.

ROSE: Well, I don't think it's right for her to overcharge. That's all I was saying.

BONO: Look here…I got to get on. Lucille going to be raising all kind of hell.

TROY: Where you going, nigger? We ain't finished this pint. Come here, finish this pint.

BONO: Well, hell, I am…if you ever turn the bottle loose.

TROY: (Hands him the bottle.) The only thing I say about the A&P is I'm glad Cory got that job down there. Help him take care of his school clothes and things. Gabe done moved out and things getting tight around here. He got that job…. He can start to look out for himself.

ROSE: Cory done went and got recruited by a college football team.

TROY: I told that boy about that football stuff. The white man ain't gonna let him get nowhere with that football. I told him when he first come to me with it. Now you come telling me he done went and got more tied up in it. He ought to go and get recruited in how to fix cars or something where he can make a living.

ROSE: He ain't talking about making no living playing football. It's just something the boys in school do. They gonna send a recruiter by to talk to you. He'll tell you he ain't talking about making no living playing football. It's a honor to be recruited.

TROY: It ain't gonna get him nowhere. Bono'll tell you that.

BONO: If he be like you in the sports…he's gonna be alright. Ain't but two men ever played baseball as good as you. That's Babe Ruth and Josh Gibson. Them's the only two men ever hit more home runs than you.

TROY: What it ever get me? Ain't got a pot to piss in or a window to throw it out of.

ROSE: Times have changed since you was playing baseball, Troy. That was before the war. Times have changed a lot since then.

TROY: How in hell they done changed?

ROSE: They got lots of colored boys playing ball now. Baseball and football.

BONO: You right about that, Rose. Times have changed, Troy. You just come along too early.

TROY: There ought not never have been no time called too early! Now you take that fellow…what's that fellow they had playing right field for the Yankees back then? You know who I'm talking about, Bono. Used to play right field for the Yankees.

ROSE: Selkirk?

TROY: Selkirk! That's it! Man batting .269, understand? .269. What kind of sense that make? I was hitting .432 with thirty-seven home runs! Man batting .269 and playing right field for the Yankees! I saw Josh Gibson's daughter yesterday. She walking around with raggedy shoes on her feet. Now I bet you Selkirk's daughter ain't walking around with raggedy shoes on her feet! I bet you that!

ROSE: They got a lot of colored baseball players now. Jackie Robinson was the first. Folks had to wait for Jackie Robinson.

TROY: I done seen a hundred niggers play baseball better than Jackie Robinson. Hell, I know some teams Jackie Robinson couldn't even make! What you talking about Jackie Robinson. Jackie Robinson wasn't nobody. I'm talking about if you could play ball then they ought to have let you play. Don't care what color you were. Come telling me I come along too early. If you could play… then they ought to have let you play.

TROY *takes a long drink from the bottle.*

ROSE: You gonna drink yourself to death. You don't need to be drinking like that.

TROY: Death ain't nothing. I done seen him. Done wrassled with him. You can't tell me nothing about death. Death ain't nothing but a fastball on the outside corner. And you know what I'll do to that! Lookee here, Bono…am I lying? You get one of them fastballs, about waist high, over the outside corner of the plate where you can get the meat of the bat on it…and good god! You can kiss it goodbye. Now, am I lying?

BONO: Naw, you telling the truth there. I seen you do it.

TROY: If I'm lying…that 450 feet worth of lying! *Pause.*

That's all death is to me. A fastball on the outside corner.

ROSE: I don't know why you want to get on talking about death.

TROY: Ain't nothing wrong with talking about death. That's part of life. Everybody gonna die. You gonna die, I'm gonna die. Bono's gonna die. Hell, we all gonna die.

ROSE: But you ain't got to talk about it. I don't like to talk about it.

TROY: You the one brought it up. Me and Bono was talking about baseball…you tell me I'm gonna drink myself to death. Ain't that right, Bono? You know I don't drink this but one night out of the week. That's Friday night. I'm gonna drink just enough to where I can handle it. Then I cuts it loose. I leave it alone. So don't you worry about me drinking myself to death. 'Cause I ain't worried about Death. I done seen him. I drone wrestled with him.

Look here, Bono…I looked up one day and Death was marching straight at me. Like Soldiers on Parade! The Army of Death was marching straight at me. The middle of July, 1941. It got real cold just like it be winter. It seem like Death himself reached out and touched me on the shoulder. He touch me just like I touch you. I got cold as ice and Death standing there grinning at me.

ROSE: Troy, why don't you hush that talk.

TROY: I say…What you want, Mr. Death? You be wanting me? You done brought your army to be getting me? I looked him dead in the eye. I wasn't fearing nothing. I was ready to tangle. Just like I'm ready to tangle now. The Bible say be ever vigilant. That's why I don't get but so drunk. I got to keep watch.

ROSE: Troy was right down there in Mercy Hospital. You remember he had pneumonia? Laying there with a fever talking plumb out of his head.

TROY: Death standing there staring at me… carrying that sickle in his hand. Finally he say, "You want bound over for another year?" See, just like that…"You want bound over for another year?" I told him, "Bound over hell! Let's settle this now!"

It seem like he kinda fell back when I said that, and all the cold went out of me. I reached down and grabbed that sickle and threw it just as far as I could throw it…and me and him commenced to wrestling.

We wrestled for three days and three nights. I can't say where I found the strength from. Every time it seemed like he was gonna get the best of me, I'd reach way down deep inside myself and find the strength to do him one better.

ROSE: Every time Troy tell that story he find different ways to tell it. Different things to make up about it.

TROY: I ain't making up nothing. I'm telling you the facts of what happened. I wrestled with Death for three days and three nights and I'm standing here to tell you about it.

Pause.

Alright. At the end of the third night we done weakened each other to where we can't hardly move. Death stood up, throwed on his robe…had him a white robe with a hood on it. He throwed on that robe and went off to look for his sickle. Say, "I'll be back." Just like that. "I'll be back." I told him, say, "Yeah, but…you gonna have to find me!" I wasn't no fool. I wasn't going looking for him. Death ain't nothing to play with. And I know he's gonna get me. I know I got to join his army…his camp followers. But as long as I keep my strength and see him coming…as long as I keep up my vigilance …he's gonna have to fight to get me. I ain't going easy.

BONO: Well, look here, since you got to keep up your vigilance…let me have the bottle.

TROY: Aw hell, I shouldn't have told you that part. I should have left out that part.

ROSE: Troy be talking that stuff and half the time don't even know what he be talking about.

TROY: Bono know me better than that.

BONO: That's right. I know you. I know you got some Uncle Remus in your blood. You got more stories than the devil got sinners.

TROY: Aw hell, I done seen him too! Done talked with the devil.

ROSE: Troy, don't nobody wanna be hearing all that stuff.

LYONS *enters the yard from the street. Thirty-four years old,* TROY'S *son by a previous marriage, he sports a neatly trimmed goatee, sport coat, white shirt, tieless and buttoned at the collar. Though he fancies himself a musician, he is more caught up in the rituals and "idea" of being a musician than in the actual practice of the music. He has come to borrow money from* TROY, *and while he knows he will be successful, he is uncertain as to what extent his lifestyle will be held up to scrutiny and ridicule.*

LYONS: Hey, Pop.

TROY: What you come "Hey, Popping" me for?

LYONS: How you doing, Rose?

He kisses her.

Mr. Bono. How you doing?

BONO: Hey, Lyons…how you been?

TROY: He must have been doing alright. I ain't seen him around here last week.

ROSE: Troy, leave your boy alone. He come by to see you and you wanna start all that nonsense.

TROY: I ain't bothering Lyons.

Offers him the bottle.

Here…get you a drink. We got an understanding. I know why he come by to see me and he know I know.

LYONS: Come on, Pop…I just stopped by to say hi…see how you was doing.

TROY: You ain't stopped by yesterday.

ROSE: You gonna stay for supper, Lyons? I got some chicken cooking in the oven.

LYONS: No, Rose…thanks. I was just in the neighborhood and thought I'd stop by for a minute.

TROY: You was in the neighborhood alright, nigger. You telling the truth there. You was in the neighborhood cause it's my payday.

LYONS: Well, hell, since you mentioned it…let me have ten dollars.

TROY: I'll be damned! I'll die and go to hell and play blackjack with the devil before I give you ten dollars.

BONO: That's what I wanna know about…that devil you done seen.

LYONS: What…Pop done seen the devil? You too much, Pops.

TROY: Yeah, I done seen him. Talked to him too!

ROSE: You ain't seen no devil. I done told you that man ain't had nothing to do with the devil. Anything you can't understand, you want to call it the devil.

TROY: Look here, Bono…I went down to see Hertzberger about some furniture. Got three rooms for two-ninety-eight. That what it say on the radio. "Three rooms…two-ninety-eight." Even made up a little song about it. Go down there…man tell me I can't get no credit. I'm working every day and can't get no credit. What to do? I got an empty house with some raggedy furniture in it. Cory ain't got no bed. He's sleeping on a pile of rags on the floor. Working every day and can't get no credit. Come back here—Rose'll tell you—madder than hell. Sit down…try to figure what I'm gonna do. Come a knock on the door. Ain't been living here but three days. Who know I'm here? Open the door…devil standing there bigger than life. White fellow…got on good clothes and everything. Standing there with a clipboard in his hand. I ain't had to say nothing. First words come out of his mouth was…"I understand you need some furniture and can't get no credit." I liked to fell over. He say "I'll give you all the credit you want, but you got to pay the interest on it." I told him, "Give me three rooms worth and charge whatever you want." Next day a truck pulled up here and two men unloaded them three rooms. Man what drove the truck give me a book. Say send ten dollars, first of every month to the address in the book and everything will be alright. Say if I miss a payment the devil was coming back and it'll be hell to pay. That was fifteen years ago. To this day…the first of the month I send my ten dollars, Rose'll tell you.

ROSE: Troy lying.

TROY: I ain't never seen that man since. Now you tell me who else that could have been but the devil? I ain't sold my soul or nothing like that, you understand. Naw, I wouldn't have truck with the devil about nothing like that. I got my furniture and pays my ten dollars the first of the month just like clockwork.

BONO: How long you say you been paying this ten dollars a month?

TROY: Fifteen years!

BONO: Hell, ain't you finished paying for it yet? How much the man done charged you.

TROY: Aw hell, I done paid for it. I done paid for it ten times over! The fact is I'm scared to stop paying it.

ROSE: Troy lying. We got that furniture from Mr. Glickman. He ain't paying no ten dollars a month to nobody.

TROY: Aw hell, woman. Bono know I ain't that big a fool.

LYONS: I was just getting ready to say…I know where there's a bridge for sale.

TROY: Look here, I'll tell you this…it don't matter to me if he was the devil. It don't matter if the devil give credit. Somebody has got to give it.

ROSE: It ought to matter. You going around talking about having truck with the devil… God's the one you gonna have to answer to. He's the one gonna be at the Judgment.

LYONS: Yeah, well, look here, Pop…let me have that ten dollars. I'll give it back to you. Bonnie got a job working at the hospital.

TROY: What I tell you, Bono? The only time I see this nigger is when he wants something. That's the only time I see him.

LYONS: Come on, Pop, Mr. Bono don't want to hear all that. Let me have the ten dollars. I told you Bonnie working.

TROY: What that mean to me? "Bonnie working." I don't care if she working. Go ask her for the ten dollars if she working. Talking about "Bonnie working." Why ain't you working?

LYONS: Aw, Pop, you know I can't find no decent job. Where am I gonna get a job at? You know I can't get no job.

TROY: I told you I know some people down there. I can get you on the rubbish if you want to work. I told you that the last time you came by here asking me for something.

LYONS: Naw, Pop…thanks. That ain't for me. I don't wanna be carrying nobody's rubbish. I don't wanna be punching nobody's time clock.

TROY: What's the matter, you too good to carry people's rubbish? Where you think that ten dollars you talking about come from? I'm just supposed to haul people's rubbish and give my money to you cause you too lazy to work. You too lazy to work and wanna know why you ain't got what I got.

ROSE: What hospital Bonnie working at? Mercy?

LYONS: She's down at Passavant working in the laundry.

TROY: I ain't got nothing as it is. I give you that ten dollars and I got to eat beans the rest of the week. Naw…you ain't getting no ten dollars here.

LYONS: You ain't got to be eating no beans. I don't know why you wanna say that.

TROY: I ain't got no extra money. Gabe done moved over to Miss Pearl's paying her the rent and things done got tight around here. I can't afford to be giving you every payday.

LYONS: I ain't asked you to give me nothing. I asked you to loan me ten dollars. I know you got ten dollars.

TROY: Yeah, I got it. You know why I got it? Cause I don't throw my money away out there in the streets. You living the fast life… wanna be a musician…running around in them clubs and things…then, you learn to take care of yourself. You ain't gonna find me going and asking nobody for nothing. I done spent too many years without.

LYONS: You and me is two different people, Pop.

TROY: I done learned my mistake and learned to do what's right by it. You still trying to get something for nothing. Life don't owe you nothing. You owe it to yourself. Ask Bono. He'll tell you I'm right.

LYONS: You got your way of dealing with the world…I got mine. The only thing that matters to me is the music.

TROY: Yeah, I can see that! It don't matter how you gonna eat…where your next dollar is coming from. You telling the truth there.

LYONS: I know I got to eat. But I got to live too. I need something that gonna help me to get out of the bed in the morning. Make me feel like I belong in the world. I don't bother nobody. I just stay with my music cause that's the only way I can find to live in the world. Otherwise there ain't no telling what I might do. Now I don't come criticizing you and how you live. I just come by to ask you for ten dollars. I don't wanna hear all that about how I live.

TROY: Boy, your mama did a hell of a job raising you.

LYONS: You can't change me, Pop. I'm thirty-four years old. If you wanted to change me, you should have been there when I was growing up. I come by to see you…ask for ten dollars and you want to talk about how I was raised. You don't know nothing about how I was raised.

ROSE: Let the boy have ten dollars, Troy.

TROY: (*To* LYONS.) What the hell you looking at me for? I ain't got no ten dollars. You know what I do with my money.
(*To* ROSE.)
Give him ten dollars if you want him to have it.

ROSE: I will. Just as soon as you turn it loose.

TROY: (*Handing* ROSE *the money.*) There it is. Seventy-six dollars and forty-two cents. You see this, Bono? Now, I ain't gonna get but six of that back.

ROSE: You ought to stop telling that lie. Here, Lyons.
She hands him the money.

LYONS: Thanks, Rose. Look…I got to run…I'll see you later.

TROY: Wait a minute. You gonna say, "thanks, Rose" and ain't gonna look to see where she got that ten dollars from? See how they do me, Bono?

LYONS: I know she got it from you, Pop. Thanks. I'll give it back to you.

TROY: There he go telling another lie. Time I see that ten dollars…he'll be owing me thirty more.

LYONS: See you, Mr. Bono.

BONO: Take care, Lyons!

LYONS: Thanks, Pop. I'll see you again.

LYONS *exits the yard.*

TROY: I don't know why he don't go and get him a decent job and take care of that woman he got.

BONO: He'll be alright, Troy. The boy is still young.

TROY: The *boy* is thirty-four years old.

ROSE: Let's not get off into all that.

BONO: Look here…I got to be going. I got to be getting on. Lucille gonna be waiting.

TROY: (*Puts his arm around* ROSE.) See this woman, Bono? I love this woman. I love this woman so much it hurts. I love her so much…I done run out of ways of loving her. So I got to go back to basics. Don't you come by my house Monday morning talking about time to go to work…'cause I'm still gonna be stroking!

ROSE: Troy! Stop it now!

BONO: I ain't paying him no mind, Rose. That ain't nothing but gin-talk. Go on, Troy. I'll see you Monday.

TROY: Don't you come by my house, nigger! I done told you what I'm gonna be doing.

The lights go down to black.

SCENE TWO

The lights come up on ROSE *hanging up clothes. She hums and sings softly to herself. It is the following morning.*

ROSE: (*Sings*) Jesus, be a fence all around me every day

    Jesus, I want you to protect me as I travel on my way.

    Jesus, be a fence all around me every day.

TROY *enters from the house*

ROSE (*continued*): Jesus, I want you to protect me

    As I travel on my way.

To TROY.

'Morning. You ready for breakfast? I can fix it soon as I finish hanging up these clothes?

TROY: I got the coffee on. That'll be alright. I'll just drink some of that this morning.

ROSE: That 651 hit yesterday. That's the second time this month. Miss Pearl hit for a dollar …seem like those that need the least always get lucky. Poor folks can't get nothing.

TROY: Them numbers don't know nobody. I don't know why you fool with them. You and Lyons both.

ROSE: It's something to do.

TROY: You ain't doing nothing but throwing your money away.

ROSE: Troy, you know I don't play foolishly. I just play a nickel here and a nickel there.

TROY: That's two nickels you done thrown away.

ROSE: Now I hit sometimes…that makes up for it. It always comes in handy when I do hit. I don't hear you complaining then.

TROY: I ain't complaining now. I just say it's foolish. Trying to guess out of six hundred ways which way the number gonna come. If I had all the money niggers, these Negroes, throw away on numbers for one week—just one week—I'd be a rich man.

ROSE: Well, you wishing and calling it foolish ain't gonna stop folks from playing numbers. That's one thing for sure. Besides… some good things come from playing numbers. Look where Pope done bought him that restaurant off of numbers.

TROY: I can't stand niggers like that. Man ain't had two dimes to rub together. He walking around with his shoes all run over bumming money for cigarettes. Alright. Got lucky there and hit the numbers…

ROSE: Troy, I know all about it.

TROY: Had good sense, I'll say that for him. He ain't throwed his money away. I seen niggers hit the numbers and go through two thousand dollars in four days. Man bought him that restaurant down there…fixed it up real nice…and then didn't want nobody to come in it! A Negro go in there and can't get no kind of service. I seen a white fellow come in there and order a bowl of stew. Pope picked all the meat out the pot for him. Man ain't had nothing but a bowl of meat! Negro come behind him and ain't got nothing but the potatoes and carrots. Talking about what numbers do for people, you picked a wrong example. Ain't done nothing but make a worser fool out of him than he was before.

ROSE: Troy, you ought to stop worrying about what happened at work yesterday.

TROY: I ain't worried. Just told me to be down there at the Commissioner's office on Friday. Everybody think they gonna fire me. I ain't worried about them firing me. You ain't got to worry about that.

(*Pause.*)

Where's Cory? Cory in the house? (*Calls.*) Cory?

ROSE: He gone out.

TROY: Out, huh? He gone out 'cause he know I want him to help me with this fence. I know how he is. That boy scared of work.

GABRIEL *enters. He comes halfway down the alley and, hearing* TROY's *voice, stops.*

TROY (*continues*): He ain't done a lick of work in his life.

ROSE: He had to go to football practice. Coach wanted them to get in a little extra practice before the season start.

TROY: I got his practice…running out of here before he get his chores done.

ROSE: Troy, what is wrong with you this morning? Don't nothing set right with you. Go on back in there and go to bed…get up on the other side.

TROY: Why something got to be wrong with me? I ain't said nothing wrong with me.

ROSE: You got something to say about everything. First it's the numbers…then it's the way the man runs his restaurant…then you done got on Cory. What's it gonna be next? Take a look up there and see if the weather suits you…or is it gonna be how you gonna put up the fence with the clothes hanging in the yard.

TROY: You hit the nail on the head then.

ROSE: I know you like I know the back of my hand. Go on in there and get you some coffee…see if that straighten you up. 'Cause you ain't right this morning.

TROY *starts into the house and sees* GABRIEL. GABRIEL *starts singing.* TROY's *brother, he is seven years younger than* TROY. *Injured in* World War II, *he has a metal plate in his head. He carries an old trumpet tied around his waist and believes with every fiber of his being that he is the Archangel Gabriel. He carries a chipped basket with an assortment of discarded fruits and vegetables he has picked up in the strip district and which he attempts to sell.*

GABRIEL: (*Singing.*)

Yes, ma'am, I got plums
You ask me how I sell them
Oh ten cents apiece
Three for a quarter
Come and buy now
'Cause I'm here today
And tomorrow I'll be gone

GABRIEL *enters.*

Hey, Rose!

ROSE: How you doing, Gabe?

GABRIEL: There's Troy…Hey, Troy!

TROY: Hey, Gabe.

Exit into kitchen.

ROSE: (*To* GABRIEL.) What you got there?

GABRIEL: You know what I got, Rose. I got fruits and vegetables.

ROSE: (*Looking in basket.*) Where's all these plums you talking about?

GABRIEL: I ain't got no plums today, Rose. I was just singing that. Have some tomorrow. Put me in a big order for plums. Have enough plums tomorrow for St. Peter and everybody.

TROY *re-enters from kitchen, crosses to steps.*

To ROSE.

Troy's mad at me.

TROY: I ain't mad at you. What I got to be mad at you about? You ain't done nothing to me.

GABRIEL: I just moved over to Miss Pearl's to keep out from in your way. I ain't mean no harm by it.

TROY: Who said anything about that? I ain't said anything about that.

GABRIEL: You ain't mad at me, is you?

TROY: Naw…I ain't mad at you, Gabe. If I was mad at you I'd tell you about it.

GABRIEL: Got me two rooms. In the basement. Got my own door too. Wanna see my key?

He holds up a key.

That's my own key! Ain't nobody else got a key like that. That's my key! My two rooms!

TROY: Well, that's good, Gabe. You got your own key…that's good.

ROSE: You hungry, Gabe? I was just fixing to cook Troy his breakfast.

GABRIEL: I'll take some biscuits. You got some biscuits? Did you know when I was in heaven…every morning me and St. Peter would sit down by the gate and eat some big fat biscuits? Oh, yeah! We had us a good time. We'd sit there and eat us them biscuits and then St. Peter would go off to sleep and tell me to wake him up when it's time to open the gates for the judgment.

ROSE: Well, come on…I'll make up a batch of biscuits.

ROSE *exits into the house.*

GABRIEL: Troy…St. Peter got your name in the book. I seen it. It say…Troy Maxson. I say… I know him! He got the same name like what I got. That's my brother!

TROY: How many times you gonna tell me that, Gabe?

GABRIEL: Ain't got my name in the book. Don't have to have my name. I done died and went to heaven. He got your name though. One morning St. Peter was looking at his book…marking it up for the judgment… and he let me see your name. Got it in there under M. Got Rose's name…I ain't seen it like I seen yours…but I know it's in there. He got a great big book. Got everybody's name what was ever been born. That's what he told me. But I seen your name. Seen it with my own eyes.

TROY: Go on in the house there. Rose going to fix you something to eat.

GABRIEL: Oh, I ain't hungry. I done had breakfast with Aunt Jemimah. She come by and cooked me up a whole mess of flapjacks. Remember how we used to eat them flapjacks?

TROY: Go on in the house and get you something to eat now.

GABRIEL: I got to go sell my plums. I done sold some tomatoes. Got me two quarters. Wanna see?

He shows TROY *his quarters.*

I'm gonna save them and buy me a new horn so St. Peter can hear me when it's time to open the gates.

GABRIEL *stops suddenly. Listens.*

Hear that? That's the hellhounds. I got to chase them out of here. Go on get out of here! Get out!

GABRIEL *exits singing.*

Better get ready for the judgment
Better get ready for the judgment
My Lord is coming down

ROSE *enters from the house.*

TROY: He gone off somewhere.

GABRIEL: (*Offstage*)

Better get ready for the judgment
Better get ready for the judgment morning
Better get ready for the judgment
My God is coming down

ROSE: He ain't eating right. Miss Pearl say she can't get him to eat nothing.

TROY: What you want me to do about it, Rose? I done did everything I can for the man. I can't make him get well. Man got half his head blown away…what you expect?

ROSE: Seem like something ought to be done to help him.

TROY: Man don't bother nobody. He just mixed up from that metal plate he got in his head. Ain't no sense for him to go back into the hospital.

ROSE: Least he be eating right. They can help him take care of himself.

TROY: Don't nobody wanna be locked up, Rose. What you wanna lock him up for? Man go over there and fight the war…messin' around with them Japs, get half his head blown off…and they give him a lousy three thousand dollars. And I had to swoop down on that.

ROSE: Is you fixing to go into that again?

TROY: That's the only way I got a roof over my head…cause of that metal plate.

ROSE: Ain't no sense you blaming yourself for nothing. Gabe wasn't in no condition to manage that money. You done what was right by him. Can't nobody say you ain't done what was right by him. Look how long you took care of him…till he wanted to have his own place and moved over there with Miss Pearl.

TROY: That ain't what I'm saying, woman! I'm just stating the facts. If my brother didn't have that metal plate in his head…I wouldn't have a pot to piss in or a window to throw it out of. And I'm fifty-three years old. Now see if you can understand that!

TROY gets up from the porch and starts to exit the yard.

ROSE: Where you going off to? You been running out of here every Saturday for weeks. I thought you was gonna work on this fence?

TROY: I'm gonna walk down to Taylors'. Listen to the ball game. I'll be back in a bit. I'll work on it when I get back.

He exits the yard. The lights go to black.

SCENE THREE

The lights come up on the yard. It is four hours later. ROSE is taking down the clothes from the line. CORY enters carrying his football equipment.

ROSE: Your daddy like to had a fit with you running out of here this morning without doing your chores.

CORY: I told you I had to go to practice.

ROSE: He say you were supposed to help him with this fence.

CORY: He been saying that the last four or five Saturdays, and then he don't never do nothing, but go down to Taylors'. Did you tell him about the recruiter?

ROSE: Yeah, I told him.

CORY: What he say?

ROSE: He ain't said nothing too much. You get in there and get started on your chores before he gets back. Go on and scrub down them steps before he gets back here hollering and carrying on.

CORY: I'm hungry. What you got to eat, Mama?

ROSE: Go on and get started on your chores. I got some meat loaf in there. Go on and make you a sandwich…and don't leave no mess in there.

CORY exits into the house. ROSE continues to take down the clothes. TROY enters the yard and sneaks up and grabs her from behind.

Troy! Go on, now. You liked to scared me to death. What was the score of the game? Lucille had me on the phone and I couldn't keep up with it.

TROY: What I care about the game? Come here, woman. (*He tries to kiss her.*)

ROSE: I thought you went down Taylors' to listen to the game. Go on, Troy! You supposed to be putting up this fence.

TROY: (*Attempting to kiss her again.*) I'll put it up when I finish with what is at hand.

ROSE: Go on, Troy. I ain't studying you.

TROY: (*Chasing after her.*) I'm studying you… fixing to do my homework!

ROSE: Troy, you better leave me alone.

TROY: Where's Cory? That boy brought his butt home yet?

ROSE: He's in the house doing his chores.

TROY: (*Calling.*) Cory! Get your butt out here, boy!

ROSE exits into the house with the laundry. TROY goes over to the pile of wood, picks up a board, and starts sawing. CORY enters from the house.

TROY: You just now coming in here from leaving this morning?

CORY: Yeah, I had to go to football practice.

TROY: Yeah, what?

CORY: Yessir.

TROY: I ain't but two seconds off you noway. The garbage sitting in there overflowing…you ain't done none of your chores…and you come in here talking about "Yeah."

CORY: I was just getting ready to do my chores now, Pop…

TROY: Your first chore is to help me with this fence on Saturday. Everything else come after that. Now get that saw and cut them boards.

CORY takes the saw and begins cutting the boards. TROY continues working. There is a long pause.

CORY: Hey, Pop…why don't you buy a TV?

TROY: What I want with a TV? What I want one of them for?

CORY: Everybody got one. Earl, Ba Bra…Jesse!

TROY: I ain't asked you who had one. I say what I want with one?

CORY: So you can watch it. They got lots of things on TV. Baseball games and everything. We could watch the World Series.

TROY: Yeah…and how much this TV cost?

CORY: I don't know. They got them on sale for around two hundred dollars.

TROY: Two hundred dollars, huh?

CORY: That ain't that much, Pop.

TROY: Naw, it's just two hundred dollars. See that roof you got over your head at night? Let me tell you something about that roof. It's been over ten years since that roof was last tarred. See now…the snow come this winter and sit up there on that roof like it is …and it's gonna seep inside. It's just gonna be a little bit…ain't gonna hardly notice it. Then the next thing you know, it's gonna be leaking all over the house. Then the wood rot from all that water and you gonna need a whole new roof. Now, how much you think it cost to get that roof tarred?

CORY: I don't know.

TROY: Two hundred and sixty-four dollars… cash money. While you thinking about a TV, I got to be thinking about the roof…and whatever else go wrong around here. Now if you had two hundred dollars, what would you do…fix the roof or buy a TV?

CORY: I'd buy a TV. Then when the roof started to leak…when it needed fixing…I'd fix it.

TROY: Where you gonna get the money from? You done spent it for a TV. You gonna sit up and watch the water run all over your brand new TV.

CORY: Aw, Pop. You got money. I know you do.

TROY: Where I got it at, huh?

CORY: You got it in the bank.

TROY: You wanna see my bankbook? You wanna see that seventy-three dollars and twenty-two cents I got sitting up in there?

CORY: You ain't got to pay for it all at one time. You can put a down payment on it and carry it on home with you.

TROY: Not me. I ain't gonna owe nobody nothing if I can help it. Miss a payment and they come and snatch it right out your house. Then what you got? Now, soon as I get two hundred dollars clear, then I'll buy a TV. Right now, as soon as I get two hundred and sixty-four dollars, I'm gonna have this roof tarred.

CORY: Aw…Pop!

TROY: You go on and get you two hundred dollars and buy one if ya want it. I got better things to do with my money.

CORY: I can't get no two hundred dollars. I ain't never seen two hundred dollars.

TROY: I'll tell you what…you get you a hundred dollars and I'll put the other hundred with it.

CORY: Alright, I'm gonna show you.

TROY: You gonna show me how you can cut them boards right now.

CORY begins to cut the boards. There is a long pause.

CORY: The Pirates won today. That makes five in a row.

TROY: I ain't thinking about the Pirates. Got an all-white team. Got that boy…that Puerto Rican boy…Clemente. Don't even half-play him. That boy could be something if they give him a chance. Play him one day and sit him on the bench the next.

CORY: He gets a lot of chances to play.

TROY: I'm talking about playing regular. Playing every day so you can get your timing. That's what I'm talking about.

CORY: They got some white guys on the team that don't play every day. You can't play everybody at the same time.

TROY: If they got a white fellow sitting on the bench…you can bet your last dollar he can't play! The colored guy got to be twice as good before he get on the team. That's why I don't want you to get all tied up in them sports. Man on the team and what it get him? They got colored on the team and don't use them. Same as not having them. All them teams the same.

CORY: The Braves got Hank Aaron and Wes Covington. Hank Aaron hit two home runs today. That makes forty-three.

TROY: Hank Aaron ain't nobody. That's what you supposed to do. That's how you supposed to play the game. Ain't nothing to it. It's just a matter of timing…getting the right follow-through. Hell, I can hit forty-three home runs right now!

CORY: Not off no major-league pitching, you couldn't.

TROY: We had better pitching in the Negro leagues. I hit seven home runs off of Satchel Paige. You can't get no better than that!

CORY: Sandy Koufax. He's leading the league in strikeouts.

TROY: I ain't thinking of no Sandy Koufax.

CORY: You got Warren Spahn and Lew Burdette. I bet you couldn't hit no home runs off of Warren Spahn.

TROY: I'm through with it now. You go on and cut them boards.

(*Pause.*)

Your mama tell me you done got recruited by a college football team? Is that right?

CORY: Yeah. Coach Zellman say the recruiter gonna be coming by to talk to you. Get you to sign the permission papers.

TROY: I thought you supposed to be working down there at the A&P. Ain't you suppose to be working down there after school?

CORY: Mr. Stawicki say he gonna hold my job for me until after the football season. Say starting next week I can work weekends.

TROY: I thought we had an understanding about this football stuff? You suppose to keep up with your chores and hold that job down at the A&P. Ain't been around here all day on a Saturday. Ain't none of your chores done …and now you telling me you done quit your job.

CORY: I'm gonna be working weekends.

TROY: You damn right you are! And ain't no need for nobody coming around here to talk to me about signing nothing.

CORY: Hey, Pop…you can't do that. He's coming all the way from North Carolina.

TROY: I don't care where he coming from. The white man ain't gonna let you get nowhere with that football noway. You go on and get your book-learning so you can work yourself up in that A&P or learn how to fix cars or build houses or something, get you a trade. That way you have something can't nobody take away from you. You go on and learn how to put your hands to some good use. Besides hauling people's garbage.

CORY: I get good grades, Pop. That's why the recruiter wants to talk with you. You got to keep up your grades to get recruited. This way I'll be going to college. I'll get a chance…

TROY: First you gonna get your butt down there to the A&P and get your job back.

CORY: Mr. Stawicki done already hired somebody else 'cause I told him I was playing football.

TROY: You a bigger fool than I thought…to let somebody take away your job so you can play some football. Where you gonna get your money to take out your girlfriend and whatnot? What kind of foolishness is that to let somebody take away your job?

CORY: I'm still gonna be working weekends.

TROY: Naw…naw. You getting your butt out of here and finding you another job.

CORY: Come on, Pop! I got to practice. I can't work after school and play football too. The team needs me. That's what Coach Zellman say…

TROY: I don't care what nobody else say. I'm the boss…you understand? I'm the boss around here. I do the only saying what counts.

CORY: Come on, Pop!

TROY: I asked you…did you understand?

CORY: Yeah…

TROY: What?!

CORY: Yessir.

TROY: You go on down there to that A&P and see if you can get your job back. If you can't do both…then you quit the football team. You've got to take the crookeds with the straights.

CORY: Yessir.

(*Pause.*)

Can I ask you a question?

TROY: What the hell you wanna ask me? Mr. Stawicki the one you got the questions for.

CORY: How come you ain't never liked me?

TROY: Liked you? Who the hell say I got to like you? What law is there say I got to like you?

Wanna stand up in my face and ask a damn fool-ass question like that. Talking about liking somebody. Come here, boy, when I talk to you.

CORY *comes over to where* TROY *is working. He stands slouched over and* TROY *shoves him on his shoulder.*

Straighten up, goddammit! I asked you a question…what law is there say I got to like you?

CORY: None.

TROY: Well, alright then! Don't you eat every day? (*Pause.*)

Answer me when I talk to you! Don't you eat every day?

CORY: Yeah.

TROY: Nigger, as long as you in my house, you put that sir on the end of it when you talk to me!

CORY: Yes…sir.

TROY: You eat every day.

CORY: Yessir!

TROY: Got a roof over your head.

CORY: Yessir!

TROY: Got clothes on your back.

CORY: Yessir.

TROY: Why you think that is?

CORY: Cause of you.

TROY: Aw, hell I know it's 'cause of me…but why do you think that is?

CORY: (*Hesitant.*) Cause you like me.

TROY: Like you? I go out of here every morning …bust my butt…putting up with them crackers every day…cause I like you? You about the biggest fool I ever saw. (*Pause.*)

It's my job. It's my responsibility! You understand that? A man got to take care of his family. You live in my house…sleep you behind on my bedclothes…fill you belly up with my food…cause you my son. You my flesh and blood. Not 'cause I like you! Cause it's my duty to take care of you. I owe a responsibility to you! Let's get this straight right here…before it go along any further…I ain't got to like you. Mr. Rand don't give me my money come payday cause he likes me. He gives me cause he owe me. I done give you everything I had to give you. I gave you your life! Me and your mama worked that out between us. And liking your black ass wasn't part of the bargain. Don't you try and go through life worrying about if somebody like you or not. You best be making sure they doing right by you. You understand what I'm saying, boy?

CORY: Yessir.

TROY: Then get the hell out of my face, and get on down to that A&P.

ROSE *has been standing behind the screen door for much of the scene. She enters as* CORY *exits.*

ROSE: Why don't you let the boy go ahead and play football, Troy? Ain't no harm in that. He's just trying to be like you with the sports.

TROY: I don't want him to be like me! I want him to move as far away from my life as he can get. You the only decent thing that ever happened to me. I wish him that. But I don't wish him a thing else from my life. I decided seventeen years ago that boy wasn't getting involved in no sports. Not after what they did to me in the sports.

ROSE: Troy, why don't you admit you was too old to play in the major leagues? For once… why don't you admit that?

TROY: What do you mean too old? Don't come telling me I was too old. I just wasn't the right color. Hell, I'm fifty-three years old and can do better than Selkirk's .269 right now!

ROSE: How's was you gonna play ball when you were over forty? Sometimes I can't get no sense out of you.

TROY: I got good sense, woman. I got sense enough not to let my boy get hurt over playing no sports. You been mothering that boy too much. Worried about if people like him.

ROSE: Everything that boy do…he do for you. He wants you to say "Good job, son." That's all.

TROY: Rose, I ain't got time for that. He's alive. He's healthy. He's got to make his own way. I made mine. Ain't nobody gonna hold his hand when he get out there in that world.

ROSE: Times have changed from when you was young, Troy. People change. The world's changing around you and you can't even see it.

TROY: (*Slow, methodical.*) Woman…I do the best I can do. I come in here every Friday. I carry a sack of potatoes and a bucket of lard. You all line up at the door with your hands out. I give you the lint from my pockets. I give you my sweat and my blood. I ain't got no tears. I done spent them. We go upstairs in that room at night…and I fall down on you and try to blast a hole into forever. I get up Monday morning…find my lunch on the table. I go out. Make my way. Find my strength to carry me through to the next Friday.
(*Pause.*)
That's all I got, Rose. That's all I got to give. I can't give nothing else.
TROY *exits into the house. The lights go down to black.*

SCENE FOUR

It is Friday. Two weeks later. CORY *starts out of the house with his football equipment. The phone rings.*

CORY: (*Calling.*) I got it!
He answers the phone and stands in the screen door talking.
Hello? Hey, Jesse. Naw…I was just getting ready to leave now.
ROSE: (*Calling.*) Cory!
CORY: I told you, man, them spikes is all tore up. You can use them if you want, but they ain't no good. Earl got some spikes.
ROSE: (*Calling.*) Cory!
CORY: (*Calling to* ROSE.) Mam? I'm talking to Jesse. (*Into phone.*)
When she say that? (*Pause.*) Aw, you lying, man. I'm gonna tell her you said that.
ROSE: (*Calling.*) Cory, don't you go nowhere!
CORY: I got to go to the game, Ma!
(*Into the phone.*)
Yeah, hey, look, I'll talk to you later. Yeah, I'll meet you over Earl's house. Later. Bye, Ma.
CORY *exits the house and starts out the yard.*
ROSE: Cory, where you going off to? You got that stuff all pulled out and thrown all over your room.

CORY: (*In the yard.*) I was looking for my spikes. Jesse wanted to borrow my spikes.
ROSE: Get up there and get that cleaned up before your daddy get back in here.
CORY: I got to go to the game! I'll clean it up *when I get back.*
CORY *exits.*
ROSE: That's all he need to do is see that room all messed up.
ROSE *exits into the house.* TROY *and* BONO *enter the yard.* TROY *is dressed in clothes other than his work clothes.*
BONO: He told him the same thing he told you. Take it to the union.
TROY: Brownie ain't got that much sense. Man wasn't thinking about nothing. He wait until I confront them on it…then he wanna come crying seniority.
(*Calls.*)
Hey, Rose!
BONO: I wish I could have seen Mr. Rand's face when he told you.
TROY: He couldn't get it out of his mouth! Liked to bit his tongue! When they called me down there to the Commissioner's office… he thought they was gonna fire me. Like everybody else.
BONO: I didn't think they was gonna fire you. I thought they was gonna put you on the warning paper.
TROY: Hey, Rose!
(*To* BONO.)
Yeah, Mr. Rand like to bit his tongue.
TROY *breaks the seal on the bottle, takes a drink, and hands it to* BONO.
BONO: I see you run right down to Taylors' and told that Alberta gal.
TROY: (*Calling.*) Hey Rose! (*To* BONO.) I told everybody. Hey, Rose! I went down there to cash my check.
ROSE: (*Entering from the house.*) Hush all that hollering, man! I know you out here. What they say down there at the Commissioner's office?
TROY: You supposed to come when I call you, woman. Bono'll tell you that.
(*To* BONO.)
Don't Lucille come when you call her?

ROSE: Man, hush your mouth. I ain't no dog… talk about "come when you call me."

TROY: (*Puts his arm around* ROSE.) You hear this, Bono? I had me an old dog used to get uppity like that. You say, "C'mere, Blue!"… and he just lay there and look at you. End up getting a stick and chasing him away trying to make him come.

ROSE: I ain't studying you and your dog. I remember you used to sing that old song.

TROY: (*He sings.*) Hear it ring! Hear it ring! I had a dog his name was Blue.

ROSE: Don't nobody wanna hear you sing that old song.

TROY: (*Sings.*) You know Blue was mighty true.

ROSE: Used to have Cory running around here singing that song.

BONO: Hell, I remember that song myself.

TROY: (*Sings.*) You know Blue was a good old dog.
Blue treed a possum in a hollow log.
That was my daddy's song. My daddy made up that song.

ROSE: I don't care who made it up. Don't nobody wanna hear you sing it.

TROY: (*Makes a song like calling a dog.*) Come here, woman.

ROSE: You come in here carrying on, I reckon they ain't fired you. What they say down there at the Commissioner's office?

TROY: Look here, Rose…Mr. Rand called me into his office today when I got back from talking to them people down there…it come from up top…he called me in and told me they was making me a driver.

ROSE: Troy, you kidding!

TROY: No I ain't. Ask Bono.

ROSE: Well, that's great, Troy. Now you don't have to hassle them people no more.
LYONS *enters from the street.*

TROY: Aw hell, I wasn't looking to see you today. I thought you was in jail. Got it all over the front page of the *Courier* about them raiding Sefus' place…where you be hanging out with all them thugs.

LYONS: Hey, Pop…that ain't got nothing to do with me. I don't go down there gambling. I go down there to sit in with the band. I ain't

got nothing to do with the gambling part. They got some good music down there.

TROY: They got some rogues…is what they got.

LYONS: How you been, Mr. Bono? Hi, Rose.

BONO: I see where you playing down at the Crawford Grill tonight.

ROSE: How come you ain't brought Bonnie like I told you. You should have brought Bonnie with you, she ain't been over in a month of Sundays.

LYONS: I was just in the neighborhood…thought I'd stop by.

TROY: Here he come…

BONO: Your daddy got a promotion on the rubbish. He's gonna be the first colored driver. Ain't got to do nothing but sit up there and read the paper like them white fellows.

LYONS: Hey, Pop…if you knew how to read you'd be alright.

BONO: Naw…naw…you mean if the nigger knew how to *drive* he'd be all right. Been fighting with them people about driving and ain't even got a license. Mr. Rand know you ain't got no driver's license?

TROY: Driving ain't nothing. All you do is point the truck where you want it to go. Driving ain't nothing.

BONO: Do Mr. Rand know you ain't got no driver's license? That's what I'm talking about. I ain't asked if driving was easy. I asked if Mr. Rand know you ain't got no driver's license.

TROY: He ain't got to know. The man ain't got to know my business. Time he find out, I have two or three driver's licenses.

LYONS: (*Going into his pocket.*) Say, look here, Pop…

TROY: I knew it was coming. Didn't I tell you, Bono? I know what kind of "Look here, Pop" that was. The nigger fixing to ask me for some money. It's Friday night. It's my payday. All them rogues down there on the avenue…the ones that ain't in jail…and Lyons is hopping in his shoes to get down there with them.

LYONS: See, Pop…if you give somebody else a chance to talk sometime, you'd see that I was fixing to pay you back your ten dollars like I told you. Here…I told you I'd pay you when Bonnie got paid.

TROY: Naw…you go ahead and keep that ten dollars. Put it in the bank. The next time you feel like you wanna come by here and ask me for something…you go on down there and get that.

LYONS: Here's your ten dollars, Pop. I told you I don't want you to give me nothing. I just wanted to borrow ten dollars.

TROY: Naw…you go on and keep that for the next time you want to ask me.

LYONS: Come on, Pop…here go your ten dollars.

ROSE: Why don't you go on and let the boy pay you back, Troy?

LYONS: Here you go, Rose. If you don't take it I'm gonna have to hear about it for the next six months.

He hands her the money.

ROSE: You can hand yours over here too, Troy.

TROY: You see this, Bono. You see how they do me.

BONO: Yeah, Lucille do me the same way.

GABRIEL *is heard singing offstage. He enters.*

GABRIEL: Better get ready for the Judgment! Better get ready for…Hey!…Hey!…There's Troy's boy!

LYONS: How you doing, Uncle Gabe?

GABRIEL: Lyons…The King of the Jungle! Rose …hey, Rose. Got a flower for you.

He takes a rose from his pocket.

Picked it myself. That's the same rose like you is!

ROSE: That's right nice of you, Gabe.

LYONS: What you been doing, Uncle Gabe?

GABRIEL: Oh, I been chasing hellhounds and waiting on the time to tell St. Peter to open the gates.

LYONS: You been chasing hellhounds, huh? Well …you doing the right thing, Uncle Gabe. Somebody got to chase them.

GABRIEL: Oh, yeah…I know it. The devil's strong. The devil ain't no pushover. Hellhounds snipping at everybody's heels. But I got my trumpet waiting on the judgment time.

LYONS: Waiting on the Battle of Armageddon, huh?

GABRIEL: Ain't gonna be too much of a battle when God get to waving that Judgment sword. But the people's gonna have a hell of a time trying to get into heaven if them gates ain't open.

LYONS: (*Putting his arm around* GABRIEL.) You hear this, Pop. Uncle Gabe, you alright!

GABRIEL: (*Laughing with* LYONS.) Lyons! King of the Jungle.

ROSE: You gonna stay for supper, Gabe. Want me to fix you a plate?

GABRIEL: I'll take a sandwich, Rose. Don't want no plate. Just wanna eat with my hands. I'll take a sandwich.

ROSE: How about you, Lyons? You staying? Got some short ribs cooking.

LYONS: Naw, I won't eat nothing till after we finished playing.

(*Pause.*)

You ought to come down and listen to me play, Pop.

TROY: I don't like that Chinese music. All that noise.

ROSE: Go on in the house and wash up, Gabe …I'll fix you a sandwich.

GABRIEL: (*To* LYONS, *as he exits.*) Troy's mad at me.

LYONS: What you mad at Uncle Gabe for, Pop.

ROSE: He thinks Troy's mad at him cause he moved over to Miss Pearl's.

TROY: I ain't mad at the man. He can live where he want to live at.

LYONS: What he move over there for? Miss Pearl don't like nobody.

ROSE: She don't mind him none. She treats him real nice. She just don't allow all that singing.

TROY: She don't mind that rent he be paying… that's what she don't mind.

ROSE: Troy, I ain't going through that with you no more. He's over there cause he want to have his own place. He can come and go as he please.

TROY: Hell, he could come and go as he please here. I wasn't stopping him. I ain't put no rules on him.

ROSE: It ain't the same thing, Troy. And you know it.

GABRIEL *comes to the door.*

Now, that's the last I wanna hear about that. I don't wanna hear nothing else about Gabe and Miss Pearl. And next week…

GABRIEL: I'm ready for my sandwich, Rose.

ROSE: And next week…when that recruiter come from that school…I want you to sign that paper and go on and let Cory play football. Then that'll be the last I have to hear about that.

TROY: (*To* ROSE *as she exits into the house.*) I ain't thinking about Cory nothing.

LYONS: What…Cory got recruited? What school he going to?

TROY: That boy walking around here smelling his piss…thinking he's grown. Thinking he's gonna do what he want, irrespective of what I say. Look here, Bono…I left the Commissioner's office and went down to the A&P…that boy ain't working down there. He lying to me. Telling me he got his job back…telling me he working weekends …telling me he working after school…Mr. Stawicki tell me he ain't working down there at all!

LYONS: Cory just growing up. He's just busting at the seams trying to fill out your shoes.

TROY: I don't care what he's doing. When he get to the point where he wanna disobey me… then it's time for him to move on. Bono'll tell you that. I bet he ain't never disobeyed his daddy without paying the consequences.

BONO: I ain't never had a chance. My daddy came on through…but I ain't never knew him to see him…or what he had on his mind or where he went. Just moving on through. Searching out the New Land. That's what the old folks used to call it. See a fellow moving around from place to place…woman to woman…called it searching out the New Land. I can't say if he ever found it. I come along, didn't want no kids. Didn't know if I was gonna be in one place long enough to fix on them right as their daddy. I figured I was going searching too. As it turned out I been hooked up with Lucille near about as long as your daddy been with Rose. Going on sixteen years.

TROY: Sometimes I wish I hadn't known my daddy. He ain't cared nothing about no kids. A kid to him wasn't nothing. All he wanted was for you to learn how to walk so he could start you to working. When it come time for eating…he ate first. If there was anything left over, that's what you got. Man would sit down and eat two chickens and give you the wing.

LYONS: You ought to stop that, Pop. Everybody feed their kids. No matter how hard times is…everybody care about their kids. Make sure they have something to eat.

TROY: The only thing my daddy cared about was getting them bales of cotton in to Mr. Lubin. That's the only thing that mattered to him. Sometimes I used to wonder why he was living. Wonder why the devil hadn't come and got him. "Get them bales of cotton in to Mr. Lubin" and find out he owe him money…

LYONS: He should have just went on and left when he saw he couldn't get nowhere. That's what I would have done.

TROY: How he gonna leave with eleven kids? And where he gonna go? He ain't knew how to do nothing but farm. No, he was trapped and I think he knew it. But I'll say this for him…he felt a responsibility toward us. Maybe he ain't treated us the way I felt he should have…but without that responsibility he could have walked off and left us…made his own way.

BONO: A lot of them did. Back in those days what you talking about…they walk out their front door and just take on down one road or another and keep on walking.

LYONS: There you go! That's what I'm talking about.

BONO: Just keep on walking till you come to something else. Ain't you never heard of nobody having the walking blues? Well, that's what you call it when you just take off like that.

TROY: My daddy ain't had them walking blues! What you talking about? He stayed right there with his family. But he was just as evil as he could be. My mama couldn't stand him. Couldn't stand that evilness. She run off when I was about eight. She sneaked off one night after he had gone to sleep. Told me she was coming back for me. I ain't never seen her no more. All his women run off and left him. He wasn't good for nobody. When my turn come to head out, I was fourteen and got to sniffing around Joe Canewell's daughter. Had us an old mule we called Greyboy. My daddy sent me out to do some plowing and I tied up Greyboy and went to fooling around with Joe Canewell's daughter. We done found us a nice little spot, got real cozy with each other. She about thirteen and we done figured we was grown anyway…so we down there enjoying ourselves…ain't thinking about nothing. We didn't know Greyboy had got loose and wandered back to the house and my daddy was looking for me. We down there by the creek enjoying ourselves when my daddy come up on us. Surprised us. He had them leather straps off the mule and commenced to whupping me like there was no tomorrow. I jumped up, mad and embarrassed. I was scared of my daddy. When he commenced to whupping on me…quite naturally I run to get out of the way.

(*Pause.*)

Now I thought he was mad cause I ain't done my work. But I see where he was chasing me off so he could have the gal for himself. When I see what the matter of it was, I lost all fear of my daddy. Right there is where I become a man…at fourteen years of age.

(*Pause.*)

Now it was my turn to run him off. I picked up them same reins that he had used on me. I picked up them reins and commenced to whupping on him. The gal jumped up and run off…and when my daddy turned to face me, I could see why the devil had never come to get him…cause he was the devil himself. I don't know what happened. When I woke up, I was laying right there by the creek, and Blue…this old dog we had…was licking my face. I thought I was blind. I couldn't see nothing. Both my eyes were swollen shut. I layed there and cried. I didn't know what I was gonna do. The only thing I knew was the time had come for me to leave my daddy's house. And right there the world suddenly got big. And it was a long time before I could cut it down to where I could handle it.

Part of that cutting down was when I got to the place where I could feel him kicking in my blood and knew that the only thing that separated us was the matter of a few years.

GABRIEL *enters from the house with a sandwich.*

LYONS: What you got there, Uncle Gabe?

GABRIEL: Got me a ham sandwich. Rose gave me a ham sandwich.

TROY: I don't know what happened to him. I done lost touch with everybody except Gabriel. But I hope he's dead. I hope he found some peace.

LYONS: That's a heavy story, Pop. I didn't know you left home when you was fourteen.

TROY: And didn't know nothing. The only part of the world I knew was the forty-two acres of Mr. Lubin's land. That's all I knew about life.

LYONS: Fourteen's kinda young to be out on your own. (*Phone rings.*) I don't even think I was ready to be out on my own at fourteen. I don't know what I would have done.

TROY: I got up from the creek and walked on down to Mobile. I was through with farming. Figured I could do better in the city. So I walked the two hundred miles to Mobile.

LYONS: Wait a minute…you ain't walked no two hundred miles, Pop. Ain't nobody gonna walk no two hundred miles. You talking about some walking there.

BONO: That's the only way you got anywhere back in them days.

LYONS: Shhh. Damn if I wouldn't have hitched a ride with somebody!

TROY: Who you gonna hitch it with? They ain't had no cars and things like they got now. We talking about 1918.

ROSE: (*Entering.*) What you all out here getting into?

TROY: (*To* ROSE.) I'm telling Lyons how good he got it. He don't know nothing about this I'm talking.

ROSE: Lyons, that was Bonnie on the phone. She say you supposed to pick her up.

LYONS: Yeah, okay, Rose.

TROY: I walked on down to Mobile and hitched up with some of them fellows that was heading this way. Got up here and found out…not only couldn't you get a job…you couldn't find no place to live. I thought I was in freedom. Shhh. Colored folks living down there on the riverbanks in whatever kind of shelter they could find for themselves. Right down there under the Brady Street Bridge. Living in shacks made of sticks and tarpaper. Messed around there and went from bad to worse. Started stealing. First it was food. Then I figured, hell, if I steal money I can buy me some food. Buy me some shoes too! One thing led to another. Met your mama. I was young and anxious to be a man. Met your mama and had you. What I do that for? Now I got to worry about feeding you and her. Got to steal three times as much. Went out one day looking for somebody to rob…that's what I was, a robber. I'll tell you the truth. I'm ashamed of it today. But it's the truth. Went to rob this fellow…pulled out my knife… and he pulled out a gun. Shot me in the chest. It felt just like somebody had taken a hot branding iron and laid it on me. When he shot me I jumped at him with my knife. They told me I killed him and they put me in the penitentiary and locked me up for fifteen years. That's where I met Bono. That's where I learned how to play baseball. Got out that place and your mama had taken you and went on to make life without me. Fifteen years was a long time for her to wait. But that fifteen years cured me of that robbing stuff. Rose'll tell you. She asked me when I met her if I had gotten all that foolishness out of my system. And I told her,

"Baby, it's you and baseball all what count with me." You hear me, Bono? I meant it too. She say, "Which one comes first?" I told her, "Baby, ain't no doubt it's baseball…but you stick and get old with me and we'll both outlive this baseball." Am I right, Rose? And it's true.

ROSE: Man, hush your mouth. You ain't said no such thing. Talking about, "Baby, you know you'll always be number one with me." That's what you was talking.

TROY: You hear that, Bono. That's why I love her.

BONO: Rose'll keep you straight. You get off the track, she'll straighten you up.

ROSE: Lyons, you better get on up and get Bonnie. She waiting on you.

LYONS: (*Gets up to go.*) Hey, Pop, why don't you come on down to the Grill and hear me play?

TROY: I ain't going down there. I'm too old to be sitting around in them clubs.

BONO: You got to be good to play down at the Grill.

LYONS: Come on, Pop…

TROY: I got to get up in the morning.

LYONS: You ain't got to stay long.

TROY: Naw, I'm gonna get my supper and go on to bed.

LYONS: Well, I got to go. I'll see you again.

TROY: Don't you come around my house on my payday.

ROSE: Pick up the phone and let somebody know you coming. And bring Bonnie with you. You know I'm always glad to see her.

LYONS: Yeah, I'll do that, Rose. You take care now. See you, Pop. See you, Mr. Bono. See you, Uncle Gabe.

GABRIEL: Lyons! King of the Jungle!

LYONS *exits.*

TROY: Is supper ready, woman? Me and you got some business to take care of. I'm gonna tear it up too.

ROSE: Troy, I done told you now!

TROY: (*Puts his arm around* BONO.) Aw hell, woman…this is Bono. Bono like family. I done known this nigger since…how long I done know you?

BONO: It's been a long time.

TROY: I done known this nigger since Skippy was a pup. Me and him done been through some times.

BONO: You sure right about that.

TROY: Hell, I done know him longer than I known you. And we still standing shoulder to shoulder. Hey, look here, Bono…a man can't ask for no more than that.
Drinks to him.
I love you, nigger.

BONO: Hell, I love you too…but I got to get home see my woman. You got yours in hand. I got to go get mine.
BONO *starts to exit as* CORY *enters the yard, dressed in his football uniform. He gives* TROY *a hard, uncompromising look.*

CORY: What you do that for, Pop?
He throws his helmet down in the direction of TROY.

ROSE: What's the matter? Cory…what's the matter?

CORY: Papa done went up to the school and told Coach Zellman I can't play football no more. Wouldn't even let me play the game. Told him to tell the recruiter not to come.

ROSE: Troy…

TROY: What you Troying me for. Yeah, I did it. And the boy know why I did it.

CORY: Why you wanna do that to me? That was the one chance I had.

ROSE: Ain't nothing wrong with Cory playing football, Troy.

TROY: The boy lied to me. I told the nigger if he wanna play football…to keep up his chores and hold down that job at the A&P. That was the conditions. Stopped down there to see Mr. Stawicki…

CORY: I can't work after school during the football season, Pop! I tried to tell you that Mr. Stawicki's holding my job for me. You don't never want to listen to nobody. And then you wanna go and do this to me!

TROY: I ain't done nothing to you. You done it to yourself.

CORY: Just cause you didn't have a chance! You just scared I'm gonna be better than you, that's all.

TROY: Come here.

ROSE: Troy…

CORY *reluctantly crosses over to* TROY.

TROY: Alright! See. You done made a mistake.

CORY: I didn't even do nothing!

TROY: I'm gonna tell you what your mistake was. See…you swung at the ball and didn't hit it. That's strike one. See, you in the batter's box now. You swung and you missed. That's strike one. Don't you strike out!
Lights fade to black.

ACT TWO

SCENE ONE

The following morning. CORY *is at the tree hitting the ball with the bat. He tries to mimic* TROY, *but his swing is awkward, less sure.* ROSE *enters from the house.*

ROSE: Cory, I want you to help me with this cupboard.

CORY: I ain't quitting the team. I don't care what Poppa say.

ROSE: I'll talk to him when he gets back. He had to go see about your Uncle Gabe. The police done arrested him. Say he was disturbing the peace. He'll be back directly. Come on in here and help me clean out the top of this cupboard.
CORY *exits into the house.* ROSE *sees* TROY *and* BONO *coming down the alley.*
Troy…what they say down there?

TROY: Ain't said nothing. I give them fifty dollars and they let him go. I'll talk to you about it. Where's Cory?

ROSE: He's in there helping me clean out these cupboards.

TROY: Tell him to get his butt out here.
TROY *and* BONO *go over to the pile of wood.* BONO *picks up the saw and begins sawing.*

TROY: (*To* BONO.) All they want is the money. That makes six or seven times I done went down there and got him. See me coming they stick out their *hands.*

BONO: Yeah. I know what you mean. That's all they care about…that money. They don't care about what's right.
(*Pause.*)

Nigger, why you got to go and get some hard wood? You ain't doing nothing but building a little old fence. Get you some soft pine wood. That's all you need.

TROY: I know what I'm doing. This is outside wood. You put pine wood inside the house. Pine wood is inside wood. This here is outside wood. Now you tell me where the fence is gonna be?

BONO: You don't need this wood. You can put it up with pine wood and it'll stand as long as you gonna be here looking at it.

TROY: How you know how long I'm gonna be here, nigger? Hell, I might just live forever. Live longer than old man Horsely.

BONO: That's what Magee used to say.

TROY: Magee's a damn fool. Now you tell me who you ever heard of gonna pull their own teeth with a pair of rusty pliers.

BONO: The old folks…my granddaddy used to pull his teeth with pliers. They ain't had no dentists for the colored folks back then.

TROY: Get clean pliers! You understand? Clean pliers! Sterilize them! Besides we ain't living back then. All Magee had to do was walk over to Doc Goldblum's.

BONO: I see where you and that Tallahassee gal …that Alberta…I see where you all done got tight.

TROY: What you mean "got tight"?

BONO: I see where you be laughing and joking with her all the time.

TROY: I laughs and jokes with all of them, Bono. You know me.

BONO: That ain't the kind of laughing and joking I'm talking about.

CORY *enters from the house.*

CORY: How you doing, Mr. Bono?

TROY: Cory? Get that saw from Bono and cut some wood. He talking about the wood's too hard to cut. Stand back there, Jim, and let that young boy show you how it's done.

BONO: He's sure welcome to it.

CORY *takes the saw and begins to cut the wood.*
Whew-e-e! Look at that. Big old strong boy. Look like Joe Louis. Hell, must be getting old the way I'm watching that boy whip through that wood.

CORY: I don't see why Mama want a fence around the yard noways.

TROY: Damn if I know either. What the hell she keeping out with it? She ain't got nothing nobody want.

BONO: Some people build fences to keep people out…and other people build fences to keep people in. Rose wants to hold on to you all. She loves you.

TROY: Hell, nigger, I don't need nobody to tell me my wife loves me. Cory…go on in the house and see if you can find that other saw.

CORY: Where's it at?

TROY: I said find it! Look for it till you find it!

CORY *exits into the house.*
What's that supposed to mean? Wanna keep us in?

BONO: Troy…I done known you seem like damn near my whole life. You and Rose both. I done know both of you all for a long time. I remember when you met Rose. When you was hitting them baseball out the park. A lot of them old gals was after you then. You had the pick of the litter. When you picked Rose, I was happy for you. That was the first time I knew you had any sense. I said…My man Troy knows what he's doing…I'm gonna follow this nigger…he might take me somewhere. I been following you too. I done learned a whole heap of things about life watching you. I done learned how to tell where the shit lies. How to tell it from the alfalfa. You done learned me a lot of things. You showed me how to not make the same mistakes…to take life as it comes along and keep putting one foot in front of the other. (*Pause.*)
Rose a good woman, Troy.

TROY: Hell, nigger, I know she a good woman. I been married to her for eighteen years. What you got on your mind, Bono?

BONO: I just say she a good woman. Just like I say anything. I ain't got to have nothing on my mind.

TROY: You just gonna say she a good woman and leave it hanging out there like that? Why you telling me she a good woman?

BONO: She loves you, Troy. Rose loves you.

TROY: You saying I don't measure up. That's what you trying to say. I don't measure up cause I'm seeing this other gal. I know what you trying to say.

BONO: I know what Rose means to you, Troy. I'm just trying to say I don't want to see you mess up.

TROY: Yeah, I appreciate that, Bono. If you was messing around on Lucille I'd be telling you the same thing.

BONO: Well, that's all I got to say. I just say that because I love you both.

TROY: Hell, you know me…I wasn't out there looking for nothing. You can't find a better woman than Rose. I know that. But seems like this woman just stuck onto me where I can't shake her loose. I done wrestled with it, tried to throw her off me…but she just stuck on tighter. Now she's stuck on for good.

BONO: You's in control…that's what you tell me all the time. You responsible for what you do.

TROY: I ain't ducking the responsibility of it. As long as it sets right in my heart…then I'm okay. Cause that's all I listen to. It'll tell me right from wrong every time. And I ain't talking about doing Rose no bad turn. I love Rose. She done carried me a long ways and I love and respect her for that.

BONO: I know you do. That's why I don't want to see you hurt her. But what you gonna do when she find out? What you got then? If you try and juggle both of them…sooner or later you gonna drop one of them. That's common sense.

TROY: Yeah, I hear what you saying, Bono. I been trying to figure a way to work it out.

BONO: Work it out right, Troy. I don't want to be getting all up between you and Rose's business…but work it so it come out right.

TROY: Aw hell, I get all up between you and Lucille's business. When you gonna get that woman that refrigerator she been wanting? Don't tell me you ain't got no money now. I know who your banker is. Mellon don't need that money bad as Lucille want that refrigerator. I'll tell you that.

BONO: Tell you what I'll do…when you finish building this fence for Rose…I'll buy Lucille that refrigerator.

TROY: You done stuck your foot in your mouth now!

TROY *grabs up a board and begins to saw.* BONO *starts to walk out the yard.*

Hey, nigger…where you going?

BONO: I'm going home. I know you don't expect me to help you now. I'm protecting my money. I wanna see you put that fence up by yourself. That's what I want to see. You'll be here another six months without me.

TROY: Nigger, you ain't right.

BONO: When it comes to my money…I'm right as fireworks on the Fourth of July.

TROY: Alright, we gonna see now. You better get out your bankbook.

BONO *exits, and* TROY *continues to work.* ROSE *enters from the house.*

ROSE: What they say down there? What's happening with Gabe?

TROY: I went down there and got him out. Cost me fifty dollars. Say he was disturbing the peace. Judge set up a hearing for him in three weeks. Say to show cause why he shouldn't be re-committed.

ROSE: What was he doing that cause them to arrest him?

TROY: Some kids was teasing him and he run them off home. Say he was howling and carrying on. Some folks seen him and called the police. That's all it was.

ROSE: Well, what's you say? What'd you tell the judge?

TROY: Told him I'd look after him. It didn't make no sense to recommit the man. He stuck out his big greasy palm and told me to give him fifty dollars and take him on home.

ROSE: Where's he at now? Where'd he go off to?

TROY: He's gone on about his business. He don't need nobody to hold his hand.

ROSE: Well, I don't know. Seem like that would be the best place for him if they did put him into the hospital. I know what you're gonna say. But that's what I think would be best.

TROY: The man done had his life ruined fighting for what? And they wanna take and lock him up. Let him be free. He don't bother nobody.

ROSE: Well, everybody got their own way of looking at it I guess. Come on and get your lunch. I got a bowl of lima beans and some cornbread in the oven. Come on get something to eat. Ain't no sense you fretting over Gabe.
ROSE *turns to go into the house.*

TROY: Rose…got something to tell you.

ROSE: Well, come on…wait till I get this food on the table.

TROY: Rose!
She stops and turns around.
I don't know how to say this.
(*Pause.*)
I can't explain it none. It just sort of grows on you till it gets out of hand. It starts out like a little bush…and the next thing you know it's a whole forest.

ROSE: Troy…what is you talking about?

TROY: I'm talking, woman, let me talk. I'm trying to find a way to tell you…I'm gonna be a daddy. I'm gonna be somebody's daddy.

ROSE: Troy…you're not telling me this? You're gonna be…what?

TROY: Rose…now…see…

ROSE: You telling me you gonna be somebody's daddy? You telling your *wife* this?
GABRIEL *enters from the street. He carries a rose in his hand.*

GABRIEL: Hey, Troy! Hey, Rose!

ROSE: I have to wait eighteen years to hear something like this.

GABRIEL: Hey, Rose…I got a flower for you.
He hands it to her.
That's a rose. Same rose like you is.

ROSE: Thanks, Gabe.

GABRIEL: Troy, you ain't mad at me is you? Them bad mens come and put me away. You ain't mad at me is you?

TROY: Naw, Gabe, I ain't mad at you.

ROSE: Eighteen years and you wanna come with this.

GABRIEL: (*Takes a quarter out of his pocket.*) See what I got? Got a brand new quarter.

TROY: Rose…it's just…

ROSE: Ain't nothing you can say, Troy. Ain't no way of explaining that.

GABRIEL: Fellow that give me this quarter had a whole mess of them. I'm gonna keep this quarter till it stop shining.

ROSE: Gabe, go on in the house there. I got some watermelon in the frigidaire. Go on and get you a piece.

GABRIEL: Say, Rose…you know I was chasing hellhounds and them bad mens come and get me and take me away. Troy helped me. He come down there and told them they better let me go before he beat them up. Yeah, he did!

ROSE: You go on and get you a piece of watermelon, Gabe. Them bad mens is gone now.

GABRIEL: Okay, Rose…gonna get me some watermelon. The kind with the stripes on it.
GABRIEL *exits into the house.*

ROSE: Why, Troy? Why? After all these years to come dragging this in to me now. It don't make no sense at your age. I could have expected this ten or fifteen years ago, but not now.

TROY: Age ain't got nothing to do with it, Rose.

ROSE: I done tried to be everything a wife should be. Everything a wife could be. Been married eighteen years and I got to live to see the day you tell me you been seeing another woman and done fathered a child by her. And you know I ain't never wanted no half nothing in my family. My whole family is half. Everybody got different fathers and mothers…my two sisters and my brother. Can't hardly tell who's who. Can't never sit down and talk about Papa and Mama. It's your papa and your mama and my papa and my mama…

TROY: Rose…stop it now.

ROSE: I ain't never wanted that for none of my children. And now you wanna drag your behind in here and tell me something like this.

TROY: You ought to know. It's time for you to know.

ROSE: Well, I don't want to know, goddamn it!

TROY: I can't just make it go away. It's done now. I can't wish the circumstance of the thing away.

ROSE: And you don't want to either. Maybe you want to wish me and my boy away. Maybe that's what you want? Well, you can't wish us away. I've got eighteen years of my life invested in you. You ought to have stayed upstairs in my bed where you belong.

TROY: Rose…now listen to me…we can get a handle on this thing. We can talk this out… come to an understanding.

ROSE: All of a sudden it's "we." Where was "we" at when you was down there rolling around with some god-forsaken woman? "We" should have come to an understanding before you started making a damn fool of yourself. You're a day late and a dollar short when it comes to an understanding with me.

TROY: It's just…She gives me a different idea…a different understanding about myself. I can step out of this house and get away from the pressures and problems…be a different man. I ain't got to wonder how I'm gonna pay the bills or get the roof fixed. I can just be a part of myself that I ain't never been.

ROSE: What I want to know…is do you plan to continue seeing her. That's all you can say to me.

TROY: I can sit up in her house and laugh. Do you understand what I'm saying. I can laugh out loud…and it feels good. It reaches all the way down to the bottom of my shoes.
(Pause.)
Rose, I can't give that up.

ROSE: Maybe you ought to go on and stay down there with her…if she a better woman than me.

TROY: It ain't about nobody being a better woman or nothing. Rose, you ain't the blame. A man couldn't ask for no woman to be a better wife than you've been. I'm responsible for it. I done locked myself into a pattern trying to take care of you all that I forgot about myself.

ROSE: What the hell was I there for? That was my job, not somebody else's.

TROY: Rose, I done tried all my life to live decent …to live a clean…hard…useful life. I tried to be a good husband to you. In every way I knew how. Maybe I come into the world backwards, I don't know. But…you born with two strikes on you before you come to the plate. You got to guard it closely…always looking for the curve-ball on the inside corner. You can't afford to let none get past you. You can't afford a call strike. If you going down…you going down swinging. Everything lined up against you. What you gonna do. I fooled them, Rose. I bunted. When I found you and Cory and a halfway decent job…I was safe. Couldn't nothing touch me. I wasn't gonna strike out no more. I wasn't going back to the penitentiary. I wasn't gonna lay in the streets with a bottle of wine. I was safe. I had me a family. A job. I wasn't gonna get that last strike. I was on first looking for one of them boys to knock me in. To get me home.

ROSE: You should have stayed in my bed, Troy.

TROY: Then when I saw that gal…she firmed up my backbone. And I got thinking that if I tried…I just might be able to steal second. Do you understand after eighteen years I wanted to steal second.

ROSE: You should have held me tight. You should have grabbed me and held on.

TROY: I stood on first base for eighteen years and I thought…well, goddamn it…go on for it!

ROSE: We're not talking about baseball! We're talking about you going off to lay in bed with another woman…and then bring it home to me. That's what we're talking about. We ain't talking about no baseball.

TROY: Rose, you're not listening to me. I'm trying the best way I can to explain it to you. It's not easy for me to admit that I been standing in the same place for eighteen years.

ROSE: I been standing with you! I been right here with you, Troy. I got a life too. I gave eighteen years of my life to stand in the same spot with you. Don't you think I ever wanted other things? Don't you think I had dreams and hopes? What about my life? What about me? Don't you think it ever crossed my mind to want to know other men? That I wanted to lay up somewhere and forget about my responsibilities? That I wanted someone to make me laugh so I could feel good? You not the only one who's got wants and needs.

But I held on to you, Troy. I took all my feelings, my wants and needs, my dreams… and I buried them inside you. I planted a seed and watched and prayed over it. I planted myself inside you and waited to bloom. And it didn't take me no eighteen years to find out the soil was hard and rocky and it wasn't never gonna bloom.

But I held on to you, Troy. I held you tighter. You was my husband. I owed you everything I had. Every part of me I could find to give you. And upstairs in that room…with the darkness falling in on me…I gave everything I had to try and erase the doubt that you wasn't the finest man in the world. And wherever you was going…I wanted to be there with you. Cause you was my husband. Cause that's the only way I was gonna survive as your wife. You always talking about what you give…and what you don't have to give. But you take too. You take… and don't even know nobody's giving!

ROSE *turns to exit into the house;* TROY *grabs her arm.*

TROY: You say I take and don't give!

ROSE: Troy! You're hurting me!

TROY: You say I take and don't give.

ROSE: Troy…you're hurting my arm! Let go!

TROY: I done give you everything I got. Don't you tell that lie on me.

ROSE: Troy!

TROY: Don't you tell that lie on me!

CORY *enters from the house.*

CORY: Mama!

ROSE: Troy. You're hurting me.

TROY: Don't you tell me about no taking and giving.

CORY *comes up behind* TROY *and grabs him.* TROY, *surprised, is thrown off balance just as* CORY *throws a glancing blow that catches him on the chest and knocks him down.* TROY *is stunned, as is* CORY.

ROSE: Troy. Troy. No!

TROY *gets to his feet and starts at* CORY. Troy…no. Please! Troy!

ROSE *pulls on* TROY *to hold him back.* TROY *stops himself.*

TROY: (*To* CORY.) Alright. That's strike two. You stay away from around me, boy. Don't you strike out. You living with a full count. Don't you strike out.

TROY *exits out the yard as the lights go down.*

SCENE TWO

It is six months later, early afternoon. TROY *enters from the house and starts to exit the yard.* ROSE *enters from the house.*

ROSE: Troy, I want to talk to you.

TROY: All of a sudden, after all this time, you want to talk to me, huh? You ain't wanted to talk to me for months. You ain't wanted to talk to me last night. You ain't wanted no part of me then. What you wanna talk to me about now?

ROSE: Tomorrow's Friday.

TROY: I know what day tomorrow is. You think I don't know tomorrow's Friday? My whole life I ain't done nothing but look to see Friday coming and you got to tell me it's Friday.

ROSE: I want to know if you're coming home.

TROY: I always come home, Rose. You know that. There ain't never been a night I ain't come home.

ROSE: That ain't what I mean…and you know it. I want to know if you're coming straight home after work.

TROY: I figure I'd cash my check…hang out at Taylors' with the boys…maybe play a game of checkers…

ROSE: Troy, I can't live like this. I won't live like this. You livin' on borrowed time with me. It's been going on six months now you ain't been coming home.

TROY: I be here every night. Every night of the year. That's 365 days.

ROSE: I want you to come home tomorrow after work.

TROY: Rose…I don't mess up my pay. You know that now. I take my pay and I give it to you.

I don't have no money but what you give me back. I just want to have a little time to myself...a little time to enjoy life.

ROSE: What about me? When's my time to enjoy life?

TROY: I don't know what to tell you, Rose. I'm doing the best I can.

ROSE: You ain't been home from work but time enough to change your clothes and run out ...and you wanna call that the best you can do?

TROY: I'm going over to the hospital to see Alberta. She went into the hospital this afternoon. Look like she might have the baby early. I won't be gone long.

ROSE: Well, you ought to know. They went over to Miss Pearl's and got Gabe today. She said you told them to go ahead and lock him up.

TROY: I ain't said no such thing. Whoever told you that is telling a lie. Pearl ain't doing nothing but telling a big fat lie.

ROSE: She ain't had to tell me. I read it on the papers.

TROY: I ain't told them nothing of the kind.

ROSE: I saw it right there on the papers.

TROY: What it say, huh?

ROSE: It said you told them to take him.

TROY: Then they screwed that up, just the way they screw up everything. I ain't worried about what they got on the paper.

ROSE: Say the government send part of his check to the hospital and the other part to you.

TROY: I ain't got nothing to do with that if that's the way it works. I ain't made up the rules about how it work.

ROSE: You did Gabe just like you did Cory. You wouldn't sign the paper for Cory...but you signed for Gabe. You signed that paper.

The telephone is heard ringing inside the house.

TROY: I told you I ain't signed nothing, woman! The only thing I signed was the release form. Hell, I can't read, I don't know what they had on that paper! I ain't signed nothing about sending Gabe away.

ROSE: I said send him to the hospital...you said let him be free...now you done went down there and signed him to the hospital for half his money. You went back on yourself, Troy. You gonna have to answer for that.

TROY: See now...you been over there talking to Miss Pearl. She done got mad cause she ain't getting Gabe's rent money. That's all it is. She's liable to say anything.

ROSE: Troy, I seen where you signed the paper.

TROY: You ain't seen nothing I signed. What she doing got papers on my brother anyway? Miss Pearl telling a big fat lie. And I'm gonna tell her about it too! You ain't seen nothing I signed. Say...you ain't seen nothing I signed.

ROSE *exits into the house to answer the telephone. Presently she returns.*

ROSE: Troy...that was the hospital. Alberta had the baby.

TROY: What she have? What is it?

ROSE: It's a girl.

TROY: I better get on down to the hospital to see her.

ROSE: Troy...

TROY: Rose...I got to go see her now. That's only right...what's the matter...the baby's alright, ain't it?

ROSE: Alberta died having the baby.

TROY: Died...you say she's dead? Alberta's dead?

ROSE: They said they done all they could. They couldn't do nothing for her.

TROY: The baby? How's the baby?

ROSE: They say it's healthy. I wonder who's gonna bury her.

TROY: She had a family, Rose. She wasn't living in the world by herself.

ROSE: I know she wasn't living in the world by herself.

TROY: Next thing you gonna want to know if she had any insurance.

ROSE: Troy, you ain't got to talk like that.

TROY: That's the first thing that jumped out of your mouth. "Who's gonna bury her?" Like I'm fixing to take on that task for myself.

ROSE: I am your wife. Don't push me away.

TROY: I ain't pushing nobody away. Just give me some space. That's all. Just give me some room to breathe.

ROSE *exits into the house.* TROY *walks about the yard.*

TROY: (*With a quiet rage that threatens to consume him.*) Alright...Mr. Death. See now...I'm gonna tell you what I'm gonna do. I'm gonna take and build me a fence around this yard. See? I'm gonna build me a fence around what belongs to me. And then I want you to stay on the other side. See? You stay over there until you're ready for me. Then you come on. Bring your army. Bring your sickle. Bring your wrestling clothes. I ain't gonna fall down on my vigilance this time. You ain't gonna sneak up on me no more. When you ready for me...when the top of your list say Troy Maxson...that's when you come around here. You come up and knock on the front door. Ain't nobody else got nothing to do with this. This is between you and me. Man to man. You stay on the other side of that fence until you are ready for me. Then you come up and knock on the front door. Anytime you want. I'll be ready for you.

The lights go down to black.

SCENE THREE

The lights come up on the porch. It is late evening three days later. ROSE *sits listening to the ball game waiting for* TROY. *The final out of the game is made and* ROSE *switches off the radio.* TROY *enters the yard carrying an infant wrapped in blankets. He stands back from the house and calls.*

ROSE *enters and stands on the porch. There is a long, awkward silence, the weight of which grows heavier with each passing second.*

TROY: Rose...I'm standing here with my daughter in my arms. She ain't but a wee bittie little old thing. She don't know nothing about grownups' business. She innocent...and she ain't got no mama.

ROSE: What you telling me for, Troy?

She turns and exits into the house.

TROY: Well...I guess we'll just sit out here on the porch.

He sits down on the porch. There is an awkward indelicateness about the way he handles the baby. His largeness engulfs and seems to swallow it. He speaks loud enough for ROSE *to hear.*

A man's got to do what's right for him. I ain't sorry for nothing I done. It felt right in my heart.

To the baby.

What you smiling at? Your daddy's a big man. Got these great big old hands. But sometimes he's scared. And right now your daddy's scared cause we sitting out here and ain't got no home. Oh, I been homeless before. I ain't had no little baby with me. But I been homeless. You just be out on the road by your lonesome and you see one of them trains coming and you just kinda go like this...

He sings as a lullaby.

Please, Mr. Engineer let a man ride the line
Please, Mr. Engineer let a man ride the line
I ain't got no ticket please let me ride the blinds

ROSE *enters from the house.* TROY *hearing her steps behind him, stands and faces her.*

She's my daughter, Rose. My own flesh and blood. I can't deny her no more than I can deny them boys.

(*Pause.*)

You and them boys is my family. You and them and this child is all I got in the world. So I guess what I'm saying is...I'd appreciate it if you'd help me take care of her.

ROSE: Okay, Troy...you're right. I'll take care of your baby for you...cause...like you say... she's innocent...and you can't visit the sins of the father upon the child. A motherless child has got a hard time.

She takes the baby from him.

From right now...this child got a mother. But you a womanless man.

ROSE *turns and exits into the house with the baby. Lights go down to black.*

SCENE FOUR

It is two months later. LYONS *enters from the street. He knocks on the door and calls.*

LYONS: Hey, Rose! (*Pause.*) Rose!

ROSE: (*From inside the house.*) Stop that yelling. You gonna wake up Raynell. I just got her to sleep.

LYONS: I just stopped by to pay Papa this twenty dollars I owe him. Where's Papa at?

ROSE: He should be here in a minute. I'm getting ready to go down to the church. Sit down and wait on him.

LYONS: I got to go pick up Bonnie over her mother's house.

ROSE: Well, sit it down there on the table. He'll get it.

LYONS: (*Enters the house and sets the money on the table.*) Tell Papa I said thanks. I'll see you again.

ROSE: Alright, Lyons. We'll see you.

LYONS *starts to exit as* CORY *enters.*

CORY: Hey, Lyons.

LYONS: What's happening, Cory. Say man, I'm sorry I missed your graduation. You know I had a gig and couldn't get away. Otherwise, I would have been there, man. So what you doing?

CORY: I'm trying to find a job.

LYONS: Yeah I know how that go, man. It's rough out here. Jobs are scarce.

CORY: Yeah, I know.

LYONS: Look here, I got to run. Talk to Papa…he know some people. He'll be able to help you get a job. Talk to him…see what he say.

CORY: Yeah…alright, Lyons.

LYONS: You take care. I'll talk to you soon. We'll find some time to talk.

LYONS *exits the yard.* CORY *wanders over to the tree, picks up the bat and assumes a batting stance. He studies an imaginary pitcher and swings. Dissatisfied with the result, he tries again.* TROY *enters. They eye each other for a beat.* CORY *puts the bat down and exits the yard.* TROY *starts into the house as* ROSE *exits with* RAYNELL. *She is carrying a cake.*

TROY: I'm coming in and everybody's going out.

ROSE: I'm taking this cake down to the church for the bakesale. Lyons was by to see you. He stopped by to pay you your twenty dollars. It's laying in there on the table.

TROY: (*Going into his pocket.*) Well…here go this money.

ROSE: Put it in there on the table, Troy. I'll get it.

TROY: What time you coming back?

ROSE: Ain't no use in you studying me. It don't matter what time I come back.

TROY: I just asked you a question, woman. What's the matter…can't I ask you a question?

ROSE: Troy, I don't want to go into it. Your dinner's in there on the stove. All you got to do is heat it up. And don't you be eating the rest of them cakes in there. I'm coming back for them. We having a bakesale at the church tomorrow.

ROSE *exits the yard.* TROY *sits down on the steps, takes a pint bottle from his pocket, opens it and drinks. He begins to sing.*

TROY: Hear it ring! Hear it ring!
Had an old dog his name was Blue
You know Blue was mighty true
You know Blue was a good old dog
Blue trees a possum in a hollow log
You know from that he was a good old dog

BONO *enters the yard.*

BONO: Hey, Troy.

TROY: Hey, what's happening, Bono?

BONO: I just thought I'd stop by to see you.

TROY: What you stop by and see me for? You ain't stopped by in a month of Sundays. Hell, I must owe you money or something.

BONO: Since you got your promotion I can't keep up with you. Used to see you everyday. Now I don't even know what route you working.

TROY: They keep switching me around. Got me out in Greentree now…hauling white folk's garbage.

BONO: Greentree, huh? You lucky, at least you ain't got to be lifting them barrels. Damn if they ain't getting heavier. I'm gonna put in my two years and call it quits.

TROY: I'm thinking about retiring myself.

BONO: You got it easy. You can *drive* for another five years.

TROY: It ain't the same, Bono. It ain't like working the back of the truck. Ain't got nobody to talk to…feel like you working by yourself. Naw, I'm thinking about retiring. How's Lucille?

BONO: She alright. Her arthritis get to acting up on her sometime. Saw Rose on my way in. She going down to the church, huh?

TROY: Yeah, she took up going down there. All them preachers looking for somebody to fatten their pockets.
(*Pause.*)
Got some gin here.

BONO: Naw, thanks. I just stopped by to say hello.

TROY: Hell, nigger…you can take a drink. I ain't never known you to say no to a drink. You ain't got to work tomorrow.

BONO: I just stopped by. I'm fixing to go over to Skinner's. We got us a domino game going over his house every Friday.

TROY: Nigger, you can't play no dominoes. I used to whup you four games out of five.

BONO: Well, that learned me. I'm getting better.

TROY: Yeah? Well, that's alright.

BONO: Look here…I got to be getting on. Stop by sometime, huh?

TROY: Yeah, I'll do that, Bono. Lucille told Rose you bought her a new refrigerator.

BONO: Yeah, Rose told Lucille you had finally built your fence…so I figured we'd call it even.

TROY: I knew you would.

BONO: Yeah…okay. I'll be talking to you.

TROY: Yeah, take care, Bono. Good to see you. I'm gonna stop over.

BONO: Yeah. Okay, Troy.

BONO *exits.* TROY *drinks from the bottle.*

TROY: Old Blue died and I dig his grave
Let him down with a golden chain
Every night when I hear old Blue bark
I know Blue treed a possum in Noah's Ark.
Hear it ring! Hear it ring!
CORY *enters the yard. They eye each other for a beat.* TROY *is sitting in the middle of the steps.* CORY *walks over.*

CORY: I got to get by.

TROY: Say what? What's you say?

CORY: You in my way. I got to get by.

TROY: You got to get by where? This is my house. Bought and paid for. In full. Took me fifteen years. And if you wanna go in my house and I'm sitting on the steps…you say excuse me. Like your mama taught you.

CORY: Come on, Pop…I got to get by.

CORY *starts to maneuver his way past* TROY. TROY *grabs his leg and shoves him back.*

TROY: You just gonna walk over top of me?

CORY: I live here too!

TROY: (*Advancing toward him.*) You just gonna walk over top of me in my own house?

CORY: I ain't scared of you.

TROY: I ain't asked if you was scared of me. I asked you if you was fixing to walk over top of me in my own house? That's the question. You ain't gonna say excuse me? You just gonna walk over top of me?

CORY: If you wanna put it like that.

TROY: How else am I gonna put it?

CORY: I was walking by you to go into the house cause you sitting on the steps drunk, singing to yourself. You can put it like that.

TROY: Without saying excuse me???
CORY *doesn't respond.*
I asked you a question. Without saying excuse me???

CORY: I ain't got to say excuse me to you. You don't count around here no more.

TROY: Oh, I see…I don't count around here no more. You ain't got to say excuse me to your daddy. All of a sudden you done got so grown that your daddy don't count around here no more…Around here in his own house and yard that he done paid for with the sweat of his brow. You done got so grown to where you gonna take over. You gonna take over my house. Is that right? You gonna wear my pants. You gonna go in there and stretch out on my bed. You ain't got to say excuse me cause I don't count around here no more. Is that right?

CORY: That's right. You always talking this dumb stuff. Now, why don't you just get out my way.

TROY: I guess you got someplace to sleep and something to put in your belly. You got that, huh? You got that? That's what you need. You got that, huh?

CORY: You don't know what I got. You ain't got to worry about what I got.

TROY: You right! You one hundred percent right! I done spent the last seventeen years worrying about what you got. Now it's your turn, see? I'll tell you what to do. You grown…we done established that. You a man. Now, let's see you act like one. Turn your behind around and walk out this yard. And when you get out there in the alley…you can forget about this house. See? Cause this is my house. You go on and be a man and get your own house. You can forget about this. 'Cause this is mine. You go on and get yours cause I'm through with doing for you.

CORY: You talking about what you did for me… what'd you ever give me?

TROY: Them feet and bones! That pumping heart, nigger! I gave you more than anybody else is ever gonna give you.

CORY: You ain't never gave me nothing! You ain't never done nothing but hold me back. Afraid I was gonna be better than you. All you ever did was try to make me scared of you. I used to tremble every time you called my name. Every time I heard your footsteps in the house. Wondering all the time… what's Papa gonna say if I do this?…What's he gonna say if I do that?…What's Papa gonna say if I turn on the radio? And Mama, too…she tries…but she's scared of you.

TROY: You leave your mama you of this. She ain't got nothing to do with this.

CORY: I don't know how she stand you…after what you did to her.

TROY: I told you to leave your Mama out of this! *He advances toward CORY.*

CORY: What you gonna do…give me a whupping? You can't whup me no more. You're too old. You just an old man.

TROY: (*Shoves him on his shoulder.*) Nigger! That's what you are. You just another nigger on the street to me!

CORY: You crazy! You know that?

TROY: Go on now! You got the devil in you. Get on away from me!

CORY: You just a crazy old man…talking about I got the devil in me.

TROY: Yeah, I'm crazy! If you don't get on the other side of that yard…I'm gonna show you how crazy I am! Go on…get the hell out of my yard.

CORY: It ain't your yard. You took Uncle Gabe's money he got from the army to buy this house and then you put him out.

TROY: (TROY *advances on* CORY.) Get your black ass out of my yard!

TROY's advance backs CORY up against the tree. CORY grabs up the bat.

CORY: I ain't going nowhere! Come on…put me out! I ain't scared of you.

TROY: That's my bat!

CORY: Come on!

TROY: Put my bat down!

CORY: Come on, put me out.

CORY swings at TROY, who backs across the yard. What's the matter? You so bad…put me out! TROY advances toward CORY.

CORY: (*Backing up.*) Come on! Come on!

TROY: You're gonna have to use it! You wanna draw that bat back on me…you're gonna have to use it.

CORY: Come on!…Come on!

CORY swings the bat at TROY a second time. He misses. TROY continues to advance toward him.

TROY: You're gonna have to kill me! You wanna draw that bat back on me. You're gonna have to kill me.

CORY, backed up against the tree, can go no farther. TROY taunts him. He sticks out his head and offers him a target.

Come on! Come on!

CORY is unable to swing the bat. TROY grabs it.

TROY: Then I'll show you.

CORY and TROY struggle over the bat. The struggle is fierce and fully engaged. TROY ultimately is the stronger, and takes the bat from CORY and stands over him ready to swing. He stops himself.

Go on and get away from around my house. *CORY, stung by his defeat, picks himself up, walks slowly out of the yard and up the alley.*

CORY: Tell Mama I'll be back for my things.

TROY: They'll be on the other side of that fence.

CORY exits.

TROY: I can't taste nothing. Helluljah! I can't taste nothing no more. (TROY *assumes a batting posture and begins to taunt Death, the fastball in the outside corner.*) Come on! It's between you and me now! Come on! Anytime you want! Come on! I be ready for you…but I ain't gonna be easy.

The lights go down on the scene.

SCENE FIVE

The time is 1965. The lights come up in the yard. It is the morning of TROY's *funeral. A funeral plaque with a light hangs beside the door. There is a small garden plot off to the side. There is noise and activity in the house as* ROSE, LYONS *and* BONO *have gathered. The door opens and* RAYNELL, *seven years old, enters dressed in a flannel nightgown. She crosses to the garden and pokes around with a stick.* ROSE *calls from the house.*

ROSE: Raynell!

RAYNELL: Mam?

ROSE: What you doing out there?

RAYNELL: Nothing.

> ROSE *comes to the door.*

ROSE: Girl, get in here and get dressed. What you doing?

RAYNELL: Seeing if my garden growed.

ROSE: I told you it ain't gonna grow overnight. You got to wait.

RAYNELL: It don't look like it never gonna grow. Dag!

ROSE: I told you a watched pot never boils. Get in here and get dressed.

RAYNELL: This ain't even no pot, Mama.

ROSE: You just have to give it a chance. It'll grow. Now you come on and do what I told you. We got to be getting ready. This ain't no morning to be playing around. You hear me?

RAYNELL: Yes, mam.

> ROSE *exits into the house.* RAYNELL *continues to poke at her garden with a stick.* CORY *enters. He is dressed in a Marine corporal's uniform, and carries a duffel bag. His posture is that of a military man, and his speech has a clipped sternness.*

CORY: (*To* RAYNELL.) Hi.

> (*Pause.*)
> I bet your name is Raynell.

RAYNELL: Uh huh.

CORY: Is your mama home?

> RAYNELL *runs up on the porch and calls through the screendoor.*

RAYNELL: Mama...there's some man out here. Mama?

> ROSE *comes to the door.*

ROSE: Cory? Lord have mercy! Look here, you all!

> ROSE *and* CORY *embrace in a tearful reunion as* BONO *and* LYONS *enter from the house dressed in funeral clothes.*

BONO: Aw, looka here...

ROSE: Done got all grown up!

CORY: Don't cry, Mama. What you crying about?

ROSE: I'm just so glad you made it.

CORY: Hey Lyons. How you doing, Mr. Bono.

> LYONS *goes to embrace* CORY.

LYONS: Look at you, man. Look at you. Don't he look good, Rose. Got them Corporal stripes.

ROSE: What took you so long.

CORY: You know how the Marines are, Mama. They got to get all their paperwork straight before they let you do anything.

ROSE: Well, I'm sure glad you made it. They let Lyons come. Your Uncle Gabe's still in the hospital. They don't know if they gonna let him out or not. I just talked to them a little while ago.

LYONS: A Corporal in the United States Marines.

BONO: Your daddy knew you had it in you. He used to tell me all the time.

LYONS: Don't he look good, Mr. Bono?

BONO: Yeah, he remind me of Troy when I first met him.

> (*Pause.*)
> Say, Rose, Lucille's down at the church with the choir. I'm gonna go down and get the pallbearers lined up. I'll be back to get you all.

ROSE: Thanks, Jim.

CORY: See you, Mr. Bono.

LYONS: (*With his arm around* RAYNELL.) Cory... look at Raynell. Ain't she precious? She gonna break a whole lot of hearts.

ROSE: Raynell, come and say hello to your brother. This is your brother, Cory. You remember Cory.

RAYNELL: No, Mam.

CORY: She don't remember me, Mama.

ROSE: Well, we talk about you. She heard us talk about you.

> (*To* RAYNELL.) This is your brother, Cory. Come on and say hello.

RAYNELL: Hi.

CORY: Hi. So you're Raynell. Mama told me a lot about you.

ROSE: You all come on into the house and let me fix you some breakfast. Keep up your strength.

CORY: I ain't hungry, Mama.

LYONS: You can fix me something, Rose. I'll be in there in a minute.

ROSE: Cory, you sure you don't want nothing. I know they ain't feeding you right.

CORY: No, Mama…thanks. I don't feel like eating. I'll get something later.

ROSE: Raynell…get on upstairs and get that dress on like I told you.

ROSE and RAYNELL *exit into the house.*

LYONS: So…I hear you thinking about getting married.

CORY: Yeah, I done found the right one, Lyons. It's about time.

LYONS: Me and Bonnie been split up about four years now. About the time Papa retired. I guess she just got tired of all them changes I was putting her through.

(*Pause.*)

I always knew you was gonna make something out yourself. Your head was always in the right direction. So…you gonna stay in… make it a career…put in your twenty years?

CORY: I don't know. I got six already, I think that's enough.

LYONS: Stick with Uncle Sam and retire early. Ain't nothing out here. I guess Rose told you what happened with me. They got me down the workhouse. I thought I was being slick cashing other people's checks.

CORY: How much time you doing?

LYONS: They give me three years. I got that beat now. I ain't got but nine more months. It ain't so bad. You learn to deal with it like anything else. You got to take the crookeds with the straights. That's what Papa used to say. He used to say that when he struck out. I seen him strike out three times in a row …and the next time up he hit the ball over the grandstand. Right out there in Homestead Field. He wasn't satisfied hitting in the seats…he want to hit it over everything! After the game he had two hundred people standing around waiting to shake his hand. You got to take the crookeds with the straights. Yeah, Papa was something else.

CORY: You still playing?

LYONS: Cory…you know I'm gonna do that. There's some fellows down there we got us a band…we gonna try and stay together when we get out…but yeah, I'm still playing. It still helps me to get out of bed in the morning. As long as it do that I'm gonna be right there playing and trying to make some sense out of it.

ROSE: (*Calling.*) Lyons, I got these eggs in the pan.

LYONS: Let me go on and get these eggs, man. Get ready to go bury Papa.

(*Pause.*)

How you doing? You doing alright?

CORY *nods.* LYONS *touches him on the shoulder and they share a moment of silent grief.* LYONS *exits into the house.* CORY *wanders about the yard.* RAYNELL *enters.*

RAYNELL: Hi.

CORY: Hi.

RAYNELL: Did you used to sleep in my room?

CORY: Yeah…that used to be my room.

RAYNELL: That's what Papa call it. "Cory's room." It got your football in the closet.

ROSE *comes to the door.*

ROSE: Raynell, get in there and get them good shoes on.

RAYNELL: Mama, can't I wear these. Them other one hurt my feet.

ROSE: Well, they just gonna have to hurt your feet for a while. You ain't said they hurt your feet when you went down to the store and got them.

RAYNELL: They didn't hurt then. My feet done got bigger.

ROSE: Don't you give me no backtalk now. You get in there and get them shoes on.

RAYNELL *exits into the house.*

Ain't too much changed. He still got that piece of rag tied to that tree. He was out here swinging that bat. I was just ready to go back in the house. He swung that bat and then just fell over. Seem like he swung it and stood there with this grin on his face…and then he just fell over. They carried him on down to the hospital but I knew there wasn't no need…why don't you come on in the house?

CORY: Mama…I got something to tell you. I don't know how to tell you this…but I've got to tell you…I'm not going to Papa's funeral.

ROSE: Boy, hush your mouth. That's your daddy you talking about. I don't want hear that kind of talk this morning. I done raised you to come to this? You standing there all healthy and grown talking about you ain't going to your daddy's funeral?

CORY: Mama…listen…

ROSE: I don't want to hear it, Cory. You just get that thought out of your head.

CORY: I can't drag Papa with me everywhere I go. I've got to say no to him. One time in my life I've got to say no.

ROSE: Don't nobody have to listen to nothing like that. I know you and your daddy ain't seen eye to eye, but I ain't got to listen to that kind of talk this morning. Whatever was between you and your daddy…the time has come to put it aside. Just take it and set it over there on the shelf and forget about it. Disrespecting your daddy ain't gonna make you a man, Cory. You got to find a way to come to that on your own. Not going to your daddy's funeral ain't gonna make you a man.

CORY: The whole time I was growing up…living in his house…Papa was like a shadow that followed you everywhere. It weighed on you and sunk into your flesh. It would wrap around you and lay there until you couldn't tell which one was you anymore. That shadow digging in your flesh. Trying to crawl in. Trying to live through you. Everywhere I looked, Troy Maxson was staring back at me…hiding under the bed…in the closet. I'm just saying I've got to find a way to get rid of that shadow, Mama.

ROSE: You just like him. You got him in you good.

CORY: Don't tell me that, Mama.

ROSE: You Troy Maxson all over again.

CORY: I don't want to be Troy Maxson. I want to be me.

ROSE: You can't be nobody but who you are, Cory. That shadow wasn't nothing but you growing into yourself. You either got to grow into it or cut it down to fit you. But that's all you got to make life with. That's all you got to measure yourself against that world out there. Your daddy wanted you to be everything he wasn't…and at the same time he tried to make you into everything he was. I don't know if he was right or wrong…but I do know he meant to do more good than he meant to do harm. He wasn't always right. Sometimes when he touched he bruised. And sometimes when he took me in his arms he cut. When I first met your daddy I thought…Here is a man I can lay down with and make a baby. That's the first thing I thought when I seen him. I was thirty years old and had done seen my share of men. But when he walked up to me and said, "I can dance a waltz that'll make you dizzy," I thought, Rose Lee, here is a man that you can open yourself up to and be filled to bursting. Here is a man that can fill all them empty spaces you been tipping around the edges of. One of them empty spaces was being somebody's mother.

I married your daddy and settled down to cooking his supper and keeping clean sheets on the bed. When your daddy walked through the house he was so big he filled it up. That was my first mistake. Not to make him leave some room for me. For my part in the matter. But at that time I wanted that. I wanted a house that I could sing in. And that's what your daddy gave me. I didn't know to keep up his strength I had to give up little pieces of mine. I did that. I took on his life as mine and mixed up the pieces so that you couldn't hardly tell which was which anymore. It was my choice. It was my life and I didn't have to live it like that. But that's what life offered me in the way of being a woman and I took it. I grabbed hold of it with both hands.

By the time Raynell came into the house, me and your daddy had done lost touch with one another. I didn't want to make my blessing off of nobody's misfortune…but I took on to Raynell like she was all them babies I had wanted and never had.

The phone rings.

Like I'd been blessed to relive a part of my life. And if the Lord see fit to keep up my strength…I'm gonna do her just like your daddy did you…I'm gonna give her the best of what's in me.

RAYNELL: (*Entering, still with her old shoes.*) Mama …Reverend Tollivier on the phone.

ROSE *exits into the house.*

RAYNELL: Hi.

CORY: Hi.

RAYNELL: You in the Army or the Marines?

CORY: Marines.

RAYNELL: Papa said it was the Army. Did you know Blue?

CORY: Blue? Who's Blue?

RAYNELL: Papa's dog what he sing about all the time.

CORY: (*Singing.*) Hear it ring! Hear it ring!
    I had a dog his name was Blue
    You know Blue was mighty true
    You know Blue was a good old dog
    Blue treed a possum in a hollow log
    You know from that he was a good old dog.
    Hear it ring! Hear it ring!

RAYNELL *joins in singing.*

CORY AND RAYNELL: Blue treed a possum out on a limb
    Blue looked at me and I looked at him
    Grabbed that possum and put him in a sack
    Blue stayed there till I came back
    Old Blue's feets was big and round
    Never allowed a possum to touch the ground.
    Old Blue died and I dug his grave
    I dug his grave with a silver spade
    Let him down with a golden chain
    And every night I call his name
    Go on Blue, you good dog you
    Go on Blue, you good dog you

RAYNELL: Blue laid down and died like a man
    Blue laid down and died…

BOTH: Blue laid down and died like a man
    Now he's treeing possums in the Promised Land
    I'm gonna tell you this to let you know
    Blue's gone where the good dogs go

    When I hear old Blue bark
    When I hear old Blue bark
    Blue treed a possum in Noah's Ark
    Blue treed a possum in Noah's Ark.

ROSE *comes to the screen door.*

ROSE: Cory, we gonna be ready to go in a minute.

CORY: (*To* RAYNELL.) *You go on in the house and change them shoes like Mama told you so we can go to Papa's funeral.*

RAYNELL: Okay, I'll be back.

RAYNELL *exits into the house.* CORY *gets up and crosses over to the tree.* ROSE *stands in the screen door watching him.* GABRIEL *enters from the alley.*

GABRIEL: (*Calling.*) Hey, Rose!

ROSE: Gabe?

GABRIEL: I'm here, Rose. Hey Rose, I'm here!

ROSE *enters from the house.*

ROSE: Lord…Look here, Lyons!

LYONS: See, I told you, Rose…I told you they'd let him come.

CORY: How you doing, Uncle Gabe?

LYONS: How you doing, Uncle Gabe?

GABRIEL: Hey, Rose. It's time. It's time to tell St. Peter to open the gates. Troy, you ready? You ready, Troy. I'm gonna tell St. Peter to open the gates. You get ready now.

GABRIEL, *with great fanfare, braces himself to blow. The trumpet is without a mouthpiece. He puts the end of it into his mouth and blows with great force, like a man who has been waiting some twenty-odd years for this single moment. No sound comes out of the trumpet. He braces himself and blows again with the same result. A third time he blows. There is a weight of impossible description that falls away and leaves him bare and exposed to a frightful realization. It is a trauma that a sane and normal mind would be unable to withstand. He begins to dance. A slow, strange dance, eerie and life-giving. A dance of atavistic signature and ritual.* LYONS *attempts to embrace him.* GABRIEL *pushes* LYONS *away. He begins to howl in what is an attempt at song, or perhaps a song turning back into itself in an attempt at speech. He finishes his dance and the gates of heaven stand open as wide as God's closet.*

That's the way that go!

BLACKOUT

PERFORMING *FENCES*

August Wilson's *Fences,* written in 1983, was given a staged reading that year at the Eugene O'Neill Center in Waterford, Connecticut. Lloyd Richards, then Dean of the Yale Drama School and Artistic Director of the Yale Repertory Theatre, directed the first production of *Fences* at the Yale Rep in May of 1985. Two remarkable performers—James Earl Jones as Troy Maxson and Mary Alice as Troy's wife Rose—created the central roles and gave presence and voice to the play's dialogue and culture.

James Earl Jones drew on his experiences as a boy growing up in Mississippi and Michigan with his maternal grandfather. Mary Alice used her acquaintances in 1950s Chicago to identify with Rose and other women who were waiting to bloom; many, like Wilson's Rose, never did. Both actors acknowledged that Wilson's play required extraordinary concentration and energy that left them physically and emotionally drained long after they left the theater.[10]

Fences toured to Chicago, San Francisco, and Seattle before arriving at Broadway's Forty-Eighth Street Theater on March 26, 1987, with supporting actors Ray Aranha, Charles Brown, Frankie R. Faison, and Courtney B. Vance. The play won four Tony Awards for best play, best actor (James Earl Jones), best supporting actress (Mary Alice), and best director (Lloyd Richards). The work of August Wilson, James Earl Jones, Mary Alice, and Lloyd Richards was acknowledged and celebrated by the American theater community. One critic congratulated James Earl Jones for finding what was possibly the finest role of his career in a performance that embraced Troy Maxson's contradictions as black, male, and American.[11]

Like many of August Wilson's award winning plays, *Fences* has been popular in regional theaters from Pittsburgh to Seattle and has been published in numerous play collections.

CRITICS' NOTEBOOK

Critical assessments of August Wilson's plays are to be found in increasing numbers over the last two decades, beginning with the Broadway success of *Ma Rainey's Black Bottom* in 1981. Wilson is currently one of the most produced and written-about playwrights in America. The published commentaries on his works include theater reviews and interviews with the playwright, articles found in literature and theater journals, and full-length studies of the playwright's work. The most engaging full-length studies to date are Mary L. Bogumil's *Understanding August Wilson* (1999), Yvonne Shafer's *August Wilson: A Research and Production Sourcebook* (1998), Quin Wang's *An In-Depth Study of the Major Plays of African American Playwright August Wilson: Vernacularizing the Blues on Stage* (1999), and Alan Nadel's collection of essays called *May All Your Fences Have Gates: Essays on the Drama of August Wilson* (1994).

In his examination of modern American drama in *Modern American Drama, 1945–1990,* C. W. E. Bigsby looks at the playwrights who shaped the post-war theater in the United States, including Eugene O'Neill, Tennessee Williams, Arthur Miller, Edward Albee, David Mamet, and Sam Shepard. Lorraine Hansberry and August Wilson are central to his discussion of politics, race, and gender in the Broadway theater.

August Wilson talked about himself and his work during a session at the Poetry Center of the 92nd Street Y in New York City in 1990. His reflections throw light on how he writes plays and his concentration on black American history and culture.

C. W. E. Bigsby, from *Modern American Drama, 1945–1990**

August Wilson chooses deliberately to situate his characters historically, but his are not historical dramas in the sense that the past is treated as icon, faithfully reconstructed in its detailed real-

---

*C. W. E. Bigsby, *Modern American Drama, 1945–1990* (New York: Cambridge University Press, 1992): 286–287, 291–292.

ism. For him the past constitutes something more than a series of way-stations on a journey towards the present, though it is that, too. The past is the present. It provides the images, the language, the myths which we inhabit, with which we debate and against which we define ourselves. He has set himself to recreate the emotional, psychological and spiritual history of a people, to identify the way in which the individual has struggled to sustain a sense of self in the face of pressures, internal and external....

❧ ❧ ❧

It is tempting to see August Wilson as doing for a black underclass what Lorraine Hansberry did for the aspiring middle class. But where she created characters who self-consciously forged their frustrations and dreams into social action or political significance, he does not. There is an anger in the plays but it never shapes itself into polemic. Indeed, he is interested precisely in that space between suffering and its articulation, between need and its expression. His characters seldom make a connection between their individual sufferings and the necessity for social transformation. Their lives express that need; their words, their actions, seldom do. They want to be at ease with themselves and their world but fail in that ambition. They are fenced in and if, unlike Lorraine Hansberry's family in A Raisin in the Sun, they do not choose to break through that containment in a public way, finding the meaning of their lives in that conflict, they are aware that a barrier exists. As a result the anger and aggression bounce back and are turned inwards. The barriers are so implacable they seem organic. Troy questions the practices of his employer but his victory is to move himself from the rear to the front of the garbage truck. In the end that victory is far less important than others. He leaves behind a child, his daughter Raynell, and when he is dead the son he had alienated joins with his illegitimate half-sister to sing his father's song—a song that had grown out of his experience. The man who had spent his life seeking his 'song', his identity, the shape to his life, was that song....

❧ ❧ ❧

From the perspective of the 1960s such writing would seem conservative. It explores and in some senses celebrates the given. Lives are not shaped into weapons nor laments into diatribes. His characters do not serve meaning; they are not subordinated to social purpose. They speak their lives and sometimes sing them. The music is the blues, not the protest song.

August Wilson, from "How to Write a Play Like August Wilson"*

❦

I start—generally I have an idea of something I want to say—but I start with a line of dialogue. I have no idea half the time who's speaking or what they're saying. I'll start with the line, and the more dialogue I write, the better I get to know the characters. For instance, in writing the play "The Piano Lesson," one of the characters, Berniece, says something to Boy Willie, her brother, and he talks about how "Sutter fell in the well." Well this is a surprise to *me*. I didn't know that.

Then I say, "Well, who is Sutter?" You see, if you have a character in a play, the character who knows everything, then you won't have any problem. Whenever you get stuck you ask them a question. I have learned that if you trust them and simply do not even think about what they're saying, it doesn't matter. They say things like, "Sutter fell in the well." You just write it down and make it all make sense later. So I use those characters a lot. Anything you want to know you ask the characters.

Part of my process is that I assemble all these things and later try to make sense out of them and sort of plug them in to what is my larger artistic agenda. That agenda is answering James Baldwin when he called for "a profound articulation of the black tradition," which he defined as "that field of manners and ritual of

*August Wilson, "How to Write A Play Like August Wilson," *The New York Times* (March 10, 1991):H5, 17.

intercourse that will sustain a man once he's left his father's house."

So I say, O.K., that field of manners and ritual of intercourse is what I'm trying to put on stage. And I best learn about that through the blues. I discovered everything there. So I have an agenda. Someone asked the painter Romare Bearden about his work and he said, "I try to explore, in terms of the life I know best, those things which are common to all cultures."

So I say, O.K., culture and the commonalities of culture.

Using those two things and having the larger agenda, I take all this material, no matter what it is, and later, I sit down and assemble it. And I discovered—and I admire Romare Bearden a lot; he's a collagist, he pieces things together—I discovered that that's part of my process, what I do. I piece it all together, and, hopefully, have it make sense, the way a collage would.

As for the characters, they are all invented. At the same time they are all made up out of myself. So they're all me, different aspects of my personality, I guess. But I don't say, "Oh, I know a guy like this. I'm going to write Joe." Some people do that. I can't do that. So I write different parts of myself and I try to invent or discover some other parts.

And I think that we as black Americans need to go back and make the connection that we allowed to be severed when we moved from the South to the North, the great migration starting in 1915. For the most part, the culture that was growing and developing in the Southern part of the United States for 200 and some years, we more or less abandoned. And we have a situation where in 1991 kids do not know who they are because they cannot make the connection with their grandparents—and therefore the connection with their political history in America.

REVISITING MODERN REALISM

As a principal writing and performance style for more than a century, *realism* implies a conception of dramatic reality different from that found in earlier works by Sophocles, Shakespeare, or Oscar Wilde. Regardless of the times in which they live, all playwrights have their concepts of the "real" in human behavior and events, as we have seen in *Oedipus the King, Hamlet,* and *The Importance of Being Earnest.* The means of imitating that conception of reality changes with each writer and age. However, realism in the mind of its European pioneers in the 1860s implied a candid representation of the world around them. Along with their efforts to bring a new truth into the dramatic text (and hence onto the stage), came new subjects, characters, environments, language, and life styles taken from contemporary life. A new tragic hero, the somewhat ordinary individual, struggling for selfhood and dignity, emerged from living rooms, kitchens, flophouses, and streets to indict society. Early on, heredity and environment became the verifiable enemies of individual expression and freedom and the *causes célèbres* more so of the naturalists than the realists.

The realists tried to put on stage only what could be verified by observing ordinary life. The naturalistic movement, spearheaded by Emile Zola, was committed to presenting an even narrower view of reality by focusing on the sordid and squalid in contemporary life. The naturalists tried to show those powerful forces governing human lives over which we exercise little awareness or control. In their work, heredity and environment reached new pinnacles of importance. Eventually, the loss of individuality in dramatic character and the repetition of sordid situations and themes lessened interest in their work.

The nineteenth-century realists rendered setting, character, and dialogue so close to actual life that audiences were convinced by the illusion of contemporary reality. Audiences responded to ordinary lives made both significant and universal. What seemed small, inconsequential, and overlooked became important and urgent. As a consequence, familiar events became dramatic fictions. The great realists, Ibsen, Strindberg, Shaw, and Chekhov, put their understanding of the world around them into dramatic form—often a variant of the well-made-play format—and held a dramatic magnifying glass up to commonplace realities.

Today, the goals of realistic writers have changed very little from those of their predecessors. Writing within the realistic tradition, Arthur Miller, David Mamet, Marsha Norman, and August Wilson construct verifiable worlds, exploring recognizable relationships, illuminating the social and the familial, and plunging beneath the surfaces of ordinary mid-twentieth-century life to arrive at the troubling relevances of human and social themes. The fact that realism holds a mirror up to humanity's insignificance and gives the ordinary and commonplace a new dimension is the source of its popular appeal.

Writing styles that *revolted* against the "illusion of the real" in the theater span a period from the early 1900s to the present. These experiments involved some of the most influential playwrights of our time, especially Bertolt Brecht and Samuel Beckett, whose plays are the subject of the next chapters.

NOTES

1. Emile Zola, *Le Naturalism au Théâtre* in *Les Oeuvres Completes,* Vol. 42 (Paris: Francois Bernouard, 1927): 17.

2. Eric Bentley, *The Playwright as Thinker: A Study of Drama in Modern Times* (New York: Harcourt, Brace, Jovanovich, 1987): 4.

3. Joseph Wood Krutch, *"Modernism" in Modern Drama: A Definition and an Estimate* (Ithaca, N.Y.: Cornell University Press, 1953): 22.

4. August Strindberg, "Preface" to *Miss Julie,* in *Six Plays of August Strindberg,* trans. Elizabeth Sprigge (New York: Doubleday & Company, 1955): 65–66.

5. Frederick Marker and Lise-Lone Marker, *The Scandinavian Theatre: A Short History* (Totowa, N.J.: Rowman and Littlefield, 1975): 154.

6. Zola 17.

7. *Conversations with Lillian Hellman,* ed. Jackson R. Bryer (Jackson, MI: University of Mississippi Press, 1986): 115.

8. Eugene Scribe, *Oeuvres Completes de Eugène Scribe,* ed. E. Dentu (Paris, 1874): I, xxiv.

9. August Wilson, "Interview," *In Their Own Words Contemporary American Playwrights: Interviews,* ed. David Savran (New York: Theatre Communications Group, 1988): 299.

10. Heather Henderson, "Building *Fences*: An Interview with Mary Alice and James Earl Jones, *Theater,* No. XVI, No. 3 (Summer/Fall 1985): 67–70.

11. Frank Rich, "Barrier Riffs: *Fences,*" *The New York Times* (March 27, 1987): C3: 1.

PART FIVE

UNDERSTANDING
THEATRICALISM

CHAPTER 11

UNDERSTANDING THEATRICALISM AND EPIC THEATER

Brian Dennehy in the title role in the Goodman Theatre's 1986 production of *Galileo*, directed by Robert Falls. (Photo © 1986 Kevin Horan.)

...the inflexible rule that the proof of the pudding is in the eating.
—Bertolt Brecht

THE STAGE AS PLATFORM

Expressionism in Germany as early as 1912 was highly influential in the arts, most especially in writing and performance styles for the theater. With antecedents in romanticism and symbolism, the expressionists as a group, which included the young Bertolt Brecht, were defined by their revolt against established writing conventions and by their bold distortion of reality. In the German theater, such expressionist writers as George Kaiser and Ernst Toller led the way. They rejected the conventions of the well-made play and the plausibility of stage realism. In their place, we find disjointed plots, bizarre events, staccato dialogue, visual images symbolizing mental states, and characters signifying social functions. Themes dealt with humanitarian causes, pacificism, and progressive social reforms. The villains were industrial magnates, military-industrial institutions, and a self-satisfied middle class. The stage was treated as a platform, not as someone's living room, and was used to comment on the social, economic, and political issues of the times. Bertolt Brecht and his chief mentor Erwin Piscator owe their theories and practices of epic theater to the expressionists, music hall routines, film technology, and to the political and economic turmoil of Germany in the 1920s and 1930s.

EPIC THEORY AND PRACTICE

As evolved by Piscator and Brecht, epic theory was both a new way of writing for the theater and a different style of performance. A left-wing experimenter in *agitprop,* or propaganda theater, Piscator perfected many of the techniques associated with Brecht's epic theater. *The Good Soldier Schweik,* staged by Piscator in 1928, climaxed his earlier experiments. He used conveyor belts for bringing on short sequential scenes; translucent backgrounds or screens for projections; slide and movie projectors for photographs, cartoons, and explanatory captions; musical revue numbers; and announcements through loudspeakers. His staging techniques, combined with a loosely constructed series of scenes, shaped a serious theatrical revue which he called "epic theater." Piscator's productions were political, technological, and episodic in scope, thereby presenting a world in economic and political chaos. Bertolt Brecht was highly influenced by this bold staging designed to make blatant political statements about contemporary events.

Developed over forty years, Brecht's own ideas of "epic theater" were more complex and ambitious than those of Piscator. Like Piscator, he set about to represent historical process in the theater. He argued that the stage should be used as an undisguised *platform* on which political and social issues could be debated.

As a playwright, Brecht thought of drama as *episodic* and *narrative:* a sequence of incidents or events narrated without artificial restrictions as to time, place, or formal plot. He reminded us that history does not have beginnings, middles, and endings. Rather, history moves from episode to episode and a play's structure and action should reflect this process. Brecht's plays, therefore, were built of a series of loosely knit scenes, each complete in itself, and introduced by signs, placards, or announcements. The total effect was achieved through the juxtaposition of contrasting *episodes* moving in a forward, linear motion. In the same way, nonliterary elements of production—cacophonous music, harsh lighting, moving scenery, and gestural acting—retained their separate identities while contributing to the total effect.

As pioneers and iconoclasts, Piscator and Brecht conceived of epic theater as a way to teach lessons about history and to call directly upon audiences to learn the processes by which the modern world, if not halted, was moving toward Armageddon. While his staging practices resembled Piscator's, Brecht's have been far more influential, especially during the seven years after the Second World War when he directed the Berliner Ensemble (1949–56), located at that time in East Berlin. As a playwright, Brecht wrote some of the great plays of the modern theater, one of the major being *Galileo*, which embodies his theories on epic theater.

Galileo

BERTOLT BRECHT

Bertolt Brecht (1898–1956) was born in Augsburg, Germany, where he spent his youth. In 1918, while studying medicine at Munich University, he was called up for military service as a medical orderly. His early poems about the horrors of war and his first play, Baal *(1918), date from this experience.*

At the war's end, Brecht drifted into the Bohemian world of theater and literature in Munich and Berlin. During the 1920s, Brecht seriously entered the theater world as a reviewer and playwright. Working with Erwin Piscator, he solidified his own theories of epic theater and in 1928 wrote The Threepenny Opera *(in collaboration with composer Kurt Weill). An overnight success, the play made both Brecht and Weill famous.*

With the rise of the Nazi movement in the 1930s, many artists and intellectuals fled Germany, including Kurt Weill and his actress-wife Lotte Lenya. In 1933, Brecht fled with his family to Scandinavia and then to America, where he resided until 1947. As an immigrant member of the motion picture industry, Brecht was subpoenaed in 1947 to appear before the House Committee on Un-American Activities (HUAC) to testify on the "Communist infiltration" of Hollywood. The day following his testimony, he left the United States and settled in Switzerland and eventually worked in what was then East Berlin where he founded the Berliner Ensemble in 1949.

Brecht's writings on epic theory and practice span a period of forty years. However, his greatest plays were written during his years of exile from his native Germany (1933–48). They are The Good Person of Setzuan, Galileo, The Caucasian Chalk Circle, *and* Mother Courage and Her Children.

CRITICAL INTRODUCTION TO *GALILEO*

Brecht's only play based on a historical figure, the seventeenth-century Italian astronomer and physicist, Galileo Galilei (1564–1642), who challenged prevailing notions of astronomy by suggesting that the earth was not the center of the universe but rather revolved around the sun, was written in three versions over a period of nineteen years. He wrote the first version (the early title was *The Earth Moves*) in Denmark in 1938–39 while fleeing Hitler's Germany. This text was performed in Zurich in 1943. The second, the American version reprinted here, was written in 1945–46 in collaboration with British actor Charles Laughton, who played Galileo in a 1947 production in Beverly Hills, California, and again on Broadway in 1948. The third and final version (retitled *The Life of Galileo* and based on the English text) was written with Brecht's collaborators at the Berliner Ensemble in East Berlin and produced with Ernst Busch in the title role in 1957, shortly following Brecht's death in the previous year.

Each time Brecht revised *Galileo,* his emphases changed with his maturity as an artist and political thinker, and with the cataclysm of world history that evolved into a world war, the partition of Western Europe, and the advent of the nuclear age.

At the outset, Brecht's Galileo was an intellectual figure in history who outsmarted reactionary authority (the Inquisition), and, experiencing near blindness, completed his great scientific work, the *Discorsi,* and smuggled the manuscript out of Italy with the assistance of his pupil, Andrea Sarti. Thus, the individual's subversive political action against reactionary authority, Brecht concluded, caused a light to dawn in the darkness of his age.

In the 1930s what commended the subject of Galileo to Brecht was the analogy between the seventeenth-century scientist's underground activities against the authority of the Roman Catholic Church and those of the twentieth-century opponents to Hitler's Germany. In all instances, Brecht insisted that the play was neither an attack on the church nor the priesthood, but rather on reactionary authority in any age. In Galileo's time, science was a branch of theology. The church as the intellectual authority of the day was, therefore, the ultimate scientific, political, and spiritual court of appeal. Galileo's struggle in the name of intellectual freedom gives thinly disguised attention to present-day reactionary authorities of a totally secular kind.[1]

In the American version, written six years later as Brecht continued his exile in California, the nuclear age (the logical progression of Galileo's earlier discoveries) had dawned with new weapons of destruction and all of its attendant horrors. As Brecht was writing the first-draft version of his play in 1938–39, the German physicist Nils Bohr was making his discoveries in atomic theory that resulted in the splitting of the uranium atom; in 1945, as Brecht was working with Charles Laughton on a second script, the United States exhibited the atomic bomb's destructive possibilities on the Japanese cities of Hiroshima and Nagasaki. The playwright then faced the fact that the nuclear age was a product of the new science founded by Galileo at the beginning of the "scientific age" three hundred years prior. Brecht then set about to condemn Galileo as a traitor because the atomic bomb, in Brecht's view, had made the relationship between society and science into a matter of life and death for the human race.[2] In this second and darker version of the Galileo story, Brecht's admiration for his clever scientist is altered and Galileo is depicted as a gluttonous, self-serving, and unethical (if not "criminal") intellectual who has betrayed humankind. In the second text, Brecht set about to demand not just freedom to research and teach, but a sense of social and moral responsibility toward humankind from the world's scientists. The point in 1947 was to demand from those who viewed scientific advances "as an end in itself," thus playing into the hands of those in power, a change and advancement of a utilitarian concept of science.[3] What

Brecht has to say about his collaboration with Charles Laughton (and his thoughts on what the revised work has to say about modern science in 1945) is contained in a foreword to the German edition entitled "Building up a Part: Laughton's Galileo."

As a playwright, Brecht used historical material—what he called *historification*—drawn from other times and places (ancient China in *The Caucasian Chalk Circle*, Germany's Thirty Years' War in *Mother Courage and Her Children*, the church-dominated Italy of the seventeenth century in *Galileo*) in order to get audiences to reflect upon oppressive social and political problems and events of the present time. Brecht argued that the theater should not treat contemporary subjects in a direct way, but by putting similar events of the past on stage and by distancing us from immediate problems get us to see the parallels in history and to understand what actions should have been taken in the past (and were not), but can be undertaken in the present to correct social and political problems.

As a historical scientific figure, Galileo's life embraced a twofold responsibility: to the work to be achieved and then to humankind, which the work serves. In his lecherous and gluttonous character, Brecht has at hand a genius whose most powerful instinct is curiosity and whose greatest sensual pleasure is the pleasure of discovery, whether of a well-cooked goose or of Jupiter's moons. To be able to indulge his appetites, Galileo is prepared to commit the basest acts: He cheats the Venetians by selling them the telescope he has not invented but merely reproduced from a traveller's description. He writes servile letters to the Medici prince whose tyrannies he despises. And, with the physical cowardice of the sensuous man, he recants his theories when merely shown the instruments of torture. In the earlier version of the play, Galileo's recantation was made to appear excusable as a deliberate and calculating act: By recanting he saved his life and gained the time to complete his treatise which was then smuggled out to the free world. Nevertheless, Brecht came increasingly to view the Galileos of the world as serving pure research devoid of ethical responsibility to humanity. In the Berlin text, he labels Galileo as a "social criminal, a complete rogue."[4] Galileo becomes a "criminal," in Brecht's harsher view of scientific progress, because by his cowardice he has established the tradition of the scientist's subservence to the state—the tradition that, according to Brecht, reached its culmination in the production of the atomic bomb for military purposes, which science then put at the disposal of nonscientific people to serve their power politics.

EPIC DEVICES

Brecht described his ideal theater as using three key devices: *historification, epic,* and *alienation.* Brecht's theory of epic staging, as found in his writings, included progressive scenes with no act divisions to show the ascending or declining fortunes of the central figure. In the epic style, each scene of *Galileo* begins with titles, or legends, written on placards and other images suspended above the stage or projected on screens. For example, a sign—located above the stage and written in crude letters on a frame—depicts the changing years and places in Galileo's life. In pursuit of his researches and new patrons, he moves from Venice to Florence to Rome and back to Florence. Subsequent titles describe years, seasons, and Galileo's machinations, discoveries, and political fortunes. The scene titles are thematically consistent, describing Galileo in relation to three things: research, materialism, and authority.

> *Eight long years with tongue in cheek*
> *Of what he knew he did not speak*
> *Then temptation grew too great*
> *And Galileo challenged fate. (8)*

In the American version, sketches of Jupiter's moons, Leonardo da Vinci's technical drawings, and a Venetian warship were projected on screens to assist in the telling of the story.

The epic devices allow Brecht to express his political, sociological, and economic arguments, such as the connections between science and industry, individuals and governments, and the ultimate victimization of common humanity by both. Galileo vacillates between life's contradictions (an important point in Brecht's immersion in Marxist theory): the necessities of research and family, pure research and materialism, science and religion, profit and loss, hunger and gratification, and so on. In the downward spiral of Galileo's life (his isolation, poverty, poor health, and near blindness), Brecht offers a general judgment at the end of Scene 13 that Galileo failed his ethical responsibilities to humankind. Galileo explains to his former pupil:

> *As a scientist I had an almost unique opportunity …I surrendered my knowledge to the powers that be, to use it, no, not use it, abuse it, as it suits their ends. I have betrayed my profession. Any man who does what I have done must not be tolerated in the ranks of science. (13)*

Caught up in Galileo's plight and "heroic" passing of his forbidden writings to his pupil for future generations, few audiences have realized that this was the bitterest and most meaningful lesson of the play. Brecht's condemnation of his exemplar as hero and criminal is also an indictment of modern scientific-industrial-political power systems and those individuals in positions of influence.

What is clear in the epic style is that Brecht is concerned neither with biography nor the history of the seventeenth century, but with the historical and human problems of the twentieth century. The recantation scene (12) is the crisis scene of the play (all of the previous scenes have been arranged to build to this moment). The arrangement of the episodes permits us to interpret Galileo's behavior in recanting under pressure from the Inquisition. He has proved over and over again that he has only judged the powers of the world in so far as they were advantageous or detrimental to his researches. He has sacrificed his daughter's marriage (Scene 8), security for himself by rejecting the iron founder's offer of sanctuary (Scene 10), and his eyesight and reputation as a man of integrity (Scenes 12 and 13). In all things, though, Brecht's character is consistent. The inner makeup of Brecht's Galileo is determined by a hedonistic indulgence of life's pleasures and an excessive joy in scientific experimentation and discovery. Nothing else matters, including the social importance of his discoveries. For this, Brecht increasingly condemns his scientist in the play's two later versions.

I AM BECOME DEATH, THE DESTROYER OF WORLDS

The 1945–46 version of *Galileo* only slightly masks the theme of the relationship of scientific research to the most profound moral and social questions illuminated by the explosions on Hiroshima and Nagasaki. In the second text, Brecht has taken a bleak vision of "scientific progress," echoed in J. Robert Oppenheimer's famous cry—words from the Indian epic, the *Bhagavad Gita*—as he watched the first test explosion of an atomic weapon: "I am become death, the destroyer of worlds." By 1947, Brecht had a wholly negative view of Galileo whom he now regarded as an "intellectual prostitute."[5] The recantation scene becomes thereby not an example of practical behavior but a clear case of the scientist allowing the powers that be to use him for their own nonhumanistic ends. What was frustrating for Brecht was that, despite his distancing devices, audiences refused to condemn the physicist's behavior before the Inquisition and his secret efforts to preserve his writings elicited sympathy and highly emotional responses. Brecht concluded that "Technically, *Life of Galileo* is a great step backwards…" because he had been unable to distance the audience emotionally from Galileo's plight.[6]

Brecht's concept of alienation (or distancing) is at work on two principal levels in the play: Galileo himself finds his world of 1600 to be unfamiliar, outdated, and in need of explanation. This fact accounts for the historical character's novelty, strangeness, and difference.[7] Audiences also sympathized with the character's strong lust for living, and, despite Brecht's many efforts to censor Galileo, they continued to applaud the scientist's struggles against reactionary authority.

Despite the epic devices, *Galileo* remained an old-fashioned play (almost classical) centered on the central figure's choices under pressure during which he has campaigned to change the world and has capitulated unheroically when faced with physical pain. Disillusioned by Galileo's recantation ("I, Galileo Galilei, Teacher of Mathematics and Physics, do hereby publicly renounce my teaching that the earth moves."), his student, Andrea Sarti, rejects his teacher with the famous line, "Unhappy is the land that breeds no heroes." Galileo replies, "Unhappy is the land that needs a hero." Galileo has not fulfilled the heroic role his pupil envisioned for him, for, in the horror of the moment, he has fallen victim to human frailty.

> **GALILEO:** They showed me the instruments.
> **ANDREA:** It was not a plan?
> **GALILEO:** It was not. (13)

Eric Bentley called the play a tragicomedy of "heroic combat followed by unheroic capitulation." In the writing tradition of great tragicomic plays, he continued, there is in *Galileo* no noble contrition, no belated rebellion, but rather only undisguised self-loathing.[8] In explanation to Sarti at the play's end, Galileo says, "I have come to believe that I was never in real danger; for some years I was as strong as the authorities and I surrendered my knowledge to the powers that be" (Scene 13). In the new version, Galileo is given a long tirade of self-condemnation. Sarti is also placed in the wrong because he argues that "science has only one commandment: contribution." Galileo's retort is: "Then welcome to the gutter, dear colleague in science and brother in betrayal: I sold out, you are a buyer" (Scene 13).

DIALECTICAL THEATER

In his theoretical writings, set down between 1948 and 1956, Brecht referred to his theater and plays as "dialectical," further stressing the collision of conflicting ideas and social forces in his plays. The ultimate source of Brecht's dialectic in *Galileo* is the central figure of his corpulent and vociferous scientist whose greatness and enormous failure intrigued Brecht as a subject for epic theater. The figure of the historical genius provided dialectical argument about the ultimate cost of scientific progress for humanity and the ethical responsibility to humankind of those individuals responsible for discoveries and inventions that have resulted not only in Chernobyl-like disasters but also in space exploration and detection of black holes in the universe.

The premiere of the English language version prepared jointly by Brecht and actor Charles Laughton, who played the lead and co-directed the play with Brecht (though the director of record was Joseph Losey), opened in Los Angeles at the Coronet Theatre on July 30, 1947. The production proceeded to Broadway following its successful California run, and opened at the Maxine Elliott Theater on December 7, 1947 (the date on which the Japanese bombed Pearl Harbor six years earlier). By the time the play opened in New York, Brecht, following his appearance before the House Un-American Activities Committee in Washington, D.C., had returned to Europe. He had been subpoenaed to testify on the issue of Communist infiltration into the motion picture industry and played a role not unlike Galileo's before the Inquisition. Brecht prevaricated, entertained, and escaped to Europe, never to return to the United States.

Galileo is an important document as the last (if unfinished) aesthetic testament of Bertolt Brecht as a playwright and director. Unable to complete work on the Berliner Ensemble version of the text, he turned rehearsals over to Eric Engel and the play was produced in its third version on January 15, 1957, five months following Brecht's death.

Galileo

TRANSLATED BY CHARLES LAUGHTON

It is my opinion that the earth is very noble and admirable by reason of so many and so different alterations and generations which are incessantly made therein.

—Galileo Galilei

CHARACTERS

GALILEO GALILEI

ANDREA SARTI, *two actors: boy and man*

MRS. SARTI

LUDOVICO MARSILI

PRIULI, THE CURATOR

SAGREDO, *Galileo's friend*

VIRGINIA GALILEI

TWO SENATORS

MATTI, *an iron founder*

PHILOSOPHER, *later, Rector of the University*

ELDERLY LADY

YOUNG LADY

FEDERZONI, *assistant to Galileo*

MATHEMATICIAN

LORD CHAMBERLAIN

FAT PRELATE

TWO SCHOLARS

TWO MONKS

INFURIATED MONK

OLD CARDINAL

ATTENDANT MONK

CHRISTOPHER CLAVIUS

LITTLE MONK

TWO SECRETARIES

CARDINAL BELLARMIN

CARDINAL BARBERINI

CARDINAL INQUISITOR

YOUNG GIRL

HER FRIEND

GIUSEPPE

STREET SINGER

HIS WIFE

REVELLER

A LOUD VOICE

INFORMER

TOWN CRIER

OFFICIAL

PEASANT

CUSTOMS OFFICER

BOY

SENATORS, OFFICIALS, PROFESSORS, LADIES, GUESTS, CHILDREN

There are two wordless roles: The Doge in scene 2 and Prince Cosmo de Medici in scene 4. The ballad of scene 9 is filled out by a pantomime: among the individuals in the pantomimic crowd are three extras (including the "King of Hungary"), Cobbler's Boy, Three Children, Peasant Woman, Monk, Rich Couple, Dwarf, Beggar, and Girl.

SCENE 1

In the year sixteen hundred and nine
Science' light began to shine.
At Padua City in a modest house
Galileo Galilei set out to prove
The sun is still, the earth is on the move.

(GALILEO's *scantily furnished study. Morning.* GALILEO *is washing himself. A barefooted boy,* ANDREA, *son of his housekeeper,* MRS. SARTI, *enters with a big astronomical model.*)

GALILEO: Where did you get that thing?

ANDREA: The coachman brought it.

GALILEO: Who sent it?

ANDREA: It said "From the Court of Naples" on the box.

GALILEO: I don't want their stupid presents. Illuminated manuscripts, a statue of Hercules the size of an elephant—they never send money.

ANDREA: But isn't this an astronomical instrument, Mr. Galilei?

GALILEO: That is an antique too. An expensive toy.

ANDREA: What's it for?

GALILEO: It's a map of the sky according to the wise men of ancient Greece. Bosh! We'll try and sell it to the university. They still teach it there.

ANDREA: How does it work, Mr. Galilei?

GALILEO: It's complicated.

ANDREA: I think I could understand it.

GALILEO (*interested*): Maybe. Let's begin at the beginning. Description!

ANDREA: There are metal rings, a lot of them.

GALILEO: How many?

ANDREA: Eight.

GALILEO: Correct. And?

ANDREA: There are words painted on the bands.

GALILEO: What words?

ANDREA: The names of stars.

GALILEO: Such as?

ANDREA: Here is a band with the sun on it and on the inside band is the moon.

GALILEO: Those metal bands represent crystal globes, eight of them.

ANDREA: Crystal?

GALILEO: Like huge soap bubbles one inside the other and the stars are supposed to be tacked on to them. Spin the band with the sun on it. (ANDREA *does.*) You see the fixed ball in the middle?

ANDREA: Yes.

GALILEO: That's the earth. For two thousand years man has chosen to believe that the sun and all the host of stars revolve about him. Well. The Pope, the Cardinals, the princes, the scholars, captains, merchants, housewives, have pictured themselves squatting in the middle of an affair like that.

ANDREA: Locked up inside?

GALILEO (*triumphant*): Ah!

ANDREA: It's like a cage.

GALILEO: So you sensed that. (*Against the model.*) I like to think the ships began it.

ANDREA: Why?

GALILEO: They used to hug the coasts and then all of a sudden they left the coasts and spread over the oceans. A new age was coming. I was on to it years ago. I was a young man, in Siena. There was a group of masons arguing. They had to raise a block of granite. It was hot. To help matters, one of them wanted to try a new arrangement of ropes. After five minutes' discussion, out went a method which had been employed for a thousand years. The millennium of faith is ended, said I, this is the millennium of doubt. And we are pulling out of that contraption. The sayings of the wise men won't wash anymore. Everybody, at last, is getting nosy. I predict that in our time astronomy will become the gossip of the marketplace and the sons of fish-wives will pack the schools.

ANDREA: You're off again, Mr. Galilei. Give me the towel. (*He wipes some soap from Galilei's back.*)

GALILEO: By that time, with any luck, they will be learning that the earth rolls round the sun, and that their mothers, the captains, the scholars, the princes, and the Pope are rolling with it.

ANDREA: That turning-round-business is no good. I can see with my own eyes that the sun comes up in one place in the morning and goes down in a different place in the evening. It doesn't stand still, I can see it move.

GALILEO: You see nothing, all you do is gawk. Gawking is not seeing. (*He puts the iron washstand in the middle of the room.*) Now: that's the sun. Sit down. (ANDREA *sits on a chair.* GALILEO *stands behind him.*) Where is the sun, on your right or on your left?

ANDREA: Left.

GALILEO: And how will it get to the right?

ANDREA: By your putting it there, of course.

GALILEO: Of course? (*He picks* ANDREA *up, chair and all, and carries him round to the other side of the washstand.*) *Now* where is the sun?

ANDREA: On the right.

GALILEO: And did it move?

ANDREA: I did.

GALILEO: Wrong. Stupid! The chair moved.

ANDREA: But I was on it.

GALILEO: Of course. The chair is the earth, and you're sitting on it.

(MRS. SARTI, *who has come in with a glass of milk and a roll, has been watching.*)

MRS. SARTI: What are you doing with my son, Mr. Galilei?

ANDREA: Now, mother, you don't understand.

MRS. SARTI: You understand, don't you? Last night he tried to tell me that the earth goes round the sun. You'll soon have him saying that two times two is five.

GALILEO (*eating his breakfast*): Apparently we are on the threshold of a new era, Mrs. Sarti.

MRS. SARTI: Well, I hope we can pay the milkman in this new era. A young gentleman is here to take private lessons and he is well-dressed and don't you frighten him away like you did the others. Wasting your time with Andrea! (*To* ANDREA.) How many times have I told you not to wheedle free lessons out of Mr. Galilei? (MRS. SARTI *goes.*)

GALILEO: So you thought enough of the turning-round-business to tell your mother about it.

ANDREA: Just to surprise her.

GALILEO: Andrea, I wouldn't talk about our ideas outside.

ANDREA: Why not?

GALILEO: Certain of the authorities won't like it.

ANDREA: Why not, if it's the truth?

GALILEO (*laughs*): Because we are like the worms who are little and have dim eyes and can hardly see the stars at all, and the new astronomy is a framework of guesses or very little more—yet.

(MRS. SARTI *shows in* LUDOVICO MARSILI, *a presentable young man.*)

GALILEO: This house is like a marketplace. (*Pointing to the model.*) Move that out of the way! Put it down there!

(LUDOVICO *does.*)

LUDOVICO: Good morning, sir. My name is Ludovico Marsili.

GALILEO (*reading a letter of recommendation he has brought*): You came by way of Holland and your family lives in the Campagna? Private lessons, thirty scudi a month.

LUDOVICO: That's all right, of course, sir.

GALILEO: What is your subject?

LUDOVICO: Horses.

GALILEO: Aha.

LUDOVICO: I don't understand science, sir.

GALILEO: Aha.

LUDOVICO: They showed me an instrument like that in Amsterdam. You'll pardon me, sir, but it didn't make sense to me at all.

GALILEO: It's out of date now.

(ANDREA *goes.*)

LUDOVICO: You'll have to be patient with me, sir. Nothing in science makes sense to me.

GALILEO: Aha.

LUDOVICO: I saw a brand new instrument° in Amsterdam. A tube affair. "See things five times as large as life!" It had two lenses, one at each end, one lens bulged and the other was like that. (*Gesture.*) Any normal person would think that different lenses cancel each other out. They didn't! I just stood and looked a fool.

GALILEO: I don't quite follow you. What does one see enlarged?

LUDOVICO: Church steeples, pigeons, boats. Anything at a distance.

GALILEO: Did you yourself—see things enlarged?

LUDOVICO: Yes, sir.

GALILEO: And the tube had two lenses? Was it like this? (*He has been making a sketch.*)

(LUDOVICO *nods.*)

GALILEO: A recent invention?

brand new intrument: The telescope was thought erroneously to have been invented by Hans Lippershey, who made and sold telescopes in Middelburg, Netherlands, in 1608. When he applied for a patent, he was refused on the grounds that the idea was widespread. Telescopes were available for sale in Paris in 1609, then Germany, Italy, and London in the same year. Galileo reinvented the instrument by calculating the mathematical relationship of the focal lengths of lenses. His versions were on the order of ten times more powerful than those available, and they also permitted the viewer to see things right side up, which Lippershey's did not.

LUDOVICO: It must be. They only started peddling it on the streets a few days before I left Holland.

GALILEO (*starts to scribble calculations on the sketch; almost friendly*): Why do you bother your head with science? Why don't you just breed horses?

(*Enter* MRS. SARTI. GALILEO *doesn't see her. She listens to the following.*)

LUDOVICO: My mother is set on the idea that science is necessary nowadays for conversation.

GALILEO: Aha. You'll find Latin or philosophy easier. (MRS. SARTI *catches his eye.*) I'll see you on Tuesday afternoon.

LUDOVICO: I shall look forward to it, sir.

GALILEO: Good morning. (*He goes to the window and shouts into the street.*) Andrea! Hey, Redhead, Redhead!

MRS. SARTI: The curator of the museum is here to see you.

GALILEO: Don't look at me like that. I took him, didn't I?

MRS. SARTI: I caught your eye in time.

GALILEO: Show the curator in.

(*She goes. He scribbles something on a new sheet of paper. The* CURATOR *comes in.*)

CURATOR: Good morning, Mr. Galilei.

GALILEO: Lend me a scudo. (*He takes it and goes to the window, wrapping the coin in the paper on which he has been scribbling.*) Redhead, run to the spectacle-maker and bring me two lenses; here are the measurements. (*He throws the paper out of the window. During the following scene* GALILEO *studies his sketch of the lenses.*)

CURATOR: Mr. Galilei, I have come to return your petition for an honorarium. Unfortunately I am unable to recommend your request.

GALILEO: My good sir, how can I make ends meet on five hundred scudi?

CURATOR: What about your private students?

GALILEO: If I spend all my time with students, when am I to study? My particular science is on the threshold of important discoveries. (*He throws a manuscript on the table.*) Here are my findings on the laws of failing bodies. That should be worth two hundred scudi.

CURATOR: I am sure that any paper of yours is of infinite worth, Mr. Galilei....

GALILEO: I was limiting it to two hundred scudi.

CURATOR (*cool*): Mr. Galilei, if you want money and leisure, go to Florence. I have no doubt Prince Cosmo de Medici will be glad to subsidize you, but eventually you will be forbidden to think—in the name of the Inquisition. (GALILEO *says nothing.*) Now let us not make a mountain out of a molehill. You are happy here in the Republic of Venice but you need money. Well, that's human, Mr. Galilei, may I suggest a simple solution? You remember that chart you made for the army to extract cube roots without any knowledge of mathematics? Now that was practical!

GALILEO: Bosh!

CURATOR: Don't say bosh about something that astounded the Chamber of Commerce. Our city elders are businessmen. Why don't you invent something useful that will bring them a little profit?

GALILEO (*playing with the sketch of the lenses; suddenly*): I see. Mr. Priuli, I may have something for you.

CURATOR: You don't say so.

GALILEO: It's not quite there yet, but...

CURATOR: You've never let me down yet, Galilei.

GALILEO: You are always an inspiration to me, Priuli.

CURATOR: You are a great man: a discontented man, but I've always said you are a great man.

GALILEO (*tartly*): My discontent, Priuli, is for the most part with myself. I am forty-six years of age and have achieved nothing which satisfies me.

CURATOR: I won't disturb you any further.

GALILEO: Thank you. Good morning.

CURATOR: Good morning. And thank you.

(*He goes.* GALILEO *sighs.* ANDREA *returns, bringing lenses.*)

ANDREA: One scudo was not enough. I had to leave my cap with him before he'd let me take them away.

GALILEO: We'll get it back someday. Give them to me. (*He takes the lenses over to the window, holding them in the relation they would have in a telescope.*)

ANDREA: What are those for?

GALILEO: Something for the senate. With any luck, they will rake in two hundred scudi. Take a look!

ANDREA: My, things look close! I can read the copper letters on the bell in the Campanile. And the washerwomen by the river, I can see their washboards!

GALILEO: Get out of the way. (*Looking through the lenses himself.*) Aha!

SCENE 2

No one's virtue is complete:
Great Galileo liked to eat.
You will not resent, we hope,
The truth about his telescope.

(*The great arsenal of Venice, overlooking the harbor full of ships.* SENATORS *and* OFFICIALS *on one side,* GALILEO, *his daughter* VIRGINIA, *and his friend* SAGREDO *on the other side. They are dressed in formal, festive clothes.* VIRGINIA *is fourteen and charming. She carries a velvet cushion on which lies a brand new telescope. Behind* GALILEO *are some Artisans from the arsenal. There are onlookers,* LUDOVICO *amongst them.*)

CURATOR (*announcing*): Senators, Artisans of the Great Arsenal of Venice; Mr. Galileo Galilei, professor of mathematics at your University of Padua.

(GALILEO *steps forward and starts to speak.*)

GALILEO: Members of the High Senate! Gentlemen: I have great pleasure, as director of this institute, in presenting for your approval and acceptance an entirely new instrument originating from this our great arsenal of the Republic of Venice. As professor of mathematics at your University of Padua, your obedient servant has always counted it his privilege to offer you such discoveries and inventions as might prove lucrative to the manufacturers and merchants of our Venetian Republic. Thus, in all humility, I tender you this, my optical tube, or telescope, constructed, I assure you, on

the most scientific and Christian principles, the product of seventeen years patient research at your University of Padua.

(GALILEO *steps back. The* SENATORS *applaud.*)

SAGREDO (*aside to* GALILEO): Now you will be able to pay your bills.

GALILEO: Yes. It will make money for them. But you realize that it is more than a money-making gadget?—I turned it on the moon last night…

CURATOR (*in his best chamber-of-commerce manner*): Gentlemen: Our Republic is to be congratulated not only because this new acquisition will be one more feather in the cap of Venetian culture…(*polite applause*)… not only because our own Mr. Galilei has generously handed this fresh product of his teeming brain entirely over to you, allowing you to manufacture as many of these highly salable articles as you please…. (*Considerable applause.*) But Gentlemen of the Senate, has it occurred to you that—with the help of this remarkable new instrument—the battle fleet of the enemy will be visible to us a full two hours before we are visible to him? (*Tremendous applause.*)

GALILEO (*aside to* SAGREDO): We have been held up three generations for lack of a thing like this. I want to go home.

SAGREDO: What about the moon?

GALILEO: Well, for one thing, it doesn't give off its own light.

CURATOR (*continuing his oration*): And now, Your Excellency, and Members of the Senate, Mr. Galilei entreats you to accept the instrument from the hands of his charming daughter Virginia.

(*Polite applause. He beckons to* VIRGINIA *who steps forward and presents the telescope to the* DOGE.)

CURATOR (*during this*): Mr. Galilei gives his invention entirely into your hands, Gentlemen, enjoining you to construct as many of these instruments as you may please.

(*More applause. The* SENATORS *gather round the telescope, examining it, and looking through it.*)

GALILEO (*aside to* SAGREDO): Do you know what the Milky Way is made of?

SAGREDO: No.

GALILEO: I do.

CURATOR (*interrupting*): Congratulations, Mr. Galilei. Your extra five hundred scudi a year are safe.

GALILEO: Pardon? What? Of course, the five hundred scudi! Yes!

(*A prosperous man is standing beside the* CURATOR.)

CURATOR: Mr. Galilei, Mr. Matti of Florence.

MATTI: You're opening new fields, Mr. Galilei. We could do with you at Florence.

CURATOR: Now, Mr. Matti, leave something to us poor Venetians.

MATTI: It is a pity that a great republic has to seek an excuse to pay its great men their right and proper dues.

CURATOR: Even a great man has to have an incentive. (*He joins the* SENATORS *at the telescope.*)

MATTI: I am an iron founder.

GALILEO: Iron founder!

MATTI: With factories at Pisa and Florence. I wanted to talk to you about a machine you designed for a friend of mine in Padua.

GALILEO: I'll put you on to someone to copy it for you, I am not going to have the time.—How are things in Florence?

(*They wander away.*)

FIRST SENATOR (*peering*): Extraordinary! They're having their lunch on that frigate. Lobsters! I'm hungry!

(*Laughter.*)

SECOND SENATOR: Oh, good heavens, look at her! I must tell my wife to stop bathing on the roof. When can I buy one of these things?

(*Laughter.* VIRGINIA *has spotted* LUDOVICO *among the onlookers and drags him to* GALILEO.)

VIRGINIA (*to* LUDOVICO): Did I do it nicely?

LUDOVICO: I thought so.

VIRGINIA: Here's Ludovico to congratulate you, father.

LUDOVICO (*embarrassed*): Congratulations, sir.

GALILEO: I improved it.

LUDOVICO: Yes, sir. I am beginning to understand science.

(GALILEO *is surrounded.*)

VIRGINIA: Isn't father a great man?

LUDOVICO: Yes.

VIRGINIA: Isn't that new thing father made pretty?

LUDOVICO: Yes, a pretty red. Where I saw it first it was covered in green.

VIRGINIA: What was?

LUDOVICO: Never mind. (*A short pause.*) Have you ever been to Holland?

(*They go. All Venice is congratulating* GALILEO, *who wants to go home.*)

SCENE 3

January ten, sixteen ten;
Galileo Galilei abolishes heaven.

(GALILEO's *study at Padua. It is night.* GALILEO *and* SAGREDO *at a telescope.*)

SAGREDO (*softly*): The edge of the crescent is jagged. All along the dark part, near the shiny crescent, bright particles of light keep coming up, one after the other and growing larger and merging with the bright crescent.

GALILEO: How do you explain those spots of light?

SAGREDO: It can't be true…

GALILEO: It *is* true: they are high mountains.

SAGREDO: On a star?

GALILEO: Yes. The shining particles are mountain peaks catching the first rays of the rising sun while the slopes of the mountains are still dark, and what you see is the sunlight moving down from the peaks into the valleys.

SAGREDO: But this gives the lie to all the astronomy that's been taught for the last two thousand years.

GALILEO: Yes. What you are seeing now has been seen by no other man beside myself.

SAGREDO: But the moon can't be an earth with mountains and valleys like our own any more than the earth can be a star.

GALILEO: The moon *is* an earth with mountains and valleys—and the earth *is* a star. As the moon appears to us, so we appear to the moon. From the moon, the earth looks sometimes like a crescent, sometimes like a half-globe, sometimes a full globe, and sometimes it is not visible at all.

SAGREDO: Galileo, this is frightening.

(*An urgent knocking on the door.*)

GALILEO: I've discovered something else, something even more astonishing.

(*More knocking.* GALILEO *opens the door and the* CU-RATOR *comes in.*)

CURATOR: There it is—your "miraculous optical tube." Do you know that this invention he so picturesquely termed "the fruit of seventeen years research" will be on sale tomorrow for two scudi apiece at every street corner in Venice? A shipload of them has just arrived from Holland.

SAGREDO: Oh, dear!

(GALILEO *turns his back and adjusts the telescope.*)

CURATOR: When I think of the poor gentlemen of the senate who believed they were getting an invention they could monopolize for their own profit.... Why, when they took their first look through the glass, it was only by the merest chance that they didn't see a peddler, seven times enlarged, selling tubes exactly like it at the corner of the street.

SAGREDO: Mr. Priuli, with the help of this instrument, Mr. Galilei has made discoveries that will revolutionize our concept of the universe.

CURATOR: Mr. Galilei provided the city with a first rate water pump and the irrigation works he designed function splendidly. How was I to expect this?

GALILEO (*still at the telescope*): Not so fast, Priuli. I may be on the track of a very large gadget. Certain of the stars appear to have regular movements. If there were a clock in the sky, it could be seen from anywhere. That might be useful for your shipowners.

CURATOR: I won't listen to you. I listened to you before, and as a reward for my friendship you have made me the laughingstock of the town. You can laugh—you got your money. But let me tell you this: you've destroyed my faith in a lot of things, Mr. Galilei. I'm disgusted with the world. That's all I have to say. (*He storms out.*)

GALILEO (*embarrassed*): Businessmen bore me, they suffer so. Did you see the frightened look in his eyes when he caught sight of a world not created solely for the purpose of doing business?

SAGREDO: Did you know that telescopes had been made in Holland?

GALILEO: I'd heard about it. But the one I made for the Senators was twice as good as any Dutchman's. Besides, I needed the money. How can I work, with the tax collector on the doorstep? And my poor daughter will never acquire a husband unless she has a dowry, she's not too bright. And I like to buy books—all kinds of books. Why not? And what about my appetite? I don't think well unless I eat well. Can I help it if I get my best ideas over a good meal and a bottle of wine? They don't pay me as much as they pay the butcher's boy. If only I could have five years to do nothing but research! Come on. I am going to show you something else.

SAGREDO: I don't know that I want to look again.

GALILEO: This is one of the brighter nebulae of the Milky Way. What do you see?

SAGREDO: But it's made up of stars—countless stars.

GALILEO: Countless worlds.

SAGREDO (*hesitating*): What about the theory that the earth revolves round the sun? Have you run across anything about that?

GALILEO: No. But I noticed something on Tuesday that might prove a step towards even that. Where's Jupiter? There are four lesser stars near Jupiter. I happened on them on Monday but didn't take any particular note of their position. On Tuesday I looked again. I could have sworn they had moved. They have changed again. Tell me what you see.

SAGREDO: I only see three.

GALILEO: Where's the fourth? Let's get the charts and settle down to work.

(*They work and the lights dim. The lights go up again. It is near dawn.*)

GALILEO: The only place the fourth can be is round at the back of the larger star where we cannot see it. This means there are small stars revolving around a big star. Where are the crystal shells now that the stars are supposed to be fixed to?

SAGREDO: Jupiter can't be attached to anything: there are other stars revolving round it.

GALILEO: There is no support in the heavens. (SAGREDO *laughs awkwardly.*) Don't stand there looking at me as if it weren't true.

SAGREDO: I suppose it is true. I'm afraid.

GALILEO: Why?

SAGREDO: What do you think is going to happen to you for saying that there is another sun around which other earths revolve? And that there are only stars and no difference between earth and heaven? Where is God then?

GALILEO: What do you mean?

SAGREDO: God? Where is God?

GALILEO (*angrily*): Not there! Any more than he'd be here—if creatures from the moon came down to look for him!

SAGREDO: Then where is He?

GALILEO: I'm not a theologian: I'm a mathematician.

SAGREDO: You are a human being! (*Almost shouting.*) Where is God in your system of the universe?

GALILEO: Within ourselves. Or—nowhere.

SAGREDO: Ten years ago a man was burned at the stake for saying that.

GALILEO: Giordano Bruno° was an idiot: he spoke too soon. He would never have been condemned if he could have backed up what he said with proof.

Giordano Bruno: Bruno (1548–1600), one of the most distinguished Italian Renaissance thinkers, lectured in England, France, Germany, and other countries in Europe before being imprisoned for heresy by the Inquisition. After a period of confinement and a lengthy trial, he was burned at the stake. He believed, like Galileo, in the Copernican view of astronomy, which asserted that the earth rotated around the sun.

SAGREDO (*incredulously*): Do you really believe proof will make any difference?

GALILEO: I believe in the human race. The only people that can't be reasoned with are the dead. Human beings are intelligent.

SAGREDO: Intelligent—or merely shrewd?

GALILEO: I know they call a donkey a horse when they want to sell it, and a horse a donkey when they want to buy it. But is that the whole story? Aren't they susceptible to truth as well? (*He fishes a small pebble out of his pocket.*) If anybody were to drop a stone …(*drops the pebble*)…and tell them that it didn't fall, do you think they would keep quiet? The evidence of your own eyes is a very seductive thing. Sooner or later everybody must succumb to it.

SAGREDO: Galileo, I am helpless when you talk.

(*A church bell has been ringing for some time, calling people to Mass. Enter* VIRGINIA, *muffled up for Mass, carrying a candle, protected from the wind by a globe.*)

VIRGINIA: Oh, father, you promised to go to bed tonight, and it's five o'clock again.

GALILEO: Why are you up at this hour?

VIRGINIA: I'm going to Mass with Mrs. Sarti. Ludovico is going too. How was the night, father?

GALILEO: Bright.

VIRGINIA: What did you find through the tube?

GALILEO: Only some little specks by the side of a star. I must draw attention to them somehow. I think I'll name them after the Prince of Florence. Why not call them the Medicean planets? By the way, we may move to Florence. I've written to His Highness, asking if he can use me as Court Mathematician.

VIRGINIA: Oh, father, we'll be at the court!

SAGREDO (*amazed*): Galileo!

GALILEO: My dear Sagredo, I must have leisure. My only worry is that His Highness after all may not take me. I'm not accustomed to writing formal letters to great personages. Here, do you think this is the right sort of thing?

SAGREDO (*reads and quotes*): "Whose sole desire is to reside in Your Highness' presence—the rising sun of our great age." Cosmo de Medici is a boy of nine.

GALILEO: The only way a man like me can land a good job is by crawling on his stomach. Your father, my dear, is going to take his share of the pleasures of life in exchange for all his hard work, and about time too. I have no patience, Sagredo, with a man who doesn't use his brains to fill his belly. Run along to Mass now.

(VIRGINIA *goes.*)

SAGREDO: Galileo, do not go to Florence.

GALILEO: Why not?

SAGREDO: The monks are in power there.

GALILEO: Going to Mass is a small price to pay for a full belly. And there are many famous scholars at the court of Florence.

SAGREDO: Court monkeys.

GALILEO: I shall enjoy taking them by the scruff of the neck and making them look through the telescope.

SAGREDO: Galileo, you are traveling the road to disaster. You are suspicious and skeptical in science, but in politics you are as naive as your daughter! How can people in power leave a man at large who tells the truth, even if it be the truth about the distant stars? Can you see the Pope scribbling a note in his diary: "10th of January, 1610, Heaven abolished"? A moment ago, when you were at the telescope, I saw you tied to the stake, and when you said you believed in proof, I smelt burning flesh!

GALILEO: I am going to Florence.

Before the next scene a curtain with the following legend on it is lowered:

By setting the name of Medici in the sky, I am bestowing immortality upon the stars. I commend myself to you as your most faithful and devoted servant, whose sole desire is to reside in Your Highness' presence, the rising sun of our great age.

—GALILEO GALILEI

SCENE 4

(GALILEO'S *house at Florence. Well-appointed.* GALILEO *is demonstrating his telescope to* PRINCE COSMO DE MEDICI, *a boy of nine, accompanied by his* LORD CHAMBERLAIN, LADIES *and* GENTLEMEN *of the Court, and an assortment of university* PROFESSORS. *With* GALILEO *are* ANDREA *and* FEDERZONI, *the new assistant (an old man).* MRS. SARTI *stands by. Before the scene opens the voice of the* PHILOSOPHER *can be heard.*)

VOICE OF THE PHILOSOPHER: Quaedam miracula universi. Orbes mystice canorae, arcus crystallini, circulatio corporum coelestium. Cyclorum epicyclorumque intoxicatio, integritas tabulae chordarum et architectura elata globorum coelestium.

GALILEO: Shall we speak in everyday language? My colleague Mr. Federzoni does not understand Latin.

PHILOSOPHER: Is it necessary that he should?

GALILEO: Yes.

PHILOSOPHER: Forgive me. I thought he was your mechanic.

ANDREA: Mr. Federzoni is a mechanic and a scholar.

PHILOSOPHER: Thank you, young man. If Mr. Federzoni insists…

GALILEO: I insist.

PHILOSOPHER: It will not be as clear, but it's your house. Your Highness…(*The* PRINCE *is ineffectually trying to establish contact with* ANDREA.) I was about to recall to Mr. Galilei some of the wonders of the universe as they are set down for us in the Divine Classics. (*The* LADIES *"ah."*) Remind him of the "mystically musical spheres, the crystal arches, the circulation of the heavenly bodies—"

ELDERLY LADY: Perfect poise!

PHILOSOPHER: "—the intoxication of the cycles and epicycles, the integrity of the tables of chords and the enraptured architecture of the celestial globes."

ELDERLY LADY: What diction!

PHILOSOPHER: May I pose the question: Why should we go out of our way to look for things that can only strike a discord in this ineffable harmony?

(*The* LADIES *applaud.*)

FEDERZONI: Take a look through here—you'll be interested.

ANDREA: Sit down here, please.

(*The* PROFESSORS *laugh.*)

MATHEMATICIAN: Mr. Galilei, nobody doubts that your brain child—or is it your adopted brain child?—is brilliantly contrived.

GALILEO: Your Highness, one can see the four stars as large as life, you know.

(*The* PRINCE *looks to the* ELDERLY LADY *for guidance.*)

MATHEMATICIAN: Ah. But has it occurred to you that an eyeglass through which one sees such phenomena might not be a too reliable eyeglass?

GALILEO: How is that?

MATHEMATICIAN: If one could be sure you would keep your temper, Mr. Galilei, I could suggest that what one sees in the eyeglass and what is in the heavens are two entirely different things.

GALILEO (*quietly*): You are suggesting fraud?

MATHEMATICIAN: No! How could I, in the presence of His Highness?

ELDERLY LADY: The gentlemen are just wondering if Your Highness' stars are really, really there!

(*Pause.*)

YOUNG LADY (*trying to be helpful*): Can one see the claws on the Great Bear?

GALILEO: And everything on Taurus the Bull.

FEDERZONI: Are you going to look through it or not?

MATHEMATICIAN: With the greatest of pleasure.

(*Pause. Nobody goes near the telescope. All of a sudden the boy* ANDREA *turns and marches pale and erect past them through the whole length of the room. The* GUESTS *follow with their eyes.*)

MRS. SARTI (*as he passes her*): What is the matter with you?

ANDREA (*shocked*): They are wicked.

PHILOSOPHER: Your Highness, it is a delicate matter and I had no intention of bringing it up, but Mr. Galilei was about to demonstrate the impossible. His new stars would have broken the outer crystal sphere—which we know of on the authority of Aristotle. I am sorry.

MATHEMATICIAN: The last word.

FEDERZONI: He had no telescope.

MATHEMATICIAN: Quite.

GALILEO (*keeping his temper*): "Truth is the daughter of Time, not of Authority." Gentlemen, the sum of our knowledge is pitiful. It has been my singular good fortune to find a new instrument which brings a small patch of the universe a little bit closer. It is at your disposal.

PHILOSOPHER: Where is all this leading?

GALILEO: Are we, as scholars, concerned with where the truth might lead us?

PHILOSOPHER: Mr. Galilei, the truth might lead us anywhere!

GALILEO: I can only beg you to look through my eyeglass.

MATHEMATICIAN (*wild*): If I understand Mr. Galilei correctly, he is asking us to discard the teachings of two thousand years.

GALILEO: For two thousand years we have been looking at the sky and didn't see the four moons of Jupiter, and there they were all the time. Why defend shaken teachings? You should be doing the shaking. (*The* PRINCE *is sleepy.*) Your Highness! My work in the Great Arsenal of Venice brought me in daily contact with sailors, carpenters, and so on. These men are unread. They depend on the evidence of their senses. But they taught me many new ways of doing things. The question is whether these gentlemen here want to be found out as fools by men who might not have had the advantages of a classical education but who are not afraid to use their eyes. I tell you that our dockyards are stirring with that same high curiosity which was the true glory of Ancient Greece.

(*Pause.*)

PHILOSOPHER: I have no doubt Mr. Galilei's theories will arouse the enthusiasm of the dockyards.

CHAMBERLAIN: Your Highness, I find to my amazement that this highly informative discussion has exceeded the time we had allowed for it. May I remind Your Highness that the State Ball begins in three-quarters of an hour?

(*The Court bows low.*)

ELDERLY LADY: We would really have liked to look through your eyeglass, Mr. Galilei, wouldn't we, Your Highness?

(*The* PRINCE *bows politely and is led to the door.* GALILEO *follows the* PRINCE, CHAMBERLAIN, *and* LADIES *towards the exit. The* PROFESSORS *remain at the telescope.*)

GALILEO (*almost servile*): All anybody has to do is look through the telescope, Your Highness.

(MRS. SARTI *takes a plate with candies to the* PRINCE *as he is walking out.*)

MRS. SARTI: A piece of homemade candy, Your Highness?

ELDERLY LADY: Not now. Thank you. It is too soon before His Highness' supper.

PHILOSOPHER: Wouldn't I like to take that thing to pieces.

MATHEMATICIAN: Ingenious contraption. It must be quite difficult to keep clean. (*He rubs the lens with his handkerchief and looks at the handkerchief*)

FEDERZONI: We did not paint the Medicean stars on the lens.

ELDERLY LADY (*to the* PRINCE, *who has whispered something to her*): No, no, no, there is nothing the matter with your stars!

CHAMBERLAIN (*across the stage to* GALILEO): His Highness will of course seek the opinion of the greatest living authority: Christopher Clavius, Chief Astronomer to the Papal College in Rome.

SCENE 5

Things take indeed a wondrous turn
When learned men do stoop to learn.
Clavius, we are pleased to say,
Upheld Galileo Galilei.

(*A burst of laughter is heard and the curtains reveal a hall in the Collegium Romanum.* HIGH CHURCHMEN, MONKS, *and* SCHOLARS *standing about talking and laughing.* GALILEO *by himself in a corner.*)

FAT PRELATE (*shaking with laughter*): Hopeless! Hopeless! Hopeless! Will you tell me something people won't believe?

A SCHOLAR: Yes, that you don't love your stomach!

FAT PRELATE: They'd believe that. They only do not believe what's good for them. They doubt the devil, but fill them up with some fiddle-de-dee about the earth rolling like a marble in the gutter and they swallow it hook, line, and sinker. Sancta simplicitas!

(*He laughs until the tears run down his cheeks. The others laugh with him. A group has formed whose members boisterously begin to pretend they are standing on a rolling globe.*)

A MONK: It's rolling fast, I'm dizzy. May I hold on to you, Professor? (*He sways dizzily and clings to one of the scholars for support.*)

THE SCHOLAR: Old Mother Earth's been at the bottle again. Whoa!

MONK: Hey! Hey! We're slipping off! Help!

SECOND SCHOLAR: Look! There's Venus! Hold me, lads. Whee!

SECOND MONK: Don't, don't hurl us off on to the moon. There are nasty sharp mountain peaks on the moon, brethren!

VARIOUSLY: Hold tight! Hold tight! Don't look down! Hold tight! It'll make you giddy!

FAT PRELATE: And we cannot have giddy people in Holy Rome.

(*They rock with laughter. An* INFURIATED MONK *comes out from a large door at the rear holding a Bible in his hand and pointing out a page with his finger.*)

INFURIATED MONK: What does the Bible say— "Sun, stand thou still on Gideon and thou, moon, in the valley of Ajalon." Can the sun come to a standstill if it doesn't ever move? Does the Bible lie?

FAT PRELATE: How did Christopher Clavius, the greatest astronomer we have, get mixed up in an investigation of this kind?

INFURIATED MONK: He's in there with his eye glued to that diabolical instrument.

FAT PRELATE (*to* GALILEO, *who has been playing with his pebble and has dropped it*): Mr. Galilei, something dropped down.

GALILEO: Monsignor, are you sure it didn't drop up?

INFURIATED MONK: As astronomers we are aware that there are phenomena which are beyond us, but man can't expect to understand everything!

(*Enter a very old* CARDINAL *leaning on a* MONK *for support. Others move aside.*)

OLD CARDINAL: Aren't they out yet? Can't they reach a decision on that paltry matter? Christopher Clavius ought to know his astronomy after all these years. I am informed that Mr. Galilei transfers mankind from the center of the universe to somewhere on the outskirts. Mr. Galilei is therefore an enemy of mankind and must be dealt with as such. Is it conceivable that God would trust this most precious fruit of His labor to a minor frolicking star? Would He have sent His Son to such a place? How can there be people with such twisted minds that they believe what they're told by the slave of a multiplication table?

FAT PRELATE (*quietly to* CARDINAL): The gentleman is over there.

OLD CARDINAL: So you are the man. You know my eyes are not what they were, but I can see you bear a striking resemblance to the man we burned. What was his name?

MONK: Your Eminence must avoid excitement the doctor said…

OLD CARDINAL (*disregarding him*): So you have degraded the earth despite the fact that you live by her and receive everything from her. I won't have it! I won't have it! I won't be a nobody on an inconsequential star briefly twirling hither and thither. I tread the earth, and the earth is firm beneath my feet, and there is no motion to the earth, and the earth is the center of all things, and I am the center of the earth, and the eye of the creator is upon me. About me revolve, affixed to their crystal shells, the lesser lights of the stars and the great light of the sun, created to give light upon me that God might see me— Man, God's greatest effort, the center of creation. "In the image of God created He

him." Immortal…(*His strength fails him and he catches for the* MONK *for support.*)

MONK: You mustn't overtax your strength, Your Eminence.

(*At this moment the door at the rear opens and* CHRISTOPHER CLAVIUS *enters followed by his* AS- TRONOMERS. *He strides hastily across the hall, looking neither to right nor left. As he goes by we hear him say—*)

CLAVIUS: He is right.

(*Deadly silence. All turn to* GALILEO.)

OLD CARDINAL: What is it? Have they reached a decision?

(*No one speaks.*)

MONK: It is time that Your Eminence went home.

(*The hall is emptying fast. One little* MONK *who had entered with* CLAVIUS *speaks to* GALILEO.)

LITTLE MONK: Mr. Galilei, I heard Father Clavius say: "Now it's for the theologians to set the heavens right again." You have won.

Before the next scene a curtain with the following legend on it is lowered:

>…As these new astronomical charts enable us to determine longitudes at sea and so make it possible to reach the new continents by the shortest routes, we would beseech Your Excellency to aid us in reaching Mr. Galilei, mathematician to the Court of Florence, who is now in Rome…
>
>—From a letter written by a member of the Genoa Chamber of Commerce and Navigation to the Papal Legation

SCENE 6

When Galileo was in Rome
A Cardinal asked him to his home
He wined and dined him as his guest
And only made one small request.

(CARDINAL BELLARMIN'S *house in Rome. Music is heard and the chatter of many guests.* TWO SECRE- TARIES *are at the rear of the stage at a desk.* GALILEO, *his daughter* VIRGINIA, *now twenty-one, and* LU-

DOVICO MARSILI, *who has become her fiancé, are just arriving. A few* GUESTS, *standing near the entrance with masks in their hands, nudge each other and are suddenly silent.* GALILEO *looks at them. They applaud him politely and bow.*)

VIRGINIA: O father! I'm so happy. I won't dance with anyone but you, Ludovico.

GALILEO (*to a* SECRETARY): I was to wait here for His Eminence.

FIRST SECRETARY: His Eminence will be with you in a few minutes.

VIRGINIA: Do I look proper?

LUDOVICO: You are showing some lace.

(GALILEO *puts his arms around their shoulders.*)

GALILEO (*quoting mischievously*): Fret not, daughter, if perchance
You attract a wanton glance.
The eyes that catch a trembling lace
Will guess the heartbeat's quickened pace.
Lovely woman still may be
Careless with felicity.

VIRGINIA (*to* GALILEO): Feel my heart.

GALILEO (*to* LUDOVICO): It's thumping.

VIRGINIA: I hope I always say the right thing.

LUDOVICO: She's afraid she's going to let us down.

VIRGINIA: Oh, I want to look beautiful.

GALILEO: You'd better. If you don't they'll start saying all over again that the earth doesn't turn.

LUDOVICO (*laughing*): It *doesn't* turn, sir.

(GALILEO *laughs.*)

GALILEO: Go and enjoy yourselves. (*He speaks to one of the* SECRETARIES.) A large fête?

FIRST SECRETARY: Two hundred and fifty guests, Mr. Galilei. We have represented here this evening most of the great families of Italy, the Orsinis, the Villanis, the Nuccolis, the Soldanieris, the Canes, the Lecchis, the Estensis, the Colombinis, the…

(VIRGINIA *comes running back.*)

VIRGINIA: Oh father, I didn't tell you: you're famous.

GALILEO: Why?

VIRGINIA: The hairdresser in the Via Vittorio kept four other ladies waiting and took me first. (*Exit.*)

GALILEO (*at the stairway, leaning over the well*): Rome!

(*Enter* CARDINAL BELLARMIN, *wearing the mask of a lamb, and* CARDINAL BARBERINI, *wearing the mask of a dove.*)

SECRETARIES: Their Eminences, Cardinals Bellarmin and Barberini.

(*The* CARDINALS *lower their masks.*)

GALILEO (*to* BELLARMIN): Your Eminence.

BELLARMIN: Mr. Galilei, Cardinal Barberini.

GALILEO: Your Eminence.

BARBERINI: So you are the father of that lovely child!

BELLARMIN: Who is inordinately proud of being her father's daughter.

(*They laugh.*)

BARBERINI (*points his finger at* GALILEO): "The sun riseth and setteth and returneth to its place," saith the Bible. What saith Galilei?

GALILEO: Appearances are notoriously deceptive, Your Eminence. Once when I was so high, I was standing on a ship that was pulling away from the shore and I shouted, "The shore is moving!" I know now that it was the ship which was moving.

BARBERINI (*laughs*): You can't catch that man. I tell you, Bellarmin, his moons around Jupiter are hard nuts to crack. Unfortunately for me I happened to glance at a few papers on astronomy once. It is harder to get rid of than the itch.

BELLARMIN: Let's move with the times. If it makes navigation easier for sailors to use new charts based on a new hypothesis let them have them. We only have to scotch doctrines that contradict Holy Writ.

(*He leans over the balustrade of the well and acknowledges various* GUESTS.)

BARBERINI: But Bellarmin, you haven't caught on to this fellow. The scriptures don't satisfy him. Copernicus does.

GALILEO: Copernicus? "He that withholdeth corn the people shall curse him." Book of Proverbs.

BARBERINI: "A prudent man concealeth knowledge." Also Book of Proverbs.

GALILEO: "Where no oxen are, the stable is clean, but much increase is by the strength of the ox."

BARBERINI: "He that ruleth his spirit is better than he that taketh a city."

GALILEO: "But a broken spirit drieth up the bones." (*Pause.*) "Doth not wisdom cry?"

BARBERINI: "Can one walk on hot coals and his feet not be scorched?"—Welcome to Rome, Friend Galileo. You recall the legend of our city's origin? Two small boys found sustenance and refuge with a she-wolf and from that day we have paid the price for the she-wolf's milk. But the place is not bad. We have everything for your pleasure—from a scholarly dispute with Bellarmin to ladies of high degree. Look at that woman flaunting herself. No? He wants a weighty discussion! All right! (*To* GALILEO.) You people speak in terms of circles and ellipses and regular velocities—simple movements that the human mind can grasp—very convenient—but suppose Almighty God had taken it into his head to make the stars move like that…(*he describes an irregular motion with his fingers through the air*)…then where would you be?

GALILEO: My good man—the Almighty would have endowed us with brains like that… (*repeats the movement*)…so that we could grasp the movements…(*repeats the movement*)…like that. I believe in the brain.

BARBERINI: I consider the brain inadequate. He doesn't answer. He is too polite to tell me he considers *my* brain inadequate. What is one to do with him? Butter wouldn't melt in his mouth. All he wants to do is to prove that God made a few boners in astronomy. God didn't study his astronomy hard enough before he composed Holy Writ. (*To the* SECRETARIES.) Don't take anything down. This is a scientific discussion among friends.

BELLARMIN (*to* GALILEO): Does it not appear more probable—even to you—that the Creator knows more about his work than the created?

GALILEO: In his blindness man is liable to misread not only the sky but also the Bible.

BELLARMIN: The interpretation of the Bible is a matter for the ministers of God. (GALILEO *remains silent.*) At last you are quiet. (*He gestures to the* SECRETARIES. *They start writing.*) Tonight the Holy Office has decided that the theory according to which the earth goes around the sun is foolish, absurd, and a heresy. I am charged, Mr. Galilei, with cautioning you to abandon these teachings. (*To the* FIRST SECRETARY.) Would you repeat that?

FIRST SECRETARY (*reading*): "His Eminence, Cardinal Bellarmin, to the aforesaid Galilei: The Holy Office has resolved that the theory according to which the earth goes around the sun is foolish, absurd, and a heresy. I am charged, Mr. Galilei, with cautioning you to abandon these teachings."

GALILEO (*rocking on his base*): But the facts!

BARBERINI (*consoling*): Your findings have been ratified by the Papal Observatory, Galilei. That should be most flattering to you…

BELLARMIN (*cutting in*): The Holy Office formulated the decree without going into details.

GALILEO (*to* BARBERINI): Do you realize, the future of all scientific research is…

BELLARMIN (*cutting in*): Completely assured, Mr. Galilei. It is not given to man to know the truth: it is granted to him to seek after the truth. Science is the legitimate and beloved daughter of the Church. She must have confidence in the Church.

GALILEO (*infuriated*): I would not try confidence by whistling her too often.

BARBERINI (*quickly*): Be careful what you're doing—you'll be throwing out the baby with the bath water, friend Galilei. (*Serious.*) We need you more than you need us.

BELLARMIN: Well, it is time we introduced our distinguished friend to our guests. The whole country talks of him!

BARBERINI: Let us replace our masks, Bellarmin. Poor Galilei hasn't got one.

(*He laughs. They take* GALILEO *out.*)

FIRST SECRETARY: Did you get his last sentence?

SECOND SECRETARY: Yes. Do you have what he said about believing in the brain?

(*Another cardinal—the* INQUISITOR—*enters.*)

INQUISITOR: Did the conference take place?

(*The* FIRST SECRETARY *hands him the papers and the* INQUISITOR *dismisses the* SECRETARIES. *They go. The* INQUISITOR *sits down and starts to read the transcription. Two or three* YOUNG LADIES *skitter across the stage; they see the* INQUISITOR *and curtsy as they go.*)

YOUNG GIRL: Who was that?

HER FRIEND: The Cardinal Inquisitor.

(*They giggle and go. Enter* VIRGINIA. *She curtsies as she goes. The* INQUISITOR *stops her.*)

INQUISITOR: Good evening, my child. Beautiful night. May I congratulate you on your betrothal? Your young man comes from a fine family. Are you staying with us here in Rome?

VIRGINIA: Not now, Your Eminence. I must go home to prepare for the wedding.

INQUISITOR: Ah. You are accompanying your father to Florence. That should please him. Science must be cold comfort in a home. Your youth and warmth will keep him down to earth. It is easy to get lost up there. (*He gestures to the sky.*)

VIRGINIA: He doesn't talk to me about the stars, Your Eminence.

INQUISITOR: No. (*He laughs.*) They don't eat fish in the fisherman's house. I can tell you something about astronomy. My child, it seems that God has blessed our modern astronomers with imaginations. It is quite alarming! Do you know that the earth—which we old fogies supposed to be so large—has shrunk to something no bigger than a walnut, and the new universe has grown so vast that prelates—and even cardinals—look like ants. Why, God Almighty might lose sight of a Pope! I wonder if I know your Father Confessor.

VIRGINIA: Father Christopherus, from Saint Ursula's at Florence, Your Eminence.

INQUISITOR: My dear child, your father will need you. Not so much now perhaps, but one of these days. You are pure, and there is strength in purity. Greatness is sometimes, indeed often, too heavy a burden for those to whom God has granted it. What man is so great that he has no place in a prayer? But I am keeping you, my dear. Your fiancé will be jealous of me, and I am afraid your father will never forgive me for holding forth on astronomy. Go to your dancing and remember me to Father Christopherus.

(VIRGINIA *kisses his ring and runs off. The* INQUISITOR *resumes his reading.*)

SCENE 7

Galileo, feeling grim,
A young monk came to visit him.
The monk was born of common folk.
It was of science that they spoke.

(*Garden of the Florentine Ambassador in Rome. Distant hum of a great city.* GALILEO *and the* LITTLE MONK *of scene 5 are talking.*)

GALILEO: Let's hear it. That robe you're wearing gives you the right to say whatever you want to say. Let's hear it.

LITTLE MONK: I have studied physics, Mr. Galilei.

GALILEO: That might help us if it enabled you to admit that two and two are four.

LITTLE MONK: Mr. Galilei, I have spent four sleepless nights trying to reconcile the decree that I have read with the moons of Jupiter that I have seen. This morning I decided to come to see you after I had said Mass.

GALILEO: To tell me that Jupiter has no moons?

LITTLE MONK: No, I found out that I think the decree a wise decree. It has shocked me into realizing that free research has its dangers. I have had to decide to give up astronomy. However, I felt the impulse to confide in you some of the motives which have impelled even a passionate physicist to abandon his work.

GALILEO: Your motives are familiar to me.

LITTLE MONK: You mean, of course, the special powers invested in certain commissions of the Holy Office? But there is something else. I would like to talk to you about my family. I do not come from the great city. My parents are peasants in the Campagna, who know about the cultivation of the olive tree, and not much about anything else. Too often these days when I am trying to concentrate on tracking down the moons of Jupiter, I see my parents. I see them sitting by the fire with my sister, eating their curded cheese. I see the beams of the ceiling above them, which the smoke of centuries has blackened, and I can see the veins stand out on their toil-worn hands, and the little spoons in their hands. They scrape a living, and underlying their poverty there is a sort of order. There are routines. The routine of scrubbing the floors, the routine of the seasons in the olive orchard, the routine of paying taxes. The troubles that come to them are recurrent troubles. My father did not get his poor bent back all at once, but little by little, year by year, in the olive orchard; just as year after year, with unfailing regularity, childbirth has made my mother more and more sexless. They draw the strength they need to sweat with their loaded baskets up the stony paths, to bear children, even to eat, from the sight of the trees greening each year anew, from the reproachful face of the soil, which is never satisfied, and from the little church and Bible texts they hear there on Sunday. They have been told that God relies upon them and that the pageant of the world has been written around them that they may be tested in the important or unimportant parts handed out to them. How could they take it, were I to tell them that they are on a lump of stone ceaselessly spinning in empty space, circling around a second-rate star? What, then, would be the use of their patience, their acceptance of misery? What comfort, then, the Holy Scriptures, which have mercifully explained their crucifixion? The Holy Scriptures would then be proved full of mistakes. No, I see them be-gin to look frightened. I see them slowly put their spoons down on the table. They would feel cheated. "There is no eye watching over us, after all," they would say. "We have to start out on our own, at our time of life. Nobody has planned a part for us beyond this wretched one on a worthless star. There is no meaning in our misery. Hunger is just not having eaten. It is no test of strength. Effort is just stooping and carrying. It is not a virtue." Can you understand that I read into the decree of the Holy Office a noble motherly pity and a great goodness of the soul?

GALILEO (*embarrassed*): Hm, well at least you have found out that it is not a question of the satellites of Jupiter, but of the peasants of the Campagna! And don't try to break me down by the halo of beauty that radiates from old age. How does a pearl develop in an oyster? A jagged grain of sand makes its way into the oyster's shell and makes its life unbearable. The oyster exudes slime to cover the grain of sand and the slime eventually hardens into a pearl. The oyster nearly dies in the process. To hell with the pearl, give me the healthy oyster! And virtues are not exclusive to misery. If your parents were prosperous and happy, they might develop the virtues of happiness and prosperity. Today the virtues of exhaustion are caused by the exhausted land. For that my new water pumps could work more wonders than their ridiculous superhuman efforts. Be fruitful and multiply: for war will cut down the population, and our fields are barren! (*A pause.*) Shall I lie to your people?

LITTLE MONK: We must be silent from the highest of motives: the inward peace of less fortunate souls.

GALILEO: My dear man, as a bonus for not meddling with your parents' peace, the authorities are tendering me, on a silver platter, persecution-free, my share of the fat sweated from your parents, who, as you know, were made in God's image. Should I condone this decree, my motives might not be disinterested: easy life, no persecution, and so on.

LITTLE MONK: Mr. Galilei, I am a priest.

GALILEO: You are also a physicist. How can new machinery be evolved to domesticate the river water if we physicists are forbidden to study, discuss, and pool our findings about the greatest machinery of all, the machinery of the heavenly bodies? Can I reconcile my findings on the paths of falling bodies with the current belief in the tracks of witches on broom sticks? (*A pause.*) I am sorry—I shouldn't have said that.

LITTLE MONK: You don't think that the truth, if it is the truth, would make its way without us?

GALILEO: No! No! No! As much of the truth gets through as we push through. You talk about the Campagna peasants as if they were the moss on their huts. Naturally, if they don't get a move on and learn to think for themselves, the most efficient of irrigation systems cannot help them. I can see their divine patience, but where is their divine fury?

LITTLE MONK (*helpless*): They are old!

(GALILEO *stands for a moment, beaten; he cannot meet the* LITTLE MONK'S *eyes. He takes a manuscript from the table and throws it violently on the ground.*)

LITTLE MONK: What is that?

GALILEO: Here is writ what draws the ocean when it ebbs and flows. Let it lie there. Thou shalt not read. (LITTLE MONK *has picked up the manuscript.*) Already! An apple of the tree of knowledge, he can't wait, he wolfs it down. He will rot in hell for all eternity. Look at him, where are his manners?—Sometimes I think I would let them imprison me in a place a thousand feet beneath the earth where no light could reach me, if in exchange I could find out what stuff that is: "Light." The bad thing is that, when I find something, I have to boast about it like a lover or a drunkard or a traitor. That is a hopeless vice and leads to the abyss. I wonder how long I shall be content to discuss it with my dog!

LITTLE MONK (*immersed in the manuscript*): I don't understand this sentence.

GALILEO: I'll explain it to you, I'll explain it to you.

(*They are sitting on the floor.*)

SCENE 8

Eight long years with tongue in cheek
Of what he knew he did not speak.
Then temptation grew too great
And Galileo challenged fate.

(GALILEO'S *house in Florence again. Galileo is supervising his Assistants* ANDREA, FEDERZONI, *and the* LITTLE MONK *who are about to prepare an experiment.* MRS. SARTI *and* VIRGINIA *are at a long table sewing bridal linen. There is a new telescope, larger than the old one. At the moment it is covered with a cloth.*)

ANDREA (*looking up a schedule*): Thursday. Afternoon. Floating bodies again. Ice, bowl of water, scales, and it says here an iron needle. Aristotle.

VIRGINIA: Ludovico likes to entertain. We must take care to be neat. His mother notices every stitch. She doesn't approve of father's books.

MRS. SARTI: That's all a thing of the past. He hasn't published a book for years.

VIRGINIA: That's true. Oh Sarti, it's fun sewing a trousseau.

MRS. SARTI: Virginia, I want to talk to you. You are very young, and you have no mother, and your father is putting those pieces of ice in water, and marriage is too serious a business to go into blind. Now you should go to see a real astronomer from the university and have him cast your horoscope so you know where you stand. (VIRGINIA *giggles.*) What's the matter?

VIRGINIA: I've been already.

MRS. SARTI: Tell Sarti.

VIRGINIA: I have to be careful for three months now because the sun is in Capricorn, but after that I get a favorable ascendant, and I can undertake a journey if I am careful of Uranus, as I'm a Scorpion.

MRS. SARTI: What about Ludovico?

VIRGINIA: He's a Leo, the astronomer said. Leos are sensual. (*Giggles.*)

(*There is a knock at the door, it opens. Enter the* RECTOR *of the University, the philosopher of scene 4, bringing a book.*)

RECTOR (*to* VIRGINIA): This is about the burning issue of the moment. He may want to glance over it. My faculty would appreciate his comments. No, don't disturb him now, my dear. Every minute one takes of your father's time is stolen from Italy. (*He goes.*)

VIRGINIA: Federzoni! The rector of the university brought this.

(FEDERZONI *takes it.*)

GALILEO: What's it about?

FEDERZONI (*spelling*): DE MACULIS IN SOLE.

ANDREA: Oh, it's on the sun spots!

(ANDREA *comes one side, and the* LITTLE MONK *the other, to look at the book.*)

ANDREA: A new one!

(FEDERZONI *resentfully puts the book into their hands and continues with the preparation of the experiment.*)

ANDREA: Listen to this dedication. (*Quotes.*) "To the greatest living authority on physics, Galileo Galilei."—I read Fabricius' paper the other day. Fabricius says the spots are clusters of planets between us and the sun.

LITTLE MONK: Doubtful.

GALILEO (*noncommittal*): Yes?

ANDREA: Paris and Prague hold that they are vapors from the sun. Federzoni doubts that.

FEDERZONI: Me? You leave me out. I said "hm," that was all. And don't discuss new things before me. I can't read the material, it's in Latin. (*He drops the scales and stands trembling with fury.*) Tell me, can I doubt anything?

(GALILEO *walks over and picks up the scales silently. Pause.*)

LITTLE MONK: There is happiness in doubting, I wonder why.

ANDREA: Aren't we going to take this up?

GALILEO: At the moment we are investigating floating bodies.

ANDREA: Mother has baskets full of letters from all over Europe asking his opinion.

FEDERZONI: The question is whether you can afford to remain silent.

GALILEO: I cannot afford to be smoked on a wood fire like a ham.

ANDREA (*surprised*): Ah. You think the sun spots may have something to do with that again? (GALILEO *does not answer.*)

ANDREA: Well, we stick to fiddling about with bits of ice in water. That can't hurt you.

GALILEO: Correct.—Our thesis!

ANDREA: All things that are lighter than water float, and all things that are heavier sink.

GALILEO: Aristotle says—

LITTLE MONK (*reading out of a book, translating*): "A broad and flat disk of ice, although heavier than water, still floats, because it is unable to divide the water."

GALILEO: Well. Now I push the ice below the surface. I take away the pressure of my hands. What happens?

(*Pause.*)

LITTLE MONK: It rises to the surface.

GALILEO: Correct. It seems to be able to divide the water as it's coming up, doesn't it?

LITTLE MONK: Could it be lighter than water after all?

GALILEO: Aha!

ANDREA: Then all things that are lighter than water float, and all things that are heavier sink. Q.e.d.°

GALILEO: Not at all. Hand me that iron needle. Heavier than water? (*They all nod.*) A piece of paper.
(*He places the needle on a piece of paper and floats it on the surface of the water. Pause.*) Do not be hasty with your conclusion. (*Pause.*) What happens?

FEDERZONI: The paper has sunk, the needle is floating.

VIRGINIA: What's the matter?

MRS. SARTI: Every time I hear them laugh it sends shivers down my spine.

Q.e.d.: In Latin, *quod erat demonstrandum,* "which was to be demonstrated," the usual ending on a logical examination using Aristotelian logic. The point is that it is not demonstrated; the experiment with the needle and the paper demonstrates the power of surface tension, which contradicts Andrea's earlier statement. Experimentation, in other words, is the final arbiter of what is true, not rules such as Andrea establishes.

(*There is a knocking at the outer door.*)

MRS. SARTI: Who's that at the door?

(*Enter* LUDOVICO. VIRGINIA *runs to him. They embrace.* LUDOVICO *is followed by a* SERVANT *with baggage.*)

MRS. SARTI: Well!

VIRGINIA: Oh! Why didn't you write that you were coming?

LUDOVICO: I decided on the spur of the moment. I was over inspecting our vineyards at Bucciole. I couldn't keep away.

GALILEO: Who's that?

LITTLE MONK: Miss Virginia's intended. What's the matter with your eyes?

GALILEO (*blinking*): Oh yes, it's Ludovico, so it is. Well! Sarti, get a jug of that Sicilian wine, the old kind. We celebrate.

(*Everybody sits down.* MRS. SARTI *has left, followed by Ludovico's* SERVANT.)

GALILEO: Well, Ludovico, old man. How are the horses?

LUDOVICO: The horses are fine.

GALILEO: Fine.

LUDOVICO: But those vineyards need a firm hand. (*To* VIRGINIA.) You look pale. Country life will suit you. Mother's planning on September.

VIRGINIA: I suppose I oughtn't, but stay here, I've got something to show you.

LUDOVICO: What?

VIRGINIA: Never mind. I won't be ten minutes. (*She runs out.*)

LUDOVICO: How's life these days, sir?

GALILEO: Dull.—How was the journey?

LUDOVICO: Dull.—Before I forget, mother sends her congratulations on your admirable tact over the latest rumblings of science.

GALILEO: Thank her from me.

LUDOVICO: Christopher Clavius had all Rome on its ears. He said he was afraid that the turning-around-business might crop up again on account of these spots on the sun.

ANDREA: Clavius is on the same track! (*To* LUDOVICO.) My mother's baskets are full of letters from all over Europe asking Mr. Galilei's opinion.

GALILEO: I am engaged in investigating the habits of floating bodies. Any harm in that?

(MRS. SARTI *reenters, followed by the* SERVANT. *They bring wine and glasses on a tray.*)

GALILEO (*hands out the wine*): What news from the Holy City, apart from the prospect of my sins?

LUDOVICO: The Holy Father is on his death bed. Hadn't you heard?

LITTLE MONK: My goodness! What about the succession?

LUDOVICO: All the talk is of Barberini.

GALILEO: Barberini?

ANDREA: Mr. Galilei knows Barberini.

LITTLE MONK: Cardinal Barberini is a mathematician.

FEDERZONI: A scientist in the chair of Peter!

(*Pause.*)

GALILEO (*cheering up enormously*): This means change. We might live to see the day, Federzoni, when we don't have to whisper that two and two are four. (*To* LUDOVICO.) I like this wine. Don't you, Ludovico?

LUDOVICO: I like it.

GALILEO: I know the hill where it is grown. The slope is steep and stony, the grape almost blue. I am fond of this wine.

LUDOVICO: Yes, sir.

GALILEO: There are shadows in this wine. It is almost sweet but just stops short.—Andrea, clear that stuff away, ice, bowl and needle.—I cherish the consolations of the flesh. I have no patience with cowards who call them weaknesses. I say there is a certain achievement in enjoying things.

(*The* PUPILS *get up and go to the experiment table.*)

LITTLE MONK: What are we to do?

FEDERZONI: He is starting on the sun.

(*They begin with clearing up.*)

ANDREA (*singing in a low voice*): The Bible proves the earth stands still,
The Pope, he swears with tears:
The earth stands still. To prove it so
He takes it by the ears.

LUDOVICO: What's the excitement?

MRS. SARTI: You're not going to start those hellish goings-on again, Mr. Galilei?

ANDREA: And gentlefolk, they say so too. Each learned doctor proves,
(If you grease his palm): The earth stands still.
And yet—and yet it moves.

GALILEO: Barberini is in the ascendant, so your mother is uneasy, and you're sent to investigate me. Correct me if I am wrong, Ludovico. Clavius is right: These spots on the sun interest me.

ANDREA: We might find out that the sun also revolves. How would you like that, Ludovico?

GALILEO: Do you like my wine, Ludovico?

LUDOVICO: I told you I did, sir.

GALILEO: You really like it?

LUDOVICO: I like it.

GALILEO: Tell me, Ludovico, would you consider going so far as to accept a man's wine or his daughter without insisting that he drop his profession? I have no wish to intrude, but have the moons of Jupiter affected Virginia's bottom?

MRS. SARTI: That isn't funny, it's just vulgar. I am going for Virginia.

LUDOVICO (keeps her back): Marriages in families such as mine are not arranged on a basis of sexual attraction alone.

GALILEO: Did they keep you back from marrying my daughter for eight years because I was on probation?

LUDOVICO: My future wife must take her place in the family pew.

GALILEO: You mean, if the daughter of a bad man sat in your family pew, your peasants might stop paying the rent?

LUDOVICO: In a sort of way.

GALILEO: When I was your age, the only person I allowed to rap me on the knuckles was my girl.

LUDOVICO: My mother was assured that you had undertaken not to get mixed up in this turning-around-business again, sir.

GALILEO: We had a conservative Pope then.

MRS. SARTI: Had! His Holiness is not dead yet!

GALILEO (with relish): Pretty nearly.

MRS. SARTI: That man will weigh a chip of ice fifty times, but when it comes to something that's convenient, he believes it blindly. "Is His Holiness dead?"—"Pretty nearly!"

LUDOVICO: You will find, sir, if His Holiness passes away, the new Pope, whoever he turns out to be, will respect the convictions held by the solid families of the country.

GALILEO (to ANDREA): That remains to be seen.—Andrea, get out the screen. We'll throw the image of the sun on our screen to save our eyes.

LITTLE MONK: I thought you'd been working at it. Do you know when I guessed it? When you didn't recognize Mr. Marsili.

MRS. SARTI: If my son has to go to hell for sticking to you, that's my affair, but you have no right to trample on your daughter's happiness.

LUDOVICO (to his SERVANT): Giuseppe, take my baggage back to the coach, will you?

MRS. SARTI: This will kill her. (She runs out, still clutching the jug.)

LUDOVICO (politely): Mr. Galilei, if we Marsilis were to countenance teachings frowned on by the church, it would unsettle our peasants. Bear in mind: these poor people in their brute state get everything upside down. They are nothing but animals. They will never comprehend the finer points of astronomy. Why, two months ago a rumor went around, an apple had been found on a pear tree, and they left their work in the fields to discuss it.

GALILEO (interested): Did they?

LUDOVICO: I have seen the day when my poor mother has had to have a dog whipped before their eyes to remind them to keep their place. Oh, you may have seen the waving corn from the window of your comfortable coach. You have, no doubt, nibbled our olives, and absentmindedly eaten our cheese, but you can have no idea how much responsibility that sort of thing entails.

GALILEO: Young man, I do not eat my cheese absentmindedly. (To ANDREA.) Are we ready?

ANDREA: Yes, sir.

GALILEO (leaves LUDOVICO and adjusts the mirror): You would not confine your whippings to dogs to remind your peasants to keep their places, would you, Marsili?

LUDOVICO (*after a pause*): Mr. Galilei, you have a wonderful brain, it's a pity.

LITTLE MONK (*astonished*): He threatened you.

GALILEO: Yes. And he threatened you too. We might unsettle his peasants. Your sister, Fulganzio, who works the lever of the olive press, might laugh out loud if she heard the sun is not a gilded coat of arms but a lever too. The earth turns because the sun turns it.

ANDREA: That could interest his steward too and even his money lender—and the seaport towns…

FEDERZONI: None of them speak Latin.

GALILEO: I might write in plain language. The work we do is exacting. Who would go through the strain for less than the population at large!

LUDOVICO: I see you have made your decision. It was inevitable. You will always be a slave of your passions. Excuse me to Virginia, I think it's as well I don't see her now.

GALILEO: The dowry is at your disposal at any time.

LUDOVICO: Good afternoon. (*He goes followed by the* SERVANT.)

ANDREA: Exit Ludovico. To hell with all Marsilis, Villanis, Orsinis, Canes, Nuccolis, Soldanieris…

FEDERZONI: …who ordered the earth stand still because their castles might be shaken loose if it revolves…

LITTLE MONK: …and who only kiss the Pope's feet as long as he uses them to trample on the people. God made the physical world, God made the human brain. God will allow physics.

ANDREA: They will try to stop us.

GALILEO: Thus we enter the observation of these spots on the sun in which we are interested, at our own risk, not counting on protection from a problematical new Pope…

ANDREA: …but with great likelihood of dispelling Fabrizius' vapors, and the shadows of Paris and Prague, and of establishing the rotation of the sun…

GALILEO: …and with *some* likelihood of establishing the rotation of the sun. My intention is not to prove that I was right but to find out *whether* I was right. "Abandon hope all ye who enter—an observation." Before assuming these phenomena are spots, which would suit us, let us first set about proving that they are not—fried fish. We crawl by inches. What we find today we will wipe from the blackboard tomorrow and reject it—unless it shows up again the day after tomorrow. And if we find anything which would suit us, that thing we will eye with particular distrust. In fact, we will approach this observing of the sun with the implacable determination to prove that the earth stands still and only if hopelessly defeated in this pious undertaking can we allow ourselves to wonder if we may not have been right all the time: the earth revolves. Take the cloth off the telescope and turn it on the sun.

(*Quietly they start work. When the corruscating image of the sun is focused on the screen,* VIRGINIA *enters hurriedly, her wedding dress on, her hair disheveled,* MRS. SARTI *with her, carrying her wedding veil. The two women realize what has happened.* VIRGINIA *faints.* ANDREA, LITTLE MONK, *and* GALILEO *rush to her.* FEDERZONI *continues working.*)

SCENE 9

On April Fool's Day, thirty two,
Of science there was much ado.
People had learned from Galilei:
They used his teaching in their way.

(*Around the corner from the marketplace a* STREET SINGER *and his* WIFE, *who is costumed to represent the earth in a skeleton globe made of thin bands of brass, are holding the attention of a sprinkling of representative citizens, some in musquerade who were on their way to see the carnival procession. From the marketplace the noise of an impatient crowd.*)

BALLAD SINGER (*accompanied by his* WIFE *on the guitar*): When the Almighty made the universe He made the earth and then he made the sun.
Then round the earth he bade the sun to turn—
That's in the Bible, Genesis, Chapter One.

And from that time all beings here below
Were in obedient circles meant to go:

Around the Pope the cardinals
Around the cardinals the bishops
Around the bishops the secretaries
Around the secretaries the aldermen
Around the aldermen the craftsmen
Around the craftsmen the servants
Around the servants the dogs, the chickens,
and the beggars.

(*A conspicuous reveller—henceforth called the*
SPINNER—*has slowly caught on and is exhibiting his
idea of spinning around. He does not lose dignity, he
faints with mock grace.*)

BALLAD SINGER: Up stood the learned Galileo
Glanced briefly at the sun
And said: "Almighty God was wrong
In Genesis, Chapter One!"

Now that was rash, my friends, it is no matter small
For heresy will spread today like foul
diseases.
Change Holy Writ, forsooth? What will be
left at all?
Why: each of us would say and do just what
he pleases!

(*Three wretched* EXTRAS, *employed by the chamber of
commerce, enter. Two of them, in ragged costumes,
moodily bear a litter with a mock throne. The third
sits on the throne. He wears sacking, a false beard, a
prop crown, he carries a prop orb and sceptre, and
around his chest the inscription* "THE KING OF HUN-
GARY." *The litter has a card with* "No. 4" *written on
it. The litter bearers dump him down and listen to
the* BALLAD SINGER.)

BALLAD SINGER: Good people, what will come to
pass
If Galileo's teachings spread?
No altar boy will serve the Mass
No servant girl will make the bed.

Now that is grave, my friends, it is no matter small:
For independent spirit spreads like foul
diseases!

(Yet life is sweet and man is weak and after
all—
How nice it is, for a little change, to do just
as one pleases!)

(*The* BALLAD SINGER *takes over the guitar. His* WIFE
*dances around him, illustrating the motion of the
earth. A* COBBLER'S BOY *with a pair of resplendent
lacquered boots hung over his shoulder has been
jumping up and down in mock excitement. There are
three more children, dressed as grownups among the
spectators, two together and a single one with mother.
The* COBBLER'S BOY *takes the three* CHILDREN *in
hand, forms a chain, and leads it, moving to the music, in and out among the spectators, "whipping" the
chain so that the last child bumps into people. On the
way past a* PEASANT WOMAN, *he steals an egg from
her basket. She gestures to him to return it. As he
passes her again he quietly breaks the egg over her
head. The* KING OF HUNGARY *ceremoniously hands
his orb to one of his bearers, marches down with mock
dignity, and chastises the* COBBLER'S BOY. *The parents remove the three* CHILDREN. *The unseemliness
subsides.*)

BALLAD SINGER: The carpenters take wood and
build
Their houses—not the church's pews.
And members of the cobblers' guild
Now boldly walk the streets—in shoes.
The tenant kicks the noble lord
Quite off the land he owned—like that!
The milk his wife once gave the priest
Now makes (at last!) her children fat.

Ts, ts, ts, ts, my friends, this is no matter
small
For independent spirit spreads like foul
diseases
People must keep their place, some down
and some on top!
(Though it is nice, for a little change, to do
just as one pleases!)

(*The* COBBLER'S BOY *has put on the lacquered boots
he was carrying. He struts off. The* BALLAD SINGER
takes over the guitar again. His WIFE *dances around
him in increased tempo. A* MONK *has been standing
near a rich* COUPLE, *who are in subdued costly
clothes, without masks: shocked at the song, he now*

leaves. A DWARF *in the costume of an astronomer turns his telescope on the departing* MONK, *thus drawing attention to the rich* COUPLE. *In imitation of the* COBBLER'S BOY, *the* SPINNER *forms a chain of grownups. They move to the music, in and out, and between the rich* COUPLE. *The* SPINNER *changes the* GENTLEMAN'S *bonnet for the ragged hat of a* BEGGAR. *The* GENTLEMAN *decides to take this in good part, and a* GIRL *is emboldened to take his dagger. The* GENTLEMAN *is miffed, throws the* BEGGAR'S *hat back. The* BEGGAR *discards the* GENTLEMAN'S *bonnet and drops it on the ground. The* KING OF HUNGARY *has walked from his throne, taken an egg from the* PEASANT WOMAN, *and paid for it. He now ceremoniously breaks it over the* GENTLEMAN'S *head as he is bending down to pick up his bonnet. The* GENTLEMAN *conducts the* LADY *away from the scene. The* KING OF HUNGARY, *about to resume his throne, finds one of the* CHILDREN *sitting on it. The* GENTLEMAN *returns to retrieve his dagger. Merriment. The* BALLAD SINGER *wanders off. This is part of his routine. His* WIFE *sings to the* SPINNER.)

WIFE: Now speaking for myself I feel
That I could also do with a change.
You know, for me…(*Turning to a reveller*)
…*you* have appeal
Maybe tonight we could arrange…

(*The* DWARF-ASTRONOMER *has been amusing the people by focusing his telescope on her legs. The* BALLAD SINGER *has returned.*)

BALLAD SINGER: No, no, no, no, no, stop, Galileo, stop!
For independent spirit spreads like foul diseases
People must keep their place, some down and some on top!
(Though it is nice, for a little change, to do just as one pleases!)

(*The* SPECTATORS *stand embarrassed. A* GIRL *laughs loudly.*)

BALLAD SINGER AND HIS WIFE: Good people who have trouble here below
in serving cruel lords and gentle Jesus
Who bids you turn the other cheek just so…
(*With mimicry.*)

While they prepare to strike the second blow:
Obedience will never cure your woe
So each of you wake up and do just as he pleases!

(*The* BALLAD SINGER *and his* WIFE *hurriedly start to try to sell pamphlets to the spectators.*)

BALLAD SINGER: Read all about the earth going round the sun, two centesemi only. As proved by the great Galileo. Two centesemi only. Written by a local scholar. Understandable to one and all. Buy one for your friends, your children and your aunty Rosa, two centesimi only. Abbreviated but complete. Fully illustrated with pictures of the planets, including Venus, two centesimi only.

(*During the speech of the* BALLAD SINGER *we hear the carnival procession approaching followed by laughter. A* REVELLER *rushes in.*)

REVELLER: The procession!

(*The litter bearers speedily joggle out the* KING OF HUNGARY. *The* SPECTATORS *turn and look at the first float of the procession, which now makes its appearance. It bears a gigantic figure of* GALILEO, *holding in one hand an open Bible with the pages crossed out. The other hand points to the Bible, and the head mechanically turns from side to side as if to say "No! No!"*)

A LOUD VOICE: Galileo, the Bible killer!

(*The laughter from the marketplace becomes uproarious. The* MONK *comes flying from the marketplace followed by delighted* CHILDREN.)

SCENE 10

*The depths are hot, the heights are chill
The streets are loud, the court is still.*

(*Antechamber and staircase in the Medicean palace in Florence.* GALILEO, *with a book under his arm, waits with his* DAUGHTER *to be admitted to the presence of the* PRINCE.)

VIRGINIA: They are a long time.
GALILEO: Yes.
VIRGINIA: Who is that funny-looking man? (*She indicates the* INFORMER *who has entered casually*

and seated himself in the background, taking no apparent notice of GALILEO.)

GALILEO: I don't know.

VIRGINIA: It's not the first time I have seen him around. He gives me the creeps.

GALILEO: Nonsense. We're in Florence, not among robbers in the mountains of Corsica.

VIRGINIA: Here comes the Rector.

(*The* RECTOR *comes down the stairs.*)

GALILEO: Gaffone is a bore. He attaches himself to you.

(*The* RECTOR *passes, scarcely nodding.*)

GALILEO: My eyes are bad today. Did he acknowledge us?

VIRGINIA: Barely. (*Pause.*) What's in your book? Will they say it's heretical?

GALILEO: You hang around church too much. And getting up at dawn and scurrying to Mass is ruining your skin. You pray for me, don't you?

(*A* MAN *comes down the stairs.*)

VIRGINIA: Here's Mr. Matti. You designed a machine for his iron foundries.

MATTI: How were the squabs, Mr. Galilei? (*Low.*) My brother and I had a good laugh the other day. He picked up a racy pamphlet against the Bible somewhere. It quoted you.

GALILEO: The squabs, Matti, were wonderful, thank you again. Pamphlets I know nothing about. The Bible and Homer are my favorite reading.

MATTI: No necessity to be cautious with me, Mr. Galilei. I am on your side. I am not a man who knows about the motions of the stars, but you have championed the freedom to teach new things. Take that mechanical cultivator they have in Germany which you described to me. I can tell you, it will never be used in this country. The same circles that are hampering you now will forbid the physicians at Bologna to cut up corpses for research. Do you know, they have such things as money markets in Amsterdam and in London? Schools for business, too. Regular papers with news. Here we are not even free

to make money. I have a stake in your career. They are against iron foundries because they say the gathering of so many workers in one place fosters immorality! If they ever try anything, Mr. Galilei, remember you have friends in all walks of life including an iron founder. Good luck to you. (*He goes.*)

GALILEO: Good man, but need he be so affectionate in public? His voice carries. They will always claim me as their spiritual leader particularly in places where it doesn't help me at all. I have written a book about the mechanics of the firmament, that is all. What they do or don't do with it is not my concern.

VIRGINIA (*loud*): If people only knew how you disagreed with those goings-on all over the country last All Fools day.

GALILEO: Yes. Offer honey to a bear, and lose your arm if the beast is hungry.

VIRGINIA (*low*): Did the prince ask you to come here today?

GALILEO: I sent word I was coming. He will want the book, he has paid for it. My health hasn't been any too good lately. I may accept Sagredo's invitation to stay with him in Padua for a few weeks.

VIRGINIA: You couldn't manage without your books.

GALILEO: Sagredo has an excellent library.

VIRGINIA: We haven't had this month's salary yet—

GALILEO: Yes. (*The* CARDINAL INQUISITOR *passes down the staircase. He bows deeply in answer to* GALILEO's *bow.*) What is he doing in Florence? If they try to do anything to me, the new Pope will meet them with an iron NO. And the Prince is my pupil, he would never have me extradited.

VIRGINIA: Psst. The Lord Chamberlain.

(*The* LORD CHAMBERLAIN *comes down the stairs.*)

LORD CHAMBERLAIN: His Highness had hoped to find time for you, Mr. Galilei. Unfortunately, he has to leave immediately to judge the parade at the Riding Academy. On what business did you wish to see His Highness?

GALILEO: I wanted to present my book to His Highness.

LORD CHAMBERLAIN: How are your eyes today?

GALILEO: So, so. With His Highness' permission, I am dedicating the book…

LORD CHAMBERLAIN: Your eyes are a matter of great concern to His Highness. Could it be that you have been looking too long and too often through your marvelous tube? (*He leaves without accepting the book.*)

VIRGINIA (*greatly agitated*): Father, I am afraid.

GALILEO: He didn't take the book, did he? (*Low and resolute.*) Keep a straight face. We are not going home, but to the house of the lens-grinder. There is a coach and horses in his backyard. Keep your eyes to the front, don't look back at that man.

(*They start. The* LORD CHAMBERLAIN *comes back.*)

LORD CHAMBERLAIN: Oh, Mr. Galilei! His Highness has just charged me to inform you that the Florentine Court is no longer in a position to oppose the request of the Holy Inquisition to interrogate you in Rome.

SCENE 11

The Pope

(*A chamber in the Vatican. The Pope, Urban VIII—formerly* CARDINAL BARBERINI—*is giving audience to the* CARDINAL INQUISITOR. *The trampling and shuffling of many feet is heard throughout the scene from the adjoining corridors. During the scene the Pope is being robed for the conclave he is about to attend: at the beginning of the scene he is plainly* BARBERINI, *but as the scene proceeds he is more and more obscured by grandiose vestments.*)

POPE: No! No! No!

INQUISITOR (*referring to the owners of the shuffling feet*): Doctors of all chairs from the universities, representatives of the special orders of the church, representatives of the clergy as a whole who have come believing with child-like faith in the word of God as set forth in the scriptures, who have come to hear Your Holiness confirm their faith: and Your Holiness is really going to tell them that the Bi-

ble can no longer be regarded as the alphabet of truth?

POPE: I will not set myself up against the multiplication table. No!

INQUISITOR: Ah, that is what these people say, that it is the multiplication table. Their cry is, "The figures compel us," but where do these figures come from? Plainly they come from doubt. These men doubt everything. Can society stand on doubt and not on faith? "Thou art my master, but I doubt whether it is for the best." "This is my neighbor's house and my neighbor's wife, but why shouldn't they belong to me?" After the plague, after the new war, after the unparalleled disaster of the Reformation, your dwindling flock look to their shepherd, and now the mathematicians turn their tubes on the sky and announce to the world that you have not the best advice about the heavens either—up to now your only uncontested sphere of influence. This Galilei started meddling in machines at an early age. Now that men in ships are venturing on the great oceans—I am not against that of course—they are putting their faith in a brass bowl they call a compass and not in Almighty God.

POPE: This man is the greatest physicist of our time. He is the light of Italy, and not just any muddle-head.

INQUISITOR: Would we have had to arrest him otherwise? This bad man knows what he is doing, not writing his books in Latin, but in the jargon of the marketplace.

POPE (*occupied with the shuffling feet*): That was not in the best of taste. (*A pause.*) These shuffling feet are making me nervous.

INQUISITOR: May they be more telling than my words, Your Holiness. Shall all these go from you with doubt in their hearts?

POPE: This man has friends. What about Versailles?° What about the Viennese court?

Versailles: This reference to the French court is an anachronism. The palace housing the court had not yet been built at Versailles. In Galileo's time, it was in Paris.

They will call Holy Church a cesspool for defunct ideas. Keep your hands off him.

INQUISITOR: In practice it will never get far. He is a man of the flesh. He would soften at once.

POPE: He has more enjoyment in him than any man I ever saw. He loves eating and drinking and thinking. To excess. He indulges in thinking bouts! He cannot say no to an old wine or a new thought. (*Furious.*) I do not want a condemnation of physical facts. I do not want to hear battle cries: Church, church, church! Reason, reason, reason! (*Pause.*) These shuffling feet are intolerable. Has the whole world come to my door?

INQUISITOR: Not the whole world, Your Holiness. A select gathering of the faithful.

(*Pause.*)

POPE (*exhausted*): It is clearly understood: he is not to be tortured. (*Pause.*) At the very most, he may be shown the instruments.

INQUISITOR: That will be adequate, Your Holiness. Mr. Galilei understands machinery.

(*The eyes of* BARBERINI *look helplessly at the* CARDINAL INQUISITOR *from under the completely assembled panoply of Pope Urban VIII.*)

SCENE 12

June twenty-second, sixteen thirty-three,
A momentous date for you and me.
Of all the days that was the one
An age of reason could have begun.

(*Again the garden of the Florentine Ambassador at Rome, where* GALILEO'S *assistants wait the news of the trial. The* LITTLE MONK *and* FEDERZONI *are attempting to concentrate on a game of chess.* VIRGINIA *kneels in a corner, praying and counting her beads.*)

LITTLE MONK: The Pope didn't even grant him an audience.

FEDERZONI: No more scientific discussions.

ANDREA: The "Discorsi" will never be finished. The sum of his findings. They will kill him.

FEDERZONI (*stealing a glance at him*): Do you really think so?

ANDREA: He will never recant.

(*Silence.*)

LITTLE MONK: You know when you lie awake at night how your mind fastens on to something irrelevant. Last night I kept thinking: if only they would let him take his little stone in with him, the appeal-to-reason-pebble that he always carries in his pocket.

FEDERZONI: In the room *they'll* take him to, he won't have a pocket.

ANDREA: But he will not recant.

LITTLE MONK: How can they beat the truth out of a man who gave his sight in order to see?

FEDERZONI: Maybe they can't.

(*Silence.*)

ANDREA (*speaking about* VIRGINIA): She is praying that he will recant.

FEDERZONI: Leave her alone. She doesn't know whether she's on her head or on her heels since they got hold of her. They brought her Father Confessor from Florence.

(*The* INFORMER *of scene 10 enters.*)

INFORMER: Mr. Galilei will be here soon. He may need a bed.

FEDERZONI: Have they let him out?

INFORMER: Mr. Galilei is expected to recant at five o'clock. The big bell of Saint Marcus will be rung and the complete text of his recantation publicly announced.

ANDREA: I don't believe it.

INFORMER: Mr. Galilei will be brought to the garden gate at the back of the house, to avoid the crowds collecting in the streets. (*He goes.*)

(*Silence.*)

ANDREA: The moon is an earth because the light of the moon is not her own. Jupiter is a fixed star, and four moons turn around Jupiter, therefore we are not shut in by crystal shells. The sun is the pivot of our world, therefore the earth is not the center. The earth moves, spinning about the sun. And he showed us. You can't make a man unsee what he has seen.

(*Silence.*)

FEDERZONI: Five o'clock is one minute.

(VIRGINIA *prays louder.*)

ANDREA: Listen all of you, they are murdering the truth.

(*He stops up his ears with his fingers. The two other pupils do the same.* FEDERZONI *goes over to the* LITTLE MONK, *and all of them stand absolutely still in cramped positions. Nothing happens. No bell sounds. After a silence, filled with the murmur of* VIRGINIA's *prayers,* FEDERZONI *runs to the wall to look at the clock. He turns around, his expression changed. He shakes his head. They drop their hands.*)

FEDERZONI: No. No bell. It is three minutes after.

LITTLE MONK: He hasn't.

ANDREA: He held true. It is all right, it is all right.

LITTLE MONK: He did not recant.

FEDERZONI: No.

(*They embrace each other, they are delirious with joy.*)

ANDREA: So force cannot accomplish everything. What has been seen can't be unseen. Man is constant in the face of death.

FEDERZONI: June 22, 1633: dawn of the age of reason. I wouldn't have wanted to go on living if he had recanted.

LITTLE MONK: I didn't say anything, but I was in agony. Oh, ye of little faith!

ANDREA: I was sure.

FEDERZONI: It would have turned our morning to night.

ANDREA: It would have been as if the mountain had turned to water.

LITTLE MONK (*kneeling down, crying*): Oh God, I thank Thee.

ANDREA: Beaten humanity can lift its head. A man has stood up and said "no."

(*At this moment the bell of Saint Marcus begins to toll. They stand like statues.* VIRGINIA *stands up.*)

VIRGINIA: The bell of Saint Marcus. He is not damned.

(*From the street one hears the* TOWN CRIER *reading* GALILEO's *recantation.*)

TOWN CRIER: I, Galileo Galilei, Teacher of Mathematics and Physics, do hereby publicly renounce my teaching that the earth moves. I foreswear this teaching with a sincere heart and unfeigned faith and detest and curse this and all other errors and heresies repugnant to the Holy Scriptures.

(*The lights dim; when they come up again the bell of Saint Marcus is petering out.* VIRGINIA *has gone but the* SCHOLARS *are still there waiting.*)

ANDREA (*loud*): The mountain did turn to water.

(GALILEO *has entered quietly and unnoticed. He is changed, almost unrecognizable. He has heard* ANDREA. *He waits some seconds by the door for somebody to greet him. Nobody does. They retreat from him. He goes slowly and, because of his bad sight, uncertainly, to the front of the stage where he finds a chair, and sits down.*)

ANDREA: I can't look at him. Tell him to go away.

FEDERZONI: Steady.

ANDREA (*hysterically*): He saved his big gut.

FEDERZONI: Get him a glass of water.

(*The* LITTLE MONK *fetches a glass of water for* ANDREA. *Nobody acknowledges the presence of* GALILEO, *who sits silently on his chair listening to the voice of the* TOWN CRIER, *now in another street.*)

ANDREA: I can walk. Just help me a bit.

(*They help him to the door.*)

ANDREA (*in the door*): "Unhappy is the land that breeds no hero."

GALILEO: No, Andrea: "Unhappy is the land that needs a hero."

Before the next scene a curtain with the following legend on it is lowered:

You can plainly see that if a horse were to fall from a height of three or four feet, it could break its bones, whereas a dog would not suffer injury. The same applies to a cat from a height of as much as eight or ten feet, to a grasshopper from the top of a tower, and to an ant falling down from the moon. Nature could not allow a horse to become as big as twenty horses nor a giant as big as ten men, unless she were to change the proportions of all its members, particularly the bones. Thus the common assumption that great and small structures are equally tough is obviously wrong.

—From the *Discorsi*

SCENE 13

1633–1642.

*Galileo Galilei remains a prisoner
of the Inquisition until his death.*

(*A country house near Florence. A large room simply
furnished. There is a huge table, a leather chair, a
globe of the world on a stand, and a narrow bed. A
portion of the adjoining anteroom is visible, and the
front door which opens into it.*)

   (*An* OFFICIAL *of the Inquisition sits on guard in
the anteroom.*)

   (*In the large room,* GALILEO *is quietly experiment-
ing with a bent wooden rail and a small ball of wood.
He is still vigorous but almost blind.*)

   (*After a while there is a knocking at the outside
door. The* OFFICIAL *opens it to a* PEASANT *who brings
a plucked goose.* VIRGINIA *comes from the kitchen.
She is past forty.*)

PEASANT (*handing the goose to* VIRGINIA): I was
   told to deliver this here.

VIRGINIA: I didn't order a goose.

PEASANT: I was told to say it's from someone
   who was passing through.

(VIRGINIA *takes the goose, surprised. The* OFFICIAL
*takes it from her and examines it suspiciously. Then,
reassured, he hands it back to her. The* PEASANT *goes.*
VIRGINIA *brings the goose in to* GALILEO.)

VIRGINIA: Somebody who was passing through
   sent you something.

GALILEO: What is it?

VIRGINIA: Can't you see it?

GALILEO: No. (*He walks over.*) A goose. Any name?

VIRGINIA: No.

GALILEO (*weighing the goose*): Solid.

VIRGINIA (*cautiously*): Will you eat the liver, if I
   have it cooked with a little apple?

GALILEO: I had my dinner. Are you under orders
   to finish me off with food?

VIRGINIA: It's not rich. And what is wrong with
   your eyes again? You should be able to see it.

GALILEO: You were standing in the light.

VIRGINIA: I was not.—You haven't been writing
   again?

GALILEO (*sneering*): What do you think?

(VIRGINIA *takes the goose out into the anteroom and
speaks to the* OFFICIAL.)

VIRGINIA: You had better ask Monsignor Carp-
   ula to send the doctor. Father couldn't see
   this goose across the room.—Don't look at
   me like that. He has not been writing. He
   dictates everything to me, as you know.

OFFICIAL: Yes?

VIRGINIA: He abides by the rules. My father's repentance is sincere. I keep an eye on him.
   (*She hands him the goose.*) Tell the cook to fry
   the liver with an apple and an onion. (*She
   goes back into the large room.*) And you have
   no business to be doing that with those eyes
   of yours, father.

GALILEO: You may read me some Horace.

VIRGINIA: We should go on with your weekly
   letter to the Archbishop. Monsignor Carp-
   ula to whom we owe so much was all
   smiles the other day because the Archbishop had expressed his pleasure at your
   collaboration.

GALILEO: Where were we?

VIRGINIA (*sits down to take his dictation*): Paragraph four.

GALILEO: Read what you have.

VIRGINIA: "The position of the church in the matter of the unrest at Genoa. I agree with Cardinal Spoletti in the matter of the unrest
   among the Venetian ropemakers..."

GALILEO: Yes. (*Dictates.*) I agree with Cardinal
   Spoletti in the matter of the unrest among the
   Venetian ropemakers: it is better to distribute
   good nourishing food in the name of charity
   than to pay them more for their bellropes. It
   being surely better to strengthen their faith
   than to encourage their acquisitiveness. St.
   Paul says: Charity never faileth.—How is
   that?

VIRGINIA: It's beautiful, father.

GALILEO: It couldn't be taken as irony?

VIRGINIA: No. The Archbishop will like it. It's so
   practical.

GALILEO: I trust your judgment. Read it over
   slowly.

VIRGINIA: "The position of the Church in the
   matter of the unrest..."

(*There is a knocking at the outside door.* VIRGINIA
goes into the anteroom. The OFFICIAL *opens the door.
It is* ANDREA.)

ANDREA: Good evening. I am sorry to call so late, I'm on my way to Holland. I was asked to look him up. Can I go in?

VIRGINIA: I don't know whether he will see you. You never came.

ANDREA: Ask him.

(GALILEO *recognizes the voice. He sits motionless.* VIRGINIA *comes in to* GALILEO.)

GALILEO: Is that Andrea?

VIRGINIA: Yes. (*Pause.*) I will send him away.

GALILEO: Show him in.

(VIRGINIA *shows* ANDREA *in.* VIRGINIA *sits,* ANDREA *remains standing.*)

ANDREA (*cool*): Have you been keeping well, Mr. Galilei?

GALILEO: Sit down. What are you doing these days? What are you working on? I heard it was something about hydraulics in Milan.

ANDREA: As he knew I was passing through, Fabricius of Amsterdam asked me to visit you and inquire about your health.

(*Pause.*)

GALILEO: I am very well.

ANDREA (*formally*): I am glad I can report you are in good health.

GALILEO: Fabricius will be glad to hear it. And you might inform him that, on account of the depth of my repentance, I live in comparative comfort.

ANDREA: Yes, we understand that the church is more than pleased with you. Your complete acceptance has had its effect. Not one paper expounding a new thesis has made its appearance in Italy since your submission.

(*Pause.*)

GALILEO: Unfortunately there are countries not under the wing of the church. Would you not say the erroneous condemned theories are still taught—there?

ANDREA (*relentless*): Things are almost at a standstill.

GALILEO: Are they? (*Pause.*) Nothing from Descartes in Paris?

ANDREA: Yes. On receiving the news of your recantation, he shelved his treatise on the nature of light.

GALILEO: I sometimes worry about my assistants whom I led into error. Have they benefited by my example?

ANDREA: In order to work I have to go to Holland.

GALILEO: Yes.

ANDREA: Federzoni is grinding lenses again, back in some shop.

GALILEO: He can't read the books.

ANDREA: Fulganzio, our little monk, has abandoned research and is resting in peace in the church.

GALILEO: So. (*Pause.*) My superiors are looking forward to my spiritual recovery. I am progressing as well as can be expected.

VIRGINIA: You are doing well, father.

GALILEO: Virginia, leave the room.

(VIRGINIA *rises uncertainly and goes out.*)

VIRGINIA (*to the* OFFICIAL): He was his pupil, so now he is his enemy.—Help me in the kitchen.

(*She leaves the anteroom with the* OFFICIAL.)

ANDREA: May I go now, sir?

GALILEO: I do not know why you came, Sarti. To unsettle me? I have to be prudent.

ANDREA: I'll be on my way.

GALILEO: As it is, I have relapses. I completed the "Discorsi."

ANDREA: You completed what?

GALILEO: My "Discorsi."

ANDREA: How?

GALILEO: I am allowed pen and paper. My superiors are intelligent men. They know the habits of a lifetime cannot be broken abruptly. But they protect me from any unpleasant consequences: they lock my pages away as I dictate them. And I should know better than to risk my comfort. I wrote the "Discorsi" out again during the night. The manuscript is in the globe. My vanity has up to now prevented me from destroying it. If you consider taking it, you will shoulder the entire risk. You will say it was pirated from the original in the hands of the Holy Office.

(ANDREA, *as in a trance, has gone to the globe. He lifts the upper half and gets the book. He turns the pages as if wanting to devour them. In the background the opening sentences of the* Discorsi *appear:*

MY PURPOSE IS TO SET FORTH A VERY NEW
SCIENCE DEALING WITH A VERY ANCIENT
SUBJECT—MOTION.... AND I HAVE
DISCOVERED BY EXPERIMENT SOME PROPER
TIES OF IT WHICH ARE WORTH KNOWING....)

GALILEO: I had to employ my time somehow.

(*The text disappears.*)

ANDREA: Two new sciences! This will be the foundation stone of a new physics.

GALILEO: Yes. Put it under your coat.

ANDREA: And we thought you had deserted. (*In a low voice.*) Mr. Galilei, how can I begin to express my shame. Mine has been the loudest voice against you.

GALILEO: That would seem to have been proper. I taught you science and I decried the truth.

ANDREA: Did you? I think not. Everything is changed!

GALILEO: What is changed?

ANDREA: You shielded the truth from the oppressor. Now I see! In your dealings with the Inquisition you used the same superb common sense you brought to physics.

GALILEO: Oh!

ANDREA: We lost our heads. With the crowd at the street corners we said: "He will die, he will never surrender!" You came back: "I surrendered but I am alive." We cried: "Your hands are stained!" You say: "Better stained than empty."

GALILEO: "Better stained than empty."—It sounds realistic. Sounds like me.

ANDREA: And I of all people should have known. I was twelve when you sold another man's telescope to the Venetian Senate, and saw you put it to immortal use. Your friends were baffled when you bowed to the Prince of Florence: Science gained a wider audience. You always laughed at heroics. "People who suffer bore me," you said. "Misfortunes are due mainly to miscalculations." And: "If there are obstacles, the shortest line between two points may be the crooked line."

GALILEO: It makes a picture.

ANDREA: And when you stooped to recant in 1633, I should have understood that you were again about your business.

GALILEO: My business being?

ANDREA: Science. The study of the properties of motion, mother of the machines which will themselves change the ugly face of the earth.

GALILEO: Aha!

ANDREA: You gained time to write a book that only you could write. Had you burned at the stake in a blaze of glory they would have won.

GALILEO: They have won. And there is no such thing as a scientific work that only one man can write.

ANDREA: Then why did you recant, tell me that!

GALILEO: I recanted because I was afraid of physical pain.

ANDREA: No!

GALILEO: They showed me the instruments.

ANDREA: It was not a plan?

GALILEO: It was not.

(*Pause.*)

ANDREA: But you have contributed. Science has only one commandment: contribution. And you have contributed more than any man for a hundred years.

GALILEO: Have I? Then welcome to my gutter, dear colleague in science and brother in treason: I sold out, you are a buyer. The first sight of the book! His mouth watered and his scoldings were drowned. Blessed be our bargaining, whitewashing, death-fearing community!

ANDREA: The fear of death is human.

GALILEO: Even the church will teach you that to be weak is not human. It is just evil.

ANDREA: The church, yes! But science is not concerned with our weaknesses.

GALILEO: No? My dear Sarti, in spite of my present convictions, I may be able to give you a few pointers as to the concerns of your chosen profession.

(*Enter* VIRGINIA *with a platter.*)

In my spare time, I happen to have gone over this case. I have spare time.—Even a man who sells wool, however good he is at buying wool cheap and selling it dear, must be concerned with the standing of the wool trade. The practice of science would seem to call for valor. She trades in knowledge, which is the product of doubt. And this new art of doubt has enchanted the public. The plight of the multitude is old as the rocks, and is believed to be basic as the rocks. But now they have learned to doubt. They snatched the telescopes out of our hands and had them trained on their tormentors: prince, official, public moralist. The mechanism of the heavens was clearer, the mechanism of their courts was still murky. The battle to measure the heavens is won by doubt; by credulity the Roman housewife's battle for milk will always be lost. Word is passed down that this is of no concern to the scientist who is told he will only release such of his findings as do not disturb the peace, that is, the peace of mind of the well-to-do. Threats and bribes fill the air. Can the scientist hold out on the numbers?—For what reason do you labor? I take it the intent of science is to ease human existence. If you give way to coercion, science can be crippled, and your new machines may simply suggest new drudgeries. Should you then, in time, discover all there is to be discovered, your progress must then become a progress away from the bulk of humanity. The gulf might even grow so wide that the sound of your cheering at some new achievement would be echoed by a universal howl of horror.—As a scientist I had an almost unique opportunity. In my day astronomy emerged into the marketplace. At that particular time, had one man put up a fight, it could have had wide repercussions. I have come to believe that I was never in real danger; for some years I was as strong as the authorities, and I surrendered my knowledge to the powers that be, to use it, no, not *use* it, *abuse* it, as it suits their ends. I have betrayed my profession. Any man who does what I have done must not be tolerated in the ranks of science.

(VIRGINIA, *who has stood motionless, puts the platter on the table.*)

VIRGINIA: You are accepted in the ranks of the faithful, father.

GALILEO (*sees her*): Correct. (*He goes over to the table.*) I have to eat now.

VIRGINIA: We lock up at eight.

ANDREA: I am glad I came. (*He extends his hand.* GALILEO *ignores it and goes over to his meal.*)

GALILEO (*examining the plate; to* ANDREA): Somebody who knows me sent me a goose. I still enjoy eating.

ANDREA: And your opinion is now that the "new age" was an illusion?

GALILEO: Well.—This age of ours turned out to be a whore, spattered with blood. Maybe, new ages look like blood-spattered whores. Take care of yourself.

ANDREA: Yes. (*Unable to go.*) With reference to your evaluation of the author in question— I do not know the answer. But I cannot think that your savage analysis is the last word.

GALILEO: Thank you, sir.

(OFFICIAL *knocks at the door.*)

VIRGINIA (*showing* ANDREA *out*): I don't like visitors from the past, they excite him.

(*She lets him out. The* OFFICIAL *closes the iron door.* VIRGINIA *returns.*)

GALILEO (*eating*): Did you try and think who sent the goose?

VIRGINIA: Not Andrea.

GALILEO: Maybe not. I gave Redhead his first lesson; when he held out his hand, I had to remind myself he is teaching now.—How is the sky tonight?

VIRGINIA (*at the window*): Bright.

(GALILEO *continues eating.*)

SCENE 14

*The great book o'er the border went
And, good folk, that was the end.
But we hope you'll keep in mind
You and I were left behind.*

(*Before a little Italian customs house early in the morning.* ANDREA *sits upon one of his traveling* trunks at the barrier and reads GALILEO's book. The window of a small house is still lit, and a big grotesque shadow, like an old witch and her cauldron, falls upon the house wall beyond. Barefoot CHILDREN in rags see it and point to the little house.)

CHILDREN (singing): One, two, three, four, five, six, Old Marina is a witch.
At night, on a broomstick she sits
And on the church steeple she spits.
CUSTOMS OFFICER (to ANDREA): Why are you making this journey?
ANDREA: I am a scholar.
CUSTOMS OFFICER (to his CLERK): Put down under "reason for leaving the country": Scholar. (He points to the baggage.) Books! Anything dangerous in these books?
ANDREA: What is dangerous?
CUSTOMS OFFICER: Religion. Politics.
ANDREA: These are nothing but mathematical formulas.
CUSTOMS OFFICER: What's that?
ANDREA: Figures.
CUSTOMS OFFICER: Oh, figures. No harm in figures. Just wait a minute, sir, we will soon have your papers stamped. (He exits with CLERK.)

(Meanwhile, a little council of war among the CHILDREN has taken place. ANDREA quietly watches. One of the BOYS, pushed forward by the others, creeps up to the little house from which the shadow comes and takes the jug of milk on the doorstep.)

ANDREA (quietly): What are you doing with that milk?
BOY (stopping in mid-movement): She is a witch.

(The other CHILDREN run away behind the customs house. One of them shouts, "Run, Paolo!")

ANDREA: Hmm!—And because she is a witch she mustn't have milk. Is that the idea?
BOY: Yes.
ANDREA: And how do you know she is a witch?
BOY (points to shadow on house wall): Look!
ANDREA: Oh! I see.
BOY: And she rides on a broomstick at night—and she bewitches the coachman's horses. My cousin Luigi looked through the hole in the stable roof, that the snowstorm made,

and heard the horses coughing something terrible.
ANDREA: Oh!—How big was the hole in the stable roof?
BOY: Luigi didn't tell. Why?
ANDREA: I was asking because maybe the horses got sick because it was cold in the stable. You had better ask Luigi how big that hole is.
BOY: You are not going to say Old Marina isn't a witch, because you can't.
ANDREA: No, I can't say she isn't a witch. I haven't looked into it. A man can't know about a thing he hasn't looked into, or can he?
BOY: No!—But THAT! (He points to the shadow.) She is stirring hell-broth.
ANDREA: Let's see. Do you want to take a look? I can lift you up.
BOY: You lift me to the window, mister! (He takes a sling shot out of his pocket.) I can really bash her from there.
ANDREA: Hadn't we better make sure she is a witch before we shoot? I'll hold that.

(The BOY puts the milk jug down and follows him reluctantly to the window. ANDREA lifts the boy up so that he can look in.)

ANDREA: What do you see?
BOY (slowly): Just an old girl cooking porridge.
ANDREA: Oh! Nothing to it then. Now look at her shadow, Paolo.

(The BOY looks over his shoulder and back and compares the reality and the shadow.)

BOY: The big thing is a soup ladle.
ANDREA: Ah! A ladle! You see, I would have taken it for a broomstick, but I haven't looked into the matter as you have, Paolo. Here is your sling.
CUSTOMS OFFICER (returning with the CLERK and handing ANDREA his papers): All present and correct. Good luck, sir.

(ANDREA goes, reading GALILEO's book. The CLERK starts to bring his baggage after him. The barrier rises. ANDREA passes through, still reading the book. The BOY kicks over the milk jug.)

BOY (shouting after ANDREA): She is a witch! She is a witch!

ANDREA: You saw with your own eyes: think it over!

(*The* BOY *joins the others. They sing.*)

One, two, three, four, five, six,
Old Marina is a witch.
At night, on a broomstick she sits
And on the church steeple she spits.

(*The* CUSTOMS OFFICERS *laugh.* ANDREA *goes.*)

PERFORMING *GALILEO*

Brecht's *Galileo* (the final version was retitled *The Life of Galileo*) was first produced in Zurich, Switzerland, in 1943 with Leonard Steckel in the title role. Brecht was then in exile from Hitler's armies and living in California. The American version was developed in a remarkable collaboration between the playwright and the actor Charles Laughton and first staged at the Los Angeles Coronet Theater on July 30, 1947. This version with music by Hanns Eisler was directed by Brecht and Joseph Losey and produced by T. Edward Hambleton. The production transferred to Broadway's Maxine Elliott Theater on December 7, 1947. Neither of the American productions in the 1940s was received with great enthusiasm but Charles Laughton's performance was considered a remarkable achievement.

Once Brecht was relocated in East Berlin in the late 1940s, he became head of a new company, called the Berliner Ensemble. Shortly before his death in 1956, he was working on the third and final version of the script with the celebrated German actor Ernst Busch. *The Life of Galileo* was in rehearsal at the time of his death. Brecht's longtime collaborator, Erich Engel, staged *The Life of Galileo* with scenery by Caspar Neher and music by Hanns Eisler. It opened at the Theater am Schiffbauerdamm (the home of the Berliner Ensemble) in January of 1957. Brecht had changed the ending of the last scene to emphasize the precarious nature of human circumstances and the hope for a changing world. (In the final version, Andrea's last line is, "We've hardly begun.")

The Life of Galileo was revived again at the Berliner Ensemble in 1978, directed by Manfred Wekwerth and Joachim Tenschert with Ekkehard Schall as Galileo. The production remained in the theater's repertoire into the 1990s.

Like Brecht's other major plays (*Mother Courage and Her Children, The Caucasian Chalk Circle,* and *The Good Person of Setzuan*), *Galileo* requires a leading actor of great physical stamina and versatility along with an exceptionally large cast. In England and the United States, large "physical" actors with rich, commanding voices have assayed the role. Michael Gambon performed the role at London's Royal National Theater in 1979 and Brian Dennehy played Galileo in the Goodman Theatre production in 1986. The demanding title role and cast size have limited productions of the play in commercial and nonprofit theaters in the United States.

CRITICS' NOTEBOOK

Bertolt Brecht's plays, theoretical writings, and production notes were first introduced to English-language readers in the late fifties when the Brecht Archives were opened in Berlin in 1957. John Willett, Ralph Manheim, and Eric Bentley were instrumental in translating and publishing Brecht's work in English.

The most accessible works on Brecht in English are found in *Collected Plays,* volumes I to VIII, edited and annotated by John Willett and Ralph Manheim (first published in 1970); John Willett's *Brecht on Theatre: The Development of an Aesthetic* (1964) and *The Theatre of Bertolt Brecht: A Study from Eight Aspects* (1977); and Eric Bentley's *The Brecht Commentaries* (1981). Also, Hubert Witt edited *Brecht As They Knew Him* (1975), a group of thirty-four recollections by writers, actors, collaborators, and friends who worked with Brecht.

The unlikely collaboration between the German playwright who spoke little English and the British-born stage and film actor Charles Laughton who spoke no German nonetheless resulted in the American version of Brecht's *Galileo.* Brecht's notes, called "Building up a Part," convey insight into the way their unusual process resulted in a performance text.

Building up a Part: Laughton's Galileo (c. 1945)* Translated by John Willett

❦

We usually met in L.'s [Laughton's] big house above the Pacific, as the dictionaries of synonyms were too big to cart about. He had continual and inexhaustibly patient recourse to these tomes, and used in addition to fish out the most varied literary texts in order to examine this or that gest, or some particular mode of speech: Aesop, the Bible, Molière, Shakespeare. In my house he gave readings of Shakespeare's works to which he would devote perhaps a fortnight's preparation. In this way he read *The Tempest* and *King Lear,* simply for himself and one or two guests who happened to have dropped in. After that we would briefly discuss what seemed relevant, an 'aria' perhaps, or an effective scene opening. These were exercises, and he would pursue them in various directions, assimilating them in the rest of his work. If he had to give a reading on the radio he would get me to hammer out the syncopated rhythms of [Walt] Whitman's poems (which he found somewhat strange) on a table with my fists.... We needed such broadly ramified studies, because he spoke no German whatever and we had to decide the gest of each piece of dialogue by my acting it all in bad English or even in German and his then acting it back in proper English in a variety of ways until I could say: that's it. The result he would write down sentence by sentence in longhand. Some sentences, indeed many, he carried around for days, changing them continually. This system of performance-and-repetition had one immense advantage in that psychological discussions were almost entirely avoided. Even the most fundamental gests, such as Galileo's way of observing, or his showmanship, or his craze for pleasure, were established in three dimensions by actual performance. Our first concern throughout was for the smallest fragments, for sentences, even for exclamations—

Brecht on Theatre: The Development of an Aesthetic, ed. and trans. John Willett (New York: Hill and Wang, 1964): 165–168.

each treated separately, each needing to be given the simplest, freshly fitted form, giving so much away, hiding so much or leaving it open. More radical attacks on the structure of entire scenes or of the work itself were meant to help the story to move and to bring out fairly general conclusions about people's attitude to the great physicist. But this reluctance to tinker with the psychological aspect remained with L. all through our long period of collaboration, even when a rough draft of the play was ready and he was giving various readings in order to test reactions, and even during the rehearsals.

The awkward circumstance that one translator knew no German and the other scarcely any English compelled us, as can be seen, from the outset to use acting as our means of translation. We were forced to do what better equipped translators should do too: to translate gests. For language is theatrical in so far as it primarily expresses the mutual attitude of the speakers....

REVISITING EPIC THEATER

The work of Erwin Piscator and Bertolt Brecht changed the course of modern European theater. Their sphere of influence was exceptional. Following the work of the expressionists in Germany in the 1910s, their theories and experimentation reframed the harsh politics of class struggle and capitalistic inequities on a stage that demonstrated the dehumanizing plight of the average citizen caught up in the struggle for power and money. Along with Erwin Piscator, Brecht advocated the use of new technologies in the theater to develop a kind of performance style (called *epic theater*) that responded to the mechanized and accelerated routines of modern life. Brecht's serious reading of Karl Marx in the 1920s gave rise to his treatment of the class struggle in politics and his condemnation of bourgeois "realism" in theater. He went so far as to redefine Marx's concept of "alienation" as a mode of theatrical practice. In *Das Kapital,* Marx argued that the division of labor in modern industrial production created a separation (a distance) between the worker and the product. Workers, therefore, became dehumanized, mechanized, alienated from their work, the commodity, and society. Brecht's theater sets out to "alienate" or "estrange" the audience from the seamless illusion of the realistic stage in order to train us to reflect upon and question the world, its politicians, its social and financial institutions.

Brecht's experiments with epic writing and staging resulted in both episodic and narrative plays, the aims of which were to show social and political contradictions at work in the world. His goal was to encourage audiences to learn from the lessons of history, such as the sad destinies of those perennial small-time profiteers, like Mother Courage, or the despised ends of those giant shapers of human destiny like Galileo Galilei.

Writing styles that *revolted* against the "illusion of the real" in the theater span a period from the early 1900s to the present. In addition to the new writing and staging experiments in Germany, another singular group of highly influential playwrights in France, England, and the United States called, collectively, *the theater of the absurd* emerged at mid-century. Samuel Beckett and Eugène Ionesco led the way.

NOTES

1. Bertolt Brecht, *Collected Plays Volume 5,* edited by Ralph Manheim and John Willett (New York: Vintage Books, 1972): 216–217.
2. Ronald Hayman, *Brecht: A Biography* (New York: Oxford University Press, 1938): 296.
3. Eric Bentley, *The Brecht Commentaries* (London: Methuen, 1981): 190.
4. Martin Esslin, *Brecht: A Choice of Evils,* Fourth Edition (New York: Methuen, 1984): 234.
5. John Fuegi, *The Essential Brecht* (Los Angeles: Hennessey and Ingalls, 1972): 162.
6. Brecht 267.
7. Brecht 219.
8. Bentley 196.

CHAPTER 12

UNDERSTANDING MINIMALISM
AND THE ABSURD

Billie Whitelaw in a scene from the Samuel Beckett Theatre production of
Footfalls, directed by Alan Schneider. (Photo © Martha Swope.)

...you're on earth, there's no cure for that!
—Samuel Beckett

BACKGROUND

Postwar trends in European and American theater, from the end of the first world war to the present, reflect what sociologist Christopher Lasch called a "schizoid society." Plays written in our time have in a similar way represented the multiple faces and styles of our contemporary world. However, two broad performance styles—realism and theatricalism—have dominated the modern theater. One adheres to a candid representation of everyday reality, and the other uses the stage to call attention to life's theatricality. Playwrights, responding to changing philosophical, economic, social, and theatrical ideas, developed new dramaturgical conventions to express their changing vision of the universe. We have seen Erwin Piscator and Bertolt Brecht, beginning in the 1920s, turn to more theatrical modes of expression—open stages, revolving stages, minimal scenery, and the music hall revue—to address the social and political conditions of postwar worlds.

In the 1950s in France, Eugène Ionesco, Samuel Beckett, Arthur Adamov, and Jean Genet also pioneered new ways of expressing their vision of an "absurd" universe that resulted in another full-fledged theater movement—the theater of the absurd.

ABSURDIST THEORY

Martin Esslin coined the term the *theater of the absurd* in his landmark book of that name, written in 1961, and applied it to a new group of European writers, most notably, Samuel Beckett, Eugène Ionesco, Arthur Adamov, Jean Genet, Harold Pinter, and Fernando Arrabal. Esslin had observed certain common attitudes toward the human predicament in writings by this group of dramatists following the Second World War. Albert Camus had earlier summarized that predicament as "absurd" in his essay *The Myth of Sisyphus* (1941), which diagnosed humanity's

plight as purposelessness in an existence out of harmony with its surroundings. In most dictionary definitions, *absurd* means "out of harmony with reason and propriety." Esslin added ridiculous, incongruous, and unreasonable.[1] In *Notes and Counter Notes: Writings on the Theatre*, Ionesco redefined *absurd* as "anything without a goal...when man is cut off from his religious or metaphysical roots, he is lost; all his struggles become senseless, futile and oppressive."[2]

Absurdist writers, as this group has come to be called, not only shared similar concerns about the ideas that shaped their work but also shared the means whereby they transferred the irrationality and emptiness of experience to the stage.

THE STAGE AS EXISTENTIAL VOID

Absurdist playwrights neither argue nor debate life's absurdities. Rather, they "show" in concrete stage images and in language emptied of formal meaning a *dramatic metaphor* of an absurd universe. Martin Esslin insisted that it was not essential for audiences to decode the story lines but rather to take home with them the *overall impact* of a single overwhelmingly powerful image, composed of startling visual elements, strange murmurs of subdued voices in dim half-light, and the magical effect of the relentless flow of poetic phrasing and rich images.[3]

The playwrights of the absurd made their breakthrough in dramatic form by *presenting,* without comment or moral judgment, situations showing life's senselessness and irrationality. Ionesco called his first work, *The Bald Soprano* (written in 1948 and performed in 1950), an "antiplay" to point up his rebellion against conventional drama, especially the well-made play. His plays of the fifties parody materialistic bourgeois society, clichés of language and thought, and human irrationality. In his full-length plays of the sixties—*Rhinoceros, Victims of Duty, Exit the King*—his protagonists struggle against social and political conformity, although they can offer no rational basis for their actions. In more recent plays, Ionesco has written parables on human evil, the will to power, and the inevitability of death.

With the absurdist plays of the early fifties came a startling change in playwriting that challenged conventional ideas about plot, action, character, and language. *The Bald Soprano* and *Waiting for Godot,* produced three years apart in Paris, changed the direction of avant garde writing for the theater. New dramatic conventions were introduced: no recognizable plots, puppet-like characters, mechanical behavior and language, illogical acts, dreams and nightmares replacing social commentary. In a world where people are cut off from religious or transcendental roots, all human actions, including speech, become senseless, useless, absurd. Their plays projected this vision of the world's absurdity.

Footfalls

SAMUEL BECKETT

Samuel Beckett (1906–1989) was born near Dublin, Ireland, where he grew up. He attended Trinity College, Dublin, where he received two degrees in literature and began a teaching career. In 1932, he left his teaching position at Trinity and spent time on the continent and in London. He published his first novel (More Pricks Than Kicks) *in 1934, and wrote his first poems in French. In 1937, he settled in Paris, renewing an earlier friendship with novelist James Joyce. During the Second World War he worked with the French Resistance and barely escaped capture by the Nazis. Beckett continued until his death to live in Paris writing novels, plays, and poems in French. He was awarded the Nobel Prize for Literature in 1970.*

Beckett wrote some thirty theatrical pieces, including radio plays, monodramas, and four full-length plays (Waiting for Godot, Endgame, Krapp's Last Tape, *and* Happy Days). *Beckett's final plays have been called* minimalist. Not I *(1973) consists of eight pages of text,* Rockaby *(1981) is a fifteen-minute performance, and* Footfalls *(1976) has 132 lines of dialogue. However, with these brief pieces, Beckett constructed a theatrical image of how we, in a lifetime, fill a void on this earth and then vanish without a trace.*

CRITICAL INTRODUCTION TO *FOOTFALLS*

Virtually unknown at the age of fifty, Samuel Beckett premiered *Waiting for Godot* in 1953 in Paris and revolutionized the theater. *Godot* has since become one of the most influential plays of our time.

Beckett's writing has its source in French novelist Albert Camus's vision of the absurd: a universe that no longer makes sense because there is no God to resolve the contradictions between new hopes and dreams on the one hand and our experiences on the other. As early as 1941, Camus wrote in *The Myth of Sisyphus* that a universe in which human beings feel alien and deprived of memory and hope is absurd: "This divorce between man and his life, the actor and his setting, is properly the feeling of absurdity."[4] Beckett's absurd universe depicts human isolation (especially as attributed to the infirmities of aging and dying) and its counterpart, physical and psychic emptiness. Beckett's characters repeat endlessly that there is "nothing to be done," and yet they go on doing. Vladimir and Estragon in *Waiting for Godot* keep waiting; Clov in *Endgame* threatens to leave his master but always stops just short of the doorsill; the woman in the final fifteen minutes of her life in *Rockaby* asks for "more."

Beckett's late works, including *Footfalls,* are monologues (solo performances) dealing with the immobility that comes with aging, with strokes, or with other incapacities. Only the characters' minds have free play, but they have turned inward to contemplate physical aches, feebleness, and partial memories of happier times.

Beckett's plays have no endings and no beginnings, for the *existential void* that he perceives has no parameters. Rather, Beckett condenses life into a single stunning image that is both visual and aural: an old man listening without comprehension to tapes made in his youth, a woman's two large red lips emitting a relentless torrent of words, a daughter measuring out her mother's dying and her own habituated life in ceaseless pacing. Located in the void of the stage cavity, Beckett's minimalist staging captures significant aspects of our humanness: crying, speaking, moving, walking, joking, waiting, remembering. The context is frustration, anxiety, dependency, habituation, and loss.

Footfalls, first performed at the Royal Court Theatre, London, in 1976, repeats Beckett's use of a darkened boxlike stage as a basic metaphor for the circumscribed life. May, some forty years old, carries on a dialogue in her mind ("revolving it all") with the disembodied voice of her dying or dead mother. It is never clear whether or not the dialogue takes place only in May's head, though we can hear the Mother's voice (*"from dark upstage"*) and May's spoken responses. The stage lights are concentrated on a strip of light on the floor over which May's feet are seen and her footsteps heard as she passes to and fro. May paces on a line parallel to the audience (a length of nine steps) left to right with a clearly audible tread. As she walks back and forth, she inquires how she can be of service to her mother "again." Their broken dialogue touches upon such topics as physical distress, illness, age, birth, disappointment, and memories.

Beckett's text is divided by lighting and sound effects into four segments. At the end of each segment, the stage directions require the lights to fade into darkness, steps to cease, and after a long pause, a chime to ring and lights to come up but with less intensity each time. The technique is to give audiences the sensation that time is passing—a life is being measured out by a succession of days filled with sameness, routine, starts and stops as day turns to night and back again to day for a lifetime.

The character, May, has grey hair and a grey wrap. She is first seen in dim light pacing out her measured steps: a visible metaphor for a half-lived life. This sequence occurs three times. Part four is the terminus: chime very faint, light even less; there is no trace of May. Then a fade out. In some 132 lines of dialogue, Beckett evokes a nearly silent life with no brightness, color, happiness, joy, or activity. May's pacing figure is barely visible in the dimness of an unfulfilled life. Behind the stage picture lies the sound of the Mother's voice reviewing their lives, presumably at the moment of her death, or possibly as May's memory of her voice. May's measured tread signifies her own predictable life of servitude, dependency, and distress. Her only protest against life has been, "This is not enough."

Beckett's rejection of movement, emotion, color, light, and complete sentences diminishes the character's presence and the actor's mobility. All the while a story is being told that reflects the incompleteness and destitution of two lives lived in habituation and dependency. Identity (except for May's name) and emotion are eliminated. The Mother's voice denies knowledge of why their lives seem unfulfilled. She refers to "it all"—the totality of their lives—some ten times until the figure and the voice, the visible and the invisible, disappear into the darkness of nonbeing. In the audience we are left with questions: What does it all mean? When did May's mother die? Is May's story autobiographical? Who is Amy (an anagram for May)? Why did May's mother have her so "late" in life? How old is May now? Why do May and Voice invent stories? Why does the illuminated stage space grow smaller after each fade-out? Is *May* dead? Our questions about this drama, as about life, prove endless and go unanswered. What we perceive is a presence; what we hear are sounds of voices and footfalls; what we know, finally, is that human experience is composed of presence and absence. In the single figure of May pacing back and forth, Beckett slowly builds an image of life as sound in motion.

The aim of Beckett's minimalist art is to communicate an experience of existential totality. To do so, the dramatic text is reduced to a piece of monologue stripped of nonessentials like color, movement, music, and scenery. The authentic experience in the theater for Beckett comes with the totality of being in its most concentrated form. For example, an aging woman pacing, split into perceiver and perceived, the speaker and the spoken to, but changing through time from moment to moment as she moves about. With death comes the only release from routine and disappointment.

The four segments of *Footfalls* summarize Beckett's vision of human experience: aging, dying, measuring; questions about birth ("Where it all began"); protests about insufficiencies ("not enough"); survival ("the semblance") and silence; memory ("revolving it all") and regret; dimness, darkness, and obliteration.

With economy of action and language, the playwright has sketched diminishing images of two lives whose resonances (footfalls and voices) are applicable to us all—being born, surviving mechanically, experiencing time, remembering others, questioning life's meaning, and experiencing loss. Like May's footfalls, we eventually become, with time, only dim echoes of our former selves. And then it is over.

Footfalls

MAY (M), *dishevelled grey hair, worn grey wrap hiding feet, trailing.*

WOMAN'S VOICE (V) *from dark upstage.*

Strip: downstage, parallel with front, length nine steps, width one metre, a little off centre audience right.

$$L\genfrac{}{}{0.5pt}{}{r\,l\,r\,l\,r\,l\,r}{l\,r\,l\,r\,l\,r\,l}R$$

Pacing: starting with right foot (r) from right (R) to left (L), with left foot (l) from L to R.

> *Turn: rightabout at L, leftabout at R.*
> *Steps: clearly audible rhythmic tread.*
> *Lighting: dim, strongest at floor level, less on body, least on head.*
> *Voices: both low and slow throughout.*

Curtain. Stage in darkness. Faint single chime. Pause as echoes die. Fade up to dim on strip. Rest in darkness. M *discovered pacing approaching L. Turns at L, paces three more lengths, halts facing front at R.*
> *Pause.*

M: Mother. (*Pause. No louder.*) Mother.
> *Pause.*

V: Yes, May.

M: Were you asleep?

V: Deep asleep. (*Pause.*) I heard you in my deep sleep. (*Pause.*) There is no sleep so deep I would not hear you there. (*Pause.* M *resumes pacing. Four lengths. After first length, synchronous with steps.*)........seven eight nine wheel........seven eight nine wheel. (*Free.*) Will you not try to snatch a little sleep?
> M *halts facing front at R. Pause.*

M: Would you like me to inject you…again?

V: Yes, but it is too soon.
> *Pause.*

M: Would you like me to change your position… again?

V: Yes, but it is too soon.
> *Pause.*

M: Straighten your pillows? (*Pause.*) Change your drawsheet? (*Pause.*) Pass you the bedpan? (*Pause.*) The warming-pan? (*Pause.*) Dress your sores? (*Pause.*) Sponge you down? (*Pause.*) Moisten your poor lips? (*Pause.*) Pray with you? (*Pause.*) For you? (*Pause.*) Again.
> *Pause.*

V: Yes, but it is too soon.
> *Pause.* M *resumes pacing, after one length halts facing front at L. Pause.*

M: What age am I now?

V: And I? (*Pause. No louder.*) And I?

M: Ninety.

V: So much?

M: Eighty-nine, ninety.

V: I had you late. (*Pause.*) In life. (*Pause.*) Forgive me…again. (*Pause. No louder.*) Forgive me …again.
> *Pause.*

M: What age am I now?

V: In your forties.

M: So little?

V: I'm afraid so. (*Pause.* M *resumes pacing. After first turn at R.*) May. (*Pause. No louder.*) May.

M (*pacing*): Yes, Mother.

V: Will you never have done? (*Pause.*) Will you never have done…revolving it all?

M (*halting*): It?

V: It all. (*Pause.*) In your poor mind. (*Pause.*) It all. (*Pause.*) It all.
> M *resumes pacing. Five seconds. Fade out on strip. All in darkness. Steps cease.*
> *Long pause.*
> *Chime a little fainter. Pause for echoes. Fade up to a little less on strip. Rest in darkness.* M *discovered facing front at R.*
> *Pause.*

v: I walk here now. (*Pause.*) Rather I come and stand. (*Pause.*) At nightfall. (*Pause.*) She fancies she is alone. (*Pause.*) See how still she stands, how stark, with her face to the wall. (*Pause.*) How outwardly unmoved. (*Pause.*) She has not been out since girlhood. Not out since girlhood. (*Pause.*) Where is she, it may be asked. (*Pause.*) Why, in the old home, the same where she—(*Pause.*) The same where she began. (*Pause.*) Where it began. (*Pause.*) It all began. (*Pause.*) But this, this, when did this begin? (*Pause.*) When other girls of her age were out at…lacrosse she was already here. (*Pause.*) At this. (*Pause.*) The floor here, now bare, once was—(M *begins pacing. Steps a little slower.*) But let us watch her move, in silence. (M *paces. Towards end of second length.*) Watch how fast she wheels. (M *turns, paces. Synchronous with steps third length.*) Seven eight nine wheel. (M *turns at L, paces one more length, halts facing front at R.*) I say the floor here, now bare, this strip of floor, once was carpeted, a deep pile. Till one night, while still little more than a child, she called her mother and said, Mother, this is not enough. The mother: Not enough? May—the child's given name—May: Not enough. The mother: What do you mean, May, not enough, what can you possibly mean, May, not enough? May: I mean, Mother, that I must hear the feet, however faint they fall. The mother: The motion alone is not enough? May: No, Mother, the motion alone is not enough, I must hear the feet, however faint they fall. (*Pause.* M *resumes pacing. With pacing.*) Does she still sleep, it may be asked? Yes, some nights she does, in snatches, bows her poor head against the wall and snatches a little sleep. (*Pause.*) Still speak? Yes, some nights she does, when she fancies none can hear. (*Pause.*) Tells how it was. (*Pause.*) Tries to tell how it was. (*Pause.*) It all. (*Pause.*) It all.

M *continues pacing. Five seconds. Fade out on strip. All in darkness. Steps cease. Long pause. Chime a little fainter still. Pause for echoes. Fade up to a little less still on strip.*

Rest in darkness. M *discovered facing front at R. Pause.*

M: Sequel. (M *begins pacing, after two lengths halts facing front at R.*) Sequel. A little later, when she was quite forgotten, she began to— (*Pause.*) A little later, when as though she had never been, it never been, she began to walk. (*Pause.*) At nightfall. (*Pause.*) Slip out at nightfall and into the little church by the north door, always locked at that hour, and walk, up and down, up and down, His poor arm. (*Pause.*) Some nights she would halt, as one frozen by some shudder of the mind, and stand stark still till she could move again. But many also were the nights when she paced without pause, up and down, up and down, before vanishing the way she came. (*Pause.*) No sound. (*Pause.*) None at least to be heard. (*Pause.*) The semblance. (*Pause. Resumes pacing. Steps a little slower still. After two lengths halts facing front at R.*) The semblance. Faint, though by no means invisible, in a certain light. (*Pause.*) Given the right light. (*Pause.*) Grey rather than white, a pale shade of grey. (*Pause.*) Tattered. (*Pause.*) A tangle of tatters. (*Pause.*) A faint tangle of pale grey tatters. (*Pause.*) Watch it pass—(*pause*)—watch her pass before the candelabrum how its flames, their light…like moon through passing…rack. (*Pause.*) Soon then after she was gone, as though never there, began to walk, up and down, up and down, that poor arm. (*Pause.*) At nightfall. (*Pause.*) That is to say, at certain seasons of the year, during Vespers. (*Pause.*) Necessarily. (*Pause. Resumes pacing. After one length halts facing front at L. Pause.*) Old Mrs. Winter, whom the reader will remember, old Mrs. Winter, one late autumn Sunday evening, on sitting down to supper with her daughter after worship, after a few half-hearted mouthfuls laid down her knife and fork and bowed her head. What is it, Mother, said the daughter, a most strange girl, though scarcely a girl any more… (*brokenly*)…dreadfully un—(*Pause. Normal voice.*) What is it, Mother, are you not feeling

yourself? (*Pause.*) Mrs. W. did not at once re-ply. But finally, raising her head and fixing Amy—the daughter's given name, as the reader will remember—raising her head and fixing Amy full in the eye she said—(*pause*)—she murmured, fixing Amy full in the eye she murmured, Amy, did you observe anything...strange at Evensong? Amy: No, Mother, I did not. Mrs. W: Perhaps it was just my fancy. Amy: Just what exactly, Mother, did you perhaps fancy it was? (*Pause.*) Just what exactly, Mother, did you perhaps fancy this...strange thing was you observed? (*Pause.*) Mrs. W: You yourself observed nothing...strange? Amy: No, Mother, I myself did not, to put it mildly. Mrs. W: What do you mean, Amy, to put it mildly, what can you possibly mean, Amy, to put it mildly? Amy: I mean, Mother, that to say I observed nothing...strange is indeed to put it mildly. For I observed nothing of any kind, strange or otherwise. I saw nothing, heard nothing, of any kind. I was not there. Mrs. W: Not there? Amy: Not there. Mrs. W: But I heard you respond. (*Pause.*) I heard you say Amen. (*Pause.*) How could you have responded if you were not there? (*Pause.*) How could you possibly have said Amen if, as you claim, you were not there? (*Pause.*) The love of God, and the fellowship of the Holy Ghost, be with us all, now, and for evermore. Amen. (*Pause.*) I heard you distinctly. (*Pause. Resumes pacing. After five steps halts without facing front. Long pause. Resumes pacing, halts facing front at R. Long pause.*) Amy. (*Pause. No louder.*) Amy. (*Pause.*) Yes, Mother. (*Pause.*) Will you never have done? (*Pause.*) Will you never have done...re-volving it all? (*Pause.*) It? (*Pause.*) It all. (*Pause.*) In your poor mind. (*Pause.*) It all. (*Pause.*) It all.
Pause. Fade out on strip. All in darkness.
Pause.
Chime even a little fainter. Pause for echoes. Fade up to even a little less still on strip. No trace of May. Hold fifteen seconds. Fade out. Curtain.

PERFORMING *FOOTFALLS*

Samuel Beckett wrote *Footfalls* in English in 1975 and translated the play into French. The first production of *Footfalls* was at the Royal Court Theatre in London in 1976 with Beckett directing British actress Billie Whitelaw. Alan Schneider, who had directed the first American production of *Waiting for Godot*, staged *Footfalls* at Arena Stage in Washington, D.C., in December of that year. Schneider also staged the New York revival of the minimalist play at the Samuel Beckett Theater in New York in 1984.

Billie Whitelaw has been the chief interpreter of Beckett's women on the English stage. The playwright turned to her over and over again to give presence to his spectral creatures, including Winnie encased in a mound of dirt (*Happy Days*), as the mouth and moving lips (*Not I*), as the woman rocking into oblivion (*Rockaby*), and as the solitary daughter pacing out her life in measured steps (*Footfalls*).

Only once did the actress ask the playwright a question about the character of May. As they were rehearsing *Footfalls* in London, Whitelaw asked, "Am I dead?" Beckett replied, "Let's just say, you're not quite there."[5]

CRITICS' NOTEBOOK

Martin Esslin coined the phrase "theater of the absurd" in his seminal book, first published in 1961, in which he defined a body of avant-garde work appearing on stages in France and England. Esslin's critical perspective has become a standard for categorizing works by Eugène Ionesco, Samuel Beckett, Jean Genet, and others. For almost a half century, Ruby Cohn's landmark writings—*Samuel Beckett: The Comic Gamut* (1962), *Casebook on Waiting for Godot* (1967), and *Back to Beckett* (1973)—opened up avenues of American scholarship on the theater of Samuel Beckett.

Alan Schneider became the foremost director of Beckett's plays in the United States. In 1956, he directed the first American production of *Waiting for Godot* at the Coconut Grove

Playhouse in Miami and followed that production with *Krapp's Last Tape, Happy Days, Endgame, Play, Come and Go, Not I, Act Without Words I and II, Rockaby, Footfalls, Catastrophe,* and *Ohio Impromptu* in Washington, D.C., New York, London, and Edinburgh. Schneider died in a traffic accident in London in 1984 before writing a book on his considerable experiences with Beckett's plays. His lecture in 1976 on the "Beckett trio"—*Play, That Time,* and *Footfalls*—is reprinted here to give insight into the director's sensibility and process.

Martin Esslin, from *The Theatre of the Absurd**

❦

...The Theatre of the Absurd, however, can be seen as the reflection of what seems to be the attitude most genuinely representative of our own time.

The hallmark of this attitude is its sense that the certitudes and unshakable basic assumptions of former ages have been swept away, that they have been tested and found wanting, that they have been discredited as cheap and somewhat childish illusions. The decline of religious faith was masked until the end of the Second World War by the substitute religions of faith in progress, nationalism, and various totalitarian fallacies. All this was shattered by the war. By 1942, Albert Camus was calmly putting the question why, since life had lost all meaning, man should not seek escape in suicide. In one of the great, seminal heart-searchings of our time, *The Myth of Sisyphus,* Camus tried to diagnose the human situation in a world of shattered beliefs:

> A world that can be explained by reasoning, however faulty, is a familiar world. But in a universe that is suddenly deprived of illusions and of light, man feels a stranger. His is an irremediable exile, because he is deprived of memories of a lost homeland as much as he lacks the hope of a promised land to come. This divorce between man and his life, the actor and his setting, truly constitutes the feeling of Absurdity.

*'Absurd' originally means 'out of harmony,' in a musical context. Hence its dictionary definition: 'out of harmony with reason or propriety; incongruous, unreasonable, illogical'. In common usage, 'absurd' may simply mean 'ridiculous', but this is not the sense in which Camus uses the word, and in which it is used when we speak of the Theatre of the Absurd. In an essay on Kafka, Ionesco defined his understanding of the term as follows: 'Absurd is that which is devoid of purpose.... Cut off from his religious, metaphysical, and transcendental roots, man is lost; all his actions become senseless, absurd, useless.'

This sense of metaphysical anguish at the absurdity of the human condition is, broadly speaking, the theme of the plays of Beckett, Adamov, Ionesco, Genet....

❧ ❧ ❧

This is an inner contradiction that the dramatists of the Absurd are trying, by instinct and intuition rather than by conscious effort, to overcome and resolve. The Theatre of the Absurd has renounced arguing *about* the absurdity of the human condition; it merely *presents* it in being—that is, in terms of concrete stage images. This is the difference between the approach of the philosopher and that of the poet....

❧ ❧ ❧

It is the striving for an integration between the subject-matter and the form in which it is expressed that separates the Theatre of the Absurd from the Existentialist theatre.

Alan Schneider, "On *Play* and Other Plays"*

❦

So, following [Preston Jones's] *A Texas Trilogy's* somewhat less than triumphant tour of New York, I'm back in Washington once more—this

---

*Martin Esslin, *The Theatre of the Absurd* (New York: Penguin Books, Inc., 1961): 22–25.

*This 1976 lecture by Alan Schneider is held in the Alan Schneider Papers (MSS 103), Mandeville Special Collections Library, University of California–San Diego. Reprinted by permission of Mrs. Alan Schneider.

time with a Beckett trio. And, as always, since Sam [Beckett] won't come over here (he doesn't like the way we treat writers, I guess), I've just gone to Berlin to talk with him, see his own staged versions of the plays in question, and try to clear up a few of the normal mysteries involved in their stage production.

What can I tell you? That these three very small and quite special pieces are going to be easy to "understand"? (They are and are not.) That actually, as with all of Beckett, from that once baffling and now practically all-too-clear foursome in *Godot* to that mystically enigmatic and eventually lucid *Not I* you watched Jessica Tandy mouthing at the Kreeger a couple of seasons back, they should be experienced and felt, rather than figured out or explained in orderly, rational, nonpoetic terms. (They should.) That with all of Beckett, as with so many contemporary artists, content comes from the form itself, that in Beckett meaning depends on the sounds and images that are evoked. That it is precisely from within his ambiguities and overtones that his dramatic tension arises. (It does.) All of which has, of course, been said over and over again before.

In the twenty years or so in which I have had the good fortune to begin work on a new Beckett script, the process has always involved a spirit of adventure and exaltation—as well as trepidation. But, always, the adventure has led to a series of deepening discoveries—not only of the plays themselves but of their performers and of my own innermost depths. To me, Sam Beckett has always been and remains now a true poet of the theater, his creative imagination totally attuned to the essential nature and constantly shifting limits of dramatic expression. With each new work, he has propelled those limits farther than any other playwright of our time; yet he remains aloof from the struggles and pain of the marketplace, personally vulnerable, gentle, unsure of his own achievement.

These three short plays, each less than half an hour in length, the latter two being presented at the Arena Stage for the first time in the American theater, represent a kind of theatrical chamber music. In each of them, and in very different ways, sounds and silences, cadences and

rhythm, are selected, arranged, balanced, and counterpointed, as are the plots and counterplots, characters and dialogue, of more conventional playwrights. Together the three concern themselves with the obsessive influence of the past; of our constant, unsuccessful, yet all-too-human need to deny the void surrounding human existence. Each one suggests a kind of metaphor, at once unique and universal, speaking to us all in a small but insistently clear voice of our mystical mortality and facing that mortality with courage—and, occasionally, even humor.

These are not easy plays to come to, or to face. But then *Godot,* twenty years back, was not exactly easy to take—more than half of its original American audiences at Miami Beach walked out (and lived to rue the day or night, because *Godot* has survived that experience to become a world classic in its own time). Nor was *Endgame*—although it is now considered a modern *Lear.* Nor *Happy Days* nor *Krapp's Last Tape,* dramatic monologues without peers in all of world drama. *Not I* when first presented at the Lincoln Center had almost the same percentage of walkouts as the original *Godot;* many of those who left came back to admire and be moved. And *Play,* where for the first and only time in my career I actually betrayed the author's stated intention (to have it played through twice at top speed), because my producers felt that New York audiences were too "sophisticated" or jaded, has survived to prove all over the world that both those producers and those first audiences were wrong.

Each of these three plays seems to strip the stage bare, even as each one drives unerringly to absorb the spectator's senses and mind. As in Tiffany's windows, the process of selection is unerringly ultimate. In *Play,* ashened faces are frozen in their funeral urns and are doomed for always to repeat and repeat their banal stories of a love triangle no longer real. In *That Time,* someone is visited by and tormented by constantly changing visions of his past floating up to him from his uncertain past; but this time the image is not that of a decrepit old man crouched beside an equally ancient tape recorder but simply that of a human head floating somewhere in space— as well as time. (The process of greater and greater selection never stops.) And, finally, in *Footfalls*, one ghostly figure and a distant voice come together in a ghost story about the nature of reality. Is she really there, or has she ever been there? Is the mother listening, or is the daughter imagining everything? Who is imagining whom? Beckett seems to be asking. And to me the joy, as always, is not so much in answering that question beyond a reasonable doubt but in sharing in the eloquence of the question itself. After all, as everyone knows by now, it doesn't matter who or what Godot is—if Beckett had known, he would have told us immediately—what matters is that we are all waiting.

For me, each new Beckett play, through its compassionate view of humanity, through the intensity and scope of its vision, through its musicality and poetic intensity, enlarges and enriches the whole of theater, the whole of life. Even Buster Keaton, not exactly an avant-garde enthusiast, seemed to sense that when, in the middle of a Beckett film I once directed in which he had not one line of dialogue, he burst out with "Now, I'm getting this Shakespearian stuff." Buster knew what he was talking about. For these three plays, two new and one not so old, silence and inscrutability and whatever else they may offer up to audiences willing enough and patient enough to accept them on some basis, are classic in their structure as well as eternal in their truths about our all-too-human nature....

REVISITING ABSURDIST THEATER

Our discussions of recent writing styles have touched on two major stylistic movements, spanning seventy years of the twentieth century, that resulted in new subjects and dramatic forms for the modern theater. The epic and absurdist movements represent special attitudes toward our life and times—one representing a socially constructive theater and the other a theater of existential situations.

Absurdist writers turned away from socioeconomic and political concerns in an apocalyp-

tic vision of humanity caught up in a senseless, futile, and oppressive existence. They called their vision *absurd*. They pioneered a dramaturgy that did not debate or moralize issues, but rather *presented* an absurd universe by using concrete stage images and language emptied of meaning. For over thirty-five years, Samuel Beckett was the leading spokesman for the theatrical absurd. His plays present the world as a terminal "void" and humanity's place in it as purposeless. We are born, we die, and in between we exist. Beckett's plays condense life's absurdness into remarkable images of existence in the void. In Beckett's minimalist art, the actor's presence effectively becomes the play.

To analyze plays by Bertolt Brecht and Samuel Beckett, we must comprehend the *writer's vision* of modern society and the universe, along with the forms, conventions, and techniques used to convey their statements about the human condition. More recently, feminists, interculturalists, performance artists, and postmodernists have influenced politics and art in the United States. Beginning in the 1980s, the new writing has had a huge impact on American, British, and French theater. The next chapters examine these new theatrical forms and their perspectives on contemporary culture and society at the millennium.

NOTES

1. Martin Esslin, *The Theatre of the Absurd*, 3rd Edition (New York: Pelican Books, 1983): 23.
2. Eugène Ionesco, *Notes and Counter Notes: Writings on the Theatre*, trans. Donald Watson (New York: Grove Press, 1964): 257.
3. Martin Esslin, *Mediations: Essays on Brecht, Beckett, and the Media* (Baton Rouge: Louisiana State University Press, 1980): 123–124.
4. Albert Camus, *The Myth of Sisyphus and Other Essays* (New York: Vintage Books, 1955): 5.
5. From an unscripted video interview with Billie Whitelaw, in *Changing Stages*, created and directed by Richard Eyre, Public Broadcasting Company, 2001.

PART SIX

PLAYWRITING AT THE MILLENNIUM

CHAPTER 13

UNDERSTANDING FEMINIST DRAMA

Mary-Louise Parker as Lil' Bit and David Morse as Uncle Peck in *How I Learned to Drive* by Paula Vogel, directed by Mark Brokaw, in the Vineyard Theatre production, Century Theatre, New York City, 1997. (Photo © Carol Rosegg.)

> *In this time of political correctness, you have to go against the grain. If audiences don't embrace both sides of an issue, there can be no real political dialogue. In my sense of political, you can never be politically correct. To be political means to open up a dialogue, not to be "correct."*[1]
> —Paula Vogel

GENDER, ART, AND POLITICS

In 1970, Kate Millet wrote the influential *Sexual Politics*, which called attention to gender bias in politics and in art. She illustrated ways of recognizing and interpreting the "image of woman" in literature written by men as misogynistic and subversive to women's interests. The new view linked art with politics and history with male-dominated or patriarchal cultures. For theater studies, historians and critics were prompted to distinguish between historical women and the cultural fictions of "woman" as found in plays written by men dating from the Greeks to the present.

Feminism is defined as a critique of prevailing social conditions which have excluded women from dominant male cultural, social, sexual, political, and intellectual discourse and pursuits. Initial feminist observations on the history of theater, according to Sue-Ellen Case, noted the absence of women as playwrights and the biased treatment of women as characters of fiction and drama.[2] Hrosvitha of Gandersheim, a mid-tenth-century nun, and Aphra Behn, a seventeenth-century English writer, were stepping stones in the late emergence of women as playwrights in Western culture. Hrosvitha, writing during the Holy Roman Empire, in what is now known as Germany, set about in six plays to revise the "licentious" image of women found in classical drama and "to glorify the laudable chastity" of Christian women. Some 700 years later, Aphra Behn (1640–1689) became the first woman to earn her living as a playwright. She wrote eighteen plays staged in London's commercial theaters, including the popular *The Rover*, which held the stage from 1677 to 1760. Aphra Behn described herself as "an author who is forced to write for bread and not ashamed to own it." In her bawdy comedies, she showed women in their spheres of personal power and influence (bedrooms and brothels), and celebrated their accomplishments against social odds. Behn's struggles and successes as a commercial playwright set a model for professional women writers, novelists, and playwrights who came after her.

For another two centuries, women writers participated in creating a literature of shared subjects and concerns. The most famous woman playwright of her era in America was Anna Cora Mowatt who wrote the satiric comedy *Fashion* in 1845. Although American playwriting was male dominated, as it is today, a number of commercially successful women writers followed Mowatt. Ann Nichols wrote *Abie's Irish Rose* (1922), one of the longest running plays on the American stage. Rachel Crothers (1878–1938), Zöe Akins (1886–1958), Susan Glaspell (1881–1948), and Sophie Treadwell (1890?–1970) found commercial success as playwrights and novelists. Gertrude Stein, a truly original writer, experimented with language, syntax, and musical forms. In Stein's early feminist view, modern woman is tormented with ambivalence; the figure of Susan B. Anthony in *The Mother of Us All*, the opera written in 1945, with music by Virgil Thomson, is Stein's dramatic image of *modern* pioneering woman.

In the 1930s, Lillian Hellman achieved commercial and literary success with *The Children's Hour* and *The Little Foxes*. Her frank treatment of women's lives was often controversial. *The Children's Hour* (1934) dramatizes oppressive attitudes, now dated, toward lesbianism. *The Little Foxes* (1939) tells the story of four women: Regina, the rapacious sister who dominates her brothers and husband; Alexandra, the young daughter seeking her own identity within a family of "little foxes"; Birdie, the vulnerable and compassionate aunt; and Abby, a woman of color who serves the Hubbard family with moral strength and iron practicality.

In the 1950s, Hellman's contemporaries, who included Carson McCullers (*A Member of the Wedding*), Alice Childress (*Trouble in Mind*), Jane Bowles (*In the Summerhouse*), and Lorraine Hansberry (*A Raisin in the Sun*), demonstrated the presence of women playwrights in the American commercial theater. The Vietnam war decade produced a generation of Off and Off Off Broadway writers whose subjects, attitudes, and styles predated the women's movement of the 1970s. Rosalyn Drexler, María Irene Fornés, Adrienne Kennedy, Rochelle Owens, and Megan Terry began important careers writing from their own experiences. As pioneers of feminist drama, they rejected the well-made play as a male province and communicated the inner drama of their lives in highly original dramatic forms. In representing their own, often fragmented experiences in their plays, they raised the consciousness of audiences and readers about women's lives, feelings, needs, and ambitions. Today's feminist drama is a further articulation of women's viewpoints and new dramatic forms for mirroring the special rhythms, emotions, and experiences of women.

Beginning in the early 1970s, the feminist perspective produced a number of plays by new women writers and biographies recording the lives of earlier women playwrights as well. Also, in the seventies, women playwrights, directors, and designers emerged in the regional theaters, Off Off Broadway, and in grass-roots collectives as alternatives to the commercial tradition of Broadway. Marsha Norman, Beth Henley, and Paula Vogel emerged from the regional theaters; Julie Bovasso, María Irene Fornés, Tina Howe, and Suzan-Lori Parks came from Off Off Broadway; and others grew out of collectives and performance art dedicated to the radical feminist position that patriarchy is the primary cause of oppression of women. In their work, women's biologism (cycles, intuition, fertility, bonding, nurturing) and such social issues as pedophilia, rape, domestic violence, and discrimination serve as ultimate signs of women's oppression and victimization by men.

The feminist movement—political, social, sexual, and artistic—led to identifiable practices, thought, and criticism in the contemporary theater. "Feminist" plays and performance art explore issues of women's oppression and rights based on sex- and gender-related issues. Often the writers are committed to radical social change and direct political action. Since the 1970s, such distinct feminist positions as radical feminism, lesbian feminism, and materialist feminism have emerged. Radical feminism is based on the belief that patriarchy, or all systems of male dominance, is the primary source of the oppression of women and remains the predominant critical approach in the United States among women writers.

Lesbian feminism resists both patriarchy and compulsory heterosexuality and celebrates the lesbian experience and perspective. This viewpoint also includes an acknowledgment of the invisibility or unmarked identity of women in modern cultures and social groups. Materialist feminism, a large term covering common elements of "Marxist" and "socialist" feminism, underscores the roles of class and history in the oppression of women. In the materialist view, the primacy of class and socioeconomic factors are considered the exploitative forces among women, not gender. Many feminists embrace a combination of these viewpoints that shape their writing in theory and in practice.

FEMINIST THEORY

Feminist theory rose to prominence in the 1980s within the women's movement and within general theater practice and criticism. The strategies of feminist theory are largely focused on politics, patriarchal prejudice, sexual oppression, wage inequities, discriminatory hiring practices, and women's invisibility within a male-dominated culture.

Feminist critics, historians, and writers have taken a two-edged approach to their critique of drama's history and writing. First, there is an effort to reconstruct the history of women in theater and to recover plays and materials suppressed over centuries. Second, playwrights, critics, and scholars evolved new writing styles compatible with radical feminism. The feminist critics recognized today in the United States for their pioneering writing on theater and performance are Sue-Ellen Case, Gayle Austin, Lynda Hart, Jill Dolan, Peggy Phelan, and Elin Diamond.

Feminist writing of the 1970s and 1980s has the raising of women's (and society's) consciousness as central to the social and political movement. A coalition of social activists, theorists, artists, historians, and critics evolved whose aim was to understand modes of perception, psychological factors, and patterns of thought. In writing for the theater, feminist playwrights introduced new subjects, vocabularies, characters, forms, and alternative modes of perception. Their influence on writing, performance, and criticism at the new millennium has been remarkable in several ways.

First, feminist writers moved drama's boundaries, taking a revisionist approach to women's roles in dramatic texts. Feminist plays identify the psychological, social, cultural, and educational controls to which women are subject. Hence the plays have a consciousness-raising function. Both feminist playwrights and critics purposely set about to construct new critical models and dramatic methods to accommodate the presence of women in art, to reveal the cultural fictions about the female gender, and to expose the historic "valorization" of the male gender in history and literature.[3] The result was, especially in France, England, and the United States, a new mode of writing for the theater. Led by such playwrights as Simone Benmussa, Hélène Cixous, Caryl Churchill, Pam Gems, Adrienne Kennedy, and María Irene Fornés, women emerged in drama as subjects rather than objects; further, these writers concentrated by and large on women's alienation and repression in modern society.

In *Cloud Nine* (1979), Caryl Churchill illustrated women's social and cultural alienation created by distinctions between the "real" woman and how she is perceived as the "other" in a male-dominated society. In Act One, Betty, the wife-mother, is played by a male actor in drag. Betty, the female "character," is, therefore, everything men want her to be since her social identity is a fiction of the male gaze. By substituting the male actor for the female, no real woman exists under the layers of costume, makeup, and gesture. Churchill's point about the "colonizing" of women, the privilege of gender and class, is doubly reinforced by actor-in-costume and character-in-fiction in her celebrated play.

In *The Conduct of Life* (1985), María Irene Fornés represents three views of women's victimization in a patriarchal culture dominated by a South American petty tyrant who is both soldier and husband. Moreover, she also shows men as equally conditioned and victimized by historical social forces and prescribed gender roles. Orlando's "wife" and his "housekeeper" are objects of his domestic needs and tranquility while his "slave," a twelve-year-old female prisoner, is the object of his sexual desire. In Fornés' view, all (women and men) are objects and victims of patriarchy. Fornés effectively dramatizes the attitudes, conditions, and demands of the contemporary world on individuals of both sexes—all are victims of socially conditioned attitudes regarding gender roles and class distinctions.

In one sense, feminist theory is an expansion of psychoanalytic theories of both Sigmund Freud and Lucian Laçan to include the identity formation of women and their complex sexualities. Feminist writers have rejected traditions of Western psychiatry that emphasized male development. In turn, they elevated women from a subordinate, derivative, and apolitical position in the family unit in particular and in society in general. Many feminist plays take as their setting women's time-honored environs, the domestic setting: living room, dining room, kitchen, bedroom. Within the family unit, women are portrayed as confined to the domestic setting, dependent on husband and other male companions, and denied opportunities for growth and change. In this setting, woman is betrayed, brutalized, habituated, and imprisoned. Such American playwrights as Marsha Norman in *Getting Out* and *'Night, Mother* and Wendy Wasserstein in *Uncommon Women and Others, The Heidi Chronicles*, and *The Sisters Rosensweig* have explored these themes in domestic settings.

FEMINIST PLAY STRUCTURE

As seen in epic and absurdist writing for the theater, new perspectives require new dramatic forms. Evolving new forms, feminist writers rejected a linear, forward-moving action in favor of *contiguity*, or a series of scenes in continuous connection. Drama's forms in feminist writing abandon hierarchical organizing principles of traditional playwriting which proceed from complication to climax to resolution. Feminists argue that this type of plot organization is tied to the male experience; that is, it is phallocentric. Women's experiences, they argue, are rather disjointed, broken, and disconnected without clear lines of development.

If there is a discernible dramatic structure for feminist plays, it is deduced from female biology and from the feminine sexual experience. Feminist play structure has a contiguous organization characterized by nonlinear narrative, fragmentary scenes, elliptical forms, indirect dialogue, ambiguity rather than clarity, and interrupted rather than completed action. One argument for a recurrent line of dramatic action is that women's lives are in themselves fragmented; their experience of time and relationships is one of constant interruption. In general, women experience a thousand demands on their time, attention, and energy throughout a single day. In the domestic world these activities include household chores, errands, meals, purchases, car pools, child care, and so on. Consequently, plays written from their perspective are shaped by contiguous scenes that show these myriad demands and frenetic behavior responses as one demand after the next is met. On another level, dramatic form and language as presented by feminist writers raise large issues about women's lives, such as gender, race, and class. Paula Vogel centers her Pulitzer prize-winning play, *How I Learned to Drive* (1997), on issues of gender, female puberty, sexual molestation, and family and community responsibility in the abuse of women within society.

How I Learned to Drive

PAULA VOGEL

Paula Vogel (b. 1951) grew up in a working-class family in suburban Maryland and arrived as a playwright on the national scene with such highly charged issues as gender bias, gay parenthood, AIDS, pedophilia, incest, pornography, and domestic violence. Unlike most writers on political issues, she is not interested in persuading audiences to adopt political or moral positions, but rather to understand that there are no easy answers to complex social, moral, and political issues.

Vogel was educated at Bryn Mawr College and Catholic University in Washington, D.C., where she earned a B.A. degree in theater in 1974. She then applied to the Yale Drama School but was rejected and attended Cornell University in Ithaca, New York, where she completed all but the dissertation for a doctoral degree. She has been both a lecturer and an instructor of theater arts at Cornell (1977–82). She began teaching in 1984 at Brown University in Providence, Rhode Island, and served as head of the M.F.A. playwriting program there until 1998. She has received numerous awards, including a 1995 Guggenheim Fellowship and a three-year playwriting residency (along with the commission of two new plays) at Arena Stage in Washington, D.C.

Vogel wrote her first play, Meg, *in 1977 at Cornell. She came to national attention some fifteen years later with* Baltimore Waltz, *a play about a schoolteacher (Vogel's alter ego) and a dying AIDS patient. Vogel's beloved brother (Carl) also died of AIDS and she wrote* Baltimore Waltz *to use her feelings and experiences with his death to show how larger political, social, and moral issues (homophobia and national prejudice, in this instance) affect individuals. She has said that she only writes about things that directly impact her life. "When I write," she said, "there's a pain that I have to reach, and a release that I have to work toward from myself. So it's really a question of the particular emotional circumstances*

that I want to express, a character appears, a moment in time, and then I write the play backwards."[4]

Baltimore Waltz is a journey through the character Anna's imagination as Carl lies dying of AIDS in a hospital room in Baltimore. The play won an Off Broadway "Obie" award for Best Play and has been produced in many prominent regional theaters throughout the country.

How I Learned to Drive, *produced in 1997, is the most successful of Vogel's twenty-odd plays, having won a number of prestigious awards along with the 1998 Pulitzer Prize for Drama. Its bold subject matter centered around a pedophilic relationship. Critics unanimously praised Vogel's skills in bringing the uncomfortable subject matter to the stage with sensitivity, humor, and compelling characters.*

Vogel's work was first seen in regional theaters across America and Off Broadway. Her plays have been produced by the Perseverance Theater (Alaska), the American Repertory Theater (Cambridge, MA), the Alley Theater (Houston), the Goodman Theatre (Chicago), Center Stage (Baltimore), Arena Stage (Washington, D.C.), and Off Broadway at the Lucile Lortel Theater, Circle in the Square, the Vineyard Theater, and the Century Theater. Other plays written by Vogel include Desdemona: A Play About a Handkerchief *(1980),* And Baby Makes Seven *(1984),* The Oldest Profession *(1988),* Hot 'n' Throbbing *(1994),* The Mineola Twins *(1996) and* The Long Christmas Ride Home *(2003).* How I Learned to Drive *and* The Mineola Twins *make up what Vogel calls* The Mammary Plays. *She is also at work on screenplays for* The Oldest Profession *and* How I Learned to Drive.

Paula Vogel is a feminist/lesbian writer with a balanced point of view that incorporates stringent commentary on such contemporary topics as gender issues, domestic violence, homophobia, and nontraditional families. In his observations on Vogel's ca-

reer, David Savran writes, "For as a feminist writer, Vogel not only attends to the deeply contradictory representations of women in our culture, but also delineates female characters who are prepared to use their physical charms (if need be) to wrest control of their lives."[5]

CRITICAL INTRODUCTION TO
HOW I LEARNED TO DRIVE

Paula Vogel writes as a radical feminist with women as the center of situations that portray the effects of male domination and abusive behavior toward women. *How I Learned to Drive* brings into focus Vogel's twin themes of incest and pedophilia, which "drive" the play. The play was inspired by Vogel's reading of Vladimir Nabokov's novel *Lolita* about a relationship between a man in his forties and a pre-teen girl. What fascinated her was the novelist's even-handed and neutral treatment of the relationship between the man and the girl. "I couldn't stop thinking about what would happen," she said, "if a woman wrote the story from Lolita's point of view."[6] *How I Learned to Drive* is Vogel's response to a culture that, she says, "trains us to be pedophiles. The eroticism of children is all around us. It's on film, on television, it's in those Calvin Klein ads," she told Steven Drukman.[7]

Vogel's nonlinear narrative is madeup of nineteen scenes that portray the sexual initiation of Li'l Bit, beginning at age eleven and continuing to age eighteen. The scenes, marked only by titles, are interspersed with choral interludes on "men, sex, and women" that portray the ways in which society conditions sexual behavior in young women and the influence of mothers, grandmothers, and girl friends. Vogel does not tell the story of Li'l Bit's sexual molestation in chronological order. Like Tennessee Williams's *The Glass Menagerie*, *How I Learned to Drive* is a memory play, and, like Williams's narrator Tom Wingfield, Li'l Bit exists both without and within the play. She narrates her memories of growing up in a small Maryland rural community. She controls time past and present, moving forward and backward in memory, as she tells her story of betrayal, abuse, isolation, and recovery. As nar-

rator, Li'l Bit's imagination drifts among different periods of her relationship with her uncle; her narration is subject more to her streaming of consciousness than to chronological sequence. As Vogel told Stephanie Coen, "Theater is about structure, sequence, and not about words."[8] Vogel allows memory to create the structure and sequencing of the unrelenting tale of Li'l Bit's seven-year sexual molestation by her Uncle Peck.

Li'l Bit's family and friends (portrayed by the three-person chorus) form the backdrop to explain her socially conditioned responses to her sexual initiation by an adult relative. The story's complexity is enlarged by Peck, whose personal history is that of pedophile, voyeur, and sexual deviant.

Vogel's memory play also has another connection to Tennessee Williams's staging techniques found in *The Glass Menagerie*. In addition to the device of narrator to tell the story, Williams used such expressionistic staging devices as projections or "legends," as he called them, to label scenes with captions and images. Vogel calls for announcements of the driving lesson through the theater's sound system to mark the various stages of Li'l Bit's sexual initiation. In Vogel's terms, learning to drive a car becomes a complex metaphor for sexual initiation. We hear announcements of "Shifting Forward from First to Second Gear" or "Idling in Neutral Gear" and imagine the emotional alterations and changes in the relationship between the adolescent and her seducer that are to be played out. Peck is a thoughtful seducer and welcome confidant; he is patient, careful never to hurt Li'l Bit, and, in his mind, never pushes her to do anything that she doesn't wish to do. Nonetheless, his wife tells us that he "has a way" with adolescent girls. Peck takes advantage of Li'l Bit starting at age eleven and continues until she is in college.

The play begins with Li'l Bit (all family nicknames are derived from their sexual features and her nickname derives from the family's discovery at birth that the baby's genitals are "just a little bit") at age thirty-something reflecting on the "secret" of her forbidden sexual life when she was an adolescent. Li'l Bit sets the play's cultural and emotional landscape with her opening monologue (announced as "Safety First—You and Driver Education"), which begins: "Sometimes to tell a secret, you first have to teach a lesson." Vogel situates the first scene of the play in a parking lot of modern-day Maryland with its concrete highway in the distance lined by porno drive-ins, revival churches, and boarded-up motels. A portion of the countryside preserved by the U.S. Department of Agriculture is redolent with the smell of clover and farm animals. The sensuousness of the farmland odors are mixed with the smells of the leather dashboard of the car where Li'l Bit resides in her memories. She conjures another time that Southerners tend to romanticize, when farmhouses dotting the fields where the Civil War raged over the countryside, long before the concrete malls took over and obliterated the rural landscape. The smells, the moon, the tranquil air spin into memories of an early summer night when a seventeen-year-old Li'l Bit parked off a dark lane with a married man. The memories of Li'l Bit's many "driving" lessons are brought into focus in her opening monologue. The innocent jargon of learning to drive a car (ordinarily a universal adolescent experience) teems with sexual innuendo. The provocative "learning to drive" metaphor of the play's title and subject matter underscores the perverse sexual education of the young girl in the 1960s.

The play is framed by Li'l Bit's two monologues, which set the emotional and physical landscape for the adolescent's sexual molestation. The first introduces the situation as it has evolved for seven years with Peck's gradual sexual advances. The final monologue finds Li'l Bit alone with her understanding of what her younger self lost along the way (family connections, her innocence, her teenage years) together with her own complicity in the relationship with Peck. At the play's end, the thirty-something Li'l Bit prepares to drive several hundred miles to recapture what for her is the most sensuous experience in her adult life: "flight in the body"—driving a car. Just as she was conditioned by Peck's lessons in her long-ago adolescent life, she completes the manual check of the car preparatory to driving: tires, oil, gasoline. Echoing her uncle, she says of the car: "You've got to treat her with respect." The car radio blares out sexual clichés voiced by the Greek chorus that reprise her adolescent angst ("Am I doing it right?") and segue into Roy Orbison's languid "Sweet Dreams."

Li'l Bit's unspoken lesson is the residual effects, twenty years later, of her seven-year sexual molestation during her formative adolescent years. She is suspended in a condition of alienation from others, having become the perpetual outsider and able to feel sensations only when she is driving a car. Nonetheless, she is not alone. As she looks in the rearview mirror, she sees in her mind's eye a fantasy Peck sitting on the back seat of the car accompanying her on yet another trip. Caressed by the familiar sensations evoked by leather seats, gear shift, warm enclosure, and romantic pop music, she is happy again in the possibility of a long drive through her memories with Peck. She is also learning forgiveness of self that, for Vogel, is essential to her moving forward in life.

In her theory of memory, Paula Vogel puts weight on the sensory dimensions of L'il Bit's recollections—warm nights, full moon, and the fragrance of leather car seats pressing against her. Li'l Bit is one of Vogel's memory-obsessed adults who are often refugees from ugly childhood experiences. The oppression is over but the memory (seen in the rearview mirror of her mind) keeps the good part alive and with her in the present. One writer says that Vogel's characters "bring to the stage exilic memories of loss. Remembering how it felt to be abused or deprived, they frequently resurrect incarnations of their much younger selves."[9]

As the narrator, Li'l Bit's control of the narrative development (her drive up and down memory lane) affords her (and the actress) a creative role as she puts a figurative hand into her memory bank and pulls out the sexual initiations of her youth. The audience is asked to review the warnings, the cries for help, the inappropriate behaviors of both children and adults. In her adult freedom, Li'l Bit asks the question: "Who did it to you, Uncle Peck? How old were you? Were you eleven?" Significant plays like *How I Learned to Drive* pose questions on large and even painful issues and provoke audiences to consider possible answers within the framework of their own lives and societies.

Music, like sound effects, is an important feature of Vogel's work. She tells us that before she sits down to write a play, she makes a tape of songs and music to play continuously throughout her process. She wrote sections of *How I Learned to Drive* listening to Roy Orbison's "Dream Baby" and "Sweet Dreams" and to the music of the Beach Boys and the Mamas and the Papas. Late in the play, Li'l Bit introduces Richard Wagner's opera "The Flying Dutchman" as she contemplates Peck's death seven years after she refused to see him again. She thinks of her uncle "as a kind of Flying Dutchman," Wagner's tortured hero, and of Wagner's love-possessed heroine as a version of her earlier self. She says, "In the opera, the phantom Dutchman is doomed to wander the sea; but every seven years he can come ashore, and if he finds a maiden who will love him of her own free will— he will be released." Li'l Bit uses the analogy to illuminate her own complicity in her seduction as well as the curse of deviancy that Peck has carried within him since childhood.

Paula Vogel's work, including *Baltimore Waltz, The Oldest Profession, How I Learned to Drive,* and *The Mineola Twins,* takes us into a topos of memories that explore such feminist issues as women's (and men's) victimization by other men and women. Li'l Bit and Peck are victimized by historical social forces and by prescribed gender roles in a largely patriarchal society—the American South. In this setting, women in particular are betrayed, brutalized, habituated, and oppressed. Under the scrutiny of the male gaze of both pubescent boys and adult men, women become self-conscious about their bodies and, like Li'l Bit, avoid situations where she would likely call attention to her breasts, for instance. She refuses to dance at the high school prom because her breasts "jiggle" and thus rivet the male gaze of the high school population.

Nonetheless, Vogel's is a balanced view of her feminist landscape. In her freedom (Peck has been dead for seven years at the play's end), Li'l Bit muses on her secret past and wonders who initiated Peck and created the pedophile that he became. Memory unlocks self-awareness. The day Peck molested her in the automobile, she recognizes as "the last day I lived in my body. I retreated above the neck, and I've lived inside the 'fire' in my head ever since."

For Vogel, the stage with its capacity for metaphor and live performance is a vibrant site for demonstrating the human act of remembering. This play itself is an act of remembering presided over by a Greek chorus. Li'l Bit enacts her memories of Peck's seduction, the maternal relatives' advice on men, sex, and women, and her high school friends' behaviors. The processes of imposing narrative order on remembering and tying together sequences of what were once thought unrelated moments ("the last time she was in her body") are Li'l Bit's strategies for understanding and distancing the pain of the past. She has escaped her predator, but, like the Civil War soldiers on those long-ago battlefields, she carries the emotional wounds and the scars. She has left the battlefield but the adult Li'l Bit roils in her efforts to find freedom in self-forgiveness. At the play's end as she repeats the old pattern of checking the car before driving off, she admits the pleasure, sensations, and contentment that she finds in the physical act of driving. The act of driving places her in control of the car; but there is always the secretive pleasure in the rearview mirror—in the backward motion of her memory—of imagining that she and Peck are happy to be going on a long ride together. In her memory state, Peck is no longer seated beside her but is relegated to the back seat and she is in control of the car and her life. At the play's end, she is moving forward.

Vogel's ending is problematic. The final scene (labeled "Driving in Today's World") suggests that Li'l Bit cannot fully escape the consequences of her abusive past. She has been damaged but she can come to an understanding of her relationship with Peck. As she works toward finding self-forgiveness, understanding, and peace, she is effectively getting on with her life.

How I Learned to Drive

CHARACTERS

LI'L BIT—A woman who ages forty-something to eleven years old.

PECK—Attractive man in his forties. Despite a few problems, he should be played by an actor one might cast in the role of Atticus in *To Kill A Mockingbird*.

THE GREEK CHORUS If possible, these three members should be able to sing three-part harmony.

MALE GREEK CHORUS—Plays Grandfather, Waiter, High School Boys. Thirties–forties.

FEMALE GREEK CHORUS—Plays Mother, Aunt Mary, High School Girls. Thirty–fifty.

TEENAGE GREEK CHORUS—Plays Grandmother, High School Girls, and the voice of eleven-year-old Li'l Bit. Note on the casting of this actor: I would strongly recommend casting a young woman who is "of legal age," that is, twenty-one to twenty-five years old who can look as close to eleven as possible. The contrast with the other cast members will help. If the actor is too young, the audience may feel uncomfortable.

As the house lights dim, a Voice announces:
Safety First—You and Driver Education.

Then the sound of a key turning the ignition of a car. Li'l Bit steps into a spotlight on the stage; "well-endowed," she is a softer-looking woman in the present time than she was at seventeen.

LI'L BIT: Sometimes to tell a secret, you first have to teach a lesson. We're going to start our lesson tonight on an early, warm summer evening.

In a parking lot overlooking the Beltsville Agricultural Farms in suburban Maryland.

Less than a mile away, the crumbling concrete of U.S. One wends its way past one-room revival churches, the porno drive-in, and boarded up motels with For Sale signs tumbling down.

Like I said, it's a warm summer evening.

Here on the land the Department of Agriculture owns, the smell of sleeping farm animals is thick on the air. The smells of clover and hay mix in with the smells of the leather dashboard. You can still imagine how Maryland used to be, before the malls took over. This countryside was once dotted with farmhouses—from their porches you could have witnessed the Civil War raging in the front fields.

Oh yes. There's a moon over Maryland tonight, that spills into the car where I sit beside a man old enough to be—did I mention how still the night is? Damp soil and tranquil air. It's the kind of night that makes a middle-aged man with a mortgage feel like a country boy again.

It's 1969. And I am very old, very cynical of the world, and I know it all. In short, I am seventeen years old, parking off a dark lane with a married man on an early summer night.

(Lights up on two chairs facing front—or a Buick Riviera, if you will. Waiting patiently, with a smile on his face, Peck sits sniffing the night air. Li'l Bit climbs in beside him, seventeen years old and tense. Throughout the following, the two sit facing directly

front. They do not touch. Their bodies remain passive. Only their facial expressions emote.)

PECK: Ummm. I love the smell of your hair.

LI'L BIT: Uh-huh.

PECK: Oh, Lord. Ummmm. (*Beat.*) A man could die happy like this.

LI'L BIT: Well, *don't.*

PECK: What shampoo is this?

LI'L BIT: Herbal Essence.

PECK: Herbal Essence. I'm gonna buy me some. Herbal Essence. And when I'm all alone in the house, I'm going to get into the bathtub, and uncap the bottle and—

LI'L BIT: —Be good.

PECK: What?

LI'L BIT: Stop being…bad.

PECK: What did you think I was going to say? What do you think I'm going to do with the shampoo?

LI'L BIT: I don't want to know. I don't want to hear it.

PECK: I'm going to wash my hair. That's all.

LI'L BIT: Oh.

PECK: What did you think I was going to do?

LI'L BIT: Nothing…I don't know. Something…nasty.

PECK: With shampoo? Lord, gal—your mind!

LI'L BIT: And whose fault is it?

PECK: Not mine. I've got the mind of a boy scout.

LI'L BIT: Right. A horny boy scout.

PECK: Boy scouts are always horny. What do you think the first Merit Badge is for?

LI'L BIT: There. You're going to be nasty again.

PECK: Oh, no. I'm good. Very good.

LI'L BIT: It's getting late.

PECK: Don't change the subject. I was talking about how good I am. (*Beat.*) Are you ever gonna let me show you how good I am?

LI'L BIT: Don't go over the line now.

PECK: I won't. I'm not gonna do anything you don't want me to do.

LI'L BIT: That's right.

PECK: And I've been good all week.

LI'L BIT: You have?

PECK: Yes. All week. Not a single drink.

LI'L BIT: Good boy.

PECK: Do I get a reward? For not drinking?

LI'L BIT: A small one. It's getting late.

PECK: Just let me undo you. I'll do you back up.

LI'L BIT: All right. But be quick about it. (*Peck pantomimes undoing Li'l Bit's brassiere with one hand.*) You know, that's amazing. The way you can undo the hooks through my blouse with one hand.

PECK: Years of practice.

LI'L BIT: You would make an incredible brain surgeon with that dexterity.

PECK: I'll bet Clyde—what's the name of the boy taking you to the prom?

LI'L BIT: Claude Souders.

PECK: Claude Souders. I'll bet it takes him two hands, lights on, and you helping him on to get to first base.

LI'L BIT: Maybe. (*Beat.*)

PECK: Can I…kiss them? Please?

LI'L BIT: I don't know.

PECK: Don't make a grown man beg.

LI'L BIT: Just one kiss.

PECK: I'm going to lift your blouse.

LI'L BIT: It's a little cold. (*Peck laughs gently.*)

PECK: That's not why you're shivering. (*They sit, perfectly still, for a long moment of silence. Peck makes gentle, concentric circles with has thumbs in the air in front of him.*) How does that feel? (*Li'l Bit closes her eyes, carefully keeps her voice calm.*)

LI'L BIT: It's…okay. (*Sacred music, organ music or a boy's choir swells beneath the following.*)

PECK: I tell you, you can keep all the cathedrals of Europe. Just give me a second with these— these celestial orbs—(*Peck bozos his head as if praying. But he is kissing her nipple. Li'l Bit, eyes still closed, rears back her head on the leather Buick car seat.*)

LI'L BIT: Uncle Peck —we've got to go. I've got graduation rehearsal at school tomorrow morning. And you should get on home to Aunt Mary—

PECK: —All right, Li'l Bit.

LI'L BIT: —*Don't* call me that no more. (*Calmer.*) Any more. I'm a big girl now, Uncle Peck. As you know. (*Li'l Bit pantomimes refastening her bra behind her back.*)

PECK: That you are. Going on eighteen. Kittens will turn into cats. (*Sighs.*) I live all week long for these few minutes with you—you know that?

LI'L BIT: I'll drive. (*A Voice cuts in with:*)

Idling in the Neutral Gear.

(*Sound of car revving cuts off the sacred music; Li'l Bit, now an adult, rises out of the car and comes to us.*)

LI'L BIT: In most families, relatives get names like "Junior," or "Brother," or "Bubba." In my family, if we call someone "Big Papa," it's not because he's tall. In my family, folks tend to get nicknamed for their genitalia. Uncle Peck, for example. My mama's adage was "the titless wonder," and my cousin Bobby got branded for life as "B.B." (*In unison with Greek Chorus.*)

LI'L BIT:	GREEK CHORUS:
For blue balls.	For blue balls.

FEMALE GREEK CHORUS: (*As Mother.*) And of course, we were so excited to have a baby girl that when the nurse brought you in and said, "It's a girl! It's a baby girl!" I just had to see for myself. So we whipped your diapers down and parted your chubby little legs—and right between your legs there was—(*Peck has come over during the above and chimes along:*)

PECK:	GREEK CHORUS:
Just a little bit.	Just a little bit.

FEMALE GREEK CHORUS: (*As Mother.*) And when you were born, you were so tiny that you fit in Uncle Peck's outstretched hand. (*Peck stretches his hand out.*)

PECK: Now that's a fact. I held you, one day old, right in this hand. (*A traffic signal is projected of a bicycle in a circle with a diagonal red slash.*)

LI'L BIT: Even with my family background, I was sixteen or so before I realized that pedophilia did not mean people who loved to bicycle…

(*A Voice intrudes:*)

Driving in First Gear.

LI'L BIT: 1969. A typical family dinner.

FEMALE GREEK CHORUS: (*As Mother.*) Look, Grandma. Li'l Bit's getting to be as big in the bust as you are.

LI'L BIT: Mother! Could we please change the subject?

TEENAGE GREEK CHORUS: (*As Grandmother.*) Well, I hope you are buying her some decent bras. I never had a decent bra, growing up in the Depression, and now my shoulders are just crippled—crippled from the weight hanging on my shoulders—the dents from my bra straps are big enough to put your finger in.—Here, let me show you—(*As Grandmother starts to open her blouse:*)

LI'L BIT: Grandma! Please don't undress at the dinner table.

PECK: I thought the entertainment came *after* the dinner.

LI'L BIT: (*To the audience.*) This is how it always starts. My grandfather, Big Papa, will chime in next with—

MALE GREEK CHORUS: (*As Grandfather.*) Yup. If Li'l Bit gets any bigger, we're gonna haveta buy her a wheelbarrow to carry in front of her—

LI'L BIT: —Damn it—

PECK: —How about those Redskins on Sunday, Big Papa?

LI'L BIT: (*To the audience.*) The only sport Big Papa followed was chasing Grandma around the house—

MALE GREEK CHORUS: (*As Grandfather.*)—Or we could write to Kate Smith. Ask her for somma her used brassieres she don't want anymore—she could maybe give to Li'l Bit here—

LI'L BIT: —I can't stand it. I can't.

PECK: Now, honey, that's just their way—

FEMALE GREEK CHORUS: (*As Mother.*) I tell you, Grandma, Li'l Bit's at that age. She's so sensitive, you can't say boo—

LI'L BIT: I'd like some privacy, that's all. Okay? Some goddamn privacy—

PECK: —Well, at least she didn't use the savior's name—

LI'L BIT: (*To the audience.*) And Big Papa wouldn't let a dead dog lie. No sirree.

MALE GREEK CHORUS: (*As Grandfather.*) Well, she'd better stop being so sensitive. 'Cause five minutes before Li'l Bit turns the corner, her tits turn first—

LI'L BIT: (*Starting to rise from the table.*)—That's it. That's it.

PECK: Li'l Bit, you can't let him get to you. Then he wins.

LI'L BIT: I hate him. *Hate* him.

PECK: That's fine. But hate him and eat a good dinner at the same time. (*Li'l Bit calms down and sits with perfect dignity.*)

LI'L BIT: The gumbo is really good, Grandma.

MALE GREEK CHORUS: (*As Grandfather.*) A'course, Li'l Bit's got a big surprise coming for her when she goes to that fancy college this fall—

PECK: Big Papa—let it go.

MALE GREEK CHORUS: (*As Grandfather.*) What does she need a college degree for? She's got all the credentials she'll need on her chest—

LI'L BIT: —Maybe I want to learn things. Read. Rise above my cracker background—

PECK: —Whoa, now, Li'l Bit—

MALE GREEK CHORUS: (*As Grandfather.*) What kind of things do you want to read?

LI'L BIT: There's a whole semester course, for example, on Shakespeare—(*Male Greek Chorus, as Grandfather, laughs until he weeps.*)

MALE GREEK CHORUS: (*As Grandfather.*) Shakespeare. That's a good one. Shakespeare is really going to help you in life.

PECK: I think it's wonderful. And on scholarship!

MALE GREEK CHORUS: (*As Grandfather.*) How is Shakespeare going to help her lie on her back in the dark? (*Li'l Bit is on her feet.*)

LI'L BIT: You're getting old, Big Papa. You are going to die—very very soon. Maybe even *tonight*. And when you get to heaven, God's going to be a beautiful black woman in a long white robe. She's gonna look at your chart and say: Uh-oh. Fornication. Dogugly mean with blood relatives. Oh. Uh-oh. Voted for George Wallace. Well, one last chance: If you can name the play, all will be forgiven. And then she'll quote: "The quality of mercy is not strained." Your answer? Oh, too bad—*Merchant of Venice*: Act IV, Scene iii. And then she'll send your ass to fry in hell with all the other crackers. Excuse me, please.

(*To the audience.*) And as I left the house, I would always hear Big Papa say:

MALE GREEK CHORUS: (*As Grandfather.*) Lucy, your daughter's got a mouth on her. Well, no sense in wasting good gumbo. Pass me her plate, Mama.

LI'L BIT: And Aunt Mary would come up to Uncle Peck:

FEMALE GREEK CHORUS: (*As Aunt Mary.*) Peck, go after her, will you? You're the only one she'll listen to when she gets like this.

PECK: She just needs to cool off.

FEMALE GREEK CHORUS: (*As Aunt Mary.*) Please, honey—Grandma's been on her feet cooking all day.

PECK: All right.

LI'L BIT: And as he left the room, Aunt Mary would say:

FEMALE GREEK CHORUS: (*As Aunt Mary.*) Peck's so good with them when they get to be this age. (*Li'l Bit has stormed to another part of the stage, her back turned, weeping with a teenage fury. Peck, cautiously, as if stalking a deer, comes to her. She turns away even more. He waits a bit.*)

PECK: I don't suppose you're talking to family. (*No response.*) Does it help that I'm in-law?

LI'L BIT: Don't you dare make fun of this.

PECK: I'm not. There's nothing funny about this. (*Beat.*) Although I'll bet when Big Papa is about to meet his maker, he'll remember *The Merchant of Venice*.

LI'L BIT: I've got to get away from here.

PECK: You're going away. Soon. Here, take this. (*Peck hands her his folded handkerchief. Li'l Bit uses it, noisily. Hands it back. Without her seeing, he reverently puts it back.*)

LI'L BIT: I hate this family.

PECK: Your grandfather's ignorant. And you're right—he's going to die soon. But he's family. Family is…family.

LI'L BIT: Grown-ups are always saying that. Family.

PECK: Well, when you get a little older, you'll see what we're saying.

LI'L BIT: Uh-huh. So family is another acquired taste, like French kissing?

PECK: Come again?

LI'L BIT: You know, at first it really grosses you out, but in time you grow to like it?

PECK: Girl, you are…a handful.

LI'L BIT: Uncle Peck—you have the keys to your car?

PECK: Where do you want to go?

LI'L BIT: Just up the road.

PECK: I'll come with you.

LI'L BIT: No—please? I just need to…to drive for a little bit. Alone. (*Peck tosses her the keys.*)

PECK: When can I see you alone again?

LI'L BIT: Tonight. (*Li'l Bit crosses to C. while the lights dim around her.*

A Voice directs:)

Shifting Forward from First to Second Gear.

LI'L BIT: There were a lot of rumors about why I got kicked out of that fancy school in 1970. Some say I got caught with a man in my room. Some say as a kid on scholarship I fooled around with a rich man's daughter. (*Li'l Bit smiles innocently at the audience.*)

I'm not talking.

But the real truth was I had a constant companion in my dorm room—who was less than discrete. Canadian V.O. A fifth a day.

1970. A Nixon recession. I slept on the floors of friends who were out of work themselves. Took factory work when I could find it. A string of dead-end day jobs that didn't last very long.

What I did, most nights, was cruise the Beltway and the back roads of Maryland, where there was still country, past the battle-fields and farm houses. Racing in a 1965 Mustang—and as long as I had gasoline for my car and whiskey for me, the nights would pass. Fully tanked, I would speed past the churches and the trees on the bend, thinking just one notch of the steering wheel would be all it would take, and yet some…reflex took over. My hands on the wheel in the nine and three o'clock position—I never so much as got a ticket. He taught me well.

(*A Voice announces:*)

You and the Reverse Gear.

LI'L BIT: Back up. 1968. On the Eastern Shore. A celebration dinner. (*Li'l Bit joins Peck at a table in a restaurant.*)

PECK: Feeling better, missy?

LI'L BIT: The bathroom's really amazing here, Uncle Peck! They have these little soaps—instead of borax or something—and they're in the shape of shells.

PECK: I'll have to take a trip to the gentleman's room just to see.

LI'L BIT: How did you know about this place?

PECK: This inn is famous on the Eastern Shore—it's been open since the seventeenth century. And I know how you like history…(*Li'l Bit is shy and pleased.*)

LI'L BIT: It's great.

PECK: And you've just done your first, legal, long-distance drive. You must be hungry.

LI'L BIT: I'm starved.

PECK: I would suggest a dozen oysters to start, and the crab imperial…(*Li'l Bit is genuinely agog.*) You might be interested to know the town history. When the British sailed up this very river in the dead of night—see outside where I'm pointing?—they were going to bombard the heck out of this town. But the town fathers were ready for them. They crept up all the trees with lanterns so that the British would think they saw the town lights and they aimed their cannons too high. And that's why the inn is still here for business today.

LI'L BIT: That's a great story.

PECK: (*Casually.*) Would you like to start with a cocktail?

LI'L BIT: You're not…you're not going to start drinking, are you, Uncle Peck?

PECK: Not me. I told you, as long as you're with me, I'll never drink. I asked you if *you'd* like a cocktail before dinner. It's nice to have a little something with the oysters.

LI'L BIT: But…I'm not…legal. We could get arrested. Uncle Peck, they'll never believe I'm twenty-one!

PECK: So? Today we celebrate your driver's license—on the first try. This establishment reminds me a lot of places back home.

LI'L BIT: What does that mean?

PECK: In South Carolina, like here on the Eastern Shore, they're…(*Searches for the right euphemism.*)…"European." Not so puritanical. And very understanding if gentlemen wish to escort very attractive young ladies who might want a before-dinner cocktail. If you want one, I'll order one.

LI'L BIT: Well—sure. Just…one. (*The Female Greek Chorus appears in a spot.*)

FEMALE GREEK CHORUS: (*As Mother.*) A Mother's Guide to Social Drinking:

A lady never gets sloppy—she may, however, get tipsy and a little gay.

Never drink on an empty stomach. Avail yourself of the bread basket and generous portions of butter. *Slather* the butter on your bread.

Sip your drink, slowly, let the beverage linger in your mouth—interspersed with interesting, fascinating conversation. Sip, never…slurp or gulp. Your glass should always be three-quarters full when his glass is empty.

Stay away from *ladies'* drinks: drinks like pink ladies, slow gin fizzes, daiquiris, gold cadillacs, Long Island iced teas, margaritas, piña coladas, mai tais, planters punch, white Russians, black Russians, red Russians, melon balls, blue balls, hummingbirds, hemorrhages and hurricanes. In short, avoid anything with sugar, or anything with an umbrella. Get your vitamin C from *fruit*. Don't order anything with Voodoo or Vixen in the title or sexual positions in the name like Dead Man Screw or the Missionary. (*She sort of titters.*)

Believe me, they are lethal…I think you were conceived after one of those.

Drink, instead, like a man: straight up or on the rocks, with plenty of water in between.

Oh, yes. And never mix your drinks. Stay with one all night long, like the man you came in with: bourbon, gin, or tequila till dawn, damn the torpedoes, full speed ahead! (*As the Female Greek Chorus retreats, the Male Greek Chorus approaches the table as a Waiter.*)

MALE GREEK CHORUS: (*As Waiter.*) I hope you all are having a pleasant evening. Is there something I can bring you, sir, before you order? (*Li'l Bit waits in anxious fear. Carefully, Uncle Peck says with command:*)

PECK: I'll have a plain iced tea. The lady would like a drink, I believe. (*The Male Greek Chorus does a double take; there is a moment when Uncle Peck and he are in silent communication.*)

MALE GREEK CHORUS: (*As Waiter.*) Very good. What would the…lady like?

LI'L BIT: (*A bit flushed.*) Is there…is there any sugar in a martini?

PECK: None that I know of.

LI'L BIT: That's what I'd like then—a dry martini. And could we maybe have some bread?

PECK: A drink fit for a woman of the world.— Please bring the lady a dry martini, be generous with the olives, straight up. (*The Male Greek Chorus anticipates a large tip.*)

MALE GREEK CHORUS: (*As Waiter.*) Right away. Very good, sir. (*The Male Greek Chorus returns with an empty martini glass which he puts in front of Li'l Bit.*)

PECK: Your glass is empty. Another martini, madam?

LI'L BIT: Yes, thank you. (*Peck signals the Male Greek Chorus, who nods.*) So why did you leave South Carolina, Uncle Peck?

PECK: I was stationed in D.C. after the war, and decided to stay. Go North, Young Man, someone might have said.

LI'L BIT: What did you do in the service anyway?

PECK: (*Suddenly taciturn.*) I…I did just this and that. Nothing heroic or spectacular.

LI'L BIT: But did you see fighting? Or go to Europe?

PECK: I served in the Pacific Theater. It's really nothing interesting to talk about.

LI'L BIT: It is to me. (*The Waiter has brought another empty glass.*) Oh, goody. I love the color of the swizzle sticks. What were we talking about?

PECK: Swizzle sticks.

LI'L BIT: Do you ever think of going back?

PECK: To the Marines?

LI'L BIT: No—to South Carolina.

PECK: Well, we do go back. To visit.

LI'L BIT: No, I mean to live.

PECK: Not very likely. I think it's better if my mother doesn't have a daily reminder of her disappointment.

LI'L BIT: Are these floorboards slanted?

PECK: Yes, the floor is very slanted. I think this is the original floor.

LI'L BIT: Oh, good. (*The Female Greek Chorus as Mother enters swaying a little, a little past tipsy.*)

FEMALE GREEK CHORUS: (*As Mother.*) Don't leave your drink unattended when you visit the ladies' room. There is such a thing as white slavery; the modus operandi is to spike an unsuspecting young girl's drink with a "mickey" when she's left the room to powder her nose.

But if you feel you have had more than your sufficiency in liquor, do go to the ladies' room—often. Pop your head out of doors for a refreshing breath of the night air. If you must, wet your face and head with tap water. Don't be afraid to dunk your head if necessary. A wet woman is still less conspicuous than a drunk woman. (*The Female Greek Chorus stumbles a little; conspiratorially.*)

When in the course of human events it becomes necessary, go to a corner stall and insert the index and middle finger down the throat almost to the epiglottis. Divulge your stomach contents by such persuasion, and then wait a few moments before rejoining your beau waiting for you at your table.

Oh, no. Don't be shy or embarrassed. In the very best of establishments, there's always one or two debutantes crouched in the corner stalls, their beaded purses tossed willy-nilly, sounding like cats in heat, heaving up the contents of their stomachs. (*The Female Greek Chorus begins to wander off.*)

I wonder what it is they do in the men's rooms…

LI'L BIT: So why is your mother disappointed in you, Uncle Peck?

PECK: Every mother in Horry County has Great Expectations.

LI'L BIT: —Could I have another mar-ti-ni, please?

PECK: I think this is your last one. (*Peck signals the Waiter. The Waiter looks at Li'l Bit and shakes his head no. Peck raises his eyebrow, raises his finger to indicate one more, and then rubs his fingers together. It looks like a secret code. The Waiter sighs, shakes his head sadly, and brings*

over another empty martini glass. He glares at Peck.)

LI'L BIT: The name of the county where you grew up is "Horry?" (*Li'l Bit, plastered, begins to laugh. Then she stops.*) I think your mother should be proud of you. (*Peck signals for the check.*)

PECK: Well, missy, she wanted me to do—to *be* everything my father was not. She wanted me to amount to something.

LI'L BIT: But you have! You've amounted a lot…

PECK: I'm just a very ordinary man. (*The Waiter has brought the check and waits. Peck draws out a large bill and hands it to the Waiter. Li'l Bit is in the soppy stage.*)

LI'L BIT: I'll bet your mother loves you, Uncle Peck. (*Peck freezes a bit. To Male Greek Chorus as Waiter:*)

PECK: Thank you. The service was exceptional. Please keep the change.

MALE GREEK CHORUS: (*As Waiter, in a tone that could freeze.*) Thank you, sir. Will you be needing any help?

PECK: I think we can manage, thank you. (*Just then, the Female Greek Chorus as Mother lurches on stage; the Male Greek Chorus as Waiter escorts her off as she delivers:*)

FEMALE GREEK CHORUS: (*As Mother.*) Thanks to judicious planning and several trips to the ladies' loo, your mother once out-drank an entire regiment of British officers on a goodwill visit to Washington! Every last man of them! Milquetoasts! How'd they ever kick Hitler's cahones, huh? No match for an American lady—I could drink every man in here under the table. (*She delivers one last crucial hint before she is gently "bounced."*) As a last resort, when going out for an evening on the town, be sure to wear a skin-tight girdle—so tight that only a surgical knife or acetylene torch can get it off you—so that if you do pass out in the arms of your escort, he'll end up with rubber burns on his fingers before he can steal your virtue—

(*A Voice punctuates the interlude with:*)

Vehicle Failure.

Even with careful maintenance and preventive operation of your automobile, it is

all too common for us to experience an unexpected breakdown. If you are driving at any speed when a breakdown occurs, you must slow down and guide the automobile to the side of the road.

(*Peck is slowly propping up Li'l Bit as they work their way to his car in the parking lot of the inn.*)

PECK: How are you doing, missy?

LI'L BIT: It's so far to the car, Uncle Peck. Like the lanterns in the trees the British fired on… (*Li'l Bit stumbles. Peck swoops her up in his arms.*)

PECK: Okay. I think we're going to take a more direct route. (*Li'l Bit closes her eyes.*) Dizzy? (*She nods her head.*) Don't look at the ground. Almost there—do you feel sick to your stomach? (*Li'l Bit nods. They reach the "car." Peck gently deposits her on the front seat.*) Just settle here a little while until things stop spinning. (*Li'l Bit opens her eyes.*)

LI'L BIT: What are we doing?

PECK: We're just going to sit here until your tummy settles down.

LI'L BIT: It's such nice upholst'ry—

PECK: Think you can go for a ride, now?

LI'L BIT: Where are you taking me?

PECK: Home.

LI'L BIT: You're not taking me—upstairs? There's no room at the inn? (*Li'l Bit giggles.*)

PECK: Do you want to go upstairs? (*Li'l Bit doesn't answer.*) Or home?

LI'L BIT: —This isn't right, Uncle Peck.

PECK: What isn't right?

LI'L BIT: What we're doing. It's wrong. It's very wrong.

PECK: What are we doing? (*Li'l Bit does not answer.*) We're just going out to dinner.

LI'L BIT: You know. It's not nice to Aunt Mary.

PECK: You let me be the judge of what's nice and not nice to my wife. (*Beat.*)

LI'L BIT: Now you're mad.

PECK: I'm not mad. It's just that I thought you… understood me, Li'l Bit. I think you're the only one who does.

LI'L BIT: Someone will get hurt.

PECK: Have I forced you to do anything? (*There is a long pause as Li'l Bit tries to get sober enough to think this through.*)

LI'L BIT: …I guess not.

PECK: We are just enjoying each other's company. I've told you, nothing is going to happen between us until you want it to. Do you know that?

LI'L BIT: Yes.

PECK: Nothing is going to happen until you want it to. (*A second more, with Peck staring ahead at the river while seated at the wheel of his car. Then, softly:*) Do you want something to happen? (*Peck reaches over and strokes her face, very gently. Li'l Bit softens, reaches for him, and buries her head in his neck. Then she kisses him. Then she moves away, dizzy again.*)

LI'L BIT: I don't know. (*Peck smiles, this has been good news for him—it hasn't been a "no."*)

PECK: Then I'll wait. I'm a very patient man. I've been waiting for a long time. I don't mind waiting.

LI'L BIT: Someone is going to get hurt.

PECK: No one is going to get hurt. (*Li'l Bit closes her eyes.*) Are you feeling sick?

LI'L BIT: Sleepy. (*Carefully, Peck props Li'l Bit up on the seat.*)

PECK: Stay here a second.

LI'L BIT: Where're you going?

PECK: I'm getting something from the back seat.

LI'L BIT: (*Scared; too loud.*) What? What are you going to do? (*Peck reappears in the front seat with a lap rug.*)

PECK: Shhhh. (*Peck covers Li'l Bit. She calms down.*) There. Think you can sleep? (*Li'l Bit nods. She slides over to rest on his shoulder. With a look of happiness, Peck turns the ignition key. Beat. Peck leaves Li'l Bit sleeping in the car and strolls down to the audience. Wagner's* Flying Dutchman *comes up faintly. A Voice interjects:*)

Idling in the Neutral Gear.

TEENAGE GREEK CHORUS: Uncle Peck Teaches Cousin Bobby How to Fish.

PECK: I get back once or twice a year—supposedly to visit Mama and the family, but the real truth is to fish. I miss this the most of all. There's a smell in the Low Country—where the swamp and fresh inlet join the saltwater—a scent of sand and cypress, that I haven't found anywhere yet.

I don't say this very often up North because it will just play into the stereotype everyone has, but I will tell you: I didn't wear shoes in the summertime until I was sixteen. It's unnatural down here to pen up your feet in leather. Go ahead—take 'em off. Let yourself breathe—it really will make you feel better.

We're going to aim for some pompano today—and I have to tell you, they're a very shy, mercurial fish. Takes patience, and psychology. You have to believe it doesn't matter if you catch one or not.

Sky's pretty spectacular—there's some beer in the cooler next to the crab salad I packed, so help yourself if you get hungry. Are you hungry? Thirsty? Holler if you are.

Okay. You don't want to lean over the bridge like that—pompano feed in shallow water, and you don't want to get too close— they're frisky and shy little things—wait, check your line. Yep, something's been munching while we were talking.

Okay, look: We take the sand flea and you take the hook like this—right through his little sand flea rump. Sand fleas should always keep their backs to the wall. Okay. Cast it in, like I showed you. That's great! I can taste that pompano now, sautéed with some pecans and butter, a little bourbon— now—let it lie on the bottom—now, reel, jerk, reel, jerk—

Look—look at your line. There's something calling, all right. Okay, tip the rod up—not too sharp—hook it—all right, now easy, reel and then rest—let it play. And reel—play it out, that's right—really good! I can't believe it! It's a pompano.—Good work! Way to go! You are an official fisherman now. Pompano are hard to catch. We are going to have a delicious little—

What? Well, I don't know how much pain a fish feels—you can't think of that. Oh, no, don't cry, come on now, it's just a fish—the other guys are going to see you.— No, no, you're just real sensitive, and I think that's wonderful at your age—look, do you want me to cut it free? You do?

Okay, hand me those pliers—look—I'm cutting the hook—okay? And we're just going to drop it in—no I'm not mad. It's just for fun, okay? There—it's going to swim back to its lady friend and tell her what a terrible day it had and she's going to stroke him with her fins until he feels better, and then they'll do something alone together that will make them both feel good and sleepy...

(*Peck bends down, very earnest.*) I don't want you to feel ashamed about crying. I'm not going to tell anyone, okay? I can keep secrets. You know, men cry all the time. They just don't tell anybody, and they don't let anybody catch them. There's nothing you could do that would make me feel ashamed of you. Do you know that? Okay. (*Peck straightens up, smiles.*)

Do you want to pack up and call it a day? I tell you what—I think I can still remember—there's a really neat tree house where I used to stay for days. I think it's still here—it was the last time I looked. But it's a secret place—you can't tell anybody we've gone there—least of all your mom or your sisters.—This is something special just between you and me. Sound good? We'll climb up there and have a beer and some crab salad—okay, B.B.? Bobby? Robert... (*Li'l Bit sits at a kitchen table with the two Female Greek Chorus members.*)

LI'L BIT: (*To the audience.*) Three women, three generations, sit at the kitchen table.

On Men, Sex, and Women: Part I:

FEMALE GREEK CHORUS: (*As Mother.*) Men only want one thing.

LI'L BIT: (*Wide-eyed.*) But what? What is it they want?

FEMALE GREEK CHORUS: (*As Mother.*) And once they have it, they lose all interest. So Don't Give It to Them.

TEENAGE GREEK CHORUS: (*As Grandmother.*) I never had the luxury of the rhythm method. Your grandfather is just a big bull. A big bull. Every morning, every evening.

FEMALE GREEK CHORUS: (*As Mother, whispers to Li'l Bit.*) And he used to come home for lunch every day.

LI'L BIT: My god, Grandma!

TEENAGE GREEK CHORUS: (*As Grandmother.*) Your grandfather only cares that I do two things: have the table set and the bed turned down.

FEMALE GREEK CHORUS: (*As Mother.*) And in all that time, Mother, you never have experienced—?

LI'L BIT: (*To the audience.*)—Now my grandmother believed in all the sacraments of the church, to the day she died. She believed in Santa Claus and the Easter Bunny until she was fifteen. But she didn't believe in—

TEENAGE GREEK CHORUS: (*As Grandmother.*)—Orgasm! That's just something you and Mary have made up! I don't believe you.

FEMALE GREEK CHORUS: (*As Mother.*) Mother, it happens to women all the time—

TEENAGE GREEK CHORUS: (*As Grandmother.*)—Oh, now you're going to tell me about the G force!

LI'L BIT: No, Grandma, I think that's astronauts—

FEMALE GREEK CHORUS: (*As Mother.*) Well, Mama, after all, you were a child bride when Big Papa came and got you—you were a married woman and you still believed in Santa Claus.

TEENAGE GREEK CHORUS: (*As Grandmother.*) It was legal, what Daddy and I did! I was fourteen and in those days, fourteen was a grown-up woman—(*Big Papa shuffles in the kitchen for a cookie.*)

MALE GREEK CHORUS: (*As Grandfather.*)—Oh, now we're off on Grandma and the Rape of the Sa-bean Women!

TEENAGE GREEK CHORUS: (*As Grandmother.*) Well, you were the one in such a big hurry—

MALE GREEK CHORUS: (*As Grandfather to Li'l Bit.*)—I picked your grandmother out of that herd of sisters just like a lion chooses the gazelle—the plump, slow, flaky gazelle dawdling at the edge of the herd—your sisters were too smart and too fast and too scrawny—

LI'L BIT: (*To the audience.*)—The family story is that when Big Papa came for Grandma, my Aunt Lily was waiting for him with a broom—and she beat him over the head all the way down the stairs as he was carrying out Grandma's hope chest—

MALE GREEK CHORUS: (*As Grandfather.*)—And they were *mean*. 'Specially Lily.

FEMALE GREEK CHORUS: (*As Mother.*) Well, you were robbing the baby of the family!

TEENAGE GREEK CHORUS: (*As Grandmother.*) I still keep a broom handy in the kitchen! And I know how to use it! So get your hand out of the cookie jar and don't you spoil your appetite for dinner—out of the kitchen! (*Male Greek Chorus as Grandfather leaves chuckling with a cookie.*)

FEMALE GREEK CHORUS: (*As Mother.*) Just one thing a married woman needs to know how to use—the rolling pin or the broom. I prefer a heavy, cast-iron fry pan—they're great on a man's head, no matter how thick the skull is.

TEENAGE GREEK CHORUS: (*As Grandmother.*) Yes, sir, your father is ruled by only two bosses! Mr. Gut and Mr. Peter! And sometimes, first thing in the morning, Mr. Sphincter Muscle!

FEMALE GREEK CHORUS: (*As Mother.*) It's true. Men are like children. Just like little boys.

TEENAGE GREEK CHORUS: (*As Grandmother.*) Men are bulls! Big bulls! (*The Greek Chorus is getting aroused.*)

FEMALE GREEK CHORUS: (*As Mother.*) They'd still be crouched on their haunches over a fire in a cave if we hadn't cleaned them up!

TEENAGE GREEK CHORUS: (*As Grandmother, flushed.*) Coming in smelling of sweat—

FEMALE GREEK CHORUS: (*As Mother.*)—Looking at those naughty pictures like boys in a dime store with a dollar in their pockets!

TEENAGE GREEK CHORUS: (*As Grandmother; raucous.*) No matter to them what they smell like! They've got to have it, right then, on the spot, right there! Nasty!—

FEMALE GREEK CHORUS: (*As Mother.*)—Vulgar!

TEENAGE GREEK CHORUS: (*As Grandmother.*) Primitive!—

FEMALE GREEK CHORUS: (*As Mother.*)—Hot!—

LI'L BIT: And just about then, Big Papa would shuffle in with—

MALE GREEK CHORUS: (*As Grandfather.*)—What are you all cackling about in here?

TEENAGE GREEK CHORUS: (*As Grandmother.*) Stay out of the kitchen! This is just for girls! (*As Grandfather leaves:*)

MALE GREEK CHORUS: (*As Grandfather.*) Lucy, you'd better not be filling Mama's head with sex! Every time you and Mary come over and start in about sex, when I ask a simple question like, "What time is dinner going to be ready?," Mama snaps my head off!

TEENAGE GREEK CHORUS: (*As Grandmother.*) Dinner will be ready when I'm good and ready! Stay out of this kitchen! (*Li'l Bit steps out. A Voice directs:*)

When Making a Left Turn, You Must Downshift While Going Forward.

LI'L BIT: 1979. A long bus trip to Upstate New York. I settled in to read, when a young man sat beside me.

MALE GREEK CHORUS: (*As Young Man; voice cracking.*) "What are you reading?"

LI'L BIT: He asked. His voice broke into that miserable equivalent of vocal acne, not quite falsetto and not tenor, either. I glanced a side view. He was appealing in an odd way, huge ears at a defiant angle springing forward at ninety degrees. He must have been shaving, because his face, with a peach sheen, was speckled with nicks and styptic. "I have a class tomorrow," I told him.

MALE GREEK CHORUS: (*As Young Man.*) "You're taking a class?"

LI'L BIT: "I'm teaching a class." He concentrated on lowering his voice.

MALE GREEK CHORUS: (*As Young Man.*) "I'm a senior. Walt Whitman High."

LI'L BIT: The light was fading outside, so perhaps he was—with a very high voice.

I felt his "interest" quicken. Five steps ahead of the hopes in his head, I slowed down, waited, pretended surprise, acted at listening, all the while knowing we would get off the bus, he would just then seem to think to ask me to dinner, he would chivalrously insist on walking me home, he would continue to converse in the street until I would casually invite him up to my room—and—I was only into the second moment of conversation and I could see the whole evening before me.

And dramaturgically speaking, after the faltering and slightly comical "first act,"

there was the very briefest of intermissions, and an extremely capable and forceful and *sustained* second act. And after the second act climax and a gentle denouement—before the post-play discussion—I lay on my back in the dark and I thought about you, Uncle Peck. Oh. Oh—this is the allure. Being older. Being the first. Being the translator, the teacher, the epicure, the already jaded. This is how the giver gets taken.

(*Li'l Bit changes her tone.*) On Men, Sex, and Women: Part II: (*Li'l Bit steps back into the scene as a fifteen year old, gawky and quiet, as the gazelle at the edge of the herd.*)

TEENAGE GREEK CHORUS: (*As Grandmother; to Li'l Bit.*) You're being mighty quiet, missy. Cat Got Your Tongue?

LI'L BIT: I'm just listening. Just thinking.

TEENAGE GREEK CHORUS: (*As Grandmother.*) Oh, yes, Little Miss Radar Ears? Soaking it all in? Little Miss Sponge? Penny for your thoughts? (*Li'l Bit hesitates to ask but she really wants to know.*)

LI'L BIT: Does it—when you do it—you know, theoretically when I do it and I haven't done it before—I mean—does it hurt?

FEMALE GREEK CHORUS: (*As Mother.*) Does what hurt, honey?

LI'L BIT: When a…when a girl does it for the first time—with a man—does it hurt?

TEENAGE GREEK CHORUS: (*As Grandmother; horrified.*) *That's* what you're thinking about?

FEMALE GREEK CHORUS: (*As Mother; calm.*) Well, just a little bit. Like a pinch. And there's a little blood.

TEENAGE GREEK CHORUS: (*As Grandmother.*) Don't tell her that! She's too young to be thinking those things!

FEMALE GREEK CHORUS: (*As Mother.*) Well, if she doesn't find out from me, where is she going to find out? In the street?

TEENAGE GREEK CHORUS: (*As Grandmother.*) Tell her it hurts! It's agony! You think you're going to die! Especially if you do it before marriage!

FEMALE GREEK CHORUS: (*As Mother.*) Mama! I'm going to tell her the truth! Unlike you, you left me and Mary completely in the dark with fairy tales and told us to go to the priest! What does an eighty-year-old priest know about lovemaking with girls!

LI'L BIT: (*Getting upset.*) It's not fair!

FEMALE GREEK CHORUS: (*As Mother.*) Now, see, she's getting upset—you're scaring her.

TEENAGE GREEK CHORUS: (*As Grandmother.*) Good! Let her be good and scared! It hurts! You bleed like a stuck pig! And you lay there and say, "Why, O Lord, have you forsaken me?"

LI'L BIT: It's not fair! Why does everything have to hurt for girls? Why is there always blood?

FEMALE GREEK CHORUS: (*As Mother.*) It's not a lot of blood—and it feels wonderful after the pain subsides…

TEENAGE GREEK CHORUS: (*As Grandmother.*) You're encouraging her to just go out and find out with the first drugstore joe who buys her a milk shake!

FEMALE GREEK CHORUS: (*As Mother.*) Don't be scared. It won't hurt you—if the man you go to bed with really loves you. It's important that he loves you.

TEENAGE GREEK CHORUS: (*As Grandmother.*)—Why don't you just go out and rent a motel room for her, Lucy?

FEMALE GREEK CHORUS: (*As Mother.*) I believe in telling my daughter the truth! We have a very close relationship! I want her to be able to ask me anything—I'm not scaring her with stories about Eve's sin and snakes crawling on their bellies for eternity and women bearing children in mortal pain—

TEENAGE GREEK CHORUS: (*As Grandmother.*)—If she stops and thinks before she takes her knickers off, maybe someone in this family will finish high school! (*Li'l Bit knows what is about to happen and starts to retreat from the scene at this point.*)

FEMALE GREEK CHORUS: (*As Mother.*) Mother! If you and Daddy had helped me—I wouldn't have had to marry that—that no-good-son-of-a—

TEENAGE GREEK CHORUS: (*As Grandmother.*)—He was good enough for you on a full moon! I hold you responsible!

FEMALE GREEK CHORUS: (*As Mother.*)—You could have helped me! You could have told me something about the facts of life!

TEENAGE GREEK CHORUS: (*As Grandmother.*)—I told you what my mother told me! A girl with her skirt up can outrun a man with his pants down! (*The Male Greek Chorus enters the fray; L'il Bit edges further D.*)

FEMALE GREEK CHORUS: (*As Mother.*) And when I turned to you for a little help, all I got afterwards was—

MALE GREEK CHORUS: (*As Grandfather.*) You Made Your Bed; Now Lie On It! (*The Greek Chorus freezes, mouths open, argumentatively.*)

LI'L BIT: (*To the audience.*) Oh, please! I still can't bear to listen to it, after all these years—(*The Male Greek Chorus "unfreezes," but out of his open mouth, as if to his surprise, comes a base refrain from a Motown* song.*)

MALE GREEK CHORUS: "Do-Bee-Do-Wah!" (*The Female Greek Chorus member is also surprised; but she, too, unfreezes.*)

FEMALE GREEK CHORUS: "Shoo-doo-be-doo-be-doo; shoo-doo-be-doo-be-doo." (*The Male and Female Greek Chorus members continue with their harmony, until the Teenage member of the Chorus starts in with Motown lyrics such as "Dedicated to the One I Love," or "In the Still of the Night," or "Hold Me"—any Sam Cooke will do. The three modulate down into three part harmony, softly, until they are submerged by the actual recording playing over the radio in the car in which Uncle Peck sits in the driver's seat, waiting. Li'l Bit sits in the passenger's seat.*)

LI'L BIT: Ahh. That's better. (*Uncle Peck reaches over and turns the volume down; to Li'l Bit.*)

PECK: How can you hear yourself think? (*Li'l Bit does not answer.*

A Voice insinuates itself in the pause:)

Before You Drive.

Always check under your car for obstructions—broken bottles, fallen tree branches, and the bodies of small children. Each year hundreds of children are crushed beneath the wheels of unwary drivers in their own driveways. Children depend on *you* to watch them.

(*Pause. The Voice continues.*)

You and the Reverse Gear.

(*In the following section, it would be nice to have slides of erotic photographs of women and cars:*

women posed over the hood; women draped along the sideboards; women with water hoses spraying the car; and the actress playing Li'l Bit with a Bel Air or any 1950s car one can find for the finale.)

LI'L BIT: 1967. In a parking lot of the Beltsville Agricultural Farms. The Initiation into a Boy's First Love.

PECK: (*With a soft look on his face.*) Of course, my favorite car will always be the '56 Bel Air Sports Coupe. Chevy sold more '55s, but the '56!—a V-8 with Corvette option, 225 horsepower; went from zero to sixty miles per hour in 8.9 seconds.

LI'L BIT: (*To the audience.*) Long after a mother's tits, but before a woman's breasts:

PECK: Super-Turbo-Fire! What a Power Pack—mechanical lifters, twin four-barrel carbs, lightweight valves, dual exhausts—

LI'L BIT: (*To the audience.*) After the milk but before the beer:

PECK: A specific intake manifold, higher-lift camshaft, and the tightest squeeze Chevy had ever made—

LI'L BIT: (*To the audience.*) Long after he's squeezed down the birth canal but before he's pushed his way back in: The boy falls in love with the thing that bears his weight with speed.

PECK: I want you to know your automobile inside and out.—Are you there? Li'l Bit? (*Slides end here.*)

LI'L BIT: —What?

PECK: You're drifting. I need you to concentrate.

LI'L BIT: Sorry.

PECK: Okay. Get into the driver's seat. (*Li'l Bit does.*) Okay. Now. Show me what you're going to do before you start the car. (*Li'l Bit sits, with her hands in her lap. She starts to giggle.*)

LI'L BIT: I don't know, Uncle Peck.

PECK: Now, come on. What's the first thing you're going to adjust?

LI'L BIT: My bra strap?—

PECK: —Li'l Bit. What's the most important thing to have control of on the inside of the car?

LI'L BIT: —That's easy. The radio. I tune the radio from Mama's old fart tunes to—(*Li'l Bit*

turns the radio up so we can hear a 1960s tune. With surprising firmness, Peck commands.)

PECK: —Radio off. Right now. (*Li'l Bit turns the radio off.*) When you are driving your car, with your license, you can fiddle with the stations all you want. But when you are driving with a learner's permit in my car, I want all your attention to be on the road.

LI'L BIT: Yes, sir.

PECK: Okay. Now the seat—forward and up. (*Li'l Bit pushes it forward.*) Do you want a cushion?

LI'L BIT: No—I'm good.

PECK: You should be able to reach all the switches and controls. Your feet should be able to push the accelerator, brake and clutch all the way down. Can you do that?

LI'L BIT: Yes.

PECK: Okay, the side mirrors. You want to be able to see just a bit of the right side of the car in the right mirror—can you?

LI'L BIT: Turn it out more.

PECK: Okay. How's that?

LI'L BIT: A little more…Okay, that's good.

PECK: Now the left—again, you want to be able to see behind you—but the left lane—adjust it until you feel comfortable. (*Li'l Bit does so.*) Next. I want you to check the rearview mirror. Angle it so you have a clear vision of the back. (*Li'l Bit does so.*) Okay. Lock your door. Make sure all the doors are locked.

LI'L BIT: (*Making a joke of it.*) But then I'm locked in with you.

PECK: Don't fool.

LI'L BIT: All right. We're locked in.

PECK: We'll deal with the air vents and defroster later. I'm teaching you on a manual—once you learn manual, you can drive anything. I want you to be able to drive any car, any machine. Manual gives you *control.* In ice, if your brakes fail, if you need more power—okay? It's a little harder at first, but then it becomes like breathing. Now. Put your hands on the wheel. I never want to see you driving with one hand. Always two hands. (*Lid Bit hesitates.*) What? What is it now?

LI'L BIT: If I put my hands on the wheel—how do I defend myself?

PECK: (*Softly.*) Now listen. Listen up close. We're not going to fool around with this. This is serious business. I will never touch you when you are driving a car. Understand?

LI'L BIT: Okay.

PECK: Hands on the nine o'clock and three o'clock position gives you maximum control and turn. (*Peck goes silent for a while. Li'l Bit waits for more instruction.*)

Okay. Just relax and listen to me, Li'l Bit, okay? I want you to lift your hands for a second and look at them. (*Li'l Bit feels a bit silly, but does it.*)

Those are your two hands. When you are driving, your life is in your own two hands. Understand? (*Li'l Bit nods.*)

I don't have any sons. You're the nearest to a son I'll ever have—and I want to give you something. Something that really matters to me.

There's something about driving—when you're in control of the car, just you and the machine and the road—that nobody can take from you. A power. I feel more myself in my car than anywhere else. And that's what I want to give to you.

There's a lot of assholes out there. Crazy men, arrogant idiots, drunks, angry kids, geezers who are blind—and you have to be ready for them. I want to teach you to drive like a man.

LI'L BIT: What does that mean?

PECK: Men are taught to drive with confidence—with aggression. The road belongs to them. They drive defensively—always looking out for the other guy. Women tend to be polite—to hesitate. And that can be fatal.

You're going to learn to think what the other guy is going to do before he does it. If there's an accident, and ten cars pile up, and people get killed, you're the one who's gonna steer through it, put your foot on the gas if you have to, and be the only one to walk away. I don't know how long you or I are going to live, but we're for damned sure not going to die in a car.

So if you're going to drive with me, I want you to take this very seriously.

LI'L BIT: I will, Uncle Peck. I want you to teach me to drive.

PECK: Good. You're going to pass your test on the first try. Perfect score. Before the next four weeks are over, you're going to know this baby inside and out. Treat her with respect.

LI'L BIT: Why is it a "she?"

PECK: Good question. It doesn't have to be a "she"—but when you close your eyes and think of someone who responds to your touch—someone who performs just for you and gives you what you ask for—I guess I always see a "she." You can call her what you like.

LI'L BIT: (*To the audience.*) I closed my eyes—and decided not to change the gender. (*A Voice:*)

Defensive driving involves defending yourself from hazardous and sudden changes in your automotive environment. By thinking ahead, the defensive driver can adjust to weather, road conditions and road kill. Good defensive driving involves mental and physical preparation. Are you prepared?

(*Another Voice chimes in:*)

You and the Reverse Gear.

LI'L BIT: 1966. The Anthropology of the Female Body in Ninth Grade—Or A Walk Down Mammary Lane. (*Throughout the following, there is occasional rhythmic beeping, like a transmitter signalling. Li'l Bit is aware of it, but can't figure out where it is coming from. No one else seems to hear it.*)

MALE GREEK CHORUS: In the hallway of Francis Scott Key Middle School. (*A bell rings; the Greek Chorus is changing classes and meets in the hall, conspiratorially.*)

TEENAGE GREEK CHORUS: She's coming! (*Li'l Bit enters the scene; the Male Greek Chorus member has a sudden, violent sneezing and lethal allergy attack.*)

FEMALE GREEK CHORUS: Jerome? Jerome? Are you all right?

MALE GREEK CHORUS: I—don't—know. I can't breathe—get Li'l Bit—

TEENAGE GREEK CHORUS: —He needs oxygen!—

FEMALE GREEK CHORUS: —Can you help us here?

LI'L BIT: What's wrong? Do you want me to get the school nurse—(*The Male Greek Chorus member wheezes, grabs his throat and sniffs at Li'l Bit's chest, which is beeping away.*)

MALE GREEK CHORUS: No—it's okay—I only get this way when I'm around an allergy trigger—

LI'L BIT: Golly. What are you allergic to?

MALE GREEK CHORUS: (*With a sudden grab of her breast.*) Foam rubber. (*The Greek Chorus members break up with hilarity; Jerome leaps away from Liz Bit's kicking rage with agility; as he retreats:*)

LI'L BIT: Jerome! Creep! Cretin! Cro-Magnon!

TEENAGE GREEK CHORUS: Rage is not attractive in a girl.

FEMALE GREEK CHORUS: Really. Get a Sense of Humor. (*A Voice echoes:*)

Good defensive driving involves mental and physical preparation. Were You Prepared?

FEMALE GREEK CHORUS: Gym Class: In the showers. (*The sudden sound of water; the Female Greek Chorus members and Li'l Bit, while fully clothed, drape towels across their fronts, miming nudity. They stand, hesitate, at an imaginary shower's edge.*)

LI'L BIT: Water looks hot.

FEMALE GREEK CHORUS: Yesss…(*Female Greek Chorus members are not going to make the first move. One dips a tentative toe under the water, clutching the towel around her.*)

LI'L BIT: Well, I guess we'd better shower and get out of here.

FEMALE GREEK CHORUS: Yep. You go ahead. I'm still cooling off.

LI'L BIT: Okay.—Sally? Are you gonna shower?

TEENAGE GREEK CHORUS: After you—(*Li'l Bit takes a deep breath for courage, drops the towel and plunges in: The two Female Greek Chorus members look at Li'l Bit in the all together, laugh, gasp and high-five each other.*) Oh my god! Can you believe—

FEMALE GREEK CHORUS: Told you! It's not foam rubber! I win! Jerome owes me fifty cents! (*A Voice editorializes:*)

Were You Prepared?

(*Li'l Bit tries to cover up, she is exposed, as suddenly 1960s Motown fills the room and we segue into:*)

FEMALE GREEK CHORUS: The Sock Hop. (*Li'l Bit stands up against the wall with her female classmates. Teenage Greek Chorus is mesmerized by the music and just sways alone, lipsynching the lyrics.*)

LI'L BIT: I don't know. Maybe it's just me—but—do you ever feel like you're just a walking Mary Jane joke?

FEMALE GREEK CHORUS: I don't know what you mean.

LI'L BIT: You haven't heard the Mary Jane jokes? (*Female Greek Chorus member shakes her head no.*) Okay. "Little Mary Jane is walking through the woods, when all of a sudden this man who was hiding behind a tree *jumps* out, *rips* open Mary Jane's blouse, and *plunges* his hands on her breasts. And Little Mary Jane just laughed and laughed because she knew her money was in her shoes." (*Li'l Bit laughs, the Female Greek Chorus does not.*)

FEMALE GREEK CHORUS: You're weird. (*In another space, in a strange light, Uncle Peck stands and stares at Li'l Bit's body. He is setting up a tripod, but he just stands, appreciative, watching her.*)

LI'L BIT: Well, don't you ever feel…self-conscious? Like you're being looked at all the time?

FEMALE GREEK CHORUS: That's not a problem for me.—Oh—look—Greg's coming over to ask you to dance. (*Teenage Greek Chorus becomes attentive, flustered. Male Greek Chorus member; as Greg, bends slightly as a very short young man, whose head is at Li'l Bit's chest level. Ardent, sincere and socially inept, Greg will become a successful gynecologist.*)

TEENAGE GREEK CHORUS: (*Softly.*) Hi, Greg. (*Greg does not hear. He is intent on only one thing.*)

MALE GREEK CHORUS: (*As Greg, to Li'l Bit.*) Good Evening. Would you care to dance?

LI'L BIT: (*Gently.*) Thank you very much, Greg—but I'm going to sit this one out.

MALE GREEK CHORUS: (*As Greg.*) Oh. Okay. I'll try my luck later. (*He disappears.*)

TEENAGE GREEK CHORUS: Oohhh. (*Li'l Bit relaxes. Then she tenses, aware of Peck's gaze.*)

FEMALE GREEK CHORUS: Take pity on him. Someone should.

LI'L BIT: But he's so short.

TEENAGE GREEK CHORUS: He can't help it.

LI'L BIT: But his head comes up to (*Li'l Bit gestures.*) here. And I think he asks me on the fast dances so he can watch me—you know—jiggle.

FEMALE GREEK CHORUS: I wish I had your problems. (*The tune changes; Greg is across the room in a flash.*)

MALE GREEK CHORUS: (*As Greg.*) Evening again. May I ask you for the honor of a spin on the floor?

LI'L BIT: I'm…very complimented, Greg. But I…I just don't do fast dances.

MALE GREEK CHORUS: (*As Greg.*) Oh. No problem. That's okay. (*He disappears. Teenage Greek Chorus watches him go.*)

TEENAGE GREEK CHORUS: That is just so—*sad.* (*Li'l Bit becomes aware of Peck waiting.*)

FEMALE GREEK CHORUS: You know, you should take it as a compliment that the guys want to watch you jiggle. They're guys. That's what they're supposed to do.

LI'L BIT: I guess you're right. But sometimes I feel like these alien life forces, these two mounds of flesh have grafted themselves onto my chest, and they're using me until they can "propagate" and take over the world and they'll just keep growing, with a mind of their own until I collapse under their weight and they suck all the nourishment out of my body and I finally just waste away while they get bigger and bigger and—(*Li'l Bit's classmates are just staring at her in disbelief.*)

FEMALE GREEK CHORUS: —You are the strangest girl I have ever met. (*Li'l Bit's trying to joke but feels on the verge of tears.*)

LI'L BIT: Or maybe someone's implanted radio transmitters in my chest at a frequency I can't hear, that girls can't detect, but they're sending out these signals to men who get mesmerized, like sirens, calling them to dash themselves on these "rocks"—(*Just then, the music segues into a slow dance, perhaps a Beach Boys tune like "Little Surfer," but over the music there's a rhythmic, hypnotic beeping transmitted, which both Greg and Peck hear. Li'l Bit hears it too, and in horror she stares at her chest. She, too, is almost hypnotized. In a trance, Greg responds to the signals and is called to her side—actually, her front. Like a zombie, he stands in front of her, his eyes planted on her two orbs.*)

MALE GREEK CHORUS: (*As Greg.*) This one's a slow dance. I hope your dance card isn't…filled? (*Li'l Bit is aware of Peck; but the signals are calling her to him. The signals are no longer transmitters, but an electromagnetic force, pulling Li'l Bit to his side, where he again waits for her to join him. She must get away from the dance floor.*)

LI'L BIT: Greg—you really are a nice boy. But I don't like to dance.

MALE GREEK CHORUS: (*As Greg.*) That's okay. We don't have to move or anything. I could just hold you and we could just *sway* a little—

LI'L BIT: —No! I'm sorry—but I think I have to leave; I hear someone calling me—(*Li'l Bit starts across the dance floor, leaving Greg behind. The beeping stops. The lights change, although the music does not. As Li'l Bit talks to the audience, she continues to change and prepare for the coming session. She should be wearing a tight tank top or a sheer blouse and very tight pants. To the audience.*)

In every man's home some small room, some zone in his house, is set aside. It might be the attic, or the study, or a den. And there's an invisible sign as if from the old treehouse: Girls Keep Out.

Here, away from female eyes, lace doilies and crochet, he keeps his manly toys: the Vargas pinups, the tackle. A scent of tobacco and WD-40. (*She inhales deeply.*) A dash of his Bay Rum. Ahhh…(*Li'l Bit savors it for just a moment more.*)

Here he keeps his secrets: a violin or saxophone, drum set or darkroom, and the stacks of *Playboy*. (*In a whisper.*) Here, in my aunt's home, it was the basement. Uncle Peck's turf.

(*A Voice commands:*)

You and the Reverse Gear.

LI'L BIT: 1965. The Photo Shoot. (*Li'l Bit steps into the scene as a nervous but curious thirteen year old. Music, from the previous scene, continues to play, changing into something like Roy Orbison later—something seductive with a beat. Peck fiddles, all business, with his camera. As in the driving lesson, he is all competency and concentration. Li'l Bit stands awkwardly. He looks through the Leica camera on the tripod, adjusts the back lighting, etc.*)

PECK: Are you cold? The lights should heat up some in a few minutes—

LI'L BIT: —Aunt Mary is?

PECK: At the National Theatre matinee. With your mother. We have time.

LI'L BIT: But—what if—

PECK: —And so what if they return? I told them you and I were going to be working with my camera. They won't come down. (*Li'l Bit is quiet, apprehensive.*)—Look, are you sure you want to do this?

LI'L BIT: I said I'd do it. But—

PECK: —I know. You've drawn the line.

LI'L BIT: (*Reassured.*) That's right. No frontal nudity.

PECK: Good heavens, girl, where did you pick that up?

LI'L BIT: (*Defensive.*) I *read*. (*Peck tries not to laugh.*)

PECK: And I read *Playboy* for the interviews. Okay. Let's try some different music. (*Peck goes to an expensive reel-to-reel and forwards. Something like "Sweet Dreams" begins to play.*)

LI'L BIT: I didn't know you listened to this.

PECK: I'm not dead, you know. I try to keep up. Do you like this song? (*Li'l Bit nods with pleasure.*) Good. Now listen—at professional photo shoots, they always play music for the models. Okay? I want you to just enjoy the music. Listen to it with your body, and just—respond.

LI'L BIT: Respond to the music with my…body?

PECK: Right. Almost like dancing. Here—let's get you on the stool, first. (*Peck comes over and helps her up.*)

LI'L BIT: But nothing showing—(*Peck firmly, with his large capable hands, brushes back her hair, angles her face. Li'l Bit turns to him like a plant to the sun.*)

PECK: Nothing showing. Just a peek. (*He holds her by the shoulder, looking at her critically. Then he unbuttons her blouse to the mid-point, and runs his hands over the flesh of her exposed sternum, arranging the fabric, just touching her. Deliberately, calmly. Asexually. Li'l Bit quiets, sits perfectly still, and closes her eyes.*) Okay?

LI'L BIT: Yes. (*Peck goes back to his camera.*)

PECK: I'm going to keep talking to you. Listen without responding to what I'm saying; you want to *listen* to the music. Sway, move just your torso or your head—I've got to check the light meter.

LI'L BIT: But—you'll be watching.

PECK: No—I'm not here—just my voice. Pretend you're in your room all alone on a Friday night with your mirror—and the music feels good—just move for me, Li'l Bit—(*Li'l Bit closes her eyes. At first self-conscious; then she gets more into the music and begins to sway. We hear the camera start to whir. Through-out the shoot, there can be a slide montage of actual shots of the actor playing Li'l Bit—interspersed with other models à la Playboy, Calvin Klein and Victoriana/Lewis Carroll's Alice Liddell.*)

That's it. That looks great. Okay. Just keep doing that. Lift your head up a bit more, good, good, just keep moving, that a girl—you're a very beautiful young woman. Do you know that? (*Li'l Bit looks up, blushes. Peck shoots the camera. The audience should see this shot on the screen.*)

LI'L BIT: No. I don't know that.

PECK: Listen to the music. (*Li'l Bit closes her eyes again.*) Well you are. For a thirteen-year-old, you have a body a twenty-year-old woman would die for.

LI'L BIT: The boys in school don't think so.

PECK: The boys in school are little Neanderthals in short pants. You're ten years ahead of them in maturity; it's gonna take a while for them to catch up. (*Peck clicks another shot; we see a faint smile on Li'l Bit on the screen.*)

Girls turn into women long before boys turn into men.

LI'L BIT: Why is that?

PECK: I don't know, Li'l Bit. But it's a blessing for men. (*Li'l Bit turns silent.*) Keep moving. Try arching your back on the stool, hands behind you, and throw your head back. (*The slide shows a* Playboy *model in this pose.*) Oohh, great. That one was great. Turn your head away, same position. (*Whir.*) Beautiful. (*Li'l Bit looks at him a bit defiantly.*)

LI'L BIT: I think Aunt Mary is beautiful. (*Peck stands still.*)

PECK: My wife is a very beautiful woman. Her beauty doesn't cancel yours out. (*More casually; he returns to the camera.*) All the women in your family are beautiful. In fact, I think all women are. You're not listening to the music. (*Peck shoots some more film in silence.*) All right, turn your head to the left. Good. Now take the back of your right hand and put in on your right cheek—your elbow angled up—now slowly, slowly, stroke your cheek, draw back your hair with the back of your hand. (*Another classic* Playboy *or Vargas.*) Good. One hand above and behind your head; stretch your body; smile. (*Another pose.*)

Li'l Bit. I want you to think of something that makes you laugh—

LI'L BIT: I can't think of anything.

PECK: Okay. Think of Big Papa chasing Grandma around the living room. (*Li'l Bit lifts her head and laughs. Click. We should see this shot.*) Good. Both hands behind your head. Great! Hold that. (*From behind his camera.*) You're doing great work. If we keep this up, in five years we'll have a really professional portfolio. (*Li'l Bit stops.*)

LI'L BIT: What do you mean in five years?

PECK: You can't submit work to *Playboy* until you're eighteen.—(*Peck continues to shoot; he knows he's made a mistake.*)

LI'L BIT: —Wait a minute. You're joking, aren't you, Uncle Peck?

PECK: Heck, no. You can't get into *Playboy* unless you're the very best. And you are the very best.

LI'L BIT: I would never do that! (*Perk stops shooting. He turns off the music.*)

PECK: Why? There's nothing wrong with *Playboy*—it's a very classy maga—

LI'L BIT: (*More upset.*) But I thought you said I should go to college!

PECK: Wait—Li'l Bit—it's nothing like that. Very respectable women model for *Playboy*—actresses with major careers—women in college—there's an Ivy League issue every—

LI'L BIT: —I'm never doing anything like that! You'd show other people these—other *men*—these—what I'm doing.—Why would you do that?! Any *boy* around here could just pick up, just go into The Stop & Go and *buy*—Why would you ever want to—to share—

PECK: —Whoa, whoa. Just stop a second and listen to me. Li'l Bit. Listen. There's nothing wrong in what we're doing. I'm very proud of you. I think you have a wonderful body and an even more wonderful mind. And of course I want other people to *appreciate* it. It's not anything shameful.

LI'L BIT: (*Hurt.*) But this is something—that I'm only doing for you. This is something—that you said was just between us.

PECK: It is. And if that's how you feel, five years from now, it will remain that way. Okay? I know you're not going to do anything you don't feel like doing.

(*He walks back to the camera.*) Do you want to stop now? I've got just a few more shots on this roll—

LI'L BIT: I don't want anyone seeing this.

PECK: I swear to you. No one will. I'll treasure this—that you're doing this only for me. (*Li'l Bit, still shaken, sits on the stool. She closes her eyes.*) Li'l Bit? Open your eyes and look at me. (*Li'l Bit shakes her head no.*) Come on. Just open your eyes, honey.

LI'L BIT: If I look at you—if I look at the camera: You're gonna know what I'm thinking. You'll see right through me—

PECK: —No, I won't. I want you to look at me. All right, then. I just want you to listen. Li'l Bit. (*She waits.*) I love you. (*Li'l Bit opens her eyes; she is startled. Peck captures the shot. On the screen we see right though her. Peck says softly.*) Do you know that? (*Li'l Bit nods her head yes.*) I have loved you every day since the day you were born.

LI'L BIT: Yes. (*Li'l Bit and Peck just look at each other. Beat. Beneath the shot of herself on the screen, Li'l Bit, still looking at her uncle, begins to unbutton her blouse.*

    A neutral Voice cuts off the above scene with:) **Implied Consent.**

As an individual operating a motor vehicle in the state of Maryland, you must abide by "Implied Consent." If you do not consent to take the blood alcohol content test, there may be severe penalties: a suspension of license, a fine, community service and a possible *jail* sentence.

(*The Voice shifts tone.*)

Idling in the Neutral Gear.

MALE GREEK CHORUS: (*Announcing.*) Aunt Mary on behalf of her husband. (*Female Greek Chorus checks her appearance, and with dignity comes to the front of the stage and sits down to talk to the audience.*)

FEMALE GREEK CHORUS: (*As Aunt Mary.*) My husband was such a good man—is. Is such a good man. Every night, he does the dishes. The second he comes home, he's taking out the garbage, or doing yard work, lifting the heavy things I can't. Everyone in the neighborhood borrows Peck—it's true—women with husbands of their own, men who just don't have Peck's abilities—there's always a knock on our door for a jump start on cold mornings, when anyone needs a ride, or help shoveling the sidewalk—I look out, and there Peck is, without a coat, pitching in.

I know I'm lucky. The man works from dawn to dusk. And the overtime he does every year—my poor sister. She sits every Christmas when I come to dinner with a new stole, or diamonds, or with the tickets to Bermuda.

I know he has troubles. And we don't talk about them. I wonder, sometimes, what happened to him during the war. The men who fought World War II didn't have "rap sessions" to talk about their feelings. Men in his generation were expected to be quiet about it and get on with their lives. And sometimes I can feel him just fighting the trouble—whatever has burrowed deeper than the scar tissue—and we don't talk about it. I know he's having a bad spell because he comes looking for me in the house, and just hangs around me until it passes. And I keep my banter light—I discuss a new recipe, or sales, or gossip—because I think domesticity can be a balm for men when they're lost. We sit in the house and listen to the peace of the clock ticking in his well-ordered living room, until it passes.

(*Sharply.*) I'm not a fool. I know what's going on. I wish you could feel how hard Peck fights against it—he's swimming against the tide, and what he needs is to see me on the shore, believing in him, knowing he won't go under, he won't give up—

And I want to say this about my niece. She's a sly one, that one is. She knows exactly what she's doing; she's twisted Peck around her little finger and thinks it's all a big secret. Yet another one who's borrowing my husband until it doesn't suit her anymore.

Well. I'm counting the days until she goes away to school. And she manipulates someone else. And then he'll come back again, and sit in the kitchen while I bake, or beside me on the sofa when I sew in the evenings. I'm a very patient woman. But I'd like my husband back.

I am counting the days.

(*A Voice repeats:*)

You and the Reverse Gear.

MALE GREEK CHORUS: Li'l Bit's Thirteenth Christmas. Uncle Peck Does the Dishes. Christmas 1964. (*Peck stands in a dress shirt and tie, nice pants, with an apron. He is washing dishes. He's in a mood we haven't seen. Quiet, brooding. Li'l Bit watches him a moment before seeking him out.*)

LI'L BIT: Uncle Peck? (*He does not answer. He continues to work on the pots.*) I didn't know where you'd gone to. (*He nods. She takes this as a sign to come in.*) Don't you want to sit with us for a while?

PECK: No. I'd rather do the dishes. (*Pause. Li'l Bit watches him.*)

LI'L BIT: You're the only man I know who does dishes. (*Peck says nothing.*) I think it's really nice.

PECK: My wife has been on her feet all day. So's your grandmother and your mother.

LI'L BIT: I know. (*Beat.*) Do you want some help?

PECK: No. (*He softens a bit towards her.*) You can help by just talking to me.

LI'L BIT: Big Papa never does the dishes. I think it's nice.

PECK: I think men should be nice to women. Women are always working for us. There's nothing particularly manly in wolfing down food and then sitting around in a stupor while the women clean up.

LI'L BIT: That looks like a really neat camera that Aunt Mary got you.

PECK: It is. It's a very nice one. (*Pause, as Peck works on the dishes and some demon that Li'l Bit intuits.*)

LI'L BIT: Did Big Papa hurt your feelings?

PECK: (*Tired.*) What? Oh, no—it doesn't hurt me. Family is family. I'd rather have him picking on me than—I don't pay him any mind, Li'l Bit.

LI'L BIT: Are you angry with us?

PECK: No, Li'l Bit. I'm not angry. (*Another pause.*)

LI'L BIT: We missed you at Thanksgiving...I did. I missed you.

PECK: Well, there were..."things" going on. I didn't want to spoil anyone's Thanksgiving.

LI'L BIT: Uncle Peck? (*Very carefully.*) Please don't drink anymore tonight.

PECK: I'm not...overdoing it.

LI'L BIT: I know. (*Beat.*) Why do you drink so much? (*Peck stops and thinks, carefully.*)

PECK: Well, Li'l Bit—let me explain it this way. There are some people who have a...a "fire" in the belly. I think they go to work on Wall Street or they run for office. And then there are people who have a "fire" in their heads—and they become writers or scientists or historians. (*He smiles a little at her.*) You. You've got a "fire" in the head. And then there are people like me.

LI'L BIT: Where do you have...a fire?

PECK: I have a fire in my heart. And sometimes the drinking helps.

LI'L BIT: There's got to be other things that can help.

PECK: I suppose there are.

LI'L BIT: Does it help—to talk to me?

PECK: Yes. It does. (*Quiet.*) I don't get to see you very much.

LI'L BIT: I know. (*Li'l Bit thinks.*) You could talk to me more.

PECK: Oh?

LI'L BIT: I could make a deal with you, Uncle Peck.

PECK: I'm listening.

LI'L BIT: We could meet and talk—once a week. You could just store up whatever's bothering you during the week—and then we could talk.

PECK: Would you like that?

LI'L BIT: As long as you don't drink. I'd meet you somewhere for lunch or for a walk—on the weekends—as long as you stop drinking. And we could talk about whatever you want.

PECK: You would do that for me?

LI'L BIT: I don't think I'd want Mom to know. Or Aunt Mary. I wouldn't want them to think—

PECK: —No. It would just be us talking.

LI'L BIT: I'll tell Mom I'm going to a girlfriend's. To study. Mom doesn't get home until six, so you can call me after school and tell me where to meet you.

PECK: You get home at four?

LI'L BIT: We can meet once a week. But only in public. You've got to let me—draw the line. And once it's drawn, you mustn't cross it.

PECK: Understood.

LI'L BIT: Would that help? (*Peck is very moved.*)

PECK: Yes. Very much.

LI'L BIT: I'm going to join the others in the living room now. (*Li'l Bit turns to go.*)

PECK: Merry Christmas, Li'l Bit. (*Li'l Bit bestows a very warm smile on him.*)

LI'L BIT: Merry Christmas, Uncle Peck.

(*A Voice dictates:*)

Shifting Forward from Second to Third Gear.

(*The Male and Female Creek Chorus members come forward.*)

MALE GREEK CHORUS: 1969. Days and Gifts: A Countdown:

FEMALE GREEK CHORUS: A note. "September 3, 1969. Li'l Bit: You've only been away two days and it feels like months. Hope your dorm room is cozy. I'm sending you this tape cassette—it's a new model—so you'll have some music in your room. Also that music you're reading about for class—*Carmina Burana.* Hope you enjoy. Only ninety days to go!—Peck."

MALE GREEK CHORUS: September 22. A bouquet of roses. A note: "Miss you like crazy. Sixty-nine days…"

TEENAGE GREEK CHORUS: September 25. A box of chocolates. A card: "Don't worry about the weight gain. You still look great. Got a post office box—write to me there. Sixty-six days.—Love, your candy man."

MALE GREEK CHORUS: October 16. A note: "Am trying to get through the Jane Austin you're reading—*Emma*—here's a book in return: *Liaisons Dangereuses.* Hope you're saving time for me." Scrawled in the margin the number: "47."

FEMALE GREEK CHORUS: November 16. "Sixteen days to go!—Hope you like the perfume.—Having a hard time reaching you on the dorm phone. You must be in the library a lot. Won't you think about me getting you your own phone so we can talk?"

TEENAGE GREEK CHORUS: November 18. "Li'l Bit—got a package returned to the P.O. Box. Have you changed dorms? Call me at work or write to the P.O. Am still on the wagon. Waiting to see you. Only two weeks more!"

MALE GREEK CHORUS: November 23. A letter. "Li'l Bit. So disappointed you couldn't come home for the turkey. Sending you some money for a nice dinner out—nine days and counting!"

GREEK CHORUS: (*In unison.*) November 25th. A letter:

LI'L BIT: "Dear Uncle Peck: I am sending this to you at work. Don't come up next weekend for my birthday. I will not be here—"

(*A Voice directs:*)

Shifting Forward from Third to Fourth Gear.

MALE GREEK CHORUS: December 10, 1969. A hotel room. Philadelphia. There is no moon tonight. (*Peck sits on the side of the bed while Li'l Bit paces. He can't believe she's in his room, but there's a desperate edge to his happiness. Li'l Bit is furious, edgy. There is a bottle of champagne in an ice bucket in a very nice hotel room.*)

PECK: Why don't you sit?

LI'L BIT: I don't want to.—What's the champagne for?

PECK: I thought we might toast your birthday—

LI'L BIT: —I am so pissed off at you, Uncle Peck.

PECK: Why?

LI'L BIT: I mean, are you crazy?

PECK: What did I do?

LI'L BIT: You scared the holy crap out of me—sending me that stuff in the mail—

PECK: They were gifts! I just wanted to give you some little perks your first semester—

LI'L BIT: —Well, what the hell were those numbers all about! Forty-four days to go—only two more weeks.—And then just numbers—69—68—67—like some serial killer!

PECK: Li'l Bit! Whoa! This is me you're talking to—I was just trying to pick up your spirits, trying to celebrate your birthday.

LI'L BIT: My *eighteenth* birthday. I'm not a child, Uncle Peck. You were counting down to my eighteenth birthday.

PECK: So?

LI'L BIT: So? So statutory rape is not in effect when a young woman turns eighteen. And you and I both know it. (*Peck is walking on ice.*)

PECK: I think you misunderstand.

LI'L BIT: I think I understand all too well. I know what you want to do five steps ahead of you doing it. Defensive Driving 101.

PECK: Then why did you suggest we meet here instead of the restaurant?

LI'L BIT: I don't want to have this conversation in public.

PECK: Fine. Fine. We have a lot to talk about.

LI'L BIT: Yeah. We do. (*Li'l Bit doesn't want to do what she has to do.*) Could I...have some of that champagne?

PECK: Of course, madam! (*Peck makes a big show of it.*) Let me do the honors. I wasn't sure which you might prefer—Taittingers or Veuve Clicquot—so I thought we'd start out with an old standard—Perrier Jouet. (*The bottle is popped.*)

Quick—Li'l Bit—your glass! (*Uncle Peck fills Li'l Bit's glass. He puts the bottle back in the ice and goes for a can of ginger ale.*) Let me get some of this ginger ale—my bubbly—and toast you. (*He turns and sees that Li'l Bit has not waited for him.*)

LI'L BIT: Oh—sorry, Uncle Peck. Let me have another. (*Peck fills her glass and reaches for his ginger ale; she stops him.*) Uncle Peck—maybe you should join me in the champagne.

PECK: You want me to—drink?

LI'L BIT: It's not polite to let a lady drink alone.

PECK: Well, missy, if you insist...(*Peck hesitates.*)—Just one. It's been a while. (*Peck fills another flute for himself.*) There. I'd like to propose a toast to you and your birthday! (*Peck sips it tentatively.*) I'm not used to this anymore.

LI'L BIT: You don't have anywhere to go tonight, do you? (*Peck hopes this is a good sign.*)

PECK: I'm all yours.—God, it's good to see you! I've gotten so used to...to...talking to you in my head. I'm used to seeing you every week—there's so much—I don't quite know where to begin. How's school, Li'l Bit?

LI'L BIT: I—it's hard. Uncle Peck. Harder than I thought it would be. I'm in the middle of exams and papers and—I don't know.

PECK: You'll pull through. You always do.

LI'L BIT: Maybe. I...might be flunking out.

PECK: You always think the worse, Li'l Bit, but when the going gets tough—(*Li'l Bit shrugs and pours herself another glass.*)—Hey, honey, go easy on that stuff, okay?

LI'L BIT: Is it very expensive?

PECK: Only the best for you. But the cost doesn't matter—champagne should be "sipped." (*Li'l Bit is quiet.*) Look—if you're in trouble in school—you can always come back home for a while.

LI'L BIT: *No*—(*Li'l Bit tries not to be so harsh.*)—Thanks, Uncle Peck, but I'll figure some way out of this.

PECK: You're supposed to get in scrapes, your first year away from home.

LI'L BIT: Right. How's Aunt Mary?

PECK: She's fine. (*Pause.*) Well—how about the new car?

LI'L BIT: It's real nice. What is it, again?

PECK: It's a Cadillac El Dorado.

LI'L BIT: Oh. Well, I'm real happy for you, Uncle Peck.

PECK: I got it for you.

LI'L BIT: What?

PECK: I always wanted to get a Cadillac—but I thought, Peck, wait until Li'l Bit's old enough—and thought maybe you'd like to drive it, too.

LI'L BIT: (*Confused.*) Why would I want to drive your car?

PECK: Just because it's the best—I want you to have the best. (*They are running out of "gas"; small talk.*)

LI'L BIT:	PECK:
Listen, Uncle Peck,	I have been thinking
I don't know how	of how to say this
to begin this,	in my head, over
but—	and over—

PECK: Sorry.

LI'L BIT: You first.

PECK: Well, your going away—has just made me realize how much I miss you. Talking to you and being alone with you. I've really come to depend on you, Li'l Bit. And it's been so hard to get in touch with you lately—the distance and—and you're never in when I call—I guess you've been living in the library—

LI'L BIT: —No—the problem is, I haven't been in the library—

PECK: —Well, it doesn't matter—I hope you've been missing me as much.

LI'L BIT: Uncle Peck—I've been thinking a lot about this—and I came here tonight to tell you that—I'm not doing very well. I'm getting very confused—I can't concentrate on my work—and now that I'm away—I've been going over and over it in my mind—and I don't want us to "see" each other anymore. Other than with the rest of the family.

PECK: (*Quiet.*) Are you seeing other men?

LI'L BIT: (*Getting agitated.*) I—no, that's not the reason—I—well, yes, I am seeing other—listen, it's not really anybody's business!

PECK: Are you in love with anyone else?

LI'L BIT: That's not what this is about.

PECK: Li'l Bit—you're scared. Your mother and your grandparents have filled your head with all kinds of nonsense about men—I hear them working on you all the time—and you're scared. It won't hurt you—if the man you go to bed with really loves you. (*Li'l Bit is scared. She starts to tremble.*) And I have loved you since the day I held you in my hand. And I think everyone's just gotten you frightened to death about something that is just like breathing—

LI'L BIT: Oh, my god—(*She takes a breath.*) I can't see you anymore, Uncle Peck. (*Peck downs the rest of his champagne.*)

PECK: Li'l Bit. Listen. Listen. Open your eyes and look at me. Come on. Just open your eyes, honey. (*Li'l Bit, eyes squeezed shut, refuses.*) All right then. I just want you to listen. Li'l Bit—I'm going to ask you just this once. Of your own free will. Just lie down on the bed with me—our clothes on—just lie down with me, a man and a woman …and let's… hold one another. Nothing else. Before you say anything else. I want

the chance to… hold you. Because sometimes the body knows things that the mind isn't listening to …and after I've held you, then I want you to tell me what you feel.

LI'L BIT: You'll just…hold me?

PECK: Yes. And then you can tell me what you're feeling. (*Li'l Bit—half wanting to run, half wanting to get it over with, half wanting to be held by him.*)

LI'L BIT: Yes. All right. Just hold. Nothing else. (*Peck lies down on the bed and holds his arms out to her. Li'l Bit lies beside him, putting her head on his chest. He looks as if he's trying to soak her into his pores by osmosis. He strokes her hair, and she lies very still. The Male Greek Chorus member and the Female Greek Chorus member as Aunt Mary come into the room.*)

MALE GREEK CHORUS: Recipe for a Southern Boy:

FEMALE GREEK CHORUS: (*As Aunt Mary.*) A drawl of molasses in the way he speaks.

MALE GREEK CHORUS: A gumbo of red and brown mixed in the cream of his skin. (*While Peck lies, his eyes closed, Li'l Bit rises in the bed and responds to her aunt.*)

LI'L BIT: Warm brown eyes—

FEMALE GREEK CHORUS: (*As Aunt Mary.*) Bedroom eyes—

MALE GREEK CHORUS: A dash of Southern Baptist Fire and Brimstone—

LI'L BIT: A curl of Elvis on his forehead—

FEMALE GREEK CHORUS: (*As Aunt Mary.*) A splash of Bay Rum—

MALE GREEK CHORUS: A closely shaven beard that he razors just for you—

FEMALE GREEK CHORUS: (*As Aunt Mary.*) Large hands—rough hands—

LI'L BIT: Warm hands—

MALE GREEK CHORUS: The steel of the military in his walk—

LI'L BIT: The slouch of the fishing skiff in his walk—

MALE GREEK CHORUS: Neatly pressed khakis—

FEMALE GREEK CHORUS: (*As Aunt Mary.*) And under the wide leather of the belt—

LI'L BIT: Sweat of cypress and sand—

MALE GREEK CHORUS: Neatly pressed khakis—

LI'L BIT: His heart beating Dixie—

FEMALE GREEK CHORUS: (*As Aunt Mary.*) The whisper of the zipper—you could reach out with your hand and—

LI'L BIT: His mouth—

FEMALE GREEK CHORUS: (*As Aunt Mary.*) You could just reach out and—

LI'L BIT: Hold him in your hand—

FEMALE GREEK CHORUS: (*As Aunt Mary.*) And his mouth—(*Li'l Bit rises above her uncle and looks at his mouth; she starts to lower herself to kiss him—and wrenches herself free. She gets up from the bed.*)

LI'L BIT: —I've got to get back.

PECK: Wait—Li'l Bit. Did you…feel nothing?

LI'L BIT: (*Lying.*) No. Nothing.

PECK: Do you—do you think of me? (*The Greek Chorus whispers.*)

FEMALE GREEK CHORUS: (*As Aunt Mary.*) Khakis—

MALE GREEK CHORUS: Bay Rum—

FEMALE GREEK CHORUS: (*As Aunt Mary.*) The whisper of the—

LI'L BIT: —No. (*Peck, in a rush, trembling, gets something out of his pocket.*)

PECK: I'm forty-five. That's not old for a man. And I haven't been able to do anything else but think of you. I can't concentrate on my work—Li'l Bit. You've got to—I want you to think about what I am about to ask you.

LI'L BIT: I'm listening. (*Peck opens a small ring box.*)

PECK: I want you to be my wife.

LI'L BIT: This isn't happening.

PECK: I'll tell Mary I want a divorce. We're not blood-related. It would be legal—

LI'L BIT: —What have you been thinking! You are married to my aunt, Uncle Peck. She's my family. You have—you have gone way over the line. Family is family. (*Quickly, Li'l Bit flies through the room, gets her coat.*) I'm leaving. Now. I am not seeing you. Again. (*Peck lies down on the bed for a moment, trying to absorb the terrible news. For a moment, he almost curls into a fetal position.*)

I'm not coming home for Christmas. You should go home to Aunt Mary. Go home now, Uncle Peck. (*Peck gets control, and sits, rigid.*)

Uncle Peck?—I'm sorry but I have to go. (*Pause.*)

Are you all right. (*With a discipline that comes from being told that boys don't cry, Peck stands upright.*)

PECK: I'm fine. I just think—I need a real drink. (*The Male Greek Chorus has become a bartender. At a small counter, he is lining up shots for Peck. As Li'l Bit narrates, we see Peck sitting, carefully and calmly downing shot glasses.*)

LI'L BIT: (*To the audience.*) I never saw him again. I stayed away from Christmas and Thanksgiving for years after.

It took my uncle seven years to drink himself to death. First he lost his job, then his wife, and finally his driver's license. He retreated to his house, and had his bottles delivered. (*Peck stands, and puts his hands in front of him—almost like Superman flying.*)

One night he tried to go downstairs to the basement—and he flew down the steep basement stairs. My aunt came by weekly to put food on the porch, and she noticed the mail and the papers stacked up, uncollected.

They found him at the bottom of the stairs. Just steps away from his dark room.

Now that I'm old enough, there are some questions I would have liked to have asked him. Who did it to you, Uncle Peck? How old were you? Were you eleven? (*Peck moves to the driver's seat of the car and waits.*)

Sometimes I think of my uncle as a kind of Flying Dutchman. In the opera, the Dutchman is doomed to wander the sea; but every seven years he can come ashore, and if he finds a maiden who will love him of her own free will—he will be released.

And I see Uncle Peck in my mind, in his Chevy '56, a spirit driving up and down the back roads of Carolina—looking for a young girl who, of her own free will, will love him. Release him.

(*A Voice states:*)

You and the Reverse Gear

LI'L BIT: The summer of 1962. On Men, Sex, and Women: Part III: (*Li'l Bit steps, as an eleven year old, into:*)

FEMALE GREEK CHORUS: (*As Mother.*) It is out of the question. End of Discussion.

LI'L BIT: But why?

FEMALE GREEK CHORUS: (*As Mother.*) Li'l Bit—we are not discussing this. I said no.

LI'L BIT: But I could spend an extra week at the beach! You're not telling me why!

FEMALE GREEK CHORUS: (*As Mother.*) Your uncle pays entirely too much attention to you.

LI'L BIT: He listens to me when I talk. And—and he talks to me. He teaches me about things. Mama—he knows an awful lot.

FEMALE GREEK CHORUS: (*As Mother.*) He's a small town hick who's learned how to mix drinks from Hugh Hefner.

LI'L BIT: Who's Hugh Hefner? (*Beat.*)

FEMALE GREEK CHORUS: (*As Mother.*) I am not letting an eleven-year-old girl spend seven hours alone in the car with a man...I don't like the way your uncle looks at you.

LI'L BIT: For god's sake, mother! Just because you've gone through a bad time with my father—you think every man is evil!

FEMALE GREEK CHORUS: (*As Mother.*) Oh no, Li'l Bit—not all men...We...we just haven't been very lucky with the men in our family.

LI'L BIT: Just because you lost your husband—I still deserve a chance at having a father! Someone! A man who will look out for me! Don't I get a chance?

FEMALE GREEK CHORUS: (*As Mother.*) I will feel terrible if something happens.

LI'L BIT: Mother! It's in your head! Nothing will happen! I can take care of myself. And I can certainly handle Uncle Peck.

FEMALE GREEK CHORUS: (*As Mother.*) All right. But I'm warning you—if anything happens, I hold you responsible. (*Li'l Bit moves out of this scene and toward the car.*)

LI'L BIT: 1962. On the Back Roads of Carolina: The First Driving Lesson. (*The Teenage Greek Chorus member stands apart on stage. She will speak all of Li'l Bit's lines. Li'l Bit sits beside Peck in the front seat. She looks at him closely, remembering.*)

PECK: Li'l Bit? Are you getting tired?

TEENAGE GREEK CHORUS: A little.

PECK: It's a long drive. But we're making really good time. We can take the back road from here and see...a little scenery. Say—I've got an idea—(*Peck checks his rearview mirror.*)

TEENAGE GREEK CHORUS: Are we stopping, Uncle Peck?

PECK: There's no traffic here. Do you want to drive?

TEENAGE GREEK CHORUS: I can't drive.

PECK: It's easy. I'll show you how. I started driving when I was your age. Don't you want to?—

TEENAGE GREEK CHORUS: —But it's against the law at my age!

PECK: And that's why you can't tell anyone I'm letting you do this—

TEENAGE GREEK CHORUS: —But—I can't reach the pedals.

PECK: You can sit in my lap and steer. I'll push the pedals for you. Did your father ever let you drive his car?

TEENAGE GREEK CHORUS: No way.

PECK: Want to try?

TEENAGE GREEK CHORUS: Okay. (*Li'l Bit moves into Peck's lap. She leans against him, closing her eyes.*)

PECK: You're just a little thing, aren't you? Okay—now think of the wheel as a big clock—I want you to put your right hand on the clock where three o'clock would be; and your left hand on the nine—(*Li'l Bit puts one hand to Peck's face, to stroke him. Then, she takes the wheel.*)

TEENAGE GREEK CHORUS: Am I doing it right?

PECK: That's right. Now, whatever you do, don't let go of the wheel. You tell me whether to go faster or slower—

TEENAGE GREEK CHORUS: Not so fast, Uncle Peck!

PECK: Li'l Bit—I need you to watch the road—(*Peck puts his hands on Li'l Bit's breasts. She relaxes against him, silent, accepting his touch.*)

TEENAGE GREEK CHORUS: Uncle Peck—what are you doing?

PECK: Keep driving. (*He slips his hands under her blouse.*)

TEENAGE GREEK CHORUS: Uncle Peck—please don't do this—

PECK: —Just a moment longer…(*Peck tenses against Li'l Bit.*)

TEENAGE GREEK CHORUS. (*Trying not to cry.*) This isn't happening. (*Peck tenses more, sharply. He buries his face in Li'l Bit's neck, and moans softly. The Teenage Greek Chorus exits, and Li'l Bit steps out of the car. Peck, too, disappears.*

    A Voice reflects:)

Driving in Today's World.

LI'L BIT: That day was the last day I lived in my body. I retreated above the neck, and I've lived inside the "fire" in my head ever since.

    And now that seems like a long, long time ago. When we were both very young.

    And before you know it, I'll be thirty-five. That's getting up there for a woman. And I find myself believing in things that a younger self vowed never to believe in. Things like family and forgiveness.

    I know I'm lucky. Although I still have never known what it feels like to jog or dance. Anything that…"jiggles." I do like to watch people on the dance floor, or out on the running paths, just jiggling away. And I say—good for them. (*Li'l Bit moves to the car with pleasure.*)

    The nearest sensation I feel—of flight in the body—I guess I feel when I'm driving. On a day like today. It's five A.M. The radio says it's going to be clear and crisp. I've got five hundred miles of highway ahead of me—and some back roads too. I filled the tank last night, and had the oil checked. Checked the tires, too. You've got to treat her…with respect.

    First thing I do is: Check under the car. To see if any two year olds or household cats have crawled beneath, and strategically placed their skulls behind my back tires. (*Li'l Bit crouches.*)

    Nope. Then I get in the car. (*Li'l Bit does so.*)

I lock the doors. And turn the key. Then I adjust the most important control on the dashboard—the radio—(*Li'l Bit turns the radio on: We hear all of the Greek Chorus overlapping, and static.*)

FEMALE GREEK CHORUS: (*Overlapping.*)—"You were so tiny you fit in his hand—"

MALE GREEK CHORUS: (*Overlapping.*)—"How is Shakespeare gonna help her lie on her back in the—"

TEENAGE GREEK CHORUS: (*Overlapping.*)—"Am I doing it right?" (*Li'l Bit fine-tunes the radio station. A song like "Dedicated to the One I Love" or Orbison's "Sweet Dreams" comes on, and cuts off the Greek Chorus.*)

LI'L BIT: Ahh…(*Beat.*) I adjust my seat. Fasten my seat belt. Then I check the right side mirror—check the left side. (*She does.*) Finally, I adjust the rearview mirror. (*As Li'l Bit adjusts the rearview mirror, a faint light strikes the spirit of Uncle Peck, who is sitting in the back seat of the car. She sees him in the mirror. She smiles at him, and he nods at her. They are happy to be going for a long drive together. Li'l Bit slips the car into first gear; to the audience.*) And then—I floor it. (*Sound of a car taking off. Blackout.*)

    END OF PLAY

PERFORMING *HOW I LEARNED TO DRIVE*

Paula Vogel's award-winning play, *How I Learned to Drive,* was developed at the Perseverance Theater in Juneau, Alaska, under the direction of Molly Smith, now artistic director of Arena Stage in Washington, D.C. The play had its New York production Off Broadway at the Vineyard Theater in February 1997 under the direction of Mark Brokaw with Mary-Louise Parker and David Morse playing Li'l Bit and Uncle Peck. The production moved to the larger Century Theater in April. The play has since been performed in numerous regional theaters and in London.

    Vogel wrote *How I Learned to Drive* to be performed by five actors without an intermission. Using the device of a Greek chorus, three actors play the male, female, and teenage choruses.

The chorus fills in the environment and becomes members of Li'l Bit's family—grandfather, grandmother, mother, Aunt Mary, waiter, and high school students. Vogel designated that the script's bold-faced titles should be spoken in a neutral voice ("the type of voice that driver education films employ") as announcements over the theater's sound system: "Safety First—You and Driver Education." In some productions the titles have been assigned to members of the Greek chorus and announced by the actors from the stage. The various automobile sounds (key turning in the ignition, sounds of a car accelerating, a car radio playing 1960s tunes, etc.) underscore the play's action—the driving lesson and Li'l Bit's sexual initiation. In addition, Vogel provides notations for slides and projections in the script but accepts the fact that the play can be performed without the images. With awareness of the practical issues of staging, she writes, "...it would be nice to have slides of erotic photographs women and cars..." Projections were not used in the original New York production.

Vogel created the role of Li'l Bit for an actress whose age ranges from eleven years old to forty-something. However, when the twenty-something Mary-Louise Parker was cast in the New York production, Vogel conceded that the age range was flexible. She changed the age of Li'l Bit in the last monologue to thirty-five to accommodate the actress's age-range and noted the appropriate change in the dialogue ("And before you know it, I'll be thirty-five"). As for Peck, Vogel called for a man in his forties. Envisioning a handsome, avuncular Gregory Peck, she said that Uncle Peck should be played by an actor one might cast in the role of Atticus in Harper Lee's *To Kill A Mockingbird*. In all instances, Vogel resisted turning the play into a contest between predator and prey.

Jill Dolan reviewed the Vineyard Theater production of *How I Learned to Drive* and wrote about Vogel's dramaturgy as "at once creative, highly imaginative, and brutally honest." She concluded, "Vogel's play is about forgiveness and family, about the instability of sexuality, about the unpredictable ways in which we learn who we are, how we desire, and how our growth is built on loss."[10]

CRITICS' NOTEBOOK

As a body of feminist playwriting and practice became evident, scholars set about creating a field of criticism on feminist drama and theater. Jill Dolan's work on the feminist spectator, written in 1991, presents a unique perspective on feminist performance criticism. The interview is another strategy of feminist criticism. Alexis Greene's interview with Paula Vogel is a variation on feminist writing as playwrights and practitioners talk about their process in a semi-public forum.

Jill Dolan, from *The Feminist Spectator as Critic**

In the illusionist tradition that dominates American theatre practice, performers and spectators are separated by a curtain of light that helps maintain the fictitious fourth wall. Performers facing the audience are blinded by the workings of the apparatus that frames them. The blinding lights set them apart from the sea of silhouetted heads without faces toward whom their words flow. The spectators' individuality is subsumed under an assumption of commonality; their differences from each other are disguised by anonymity. The spectators become the audience whom the performers address—albeit obliquely, given realist theatre conventions—as a singular mass.

The performance apparatus that directs the performer's address, however, works to constitute that amorphous, anonymous mass as a particular subject position. The lighting, setting, costumes, blocking, text—all the material aspects of theatre—are manipulated so that the performance's meanings are intelligible to a particular spectator, constructed in a particular way by the terms of its address. Historically, in North American culture, this spectator has been assumed to be white, middle-class, heterosexual,

---

*Jill Dolan, *The Feminist Spectator as Critic* (Ann Arbor: The University of Michigan Press, 1991): 1–2.

and male. That theatre creates an ideal spectator carved in the likeness of the dominant culture whose ideology he represents is the motivating assumption behind the discourse of feminist performance criticism.

Since the resurgence of American feminism in the 1960s, feminist theatre makers and critics have worked to expose the gender-specific nature of theatrical representation, and to radically modify its terms. Denaturalizing the position of the ideal spectator as a representative of the dominant culture enables the feminist critic to point out that every aspect of theatrical production, from the types of plays and performances produced to the texts that are ultimately canonized, is determined to reflect and perpetuate the ideal spectator's ideology.

Because its critique centers on the ideological assumptions that create an ideal spectator for representation, feminist performance criticism is subversive by nature. It is grounded in the belief that representation—visual art, theatre and performance, film and dance—creates from an ideological base meanings that have very specific, material consequences.

The feminist critic can be seen as a "resistant reader," who analyzes a performance's meaning by reading against the grain of stereotypes and resisting the manipulation of both the performance text and the cultural text that it helps to shape. By exposing the ways in which dominant ideology is naturalized by the performance's address to the ideal spectator, feminist performance criticism works as political intervention in an effort toward cultural change....

Alexis Greene, from an Interview with Paula Vogel*

❦

AG: What does it mean to you, at the beginning of this century, to be a woman who writes plays in America?

*Alexis Greene, ed. *Women Who Write Plays: Interviews with American Dramatists* (Hanover, NH: Smith and Kraus, Inc., 2001): 426.

PV: I don't think I have a single goal when writing. But I do have a desire to see an American identity forged by as many writers of as many ethnicities, races, women, and in terms of sexuality, gays and lesbians, as possible. I do have a desire to see identity forged outside of the mainstream, outside of the status quo. So that's one of my desires and one of my goals. I'd like to see women looking at and defining male identity as women writers. I'd like to see women looking at female desire and sexuality.

My fear is that before we embrace this rainbow coalition of writers and viewpoints, we will have a backlash. As a theater and entertainment industry, I think we will have a last gasp of exclusion. I am hoping that the twenty-first century is not a male world anymore. I'm hoping it's not a white world anymore. I'm hoping it's an inclusive world. But I fear a circling-the-wagons mentality. This is happening right now on Broadway.

AG: A backlash arising from what?

PV: Fear and the politics of fear. Time and again, the political Right in this country turns us back. I have been noticing with some pain, in terms of Broadway and the industry in New York, that American playwrights are being excluded from the notion not only of what is popular entertainment, but the notion of what is high culture. At this point in time, that we still have an internalized self-hatred and esteem problem—a cultural inferiority complex—is very depressing. I think the majority of American playwrights, my colleagues, have been dismayed and depressed in the last seasons by the definitions of what is commercial and what will appeal to audiences. England is not my mother country. I don't recognize it as my mother tongue or my motherland. I would rather have a mother tongue and a motherland forged by people like José Rivera, Philip Kan Gotanda, Suzan-Lori Parks, and Nilo Cruz. There is a notion of American identity that is coming in an exciting way not only from regional theater but also from off Broadway and off-off Broadway. That is the twenty-first century. How long, however, there will be resistance to it, I don't know.

REVISITING FEMINIST DRAMA

The feminist movement, which emerged in the in the 1970s, has had an enormous impact on politics and art in the United States and Western Europe. Examining the gender-biased "image of woman" in patriarchal cultures, feminist playwrights have militantly and didactically centered "woman" as drama's subject and evolved play forms analogous to women's biological cycles, sexual experiences, domestic routines. In general, their subjects are the alienation and repression of women throughout history. A playwright, like María Irene Fornés, who confronts the contemporary social conditioning and abusive behavior of women *and* men has been both embraced by the feminists and rejected by them. Fornés herself rejects the categorizing of her work. She has remarked that to read *The Conduct of Life* as being about the subjugation of Latin American women is to limit the scope of the work. She has said of her writing that if her expression is "honest," it is "inevitable that it will often speak in a feminine way," but that she has never set about to write in a particular manner or about a particular subject.[11]

Fornés' work underscores the misunderstandings and contradictions inherent in feminist writing today. Women artists write from their personal perspectives which may or may not be philosophical and political observations about the role of women in Western society. Since the women's movement is over twenty years old, certain assumptions are brought to their work by readers and audiences; that is, women as subjects are expected to be shown in traditional or nontraditional roles, or in roles of subservience, subjugation, or dominance to illustrate certain themes. However, feminine voices, in particular playwrights and performance artists, entering the mainstream of theater today introduce not only women's perspectives but unexpected agendas and new dramatic forms. By enlarging the parameters of Western drama, feminist writing reaches beyond narrow categories and brings a different sensibility to examine age-old questions about human choice, history, suffrage, and liberation.

One vital new direction of *modernist* writing in the last decade of the twentieth century has been theatrical work that addresses issues of cultural diversity in a Western Eurocentric society such as the United States has been since its founding. *Multiculturalism* and *interculturalism* are labels used to describe the rich diversity of American society and the fractures that appear at the seams of cultural hegemony as well. An unusually large number of playwrights and performance artists have emerged on the American scene in the last three decades. They address their ethnic identities and cultural differences and make art out of some of the most timely social and political issues of the new millennium.

NOTES

1. Steven Drukman, "Interview with Paula Vogel," *The New York Times* (March 16, 1997): II 6:1.
2. Sue-Ellen Case, *Feminism and Theatre* (New York: Methuen, 1988): 5–27.
3. Case 114–115.
4. Kathy Sova, "Time to Laugh: An Interview with the Playwright," *American Theatre,* 14.2 (February 1997): 24.
5. David Savran, "Paula Vogel," from *The Playwright's Voice: American Dramatists on Memory, Writing and the Politics of Culture* (New York: Theatre Communications Group, 1999): 265.
6. "Vogel, Paula," *1998 Current Biography Yearbook* (New York: The H. W. Wilson Company, 1998): 589.
7. *The New York Times* (March 16, 1997).
8. Stephanie Coen, "Interview with Paula Vogel," *American Theatre,* 10.4 (April 1993): 26–27.
9. Alan Shepard and Mary Lamb, "The Memory Palace in Paula Vogel's Plays," *Southern Women Playwrights: New Essays in Literary History and Criticism,* Eds. Robert L. McDonald and Linda Rohrer Paige (Tuscaloosa, AL: The University of Alabama Press, 2002): 214.
10. Jill Dolan, "Review of *How I Learned to Drive,*" *Theatre Journal,* 50 (March 1988): 128.
11. María Irene Fornés, "Creative Danger," *American Theater,* 2, No. 5 (September 1985): 13, 15.

CHAPTER 14

UNDERSTANDING THE "NEW" DOCUDRAMA

(Left to right) Mercedes Herrero, Greg Pierotti (back to camera and on video monitors), Kelli Simpkins, and Barbara Pitts in The Denver Center Theatre Company/Tectonic Theater Project World Premiere (2000) of *The Laramie Project* by Moisés Kaufman. (Photo by Dan McNeil.)

Artists are recording our times…
—Robert Wilson

RECONSTRUCTING MODERN HISTORY IN THE EPIC STYLE

German-born Erwin Piscator (1893–1966), the leading exponent of political theater in the Weimar Republic following his experiences in the trenches during the First World War, initiated a cinematic style for documenting current events in the theater. Dismissed from the Volksbühne in Berlin for promoting political ideas, he created his own working-class theater (the Piscator Theater) in 1927 and an "agit-prop" style (short for agitation-propaganda) for the presentation of documentary revues that held up current social and political events for examination and reform.

As early as 1925, he had fully developed a documentary style for creating and staging scripts. *In Spite of Everything* featured a documentary revue of events from the outbreak of the First World War to the assassinations of Karl Liebknecht and Rosa Luxemburg in 1919. Nonetheless, it would be another forty years before playwrights wrote documentary plays that utilized Piscator's innovations.

Piscator's early scripts were pasted up from newspapers, parliamentary speeches, personal memoirs, and backed up with projections from films and newsreels of the day. He soon developed elaborate machinery (moving treadmills, rear projections, large cycloramas) to show historical process in the making. For a production of Ernst Toller's *Hurrah, We Live!* (1927), Piscator presented a cross-section of Weimar society on a four-story set with rear-projections of décor. In reworking Alexey Tolstoy's *Rasputin* (1927), he showed the historical events that led up to the 1917 Russian revolution by making use of segments with actors and settings, screens lowered for illustrative projections, and side screens for the projection of carefully researched data on the chronology of social, political, and military events leading up to the revolution.

The adaptation of Jaroslav Haček's satirical novel about the First World War, *The Good Soldier Schweik*, was Piscator's best-known and most influential work from this period. Bertolt Brecht worked on the script for *Schweik* and later appropriated Piscator's use of the term *epic* theater, which Piscator had defined as expanding the dramatic text to expose its sociopolitical context. Mordecai Gorelik credits Piscator with shaping epic theater in practice in the 1920s and Brecht with shaping the artistic theory.[1]

In the celebrated 1928 production of *The Good Soldier Schweik*, which established Piscator as an innovator, he introduced two conveyor belts as treadmills, whose combined width formed the depth of the stage and made possible the perpetual motion of troops and machinery. Three thin portals spanned the depth of the stage, which was closed in with a translucent drop in the rear. Czech folksongs were played on a hurdy-gurdy and cartoons drawn by artist Georg Grosz were projected onto the backdrop as animations to satirize Austro-Hungarian officials in the First World War. *Schweik* recounts the adventures of a common foot soldier, a Sancho Panza-type figure from *Don Quixote*, who, from the time he is conscripted, absorbs all the lessons that the war has to offer about imperialism, devastation, demoralization, and economic hardship. The "conveyor belt" effect supported the story of the wandering soldier by literally transporting the central character (played by the great comic actor Max Pallenberg) from place to place and reinforcing the effects of the relentless war machine on the common soldier and citizens.

Accused of turning art into propaganda, Piscator responded that his audiences were in the middle of life and death struggles for survival following a devastating war and were looking to the theater for guidance. That theater, in Piscator's view, was the epic theater that moved beyond emotional titillation to teach opposition to the cruelty and stupidity fostered by governments in their citizens. The Austrian war machine in *Schweik* was portrayed as the prototype for all war machines that grind out war propaganda, police spying, conscription of ill-suited soldiers, mobilization, transportation, bombardment, and multitudes of dead. At the play's end, Schweik dies following a shell burst. From the upper corner of the rear screen, a procession of crosses moves toward the audience; the effect was a marching rain of crosses moving closer and closer to the spectators.

In 1931, Piscator went to the Soviet Union to make a film and then moved to the United States in 1938 as Stalin's purges began to engulf Soviet artists. In New York City, he set up the Dramatic Workshop at the New School for Social Research where he taught and staged a number of plays, including a 1942 adaptation of Leo Tolstoy's *War and Peace*. In 1951, he returned to Germany as a freelance director and in 1962 became head of the new Freie Volksbühne in West Berlin. Here, he applied the techniques he had devised for staging epic theater to the new "documentary" drama written in the 1960s with the purpose of investigating large historical events that shaped modern history. Piscator staged productions of Rolf Hochhuth's *The Representative* (1963, called *The Deputy* in the United States), which examined Pope Pius XII's complicity in the Holocaust; Heinar Kipphardt's *In the Matter of J. Robert Oppenheimer* (1964), derived from transcripts of the hearings at which the physicist who developed the U.S. atomic bomb was charged with treason; and Peter Weiss's *The Investigation* (1965), based on transcripts of the 1963–65 Auschwitz trials in Frankfurt, Germany.

Piscator's staging practices in the creation of a documentary drama and a hard-edged production style influenced the "living newspaper" productions of the Federal Theater Project in the United States in the 1930s and Joan Littlewood's work at the Theater Workshop in East London beginning in 1945. In the 1990s, the works of Emily Mann and Moisés Kaufman owe a great debt to Erwin Piscator's documentary style, to the Federal Theater Project's "living newspaper," and to the playwrights in the sixties who turned to historical records, film clips, tape recordings, and projected newspaper headlines to create documentary plays.

THE LIVING NEWSPAPER

Out of the Great Depression in the United States in the 1930s a uniquely indigenous documentary theater emerged under the auspices of the Federal Theater Project. Established under the Works Progress Administration (WPA) in 1935 by an Act of the U.S. Congress, the Federal Theater Project became the first federally funded and sponsored theater in America. Hallie Flanagan Davis (1890–1969) was then head of the experimental theater at Vassar College in Poughkeepsie, New York, and was named director of the Federal Theater Project. The mandate was twofold: (1) to give meaningful employment to out-of-work theater professionals and (2) to provide "free, adult, uncensored theater" to audiences throughout the country. At its peak, 10,000 people were employed with theaters in forty states. During its four years of existence (1935–39), twelve million people saw a diversity of performers and plays ranging from classics and children's theater to musicals, religious works, and African-American plays. Of the new work developed under the FTP, the most innovative and controversial was the Living Newspaper, suggested by playwright Elmer Rice and sponsored by the national union of newspaper workers (the American Newspaper Guild). The Living Newspaper, like Piscator's political theater and the theatrical bulletins of the earlier Bolshevik revolutionary government, proposed to dramatize the important social and political issues of the day by utilizing documented facts and statistics, newspaper headlines and loudspeakers, large casts, and sparse settings.

Now celebrated for developing a cinematic form that integrated factual data on current social problems with dramatic scenes, the Living Newspaper in the United States called attention to current social issues. The documentary method defined a problem and then called for a specific action to be taken. The theatrical techniques incorporated short episodic scenes, visual projections, musical interludes, and parts of authentic speeches, documents, and maps. The most successful productions were based on strong, well-crafted scripts that addressed such diverse problems as public housing, health care, utility companies, farm subsidies, and environmental issues. Arthur Arent wrote the three most successful Living Newspaper scripts: *Triple-A Plowed Under* (1936) dealt with agriculture and the need for farmers and consumers to unite to improve their incomes and provide cheaper food; *Power* (1937) with rural electrification and the plea for public ownership of utilities; and *One-Third of a Nation* (1939) with the dire state of urban housing for the poor and working-class.

Arthur Arent devised scripts that focused on a social problem and a central character, an Everyman figure, to serve as a guide leading to an understanding of the subject and its human dimensions. The background to the problem was explored with facts and figures, the dire human consequences depicted in human terms, and possible solutions set forth. In the manner of epic writing, the dialogue was taken from speeches, newspaper stories, government data, and other documents, and the staging techniques were adapted from the presentational style of epic theater. The off-stage Voice of the Living Newspaper, for example, established date, time, and location of the social issue and interrupted and commented on the stage events.

Under the auspices of the Federal Theater Project, the first Living Newspaper production, called *Triple-A Plowed Under,* opened with twenty-six scenes each based on undisputed newspaper accounts and published statements accompanied by projected images, contrapuntal music, and announcements and speeches delivered over a loudspeaker system. The play traced the origins of President Franklin D. Roosevelt's New Deal Agricultural Adjustment Administration, the problems resulting from the invalidation of the new administrative unit by the U.S. Supreme Court, and the economic consequences of the Court's action. The economic crisis in the life of the nation was documented in speeches, statistics, and reenactments of news events. In the ever-spreading panorama of crisis on the nation's farms and markets, one projection showed hog farms and the dwindling size of the farms and the animals accompanied by an announcer's voice on the loudspeaker: "To curtail

production, Hog production was cut from sixty million in 1933 to thirty-seven million in 1935…." The final scene depicted farmers and unemployed workers arriving at an understanding of their common needs; the broadcast on the loudspeaker announced the formation of a farmer-labor political alliance.

One-Third of a Nation, the most powerful and successful of the Living Newspapers, critiqued slum housing conditions and generated moral outrage in every city where it was staged. For the New York production, Howard Bay used steel scaffolding to reproduce a four-story tenement building seventy feet high with windows, balconies, and fire escapes. To make its point, the play began with the noise, smoke, and panic of a simulated tenement fire that focused the reality of slum life.

The Living Newpaper's outspoken criticism of social problems (and their antiestablishment solutions) was eventually interpreted by congressional conservatives as left-wing (or worse) and ultimately led to a heated debate in Congress and to the eventual refusal of Congress to appropriate funds for the continuance of the Federal Theater Project. Hallie Flanagan said, "It was ended because Congress, in spite of protests from many of its own members, treated the Federal Theater not as a human issue or a cultural issue, but as a political issue."[2]

Deprived of funding, the Federal Theater Project disbanded on June 30, 1939. The many outcomes of this vibrant experiment included Hallie Flanagan's account, called *Arena* (1940), of the convoluted history of the Federal Theater Project, followed in 1974 by the establishment of the Federal Theater Project Research Center at George Mason University in New Jersey, although original material in the archive was moved to the Library of Congress in 1994. In addition, the "theater of fact," another version of docudrama, was revived in the sixties with protests against the Vietnam War and memories of the Holocaust in Europe. Again, beginning in the 1980s, playwrights addressed concerns for the deep roots of racism and homophobia in American society in the documentary style. Emily Mann's *Still Life* (1980) and Moisés Kaufman's *The Laramie Project* (1998–2000) used a documentary style of writing and performance to confront issues of questionable wars, racism, and homophobia. The terms now used to describe the new work are *documentary plays* and *docudrama*.

THE "NEW" DOCUMENTARY PLAY

Although it is possible to show that epic theater is the predecessor of documentary films and the learning plays of the Living Newspaper, it would be an exaggeration to suggest that all plays that inquire into social and political data are indebted to the work of Erwin Piscator and Bertolt Brecht. Art has always tried to be instructive and to teach audiences about truth and the exigencies of human behavior.

Journalist Sophie Treadwell's play *Machinal* (1928) was based on a real-life murder trial and the execution of Ruth Snyder, but the scenes, design, and performance style were more expressionistic than documentary in telling the semifictionalized story of a woman who is robotized by family, work, husband, lover, and life.

Playwright and director Emily Mann (b. 1952) prefers to call her plays documentaries—even theater of testimony—rather than docudrama. Beginning with interviews with people who witnessed the event, she distills their testimonies and uses their words to advocate their viewpoints to audiences. *Annulla, An Autobiography* (1977, revised 1985) tells the story of Holocaust survivors through interviews and records. *Still Life* uses the traumatic memories of a Vietnam veteran, his wife, and girlfriend to talk about violence in America and the casualties of violence and war. *Execution of Justice* (1984) is based on interviews and the transcripts of the trial of Dan White for the murders of George Moscone and Harvey Milk in a hate crime against homosexuals. *Greensboro (A Requiem)* (1996) takes as its subject the murder of five people by members of the Ku Klux Klan and the American Nazi Party in Greensboro, North Carolina, in 1979. *Having Our Say: The Delany Sisters' First 100 Years* (1995), based on a popular memoir by Sadie and Bessie Delany published in

1993, provides an oral history of race and politics in America delivered by two African-American women of 103 and 105 years of age in the kitchen of their home as they prepare their late father's favorite birthday meal and discourse on a hundred years of black history.

Once she decides upon the story to be investigated, Mann sits down with tape recorder, notepad, and pencil and interviews people central to the story. Over many months taping interviews, studying transcripts, newspapers, and news videos, and writing several drafts of the manuscript (*Having Our Say* had seven drafts), she crafts the source material into what she calls "the language of real life." She steadfastly resists fictionalizing the individuals in the historical moment but allows their voices—conflicting viewpoints and passions—to distill into the poetry of real life. "I use their words," she says. "This is why I call my plays documentaries."[3]

Emily Mann, artistic director of the McCarter Theater Center for the Performing Arts, located on the campus of Princeton University, New Jersey, staged the original production of Anna Deavere Smith's award-winning solo performance text called *Fires in the Mirror: Crown Heights, Brooklyn and Other Identities*. Unlike Emily Mann's plays, Anna Deavere Smith's (b. 1951) are solo pieces created in the documentary style. *Fires in the Mirror* (1992) documents the events surrounding the 1991 stabbing of a Hasidic scholar by a group of young black men in Brooklyn following the accidental death of a Guyanan child by a car carrying the Lubavitcher Hasidic *rebbe* (spiritual leader). Smith's solo text grew out of one hundred interviews with a variety of participants and witnesses from the black and Lubavitcher communities in Crown Heights. She followed *Fires in the Mirror* with *Twilight: Los Angeles, 1992* based on the racial divisions and riots in Los Angeles following the Rodney King incident and the federal trial and conviction of two Los Angeles policemen for violating King's civil rights.

Both *Fires in the Mirror* and *Twilight* are documentary in style and political in intention. Using original interviews, newsroom videotapes, court records, news reports, and public speeches, she captures a multiracial America at those explosive historical moments where the fuses are ignited by racism and classism. Smith is a writer who distills the many interviews into ninety-minute solo performances in which she assumes the personas (male and female, black and Jewish, activist and resident, parent and teacher) of the participants in the conflict speaking their own words and reflecting their own differences.

Anna Deavere Smith's "search for American character," her label for a series of work begun in 1983, brings onstage a multicultural America whose many voices document American character and identity in the late twentieth century. Another leading writer of documentary plays, Moisés Kaufman, in collaboration with the Tectonic Theater Project (a group of eight actors plus designers and dramaturgs), reminded audiences in *Gross Indecency: The Three Trials of Oscar Wilde* and *The Laramie Project* that political theater is a persuasive vehicle for social change.

TEXT AS THEATRICAL DOCUMENT

Whether created for the solo performer or a number of actors, the new documentary text is cinematic in style and defined by the voices of real people engaged in narrating, reporting, reflecting, judging, and analyzing. There is a linear flow of short scenes or segments (Moisés Kaufman calls them "moments" of theatrical time) that trace the historical subject (unjust wars and hate crimes) in a mode aimed toward political discourse.

The text itself is a composite of dialogue, voiceovers, and notes for sounds, projections, and images. The stage dialogue replicates words recorded in interviews, language found in trial transcripts, interpretations of eyewitnesses, and reportage found in newspapers, television journalism, and documentary footage recorded by television cameras.

The primary materials of the documentary writer are largely the witnesses to the historical event. For many documentary playwrights, the model is Bertolt Brecht's "The Street Scene" in which he describes the model for epic theater in terms of "an eyewitness" on a street corner demonstrating to a collection of people what he or she observed—how a traffic accident took place. Brecht argued,

> The bystanders may not have observed what happened, or they may simply not agree with him, may "see things a different way"; the point is that the demonstrator acts the behaviour of driver or victim or both in such a way that the bystanders are able to form an opinion about the accident.[4]

Brecht insisted that this kind of street corner demonstration was the basis for what he called "theater for a scientific age," meaning epic theater. Most important to Brecht was the clear social function that this type of theater presented.

The writer's secondary materials are usually a combination of documents, memories, tapes, photographs, and transcripts. Emily Mann begins with an idea, story, or person whose presence demands investigation and proceeds to explore in interviews, court records, and newspaper accounts the hard, unavoidable truths of a complex story.

The process of collecting materials and artistic creation is as varied as the writer's choice of subject. The job of transcribing hundreds of hours of audiotapes is grueling. The creative process begins with selection—the cutting and pasting of important materials relevant to the story to be told persuasively and theatrically. Some playwrights, like Emily Mann, work in a solitary way to create the text. Others, like Caryl Churchill and Moisés Kaufman, form collaborative teams of actors, dramaturgs, and designers to select the materials to be used on stage and to assist with the organization of the segments. However, one facet common to all documentary texts is the carefully crafted interplay between individual perspectives and the larger social matrix of which they are a part. In the presentation of the real-life encounters with historical events, the playwright as final arbiter forces the spectator to confront his or her own attitudes and beliefs—toward racism or homophobia or hate crimes—and encourages a reevaluation of deeply troubling issues in society at large. The ultimate goal of the documentary text, as it is written today, is to make a theatrical contribution to the nation's political discourse on difference, identity, tolerance, and acceptance.

Ordinarily, the documentary play has a rigorous form. The playwright is restricted to the facts of the case—not siding with the victims and not excoriating the monsters, nor fictionalizing events for theatrical effect and didactic purpose. The writer has a responsibility to balance the points of view; otherwise, the text becomes propaganda. The style of presentation is often rigorous as well. The actors-as-characters oftentimes do not interact with one another but perform alone on a crowded stage suspended within their thoughts and attitudes.

What is the appeal of documentary playwriting at the millennium? Many writers say that they are motivated by the pain of the story and by the disrupted lives connected to it to draw a comprehensive picture of American society that goes beyond nightly televised sound bites. Their aim is to depict the society as a whole in all the facts and contradictions of its violence, coercion, and fragmentation.

The Laramie Project

MOISÉS KAUFMAN

Moisés Kaufman (b. 1964) was born in Caracas, Venezuela, into a Jewish family and has lived in the United States since 1987. Kaufman started his theater career as an actor with the Thespis Theater Ensemble, a prominent experimental company in Venezuela. After moving to New York City in the eighties, he studied at New York University's Experimental Theater Wing and founded the Tectonic Theater Project, a New York–based company dedicated to exploring theatrical language and forms, where he has served as artistic director since 1991. He has also directed regularly with Working Classroom, a multiethnic arts program that showcases original work written and performed by residents of Albuquerque, New Mexico.

For Tectonic, Kaufman directed short plays by Samuel Beckett, Tennessee Williams, Sophie Treadwell, and Franz Xaver Kroetz's The Nest, which was named by the Village Voice as one of the best ten Off Broadway works of the 1994–95 season. Evolving a personalized documentary approach to writing for the theater, Kaufman developed two remarkable theatrical pieces incorporating oral history, memoirs, letters, newspaper accounts, and other kinds of texts to "reconstruct" history. The success of Gross Indecency: The Three Trials of Oscar Wilde (1997) and The Laramie Project (2000) garnered Kaufman and the company numerous awards in New York, Los Angeles, Denver, San Francisco, Toronto, London, and elsewhere. The Laramie Project was filmed for television by HBO and released in 2002.

Moisés Kaufman is noted for his abilities as a writer and stage director to transform moments in history into a theater that uses the prevailing ideas and voices of individuals to illumine the frissons of an entire culture, whether that culture is England of the 1890s or Laramie, Wyoming, of 1998.

CRITICAL INTRODUCTION TO THE LARAMIE PROJECT

In November of 1998, Moisés Kaufman and his theater company (called the Tectonic Theater Project) traveled to Laramie, Wyoming, to investigate the brutal murder of a gay man. They set out on the journey to determine if the crime would serve as a lightning rod to warrant a theatrical piece in support of a national dialogue on hate crimes.

"Tectonic" refers to deformations in the earth's crust that set up movements of faults within the earth, which result in earthquakes. The Laramie Project suggests that similar deformities among human beings cause catastrophic effects for individuals, communities, and even nations. Matthew Shepard, the twenty-three year-old Wyoming college student, who was brutally beaten and crucified against a wire fence, was the lightning rod that set the company on its journey to examine human "faults" as a means of participating in a national dialogue on current issues of sexual politics, education, race, violence, and so on.

Moisés Kaufman, as the artistic leader of the Tectonic Theater Project, thinks that the theater is uniquely situated to contribute to a national dialogue on current events, especially one that incorporates a documentary style into its aesthetic. His company was formed with two objectives—one is cultural/political and the other artistic. Their first aim was to examine and record the subject as source material for performance and the second was to explore theatrical language and form. Both Gross Indecency and The Laramie Project mirror the twin missions of the company and use the techniques of documentary writing and performance.

The developmental process for *The Laramie Project* required that the company travel to Laramie, talk with people over a period of weeks, and return to their New York base with what they saw and heard in order to create the play. Their journey began four weeks after the death of Matthew Shepard and required two and a half years, two hundred interviews, and six trips to Laramie.

The first trip involved the entire company (Kaufman and eight actors) in an effort to learn more about the town, to meet and interview a cross-section of the townspeople, and to gather information on the perpetrators. The group was extremely sensitive to the fact that they would be perceived as intruders—as outsiders. Moreover, they were troubled by concerns for the ethics of conducting interviews with individuals who were still in states of shock and grief. As they talked with the community, they discovered a rich and varied collection of community voices, ranging from the bewildered bartender who served Shepard and his killers that evening, to the Islamic feminist from Bangladesh, the right-wing Christian leadership, the conflicted Catholic priest, Shepard's family and friends, and the policewoman traumatized by the fact that she handled Shepard's body and got his HIV-contaminated blood on her hands.

Following these initial interviews, Tectonic returned to New York City with nearly eighty interviews and conducted a three-week workshop to begin the process of selecting and shaping the Laramie story. Kaufman found the actors (joined by dramaturgs) arguing strongly for the inclusion in the final text of the people they had personally interviewed.

In April 1999, the Tectonic group returned for a second time to Laramie for the trial of Russell Henderson, the confessed killer of Matthew Shepard and encountered a media frenzy that eventually made its way into the staging. Part of the company made four more trips to Laramie—one on the anniversary of Shepard's death, two others to cover the trial of Aaron McKinney, and the last to hold follow-up interviews.

As a documentary play dealing with a hate crime at the end of the millennium, *The Laramie Project* is shaped by fifty *moments* (Kaufman's term for a theatrical unit of time) and written for the eight Tectonic actors who play thirty-one characters as well as the ensemble. The text is divided into three acts; within the act divisions, the fifty moments are labeled along with the narrator's speeches, the characters and company members, music, and special staging devices. The juxtaposition of the moments creates the unity and effectiveness of the play.

The performance style is presentational. There are factual accounts of events that took place on the night of Shepard's beating, the three-day vigil before he died is staged, and the trials of his two assailants are documented. The company made the decision not to represent Matthew Shepard on stage. Aware that the unseen presence of Matthew Shepard was more powerful and mysterious than any representation, Kaufman decided against depicting the central figure of the event in order to avoid the sentimental and maudlin.

Kaufman talked in an interview about his concern for creating a stage document that would illuminate homophobia in American culture and the hate crimes that resulted from it:

> My idea was that if we went to Laramie and we interviewed the people of the town, we might be able to create a document not only about how Laramie was feeling at the end of the millennium, but about how the whole country was feeling and thinking and talking—not only about homosexuality, but also about class and education and violence. So the impetus behind going to Laramie had to do with trying to gather a document that was an X-ray of where we were at the end of the millennium....[5]

Kaufman and the company had come to view the brutality of Matthew Shepard's death as a resonant turning point in American culture. The staging—in particular, the allusion to Thornton Wilder's *Our Town*, replete with graveside and townspeople with black umbrellas—suggested that Kaufman viewed the Laramie experience as a microcosm reflective of the American condition. The small Western town with its cross section of American attitudes and beliefs and with its horrendous unlooked-for crime took on a larger significance for the whole of society.

In all of the writings on *The Laramie Project* thus far, the focus has been on the collaborative methods of the company more than on the strategies of the text-as-documentation. There are few commentaries on the theatrical influences on Kaufman's work even though he has often stated that his work is grounded in the theories and staging of Erwin Piscator and Bertolt Brecht. The company entered into the presentational style described by Bertolt Brecht as street corner theater where actors demonstrate their parts as though they were eyewitnesses to a "traffic accident." In Brecht's model for epic theater, the demonstration must also take on socially practical significance for the spectator.[6]

In the documentary writing and performance style for *The Laramie Project,* the persons of the play and the dialogue are factual, the voices authentic, the emotional responses of individuals derived from interviews, and the acting style reflective of the eyewitness to the event. Nonetheless, in the classic Brechtian strategy, spectators are also distanced by their awareness that they are observing an artificially contrived theatrical event while at the same time seeing clearly the moral investigation that is thrusting toward them. There is no pretense that the spectator is anywhere else than in the theater. In general, the narrator introduces a member of the company who then introduces the character that he or she becomes with the addition of a hat, glasses, or jacket. At the start of the performance, the Narrator introduces "Company member Greg Pierotti" who announces, "My first interview was with Detective Sergeant Hing of the Laramie Police Department." Then, the actor-as-narrator transforms into the detective and begins speaking, "I was born and raised here...." As the moments progress, Kaufman aptly places conflicting points of view before the spectators and invites them to synthesize the material themselves and reach their own conclusions about truth and difference in American society.

The final speech of the text delivered by the Catholic priest reinforces the Tectonic Theater Project's challenge. "I trust that if you write a play of this," says Father Roger Schmidt, "that you say it right. You need to do your best to say it correct." It is left to the audience to answer the implied question about the truth and justice of the stage record and about society's role in the Laramie incident and others taking place elsewhere.

The Laramie Project

CHARACTERS

SHERRY AANENSON Russell Henderson's landlord, in her forties.

ANONYMOUS Friend of Aaron McKinney, in his twenties; works for the railroad.

BAILIFF

BAPTIST MINISTER Originally from Texas, in his fifties.

BAPTIST MINISTER'S WIFE In her late forties.

STEPHEN BELBER Member of Tectonic Theater Project.

DR. CANTWAY Emergency room doctor at Ivinson Memorial Hospital in Laramie, in his fifties.

CATHERINE CONNOLLY Out lesbian professor at the university, in her forties.

MURDOCK COOPER Rancher, in his fifties; resident of Centennial, a nearby town.

ROB DEBREE Detective sergeant for the Albany County Sheriff's Department, in his forties; chief investigator of Matthew's murder.

KERRY DRAKE Reporter with the *Casper Star-Tribune*, in his forties.

PHILIP DUBOIS President of the University of Wyoming, in his forties.

TIFFANY EDWARDS Local reporter, in her twenties.

E-MAIL WRITER

GIL AND EILEEN ENGEN Ranchers; he is in his sixties; she is in her fifties.

REGGIE FLUTY The policewoman who responded to the 911 call and discovered Matthew at the fence, in her late thirties.

LEIGH FONDAKOWSKI Member of Tectonic Theater Project.

MATT GALLOWAY Bartender at the Fireside, in his twenties; student at the University of Wyoming.

GOVERNOR JIM GERINGER Republican governor of Wyoming, forty-five years old.

ANDREW GOMEZ Latino from Laramie, in his twenties.

AMANDA GRONICH Member of Tectonic Theater Project.

RUSSELL HENDERSON One of the perpetrators, twenty-one years old.

REBECCA HILLIKER Head of the theater department at the University of Wyoming, in her forties; midwestern accent.

SERGEANT HING Detective at the Laramie Police Department, in his forties.

JEN A friend of Aaron McKinney, in her early twenties.

SHERRY JOHNSON Administrative assistant at the university, in her forties.

STEPHEN MEAD JOHNSON Unitarian minister, in his fifties.

TWO JUDGES

JURORS AND FOREPERSON

MOISÉS KAUFMAN Member of Tectonic Theater Project.

AARON KREIFELS University student, nineteen years old.

PHIL LABRIE Friend of Matthew Shepard, in his late twenties; eastern European accent.

DOUG LAWS State Ecclesiastical leader for the Mormon Church in Laramie, in his fifties.

JEFFREY LOCKWOOD Laramie resident, in his forties.

AARON MCKINNEY One of the perpetrators, twenty-one years old.

BILL MCKINNEY Father of Aaron McKinney, in his forties; truck driver.

ALISON MEARS Volunteer for a social service agency in town, in her fifties; very good friend of Marge Murray.

MEDIA/NEWSPAPER PEOPLE

MATT MICKELSON Owner of the Fireside, in his thirties.

CONRAD MILLER   Car mechanic, in his thirties.

MORMON HOME TEACHER TO RUSSELL HENDERSON   In his sixties.

MARGE MURRAY   Reggie Fluty's mother, in her seventies; has emphysema but continues to smoke.

DOC O'CONNOR   Limousine driver and local entrepreneur, in his fifties.

ANDY PARIS   Member of Tectonic Theater Project.

ROMAINE PATTERSON   Lesbian, twenty-one years old.

JON PEACOCK   Matthew Shepard's academic adviser, in his thirties; political science professor.

REVEREND FRED PHELPS   Minister from Kansas, in his sixties.

GREG PIEROTTI   Member of Tectonic Theater Project.

BARBARA PITTS   Member of Tectonic Theater Project.

KRISTIN PRICE   Girlfriend of Aaron McKinney, in her twenties; has a son with Aaron; Tennessee accent.

PRIEST AT THE FUNERAL

CAL RERUCHA   Prosecuting attorney, in his fifties.

ZACKIE SALMON   Administrator at the University of Wyoming, in her forties; lesbian; Texas accent.

FATHER ROGER SCHMIT   Catholic priest, in his forties; very outspoken.

JEDADIAH SCHULTZ   University student, nineteen years old.

SHADOW   DJ at the Fireside; African American man, in his thirties.

SHANNON   A friend of Aaron McKinney, in his early twenties.

DENNIS SHEPARD   Father of Matthew Shepard, in his forties; Wyoming native.

APRIL SILVA   Bisexual university student, nineteen years old.

JONAS SLONAKER   Gay man, in his forties.

RULON STACEY   CEO Poudre Valley Hospital in Fort Collins, Colorado, in his forties; a Mormon.

TRISH STEGER   Romaine Patterson's sister, in her forties; owner of a shop in town.

LUCY THOMPSON   Grandmother of Russell Henderson, in her sixties; working-class woman who provided a popular day-care service for the town.

ZUBAIDA ULA   Muslim woman, in her twenties.

WAITRESS (DEBBIE REYNOLDS)

HARRY WOODS   Gay Laramie resident, fifty-two years old.

Note: When a character is not named (for example, friend of Aaron McKinney, "Baptist minister"), it is at the person's request.

PLACE:
Laramie, Wyoming, U.S.A.

TIME:
1998–99

ABOUT THE STAGING
The set is a performance space. There are a few tables and chairs. Costumes and props are always visible. The basic costumes are the ones worn by the company of actors. Costumes to portray the people of Laramie should be simple: a shirt, a pair of glasses, a hat. The desire is to suggest, not re-create. Along the same lines, this should be an actor-driven event. Costume changes, set changes, and anything else that happens on the stage should be done by the company of actors.

ABOUT THE TEXT
When writing this play, we used a technique I developed called moment work. It is a method to create and analyze theater from a structuralist (or tectonic) perspective. For that reason, there are no scenes in this play, only moments. A moment does not mean a change of locale or an entrance or exit of actors or characters. It is simply a unit of theatrical time that is then juxtaposed with other units to convey meaning.

ACT I

MOMENT: A DEFINITION

NARRATOR: On November 14, 1998, the members of Tectonic Theater Project traveled to Laramie, Wyoming, and conducted interviews with the people of the town. During the next year, we would return to Laramie several times and conduct over two hundred interviews. The play you are about to see is edited from those interviews, as well as from journal entries by members of the company and other found texts. Company member Greg Pierotti:

GREG PIEROTTI: My first interview was with Detective Sergeant Hing of the Laramie Police Department. At the start of the interview he was sitting behind his desk, sitting something like this (*he transforms into Sergeant Hing*):

I was born and raised here.
My family is, uh, third generation.
My grandparents moved here in the early nineteen hundreds.
We've had basically three, well, my daughter makes it fourth generation.
Quite a while.... It's a good place to live. Good people—lots of space.

Now, all the towns in southern Wyoming are laid out and spaced because of the railroad came through.
It was how far they could go before having to refuel and rewater.
And, uh, Laramie was a major stopping point.
That's why the towns are spaced so far apart.
We're one of the largest states in the country, and the least populated.

REBECCA HILLIKER: There's so much space between people and towns here, so much time for reflection.

NARRATOR: Rebecca Hilliker, head of the theater department at the University of Wyoming:

REBECCA HILLIKER: You have an opportunity to be happy in your life here. I found that people here were nicer than in the Midwest, where I used to teach, because they were happy. They were glad the sun was shining. And it shines a lot here.

SERGEANT HING: What you have is, you have your old-time traditional-type ranchers, they've been here forever—Laramie's been

the hub of where they come for their supplies and stuff like that.

EILEEN ENGEN: Stewardship is one thing all our ancestors taught us.

NARRATOR: Eileen Engen, rancher:

EILEEN ENGEN: If you don't take care of the land, then you ruin it and you lose your living. So you first of all have to take care of your land and do everything you can to improve it.

DOC O'CONNOR: I love it here.

NARRATOR: Doc O'Connor, limousine driver:

DOC O'CONNOR: You couldn't put me back in that mess out there back east. Best thing about it is the climate. The cold, the wind. They say the Wyoming wind'll drive a man insane. But you know what? It don't bother me. Well, some of the times it bothers me. But most of the time it don't.

SERGEANT HING: And then you got, uh, the university population.

PHILIP DUBOIS: I moved here after living in a couple of big cities.

NARRATOR: Philip Dubois, president of the University of Wyoming:

PHILIP DUBOIS: I loved it there. But you'd have to be out of your mind to let your kids out after dark. And here, in the summertime, my kids play out at night till eleven and I don't think twice about it.

SERGEANT HING: And then you have the people who live in Laramie, basically.

ZACKIE SALMON: I moved here from rural Texas.

NARRATOR: Zackie Salmon, Laramie resident:

ZACKIE SALMON: Now, in Laramie, if you don't know a person, you will definitely know someone they know. So it can only be one degree removed at most. And for me—I love it! I mean, I love to go to the grocery store 'cause I get to visit with four or five or six people every time I go. And I don't really mind people knowing my business— 'cause what's my business? I mean, my business is basically good.

DOC O'CONNOR: I like the trains, too. They don't bother me. Well, some of the times they bother me, but most times they don't. Even though one goes by every thirteen minutes out where I live....

NARRATOR: Doc actually lives up in Bossler. But everybody in Laramie knows him. He's also not really a doctor.

DOC O'CONNOR: They used to carry cattle...them trains. Now all they carry is diapers and cars.

APRIL SILVA: I grew up in Cody, Wyoming.

NARRATOR: April Silva, university student:

APRIL SILVA: Laramie is better than where I grew up. I'll give it that.

SERGEANT HING: It's a good place to live. Good people, lots of space. Now, when the incident happened with that boy, a lot of press people came here. And one time some of them followed me out to the crime scene. And uh, well, it was a beautiful day, absolutely gorgeous day, real clear and crisp and the sky was that blue that, uh...you know, you'll never be able to paint, it's just sky blue—it's just gorgeous. And the mountains in the background and a little snow on 'em, and this one reporter, uh, lady...person, that was out there, she said...

REPORTER: Well, who found the boy, who was out here anyway?

SERGEANT HING: And I said, "Well, this is a really popular area for people to run, and mountain biking's really big out here, horseback riding, it's just, well, it's close to town." And she looked at me and she said:

REPORTER: Who in the hell would want to run out here?

SERGEANT HING: And I'm thinking, "Lady, you're just missing the point." You know, all you got to do is turn around, see the mountains, smell the air, listen to the birds, just take in what's around you. And they were just—nothing but the story. I didn't feel judged, I felt that they were stupid. They're, they're missing the point—they're just missing the whole point.

JEDADIAH SCHULTZ: It's hard to talk about Laramie now, to tell you what Laramie is, for us.

NARRATOR: Jedadiah Schultz:

JEDADIAH SCHULTZ: If you would have asked me before, I would have told you Laramie is a beautiful town, secluded enough that you can have your own identity.... A town with a strong sense of community—everyone knows everyone.... A town with a personality that most larger cities are stripped of. Now, after Matthew, I would say that Laramie is a town defined by an accident, a crime. We've become Waco, we've become Jasper. We're a noun, a definition, a sign. We may be able to get rid of that...but it will sure take a while.

MOMENT: JOURNAL ENTRIES

NARRATOR: Journal entries—members of the company. Andy Paris:

ANDY PARIS: Moisés called saying he had an idea for his next theater project. But there was a somberness to his voice, so I asked what it was all about and he told me he wanted to do a piece about what's happening in Wyoming.

NARRATOR: Stephen Belber:

STEPHEN BELBER: Leigh told me the company was thinking of going out to Laramie to conduct interviews and that they wanted me to come. But I'm hesitant. I have no real interest in prying into a town's unraveling.

NARRATOR: Amanda Gronich:

AMANDA GRONICH: I've never done anything like this in my life. How do you get people to talk to you? What do you ask?

NARRATOR: Moisés Kaufman:

MOISÉS KAUFMAN: The company has agreed that we should go to Laramie for a week and interview people.

Am a bit afraid about taking ten people in a trip of this nature. Must make some safety rules. No one works alone. Everyone carries cell phones. Have made some preliminary contacts with Rebecca Hilliker, head of the theater department at the University of Wyoming. She is hosting a party for us our first night in Laramie and has promised to introduce us to possible interviewees.

MOMENT: REBECCA HILLIKER

REBECCA HILLIKER: I must tell you that when I first heard that you were thinking of coming here, when you first called me, I wanted to say, You've just kicked me in the stomach. Why are you doing this to me?

But then I thought, That's stupid, you're not doing this to me. And, more important, I thought about it and decided that we've had so much negative closure on this whole thing. And the students really need to talk. When this happened they started talking about it, and then the media descended and all dialogue stopped.

You know, I really love my students because they are free thinkers. And you may not like what they have to say, and you may not like their opinions, because they can be very redneck, but they are honest and they're truthful—so there's an excitement here, there's a dynamic here with my students that I never had when I was in the Midwest or in North Dakota, because there, there was so much Puritanism that dictated how people looked at the world that a lot of times they didn't have an opinion, you couldn't get them to express an opinion. And, quite honestly, I'd rather have opinions that I don't like—and have that dynamic in education.

There's a student I think you should talk to. His name is Jedadiah Schultz.

MOMENT: *ANGELS IN AMERICA*

JEDADIAH SCHULTZ: I've lived in Wyoming my whole life. The family has been in Wyoming, well…for generations. Now when it came time to go to college, my parents can't—couldn't afford to send me to college. I wanted to study theater. And I knew that if I was going to go to college I was going to have to get on a scholarship—and so, uh, they have this competition each year, this Wyoming state high school competition. And I knew that if I didn't take first place in, uh, duets that I wasn't gonna get a scholarship. So I went to the theater department of the university looking for good scenes, and I asked one of the professors—I was like, "I need—I need a killer scene," and he was like, "Here you go, this is it." And it was from *Angels in America*.

So I read it and I knew that I could win best scene if I did a good enough job.

And when the time came I told my mom and dad so that they would come to the competition. Now you have to understand, my parents go to everything—every ball game, every hockey game—everything I've ever done.

And they brought me into their room and told me that if I did that scene, that they would not come to see me in the competition. Because they believed that it is wrong—that homosexuality is wrong—they felt that strongly about it that they didn't want to come see their son do probably the most important thing he'd done to that point in his life. And I didn't know what to do.

I had never, ever gone against my parents' wishes. So I was kind of worried about it. But I decided to do it.

And all I can remember about the competition is that when we were done, me and my scene partner, we came up to each other and we shook hands and there was a standing ovation.

Oh, man, it was amazing! And we took first place and we won. And that's how come I can afford to be here at the university, because of that scene. It was one of the best moments of my life. And my parents weren't there. And to this day, that was the one thing that my parents didn't see me do.

And thinking back on it, I think, why did I do it? Why did I oppose my parents? 'Cause I'm not gay. So why did I do it? And I guess the only honest answer I can give is that, well (*he chuckles*) I wanted to win. It was such a good scene; it was like the best scene!

Do you know Mr. Kushner? Maybe you can tell him.

MOMENT: JOURNAL ENTRIES

NARRATOR: Company member Greg Pierotti:

GREG PIEROTTI: We arrived today in the Denver Airport and drove to Laramie. The moment we crossed the Wyoming border I swear I saw a herd of buffalo. Also, I thought it was strange that the Wyoming sign said: WYOMING—LIKE NO PLACE ON EARTH instead of WYOMING—LIKE NO PLACE ELSE ON EARTH.

NARRATOR: Company member Leigh Fondakowski:

LEIGH FONDAKOWSKI: I stopped at a local inn for a bite to eat. And my waitress said to me:

WAITRESS: Hi, my name is Debbie. I was born in nineteen fifty-four and Debbie Reynolds was big then, so, yes, there are a lot of us around, but I promise that I won't slap you if you leave your elbows on the table.

MOISÉS KAUFMAN: Today Leigh tried to explain to me to no avail what chicken fried steak was.

WAITRESS: Now, are you from Wyoming? Or are you just passing through?

LEIGH FONDAKOWSKI: We're just passing through.

NARRATOR: Company member Barbara Pitts:

BARBARA PITTS: We arrived in Laramie tonight. Just past the WELCOME TO LARAMIE sign—POPULATION 26,687—the first thing to greet us was Wal-Mart. In the dark, we could be on any main drag in America—fast-food chains, gas stations. But as we drove into the downtown area by the railroad tracks, the buildings still look like a turn-of-the-century western town. Oh, and as we passed the University Inn, on the sign where amenities such as heated pool or cable TV are usually touted, it said: HATE IS NOT A LARAMIE VALUE.

NARRATOR: Greg Pierotti:

MOMENT: ALISON AND MARGE

GREG PIEROTTI: I met today with two longtime Laramie residents, Alison Mears and Marge Murray, two social service workers who taught me a thing or two.

ALISON MEARS: Well, what Laramie used to be like when Marge was growing up, well, it was mostly rural.

MARGE MURRAY: Yeah, it was. I enjoyed it, you know. My kids all had horses.

ALISON MEARS: Well, there was more land, I mean, you could keep your pet cow. Your horse. Your little chickens. You know, just have your little bit of acreage.

MARGE MURRAY: Yeah, I could run around the house in my all togethers, do the housework while the kids were in school. And nobody could see me. And if they got that close…

ALISON MEARS: Well, then that's their problem.

MARGE MURRAY: Yeah.

GREG PIEROTTI: I just want to make sure I got the expression right: in your all togethers?

MARGE MURRAY: Well, yeah, honey, why wear clothes?

ALISON MEARS: Now, how's he gonna use that in his play?

GREG PIEROTTI: So this was a big ranching town?

ALISON MEARS: Oh, not just ranching, this was a big railroad town at one time. Before they moved everything to Cheyenne and Green River and Omaha. So now, well, it's just a drive through spot for the railroad—because even, what was it, in the fifties? Well, they had one big roundhouse, and they had such a shop they could build a complete engine.

MARGE MURRAY: They did, my mom worked there.

GREG PIEROTTI: Your mom worked in a roundhouse?

MARGE MURRAY: Yep. She washed engines. Her name was Minnie. We used to, you know, sing that song for her, you know that song.

GREG PIEROTTI: What song?

MARGE MURRAY: "Run for the roundhouse, Minnie, they can't corner you there."

(*They crack up.*)

ALISON MEARS: But I'll tell you, Wyoming is bad in terms of jobs. I mean, the university has the big high whoop-de-do jobs. But Wyoming, unless you're a professional, well, the bulk of the people are working minimum-wage jobs.

MARGE MURRAY: Yeah, I've been either in the service industry or bartending most of my life. Now I know everybody in town.

ALISON MEARS: And she does.

MARGE MURRAY: And I do. Now that I'll tell ya, here in Laramie there is a difference and there always has been. What it is is a class distinction. It's about the well-educated and the ones that are not. And the educated don't understand why the ones that are not don't get educated. That's why I told you before my kids had to fight because their mother was a bartender. Never mind I was the best damn bartender in town.

ALISON MEARS: And she was.

MARGE MURRAY: That's not bragging, that's fact.

ALISON MEARS: But here in Laramie, if it weren't for the university, we'd just be S.O.L.

GREG PIEROTTI: What's S.O.L.?

ALISON MEARS: Well, do I have to say it? Well, it's shit outta luck. (*She cracks up.*) Oh Lordy, you've got that on your tape. Boy, you are getting an education today.

GREG PIEROTTI: Yeah, I guess I am. So, let me just ask you—what was your response when this happened to Matthew Shepard?

MARGE MURRAY: Well, I've been close enough to the case to know many of the people. I have a daughter that's on the Sheriff's Department.

As far as the gay issue, I don't give a damn one way or the other as long as they don't bother me. And even if they did, I'd just say no thank you. And that's the attitude of most of the Laramie population. They might poke one, if they were in a bar situation, you know, they had been drinking, they might actually smack one in the mouth, but then they'd just walk away. Most of 'em, they would just say, "I don't swing that way," and whistle on about their business. Laramie is live and let live.

ALISON MEARS: I'd say that Marge probably knows a lot more except she's even willing to say, and we have to respect her for that.

MARGE MURRAY: Well, uh, where are you going with this story?

GREG PIEROTTI: Oh, well, we still haven't decided. When we've finished, we are going to try to bring it around to Laramie.

MARGE MURRAY: Okay, then, there are parts I won't tell you.

MOMENT: MATTHEW

NARRATOR: Company member Andy Paris:

ANDY PARIS: Today, for the first time, we met someone who actually knew Matthew

Shepard. Trish Steger, owner of a shop in town, referred to him as Matt.

TRISH STEGER: Matt used to come into my shop—that's how I knew him.

ANDY PARIS: It was the first time I heard him referred to as Matt instead of Matthew. Did he go by Matt to everyone?

DOC O'CONNOR: Well, on the second of October, I get a phone call about, uh, ten after seven.

NARRATOR: Doc O'Connor:

DOC O'CONNOR: It was Matthew Shepard. And he said, "Can you pick me up at the corner of Third and Grand?" So, anyhow, I pull up to the corner, to see who Matthew Shepard is, you know. It's a little guy, about five-two, soakin' wet, I betcha ninety-seven pounds tops. They say he weighed a hundred and ten, but I wouldn't believe it. They also said he was five-five in the newspapers, but this man, he was really only about five-two, maybe five-one. So he walks up to the window—I'm gonna try and go in steps so you can better understand the principle of this man. So he walks up to the window, and I say, "Are you Matthew Shepard?" And he says, "Yeah, I'm Matthew Shepard. But I don't want you to call me Matthew, or Mr. Shepard. I don't want you to call me anything. My name is Matt. And I want you to know, I am gay and we're going to go to a gay bar. Do you have a problem with that?" And I said, "How're you paying?"

The fact is…Laramie doesn't have any gay bars…and for that matter neither does Wyoming…so he was hiring me to take him to Fort Collins, Colorado, about an hour away.

Matt was a blunt little shit, you know what I'm sayin'? But I liked him 'cause he was straightforward, you see what I'm saying? Maybe gay but straightforward, you see what I'm saying?

TRISH STEGER: I don't know, you know, how does any one person ever tell about another? You really should talk to my sister Romaine. She was a very close friend of Matthew's.

ROMAINE PATTERSON: We never called him Matthew, actually, most of the time we called him Choo-choo. You know, because we used to call him Mattchew, and then we just called him Choo-choo.

And whenever I think of Matthew, I always think of his incredible beaming smile. I mean, he'd walk in and he'd be like (*demonstrates*) you know, and he'd smile at everyone…he just made you feel great.… And he—would like stare people down in the coffee shop…'cause he always wanted to sit on the end seat so that he could talk to me while I was working. And if someone was sitting in that seat, he would just sit there and stare at them. Until they left. And then he would claim his spot.

But Matthew definitely had a political side to him.… I mean, he really wanted to get into political affairs…that's all his big interest was, was watching CNN and MSNBC, I mean, that's the only TV station I ever saw his TV tuned in to. He was just really smart in political affairs, but not too smart on like commonsense things…

So, he moves to Laramie to go to school.

JON PEACOCK: Matthew was very shy when he first came in.

NARRATOR: Jon Peacock, Matthew Shepard's academic adviser:

JON PEACOCK: To the point of being somewhat mousy I'd almost say. He was having some difficulties adjusting, but this was home for him and he made that quite clear. And so his mousiness, his shyness gave way to a person who was excited about this track that he was going to embark on. He was just figuring out wanting to work on human rights, how he was going to do that. And when that happens this person begins to bloom a little bit. He was starting to say, "Wow, there are opportunities here. There are things I can do in this world. I can be important."

ROMAINE PATTERSON: I did hear from Matthew about forty-eight hours before his attack. And he told me that he had joined the gay and lesbian group on campus, and he said he was enjoying it, you know, he was getting ready for Pride Week and whatnot. I mean, he was totally stoked about school—

yeah, he was really happy about being there.

JON PEACOCK: And in retrospect and I can only say this in retrospect of course—I think that's where he was heading, towards human rights. Which only adds to the irony and tragedy of this.

MOMENT: WHO'S GETTING WHAT?

DOC O'CONNOR: Let me tell you something else here. There's more gay people in Wyoming than meets the eye. I know, I know for a fact. They're not particularly, ah, the whattayou call them, the queens, the gay people, queens, you know, runaround faggot-type people. No, they're the ones that throw bails of hay, jump on horses, brand 'em, and kick ass, you see what I'm saying? As I always say, Don't fuck with a Wyoming queer, 'cause they will kick you in your fucking ass, but that's not the point of what I'm trying to say. 'Cause I know a lot of gay people in Wyoming, I know a lot of people period. I've been lived up here some forty-odd years, you see what I'm saying?

And I don't think Wyoming people give a damn one way or another if you're gay or straight, that's just what I just said, doesn't matter. If there's eight men and one woman in a Wyoming bar, which is often the case, now you stop and think—who's getting what? You see what I'm saying? Now jeez, it don't take a big intelligent mind to figure that one out.

MOMENT: EASIER SAID THAN DONE

CATHERINE CONNOLLY: My understanding when I first came here…

NARRATOR: Catherine Connolly:

CATHERINE CONNOLLY: …is that I was the first "out" lesbian or gay faculty member on campus. And that was in nineteen ninety-two. So, that wasn't that long ago. Um, I was asked at my interview what my husband did, um, and so I came out then.… Do you want a funny story?

When you first get here as a new faculty member, there's all these things you have to do. And so, I was in my office and I noticed that this woman called.... I was expecting, you know, it was a health insurance phone call, something like that, and so I called her back. And I could hear her, she's working on her keyboard, clicking away. I said, you know, "This is Cathy Connolly returning your phone call." And she said, "Oh. It's you." And I thought, "This is bizarre." And she said, "I hear—I hear—I hear you're gay. I hear you are." I was like, "Uh huh." And she said, "I hear you came as a couple. I'm one too. Not a couple, just a person." And so—she was—a kind of lesbian who knew I was coming and she wanted to come over and meet me immediately. And she later told me that there were other lesbians that she knew who wouldn't be seen with me. That I would irreparably taint them, that just to be seen with me could be a problem.

JONAS SLONAKER: When I came here I knew it was going to be hard as a gay man.

NARRATOR: Jonas Slonaker:

JONAS SLONAKER: But I kept telling myself: People should live where they want to live. And there would be times I would go down to Denver and I would go to gay bars and, um, people would ask where I was from and I'd say, "Laramie, Wyoming." And I met so many men down there from Wyoming. So many gay men who grew up here, and they're like: "This is not a place where I can live, how can you live there, I had to get out, grrr, grrr, grrr." But every once in a while there would be a guy, "Oh gosh, I miss Laramie. I mean I really love it there, that's where I want to live." And they get this starry-eyed look and I'm like: If that's where you want to live, do it. I mean, imagine if more gay people stayed in small towns. But it's easier said than done of course.

MOMENT: JOURNAL ENTRIES

MOISÉS KAUFMAN: Today we are moving from our motel and heading for the Best Western.

NARRATOR: Moisés Kaufman:

MOISÉS KAUFMAN: My hope is that it is a better Western.

NARRATOR: Amanda Gronich:

AMANDA GRONICH: Today we divided up to go to different churches in the community. Moisés and I were given a Baptist church. We were welcomed into the services by the reverend himself standing at the entrance to the chapel. This is what I remember of his sermon that morning.

MOMENT: THE WORD

BAPTIST MINISTER: My dear brothers and sisters: I am here today to bring you the Word of the Lord. Now, I have a simple truth that I tell to my colleagues and I'm gonna tell it to you today: The word is either sufficient or it is not.

Scientists tell me that human history, that the world is five billion or six billion years old—after all, what's a billion years give or take? The Bible tells me that human history is six thousand years old.

The word is either sufficient or it is not.

STEPHEN MEAD JOHNSON: Ah, the sociology of religion in the West...

NARRATOR: Stephen Mead Johnson, Unitarian minister:

STEPHEN MEAD JOHNSON: Dominant religious traditions in this town: Baptist, Mormon—they're everywhere, it's not just Salt Lake, you know, they're all over—they're like jam on roast down here.

DOUG LAWS: The Mormon Church has a little different thing going that irritates some folks.

NARRATOR: Doug Laws, Stake Ecclesiastical leader for the Mormon Church:

DOUG LAWS: And that is that we absolutely believe that God still speaks to man. We don't think that it happened and some folks wrote it in the Bible. God speaks to us today, and we believe that. We believe that the prophet of the church has the authority to receive inspiration and revelation from God.

STEPHEN MEAD JOHNSON: So, the spectrum would be—uh, on the left side of that panel: So far left that I am probably sitting by myself, is me—and the Unitarian Church. Unitarians are by and large humanists, many of whom are atheists. I mean—we're, you know, we're not even sure we're a religion. And to my right on the spectrum, to his credit, Father Roger, Catholic priest, who is well-established here, and God bless him—he did not equivocate at all when this happened—he hosted the vigil for Matthew that night.

FATHER ROGER SCHMIT: I was really jolted because, you know, when we did the vigil—we wanted to get other ministers involved and we called some of them, and they were not going to get involved. And it was like, "We are gonna stand back and wait and see which way the wind is blowing." And that angered me immensely. We are supposed to stand out as leaders. I thought, "Wow, what's going on here?"

DOUG LAWS: God has set boundaries. And one of our responsibilities is to learn: What is it that God wants? So you study Scripture, you look to your leaders. Then you know what the bounds are. Now once you kinda know what the bounds are, then you sorta get a feel for what's out-of-bounds.

There is a proclamation that came out on the family. A family is defined as one woman and one man and children. That's a family. That's about as clear as you can state it. There's no sexual deviation in the Mormon Church. No—no leniency. We just think it's out-of-bounds.

BAPTIST MINISTER: I warn you: You will be mocked! You will be ridiculed for the singularity of your faith! But you let the Bible be your guide. It's in there. It's all in there.

STEPHEN MEAD JOHNSON: The Christian pastors, many of the conservative ones, were silent on this. Conservative Christians use the Bible to show the rest of the world, It says here in the Bible. And most Americans believe, and they do, that the Bible is the word of God, and how you gonna fight that?

BAPTIST MINISTER: I am a Biblicist. Which means: The Bible doesn't need me to be true. The Bible is true whether I believe it or not. The word is either sufficient or it is not.

STEPHEN MEAD JOHNSON: I arrived in Laramie on September fifteenth. I looked around—tumbleweed, cement factory—and said, "What in the hell am I doing in Wyoming?" Three weeks later, I found out what the hell I'm doing in Wyoming.

MOMENT: A SCARF

STEPHEN BELBER: I had breakfast this morning with a university student named Zubaida Ula. She is an Islamic feminist who likes to do things her own way.

ZUBAIDA ULA: I've lived in Laramie since I was four. Yeah. My parents are from Bangladesh. Two years ago, because I'm Muslim, I decided to start wearing a scarf. That's really changed my life in Laramie. Yeah.

Like people say things to me like, "Why do you have to wear that thing on your head?" Like when I go to the grocery store, I'm not looking to give people Islam 101, you know what I mean? So I'll be like, "Well, it's part of my religion," and they'll be—this is the worst part cuz they'll be like, "I know it's part of your religion, but why?" And it's—how am I supposed to go into the whole doctrine of physical modesty and my own spiritual relationship with the Lord, standing there with my pop and chips? You know what I mean?

STEPHEN BELBER: Yeah.

ZUBAIDA ULA: You know, it's so unreal to me that, yeah, that a group from New York would be writing a play about Laramie. And then I was picturing like you're gonna be in a play about my town. You're gonna be onstage in New York and you're gonna be acting like you're us. That's so weird.

MOMENT: LIFESTYLE 1

BAPTIST MINISTER'S WIFE: Hello?

AMANDA GRONICH: Yes, hello. My name is Amanda Gronich and I am here in Laramie working with a theater company. I went to the reverend's, your husband's church on Sunday, and I was extremely interested in talking with the reverend about some of his thoughts about recent events.

BAPTIST MINISTER'S WIFE: Well, I don't think he'll want to talk to you. He has very biblical views about homosexuality—he doesn't condone that kind of violence. But he doesn't condone that kind of lifestyle, you know what I mean? And he was just bombarded with press after this happened and the media has been just terrible about this whole thing.

AMANDA GRONICH: Oh, I know, I really understand, it must have just been terrible.

BAPTIST MINISTER'S WIFE: Oh, yes, I think we are all hoping this just goes away.

AMANDA GRONICH: Well, um, do you think maybe I could call back and speak with your husband just briefly?

BAPTIST MINISTER'S WIFE: Well, all right, you can call him back tonight at nine.

AMANDA GRONICH: Oh, thank you so much. I'll do that.

MOMENT: THE FIRESIDE

STEPHEN BELBER: Today Barbara and I went to the Fireside Bar, which is the last place Matthew was seen in public.

BARBARA PITTS: The Fireside—definitely feels like a college bar, with a couple of pool tables and a stage area for karaoke. Still, the few regulars in the late afternoon were hardly the college crowd.

STEPHEN BELBER: First person we talked to was Matt Mickelson, the owner.

MATT MICKELSON: My great-great-grandfather moved here in eighteen sixty-two, he owned Laramie's first opera house, it was called Old Blue Front, and in eighteen seventy Louisa Grandma Swain cast the first woman's ballot in any free election in the world, and that's why Wyoming is the Equality State, so what I want to do is reestablish my bar business as the Old Blue Front Opera House and Good Time Emporium, you know, I want to have a restaurant, I want to have a gift shop, I want to have a pool hall, and do all this shit, you know… every night's ladies' night…

So the Fireside is the first step towards the Old Blue Front Opera House and Good Time Emporium.

BARBARA PITTS: So, what about the night Matthew Shepard was here?

MATT MICKELSON: We had karaoke that night, twenty or thirty people here—Matthew Shepard came in, sitting right—right where you're sitting, just hanging out…. I mean, if you wanna talk to somebody, you should talk to Matt Galloway, he was the kid that was bartending that night. You'd have to meet him, his character stands for itself.

(Calling) Hey, is Galloway bartending tonight?

MATT GALLOWAY: Okay. I'm gonna make this brief, quick, get it over with, but it will be everything—factual. Just the facts. Here we go. Ten o'clock. I clock in, usual time, Tuesday nights. Ten-thirty—Matthew Shepard shows up—alone—sits down, orders a Heineken.

NARRATOR: Phil Labrie, friend of Matthew Shepard:

PHIL LABRIE: Matt liked to drink Heineken and nothing else. Heineken even though you have to pay nine-fifty for a six-pack. He'd always buy the same beer.

MATT GALLOWAY: So what can I tell you about Matt?

If you had a hundred customers like him it'd be the—the most perfect bar I've ever been in. Okay? And nothing to do with sexual orientation. Um, absolute mannerisms. Manners. Politeness, intelligence.

Taking care of me, as in tips. Everything—conversation, uh, dressed nice, clean-cut. Some people you just know, sits down, "Please," "Thank you"—offers intellect, you know, within—within—within their vocabulary.

Um, so, he kicks it there. Didn't seem to have any worries, or like he was looking for anyone. Just enjoy his drink and the company around.

Now approximately eleven forty-five, eleven-thirty—eleven forty-five, Aaron McKinney and Russell Henderson come in—I didn't know their names then, but they're the accused, they're the perps, they're the accused. They walked in, just very stone-faced, you know. Dirty. Grungy.

Rude. "Gimme." That type of thing. They walked up to the bar, uh, and, as you know, paid for a pitcher with dimes and quarters, uh, which is something that I mean you don't forget. You don't forget that. Five-fifty in dimes and quarters. That's a freakin' nightmare.

Now Henderson and McKinney, they didn't seem intoxificated at all. They came in—they just ordered a beer, took the pitcher with them back there into the pool room, and kept to themselves. Next thing I knew, probably a half hour later, they were kind of walking around—no beer. And I remember thinking to myself that I'm not gonna ask them if they want another one, because obviously they just paid for a pitcher with dimes and quarters, I have a real good feeling they don't have any more money.

NARRATOR: Romaine Patterson:

ROMAINE PATTERSON: Money meant nothing to Matthew, because he came from a lot of it. And he would like hand over his wallet in two seconds—because money meant nothing. His—shoes—might have meant something. They can say it was robbery…I don't buy it. For even an iota of a second.

MATT GALLOWAY: Then a few moments later I looked over and Aaron and Russell had been talking to Matthew Shepard.

KRISTIN PRICE: Aaron said that a guy walked up to him and said that he was gay, and wanted to get with Aaron and Russ.

NARRATOR: Kristin Price, girlfriend of Aaron McKinney:

KRISTIN PRICE: And Aaron got aggravated with it and told him that he was straight and didn't want anything to do with him and walked off. He said that is when he and Russell went to the bathroom and decided to pretend they were gay and get him in the truck and rob him. They wanted to teach him a lesson not to come on to straight people.

MATT GALLOWAY: Okay, no. They stated that Matt approached them, that he came on to them. I absolutely, positively disbelieve and refute the statement one hundred percent.

Refute it. I'm gonna give you two reasons why.

One. Character reference.

Why would he approach them? Why them? He wasn't approaching anybody else in the bar. They say he's gay, he was a flaming gay, he's gonna come on to people like that. Bullshit. He never came on to me. Hello?!? He came on to them? I don't believe it.

Two. Territorialism is—is—is the word I will use for this. And that's the fact that Matt was sitting there. Russell and Aaron were in the pool area. Upon their first interaction, they were in Matt's area, in the area that Matt had been seen all night. So who approached who by that?

ROMAINE PATTERSON: But Matthew was the kind of person…like, he would never not talk to someone for any reason. If someone started talking to him, he'd just be like, "Oh, blah, blah, blah." He never had any problem just striking up a conversation with anybody.

PHIL LABRIE: Matt did feel lonely a lot of times. Me knowing that—and knowing how gullible Matt could be…he would have walked right into it. The fact that he was at the bar alone without any friends made him that much more vulnerable.

MATT GALLOWAY: So the only thing is—and this is what I'm testifying to—'cause, you know, I'm also, basically, the key eyewitness in this case, uh (pause) basically what I'm testifying is that I saw Matthew leave. I saw two individuals leave with Matthew. I didn't see their faces, but I saw the back of their heads. At the same time, McKinney and Henderson were no longer around. You do the math.

MATT MICKELSON: Actually, I think the DJ was the last one to talk to him on his way out that night…gave him a cigarette or something. His name is Shadow

SHADOW: I was the last person that Matt talked to before he left the Fireside.… I was just bullshittin' around with my shit, and he stopped me, I stopped him actually, and he's like, "Hey, Shadow, da da da," and I was like, "What, man, you gettin' ready to leave?" he's like, "Yeah, man, and this an' that." But then I noticed them two guys and they stood outside, you could see, you could see it, they were standing there, you know, and he was looking over to them, and they were looking back at him. And I stood and talked to Matt for like a good ten minutes and you seen the guys with him, you seen 'em getting like, you seen 'em like worried, like, you know, anxious to leave and shit.... So when they took off, I seen it, when they took off, it was in a black truck, it was a small truck, and the three of them sat in the front seat and Matt sat in the middle.

And I didn't think nothin' of it, you know. I didn't figure them guys was gonna be like that.

MOMENT: MCKINNEY AND HENDERSON

NARRATOR: A friend of Aaron McKinney:

ANONYMOUS: Oh, I've known Aaron a long time. Aaron was a good kid, I liked Aaron a lot, that's why I was shocked when I heard this, I'm like...I know he was, he was living out far...at his trailer house is what he told me, with his girl...they just started dating last summer...they musta gotten pregnant as soon as they started dating, you know, 'cause they had a kid. He was only twenty-one years old, but he was running around with a kid.... You see, that's the kinda person Aaron was, just like he always dressed in like big clothes, you know like, in like Tommy "Hile-figer," Polo, Gucci...

At the time I knew him, he was just, he was just a young kid trying to, you know, he just wanted to fit in, you know, acting tough, acting cool, but, you know, you could get in his face about it and he would back down, like he was some kinda scared kid.

NARRATOR: Sherry Aanenson:

SHERRY AANENSON: Russell was just so sweet. He was the one who was the Eagle Scout. I mean, his whole presence was just quiet and sweet. So of course it doesn't make sense to me and I know people snap and whatever

and like it wasn't a real intimate relationship, I was just his landlord. I did work with him at the Chuck Wagon too. And I remember like at the Christmas party he was just totally drunk out of his mind, like we all were pretty much just party-party time.... And he wasn't belligerent, he didn't change, his personality didn't change. He was still the same little meek Russell, I remember him coming up to me and saying, "When you get a chance, Sherry, can I have a dance?" Which we never did get around to doing that but...Now I just want to shake him, you know—What were you thinking? What in the hell were you thinking?

MOMENT: THE FENCE

STEPHEN MEAD JOHNSON: The fence—I've been out there four times, I've taken visitors. That place has become a pilgrimage site. Clearly that's a very powerful personal experience to go out there. It is so stark and so empty and you can't help but think of Matthew out there for eighteen hours in nearly freezing temperatures, with that view up there isolated, and, the "God, my God, why have you forsaken me" comes to mind.

NARRATOR: Company member Greg Pierotti:

GREG PIEROTTI: Phil Labrie, a friend of Matthew's, took us to the fence this morning. I broke down the minute I touched it. I feel such a strong kinship with this young man. On the way back, I made sure that no one saw me crying.

NARRATOR: Leigh Fondakowski:

LEIGH FONDAKOWSKI: Greg was crying on the way back. I couldn't bring myself to tears, but I felt the same way. I have an interview this afternoon with Aaron Kreifels. He's the boy who found Matthew out there at the fence. I don't think I'm up for it right now. I'll see if someone else can do it.

MOMENT: FINDING MATTHEW SHEPARD

AARON KREIFELS: Well I, uh, I took off on my bicycle about five P.M. on Wednesday from my dorm. I just kinda felt like going for a ride. So I—I went up to the top of Cactus

Canyon, and I'm not superfamiliar with that area, so on my way back down, I didn't know where I was going, I was just sort of picking the way to go, which now…it just makes me think that God wanted me to find him because there's no way that I was going to go that way.

So I was in some deep-ass sand, and I wanted to turn around—but for some reason, I kept going. And, uh, I went along. And there was this rock, on the—on the ground—and I just drilled it. I went—over the handlebars and ended up on the ground.

So, uh, I got up, and I was just kind of dusting myself off, and I was looking around and I noticed something—which ended up to be Matt, and he was just lying there by a fence, and I—I just thought it was a scarecrow. I was like, Halloween's coming up, thought it was a Halloween gag, so I didn't think much of it, so I got my bike, walked it around the fence that was there, it was a buck-type fence. And, uh, got closer to him, and I noticed his hair—and that was a major key to me noticing it was a human being—was his hair. 'Cause I just thought it was a dummy, seriously, I noticed—I even noticed the chest going up and down, I still thought it was a dummy, you know. I thought it was just like some kind of mechanism.

But when I saw hair, well, I knew it was a human being.

So…I ran to the nearest house and—I just ran as fast as I could…and called the police.

REGGIE FLUTY: I responded to the call.

NARRATOR: Officer Reggie Fluty:

REGGIE FLUTY: When I got there, the first—at first the only thing I could see was partially somebody's feet, and I got out of my vehicle and raced over—I seen what appeared to be a young man, thirteen, fourteen years old because he was so tiny laying on his back and he was tied to the bottom end of a pole.

I did the best I could. The gentleman that was laying on the ground, Matthew Shepard, he was covered in dry blood all over his head, there was dry blood underneath him and he was barely breathing…he was doing the best he could.

I was going to breathe for him and I couldn't get his mouth open—his mouth wouldn't open for me.

He was covered in, like I said, partially dry blood and blood all over his head—the only place that he did not have any blood on him, on his face, was what appeared to be where he had been crying down his face.

His head was distorted—you know, it did not look normal—he looked as if he had a real harsh head wound.

DR. CANTWAY: I was working the emergency room the night Matthew Shepard was brought in. I don't think that any of us, ah, can remember seeing a patient in that condition for a long time—those of us who've worked in big city hospitals have seen this. Ah, but we have some people here who've not worked in a big city hospital. And, ah, it's not something you expect here.

Ah, you expect it, you expect this kind of injuries to come from a car going down a hill at eighty miles an hour. You expect to see gross injuries from something like that—this horrendous, terrible thing. Ah, but you don't expect to see that from someone doing this to another person.

The ambulance report said it was a beating, so we knew.

AARON KREIFELS: There was nothing I could do. I mean, if there was anything that I could of done to help him I would've done it but there was nothing.

And I, I was yelling at the top of my lungs at him, trying to get something outta him.

Like: "Hey, wake up," "HELLO!"

But he didn't move, he didn't flinch, he didn't anything…

REGGIE FLUTY: He was tied to the fence—his hands were thumbs out in what we call a cuffing position—the way we handcuff people. He was bound with a real thin white rope, it went around the bottom of the pole, about four inches up off the ground.

His shoes were missing.

He was tied extremely tight—so I used my boot knife and tried to slip it between the rope and his wrist—I had to be extremely careful not to harm Matthew any further.

DR. CANTWAY: Your first thought is…well, certainly you'd like to think that it's somebody from out of town, that comes through and beats somebody. I mean, things like this happen, you know, shit happens, and it happens in Laramie. But if there's been somebody who has been beaten repeatedly, ah, certainly this is something that offends us. I think that's a good word. It offends us!

REGGIE FLUTY: He was bound so tight—I finally got the knife through there—I'm sorry—we rolled him over to his left side—when we did that he quit breathing. Immediately, I put him back on his back—and that was just enough of an adjustment—it gave me enough room to cut him free there—

I seen the EMS unit trying to get to the location, once the ambulance got there we put a neck collar on him, placed him on a back board, and scooted him from underneath the fence—then Rob drove the ambulance to Ivinson Hospital's emergency room…

DR. CANTWAY: Now, the strange thing is, twenty minutes before Matthew came in, Aaron McKinney was brought in by his girlfriend. Now I guess he had gotten into a fight later on that night back in town, so I am working on Aaron and the ambulance comes in with Matthew. Now at this point I don't know that there's a connection—at all. So I tell Aaron to wait and I go and treat Matthew. So there's Aaron in one room of the ER and Matthew in another room two doors down.

Now as soon as we saw Matthew…It was very obvious that his care was beyond our capabilities. Called the neurosurgeon at Poudre Valley, and he was on the road in an hour and fifteen minutes, I think.

REGGIE FLUTY: They showed me a picture…days later I saw a picture of Matthew…I would have never recognized him.

DR. CANTWAY: Then two days later I found out the connection and I was…very…struck!!! They were two kids!!!!! They were both my patients and they were two kids. I took care of both of them…. Of both their bodies. And…for a brief moment I wondered if this is how God feels when he looks down at us. How we are all his kids…. Our bodies…. Our souls…. And I felt a great deal of compassion…. For both of them….

END OF ACT ONE

ACT II

MOMENT: A LARAMIE MAN

NARRATOR: This is Jon Peacock, Matthew's academic adviser.

JON PEACOCK: Well, the news reports started trickling out on Thursday, but no names were mentioned, the brutality of the crime was not mentioned. All that was mentioned was that there was a man, Laramie man, found beaten, out on the prairie basically. Later on in the evening they mentioned his name. It was like, That can't, that's not the Matthew Shepard I know, that's not my student, that's not this person who I've been meeting with.

ROMAINE PATTERSON: I was in the coffee shop.

NARRATOR: Romaine Patterson:

ROMAINE PATTERSON: And someone pulled me aside and said: "I don't know much, but they say that there's been a young man who's been beaten in Laramie. And they said his name was Matthew Shepard." And he said, "Do you think this could be our Matthew?"

And I said, "Well, yeah, it sounds like it could be our Matthew."

So I called up my sister Trish and I said, "Tell me what you know" I'm just like, "I need to know anything you know because I don't know anything."

TRISH STEGER: So I'm talking to my sister on the phone and that's when the whole story came up on Channel 5 news and it was just like *baboom.*

JON PEACOCK: And the news reports kept rolling in, young University of Wyoming student, his age, his description, it's like, "Oh my God."

TRISH STEGER: And, uh (*pause*) I—I felt sick to my stomach…it's just instantly sick to my stomach. And I had to tell Romaine, "Yes, it was Matthew. It was your friend."

MATT GALLOWAY: Well, I'll tell you—I'll tell you what is overwhelming.

NARRATOR: Matt Galloway:

MATT GALLOWAY: Friday morning I first find out about it. I go to class, walk out, boom there it is—in the *Branding Iron*. So immediately I drive to the nearest newsstand, buy a *Laramie Boomerang* 'cause I want more details, buy that—go home…before I can even open the paper, my boss calls me, he says:

MATT MICKELSON: Did you hear about what happened?

MATT GALLOWAY: I'm like, "Yeah."

MATT MICKELSON: Was he in the bar Tuesday night?

MATT GALLOWAY: I go, "Yes, yes he was."

MATT MICKELSON: You've got to get down to the bar right now, we've got to talk about this, we've got to discuss what's going to go on.

JON PEACOCK: By this time, I was starting to get upset, but still the severity wasn't out yet.

RULON STACEY: It was Thursday afternoon.

NARRATOR: Rulon Stacey at Poudre Valley Hospital:

RULON STACEY: I got a call: "We just got a kid in from Wyoming and it looks like he may be the victim of a hate crime. We have a couple of newspaper reporters here asking questions." And so, we agreed that we needed one spokesperson: As CEO, I'll do that and we'll try and gather all the information that we can.

ROMAINE PATTERSON: And then I watched the ten o'clock news that night, where they started speaking about the nature and the seriousness of it…

MATT GALLOWAY: So I'm on the phone with Mickelson and he's like:

MATT MICKELSON: We need to go to the arraignment so we can identify these guys, and make sure these guys were in the bar.

MATT GALLOWAY: So we go to the arraignment.

MOMENT: THE ESSENTIAL FACTS

NEWSPERSON: Our focus today turns to Laramie, Wyoming, and the Albany County Courthouse, where Aaron James McKinney and Russell Arthur Henderson are being charged with the brutal beating of Matthew Shepard, a gay University of Wyoming student.

NARRATOR: Catherine Connolly:

CATHERINE CONNOLLY: The arraignment was on Friday. Right around lunchtime. And I said, "I'm just going." I just took off—it's just down the street. So I walked a few blocks and I went. Has anybody told you about the arraignment?

There were probably about a hundred people from town and probably as many news media. By that point, a lot more of the details had come out. The fact that the perpetrators were kids themselves, local kids, that everyone who's from around here has some relationship to. And what—Everyone was really I think waiting on pins and needles for what would happen when the perpetrators walked in. And what happened—there's two hundred people in the room at this point…they walked in in their complete orange jumpsuits and their shackles, and, you could have heard a pin drop.

It was incredibly solemn.

I mean, lots of people were teary at that point. Then the judge came in and did a reading—there was a reading of the evidence that the prosecution has and—it's just a—it's a statement of facts, and the reading of the facts was…

JUDGE: The essential facts are that the defendants, Aaron James McKinney and Russell Arthur Henderson, met Matthew Shepard at the Fireside Bar, and after Mr. Shepard confided he was gay, the subjects deceived Mr. Shepard into leaving with them in their vehicle to a remote area. Upon arrival at said area, both subjects tied their victim to a buck fence, robbed him, tortured him, and beat him.... Both defendants were later contacted by officers of the Laramie Police Department, who observed inside the cab of their pickup a credit card and a pair of black patent leather shoes belonging to the victim, Matthew Shepard.

(*The* JUDGE *goes sotto voce here while* CATHERINE CONNOLLY *speaks.*)

The subjects took the victim's credit card, wallet containing twenty dollars in cash, his shoes, and other items, and obtained the victim's address in order to later burglarize his home.

CATHERINE CONNOLLY: I don't think there was any person who was left in that courtroom who wasn't crying at the end of it. I mean it lasted—five minutes, but it kept on getting more and more horrific, ending with:

JUDGE: Said defendants left the victim begging for his life.

MOMENT: LIVE AND LET LIVE

NARRATOR: Sergeant Hing:

SERGEANT HING: How could this happen? I—I think a lot of people just don't understand, and even I don't really understand, how someone can do something like that. We have one of the most vocal populations of gay people in the state.... And it's pretty much: Live and let live.

NARRATOR: Laramie resident Jeffrey Lockwood:

JEFFREY LOCKWOOD: My secret hope was that they were from somewhere else, that then of course you can create that distance: We don't grow children like that here. Well, it's pretty clear that we do grow children like that here...

CATHERINE CONNOLLY: So that was the arraignment, and my response—was pretty catatonic—not sleeping, not eating. Don't—you know, don't leave me alone right now.

JON PEACOCK: More and more details came in about the sheer brutality, um, motivations, how this happened. And then quite frankly the media descended and there was no time to reflect on it anymore.

MOMENT: THE GEM CITY OF THE PLAINS

(*Many reporters enter the stage, followed by media crews carrying cameras, microphones, and lights. They start speaking into the cameras. Simultaneously, television monitors enter the space—in our production they flew in from above the light grid. In the monitors, one can see in live feed the reporters speaking as well as other media images. The texts overlap to create a kind of media cacophony. This moment should feel like an invasion and should be so perceived by the other actors onstage.*)

NEWSPERSON 1: Laramie, Wyoming—often called the Gem City of the Plains—is now at the eye of the storm.

(*Enter* NEWSPERSON 2. NEWSPERSON 1 *goes sotto voce.*)

The cowboy state has its rednecks and yahoos for sure, but there are no more bigots per capita in Wyoming than there are in New York, Florida, or California. The difference is that in Wyoming there are fewer places to blend in if you're anything other than prairie stock.

NEWSPERSON 2: Aaron McKinney and his friend Russell Henderson came from the poor side of town.

(*Enter* NEWSPERSON 3. NEWSPERSON 2 *goes sotto voce.*)

Both were from broken homes and as teenagers had had run-ins with the law. They lived in trailer parks and scratched out a living working at fast-food restaurants and fixing roofs.

NEWSPERSON 3: As a gay college student lay hospitalized in critical condition after a severe beating...this small city, which bills itself as Wyoming's Hometown, wrestled with its attitudes toward gay men.

(*Enter* NEWSPERSON 4. NEWSPERSON 3 *goes sotto voce.*)

NEWSPERSON 4: People would like to think that what happened to Matthew was an exception to the rule, but it was an extreme version of what happens in our schools on a daily basis.

(*The voices and sounds have escalated to a high pitch. And the last text we hear is:*)

NEWSPERSON 1: It's a tough business, as Matt Shepard knew, and as his friends all know, to be gay in cowboy country.
(*These reporters continue speaking into the cameras sotto voce over the next texts.*)

JON PEACOCK: It was huge. Yeah. It was herds and—and we're talking hundreds of reporters, which makes a huge dent in this town's population. There's reporters everywhere, news trucks everywhere on campus, everywhere in the town. And we're not used to that type of attention to begin with, we're not used to that type of exposure.

NARRATOR: Tiffany Edwards, local reporter:

TIFFANY EDWARDS: These people are predators. Like this one journalist actually caught one of the judges in the bathroom at the urinal and was like asking him questions. And the judge was like, "Excuse me, can I please have some privacy?" And the journalist was like *OFFENDED* that he asked for privacy. I mean, this is not how journalism started, like the Gutenberg press, you know.

DOC O'CONNOR: I'll tell you what, when *Hard Copy* came and taped me, I taped them at the exact same time. I have every word I ever said on tape so if they ever do anything funny they better watch their fuckin' ass.

NEWSPERSON: Wyoming governor Jim Geringer, a first-term Republican up for reelection:

GOVERNOR GERINGER: I am outraged and sickened by the heinous crime committed on Matthew Shepard. I extend my most heartfelt sympathies to the family.

NEWSPERSON: Governor, you haven't pushed hate crime legislation in the past.

GOVERNOR GERINGER: I would like to urge the people of Wyoming against overreacting in a way that gives one group "special rights over others."

We will wait and see if the vicious beating and torture of Matthew Shepard was motivated by hate.

SERGEANT HING: You've got the beginning of the news story where they have the graphics in the background, and they've got: "Murder in Wyoming," and Wyoming's dripping red like it's got blood on it or something, and

it's like, what's the—what is this, this is sensationalism. And…we're here going, "Wait a minute. We had the guys in jail in less than a day. I think that's pretty damn good."

EILEEN ENGEN: And for us to be more or less maligned.

NARRATOR: Eileen and Gil Engen:

EILEEN ENGEN: That we're not a good community and we are—The majority of people here are good people.

GIL ENGEN: You get bad apples once in a while. And I think that the gay community took this as an advantage, said this is a good time for us to exploit this.

NEWSPERSON: Bill McKinney, father of one of the accused:

BILL MCKINNEY: Had this been a heterosexual these two boys decided to take out and rob, this never would have made the national news. Now my son is guilty before he's even had a trial.

TIFFANY EDWARDS: Look, I do think that, um, the media actually made people accountable. Because they made people think. Because people were sitting in their homes, like watching TV and listening to CNN and watching Dan Rather and going, "Jesus Christ, well that's not how it is here." Well how is it here?

MOMENT: MEDICAL UPDATE

NARRATOR: Matthew Shepard update at three P.M., Saturday, October tenth.

RULON STACEY: By this point, I looked out there and where there had been two or three reporters…it must have been ten or fifteen still photographers, another twenty or thirty reporters, and ten video cameras. The parents had just arrived. I had barely introduced myself to them. I looked out there and I thought, "My gosh. What am I going to do?" (*He crosses to the area where the reporters are gathered with their cameras. As he arrives, several camera flashes go off. He speaks straight into the camera. We see his image on the monitors around the stage.*)

Matthew Shepard was admitted in critical condition approximately nine-fifteen

P.M., October seventh. When he arrived, he was unresponsive, and breathing support was being provided.

Matthew's major injuries upon arrival consisted of hypothermia and a fracture from behind his head to just in front of the right ear. This has caused bleeding in the brain, as well as pressure on the brain. There were also several lacerations on his head, face, and neck.

Matthew's temperature has fluctuated over the last twenty-four hours, ranging from ninety-eight to one hundred and six degrees. We have had difficulty controlling his temperature.

Matthew's parents arrived at seven P.M., October ninth, and are now at his bedside. The following is a statement from them:

First of all, we want to thank the American public for their kind thoughts about Matthew and their fond wishes for his speedy recovery. We appreciate your prayers and goodwill, and we know that they are something Matthew would appreciate, too.

We also have a special request for the members of the media. Matthew is very much in need of his family at this time, and we ask that you respect our privacy as well as Matthew's, so we can concentrate all of our efforts, thoughts, and love on our son.

Thank you very much.

MOMENT: SEEING MATTHEW

NARRATOR: Both Aaron McKinney and Russell Henderson pled not guilty to charges. Their girlfriends, Chastity Pasley and Kristin Price, also pled not guilty after being charged as accessories after the fact. On our next trip, we spoke to the chief investigating officer on the case, Detective Rob DeBree of the Albany County Sheriff's Department.

ROB DEBREE: I guess the thing that bothered me the most was when I went down to Poudre Valley, where Matthew was, and the thing that bothered me the most is seeing him, touching him. As a homicide detective, you look at bodies…. This poor boy is sitting here, fighting all his life, trying to make it. I wanted it so by the book you know.

AARON KREIFELS: I keep seeing that picture in my head when I found him…

NARRATOR: Aaron Kreifels:

AARON KREIFELS: …and it's not pleasant whatsoever. I don't want it to be there. I wanna like get it out. That's the biggest part for me is seeing that picture in my head. And it's kind of unbelievable to me, you know, that—I happened to be the person who found him—because the big question with me, like with my religion, is like, Why did God want ME to find him?

CATHERINE CONNOLLY: I know how to take care of myself, and I was irrationally terrified.

NARRATOR: Catherine Connolly:

CATHERINE CONNOLLY: So what that means is, not letting my twelve-year-old son walk the streets, seeing a truck do a U-turn and thinking it's coming after me. Having to stop because I'm shaking so bad. And, in fact, the pickup truck did not come after me, but my reaction was to have my heart in my mouth.

MATT GALLOWAY: Ultimately, no matter how you dice it, I did have an opportunity.

NARRATOR: Matt Galloway:

MATT GALLOWAY: If I had—amazing hindsight of 20/20—to have stopped—what occurred …and I keep thinkin', "I shoulda noticed. These guys shouldn'ta been talking to this guy. I shoulda not had my head down when I was washing dishes for those twenty seconds. Things I coulda done. What the hell was I thinking?"

ROB DEBREE: So you do a lot of studying, you spend hours and hours and hours. You study and study and study…talking to the officers, making sure they understand, talk to your witnesses again, and then always coming back to I get this flash of seeing Matthew…I wanted it so tight that there was no way that they were gonna get out of this.

REGGIE FLUTY: One of the things that happened when I got to the fence…

NARRATOR: Reggie Fluty:

REGGIE FLUTY: …It was just such an overwhelming amount of blood…and we try to wear protective gloves, but we had a really cheap sheriff at the time, and he bought us shit gloves, you know, you put 'em on, you put 'em on, and they kept breaking, so finally you just ran out of gloves, you know. So, you figure, well, you know, "Don't hesitate," you know, that's what your mind tells you all the time—Don't hesitate—and so you just keep moving and you try to help Matthew and find an airway and, you know, that's what you do, you know.

MARGE MURRAY: The thing I wasn't telling you before is that Reggie is my daughter.

NARRATOR: Marge Murray:

MARGE MURRAY: And when she first told me she wanted to be a police officer, well, I thought there was not a better choice for her. She could handle whatever came her way.…

REGGIE FLUTY: Probably a day and a half later, the hospital called me and told me Matthew had HIV. And the doctor said, "You've been exposed, and you've had a bad exposure," because, you see, I'd been—been building—building a, uh, lean-to for my llamas, and my hands had a bunch of open cuts on 'em, so I was kinda screwed (she laughs) you know, and you think, "Oh, shoot," you know.

MARGE MURRAY: Would you like to talk about losing sleep?

REGGIE FLUTY: So I said to the doctor, "Okay, what do I do?" And they said, "Get up here." So, I got up there and we started the ATZ [sic] drugs. Immediately.

MARGE MURRAY: Now they told me that's a medication that if it's administered thirty-six hours after you've been exposed…it can maybe stop your getting the disease…

REGGIE FLUTY: That is a mean nasty medicine. Mean. I've lost ten pounds and a lot of my hair. Yeah…

MARGE MURRAY: And quite frankly I wanted to lash out at somebody. Not at Matthew, please understand that, not one of us was mad at Matthew. But we maybe wanted to squeeze McKinney's head off. And I think about Henderson. And, you know, two absolutely human beings cause so much grief for so many people.… It has been terrible for my whole family, but mostly for her and her kids.

REGGIE FLUTY: I think it brought home to my girls what their mom does for a living.

MARGE MURRAY: Well, Reggie, you know what I'm gonna tell you now.

REGGIE FLUTY: And my parents told me, you know, they both said the same damn thing.

MARGE MURRAY: You're quitting this damn job!

REGGIE FLUTY: And it's just a parent thing, you know, and they're terribly proud of you, 'cause you do a good job whether it's handling a drunk or handling a case like this, but you're, you know, they don't want you getting hurt—

MARGE MURRAY: Like I said, there's a right way, a wrong way, and then there's Reggie's way.

REGGIE FLUTY: So finally I said, "Oh, for God's sakes, lighten up, Francis!"

MARGE MURRAY: You are so stubborn!

REGGIE FLUTY: They say I'm stubborn, and I don't believe them, but I just think, you know, okay, I've heard your opinion and now here's mine. I'm thirty-nine years old, you know, what are they gonna do, spank me?

MARGE MURRAY: Reggie, don't give me any ideas.

REGGIE FLUTY: It'd look pretty funny. You know, what can they say?

MARGE MURRAY: I just hope she doesn't go before me. I just couldn't handle that.

MOMENT: E-MAIL

NARRATOR: University of Wyoming president Philip Dubois:

PHILIP DUBOIS: Well, this is a young person—who read my statement on the *Denver Post* story, and sent me an e-mail, to me directly, and said:

E-MAIL WRITER: You and the straight people of Laramie and Wyoming are guilty of the beating of Matthew Shepard just as the Germans who looked the other way are guilty of the deaths of the Jews, the Gypsies, and the homosexuals. You have taught your straight children to hate their gay and lesbian brothers and sisters. Unless and until you acknowledge that Matt Shepard's beating is not just a random occurrence, not just the work of a couple of random crazies, you have Matthew's blood on your hands.

PHILIP DUBOIS: And uh, well, I just can't begin to tell you what that does to you. And it's like, you can't possibly know what I'm thinking, you can't possibly know what this has done to me and my family and my community.

MOMENT: VIGILS

(*We see images of the vigils taking place around the country in the monitors as.*)

NARRATOR: That first week alone, vigils were held in Laramie, Denver, Fort Collins, and Colorado Springs. Soon after in Detroit, Chicago, San Francisco, Washington, D.C., Atlanta, Nashville, Minneapolis, and Portland, Maine, among others. In Los Angeles, five thousand people gathered, and in New York City a political rally ended in civil disobedience and hundreds of arrests. And the Poudre Valley Hospital Web site received close to a million visitors from across the country and around the world, all expressing hope for Matthew's recovery.

MOMENT: MEDICAL UPDATE

NARRATOR: Matthew Shepard medical update at nine A.M., Sunday, October eleventh. (RULON STACEY *is in front of the cameras. We see him on the monitors.*)

RULON STACEY: As of nine A.M. today, Matthew Shepard remains in critical condition. The family continues to emphasize that the media respect their privacy. The family also wants to thank the American public for their kind thoughts and concern for Matthew.

MOMENT: LIVE AND LET LIVE

JEDADIAH SCHULTZ: There are certain things when I sit in church.

NARRATOR: Jedadiah Schultz:

JEDADIAH SCHULTZ: And the reverend will tell you flat out he doesn't agree with homosexuality—and I don't know—I think right now, I'm going through changes, I'm still learning about myself and—you know I don't feel like I know enough about certain things to make a decision that says, "Homosexuality is right." When you've been raised your whole life that it's wrong—and right now, I would say that I don't agree with it yeah, that I don't agree with it but—maybe that's just because I couldn't do it—and speaking in religious terms—I don't think that's how God intended it to happen. But I don't hate homosexuals and, I mean—I'm not going to persecute them or anything like that. At all—I mean, that's not gonna be getting in the way between me and the other person at all.

CONRAD MILLER: Well, it's preached in schools that being gay is okay.

NARRATOR: Conrad Miller:

CONRAD MILLER: And if my kids asked me, I'd set them down and I'd say, "Well, this is what gay people do. This is what animals do. Okay?" And I'd tell 'em, "This is the life, this is the lifestyle, this is what they do." And I'd say, "This is why I believe it's wrong."

MURDOCK COOPER: There's more gay people around than what you think.

NARRATOR: Murdock Cooper:

MURDOCK COOPER: It doesn't bother anybody because most of 'em that are gay or lesbian they know damn well who to talk to. If you step out of line you're asking for it. Some people are saying he made a pass at them. You don't pick up regular people. I'm not excusing their actions, but it made me feel better because it was partially Matthew Shepard's fault and partially the guys who did it…you know, maybe it's fifty-fifty.

ZACKIE SALMON: Yes, as a lesbian I was more concerned for my safety.

NARRATOR: Zackie Salmon:

ZACKIE SALMON: I think we all were. And I think it's because somewhere inside we know it could happen to us anytime, you know. I mean, I would be afraid to walk down the street and display any sort of physical affection for my partner. You don't do that here in Laramie.

JONAS SLONAKER: Well, there's this whole idea: You leave me alone, I leave you alone.

NARRATOR: Jonas Slonaker:

JONAS SLONAKER: And it's even in some of the western literature, you know, live and let live. That is such crap. I tell my friends that—even my gay friends bring it up sometimes. I'm like, "That is crap, you know?" I mean, basically what it boils down to: If I don't tell you I'm a fag, you won't beat the crap out of me. I mean, what's so great about that? That's a great philosophy?

MOMENT: IT HAPPENED HERE

ZUBAIDA ULA: We went to the candle vigil.

NARRATOR: Zubaida Ula:

ZUBAIDA ULA: And it was so good to be with people who felt like shit. I kept feeling like I don't deserve to feel this bad, you know? And someone got up there and said, "C'mon, guys, let's show the world that Laramie is not this kind of a town." But it is that kind of a town. If it wasn't this kind of a town, why did this happen here? I mean, you know what I mean, like—that's a lie. Because it happened here. So how could it not be a town where this kind of thing happens? Like, that's just totally—like, looking at an Escher painting and getting all confused, like, it's just totally like circular logic like how can you even say that? And we have to mourn this and we have to be sad that we live in a town, a state, a country where shit like this happens. And I'm not going to step away from that and say, "We need to show the world this didn't happen." I mean, these are people trying to distance themselves from this crime. And we need to own this crime. I feel. Everyone needs to own it. We are like this. We ARE like this. WE are LIKE this.

MOMENT: SHANNON AND JEN

STEPHEN BELBER: I was in the Fireside one afternoon and I ran into two friends of Aaron McKinney, Shannon and Jen. (*To Shannon and Jen*) You knew Aaron well, right?

SHANNON: Yeah, we both did. When I first found out about this, I thought it was really really awful. I don't know whether Aaron was fucked up or whether he was coming down or what, but Matthew had money. Shit, he had better clothes than I did. Matthew was a little rich bitch.

JEN: You shouldn't call him a rich bitch though, that's not right.

SHANNON: Well, I'm not saying he's a bad guy either, because he was just in the wrong place at the wrong time, said the wrong things. And I don't know, I won't lie to you. There was times that I was all messed up on meth and I thought about going out and robbing. I mean, I never did. But yeah, it was there. It's easy money.

JEN: Aaron's done that thing before. They've both done it. I know one night they went to Cheyenne to go do it and they came back with probably three hundred dollars. I don't know if they ever chose like gay people as their particular targets before, but anyone that looked like they had a lot of money and that was you know, they could outnumber, or overpower, was fair game.

STEPHEN BELBER: But do you think there was any homophobia involved in this that contributed to some of it?

JEN: Probably. It probably would've pissed him off that Matthew was gay 'cause he didn't like—the gay people that I've seen him interact with, he was fine as long as, you know, they didn't hit on him. As long as it didn't come up.

SHANNON: Yeah, as long as they weren't doing it in front of him.

STEPHEN BELBER: Do you get the impression that Aaron knew other gay people?

SHANNON: I'm sure that he knew people that are gay. I mean, he worked up at KFC and there was a couple people up there that—yeah (*he laughs*)—and I'm not saying it's bad or anything 'cause I don't know, half the people I know in Laramie are gay.

STEPHEN BELBER: What would you guys say to Aaron if you saw him right now?

SHANNON: First of all, I'd ask him if he'd ever do anymore tweak.

JEN: He wouldn't I bet. If I saw Aaron now, I'd be like, "Man, why'd you fuck up like that?" But, I'd want to make sure he's doing good in there. But, I'm sure he is though. I'd probably just want to like hang out with him.

SHANNON: Smoke a bowl with him.

JEN: I bet he wants one so bad.

STEPHEN BELBER: So, you guys both went to Laramie High?

SHANNON: Yeah. Can't you tell? We're a product of our society.

MOMENT: HOMECOMING

NEWSPERSON: On a day that is traditionally given over to nothing more profound than collegiate exuberance and the fortunes of the University of Wyoming football team, this community on the high plains had a different kind of homecoming Saturday, as many searched their souls in the wake of a vicious, apparent antigay hate crime.

NARRATOR: University president Philip Dubois:

PHILIP DUBOIS: This was homecoming weekend. There were a lot of people in town, and there's a homecoming parade that was scheduled, and then the students organized to tag onto the back of it—you know, behind the banner supporting Matt, and everybody wearing the armbands that the students had created…

HARRY WOODS: I live in the center of town.

NARRATOR: Harry Woods:

HARRY WOODS: And my apartment has windows on two opposite streets. One goes north and one goes south. And that is exactly the homecoming parade route. Now, on the day of the parade, I had a cast on my leg because of a fall. So I was very disappointed because I really wanted to walk with the people that were marching for Matthew. But I couldn't. So I watched from my window. And it was …it was just…I'm fifty-two years old and I'm gay. I have lived here for many years and I've seen a lot. And I was very moved when I saw the tag on the end of the home-

coming parade. About a hundred people walking behind a banner for Matthew Shepard.

So then the parade went down to the end of the block to make a U-turn, and I went to the other side of my apartment to wait for it to come south down the other street.

MATT GALLOWAY: I was right up in front there where they were holding the banner for Matthew, and let me tell you…I've never had goose bumps so long in my life. It was incredible. A mass of people. Families—mothers holding their six-year-old kids, tying these armbands around these six-year-old kids and trying to explain to them why they should wear an armband. just amazing. I mean it was absolutely one of the most—beautiful things I've ever done in my life.

HARRY WOODS: Well, about ten minutes went by, and sure enough the parade started coming down the street. And then I noticed the most incredible thing…as the parade came down the street…the number of people walking for Matthew Shepard had grown five times. There were at least five hundred people marching for Matthew. Five hundred people. Can you imagine? The tag at the end was larger than the entire parade. And people kept joining in. And you know what? I started to cry. Tears were streaming down my face. And I thought, "Thank God that I got to see this in my lifetime." And my second thought was, "Thank you, Matthew."

MOMENT: ONE OF OURS

SHERRY JOHNSON: I really haven't been all that involved, per se. My husband's a highway patrolman, so that's really the only way that I've known about it.

Now when I first found out I just thought it was horrible. I just, I can't… Nobody deserves that! I don't care who ya are.

But, the other thing that was not brought out—at the same time this happened that patrolman was killed. And there was nothing. Nothing. They didn't say any-thing about the old man that killed him. He was driving down the road and he shouldn't have been driving and killed him. It was just a little piece in the paper. And we lost one of our guys.

You know, my husband worked with him. This man was brand-new on the force. But, I mean, here's one of ours, and it was just a little piece in the paper.

And a lot of it is my feeling that the me-dia is portraying Matthew Shepard as a saint. And making him as a martyr. And I don't think he was. I don't think he was that pure.

Now, I didn't know him, but...there's just so many things about him that I found out that I just, it's scary. You know about his character and spreading AIDS and a few other things, you know, being the kind of person that he was. He was, he was just a barfly, you know. And I think he pushed himself around. I think he flaunted it.

Everybody's got problems. But why they exemplified him I don't know. What's the difference if you're gay? A hate crime is a hate crime. If you murder somebody you hate 'em. It has nothing to do with if you're gay or a prostitute or whatever.

I don't understand. I don't understand.

MOMENT: TWO QUEERS
AND A CATHOLIC PRIEST

NARRATOR: Company member Leigh Fonda-kowski:

LEIGH FONDAKOWSKI: This is one of the last days on our second trip to Laramie. Greg and I have been conducting interviews nonstop and we are exhausted.

GREG PIEROTTI: We are to meet Father Roger at seven-thirty in the morning. I was wishing we could skip it all together, but we have to follow through to the end. So here we go: seven-thirty A.M., two queers and a Catholic priest.

FATHER ROGER SCHMIT: Matthew Shepard has served us well. You realize that? He has served us well. And I do not mean to condemn

Matthew to perfection, but I cannot men-tion any one who has done more for this community than Matthew Shepard.

And I'm not gonna sit here and say, "I was just this bold guy—no fear." I was scared. I was very vocal in this community when this happened—and I thought, "You know, should we, uh, should we call the bishop and ask him permission to do the vigil?" And I was like, "Hell, no, I'm not going to do that." His permission doesn't make it correct, you realize that? And I'm not knocking bishops, but what is correct is correct.

You people are just out here on a search, though. I will do this. I will trust you people that if you write a play of this, that you (*pause*) say it right, say it correct. I think you have a responsibility to do that.

Don't—don't—don't, um (*pause*) don't make matters worse.... You think violence is what they did to Matthew—they did do violence to Matthew—but you know, every time that you are called a fag, or you are called a you know, a lez or whatever...

LEIGH FONDAKOWSKI: Or a dyke.

FATHER ROGER SCHMIT: Dyke, yeah, dyke. Do you realize that is violence? That is the seed of vi-olence. And I would resent it immensely if you use anything I said, uh, you know, to—to somehow cultivate that kind of violence, even in its smallest form. I would resent it immensely. You need to know that.

LEIGH FONDAKOWSKI: Thank you, Father, for saying that.

FATHER ROGER SCHMIT: Just deal with what is true. You know what is true. You need to do your best to say it correct.

MOMENT: CHRISTMAS

NARRATOR: Andrew Gomez:

ANDREW GOMEZ: I was in there, I was in jail with Aaron in December. I got thrown in over Christmas. Assault and battery, two counts. I don't wanna talk about it. But we were sit-tin' there eatin' our Christmas dinner, tryin' to eat my stuffing, my motherfucking bread, my little roll and whatnot, and I asked him, I was like, "Hey, homey, tell me something, tell me something please, why did you—" Okay, I'm thinking how I worded this, I was like, "Why did you kill a faggot if you're gonna be destined to BE a faggot later?" You know? I mean, think about it, he's either gonna get humped a lot or he's gonna die. So why would you do that, think about that. I don't understand that.

And you know what he told me? Honest to God, this is what he said, he goes: "He tried to grab my dick." That's what he said, man! He's dumb, dog, he don't even act like it was nothin'.

Now I heard they was auctioning those boys off. Up there in the max ward, you know, where the killers go, I heard that when they found out Aaron was coming to prison, they were auctioning those boys off "I want him. I'll put aside five, six, seven cartons of cigarettes." Auction his ass off. I'd be scared to go to prison if I was those two boys.

MOMENT: LIFESTYLE 2

BAPTIST MINISTER: Hello.

AMANDA GRONICH: Reverend?

BAPTIST MINISTER: Yes, hello.

AMANDA GRONICH: I believe your wife told you a bit about why I'm contacting you.

BAPTIST MINISTER: Yes, she did. And let me tell you—uh—I don't know that I really want to talk to anyone about any of this incident—uh—I am somewhat involved and I just don't think—

AMANDA GRONICH: Yes, I completely understand and I don't blame you. You know, I went to your service on Sunday.

BAPTIST MINISTER: You went to the services on Sunday?

AMANDA GRONICH: Yes, I did.

BAPTIST MINISTER: On Sunday?

AMANDA GRONICH: Yes, this past Sunday.

BAPTIST MINISTER: Did I meet you?

AMANDA GRONICH: Yes, you welcomed me at the beginning, I believe.

BAPTIST MINISTER: I see. Well, let me tell you. I am not afraid to be controversial or to speak my mind, and that is not necessarily the views of my congregation per se. Now as I said, I am somewhat involved—that half the people in the case—well, the girlfriend of the accused is a member of our congregation, and one of the accused has visited.

AMANDA GRONICH: Mmmmmm.

BAPTIST MINISTER: Now, those two people, the accused, have forfeited their lives. We've been after the two I mentioned for ages, trying to get them to live right, to do right. Now, one boy is on suicide watch and I am working with him—until they put him in the chair and turn on the juice I will work for his salvation. Now I think they deserve the death penalty—I will try to deal with them spiritually.

AMANDA GRONICH: Right, I understand.

BAPTIST MINISTER: Now, as for the victim, I know that that lifestyle is legal, but I will tell you one thing: I hope that Matthew Shepard as he was tied to that fence, that he had time to reflect on a moment when someone had spoken the word of the Lord to him—and that before he slipped into a coma he had a chance to reflect on his lifestyle.

AMANDA GRONICH: Thank you, Reverend, I appreciate your speaking with me.

(*Rain begins to fall on the stage.*)

MOMENT: THAT NIGHT

RULON STACEY: About eleven-thirty that night, I had just barely gone to bed, and Margo, our chief operating officer, called and said, "His blood pressure has started to drop." "Well, let's wait and see." She called me about ten after—he just died. So I quick got dressed and came in, and uh went into the ICU where the family was, and Judy came up and she put her arms around me and I put my arms around her and we just stood there—honestly, for about ten minutes just—'cause what else do you do?

And then we had to sit and talk about things that you just—"Dennis, it's now public knowledge.... And I'm gonna go out there now and tell the whole world that this has happened."

'Cause by this point it was clear to us that it was the world—it was the whole world.

And so Judy told me what she wanted me to say. And I went out at four A.M. (*He crosses to the camera.*)

MOMENT: MEDICAL UPDATE

NARRATOR: Matthew Shepard medical update for four-thirty A.M., Monday, October twelfth.

RULON STACEY: At twelve midnight on Monday, October twelfth, Matthew Shepard's blood pressure began to drop. We immediately notified his family, who were already at the hospital.

At twelve fifty-three A.M. Matthew Shepard died. His family was at his bedside.

The family did release the following statement,

The family again asked me to express their sincerest gratitude to the entire world for the overwhelming response for their son.

The family was grateful that they did not have to make a decision regarding whether or not to continue life support for their son. Like a good son, he was caring to the end and removed guilt or stress from the family.

He came into the world premature and left the world premature.

Matthew's mother said:

Go home, give your kids a hug, and don't let a day go by without telling them that you love them.

MOMENT: MAGNITUDE

RULON STACEY: And—I don't know *how* I let that happen—I lost it on national television, but, you know, we had been up for like seventy-two hours straight and gone home and gone to sleep for half an hour and had to get up and come in—and maybe I was just way—I don't know—but (*pause*) in a moment of complete brain-deadness, while I was out there reading that statement I thought about my own four daughters—

and go home, hug your kids (*he begins to cry*) and, oh, she doesn't have her kid anymore.

And there I am and I'm thinking, "This is so lame."

Um, and then we started to get people sending us e-mails and letters. And most of them were just generally very kind. But I did get this one. This guy wrote me and said, "Do you cry like a baby on TV for all of your patients or just the faggots?" And as I told you before, homosexuality is not a lifestyle with which I agree. Um, but having been thrown into this (*pause*) I guess I didn't understand the magnitude with which some people hate. And of all the letters that we got, there were maybe two or three that were like that, most of them were, Thank you for your caring and compassion, and Matthew had caring and compassion from the moment he got here.

MOMENT: H-O-P-E

STEPHEN BELBER: I spoke with Doc today and told him we would soon be coming back out for the upcoming trials of Russell Henderson and Aaron McKinney, and this is what he had to say.

DOC O'CONNOR: I'll tell you what, if they put those two boys to death, that would defeat everything Matt would be thinking about on them. Because Matt would not want those two to die. He'd want to leave them with hope. (*Spelling*) H-O-P-E. Just like the whole world hoped that Matt would survive. The whole thing, you see, the whole thing, ropes around hope, H-O-P-E.
END OF ACT II

ACT III

(*The stage is now empty except for several chairs stage right. They occupy that half of the stage. They are all facing the audience and arranged in rows as if to suggest a church or a courthouse. As the lights come up, several actors are sitting there dressed in black. Some of them have umbrellas. A few beats with just this image in silence Then* MATT GALLOWAY *enters stage left. Looks at them and says:*)

MOMENT: SNOW

MATT GALLOWAY: The day of the funeral, it was snowing so bad, big huge wet snowflakes. And when I got there, there were thousands of people in just black, with umbrellas everywhere. And there were two churches—one for the immediate family, uh, invited guests, people of that nature, and then one church for everybody else who wanted to be there. And then, still, hundreds of people outside that couldn't fit into either of the churches. And there was a big park by the church, and that's where these people were. And this park was full.

PRIEST: The liturgy today is an Easter liturgy. It finds its meaning in the Resurrection. The service invites your full participation.

PRIEST: The Lord be with you.

PEOPLE: And also with you.

PRIEST: Let us pray.

TIFFANY EDWARDS: And I guess it was like the worst storm that they have had.

NARRATOR: Tiffany Edwards:

TIFFANY EDWARDS: Like that anybody could ever tell, like trees fell down and the power went out for a couple of days because of it and I just thought, "It's like the forces of the universe at work, you know." Whatever higher spirit, you know, is like that blows storms, was blowin' this storm.

PRIEST: For our brother, Matthew, let us pray to our Lord Jesus Christ, who said, "I am the Resurrection and the Life." We pray to the Lord.

PEOPLE: HEAR US, LORD.

(*The* PRIEST *begins and goes into sotto voce.*)

PRIEST: Lord, you who consoled Martha and Mary in their distress: draw near to us who mourn for Matthew, and dry the tears of those who weep. We pray to the Lord.

PEOPLE: HEAR US, LORD.

PRIEST: You wept at the grave of Lazarus, your friend: comfort us in our sorrow. We pray to the Lord.

PEOPLE: HEAR US, LORD.

PRIEST: You raised the dead to life: give to our brother eternal life. We pray to the Lord.

PEOPLE: HEAR US, LORD.

PRIEST: You promised paradise to the thief who repented: bring our brother the joys of heaven. We pray to the Lord.

PEOPLE: HEAR US, LORD.

PRIEST: He was nourished with your Body and Blood; grant him a place at the table in your heavenly kingdom. We pray to the Lord.

PEOPLE: HEAR US, LORD.

PRIEST: Comfort us in our sorrows at the death of our brother; let our faith be our consolation, and eternal life our hope. We pray to the Lord.

KERRY DRAKE: My most striking memory from the funeral…

NARRATOR: Kerry Drake, *Casper Star-Tribune*.

KERRY DRAKE: …is seeing the Reverend Fred Phelps from Kansas…that scene go up in the park.

REVEREND FRED PHELPS: Do you believe the Bible? Do you believe you're supposed to separate the precious from the vile? You don't believe that part of the Bible? You stand over there ignorant of the fact that the Bible—two times for every verse it talks about God's love it talks about God's hate.

(REVEREND FRED PHELPS *continues sotto voce.*)

KERRY DRAKE: A bunch of high school kids who got out early came over and started yelling at some of these people in the protest—the Fred Phelps people—and across the street you had people lining up for the funeral…. Well, I remember a guy, this skinhead coming over, and he was dressed in leather and spikes everywhere, and he came over from across the street where the protest was and he came into the crowd and I just thought, "Oh, this is gonna be a really ugly confrontation" BUT instead he came over and he started leading them in "Amazing Grace."

(*The people sing "Amazing Grace."*)

REVEREND FRED PHELPS: We wouldn't be here if this was just another murder the state was gonna deal with. The state deals with hundreds of murders every single day. But this murder is different, because the fags are bringing us out here trying to make Matthew Shepard into a poster boy for the gay lifestyle. And were going to answer it. It's just that simple.

(REVEREND FRED PHELPS *continues sotto voce.*)

NARRATOR: Six months later, the company returned to Laramie for the trial of Russell Henderson, the first of the two perpetrators. It was to be a capital murder trial. When we got to the Albany County Courthouse, Fred Phelps was already there.

REVEREND FRED PHELPS: You don't like that attribute of God.

NARRATOR: But so was Romaine Patterson.

REVEREND FRED PHELPS: That perfect attribute of God. Well, WE love that attribute of God, and we're going to preach it. Because God's hatred is pure. It's a determination—it's a determination that he's gonna send some people to hell. That's God's hatred…

(*Continues sotto voce.*)

We're standing here with God's message. We're standing here with God's message. Is homosexuality—is being a fag okay? What do you mean it's not for you to judge? If God doesn't hate fags, why does he put 'em in hell?…You see the barrenness and sterility of your silly arguments when set over against some solid gospel truth? Barren and sterile. Like your lifestyle. Your silly arguments.

ROMAINE PATTERSON: After seeing Fred Phelps protesting at Matthew's funeral and finding out that he was coming to Laramie for the trial of Russell Henderson, I decided that someone needed to stand toe-to-toe with this guy and show the differences. And I think at times like this, when we're talking about hatred as much as the nation is right now, that someone needs to show that there is a better way of dealing with that kind of hatred.

So our idea is to dress up like angels. And so we have designed an angel outfit—for our wings are huge—they're like big-ass wings—and there'll be ten to twenty of us that are angels and what we're gonna do is we're gonna encircle Phelps…and because of our big wings—we are gonna com-plete-ly block him.

So this big-ass band of angels comes in, we don't say a fuckin' word, we just turn our backs to him and we stand there…. And we are a group of people bringing forth a message of peace and love and compassion. And we're calling it "Angel Action."

Yeah, this twenty-one-year-old little lesbian is ready to walk the line with him.

REVEREND FRED PHELPS: When those old preachers laid their hands on me it's called an ordination. Mine was from Isaiah fifty-eight: one—"Cry aloud. Spare not. Lift up thy voice like a trumpet and show my people their transgressions."

ROMAINE PATTERSON: And I knew that my angels were gonna be taking the brunt of everything he had to yell and say. I mean, we were gonna be blocking his view and he was gonna be liked pissed off to all hell…. So I went out and bought all my angels earplugs. (*"Amazing Grace" ends.*)

MOMENT: JURY SELECTION

BAILIFF: The court is in session.

(*All stand.*)

NARRATOR: Romaine Patterson's sister, Trish Steger:

TRISH STEGER: As soon as they started jury selection, you know, everybody was coming into my shop with "I don't want to be on this trial. I hope they don't call me." Or, "Oh my God, I've been called. How do I get off?" Just wanting to get as far away from it as they could…very fearful that they were going to have to be part of that jury.

And then I heard…Henderson had to sit in the courtroom while they question the prospective jurors. And one of the questions that they ask is: Would you be willing to put this person to death?

And I understand that a lot of the comments were: "Yes, I would."

JUROR: Yes, I would, Your Honor.

JUROR: Yes, sir.

JUROR: Absolutely.

JUROR: Yes, sir!

(*Jurors continue underneath.*)

JUROR: No problem.

JUROR: Yep.

TRISH STEGER: Well, can you imagine hearing that? You know, juror after juror after juror…

MOMENT: RUSSELL HENDERSON

(*"Amazing Grace" begins again.*)

JUDGE: You entered a not guilty plea earlier, Mr. Henderson. But I understand you wish to change your plea today. Is that correct?

RUSSELL HENDERSON: Yes, sir.

JUDGE: You understand, Mr. Henderson, that the recommended sentence here is two life sentences?

RUSSELL HENDERSON: Yes, Sir.

JUDGE: Do you understand that those may run concurrently or they may run consecutively?

RUSSELL HENDERSON: Yes, sir.

JUDGE: Mr. Henderson, I will now ask you how you wish to plead. Guilty or not guilty?

RUSSELL HENDERSON: Guilty.

JUDGE: Before the Court decides whether the sentences will be concurrent or consecutive, I understand that there are statements to be made by at least one individual.

NARRATOR: This is an excerpt from a statement made to the court by Lucy Thompson.

MS. THOMPSON: As the grandmother and the person who raised Russell, along with my family, we have written the following statement: Our hearts ache for the pain and suffering that the Shepards have went through. We have prayed for your family since the very beginning. Many times throughout the day I have thought about Matt. And you will continue to be in our thoughts and prayers, as we know that your pain will never go away. You have showed such mercy in allowing us to have this plea, and we are so grateful that you are giving us all the opportunity to live. Your Honor, we, as a family, hope that as you sentence Russell, that you will do it concurrently two life terms. For the Russell we know and love, we humbly plead, Your Honor, to not take Russell completely out of our lives forever.

JUDGE: Thank you. Mr. Henderson, you have a constitutional right to make a statement if you would like to do so. Do you have anything you would like to say?

RUSSELL HENDERSON: Yes, I would, Your Honor. Mr. and Mrs. Shepard, there is not a moment that goes by that I don't see what happened that night. I know what I did was very wrong, and I regret greatly what I did. You have my greatest sympathy for what happened. I hope that one day you will be able to find it in your hearts to forgive me. Your Honor, I know what I did was wrong. I'm very sorry for what I did, and I'm ready to pay my debt for what I did.

JUDGE: Mr. Henderson, you drove the vehicle that took Matthew Shepard to his death. You bound him to that fence in order that he might be more savagely beaten and in order that he might not escape to tell his tale. You left him out there for eighteen hours, knowing full well that he was there, perhaps having an opportunity to save his life, and you did nothing. Mr. Henderson, this Court does not believe that you really feel any true remorse for your part in this matter. And I wonder, Mr. Henderson, whether you fully realize the gravity of what you've done.

The Court finds it appropriate, therefore, that sentence be ordered as follows: As to Count Three, that being felony murder with robbery, you are to serve a period of imprisonment for the term of your natural life. On Count One, kidnapping, that you serve a period of imprisonment for the term of your natural life. Sentencing for Count One to run consecutive to sentencing for Count Three.

NARRATOR: After the hearing, we spoke with Russell Henderson's Mormon home teacher.

MORMON HOME TEACHER: I've known Russell's family for thirty-eight years. Russell's only twenty-one, so I've known him his entire life. I ordained Russell a priest of the Mormon Church, so when this happened, you can imagine—disbelief…. After the sentencing…the church held a disciplinary council, and the result of that meeting was to excommunicate Russell from the Mormon Church. And what that means is that your name is taken off the records of the church, so you just disappear.

Russell's reaction to that was not positive, it hurt him, it hurt him to realize how serious a transgression he had committed.

But I will not desert Russell. That's a matter of my religion and my friendship with the family.

(*All exit. Lights fade on* RUSSELL, *his grandmother, and his home teacher.*)

MOMENT: *ANGELS IN AMERICA*

NARRATOR: Before we left Laramie, we met again with Rebecca Hilliker at the theater department. She is producing *Angels in America* this year at the university.

REBECCA HILLIKER: I think that's the focus the university has taken—is that we have a lot of work to do. That we have an obligation to find ways to reach our students.... And the question is, How do we move—how do we reach a whole state where there is some really deep-seated hostility toward gays? How do you reach them?

This is the beginning...and guess who's auditioning for the lead?

JEDADIAH SCHULTZ: MY PARENTS!

NARRATOR: Jedadiah Schultz:

JEDADIAH SCHULTZ: My parents were like, "So what plays are you doing this year at school?" And I was like, "*Angels in America*," and I told them the whole list of plays. And they're like, "*Angels in America?* Is that...that play you did in high school? That scene you did in high school?" And I was like, "Yeah." And she goes: "Huh. So are you gonna audition for it?" And I was like, "Yeah." And we got in this huge argument...and my best, the best thing that I knew I had them on is it was just after they had seen me in a performance of *Macbeth*, and onstage like I murdered like a little kid, and Lady Macduff and these two other guys and like and she goes, "Well, you know homosexuality is a sin"—she kept saying that—and I go, "Mom, I just played a murderer tonight. And you didn't seem to have a problem with that..."

I tell you. I've never prepared myself this much for an audition in my life. Never ever. Not even close.

ROB DEBREE: Not having to deal that much with the gay society here in Laramie.

NARRATOR: Detective Sergeant Rob DeBree:

ROB DEBREE: Well, once we started working into the case, and actually speaking to the people that were gay and finding out what their underlying fears were, well, then it sort of hit home. This is America. You don't have the right to feel that fear.

And we're still going to have people who hold with the old ideals, and I was probably one of them fourteen months ago. I'm not gonna put up with it, and I'm not going to listen to it. And if they don't like my views on it, fine. The door goes both ways. I already lost a couple of buddies. I don't care. I feel more comfortable and I can sleep at night.

REGGIE FLUTY: Well, you're tested every three months.

NARRATOR: Reggie Fluty:

REGGIE FLUTY: And I was able to have the DNA test done. And so they got me to Fort Collins, they drew the blood there, flew it to Michigan, and did all the DNA work there and—which was—a week later...I knew I was negative for good.

MARGE MURRAY: I'll tell ya, we were all on our knees saying Hail Marys.

REGGIE FLUTY: You were just elated, you know, and you think, "Thank God!"

MARGE MURRAY: So what's the first thing she does?

REGGIE FLUTY: I stuck my tongue right in my husband's mouth. I was just happy, you know, you're just so happy. You think, "Yeah, I hope I did this service well," you know, I hope I did it with some kind of integrity. So, you're just really happy...and my daughters just bawled.

MARGE MURRAY: They were so happy.

REGGIE FLUTY: And the force...

MARGE MURRAY: Oh boy...

REGGIE FLUTY: We went out and got shitfaced.

MARGE MURRAY: (*Simultaneous*) Shitfaced.

REGGIE FLUTY: They all bought me drinks too, it was great...and everybody hugged and cried, and, you know, I kissed everybody who walked through the door...

MARGE MURRAY: Reggie, they don't need to know that.

REGGIE FLUTY: I didn't care if they were male or female, they each got a kiss on the lips. (REGGIE *and* MARGE *exit together, arguing as they go.*)

MARGE MURRAY: Now what part of what I just said didn't you understand?

REGGIE FLUTY: Oh, get over it, Maw!

MOMENT: A DEATH PENALTY CASE

NARRATOR: Almost a year to the day that Matthew Shepard died, the trial for Aaron James McKinney was set to begin.

CAL RERUCHA: Probably the question that most of you have in your mind is ah, ah, how the McKinney case will proceed.

NARRATOR: Cal Rerucha, prosecuting attorney:

CAL RERUCHA: And it's the decision of the county attorney's office that that will definitely be a death penalty case.

MARGE MURRAY: Part of me wants McKinney to get it. But I'm not very proud of that. I was on and off, off and on. I can't say what I would do...I'm too personally involved.

ZACKIE SALMON: Oh, I believe in the death penalty one hundred percent. You know, because I want to make sure that guy's ass dies. This is one instance where I truly believe with all my heart an eye for an eye, a tooth for a tooth.

MATT MICKELSON: I don't know about the death penalty. But I don't ever want to see them ever walk out of Rawlins Penitentiary. I'll pay my nickel, or whatever, my little percentage of tax, nickel a day to make sure that his ass stays in there and never sees society again and definitely never comes into my bar again.

MATT GALLOWAY: I don't believe in the death penalty. It's too much for me. I don't believe that one person should be killed as redemption for his having killed another. Two wrongs don't make a right.

ZUBAIDA ULA: How can I protest, if the Shepards want McKinney dead? I just can't interfere in that. But on a personal level, I knew Aaron in grade school. We never called him Aaron, he was called A.J.... How can we put A.J. McKinney—how can we put A.J. McKinney to death?

FATHER ROGER SCHMIT: I think right now our most important teachers must be Russell Henderson and Aaron McKinney. They have to be our teachers. How did you learn? What did we as a society do to teach you that? See, I don't know if many people will let them be their teachers. I think it would be wonderful if the judge said: "In addition to your sentence, you must tell your story, you must tell your story."

BAILIFF: All rise. State of Wyoming versus Aaron James McKinney, docket number 6381. The Honorable Barton R. Voigt presiding. The Court is in session.

MOMENT: AARON MCKINNEY

NARRATOR: During the trial of Aaron McKinney, the prosecution played a tape recording of his confession.

ROB DEBREE: My name is Rob DeBree, sergeant for the Sheriff's Office. You have the right to remain silent. Anything you say can and may be used against you in a court of law.

NARRATOR: The following is an excerpt of that confession.

ROB DEBREE: Okay, so you guys, you and Russ go to the Fireside. So you're at the Fireside by yourselves, right?

AARON MCKINNEY: Yeah.

ROB DEBREE: Okay, where do you go after you leave the Fireside?

AARON MCKINNEY: Some kid wanted a ride home.

ROB DEBREE: What's he look like?

AARON MCKINNEY: Mmm, like a queer. Such a queer dude.

ROB DEBREE: He looks like a queer?

AARON MCKINNEY: Yeah, like a fag, you know?

ROB DEBREE: Okay. How did you meet him?

AARON MCKINNEY: He wanted a ride home and I just thought, well, the dude's drunk, let's just take him home.

ROB DEBREE: When did you and Russ talk about jacking him up?

AARON MCKINNEY: We kinda talked about it at the bar.

ROB DEBREE: Okay, what happened next?

AARON MCKINNEY: We drove him out past Wal-Mart. We got over there, and he starts grabbing my leg and grabbing my genitals. I was like, "Look, I'm not a fuckin' faggot. If you touch me again you're gonna get it." I don't know what the hell he was trying to do but I beat him up pretty bad. Think I killed him.

ROB DEBREE: What'd you beat him with?

AARON MCKINNEY: Blacked out. My fist. My pistol. The butt of the gun. Wondering what happened to me. I had a few beers and, I don't know. It's like I could see what was going on, but I don't know, but I don't know, it was like somebody else was doing it.

ROB DEBREE: What was the first thing that he said or that he did in the truck that made you hit him?

AARON MCKINNEY: Well, he put his hand on my leg, slid his hand like as if he was going to grab my balls.

MOMENT: GAY PANIC

ZACKIE SALMON: When that defense team argued that McKinney did what he did because Matthew made a pass at him…I just wanted to vomit, because that's like saying that it's okay. It's like the "Twinkie Defense," when the guy killed Harvey Milk and Moscone. It's the same thing.

REBECCA HILLIKER: As much as, uh, part of me didn't want the defense of them saying that it was a gay bashing or that it was gay panic, part of me is really grateful. Because I was really scared that in the trial they were going to try and say that it was a robbery, or it was about drugs. So when they used "gay panic" as their defense, I felt, this is good, if nothing else the truth is going to be told… the truth is coming out.

MOMENT: AARON MCKINNEY
(continued)

ROB DEBREE: Did he ever try to defend himself against you or hit you back?

AARON MCKINNEY: Yeah, sort of. He tried his little swings or whatever but he wasn't very effective.

ROB DEBREE: Okay. How many times did you hit him inside the truck before you guys stopped where you left him?

AARON MCKINNEY: I'd say I hit him two or three times, probably three times with my fists and about six times with the pistol.

ROB DEBREE: Did he ask you to stop?

AARON MCKINNEY: Well, yeah. He was getting the shit kicked out of him.

ROB DEBREE: What did he say?

AARON MCKINNEY: After he asked me to stop most all he was doing was screaming.

ROB DEBREE: So Russ kinda dragged him over to the fence, I'm assuming, and tied him up?

AARON MCKINNEY: Something like that. I just remember Russ was laughing at first but then he got pretty scared.

ROB DEBREE: Was Matthew conscious when Russ tied him up?

AARON MCKINNEY: Yeah. I told him to turn around and don't look at my license plate number 'cause I was scared he would tell the police. And then I asked him what my license plate said. He read it and that's why I hit him a few more times.

ROB DEBREE: Just to be sure? (*Pause*) So obviously you don't like gay people?

AARON MCKINNEY: No, I don't.

ROB DEBREE: Would you say you hate them?

AARON MCKINNEY: Uh, I really don't hate them but, you know, when they start coming on to me and stuff like that I get pretty aggravated.

ROB DEBREE: Did he threaten you?

AARON MCKINNEY: This gay dude?

ROB DEBREE: Yeah.

AARON MCKINNEY: Not really.

ROB DEBREE: Can you answer me one thing? Why'd you guys take his shoes?

AARON MCKINNEY: I don't know. (*Pause*) Now I'm never going to see my son again.

ROB DEGREE: I don't know. You'll probably go to court sometime today.

AARON MCKINNEY: Today? So I'm gonna go in there and just plead guilty or not guilty today?

ROB DEGREE: No, no, you're just going to be arraigned today.

AARON MCKINNEY: He is gonna die for sure?

ROB DEBREE: There is no doubt that Mr. Shepard is going to die.

AARON MCKINNEY: So what are they going to give me, twenty-five to life or just the death penalty and get it over with?

ROB DEBREE: That's not our job. That's the judge's job and the jury.

MOMENT: THE VERDICT

NARRATOR: Has the jury reached a verdict?

FOREPERSON: We have, Your Honor.

We the jury, impaneled and sworn to try the above entitled case, after having well and truly tried the matter, unanimously find as follows:

As to the charge of kidnapping, we find the defendant, Aaron James McKinney, guilty.

As to the charge of aggravated robbery, we find the defendant, Aaron James McKinney, guilty.

As to the charge of first-degree felony murder (kidnapping), we find the defendant, Aaron James McKinney, guilty.

(*Verdict goes sotto voce. Narration begins.*)

As to the charge of first-degree felony murder (robbery), we find the defendant, Aaron James McKinney, guilty.

As to the charge of premeditated first-degree murder, we find the defendant, Aaron James McKinney, not guilty.

As to the lesser-included offense of second-degree murder, we find the defendant, Aaron James McKinney, guilty.

MOMENT: DENNIS SHEPARD'S STATEMENT

NARRATOR: Aaron McKinney was found guilty of felony murder, which meant the jury could give him the death penalty. That evening, Judy and Dennis Shepard were approached by McKinney's defense team, who pled for their client's life. The following morning, Dennis Shepard made a statement to the Court. Here is some of what he said.

DENNIS SHEPARD: My son Matthew did not look like a winner. He was rather uncoordinated and wore braces from the age of thirteen un-til the day he died. However, in his all too brief life he proved that he was a winner. On October 6, 1998, my son tried to show the world that he could win again. On October 12, 1998, my firstborn son and my hero lost. On October 12, 1998, my firstborn son and my hero died, fifty days before his twenty-second birthday.

I keep wondering the same thing that I did when I first saw him in the hospital. What would he have become? How could he have changed his piece of the world to make it better?

Matt officially died in a hospital in Fort Collins, Colorado. He actually died on the outskirts of Laramie, tied to a fence. You, Mr. McKinney, with your friend Mr. Henderson left him out there by himself, but he wasn't alone. There were his lifelong friends with him, friends that he had grown up with. You're probably wondering who these friends were. First he had the beautiful night sky and the same stars and moon that we used to see through a telescope. Then he had the daylight and the sun to shine on him. And through it all he was breathing in the scent of pine trees from the snowy range. He heard the wind, the ever-present Wyoming wind, for the last time. He had one more friend with him, he had God. And I feel better knowing he wasn't alone.

Matt's beating, hospitalization, and funeral focused world-wide attention on hate. Good is coming out of evil. People have said enough is enough. I miss my son, but I am proud to be able to say that he is my son.

Judy has been quoted as being against the death penalty. It has been stated that Matt was against the death penalty. Both of these statements are wrong. Matt believed that there were crimes and incidents that justified the death penalty. I too believe in the death penalty. I would like nothing better than to see you die, Mr. McKinney. However, this is the time to begin the healing process. To show mercy to someone who refused to show any mercy. Mr. McKinney, I am going to grant you life, as hard as it is for me to do so, because of Matthew. Every time you celebrate Christmas, a birthday, the Fourth of July, remember that Matt isn't. Every time you wake up in your prison cell, remember that you had the opportunity and the ability to stop your actions that night. You robbed me of something very precious, and I will never forgive you for that. Mr. McKinney, I give you life in the memory of one who no longer lives. May you have a long life, and may you thank Matthew every day for it.

MOMENT: AFTERMATH

REGGIE FLUTY: Me and DeBree hugged and cried.... And, you know, everybody had tears in their eyes, and you're just so thankful, you know, and Mr. Shepard was cryin', and then that got me bawlin' and everybody just—

ROB DEBREE: This is all we've lived and breathed for a year. Daily. This has been my case daily. And now it's over.

REGGIE FLUTY: Maybe now we can go on and we can quit being stuck, you know?

AARON KREIFELS: It just hit me today, the minute that I got out of the courthouse. That the reason that God wanted me to find him is, for he didn't have to die out there alone, you know. And if I wouldn't of came along, they wouldn't of found him for a couple of weeks at least. So it makes me feel really good that he didn't have to die out there alone.

MATT GALLOWAY: I'm just glad it's over. I really am. Testifying in that trial was one of the hardest things I've ever done. And don't get me wrong, I love the stage, I really do, I love it. But it's tricky, because basically what you have is lawyers questioning you from this angle but the answers need to be funneling this way, to the jury. So what you have to do is establish a funneling system. And that's hard for me because I'm a natural conversationalist, so it's just natural instinct that when someone asks you a question, you look at that person to make eye contact. But it's kind of tough when you literally have to scoot over—change your position, in effect, funnel over to where the jury is. But I was

able to do that several times over the course of my testimony.

(*Everyone is amused and baffled by this last text.*)

REGGIE FLUTY: It's time to move on. And I think even the citizens are having the town painted red so to speak. They're gonna just be glad to maybe get moved on.

MOMENT: EPILOGUE

ANDY PARIS: On our last trip, I had the good fortune of seeing Jedadiah Schultz play the role of Prior in *Angels in America*. After a performance, we spoke.

JEDADIAH SCHULTZ: I didn't for the longest time let myself become personally involved in the Matthew Shepard thing. It didn't seem real, it just seemed way blown out of proportion. Matthew Shepard was just a name instead of an individual....

I don't know, it's weird. It's so weird, man. I just—I just feel bad. Just for all that stuff I told you, for the person I used to be. That's why I want to hear those interviews from last year when I said all that stuff. I don't know. I just can't believe I ever said that stuff about homosexuals, you know. How did I ever let that stuff make me think that you were different from me?

NARRATOR: This is Romaine Patterson.

ROMAINE PATTERSON: Well, a year ago, I wanted to be a rock star. That was my goal. And now, um, well, now it's obviously changed in the fact that, um, throughout the last year I—I've really realized my role in, um, in taking my part. And, um, so now instead of going to school to be in music, I'm gonna go to school for communications and political science. Um, because I have a career in political activism.

Actually, I just recently found out I was gonna be honored in Washington, D.C., from the Anti-Defamation League. And whenever I think about the angels or any of the speaking that I've done, you know... Matthew gave me—Matthew's like guiding this little path with his light for me to walk down. And he just—every time we get to like a door, he opens it. And he just says, "Okay, next step."

And if I get to be a rock star on the side, okay.

NARRATOR: This is Jonas Slonaker.

JONAS SLONAKER: Change is not an easy thing, and I don't think people were up to it here. They got what they wanted. Those two boys got what they deserve, and we look good now. Justice has been served. The OK Corral. We shot down the villains. We sent the prostitutes on the train. The town's cleaned up, and we don't need to talk about it anymore.

You know, it's been a year since Matthew Shepard died, and they haven't passed shit in Wyoming…at a state level, any town, nobody anywhere, has passed any kind of laws, antidiscrimination laws or hate crime legislation, nobody has passed anything anywhere. What's come out of it? What's come out of this that's concrete or lasting?

NARRATOR: We all said we would meet again—one last time at the fence.

DOC O'CONNOR: I been up to that site in my limousine, okay? And I remembered to myself the night he and I drove around together, he said to me, "Laramie sparkles, doesn't it?" And where he was up there, if you sit exactly where he was, up there, Laramie sparkles from there, with a low-lying cloud…. it's the blue lights that's bouncing off the clouds from the airport, and it goes *tst tst tst tst*…right over the whole city. I mean, it blows you away…Matt was right there in that spot, and I can just picture in his eyes, I can just picture what he was seeing. The last thing he saw on this earth was the sparkling lights.

MOMENT: DEPARTURE

MOISÉS KAUFMAN: We've spent the last two days packing a year's worth of materials and saying our good-byes. We've been here six times and conducted over two hundred interviews. Jedadiah cried when he said good-bye.

LEIGH FONDAKOWSKI: Marge wished us luck, and when we asked her how Laramie would feel seeing a play about itself, she said:

MARGE MURRAY: I think we'd enjoy it. To show it's not the hellhole of the earth would be nice, but that is up to how you portray us. And that in turn is up to how Laramie behaves.

GREG PIEROTTI: As we were getting off the phone she said to me:

MARGE MURRAY: Now, you take care. I love you, honey.

STEPHEN BELBER: Doc asked me if I wanted to ghostwrite a book about the whole event. Galloway offered me or anyone else a place to stay if and when we come back to Laramie. He also seemed interested as to whether there'd be any open auditions for this play.

ANDY PARIS: We left Laramie at about seven in the evening. On the way to Denver, I looked in my rearview mirror to take one last look at the town.

FATHER ROGER SCHMIT: And I will speak with you, I will trust that if you write a play of this, that you say it right. You need to do your best to say it correct.

ANDY PARIS: And in the distance I could see the sparkling lights of Laramie, Wyoming.

END OF PLAY

PERFORMING *THE LARAMIE PROJECT*

The Laramie Project had a two-and-a-half-year development process that began in 1998 and concluded with the professional premiere at the Denver Theater Center in February of 2000. In November, the Tectonic production was restaged Off Broadway at the Union Square Theater. Several developmental workshops sponsored by the Sundance Institute Theater Laboratory and the New York Theater Workshop preceded the Denver opening.

It was important to Moisés Kaufman and the Tectonic company that the play receive its premiere in the West since the story had taken place there. Kaufman approached Donovan Marley at the Denver Theater Center for the chief reason that the townspeople of Laramie,

Wyoming, were about two and a half hours away from Denver and that those portrayed (and others) would have an opportunity to see the first production.

Kaufman's aesthetic requires that the stage itself be treated as a performance space. The stage is exposed in its bare minimalism—there are a few tables and chairs to be moved about as needed by the actors and the costumes and properties are always visible—and the performance style is starkly presentational. The performance begins with actors playing themselves grouped around the tables sharing the results of their investigations into Matthew Shepard's murder. As the play opens up, we meet the people of Laramie in various locations designated by actors moving the tables and chairs about the stage. For the New York production, designer Robert Brill introduced theatrical touches by spotlighting a window box of cornstalks to suggest the Wyoming prairie. At another time a screen showed footage of a two-lane highway late at night as seen in the headlights of a lonely vehicle. As the media descended upon Laramie, television monitors dropped from the ceiling and the audience sees juxtaposed images of the actors-as-television journalists repeated on the monitors as the stage actors "announce" their coverage of the first trial. The performative style and the use of screens and television monitors distance the audience from the horror of the unfolding story.

As an actor-driven performance without a central character present on stage, the actors as themselves establish an almost personal contact with the audience as they introduce the citizens of Laramie and represent them as recognizable people. The audience never loses sight of the actors as they slip in and out of the thirty-one roles.

As the director, Moisés Kaufman faced the problem of how to create a whole town on a stage with only eight people. He frequently held conversations with the company to determine if one approach would work better than another as they staged the piece. In one instance, Kaufman turned to staging techniques by the influential Russian director Vsevelod Meyerhold (1874–1940) noted for his experiments with physicalization and nonrepresentational space. *The Laramie Project* has its Meyerholdian moment, as Kaufman called it, when the men arrested for beating Shepard were arraigned. The actors as townspeople are seated in chairs arranged sideways as the officer reads aloud the details of the crime. The bodies of the listeners collapse inwardly as the horror of Shepard's beating and death sink in.[7]

Following the Denver and New York productions of *The Laramie Project*, the play was seen in Laramie and in numerous regional theaters across the United States. The Tectonic Theater Company has achieved an international reputation with productions of both *Gross Indecency: The Three Trials of Oscar Wilde* and *The Laramie Project* in London, Paris, Stockholm, Mexico City, Budapest, Toronto, and Montreal. The *Laramie Project* was filmed for television in 2002.

CRITICS' NOTEBOOK

The writings of stage practitioners and theorists on documentary drama (also called docudrama) date from Erwin Piscator's work in Germany in the 1920s that resulted in his influential book *Political Theater* (1929) and Bertolt Brecht's later discussions of models for epic theater. Brecht's staging practices and writings were discussed by British author and translator John Willett in *The Theatre of Bertolt Brecht: A Study of Eight Aspects* (1959) and later translated and published by Willett in *Brecht on Theatre: The Development of an Aesthetic* (1964). Stage designer Mordecai Gorelik's seminal book, called *New Theatres for Old* (1957), examined the effects of political movements on new playwriting and staging practices. His chapter on "Theatre Is a Tribunal" is especially relevant to understanding the development of the documentary style in modern theater practice.

The work in the late 1930s of the Living Newspaper under the auspices of the Federal Theater Project has been documented by Hallie Flanagan in *Arena* (1940) and by scholars working with the Federal Theater archives, most notably Lorraine Brown (*Free, Adult, Uncensored: The History of the Federal Theatre Project*, 1978, with John O'Conner; and *Liberty Deferred and Other Living Newspapers of the 1930s,* 1989).

More recently, the writings and practices of contemporary documentary playwrights have received the most attention from theater reviewers, from writers for *American Theatre* magazine, and in published interviews with the creators themselves.

The two documents appended here represent Brecht's thoughts on his model for epic theater, called *The Street Scene,* and reflections on *The Laramie Project* prepared by dramaturg Karen Blansfield for a production of Moisés Kaufman's play by a regional theater.

Bertolt Brecht, from "The Street Scene: A Basic Model for Epic Theater" (1938–1940)*

❦

In the decade and a half that followed the [First] World War a comparatively new way of acting was tried out in a number of German theatres. Its qualities of clear description and reporting and its use of choruses and projections as a means of commentary earned it the name of 'epic'. The actor used a somewhat complex technique to detach himself from the character portrayed; he forced the spectator to look at the play's situations from such an angle that they necessarily became subject to his criticism. Supporters of this epic theatre argued that the new subject-matter, the highly involved incidents of the class war in its acutest and most terrible stage, would be mastered more easily by such a method, since it would thereby become possible to portray social processes as seen in their causal relationships. But the result of these experiments was that aesthetics found itself up against a whole series of substantial difficulties.

*Bertolt Brecht, "The Street Scene," in *Brecht on Theatre: The Development of an Aesthetic,* trans. John Willett (New York: Hill and Wang Publishers, 1964): 121–128.

It is comparatively easy to set up a basic model for epic theatre. For practical experiments I usually picked as my example of completely simple, 'natural' epic theatre an incident such as can be seen at any street corner: an eyewitness demonstrating to a collection of people how a traffic accident took place. The bystanders may not have observed what happened, or they may simply not agree with him, may 'see things a different way'; the point is that the demonstrator acts the behaviour of driver or victim or both in such a way that the bystanders are able to form an opinion about the accident.

Such an example of the most primitive type of epic theatre seems easy to understand. Yet experience has shown that it presents astounding difficulties to the reader or listener as soon as he is asked to see the implications of treating this kind of street corner demonstration as a basic form of major theatre, theatre for a scientific age. What this means of course is that the epic theatre may appear richer, more intricate and complex in every particular, yet to be major theatre it need at bottom only contain the same elements as a street-corner demonstration of this sort; nor could it any longer be termed epic theatre if any of the main elements of the street-corner demonstration were lacking. Until this is understood it is impossible really to understand what follows. Until one understands the novelty, unfamiliarity and direct challenge to the critical faculties of the suggestion that street-corner demonstration of this sort can serve as a satisfactory basic model of major theatre one cannot really understand what follows....

❧ ❧ ❧

One essential element of the street scene must also be present in the theatrical scene if this is to qualify as epic, namely that the demonstration should have a socially practical significance. Whether our street demonstrator is out to show that one attitude on the part of driver or pedestrian makes an accident inevitable where another would not, or whether he is demonstrating with a view to fixing the responsibility, his demonstration has a practical purpose, intervenes socially.

Karen Blansfield, from "The Healing Power of Theatre"*

❧

In October 1998, the brutal murder of a young, gay college student in Laramie, Wyoming stunned the nation. While people everywhere struggled to comprehend such random, senseless hatred, Laramie itself was caught in the glare of publicity and forced to confront the grim reality that such a thing *"can* happen here."

In this juncture of private and public shock, playwright Moisés Kaufman sensed a crucial cultural moment that would long reverberate. "The idea of listening to the citizens talk really interested me," says Kaufman. "How is Laramie different from the rest of the country and how is it similar?"

In quest of answers, Kaufman and his New York company, Tectonic Theater Project, traveled to Wyoming several times during the ensuing months and interviewed dozens of the town's residents. The result was a startling, innovative, and moving theatre piece, *The Laramie Project,* which premiered in Denver in 1999 and went on to a highly praised New York run and a special Obie Award for innovative achievement.

The Laramie Project focuses not on the crime but rather its effect on a quiet community, as well as on broader issues such as the nature of community and the genesis of hate. In the process, it not only offers a cathartic exploration of a somber event, it also illuminates the extraordinary healing possibilities theatre can offer in this new, uneasy millennium.

Barely a month after Shepard's death, just as the media onslaught was dying down, Kaufman and his group made the first of half a dozen trips to Wyoming. Initially, they were fearful; no one traveled alone, and everyone carried cell phones. But they found people remarkably willing to talk and gradually forged bonds of trust;

over the course of a year and a half, they interviewed some two hundred people and amassed about four hundred hours of interviews. The transcripts of these numerous conversations, interspersed with commentary and journal entries from the actors themselves, form the fabric of *The Laramie Project.*

❧ ❧ ❧

The voices of *The Laramie Project* represent a striking array of Laramie citizens: friends and acquaintances of Shepard, law enforcement officials, a bartender, a rancher, an Islamic feminist, the limousine driver Shepard hired, University faculty and administrators, and religious clergy—Baptist, Unitarian, Mormon, Catholic. Matthew Shepard himself is not a character in the play, though his unseen presence is more powerful than any stage portrayal could be. Nor is Shepard romanticized in any way: he is remembered as polite and joyous but also as blunt and determined.

What is remarkable about *The Laramie Project* is that only eight actors fill the roles of more than sixty citizens of Laramie. Such challenges are the domain of Tectonic Theater Project. "Tectonic refers to the art and science of structure," says Kaufman. "We're interested in doing plays that explore language and form." Having actors play multiple roles yields a blending and blurring of identities that reinforces the thematic idea of community and challenges the audience to synthesize the material themselves. In the spirit of another community play, Thornton Wilder's *Our Town, The Laramie Project* also features narration and direct address to guide the audience through the play's events.

The intriguing fusion of public events and dramatic form invests theatre with a social consciousness and a communal social power that harks back to it beginnings in Western culture. In 5th century B.C. Athens, theatre, politics, and society were inextricably intertwined, and Kaufman rediscovered this integrity in developing *The Laramie Project.* "The origin of theatre is a community talking to itself," he says. "It was a

---

*Karen Blansfield, "The Healing Power of Theatre," *Spotlight: PlayMakers Repertory Company Magazine* (Chapel Hill, NC: PlayMakers Repertory Company, 2001): 4–5.

striking experience to think that in Greek times, theatre was about 'us' or an idea of 'us.' It was a shock, really, to think 'Oh, so this is what theatre is supposed to do!' "

The need for communities to talk to themselves is perhaps more vital now than ever. Torn apart by hate crimes and racial strife, and now shattered by the horror of the September 11 terrorist attacks, communities reach out as a way of bonding and restoration. Just as the poignant tales of farewell phone calls from the World Trade Center and the doomed airline flights put a human face on this colossal tragedy, so does the story of Laramie bring us into contact with human beings we can recognize, and their courage and decency in the fact of brutality, intolerance, and hatred can inspire us.

The attack on America galvanized the country into reawakened unity, searing into it memory moments no one will forget. So too, the murder of Matthew Shepard marked, in Kaufman's view, a watershed episode in the national consciousness. "There are moments in history when a particular event brings the various ideologies and beliefs prevailing in a culture into sharp focus," says Kaufman. "At these junctures, the event becomes a lightning rod of sorts, attracting and distilling the essence of these philosophies and convictions. By paying careful attention in moments like these to people's words, one is able to hear the way these prevailing ideas affect not only individual lives, but also the culture at large."

"The Laramie Project is one of the most important works in the contemporary theatre," PlayMakers Repertory Company Artistic Director David Hammond comments. "It utilizes the words of ordinary people to create a composite picture of a community healing itself in the face of the unspeakable. We see courage, gallantry, and even heroism emerging in the townspeople, and we know that hatred and evil cannot prevail when people look honestly into their own hearts. I think that play speaks to the best instincts in all of us. It becomes a healing event for the audience as well as for the people depicted on stage."

Through theatre, something nourishing can be born of tragedy, and through theatre, communities can rediscover a vital and ancient unity. Such a work as *The Laramie Project* offers at once a means of understanding one another, the opportunities for connections, and the hope of transforming grief and bewilderment into acceptance, endurance, and growth.

REVISITING DOCUMENTARY THEATER

Modern documentary plays derive largely from the stage practices of Erwin Piscator in Germany in the 1920s and from Bertolt Brecht's theoretical writings on epic theater. From the outset, *documentary* theater has been *political* theater. The creators take a historic event, usually contemporary to them, and through personal interviews, memoirs, transcripts of trials, newspaper coverage, and other sources, they construct a theatrical document that gives a factual account of the event and fosters an agenda for political and social change.

The playwright, often in collaboration with other artists, crafts a text that tells the story of an outrage against persons and society for purposes of social reform. Documentary theater, whose purpose is showing and persuading, combines history, technology, personal viewpoints, and other documentation to demonstrate the complex truths of human behavior along with the need to change encrusted political and legal systems to avoid the reoccurrences of outrage and horror against the helpless and the innocent.

In the latter part of the twentieth century, social and political issues emerged from another perspective and found their way onto contemporary stages. A large number of playwrights, confronting a multicultural society with similar frissons, set about creating performance pieces for solo artists and also writing plays in more traditional dramatic forms but with equally loud social and political messages. Deb Margolin, Eduardo Machado, and David Henry Hwang are three contemporary voices confronting a changing American landscape.

NOTES

1. Moredicai Gorelik, *New Theatres for Old* (New York: Samuel French, 1957): 381.

2. Hallie Flanagan, *Arena: The History of the Federal Theatre* (New York: Benjamin Blom, 1965): 334–335.

3. "Emily Mann on the Craft of Documentary Plays," *The Dramatists Guild Quarterly* (Spring 1995): 10.

4. Bertolt Brecht, "The Street Scene," *Brecht on Theatre: The Development of an Aesthetic*, trans. by John Willett (New York: Hill and Wang Publishers, 1964): 121.

5. www.time.com./time/classroom/laramie/qa_kaufman.html.

6. Brecht, "The Street Scene," 121–129.

7. Don Shewey, "Town in a Mirror: The Laramie Project Revisits an American Tragedy," *American Theatre* 17.5 (May/June 2000): 68.

CHAPTER 15

UNDERSTANDING THE SOLO
PERFORMANCE TEXT

Deb Margolin performing "The Secaucas Monologue" from *Of Mice, Bugs and Women*.
(Photo © Dona Ann McAdams.)

*I use language as a way to feel less alone with the constant intense and
beautiful and humorous and ridiculous experiences that I have.[1]*
—Deb Margolin

PERFORMANCE: A DEFINITION IN THREE KEYS

Three key terms to consider here are *performance, performance art,* and *solo performance. Performance,* as Marvin Carlson tells us, has come into popular usage in recent years to describe a wide range of activities in the arts, literature, and the social sciences.[2] As its popularity increased in artistic and educational circles, a number of cultural anthropologists, modern ethnographers, radical/lesbian feminists, psychologists, sociologists, and theater scholars engaged in efforts to analyze and understand performance as human activity. Richard Schechner (*Between Theater and Anthropology*), Victor Turner (*Dramas, Fields, and Metaphors*), Irving Goffman (*The Presentation of Self in Everyday Life*), Eugenio Barba (*The Secret Art of the Performer*), and Jill Dolan (*Geographies of Learning: Theater Studies, Performance, and the Performative*) have all written varying studies on performance.

Following the interest of scholars in the subject, performance studies departments evolved in universities in the United States to address a growing body of theory and literature that connected performance in everyday life to structures of sports events and ritual behaviors, to modes of communication, and to theories of behavior, human interactions, and acting out. Performance art and solo performance attracted the interest of artists, writers, and theater scholars in the practices, trends, and issues evolving around this new type of theatrical activity.

It is our purpose here to give attention to "theatrical" performance art in general and to "solo" performance art in particular. *Performance* in its theatrical (or performative) context is associated with doing and with redoing on the part of performers (one or many) in the presence of spectators.

PERFORMANCE ART

Performance art has its roots in early twentieth-century avant-garde experiments in the art world. Contemporary performance art has its antecedents in surrealism, dadaism, cubism, and futurism; in innovations in painting, music, and dance; and in the theater theories of Antonin Artaud in France and Jerzy Grotowski in Poland. Early twentieth-century performance artists raised radical voices of dissent against social and political institutions and reactionary values of the art world. Despite their many differences of medium and style, what these artists shared in common were attacks on traditional artistic values and forms and provocations of shock and outrage.

During the 1960s in the United States, various strands from the visual arts (especially painting and sculpture), from experimental music and dance, and from the traditions of avant-garde theater combined to offer a varied mix of artistic activity, much of it taking place in New York City. Nonetheless, it was not until the 1970s that the terms "performance" and "performance art" began to be widely used by artists and writers to describe much of the experimental work of the new decade. For one thing, artists first rejected the term "performance" as too loosely associated with the text-bound traditional theater. Combined with the influences of earlier experimental theater, music, dance, and popular culture (clowns, monologists, and stand-up comedians), several common features emerged among the new artists: expressions of the human body closely related to dance, focus on stereotypes and self-definition, and exploitation of taboo subjects and political outrage.

Within the decade performance art shifted to movement-based work under the influence of modern dance choreographers and Grotowski's theories of physicality and ritualistic staging. Most influential in the United States were Alan Kaprow's "staged happenings," the "new" dance of Anna Halprin, painter Claes Oldenburg's "collages," and the dance/movement of choreographer Merce Cunningham allied with the music experimentations of John Cage. Their evolving activity, called "happenings," "avant-garde" experiments, "painting" constructions, "multi-media" spectacles, and "staged performances," stressed several common elements:

- the artist's physical presence and events
- reduced emphasis on literary text and speech
- rejection of traditional narrative, psychology, and familiar referents in writing
- blurring of boundaries between art and life
- dispensing with traditional art's unity and coherence.[3]

Changes in performance art in the United States occurred in the 1980s, when artists with political and social agendas were attracted to minimalist "staged" performances. Outcries of the disenfranchised—lesbians, gays, ethnic minorities—over civil liberties and sexual orientations prompted individual artists and small theater companies to respond to the larger national debate over voting rights, equal opportunity, and affirmative action. Representing the new pluralism, African American, Hispanic, and Asian American performance artists led the American theater's avant-garde in the late twentieth century to address the plight of the excluded, the ostracized, the isolated, and the abandoned in the world's richest country.

Performance artists called attention to the marginalized in American society: the poor, nonwhite, gay, old, young, ill, homeless, and abused. Their "stages" were nontraditional performance spaces, or, as Jill Dolan calls them, "stark, ascetic 'spaces'": art galleries, rooms, clubs, church basements, warehouses, and converted public school buildings.[4] Many performance artists found homes in Off Off Broadway sites, including the W. O. W. Café, a women's experimental theater club, and P.S. 122, a con-

verted public school in the East Village in lower Manhattan. Museums, such as the Walker Museum in Minneapolis and the Museum of Contemporary Art in Chicago, provided spaces for performance art.

Historically, the solo performer has always existed on the fringes of the establishment, that is, the commercial theater, established cultural institutions, or the larger political system. In form and substance, the solo performer's antecedents stretch back to the solitary performer of shamanistic practices in early societies and forward to the mimes, jugglers, minstrels, rope-dancers (arielists), court clowns, and jesters of medieval and Renaissance marketplaces, great houses, fairs, and taverns. Popular forms of entertainment merged with esoteric avant-garde experiments in the twentieth century to create a spirited search for inspiration and new approaches to performance art. In more recent times, vaudeville, cabaret, variety shows, and stand-up comedy along with poetry readings and dance and music concerts, provided background for experiments in performance art.

In the late twentieth century, performance artists shared in common their singular presence and their active participation with audiences. The solo explorations of Laurie Anderson, Eric Bogosian, Eve Ensler, Karen Finley, Guillermo Gómez-Peña, Spalding Gray, Holly Hughes, Deb Margolin, and Anna Deavere Smith—as challenging as their work might seem artistically—are functions of their overriding concerns with class, ethnicity, gender, sexuality, racial unrest, environmental abuses, and, indeed, with the entire political, social, cultural, and environmental spectrum of American life.

SOLO PERFORMANCE: THEORY AND PRACTICE

Director Jo Bonney, editor of a collection of performance texts (called *Extreme Exposure*), responds to the question: Why is the solo show so endemic in the 1990s? Her answer downplays the economic factors of production costs and the showcase mentality that searches for recognition within the industry. She writes,

> It would miss the heart of the artist's impulse to create solo work to simply echo the oft-cited bottom-line reasons—diminishing government funding for the arts, paucity of ensemble-size venues, the obvious showcase potential for an actor as a stepping stone to larger or more commercial work. Perhaps the primary reason for the proliferation of solo work in this decade is in the great appeal for artists of having total aesthetic control of their material....[5]

The materials of most solo performance artists in the late twentieth century, with some exceptions, are autobiographical. These artists focus on their life experiences, concerned with identity and with the impulse to unsettle or confound the fixed order of things (personal, social, and political). They perceive themselves as both subjects and objects, as acting on and being acted on by family, friends, and society.[6] Robbie McCauley performed nude as her great-great grandmother, a slave on an auction block, to rage about racial injustice in *Alice's Rape* (1989); Karen Finley and Holly Hughes, whose grants were rescinded by the National Endowment for the Arts for reasons of nudity and obscene language, have continued to challenge ultra-conservative religious and political groups in their often controversial representations of feminist and civil libertarian causes.

Following the influences of significant avant-garde activities in Europe, the first key to the theory and practice of solo performance is the rejection of the concept of the performer as an interpreter of an already existing literary text.[7] The performer/artist is at once and interchangeably author, creator, subject, and performer. Whether we are experiencing Spalding Gray's self-searching, psychoanalytic monologues (*Gray's Anatomy*), or Anna Deavere Smith's solo reportage of conversations with the black and Lubavitcher communities of Crown Heights in Brooklyn (*Fires in the Mirror*), or John Leguizamo's serio-comic perspective on growing up in an Hispanic neighborhood in Jackson Heights, Queens, NY (*Freak*), the singular artist in the performance space is at once a vulnerable presence, a con-

sciousness, and a political activist. As artists, they engage in a performative journey of autobiography, self-reflection, identity, gender, race, and class. We, the spectators, become participants with them in their journey to define America.

In the 1970s, the emergence of autobiographical-oriented performance art coincided with the women's movement. The public expression of personal material introduced taboo subjects, personal and collective histories, and new forms of presenting. Jill Dolan grouped the varieties of feminist performance into three divisions discussed in the earlier chapter on feminist drama. These divisions are roughly found in the creative and ideological materials of Karen Finley, Holly Hughes, Anna Deavere Smith, and Deb Margolin—to name only four. Depending on their viewpoints, these performance artists confront sexual inequality (liberal feminism), the separateness and difference of women (cultural or radical feminism), or the role of class and history in creating the oppression of women (materialist feminism). Catherine Elwes, herself a performance artist, explains that when a woman speaks in performance, she combines authorship with the medium (the stage) to assert her feminist presence.[8]

Although women have dominated U.S. performance art since the 1980s, it is clear at the new millennium that women and men of color have turned to performance art to find self-definition and to explore specific social, cultural, and ethnic concerns. Guillermo Gómez-Peña, a talented and articulate artist born in Mexico, is a central representative of the new orientation in performance. The goal is no longer "the mainstreaming of radical ideas," as Karen Finley expressed it in the 1980s. Focusing on the Latino/a experience in the United States, Gómez-Peña refers to himself as an "intercultural interpreter." He views his work as expressing multiple identities, including Chicano, Mexican, Latin American, or American.[9] He also looks on performance art as the place where boundaries can be crossed and artists of color need no longer be marginalized.[10]

Performance art, as Lenora Champagne remarks, ranges from highly personal solo monologues to stand-up comedy routines, to large multimedia collaborations between artists from different disciplines.[11] Holly Hughes transforms her experiences into myths presenting the possibility of women's power and pleasure; Dennis Miller does stand-up riffs on social deviance and political subterfuge; and Laurie Anderson creates a multimedia voyage into her interpretation of Herman Melville's famous novel *Moby-Dick.*

Traditionally, theater professionals have dismissed performance art because it tends to favor presentation rather than representation and confrontational style rather than familiar playwriting conventions. Nonetheless, Lenora Champagne argues that as artists used performance for four decades to explore and clarify self-definition and aesthetic issues, they made significant contributions to revitalizing theater.[12] No longer just an Off Off Broadway, comedy club, or East Village phenomenon, we find solo artists invading Broadway and television (Lily Tomlin, Whoopi Goldberg, Bill Irwin, John Leguizamo, and Robin Williams), and European and American opera houses and world festivals welcoming the large multimedia productions of Robert Wilson and Philip Glass.

SHAPING THE SOLO PERFORMANCE TEXT

Deb Margolin calls solo performance "a perfect Theater for One."[13] Such performance artists as Spalding Gray, John Leguizamo, and Deb Margolin take personal experiences as their starting point and delve into their private resources (memories, desires, obsessions, images, dreams, overheard conversations, and fantasies) to make art out of life experience.

Although in its creation and staging, there is an improvisatory quality to performance art, the truth of the matter is that solo artists work from self-created compositions or texts that may or may not be initially improvised. Deb Margolin "composes" her personal experiences and images into theater pieces reflecting her feminist outlook, Jewish identity, and lived experiences in urban America.

At the outset, Spalding Gray improvises his memories, free associations, private emotions, and ideas of childhood and family relationships.

In the early phases, Gray's methods are largely improvisational—a series of simple actions using free associations as building blocks to turn a series of memories, everyday experiences, and interactions with family, friends, and strangers into art. Once he has developed and given shape to his autobiographical sketches, he discusses the piece with a director (usually Elizabeth LeCompte of The Wooster Group) and introduces the material to small audiences in "an act of public memory." Once satisfied with the performance piece, Gray "sets" the text and takes only the outline written down in a notebook into the performance space. There, he places his notebook and a glass of water before him on the table where he sits throughout the delivery of the monologue. In *It's a Slippery Slope* (1996), he "talks" about his life after fifty and regaining one's personal equilibrium through the joys and terrors of learning to ski.

Anna Deavere Smith's solo texts are highly personal responses to large social and political issues that have occurred in the nation's experience. They serve as her means of speaking directly to America's collective conscience. She began a series of solo performances, entitled *On the Road: A Search for American Character,* which has taken her to Brooklyn Heights and to Los Angeles in her search for materials to explore race, class, and politics in contemporary America. Her method is to hold hundreds of interviews with those persons central to an event like the 1991 riots in Los Angeles following the Rodney King incident. She shaped the interviews into a solo performance called *Twilight: Los Angeles 1992.*

Smith creates her performance pieces out of the many personas and voices of the participants and witnesses she interviews. Using their words, taken from her taped interviews, she develops a sequence of the real-life incidents and contradictory insights into a complex event. For example, in *Fires in the Mirror* (1992) based on the 1991 Crown Heights riots in Brooklyn, New York, she variously became the personas/voices of the Reverend Al Sharpton, civil rights activist; Roz Malamud, a Crown Heights resident; Robert Sherman, New York City's Commissioner on Human Rights; and so on.

Anna Deavere Smith distilled the many hours of the Crown Heights taped interviews into a ninety-minute solo performance, called *Fires in the Mirror,* in which she shares with audiences the words, thoughts, emotions, photographs, and film clips of eighteen people—female and male, black and Jewish, activist and resident, parent and teacher. She says, "I try to represent multiple points of view and to capture the personality of a place by showing its individuals." As a politically aware performance artist, she aims to encapsulate the racial incident within a framework larger than that of Los Angeles or Brooklyn Heights. Critic John Lahr points out that she creates a new framework from which to assess race and class in America.[14]

In general, solo performance art as it evolved in the United States is a shared creative effort between the writer's process and the performer's methods. The material comes from memories, images, lived experiences, and personal responses to national issues and events. Given the many personalities and differences among performance artists, there is no single determinate as to how the solo artist creates the text and the performance.

What we glean is this: those interstitial moments of personal experience get sketched out, improvised, written down, ordered, sequenced, and performed. There must be a beginning and ending. The lights go up, the lights go down. In between, the performer takes over the space and expresses a range of voices, personas, subjects, political positions, and life experiences. John Leguizamo takes us through his conflicts with his father; Spalding Gray reflects upon his acting career and his mother's psychiatric treatment and suicide; Karen Finley smears her nude body with chocolate to protest government censorship of the arts.

Performance art is a creative act of consciousness where performance is made out of streams of individual experiences, viable imagery, overheard conversations, remembered dreams, recalled headlines, and lines of poetry. The act of composing involves words, images, listening to inner and outer voices, and visualizing the body's potential for gesture. In the process, the text is formed; strong visual images appear; themes take shape; "talking pieces" emerge. In the process, boundaries collapse between the personal and the larger world, between the writer and the performer.

Unlike most American actors trained to *become* the character, the performance artist (many of them, like Spalding Gray and Anna Deavere Smith, are professional actors) creates a dialectic between the self-as-performer and the characters-as-performed. Unlike the traditional actor, the performance artist allows the audience to see right through the character to the actor himself/herself. Anna Deavere Smith speaks in the persona and words of the Reverend Al Sharpton in the aftermath of the Brooklyn Heights incident, but she is clearly Anna Deavere Smith, the solo artist and civil libertarian. It is this tension between character and performer—between the character's words/gestures and the performer's intentions and personal politics—that is the fascination and complexity of performance art. As in the old Punch and Judy shows, the puppet and the puppeteer are both visible, thereby creating several levels and meaning of storytelling.

Others are often brought into the creative process in preparation for the staged performance. Before finalizing the performance piece, most solo artists work with a stage director to refine and "set" the performance in a space. Anna Deavere Smith turns to George C. Wolfe of the New York Shakespeare Festival/Public Theater, Spalding Gray consults with Elizabeth LeCompte of The Wooster Group, and Deb Margolin has worked with Kent Alexander, Jamie Leo, and Madeleine Olnek.

Then, too, there are issues of minimal properties, costumes, lighting, and setting or environment. Spalding Gray typically walks on stage casually dressed in dark slacks and a plaid shirt; he sits down at a small rustic table as though he is in a familiar New England kitchen. His props are notebook and glass of water. Sometimes he has a pointer to designate certain images in slides projected on a screen situated behind him. Anna Deavere Smith's space is often cluttered with chairs and tables that she uses throughout the performance. She usually wears dark trousers and a white long-sleeved shirt with her hair pulled back to make the changes of gender and costume pieces easier. In *Fires in the Mirror*, she exchanges hats, coats, shoes, and glasses from a nearby rack as she portrays female and male, Jewish and black, activist and resident, parent and teacher in the long-standing conflict and deadly crisis of the Crown Heights community in Brooklyn.

In conclusion, there is one truism. In solo performance art, the choices for staging are as individualistic as the material is personal and the performer distinctive.

Of Mice, Bugs and Women
The Secaucas Monologue

DEB MARGOLIN

Deb Margolin (b. 1954) was launched in the late seventies from a trade magazine writer and typesetter to playwright, performance artist, and co-founder of the Split Britches Theater Company, one of the most important feminist theater troupes of the eighties.

Margolin grew up in Westchester County, an urban community about forty-five minutes north of New York City, and was educated at New York University. After losing a writer for a show known as Split Britches *(later the name of their company), Lois Weaver and Peggy Shaw called Deb Margolin. "So I ended up writing part of the show for them," Margolin recalls, "and then the next thing I know I was in the show, and the next thing I know, that's my life."[15]*

Deb Margolin's solo career began at Dixon Place, one of New York's pioneering performance venues, at the invitation of Ellie Covan. She developed several solo pieces there and presented Of All the Nerve, *her signature performance piece, at the Soho Repertory Theater in 1988.*

Together with the other Split Britches artists (Lois Weaver and Peggy Shaw), Deb Margolin accepted invitations as an artist-in-residence at Hampshire College (Amherst, MA) and the University of Hawaii, and later as Zale writer-in-residence at Tulane University (New Orleans), which recently acquisitioned the Margolin archives. Currently, she is on the faculties of New York University and the Yale Drama School.

Deb Margolin has written solo performance pieces along with theater pieces that include other actors as well. Her work has been described as varied, highly structured, and performed with sharp intelligence and wild humor. Her monologues are crafted with the voice of a feminist consciousness, strong verbal images, and captivating insights into the paranoia and angst of contemporary urban life.

*Margolin has written and performed seven solo performance pieces written between 1984 and 2000 (*Upwardly Mobile Home; Little Women: The Tragedy; Of All the Nerve; Lesbians Who Kill; Of Mice, Bugs and Women; O Wholly Night and Other Jewish Solecisms; *and* Bill Me Later*). She has received numerous grants; performed in Los Angeles, Boston, and Philadelphia women's festivals; and been featured in* Harper's Magazine. *Her work has been aired on television's* Comedy Central *and* HBO Downtown. *In 1997, she expanded her performance pieces to include herself and other actors.* Critical Mass *(1997), written for six actors, ranges through a variety of subjects including death, beauty, time, God, sex, and desire in an effort to understand the all-too-human impulse to criticize.* Bringing the Fisherman Home *(1999), a two-person theater piece first produced at the Cleveland Playhouse, takes on the medical system and the intricacies of doctor/patient relationships.*

Margolin, who is married and has two children, lives in Montvale, New Jersey, that "distant and bizarre community in New Jersey" reached by the red and tan bus from New York's Port Authority.[16] When she was diagnosed with Hodgkin's disease, Margolin responded by writing 3 Seconds in the Key *(2001) for eight actors, a lyrical rift on time, cancer, and the New York Knicks basketball season.* Why Cleaning Fails, *a work in progress in 2002, addresses her personal response to the terrorists' attacks on New York's World Trade Center.*

Margolin's published work includes Split Britches: Lesbian Practice/Feminist Performance *(1996) and* Of All the Nerve *(1999). Many of her monologues have been anthologized in* More Monologues for Women by Women *(1996),* Out of Character *(1997),* The Ends of Performance

(1998), and Extreme Exposure: An Anthology of Solo Performance Texts from the Twentieth Century *(2000).*

As a solo performance artist, Deb Margolin's work is deeply personal and inherently political. "Margolin's special blend of comedy and the sublimity of the everyday," Lynda Hart wrote, "creates performances that are at once easily within one's grasp and yet somehow just enough beyond it to repeat the seduction."[17]

Of Mice, Bugs and Women—*a collage of her intelligence, wit, and personal response to life experiences—is typical of her highly individualized solo performance art.*

CRITICAL INTRODUCTION TO *THE SECAUCAS MONOLOGUE*

Deb Margolin calls *Of Mice, Bugs and Women,* first performed in 1994, a "rickety quartet."[18] In the four monologues that make up *Of Mice, Bugs and Women,* she consistently questions how it is possible for people to commit intimate, casual, daily acts of violence? Her probing ranges from a philosophical pest exterminator to a blocked novelist unable to write and the character "cut" from her unfinished novel, to the performer herself in the urban landscape of Secaucas,* New Jersey.

The four monologues are performed consecutively in an unchanging space with a kitchen table (with tablecloth, ashtray, coffee cup, glass of red wine, and box of Cheese Nips), two chairs (a bare wooden chair with arms and an overstuffed, sensuous armchair), a window frame with curtains suspended from the ceiling, and an open playing space downstage center. The buzzing sound of an insect—what Margolin calls her "semiotic bee"—marks the transitions between the monologues.

The casual violence in the first monologue brings Margolin onstage as the ubiquitous exter-

*Secaucus is a township in northern New Jersey about twenty-five minutes west of New York City. There is a large Panasonic plant there along with convention-center hotels and clothing warehouses that have outlets open to the public.

minator (the familiar Orkin Man from television) whose specialties are bugs and mice. He discourses on the various ways Manhattan housewives, beautiful women, executives walking to work, and the New York Port Authority order the extermination of cockroaches, mice, flies, bees, and even porcupines. Margolin's exterminator ("See, ex is Latin for out! It means out! Like EX-IT…") is part philosopher, psychiatrist, terminator, and company man. Not allowed to kill anything with his own hands, he creates an environment of death and meditates on the survival skills of the victims and survivors—bugs, mice, and human beings.

The burned-out novelist blames her distractions on flying objects (planes and flies), thus creating a transition from the exterminator's meditations on life and death to the performance artist's process of writing down random images and voices from life. The novelist, experiencing years of writer's block, lives on an airport's flight pattern. Helpless to control these outer irritations, what she can control is an irritating college-age character who invades her private thoughts by asking too many questions. Hating false intimacy with strangers on subway trains and with her fictional characters, she "cuts" the annoying character from her novel in a metaphorical act of lobotomy. Hers is as much an act of violence as teenagers fantasizing in a library about the desecration of girls by atom bombs and the violent acts of abusive parents.

In the third monologue, the "character cut from the novel" rages about the act of violence done to her by the novelist. She was axed, cut, banished, abolished. She has been transformed into a character with "no ongoing circumstances." Nonetheless, she has her revenge: she refuses to go away! She has been twenty-nine for forty-four years, sitting at a table in a black floral dress, always on the verge of smoking a cigarette. Resenting the violence done to her by the writer, she, nevertheless, loves two scenes frozen in time, like a painting, that can never be erased. These are scenes of loss: one recalls adolescent innocence and the other the sound-image of a buzzing bee caught between a window screen and the blind in an inevitable descent into death. Margolin captures here the intimacy and poignancy of Emily Dickinson's famous poem that begins, "I heard a fly buzz when I died."

The fourth in the series, the Secaucas monologue, follows as a twenty-minute unlayered look at the life of the writer/performer as a three-year resident of Secaucas. There is a shift here in Margolin's dramatic material and in the undisguised identity of the performer/persona. Having moved from the Upper West Side in Manhattan, Deb Margolin—woman, writer, performance artist, and mother—cannot fit into the surburban community that she has chosen. Out of the life of a housewife and caregiver of her three-year-old child and in response to rejections and humiliations by the residents of Secaucas, she creates a Beckett-like monologue that revolves around her difference, invisibility, and pain in contemporary America.

The range of Margolin's materials is distinctly feminist: pregnancy, childbirth, vestigial sounds of toys and television sets, Barney the purple dinosaur, and the ontological confusion of her child's "singing toothbrush." "Now if your will to go on living is THE SLIGHTEST BIT TENUOUS, this will DEFINITELY finish you off," she shouts at the audience.

Margolin's riff on Secaucas, New Jersey, is the centerpiece of the twenty-minute monologue. An alien being in the surburban culture where she has lived for three years, she experiences the unfamiliarity of mah-jongg, karaoke, and car alarms—what she calls "sitcom territory." She describes the township, ringed with highways, as a swamp converted from slaughterhouses into outlet centers. There is the potential for violence in the everydayness of her existence in Harmon Cove. There are threats from rodents, snakes, flies, and bees. There are painful, personal frissons caused by the ignorance, arrogance, and hostility of neighbors along with the mailman, the local librarian, and the crazy guy accosting her on the sidewalk as "Timmy The Tin-Man Tarantella." What comes

through the casual acts of indifference and hostility is Margolin's growing awareness of *difference*—her clothes, her screaming child, her Jewish identity. "And yet, it haunts me," she says, "who are we at the moment we choose to ignore the presence of another human being?" This *cri du coeur* (cry from the heart) is Deb Margolin at her best! In this landscape of outlet centers and upper-middle-class indifference, Margolin lets out an existential cry against the comings and goings of her habituated life measured out in routines of feedings, baths, walks, laundry, meals, and care-giving—a meaningful life dismissed by a passerby with a casual wave of the hand "as if I was a bunch of bugs."

The monologue reaches an apotheosis with Margolin's invitation to a karaoke night at the local clubhouse. When her turn comes to perform, she turns her angst into performance art and dances her *differences* to Bobby McFerrin's music and lyrics: "I'm Mad O Mad…I'm Angry, Angry…."

Unlike the historic conflicts of Anna Deavere Smith and the music spectacles of Laurie Anderson, Margolin's performance pieces are built out of the small moments, the innocent and ordinary exchanges between neighbors and strangers, that constitute our lives and make our desires and our deaths meaningful. Out of the small, familiar moments of *The Secaucas Monologue,* we surmise issues of gender, class, sexual identity, age, ethnicity, and the existential concerns for aloneness, desire, and death that are intimate premonitions within everyday existence.

As her late friend and editor Lynda Hart said, encapsulated in Deb Margolin's work are "love, passion, pleasure, fear, tenderness, longing, yearning—desire and the excruciating terror of its death."[19] The metaphors that suffuse *Of Bugs, Mice and Women,* especially the buzzing sounds of bees, are Margolin's personal and poetic responses to the ongoing circumstances of daily existence that comprise the dramatic material of her performance art.

Of Mice, Bugs and Women
The Secaucas Monologue

Lights down, and back up. Floor is now littered with costumes; a definite unit of dramatic material has been completed. This fourth monologue, SECAU-CUS, NEW JERSEY, in a break from the character-driven nature of the past three, is done more natural-istically, and seems to represent an unlayered look at the life of the actress who yearned to become the three characters that preceded.

PERFORMER: At 1:20 in the morning on December 20th the year of 1991 I had a kid.

And I still have him, and it's almost three years later. This is the most shocking thing in the world that I have ever done or will do. It is bizarre, ridiculous, other-worldly and completely banal. It is exhaust-ing, demented, exhilarating, refreshing, depressing, wretched and queer. *And no one talks about it.*

I have had vomit on my shirt, poop on my pant-legs and spit-out carrots in my hair for two years, and NO ONE TALKS ABOUT IT. Now in a world where there are race riots and ethnic cleansing, where there are guns in the schools and asbestos in the synagogue bathroom and vice versa, hav-ing a kid doesn't seem too important, so NO ONE TALKS ABOUT IT. Everyone has kids, so no one talks about it. Very few people in the performance community have kids, so there's not much talk about it.

So, screw it! I'm not going to talk about it either! I feel alienated enough! I feel often enough like my behavior is odd in some way or like I don't blend in properly in some respect! Although I'm sure no one notices! So I'm not going out on a limb to discuss

these things! I'm not going to talk about my theory that Dr. Lamaze was either a sexual sadist or a serial killer. I'm not going to talk about how laboring made me weep tears of oil during which I saw Jesus Christ and un-derstood exactly how inconvenient the cru-cifixion must have been insofar as the thorns and nails were painful but the worst pain was the deep, unrequited love he felt for the people who were killing him, and he shrieked for help while the nurses gossiped in the hallway! Or how he cried out for God his father whose answer either never came or was inaudible; a lot of angry people speak too softly, it's called passive aggression!

I'm not going to talk about how the ten-der flowers that grew up between my nerves took a shock-bath in ice water and couldn't move anymore, couldn't signal anymore; or how I sat for half a year with the beige curtains drawn and the sunlight coming through them like weak coffee while I curled up there with a hole in my ab-domen the size of the Delaware Water Gap as this tiny predator yanked and gnawed and bit on my boobies 15, 16, 17 times a day! Or how it became clearer and clearer with each passing moment that the child I had borne was a precise clone of his father in ev-ery respect, from his appearance to his mood to his sense of humor to the shape of his peepee like as if I had nothing whatso-ever to do with his composition.

Obviously this is not what people talk about. So I'm not going to discuss it.

No, no. I think instead what I would like to talk about is how funny it is that all of a sudden, as soon as my kid was born, my sense of vision had no meaning! And I am a very visual person, not because I am an artist, but because I'm an atheist. I believe what I see, that's my religious belief. Like, I never saw a snake talking to some naked gal in a garden who then gave a piece of fruit to some bumbling guy and they ended up getting dressed, leaving that municipality and opening up a bodega or a farm or something. So I'm not so sure I believe that story! Whereas sometimes what you do see is so breathtaking that it's hard not to take it spiritually! I'm a visual person!

So it was so shocking when all of a sudden, I mutated from being a visually clutchy person to being someone who never used their eyes. My eyes became vestigial. I broke up with my eyes. There was no big scene, it happened quite suddenly. Suddenly it was my *ears* bringing in the critical information.

It began in the hospital with Bobby McFerrin on the headphones; the dirty, restless river for my eyes, but for my larger being, Bobby McFerrin stinging my soul through the headphones, singing I'M MAD O MAD! I'M ANGRY, ANGRY. And I just cried until they threw me out of that hospital. I came home, I came up the stairs.

Then there were thuds and gurgling. And there was crying, and within the crying, there were different cries: there was the crackling, cry, like a knife, cry of dumb need that didn't even know what it wanted; there was the soft, social cry to be held; the long insistent, articulate cry of hunger; the short attenuated shrieks for diaper work; and the little croaks that were just games with sound.

(*Each toy or device that follows is demonstrated by the actor. Toys and music boxes are set on stage on a table, and miked for sound.*)

Then came the toy and TV cacophony. First, the tender little toy Dad brought for him, a little clown that plays 'Put on a Happy Face,' which actually seemed to amuse the little tyke. Then came the white bear that played 'Love Me Tender,' while

the animal moves its head like a junkie nodding out in an alleyway. Then came the croaking frog, then he learned to sit up.

Now once you can sit up, you're master of the Universe because it frees your hands! Your hands are free! The world around you is like Mission Control! So then comes the train-sound toy, so digital, precise and mournful, the bells and whistles, and track sounds, and then the animal-identification toy, screaming WHAT AM I? and urging the listener to match the gobble sound with the picture of the turkey, etc. WHAT AM I? WHAT AM I? And then you can combine them! Wind 'em both up and play 'Put on a Happy Face' with 'Love Me Tender,' or have the sounds of the train with the shriek of ontological confusion: WHAT AM I? WHAT AM I? I mean, which of us hasn't asked ourselves that question down at the train station from time to time, ladies and gentlemen?

Then pretty soon the TV starts vomiting purple sound into my life, with this low-I.Q. goody-goody dinosaur named Barney singing 'I love you! You love me! We're a happy family! With a great big hug and a kiss from me to you! Won't you say you love me too!' You could check right into a clinic with those lyrics! It brings up everything that went wrong! Everything that didn't happen in your childhood! You need a doctor!

Then the child hates getting his diaper changed so in order to do it, you have to get this SINGING TOOTHBRUSH! It's the only thing that works! You let him hold the fucking thing and press the button while you hose down his ass. Now if you ever wish someone was dead, you just invite him or her over to your house and you play them this song as many times as you can:

I'M YOUR FRIEND BRUSHY BRUSHY! I KEEP YOUR TEETH SHINY AND BRIGHT! PLEASE BRUSH WITH ME EVERY DAY, MORNING NOON AND NIGHT!

Now if your will to go on living is THE SLIGHTEST BIT TENUOUS, this will DEF-

INITELY finish you off! And, depending on whether he's made number one or number two, and how efficient you are at cleaning it up, you may have to listen to this song between 15 and 30 times per diaper change!

Then the song from the Shari Lewis show that brings existentialism into the realm of Dr. Jack Kevorkian.

THIS IS THE SONG THAT DOESN'T END! IT JUST GOES ON AND ON MY FRIEND! SOME PEOPLE STARTED SINGIN' IT NOT KNOWING WHAT IT WAS! AND THEY'LL CONTINUE SINGING IT FOREVER JUST BECAUSE...

Now the thing I forgot to mention is that not only all this noise came in and collapsed in the center of my life, but at the same time I moved from West 76th Street on the island of Manhattan in New York City to SECAUCUS, NEW JERSEY! Now, SECAUCUS, NEW JERSEY! Think about it! It's something you used to make FUN OF and all of a sudden it's where your MAIL GETS DELIVERED, much less your child, the stigma of it! So instead of the familiar and comforting sounds of rapes and murders and car alarms I now have mahjongg, karaoke and car alarms.

There's something very weird about Secaucus. Okay, it smells, but that's not it. The fact is, it's a swamp that got turned into a bunch of outlet centers. Secaucus is known for its outlet centers, and although it's just a swamp, people come here from very far away to buy things. But it's just a swamp and some alleged stores. And they call these stores OUTLET CENTERS. I find that so interesting. And although I have lived in Secaucus among these alleged outlet centers for three years, I've never seen a single center. You go looking for them, there are just these huge flat tracts of cement, with an occasional flattop building with a sign. It's just a scam built on a swamp! There aren't any of these stores! Although once I found one, because a Volkswagen Farvernugen full of Hasidim pulled up and asked me where Harvé Benard was, they said, it

was a fashion outlet center. And I know there's a flattop building with a sign, so I pointed them that way. Then I went there myself, and it was a big room with a rack full of hideous mustard-colored plaid wool blazers and a man in a top hat talking on the phone. I don't know. They used to slaughter pigs here in Secaucus; now the main business is these outlet centers.

And there are highways. The whole town is highways. You have a feeling here the only thing that isn't a highway is your bathroom. This cab driver told me he moonlights as a toxic waste disposal contractor man, he works putting toxic waste under the highways, they figure it's safe there because you drive right by, that's why the highways are always under construction, they're busy putting plutonium under them. And you wonder why you get so burned out by a traffic jam! You were being nuked there for half an hour while you listened to Lite FM!

Anyway, in the middle of these toxic roadways and bogus stores with hideous merchandise is this development complex where I live. It's called Harmon Cove. Harmon Cove! Isn't that a beautiful name? Harmon Cove! It implies music and resonance, gentle sailboats on a calm, clean tide! Harmon Cove! And it looks nice! Very nice! There's a pool, and some trees, and lots of different kinds of birds, and the landscaping is very meticulous, they sprinkle water all the time, even in the rain! Plenty of animals here! Unidentifiable rodents, as if all the gerbils escaped and mated with the water rats! And there are squirrels wandering around in a daze as if they just got back from Vietnam and can't find the Benefits Office! And supposedly benign snakes that grow to the size and thickness of your arm and sun themselves on top of the carefully carved bushes! And wild boars and mystical animals that wash up dead on the banks of the Hackensack River, which is a river to the same extent that these stretches of cement are outlet centers! It's very nice! Really, in a way! And precisely because it *is* so lovely, every plane taking off from the Tri-State area flies directly over us! Little Harmon Cove! Wave if you ever take the red-eye! Since it's impossible to sleep with all that horrific, crashing din that sounds like the living apocalypse, I'm sure I'll be awake to wave back!

And the library! The Secaucus library! What a living testament to the value of erudition! First of all it's attached to the firehouse, so if your work ever gets the better of you you can run across and slide down a pole! I went there one Thursday to try to find a certain John Donne poem called 'The Funeral.' It's a beautiful poem, full of strength and posture; I needed a copy of it to put in the program of some show I was directing. I drove over there, parked across from red engine Number 12 and went in. Now for openers it's the only library I ever went in that has MUZAK blasting! I get through the door, I hear WALK ON BY! DUH DUH DUH…DUH DUH DUH! WALK ON BY! FOOLISH PRIDE! I WILL NEVER GET OVER LOSIN YOU! AND SO IF I SEEM! BROKEN AND BLUE! WALK ON BY! DUH DUH…etc. Now this is the fucking library! And people are standing around drinking iced tea! All I saw was a bunch of newspapers lying around and a few copies of *Valley of the Dolls* and a notice about how senior citizens can get free Xeroxes on Wednesdays. So I said to the guy: Where is the poetry section? So he takes a sip, he was busy describing how he got stung by a bee on Saturday, and he says, Whatcha looking for, young lady? So I let that go, and I said: John Donne. So he thinks a second and he says: John Donne *what*? Eh, Pete? Ha Ha!

Now you're probably thinking I'm too snooty; that in reflecting on the snobbery of others, I've taken on an arrogance of my own. But I tried! I really tried! When we first moved to Secaucus, I made a real effort! I met my upstairs neighbor out by the mailbox, and WAS I CORDIAL! I fucking was!

and she introduced me to her dog Jellybean and she said 'LOOK! JELLYBEAN GOT A LETTER!' And she opened up a card, and made me hold the dog while she read him his Christmas card, and then she said: 'Everyone knows Jellybean. Even the mailman Earl knows Jellybean!' And the mailman for some reason rolls back his eyes and goes into a trance-like state, and he says: 'OH YES! I KNOW JELLYBEAN!' Couple days later I notice that her license plate says JELLY B! I mean what the hell is going to happen when that dog kicks the bucket? The sight of her car is going to shatter her composure!

But that's not the point! The point is that the first meeting went okay! I did very well! I mean, I played my part, I smiled, I held the dog, I read the card, I acknowledged the mailman, etcetera, but not two weeks later I blew the whole gig because I had been pulling up weeds in the front, and all of a sudden I felt something creeping on my thigh inside my pantleg, and I couldn't reach it and I thought it was a bee and I came tearing around the side of the house, kicked open the door with my foot and pulled down my pants but unfortunately my underpants came down too and my entire tushy and all its complements were hanging out there when Jellybean and the mother, the son and the father come up the stairs and see my whole predicament. So what can I tell you. We're on sitcom territory here, right?

They have a newspaper out here called the *Secaucus Reporter.* It comes out once a week whether it needs to or not, there's a limited amount of news over here. But it's free, they deliver it! And each resident gets about eight or ten copies, so it comes in handy if you're moving, you can wrap your glassware! It is a fine specimen of modern journalism! Whereas they can't get the movie times right at the local theaters, and once I had to watch *Rock-A-Doodle* because I was an hour and twenty minutes late for the adult feature, they certainly have drawn a bead on what matters in the news! For example, this compelling headline.

NO GO ON BASEMENT SWAP (*holds up paper*)

This is a real scoop! I read it with such interest! It is a groundbreaking article concerning certain shocking shenanigans going on with regard to Mayor Anthony Just's basement! Just listen:

THE BOARD OF ADJUSTMENT VOTED TO DISAPPROVE A THIRD VARIANCE ON MAYOR ANTHONY JUST'S HOME THIS WEEK, AMID BUFFETING RUMOR, SPECULATION AND QUESTIONS ABOUT PAST PRACTICES.

WHILE MAYOR JUST AND HIS SON SAID A SWAP OF BASEMENT ROOMS FOR AN OUTSIDE BUILDING HAD BEEN DONE IN GOOD FAITH, SOME BOARD MEMBERS BELIEVED IT WAS A VIOLATION.

THE HOUSE MAYOR JUST PURCHASED IN 1963 WAS BUILT ON AN UNDERSIZED LOT, BUT IT HAD A FINISHED BASEMENT IN WHICH MAYOR JUST'S SISTER LIVED!

A little Jane Eyre twist right there!

Here finally is a story worth following! This arresting piece of journalism was written by staff reporter Joe Hallivan. He is a very gifted man who I'm sure lives somewhere here in Harmon Cove, perhaps in someone's basement.

So you can see clearly that Harmon Cove is an incredible place, a little haven in the filthy mist at the elbow of New York and New Jersey. The women here are incredible, too! There's a pool, and they come to the pool with diamonds, waterproof outline lipstick and gold chains BUILT INTO THEIR BATHING SUITS! In other words, the gold chains are part of the suit! The bra straps, the bikini G-strings! They have children but they wouldn't be caught dead with them! And they play tennis all day, which keeps them fit! These are healthy women! I am the only unhealthy example in the entire community. My gold collection is limited to the L'Chaim pin I found on

Yom Kippur at the Beth Emeth Synagogue in New Rochelle 20 years ago, and I consistently commit the *faux pas* of being seen with my child not only on weekends but on the weekdays as well.

So, since I have no gold and my neighbor saw my ass, I walk my child alone. It's pretty here! We walk alone every morning, he in his stroller and me pushing him along. He only knows two letters of the alphabet: the letter B, because his name is Bennett, and the letter O, because it 'goes around and around.' And, as with all pieces of his knowledge, he likes to chant them out loud, as if they were a pin that could somehow pop the bubble of all human knowledge and open up the world! So we plod down the sidewalk, the child screaming B-O! B-O! B-O! most of the way, which I'm sure doesn't make me seem too attractive to the neighbors, and I try to act like I don't see anyone, since each person I ignore spares them the trouble of ignoring me, and these people have enough to do, God knows!

And yet, it haunts me…Who are we at the moment we choose to ignore the presence of another human being? Who are we at that moment? I was walking Bennett, okay he's screaming B-O! B-O! And my watch has stopped, and it's important! It's important for me to know what time it is because I have to get him in position every day to see the 3:45 train go by, it's critical! It makes his day! Life with a child is a critical mass of routines and, if you miss one, you pay later! So I see this woman coming towards us, okay, she's one of those in-crowd kitty-cool gold-lamé life-is-gay tennis players, but…she has a watch! We're all human beings, we'll all be dead in 50 years, and we all measure the element that ages and kills us with the same chronometer! Okay, hers was gold and mine was stainless steel, had vomit in it and had ceased to function, but that's a technicality! It's all the same! So we're going by, Bennett's with the B-O! B-O! And I said to her, excuse me! Could you please tell me what time it is? And she…I can't even do it! She...she waved me away as if I was a bunch of bugs! You know those frantic clusters of summer gnats you encounter sometimes moving in a wild cloud around each other? She turned her head as if me and my kid constituted one of those blobs of bugs and waved her hands like this, as if to totally disperse us so she could get by! And she kept on walking.

Now look! We may not be the most appealing people! But this woman LITERALLY WOULD NOT GIVE US THE TIME OF DAY! Literally would not!

So anyway, we're out on one of these cordial morning jaunts when all of a sudden I hear a man's voice say:

I DON'T KNOW HOW YOU DO IT.

I was shocked, I mean, someone spoke to me, so I whirl my head around, and there's this guy. He's about 5 foot 10 inches, paunchy, light brown hair, fuzzy blue eyes, broken blood vessels in the nose, like he drinks too much and used to be good-looking. So I said: I beg your pardon? and he says again:

I DON'T KNOW HOW YOU DO IT

So I said, DO IT? And he says, I DON'T KNOW HOW ANY OF YOU WOMEN DO IT! YOU COOK, YOU CLEAN, YOU TAKE CARE OF KIDS DAY AFTER DAY! So I said, Well, I don't cook or clean, and he says again: I DON'T SEE HOW YOU WOMEN DO IT! I'M A FEMINIST! YES SIR I AM! I STUDY FEMINISM! I STUDY FEMINISM IN A CLASS! AND FOR MILLIONS OF YEARS WOMEN HAVE DONE IT! AND I'M A FEMINIST! AND CAN YOU BELIEVE IT! AND WHEN THE TEACHER HAD TO BE ABSENT FOR A MONTH TO GET A HYSTERECTOMY, SHE ASKED ME TO TAKE OVER THE CLASS! I TOOK OVER! AND CAN YOU BELIEVE IT? YOU WOMEN ARE INCREDIBLE! I DON'T KNOW HOW YOU DO IT!

So I said thank you. And I walked away.

And then came the summer, my second summer at Harmon Cove. And the pool opened, and then came the exquisite, elongated, sensuous sessions between my body and the cool clean painted blue of that pool: afternoons clawing at that body of water like one might the body of a lover in a cheap motel; in the mornings, throwing myself in and clinging to that cold the way a sleeper in the middle of a beautiful dream clings to sleep; and then, in the evenings, my eyes clawing at the jagged edges of the rising moon, my fingers clawing at the edges of the pool, swimming back and forth and back and forth till they threw me out and locked the gate.

So then one day I'm walking my child after a particularly sensuous morning swim, when all of a sudden I hear, from behind me:

I DON'T KNOW HOW YOU WOMEN DO IT!

And I turn around, and it's the same guy! Launching the same rap! And of course at the same moment I realize he says this same thing to every woman he sees, and doesn't even remember the particular woman to whom he says it: a kind of social promiscuity, a new kind of sexism, even, ladies! So I said, DO IT? And he says: I DON'T KNOW HOW YOU WOMEN DO IT! YOU COOK, YOU CLEAN AND TAKE CARE OF KIDS DAY AFTER DAY! So I said, I don't cook or clean, and he said: I'M A FEMINIST, I STUDY FEMINISM! YES SIR I DO! AND WHEN THE TEACHER HAD TO GET A LAPAROSCOPY, SHE ASKED *ME* TO TAKE OVER THE CLASS FOR HER! I DON'T KNOW HOW YOU WOMEN DO IT!

Now this whole thing was getting very tightly on my nerves. I mean, first of all, a disquisition on feminist thinking from a paunchy pixillated white man at nine a.m. of the clock on a Wednesday morning was NOT my idea of what I had in mind for myself socially. So I said to him, Look! There are seven hundred and seventeen women living in this complex who would be *very glad* to clear this mystery up for you with hands-on training! I mean, it was a disgrace! This man was walking around with NOTHING TO DO! So he says: OH! ALLOW ME TO INTRODUCE MYSELF! MY NAME IS TIMMY 'THE TIN-MAN' TARANTELLA! So I said, How do you do? or something. And he says, What do you do? And I said, Cook, clean and take care of babies! So he says, How 'bout coming out for karaoke in the Harman Cove Clubhouse this Friday! You deserve the rest! Take the night off! You can do something! You can do something! Want to be in it? C'mon! Give it a try! So I said, Well, as a matter of fact, I am a performance artist, and maybe I can do a little something. I mean, after the knife fight that broke out during my show at Café Bustelo, I figure a little upper-middle-class hostility isn't much to cope with. So he says GREAT! And he gives me this flyer, look! I kept it! Here it is! It says:

THE RECREATION BOARD
PROUDLY PRESENTS
THE HARMON COVE VARIETY SHOW
CO-HOSTS
TIMMY 'THE TIN-MAN' TARANTELLA
AND RHONDA B. REISBAUM

Scheduled to Appear: The No Tones!
Mick & Co.!

The Harmon Cove Boy Toys!
The Vinnettes

Whitey!

AND FEATURING SPECIAL GUEST STAR
MAYOR ANTHONY JUST!

I thought I was going to die! A chance to dance karaoke with the guy who locked his sister in the basement!

And more Guest Stars and Surprises!
Call Tom or Anthony if you want to be on the bill!
THIS IS THE NIGHT YOUR STAR CAN SHINE!
TELL THE BABYSITTER
YOU'LL BE LATE!

See, there's that nice, feminist touch I've come to expect from the Tin-Man! And it finishes up,

STAG OR DRAG—YOU'LL HAVE THE
BEST TIME IN YOUR LIFE

Isn't it interesting, Stag or drag, those are the only choices?

Anyway, I went to karaoke that night in the clubhouse. I was afraid but I went. I went forward with my knees knocking. I got dressed. I put on make-up. Who knew what I would find there at the clubhouse! (*Lighting change: disco lights up, general wash down. Disco music up.*)

When I arrived, boy, what a thrill! They sure knew how to do it up! The place looked great! And everyone was there…Oh, Jeez, there's Timmy the Tin-Man dancing with Rhonda B. Reisbaum! And there's Mayor Just and his son dancing with the woman from the basement! And there's Whitey up on the dais…he must be the DJ for tonight …Oh! And there's the woman who waved me away as if I were a bunch of bugs! HI! HON! (*waving frantically*) HI!

Then the performances began! Boy that Vinny sure can sing! And those Vinnettes! What backup! And there go the Harmon Cove Boy Toys! They really are on top of things! Rhonda looks so stunning in that silverleaf bathing suit! And that Whitey! He's got a voice like Sinatra…

Then all of a sudden it was my turn. I could feel the lights come up on me. Everyone was looking at me. I knew it was my turn to…I was supposed to perform…to perform …but I just…I just…
(*Fade up: 'I'm Mad O Mad…I'm Angry, Angry…'*)
FINIS

PERFORMING *OF MICE, BUGS AND WOMEN*

Of Mice, Bugs and Women, first performed Off Off Broadway at the Atlantic Theater in 1993, is a collage of four monologues written and performed by Deb Margolin. Margolin subsequently performed the quartet, directed by Kent Alexander, at P.S. 122 in the East Village in October of 1994. This performance was reviewed by *The New York Times* and *TheaterWeek*.

As both creator and performer, Margolin is very specific about her use of theatrical space, including placement of furniture and properties, onstage costume changes, and sounds of the buzzing of her "semiotic bee." She designates how the characters plus the performer utilize the space: The Exterminator plays downstage in the empty space; the novelist sits in the wooden chair by the table; the character cut from the novel sits in the "sensuous" armchair; and the performer "encompasses all aspects, symbolic and naturalistic, of the stage setting."

Margolin appears in the first monologue as a loquacious exterminator who takes care of mice and bugs with philosophical wit and wisdom. "I'll tell you the difference between a bug and a mouse," she/he says. "*Motivation:* the bug just wants to survive, while the mouse is burdened with a will to live." The second monologue is that of an alcoholic novelist bored with her writing and bereft of "ongoing circumstances"; in the third, a fictional character who has been "cut" from the novelist's work complains about her rejection; and the final monologue delves more naturalistically into Margolin's adventures as a new mother in the strange landscape of Secaucus, New Jersey. The triptych of monologues is framed by the sound of an insect buzzing. Only the final monologue is devoid of the aural metaphor. Writing for *The New York Times*, Ben Brantley said that the "drone becomes a gnawing aural emblem of both time passing and time frozen for Ms. Margolin's ingeniously interconnected characters and the performer herself."[20]

Margolin herself says that the fourth monologue is a break from the three preceding monologues and "seems to represent an unlayered look at the life of the actress who yearned to become the three previous characters."

As the lights go down and up again for the fourth monologue, Margolin takes the stage as herself—the performer and mother of a three-year-old son who has moved from Manhattan to Secaucas and finds existential angst in her in-ability to adapt to contemporary suburban life. In one section of the monologue, she has a stinging criticism of the suburbs where the women wear diamonds and gold jewelry with their bathing suits. Nonetheless, she reserves her most venomous remarks for the "singing toothbrush" that has entered her life with her child and for her new condition as a caregiver whose *hearing* has eclipsed vision as the dominant sense in her life.

Critics *Of Mice, Bugs and Women* praised Margolin's twisted imagination, her outraged tone, and her sharp as a bee's sting wit.

CRITICS' NOTEBOOK

With the exception of Lynda Hart's exemplary writing on Deb Margolin's art, published as *Of All the Nerve* (1999), the majority of critical writing that relates to Margolin can be found in reviews and commentaries on performance art and on feminist critical theory and practice.

For purposes of exploring Deb Margolin's particular brand of performance, we included in our critics' notebook Lynda Hart's commentary on the *Secaucas Monologue* and sections from Constance K. Zaytoun's interview with the artist.

Lynda Hart, Commentary: A Little Night Music*

Of Mice, Bugs and Women is a triptych, or as Margolin says, a 'rickety quartet.' In the transition from the triptych to the 'Secaucus' monologue, Margolin has to coach her audience to hold their applause. The show is not over. As she changes out of the short, tight, flashy red dress that her character wears at the end of the triptych and into her 'Payless' shoes and a tacky polyester overall that gives her room for getting

*Lynda Hart, ed., from *Of All the Nerve: Deb Margolin Solo.* (New York: The Continuum International Publishing Group, 1999): 107–109.

pregnant or carrying a gun, she draws an invisible line with her toe and steps back and forth across it repeatedly, chanting: Life/Art, Life/Art, Life/Art. One of the distinguishing characteristics of performance art, as opposed to 'theater,' is the way in which the former muddies the distinction between life and art. When Deb visits my class to give a lecture on her work, one of my students asks me after she leaves: 'Is she really *like that all the time,* or was she performing?' Despite the fact that Margolin's lecture contained a lucid and cogent explanation of the ways in which we are all *always* already 'performing,' there remains, as Herb Blau so eloquently put it: 'a crucial particle of difference... between just breathing, eating, sleeping, loving and *performing* those functions of just living; that is, with more or less deliberation' (Herbert Blau, *The Eye of Prey: Subversions of the Postmodern,* 1987, p. 161). What most performance artists do *not* do is create the illusion of reality as do playwrights whose work takes place in the genre of dramatic realism. Perhaps performance artists could be said to reverse this formula, creating the reality of illusion.

Of Mice, Bugs and Women does mark a significant shift in Margolin's style as a performance artist. Here we have three fully developed characters, for whom she creates a referential context that appears to extend outside of or beyond their moments on stage. Her perpetually 29-year-old character cut out of the novel may have a 'character with no ongoing circumstances,' but she *is* a character, and in fact does have 'ongoing circumstances,' albeit negative ones frozen in time. Alternating between despairing and reveling in the fact of her timelessness, she lacks a narrative that is *given* to her, but she creates her own narrative out of that very lack. In a sense, she is smarter than the writer who axed her because she asked too many questions and was too smart for the author who doesn't 'suffer geniuses gladly.' It is Margolin's genius to give depth, intellectual acumen, and indeed philosophical profundity to a character who is overtly marked as vapid, narcissistic, and lacking in agency. This, indeed, is what makes *Of Mice, Bugs and Women* particu-

larly compelling. Margolin doesn't laugh *at* these characters whom one might easily find to be humorous objects; she laughs *with* them, and finds ways to identify with them. She even goes so far as to admit that she makes *herself* up by creating them. The Exterminator: a man who takes his work very seriously. Not merely efficient, he is obsessed with understanding the differences between the insects and rodents whose lives are in his hands. Well, not really in his hands *per se,* as he points out to us: it's against company policy for him to actually touch these creatures; he merely creates an atmosphere where they drop dead. As a character, the exterminator makes us laugh, but Margolin doesn't let us off with a light, comfortable glance into his world. For he is, also, a character who thinks deeply and poignantly about these mice and bugs, almost humanizing them, before he annihilates them. As in all of her work, Margolin wants to know how it is possible for people to commit the intimate, banal, casual daily acts of violence—how these realities pass as illusions. Like the woman in Secaucus who dismisses her and her child with a sweep of her hand as if they are gnats swarming under a lamppost. Margolin wants to know: 'Who are we at the moment we ignore the presence of another human being?' The exterminator's reference to 'creating an atmosphere in which they just drop dead' resonates powerfully with a post-Holocaust awareness. We might like to think that such massive extermination, on a scale that is quite literally incomprehensible, can only be understood through some recourse to a notion of 'depersonalization' or 'dehumanization.' We would like to think that unthinkable cruelties can only be performed if one's *own* humanity is somehow cut off, shut down, or missing. But that's the easy answer, and Margolin doesn't rest with it. Her exterminator is ultimately most hideous *because* he has studied and understood the differences between the creatures he kills. The persistent humming of the insect struggling to die in the night runs throughout the triptych, overlapping and connecting its parts, like a soundtrack that is not exactly a backdrop, but an intricate night music that functions as a through-line for all these characters who share the inability to rest, to sleep, but from Margolin's perspective, there is always the rub, for perchance they may dream, and dream of each other.

While these three characters in the triptych form a theatrical piece that appears to depart from the cloudy division of life and art, Margolin brings *Of Mice, Bugs and Women* back to a performative mode with the addition of the 'Secaucus' monologue. She reports her relief when a critic noticed that 'Secaucus' was not merely tacked on, but a crucial epilogue of sorts to the triptych, a piece that explained where the prior three monologues originated. On the one hand, 'Secaucus' is a monologue that addresses Margolin's own life transition: 'In two weeks, I went from being a hip and single if fat and pregnant swinging chick on the Upper West Side of the cultural urban center of the world to a married matron with a baby living in a flooded swamp that used to be a pig farm.' In itself, this would be more than enough to yield dramatic material for a twenty-minute monologue. But 'Secaucus' performs much more than its content. For it is in this piece that Margolin reinserts herself into the narrative of her characters in the triptych. Closing up the distance between herself and her 'realized characters,' she realizes that *no one* is in a position to judge others; and yet everyone is responsible for who we all become and what action we take in the world. All of us can, and do, find our lives suddenly and inexplicably altered, and in the presence of people with whom easy identifications are not possible. Margolin cannot find a way to 'fit' into the community that she has nonetheless chosen. She cannot change *into* them, nor does she desire to do so. Instead, she accepts the pain of their rejection, the humiliation of their refusal to recognize her own humanity in her differences from them. And she turns them into works of art, *without* denying their lives. So she goes to the karaoke party, and when the spotlight comes on her, she dances her differences, but fully in their midst.

Constance K. Zaytoun's, Interview with Deb Margolin*

❦

Zaytoun: Given that you have been a part of this movement since 1979, in your opinion how has women's/feminist performance art developed or changed over the past twenty-five years from when you began your work to now?

Margolin: Well, if anything, I think it has drawn more people and modalities into it. I think one of the things that was most striking, most shocking, of the so-called women's theater movement was that it was a theater of the interstitial. It was a theater of daily life. It was a theater of inclusion, and a theater that required no more than the will and the need to find a communal space for the sharing of stories.

My understanding of classical theater prior to that time was that it had certain very definite criteria in terms of what constituted drama. Drama was a story that had a very particular kind of arc and a story that was often exogenous to the daily lives of regular people. A regular woman in her kitchen trying to prepare a biscuit for a recalcitrant child would not have thought her struggle worthy of public rendition. So, the women's movement came along and in terms of theater, suddenly the moments where nothing happens in the formal sense, but much happens emotionally, and much happens interpersonally, became viable and became includable as plot. Plot turned into something that was more along the lines of transformation, instead of a car crash and a prosecution, or a rape and a resolution, or something like that.

I really feel like the origins of performance art are inherently feminine in that it was a single person talking about something that was meaningful to her. It was a way of coming together. It was a way of sharing stories. It was a way of elevating our image of importance....

❧ ❧ ❧

*Constance K. Zaytoun interviewed Deb Margolin on September 20, 2002, at the Kensington House in Chelsea, New York City.

Zaytoun: Let's discuss your personal process in developing a piece for performance. Even though you are also a dramaturg, do you ever utilize a dramaturg? And, when does the director come into your process? What does your director do for you?

Margolin: That [the role of the director] has truly been a process. In the beginning when I first started out with Split Britches, Lois Weaver was the director and also the teacher. She taught me everything. She taught me how to act; she taught me how to build characters; she taught me how to build sets. She taught me how to find the light on stage. At first, I couldn't find it; I'd stand in the dark.

Zaytoun: Nobody ever directed your solo work?

Margolin: Well, Lois [Weaver] came in and sort of tried to help me with the first piece—*Of All the Nerve*. She did a little work with me at the end of that process. But it was basically pieces that I had thrown together and brought over to my friend Amy Zorn's house and did it for her and her friend, and the cat or something and they would laugh or not.... Basically, that's how it went. I would rehearse in front of my own cat or their cat. I just thought it was the biggest kick. Then, I'd take this crazy piece...to some club, like Theater Club Funambules or Dixon Place... and just slap it up there and see what happened and generally it was fun. And generally it was revelatory. Performance was a good editor. If something seemed cumbersome to me in performance, I could adjust it. It was my play. I could just cut it right out. That's how my shows went. The audience was my editor and my dramaturg and my director.

❧ ❧ ❧

Margolin: That went on for a number of years. And then it came to *O Wholly Night and Other Jewish Solecisms* which was a piece commissioned by The Jewish Museum in 1996, I believe, as part of the All Too Jewish Exhibition they were having at the Museum and I asked Margot Lewitin, Artistic Director of the Women's Interart Theater, to please help me....

Margot is a venerable presence in the women's art scene and had directed any number of plays in her theater, and she took this project on, and that was a whole other way of working.... Margot had very definite ideas of actor's beats. A pause for Margot was a very precise thing. Timing, beats were very important to her and I was put through paces I hadn't been put through in a long time. And I remember, once desperately saying to her, "What does this look like? What do you see?" And she said, "Do you want to know if the play's any good or not?" And I said, "No. I want to know if you went up in a helicopter and looked down at this piece, like an island, what shape does it have?" Like I was in the middle of all these details, and mechanics, and I couldn't see the work. She's right. There are very precise beats in that piece. There are hairpin turns. It seems just like a casual, conversational monologue but there are hairpin emotional turns which I can now negotiate because of the work I did with her....

Zaytoun: And, to date, you have performed that piece over a period of time?

Margolin: It's been many years now, and I think the performance has gotten tighter. It's gotten better. I mean the text has not changed at all. I bring more life experience to it now, than I did then.... But those beats are as valid at this moment as they were six years ago.... Then I worked with Randy Rollison on *Car Thieves! Joy Rides!* and Randy had a heavy dramaturgical hand. Margo hadn't been focused on my work dramaturgically. Randy really helped me put that piece together. I had a bunch of monologues and we story-boarded them together. We put the piece together. And then once we put it together we figured out how to navigate our way through it physically. So he helped me with both the verbal path and the actor's path in that piece.... It's a very intimate, intense relationship you have with a director, which I'm still not the master of at all. I'm learning to take direction. I'm learning to have to get into that relationship that's so trusting, that's so profoundly, at its best, symbiotic and collaborative. It can be a magnificent thing when you're working with the right person. And it's not always easy to see your way through a relationship like that because the creative process has a lot of darkness in it, by which I mean, not sadness, but sometimes there's not a lot of light. There's a lot of heat without a lot of light. When you're in the middle of the creative process, it can be really (*sighs*) daunting.

❦ ❦ ❦

Zaytoun: Generally, do your directors come in before you actually go into rehearsal? Did your directors assist prior to rehearsal with your more recent texts, such as *Three Seconds into the Key* or *Why Cleaning Fails*?

Margolin: …The director is there with me before rehearsal so we are talking about the text. This is all very new given my origins in performance where nobody saw the piece until Amy Zorn and her cat—and then an hour later I took the piece to Dixon Place. Now, I'm in conversation usually with a director before rehearsals begin. So we're talking about text. We're talking about what might be, what vision the director has, what vision I have, what the hell this is, does it make any sense....

❦ ❦ ❦

Margolin: Although my work is very tightly scripted, people often say, "Is your work scripted?" "Did you make something up?" "Were you improvising?" No. Every word is in there. It's hard for people to believe that somebody can present themselves in such a casual conversational manner and every word is scripted…. this seems contradictory to newcomers to this style of performance....

REVISITING PERFORMANCE ART

With antecedents in earlier ages, performance art and solo performers have emerged as a theatrical phenomenon in the twentieth century. With roots in early twentieth century avant-garde experiments in the art world, performance art gained in vogue in the United States in the 1960s. Influences combined from the art,

dance, music, and theater worlds to create a plethora of experimentations labeled as happenings, multimedia spectacles, painting constructions, dance theater, and experimental theater. Performance art was now not just a label for monologists and stand-up comedians but a fine art with many performances staged in museums and galleries.

In theatrical circles, *solo* performance spun out of the more complex experiments in performance. The stages for solo work were largely converted spaces, thereby lending solo artists kinship with the theatrical avant-garde performing since the late forties in living rooms, warehouses, and garages.

As an outgrowth of the 1980s, solo performance connotes the work of a single artist who is often playwright, actor, director, *and* designer. Rejecting existing literary texts, the solo performer creates a public expression of autobiographical material and highly personal responses to taboo subjects, collective histories, and governmental policies. The text necessarily has an abbreviated format and often requires some twenty to ninety minutes to perform. Deb Margolin's *Secaucas Monologue* has 443 lines of printed text. In performance, these solo texts, or "compositions" as they are sometimes called, are as various as their writers/performers. The common thread in this new genre is the act of creation that is a shared effort between the writer's process and the performer's—what Deb Margolin calls "a perfect Theater for One."

In general, performance art has come a long and varied way from the avant-garde experiments of the dadaists and futurists in the early part of the last century. As one writer reminds us, today's performance artists in the United States are just as likely to be found at the Brooklyn Academy of Music as in P.S. 122 in lower Manhattan. The broad spectrum takes into account solo monologues, stand-up comedy routines, works with multiple actors, and large multimedia collaborations of artists from different disciplines.

Artists confronting a complex, multicultural society often in the creation of more traditional plays, many of them well-made, has been another outcome of contemporary playwriting at the millennium. Many of the new plays written by Hispanic, Latino/Latina, and Asian American playwrights have strong social and political messages highlighting issues of race, gender, class, and identity in American society. *Difference* becomes the resonant theme in works by Cuban American Eduardo Machado and Asian American David Henry Hwang writing about the intersections where their cultures collide in the American landscape.

NOTES

1. Douglas Langworthy, "Deb Margolin: Take Back Your Proscenium," *American Theatre* (May/June 1996): 38.
2. See Marvin Carlson, *Performance: A Critical Introduction* (New York: Routledge, 1996).
3. Richard Kostalentz, *On Innovative Performance(s): Three Decades of Recollections on Alternative Theater* (Jefferson, NC: McFarland, 1994): 5–7. See also Carlson, 99.
4. Jill Dolan, "Performance, Utopia, and the 'Utopian Performative,'" *Theatre Journal*, 53 (2001): 455.
5. Jo Bonney, "Fragments from the Age of the Self: Nine Artists Span the Century of the Soloist," *American Theatre*, 16, 10 (December 1999): 32.
6. Carlson 122.
7. Carlson 193.
8. Catherine Elwes, "Floating Femininity: A Look at Performance Art by Women" in *Women's Images of Men,* eds. Sarah Kent and Jacqueline Morreau (London: Writers and Readers Publishing, 1985): 165.
9. Quoted in C. Carr, *On Edge: Performance at the End of the Twentieth Century* (Middletown, CT: Wesleyan University Press, 1994): 179.
10. Quoted in Carlson 164. See also Margot Mifflin, "Performance Art: What Is It and Where Is It Going?," *Art News,* 91, 4 (1992): 84–89.
11. Lenora Champagne, "Once Upon a Time in Performance Art," in *Contemporary American Theatre,* ed. Bruce King (New York: St. Martin's Press, 1991): 183.
12. Champagne 179.
13. Deb Margolin, "A Perfect Theatre for One: Teaching 'Performance Composition,'" *The Drama Review,* 41, 2 (Summer 1997): 69.
14. John Lahr, "Under the Skin," *The New Yorker* (June 28, 1993): 90.
15. Langworthy 38.
16. Ann Daly, "Looking Underneath The Itch to Criticize," *The New York Times* (2 March 1997): 2.
17. Lynda Hart, "Introduction: A Love Letter," in *Of All the Nerve: Deb Margolin Solo* (New York: The Continuum International Publishing Group, 1999): 11.
18. Hart, "Commentary: A Little Night Music," in *Of All the Nerve,* p. 107.
19. Hart, "Introduction: A Love Letter," in *Of All the Nerve,* p. 5.
20. Ben Brantley, *The New York Times* (19 October 1994): C14.

CHAPTER 16

UNDERSTANDING INTERCULTURALISM

A scene from the Repertorio Español production of *Broken Eggs* ("Revoltillo"), with (left to right) Ofelia Gonzalez, Jose Cheo Oliveras, and Adriana Sananes. (Photo © Gerry Goodstein.)

...we cannot lose sight of the fact that we all live in a society where we have to coexist. It doesn't mean that I have to like your culture. But we have to be sensitive to each other's cultures.

—Ping Chong

BACKGROUND

Intercultural. Multicultural. These are highly de-bated terms in today's media. A dictionary defi-nition of *multicultural* is simply "of or pertaining to a society of varied cultural groups." It is used to acknowledge the rich diversity of American society and also to challenge the achievements and values of Western European culture.

In this era of concerns for representing mi-norities and all cultures in society, political groups, on campuses, and in arts institutions, such words as *multicultural, intercultural, eth-nicity,* and *fusion* abound in the new dialogue on cultural diversity. These terms bring to the foreground of our awareness the need to en-hance cultural differences; that is, to allow all cultures autonomy, self-expression, and em-powerment. It is fashionable to say that the American effort to achieve multiculturalism is the inversion of the "melting pot" idea. Cultur-ally diverse groups set about in today's world to retain their own distinct ethnic qualities: Af-rican American, Hispanic, Native American, Latino/a, Chicano/a, Asian American, Polish, Korean, Irish, Hasidic, Jamaican, and so on. The multicultural idea is not limited to ethnicity, but also includes orientations and ideologies—gay, environmental, feminist, creationist, etc.

Whereas *multicultural* celebrates the sepa-rateness and distinctions of diverse cultural groups existing side by side, *interculturalism* ex-amines the collisions of those cultures, orienta-tions, and ideologies. Interculturalists, whether artists, writers, sociologists, or journalists, probe the confrontations, ambivalences, disruptions, fears, and disturbances when and where cul-tures collide or pull away from each other. Inter-culturalists explore misunderstandings, failed communications, broken dreams, and garbled messages within and without ethnic groups.

What has not been or cannot be successfully fused is seen not as disasters or indictments of Western civilization but as "fertile rifts of cre-ative possibilities."[1] Thus, there emerge in works of art the tensions between the Islamic world and English literary practices in the nov-els of Salman Rushdie (*The Satanic Verses*), the mixing of forms, texts, and performers by direc-tor Peter Brook (*The Mahabharata*), the theater anthropology of Eugenio Barba (*The Floating Is-lands*), and the performance art of Guillermo Gómez-Peña and Anna Deavere Smith (*A Per-formance Chronicle of the Re-discovery of America by the Warrior for Gringostrioca* and *Fires in the Mir-ror: Crown Heights, Brooklyn and Other Identities*).

Whereas the multicultural generates politi-cal and scholarly writings, interculturalism has fostered new art about cultures co-existing un-easily. "Just as mountains rise where continents collide," Richard Schechner writes, "and deep ocean basins form where they pull apart, so new arts, behaviors and human interactions are ne-gotiated at the interfaces and faults connecting and separating cultures."[2] Mexican-American performance artist Gómez-Peña is a good exam-ple of an individual making art out of colliding cultures. He says, "I physically live between two cultures and two epochs. When I am on the U.S. side, I have access to high technology and spe-cialized information. When I cross back to Mex-ico, I get immersed in a rich political culture. When I return to California, I am part of the mul-ticultural thinking emerging from the interstices of the U.S.'s ethnic milieu. I walk the fibres of this transition in my everyday life, and I make art about it."[3]

THE INTERCULTURAL TEXT

The intercultural text, first, demonstrates the collision of cultures. It takes its tensions and conflicts from the cultural uneasiness defining, for example, life in the United States in the last decades of the twentieth century. Such playwrights as María Irene Fornés, Ping Chong, David Henry Hwang, Maya Angelou, Milcha Sanchez-Scott, Athol Fugard, Eduardo Machado, and Laurence Yep write about people of diverse cultural backgrounds living multiple cultural identities. Interculturalism is one of the ways to admit a general discourse on other cultures into the artistic arena. Cultures that have previously been ignored or suppressed or unknown are examined most often against the background of the dominant culture.

The intercultural text for the theater is rich and engaging in the artists' efforts to confront and explore those cultural edges where fusion has not taken place. Eduardo Machado writes most cogently in his *Floating Island Plays* of those interstices where cultures rub up against each other and frictions occur within families. The very act of addressing in art those intercultural fractures, ideological contradictions, and crumbling national myths has led to an enormous spectrum of new art—in film, theater, dance, music, painting, and performance art. Intercultural works examine questions of autonomy and empowerment. Central to the intercultural text is the notion of people of different cultures interacting and having problems in their interactions brought about by opportunities and disruptions caused by massive relocations of people from all over the globe—from Cuba to Los Angeles, Puerto Rico to New York City, Tehran to London, Hong Kong to San Francisco, and so on.

In particular, plays by Hispanic American writers examine those failed cultural fusions in lives dislocated from a familiar language, people, and customs. Many plays by Asian American playwrights, like David Henry Hwang, focus on cultural differences and racial identities that lead to generational and personal conflicts.

In our examination of intercultural texts, let us first consider *Broken Eggs* by Eduardo Machado as an example of writing that explores the frissons in the lives of Cuban Americans in suburban Los Angeles in the late seventies.

U.S. HISPANIC AND LATINO/A PLAYWRITING

Since the late sixteenth century, a Spanish-speaking theater whose purpose was to preserve Hispanic traditions and language has existed in North America. In 1965, a Chicano theater under the wing of the United Farm Workers burst onto the political scene to address the plight of migrant farm workers in California. Led by Mexican American theater artists Luis Valdez and his bilingual Chicano company El Teatro Campesino (The Farm Workers Theater), Hispanic American writing found a contemporary voice. A second generation of writers was encouraged by the experiments of activist/storyteller Luis Valdez (*Zoot Suit*), writer and teacher María Irene Fornés (*Fefu and Her Friends*), and former prison inmate Miguel Piñero (*Short Eyes*). A growing number of Latino/a playwrights, many born in the United States, followed in their footsteps: Chicano authors Josefina Lopez and Carlos Morton, Puerto Rican–born José Rivera, Latina dramatists Milcha Sanchez-Scott and Cheríe Moraga, and Cuban-born Eduardo Machado.

The new Latino/a writers who were writing in styles and subjects outside the mainstream of American traditions found stages in workshops and converted neighborhood spaces to test the waters of their new subjects: the border experience, colliding cultures, issues of ethnicity and gender, old-world taboos versus new-world lifestyles. From all over the United States, Latino/a writers came to work and study with María Irene Fornés in the Lab found at the INTAR Hispanic American Arts Center in New York City. A new wave of playwrights emerged from this creative home where nothing was forbidden and rigorous playful innovation was encouraged. Eduardo Machado, Cheríe Moraga, and Milcha Sanchez-Scott emerged from the Lab along with José Rivera, who was trained outside the Lab, as the first-wave of Latino/a playwriting in the United States. Machado's *The Modern Ladies of Guanabacoa*, Moraga's *Shadow of a Man*, Sanchez-Scott's *Roosters,* and Rivera's *The House of Ramon Iglesía* focused national attention on new voices in the American theater who were presenting new ways to understand Latino/a identity and explore issues of assimilation, marginalization, and political and artistic bias heretofore ignored by the mainstream culture and its institutions.

Broken Eggs

EDUARDO MACHADO

Eduardo Machado (1953–) was born in Havana, Cuba, and grew up in nearby Cojimar. Born on the day Fidel Castro launched the Cuban revolution, he grew up in its shadow.

When he was eight years old, his parents sent him and his younger brother to live with relatives in Miami. A year later, his parents, along with other siblings and cousins, arrived. His father, an accountant by trade, was unable to find work in Florida, so the family migrated to Canoga Park in California. In the summer of 1978, Machado was introduced to the Padua Hills Playwrights' Festival and to a "Cuban writer" whose name was María Irene Fornés. He worked as her assistant on Fefu and Her Friends and began writing and acting. Later, in New York City as part of the INTAR Hispanic American Arts Center workshop where Fornés held writing workshops, he wrote what came to be called "The Floating Island Plays"—The Modern Ladies of Guanabacoa, Fabiola, In the Eye of the Hurricane, and Broken Eggs. These are his best-known works. He returned to Cuba in 1999 as a member of a Latin American film delegation and was inspired to write a highly autobiographical play about a Cuban child exiled to the United States who returns to his homeland forty years later. The play is Havana Is Waiting (originally called When the Sea Drowns in Sand).

Eduardo Machado holds a faculty appointment in the School of the Arts at Columbia University, New York City, and heads the graduate program in playwriting there. Known primarily as a playwright, Machado works professionally as an actor and director, as a television and screenwriter, and as a filmmaker/director. He created the independent film Exiles in New York and appeared in Pollock. He has written over thirty plays, including Rosario and the Gypsies, Once Removed, Related Retreats, Crocodile Eyes, and The Cook.

CRITICAL INTRODUCTION TO *BROKEN EGGS*

Broken Eggs, the fourth play in Eduardo Machado's *Floating Island* tetralogy, was first produced in 1984 by New York's Ensemble Studio Theater. The Spanish version, entitled *Revoltillo*, was performed three years later at New York's Repertorio Español.

The earlier plays are set in Cuba in the 1920s (*The Modern Ladies of Guanabacoa*) and in the 1950s (*Fabiola* and *In the Eye of the Hurricane*). *Broken Eggs* continues the story of modern Cuba with the Marquez-Hernandez family now transplanted to a suburb of Los Angeles in 1979. The setting delineates the dominant culture: the United States, California, Woodland Hills, a country club. Three generations of the Cuban family react to their cultural isolation by language, religion, folkways; their assimilation into supermarkets, recreational drugs, divorce courts, and other ethnic families; and their existence as a universal dysfunctional family.

Written in two acts, the play examines the problems faced by a formerly wealthy Cuban family experiencing life in exile in the United States. The occasion is a wedding reception in a Southern California suburb, and the action revolves around the family's reactions to the demands made upon them during the reception. The third-generation Lizette is marrying into a Jewish family, the Rifkins. Machado's intercultural text sets the commonalities of family, religion, politics, and traditions derived from a Hispanic culture against the dominant Eurocentric culture of the United States.

The transplanted Hispanic culture of the Marquez-Hernandez family emphasizes the frissons in their lives rather than an assimilation into the dominant culture. The wedding is the playwright's occasion for bringing the family together in celebration and nostalgia: maternal grandmother, paternal grandfather, aunt, divorced parents, three siblings, and the invisible stepmother from Argentina. The play's title is taken from the adage: "You can't make an omelet without breaking a few eggs." The family has been "broken" in their experience of political exile from their Hispanic culture. Memory and nostalgia for the vanished past in the island homeland now transformed by the Castro revolution, during which an uncle remained behind and committed suicide, inform the family's expressions of regret and loss. The mother of the bride, Sonia, longs for the untroubled innocence of her adolescence:

> Why can't life be like it was? Like my coming-out party. When my father introduced me to our society in my white dress.

Her practical sister, Miriam, puts the memory in a harsher perspective: "Sonia, they threw the parties to give us away…perfect merchandising."

Broken Eggs is a play that examines the collisions of two cultures and the reactions of three generations involved in the collision. The contradictions, fears, ambivalences, misunderstandings, social disturbances, and mixed messages are played out against the age-old rituals of marriage. As family traditions, religion, politics, and opiates collide with the "Anglo" culture, we gain insight into the cultural fractures that disrupt lives and change patterns of behavior. To assuage their sense of displacement, loss, and failure to belong, the older men turn to alcohol, the younger to cocaine; the older women to Valium, the younger to sex. All have experiences of struggling to survive in a strange land where some do not speak the language and fail to understand their unhappiness.

Broken Eggs is a comedy of family values tested against an alien culture and found to be strong and enduring. Despite the anger, unhappiness, confusion, and emotional chaos, the family, although somewhat frayed, survives intact. Each member has his or her own story of the pain of survival in a world where they have

been thrust into exile by political revolution and forced to adapt. Old ways survive ("A Catholic does not get a divorce.") and new strategies emerge ("A Valium—that's the only certain thing. It reassures you."). The generational struggle for identity, empowerment, and self-expression takes different forms but the play's overriding sentiment is that ethnic qualities and pride survive the collision of cultures and each generation derives its unique strength in its own way by retaining roots in memories, dreams, and daily rituals.

As an example of the intercultural text, *Broken Eggs* sets forth the dysfunction of a Hispanic family forced to relocate to Southern California as an outcome of the Cuban revolution. Of the three generations, the grandparents and the parents have retained their language and Hispanic traditions while they have experienced the painful sense of dislocation and separation. The children of Sonia and Osvaldo have willingly assimilated the new "Anglo" culture along with its metaphors ("You look better than Elizabeth Taylor in *Father of the Bride*."), drugs (cocaine), and acceptance of crossing ethnic lines (marrying into the Jewish family). The breaking eggs of the play's title are the three generations (parents and children) whose roots have been severed by the enforced exchange of cultures. Most affected are the middle-aged family members—Sonia, her ex-husband Osvaldo, and his sister Miriam. They have "cracked" under the strain of loss and difference. Their memories of white beaches and an innocent way of life protected by wealth and social status (all lost in the transition) are in contrast to the realities of their day-to-day existence in Southern California, where to accomplish the simplest tasks such as shopping at a supermarket or asking street directions of a policeman resulted in humiliation and estrangement. The family unit has been further severed by divorce (their Roman Catholicism did not deter the divorce in the new culture or prevent Osvaldo from marrying his Argentinian mistress). The children, born in California, have wholly assimilated into the lifestyles of the culture into which they were born: Oscar flaunts his homosexuality, the unmarried Mimi is pregnant, and Lizette marries into another ethnic tradition.

The divorced parents, Sonia and Osvaldo, are at the center of Machado's intercultural story, for they exhibit the fragility and sharp edges of people existing in limbo—holding on to the past and watching helplessly the erosion of their lives in the present. They are trapped between remembrances of their past lives in Cuba before the revolution and their present dislocations in California. Machado presents a comedic analysis of the collision of cultures. The grandparents are forever separate from the new culture by inherited rituals and customs; the grandchildren have connected; but the middle-aged parents are suspended between two cultures. Their pain and fragile accommodations are the material of Machado's intercultural art.

Broken Eggs

ACT ONE

A waiting room off the main ballroom of a country club in Woodland Hills, California, a suburb of Los Angeles. The room is decorated for a wedding. Up center, sliding glass doors leading to the outside; stage right, a hallway leading to the dressing room; stage left, an archway containing the main entrance to the room and a hallway leading to the ballroom. A telephone booth in one corner. Two round tables, one set with coffee service and the other for the cake.

In the dark, we hear Mimi whistling the wedding march. As the lights come up, Lizette is practicing walking down the aisle. Mimi is drinking a Tab and watching Lizette. They are both dressed in casual clothes.

MIMI: I never thought that any of us would get married, after all—

LIZETTE: Pretend you come from a happy home.

MIMI: We were the audience to one of the worst in the history of the arrangement.

LIZETTE: Well, I'm going to pretend that Mom and Dad are together for today.

MIMI: That's going to be hard to do if that mustached bitch, whore, cunt, Argentinian Nazi shows up to your wedding.

LIZETTE: Daddy promised me that his new wife had no wish to be here. She's not going to interfere.

MIMI *starts to gag.*

Mimi, why are you doing this.

MIMI: The whole family is going to be here.

LIZETTE: They're our family. Don't vomit again, Mimi, my wedding.

MANUELA (*Offstage*): Why didn't the bakery deliver it?

MIMI: Oh, no!

LIZETTE: Oh my God.

MIMI *and* LIZETTE: *run to the offstage dressing room.*

MANUELA (*Offstage*): Who ever heard of getting up at 6 A.M.?

SONIA (*Offstage*): Mama, please—

MANUELA *and* SONIA *enter.* SONIA *is carrying two large cake boxes.* MANUELA *carries a third cake box.*

MANUELA: Well, why didn't they?

SONIA: Because the Cuban bakery only delivers in downtown L.A. They don't come out this far.

MANUELA *and* SONIA *start to assemble the cake.*

MANUELA: Then Osvaldo should have picked it up.

SONIA: It was my idea.

MANUELA: He should still pick it up, he's the man.

SONIA: He wanted to get a cake from this place, with frosting on it. But I wanted a cake to be covered with meringue, like mine.

MANUELA: You let your husband get away with everything.

SONIA: I didn't let him have a mistress.

MANUELA: Silly girl, she ended up being his wife!

SONIA: That won't last forever.

MANUELA: You were better off with a mistress. Now, you're the mistress.

SONIA: Please, help me set up the cake.... Osvaldo thought we should serve the cake on paper plates. I said no. There's nothing worse than paper plates. They only charge a dime a plate for the real ones and twenty dollars for the person who cuts it. I never saw a paper plate till I came to the USA.

MANUELA: She used witchcraft to take your husband away, and you did nothing.

SONIA: I will.

MANUELA: Then put powder in his drinks, like the witch lady told you to do.

SONIA: I won't need magic to get him back, Mama, don't put powders in his drink. It'll give him indigestion.

MANUELA: Don't worry.

SONIA: Swear to me. On my father's grave.

The cake is now assembled.

MANUELA: I swear by the Virgin Mary, Saint Teresa my patron saint and all the saints, that I will not put anything into your husband's food…as long as his slut does not show up. Here. (*She hands* SONIA *a little bottle*)

SONIA: No.

MANUELA: In case you need it.

SONIA: I won't.

MANUELA: You might want it later. It also gives you diarrhea for at least three months. For love, you kiss the bottle, and thank the Virgin Mary. For diarrhea, you do the sign of the cross twice.

SONIA: All right.

MANUELA: If your father was alive, he'd shoot him for you.

SONIA: That's true.

MANUELA: Help me roll the cake out.

SONIA: No. They'll do it. They're getting the room ready now. They don't want us in there. We wait here—the groom's family across the way.

MANUELA: The Jews?

SONIA: The Rifkins. Then we make our entrance.

MANUELA: I see.

SONIA (*Looks at cake*): Perfect. Sugary and white …pure.

MANUELA: Beautiful.

SONIA: I'm getting nervous.

MANUELA: It's your daughter's wedding. A very big day in a mother's life, believe me.

SONIA: Yes, a wedding is a big day.

MANUELA: The day you got married your father told me, "We are too far away from our little girl." I said to him, "But, Oscar, we live only a mile away" He said, "You know that empty acre on the street where she lives now?" I said "Yes" He said, "I bought it and we are building another house there, then we can still be near our little girl."

SONIA: He loved me.

MANUELA: Worshipped you.

SONIA: I worshipped him. He'll be proud.

MANUELA: Where's your ex-husband, he's late.

LIZETTE *enters and makes herself a cup of coffee.* SONIA *helps her.*

SONIA: So how do you feel, Lizette, my big girl?

LIZETTE: I'm shaking.

MANUELA: That's good. You should be scared.

LIZETTE: Why, Grandma?

MANUELA: You look dark, did you sit out in the sun again?

LIZETTE: Yes, I wanted to get a tan.

MANUELA: Men don't like that, Lizette.

LIZETTE: How do you know?

SONIA: Mama, people like tans in America.

MANUELA: Men like women with white skin.

LIZETTE: That's a lie. They don't.

MANUELA: Don't talk back to me like that.

SONIA: No fights today, please, no fights. Lizette, tell her you're sorry. I'm nervous. I don't want to get a migraine, I want to enjoy today.

LIZETTE: Give me a kiss, Grandma.

They kiss.

Everything looks so good.

SONIA: It should—eight thousand dollars.

MANUELA: We spent more on your wedding and that was twenty-nine years ago. He should spend money on his daughter.

SONIA: He tries. He's just weak.

MANUELA: Don't defend him.

SONIA: I'm not.

MANUELA: Hate him. Curse him.

SONIA: I love him.

MANUELA: Sonia! Control yourself.

LIZETTE: He's probably scared to see everybody.

MANUELA: Good, the bastard.

LIZETTE *exits to dressing room.*

SONIA: Did I do a good job? Are you pleased by how it looks? (*She looks at the corsages and boutonnieres on a table*) Purples, pinks and white ribbons...tulle. Mama, Alfredo, Pedro.... No, not Pedro's...Oscar's.... He just looks like Pedro. Pedro! He got lost. He lost himself and then we lost him.

MANUELA: Sonia!

SONIA: I'll pin yours on, Mama.

MANUELA: Later, it'll wilt if you pin it now.

MIRIAM *enters. She is wearing a beige suit and a string of pearls.*

SONIA: Miriam, you're here on time. Thank you, Miriam.

MIRIAM: Sonia, look. (*Points at pearls*) They don't match. That means expensive. I bought them for the wedding.

MANUELA: Miriam, how pretty you look!

MIRIAM: Do you think the Jews will approve?

MANUELA: They're very nice, the Rifkins. They don't act Jewish. Lizette told me they put up a Christmas tree but what for I said to her?

MIRIAM: To fit in?

MANUELA: Why? Have you seen your brother?

MIRIAM: He picked us up last night from the airport.

MANUELA: Did he say anything to you?

MIRIAM: Yes, how old he's getting.... That's all he talks about.

MANUELA: Where's your husband?

MIRIAM: He couldn't come: business.

MANUELA: That's a mistake.

MIRIAM: I'm glad I got away.

MANUELA: But is he glad to be rid of you?

SONIA: Mama, go and see if Lizette needs help, please.

MANUELA: All right. Keep your husband happy, that's the lesson to learn from all this. Keep them happy. Let them have whatever they want.... Look at Sonia. (*She exits to dressing room*)

SONIA: Thank God for a moment of silence. Osvaldo this, Osvaldo that. Powder. Curse him. Poisons, shit...

MIRIAM: Are you all right? That faggot brother of mine is not worth one more tear: coward, mongoloid, retarded creep.

SONIA: Does he look happy to you?

MIRIAM: No.

SONIA: He looks sad?

MIRIAM: He always looked sad. Now he looks old and sad.

SONIA: Fear?

MIRIAM: Doesn't the Argentinian make him feel brave?

SONIA: He'll be mine again. He'll remember what it was like before the revolution. Alfredo and you being here will remind him of that. He'll remember our wedding—how perfect it was; how everything was right...the party, the limo, walking through the rose garden late at night, sleeping in the terrace room. I'm so hot I feel like I have a fever.

MIRIAM: "My darling children, do not go near the water, the sharks will eat you up." That's the lesson we were taught.

SONIA: Today I am going to show Osvaldo who's in control. Be nice to him today.

MIRIAM: He left you three months after your father died. He went because he knew you had no defense. He went off with that twenty-nine-year-old wetback. You know, we *had* to come here, but they *want* to come here. And you still want him back?

SONIA: If he apologizes, yes.

MIRIAM: Don't hold your breath. He lets everyone go. Pedro needed him—

SONIA: Don't accuse him of that, he just forgot.

MIRIAM: What? How could he forget. Pedro was our brother.

SONIA: He got so busy here working, that he forgot, he couldn't help him anyway. He was here, Pedro stayed in Cuba, you were in Miami, and I don't think anyone should blame anyone about that. No one was to blame!

MIRIAM: Oh, I'm having an attack...(*She shows* SONIA *her hands*) See how I'm shaking? It's like having a seizure. Where's water?

SONIA *gets her a glass of water. She takes two Valium.*
You take one, too.
SONIA: No. Thank you.
MIMI enters, goes to the pay phone, dials.
MIRIAM: A Valium makes you feel like you are floating in a warm beach.
SONIA: Varadero?
MIRIAM: Varadero, the Gulf of Mexico, Santa María del Mar. It's because of these little pieces of magic that I escaped from the path. I did not follow the steps of my brothers and end up an alcoholic.
SONIA: Osvaldo never drank a lot.
MIRIAM: You forget.
SONIA: Well, drinking was not the problem.
MANUELA (*Entering*): I made Mimi call the brothel to see why your husband's late.
MIRIAM: Where's Lizette?
MANUELA: Down the hall. It says "Dressing Room."
MIRIAM: I got five hundred dollars, brand-new bills. (*She exits*)
SONIA: The world I grew up in is out of style; will we see it again, Mama?
MIMI (*Comes out of the phone booth*): She answered. She said "Yes?" I said "Where's my father?" She said "Gone." I said "Already!" She said "I'm getting ready for...." I said "For what? Your funeral?" She hung up on me. She sounded stoned.
MANUELA: Sonia, someday it will be reality again, I promise.
MIMI: What?
SONIA: Cuba. Cuba will be a reality.
MIMI: It was and is a myth. Your life there is mythical.
MANUELA: That's not true. Her life was perfect. In the mornings, after she was married, Oscar would get up at six-thirty and send one of his bus drivers ten miles to buy bread from her favorite bakery, to buy bread for his little married girl.
SONIA: At around nine, I would wake up and walk out the door through the yard to the edge of the rose garden and call, "Papa, my bread."

MANUELA: The maid would run over, cross the street and hand her two pieces of hot buttered bread...
SONIA: I'd stick my hand through the gate and she'd hand me the bread. I'd walk back—into my mother-in-law's kitchen, and my coffee and milk would be waiting for me.
MIMI: Did you read the paper?
SONIA: The papers? I don't think so.
MIMI: Did you think about the world?
SONIA: No. I'd just watch your father sleep and eat my breakfast.
MANUELA: Every morning, "Papa, my bread." (*She goes to the outside doors and stays there, staring out*)
MIMI: You will never see it again. Even if you do go back, you will seem out of place; it will never be the same.
SONIA: No? You never saw it.
MIMI: And I will never see it.
SONIA: Never say never!
MIMI: What do you mean "Never say never"?!
SONIA: Never say never. Never is not real. It is a meaningless word. Always is a word that means something. Everything will happen always. The things that you feared and made your hands shake with horror, and you thought "not to me," will happen always.
MIMI: Stop it!
SONIA: I have thoughts, ideas. Just because I don't speak English well doesn't mean that I don't have feelings. A voice—a voice that thinks, a mind that talks.
MIMI: I didn't say that.
SONIA: So never say never, dear. Be ready for anything. Don't die being afraid. Don't, my darling.
MIMI: So simple.
MIRIAM enters.
SONIA: Yes, very simple, darling.
MIRIAM: What was simple?
SONIA: Life, when we were young.
MIRIAM: A little embarrassing, a little dishonest, but without real care; that's true. A few weeks ago I read an ad. It said "Liberate Cuba through the power of Voodoo." There

was a picture of Fidel's head with three pins stuck through his temples.

MANUELA: They should stick pins in his penis.

SONIA: Mama! (*She laughs*)

MANUELA: Bastard.

MIRIAM: The idea was that if thousands of people bought the product, there would be a great curse that would surely kill him—all that for only $11.99. Twelve dollars would be all that was needed to overthrow the curse of our past.

LIZETTE *enters wearing a robe.*

MANUELA: We should try everything, anything.

LIZETTE: Today is my wedding, it is really happening in an hour, here, in Woodland Hills, California, Los Angeles. The United States of America, 1979. No Cuba today please, no Cuba today.

SONIA: Sorry.

MIMI: You want all the attention.

SONIA: Your wedding is going to be perfect. We are going to win this time.

LIZETTE: Win what?

MANUELA: The battle.

MIRIAM: "Honest woman" versus the "whore."

MIMI: But who's the "honest woman" and who's the "whore"?

MANUELA: Whores can be easily identified—they steal husbands.

MIRIAM: They're from Argentina.

SONIA: They say "yes" to everything. The good ones say "no."

LIZETTE: And we're the good ones.

SONIA: Yes. I am happy today. You are the bride, the wedding decorations came out perfect and we are having a party. Oo, oo, oo, oo, oo…*uh.*

The women all start doing the conga in a circle. They sing. OSVALDO *enters.*

Join the line.

LIZETTE: In back of me, Daddy.

MIRIAM: In front of me, Osvaldo.

They dance. MIRIAM *gooses* OSVALDO.

OSVALDO: First I kiss my daughter—(*He kisses* LIZETTE) then my other little girl—(*He kisses* MIMI) then my sister—

He and MIRIAM *blow each other a kiss.*

—then my wife. (*He kisses* SONIA)

SONIA: Your ex-wife.

OSVALDO: My daughter's mother.

SONIA: That's right.

MIRIAM *lights a cigarette and goes outside.*

MIMI: We were together once, family: my mom, my dad, my big sister, my big brother. We ate breakfast and dinner together and drove down to Florida on our vacations, looked at pictures of Cuba together.

SONIA: And laughed, right?

MIMI: And then Papa gave us up.

OSVALDO: I never gave you up.

MIMI: To satisfy his urge.

MANUELA: Stop right now.

OSVALDO: Don't ever talk like that again.

SONIA: Isn't it true?

OSVALDO: It's more complex than that.

SONIA: More complex—how? No, stop.

LIZETTE: Please stop.

MANUELA: Don't fight.

MIMI: You see, Daddy, I understand you.

OSVALDO: You don't.

MIMI: I try.

OSVALDO: So do I.

MIMI: You don't.

OSVALDO: I'm going outside.

LIZETTE: Come, sit with me.

SONIA: You have to start getting dressed.

LIZETTE: Thank you for making *me* happy.

OSVALDO: I try.

LIZETTE *and* OSVALDO *exit to dressing room.*

SONIA: Mimi, no more today. Please, no more.

MIMI: When you're born the third child, the marriage is already half apart, and being born into a family that's half over, half apart, is a disturbing thing to live with.

SONIA: Where did you read that?

MIMI: I didn't read it. It's my opinion. Based on my experience, of my life.

SONIA: We were never half apart.

MIMI: No, but that's what it felt like.

MANUELA: It's unheard of. It's unbelievable—

MIMI: What is she talking about now?

MANUELA: A Catholic does not get a divorce. They have a mistress and a wife but no divorce, a man does not leave everything.

SONIA (*To* MIMI): As difficult as it might be for you to understand, we were together, and a family when you were born. I wanted, we wanted, to have you. We had just gotten to the U.S., Lizette was ten months old. Your father had gotten his job as an accountant. We lived behind a hamburger stand between two furniture stores, away from everything we knew, afraid of everything around us. We were alone, no one spoke Spanish. Half of the people thought we were Communist, the other half traitors to a great cause; three thousand miles away from our real lives. But I wanted you and we believed in each other more than ever before. We were all we had.

MIMI: I wish it would have always stayed like that.

SONIA: So do I.

MANUELA: In Cuba, not in California, we want our Cuba back.

MIMI: It's too late for that, Grandma.

MANUELA: No.

MIMI: They like their government.

MANUELA: Who?

MIMI: The people who live there like socialism.

MANUELA: No. Who told you that?

MIMI: He's still in power, isn't he?

MANUELA: Because he oppresses them. He has the guns, Fidel has the bullets. Not the people. He runs the concentration camps. He has Russia behind him. China. We have nothing behind us. My cousins are starving there.

MIMI: At least they know who they are.

MANUELA: You don't? Well, I'll tell you. You're Manuela Sonia Marquez Hernandez. A Cuban girl. Don't forget what I just told you.

MIMI: No, Grandma. I'm Manuela Sonia Marquez, better known as Mimi Markwez. I was born in Canoga Park. I'm a first-generation white Hispanic American.

MANUELA: No you're not. You're a Cuban girl. Memorize what I just told you.

LIZETTE *and* OSVALDO *enter.* LIZETTE *is in her bra and slip.*

LIZETTE: My dress, Mama, help me, time to dress.

SONIA: The bride is finally ready, Mama, help me dress her in her wedding dress. Miriam, Mimi, she's going to put on her wedding dress.

MIRIAM *enters.*

MANUELA: You're going to look beautiful.

SONIA: And happy, right, dear?

LIZETTE: I'm happy. This is a happy day, like they tell you in church, your baptism, your first communion and your wedding. Come on, Mimi.

All the women except SONIA *exit to the dressing room.*

SONIA: That's how I felt. I felt just like her.

OSVALDO: When, Sonia?

SONIA: Twenty-nine years ago.

SONIA *exits to the dressing room.* OSVALDO *goes to the bar and pours himself a double of J&B.* ALFREDO *enters.*

ALFREDO: You the guard?

OSVALDO: No.

ALFREDO: Drinking so early in the morning.

OSVALDO: My nerves, Daddy.

ALFREDO: Nervous, you made your bed, lie in it.

OSVALDO: I do. I do lie in it.

ALFREDO: So don't complain.

OSVALDO: I'm just nervous, little Lizette is a woman now.

ALFREDO: You're lucky.

OSVALDO: Why?

ALFREDO: She turned out to be decent.

OSVALDO: Why wouldn't she?

ALFREDO: In America it's hard to keep girls decent, especially after what you did.

OSVALDO: I never deserted them.

ALFREDO: But divorce, you're an idiot. Why get married twice, once is enough. You can always have one on the side and keep your wife. But to marry your mistress is stupid, crazy and foolish. It's not done, son. It's not decent.

OSVALDO: And you know a lot about decency?!

ALFREDO: I stayed married.

OSVALDO: Daddy, she loved me. I loved her. We couldn't be away from each other. She left her husband.

ALFREDO: She wanted your money.

OSVALDO: What money?

ALFREDO: To a little immigrant you're Rockefeller.

OSVALDO: Women only wanted you for your money.

ALFREDO: I know. And I knew how to use my position.

OSVALDO: She loves me.

ALFREDO: Good, she loves you—you should have taken her out dancing. Not married her.

OSVALDO: I did what I wanted to do, that's all.

ALFREDO: You did what your mistress wanted you to do. That is all.

OSVALDO: I wanted to marry her. That's why I did it. I just didn't do what my family thought I was supposed to do.

ALFREDO: You're still a silly boy. (*Looking at wedding decorations and cake*) Well, very nice. Sonia still has taste.

OSVALDO: Yes, she does.

ALFREDO: When she was young I was always impressed by the way she dressed, by the way she looked, how she spoke. The way she treated my servants, my guests.

OSVALDO: She was very well brought up.

ALFREDO: Now your new one is common, right?

OSVALDO: She loves me. Respect her, please.

ALFREDO: So did Sonia. The only thing the new one had to offer is that she groans a little louder and played with your thing a little longer, right?

OSVALDO: That's not true.

ALFREDO: Boring you after five years?

OSVALDO: …A little.

ALFREDO: Then why?

LIZETTE *enters. She is dressed in her bride's dress.*

LIZETTE: I'm ready for my photographs, Bride and Father.

OSVALDO: You took better than Elizabeth Taylor in *Father of the Bride.*

ALFREDO: Sweetheart, you look beautiful.

LIZETTE: Thank you. He took pictures of Mama dressing me, putting on my veil. Now he wants pictures of you and me—then Mama, you and me—then Grandpa, you and me and Miriam—then Mama and me and Grandma—then with Mimi, et cetera, et cetera, et cetera, et cetera; all the combinations that make up my family.

OSVALDO: Are you excited?

LIZETTE: Yes, I am. And nervous, Daddy, I'm so excited and nervous.

SONIA (*Enters*): Time for the pictures. Mimi will call me when she needs me again.

OSVALDO: Do I look handsome?

ALFREDO: Look at this place, beautiful, Sonia, a beautiful job. (*He gives* SONIA *a little kiss*)

SONIA: Thank you.

ALFREDO: She knows how to throw parties. Hmmm, Osvaldo, with taste. With class.

OSVALDO: With class.

SONIA: Osvaldo, come here a moment. Pin my corsage.

OSVALDO *goes over to the table with the corsages on it.*

I bought myself a purple orchid. It goes with the dress. I bought your wife the one with the two white gardenias. I figured she'd be wearing white, trying to compete with the bride. She's so young and pure, hmmm…(*She laughs*)

OSVALDO: She's not coming.

SONIA: It was a joke; I was making a little joke. I can joke about it now. Laugh. Did you dream about me again last night?

OSVALDO: Shh. Not in front of Lizette.

SONIA: I want to.

OSVALDO: We spent too much money on this, don't you think?

SONIA: No, I don't. I could have used more. Mama said they spent twice as much on our wedding.

OSVALDO: Did you tell them the exact number of people that RSVP'd so that we don't have to pay money for extra food?

SONIA: Lizette did, I can't communicate with them, my English—

OSVALDO: Your English is fine. I don't want to spend extra money.

SONIA: How much did you spend on your last wedding?

OSVALDO: She paid for it, she saved her money. She works, you know. She wanted a fancy wedding. I already had one. A sixteen-thousand-dollar one, according to your mother.

SONIA: Didn't *she?* Or was she not married to the guy she left for you?

OSVALDO: She was married. She doesn't live with people.

SONIA: Fool. When you got near fifty you turned into a fool; a silly, stupid, idiotic fool.

LIZETTE: No fights today.

OSVALDO *and* LIZETTE *start to exit.*

SONIA: I'm sorry. I swear, no fights…Osvaldo…

OSVALDO: Yes?

SONIA: You look debonair.

OSVALDO: Thank you, Sonia.

ALFREDO: Don't let it go to your head.

OSVALDO: You look magnifique.

SONIA: Thank you, Osvaldo.

LIZETTE *and* OSVALDO *exit to the ballroom.*

ALFREDO: Don't let it go to your head.

SONIA: He's insecure, about his looks.

ALFREDO: I tried to talk some sense into my son.

SONIA: Today we'll be dancing every dance together, in front of everybody. And I'll be the wife again. Divorces don't really count for Catholics. We're family, him and me.

ALFREDO: When you married him and moved in with us, I always thought you were like brother and sister.

SONIA: No, lovers. Stop teasing me. He's my only friend.

ALFREDO: Even now?

SONIA: Always, Alfredo, forever.

MIRIAM (*Enters from the ballroom*): Sonia, your turn for more snapshots—Father, Mother and Bride.

SONIA: She's happy, don't you think?

MIRIAM: The bride is in heaven.

SONIA: Excuse me, Alfredo, if you want breakfast, ask the waiter.

SONIA *exits.* MIRIAM *sits down.* ALFREDO *looks at the coffee and sits down.*

ALFREDO: Go get me a cup of coffee.

MIRIAM: No. Call the waiter, he'll get it for you.

ALFREDO: You do it for me.

MIRIAM: No.

ALFREDO: When did you stop talking to waiters?

MIRIAM: When I started talking to the gardener.

ALFREDO: What a sense of humor! What wit! What a girl, my daughter.

MIRIAM: Ruthless, like her dad.

ALFREDO: Exactly like me; you need to conquer. Go! Make sure it's hot!

MIRIAM *pours the coffee.*

If I were your husband I'd punish you every night: no money for you, no vacations, no cars, no credit cards, no pills, no maid. The way you exhibit yourself in your "see-through blouses" with no bras, and your skimpy bikinis.

MIRIAM (*Teasing* ALFREDO): Ooooh!

ALFREDO: How many horns did you put on his head?

MIRIAM: It excites him.

ALFREDO: That's not true.

MIRIAM: He feels lucky when he gets me, that I did not wither like all the other girls from my class, from our country, with their backward ways. Sugar, Daddy?

ALFREDO: Two lumps. No, three, and plenty of milk.

MIRIAM: There's only cream.

ALFREDO: Yes, cream is fine.

MIRIAM: Here, Daddy.

ALFREDO (*Takes one sip and puts coffee down*): What a vile taste American coffee has.

MIRIAM: I'm used to it, less caffeine.

ALFREDO: You did keep in shape.

MIMI *enters from the ballroom in her bridesmaid's gown.*

MIRIAM: So did you. Greed and lust keep us in shape.

MIMI: Grandpa, your turn. Both sets of grandparents, the Cubans and the Jews, the bride and the groom.

ALFREDO: How do I look, sweetheart?

MIMI: Dandy, Grandpa, dandy.

ALFREDO *exits.*

Who do you lust after?

MIRIAM: Your father.

MIMI: Your own brother?!

MIRIAM: I was joking—your father's too old now. Your brother, maybe.

MIMI: You are wild.

MIRIAM: If I would have been born in this country, to be a young girl in this country, without eyes staring at you all the time. To have freedom. I would never have gotten married. I wanted to be a tightrope walker in the circus…that's what I would have wanted.

MIMI: I never feel free.

MIRIAM: Do you get to go to a dance alone?
MIMI: Naturally.
MIRIAM: Then you have more freedom than I ever did.
MIMI: How awful for you.
MIRIAM: It made you choke, you felt strangled.
MIMI: What did you do?
MIRIAM: I found revenge.
MIMI: How?
MIRIAM: I'll tell you about it, one day, when there's more time.
MIMI: Can I ask you a question? Something that I wonder about? Did Uncle Pedro kill himself, was it suicide? Did Grandpa have mistresses?
MIRIAM: How do you know?
MIMI: Information slips out in the middle of a fight.
MIRIAM: He drank himself to death.
MIMI: Oh, I thought he did it violently.
MIRIAM: And your grandpa had a whole whore-house full of wives.
  MIMI and MIRIAM laugh.
MIMI: I'm like Grandpa. I'm pregnant…
MIRIAM: Don't kid me.
MIMI: Aunt Miriam, I am.
MIRIAM: Oh God.
MIMI: What are you doing?
MIRIAM: I need this. (She takes a valium) Don't you use a pill?
MIMI: With my mother.
MIRIAM: I don't understand.
MIMI: She'd kill me.
MIRIAM: True. Why did you do it?
MIMI: Freedom.
MIRIAM: Stupidity.
MIMI: Will you help me?
  OSCAR enters.
MIRIAM: My God, a movie star.
OSCAR: No, just your nephew, Oscar.
MIRIAM: Your hair is combed. You cut your fingernails?
OSCAR: Better than that, a manicure. You two look sexy today.
MIRIAM: Thank you. She's not a virgin…
OSCAR: So?
MIMI: I'm pregnant—
MIRIAM: Don't tell him.

OSCAR: Oh, Mimi.
MIRIAM: What are you going to do?
OSCAR: Pretend she didn't say it. Poor Mimi.
MIMI: You're no saint.
OSCAR: I'm not pregnant.
MIMI: Not because you haven't tried.
OSCAR: Oh, I love you.
  MANUELA enters.
MIRIAM: You better not talk.
MANUELA: You're here. Good.
MIMI: If you tell her, I'll tell her you're a fruit.
OSCAR: I don't care.
MIMI: Swear.
OSCAR: I swear.
MANUELA: You look beautiful. Here, sit on my lap.
  OSCAR sits on MANUELA's lap.
MIRIAM: He'll get wrinkled.
MIMI: This is revolting.
MANUELA: I promised your mother that we will be polite.
MIMI: The slut is not coming.
OSCAR: Good. A curse on Argentina.
MANUELA: Oscar, if you ever see her, it is your duty to kick her in the ass. But be good to your father today. It's not his fault. We all know that your father is a decent man. We all know that she got control of him with as they say "powders."
MIMI: I think they call it "blowing."
MANUELA: Blowing? She blowed-up his ego, is that what you think?
MIMI: Right.
MANUELA: No. You are wrong. She did it with drugs. But your mother wants you not to fight with your father. She wants him back.
OSCAR: I'll have to react however I feel.
MANUELA: Your mother is weak and she cannot take another emotional scene. And these Jewish people that Lizette is marrying would never understand about witchcraft, after all they don't even believe in Christ.
OSCAR: I can't promise anything.
MANUELA: Today will be a happy day. Lizette is marrying a nice boy, he's buying her a house. And your mother has a plan.
OSCAR: Right…
MANUELA: Right, Miriam?

MIRIAM: You're right. But if I ever see that Argentinian.

MANUELA: You're going to be a good girl, right, Mimi?

MIMI: I'll do whatever the team decides.

OSCAR: Spoken like a true American.

SONIA (*Enters*): You made it in time for the pictures, thank God.

OSCAR: Do I have to pose with Dad?

SONIA: No fights.

OSCAR: All right. But I'm standing next to you.

SONIA: Thank you. Miriam, Mama, they want more pictures with you. And in ten minutes "The Family Portrait."

MIMI: That'll be a sight.

MANUELA: Is my hair all right?

SONIA: Yes. Here, put on your corsage.

MANUELA: Thank you.

MIRIAM: And for me?

SONIA: The gardenias.

> MIRIAM *and* MANUELA *exit.*
> You took neat, Oscar. Thank God. The photographer suggested a family portrait, the entire family. He said it will be something we will cherish forever.

OSCAR: Why?

> OSVALDO *enters.*

SONIA: Well, the family portrait will be a record, proof that we were really a family. That we really existed, Oscar. Oscar, my father's name.

OSCAR: I'm glad you named me after him and not Osvaldo.

SONIA: At first I thought of naming you after your father, but then I thought, "That's so old-fashioned, it's 1951, time for something new."

OSCAR: Good for you.

MIMI: What a sign of liberation.

OSVALDO: Oh?!

OSCAR: So…continue, Mama.

SONIA: You like the story?

OSCAR: Yes.

SONIA: You, Mimi?

MIMI: Fascinating.

SONIA: Well, and since your grandpa has no son, I named you after him.

OSCAR: I bet he liked that.

SONIA: It made him very happy. I keep thinking he'll show up today. He'll walk in soon, my father. "Papa, do you like it?" And he would say…

MIMI: "We have to get back to Cuba."

OSCAR: "We have to fight!"

MIMI: "Where papayas grow as large as watermelons and guayabas and mangoes grow on trees. How could anyone starve in a place like that?"

OSVALDO: Then someone took it all away.

OSCAR: He had everything. He had pride, honor—

OSVALDO: True but someone took it away.

OSCAR: That doesn't matter.

OSVALDO: Well, it does, he lost.

SONIA: You loved him, I know you did, everyone did.

OSVALDO: Yes, right, I did.

OSCAR: He fought and he knew what he believed in. He knew what his life was about.

OSVALDO: Maybe that's why he wanted to die.

SONIA: No, just a stroke.

> *Pause.*

OSCAR: Daddy, do you like my suit?

OSVALDO: Well, it's really a sports coat and pants.

OSCAR: It's linen.

OSVALDO: It'll wrinkle.

OSCAR: I wanted to look nice.

SONIA: It does.

OSVALDO: It doesn't matter.

OSCAR: No, I don't suppose it really does.

OSVALDO: It means nothing.

OSCAR: What means something, Daddy?

OSVALDO: Columns that add up, neatly. Formulas where the answer is always guaranteed!

OSCAR: Guarantees mean something?!

OSVALDO: The answer. That's what means something.

OSCAR: Then I have a meaningless life.

OSVALDO: Stop it.

OSCAR: I never found any answers.

OSVALDO: Stop your melodrama.

OSCAR: I'm going to pretend you didn't say that. I'm twenty-eight years old and I refuse to get involved with you in the emotional ways that you used to abuse our relationship.

MIMI: Time for a Cuba Libre. (*She exits*)

OSVALDO: How much did that piece of dialogue cost me?

OSCAR: Let's stop.

OSVALDO: From which quack did you get that from?

OSCAR: From the one that told me you were in the closet.

OSVALDO: What closet?

SONIA *goes to check if anyone's listening.*

OSCAR: It's an expression they have in America for men who are afraid, no, they question, no, who fears that he wants to suck cock.

OSVALDO *slaps* OSCAR.

OSVALDO: Control yourself, learn to control your tongue!

OSCAR: Did that one hit home?

OSVALDO: Spoiled brat.

OSCAR: Takes one to know one. God, I despise you.

OSVALDO: I'm ashamed of you, you're such a nervous wreck, all those doctors, all the money I spend.

OSCAR: Thanks, Daddy, I had such a fine example of Manhood from you.

OSVALDO: Bum!

OSCAR: Fool.

SONIA: No psychology today! You're both the same, you're both so selfish, think of Lizette, her fiancé's family, what if they hear this. Quiet!

OSCAR: Leave us alone.

SONIA: No. I belong in this argument too, I'm the mother and the wife.

OSCAR: The ex-wife, Mama.

SONIA: No, in this particular triangle, the wife.

OSCAR (*To* SONIA): Your life is a failure.

OSVALDO: Because of you.

SONIA: Don't say that, Osvaldo. He's our son.

OSVALDO: He's just like you.

SONIA: What do you mean by that?!

OSVALDO: An emotional wreck.

OSCAR: That's better than being emotionally dead.

OSVALDO: I hate him.

SONIA: No. Osvaldo, how dare you! (*She cries*)

OSCAR: See what you've made, turned her into?!

OSVALDO: It's because of you.

SONIA: I refuse to be the cause of this fight, today we're having a wedding, so both of you smile.

OSVALDO: You're right, Sonia, I'm sorry.

OSCAR: God.

SONIA: I'm going to be with Lizette. You two control yourselves.

OSCAR (*Whispers*): Faggot.

SONIA *exits.*

Sissy.

OSVALDO: I bet you know all about that?!

OSCAR: Yes, want to hear about it?

ALFREDO *enters.*

OSVALDO: Not in front of your grandfather.

OSCAR: There's no way to talk to you, you petty bastard. (*He starts to cry*)

OSVALDO: Exactly like her, crying.

OSCAR (*Stops crying*): Because we were both unfortunate enough to have to know you in an intimate way.

OSVALDO: Other people don't feel that way.

OSCAR: That's because they're made of ice. A lot of Nazis in Argentina.

OSVALDO: Your sister needs me today. I'm going to make sure she's happy. Men don't cry. Now stop it. (*He exits*)

OSCAR: Right.

ALFREDO: Be careful.

OSCAR: About what?

ALFREDO: You show too much. Be on your guard.

OSCAR: So what?

ALFREDO: You let him see too much of you.

OSCAR: He's my father.

ALFREDO: He's a man first, my son second, your father third.

OSCAR: That's how he feels? He told you that? Did he?!

ALFREDO: Be a little more like me. And a little less like your other grandfather. He's dead. I'm still alive.

OSCAR: He was ill. It wasn't his fault.

ALFREDO: He was a fool.

OSCAR: No. That's not true.

ALFREDO: He was foolish. He trusted mankind. Money made him flabby. He thought if you gave a starving man a plate of food, he thanks you. He didn't know that he also resents you, he also waits. No one wants to beg for food, it's humiliating.

OSCAR: Of course no one wants to.

ALFREDO: So they wait. And when they regain their strength, they stab you in the back.

OSCAR: How can you think that's true?!

ALFREDO: We are the proof of my theory—Cubans. He did it to us—Fidel, our neighbors, everybody. So never feed a hungry man.

OSCAR: You don't really believe that.

MIMI (*Enters*): The picture, Grandpa. Oscar, the family portrait!

ALFREDO: I'm on my way. Comb your hair. Fix your tie. Your suit is already wrinkled.

OSCAR: Real linen does that.

> ALFREDO *exits with* MIMI. OSCAR *takes out a bottle of cocaine—the kind that premeasures a hit. He goes outside but leaves the entrance door open. He snorts.*

Ah, breakfast.

> OSCAR *snorts again.* OSVALDO *enters but does not see* OSCAR. *He goes straight to the bar, comes back with a drink—a J&B double—and gulps it down. He looks at the corsages. We hear* OSCAR *sniffing coke.*

OSVALDO (*To himself*): White, compete with the bride…very funny, Sonia.

SONIA (*Enters*): Osvaldo, we are waiting for you. The family portrait, come.

OSVALDO: No, I can't face them.

SONIA: Don't be silly.

OSVALDO: They love you. They hate me, my sister, my father, my children, they all hate me.

SONIA: They don't. No one hates their own family. It's a sin to hate people in your immediate family.

OSVALDO: They always hated me. Till I was seventeen I thought—

SONIA: That they had found you in a trash can, I know, Osvaldo. We need a record, a family portrait. The last one was taken at Oscar's seventh birthday. It's time for a new one.

OSVALDO: You don't need me.

SONIA: It wouldn't be one without you.

OSVALDO: For who?

SONIA: For everybody. Be brave. Take my hand. I won't bite.

> OSVALDO *holds her hand.*

After all, I'm the mother and you are the father of the bride.

OSCAR (*Sticks his head in*): The Argentinian just drove up.

OSVALDO: Liar.

OSCAR: She looks drunk.

OSVALDO: Liar.

OSCAR: What do they drink in Argentina?

SONIA: Behave!

> *A car starts honking.*

OSCAR: Sounds like your car.

OSVALDO: How dare she. How can she humiliate me. How can she disobey me.

SONIA: Oscar, go out and say your father is posing with his past family. Tell her that after the portrait is taken, she can come in.

OSCAR: But she has to sit in the back.

SONIA: No, I'm going to be polite. That's what I was taught.

OSVALDO: Go and tell her.

OSCAR: Remember, Mama, I did it for you. (*He exits*)

OSVALDO: Thank you. Hold my hand.

SONIA: Kiss me.

OSVALDO: Here?

SONIA: Yes, today I'm the mother and the wife.

> OSVALDO *and* SONIA *kiss.*

OSVALDO: You did a good job.

SONIA: You do like it?

OSVALDO: I mean with our daughters. They're good girls…like their mother.

SONIA: They have a good father.

OSVALDO: That's true.

> OSVALDO *and* SONIA *exit,* OSCAR *reenters.*

OSCAR: The family portrait? This family…. My family. The Father, Jesus Christ his only son and the Holy Ghost (*Crossing himself*)…why the *fuck* did you send me to this family.

Blackout.

END OF ACT ONE

ACT TWO

Afternoon. Offstage, the band is playing "Snow," an Argentinian folksong, and a woman is singing. MIRIAM *is in the phone booth.* MIMI *is looking at the bridal bouquet and pulling it apart.* SONIA *enters eating cake.*

WOMAN'S VOICE (*Singing offstage*):
> Don't sing brother, don't sing,
> I hear Moscow is covered with snow.

And the wolves run away out of hunger.
Don't sing 'cause Olga's not coming.

Even if the sun shines again.
Even if the snow falls again.
Even if the sun shines again.
Even if the snow falls again.

Walking to Siberia tomorrow, oh,
Out goes the caravan,
Who knows if the sun
Will light our march of horror.

While in Moscow, my Olga, perhaps,
To another, her love she surrenders.
Don't sing brothers, don't sing.
For God's sake, oh God, no.

United by chains to the steppes
A thousand leagues we'll go walking.
Walking to Siberia, no.
Don't sing, I am filled with pain.
And Moscow is covered with snow.
And the snow has entered my soul.
Moscow now covered with snow.
And the snow has entered my soul.

SONIA: It's insult to injury an Argentinian song about going to Siberia, Russia. Moscow is covered with snow…what do Argentinians know about Moscow? I wish she'd go to Siberia tomorrow. (*To* MIMI) They are walking a thousand leagues to their exile…I took a plane ride ninety-nine miles, a forty-five-minute excursion to my doom.

MIRIAM (*To phone*): No, shit no! Liars.

SONIA: Don't sing, Sonia…(*She sings*) 'cause Moscow is covered with snow, right, Mimi?

MIMI: Right.

SONIA: When I first got here this place looked to me like a farm town. Are you happy, dear?

MIMI: I don't think so.

SONIA: No, say yes!

MIMI: Yes.

SONIA: That's good.

MIMI: Ciao!

MIMI *runs to the bathroom to puke.* OSVALDO *enters.*

SONIA: So, you had to play a song for her?

OSVALDO: She told the band she wanted to sing it. But it's the only Argentinian song they know.

SONIA: Good for the band! Remember when we thought Fidel was going to send us to Russia, to Moscow? Siberia, Siberia, this place is like Siberia!

OSVALDO: It's too warm to be Siberia. (*He kisses* SONIA *passionately*) It was a beautiful ceremony. (*He kisses her again*)

SONIA: Dance with me. Tell them to play a danzón.

OSVALDO: Let's dance in here.

SONIA: She'll get angry? It's our daughter's wedding.

OSVALDO: She's my wife.

SONIA: I was first.

OSVALDO: You're both my wife.

OSVALDO *and* SONIA *dance.*

SONIA: Before my sixteenth birthday your family moved to Cojimar…your cousin brought you to the club.

OSVALDO: You were singing a Rita Hayworth song called "Put the Blame on…Me"?

SONIA: No, "Mame"…I was imitating her…did I look ridiculous?

OSVALDO: No!

SONIA (*Starts to do Rita's number, substituting "Cuban" for "Frisco"*):
Put the blame on Mame, boys
Put the blame on Mame
One night she started to shim and shake
That began the Cuban quake
So-o-o, put the blame on Mame, boys
Put the blame on Mame…

OSVALDO: You look sexy.

SONIA: I let you kiss me, then you became part of the club.

OSVALDO: On your seventeenth birthday I married you.

SONIA: Well, I kissed you.

OSVALDO: Was I the only one?

SONIA: Yes.

OSVALDO: And by your eighteenth birthday we had Oscar. I should go back to the party. She'll start looking for me.

SONIA: Tell her to relax. Tell the band to stop playing that stupid song. I want to dance. I want more Cuban music.

OSVALDO: All right! What song?

SONIA: "Guantanamera."

OSVALDO: They might know "Babalú."

SONIA: That's an American song.

> MANUELA *and* ALFREDO *enter, in the middle of a conversation.* OSVALDO *exits to the ballroom.* SONIA *goes outside.*

MANUELA: The trouble is Americans are weak... they don't know how to make decisions.

ALFREDO: At least they are happy—

MANUELA: Why?

ALFREDO: Money!

MANUELA: You had that in Cuba, Alfredo, but—

ALFREDO: Look at my son—he has an accounting firm—

MANUELA: He's only a partner.

ALFREDO: He has a Lincoln Continental, a classy car; two beautiful houses, with pools and—

MANUELA: Don't talk about the prostitute's house in front of me, Alfredo, please.

ALFREDO: Forgive me.

MANUELA: We knew how to make decisions, we—

ALFREDO: Of course.

MANUELA: Fight who you don't agree with, do not doubt that you are right, and if they use force, you use force, bullets if you have to. Only right and wrong, no middle, not like Americans always asking questions, always in the middle, always maybe. Sometimes I think those Democrats are Communists—

ALFREDO: No, Manuela, you see in demo—

MANUELA: Democracy, Communism, the two don't go together, at least the Russians know that much. They don't let people complain in Russia, but here, anybody can do anything.

> *The band is playing "Guantanamera."*

At last some good music, no more of that Argentinian shit. (*She hums some of the song*)

ALFREDO: That's one of my favorite songs.

MANUELA: Yes, beautiful.

ALFREDO: May I have this dance?

MANUELA: Yes...but do I remember how?

MIMI (*Who has reentered*): It'll come back to you, Grandma.

> MANUELA, ALFREDO *and* MIMI *exit to the dance floor.* MIRIAM *is still sitting in the phone booth, smoking.* SONIA *enters.* MIRIAM *opens the phone-booth doors.*

MIRIAM: I just made a phone call to Cuba, and you can.

SONIA: They got you through?

MIRIAM: Yes. The overseas operator said, "Sometimes they answer, but only if they feel like it."

SONIA: Who did you call?

MIRIAM: My...our house.... I sometimes think that I live at the same time there as here. That I left a dual spirit there. When I go to a funeral I look through the windows as I drive and the landscapes I see are the streets outside the cemetery in Guanabacoa, not Miami. A while ago I looked out at the dance floor and I thought I was in the ballroom back home. That's why I had to call. I miss the floor, the windows, the air, the roof.

SONIA: The house is still standing, though, it is still there.

MIRIAM: But we are not.

SONIA: I saw a picture of it. It hasn't been painted in twenty years, we painted it last.

MIRIAM: Sonia, she said upstairs he's crying again.

SONIA: You're sending chills up my spine.

MIRIAM: Is it Pedro crying?

SONIA: No, she was trying to scare you. We have to hold on to it, to the way we remember it, painted.

MIRIAM: I think I heard Pedro screaming in the garden before she hung up.

SONIA: No, he's dead, he went to heaven.

MIRIAM: No, he's in hell. If there's a heaven he's in hell. Suicides go to hell. He was the only one that managed to remain, death keeps him there. Maybe the house filled with strangers is his hell.

SONIA: Why he did it I'll never understand. Maybe he had to die for us?

MIRIAM: No, he didn't do it for *me*.

SONIA: Maybe that's the way things are, maybe one of us had to die. Maybe there's an order to all these things.

MIRIAM: There's no order to things, don't you know that by now? It's chaos, only chaos.

> MIMI *enters.*

SONIA: No, there's a more important reason, that's why he did it.

MIMI: What?

SONIA: This conversation is not for your ears.

MIMI: Why not?

LIZETTE *enters.*

SONIA: Because it isn't, that's all.

LIZETTE: Mama! Daddy started dancing with her and Oscar's whistling at them, whispering "Puta, putica."

MIRIAM: The Americans won't understand what they are saying.

LIZETTE: Americans know what "puta" means. My husband is embarrassed. Other people get divorces and don't act like this. Tell him he must stop. No name-calling in Spanish or in English. This is a bilingual state.

MIMI: No, Mama, don't do it.

MIRIAM: Mimi's right, let them do whatever they want.

SONIA: Right, why should I protect her?

LIZETTE: How about me? Who's going to protect me?

SONIA: Your husband.

MIMI: Tell him to tell them to stop, you've got your husband now, your own little family unit.

LIZETTE: Fuck off, Mimi. I'm begging you, Mama, please. Just take him to the side and tell him to leave her alone, to let her have a good time.

SONIA: To let her have a good time?!

MIMI: I'll take care of it. (*She yells out to the ball-room*) Hey you slut, Miss Argentina. Don't use my sister's wedding for your crap. Come in here and fight it out with us!

MIRIAM: Mimi, she's flipping the bird at you. She's gesturing fuck you.

MIMI: Fuck yourself!

LIZETTE: Mama! Stop her! Oh God—

MIRIAM (*Yells to the ballroom*): You're just a bitch, lady.

LIZETTE (*Starts to cry*): Oh, God, oh, God—

SONIA: In a little while everybody will forget about it—

LIZETTE: Oh God, Mama. Everybody's looking at us. They are so embarrassed. You let them ruin my wedding. You promised. I hate you. It's a fiasco. I hate you, Mimi.

SONIA: Sorry, promises are something nobody keeps, including me.

LIZETTE: You're such assholes.

SONIA: Everybody's got their faults, learn to live with it!

LIZETTE: You failed me.

MIMI: That was great, Aunt Miriam.

SONIA: I'm sorry.

MIRIAM: Thanks, Mimi, it was fun.

OSVALDO (*Enters*): How could you…

MIRIAM: Careful!

OSVALDO: Help me, Sonia.

SONIA: Osvaldo, I've put up with a lot.

OSVALDO: How about me? I want you and your children to apologize to her.

SONIA: No.

MIMI: Never.

MIRIAM: She should leave the party and let the rest of us have a good time. What the hell is she doing here?

OSVALDO: For my sake, Sonia.

SONIA: I'm sorry, I can't.

OSVALDO: What am I going to do?

SONIA: Who do you love, me?

OSVALDO: Yes.

SONIA: Who do you love, her?

OSVALDO: Yes.

SONIA: So full of contradictions, so confused. I'll go tell her that. He loves both of us, Cuba and Argentina!

OSVALDO: This is not the time to kid me, look at Lizette, she's upset.

LIZETTE: I'll never be able to talk to my mother-in-law again.

MIRIAM: It's your fault, Osvaldo. He never moved from the garden.

OSVALDO: Miriam?! Who never moved from the garden?

MIRIAM: Pedro. He never left the garden.

OSVALDO: None of us have.

MIRIAM: He stayed. He took a razor blade but remained locked forever in our family's garden.

OSVALDO: He was a coward.

MIRIAM: Maybe you are the coward, you keep running away.

OSVALDO: From what?

OSCAR (*Enters, trying not to laugh*): I'm sorry. I behaved badly.

OSVALDO: Tell me, Miriam, from what? (*He exits*)

OSCAR: Don't cry, Lizette, forgive me? Hmm?

LIZETTE: Oscar, now they're starting to fight about Cuba. I just want to cry. They're going to tell my husband, "Your wife is from a crazy family. Are you sure she's not mentally disturbed?"

MIMI: Are you sure you're not mentally disturbed?

MIMI *and* OSCAR *laugh.* OSVALDO *reenters.*

OSVALDO: What do I run away from that he faced?

MIRIAM: That we lost everything.

SONIA: Everything, no.

OSVALDO: You think I don't know that?

MIRIAM: Pedro knew. He became invisible but remains in silence, as proof.

OSVALDO: As proof of what?

SONIA: That we are not a very nice family? Is that what you are saying?

OSVALDO: He had nothing to do with us, he was an alcoholic.

SONIA: He killed himself because of our sins.

OSVALDO: No, Sonia, that was Christ, Pedro was a drunk, not a Christ figure.

MIRIAM: Because of our lies, Sonia.

OSVALDO: What lies?

MIRIAM: Why did you desert him? You, his brother, you were the only one he spoke to, the only one he needed.

OSVALDO: He made me sick.

MIRIAM: You were always together, you always spent your days together.

OSVALDO: He was an alcoholic.

MIRIAM: We were all alcoholics.

SONIA: I was never an alcoholic.

MIRIAM: He needed you.

OSVALDO: He was perverted.

MIRIAM: We were all perverted. That's why the new society got rid of us.

OSVALDO: Our mother is not perverted!

MIRIAM: No, just insane.

SONIA: No, she's an honest woman, now your father—

OSVALDO: My father was just selfish, he had too many mistresses.

SONIA: Fifteen.

OSCAR: Fifteen?

MIMI: All at once?

LIZETTE: Who gives a fuck? Everybody in this family is a—

MIRIAM: I'm the one that suffered from that, not you, Osvaldo. You take after Daddy so don't complain. Why did you let Pedro kill himself?

OSVALDO: He wanted too much from me.

MIRIAM: He needed you.

OSVALDO: He wanted my mind, he wanted my…, my…, he wanted everything.

MIRIAM: You're glad he did it?

OSVALDO: I was relieved.

MIRIAM: He knew too much, ha!

SONIA: Too much of what?

MIRIAM: The perversions.

SONIA: What perversions?

MIRIAM: Too much about his perversions, darling Sonia, you married a corrupted family, you really deserved better.

OSCAR: Uh-huh.

LIZETTE: I'm closing the door.

MANUELA *and* ALFREDO *enter.*

MANUELA: I'll never forget what he said.

ALFREDO: When?

MANUELA: In 1959, after the son-of-a-bitch's first speech, he said, "That boy is going to be trouble…he's full of Commie ideals."

ALFREDO: I must say I did not suspect it. I was so bored with Batista's bullshit I thought, a revolution, good. We'll get rid of the bums, the loafers, but instead, they got rid of us.

MANUELA: I hope he rots. Rot, Fidel Castro, die of cancer of the balls.

ALFREDO: Let's hope.

MANUELA: Then they came. And they took our businesses away, one by one. And we had to let them do it. They took over each of them, one after the other. It took the milicianos three days. I looked at Oscar while they did it, for him it was like they…for him, that was his life's work, he felt like…

OSCAR: Like they were plucking out his heart. Like they were sticking pins into his brain. Like they were having birds peck out his genitals. Like he was being betrayed.

MANUELA: Yes, that's it.

ALFREDO: I hate myself for helping them, bastards.

MANUELA: All he wanted after that was—

SONIA: To fight back.

OSCAR: Right.

MIRIAM: I still do. I still want to fight somebody!

SONIA: But he did fight back. Till the day he died, he never gave up. Right, Mama?

MANUELA: "We are in an emergency," that's how he put it, "an emergency."

MIRIAM: Daddy. Daddy, I am in an emergency now. I have taken six valiums and it's only noon.

ALFREDO: Why?

MIRIAM: Because I want to strangle you every time I look at you.

LIZETTE: Quiet, they're going to want an annulment.

MANUELA: My God, Miriam!

OSCAR: Who?

ALFREDO: Why?

MIRIAM: Why?!

LIZETTE: The Jews, they're a quiet people.

ALFREDO: Yes, Miriam, why?

MIRIAM: Why did you send your mistresses' daughters to my school?!

MANUELA: Miriam, not in front of the children.

ALFREDO: Because it was a good school.

MIRIAM: People in my class wouldn't talk to me because of you!

ALFREDO: Sorry.

OSVALDO: Sorry? That's all you have to say to her?! That's the only answer you give?!

ALFREDO: I don't know, what else should I say?

OSVALDO: Why did you not once congratulate me for finishing the university?! Why did you let me drink? Why did you let Pedro drink?

ALFREDO: I never noticed that you drank.

MIMI: Why did you leave my mother, and leave me…and never came to see me play volleyball?

OSVALDO: Leave me alone, I'm talking to my father.

MIMI: And who are you to me?

MANUELA: Good girl, good question.

OSVALDO: You? Why did you make your daughter think that the only person in the world who deserved her love was your husband?!

MANUELA: He was strong.

OSVALDO: He got drunk. He was a coward when he died.

OSCAR: No. That's not true.

MANUELA: He was a real man. What are you?

LIZETTE: You mean old hag, don't you ever talk to my dad again like—

SONIA: Don't you ever call your grandmother that. She's my mother!

LIZETTE: I'm going back to the wedding. (*She exits*)

OSCAR: Why did they kick us out?
    Silence.

OSVALDO: We left. We wanted to leave.

OSCAR: No one asked me.

SONIA: We had to protect you from them.

MIRIAM: That's right.

OSVALDO: They wanted to brainwash you, to turn you into a Communist.

OSCAR: No one explained it to me. You told me I was coming here for the weekend.

OSVALDO: It was not up to you.

SONIA: You were just a child, it was up to us.

OSVALDO: That's right.

MIRIAM: And we made the right decision, believe me,

OSCAR: Miriam, why did you let me be locked out? That day in Miami, November, 1962. The day the guy from the Jehovah's Witnesses came to see you. And you took him to your room to discuss the end of the world.

MIRIAM: It was a joke. I was only twenty. I don't believe in God.

OSCAR: Well, you locked me out. And I sat outside and you laughed at me, and I sat there by a tree and I wanted to die. I wanted to kill myself at the age of ten. I wanted to beat my head against the tree, and I thought, "Please stop working, brain, even they locked me out, even my family, not just my country, my family too!" Bastards! Fidel was right. If I had a gun, I'd shoot you. I curse you, you shits. Who asked me?

OSVALDO: The revolution had nothing to do with you. You don't *really* remember it, and believe it or not, it did not happen just for you, Oscar.

OSCAR: Yeah, I didn't notice you damaged.

OSVALDO: I had to go to the market at age thirty-two and shop for the first time in my life.

MIMI: So what?

OSCAR: God.

OSVALDO: And I could not tell what fruit was ripe and what fruit was not ripe. I did not know how to figure that out. I cried at the Food King market in Canoga Park. Some people saw me. (*He cries*)

OSCAR: Big deal.

OSVALDO (*Stops crying*): And Sonia, you refused to come and help me! You made me go do it alone. And shopping is the wife's duty.

SONIA: I couldn't. I felt weak. I was pregnant with Mimi. I'm sorry, Osvaldo. (*To* OSCAR) I wanted you to live a noble life.

OSCAR: How?

SONIA: I don't know. I taught you not to put your elbows on the table. You had perfect eating habits…

OSCAR: What does that have to do with nobility?

SONIA: It shows you're not common. That's noble.

OSCAR: No, Mama, nobility—

SONIA: Yes.

OSCAR: No, nobility has to do with caring about the ugly things, seeing trash and loving it. It has to do with compassion, not table manners. It has to do with thought, not what people think about you.

SONIA: Stop picking on me.

OSCAR: I'm not picking on you.

SONIA: Everybody is always picking on me. I failed, I know I failed.

OSCAR: No, you just don't try. Why don't you try?

SONIA: Try what?

OSCAR: To do something.

SONIA: No.

OSCAR: Why?

SONIA: I'm not some whore that can go from guy to guy.

OSVALDO: Are you talking about my wife?

OSCAR: Try it.

SONIA: Don't insult me. Stop insulting me.

OSCAR: You need somebody.

SONIA: Stop it!

OSVALDO: Leave her alone.

OSVALDO *grabs* SONIA. *They walk towards the ballroom, then stop. We hear the band playing "Que Sera, Sera."*

MANUELA: I think they're going to dance.

MIRIAM: I want to see the Argentinian's expression.

SONIA *and* OSVALDO *are now dancing. The others watch.* MIMI *and* OSCAR *go into the phone booth to snort coke.*

ALFREDO: Leave all three of them alone. (*He goes outside to smoke a cigar*)

MIRIAM *and* MANUELA *walk past* SONIA *and* OSVALDO *toward the ballroom.*

MIRIAM: Why are you dancing out in the hall…afraid of Argentina?

MIRIAM *and* MANUELA *exit.*

OSVALDO: I'd like to take a big piece of wood and beat some sense into her…No, I want to beat her to death!

SONIA: She went too far…she lost control…she gets excited.

OSVALDO: They always lose control. Pedro thought there was no limit…that you did not have to stop anywhere…life was a whim…. But I knew that you have to stop yourself…that's being civilized, that's what makes us different than dogs…you can't have everything you feel you want…

SONIA: He was a tortured soul…and you loved him…

OSVALDO: My big brother. (*He starts to cry*)

SONIA: And you tried to help him…

OSVALDO: How?

SONIA: The only way you knew how, with affection.

OSVALDO: Affection?

SONIA: Yes, and that's decent.

OSVALDO: Maybe it is. Maybe I am.

SONIA *and* OSVALDO *kiss. He takes her out to the dance floor. She smiles.* OSCAR *and* MIMI *come out of the phone booth.* OSCAR *continues to snort cocaine.*

OSCAR: He did it. Well, at least he had the balls to take her out and dance. She won. You see if you have a plan and follow it…(*Sniff, sniff*) ah, hurray for the American dream.

MIMI: It's pathetic. They're still dancing. Oh God help us, she believes anything he tells her.

OSCAR: She had to endure too many things.

MIMI: What, losing her maid?

OSCAR: They never tell her the truth.

MIMI: And you do? You tell her the truth? Well, I'm gonna tell her.

OSCAR: I think you should get an abortion.

MIMI: Why should I?

OSCAR: To protect her.

MIMI: Why should I protect her.

OSCAR: I don't know. Lie to her. Tell Dad.

MIMI: Never mind. Pour me some more champagne.

LIZETTE *enters.*

I hope one of those horny Cubans just off the boat is ready to rock and roll.

LIZETTE: No more scenes, Mimi. Dad and Mom are enough.

MIMI *toasts* LIZETTE *with champagne.*

MIMI: Arrivederci. (*She exits*)

LIZETTE: They're out there dancing like they were in love or something—

OSCAR: Maybe they are.

LIZETTE: Never, he's being polite and she's showing off. And the Argentinian is complaining to me. And I don't want any part of any of you.

OSCAR: You don't! You think your husband is going to take you away from all this. Does he know about the suicides, how they drink till they explode…the violence we live with, the razor blades, the guns, the hangings, the one woman in our family who set herself on fire while her three kids watched?

ALFREDO (*Who has reentered*): We are just hot-blooded and passionate, that's all.

OSCAR: Grandpa told me a week before…"Oscar," he told me…"they'll tell you soon I'm in the hospital. That means that I'm on my way out…this life here is ridiculous."

ALFREDO: Oscar Hernandez was a fool. That's a fool's kind of suicide, that's what I told you.

OSCAR: A lot of drinks when your blood pressure is high is not a fool's kind of suicide, it's just suicide. Despair, that's always the story of people that get kicked out, that have to find refuge, you and me…us.

LIZETTE: No, you. Everybody dies on the day that they're supposed to. Forget about it.

OSCAR: How can I?

ALFREDO: You better teach yourself to.

OSCAR: How can I? Have you taught yourself? Tell me, why do you want to live? For what?

ALFREDO: Because of me…here or over there, I still need me!

OSCAR: You don't have any honor.

ALFREDO: Honor for what?

OSCAR: For our country.

ALFREDO: That little island?…Look, Oscar, when Columbus first found it there were Indians there, imagine, Indians. So we eliminated the Indians, burned all of them, cleaned up the place…. We needed somebody to do the Indians' work so we bought ourselves slaves…and then the Spaniards, that's us, and the slaves started to…well, you know.

OSCAR: I can only imagine.

ALFREDO: Well, then we started calling ourselves natives. Cubans.

LIZETTE: That's right, a name they made up!

ALFREDO: Right! And we became a nation…

OSCAR: A race.

ALFREDO: Yes. And then the U.S. came and liked it, and bought and cheated their way into this little place. They told us (*He imitates a Texan accent*) "Such a pretty place you have, a valuable piece of real estate. We will help you!" So, they bought us.

OSCAR: We should have eliminated them!

ALFREDO: Maybe. But, what we did…was sell it to them and fight against each other for decades, trying to have control of what was left of this pretty place, this valuable piece of real estate. And a bearded guy on a hill talked to us about liberty, and justice, and humanity and humility—and we bought his story. And he took everything away from everybody. And we were forced to end up here. So, we bought their real estate. Do you know how Miami was built?

LIZETTE: With sand that they shipped in from Cojimar! Right?

ALFREDO: That's right. And your other grandfather could not accept the fact that it was just real estate. So he got drunk when he knew he had high blood pressure. What a fool.

LIZETTE: He tells the truth, Oscar.

OSCAR: And Mama thinks it was her country. And someday she'd go back. And I hoped it was my country. What a laugh, huh?

LIZETTE: If you ever tell Mama this, it'll kill her.

OSCAR: Maybe it wouldn't.

LIZETTE: She can't deal with real life, believe me. I'm her daughter, I know what she's really like.

OSCAR: And you can deal with everything?

LIZETTE: Sure. I grew up here, I have a Jewish name now…Mrs. Rifkin, that's my name.

OSCAR: Well, Mrs. Rifkin, I'm jealous of you.

ALFREDO: Time for a dance. I haven't danced with the mother of the groom.
(*He exits*)

LIZETTE: Try to get away, Mrs. Rifkin!

OSCAR: And the new Mrs. Rifkin is running away. You got away.

LIZETTE: Don't be jealous, Oscar. It's still all back here. (*She points to her brain*)

OSVALDO (*Enters*): One o'clock, Lizette.

LIZETTE: One more dance.

OSCAR: Why do you have to leave so soon?

LIZETTE: It's another two thousand for the entire day.

OSCAR: God.

OSVALDO: God what?

OSCAR: You have no class.

SONIA (*Enters*): Osvaldo, I have to talk to you.

OSVALDO: Why?

SONIA: Please, just do me a favor. I have to talk to you.

LIZETTE: Want to dance?

OSCAR: All right.
    LIZETTE *and* OSCAR *exit.*

OSVALDO: What do you want, Sonia? Tell me, sweetheart.

SONIA (*Hysterical*): Don't be angry at me, there's no more wedding cake, we've run out of wedding cake. There's no more, nothing, no more wedding cake.

OSVALDO: That's all right, we should start getting them out. Tell them to start passing out the packages of rice.

SONIA: No, some people are asking for wedding cake. What do we do? What?

OSVALDO: They've had plenty to eat, a great lunch, a salad, chicken cacciatore, a pastry, all they could drink, champagne, coffee. Tell them to pass out the rice, get this over with, and let's go home.

SONIA: At a wedding, wedding cake is something people expect. I can't embarrass the groom's family again. What do we do, what are you going to do?!

OSVALDO: Let's go up to people we know…

SONIA: Only Cubans!

OSVALDO: All right, let's go up to all the Cubans we know and ask them not to eat the cake. Then serve it to the Jews. The Cubans won't care.

SONIA: You do it, I can't. I can't face them.

OSVALDO: No, do it, with me, come on.
    OSCAR *enters. He is about to eat a piece of cake.*
    SONIA *grabs it away from him.*

OSCAR: What are you doing?

SONIA: You can't eat it, there's not enough.

OSCAR: Why?

OSVALDO: Just do what your mother says. Please, let's go.

SONIA: You do it.

OSVALDO: You're not coming with me?

SONIA: No, I'm sorry. I can't, I'm too embarrassed.
    OSVALDO *exits.*

OSCAR: Okay, give it back to me now.

SONIA: No, take it to that man over there.

OSCAR: Why should I?

SONIA: He didn't get any cake. I think the waiters stole one of the layers. You take it to him. I think his name is Mr. Cohen, the man who's looking at us.

OSCAR: All right. Who?

SONIA (*Points discreetly*): The bald man.

OSCAR: Great.
    MANUELA *and* MIRIAM *enter.*

MANUELA: Oh my God; Jesus, Sonia. Osvaldo just told me that we are out of cake.

OSCAR: We are. (*He exits*)

MANUELA: We were winning.

SONIA: The stupid waiters cut the pieces too big, Mama.

MANUELA: Americans! This is one of the great follies of my life.

SONIA: Of course, Mama, this is worse than the revolution.

MANUELA *goes outside.*

MIRIAM: No, in the revolution people died.

SONIA: They really did, didn't they?

MIRIAM: Real blood was shed, real Cuban blood.

SONIA: I forget sometimes.

MIRIAM: Only when I'm calm, that's when I remember, when I'm waking up or when I'm half asleep…at those moments.

SONIA: Let's go out to the dance floor and dance like we did at the Tropicana.

LIZETTE (*Enters*): I ripped my wedding dress.

SONIA: Oh well, dear, it's only supposed to last one day. Maybe the next wedding you go to, Lizette, will be mine.

LIZETTE: Who did you find, Mama?

SONIA: Your father.

LIZETTE: Mama, Daddy can't afford another wife.

SONIA: I'm not another wife, Lizette.

LIZETTE: I hope you are right.

MIRIAM: Wait a minute. (*She gives* LIZETTE *five hundred dollars*) In case you decide you need something else when you are on your honeymoon.

LIZETTE: Another five hundred. I think we have three thousand dollars in cash.

LIZETTE *exits to the dressing room.* MIRIAM *lights two cigarettes. She gives one to* SONIA.

MIRIAM: Let's go. Remember when we thought Fidel looked sexy.

SONIA: Shh.

MIRIAM *and* SONIA *sashay off to the ballroom.* OSVALDO *and* ALFREDO *enter.* OSVALDO *is eating a big piece of cake.*

ALFREDO: All women are hysterical.

OSVALDO: I got out there, took the cake from the Cubans, who were outraged. A couple of them called me a Jew. I took it to the Jews and they were as happy as can be. I offered them the cake but nobody wanted any. She made me go through all that for nothing.

ALFREDO: They were being polite, Jews don't like to appear greedy.

OSVALDO (*Eats the cake*): Well, it's delicious.

ALFREDO: It's Cuban cake.

OSVALDO: The only thing that I like Cuban is the food.

ALFREDO: Then start acting like a man. You have one crying in the back and the other demanding in the front!

OSVALDO: I do.

ALFREDO: You don't have the energy to play it both ways.

OSVALDO: What are you talking about?

ALFREDO: Your wife…Sonia!

OSVALDO: She'll never change.

ALFREDO: Why should she?!

OSVALDO: To be acceptable.

ALFREDO *slaps* OSVALDO. MIMI *enters.*

MIMI: The rice, we have to hit her with the rice.

OSVALDO *and* ALFREDO, *glaring at each other, exit with* MIMI. LIZETTE *enters in her honeymoon outfit and goes outside. She sees* MANUELA. *They come back in.*

LIZETTE: Grandma, you've been in the sun!

MANUELA: I was taking a nap. You know when you get old you need rest.

LIZETTE: You were crying, Grandma. Don't.

MANUELA: We didn't have enough cake!

LIZETTE: Nothing turned out right, Grandma, that's the truth.

MANUELA: You're right. Oscar would have made sure that we had a good time. My husband would have spent more money. I would have been proud. Your mother would have been proud. You would have been proud.

LIZETTE: Grandma, aren't you proud of me?

MANUELA: Yes.

LIZETTE: Did you love each other?

MANUELA: Yes, dear, we did.

LIZETTE: And you never doubted it?

MANUELA: No, dear.

LIZETTE: I hope I can do it. Wish me luck, Grandma. I don't want to fail. I want to be happy.

MANUELA: I hope that you know how to fight. Everything will try to stop and corrupt your life. I hope your husband is successful and that you have enough children.

LIZETTE: And that I never regret my life.

MANUELA: That will be my prayer.

LIZETTE: That if anyone goes, it's me, that I'm the one that walks. That he'll be hooked on me forever.

MANUELA: That's right.

LIZETTE: Thank you.

MANUELA: A beautiful dress. I'll get the rice.

LIZETTE: No, we are sneaking out. I don't want rice all over my clothes. In ten minutes tell them we tricked them, that we got away.

MANUELA: Go. Don't be nervous. Tonight everything will be all right. Don't worry, have a nice vacation.

LIZETTE: It's eighty degrees in Hawaii, it's an island, like Cuba.

MANUELA: Cuba was more beautiful.

LIZETTE *exits.*

Then politicians got in the way.

LIZETTE (*Offstage*): Honey, we did it. Give me a kiss.

MANUELA *goes outside.*

ENTIRE CAST (*Offstage*): Ah! Uh-Uh! Noooooooo-ooo!

LIZETTE (*Offstage*): My God, rice, run!

SONIA *enters, covered with rice, followed by* OS-VALDO.

OSVALDO: It was a beautiful wedding.

SONIA: You're coming home with me?

OSVALDO: I can't.

SONIA: Yes, come with me.

OSVALDO: Not tonight.

SONIA: When?

OSVALDO: Never. (*Pause*) Nothing is left between you and me.

SONIA: Nothing?

OSVALDO: Nothing.

SONIA: I'm not even your mistress?

OSVALDO: That's right. Revolutions create hell for all people involved.

SONIA: Don't do this. We belong together, we were thrown out. Discarded. We stayed together, Cubans, we are Cubans. Nothing really came between us.

OSVALDO: Something did for me.

MIMI *enters.*

SONIA: What about our family? What we swore to Christ?

OSVALDO: I don't believe in anything, not even Christ.

SONIA: And me?

OSVALDO: I have another wife, she's my wife now. I have another life.

SONIA: If I was my father, I'd kill you!

MIMI (*To* OSVALDO): Your wife is waiting in the car. (*To* SONIA) She told me to tell him.

OSVALDO: Sonia, I'm starting fresh. You should too.

SONIA: I should, yes, I should. (*She takes out the bottle that* MANUELA *gave her in Act One and makes the sign of the cross twice*)

OSVALDO: That's right. (*He starts to exit*)

SONIA: Wait. One last toast.

OSVALDO: To the bride?

SONIA: No, to us. (*She goes to the fountain to pour them champagne, and puts the potion into* OS-VALDO'S *drink*)

MIMI: Osvaldo?

OSVALDO: How dare you call me that!

MIMI: Okay, Daddy, is that better? This family is the only life I know. It exists for me.

OSVALDO: This is between your mother and me.

MIMI: No, listen, Daddy, the family is continuing. I'm going to make sure of that.

OSVALDO: How? Mimi, how?

MIMI: Never mind, Osvaldo.

Sound of car horn.

OSVALDO: She's honking the horn, hurry, Sonia!

SONIA *hands* OSVALDO *the drink.*

SONIA: Money, love and the time to enjoy it, for both of us!

OSVALDO: Thanks. (*He gulps down the drink and exits*)

MIMI: Osvaldo, you jerk. Bastard!

SONIA: Don't worry, Mimi, he's going to have diarrhea till sometime in March.

MIMI: Finally.

SONIA: Put the blame on me. I don't speak the right way. I don't know how to ask the right questions.

MIMI: That's not true, Mama.

SONIA: When I first got here…I got lost. I tried to ask an old man for directions. I could not find the right words to ask him the directions. He said to me, "What's wrong with you, lady, somebody give you a lobotomy?" I repeated that word over and over to myself, "lobotomy, lobo-tomy, lo-bo-to-meee!" I looked it up. It said an insertion into the brain, for relief, of tension. I remembered people who had been lobotomized, that their minds could not express anything, they could feel nothing. They looked numb, always resting, then I realized that the old man was right.

MIMI: No. Mama.

SONIA: So I decided never to communicate or deal with this country again. Mimi, I don't know how to go back to my country. He made me realize that to him, I looked like a freak. Then I thought, but I'm still me to Osvaldo, he's trapped too. He must feel the same way too. Put the blame on me.

MIRIAM *and* OSCAR *enter.*

MIMI: Aunt Miriam, tell me, how did you find revenge?

MIRIAM: Against what?

MIMI: Your father.

MIRIAM: Oh, when my mother and father got to America, I made them live with me. I support them. Now they are old and they are dependent on me for everything.

MIMI: It's not worth it, Aunt Miriam.

MIRIAM: Yes it is.

MIMI: Grandma, I'm in the car.

MIRIAM: It's revenge.

OSCAR (*Shows* MIRIAM *the coke bottle*): My revenge!

MIRIAM: Everyone in this family's got a drug.

MANUELA (*Enters*): Mimi is taking me home?

SONIA: Yes, Mama, she's waiting in the car—

MANUELA: You didn't do it right.

SONIA: I'm sorry, Mama…I did it the way I was taught.

MANUELA *kisses* OSCAR *goodbye and then exits.* Why can't life be like it was? Like my coming-out party. When my father introduced me to our society in my white dress.

MIRIAM: Sonia, they threw the parties to give us away…perfect merchandising; Latin women dressed like American movies, doing Viennese waltzes. "Oh, beautiful stream, so clear and bright, a radiant dream we sing to you, by shores that…"

SONIA: I wonder what it would have been like if we would have stayed?

MIRIAM: They would have ridiculed us.

SONIA: We would have had a country.

MIRIAM: We didn't have a choice.

OSCAR *exits to the ballroom.*

SONIA: Miriam, Pedro took his life because of that.

MIRIAM: No. Pedro did it because of days like to-day—afternoons like this one: when you are around the people you belong with and you feel like you're choking and don't know why. (*She takes out Valium*) I'll give you a piece of magic.

SONIA: How many?

MIRIAM: One…no, two. A Valium—that's the only certain thing. It reassures you. It lets you look at the truth. That's why psychiatrists prescribe them.

SONIA: You guarantee me Varadero? I'll be floating in Varadero Beach?

MIRIAM: If you take three you get to Varadero, Cuba.

MIRIAM *and* SONIA *take the Valium. From the offstage ballroom we hear* OSCAR *speaking over the microphone.*

OSCAR (*Sniff…sniff*): …One, two, three, testing, one, three, three, two, testing. Lenin or some Commie like that said that "you cannot make an omelet without breaking a few eggs." Funny guy. Testing. All right, now from somewhere in the armpit of the world, a little tune my mother taught me. (*He sings* "Isla")
In an island
Far away from here
I left the life I knew
Island of mine
Country of mine
Mine and only mine
Terraces and houses
Country do you remember
Do you remember
Remember me?

MIRIAM (*Takes cushions from chair and puts them on the floor*): I want to float down Key Biscayne back to Varadero. Varadero, please, please come.

MIRIAM *lies on the cushions.* SONIA *looks at her.*

SONIA: Why is he making so much noise?!

MIRIAM: Shhh. I'm already there…miles and miles into the beach and the water is up to my knees…I float. The little fish nibble at my feet. I kick them. I'm in. I'm inside the place where I'm supposed to be.

OSCAR (*Singing offstage*): You were once my island
I left you all alone
I live without your houses
Beautiful houses
Houses remembered.

SONIA: Sonia is not coming back. Cojimar, Sonia will never be back.

OSCAR (*Singing offstage*): Eran mías
You were only mine
Never forget me
Don't forget me
Mi amor.

MIMI (*Enters*): Mama, what's she doing?

SONIA: Relaxing.

MIMI: Want to dance, Mama?

SONIA: Us?

MIMI: Yes.

SONIA: Yes.

OSCAR (*Singing offstage*): En una isla
Lejos de aquí
Dejé
La vida mía
Madre mía
Isla mía

MIMI: They're going to kick us out.

SONIA: That's all right, Mimi. I've been kicked out of better places.

OSCAR (*Singing offstage*): Te dejé.

SONIA *and* MIMI *begin to dance. Lights fade as we hear the end of the song.*

END OF PLAY

PERFORMING *BROKEN EGGS*

Eduardo Machado's plays and musicals have been produced since 1981 by the Ensemble Studio Theatre and Repertorio Español (New York City), the Long Wharf Theatre (CT), the Williamstown Theatre Festival (MA), the Humana Festival of Actors Theatre Louisville (KY), Cincinnati Playhouse (OH), and the Mark Taper Forum in Los Angeles. *Broken Eggs* (*Revoltillo*), the fourth play in Machado's *Floating Islands* tetralogy, was first performed in 1984 for forty-six performances at the Ensemble Studio Theatre and di-

rected by James Hammerstein. In 1995, Oskar Eustis directed the complete *Floating Islands* at the Mark Taper Forum Theatre in Los Angeles as a two-part production of four plays: Part I—*The Family Business: The Modern Ladies of Guanabacoa* and *In the Eye of the Hurricane*; Part II—*After the Revolution: Fabiola* and *Broken Eggs*. This six-hour production featured the distinguished actress Miriam Colón as Manuela in *Broken Eggs*.

Machado's "Floating Islands" in general and *Broken Eggs* in particular focus on domestic power struggles as a mirror for a society in flux. His Hispanic versions of modern political and social convolutions have been compared to Lillian Hellman's *The Little Foxes*, to García Lorca's *The House of Bernarda Alba,* and to Anton Chekhov's *The Cherry Orchard.* They all write about societies in flux.

The staging of Machado's epic tetralogy about four generations of Cubans stretching from 1929–1980 opened in October 1995 at Los Angeles' Mark Taper Forum. The reviews were mixed. One reviewer called *Floating Islands* a "small work that just happens to go on and on." Nonetheless, the distinguished critic John Lahr came to his defense, arguing that Machado's characters are political ideas in search of a performing style.[4]

CRITICS' NOTEBOOK
ON HISPANIC AMERICAN DRAMA

The theatrical diversity of the American theater has generated a plethora of scholarly books on the history of Hispanic American writing in the United States. Jorge Huerta has written on Chicano theater (*Chicano Theatre: Themes and Forms,* 1982), Joanne Pottlitzer on Hispanic theater in the United States and Puerto Rico (*Hispanic Theatre in the United States and Puerto Rico,* 1988), and Nicolas Kanellos on the origins and development of Hispanic theater (*A History of Hispanic Theatre in the United States: Origins to 1940,* 1990). Eduardo Machado's work has received most attention in the annual publications of plays produced by the Humana Festival in Louisville (KY) and by New York's Theatre Communications Group, which publishes *The Floating Island*

Plays and *On New Ground: Contemporary Hispanic-American Plays.* His plays have also been consistently reviewed in *The New York Times* and *The New Yorker.*

The following commentary by Caridad Svich, resident playwright at the Mark Taper Forum in Los Angeles and editor/translator of books on María Irene Fornés and García Lorca, traces the development of Latino/a drama by a "new" generation of playwrights who worked at New York City's INTAR (the Hispanic American Arts Center). Eduardo Machado adds in an interview his perception of prejudice within arts institutions that works against the full expression of a writer's truth.

Caridad Svich, from *Out of the Fringe**

❦

In the margins, in the black boxes, clubs, art galleries, performance spaces, garages, basements, universities, cabarets, poetry slams and other alternative spaces, a new kind of Latina/o theatre and performance aesthetic has been forged over the last ten years: a bold, frank, uncompromising, lyrical, private, metaphorical kind of work that re-visions what it is to be a Latina/o dramatist in the U.S. Created outside the mainstream of "official" culture (both Latina/o and Anglo), this new generation of theatrical writing seeks to deconstruct and reconstruct not only theatrical forms but also the boundaries by which those forms have been created. Drawing, in part, from the rich and varied exploration of a generation of novelists and visual artists from Spain and Latin America, these young dramatists have discovered new ways of shaping text, addressing the audience, working with language, and exploring and decoding the encoded taboos of the Latina/o culture. Feminist, proto-feminist, gay, lesbian, bisexual, transgressive, pagan, spiritual

and reinvented Americans, these dramatists have slowly taken their work beyond the expected and established tropes made available to them by "official" culture, and in so doing have moved out of the fringe and into the virtual center of contemporary American performance.

In the 1970s and 1980s, Latina/o dramatists were encouraged by the bold experiments of master playwright and teacher María Irene Fornés, activist and storyteller Luis Valdez, maverick playwright and pioneering publisher of Latino/a work Pedro Monge-Rafuls, and a handful of other brave writers who were testing the uncharted, previously forbidden waters of American theatrical writing. An interest in old world versus new world issues—the border experience, multiculturalism and the postmodern hold of "magic realism" on the audience's imagination—led to the support and development of new work by mostly U.S.-born Latina/o writers. Theatres actively began seeking funding for work that would specifically address issues of ethnicity and gender in the hope of discovering new voices and serving a necessary political end. No longer could the generation upon generation of Latinos in this country be ignored. These were artists to be nurtured, and a growing visible audience among them as well....

Eduardo Machado, "An Interview with the Playwright"*

A few years ago, a prominent dramaturg told me, "No matter how good your plays are, no one will do them, because what did Cubans have to do with any artistic director's life?" I told her I thought I was writing about the human condition.

Some time later, a well-meaning Broadway producer told me, "Listen, Eduardo, with your name they're expecting Carmen Miranda, and you give them the opposite."

**Out of the Fringe: Contemporary Latina/Latino Theatre and Performance,* eds. Caridad Svich and Maria Teresa Marrero (New York: Theatre Communications Group, 2000): ix–x.

*Eduardo Machado, "The Entire Canvas: An Interview with the Playwright," *American Theatre,* 14.5 (May/June 1997): 15, 59.

A year ago the Roundabout Theatre Company commissioned me to write a play. I wrote about Cuba at the turn of the century. In the play a first-generation German woman, in order to become Cuban, has to let the spirit of a black slave into her. Todd Haimes, the artistic director, told me that my play was wonderful but too much for his audience. My characters think and don't wear bananas on their heads, I thought to myself—that's still too much for his audience.

So I thought that indeed it was a matter of race.

Then, one very bleak night this year—the kind where you wonder what exactly you've been doing for the past 20 years—I came to the realization that those 65 regional theatres August Wilson recently spoke of had only used my talent to 25 percent of its capacity—and that, to me, was the ultimate prejudice: the prejudice against the full expression of an artist's talent.

The full expression of talent is anarchistic, the real enemy of institutions, society, capitalism, show biz and political correctness. *Of course* being of a different race makes you less familiar, more threatening, more unproducible.

The world I live in is too big for the stages of those 65 theatres. I have happily gone somewhere else to express myself: to independent film, to small theatre companies, to small crowds that stay awake.

But I must say that I understand that when Wilson looks into his mother's eyes, he sees the slave ship in which her ancestors were brought here. That he never looked into his father's eyes is something Wilson must answer only to himself.

But surely there must be room for my eyes, too. When I look into my eyes I see my mother's grandfather who was a Basque, my father's dark-skinned grandmother, my father's blue-eyed German grandfather, and then all the fearful, driven, paranoid Cubans who came to the States and tried to hold onto a nationality that vanished in front of their veiled eyes.

Then, inside my eyes where memory lives, I see Gena Franz burning an American flag in Van Nuys High during the Vietnam war; my socialist wife trying to find a place in a country where the Left has forgotten the world they were supposed to build; daughters and sons of the famous trying to find their place in the limelight; my friends denying they were dying of AIDS; my black cousin Alberto; the beggars on the streets; the bruises on a friend's back when she has been beaten by her husband.

Isn't it my duty to write about all that, about the entire canvas that has been my life?

But we divide ourselves in the theatre according to the color of our skin, birthplace, etc., etc., etc. Isn't idealism, either artistic or political, more binding than blood, color or gender?

To show life here on Earth. Isn't that our job? Why waste time fighting about anything else? Truth in art is individualistic, not communal. The writer's truth. This is all a playwright owes to himself, her community, and the writers that came before.

ASIAN AMERICAN PLAYWRITING

As early as the 1850s, Asian theater and opera traditions were imported by laborers from China and by Japanese and Filipino workers settling in the United States at the turn of the century. Many workers and their families remained clustered in neighborhoods within major port cities, such as San Francisco, Los Angeles, Seattle, and New York City. Many communities developed their own entertainments that featured Asian players but interest in traditional Eastern performance styles gradually diminished under the influence of Westernized life in America. The film industry stepped into the vacuum and, until the civil rights era, featured Asian players, chiefly as racial stereotypes, in films with Asian themes and exotic locations. The inscrutable detective "Charlie Chan" and the seductive "Dragon Lady" were two among many stereotypical characters found in Hollywood films. Beginning in the sixties, a cultural change occurred influenced by the civil rights movement and the Korean and Vietnam wars, during which an increased number of immigrants from Asia further enhanced awareness of Asian culture and traditions.

In order to combat the stereotyping and provide venues for their work, Asian- and

American-born writers and artists found it necessary to establish their own theaters and cultural centers. Their works, old and new, exploded narrow stereotypes and misperceptions about Asian culture, people, and traditions. In addition, such earlier international artists as Antonin Artaud in France and Bertolt Brecht in Germany drew heavily upon Asian theatrical traditions in performance and design and influenced a new generation of theater practitioners. Jerzy Grotowski, Peter Brook, Ariane Mnouchkine, Harold Prince, Andrei Serban, and Julie Taymor owe a great debt to Asian stage practice and puppet traditions. They became known as the *transculturalists* in Western art who fused Western and Eastern theater practice into new artistic expressions.

In the wake of the civil rights movement in the late sixties and early seventies, Asian American artists formed small theater companies in major cities to tell their own stories with authentic voices. The East West Players in Los Angeles, founded in 1965, was created as a home to promote Asian-Pacific American works. Under the leadership of actor-director Mako, the group concentrated on plays by Asian Americans and showcased Asian American actors in classical plays. Other companies followed—the Northwest Asian American Theater Company, the Asian American Theater Workshop, Ping Chong and Company, the Pan Asian Repertory Theater, and the Ma-Yi Theater Ensemble—in Los Angeles, Seattle, San Francisco, and New York City. These companies nurtured writers and artists and in many instances transcended geographic and ethnic boundaries. Ping Chong as a performance artist, writer, director, and choreographer has resisted being "ghettoized as an Asian-American artist" and views his company's work as an "ongoing dialogue with the twentieth century." His artistic investigations exist at the intersections where race, culture, history, art, and technology meet and are celebrated as intercultural experiments.

In the last two decades, Asian American artists have emerged as unique voices in the American theater, addressing complex issues of race, prejudice, family, compromise, identity, and struggles for self-fulfillment. David Henry Hwang's *M. Butterfly* in 1988 effectively introduced the Asian American voice into mainstream American theater. Nonprofit regional theaters across the United States have also provided creative homes for the new generation of Asian American playwrights, including Philip Kan Gotanda (*Sisters Matsumoto*), Jessica Hagedorn (*Tenement Lover*), Han Ong (*L.A. Stories*), Diana Son (*Stop Kiss*), and Wakako Yamauchi (*And the Soul Shall Dance*).

David Henry Hwang's work has been chosen here as an example of intercultural writing that reveals the collision of two cultures (East and West) and thereby exposes the rough cultural edges in the politics of race, gender, class, sexuality, and identity. *Golden Child* shows individuals caught up in the colliding of traditional Chinese culture and beliefs with Western Christian beliefs and social mores. The dualities make for a richly complex and theatrical text.

Golden Child

DAVID HENRY HWANG

David Henry Hwang (1957–) was born in Los Angeles and grew up in San Gabriel, an affluent Los Angeles suburb, as the first generation of a Chinese American fundamentalist Christian family. His father, a banker, immigrated to the United States from Shanghai in the late 1940s, and his mother, a pianist and music teacher, although born in China was reared in the Philippines.

One of three siblings, David Henry Hwang, a star debater and violinist, attended an elite preparatory academy (the Harvard School) in North Hollywood and, on graduation in 1975, went to Stanford University where he graduated Phi Beta Kappa in English. During a summer term, he attended the first Padua Hills Playwrights Festival held in Claremont, CA, and came under the influence of Sam Shepard and María Irene Fornés. There, he began work on F.O.B. (for "fresh off the boat") in which he examined the contrasting attitudes of American-born Chinese and recent Chinese immigrants. In this first play, Hwang articulated the consistent themes of his later work: issues of race, gender, sexuality, and class that highlight cultural differences and the mysteries of identity.

In 1979, Hwang submitted F.O.B. to the National Playwrights Conference at the O'Neill Theater Center in Waterford, CT, where the play was staged with professional actors. At the time, Joseph Papp, then artistic director of the New York Shakespeare Festival/Public Theater, was searching for new plays by Asian American authors and made the decision to stage F.O.B. at the Public Theater. F.O.B. won an Obie award as best play of the 1980–81 Off Broadway season. Directed by Mako of the Los Angeles–based East West Players, the production featured John Lone, a Chinese actor trained in the stylized techniques of Beijing Opera.

The following season, the Henry Street Settlement in New York City commissioned a new play by David Henry Hwang for a forthcoming ethnic heritage series; The Dance and the Railroad transferred to the Public Theater with actors John Lone and Tzi Ma as two Chinese laborers hired to build the transcontinental railroad across the United States in the mid-nineteenth century. Idled by a strike in 1867, the two workers pass the time practicing the exacting balletic movements of the Beijing Opera as they dream of returning to their homeland and careers in the Chinese theater. Praised for its sensitive characterization and inventive choreography created by John Lone, The Dance and the Railroad was still playing at the Public Theater when Hwang's third play, Family Devotions, opened there in October of 1981. The farce was based on the confrontation between members of an affluent Chinese American family when a revered uncle arrives from China and forces them to reexamine their values and "connections to the past." This broadly satiric work disappointed critics. It was followed by Sound and Beauty (two one-act plays, The Sound of a Voice and The House of Sleeping Beauties), which critics called "vibrant" and "freewheeling."

Having had four plays produced in three years, Hwang took a break and traveled to Canada, Europe, and Asia to reassess his newly acquired status as an Asian American voice in U.S. culture. "It was no longer that I was a playwright per se," he told an interviewer, "but that I was an Asian American playwright, and my Asian-Americanness became the quality that defined me to the public."[5] He credits Maxine Hong Kingston (author of Woman Warrior) with liberating his playwright's voice and enabling him to believe that his own parochial concerns could be made into literature.[6]

Hwang returned to write Rich Relations, Bondage, Face Value, and Trying to Find China Town, along with television, screenplays, and the

Tony award–winning M. Butterfly, *produced on Broadway in 1988, based on a real-life espionage case involving a French diplomat and a male Chinese agent masquerading as an actress with the Beijing Opera. British director John Dexter staged the skewered version of Puccini's opera* Madama Butterfly *with John Lithgow and B. D. Wong as diplomat and Chinese agent-actress. In this multilayered play of sexual and cultural role reversals, Hwang took up themes of "racism, sexism, and imperialism."*[7]

More recently, David Henry Hwang joined as a librettist with composer Philip Glass and stage designer Jerome Sirlin to create a "science fiction music drama" called 1000 Airplanes on the Roof, *followed by* The Voyage, *again with composer Philip Glass, commissioned by the Metropolitan Opera Company in commemoration of the five hundredth anniversary of Christopher Columbus's discovery of America, and* The Silver River, *with music by Bright Sheng.*

Hwang turned again to his contemplations on race, gender, and cultural identity in Golden Child, *produced on Broadway in 1998. He described* Golden Child *as being about "the oppositions between Christianity and ancestor worship in terms of dualities."*[8] *This play is representative of Hwang's dramaturgy that uses both Occidental and Oriental theatrical techniques, interweaving the well-made details of realistic modern American playwriting with the exotic theatricality of Eastern theater practice.*

CRITICAL INTRODUCTION TO *GOLDEN CHILD*

Playwright David Henry Hwang describes his work as a personal journey that just happens to have a "public dimension."[9] *Golden Child* combines these dual facets of the personal and the public that characterize Hwang's writing. On the personal level, Hwang creates a story out of his Chinese heritage from tales related to him by his maternal grandmother in which she experienced the ancient custom of foot binding for young girls. As Ahn, the "golden child" of Hwang's play, has her bindings removed in the pivotal action of the play, the event establishes a metaphorical dividing line between East and West. Chinese foot binding serves as the catalyst for

Hwang's reflections upon such public issues of difference as religion, gender, and racial customs.

Hwang's play had its inception in an unpublished novel, called *Only Three Generations* and based on tape-recorded conversations with his maternal grandmother about the family's history in China. The novel's title is taken from the Chinese proverb that says, "The wealth of a Chinese family lasts only three generations." Even though he was a child of ten when he recorded the stories and wrote the novel, the adult David Henry Hwang perceives a sensibility at work that sought a context for his life as an Asian American more real than the "Charlie Chans" or the "Fu Manchus" that he saw on television or in films.[10]

On several occasions, Hwang cites Anton Chekhov's *The Three Sisters* as his model for *Golden Child.* Rather than the sisters, Hwang's play features three wives (polygamy was the norm of the time in China). In contrast to Chekhov's play, *Golden Child* is basically a realistic domestic drama set in China in 1923 in which Eng Tieng-Bin's three wives contend for control of the household and the attention of their husband. Nonetheless, *Golden Child* is more than a realistic, "kitchen sink" play. It has a frame (Hwang called it a "bookend" structure) that transposes the scene from present-day New York City to Southeast China in 1918–19 and back again. It is a memory play with a narrator (the character Andrew Kwong) who, anticipating the birth of his "golden child," is awakened by the ghost of his grandmother and to memories of the family's past. Hwang told an interviewer that "family history functions in the same way as scripture, or mythology, or literature. It's only important as it is able to be interactive and reinterpreted by people who are alive. That's the way the ghosts of the past serve us."[11]

Unlike Tennessee Williams's *The Glass Menagerie* where Tom Wingfield, the narrator, plays a younger version of himself in his family story, the narrator of *Golden Child* doubles as his great-grandfather in scenes from 1918 to 1919. In the outer play, which takes place in the present, Andrew Kwong anticipates the birth of his daughter and conjures up in his imagination his

Chinese ancestors whose story has shaped his own life along with his desire to write down their struggles for the next generation to read. In Hwang's lexicon, "That's the way the ghosts of the past serve us."[12]

The inner play finds the actor playing Andrew doubling as his great-grandfather and the actress playing his wife Elizabeth doubling as Eling, a Chinese woman in her early twenties. In a variation on the theatrical device of doubling, the actress playing Eng Ahn (a role created by Tsai Chin) ranges in age from a Chinese girl of ten to an eighty-five-year-old woman. The inner play was inspired by the story of Hwang's great-grandfather, who converted to Christianity in China and set wrenching change into motion that forever altered the world of his three wives and one of his daughters.

The inner play takes place in the household of Eng Tieng-Bin in China with his three wives (Eng Siu-Young, Eng Luan, and Eng Eling) in various states of conflict within a household managed by the three women. In addition, there are customs of polygamy, dress, religion, ancestor worship, and foot binding. The three wives are studies in contrast. The First Wife is hidebound, the Second Wife grasping, and the younger Third Wife wholly in love with her husband. European ideas (monogamy, Christianity, romantic love, and child-rearing) are introduced by Eng Tieng-Bin, who returns from work in the Philippines where he has converted to Christianity. The women in the household who can adapt to new customs and ideas grow and change. The First Wife, who refuses to accede to her husband's demands for change, destroys herself with opium. The release of Ahn, her father's golden child, from the bindings functions as a theatrically symbolic moment. When the child's feet are free of the terrible bindings, so too is the household liberated for personal growth and freedoms. Eng Tieng-Bin's courageous act in the face of the time-honored, brutal custom reverses the tradition that turned women into cripples in the name of feminine beauty.[13] His act of releasing the bindings from his daughter's feet likewise serves as a public metaphor for those who dare to challenge tradition and authority. As the First Wife unbinds the wrappings from the child's feet, she speaks in rebuttal of the changes sweeping over the world in 1918: "Daughter— you do not know what a terrible gift is freedom." Hwang suggests here that the new century is on the cusp of remarkable changes in communications, air travel, scientific discovery, and the liberation of women and men, but not without struggle and conflict—personal and global.

It is not this playwright's intention to treat the encroachment of Western ideals on China as an act that contaminates or destroys a way of life. Instead, Hwang insists that the exchange of ideas creates opportunities for personal growth, for new ways of thinking, and release from such constraints as foot binding and ancestor worship that keep people anchored to the past, mired in the present, and fearful of the future. The presence of the fundamentalist missionary Reverend Baines serves to introduce a benign Christianity along with the outside, Westernized world from which Eng Tieng-Bin has just returned. Although Eng has converted to Christianity, his desire to live in a monogamous relationship with his third wife is related more to the Western ideal of romantic love than to the restoration of monogamy or to the triumph of Christian belief.

Golden Child functions as an intercultural text on several levels. In structure, it combines realistic well-made playwriting with the familiar dramatic frame of the memory play, thus creating the outer and the inner worlds of the play. The conventions of the exotic theatrical vocabulary of Eastern stagecraft are introduced in the remembered section. There are ghosts, ancient customs, exotic clothes, and household divisions. The landscape of the inner play requires individual pavilions for the three wives, whose separate living spaces with religious altars function as private cages for the women when they are away from their household chores. The Main Hall (usually the outer stage) functions as a public space, the communal room where the household sits, dines, serves tea to guests, and so on. The outer framing device takes place in a bedroom in Manhattan where Andrew Kwong sleeps and dreams beside his pregnant wife.

As an intercultural text, *Golden Child* blends cultural and theatrical traditions of East and West in this story of familial change. Hwang has said: "By confronting our ethnicity, we are simply confronting the roots of our humanity. The denial of this truth creates a bizarre world."[14] The play about the creation of a Chinese American family in the third generation of the Eng family is a blending of Eastern and Western customs and beliefs. Andrew Kwong converses with the ghost of his grandmother, who was liberated by the winds of change introduced by her father into the household. Andrew draws understanding from the ancestral spirits and acknowledges that "many of them, people not so different from myself…struggled with what to keep, and what to change—for the next generation." The fusion of Eastern and Western ideals and sensibilities in *Golden Child* serves to create a new cultural context. In the intermingling of theatrical traditions of Western writing and Eastern lifestyle, David Henry Hwang speaks with a universal voice on issues of freedom and responsibility common to all humankind.

Golden Child

CHARACTERS

ANDREW KWONG/ENG TIENG-BIN   Husband of Elizabeth/Husband of Three Wives, Ahn's father

ENG AHN   Grandmother of Andrew Kwong, daughter of Tieng-Bin and Siu-Yong

ELIZABETH KWONG/ENG ELING, THIRD WIFE   Andrew's wife/Tieng-Bin's Third Wife

ENG SIU-YONG, FIRST WIFE   Tieng-Bin's First Wife

ENG LUAN, SECOND WIFE   Tieng-Bin's Second Wife

REVEREND BAINES   A Missionary

SERVANTS/GHOSTS

PLACE

Manhattan and Eng Tieng-Bin's home village near Amoy, in Southeast China

TIME

ACT ONE: *The present and winter 1918*
ACT TWO: *Spring 1919 and the present*

ACT ONE

Fade up on Ahn, a Chinese girl of ten, who speaks in the voice of an eighty-five-year-old woman.

AHN: Andrew—you must be born again.
(Lights up on Andrew Kwong, Asian, fifties, in bed beside Elizabeth—the same actress who will later play Eling. He sits up with a start, awakening her.)

ELIZABETH: What?

ANDREW: Nothing.

AHN: Make money, not important; write successful book, not important. Only one thing important: you love Jesus.

ANDREW *(To Ahn)*: Ma? Ma?

ELIZABETH: Andrew, wake up.

ANDREW: Sorry, I thought I heard…

ELIZABETH: Did you just say, "Ma?"

AHN: Andrew—what this I hear, you no want baby?

ANDREW: It's okay, go back to sleep.
(Elizabeth goes back to sleep. Ahn sits on the edge of the bed.)

AHN: Andrew.

ANDREW: Shit! You're a Christian, Ma. Christians don't come back from the dead.

AHN: You forget—I am *Chinese* Christian. Best of East, best of West.

ANDREW: Yeah, worst of both worlds, don't remind me. What are you doing here, anyway?

AHN: To become grandmother—why I must wait so long? Now I must help you…so you not make terrible mistake.

ANDREW: Ma, I've never wanted to become a father. This pregnancy—it happened by accident.

AHN: This may be last chance God give you—to make new life.

ANDREW: You were always hounding me: have children, go to church, follow Jesus' plan. I've never wanted anything to do with that sort of life.

AHN: You never go church, this your third wife. Already you prove you are big sinner. Now, baby—on the way, Andrew. Time to cast out demon of your anger. Time you hear my story again—not with ear only, but also with spirit.

ANDREW: Sorry; but that's the last thing I need right now.

AHN: No—is only thing you need.

ANDREW: To hear how you became a religious fanatic? No thanks, I think it's time for you to get back to heaven. *(Shakes Elizabeth)* Elizabeth—

(Elizabeth sits up in bed. She's wearing ghost makeup and robes, and speaks in the voice of Eling, Third Wife, a Chinese woman in her early twenties.)

ELING: The spirit of my unborn child cries out to be remembered.

(Eling exits. Luan, a woman in her thirties, appears.)

LUAN: Ah Ying! Tell the servants to begin the feast for Husband's arrival!

(Siu-Yong, a woman in her forties, appears.)

SIU-YONG: Third Wife—you are responsible for seeing to it that the village is scrubbed and whitewashed.

(Ahn produces a Chinese man's robe from the early twentieth century. She slips it onto Andrew, and he becomes Eng Tieng-Bin, his grandfather.)

AHN: Remember? When you are little boy? You lie on my stomach, and I tell you story of our family. Winter of 1918. My father, Tieng-Bin, he make this family chosen by God. *(Pause)* My father work in Philippine, make money. But like all oversea Chinese, he leave behind most important part of life— his three wife, his children—*(Ahn begins to speak in the voice of a ten-year-old girl)*—all your future, Papa, you left behind in China. So after three years away, you got on a steamer ship, barreling across the South China Sea, towards our home village near the port of Amoy, in the province of Fukien.

SIU-YONG: Ahn! Ahn—where are you?

(Ahn exits with Andrew/Tieng-Bin. Lights come up, revealing the home of Eng Tieng-Bin. The living room of the Main Hall, surrounded in a semi-circle by three pavilions. Luan stands over a Servant.)

LUAN *(To Servant)*: What are you doing? Perhaps you don't wish to work in this house any longer? You would rather starve to death like your brothers and sisters, is that it?

(Eling enters.)

ELING: No, Second Wife! He was only following my orders.

LUAN: You act as if I was going to beat him personally. You forget, Third Wife—some of us in this house were raised as ladies.

ELING: Maybe you should talk to First Wife about this.

LUAN: Who can wait for her? There're a hundred tasks I have to complete before Husband's return. And this waste of his mother's milk failed to carry out my orders!

ELING: First Wife said I could use him to whitewash the village.

LUAN: She didn't tell me. And what is First Wife doing—reassigning domestics? That sort of disorder only confuses their simple minds. *(Siu-Yong enters.)*

SIU-YONG: Second Wife, no one creates disorder like you.

LUAN AND ELING: First Wife!

SIU-YONG: You can hear the bickering all the way across the compound. I don't care if you cut each other to ribbons, at least have the good taste to keep your voices down. What is the problem now?

ELING: She was about to punish—!

LUAN: He disobeyed my orders!

ELING: You said he could help me!

LUAN: I need all the staff I can get!

SIU-YONG: You two could give the goddess of mercy herself a headache.

(Ahn enters, as a ten-year-old girl.)

(To Ahn) Ahn, go play with your brothers and sisters. Your aunties are making peace—which is never a pretty sight.

AHN: Second Auntie, are you causing trouble again?

SIU-YONG: You must respect your auntie as a true source of wisdom. I don't care how irritating she is. Now apologize to her, or I'll have you whipped. *(Pause)* Did you hear me?

LUAN: She knows you won't whip her. You never whip her. No one whips anyone around here anymore.

(Luan crosses to Ahn, slaps her.)

SIU-YONG: Now what are you doing?

LUAN: Just helping you honor tradition, First Wife.

SIU-YONG: You have no right to strike my child! Only her nanny can do that!

(To Ahn) Ahn, go. And stop whimpering—you shouldn't give her the satisfaction. *(To Servant)* Ah Ti! Go!

(Ahn and Servant exit.)

Listen—our Husband has been away three years, and he will return to find his wives filled with love and cooperation—no matter how we feel about one another, is that clear?

LUAN: I guess I'm just too honest for that. Hypocrisy sickens me.

SIU-YONG: If you can't live with dishonesty, you have no business calling yourself a woman. Now—settle your dispute as true sisters. Or I may decide to find our Husband a Fourth Wife.

ELING: Dearest Elder Sister, forgive me for my disrespect. I know I will never be able to match the great wisdom you have gained from having lived so many more years on this earth than me.

LUAN: Thank you, Little Sister. Forgive me. When husband made you his concubine, I took a solemn vow never to remind you of your peasant birth, or the fact that you were originally brought here to be my servant. I only pray that one day you will manage to bear him a child.

SIU-YONG: That's what I like around here. True harmony. Now, everyone—back to work!
(The women exit separately. The pavilions are illuminated, revealing the three wives burning offerings to their parents. Ahn attends Siu-Yong in her pavilion.)
(To her altar) Papa, Mama—on days like today, I feel like running away from all my obligations. Thank heaven for duty: Without it, we would be forced to think for ourselves.
(She burns ghost money*) First, here's some money for you to wave in the faces of the other ghosts. Thank the heavens for inventing money—without it, what would we use to measure love? *(She holds up paper dolls)* And here are more servants—in case you were forced to beat the last bunch to death.
(She pulls out an unrecognizable paper item) And—what have we here? Ahn made these herself.

AHN: It's a steamer ship. Like the one Papa's riding on.

SIU-YONG: Oh, Ahn.

AHN: They want it. They want to be modern—like Papa.

SIU-YONG: You think you know your father so well?

AHN: From his letters. He likes modern things—not like you.

SIU-YONG: The fact that something is new simply means it has not had time to disappoint us.

AHN: Papa says, in the modern world—that they don't make girls wear bindings on their feet.

SIU-YONG: Do you want to end up a lonely spinster? Now, listen. Your father spends his time abroad trading with monkeys and devils; he may come home with all sorts of new ideas. Don't be too easily impressed.
(She burns a paper steamer ship) Papa, Mama, hear my prayer—let Husband return, if it is possible, a normal man.

LUAN *(To her altar)*: Papa, I forgive you for losing all our money, and even for selling me to be a Second Wife. All I ask in return is that Husband see myself and my son as we are: selfless, humble and modest. And reward us with absolute power.

ELING *(To her altar; burning paper robes)*: Papa, Mama—here are the silk robes you never wore in life. With Husband away, life has been hard. But what's made it bearable is the chance to give you nice things. And, please, let Husband look at me with the same eyes as when he left.
(The lights fade on the ladies' pavilions, and come up on Tieng-Bin, who enters, and kneels before the altar of his ancestors.)

TIENG-BIN: Papa, Mama, Ankong, Ama— I know I haven't been the most diligent son lately. *(He kowtows, burns paper money)* But how can I explain—what it is like for me to work in the modern world—and then return here, to my home village, where everything remains as you and your fathers decided it should be? Can you possibly understand—you who lived your entire lives within the boundaries of this country hamlet, so far removed from

---

*Ghost money is imitation money specifically intended for offerings to the dead.

any threat to your old ways? *(Pause)* Then what do I do with my doubts? Questions concerning the very traditions you taught me? When I was young, Papa, you would order me to obey, and your strong hand put an end to all discussion. How much simpler life was in those days.

(He pulls out a small crucifix, displays it to the altar) I bought a souvenir for you from a Christian temple in the Philippines. A naked man nailed to some boards. They told me for good luck, you can kiss its feet. They're very strange, the Westerners, and yet—hopeful, too. All the time talking about new inventions, new ideas. Nothing seems to excite them more than the future. *(Chinese folk music plays.)*

Well, I must prepare for the banquet. Don't worry I am still a good son. I go through all the motions, and curse myself for every deviation. In the house of his birth, a man is always a child.

(In the dimly lit Main Hall, Tieng-Bin and the ladies enact a stylized greeting ritual. They sit and begin to eat. Ahn rushes in from offstage, jumps into Tieng-Bin's lap. Lights up, music out.)
Hey, hey—who is this?

AHN: Who do you think? It's Ahn, remember? And you are my papa.

SIU-YONG: Ahn—get back to your table.

TIENG-BIN: No, you couldn't be Ahn. You must be some impostor!

AHN: But I *am* Ahn. What's wrong with you?

SIU-YONG *(To Ahn)*: Now!

TIENG-BIN: Ahn is just a baby. This person in my lap is a young lady.

AHN: Well…if you won't believe me, then you're just ignorant.

TIENG-BIN: Oh, that mouth! *You must* be Ahn!

AHN: That's what I've been trying to—

LUAN: Dear Husband, would you like to see the rest of the children, now?

SIU-YONG *(To Luan)*: No! We don't want her setting a bad example for the other children.

LUAN: It's a little late for that, don't you think?

TIENG-BIN *(To Ahn)*: See the trouble you cause? Why can't you present yourself with your brothers and sisters?

AHN: Because I am a Golden Child. Kang told me so.

TIENG-BIN: Kang?

SIU-YONG *(To Tieng-Bin)*: Her nanny's husband.

AHN: He took me gambling. Kang says he always loses, but with me beside him, he beat the whole table. So he told me I am a Golden Child.

TIENG-BIN: I need all the luck I can get. Perhaps I should take you back to the Philippines, huh?

AHN: Would that mean I could take the bindings off my feet?

SIU-YONG: Ahn!

AHN: My feet hurt so bad at night—and they stink, too!

SIU-YONG: No one ever said that feminine beauty was pretty.

AHN: It's okay. I wouldn't mind. I *want* to end up a lonely spinster.

TIENG-BIN: None of my daughters are going to end up spinsters, understand? *(To Ahn)* The world is changing. There's a whole new generation of men who will want an educated wife. Not some backwards girl hobbling around on rotting feet, filling the room with the stench of death!
(Silence; wives stare at Tieng-Sin.)
Ahn, go now.
(Ahn exits.)
First Wife—next time, I should greet the children before the banquet begins.

SIU-YONG: Of course. I hope our humble dinner meets with your satisfaction.

TIENG-BIN: Oh, yes. Yes! The…roast pig, it gets better every time. When I'm in the Philippines, all I can think of is the way you make sticky rice in this village.

SIU-YONG: All credit must be given to Second Wife. The feast was her arrangement exclusively.

TIENG-BIN: Second Wife, you honor me with your gracious attention.

LUAN: Please, Husband. This is a task any child could've performed as well as I. But your son, Yung-Bin—he is such a brilliant young scholar, his tutor tells me he can barely keep up with him…

SIU-YONG: Yes, we often see him chasing Yung-Bin across the courtyard.

LUAN: I cannot accept the suggestion that I possess even a shred of ability. The air itself is wasted on the likes of me.
(Tieng-Bin leads a toast to the smiling Luan.)

TIENG-BIN: To Second Wife—

LUAN: Oh, stop!—

TIENG-BIN: —full of diligent support for your loving sisters.

LUAN: Stop talking about me…. This is more than I can take—to a woman of my upbringing, all this praise is sheer torture—
(Siu-Yong turns to Eling.)

SIU-YONG: And did you see, dear Husband—?

ELING: First Wife! Don't!

SIU-YONG: —the brilliance of our village?

TIENG-BIN: Why, of course. The streets, they nearly shine—

ELING: No, no—there're spots and stains all over—

TIENG-BIN: When I stepped off the boat, I said: "What? Is this the Forbidden City? Or America, where the streets are paved with gold?"

ELING: You're so kind to ignore my horrible—

SIU-YONG *(To Eling)*: Shut your mouth!
(To Tieng-Bin) Some afternoons, I look out from my pavilion, and there she is, scrubbing the dung off the road as if she were still a peasant!

ELING: Once! Once, I saw some.

TIENG-BIN: To Third Wife—

ELING: So, I scooped it up, that's all.

TIENG-BIN: On every surface of this village, I see your goodness reflected.
(Tieng-Bin raises his cup. Eling points to Siu-Yong before they can drink.)

ELING: No—First Wife!

TIENG-BIN: Please—

ELING: She deserves all the credit.

SIU-YONG: Third Wife! Take your praise bravely, no matter how painful it might be!
(They drink, then Tieng-Bin adds:)

TIENG-BIN: To Eling—the sweetest and most fragrant flower.
(They drink again.)

ELING: No, no, no, no—could you all please talk about someone else, now?

LUAN: Husband, Third Wife is correct to shine the light on First Wife. Without her leadership—

SIU-YONG: Hey, hey! Stop that!

LUAN: —this entire village would've rotted away, and the first rain washed it out to sea.

SIU-YONG: What are you—retarded?

LUAN: First Wife—you said we must bear our praise bravely—

SIU-YONG: But you deserve yours.

LUAN: First Wife inspires us to work together, in the spirit of true sisterly affection.

SIU-YONG: Your mother should've drowned you before you learned to speak.

LUAN: To put aside petty feelings and focus on our common goal. Truly, First Wife supplies the wisdom which holds together this sisterhood, this family and this entire village.

SIU-YONG: Bitch.
(Tieng-Bin raises his glass toward Siu-Yong.)

TIENG-BIN: I'm well aware of what you're saying about your older sister. In my absence, she is forced to be both Wife and Husband. To First Wife—who blesses this home with wisdom.
(They drink to Siu-Yong.)

SIU-YONG: Why don't you pick up a knife and plunge it into my heart?
(They sit and resume eating.)
Nothing like a round of compliments to work up an appetite.

TIENG-BIN: I guess this is as good a time as any to share with you some of what I've been thinking lately.

SIU-YONG: Husband, we rely on you to bring home thoughts from the darkest corners of the world.

TIENG-BIN: On the boat, I met a man—an Englishman, a Christian missionary. We began talking—mostly out of curiosity. After all, the founder of our Chinese Republic, Dr. Sun Yat-Sen—he studied both Western medicine and Christianity. At any rate, this man—Reverend Baines—has come to run a mission here in Amoy. I've invited him over to continue our discussion. *(Pause)* Don't worry—I don't intend to become a Christian. But it's important to learn about new ideas—following the example of Dr. Sun.

SIU-YONG: Perhaps, then, you will also study medicine as well?

TIENG-BIN: Well, I—maybe if I were younger, I… that's a good one.

SIU-YONG: Funny the difference between Chinese and Occidental people. In China, we leave food at the altar for others. The white devils, they go to the altar and fill themselves with free bread and wine.
(The women laugh.)

TIENG-BIN: No, that's not—that's a stereotype! I wish you wouldn't act so ignorant.

SIU-YONG: Forgive us, Honored Husband. We are just backward women—hobbling around on rotting feet.
(Pause.)

TIENG-BIN: Look…what I said to Ahn—about the feet—I certainly wasn't thinking about any of you.

SIU-YONG: Oh no, of course not. The idea never even occurred to us.

LUAN: I don't even remember what you said to Ahn.

SIU-YONG: Husband is too sensitive on our behalf.

LUAN: I, for one, am very interested to hear what this reverend has to say. Perhaps I can join you sometime.

TIENG-BIN: That's not necessary, Second Wife, I don't expect you to—

LUAN: But I agree with you. I don't like the old ways.

TIENG-BIN: If the reverend comes, you're all welcome to join us. But don't feel any pressure.

LUAN: C'mon, Sisters! What've we got to lose?

SIU-YONG: Second Wife, I am constantly amazed by your rigid flexibility.
(Tieng-Bin claps his hands.)

TIENG-BIN: Now—a bit of the modern world for you each to call your own.
(Servants enter, bearing three gifts covered with cloth.)
Ah Ying! *(Servant lifts cloth off Siu-Yong's gift, revealing a cuckoo clock)*

SIU-YONG: Oh, my—what a clever Occidental clock!

TIENG-BIN: Here, let me…*(He moves forward the minute hand, causing the cuckoo to appear)* The

mechanical bird comes out every hour. I thought it would be charming, hanging on your wall.

SIU-YONG: Yes, I'm sure it will do wonders for my insomnia.

TIENG-BIN: Ah Tsun! *(He signals another servant, who carries a gift to Luan)*

LUAN: Husband, you didn't forget me?

TIENG-BIN: An ocean away, Second Wife, I found you impossible to forget.
(Servant removes cloth, revealing Luan's gift: a waffle iron.)

LUAN: Oh! It's so…shiny. What is it?

TIENG-BIN: It's a waffle iron—it makes pastries that white men eat for breakfast. I assumed— since you prepare the banquets, that you would appreciate—

LUAN: I do! In fact, it's so beautiful, I can hardly imagine actually using it.

TIENG-BIN: Good! And now—Ah Ti! *(Servant reveals Eling's gift: a phonograph player)* This is perhaps the best the outside world has to offer. *(He slips on a 78—a scratchy recording of La Traviata)* Western opera. A bit difficult to appreciate at first.

LUAN: It's so…primitive, so crude and barbaric. I like it!

TIENG-BIN: This is called *La Traviata.* The story of two lovers who only wish to be together— but their society makes this impossible.

SIU-YONG: I can see why.

TIENG-BIN: Now—I've spent three years away from the children; I won't wait a second longer. Go!
(Ladies start to exit.)

LUAN *(Calling offstage)*: Ah Ying! Warn Yung-Bin we're coming!
(Luan and Siu-Yong exit. Tieng-Bin grabs Eling before she can exit. He gives her a long kiss.)

ELING: Thank you.

TIENG-BIN: For what?

ELING: For answering my prayers.
(She exits after the other women. Lights cross fade onto Luan's pavilion. She is performing her toilette. Siu-Yong enters.)

LUAN: First Wife, aren't you supposed to be announced?

SIU-YONG: For years, you've made fun of my policy against whipping. Well, strip off your robe and come to the courtyard.

LUAN: You're growing soft.

SIU-YONG: What are you talking about?

LUAN: Even your threats don't have the usual conviction behind them.

SIU-YONG: Tonight, at dinner—you went too far.

LUAN: Really?

SIU-YONG: I won't allow it.

LUAN: Husband didn't seem to mind.

SIU-YONG: It is the simplest thing to manipulate a man. Just call him your master, and he's your slave for life.

LUAN: I, for one, trust my Husband's judgment.

SIU-YONG: How could you? Inviting us to listen to the black magic of some European witch doctor—putting us on the spot like that—

LUAN: I had to do something. You certainly weren't controlling the situation.

SIU-YONG: Me?

LUAN: You let Third Wife run wild! Far beyond her proper place at the table.

SIU-YONG: She hardly spoke a word all evening.

LUAN: Of course, I understand—the two of you have struck a bargain against me.

SIU-YONG: If there's one thing I try to be, it's fair-minded.

LUAN: And so you dishonored me at the table before our Husband—

SIU-YONG: I went to great lengths to praise you!

LUAN: —allowing Third Wife to go on forever, until he had to offer her two toasts instead of one!

SIU-YONG: So?

LUAN: One toast should've been more than enough for a slave, a concubine—but no, she went on, protesting, blushing, denying— that slut. Her modesty was absolutely shameless. And you just sat there!

SIU-YONG: I don't know why you keep track of such—

LUAN: Don't act stupid, Sister. You, of all people, should know—humility is power.

SIU-YONG: You could've gotten toasted twice. Why didn't you keep protesting your unworthiness? Should I punish Third Wife because she showed a little initiative?

LUAN: I don't flaunt my submissiveness like some people.

SIU-YONG: You know what your problem is? Deep inside, you believe the flattery is true.

LUAN: And Third Wife is different?

SIU-YONG: She's not smart enough to conceal her real emotions.

LUAN: Then why is she the one sharing her bed with Husband on his first night home?

SIU-YONG: You can't possibly take that sort of thing personally!

LUAN: I won't be content with her soggy leftovers.

SIU-YONG: Husbands always go to the bed of the youngest wife. That's what they're for. To save the rest of us all that mess and fuss.

LUAN: Has it ever occurred to you, that our Husband is different?

SIU-YONG: And that's your excuse for putting us in this position?

LUAN: If Husband becomes a Christian, then everything changes. All roles around here are up for reassignment. And the one who breaks the most rules wins.

SIU-YONG: Foreigners have been invading our country for centuries. We always change them more than they change us. It won't be any different this time.

LUAN: I'm trying to warn you, Older Sister, because I despise Third Wife even more than you. You—I find myself starting to pity.

SIU-YONG: What will it take to have some real peace in this house?

(From offstage, the recording of La Traviata *is heard.)*

LUAN: Listen. They're playing that Italian opera. He brings her music, and me a gift for the cooks.

SIU-YONG: So? I've got a bird that tells the time whether I wish to know or not.

LUAN: If it's modern Husband wants, he's looking in the wrong pavilion. No one in this house will be more modern than me ever again.

(Pause. They listen to the music from the adjoining pavilion.)

SIU-YONG: When you first came to this house, I watched Husband go to your bed and never complained. Why can't you do the same?

LUAN: When he started coming to my room, you took up the pipe.

SIU-YONG: So? I thought I'd finally earned the right to some real pleasure.

LUAN: I refuse to start taking drugs.

SIU-YONG: If you're determined to destroy yourself, there's nothing I can do to help you.

LUAN: That's why you can't see what's going on under your nose.

SIU-YONG: Stay away from the preacher. If you try to show me up by becoming a Christian, I'll see to it that you're demoted to a common concubine.

LUAN: I'm not certain I can make any such promises, First Wife.

SIU-YONG: You don't understand—the pipe makes me stronger, not weaker. It takes away the only thing that stands in the way of a woman's power—our feelings.

(Siu-Yong exits. Luan, hearing the music, looks toward Eling's pavilion.)

LUAN: No, you don't understand. Right now, feeling is the only thing our Husband desires.

(Lights fade on Luan, and come up on Eling and Tieng-Bin.)

ELING: You shouldn't have praised me so much in front of the other wives. Second Wife will be fuming for weeks.

TIENG-BIN: But just looking at you across the dinner table…

ELING: Are you going to make me blush again?

TIENG-BIN: I would never have believed my eyes could give me so much pleasure.

ELING: Just your eyes? What about your other senses?

TIENG-BIN: Well, you see, I thought I'd try out this new form of Western self-restraint.

ELING: What kind of ridiculous—? *(She reaches for him. He pulls away)*

TIENG-BIN: I'm restricting my intake of physical pleasures.

ELING: By now, your pleasure should be just about ready to explode.

TIENG-BIN: I've been living among the Christians, remember?

ELING: What does that have to do—?

TIENG-BIN: They consider abstinence a great virtue.

ELING: Says who? I hear white men stuff money into their pockets and meat down their thick throats.

TIENG-BIN: Don't be so close-minded—

ELING: Oh? Am I not—what?—*modern* enough for you? You already insulted my feet tonight.

TIENG-BIN: I'm sorry. That was just a slip of the tongue.

ELING: Where I come from, insults always get punished.

(Keeping her back to him, she crosses to the phonograph, sashaying seductively as she walks.)

So—you only want to watch? Like a good Christian? You say you are a modern man who wants a modern wife?

(Eling removes her robe, revealing Western lingerie.)

TIENG-BIN: Where did you get that outfit?

ELING: From the catalog. I've been so busy improving myself. *(Pause)* I like being modern, too. I like my new phonograph player. *(Begins to dance to the music, keeping her back to him)* I like this *Traviata*. It fills me with feelings. Modern feelings. Delicious feelings of …power.

(Tieng-Bin rises to his feet, starts toward her.)

No, no, no. Self-denial. Like a good Christian…

TIENG-BIN: Eling…

ELING: I'm your slave, remember? I can only obey your wishes.

(Eling eludes him)

TIENG-BIN: What are you—? You're going to kill me!…

ELING: You must be able to hold out longer than that, Honored Husband.

TIENG-BIN: I haven't touched a woman in three years!

ELING: You expect me to believe that? The prostitutes in Manila must be for shit.

TIENG-BIN: That's enough!

ELING: My lord and master…Sit!

TIENG-BIN: Eling!

ELING: Now, be modern. Sit! You wait for me to come to you. *(Pause)* When you're away, I would put this on and imagine your face as you lowered the straps from my shoulders…

TIENG-BIN: Now, you don't have to imagine any longer…

ELING: Not yet. Will you please struggle for me a little longer?

TIENG-BIN: But…why?

ELING: I don't know. It lets me know you care. That you suffer for me…like I suffer for you.

TIENG-BIN: Don't you believe that I want to spend every night here with you?

ELING: Yes, but you have your duty to the other wives.

TIENG-BIN: Eling…you are the first woman I was ever able to choose for myself…and you will be the last.

ELING: Now, if you like, you may touch me.
(He kisses her.)
You know I'm going to pay for every one of these kisses.

TIENG-BIN: What are you—?

ELING: When you're away, Second Wife bursts into my room whenever she feels like it, breaks—

TIENG-BIN: Eling, please. At least here, let's not talk about the others. I want to think only of you—as if you were my only wife.

ELING: That sounds so naughty.

TIENG-BIN: You're the one person from whom I want to have no secrets. This is my fantasy: that we will speak only words which are true.

ELING: Then can I tell you my secret? *(Pause)* I like it. That you come to me—that you look at me different from the other wives…I like it.

TIENG-BIN: Then look back at me. Don't avert your gaze, but look me straight in the eye. Watch me, watching you.
(They look into each other's eyes. Tieng-Bin and Eling fall into the bed, as lights fade. Lights come up on Siu-Yong's pavilion. She blows smoke from her opium pipe at her family altar.)

SIU-YONG *(Smoking on pipe; to altar)*: Papa… here's something special for you tonight. Mama, you too. A new blend made from Indian and Burmese poppies. It turns the worst insults of other wives into beautiful poetry. *(Pause)* I know I've neglected you in the days since Husband's return. But can you blame me? I prayed for normal, and what walks into my home? A bloody pagan. *(Ahn appears in the doorway to Siu-Yong's pavilion.)*
Here you are…come, come. *(Ahn crosses slowly. Siu-Yong puts her pipe down. She pulls Ahn down toward her)* Daughter—you've stopped visiting me these past few nights.

AHN: I've been getting up early. To spend time with Papa.

SIU-YONG: You are a good daughter. Headstrong, but I'll tell you a secret—I like that. Later in years, when you grow breasts and hips, you will learn to appear obedient. But you will always remember a time when your tongue was unbound. *(Pause)* I think it's wonderful that you spend time with Papa. In fact, that's why I called you here tonight. I think you should see him even more often.

AHN: Really?

SIU-YONG: Your Papa has invited a guest to visit, a white demon with skin the color of a day-old corpse. This man makes his living speaking nonsense.

AHN: Like a clown?

SIU-YONG: Only he doesn't know it. He is a clown who thinks he is a god. *(Pause)* When this clown comes, Second Auntie will join them, to try and win your father to her side. I want you there, also—to tell me everything she does.

AHN: When Papa's talking grown-up things, he always sends me away.

SIU-YONG: Just pretend you, too, wish to learn some of this rubbish. Your father will be so impressed that his daughter wishes to become a "modern woman." *(Ahn backs away from the altar)* Where are you going?

AHN: I…I don't want to lie to Papa.

SIU-YONG: You refuse your own mother? And the ghosts of all your ancestors? They're already very angry with you.

AHN: Why?

SIU-YONG: Because you complained about your foot-bindings at the banquet.

AHN: Do you think they like it when you smoke? I think you should stop.

SIU-YONG: I smoke for strength to carry out their wishes. But you—you would rather Second Auntie take over this house.

AHN: That's not true!

SIU-YONG: All right. Then you are the one who must stop her.

AHN: Why me?

SIU-YONG: Because you are a Golden Child. You said so yourself, remember? Well, if you're any sort of Golden Child at all, you should be able to hear the voices of the dead.

AHN: I don't know if I—maybe I don't want to hear them.

SIU-YONG: Ahn! To preserve the family is your first duty as a woman. If you fail, your children and grandchildren will abandon you in your old age; and when you die, your face will fade slowly from their memories, and your name will be forgotten.

AHN: Wait. I…I think I can hear them…

SIU-YONG: Of course you can.

AHN: They're saying…they're saying, "Don't be afraid…"

SIU-YONG: That sounds about right.

AHN: They're saying, "We will help you…make you brave…so you can save your whole family."

SIU-YONG: Good. You see, you are a special child. You're my daughter.

(Lights fade on scene. Lights come up on Tieng-Bin's altar. He burns offerings.)

TIENG-BIN *(To altar)*: Papa, Mama—the servants found some flowers today, which had somehow blossomed in winter. I thought you might appreciate them.

(Luan enters.)

LUAN: Husband!

TIENG-BIN: Second Wife!

LUAN: Excuse me—I didn't know you were here.

TIENG-BIN: It's hard to believe anything in this house escapes your notice.

LUAN: Oh, you flatter me. Do you mind? *(She sits beside him)*

TIENG-BIN: Actually, I was just—

LUAN: I usually come at dawn to tend your parents' altar. But last night, I couldn't sleep. Did you hear poor Ahn, crying in her room?

TIENG-BIN: Yes, I did.

LUAN: I understand First Wife recently tightened her foot-bindings.

TIENG-BIN: I thought as much.

LUAN: Husband, I am so grateful that you spoke out against foot-binding at the banquet the other night. But I must tell you, afterward, First Wife came to my pavilion hysterical, railing against everything you said.

TIENG-BIN: I don't expect First Wife to agree with me.

LUAN: As for myself, the idea of having a daughter—with beautiful, gigantic feet—it excites me. Do you want that…as much as I do?

TIENG-BIN: Actually, I do. To come home once more and see children—being turned into cripples—it makes me ashamed to be Chinese.

LUAN: I knew you would agree!

TIENG-BIN: Now, excuse me.

(Luan rises to leave; then:)

LUAN: Husband. Perhaps you would honor me later tonight?

(Luan exits.)

TIENG-BIN *(To altar)*: Papa, Mama—do I go to her? As obligation demands? Look at her—most men would jump at the opportunity. It's just that making love to Luan feels so much like doing business. And yet when it comes to foot-binding, Second Wife seems more willing to change than I. *(He calls to a servant)* At Tsun! *(To altar)* Why should we cling to a tradition that only passes down suffering from one generation to the next?

(Servant enters. To Servant:)

Fetch First Wife.

(Servant exits. To altar:)

Every day I let pass without acting, only makes the damage worse. Oh, I can hear you—and all the ancestors—crying from beyond, "Some things cannot be changed." But don't I have the right to try? I accept all responsibility, assume all consequences.

(Siu-Yong enters.)

SIU-YONG: Husband?

TIENG-BIN: It's an outdated, barbaric custom, and I won't allow it any longer.

SIU-YONG: What custom, Honored—?

(Ahn enters separately, eavesdrops from a concealed location.)

TIENG-BIN: From this day onward, foot-binding is forbidden in this home and the village beyond. I want you to remove Ahn's bindings.

SIU-YONG: One thing I have never doubted, Husband: that you are a good man.

TIENG-BIN: Let's not begin with the flattery.

SIU-YONG: Remove her bindings, and you will rescue her from pain. Isn't that your thinking?

TIENG-BIN: Do you have a point to make?

SIU-YONG: Some pains are necessary in the life of a woman. In order to spare her a lifetime of loneliness.

TIENG-BIN: All that is changing! The new government has already outlawed the practice.

SIU-YONG: Tell me, Husband—would you marry a woman with unbound feet? *(Pause)* For the sake of your daughter, answer truthfully. *(Pause)* Men. You dream of changing the world when you cannot even change yourselves. *(Pause)* Now—may I go while you consider the matter further?

(Siu-Yong starts to exit. Ahn reveals herself.)

AHN: Papa—I don't want to wear them.

(Pause.)

TIENG-BIN: Remove her bindings. Now!

SIU-YONG: Once the foot is half-trained, to release it back to its natural state—her agony will be multiplied twofold.

TIENG-BIN: If you won't obey, I will do it myself!

SIU-YONG: At least allow us to be alone.

(Mother and daughter step into Siu-Yong's pavilion. Tieng-Bin remains in the courtyard. Overlapping ghost voices fade up. Tieng-Bin hears the spirits of his ancestors.)

GHOST VOICES:

To betray your ancestors is to cut your own heart from your body.

The undutiful son reaps a harvest of famine and ruin.

Those who forsake the past enter the future without a tongue to speak or eyes to see.

His children and his children's children will be cursed to the seventh generation.

Only a fool turns his back on the wisdom of the ages.

All things worth saying have already been spoken. All things worth knowing have already been made known.

SIU-YONG *(To Ahn)*: Daughter—you do not know what a terrible gift is freedom.

(Siu-Yong unwinds strips of cloth from Ahn's feet. In the courtyard, Tieng-Bin listens to Ahn's cries of pain.)

TIENG-BIN *(To altar)*: Papa, Mama—forgive me.

(Lights fade on scene. Lights up on courtyard. Chinese folk instrumental music underscores a pantomime scene: Luan, Eling and Siu-Yong enter the courtyard to play mah-jongg. A servant brings in a calling card. Siu-Yong looks at it, the women scatter to their respective pavilions. Reverend Baines, a white man in his fifties, enters. Separately, Andrew enters with Ahn, who is again his mother, an old woman.)

AHN: Andrew—when reverend come, this first time ever I see my mother hide from any person. My father fight—bring change to our home. But when change come, come like fire. No one know—who will live, and who will be lost. *(Pause)* This, first foreigner, ever I see. White demon!

(Fade to black.)

ACT TWO

Light comes up on Ahn as a young girl, running and jumping toward the Main Hall. Then area lights come up on the Main Hall, revealing Tieng-Bin and Reverend Baines sitting over tea and pastries. Ahn enters and sits on the floor. Baines speaks brokenly with an English accent.

TIENG-BIN: Oolong.

BAINES: Oolong.

TIENG-BIN: Jasmine.

BAINES: Jasmine.

TIENG-BIN: Monkey-pick.

BAINES: Monkey-pick?

TIENG-BIN: Oolong and jasmine form the bulk of our export. But monkey-pick tea is the pride of the province.

BAINES: Why you call—?

TIENG-BIN: Because it's picked by monkeys, why else?

BAINES: I…no understand.

TIENG-BIN: The leaf grows so high that only monkeys can reach it. So we train them to harvest the plant for us. Something like among your people, I understand, there is a fungus that only pigs can dig up.

BAINES: Oh. Yes. Uh, uh—no can say in Chinese. But, not my people.

TIENG-BIN: No?

BAINES: No. I—English. Pigs—French.

TIENG-BIN: Oh, yes, yes. You're separated by a large channel of water.

BAINES: No large enough.

TIENG-BIN: We feel the same way about the Japanese. *(He toasts)* To understanding.

BAINES: Understanding. Yes, yes.

(They drink.)

Oh, oh—very good. Mmmm. Yummy. England, we cannot drink such very good tea.

TIENG-BIN: Well, you lack properly trained monkeys.

BAINES: Mon—? Oh, oh. Yes! I even learn—not to add the cream.

TIENG-BIN: Please! You might as well add cream to wine!

BAINES: Ha, ha! Tea such yummy; no need cream …and…? *(He points to the plate on the table)*

TIENG-BIN: Dan tat.

BAINES: Dan tat.

TIENG-BIN: I had a special batch made up, in honor of your visit.

BAINES: Ahn, please—you come…also cake eat? *(Ahn crosses to Baines, takes a pastry.)*

TIENG-BIN: Ahn! What do you say to the reverend?

BAINES: Please—not my house.

TIENG-BIN: You've been coming to visit us for many months.

BAINES: Not my cake.

TIENG-BIN: She must show you proper respect.

AHN *(To Baines)*: Thank you. "Yummy?" *(She pops it into her mouth)*

BAINES: Yes. Yummy. Very yummy.

(He does the same. She resumes her position on the floor.)

TIENG-BIN: I have to be honest with you, Reverend—

BAINES: Mmmm.

TIENG-BIN: I deal with a lot of white men in my business. Americans, Englishmen, Scots, Australians—

BAINES: No, no…Australians—we no think they white men.

TIENG-BIN: Well, we don't claim them as Asians, either.

BAINES: Again—understanding.

(They drink.)

TIENG-BIN: Most of the white men I meet—we do business, but deep inside, I know they look down on me.

BAINES: Mmmm.

TIENG-BIN: And yet—when I listen to them talk, watch the way they deal with each other, I must admit—there's something about them I envy.

BAINES: Envy?

TIENG-BIN: Jealousy.

BAINES: Ah, yes.

TIENG-BIN: All of us are away from our families, Reverend. Do you understand what I am saying?

BAINES: Many…temptation?

TIENG-BIN: Let's be frank. Chinese or Christian— men away from their families—are still men. Understand?

BAINES: Temptation. Men. Yes, I understand.

TIENG-BIN: But…there's a difference between myself and the Westerners. They seem… more able to forget, to pretend, even to fall in love with these other women, far from home. Whereas I—I can never forget…that my life, my duty, lies here.

BAINES: You want forget? I think, Jesus no help you here.

TIENG-BIN: No, no, it's—how can I put this? It's not that I want to forget my family, quite the opposite. But to be Chinese—means to feel a whole web of obligation—obligation?— dating back 5,000 years. I am afraid of dishonoring my ancestors, even the ones dead for centuries. All the time, I feel ghosts—sitting on my back, whispering in my ear— keeping me from living life as I see fit.

BAINES: I understand. Christian belief: we are all single person, is to say, all have own relation…

TIENG-BIN: Yes, I've seen this and it's remarkable. I'll tell you, Reverend—I once listened to some white sailors talking to each other. One said: "I can lift two hundred pounds." Another said: "I have an education." A third said: "In my life, I have saved a fortune." I was amazed.

BAINES: They brag. Not so nice.

TIENG-BIN: No, in a way, wonderful. That they feel so free to say who they are, without worrying that they're making someone else in the group feel small by their boasting.

BAINES: I see. In mission school, where learn me Chinese—they make—um, um—invent—new Chinese word, for new idea. Word is: individual.

TIENG-BIN: "Individual"?

BAINES: Meaning, each man, stand alone, choose own life.

TIENG-BIN: Yes, those sailors were individuals. Speaking the truth in their hearts, even if everyone around them disagreed!

BAINES: Okay. You try.

TIENG-BIN: What—what are you—?

BAINES: Like sailor. You try. You also, brag yourself.

TIENG-BIN: Reverend, c'mon. I mean, that sort of thing is interesting in theory, but—

BAINES: I start: my family, own many land—in beautiful country, name of Wales.

TIENG-BIN: Really? That's very impressive.

BAINES: No, no! I brag, you also. I go seminary, top of class! Now, you. You!

TIENG-BIN: I feel…okay, I run the largest Chinese-owned business in the Philippines. God, this is so—

BAINES: Good, good. God tell me: "Baines—you special man. Help China!"

TIENG-BIN: My peasants actually like me, because I try so hard to help them.

BAINES: Beautiful!

TIENG-BIN: This is incredibly self-indulgent.

BAINES: You like?

TIENG-BIN: Yes, I like.

BAINES: I am good good cook. Yummy!

TIENG-BIN: I employ good good cooks. Yummy! Yummy!

BAINES: I have daughter, most beautiful, all of world.

TIENG-BIN: One of my wives…is the most beautiful woman in the creation of any god. *(Pause)* What a luxury. To speak the truth— in my own home, of all places.
(Luan enters, dressed in Western clothing.)

LUAN: Just say the word, and I will disappear!

TIENG-BIN: Second Wife!

BAINES: Mrs. Eng—yummy!

LUAN: You are too kind, Reverend. You spoil a Chinese woman.

TIENG-BIN: You look so—

LUAN: Atrocious—

TIENG-BIN: —Exotic…

LUAN: I mean, who do I think I am?

TIENG-BIN: The mysterious Occidental.

BAINES: Very modern.

LUAN: I sent away for it about the time you started visiting us, Reverend.

BAINES: Me? Oh, oh…!

LUAN: You got us all very curious about Western ways.

TIENG-BIN: Did someone help you put that on?

LUAN: Yes, Cheng-Ming. Stupid girl. There're all sorts of strange support items—

BAINES: Oh?

LUAN: —for parts of the body that really should be able to support themselves.

BAINES: Please! Not for me hear, no, no!

LUAN: I'm sorry, was I being…immodest?

TIENG-BIN: From behind, you could be a typical white demon—oh, excuse me, Reverend.

BAINES: White demon—me—white demon.

LUAN: But I could never be as graceful as those Western women. To get into those shoes— did you realize, they actually walk on their toes?

BAINES: Chinese woman—no can?

LUAN *(To Baines)*: Well, you see, most of us lost our toes years ago…

BAINES: Oh…I see…

LUAN: Maybe I could give my Western shoes to Ahn, for when she's older.

TIENG-BIN: Second Wife! What a generous thought. *(To Ahn)* Ahn, what do you think of your auntie?

LUAN: I know what she'll say—I'm a freak.

BAINES: You look…like princess…

LUAN: What do *you* think, Husband?

TIENG-BIN: I'm amazed that you can transform yourself…into an entirely different person. *(Pause.)*

LUAN: Reverend, has Husband taken care of your tea?

BAINES: Oh, yes, yes…

LUAN: And the dan tat?

BAINES: …so much, I eat like cow…

LUAN: You mean pig?

BAINES: Huh?

LUAN: Pig…

BAINES: Oh, yes, pig, pig—my Chinese…

LUAN: Your Chinese is excellent.

AHN: Auntie, may I have the shoes? Although I do not deserve them.

LUAN *(To Baines)*: Listen to her. It's so encouraging to see even Ahn influenced by your example. *(To Ahn)* Yes, you may have them. *(To Tieng-Bin)* Your son, Yung-Bin, has asked for a Western suit.

AHN: Can I see them—now?

LUAN *(To Baines)*: So, Reverend, what lessons do you have for us today?

BAINES: Oh! Well…

AHN: I told the servants your story about the three wise men.

BAINES: My—my—? Ah, good!

TIENG-BIN: Amazing, isn't it? That her mind is so unfettered by the past.

LUAN: I am so fortunate Husband allows me to join you both. He is the most enlightened, most virtuous man in all of Fukien—no, in all of China.

TIENG-BIN: You praise me too much.

LUAN: Then let anyone in this house prove me wrong!

BAINES: He is great man—great man…

LUAN: This is what I like—honest talk! By thinking as he thinks—that's the Western way—the way of the future.

AHN: Second Auntie—

LUAN: The other wives, they don't feel so differently—

AHN: Second Auntie—

LUAN: Don't let the fact that they've never even said "hi" in eight months give you any other impression.

AHN: Second Auntie!

LUAN: What do you want!

AHN: I want my shoes!

TIENG-BIN: Ahn!

LUAN: Husband, will you please tell this girl selfishness is unworthy of your home? *(To Baines)* And it's not very Christian either, is it, Reverend?

BAINES: My Chinese…very bad…

LUAN: Well. I will forgo my lesson with the Reverend.

AHN *(To Luan)*: You said I could have them.

TIENG-BIN: Luan, where are the shoes?

LUAN: They're in my pavilion. Please allow me to—

TIENG-BIN: No! I'll go. That way, you stay here, continue your lesson with the Reverend, and Ahn will get her shoes, too.

LUAN: I really don't mind—

TIENG-BIN: I'll settle this…as always. *(To Ahn)* Thank your auntie for her generous gift.

AHN: Thank you, Second Auntie.

TIENG-BIN: Excuse us, Reverend.
(Tieng-Bin exits.)

AHN: Precious Auntie, I'm sorry your feet are so dead and rotten.
(Ahn exits.)

LUAN: Do you have enough tea?

BAINES: Oh, yes…yes…

LUAN: Here, let me warm your cup—

BAINES: Thank you, so kind—

LUAN: You know, a traditional Chinese husband would never leave his wife alone with a strange man.

BAINES: I…strange?

LUAN: The strangest. You're a foreigner. For me to be sitting here, pouring tea for you, by Chinese standards—it is absolutely indecent.

BAINES: Ha, ha, ha…I no understand.

LUAN *(Offers a plate)*: Waffle? *(Baines declines)* He loves that daughter, favors her…of course, he has no choice, she's so demanding.

BAINES: Oh, Ahn! Yes, beautiful girl…

LUAN: Not by Chinese standards. It's her inner strength that impresses me. That she's managed to remain so brave with a mother who is an opium eater. *(Pause)* Bean cake?

BAINES: Opium? You say, opium? Drug? *(He mimes smoking a pipe)*

LUAN: Oh, no—I shouldn't have even opened my—

BAINES: Ahn's mama? Opium? Mr. Eng, does he—?

LUAN: My only interest is in helping First Wife recover...the drug makes her do things she doesn't mean—to plot against myself, my Husband...you...

BAINES: Me? First Wife plot against *me*?

LUAN: But if she were not a drug addict, I know—she would never force her daughter to spy against you!

BAINES: Please, slow. Ahn—is spy? How you know?

LUAN: The servants tell me everything.

BAINES: If this true. If Ahn is spy—

LUAN (*Starts to speak as if to a child*): No—no get excited.

BAINES: Must tell Mr. Eng!

LUAN: No—please, instead, kill me!

BAINES: "Kill you"? What in devil are you—?

LUAN: Listen. If I tell Husband, he will not believe. Will become angry—at me, and you, also.

BAINES: So...no one tell him? But—

LUAN: No. Someone will tell him.

BAINES: Who?

LUAN: Third Wife—I told her Ahn is spy. She says, "I don't want to hear!" But—patience, one day, she will tell him...

BAINES: How—how you—?

LUAN: She will tell Husband because she wants to gain his favor.

BAINES: Why you tell me...all this thing?

LUAN: Reverend—when Chinese men convert to Christianity, what becomes of their many wives?

BAINES: Best idea: man choose, one woman be only true wife.

LUAN: And the rest of them?

BAINES: Can still live in house...but like—sisters, like—

LUAN: And the Christian man should have a Christian wife, yes?

BAINES: Yes, yes—this best thing.

LUAN: Well, then—will you be my advocate?

BAINES: "Advocate"?

LUAN: You understand. I think a lot more than you let on. I think we two can help each other—once you see how I can be of use to you in your work.

BAINES: You...help me?

LUAN: Husband says you have made few converts in many months. I can help you spread the word of Jesus—you see to it that I gain my rightful place.

BAINES: Yes?

LUAN: Reverend—the Chinese are a practical people. Let me arrange a great feast—for the entire village—at which the lord of the Great House pledges his allegiance to your God. You will be shocked how quickly the peasants rush to flatter my Husband by following in his footsteps. Like the good shepherd leading his flock. (*Pause*) And one more thing: when you preach, never ever say anything good about yourself—the less boastful you sound, the more you'll impress them. (*Pause*) Oh! Your cup is cold. I am the most terrible hostess this side of Australia. (*Luan pours tea*)

BAINES: You...you make Tieng-Bin...to leave room, no? So you and me...we talk, no? You make happen, no?

LUAN: Don't be ridiculous, Reverend. This is China. I nothing but woman and slave. (*Tieng-Bin enters with Ahn, the latter in too-large high-heeled pumps.*) Oh—look at her!

AHN: These are play shoes! They're too silly to wear in real life!

TIENG-BIN: But you don't seem so eager to take them off, do you?

AHN: They make me tall!—when I'm not falling over. Are you sure you do not want them, Auntie?

LUAN: I have told you many times, I cannot wear them.

AHN: Sorry. I forgot. (*Tieng-Bin crosses to Baines.*)

TIENG-BIN: Forgive me, Reverend, for leaving you—

BAINES: No—no—

TIENG-BIN: But I have absolute confidence in the ability of Second Wife—

LUAN: Oh, please—

TIENG-BIN: —to keep things interesting.

LUAN: Our time together must have exposed me as a woman of very poor character. *(Pause)* Isn't that so, Reverend?
(Pause.)

BAINES: Your wife—she teach me so much, way of your people.

LUAN: The reverend flatters me—he must have Chinese blood. The truth is, we had a very significant encounter. Now, if you will both excuse me.
(Luan exits. Ahn practices walking with the heels.)

TIENG-BIN: I settle more disputes here each day than at work during the height of the trading season. See how it is, Reverend? With such duties, how can I possibly feel like an individual?

BAINES: Christian belief: each man, individual. But also, may I?

TIENG-BIN: Please, please.

BAINES: Prophet Paul say: each individual man have only one individual wife.

TIENG-BIN: Yes, I know that's the way of your people.

BAINES: He say, your body—body of God. No join body of God with dirty thing.

TIENG-BIN: Here in China, we say, whites are simply not man enough to handle more than one woman at a time.

BAINES: What you think?

TIENG-BIN: Reverend, there were times in Manila when I would see couples strolling arm in arm—thinking only of one another. And I would wonder…what it would be like to live a simpler life. *(Pause)* One wife? You whisper the idea as if it would offend me. When the truth is, Reverend, that it's a thought so precious, I whisper it, too.

BAINES: So, agree? One wife—who also love Jesus.

TIENG-BIN: It's not that simple. You haven't the faintest notion—

BAINES: This good, natural way of God.

TIENG-BIN: No, it's wrong; it's shameful; it's the way of destruction.

BAINES: Who say this?

TIENG-BIN: The ghosts at the altar. "The righteous man holds his First Wife forever in highest honor." "The position of wives is fixed, like the bodies of the heavens."

BAINES: This—evil voice.

TIENG-BIN: My parents, my ancestors? Reverend, I couldn't even remove Ahn's foot-bindings without hearing their voices. How could I take only one wife?

BAINES: Other missionary—they tell me about you.

TIENG-BIN: What do you mean?

BAINES: Tell me, "Master Eng—not like other lords. Others, when land fail, peasant starve, they shut their gate." Correct?

TIENG-BIN: It's none of my business what the other landowners—

BAINES: Please. Brag yourself. *(Pause)* You go Philippine, make money, save village. Other lords—they do this?

TIENG-BIN: No, not usually.

BAINES: Your own father—he do this?

TIENG-BIN: My father always tried to do the best he could.

BAINES: Before I come, already you not like other lords, not like father. Already you find new way. Must not fear to speak truth you know in your soul.
(Tieng-Bin moves toward his family altar. Lights slowly dim.)

TIENG-BIN: I am an individual.

BAINES: Good. Bible say, truth shall set you free.

TIENG-BIN: And I live in a new time, much different from that of my fathers.

BAINES: Yes, must be born again.

TIENG-BIN: I should be able to make my own way, live my own life, choose the woman I love.

BAINES: Prophet Paul say, "All I do mean nothing—if I no have love."

TIENG-BIN: To act out of love…to follow only the law of my own heart…

BAINES: Now, dead—no more power over you.

TIENG-BIN: Yes. The dead are just earth and dust and bones. *(He kneels before the altar)* Papa, Mama—you gave me life. But now I am a man. And you…You are dead.
(Stage lights dim to separate spotlights on Baines and Ahn who stand apart.)

BAINES *(British accent, perfect English)*: "When I was a child, I spoke as a child, I thought as a child. But when I became a man, I put away childish things. For now we see as through a glass, darkly; but then shall we see face-to-face. And now abideth faith, hope, love, these three; but the greatest of these is love." *(Lights cross-fade to Eling's pavilion. She lies in bed, nursing a swollen belly. Tieng-Bin enters, carrying a phonograph record.)*

TIENG-BIN: Italy can never be ignored, but the future—it comes from America.

ELING: What have you got there?

(He unwraps a new 78, slips it onto the phonograph.)

TIENG-BIN: This is a different kind of opera. Where men and women dance together dreaming they are anyone they wish to be. *(He places the needle on the record. Scratchy recording of American dance music from the turn of the century.)* May I have this dance? *(He takes her hands)* In the Philippines—I took lessons.

ELING: You must've been even lonelier than I thought.

TIENG-BIN: Come. I lead. You just follow. It's the way Western men show domination over their women. *(They dance together.)*

ELING: I'll bet they didn't invent these steps for big, fat, pregnant cows with bound feet.

TIENG-BIN: Eling—the few extra inches are very erotic.

ELING: I'm swollen in places I never even knew existed. You wouldn't be like other lords, would you, and take a new wife, one who's slim and beautiful?

TIENG-BIN: Listen to the music. And try to imagine another world—better than this one. Where you…are my only wife.

ELING: You really held your teacher this close?

TIENG-BIN: Eling…

ELING: All right. My only Husband, shall we—shall we take my child up to the hills for a picnic this week?

TIENG-BIN: *Our* child. That sounds like an excellent idea.

ELING: Like a peasant family, but with money. Afterwards, we can all come here, to the American opera house.

TIENG-BIN: Except, our lives aren't only about our child. We're also two adults in love.

ELING: That's why we got married in the first place, right?

TIENG-BIN: And why we have no need—in fact, it would be impossible, illegal—for either of us to marry anyone else. *(Pause)* Eling—I think we can actually live such a life.

ELING: How? I think we would have to die and be reborn as new people.

TIENG-BIN: That's exactly right. Do you know what Reverend Baines and I have been discussing?

ELING: I'm not sure I—

TIENG-BIN: You. In a sense. He says I can pull down the family altars, live as though I had only one wife, even take you with me back to the Philippines. *(Eling pulls away front him)* Don't you like the idea? Can't you see, it's the best thing for you?

ELING: You want me to abandon my parents? Let their spirits wander alone for eternity? And if I went away with you, First Wife would lose such face. Is that what's best for us? To forget about others, and think only about ourselves?

TIENG-BIN: I thought you wanted to be modern.

ELING: I do. But does that mean I can no longer be Chinese?

(The record ends. Tieng-Bin removes the needle.)

TIENG-BIN: You know why this is so hard for you to understand? Because you've never even once attended Reverend Baines's lessons.

ELING: You said I didn't have to.

TIENG-BIN: But I—I thought you'd have wanted to come. Ahn took to the new teachings immediately.

ELING: So I hear.

TIENG-BIN: And Second Wife—

ELING: Don't start telling me about Luan.

TIENG-BIN: No, I really think even she's changing, becoming more generous—

ELING: Husband, how can you believe…?

TIENG-BIN: What? *(Pause)* Eling?

ELING: Luan runs around behind your back telling anyone who'll listen that Ahn is only pretending to be interested in your religion so she can spy for First Wife.

(Tieng-Bin stares at Eling.)

TIENG-BIN: Ahn…has been lying to me? Ahn? First Wife put her up to this?

ELING: I'm sorry, Husband, but you're the only one who believes in this new religion. For the rest of us, nothing has changed.

TIENG-BIN: And you—you kept this hidden from me—for how long?

ELING: I didn't know what to—! It was none of my business. Second Wife should have told you herself.

TIENG-BIN: This isn't about Luan. You shouldn't have left me in the dark. I'll get to the bottom of this—

ELING: No! Please don't tell First Wife you heard this from me.

TIENG-BIN: This way of life—it brings out the worst in us all.

(Tieng-Bin exits.)

ELING: Husband! Please! Don't! *(To altar)* Papa, Mama—I only tried to tell the truth.

(Lights fade on Eling's pavilion, and come up on Siu-Yong's pavilion, revealing Ahn preparing opium for her mother's pipe. Siu-Yong lies on the floor in a drug-induced fog.)

TIENG-BIN *(Offstage)*: First Wife—I am entering your pavilion!

(Siu-Yong rises unsteadily to her feet.)

SIU-YONG *(To Ahn)*: Quickly—clear the air!

(Ahn scrambles to stash the drug paraphernalia, while Siu-Yong tries absurdly to blow the smoke clear. Tieng-Bin enters, causing Ahn to freeze in her tracks.)

Oh, Honored Husband. Please excuse the untidy state of my room. Had you given me proper notice, I would've had time to prepare refreshments.

TIENG-BIN: Ahn—now—out!

AHN: But…

TIENG-BIN: Now! *(Ahn moves toward the door, trying to conceal the opium pipe)* Ahn! *(Tieng-Bin snatches the pipe from her)*

(Ahn exits from the pavilion, but remains crouched outside in the shadows, listening.)

Opium, First Wife?

SIU-YONG: Really? Where?

TIENG-BIN: How can you even ask? When I'm holding the pipe in my hand, the air smelling like shit?

SIU-YONG: Not so hard. A good wife learns to disregard any number of facts. "See no evil, smell no evil."

TIENG-BIN: How could I have been home all this time and not even noticed?

SIU-YONG: A Husband is always the last to know. Servants are always the first, by the way.

TIENG-BIN: Have you been sending Ahn to spy on my lessons with Reverend Baines?

SIU-YONG: Who told you such a thing?

TIENG-BIN: That's not important.

SIU-YONG: How dare you—do you actually imagine I would ask our daughter to spy against her own father?

TIENG-BIN: Why don't we call Ahn back? And put the question to her directly?

SIU-YONG: On the other hand, it depends on your definition of a "spy."

TIENG-BIN: I see.

SIU-YONG: She was an innocent pawn.

TIENG-BIN: This is my home! You're not going to undermine my authority. We're going to have honest dealing here, is that clear?

SIU-YONG: What is this mania for honesty?

TIENG-BIN: Is everything a joke with you? Is nothing important?

SIU-YONG: Tieng-Bin! Don't leave me like this. We were promised to each other before we were born. *(Pause)* What is family anyway, but a loose collection of people with nothing in common but blood? Does blood cause all people to think alike? To love, or even like, one another? Of course not! If we wandered wherever our emotions might take us, we would all have murdered each other ages ago. That is why blood is not sufficient for order. Blood must be reinforced—by discipline. And your precious honesty is the mortal enemy of discipline. Confucius said: "In order to rule the nation, a man must first rule himself." So rule yourself! Tell me you haven't seen or heard anything tonight which would soil the honor of our family— and then have the discipline to believe your own words.

(She lays back on her pillows) Now—how about those refreshments?

TIENG-BIN: Siu-Yong, this woman you've become, I don't even know her.

SIU-YONG: If your answer is "no," then excuse me, I have my prayers to say before bed.

TIENG-BIN: You are my wife!

SIU-YONG: And I'm trying to behave like one.

TIENG-BIN: This home is going to be a model of change! No matter what you or your damn parents say.

SIU-YONG: I have never stood in the way of change. But tell me, Honored Husband, how much change can people endure?

TIENG-BIN: And this life is better? You shoving poison into your body? Second Wife telling secrets behind your back?

SIU-YONG: Second Wife? She said I'd made Ahn a spy? And you believed her?

(Ahn leaves from outside the pavilion and exits the stage.)

(To altar) Mama, Papa—do something.

TIENG-BIN: There you go again—worshipping your parents.

SIU-YONG: Yes, at least I pray to someone I know personally.

TIENG-BIN: Denounce them—or I'll force you to!

SIU-YONG: No! Papa, Mama—

TIENG-BIN: I said, stop it!

(Tieng-Bin throws Siu-Yong away from the altar.)

SIU-YONG: You—you order me around? Listen to yourself—scratch the surface, and you're still a traditional man. Deep inside, you want a traditional wife. You want me to remain as I am, admit it!

(Tieng-Bin positions himself between Siu-Yong and the altar.)

TIENG-BIN: I'm so traditional. All right—have it your way. *(He grabs the picture of Siu-Yong's parents)* What is it—that a traditional man does? Does he lose his temper? Does he order his wife around? Then punish her? Break her precious toys?

SIU-YONG: No! Don't!

(He smashes the picture. Siu-Yong screams.)

TIENG-BIN: When she disobeys him? When she blows smoke in the faces of his children? Is this the sort of thing he does?

(He leaves the picture in a heap on the ground and stands back.)

I have made my decision. Or you've made it for me. I will be baptized. And all the family altars will come down at once. *(Pause)* The servants will search for any more of the drug you may have hidden. Then—you'll start attending Pastor Baines's lessons. We all need a fresh start, to begin a new life.

(Siu-Yong remains on the floor. Tieng-Bin exits. Siu-Yong crawls to the rubble of her parents' portrait. She cradles it in her arms.)

SIU-YONG *(To portrait)*: Papa, Mama—what terrible things did you do, that my life should go so wrong?

(Lights fade on Siu-Yong's pavilion and come up on Luan's. Luan opens her eyes and sees Ahn looking down on her. She is startled.)

LUAN: Huh? Ahn, you scared me! Idiot—have you added sleepwalking to your list of defects?

AHN: I am a Golden Child.

LUAN: "Golden Child, Golden Child."

AHN: And for your schemes against First Wife, you must now eat bitter.

LUAN: You know what Westerners say is golden? Silence. Now give me that lantern.

(Ahn snatches the lantern up before Luan can reach it.)

AHN: Your grandmother, I hear her voice. And she says: "Unworthy granddaughter, how dare you betray your sacred duties to those who gave you life."

LUAN: This is the height of—

(Luan reaches for the lantern. Ahn slaps her face.)

AHN: "Wicked granddaughter—" *(Ahn slaps her again)* "You can't spit in the face of the dead without eating the bitter fruit."

LUAN: Now give me that—

(Ahn pushes her down to the floor.)

AHN: "How dare you strike your grandmother."

LUAN: You're…not my…

AHN: "Hear our voices. We starve because you do not feed us."

LUAN: Ah Ying!

AHN: "You scheme with the foreigners to turn our family against us."

LUAN: Isn't anyone on duty here?

AHN: "As you abandoned your ancestors, so your children will abandon you after your death."

LUAN: Yung-Bin, Yung-Bin would never—

AHN: "Your son will grow ashamed of you, and future generations will not even remember your name."

LUAN: Yung-Bin will rule this family I will live to see the day.

AHN: "No, your son will curse the day you told Husband that First Wife sent a spy against him—"

LUAN: What?

AHN: "For on that day, his fortune—"

LUAN: Wait one second. I didn't.

AHN: "His fortune was lost; his anchor tether to the shore was—"

LUAN: If someone told Husband about your little assignment, it certainly wasn't me. *(Pause)* What kind of ghosts get their facts wrong, huh?

AHN: You lie—you always lie.

LUAN: I'll tell you what kind—false ghosts—who speak from the mouth of a peasant girl, whose skin reeks of opium, who calls herself a Golden Child while, deep inside, even she knows she's an ugly little liar. *(She snatches the light away from Ahn)* Ghosts have no more power over me. I'm a Christian now! So—would you like to hear *me* tell the future? I'm the only one who's been right up to this point. *(Draws back to hit Ahn, ends up patting her on the cheek, instead)* Jesus saves. He will save me and destroy your mother. He will take our miserable lives, all the injustice within these walls, and make everything born again. *(Pause)* Thank you for letting me know what happened tonight. It won't be long now before I'm First Wife—in fact, if not in name. Take my advice, Ahn—join us, forget your mother—and save yourself. Or else be washed away like the peasants in the flood.

(Ahn exits. Lights fade on Luan's pavilion. Reverend Baines enters and crosses to baptism font.)

BAINES: Resident of city of Eng…so good, see so many of you gather today, for great feast, wondrous fine festivity! One hundred thou-

sand thanks to lord of the great house, Master Eng! Who give unworthy self great fortune, meet all you honorable friends. *(Pause)* I—idiot man. My mother should have drown me in well before I learn to speak. Anyone say I smart, they no have brain. But Master Eng teach me so much, China way. Now, if any you visit ugly mission, hear my bad Chinese, I hope perhaps you find I am…tiny little bit not so stupid. *(Pause)* Now—wondrous miracle: Master Eng family—choose here, today—receive baptism, make holy water, swallow Jesus body fluid.

(Split scene: As Baines administers the sacrament of baptism, lights come up on Siu-Yong in her pavilion with Ahn. Siu-Yong produces three balls of opium hidden in her altar.)

I call Eng Tieng-Bin.

(Tieng-Bin enters, in Western suit.)

"Eng Tieng-Bin, you desire, be baptized?"

TIENG-BIN: "I do, by the grace of God."

BAINES: "You renounce Satan?"

TIENG-BIN: "I renounce Satan and all the spiritual forces of wickedness that rebel against God."

BAINES: "You renounce sin?"

TIENG-BIN: "I renounce all sinful desires that draw me from the love of God."

BAINES: "Eng Tieng-Bin, you are seal by holy spirit baptism, mark as Christ's own, forever."

(Baines makes sign of the cross on Tieng-Bin's forehead and feeds him wafer and wine.)

SIU-YONG *(To Ahn)*: "The servants will search for your opium." So pathetic. Who does your father think the servants work for? To hand me over to the missionary butchers—you must learn to put your foot down, Daughter. Such behavior is unacceptable, we mustn't allow it.

AHN: Mama…don't eat that.

SIU-YONG: Duty calls.

(Siu-Yong puts the first ball into her mouth, swallows it.)

BAINES: I call Eng Luan, receive the baptism. "Eng Luan, you desire, be baptized?"

LUAN: "I do, by the grace of God."

BAINES: "You renounce evil?"

LUAN: "I renounce the evil powers of this world which corrupt and destroy the creatures of God."

(Baines makes sign of cross on Luan's forehead and feeds her wafer and wine.)

BAINES: "Eng Luan, you are seal by Holy Spirit baptism, mark as Christ's own, forever."

SIU-YONG *(To Ahn)*: You will smile at the reverend, perhaps even kiss the Christian idol—but I know you will also worship and provide for me—in secret, where all the important things in this world happen.

(Siu-Yong eats the second ball of opium.)

BAINES: I call Eng Eling, receive the baptism. "Eng Eling, you desire, be baptized?"

ELING: "I do."

BAINES: "You believe in Jesus Christ, accept him as savior?"

ELING: "I do."

(Baines makes sign of cross on Eling's forehead and feeds her wafer and wine.)

BAINES: "Eng Eling, you are seal by Holy Spirit baptism, mark as Christ's own, forever. Amen."

(Baines blesses them.)

SIU-YONG: And you will succeed because you know the central lesson of life: that humility is power. And death is the ultimate humility.

(Siu-Yong eats the third ball.)

BAINES: "We accept you into house of God. Amen."

BAINES, TIENG-BIN, LUAN AND ELING: "Amen."

(Baines, Eling, Tieng-Bin and Luan exit.)

SIU-YONG: Now come here. And let me sing you to sleep.

(Siu-Yong takes Ahn in her arms, and rocks her while singing a lullaby:)

A brother and sister

As drought hit far and wide

They saw their parents starving

As crops around them died

These dutiful sweet children

Knew just what to do

From pieces of their own flesh

Made Mom and Dad a stew

To serve your parents

Is life's most precious goal

And if you're very lucky

They'll one day eat you whole

With a hi diddle dee

The soup gets sister's nose

And a ho ho ho…

(Siu-Yong loses consciousness.)

AHN: Ma? Ma?

(Ahn runs offstage. Fade to black.

Lights up on Eling's pavilion. Christian hymns are playing on her phonograph. She kneels before her family altar, her parents' portrait now replaced by a crucifix. Her belly is large in the final stages of pregnancy.)

ELING: "The lord is my shepherd, I shall not want." *(To altar)* Papa, Mama—I have to do this for my Husband. He saved not only me, but all your children, from poverty and hunger. *(Pause)* "He leadeth me beside the still waters…" *(Pause)* But if you see First Wife up there—

(Siu-Yong's voice is heard over the house speakers.)

SIU-YONG'S VOICE: Three tips for a well-ordered household.

ELING: Tell her, please—

SIU-YONG'S VOICE: One, the less you know about your relatives, the easier it is to love them.

ELING: Don't be angry at me, I didn't mean to tell him—

SIU-YONG'S VOICE: Two, never betray weakness in the home, it only encourages them.

ELING: I just couldn't let Husband fool himself like that.

SIU-YONG'S VOICE: And three, if, as happens in even the best families, a relative should cause your death—

ELING: Ask her to forgive me. As her sister? Bound by true affection?

SIU-YONG'S VOICE: —don't forget to return to take your revenge.

(Siu-Yong bursts into Eling's pavilion. She wears ghost robes. Hymns cross fade to Chinese opera music.)

ELING: Older Sister! I—

SIU-YONG: You learned your lessons in womanhood a little too well, I'm afraid.

ELING: No, I didn't learn a thing. I'm a fool, simple-minded, an idiot—

SIU-YONG: Quiet! You have some nerve, complimenting yourself at a time like this.

ELING: But—

SIU-YONG: Once, I actually believed you were stupid.

ELING: But I am! I must be the stupidest wife in all China!

SIU-YONG: Or the most clever. The other ghosts couldn't wait to reveal that it was you who betrayed me to Husband. It seems I grossly underestimated you.

ELING: No, I'm a good person, a humble servant, a dutiful daughter—

SIU-YONG: Dutiful?—Oh, please.

ELING: What do you know?

SIU-YONG: You forget—I'm dead. I've seen your parents.

ELING: No, you don't know them—

SIU-YONG: Now that you have stopped providing for them—

ELING: My brothers and sisters, they must be—

SIU-YONG: What can they do but sell themselves as slaves?

ELING: Slaves?

SIU-YONG: Now they work for your former neighbors, the Wongs.

ELING: Not the Wongs! The Wongs were evil people! What are they doing up there? They should be sent to hell!

SIU-YONG: Maybe that's true, but *they* have dutiful children. How many times do I have to tell you: life is not personal!

(Eling runs for the door.)

ELING: I'll call Reverend Baines—he'll send you away.

SIU-YONG: With his Chinese? I wouldn't even be able to understand his exorcism. No, the only people who can protect you from a ghost are your ancestors.

ELING: I'll pray for them. I'll burn offerings, somehow…

SIU-YONG: What if Husband should find out? He'd be so disappointed. In his old-fashioned wife.

ELING: I have to be a modern person. Just like Husband. And Second Wife. And even Ahn.

SIU-YONG: Maybe *they* are. But you will never be. *(Pause)* Some people were not created for

change. Their minds are not large enough, their souls insufficiently ruthless. These are the people left behind, their names forgotten, as time rolls on. I should know. Look into my eyes—and see yourself.

(Eling falls to her knees before the crucifix and flings it aside. She lights the candle for burning offerings. Siu-Yong moves behind Eling.)

ELING *(To altar)*: Papa, Mama, I don't know what to do.

SIU-YONG: You know you're not fit to live in Husband's new world.

ELING: I can't let you starve, but I can't disobey my Husband either.

SIU-YONG: He'll take you to the Philippines; you won't know how to live there—with each passing day, he'll grow more ashamed of you.

ELING: No, I can't let that happen.

SIU-YONG: You are not the woman he thinks you are.

ELING: Maybe I'm not. But I love him.

SIU-YONG: Love! You don't know the meaning of love! You're grateful, that is all.

ELING: Sometimes, I wish I'd never even come to this house!

SIU-YONG: Then perhaps it is time for you to leave.

(Siu-Yong waves her ghost sleeves. Eling cries out as the pains of labor begin.)

ELING: All these demands—how can I live up to them?

SIU-YONG: There is a way. To serve your parents, to serve your Husband.

ELING: How? Please, Older Sister—help me.

SIU-YONG: Come with me. You are needed elsewhere—with your parents.

(Siu-Yong shakes sleeves. Eling feels another contraction.)

ELING: But…what about my baby?

SIU-YONG: Your old thinking will only spoil his future.

(Siu-Yong leads Eling to the bed.)

ELING: Yes, you're right. It's time to prove…that I can sacrifice for others. This is the best thing for Husband.

SIU-YONG: It is best for your Husband, it is best for your parents, it is best for your child.

And to a good Chinese woman, what else could possibly matter?

(Siu-Yong shakes sleeves. Eling screams in labor. Ahn enters, runs to Eling.)

AHN *(Calling offstage)*: Papa!

(Tieng-Bin, Baines and Luan enter, and cross to Eling's bed. Hidden, Eling rolls off the back of the bed, and crosses to Siu-Yong. Siu-Yong places ghost robes on Eling and leads her into the spirit world. Baines, Luan and Ahn exit, leaving Tieng-Bin alone in Eling's pavilion.)

TIENG-BIN: Eling? Eling. *(Tieng-Bin collapses at Eling's altar. He burns offerings with increasing speed and recklessness)* How can I make you understand that I did it all for you? You must take everything now—everything with you—all my ideals, my memories of the world, my experience with far-off peoples—all the rooms I've filled to bursting with empty words—words of change, of progress—all the rooms where I had hidden our future. *(Eling's pavilion is catching on fire)* Papa, Mama—this is how you punish a disobedient son? Take from me the wife I love, even the wife I respect, leaving me with the one for whom I feel... nothing. I don't give a damn anymore about the living or the dead. Yes, by embracing the West, I have finally become... an individual.

(Ahn enters.)

AHN: All right, Papa. That's enough. Come out before you set the whole pavilion on fire.

TIENG-BIN: I can do whatever I want. Leave me alone!

AHN: "God will not test us beyond what we can bear."

TIENG-BIN: What kind of nonsense are you—?

AHN: I listened to the words of the preacher, remember? Now, rise up and walk!

TIENG-BIN: You can't talk that way to me—you are only my daughter!

AHN: That is the old way. The Bible says—

TIENG-BIN: I don't want to hear another word about this God.

AHN: "All things work together for good—"

TIENG-BIN: Get out!

AHN: "—for those that love the Lord."

TIENG-BIN: Shut your mouth! *(Tieng-Bin strikes Ahn, then pulls away, shocked. She stands her ground)* Ahn—I didn't mean to—

AHN: Papa—you can hit me, but you can't make me go away. I'm not a little girl anymore.

TIENG-BIN: I should've listened to your mother.

AHN: No—she was wrong, Papa. *(Pause)* Mama believed in our ancestors; she did everything for them. But when she called on them for help, there was nothing they could do. I watched her eat opium and die. So I'm not going to believe in them anymore. I can't end up like her. I'm going to follow this new God, the one you brought into our home. Papa, we must all be born again.

TIENG-BIN: What have I done to you all?

(She leads him out of the pavilion.)

AHN: You've thought enough for one life. It's time to let your children take over. So get up. The servants will be coming. I don't care how badly you feel; we don't try to kill ourselves in front of the help.

(Luan enters.)

LUAN: Husband, such a tragedy! We must say a prayer for Eling and the child that was lost.

TIENG-BIN: Will you leave us, Second Wife?

LUAN: Oh, slip of the tongue—my only Husband.

TIENG-BIN: Will you leave us alone...my only wife?

LUAN: Whatever you desire. *(Calling off)* Ah Ying! Ah Ying!

(Luan exits.)

TIENG-BIN: I don't know...how to go on from here.

AHN: You must go back to the Philippines. If the business fails, who cares what God we worship?

TIENG-BIN: Daughter—someday, when you are all grown, you will look back and hate me—for what I did to your mother.

AHN: Impossible, Papa. When my children ask about our family, I'll tell great stories about you—how you made us all born again. But First Wife, I will not—no, I swear, I will not even remember her name.

(Ahn begins to cry.)

TIENG-BIN: Ahn, your mother was from another time, that's all. I will always honor her name.

AHN: And I will always be grateful to you, Papa—even when I am old, even after I die.

TIENG-BIN: How can you possibly know such things?

AHN: Because I am a Golden Child.

(Lights and set transform. Tieng-Bin becomes Andrew; Ahn becomes an old woman again.)

When season change, we leave forever, home of our ancestor. Your grandfather, after this, he does not live so long. Few years later, Second Wife send me far away, to new land, call "America."

ANDREW: You see? Why I don't want to become a parent? Your father tried so hard, but he only brought tragedy to himself and everyone around him.

AHN: No. He suffer to bring family into future. Where better life, I am able to live. I first girl in family go school, choose own husband—and all the time, worship Jesus.

ANDREW: So—whenever you opened a Bible, or said a prayer to Jesus, you were actually making an offering...to your father. In spite of everything, you loved him so much.

AHN: My father, Tieng-Bin—this one thing I will never forget: you see, he is the one...who take the binding from my feet.

(In bed, Elizabeth stirs. Andrew sees her.)

ANDREW: Eling?

ELIZABETH *(Waking)*: Who's Eling?

ANDREW: Sorry. I was just remembering a story my mother used to tell me. About my grandfather.

ELIZABETH: You never told me about your grandfather.

ANDREW: He wanted to start a new family with the woman he loved. And to make that happen, he tried to move heaven and earth.

AHN: Andrew—write it down.

ANDREW: You know, I think I'll write it down.

ELIZABETH: You never write about your family.

ANDREW: I want to preserve this. For our child. Like my mother did for me.

ELIZABETH: Maybe you should talk to your mother more often.

ANDREW: Maybe I will.

AHN: Next—you must buy nice house in suburb.

ELIZABETH: Andrew, I'm really looking forward to watching our baby grow up. And you, too. Now try and get some sleep.

(She kisses him, goes to sleep. As he speaks, First Wife and Second Wife appear.)

ANDREW: I watch your mother sleeping, knowing you are growing inside her. And suddenly the room is filled with spirits—so many faces, looking down on me. And on each face, a story, some I have been told, some I can only imagine, and some I will never know at all. But many of them, people not so different from myself, who struggled with what to keep, and what to change—for the next generation. And I realize my face too will one day join this constellation. Perhaps, if I do my best, in the imagination of my descendants, I may also one day be born again. I feel the eyes of our ancestors upon us, all awaiting together the birth of you, my Golden Child.

(Elizabeth rolls over and holds him. First Wife, Second Wife and Ahn sit on their bed. Lights fade to black.)

END OF PLAY

PERFORMING *GOLDEN CHILD*

Prior to its Broadway opening on April 2, 1998, *Golden Child* had a number of developmental readings and workshops at the South Coast Repertory Theater in Costa Mesa, CA, the Trinity Repertory Company in residence at Breadloaf in Vermont, the Singapore Repertory Theatre, the American Conservatory Theatre in San Francisco, and The John F. Kennedy Center in Washington, D.C., before its premiere at The Joseph Papp Public Theater/New York Shakespeare Festival in New York City.

Golden Child, according to David Henry Hwang, was a "problem child." The material had its inception in an unpublished novel and early drafts of the play proved wordy and the structure cumbersome. Hwang said that he "pared down the contemporary monologues and hacked away at the excess dialogue."[15]

Along the way, the contemporary monologues were turned into a framing device for the historical story, scenes were added, and language trimmed. Three artists were seminal to the creative process: actors Tsai Chin and Julyana Soelistyo, who played Eng Siu-Young, the first wife, and Eng Ahn, the daughter and golden child, and director James Lapine.

Golden Child opened at the Public Theater to mixed reviews but producers stepped in and the play went into development again with an eye toward a Broadway production. A tryout production took place in Singapore in December 1997 where English-language productions reach large native audiences. The play was received with warmth and excitement but was reworked again at the American Conservatory Theatre with attention to clarifying Eng Tieng-Bin's reasons for converting to Christianity.

Golden Child reached the Longacre Theater on Broadway on April 2, 1998, with director James Lapine and designers Tony Straiges and Martin Pakledinaz. The unwinding of the binding cloth became the seminal moment that defined the painful transitions inherent in the story of a civilization in flux. Critics found the narrative force of the tale less than sensational but lavished praise on the "seemingly ageless" Julyana Soelistyo in the double role of the young and old Ahn, the indomitable life force unleashed at the same time as the golden child's feet are freed from the bindings. One critic said that Soelistyo was an actress who could magically add and subtract years with the mere "brandishing of a scarf." Others said that *Golden Child* was composed of "small moments of grace" and called it Hwang's most "sophisticated play so far."[16]

CRITICS' NOTEBOOK
ON ASIAN AMERICAN DRAMA

For many years the standard English-language sources on Asian theater practice were written by Faubion Bowers (*Japanese Theatre*, 1952) and James R. Brandon (*Theatre in Southeast Asia*, 1967). More recently, Brandon has edited *The Cambridge Guide to Asian Theatre* (1993), and such scholars as Colin Mackerras (*The Chinese Theatre in Modern Times,* 1975), Benito Ortolani (*The Japanese Theatre: From Shamanistic Ritual to Contemporary Pluralism,* 1995), and James S. Moy (*Marginal Sights: Staging the Chinese in America,* 1993) have added to our understanding of modern Asian and Asian American theater.

With the emergence of Asian American playwrights in the nonprofit and commercial theater in the United States in the last quarter of the twentieth century, anthologies of plays and collections of interviews have been added to the literature. Such anthologies as *Between Worlds: Contemporary Asian-American Plays* (1990), edited by Misha Berson, contain excellent introductions and biographical notes on Ping Chong, Philip Kan Gotanda, Jessica Hagedorn, David Henry Hwang, Wakako Yamauchi, and Laurence Yep. David Savran's interviews with contemporary playwrights collected in *In their Own Words: Contemporary American Playwrights* (1988) and *The Playwright's Voice: American Dramatists on Memory, Writing and the Politics of Culture* (1999) provide insights into the issues and sensibilities of many writers emerging from minority cultures in the United States.

Our critics' notebook provides material from Dorinne Kondo's highly original writing on race, fashion, and theater in *About Face: Performing Race in Fashion and Theater* in which she considers Japanese fashion and Asian American theater as a nexus of complex issues on gender, race, and identity. In addition, David Henry Hwang discusses his thoughts on sexism and race in an interview with Bonnie Lyons.

Dorinne Kondo, from *About Face: Performing Race in Fashion and Theater**

the narrative and performative production of home, community and identity is a particularly urgent issue in the case of asian americans. As

---

*Dorinne Kondo, *About Face: Performing Race in Fashion and Theater* (New York: Routledge, 1997): 190–192.

I noted in the introduction, the term "Asian American" itself bears the marks of the civil-rights and student struggles of the 1960s. It was created to displace the term Oriental, a word eschewed for its stereotypical associations with exoticism, despotism, and inscrutability, and for its reinscription of the East/West binary defining the East in terms of the West. Minimally, Asia names a continent, not some phantasmatic landscape. "Asian American," then, is an historically specific, constructed, political identity, a specific response to a particular historical situation in North America, where people of Asian descent are lumped together regardless of national origin, and where violence, racism, prejudice against any Asian American becomes an act of violence against all Asian Americans. "Asian American," then, is above all a coalitional and, as I have argued, a performative identity.

Given this particular sedimented history, Asian Americans have a specific relation to the notion of home. For mainland Asian Americans, surely one of the most insistent features of our particular oppression is our ineradicable foreignness. The fiftieth anniversary of the forced imprisonment of Japanese Americans was commemorated in 1992. Certainly the incarceration of Japanese Americans in concentration camps was attributable at least in part to this elision of Japanese Americans with Japanese nationals, a savagely ironic situation, given that exclusion laws prevented Issei, the immigrant generation, from becoming citizens until the passage of the MacCarran-Walter Act in 1952. No matter how many generations Asian Americans are resident here, no matter how articulate we seem, we inevitably attract the comment, "Oh, you speak English so well," or its equivalent, "Where are you from?" which somehow never seems to be adequately answered by Oregon or Illinois or New Jersey. The, question, "Where are you *really* from?" is sure to follow....

🍂 🍂 🍂

Given the continuing confusion of Asians with Asian Americans, perhaps it is not surprising that one of the most insistent themes in

Asian American literature and theater is a preoccupation with the claiming of America as home....

Bonnie Lyons, from "An Interview with David Henry Hwang"*

🐦

Lyons: *Your plays have been quite sympathetic to women characters and aware of sexism and gender issues. Any idea why?*

Hwang: I grew up with a lot of strong women. One of the funny things about being Chinese-American is that everyone else believes that Asian women are submissive and defer to men. My mom and aunt were both exceptions to that, and if everybody is an exception, then clearly something is wrong with the general rule. Traditional Chinese culture is really oppressive towards women; at the same time, growing up in a Chinese family, experientially you feel you are part of a matriarchy. I don't think Chinese women are victimized by their oppressive circumstances; I think they figure out a way to survive powerfully within those conditions. I grew up in a fundamentalist background; it was something I had to rebel against and get out of. Because of that I have been really sensitive to any kind of fundamentalism and have a kind of instinctive recoil. It seemed to me that if I was going to write about Asian characters and try to affirm their value vis-à-vis white culture, I would have to look at the entire picture, which involved me as a man trying to regard women with the same respect I would like white culture to regard me. It has never made sense to me to separate racism and sexism. Maybe that's the explanation for what you flatteringly call my sensitivity to women and gender issues.

*Bonnie Lyons, " 'Making His Muscles Work for Himself': An Interview with David Henry Hwang," *The Literary Review* 42.2 (1999): 234.

REVISITING INTERCULTURALISM

Intercultural texts demonstrate the collision of cultures as writers from minority cultures living in the West explore the contradictions, ambivalences, and difficulties of the struggle to retain ethnic, social, and ideological separateness in worlds that discourage exclusiveness. As we have used the term here, the *intercultural text* identifies and explores the conflicts, explosions, and quakes existing at the fissures where cultures rub against one another. In Eduardo Machado's *Broken Eggs*, for example, the dissonant cultural experiences in Cuba, Miami, and Canoga Park of three generations of the Marquez-Hernandez family result in disharmonies, dissolutions, and conflicts. David Henry Hwang's *Golden Child* celebrates the difficult resolution of cultural dissonances existing between Oriental and Occidental religious practices and social customs.

Conflict has been the basis of drama since its beginnings in the early Greek festivals. Intercultural dissonances are one recent source of dramatic conflict in new American playwriting since the eighties. Interculturalism is a newly recognized source of dramatic and artistic achievement related to colliding cultures within a country that once celebrated the obliteration of cultural differences into the melting pot of American democracy. The American theater today celebrates a far-flung diversity in its multicultured writers who are creating an alternative legacy of dramatic writing outside the mainstream work of the "official" culture.

Within the context of cultural diversity, efforts to combine the riches of various cultures into new artistic achievements are also celebrated under the label *transcultural*. Robert Brustein argues in "A House Divided" that "transcultural blending may be the most fully acknowledged artistic development of our time."[17] Many of today's theatrical artists—directors, actors, writers, designers—borrow forms and styles from many different cultures and create new cultural contexts. American creator Julie Taymor blends Indonesian-style puppetry and Mayan masks in *Juan Darién* based on a Uruguayan fable by Horacio Quiroga, and British-born director Peter Brook blends Eastern and Western literature and performance traditions in the twelve-hour performance of *The Mahabharata*.

Transcultural artistic expression and intercultural writing are ways contemporary writers and artists mirror their multicultural society and address global issues that affect all humankind.

NOTES

1. Richard Schechner, "An Intercultural Primer," *American Theatre*, 8.7 (October 1991): 28–31, 135–136.
2. Schechner 30.
3. Schechner 30.
4. John Lahr, "Cuban Voices," *The New Yorker* (November 14, 1994): 125–128; David Richards, "Critic's Notebook: Another Epic, With Four Plays in Six Hours," *The New York Times* (November 10, 1994): C 20; Edith Oliver, *The New Yorker* (March 5, 1984): 109.
5. "Hwang, David Henry," *1989 Current Biography Yearbook* (New York: H. W. Wilson Company, 1989): 269.
6. Bonnie Lyons, "'Making His Muscles Work for Himself': An Interview with David Henry Hwang," *The Literary Review* 42.2 (1999): 241.
7. *1989 Current Biography Yearbook*: 270.
8. Lyons 232.
9. Lyons 233.
10. David Henry Hwang, "Bringing Up 'Child,'" in *Golden Child* (New York: Theatre Communications Group, 1998): vi.
11. Lyons 241.
12. Lyons 241.
13. Hwang vii.
14. David Savran, *In Their Own Words: Contemporary American Playwrights* (New York: Theatre Communications Group, 1988): 118.
15. Hwang vii.
16. *The New York Times* (April 3, 1998); *The New York Times* (April 26, 1998); *The New York Post* (April 3, 1998).
17. Robert Brustein, "A House Divided," *American Theatre*, 8.7 (October 1991): 46.

AFTERWORD

POSTMODERNISM AND BEYOND

Postmodernism, as the term implies, follows modernism. Postmodern art has antecedents in the earlier works of the European symbolists and surrealists who shared the *subversion* of the real in poetry, painting, and theater. In the theater, this translated into the rejection of stage realism and its representational conventions of writing, design, and staging.

Postmodern artists share with their predecessors the rejection of traditional theatrical forms and dramatic materials. Robert Wilson and Laurie Anderson craft their materials out of improvisation, parody, word-sounds, multiple images, synthetic sounds, and reflexive events. Their texts are often called "assemblages" or "collages." German postmodernist and playwright Heiner Müller created short texts made up of extended monologues, paragraphs of word fragments, and notations on stage images, sensory impressions, and sounds. Best known in the United States for *Hamletmachine,* written in 1977, Müller reframed Shakespeare's play into a performative discourse on the political and ideological collapse of Western civilization in the twentieth century.

African American Pulitzer Prize–winning playwright Suzan-Lori Parks adopts postmodern strategies to re-think time, space, and history. Using surreal landscapes ("the Great Hole of History"), Parks sets out to rewrite in theatrical terms and musical "riffs" unrecorded segments of U.S. history in *The America Play* (1994), for example. Her postmodern style is apparent in fantastical landscapes, iconic characters, nonlinear narrative, academic footnotes commenting on the text, and the reimagining of history in the "great hole" of theatrical space.

In the American theater, postmodern performance has been represented in the 1990s by the visual landscape of Robert Wilson, Philip Glass, Laurie Anderson, Peter Sellars, Martha Clarke, and Anne Bogart, who function as directors-designers-composers-choreographers to create large-scale productions to raise questions about humanity's relationship to society, to the environment, to technology, and to itself. Their theatrical experiments are dominated by visual and aural images. Suzan-Lori Parks begins with the written text to reimagine historical circumstances on a smaller scale and reframe them in surreal landscapes that conflate time past and present. In both instances, the theatricality of the stage is the ideal place to demonstrate the "irreal" nature of the postmodernist's world.

The American theater at the millennium conjoins the old and the new. Revivals of popular musical and older traditional plays dominate the Broadway stages: *Oklahoma!* and *Man of La Mancha* compete with Thornton Wilder's *Our Town* and Edna Ferber's *Dinner at Eight.* Nonetheless, experimentation resides in subversive pockets of the theatrical world. As performance, theater is seductive and challenging. The theatrical is where we improvise—our personal fantasies and our quarrels with history.

The history of the theater has been a passage en route to new forms. Performance lends itself to new discourse but also to a contemplation of spectacle as a funhouse mirror to reflect back the performative nature of human experience. At this moment the theatrical avant-garde is a mix of auto-performance and world-cultural narratives. These parameters mark the millennial phase of playwriting and theater in Western culture. Because theatrical discourse is ever changing, the next rising curtain promises to alter our perspectives—on politics, ethics, and culture.

APPENDIX

PLAY ANALYSIS AND CONCEPTUALIZATION: A PROCESS*

GAYLE M. AUSTIN

WHY ANALYZE?

For the theater artist or technician it is more important to know what makes the clock tick than what time it is.[1]

Every theater practitioner and informed audience member needs to be able to analyze plays. A script is really a set of instructions for staging performances of the play and learning to understand those instructions requires work. While anyone can enjoy a skyscraper, symphony or theatrical performance, it takes more than willingness to create, or truly appreciate, one. Just as "reading" a blueprint or a musical score takes specialized knowledge and much practice, so does "reading" a play.

Because a play script is composed of words rather than drawings or symbols, it may seem that "reading" a play requires no more than basic literacy. But the words in a play are arranged in such a way as to describe an event in which sights and sounds occur simultaneously, in three-dimensional space over a fourth dimension of time. Translating a play's words into these complex images, first in the mind and then on the stage, requires a reliable technique.

Play analysis, or separating a play into its component parts, is part of a process that aids in this translation technique. Looking at one component at a time makes the enormous mental task of "seeing" a production of a play more manageable, but it is best to frame this step with two other phases.

THE FIRST PHASE: OVERVIEW

Without delving too far into the metaphor, we believe that this process is like a guide to love-making—not step-by-step instructions, but a useful list of considerations and techniques.[2]

The first reading of a script is to gain an *overview* of the play and to experience *first impressions*. Later on, the ability to see the play with fresh eyes will become increasingly difficult. These first impressions are close to what an audience will experience when seeing the play, so recording them is very important.

Try to read the play straight through, in one sitting, without taking notes. Afterwards, sit quietly and reflect back on the experience. Get down on paper as many of the impressions and images you can remember, starting with the ones that most clearly stand out in your mind. Use words and drawings (images, metaphors, colors, shapes, diagrams)—anything that will help you remember most vividly what the play did to you that first time. Your reactions may range from the emotional to the intellectual, but all of them should be recorded for possible future use.

THE SECOND PHASE: ANALYSIS

A theatre designer collecting script facts proceeds very much like a crime-scene detective

*Gayle M. Austin is an Associate Professor in the Department of Communication at Georgia State University and author of *Feminist Theories for Dramatic Criticism* (1990).

searching for physical clues and interviewing witnesses…. They look, listen, collect, and remain objective.[3]

The second phase is the process of getting more *details* from the play and afterwards doing your *analysis* by separating it into its different parts. This phase will probably take more than a single reading and definitely requires marking on the script, taking notes, and writing up the results in some form.

While doing your second reading of the play, it helps to have in your mind some scheme of the "parts" into which you are going to separate the play. If you continue to analyze plays, eventually you will probably use different schemes and develop your own. Most Western systems of play analysis are based on the six elements of drama found in Aristotle's *The Poetics*. The first three are the most important: plot, character and thought. The other three are less important and the terms describing them are often modified in some way: language, rhythm and spectacle.

In 1970, director Francis Hodge removed "spectacle" from the bottom of Aristotle's list, added a Stanislavskian term to the top and recommended seven "parts:" given circumstances, dialogue, dramatic action, characters, idea, tempos, and moods.[4] In the 1990s, from this list designer Rosemary Ingham developed an outline which asks eight questions:

    I. Where are they?
    II. When are they?
   III. Who are they?
   IV. What happened before the play began?
    V. What is the function of each character in the play?
   VI. What kinds of dialogue do the characters speak?
  VII. What happens in the play?
 VIII. What is the play's theme?[5]

Writing at about the same time, James Thomas focuses more on subdivisions of plot, and he structures his book around eight "classifications of formalist analysis": given circumstances; background story; plot actions; plot structure; character; idea; dialogue; and tempo, rhythm, and mood.[6] David Kahn and Donna Breed recommend six elements for analyzing new scripts: world of the play, story, issues, event chain, character, and patterns.[7] They also give tips for how to do a second reading: "Read the script with pencil in hand. When major events or components of the story occur, tick in the margin so you can find them again. Mark character entrances…."[8]

French Scene Chart

This last point suggests another useful device. Mark any entrance or exit, then divide the script into segments (called French scenes) based on the composition of characters seen on the stage. Draw a line across the page every time that composition changes. During and after the second reading take notes, and at some point during phase two make a chart of these French scenes. Make a grid (using "table" format in a word processor) with character names across the top and French scene numbers down the left side, then put an X or letter abbreviation for the character in each box in which a character appears. You can also make a column for the formal act: scene numbers and another for page numbers, so that any French scene can easily be found in the script.

Act:scene	Fr.Sc.	Page	Joe	Jean	Sue	Abby	Bob
Act I : 1	1	6		Je	Su		
	2	12	Jo	Je	Su		Bo
Act I : 2	3	16			Su	Ab	

This chart is invaluable, not just to directors and stage managers who are planning quick costume changes and rehearsals based on actors' availabilities, but to anyone wanting to get a visual overview of the play. Looking at the chart you can note patterns: when characters are onstage for long periods, or offstage, or always appear in pairs or groups. In a play like *Hamlet* you can underline the letter in the scene in which each character dies and know that moment for each at a glance. Scenes with only one or two characters are clearly differentiated from those with a crowd on the stage. Often the plot can be visually recalled by looking at the chart.

Horizontal Analysis

After the second reading you can begin to do a linear, *horizontal* analysis of the script by writing down notes. This form of analysis is done by considering one category of analysis at a time and tracing it as one layer through the entire length of the play. Later in the process you will probably do *vertical* analysis by slicing the play into small sections and looking at all the layers in each section; for actors these will usually be "beats." Both forms of analysis are necessary, but for this second phase, focus on horizontal elements. My suggestion for "parts" is a somewhat streamlined list: given circumstances, characters, plot, structure and themes.

First note the beginning place, specific setting, date and time of day, and make another note each time one of these elements changes over the course of the play. Second, make an annotated list of characters, giving for each their name, age (or ages over time), gender, relationships to each other, race, class and other basic information. A French scene chart made at this point will help give a visual summary of both characters and structure. Third, make a list of each major event in the play, dividing the list by act and scene. Fourth, determine if the play's structure is climactic, episodic, a combination, or other (situational, reflexive, feminine, etc.), and write down the number of acts and number of scenes in each act. Fifth, make a list of all the themes, topics or issues that the play raises.

In order to write an analysis you will need to go back and look at your ticks in the margins, your underlining and highlighting. You may need to read the play a third, fourth, fifth, or sixth time in order to collect and write down all this information. Persevere. This is the time-intensive digging necessary to know the play, but the process will take less time the more plays you analyze.

Event List

> An event in a script is a related sequence of stage activity that forms an identifiable unit of action.[9]

> An event is anything that happens. When one event causes or permits another event, the two events together comprise an action.[10]

Making a list of the things that "happen" in a play is one of the best ways to get to know it. In a play structured on the premise that every effect has its cause, each event will cause another event, which will cause another, and so on. In a play not structured on cause and effect, a list of the events that occur, in order, will enable you to look at one or two pages and begin to see the patterns that structure the piece.

A complete event list for most plays is many pages long, but a shorter list describing one event per scene, or even French scene, can be just as useful. Writing down "Act I: Scene 1" and then briefly describing, in the present tense using strong verbs, the events seen on stage in that scene means you have to have read the scene and "seen" it in your mind well enough to select a few words which will convey what "happened."

This series of events is what constitutes the *plot* of the play, as opposed to the *story* from which the plot is drawn. Many plays refer to events which take place before the play begins (in film terms its "backstory") or occur offstage in the course of the play. These are part of the story or narrative behind the play, but we need to be most concerned with those events which happen before the audience's eyes. An event list for *Oedipus the King* does not contain the line "Jocasta hangs herself," but rather "a messenger reports that Jocasta has hung herself." Since the play is based on a well-known myth we conventionally take the messenger at his word. But what if he lied? What if he were mistaken? Later, when we interpret the play for production, we may want to consider, for instance, the possibility that she lives, since she did not die in front of our eyes.

Patterns, Structure and Proportions

> There is something about human perception that causes us to look for patterns and derive meaning from the models of reality they suggest.[11]

There are patterns in each of the "parts" of a play analysis, but the pattern of events is probably the most important one. The way the events are arranged in relation to each other form the structure of the plot. The two most common plot structures are climactic (a sequence of scenes, each building upon the previous one, to a climax and resolution) and episodic (a sequence of usually shorter scenes arranged more like beads on a string, one after the other). *Oedipus the King* is the classic example of climactic structure and *Hamlet* of episodic structure. Other terms for these two structures are *intensive* and *extensive*.[12] Within any one of these structures a plot can either be linear or nonlinear, chronological or discontinuous in time.

> The structure of a play is often the most telling clue about the author's world view for that play....[13]

The arrangement of events in a play can be seen as a reflection of the view of the world held by an individual playwright, or even an entire age. The Greeks favored linear plots with a clear pattern of cause and effect, and the society as a whole was "one possessing a reassuring order, with a governing intelligence overseeing the affairs of humankind."[14] On the other hand, much drama written since the Second World War expresses "the absence of a moral order, a controlling intelligence run amok or gone away, of (alternatively) a world free of the constraints of conventional societal structures"[15] through using nonlinear and discontinuous structures of events not based on cause and effect.

Another aspect of the pattern of events in a play is the proportion of segments to each other, as well as to the whole play. When you write down the number of acts and number of scenes in each act, also note the length (in page numbers) of each scene. The column for page numbers on a French scene chart makes this an easy matter. The patterns of these sections form rhythms, which contribute to meaning. For example, multiple short scenes seem to speed up the action, while fewer, longer scenes slow it down. Placement of an intermission usually divides the experience into a longer period followed by a shorter one, but if the second act is longer than the first it may "feel" too long to an audience.

Themes

The last part of the second, or analysis, phase is to write down all the themes the play suggests to you. The themes at this point are really brief topics or issues that the play brings up. The next phase uses these topics in a kind of synthesis, or putting together of parts into a new whole. It is in the third phase that your detective-like objectivity begins to shift to artistic subjectivity; your left-brain, logical thinking shifts to a right-brain, more intuitive process.

THE THIRD PHASE: INTERPRETATION

The third phase is forming your own *interpretation* of the play, which leads to a *concept* for the intended production. Some say only the director should formulate a concept, but if everyone involved with a production comes up with a concept that can be articulated and shared with the other collaborators, the resulting production will be much richer. At preliminary meetings, production meetings, and early rehearsals, all practitioners will bring to the table not only a thorough familiarity with the play, but an ability to contribute to those formative discussions, and a good director will listen and retain at least some of those ideas to mix with her own. In cases of ensemble development of a piece, this kind of contribution from each member is expected.

To shift into interpretative mode, sit with your notes and horizontal analysis in front of you and look specifically at the last section: themes. These are probably just words, or short phrases, naming subjects the play contains: love, death, power, jealousy, greed, youth versus age, city versus country, and so on infinitely. Holding one theme in the back of your mind, think back over the play you have analyzed. Then make a leap—say what you think the play expresses about the theme. This elaboration will be subjective and through it you will begin to express your unique reaction to the play. In *Hamlet*, for instance, an initial theme of "power" might be elaborated into "maintaining power is based on manipulation." Often, especially for linear plays, this may be a statement of cause and effect: Y is caused by X or X leads to Y. Write down several of these elaborated themes and then take them, one at a time, one step further.

The Production Concept

> A production concept clarifies the specific way in which the artists working on a particular production will communicate their shared point of view to the audience…[It is] a plan that integrates and orchestrates all the elements of the production—acting, stage space, light, costume, sound, music.[16]

The production concept you develop from an elaborated theme expresses what you want to say through production about what the play expresses about the theme. Taking this second leap requires imagination. It requires all the resources you have acquired from research, training and experience. It may seem mysterious. It should suggest a style for the production: stimulate visual images in designers and character interpretations in actors. A good production concept will get collaborators together on the same page, and at the same time inspire each of them to do their own job as creatively as they can. The elaborated *Hamlet* theme "maintaining power is based on manipulation" could lead to any number of concepts concerning power and manipulation in the family, military or government; set in the Middle Ages, Renaissance England, or contemporary America.

A recent film version of the play (Ethan Hawke, 2001) seemed to be based on the concept that power manipulations in the medieval court at Elsinore are very similar to corporate manipu-

lations in New York City today. In applying this concept to production, the setting was changed to a contemporary corporate setting, with Hamlet trying to get revenge on his ambitious CEO stepfather. The film style is sleek postmodernism and Hamlet is a would-be filmmaker.

If one elaborated theme does not suggest a visual and acting style, try another. You may need to shift between the theme and concept, back and forth many times, until you are at least tentatively satisfied with your concept. Bring it with you to a first meeting or rehearsal, to throw into the pool of ideas that collects during the early phases of production. It may be made up of images, words, phrases, or full sentences; the only essential is that it can be communicated to others.

One More Reading

> …you must approach the script afresh and try to encounter the experience of the play. Put aside your close-reading techniques, allow your eyes to shift slightly out of focus, and read the play as though you were seeing it in performance.[17]

Sometime after arriving at a concept you should do another reading of the play, this time imagining how your concept might be applied to and shape the production. This reading, like the first, should be done in one sitting without taking notes. You may decide that your concept is terrible, or wonderful, or has a few things in it that can be used. Write down your responses and add them to the documentation you have already produced on the play.

> Everything I have said in this book could be summed up in the sentence "Imagine a performance as vividly as you can."[18]

After this third phase, practitioners will go on to do their own specialized work: designers sketch, actors work on characters, directors plan, and stage managers schedule. But if behind all this work is the foundation of these three phases of analysis, each individual will be more fully empowered to collaborate on the production.

NOTES

1. David Ball, *Backwards and Forwards: A Technical Manual for Reading Plays* (Carbondale: Southern Illinois UP, 1983): 3.

2. David Kahn and Donna Breed, *Scriptwork: A Director's Approach to New Play Development* (Carbondale: Southern Illinois UP, 1995): 29–30.

3. Rosemary Ingham, *From Page to Stage: How Theatre Designers Make Connections Between Scripts and Images* (Portsmouth, NH: Heinemann, 1998): 49.

4. Ingham 54.

5. Ingham 55–57.

6. James Thomas, *Script Analysis for Actors, Directors, and Designers,* 2nd ed. (Boston: Focal Press, 1999) xx–xxi.

7. Kahn and Breed 32.

8. Kahn and Breed 40.

9. Kahn and Breed 47.

10. Ball 11.

11. Kahn and Breed 63.

12. Bernard Beckerman, *Dynamics of Drama: Theory and Method of Analysis* (New York: Drama Book Specialists, 1979): 188–189.

13. Christopher Thaiss and Rick Davis, *Writing About Theatre* (Boston: Allyn and Bacon, 1999): 62.

14. Thaiss and Davis 62.

15. Thaiss and Davis 62–63.

16. Arden Fingerhut, *Theatre: Choice in Action* (New York: HarperCollins, 1995): 43.

17. Kahn and Breed 71.

18. Ronald Hayman, *How to Read a Play* (New York: Grove Press, 1977): 93.

LIST OF CRITICAL TERMS

Absurd
Act
Agitprop
Agon
Alienation/*Verfremdung*
Alienation effect/
    Verfremdungseffkt
Allegory
Anagnorisis/recognition
Antagonist
Arena stage
Aside
Avant-garde

Blank verse
Box set

Catastrophe
Catharsis
Character
Chiton
Circumstance/given
    circumstance
Climactic structure
Climax
Collage
Comedy
Comedy of manners
Comic relief
Comic vision
Commedia dell'arte
Complication
Conflict
Convention
Coryphaeus
Coup de théâtre

Dada
Decorum

Denouement
Deus ex machina
Dialogue
Didascalia
Discovery space
Distancing
Dithyramb
Docudrama
Documentary
Doubleness
Double plot
Drama
Dramatic action
Dramatic illusion
Dramatic irony
Dramatic time
Dramatist
Dramaturg
Dramaturgy
Dumbshow

Ekkyklema
Environmental theater
Epic theater
Epilogue
Episode
Episodic structure
Exit
Exodus
Exposition
Expressionism

Farce
Feminism
Foreshadowing
Fourth wall
Framing device
French scene

Genre

Hamartia
Happening
Historification
Hubris/hybris

Illusion
Image
Imitation
Impressionism
Interculturalism
Interlude
Irony

Language
Linear storytelling
Living Newspaper

Magical realism
Mechane
Melodrama
Metaphor
Meta-theater
Mime
Mimesis
Minimalism
Miracle play
Mise-en-scène
Modernism
Monologue
Morality play
Multiculturalism
Multimedia event
Musical comedy
Mystery cycles

Narrative
Narrator

Naturalism
Neoclassicism
New Comedy
Nonlinear narrative

Ode
Old Comedy
Orchestra

Pageant wagon
Pantomime
Parabasis
Paradigm
Parodos/Parodoi
Performance
Performance art
Peripety/*Peripeteia*
Presentational
Pièce à these
Pièce bien faite
Play-within-the-play
Plot
Postmodernism
Praxis
Problem play
Prologos
Prologue
Proscenium arch
Proscenium stage
Protagonist

Realism
Recognition/*Anagnorisis*

Reflexive structure
Representational
Resolution
Retrospective exposition
Revenge tragedy
Reversal/peripety
Ritual

Satire
Satyr play
Scene
Scenery
Scenography/scenographer
Sentimental drama
Setting
Sign
Situation
Skene/scene house
Slice of life
Soliloquy
Solo performance
Solo performance text
Spectacle
Stage business
Stage directions
Stage properties
Stichomythia
Stock character
Strophe/antistrophe/epode
Subplot/underplot
Subtext
Surrealism
Suspense

Suspension of disbelief
Symbol
Symbolism
Synthetic fragments

Talking pieces
Tetralogy
Theater of the Absurd
Theater of testimony
Theatricalism
Three unities
Thrust/platform stage
Thymele
Tiring house
Tragedy
Tragicomedy
Tragicomic vision
Tragic paradox
Tragic vision
Trap/trapdoor
Trilogy
Transculturalism
Trope

Unity

Verbal text
Verfremdungseffkt
Verisimilitude

Well-made play

SELECTED READINGS

Auslander, Philip. *Presence and Resistance: Postmodernism and Cultural Politics In Contemporary American Performance.* Ann Arbor, MI: University of Michigan Press, 1994.

Austin, Gayle. *Feminist Theories for Dramatic Criticism.* Ann Arbor: University Of Michigan Press, 1990.

Ball, David. *Backward and Forwards: A Technical Manual for Reading Plays.* Carbondale: Southern Illinois University Press, 1983.

Barzun, Jacques. *Darwin, Marx, Wagner: Critique of a Heritage.* Second Edition. Chicago: University of Chicago Press, 1981.

Beckerman, Bernard. *Dynamics of Drama: Theory and Method of Analysis.* New York: Drama Book Specialists, 1979.

Bentley, Eric. *The Brecht Commentaries 1943–1980.* New York: Grove Press, 1981.

———. *The Life of Drama.* New York: Applause Theatre Books, 1991.

———. *The Playwright as Thinker: A Study of Drama in Modern Times.* New York: Harcourt, Brace, Jovanovich, 1987.

Betsko, Kathleen and Rachel Koenig. *Interviews with Contemporary Women Playwrights.* New York: Beech Tree, 1987.

Bigsby, Christopher. *A Critical Introduction to Twentieth-Century American Drama.* 3 vols. New York: Cambridge University Press, 1982–85.

———. *Contemporary American Playwrights.* New York: Cambridge University Press, 1999.

———. *Modern American Drama 1945–1990.* New York: Cambridge University Press, 1992.

Bonney, Jo, ed. *Extreme Exposure: An Anthology of Solo Performance Texts from the Twentieth Century.* New York: Theatre Communications Group, 2000.

Brandon, James R., and Martin Banham, eds. *The Cambridge Guide to Asian Theatre.* New York: Cambridge University Press, 1993.

Brecht, Bertolt. *Brecht on Theatre: The Development of an Aesthetic.* Trans. and ed. John Willett. New York: Hill and Wang Publishers, 1964.

Brook, Peter. *The Empty Space.* New York: Atheneum, 1968.

———. *The Shifting Point: Forty Years of Theatrical Exploration, 1946–1987.* London: 1988.

Brown, Lorraine, and John O'Conner, eds. *Free, Adult, Uncensored: The Living History of the Federal Theatre Project.* Washington, D.C., 1978.

Butcher, S. H. *Aristotle's Theory of Poetry and Fine Art.* 4th Edition. New York: Dover, 1955.

Cardullo, Bert. *What Is Dramaturgy?* New York: Peter Lang Publishing, Inc., 1995.

Carlson, Marvin. *Performance: A Critical Introduction.* New York: Routledge, 1996.

———. *Theories of the Theatre: A Historical and Critical Survey from the Greeks to the Present.* Ithaca, NY: Cornell University Press, 1984.

Carr, C. *On Edge: Performing at the End of the Twentieth Century.* Middletown, CT: Wesleyan University Press, 1994.

Case, Sue-Ellen. *Feminism and Theatre.* New York: Methuen, 1988.

———. *Performing Feminisms: Feminist Critical Theory and Theatre.* Baltimore, MD: Johns Hopkins University Press, 1990.

Champagne, Lenora, ed. *Out from Under: Texts by Women Performance Artists.* New York: Theatre Communications Group, 1990.

Chinoy, Helen Krich, and Linda Walsh Jenkins, eds. *Women in American Theatre.* New York: Crown Publishers, 1981.

Cohn, Ruby. *Just Play: Beckett's Theater.* Princeton: Princeton University Press, 1980.

Cole, Toby, ed. *Playwrights on Playwriting: The Meaning and Making of Modern Drama from Ibsen to Ionesco.* New York: Hill and Wang, 1961.

Davidson, Cathy N., and Linda Wagner-Martin, eds. *The Oxford Companion to Women's Writing in the United States.* New York: Oxford University Press, 1995.

Davis, Hallie Flanagan. *Arena: The History of the Federal Theatre.* New York: Benjamin Blom, 1965.

Devlin, Albert J., ed. *Conversations with Tennessee Williams.* Jackson: University Press of Mississippi, 1986.

Diamond, Elin, ed. *Writing Performances.* London: Routledge, 1995.

DiGaetani, John L. *A Search for a Postmodern Theater: Interviews with Contemporary Playwrights.* New York: Greenwood Publishing Group, 1991.

Dolan, Jill. *The Feminist Spectator as Critic.* Ann Arbor, MI: The University of Michigan Press, 1988.

———. *Geographies of Learning: Theory and Practice, Activism and Performance.* Middleton, CT: Wesleyan University Press, 2001.

———. *Presence and Desire: Essays on Gender, Sexuality, Performance.* Ann Arbor, MI: University of Michigan Press, 1993.

Ellman, Richard. *Oscar Wilde: A Collection of Critical Essays.* Englewood Cliffs, NJ: Prentice Hall, 1969.

Esslin, Martin. *The Field of Drama: How the Signs of Drama Create Meaning on Stage and Screen.* London: Methuen, 1987.

———. *The Theatre of the Absurd.* 3rd Edition. New York: Pelican Books, 1983.

Fingerhut, Arden. *Theatre: Choice in Action.* New York: Harper Collins, 1995.

Fisher, James. *The Theater of Tony Kushner: Living Past Hope.* New York: Routledge, 2001.

Fortier, Mark. *Theory/Theatre: An Introduction.* New York: Routledge, 1997.

Freud, Sigmund. *Jokes and Their Relation to the Unconscious.* Trans. James Strachey. London: Heinemann, 1960.

Frye, Northrop. *The Anatomy of Criticism.* Princeton, NJ: Princeton University Press, 1957.

Fuchs, Elinor. *The Death of Character: Perspectives on Theater after Modernism.* Bloomington: Indiana University Press, 1996.

Geis, Deborah R., and Steven F. Kruger, eds. *Approaching the Millennium: Essays on Angels in America.* Ann Arbor: University of Michigan Press, 1997.

Gerould, Daniel. *Theatre Theory Theatre: The Major Critical Texts.* New York: Applause Theatre Books, 1998.

Gilman, Richard. *The Making of Modern Drama: A Study of Büchner, Ibsen, Strindberg, Chekhov, Pirandello, Brecht, Beckett, Handke.* New York: Da Capo, 1987.

Goldberg, RoseLee. *Performance Art: From Futurism to the Present.* Revised Ed. New York: Thames and Hudson Publishers, 2001.

Gómez-Peña, Guillermo. *The New World Border: Prophecies, Poems, and Loqueras For the End of the Century.* San Francisco: City Lights Books, 1996.

Gottlieb, Vera, and Paul Allain, eds. *The Cambridge Companion to Chekhov.* New York: Cambridge University Press, 2000.

Greene, Alexis, ed. *Women Who Write Plays: Interviews with American Dramatists.* Hanover, NH: Smith and Kraus, Inc., 2001.

Hart, Lynda, ed. *Making a Spectacle: Feminist Essays on Contemporary Women's Theatre.* Ann Arbor, MI: University of Michigan Press, 1989.

———, ed. *Of All the Nerve: Deb Margolin Solo.* New York: The Continuum International Publishing Group, 1999.

——— and Peggy Phelan, eds. *Acting Out: Feminist Performances.* Ann Arbor, MI: University of Michigan Press, 1994.

Hayman, Ronald. *How to Read a Play.* New York: Grove Press, 1977.

Hutcheon, Linda. *A Theory of Parody: The Teachings of Twentieth-Century Art Forms.* New York: Methuen, 1985.

Ingham, Rosemary. *From Page to Stage: How Theatre Designers Make Connections between Scripts and Images.* Portsmouth, NH: Heinemann, 1998.

Ionesco, Eugene. *Notes and Counter Notes: Writings on the Theatre.* Trans. Donald Watson. New York: Grove Press, 1964.

Kahn, David, and Donna Breed. *Scriptwork: A Director's Approach to New Play Development.* Carbondale: Southern Illinois University Press, 1995.

Kalb, Jonathan. *Beckett in Performance.* New York: Cambridge University Press, 1989.

Kent, Sarah, and Jacqueline Morreau, eds. *Women's Images of Men.* London: Writers and Readers Publishing, 1985.

King, Bruce, ed. *Contemporary American Theatre.* New York: St. Martin's Press, 1991.

Kondo, Dorinne. *About Face: Performing Race in Fashion and Theater.* New York: Routledge, 1977.

Kostalentz, Richard. *On Innovative Performance(s): Three Decades of Recollections on Alternative Theater*. Jefferson, NC: McFarland, 1994.

Krutch, Joseph Wood. *"Modernism" in Modern Drama: A Definition and an Estimate*. Ithaca, NY: Cornell University Press, 1953.

Kushner, Tony. *Thinking About the Longstanding Problems of Virtue and Happiness: Essays, A Play, Two Poems, and a Prayer*. New York: Theatre Communications Group, 1995.

Leverich, Lyle. *Tom: The Unknown Tennessee Williams*. New York: Crown Publishers, 1995.

Mahone, Sydné, ed. *Moon Marked and Touched by the Sun: Plays by African-American Women*. New York: Theatre Communications Group, 1994.

Margolin, Deb. *Of All the Nerve: Deb Margolin Solo*. Ed. Lynda Hart. New York: The Continuum International Publishing Group, 1999.

Marker, Frederick J. *Ibsen's Lively Art: A Performance Study of the Major Plays*. New York: Cambridge University Press, 1989.

Marranca, Bonnie, ed. *The Theatre of Images*. New York: Drama Book Specialists, 1997.

Martin, Carol, ed. *A Sourcebook of Feminist Theatre and Performance: On and Beyond The Stage*. New York: Routledge, 1996.

Mason, Jeffrey D., and Ellen Gainor, eds. *Performing America: Cultural Nationalism In American Theater*. Ann Arbor: University of Michigan Press, 1999.

McDonald, Robert L, and Linda Rohrer Paige, eds. *Southern Women Playwrights*. Tuscaloosa: University of Alabama Press, 2002.

Moy, James S. *Marginal Sights: Staging the Chinese in America*. Iowa City: The University of Iowa Press, 1993.

Müller, Heiner. *Hamletmachine and Other Texts for the Stage*. Ed. and trans. Carl Weber. New York: Performing Arts Journal Publications, 1984.

Murphy, Brenda. *The Cambridge Companion to American Women Playwrights*. New York: Cambridge University Press, 1999.

Nadel, Alan, ed. *May All Your Fences Have Gates: Essays on the Drama of August Wilson*. Iowa City: University of Iowa Press, 1994.

Notable Women in the American Theatre: A Biographical Dictionary. Eds. Alice M. Robinson, Vera Mowry Roberts, and Milly S. Barranger. Westport, CT: Greenwood Publishing Group, 1989.

Oppenheim, Lois. *Directing Beckett*. Ann Arbor: University of Michigan Press, 1994.

Orr, John. *Tragicomedy and Contemporary Culture: Play and Performance from Beckett to Shepard*. Ann Arbor: University of Michigan Press, 1990.

Osborn, M. Elizabeth, ed. *On New Ground: Contemporary Hispanic-American Plays*. New York: Theatre Communications Group, 1987.

Parks, Suzan-Lori. *The America Play and Other Works*. New York: Theatre Communications Group, 1995.

Pavis, Patrice. *Languages of the Stage: Essays in the Semiology of Theatre*. New York: Performing Arts Journal Publications, 1982.

Phelan, Peggy and Jill Lane. *The Ends of Performance*. New York: New York University Press, 1998.

Pirandello, Luigi. *On Humor*. Trans. Antonio Illiano and Daniel P. Tests. Chapel Hill: University of North Carolina Press, 1974.

Piscator, Erwin. *The Political Theatre: A History, 1914–1929*. Trans. Hugh Rorrison. London: Eyre Methuen, 1980.

Raby, Peter, ed. *The Cambridge Companion to Oscar Wilde*. New York: Cambridge University Press, 1997.

Scanlon, Jennifer, ed. *Significant Contemporary American Feminists: A Biographical Sourcebook*. Westport, CT: Greenwood Publishing Group, 1999.

Shafer, Yvonne. *August Wilson: A Research and Production Sourcebook*. Westport, CT: Greenwood Publishing Group, 1998.

Savran, David. *In Their Own Words Contemporary American Playwrights: Interviews*. New York: Theatre Communications Group, 1988.

———. *The Playwrights Voice: American Dramatists on Memory, Writing and The Politics of Culture*. New York: Theatre Communications Group, 1999.

Shaw, George Bernard. *The Quintessence of Ibsenism*. New York: Hill and Wang, 1957.

Schechner, Richard. *The End of Humanism: Writings on Performance*. New York: Performing Arts Journal Publications, 1982.

———. *Environmental Theater*. New York: Hawthorn, 1973.

Simmons, Ernest J. *Chekhov: A Biography*. Boston: Little, Brown & Co., 1962.

Sinfield, Alan. *Out on Stage: Lesbian and Gay Theatre in the Twentieth Century*. New Haven, CT: Yale University Press, 1999.

Sprinchorn, Evert, ed. *Ibsen Letters and Speeches.* New York: Hill and Wang, 1964.

Stanislavski, Konstantin. *My Life in Art.* New York: Routledge, 1924.

Stanton, Stephen, ed. *Tennessee Williams: A Collection of Critical Essays.* Englewood Cliffs, NJ: Prentice Hall, 1977.

Steiner, George. *The Death of Tragedy.* New York: Alfred A. Knopf, 1961.

Styan, J. L. *Chekhov in Performance.* New York: Cambridge University Press, 1971.

———. *Modern Drama in Theory and Practice.* 3 vols. New York: Cambridge University Press, 1981.

Svich, Caridad, and Maria Teresa Marrero, eds. *Out of the Fringe: Contemporary Latina/Latino Theatre and Performance.* New York: Theatre Communications Group, 2000.

Taylor, John Russell. *The Rise and Fall of the Well-Made Play.* New York: Hill & Wang, 1967.

Templeton, Joan. *Ibsen's Women.* New York: Cambridge University Press, 1997.

Thaiss, Christopher, and Rick Davis. *Writing About Theatre.* Boston, MA: Allyn & Bacon, 1999.

Thomas, James. *Script Analysis for Actors, Directors, and Designers.* Second Edition. Boston: Focal Press, 1999.

Thomson, Peter, and Glendyr Sacks, eds. *The Cambridge Companion to Brecht.* New York: Cambridge University Press, 1994.

Twentieth Century American Dramatists. Ed. Christopher J. Wheatley. 2nd Series. Detroit, MI: Gale Group, 2000.

Vorlicky, Robert ed. *Tony Kushner in Conversation.* Ann Arbor, MI: University of Michigan Press, 1998.

Willett, John. *Brecht in Context: Comparative Approaches.* 2nd edition. London: Methuen, 1998.

———. *The Theatre of Bertolt Brecht: A Study from Eight Aspects.* New York: New Directions, 1959.

Wilmeth, Don B., and Tice L. Miller, eds. *Cambridge Guide to the American Theatre.* New York: 1993.

FILM, VIDEO (DVD), AND WEB SITE RESOURCES

HAMLET AND WILLIAM SHAKESPEARE

Video:

Hamlet, by William Shakespeare. Directed by Laurence Olivier with Laurence Olivier, Eileen Herlie, Basil Sydney, and Jean Simmons. British, 1948.

Hamlet, by William Shakespeare. Directed by Kenneth Branagh with Kenneth Branagh, Richard Attenborough, and Brian Blessed. Turner Home Entertainment, 1996.

Hamlet, by William Shakespeare. Directed by Franco Zeffirelli with Mel Gibson, Glenn Close, and Alan Bates. Warner Home Video, 1990.

Hamlet. Insight Media, 1999.

Hamlet: The Readiness Is All. Insight Media, 1959.

Hamlet: Film and Stage Scenes. Insight Media, 2001.

Shakespeare: The Man and His Times. Insight Media, 1991.

Shakespeare's Language. Insight Media, 1994.

Theater in Shakespeare's Time. Insight Media, 1973.

Shakespeare: Breathing Life into Text. Insight Media, 2001.

Web Sites:

www.shakespeare.org.uk

www.Shakespeare.eb.cm/
    Shakespeare/index2.html

THE GLASS MENAGERIE AND TENNESSEE WILLIAMS

Video:

The Glass Menagerie by Tennessee Williams. With Katherine Hepburn, Sam Waterston, Michael Moriarty, and Joanna Miles. Insight Media, 1973.

The Glass Menagerie by Tennessee Williams. Directed by Paul Newman with Joanne Woodward and John Malkovich. HBO Video, 1987.

A Streetcar Named Desire by Tennessee Williams. Directed by Elia Kazan with Vivien Leigh and Marlon Brando. CBS/Fox Video, 1951.

Great Writers: Tennessee Williams. Kultur Video, 2001.

Tennessee Williams. Insight Media, 1998.

Tennessee Williams: Orpheus of the American Stage. Insight Media, 1994.

Tennessee Williams. Insight Media, 2001.

Web Sites:

The Theater of Tennessee Williams: A Virtual Fact File

www.sinc.sunysb.edu/class/thr525/
    index.htm

THE CHERRY ORCHARD AND ANTON CHEKHOV

Video:

The Cherry Orchard. Directed by Michael Cacoyannis with Charlotte Rampling, Alan Bates, and Frances De La Tour. Greek-French, 1999.

Great Russian Writers: Anton Chekhov. Kultur Video, 1999.

Andrei Serban: Experimental Theater. Interview with Margaret Croyden. Insight Media, 1978.

The Stanislavsky Century. Insight Media, 1993.

Chekhov and the Moscow Art Theater. (Includes scene from *The Cherry Orchard* at the Moscow Art Theater) Insight Media, 1982.

Web Sites:

Anton Chekhov on Writing
http://mockingbird.Creighton.edu
NCW/chekwrit.htm

OEDIPUS THE KING AND SOPHOCLES

Video:

Oedipus Rex by Sophocles. Directed by Tyrone Guthrie with Douglas Campbell as Oedipus, Stratford (Ontario) Festival production. Insight Media, 1957.
Greek Tragedy. Insight Media, 2000.

Web Sites:

Skenotheke: Images of the Ancient Stage
www.usask.ca/antharch/cnea
skenotheke.html#theaters
Greek National Theater
www.culture.gr
Theater: Honoring the Prolific Green Theater Tradition (contains images of classic and contemporary theaters)
www.istos.net.gr/theatre/menu.htm

THE IMPORTANCE OF BEING EARNEST AND OSCAR WILDE

Video:

The Importance of Being Earnest, by Oscar Wilde. Directed by Oliver Parker with Rupert Everett, Colin Firth, and Judi Dench. Walt Disney Video, 2002.
The Importance of Being Earnest, by Oscar Wilde. Directed by Anthony Asquith with Michael Redgrave, Edith Evans, and Michael Denison. Criterion, 1952.
Oscar Wilde: Spendthrift of Genius. Insight Media, 1986.

Web Sites:

www.cmgww.com/historic/wilde
www.rsc.org.uk (Royal Shakespeare Company)

THE COLORED MUSEUM AND GEORGE C. WOLFE

Video:

George C. Wolfe (Playwright and Director). Insight Media, 1995.

Panorama of African-American Theater. With scenes from *The Colored Museum.* Insight Media, 1991.

Web Sites:

BlackTheater. Includes links to black theater artists profiles and theaters.
www.bridgesweb.com/
blacktheatre.html

ANGELS IN AMERICA PART ONE: MILLENNIUM APPROACHES AND TONY KUSHNER

Web Sites:

Tony Kushner
www.goamtech.com
www.directory.infobase-intl.com
www.queertheory.com

HEDDA GABLER AND HENRIK IBSEN

Video:

Hedda Gabler by Henrik Ibsen. Directed by Trevor Nunn with Glenda Jackson, Patrick Stewart, and the Royal Shakespeare Company. British, 1975.
Hedda Gabler by Henrik Ibsen. With Fiona Shaw and Stephen Rea. British, 1993.
Ibsen's Themes. Insight Media, 1968.

Web Sites:

The Ibsen Society of America
http://ibsensociety.liu.edu

FENCES AND AUGUST WILSON

Video:

August Wilson (Interview). Insight Media, 1992.
Black Theater: The Making of a Movement. Insight Media, 1978.
Panorama of African-American Theater. (Contains scenes from *Fences*). Insight Media, 1991.

Web Sites:

August Wilson: Anthology of American Blues. (Includes Time-line for Plays, Reviews, and Other Information)
www.humboldt.edu/~ah/Wilson/
index.html

GALILEO AND BERTOLT BRECHT

Video:

> *Brecht on Stage.* Insight Media, 1992.
> *German Theater: Brecht and Schiller.* Insight Media, 1982.

Web Sites:

> The Brecht Centennial
> www.versuche.org/ie4/main.html
> The International Brecht Society
> http://polyglot.lss.wisc.edu/german/brecht

FOOTFALLS AND SAMUEL BECKETT

Video:

> *Beckett Directs Beckett* (Contains scenes from *Waiting for Godot* and *Krapp's Last Tape*) Smithsonian Institution, 1990.
> *Waiting for Beckett: A Portrait of Samuel Beckett.* Insight Media, 1993.
> *Samuel Beckett: As the Story Was Told.* (BBC production) Insight Media, 1996.
> *Samuel Beckett: Three Plays.* Insight Media, 1998. (includes *Footfalls*)
> *Samuel Beckett: Silence to Silence.* Insight Media, 1986.
> *Beckett on Film.* Ambrose Video, 2002.

Web Sites:

> The Samuel Beckett Endpage
> http://beckett.English.ucsb.edu
> The Samuel Beckett Society
> http://beckett.english.ucsb.edu/sbs/society.html

HOW I LEARNED TO DRIVE AND PAULA VOGEL

Web Sites:

> Paula Vogel
> www.search.npr.org
> www.brown.edu

THE LARAMIE PROJECT AND MOISÉS KAUFMAN

Video:

> *The Laramie Project* by Moisés Kaufman. Directed by Moisés Kaufman with Dylan Baker, Peter Fonda, Janeane Garofolo, Bill Irwin, Terry Kinney, Laura Linney, Lois Smith, and Frances Sternhagen. HBO Home Video, 2002.

OF MICE, BUGS AND WOMEN AND DEB MARGOLIN

Video:

> *Deb Margolin "Of All the Nerve."* Metropolis Media Productions, 1989.

Web Sites:

> www.notperformanceart.com
> (A video archive collection of performance art filmed in the East Village of New York City, 1987–96)

BROKEN EGGS AND EDUARDO MACHADO

Web Sites:

> Association of Hispanic Art
> http://latino.org

GOLDEN CHILD AND DAVID HENRY HWANG

Video:

> *M. Butterfly* by David Henry Hwang. Directed by David Cronenberg with Jeremy Irons, John Lone, Barbara Sukowa, and Ian Richardson. U.S.A., 1993.

Web Sites:

> Asian American Theatre Revue
> www.abcflash.com/a&e/r_tang/AATR.html

RELATED VIDEO & WEB SITE SOURCES

Peter Brook

> *Peter Brook (Interview).* Insight Media, 1973.
> *Peter Brook: The Empty Space.* Insight Media, 1975.

Dramaturgy

> www.dramaturgy.net/dramaturgy

Performance Artists

Laurie Anderson

Home of the Brave. Performed and directed by Laurie Anderson. Music Video, 1986.
One World, One Voice. BBC, 1990.
www.laurieanderson.com

Eric Bogosian

Talk Radio. Universal Pictures, 1989.
Suburbia. Castle Rock Entertainment, 1997.
www.ericbogosian.com

Guillermo Gómez-Peña

Borderstasis. Video Data Bank, 1990.
The Great Mojado Invasion. Video Data Bank, 1999.
www.mexterminator.com
www.telefonica.es/fat/egomez.html

Spalding Gray

Gray's Anatomy, by Spalding Gray. Columbia Tristar, 1996.
Monster in a Box, by Spalding Gray. New Line, 1991.
Swimming to Cambodia, by Spalding Gray. Cinecom, 1987.
Terrors of Pleasure, by Spalding Gray. HBO, 1988.
Spalding Gray (Interview)
www.altx.com/iol/gray1.html

John Leguizamo

Freak. HBO, 1998.
Spic-O-Rama. HBO, 1993.

Sexaholik. HBO, 2001.
www.johnleguizamo.com

Anna Deavere Smith

Anna Deavere Smith: In Her own Words. Audiotape, 1993.
Fires in the Mirror: Crown Heights, Brooklyn and Other Identities by Anna Deavere Smith. Directed by George C. Wolfe. PBS, 1993.
Twilight: Los Angeles, by Anna Deavere Smith. Offline, 1993.

Spiderwoman Theater

http://staff.lib.muohio.edu/nawpa/Spiderwoman.html

Postmodern Performance:

William Shakespeare

Hamlet. Directed by Michael Almereyda with Ethan Hawke, Kyle MacLachlan, Sam Shepard, Diane Venora, Bill Murray, and Julia Stiles. U.S.A. 2002.

Robert Wilson

Einstein on the Beach, a collaboration between Robert Wilson and Composer Philip Glass. Direct Cinema, 1985.
www.robertwilson.com
www.philipglass.com/einstein.html

INDEX

CREDITS

The Plays

Hamlet by William Shakespeare, edited by Sylvan Barnet, copyright © by Sylvan Barnet. Used by permission of Dutton Signet, a division of Penguin Putnam Inc.

The Glass Menagerie by Tennessee Williams, copyright 1945 by Tennessee Williams, and Edwina D. Williams; copyright renewed 1973 by Tennessee Williams. Used by permission of Random House, Inc.

The Cherry Orchard (pp. 331–398) from *Plays* by Anton Chekov, translated by Elisaveta Fen (Penguin Classics, 1954), copyright © 1951, 1954. Reprinted by permission of Penguin Books, Ltd.

Oedipus the King by Sophocles from *The Complete Greek Tragedies* (pp. 10–76). David Grene, Translator. Chicago: University of Chicago Press, 1954. Copyright © 1954 by the University of Chicago Press. Reprinted with permission.

The Colored Museum, copyright © 1985, 1987 by George C. Wolfe. Reprinted by permission of International Creative Management, Inc.

Angels in America, Part One: Millennium Approaches by Tony Kushner. Copyright 1992, 1993 by Tony Kushner. Published by Theatre Communications Group. Used by permission of Theatre Communications Group.

Hedda Gabler by Henrik Ibsen, translated by Michael Meyer. Reprinted by permission of Harold Ober Associates Incorporated. Copyright 1961, 1989 by Michael Meyer.

Fences by August Wilson, copyright © 1986 by August Wilson. Used by permission of Dutton Signet, a division of Penguin Putnam Inc.

Galileo by Bertolt Brecht, translated by Charles Laughton from *The Modern Repertoire*, Series Two (pp. 425–476), edited by Eric Bentley, © 1952. Reprinted by permission of Indiana University Press.

Footfalls by Samuel Beckett. Copyright © 1974, 1975, 1976 by Samuel Beckett. Reprinted by permission of Grove Press, Inc.

How I Learned to Drive, from *The Mammary Plays* by Paula Vogel. Copyright 1998 by Paula Vogel. Published by Theatre Communications Group. Used by permission of Theatre Communications Group.

The Laramie Project by Moisés Kaufman and The Members of Tectonic Theater Project, copyright © 2001 by Moisés Kaufman. Used by permission of Vintage Books, a division of Random House, Inc.

Broken Eggs © 1984 by Eduardo Machado.

Golden Child by David Henry Hwang. Reprinted by permission of author.

Text

p. 4: From *Pentimento: A Book of Portraits* by Lillian Hellman. Copyright © 1973, by Lillian Hellman. **pp. 10–11:** Bert Cardullo, *What Is Dramaturgy?* Reprinted with permission. **p. 20:** From Samuel Beckett, *Waiting for Godot*. Reprinted with permission. **pp. 91–93:** Margaret Webster, "Shakespeare Today" from *Shakespeare Without Tears*. Reprinted with permission. **pp. 93–95:** Essay on "Shakespearean Realism" [page 83–86] from *The Shifting Point: Theatre, Film, Opera* by Peter Brook. Copyright © 1987 by Peter Brook. Reprinted by permission of HarperCollins Publishers Inc. **pp. 142–144:** Roger B. Stein, *"The Glass Menagerie* Revisited". Reprinted with permission. **pp. 187–188:** J. L. Styan, *Modern Drama in Theory and Practice*, Vol. 1: Realism and Naturalism (pp. 81–84). Reprinted with the permission of Cambridge University Press. **p. 194:** "A National Dream-Life,"